Mitsubishi Pajero Automotive Repair Manual

by Jeff Killingsworth and John H Haynes
Member of the Guild of Motoring Writers

Models covered:
Mitsubishi Pajero - Series NL through NW
1997 through 2014

(68766 - 3U4-3)

ABCDE
FGHIJ
KL

Haynes Manuals, Inc
8/17 Willfox Street
Condell Park NSW 2200
Australia

Haynes Publishing Group
Sparkford Nr Yeovil
Somerset BA22 7JJ England

Haynes North America, Inc
859 Lawrence Drive
Newbury Park
California 91320 USA

Acknowledgements

Wiring diagrams provided by Rellim Publications.

© **Haynes North America, Inc. 2005, 2009, 2016**
With permission from J.H. Haynes & Co. Ltd.

A book in the Haynes Automotive Repair Manual Series

Printed in Malaysia

All rights reserved. No part of this book may be reproduced or transmitted in any form or by any means, electronic or mechanical, including photocopying, recording or by any information storage or retrieval system, without permission in writing from the copyright holder.

ISBN-13: 978-1-62092-139-5

ISBN-10: 1-62092-139-1

While every attempt is made to ensure that the information in this manual is correct, no liability can be accepted by the authors or publishers for loss, damage or injury caused by any errors in, or omissions from, the information given.

Contents

Introductory pages

About this manual	0-5
Introduction	0-5
Vehicle identification numbers	0-6
Recall information	0-7
Buying parts	0-8
Maintenance techniques, tools and working facilities	0-9
Booster battery (jump) starting	0-15
Jacking and towing	0-16
Automotive chemicals and lubricants	0-17
Safety first!	0-18
Conversion factors	0-19
Fraction/decimal/millimetre equivalents	0-20
Troubleshooting	0-21

Chapter 1
Tune-up and routine maintenance — 1-1

Chapter 2 Part A
V6 petrol engines — 2A-1

Chapter 2 Part B
2.8L diesel engine — 2B-1

Chapter 2 Part C
3.2L diesel engine — 2C-1

Chapter 2 Part D
General engine overhaul procedures — 2D-1

Chapter 3
Cooling, heating and air conditioning systems — 3-1

Chapter 4
Fuel and exhaust systems — 4-1

Chapter 5
Engine electrical systems — 5-1

Chapter 6
Emissions and engine control systems — 6-1

Chapter 7 Part A
Manual transmission — 7A-1

Chapter 7 Part B
Automatic transmission — 7B-1

Chapter 7 Part C
Transfer case — 7C-1

Chapter 8
Clutch and drivetrain — 8-1

Chapter 9
Brakes — 9-1

Chapter 10
Suspension and steering systems — 10-1

Chapter 11
Body — 11-1

Chapter 12
Chassis electrical system — 12-1

Wiring diagrams — 12-15

1999 NL Mitsubishi Pajero

2005 NP Mitsubishi Pajero

About this manual

Its purpose

The purpose of this manual is to help you get the best value from your vehicle. It can do so in several ways. It can help you decide what work must be done, even if you choose to have it done by a dealer service department or a repair shop; it provides information and procedures for routine maintenance and servicing; and it offers diagnostic and repair procedures to follow when trouble occurs.

We hope you use the manual to tackle the work yourself. For many simpler jobs, doing it yourself may be quicker than arranging an appointment to get the vehicle into a shop and making the trips to leave it and pick it up. More importantly, a lot of money can be saved by avoiding the expense the shop must pass on to you to cover its labor and overhead costs. An added benefit is the sense of satisfaction and accomplishment that you feel after doing the job yourself.

Using the manual

The manual is divided into Chapters. Each Chapter is divided into numbered Sections, which are headed in bold type between horizontal lines. Each Section consists of consecutively numbered paragraphs.

At the beginning of each numbered Section you will be referred to any illustrations which apply to the procedures in that Section. The reference numbers used in illustration captions pinpoint the pertinent Section and the Step within that Section. That is, illustration 3.2 means the illustration refers to Section 3 and Step (or paragraph) 2 within that Section.

Procedures, once described in the text, are not normally repeated. When it's necessary to refer to another Chapter, the reference will be given as Chapter and Section number. Cross references given without use of the word "Chapter" apply to Sections and/or paragraphs in the same Chapter. For example, "see Section 8" means in the same Chapter.

References to the left or right side of the vehicle assume you are sitting in the driver's seat, facing forward.

Even though we have prepared this manual with extreme care, neither the publisher nor the author can accept responsibility for any errors in, or omissions from, the information given.

NOTE

A **Note** provides information necessary to properly complete a procedure or information which will make the procedure easier to understand.

CAUTION

A **Caution** provides a special procedure or special steps which must be taken while completing the procedure where the Caution is found. Not heeding a Caution can result in damage to the assembly being worked on.

WARNING

A **Warning** provides a special procedure or special steps which must be taken while completing the procedure where the Warning is found. Not heeding a Warning can result in personal injury.

Introduction

Pajero models are available in two- and four-door body styles. The chassis design on these models features a separate body mounted on a boxed steel frame.

These models are equipped with either a 3.5L or 3.8L SOHC petrol engine. V6 engines use port fuel injection. In addition, four-cylinder 2.8L and 3.2L diesel engines are available. Both diesel engines are available with a turbocharger and an intercooler.

The engine drives the rear wheels through either a five-speed manual or three, four or five-speed automatic transmission via a driveshaft, differential and axles mounted in an axle housing. A transfer case and driveshaft are used to drive the front differential and driveaxles.

The front suspension on early models are composed of upper and lower control arms, shock absorbers and torsion bars. Later models use a fully independent front suspension. The solid rear axle is suspended by leaf springs and shock absorbers on earlier models. Later models use coil springs with independent rear suspension and CV-joint axles.

Early models use a steering box located to the right of the engine and is connected to the steering arms by a series of rods. Later models use rack-and pinion steering with tie-rods that connect the steering gear to the knuckles. Both systems use a power steering pump mounted on the front of the engine to assist in steering.

The brakes are vented disc on the front and solid disc on the rear. The parking brake actuator is located in the centre of the rotor.

Vehicle identification numbers

Modifications are a continuing and unpublicised process in vehicle manufacturing. Since spare parts manuals and lists are compiled on a numerical basis, the individual vehicle numbers are essential to correctly identify the component required.

Vehicle Identification Number

The Vehicle Identification Number (VIN) is found stamped on the firewall in the engine compartment (see illustration).

Vehicle information code plate

The identification plate is located on the underside of the bonnet (see illustration). It contains information such as Model code, paint and trim, as well as engine, transmission and axle information.

Vehicle data plate

The identification plate is located on the firewall (see illustration). This plate contains data such as engine number, VIN, build date, paint, trim and any special options that should be used when purchasing parts

Compliance plate

The compliance plate is located in the engine compartment on either one of the inner fenders (see illustration). This plate certifies that the vehicle complies with Australian Design Rules at the time of production.

Engine identification number

The engine model numbers are stamped into the passenger side rear of the engine block just below the cylinder head on all four-cylinder diesel engines. The engine model numbers are stamped on the drivers side lower rear engine block where the transmission meets the engine on all V6 petrol engines.

The Vehicle Identification Number is stamped into the firewall (bulkhead) in the rear of the engine compartment

The Vehicle Information Code Plate is located on the underside of the bonnet

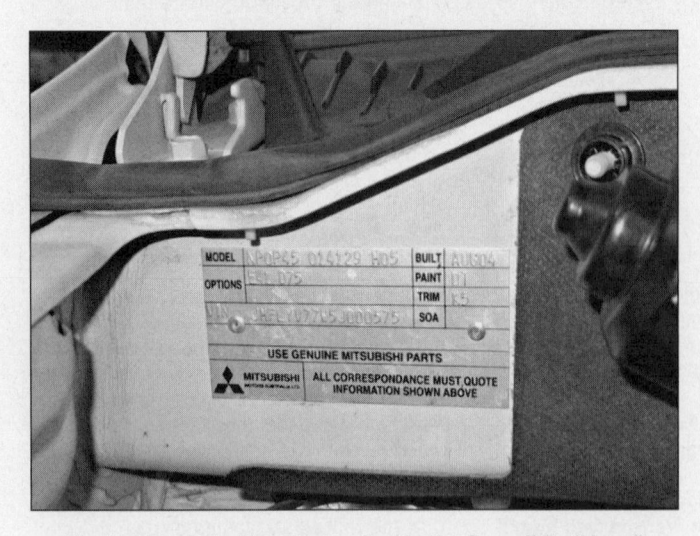

The Vehicle Data Plate is attached to the firewall (bulkhead)

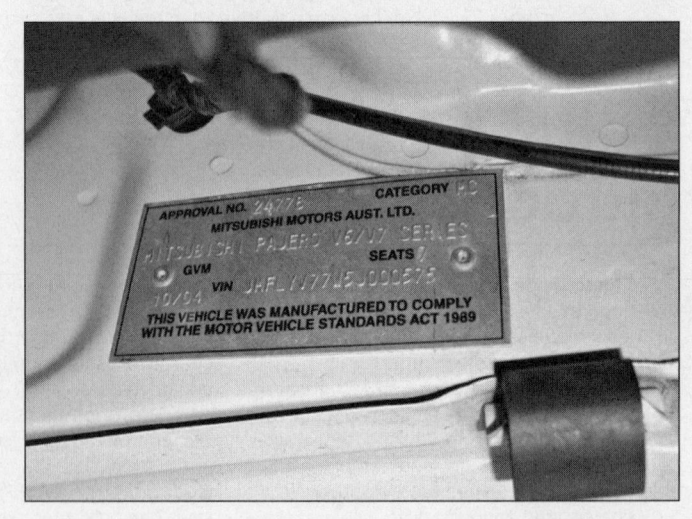

The Compliance Plate is located in the engine compartment attached to the inner fender

Recall information

Vehicle recalls are carried out by the manufacturer in the rare event of a possible safety-related defect. The vehicle's registered owner is contacted with details of the recall. Remedial work is carried out free of charge at a dealer service department.

If you are not the original owner of the vehicle and you wish to determine if a recall has been carried out, contact your local dealer and quote the vehicle identification number (VIN). The dealer will be able to inform you if there are any outstanding recalls on that particular vehicle. By law, once a recall issue has been adressed a sticker with the recall campaign number is attached to the vehicles A or B pillar — just inside the driver door — by the repairing dealer.

Most vehicles have a form in the owner's manual that can be filled out by subsequent vehicle owners. If this form is submitted to the manufacturer, the owner will receive information about any future vehicle recall notificiations.

The recall information below is current at the time of production.

To check for further recall campaings, check the Product Safety Recalls website at www.recalls.gov.au.

Recall date	Recall number – Campaign No [PRA No.]	Models affected	Concern
2nd August 2001	PRA number: 2001/4852 Reference number: 10008	NM Pajero model years 2000 to 2001"	The accumulator diaphragm on the booster may have been assembled incorrectly and if it fails will reduce the power assistance.
27th September 2001	PRA number: 2001/4958 Reference number: 10009	NM models fitted with accessory supplied towbar tongues	The parts involved were manufactured between 7 July 2000 and 20 September 2001 inclusive, and were sold separately or as part of 1200kg and 2500kg tow bar kits suitable for NM Pajero models only. The tow bar tongues subject to this recall are susceptible to embrittlement that may cause the tongue to break in service under certain circumstances.
24th July 2007	PRA number: 2007/9400 Reference number: 10036	NS automatic transmission models manufactured between 21 November 2006 and 23 March 2007	There is a possibility that the bolt welded to the manual control lever (mounted on the automatic transmission) may develop a crack when the shift cable attaching nut is tightened. If this occurs, the shift cable attaching nut torque may be reduced allowing the shift cable to move. This can result in an indicated shift position which is different to the gearshift position at the transmission. In a worse case condition if the driver selects P and or N position, actual shift position at the transmission may be R or D. If this occurs, there is a possibility of unexpected vehicle movement if the accelerator is depressed in this situation.
28th November 2007	PRA number: 2007/9678 Reference number: 10037	NS models manufactured between 20 August 2007 and 23 August 2007	A number of NS Pajero vehicles have been manufactured with the incorrect nuts used to retain the front R/H drive shaft and both front and rear propeller shafts. The threaded portion of the nut may deform on tightening, allowing the nut to become loose in operation.
18th September 2008	PRA number: 2008/10314 Reference number: JKG2008-GC28-33	NM and NP models with ABS manufactured between February 2000 and 28 July 2003.	There is the potential for the Accumulator fitted to the Hydraulic Brake Booster (HBB) to lose pressure. This may result in the following braking phenomena: Brake assistance may be delayed under rapid brake pedal application and Brake pedal effort may be increased immediately after engine start after the vehicle has been stopped for a period of time.
16th February 2015	PRA number: 2015/14559 Campaign number: 010090~010092	NS, NT, NW and NX Pajero Diesel vehicles built between 10/10/2006 to 10/03/2014	Due to inappropriate structure of the engine timing chain tensioner; abnormal noise may be generated by the lack of the tension control on the timing chain. With continued use under this condition, the timing chain may break and, in the worst case scenario, the engine could stop and not restart.

Buying parts

Spare parts are available from many sources, which generally fall into one of two categories - authorised dealer parts departments and independent retail auto parts stores. Our advice concerning these parts is as follows:

Retail auto parts stores: Good auto parts stores will stock frequently needed components which wear out relatively fast, such as clutch components, exhaust systems, brake parts, tune-up parts, etc. These stores often supply new or reconditioned parts on an exchange basis, which can save a considerable amount of money. Discount auto parts stores are often very good places to buy materials and parts needed for general vehicle maintenance such as oil, grease, filters, spark plugs, belts, touch-up paint, bulbs, etc. They also usually sell tools and general accessories, have convenient hours, charge lower prices and can often be found not far from home.

Authorised dealer parts department: This is the best source for parts which are unique to the vehicle and not generally available elsewhere (such as major engine parts, transmission parts, trim pieces, etc.).

Warranty information: If the vehicle is still covered under warranty, be sure that any renewal parts purchased - regardless of the source - do not invalidate the warranty!

To be sure of obtaining the correct parts, have engine and chassis numbers available and, if possible, take the old parts along for positive identification.

Maintenance techniques, tools and working facilities

Maintenance techniques

There are a number of techniques involved in maintenance and repair that will be referred to throughout this manual. Application of these techniques will enable the home mechanic to be more efficient, better organised and capable of performing the various tasks properly, which will ensure that the repair job is thorough and complete.

Fasteners

Fasteners are nuts, bolts, studs and screws used to hold two or more parts together. There are a few things to keep in mind when working with fasteners. Almost all of them use a locking device of some type, either a lockwasher, locknut, locking tab or thread adhesive. All threaded fasteners should be clean and straight, with undamaged threads and undamaged corners on the hex head where the spanner fits. Develop the habit of all damaged nuts and bolts with new ones. Special locknuts with nylon or fibre inserts can only be used once. If they are removed, they lose their locking ability and must be renewed.

Rusted nuts and bolts should be treated with a penetrating fluid to ease removal and prevent breakage. Some mechanics use turpentine in a spout-type oil can, which works quite well. After applying the rust penetrant, let it work for a few minutes before trying to loosen the nut or bolt. Badly rusted fasteners may have to be chiselled or sawed off or removed with a special nut breaker, available at tool stores.

If a bolt or stud breaks off in an assembly, it can be drilled and removed with a special tool commonly available for this purpose. Most automotive machine shops can perform this task, as well as other repair procedures, such as the repair of threaded holes that have been stripped out.

Flat washers and lockwashers, when removed from an assembly, should always be refitted exactly as removed. Renew any damaged washers. Never use a lockwasher on any soft metal surface (such as aluminium), thin sheet metal or plastic.

Maintenance techniques, tools and working facilities 0-9

Fastener sizes

For a number of reasons, automobile manufacturers are making wider and wider use of metric fasteners. Therefore, it is important to be able to tell the difference between standard (sometimes called US or SAE) and metric hardware, since they cannot be interchanged.

All bolts, whether standard or metric, are sized according to diameter, thread pitch and length. For example, a standard M12 - 1.75 x 25 metric bolt is 12 mm in diameter, has a thread pitch of 1.75 mm (the distance between threads) and is 25 mm long. The two bolts are nearly identical, and easily confused, but they are not interchangeable.

In addition to the differences in diameter, thread pitch and length, metric and standard bolts can also be distinguished by examining the bolt heads. To begin with, the distance across the flats on a standard bolt head is measured in inches, while the same dimension on a metric bolt is sized in millimetres (the same is true for nuts). As a result, a standard spanner should not be used on a metric bolt and a metric spanner should not be used on a standard bolt. Also, most standard bolts have slashes radiating out from the centre of the head to denote the grade or strength of the bolt, which is an indication of the amount of torque that can be applied to it. The greater the number of slashes, the greater the strength of the bolt. Grades 0 through 5 are commonly used on automobiles. Metric bolts have a property class (grade) number, rather than a slash, moulded into their heads to indicate bolt strength. In this case, the higher the number, the stronger the bolt. Property class numbers 8.8, 9.8 and 10.9 are commonly used on automobiles.

Strength markings can also be used to distinguish standard hex nuts from metric hex nuts. Many standard nuts have dots stamped into one side, while metric nuts are marked with a number. The greater the number of dots, or the higher the number, the greater the strength of the nut.

Metric studs are also marked on their ends according to property class (grade). Larger studs are numbered (the same as metric bolts), while smaller studs carry a geometric code to denote grade.

It should be noted that many fasteners, especially Grades 0 through 2, have no distinguishing marks on them. When such is the case, the only way to determine whether it is standard or metric is to measure the thread pitch or compare it to a known fastener of the same size.

Standard fasteners are often referred to as SAE, as opposed to metric. However, it should be noted that SAE technically refers to a non-metric fine thread fastener only. Coarse thread non-metric fasteners are referred to as USS sizes.

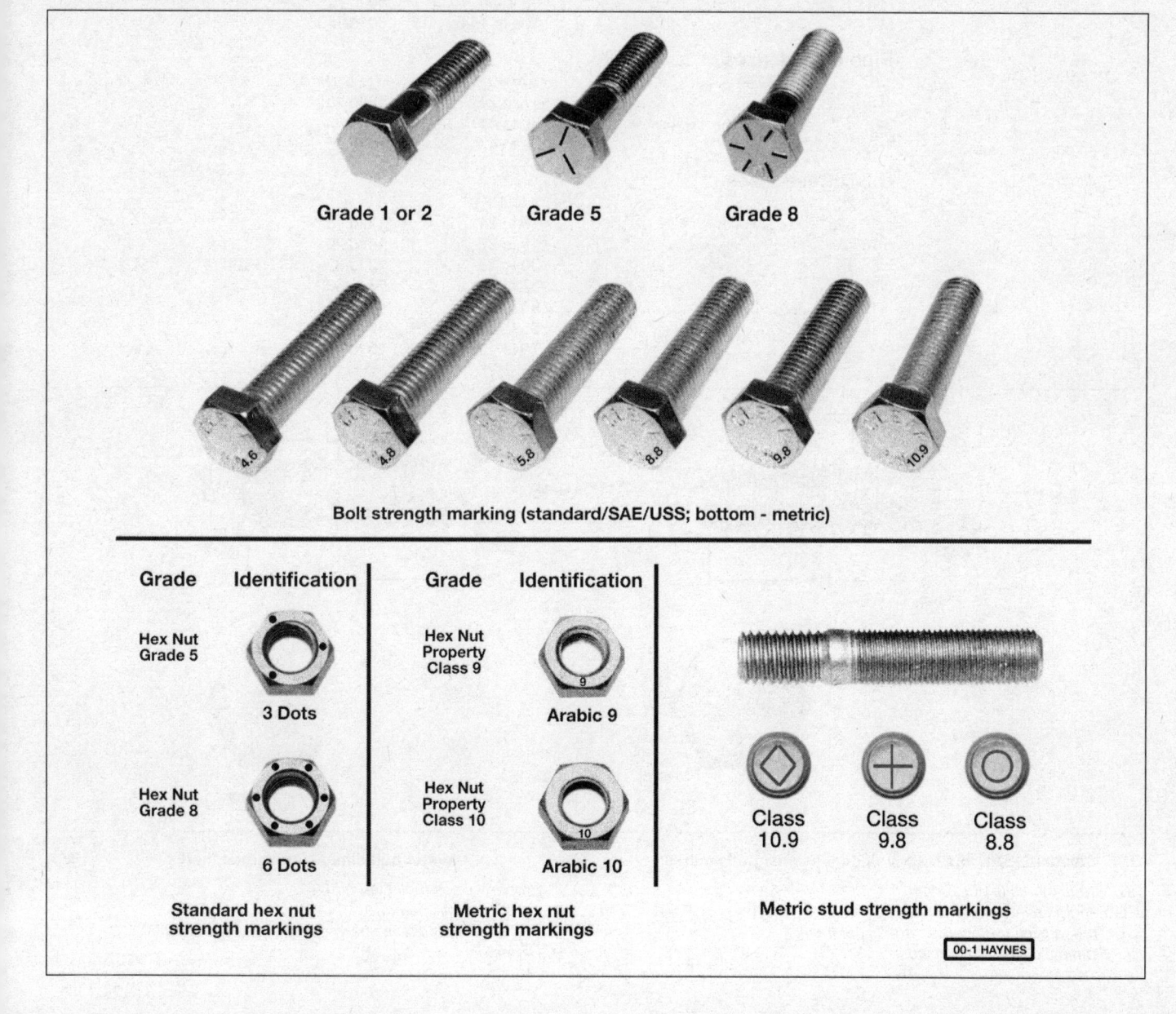

Grade 1 or 2   **Grade 5**   **Grade 8**

Bolt strength marking (standard/SAE/USS; bottom - metric)

Grade	Identification
Hex Nut Grade 5	3 Dots
Hex Nut Grade 8	6 Dots

Standard hex nut strength markings

Grade	Identification
Hex Nut Property Class 9	Arabic 9
Hex Nut Property Class 10	Arabic 10

Metric hex nut strength markings

Class 10.9   Class 9.8   Class 8.8

Metric stud strength markings

Maintenance techniques, tools and working facilities

Since fasteners of the same size (both standard and metric) may have different strength ratings, be sure to refit any bolts, studs or nuts removed from your vehicle in their original locations. Also, when renewing a fastener, make sure that the new one has a-strength rating equal to or greater than the-original.

Tightening sequences and procedures

Most threaded fasteners should be tightened to a specific torque value (torque is the twisting force applied to a threaded component such as a nut or bolt). Overtightening the fastener can weaken it and cause it to break, while undertightening can cause it to eventually come loose. Bolts, screws and studs, depending on the material they are made of and their thread diameters, have specific torque values, many of which are noted in the Specifications at the beginning of each Chapter. Be sure to follow the torque recommendations closely. For fasteners not assigned a specific torque, a general torque value chart is presented here as a guide. These torque values are for dry (unlubricated) fasteners threaded into steel or cast iron (not aluminium). As was previously mentioned, the size and grade of a fastener determine the amount of torque that can safely be applied to it. The figures listed here are approximate for Grade 2 and Grade 3 fasteners. Higher grades can tolerate higher torque values.

Fasteners laid out in a pattern, such as cylinder head bolts, sump bolts, differential cover bolts, etc., must be loosened or tightened in sequence to avoid warping the component. This sequence will normally be shown in the appropriate Chapter. If a specific pattern is not given, the following procedures can be used to prevent warping.

Initially, the bolts or nuts should be assembled finger-tight only. Next, they should be tightened one full turn each, in a criss-cross or diagonal pattern. After each one has been tightened one full turn, return to the first one and tighten them all one-half turn, following the same pattern. Finally, tighten each of them one-quarter turn at a time until each fastener has been tightened to the proper torque. To loosen and remove the fasteners, the procedure would be reversed.

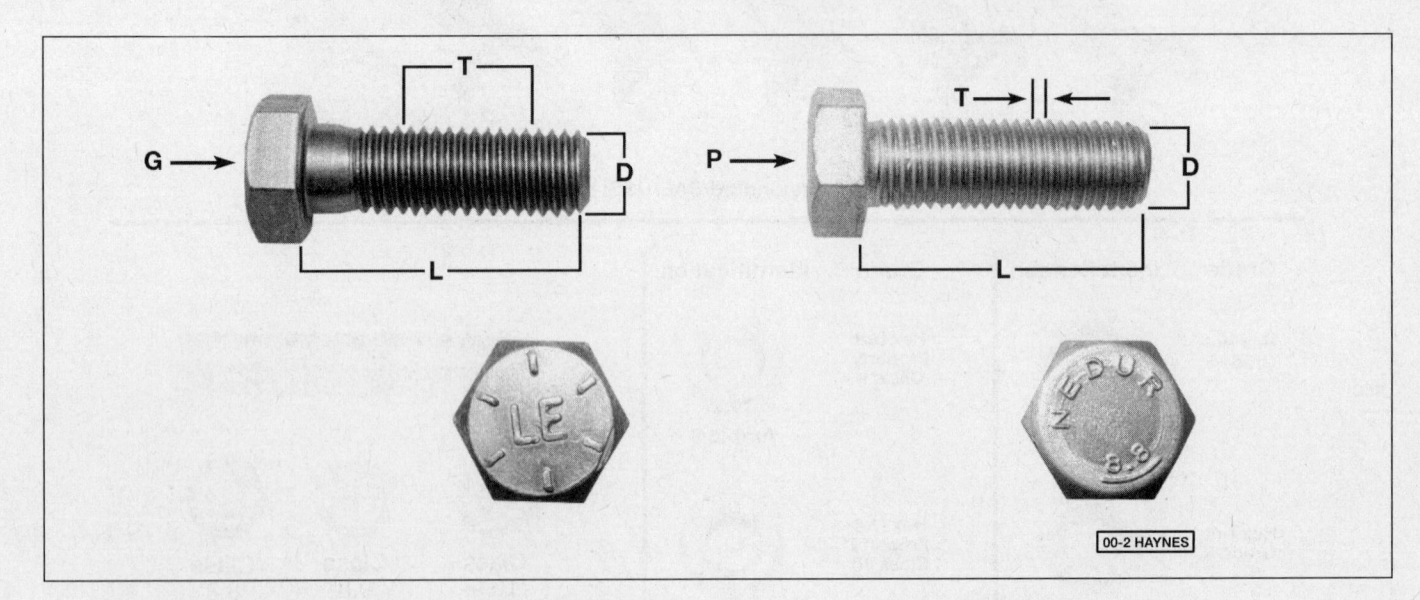

Metric thread sizes	Nm	Ft-lbs
M-6	9 to 12	6 to 9
M-8	19 to 28	14 to 21
M-10	38 to 54	28 to 40
M-12	68 to 96	50 to 71
M-14	109 to 154	80 to 140

Pipe thread sizes	Nm	Ft-lbs
1/8	7 to 10	5 to 8
1/4	17 to 24	12 to 18
3/8	30 to 44	22 to 33
1/2	34 to 47	25 to 35

U.S. thread sizes	Nm	Ft-lbs
1/4 - 20	9 to 12	6 to 9
5/16 - 18	17 to 24	12 to 18
5/16 - 24	19 to 27	14 to 20
3/8 - 16	30 to 43	22 to 32
3/8 - 24	37 to 51	27 to 38
7/16 - 14	55 to 74	40 to 55
7/16 - 20	55 to 81	40 to 60
1/2 - 13	75 to 108	55 to 80

Standard (SAE and USS) bolt dimensions/grade marks

- G Grade marks (bolt strength)
- L Length (in inches)
- T Thread pitch (number of threads per inch)
- D Nominal diameter (in inches)

Metric bolt dimensions/grade marks

- P Property class (bolt strength)
- L Length (in millimeters)
- T Thread pitch (distance between threads in millimeters)
- D Diameter

Maintenance techniques, tools and working facilities

Component disassembly

Component disassembly should be done with care and purpose to help ensure that the parts go back together properly. Always keep track of the sequence in which parts are removed. Make note of special characteristics or marks on parts that can be refit more than one way, such as a grooved-thrust washer on a shaft. It is a good idea to lay the disassembled parts out on a clean surface in the order that they were removed. It may also be helpful to make sketches or take instant photos of components before removal.

When removing fasteners from a component, keep track of their locations. Sometimes threading a bolt back in a part, or putting the washers and nut back on a stud, can prevent mix-ups later. If nuts and bolts cannot be returned to their original locations, they should be kept in a compartmented box or a series of small boxes. A cupcake or muffin tin is ideal for this purpose, since each cavity can hold the bolts and nuts from a particular area (i.e. sump bolts, valve cover bolts, engine mount bolts, etc.). A pan of this type is especially helpful when working on assemblies with very small parts, such as the carburettor, alternator, valve train or interior dash and trim pieces. The cavities can be marked with paint or tape to identify the contents.

Whenever wiring looms, harnesses or connectors are separated, it is a good idea to identify the two halves with numbered pieces of masking tape so they can be easily reconnected.

Gasket sealing surfaces

Throughout any vehicle, gaskets are used to seal the mating surfaces between two parts and keep lubricants, fluids, vacuum or pressure contained in an assembly.

Many times these gaskets are coated with a liquid or paste-type gasket sealing compound before assembly. Age, heat and pressure can sometimes cause the two parts to stick together so tightly that they are very difficult to separate. Often, the assembly can be loosened by striking it with a soft-face hammer near the mating surfaces. A regular hammer can be used if a block of wood is placed between the hammer and the part. Do not hammer on cast parts or parts that could be easily damaged. With any particularly stubborn part, always recheck to make sure that every fastener has been removed.

Avoid using a screwdriver or bar to prise apart an assembly, as they can easily mar the gasket sealing surfaces of the parts, which must remain smooth. If levering is absolutely necessary, use an old broom handle, but keep in mind that extra clean up will be necessary if the wood splinters.

After the parts are separated, the old gasket must be carefully scraped off and the gasket surfaces cleaned. Stubborn gasket material can be soaked with rust penetrant or treated with a special chemical to soften it so it can be easily scraped off.

Caution: Never use gasket removal solutions or caustic chemicals on plastic or other composite components. A scraper can be fashioned from a piece of copper tubing by flattening and sharpening one end. Copper is recommended because it is usually softer than the surfaces to be scraped, which reduces the chance of gouging the part. Some gaskets can be removed with a wire brush, but regardless of the method used, the mating surfaces must be left clean and smooth. If for some reason the gasket surface is gouged, then a gasket sealer thick enough to fill scratches will have to be used during reassembly of the components. For most applications, a non-drying (or semi-drying) gasket sealer should be used.

Hose removal tips

Warning: *If the vehicle is equipped with air conditioning, do not disconnect any of the A/C hoses without first having the system depressurised by a dealer service department or a service station.*

Hose removal precautions closely parallel gasket removal precautions. Avoid scratching or gouging the surface that the hose mates against or the connection may leak. This is especially true for radiator hoses. Because of various chemical reactions, the rubber in hoses can bond itself to the metal spigot that the hose fits over. To remove a hose, first loosen the hose clamps that secure it to the spigot. Then, with slip-joint pliers, grab the hose at the clamp and rotate it around the spigot. Work it back and forth until it is completely free, then pull it off. Silicone or other lubricants will ease removal if they can be applied between the hose and the outside of the spigot. Apply the same lubricant to the inside of the hose and the outside of the spigot to simplify refitting.

As a last resort (and if the hose is to be renewed anyway), the rubber can be slit with a knife and the hose peeled from the spigot. If this must be done, be careful that the metal connection is not damaged.

If a hose clamp is broken or damaged, do not reuse it. Wire-type clamps usually weaken with age, so it is a good idea to renew them with screw-type clamps whenever a hose is removed.

Tools

A selection of good tools is a basic requirement for anyone who plans to maintain and repair his or her own vehicle. For the owner who has few tools, the initial investment might seem high, but when compared to the spiralling costs of professional auto maintenance and repair, it is a wise one.

To help the owner decide which tools are needed to perform the tasks detailed in this manual, the following tool lists are offered: *Maintenance and minor repair*, *Repair/ overhaul* and *Special*.

The newcomer to practical mechanics should start off with the *maintenance and minor repair* tool kit, which is adequate for the simpler jobs performed on a vehicle. Then, as confidence and experience grow, the owner can tackle more difficult tasks, buying additional tools as they are needed. Eventually the basic kit will be expanded into the *repair and overhaul* tool set. Over a period of time, the experienced do-it-yourselfer will

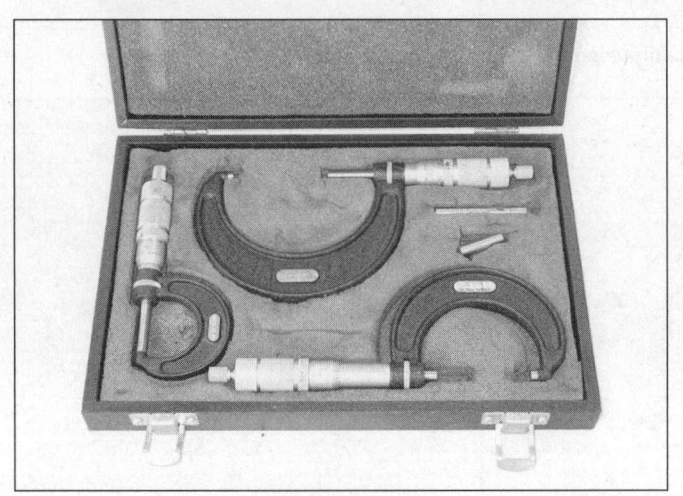

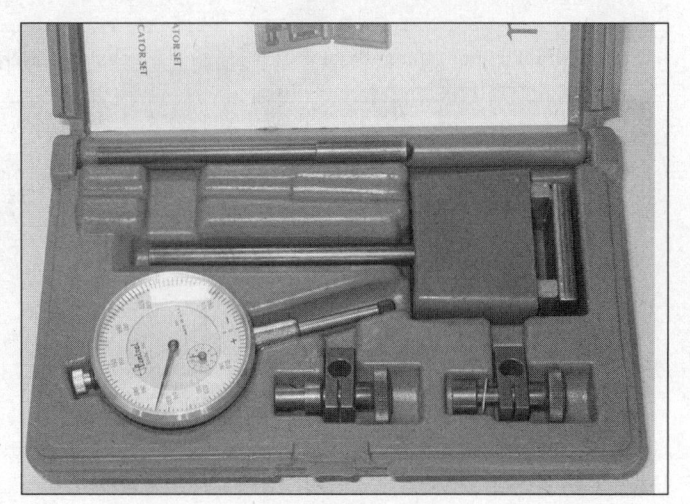

Micrometer set

Dial indicator set

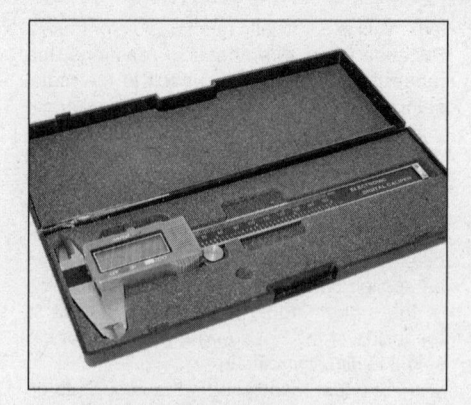

0-12　　Maintenance techniques, tools and working facilities

Dial caliper

Hand-operated vacuum pump

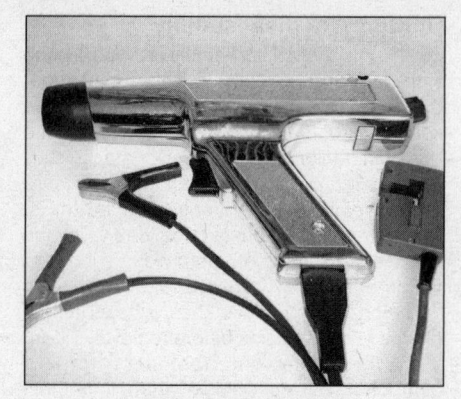

Timing light

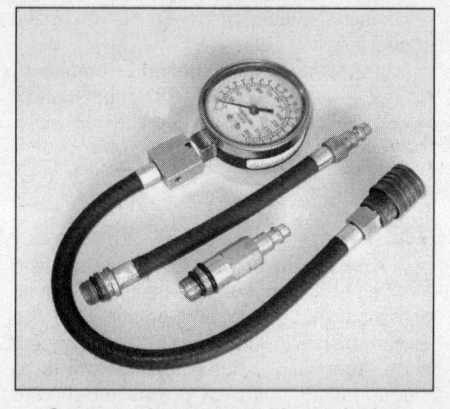

Compression gauge with spark plug hole adapter

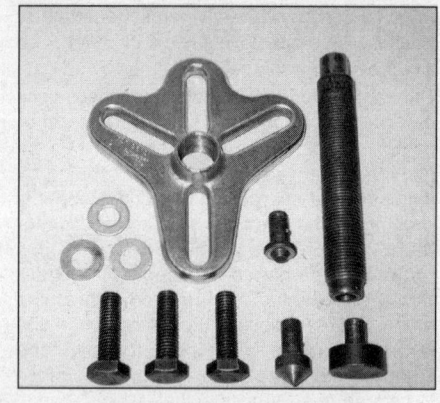

Damper/steering wheel puller

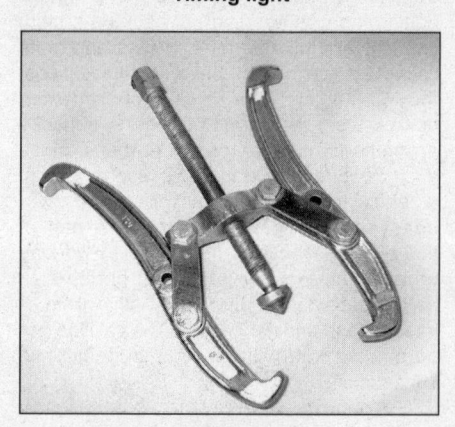

General purpose puller

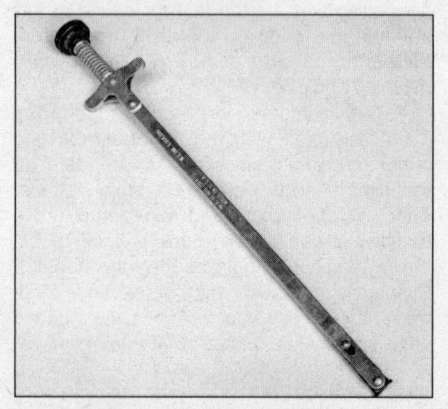

Hydraulic lifter removal tool

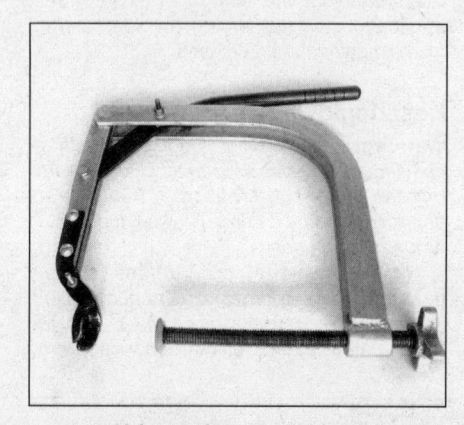

Valve spring compressor

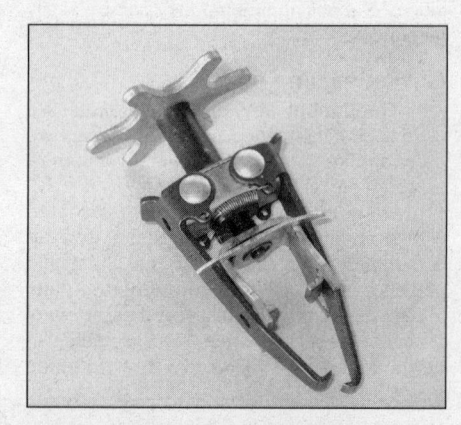

Valve spring compressor

Ridge reamer

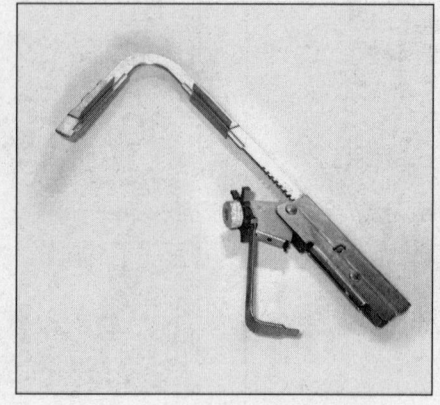

Piston ring groove cleaning tool

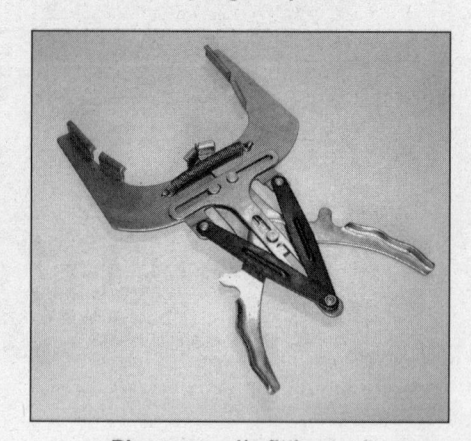

Ring removal/refitting tool

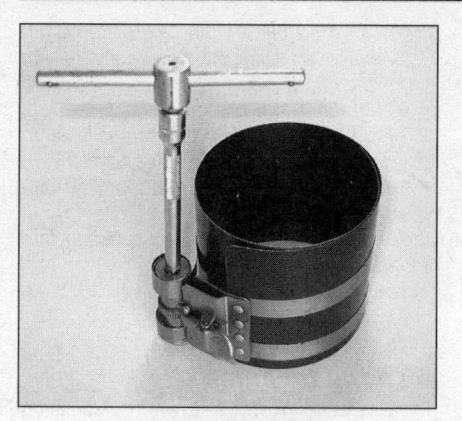

Maintenance techniques, tools and working facilities 0-13

Ring compressor

Cylinder hone

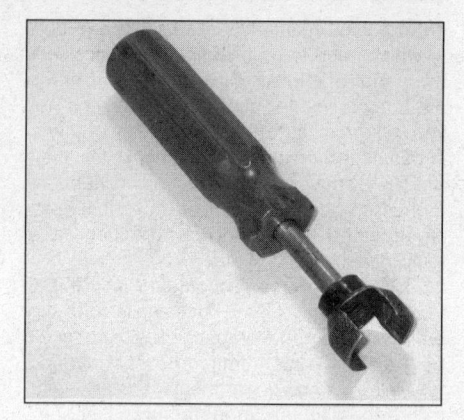

Brake hold-down spring tool

Torque angle gauge

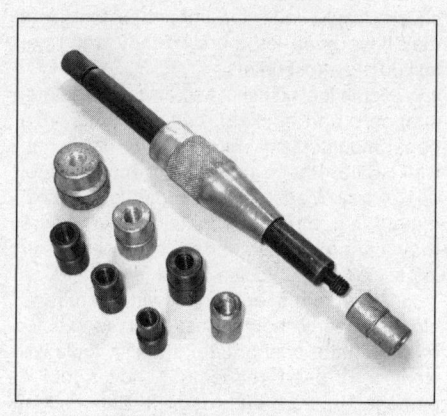

Clutch plate alignment tool

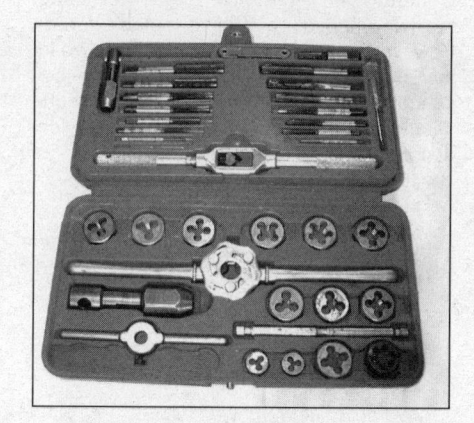

Tap and die set

assemble a tool set complete enough for most repair and overhaul procedures and will add tools from the special category when it is felt that the expense is justified by the frequency of use.

Maintenance and minor repair tool kit

The tools in this list should be considered the minimum required for performance of routine maintenance, servicing and minor repair work. We recommend the purchase of combination spanners (box-end and open-end combined in one spanner). While more expensive than open end spanners, they offer the advantages of both types of spanner.

Combination spanner set (6 mm to 19 mm)
Adjustable spanner
Spark plug spanner with rubber insert
Spark plug gap adjusting tool
Feeler gauge set
Brake bleeder spanner
Standard screwdriver
Phillips screwdriver
Combination pliers
Hacksaw and assortment of blades
Tyre pressure gauge
Grease gun
Oil can
Fine emery cloth
Wire brush

Battery post and cable cleaning tool
Oil filter spanner
Funnel (medium size)
Safety goggles
Jackstands (2)
Drain pan

Note: *If basic tune-ups are going to be part of routine maintenance, it will be necessary to purchase a good quality stroboscopic timing light and combination tachometer/dwell meter. Although they are included in the list of special tools, it is mentioned here because they are absolutely necessary for tuning most vehicles properly.*

Repair and overhaul tool set

These tools are essential for anyone who plans to perform major repairs and are in addition to those in the maintenance and minor repair tool kit. Included is a comprehensive set of sockets which, though expensive, are invaluable because of their versatility, especially when various extensions and drives are available. We recommend the 1/2-inch drive over the 3/8-inch drive. Although the larger drive is bulky and more expensive, it has the capacity of accepting a very wide range of large sockets. Ideally, however, the mechanic should have a 3/8-inch drive set and a 1/2-inch drive set.

Socket set(s)
Reversible ratchet

Extension
Universal joint
Torque wrench (same size drive as sockets)
Ball peen hammer
Soft-face hammer (plastic/rubber)
Standard screwdriver
Standard screwdriver (stubby)
Phillips screwdriver
Phillips screwdriver (stubby - No. 2)
Pliers - vise grip
Pliers - lineman's
Pliers - needle nose
Pliers - snap-ring (internal and external)
Cold chisel
Scribe
Scraper (made from flattened copper tubing)
Centrepunch
Pin punches
Steel rule/straightedge
Allen wrench set (4 mm to 10 mm)
A selection of files
Wire brush (large)
Jackstands (second set)
Jack (scissor or hydraulic type)

Note: Another tool which is often useful is an electric drill with a chuck capacity of 10 mm and a set of good quality drill bits.

Special tools

The tools in this list include those which

are not used regularly, are expensive to buy, or which need to be used in accordance with their manufacturer's instructions. Unless these tools will be used frequently, it is not very economical to purchase many of them. A consideration would be to split the cost and use between yourself and a friend or friends. In addition, most of these tools can be obtained from a tool rental shop on a temporary basis.

This list primarily contains only those tools and instruments widely available to the public, and not those special tools produced by the vehicle manufacturer for distribution to dealer service departments. Occasionally, references to the manufacturer's special tools are included in the text of this manual. Generally, an alternative method of doing the job without the special tool is offered. However, sometimes there is no alternative to their use. Where this is the case, and the tool cannot be purchased or borrowed, the work should be turned over to the dealer service department or an automotive repair shop.

Valve spring compressor
Piston ring groove cleaning tool
Piston ring compressor
Piston ring refitting tool
Cylinder compression gauge
Cylinder ridge reamer
Cylinder surfacing hone
Cylinder bore gauge
Micrometers and/or dial calipers
Hydraulic lifter removal tool
Balljoint separator
Universal-type puller
Impact screwdriver
Dial indicator set
Stroboscopic timing light (inductive pick-up)
Hand operated vacuum/pressure pump
Tachometer/dwell meter
Universal electrical multimeter
Cable hoist
Brake spring removal and refitting tools
Floor jack

Buying tools

For the do-it-yourselfer who is just starting to get involved in vehicle maintenance and repair, there are a number of options available when purchasing tools. If maintenance and minor repair is the extent of the work to be done, the purchase of individual tools is satisfactory. If, on the other hand, extensive work is planned, it would be a good idea to purchase a modest tool set from one of the large retail chain stores. A set can usually be bought at a substantial savings over the individual tool prices, and they often come with a tool box. As additional tools are needed, add-on sets, individual tools and a larger tool box can be purchased to expand the tool selection. Building a tool set gradually allows the cost of the tools to be spread over a longer period of time and gives the mechanic the freedom to choose only those tools that will actually be used.

Tool stores will often be the only source of some of the special tools that are needed, but regardless of where tools are bought, try to avoid cheap ones, especially when buying screwdrivers and sockets, because they won't last very long. The expense involved in renewing cheap tools will eventually be greater than the initial cost of quality tools.

Care and maintenance of tools

Good tools are expensive, so it makes sense to treat them with respect. Keep them clean and in useable condition and store them properly when not in use. Always wipe off any dirt, grease or metal chips before putting them away. Never leave tools lying around in the work area. Upon completion of a job, always check closely under the bonnet for tools that may have been left there so they won't get lost during a test drive.

Some tools, such as screwdrivers, pliers, spanners and sockets, can be hung on a panel mounted on the garage or workshop wall, while others should be kept in a tool box or tray. Measuring instruments, gauges, meters, etc. must be carefully stored where they cannot be damaged by weather or impact from other tools.

When tools are used with care and stored properly, they will last a very long time. Even with the best of care, though, tools will wear out if used frequently. When a tool is damaged or worn out, renew it. Subsequent jobs will be safer and more enjoyable if you do.

How to repair damaged threads

Sometimes, the internal threads of a nut or bolt hole can become stripped, usually from overtightening. Stripping threads is an all-too-common occurrence, especially when working with aluminium parts, because aluminium is so soft that it easily strips out.

Usually, external or internal threads are only partially stripped. After they've been cleaned up with a tap or die, they'll still work. Sometimes, however, threads are badly damaged. When this happens, you've got three choices:

1) *Drill and tap the hole to the next suitable oversize and refit a larger diameter bolt, screw or stud.*
2) *Drill and tap the hole to accept a threaded plug, then drill and tap the plug to the original screw size. You can also buy a plug already threaded to the original size. Then you simply drill a hole to the specified size, then run the threaded plug into the hole with a bolt and jam nut. Once the plug is fully seated, remove the jam nut and bolt.*
3) *The third method uses a patented thread repair kit like Heli-Coil or Slimsert. These easy-to-use kits are designed to repair damaged threads in straight-through holes and blind holes. Both are available as kits which can handle a variety of sizes and thread patterns. Drill the hole, then tap it with the special included tap. Fit the Heli-Coil and the hole is back to its original diameter and thread pitch.*

Regardless of which method you use, be sure to proceed calmly and carefully. A little impatience or carelessness during one of these relatively simple procedures can ruin your whole day's work and cost you a bundle if you wreck an expensive part.

Working facilities

Not to be overlooked when discussing tools is the workshop. If anything more than routine maintenance is to be carried out, some sort of suitable work area is essential.

It is understood, and appreciated, that many home mechanics do not have a good workshop or garage available, and end up removing an engine or doing major repairs outside. It is recommended, however, that the overhaul or repair be completed under the cover of a roof.

A clean, flat workbench or table of comfortable working height is an absolute necessity. The workbench should be equipped with a vise that has a jaw opening of at least 10-cm.

As mentioned previously, some clean, dry storage space is also required for tools, as well as the lubricants, fluids, cleaning solvents, etc. which soon become necessary.

Sometimes waste oil and fluids, drained from the engine or cooling system during normal maintenance or repairs, present a disposal problem. To avoid pouring them on the ground or into a sewage system, pour the used fluids into large containers, seal them with caps and take them to an authorised disposal site or recycling centre. Plastic jugs, such as old antifreeze containers, are ideal for this purpose.

Always keep a supply of old newspapers and clean rags available. Old towels are excellent for mopping up spills. Many mechanics use rolls of paper towels for most work because they are readily available and disposable. To help keep the area under the vehicle clean, a large cardboard box can be cut open and flattened to protect the garage or shop floor.

Whenever working over a painted surface, such as when leaning over a fender to service something under the bonnet, always cover it with an old blanket or bedspread to protect the finish. Vinyl covered pads, made especially for this purpose, are available at auto parts stores.

Booster battery (jump) starting

Jump starting a vehicle can be dangerous if the procedure described below is not performed correctly. If any doubt exists, it is recommended that the services of a competent mechanic be obtained.

The range of vehicles covered by this manual are equipped with complex electronic circuitry which can be damaged by voltage surges. These voltage surges can be generated when jump starting or being jump started by another vehicle.

If available, use jumper leads equipped with a surge protection device and follow the lead manufacturers instructions carefully, particularly regarding the connection and disconnection of the leads.

1 Ensure that the booster battery is 12 volts and the negative terminal is earthed.
2 Ensure that the vehicles are not touching and that the ignition and all accessories on both vehicles are switched Off.
3 Ensure that the transaxles on both vehicles are in Park or Neutral and the handbrakes are firmly applied.
4 Remove the vent caps from the battery and check the electrolyte level. Replenish with distilled water as necessary.
5 Place the vent caps loosely over the cell apertures.
6 Connect one end of the red jumper lead to the positive (+) battery terminal of the booster battery (connection 1) and the other end of the red lead to the positive (+) battery terminal of the discharged battery (connection 2).

Warning: *The battery emits hydrogen gas which is explosive. Do not expose the battery to naked flames or sparks. Do not lean over the battery when connecting the jumper leads. Do not allow the ends of the jumper leads to touch one another or any part of the vehicle.*

7 Connect one end of the black jumper lead to the negative (–) battery terminal of the booster battery (connection 3) and the other end of the black lead to a good earthing point on the engine of the vehicle with the discharged battery (connection 4).

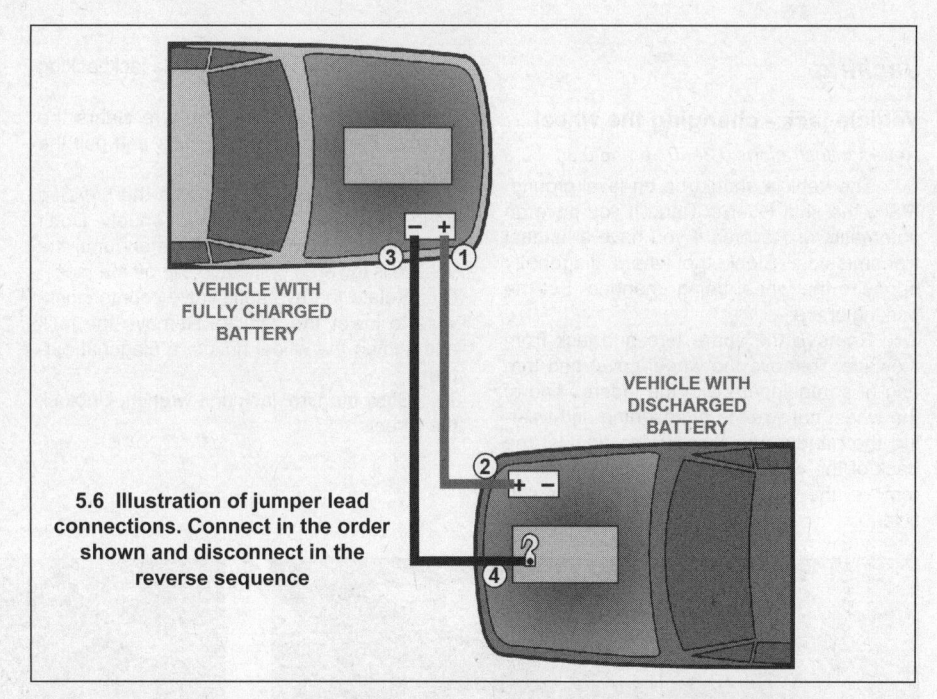

Note: *Do not connect the jumper lead directly to the negative (–) battery terminal of the discharged battery.*

8 Start the engine on the vehicle with the booster battery and run the engine at a moderate speed for a few minutes.
9 Start the engine on the vehicle with the discharged battery.
10 Leave the engines of both vehicles running for at least 10 minutes. This will partially charge the discharged battery and reduce the risk of damage to electronic circuitry from voltage surges.
11 Switch the engines of both vehicles Off and disconnect the jumper leads in the reverse order of the connecting sequence.
12 Attempt to start the engine of the vehicle with the discharged battery.
13 If the battery has not charged sufficiently to start the engine, reconnect the jumper leads as previously described and start the engines of both vehicles.
14 Switch On the headlamps of the vehicle with the discharged battery.
15 Disconnect the jumper leads in the reverse order of the connecting sequence. Switch the headlamps Off.

5.6 Illustration of jumper lead connections. Connect in the order shown and disconnect in the reverse sequence

Jacking and towing

Jacking

Vehicle jack - changing the wheel

Refer to illustrations 0.3a, 03.b and 0.3c

1 The vehicle should be on level ground. Place the shift lever in Park, if you have an automatic, or Reverse if you have a manual transmission. Block the wheel diagonally opposite the wheel being changed. Set the parking brake.
2 Remove the spare tyre and jack from stowage. Remove the wheel cover and trim ring (if so equipped) with the tapered end of the wheel nut wrench by inserting and twisting the handle and then prying against the back of the wheel cover. Loosen, but do not remove, the wheel nuts (one-half turn is sufficient).
3 Place the jack at the vehicle jack jacking points **(see illustrations)**.
4 Raise the jack until the tyre clears the ground. Remove the wheel nuts and pull the wheel off, then install the spare.
5 Install the wheel nuts with the beveled edges facing in. Tighten them snugly. Don't attempt to tighten them completely until the vehicle is lowered or it could slip off the jack.
6 Rotate the hydraulic valve counterclockwise to lower the vehicle. Remove the jack and tighten the wheel nuts in a diagonal pattern.
7 Stow the tyre, jack and wrench. Unblock the wheels.

Floor jack and chassis stands

Refer to illustrations 0.8a and 08.b

8 When the vehicle has to be raised using a floor jack, locate the lifting pad of the jack at the front or rear positions **(see illustrations)**.
9 Place wheel chocks under the rear wheels when the front end of the vehicle is raised and under the front wheels when the rear end of the vehicle is raised.
10 Place chassis stands at the illustrated vehicle jacking points **(see illustrations 0.8a and 0.8b)**.
Warning: *Never get under a vehicle that is only supported by the jack. Always support the vehicle with chassis stands at the positions shown in the illustrations. Under no circumstances use a floor jack, chassis stands or car ramps on sloping or unstable*

0.3a Front vehicle jacking points

0.3b Rear vehicle jacking points - early models with solid rear axle

Jacking and towing 0-17

0.3c Rear vehicle jacking points -- late models with independent rear axle

ground. Always use a flat solid surface, preferably concrete.

Note: Insert a wooden or rubber block between the chassis stand and the chassis when the supported surface is flat.

Towing

As a general rule, vehicles may be towed with all four wheels on the ground. If necessary, the front or rear wheels may be raised for towing. On vehicles with an automatic transmission, do not exceed 50 KPH or tow the vehicle farther than 25 kilometres (there are no speed or distance limitations on vehicles with a manual transmission).

Equipment specifically designed for towing should be used and should be attached to the main structural members of the vehicle, not the bumper or brackets. Tow hooks are attached to the frame at both ends of the vehicle. However, they are for emergency use only and should not be used for highway towing. Stand clear of vehicles when using the tow hooks - tow straps and chains may break, causing serious injury.

Safety is a major consideration when towing and all applicable state and local laws must be obeyed. A safety chain must be used for all towing (in addition to the tow bar).

While towing, the parking brake must be released, the transmission must be in Neutral and the transfer case must be in 2H. The steering must be unlocked (ignition switch in the Off position). If you're towing with the front wheels on the ground, the front hubs must be unlocked. Remember that power steering and power brakes will not work with the engine off.

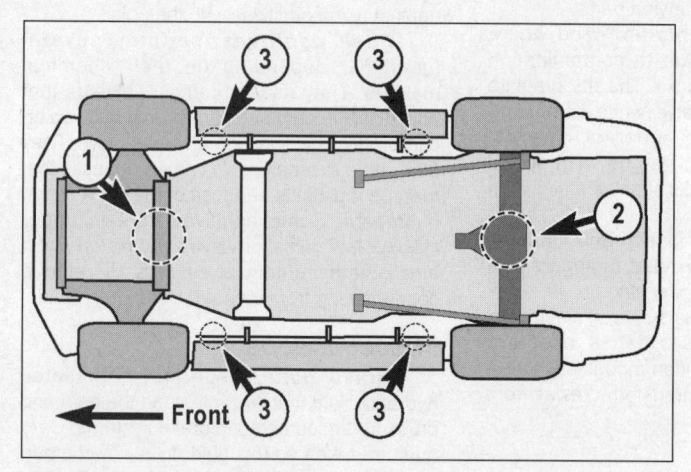

0.8a Floor jack jacking points -- early models with solid rear axle

1. Front floor jack jacking point
2. Rear floor jack jacking point
3. Chassis stand locations on the sil panel of the vehicle

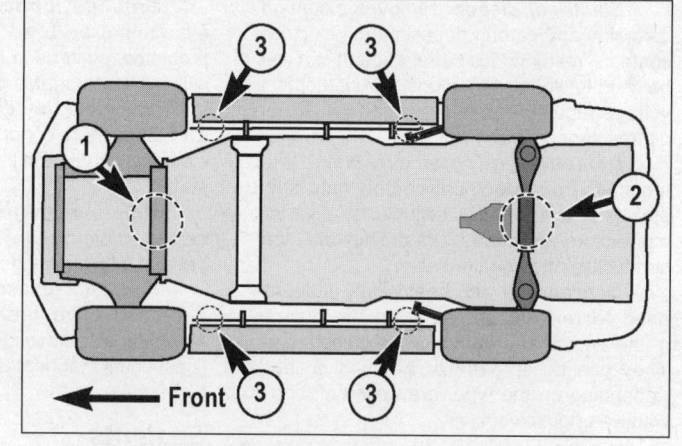

0.8b Floor jack jacking points -- late models with independent rear axle

1. Front floor jack jacking point
2. Rear floor jack jacking point
3. Chassis stand locations on the sil panel of the vehicle

Automotive chemicals and lubricants

A number of automotive chemicals and lubricants are available for use during vehicle maintenance and repair. They include a wide variety of products ranging from cleaning solvents and degreasers to lubricants and protective sprays for rubber, plastic and vinyl.

Cleaners

Carburettor cleaner and choke clean-er is a strong solvent for gum, varnish and carbon. Most carburettor cleaners leave a dry-type lubricant film which will not harden or gum up. Because of this film it is not recommended for use on electrical components.

Brake system cleaner is used to remove brake dust, grease and brake fluid from the brake system, where clean surfaces are absolutely necessary. It leaves no residue and often eliminates brake squeal caused by contaminants.

Electrical cleaner removes oxidation, corrosion and carbon deposits from electrical contacts, restoring full current flow. It can also be used to clean spark plugs, carburettor jets, voltage regulators and other parts where an oil-free surface is desired.

Demoisturants remove water and moisture from electrical components such as alternators, voltage regulators, electrical connectors and fuse blocks. They are non-conductive and non-corrosive.

Degreasers are heavy-duty solvents used to remove grease from the outside of-the engine and from chassis components. They can be sprayed or brushed on and, depending on the type, are rinsed off either with water or solvent.

Lubricants

Motor oil is the lubricant formulated for use in engines. It normally contains a wide variety of additives to prevent corrosion and reduce foaming and wear. Motor oil comes in various weights (viscosity ratings) from 0 to 50. The recommended weight of the oil depends on the season, temperature and the demands on the engine. Light oil is used in cold climates and under light load conditions. Heavy oil is used in hot climates and where high loads are encountered. Multi-viscosity oils are designed to have characteristics of both light and heavy oils and are available in a number of weights from 0W-20 to 20W-50.

Gear oil is designed to be used in differentials, manual transmissions and other areas where high-temperature lubrication is required.

Chassis and wheel bearing grease is a heavy grease used where increased loads and friction are encountered, such as for wheel bearings, balljoints, tie-rod ends and universal joints.

High-temperature wheel bearing grease is designed to withstand the extreme temperatures encountered by wheel bearings in disc brake equipped vehicles. It usually contains molybdenum disulfide (moly), which is a dry-type lubricant.

White grease is a heavy grease for metal-to-metal applications where water is a problem. White grease stays soft under both low and high temperatures (usually from -56 to +106-degrees C), and will not wash off or dilute in the presence of water.

Assembly lube is a special extreme pressure lubricant, usually containing moly, used to lubricate high-load parts (such as main and rod bearings and cam lobes) for initial start-up of a new engine. The assembly lube lubricates the parts without being squeezed out or washed away until the engine oiling system begins to function.

Silicone lubricants are used to protect rubber, plastic, vinyl and nylon parts.

Graphite lubricants are used where oils cannot be used due to contamination problems, such as in locks. The dry graphite will lubricate metal parts while remaining uncontaminated by dirt, water, oil or acids. It is electrically conductive and will not foul electrical contacts in locks such as the ignition switch.

Moly penetrants loosen and lubricate seized, rusted and corroded fasteners and prevent future rusting or freezing.

Heat-sink grease is a special electrically non-conductive grease that is used for mounting electronic ignition modules where it is essential that heat is transferred away from the module.

Sealants

RTV sealant is one of the most widely used gasket compounds. Made from silicone, RTV is air curing, it seals, bonds, waterproofs, fills surface irregularities, remains flexible, doesn't shrink, is relatively easy to remove, and is used as a supplementary sealer with almost all low and medium temperature gaskets.

Anaerobic sealant is much like RTV in that it can be used either to seal gaskets or to form gaskets by itself. It remains flexible, is solvent resistant and fills surface imperfections. The difference between an anaerobic sealant and an RTV-type sealant is in the curing. RTV cures when exposed to air, while an anaerobic sealant cures only in the absence of air. This means that an anaerobic sealant cures only after the assembly of parts, sealing them together.

Thread and pipe sealant is used for sealing hydraulic and pneumatic fittings and vacuum lines. It is usually made from a Teflon compound, and comes in a spray, a paint-on liquid and as a wrap-around tape.

Chemicals

Anti-seize compound prevents seizing, galling, cold welding, rust and corrosion in fasteners. High-temperature anti-seize, usually made with copper and graphite lubricants, is used for exhaust system and exhaust manifold bolts.

Anaerobic locking compounds are used to keep fasteners from vibrating or working loose and cure only after installation, in the absence of air. Medium strength locking compound is used for small nuts, bolts and screws that may be removed later. High-strength locking compound is for large nuts, bolts and studs which aren't removed on a regular basis.

Oil additives range from viscosity index improvers to chemical treatments that claim to reduce internal engine friction. It should be noted that most oil manufacturers caution against using additives with their oils.

Fuel additives perform several functions, depending on their chemical makeup. They usually contain solvents that help dissolve gum and varnish that build up on carburettor, fuel injection and inlet parts. They also serve to break down carbon deposits that form on the inside surfaces of the combustion chambers. Some additives contain upper cylinder lubricants for valves and piston rings, and others contain chemicals to remove condensation from the fuel tank.

Miscellaneous

Brake fluid is specially formulated hydraulic fluid that can withstand the heat and pressure encountered in brake systems. Care must be taken so this fluid does not come in contact with painted surfaces or plastics. An opened container should always be resealed to prevent contamination by water or dirt.

Weatherstrip adhesive is used to bond weatherstripping around doors, windows and luggage compartment lids. It is sometimes used to attach trim pieces.

Undercoating is a petroleum-based, tar-like substance that is designed to protect metal surfaces on the underside of the vehicle from corrosion. It also acts as a sound-deadening agent by insulating the bottom of the vehicle.

Waxes and polishes are used to help protect painted and plated surfaces from the weather. Different types of paint may require the use of different types of wax and polish. Some polishes utilise a chemical or abrasive cleaner to help remove the top layer of oxidised (dull) paint on older vehicles. In recent years many non-wax polishes that contain a wide variety of chemicals such as polymers and silicones have been introduced. These non-wax polishes are usually easier to apply and last longer than conventional waxes and polishes.

Safety first!

Regardless of how enthusiastic you may be about getting on with the job at hand, take the time to ensure that your safety is not jeopardized. A moment's lack of attention can result in an accident, as can failure to observe certain simple safety precautions. The possibility of an accident will always exist, and the following points should not be considered a comprehensive list of all dangers. Rather, they are intended to make you aware of the risks and to encourage a safety conscious approach to all work you carry out on your vehicle.

Essential DOs and DON'Ts

DON'T rely on a jack when working under the vehicle. Always use approved jackstands to support the weight of the vehicle and place them under the recommended lift or support points.

DON'T attempt to loosen extremely tight fasteners (i.e. wheel lug nuts) while the vehicle is on a jack - it may fall.

DON'T start the engine without first making sure that the transmission is in Neutral (or Park where applicable) and the parking brake is set.

DON'T remove the radiator cap from a hot cooling system - let it cool or cover it with a cloth and release the pressure gradually.

DON'T attempt to drain the engine oil until you are sure it has cooled to the point that it will not burn you.

DON'T touch any part of the engine or exhaust system until it has cooled sufficiently to avoid burns.

DON'T siphon toxic liquids such as gasoline, antifreeze and brake fluid by mouth, or allow them to remain on your skin.

DON'T inhale brake lining dust - it is potentially hazardous (see *Asbestos* below).

DON'T allow spilled oil or grease to remain on the floor - wipe it up before someone slips on it.

DON'T use loose fitting wrenches or other tools which may slip and cause injury.

DON'T push on wrenches when loosening or tightening nuts or bolts. Always try to pull the wrench toward you. If the situation calls for pushing the wrench away, push with an open hand to avoid scraped knuckles if the wrench should slip.

DON'T attempt to lift a heavy component alone - get someone to help you.

DON'T *rush or take unsafe shortcuts to finish a job.*

DON'T allow children or animals in or around the vehicle while you are working on it.

DO wear eye protection when using power tools such as a drill, sander, bench grinder, etc. and when working under a vehicle.

DO keep loose clothing and long hair well out of the way of moving parts.

DO make sure that any hoist used has a safe working load rating adequate for the job.

DO get someone to check on you periodically when working alone on a vehicle.

DO carry out work in a logical sequence and make sure that everything is correctly assembled and tightened.

DO keep chemicals and fluids tightly capped and out of the reach of children and pets.

DO remember that your vehicle's safety affects that of yourself and others. If in doubt on any point, get professional advice.

Steering, suspension and brakes

These systems are essential to driving safety, so make sure you have a qualified shop or individual check your work. Also, compressed suspension springs can cause injury if released suddenly - be sure to use a spring compressor.

Airbags

Airbags are explosive devices that can CAUSE injury if they deploy while you're working on the vehicle. Follow the manufacturer's instructions to disable the airbag whenever you're working in the vicinity of airbag components.

Asbestos

Certain friction, insulating, sealing, and other products - such as brake linings, brake bands, clutch linings, torque converters, gaskets, etc. - may contain asbestos or other hazardous friction material. Extreme care must be taken to avoid inhalation of dust from such products, since it is hazardous to health. If in doubt, assume that they do contain asbestos.

Fire

Remember at all times that gasoline is highly flammable. Never smoke or have any kind of open flame around when working on a vehicle. But the risk does not end there. A spark caused by an electrical short circuit, by two metal surfaces contacting each other, or even by static electricity built up in your body under certain conditions, can ignite gasoline vapors, which in a confined space are highly explosive. Do not, under any circumstances, use gasoline for cleaning parts. Use an approved safety solvent.

Always disconnect the battery ground (-) cable at the battery before working on any part of the fuel system or electrical system. Never risk spilling fuel on a hot engine or exhaust component. It is strongly recommended that a fire extinguisher suitable for use on fuel and electrical fires be kept handy in the garage or workshop at all times. Never try to extinguish a fuel or electrical fire with water.

Fumes

Certain fumes are highly toxic and can quickly cause unconsciousness and even death if inhaled to any extent. Gasoline vapor falls into this category, as do the vapors from some cleaning solvents. Any draining or pouring of such volatile fluids should be done in a well ventilated area.

When using cleaning fluids and solvents, read the instructions on the container carefully. Never use materials from unmarked containers.

Never run the engine in an enclosed space, such as a garage. Exhaust fumes contain carbon monoxide, which is extremely poisonous. If you need to run the engine, always do so in the open air, or at least have the rear of the vehicle outside the work area.

The battery

Never create a spark or allow a bare light bulb near a battery. They normally give off a certain amount of hydrogen gas, which is highly explosive.

Always disconnect the battery ground (-) cable at the battery before working on the fuel or electrical systems.

If possible, loosen the filler caps or cover when charging the battery from an external source (this does not apply to sealed or maintenance-free batteries). Do not charge at an excessive rate or the battery may burst.

Take care when adding water to a non maintenance-free battery and when carrying a battery. The electrolyte, even when diluted, is very corrosive and should not be allowed to contact clothing or skin.

Always wear eye protection when cleaning the battery to prevent the caustic deposits from entering your eyes.

Household current

When using an electric power tool, inspection light, etc., which operates on household current, always make sure that the tool is correctly connected to its plug and that, where necessary, it is properly grounded. Do not use such items in damp conditions and, again, do not create a spark or apply excessive heat in the vicinity of fuel or fuel vapor.

Secondary ignition system voltage

A severe electric shock can result from touching certain parts of the ignition system (such as the spark plug wires) when the engine is running or being cranked, particularly if components are damp or the insulation is defective. In the case of an electronic ignition system, the secondary system voltage is much higher and could prove fatal.

Hydrofluoric acid

This extremely corrosive acid is formed when certain types of synthetic rubber, found in some O-rings, oil seals, fuel hoses, etc. are exposed to temperatures above 750-degrees F (400-degrees C). The rubber changes into a charred or sticky substance containing the acid. *Once formed, the acid remains dangerous for years. If it gets onto the skin, it may be necessary to amputate the limb concerned.*

When dealing with a vehicle which has suffered a fire, or with components salvaged from such a vehicle, wear protective gloves and discard them after use.

Conversion factors

Length (distance)
Inches (in)	X 25.4	= Millimetres (mm)	X 0.0394	= Inches (in)
Feet (ft)	X 0.305	= Metres (m)	X 3.281	= Feet (ft)
Miles	X 1.609	= Kilometres (km)	X 0.621	= Miles

Volume (capacity)
Cubic inches (cu in; in^3)	X 16.387	= Cubic centimetres (cc; cm^3)	X 0.061	= Cubic inches (cu in; in^3)
Imperial pints (Imp pt)	X 0.568	= Litres (l)	X 1.76	= Imperial pints (Imp pt)
Imperial quarts (Imp qt)	X 1.137	= Litres (l)	X 0.88	= Imperial quarts (Imp qt)
Imperial quarts (Imp qt)	X 1.201	= US quarts (US qt)	X 0.833	= Imperial quarts (Imp qt)
US quarts (US qt)	X 0.946	= Litres (l)	X 1.057	= US quarts (US qt)
Imperial gallons (Imp gal)	X 4.546	= Litres (l)	X 0.22	= Imperial gallons (Imp gal)
Imperial gallons (Imp gal)	X 1.201	= US gallons (US gal)	X 0.833	= Imperial gallons (Imp gal)
US gallons (US gal)	X 3.785	= Litres (l)	X 0.264	= US gallons (US gal)

Mass (weight)
Ounces (oz)	X 28.35	= Grams (g)	X 0.035	= Ounces (oz)
Pounds (lb)	X 0.454	= Kilograms (kg)	X 2.205	= Pounds (lb)

Force
Ounces-force (ozf; oz)	X 0.278	= Newtons (N)	X 3.6	= Ounces-force (ozf; oz)
Pounds-force (lbf; lb)	X 4.448	= Newtons (N)	X 0.225	= Pounds-force (lbf; lb)
Newtons (N)	X 0.1	= Kilograms-force (kgf; kg)	X 9.81	= Newtons (N)

Pressure
Pounds-force per square inch (psi; lbf/in^2; lb/in^2)	X 0.070	= Kilograms-force per square centimetre (kgf/cm^2; kg/cm^2)	X 14.223	= Pounds-force per square inch (psi; lbf/in^2; lb/in^2)
Pounds-force per square inch (psi; lbf/in^2; lb/in^2)	X 0.068	= Atmospheres (atm)	X 14.696	= Pounds-force per square inch (psi; lbf/in^2; lb/in^2)
Pounds-force per square inch (psi; lbf/in^2; lb/in^2)	X 0.069	= Bars	X 14.5	= Pounds-force per square inch (psi; lbf/in^2; lb/in^2)
Pounds-force per square inch (psi; lbf/in^2; lb/in^2)	X 6.895	= Kilopascals (kPa)	X 0.145	= Pounds-force per square inch (psi; lbf/in^2; lb/in^2)
Kilopascals (kPa)	X 0.01	= Kilograms-force per square centimetre (kgf/cm^2; kg/cm^2)	X 98.1	= Kilopascals (kPa)

Torque (moment of force)
Pounds-force inches (lbf in; lb in)	X 1.152	= Kilograms-force centimetre (kgf cm; kg cm)	X 0.868	= Pounds-force inches (lbf in; lb in)
Pounds-force inches (lbf in; lb in)	X 0.113	= Newton metres (Nm)	X 8.85	= Pounds-force inches (lbf in; lb in)
Pounds-force inches (lbf in; lb in)	X 0.083	= Pounds-force feet (lbf ft; lb ft)	X 12	= Pounds-force inches (lbf in; lb in)
Pounds-force feet (lbf ft; lb ft)	X 0.138	= Kilograms-force metres (kgf m; kg m)	X 7.233	= Pounds-force feet (lbf ft; lb ft)
Pounds-force feet (lbf ft; lb ft)	X 1.356	= Newton metres (Nm)	X 0.738	= Pounds-force feet (lbf ft; lb ft)
Newton metres (Nm)	X 0.102	= Kilograms-force metres (kgf m; kg m)	X 9.804	= Newton metres (Nm)

Vacuum
Inches mercury (in. Hg)	X 3.377	= Kilopascals (kPa)	X 0.2961	= Inches mercury
Inches mercury (in. Hg)	X 25.4	= Millimetres mercury (mm Hg)	X 0.0394	= Inches mercury

Power
Horsepower (hp)	X 745.7	= Watts (W)	X 0.0013	= Horsepower (hp)

Velocity (speed)
Miles per hour (miles/hr; mph)	X 1.609	= Kilometres per hour (km/hr; kph)	X 0.621	= Miles per hour (miles/hr; mph)

*Fuel consumption**
Miles per gallon, Imperial (mpg)	X 0.354	= Kilometres per litre (km/l)	X 2.825	= Miles per gallon, Imperial (mpg)
Miles per gallon, US (mpg)	X 0.425	= Kilometres per litre (km/l)	X 2.352	= Miles per gallon, US (mpg)

Temperature
Degrees Fahrenheit = (°C x 1.8) + 32   Degrees Celsius (Degrees Centigrade; °C) = (°F - 32) x 0.56

*It is common practice to convert from miles per gallon (mpg) to litres/100 kilometres (l/100km), where mpg (Imperial) x l/100 km = 282 and mpg (US) x l/100 km = 235

DECIMALS to MILLIMETRES

Decimal	mm	Decimal	mm
0.001	0.0254	0.500	12.7000
0.002	0.0508	0.510	12.9540
0.003	0.0762	0.520	13.2080
0.004	0.1016	0.530	13.4620
0.005	0.1270	0.540	13.7160
0.006	0.1524	0.550	13.9700
0.007	0.1778	0.560	14.2240
0.008	0.2032	0.570	14.4780
0.009	0.2286	0.580	14.7320
		0.590	14.9860
0.010	0.2540		
0.020	0.5080		
0.030	0.7620		
0.040	1.0160	0.600	15.2400
0.050	1.2700	0.610	15.4940
0.060	1.5240	0.620	15.7480
0.070	1.7780	0.630	16.0020
0.080	2.0320	0.640	16.2560
0.090	2.2860	0.650	16.5100
		0.660	16.7640
0.100	2.5400	0.670	17.0180
0.110	2.7940	0.680	17.2720
0.120	3.0480	0.690	17.5260
0.130	3.3020		
0.140	3.5560		
0.150	3.8100		
0.160	4.0640	0.700	17.7800
0.170	4.3180	0.710	18.0340
0.180	4.5720	0.720	18.2880
0.190	4.8260	0.730	18.5420
		0.740	18.7960
0.200	5.0800	0.750	19.0500
0.210	5.3340	0.760	19.3040
0.220	5.5880	0.770	19.5580
0.230	5.8420	0.780	19.8120
0.240	6.0960	0.790	20.0660
0.250	6.3500		
0.260	6.6040		
0.270	6.8580	0.800	20.3200
0.280	7.1120	0.810	20.5740
0.290	7.3660	0.820	21.8280
		0.830	21.0820
0.300	7.6200	0.840	21.3360
0.310	7.8740	0.850	21.5900
0.320	8.1280	0.860	21.8440
0.330	8.3820	0.870	22.0980
0.340	8.6360	0.880	22.3520
0.350	8.8900	0.890	22.6060
0.360	9.1440		
0.370	9.3980		
0.380	9.6520		
0.390	9.9060		
		0.900	22.8600
0.400	10.1600	0.910	23.1140
0.410	10.4140	0.920	23.3680
0.420	10.6680	0.930	23.6220
0.430	10.9220	0.940	23.8760
0.440	11.1760	0.950	24.1300
0.450	11.4300	0.960	24.3840
0.460	11.6840	0.970	24.6380
0.470	11.9380	0.980	24.8920
0.480	12.1920	0.990	25.1460
0.490	12.4460	1.000	25.4000

FRACTIONS to DECIMALS to MILLIMETRES

Fraction	Decimal	mm	Fraction	Decimal	mm
1/64	0.0156	0.3969	33/64	0.5156	13.0969
1/32	0.0312	0.7938	17/32	0.5312	13.4938
3/64	0.0469	1.1906	35/64	0.5469	13.8906
1/16	0.0625	1.5875	9/16	0.5625	14.2875
5/64	0.0781	1.9844	37/64	0.5781	14.6844
3/32	0.0938	2.3812	19/32	0.5938	15.0812
7/64	0.1094	2.7781	39/64	0.6094	15.4781
1/8	0.1250	3.1750	5/8	0.6250	15.8750
9/64	0.1406	3.5719	41/64	0.6406	16.2719
5/32	0.1562	3.9688	21/32	0.6562	16.6688
11/64	0.1719	4.3656	43/64	0.6719	17.0656
3/16	0.1875	4.7625	11/16	0.6875	17.4625
13/64	0.2031	5.1594	45/64	0.7031	17.8594
7/32	0.2188	5.5562	23/32	0.7188	18.2562
15/64	0.2344	5.9531	47/64	0.7344	18.6531
1/4	0.2500	6.3500	3/4	0.7500	19.0500
17/64	0.2656	6.7469	49/64	0.7656	19.4469
9/32	0.2812	7.1438	25/32	0.7812	19.8438
19/64	0.2969	7.5406	51/64	0.7969	20.2406
5/16	0.3125	7.9375	13/16	0.8125	20.6375
21/64	0.3281	8.3344	53/64	0.8281	21.0344
11/32	0.3438	8.7312	27/32	0.8438	21.4312
23/64	0.3594	9.1281	55/64	0.8594	21.8281
3/8	0.3750	9.5250	7/8	0.8750	22.2250
25/64	0.3906	9.9219	57/64	0.8906	22.6219
13/32	0.4062	10.3188	29/32	0.9062	23.0188
27/64	0.4219	10.7156	59/64	0.9219	23.4156
7/16	0.4375	11.1125	15/16	0.9375	23.8125
29/64	0.4531	11.5094	61/64	0.9531	24.2094
15/32	0.4688	11.9062	31/32	0.9688	24.6062
31/64	0.4844	12.3031	63/64	0.9844	25.0031
1/2	0.5000	12.7000	1	1.0000	25.4000

Troubleshooting

Contents

Symptom	Section
Engine and performance	
Alternator light fails to come on when key is turned on	13
Alternator light stays on	12
Battery will not hold a charge	11
Engine backfires	18
Engine diesel (continues to run) after being turned off	21
Engine hard to start when cold	4
Engine hard to start when hot	5
Engine lacks power	17
Engine idles erratically	8
Engine misses at idle speed	9
Engine misses throughout driving speed range	4
Engine rotates but will not start	2
Engine stalls	16
Engine starts but stops immediately	7
Engine surges while holding accelerator steady	19
Engine will not rotate when attempting to start	1
Excessive fuel consumption	24
Excessively high idle speed	10
Excessive oil consumption	23
Fuel odour	25
Hesitation or stumble during acceleration	15
Low oil pressure	22
Miscellaneous engine noises	26
Pinging or knocking engine sounds when engine is under load	20
Starter motor noisy or engages roughly	6
Starter motor operates without turning engine	3
Cooling system	
Abnormal coolant loss	31
Corrosion	33
External coolant leakage	29
Internal coolant leakage	30
Overcooling	28
Overheating	27
Poor coolant circulation	32
Clutch	
Clutch pedal stays on floor when disengaged	39
Clutch slips (engine speed increases with no increase in vehicle speed)	35
Fails to release (pedal pressed to the floor - shift lever does not move freely in and out of Reverse)	34
Grabbing (chattering) as clutch is engaged	36
Squeal or rumble with clutch disengaged (pedal depressed)	38
Squeal or rumble with clutch engaged (pedal released)	37
Manual transmission	
Difficulty engaging gears	45
Noise occurs while shifting gears	46
Noisy in all gears	41
Noisy in Neutral with engine running	40
Noisy in one particular gear	42
Oil leaks	44
Slips out of gear	43
Automatic transmission	
Engine will start in gears other than Park or Neutral	50

Symptom	Section
Fluid leakage	47
General shift mechanism problems	48
Transmission slips, shifts rough, is noisy or has no drive in forward or Reverse gears	51
Transmission will not downshift with the accelerator pedal pressed to the floor	49
Driveshaft	
Knock or clunk when transmission is under initial load (just after transmission is put into gear)	53
Leaks at front of driveshaft	52
Metallic grating sound consistent with vehicle speed	54
Scraping noise	56
Vibration	55
Whining or whistling noise	57
Rear axle and differential	
Knocking sound when starting or shifting gears	59
Noise - same when in drive as when vehicle is coasting	58
Noise when turning	60
Oil leaks	62
Vibration	61
Transfer case	
Difficult shifting	64
Gear jumping out of mesh	63
Noise	65
Brakes	
Brake pedal feels spongy when depressed	69
Brake pedal pulsates during brake application	72
Brakes drag (indicated by sluggish engine performance or wheels being very hot after driving)	73
Excessive brake pedal travel	68
Excessive effort required to stop vehicle	70
Noise (high-pitched squeal)	67
Pedal travels to the floor with little resistance	71
Rear brakes lock up under heavy brake application	75
Rear brakes lock up under light brake application	74
Vehicle pulls to one side during braking	66
Suspension and steering	
Excessively stiff steering	80
Excessive pitching and/or rolling around corners or during braking	78
Excessive play in steering	81
Excessive tyre wear (not specific to one area)	87
Excessive tyre wear on inside edge	89
Excessive tyre wear on outside edge	88
Lack of power assistance	82
Miscellaneous noises	86
Noisy power steering pump	85
Shimmy, shake or vibration	77
Steering effort not the same in both directions (power system)	84
Steering wheel fails to return to straight-ahead position	83
Tyre tread worn in one place	90
Vehicle pulls to one side	76
Wandering or general instability	79

Troubleshooting   0-23

This Section provides an easy reference guide to the more common problems that may occur during the operation of your vehicle. Various symptoms and their probable causes are grouped under headings denoting components or systems, such as Engine, Cooling system, etc. They also refer to the Chapter and/or Section that deals with the problem.

Remember that successful troubleshooting isn't a mysterious black art practiced only by professional mechanics; it's simply the result of knowledge combined with an intelligent, systematic approach to a problem. Always use a process of elimination starting with the simplest solution and working through to the most complex - and never overlook the obvious. Anyone can run the fuel tank dry or leave the lights on overnight, so don't assume that you're exempt from such oversights.

Finally, always establish a clear idea why a problem has occurred and take steps to ensure that it doesn't happen again. If the electrical system fails because of a poor connection, check all other connections in the system to make sure they don't fail as well. If a particular fuse continues to blow, find out why - don't just go on renewing fuses. Remember, failure of a small component can often be indicative of potential failure or incorrect functioning of a more important component or system.

Engine and performance

1 Engine will not rotate when attempting to start

1   Battery terminal connections loose or corroded. Check the cable terminals at the battery; tighten cable clamp and/or clean off corrosion as necessary (see Chapter 1).
2   Battery discharged or faulty. If the cable ends are clean and tight on the battery posts, turn the key to the On position and switch on the headlights or windscreen wipers. If they won't run, the battery is discharged.
3   Automatic transmission not engaged in park (P) or Neutral (N).
4   Broken, loose or disconnected wires in the starting circuit. Inspect all wires and connectors at the battery, starter solenoid and ignition switch (on steering column).
5   Starter motor pinion jammed in flywheel ring gear. If manual transmission, place transmission in gear and rock the vehicle to manually turn the engine. Remove starter (Chapter 5) and inspect pinion and flywheel (Chapter 2) at earliest convenience.
6   Starter solenoid faulty (Chapter 5).
7   Starter motor faulty (Chapter 5).
8   Ignition switch faulty (Chapter 12).
9   Engine seized. Try to turn the crankshaft with a large socket and breaker bar on the pulley bolt.

2 Engine rotates but will not start

1   Fuel tank empty.
2   Battery discharged (engine rotates slowly). Check the operation of electrical components as described in previous Section.
3   Battery terminal connections loose or corroded. See previous Section.
4   Fuel not reaching fuel injector. Check for clogged fuel filter or lines and defective fuel pump. Also make sure the tank vent lines are not clogged (Chapter 4).
5   Low cylinder compression. Check as described in Chapter 2.
6   Valve clearances not properly adjusted (Chapter 1).
7   Water in fuel. Drain tank and fill with new fuel.
8   Defective ignition coil (Chapter 5).
9   Dirty or clogged fuel injector. (Chapter 4).
10 Wet or damaged ignition components (Chapters 1 and 5).
11 Worn, faulty or incorrectly gapped spark plugs (Chapter 1).
12 Broken, loose or disconnected wires in the starting circuit (see previous Section).
13 Broken, loose or disconnected wires at the ignition coil or faulty coil (Chapter 5).
14 Timing chain or belt failure or wear affecting valve timing (Chapter 2).
15 Diesel fuel cut-off solenoid faulty.
16 Diesel fuel contamination. Refer to Chapter 4.
17 Defective diesel injection pump.
18 Incorrect diesel injector pump timing.

3 Starter motor operates without turning engine

1   Starter pinion sticking. Remove the starter (Chapter 5) and inspect.
2   Starter pinion or flywheel/driveplate teeth worn or broken. Remove the inspection cover and inspect.

4 Engine hard to start when cold

1   Battery discharged or low. Check as described in Chapter 1.
2   Fuel not reaching the fuel injectors. Check the fuel filter, lines and fuel pump (Chapters 1 and 4).
3   Defective spark plugs (Chapter 1).
4   Diesel pre-heating system not operating properly.

5 Engine hard to start when hot

1   Air filter dirty (Chapter 1).
2   Fuel not reaching the fuel injectors (see Section 4). Check for a vapour lock situation, brought about by clogged fuel tank vent lines.
3   Bad engine earthing point connection.
4   Air in the fuel system, defective diesel injection pump or pump timing.

6 Starter motor noisy or engages roughly

1   Pinion or flywheel/driveplate teeth worn or broken. Remove the inspection cover on the left side of the engine and inspect.
2   Starter motor mounting bolts loose or missing.

7 Engine starts but stops immediately

1   Loose or damaged wire harness connections at coil(s) or alternator.
2   Inlet manifold vacuum leaks. Make sure all mounting bolts/nuts are tight and all vacuum hoses connected to the manifold are attached properly and in good condition.
3   Insufficient fuel flow (see Chapter 4).
4   Air in the fuel system, defective diesel injection pump or pump timing.

8 Engine idles erratically

1   Vacuum leaks. Check mounting bolts at the inlet manifold for tightness. Make sure that all vacuum hoses are connected and in good condition. Use a stethoscope or a length of fuel hose held against your ear to listen for vacuum leaks while the engine is running. A hissing sound will be heard. A soapy water solution will also detect leaks. Check the inlet manifold gasket surfaces.
2   Leaking EGR valve or clogged PCV valve (see Chapters 1 and 6).
3   Air filter clogged (Chapter 1).
4   Fuel pump not delivering sufficient fuel (Chapter 4).
5   Leaking head gasket. Perform a cylinder compression check (Chapter 2).
6   Timing chain or belt worn (Chapter 2).
7   Camshaft lobes worn (Chapter 2).
8   Valve clearance out of adjustment.
9   Valves burned or otherwise leaking (Chapter 2).
10 Ignition timing out of adjustment (Chapter 1).
11 Ignition system not operating properly (Chapters 1 and 5).
12 Thermostatic air cleaner not operating properly (Chapter 1).
13 Dirty or clogged injector(s).
14 Idle speed out of adjustment.
15 Air in the fuel system, defective diesel injection pump or pump timing.

Troubleshooting

9 Engine misses at idle speed

1 Spark plugs faulty or not gapped properly (Chapter 1).
2 Faulty spark plug wires (Chapter 1).
3 Short circuits in ignition, coil or spark plug wires.
4 Sticking or faulty emissions systems (see Chapter 6).
5 Clogged fuel filter and/or foreign matter in fuel. Remove the fuel filter (Chapter 1) and inspect.
6 Vacuum leaks at inlet manifold or hose connections. Check as described in Section 8.
7 Incorrect ignition timing.
8 Low or uneven cylinder compression. Check as described in Chapter 2.
9 Choke not operating properly (Chapter 1).
10 Clogged or dirty fuel injectors (Chapter 4).
11 Air in the fuel system, defective diesel injection pump or pump timing.

10 Excessively high idle speed

1 Sticking throttle linkage (Chapter 4).
2 Idle speed incorrectly adjusted.
3 Valve clearances incorrectly adjusted.

11 Battery will not hold a charge

1 Alternator drivebelt defective or not adjusted properly (Chapter 1).
2 Battery cables loose or corroded (Chapter 1).
3 Alternator not charging properly (Chapter 5).
4 Loose, broken or faulty wires in the charging circuit (Chapter 5).
5 Short circuit causing a continuous drain on the battery.
6 Battery defective internally.

12 Alternator light stays on

1 Fault in alternator or charging circuit (Chapter 5).
2 Alternator drivebelt defective or not properly adjusted (Chapter 1).

13 Alternator light fails to come on when key is turned on

1 Faulty bulb (Chapter 12).
2 Defective alternator (Chapter 5).
3 Fault in the printed circuit, dash wiring or bulb holder (Chapter 12).

14 Engine misses throughout driving speed range

1 Fuel filter clogged and/or impurities in the fuel system. Check fuel filter (Chapter 1) or clean system (Chapter 4).
2 Faulty or incorrectly gapped spark plugs (Chapter 1).
3 Incorrect ignition timing.
4 Defective spark plug wires (Chapter 1).
5 Emissions system components faulty (Chapter 6).
6 Low or uneven cylinder compression pressures. Check as described in Chapter 2.
7 Weak or faulty ignition coil(s) (Chapter 5).
8 Weak or faulty ignition system (Chapter 5).
9 Vacuum leaks at inlet manifold or vacuum hoses (see Section 8).
10 Dirty or clogged fuel injector (Chapter 4).
11 Leaky EGR valve (Chapter 6).
12 Idle speed out of adjustment.
13 Air in the fuel system, defective diesel injection pump or pump timing.

15 Hesitation or stumble during acceleration

1 Ignition timing incorrect.
2 Ignition system not operating properly (Chapter 5).
3 Dirty or clogged fuel injector (Chapter 4).
4 Low fuel pressure. Check for proper operation of the fuel pump and for restrictions in the fuel filter and lines (Chapter 4).
5 Air in the fuel system, defective diesel injection pump or pump timing.

16 Engine stalls

1 Idle speed incorrect (Chapter 1).
2 Fuel filter clogged and/or water and impurities in the fuel system (Chapter 1).
3 Emissions system components faulty (Chapter 6).
4 Faulty or incorrectly gapped spark plugs (Chapter 1). Also check the spark plug wires (Chapter 1).
5 Vacuum leak at the carburettor, inlet manifold or vacuum hoses. Check as described in Section 8.
6 Valve clearances incorrect.
7 Air in the fuel system, defective diesel injection pump or pump timing.

17 Engine lacks power

1 Incorrect ignition timing (Chapter 1).
2 Faulty or incorrectly gapped spark plugs (Chapter 1).
3 Air filter dirty (Chapter 1).
4 Faulty ignition coil (Chapter 5).
5 Brakes binding (Chapters 1 and 10).
6 Automatic transmission fluid level incorrect, causing slippage (Chapter 1).
7 Clutch slipping (Chapter 8).
8 Fuel filter clogged and/or impurities in the fuel system (Chapters 1 and 4).
9 EGR system not functioning properly (Chapter 6).
10 Use of sub-standard fuel. Fill tank with proper octane fuel.
11 Low or uneven cylinder compression pressures. Check as described in Chapter 2.
12 Air leak at inlet manifold (check as described in Section 8).
13 Incorrect diesel injection pump timing.

18 Engine backfires

1 EGR system not functioning properly (Chapter 6).
2 Ignition timing incorrect.
3 Thermostatic air cleaner system not operating properly (Chapter 6).
4 Vacuum leak (refer to Section 8).
5 Valve clearances incorrect.
6 Damaged valve springs or sticking valves (Chapter 2).
7 Intake air leak (see Section 8).
8 Incorrect diesel injection pump timing.

19 Engine surges while holding accelerator steady

1 Intake air leak (see Section 8).
2 Fuel pump not working properly (Chapter 4).
3 Internal diesel injection pump fault or air in the fuel system (Chapter 4).

20 Pinging or knocking engine sounds when engine is under load

1 Incorrect grade of fuel. Fill tank with fuel of the proper octane rating.
2 Ignition timing incorrect.
3 Carbon build-up in combustion chambers. Remove cylinder head(s) and clean combustion chambers (Chapter 2).
4 Incorrect spark plugs (Chapter 1).
5 Incorrect diesel injection pump timing.

21 Engine continues to run after being turned off

1 Idle speed too high.
2 Ignition timing incorrect.
3 Incorrect spark plug heat range (Chapter 1).
4 Intake air leak (see Section 8).
5 Carbon build-up in combustion chambers. Remove the cylinder head(s) and clean the combustion chambers (Chapter 2).
6 Valves sticking (Chapter 2).

Troubleshooting 0-25

7 Valve clearances incorrect.
8 EGR system not operating properly (Chapter 6).
9 Fuel shut-off system not operating properly (Chapter 6).
10 Check for causes of overheating (Section 27).
11 Faulty diesel fuel cut-off solenoid.

22 Low oil pressure

1 Improper grade of oil.
2 Oil pump worn or damaged (Chapter 2).
3 Engine overheating (refer to Section 27).
4 Clogged oil filter (Chapter 1).
5 Clogged oil strainer (Chapter 2).
6 Oil pressure gauge not working properly (Chapter 2).

23 Excessive oil consumption

1 Loose oil drain plug.
2 Loose bolts or damaged oil sump gasket (Chapter 2).
3 Loose bolts or damaged front cover gasket (Chapter 2).
4 Front or rear crankshaft oil seal leaking (Chapter 2).
5 Loose bolts or damaged rocker arm cover gasket (Chapter 2).
6 Loose oil filter (Chapter 1).
7 Loose or damaged oil pressure switch (Chapter 2).
8 Pistons and cylinders excessively worn (Chapter 2).
9 Piston rings not refitted correctly on pistons (Chapter 2).
10 Worn or damaged piston rings (Chapter 2).
11 Inlet and/or exhaust valve oil seals worn or damaged (Chapter 2).
12 Worn valve stems.
13 Worn or damaged valves/guides (Chapter 2).

24 Excessive fuel consumption

1 Dirty or clogged air filter element (Chapter 1).
2 Incorrect ignition timing.
3 Incorrect idle speed.
4 Low tyre pressure or incorrect tyre size (Chapter 11).
5 Fuel leakage. Check all connections, lines and components in the fuel system (Chapter 4).
6 Choke not operating properly (Chapter 1).
7 Dirty or clogged carburettor jets or fuel injectors (Chapter 4).
8 Air in the fuel system, defective diesel injection pump or pump timing.

25 Fuel odour

1 Fuel leakage. Check all connections, lines and components in the fuel system (Chapter 4).
2 Fuel tank overfilled. Fill only to automatic shut-off.
3 Charcoal canister filter in Evaporative Emissions Control system clogged (Chapter 1).
4 Vapour leaks from Evaporative Emissions Control system lines (Chapter 6).

26 Miscellaneous engine noises

1 A strong dull noise that becomes more rapid as the engine accelerates indicates worn or damaged crankshaft bearings or an unevenly worn crankshaft. To pinpoint the trouble spot on petrol models, remove the spark plug wire from one plug at a time and crank the engine over. If the noise stops, the cylinder with the removed plug wire indicates the problem area. Renew the bearing and/or service or renew the crankshaft (Chapter 2).
2 A similar (yet slightly higher pitched) noise to the crankshaft knocking described in the previous paragraph, that becomes more rapid as the engine accelerates, indicates worn or damaged connecting rod bearings (Chapter 2). The procedure for locating the problem cylinder on petrol models is the same as described in Paragraph 1.
3 An overlapping metallic noise that increases in intensity as the engine speed increases, yet diminishes as the engine warms up indicates abnormal piston and cylinder wear (Chapter 2). To locate the problem cylinder on petrol models, use the procedure described in Paragraph 1.
4 A rapid clicking noise that becomes faster as the engine accelerates indicates a worn piston pin or piston pin hole. This sound will happen each time the piston hits the highest and lowest points in the stroke (Chapter 2). The procedure for locating the problem piston on petrol models is described in Paragraph 1.
5 A metallic clicking noise coming from the water pump indicates worn or damaged water pump bearings or pump. Renew the water pump with a new one (Chapter 3).
6 A rapid tapping sound or clicking sound that becomes faster as the engine speed increases indicates valve 'tapping' or improperly adjusted valve clearances. This can be identified by holding one end of a section of hose to your ear and placing the other end at different spots along the rocker arm cover. The point where the sound is loudest indicates the problem valve. Adjust the valve clearance (Chapter 1). If the problem persists, you likely have a collapsed valve lifter or other damaged valve train component. Changing the engine oil and adding a high-viscosity oil treatment will sometimes cure a stuck lifter problem. If the problem still persists, the lifters and rocker arms must be removed for inspection (see Chapter 2).
7 A steady metallic rattling or rapping sound coming from the area of the timing chain cover indicates a worn, damaged or out-of-adjustment timing chain. Service or renew the chain and related components (Chapters 1 and 2).

Cooling system

27 Overheating

1 Insufficient coolant in system (Chapter 1).
2 Drivebelt defective or not adjusted properly (Chapter 1).
3 Radiator core blocked or radiator grille dirty or restricted (Chapter 3).
4 Thermostat faulty (Chapter 3).
5 Fan not functioning properly (Chapter 3).
6 Radiator cap not maintaining proper pressure. Have cap pressure tested by a repair shop.
7 Ignition timing incorrect.
8 Defective water pump (Chapter 3).
9 Improper grade of engine oil.
10 Inaccurate temperature gauge (Chapter 12).

28 Overcooling

1 Thermostat faulty (Chapter 3).
2 Inaccurate temperature gauge (Chapter 12).

29 External coolant leakage

1 Deteriorated or damaged hoses. Loose clamps at hose connections (Chapter 1).
2 Water pump seals defective. If this is the case, water will drip from the weep hole in the water pump body (Chapter 3).
3 Leakage from radiator core or coolant reservoir. This will require the radiator to be professionally repaired (see Chapter 3 for removal procedures).
4 Engine drain plugs or water jacket freeze plugs leaking (see Chapters 1 and 2).
5 Leak from coolant temperature switch (Chapter 3).
6 Leak from damaged gaskets or small cracks (Chapter 2).
7 Damaged head gasket. This can be verified by checking the condition of the engine oil as noted in Section 30.

30 Internal coolant leakage

Note: *Internal coolant leaks can usually be detected by examining the oil. Check the dipstick and inside the rocker arm cover for water deposits and an oil consistency like that of a milkshake.*

1   Leaking cylinder head gasket. Have the system pressure tested or remove the cylinder head (Chapter 2) and inspect.
2   Cracked cylinder bore or cylinder head. Dismantle engine and inspect (Chapter 2).
3   Loose cylinder head bolts (tighten as described in Chapter 2).

31 Abnormal coolant loss

1   Overfilling system (Chapter 1).
2   Coolant boiling away due to overheating (see causes in Section 27).
3   Internal or external leakage (see Sections 29 and 30).
4   Faulty radiator cap. Have the cap pressure tested.
5   Cooling system being pressurised by engine compression. This could be due to a cracked head or block or leaking head gasket(s).

32 Poor coolant circulation

1   Inoperative water pump. A quick test is to pinch the top radiator hose closed with your hand while the engine is idling, then release it. You should feel a surge of coolant if the pump is working properly (Chapter 3).
2   Restriction in cooling system. Drain, flush and refill the system (Chapter 1). If necessary, remove the radiator (Chapter 3) and have it reverse flushed or professionally cleaned.
3   Loose water pump drivebelt (Chapter 1).
4   Thermostat sticking (Chapter 3).
5   Insufficient coolant (Chapter 1).

33 Corrosion

1   Excessive impurities in the water. Soft, clean water is recommended. Distilled or rainwater is satisfactory.
2   Insufficient antifreeze solution (refer to Chapter 1 for the proper ratio of water to antifreeze).
3   Infrequent flushing and draining of system. Regular flushing of the cooling system should be carried out at the specified intervals as described in (Chapter 1).

Clutch

Note: *All clutch related service information is located in Chapter 8, unless otherwise noted.*

34 Fails to release (pedal pressed to the floor - shift lever does not move freely in and out of Reverse)

1   Freeplay incorrectly adjusted (see Chapter 1).
2   Clutch contaminated with oil. Remove clutch plate and inspect.
3   Clutch plate warped, distorted or otherwise damaged.
4   Diaphragm spring fatigued. Remove clutch cover/pressure plate assembly and inspect.
5   Leakage of fluid from clutch hydraulic system. Inspect master cylinder, operating cylinder and connecting lines.
6   Air in clutch hydraulic system. Bleed the system.
7   Insufficient pedal height. Check and adjust as necessary.
8   Piston seal in operating cylinder deformed or damaged.
9   Lack of grease on pilot bearing.

35 Clutch slips (engine speed increases with no increase in vehicle speed)

1   Worn or oil soaked clutch plate.
2   Clutch plate not broken in. It may take 30 or 40 normal starts for a new clutch to seat.
3   Diaphragm spring weak or damaged. Remove clutch cover/pressure plate assembly and inspect.
4   Flywheel warped (Chapter 2).
5   Debris in master cylinder preventing the piston from returning to its normal position.
6   Clutch hydraulic line damaged.
7   Binding in the release mechanism.

36 Grabbing (chattering) as clutch is engaged

1   Oil on clutch plate. Remove and inspect. Repair any leaks.
2   Worn or loose engine or transmission mounts. They may move slightly when clutch is released. Inspect mounts and bolts.
3   Worn splines on transmission input shaft. Remove clutch components and inspect.
4   Warped pressure plate or flywheel. Remove clutch components and inspect.
5   Diaphragm spring fatigued. Remove clutch cover/pressure plate assembly and inspect.
6   Clutch linings hardened or warped.
7   Clutch lining rivets loose.

37 Squeal or rumble with clutch engaged (pedal released)

1   Improper pedal adjustment. Adjust pedal freeplay (Chapter 1).
2   Release bearing binding on transmission shaft. Remove clutch components and check bearing. Remove any burrs or nicks, clean and relubricate before refitting.
3   Pilot bush worn or damaged.
4   Clutch rivets loose.
5   Clutch plate cracked.
6   Fatigued clutch plate torsion springs. Renew clutch plate.

38 Squeal or rumble with clutch disengaged (pedal depressed)

1   Worn or damaged release bearing.
2   Worn or broken pressure plate diaphragm fingers.

39 Clutch pedal stays on floor when disengaged

Binding linkage or release bearing. Inspect linkage or remove clutch components as necessary.

Manual transmission

Note: *All manual transmission service information is located in Chapter 7, unless otherwise noted.*

40 Noisy in Neutral with engine running

1   Input shaft bearing worn.
2   Damaged main drive gear bearing.
3   Insufficient transmission oil (Chapter 1).
4   Transmission oil in poor condition. Drain and fill with proper grade oil. Check old oil for water and debris (Chapter 1).
5   Noise can be caused by variations in engine torque. Change the idle speed and see if noise disappears.

41 Noisy in all gears

1   Any of the above causes, and/or:
2   Worn or damaged output gear bearings or shaft.

42 Noisy in one particular gear

1   Worn, damaged or chipped gear teeth.
2   Worn or damaged synchroniser.

Troubleshooting 0-27

43 Slips out of gear

1 Transmission loose on clutch housing.
2 Stiff shift lever seal.
3 Shift linkage binding.
4 Broken or loose input gear bearing retainer.
5 Dirt between clutch lever and engine housing.
6 Worn linkage.
7 Damaged or worn check balls, fork rod ball grooves or check springs.
8 Worn mainshaft or countershaft bearings.
9 Loose engine mounts (Chapter 2).
10 Excessive gear end play.
11 Worn synchronisers.

44 Oil leaks

1 Excessive amount of lubricant in transmission (see Chapter 1 for correct checking procedures). Drain lubricant as required.
2 Transfer case oil seal(s) or speedometer oil seal damaged.
3 To pinpoint a leak, first remove all built-up dirt and grime from the transmission. Degreasing agents and/or steam cleaning will achieve this. With the underside clean, drive the vehicle at low speeds so the air flow will not blow the leak far from its source. Raise the vehicle and determine where the leak is located.

45 Difficulty engaging gears

1 Clutch not releasing completely.
2 Loose or damaged shift linkage. Make a thorough inspection, renewing parts as necessary.
3 Insufficient transmission oil (Chapter 1).
4 Transmission oil in poor condition. Drain and fill with proper grade oil. Check oil for water and debris (Chapter 1).
5 Worn or damaged striking rod.
6 Sticking or jamming gears.

46 Noise occurs while shifting gears

1 Check for proper operation of the clutch (Chapter 8).
2 Faulty synchroniser assemblies.

Automatic transmission

Note: *Due to the complexity of the automatic transmission, it's difficult for the home mechanic to properly diagnose and service. For problems other than the following, the vehicle should be taken to a reputable mechanic.*

47 Fluid leakage

1 Automatic transmission fluid is a deep red colour, and fluid leaks should not be confused with engine oil which can easily be blown by air flow to the transmission.
2 To pinpoint a leak, first remove all built-up dirt and grime from the transmission. Degreasing agents and/or steam cleaning will achieve this. With the underside clean, drive the vehicle at low speeds so the air flow will not blow the leak far from its source. Raise the vehicle and determine where the leak is located. Common areas of leakage are:
a) **Fluid pan:** tighten mounting bolts and/or renew pan gasket as necessary (Chapter 1). Some models have a drain plug; make sure it's tight.
b) **Rear extension:** tighten bolts and/or renew oil seal as necessary.
c) **Filler pipe:** renew the rubber oil seal where pipe enters transmission case.
d) **Transmission oil lines:** tighten fittings where lines enter transmission case and/or renew lines.
e) **Vent pipe:** transmission overfilled and/or water in fluid (see checking procedures, Chapter 1).
f) **Speedometer connector:** renew the O-ring where speedometer cable enters transmission case.

48 General shift mechanism problems

Chapter 7 deals with checking and adjusting the shift linkage on automatic transmissions. Common problems which may be caused by out of adjustment linkage are:
a) *Engine starting in gears other than P (park) or N (Neutral).*
b) *Indicator pointing to a gear other than the one actually engaged.*
c) *Vehicle moves with transmission in P (Park) position.*

49 Transmission will not downshift with the accelerator pedal pressed to the floor

Chapter 7 deals with adjusting the throttle control cable to enable the transmission to downshift properly.

50 Engine will start in gears other than Park or Neutral

Chapter 7 deals with adjusting the Neutral start switch installed on automatic transmissions.

51 Transmission slips, shifts rough, is noisy or has no drive in forward or Reverse gears

1 There are many probable causes for the above problems, but the home mechanic should concern himself only with one possibility: fluid level.
2 Before taking the vehicle to a shop, check the fluid level and condition as described in Chapter 1. Add fluid, if necessary, or change the fluid and filter if needed. If problems persist, have a professional diagnose the transmission.

Driveshaft

Note: *Refer to Chapter 8, unless otherwise specified, for service information.*

52 Leaks at front of driveshaft

Defective transfer case rear seal. See Chapter 7 for renewal procedure. As this is done, check the splined yoke for burrs or roughness that could damage the new seal. Remove burrs with a fine file or whetstone.

53 Knock or clunk when transmission is under initial load (just after transmission is put into gear)

1 Loose or disconnected rear suspension components. Check all mounting bolts and bushes (Chapters 7 and 10).
2 Loose driveshaft bolts. Inspect all bolts and nuts and tighten them securely.
3 Worn or damaged universal joint bearings. Inspect the universal joints (Chapter 8).
4 Worn sleeve yoke and mainshaft spline.

54 Metallic grating sound consistent with vehicle speed

Pronounced wear in the universal joint bearings. Renew U-joints or renew driveshafts, as necessary.

55 Vibration

Note: *Before blaming the driveshaft, make sure the tyres are perfectly balanced and perform the following test.*

1 Install a tachometer inside the vehicle to monitor engine speed as the vehicle is driven. Drive the vehicle and note the engine speed at which the vibration (roughness) is most pronounced. Now shift the transmission to a different gear and bring the engine speed to the same point.
2 If the vibration occurs at the same engine speed (rpm) regardless of which gear

the transmission is in, the driveshaft is NOT at fault since the driveshaft speed varies.
3 If the vibration decreases or is eliminated when the transmission is in a different gear at the same engine speed, refer to the following probable causes.
4 Bent or dented driveshaft. Inspect and renew as necessary.
5 Undercoating or built-up dirt, etc. on the driveshaft. Clean the shaft thoroughly.
6 Worn universal joint bearings. Renew the U-joints or renew the driveshaft as necessary.
7 Driveshaft and/or companion flange out of balance. Check for missing weights on the shaft. Remove driveshaft and reinstall 180-degrees from original position, then recheck. Have the driveshaft balanced if problem persists.
8 Loose driveshaft mounting bolts/nuts.
9 Worn transfer case seal(s) (Chapter 7).

56 Scraping noise

Make sure the dust cover on the sleeve yoke isn't rubbing on the transmission extension housing.

57 Whining or whistling noise

Rear axle and differential

Note: *For differential servicing information, refer to Chapter 8, unless otherwise specified.*

58 Noise - same when in drive as when vehicle is coasting

1 Road noise. No corrective action available.
2 Tyre noise. Inspect tyres and check tyre pressures (Chapter 1).
3 Front wheel bearings loose, worn or damaged (Chapter 1).
4 Insufficient differential oil (Chapter 1).
5 Defective differential.

59 Knocking sound when starting or shifting gears

Defective or incorrectly adjusted differential.

60 Noise when turning

Defective differential.

61 Vibration

See probable causes under Driveshaft. Proceed under the guidelines listed for the driveshaft. If the problem persists, check the rear wheel bearings by raising the rear of the vehicle and spinning the wheels by hand. Listen for evidence of rough (noisy) bearings. Remove and inspect (Chapter 8).

62 Oil leaks

1 Pinion oil seal damaged (Chapter 8).
2 Axleshaft oil seals damaged (Chapter 8).
3 Differential cover leaking. Tighten mounting bolts or renew the gasket as required.
4 Loose filler or drain plug on differential (Chapter 1).
5 Clogged or damaged breather on differential.

Transfer case

Note: *Unless otherwise specified, refer to Chapter 7C for service and repair information.*

63 Gear jumping out of mesh

1 Incorrect control lever freeplay.
2 Interference between the control lever and the console.
3 Play or fatigue in the transfer case mounts.
4 Internal wear or incorrect adjustments.

64 Difficult shifting

1 Lack of oil.
2 Internal wear, damage or incorrect adjustment.

65 Noise

1 Lack of oil in transfer case.
2 Noise in 4H and 4L, but not in 2H indicates cause is in the front differential or front axle.
3 Noise in 2H, 4H and 4L indicates cause is in rear differential or rear axle.
4 Noise in 2H and 4H but not in 4L, or in 4L only, indicates internal wear or damage in transfer case.

Brakes

Note: *Before assuming a brake problem exists, make sure the tyres are in good condition and inflated properly, the front end alignment is correct and the vehicle is not loaded with weight in an unequal manner. All service procedures for the brakes are included in Chapter 9, unless otherwise noted.*

66 Vehicle pulls to one side during braking

1 Defective, damaged or oil contaminated brake pad on one side. Inspect as described in Chapter 1. Refer to Chapter 10 if renewal is required.
2 Excessive wear of brake pad material or disc on one side. Inspect and repair as necessary.
3 Loose or disconnected front suspension components. Inspect and tighten all bolts securely (Chapters 1 and 10).
4 Defective caliper assembly. Remove caliper and inspect for stuck piston or damage.
5 Scored or out of round rotor.
6 Loose caliper mounting bolts.
7 Incorrect wheel bearing adjustment.

67 Noise (high-pitched squeal)

1 Front brake pads worn out. This noise comes from the wear sensor rubbing against the disc. Renew pads immediately!
2 Glazed or contaminated pads.
3 Dirty or scored rotor.
4 Bent support plate.

68 Excessive brake pedal travel

1 Partial brake system failure. Inspect entire system (Chapter 1) and correct as required.
2 Insufficient fluid in master cylinder. Check (Chapter 1) and add fluid bleed system if necessary.
3 Air in system. Bleed system.
4 Excessive lateral rotor play.
5 Brakes out of adjustment. Check the operation of the automatic adjusters.
6 Defective proportioning valve. Renew valve and bleed system.

69 Brake pedal feels spongy when depressed

1 Air in brake lines. Bleed the brake system.
2 Deteriorated rubber brake hoses. Inspect all system hoses and lines. Renew parts as necessary.
3 Master cylinder mounting nuts loose. Inspect master cylinder bolts (nuts) and tighten them securely.
4 Master cylinder faulty.
5 Incorrect shoe or pad clearance.
6 Defective check valve. Renew valve and bleed system.
7 Clogged reservoir cap vent hole.
8 Deformed rubber brake lines.
9 Soft or swollen caliper seals.
10 Poor quality brake fluid. Bleed entire system and fill with new approved fluid.

Troubleshooting   0-29

70 Excessive effort required to stop vehicle

1   Power brake booster not operating properly.
2   Excessively worn linings or pads. Check and renew if necessary.
3   One or more caliper pistons seized or sticking. Inspect and rebuild as required.
4   Brake pads or linings contaminated with oil or grease. Inspect and renew as required.
5   New pads or linings fitted and not yet seated. It'll take a while for the new material to seat against the rotor or drum.
6   Worn or damaged master cylinder or caliper assemblies. Check particularly for seized pistons.
7   Also see causes listed under Section 69.

71 Pedal travels to the floor with little resistance

Little or no fluid in the master cylinder reservoir caused by leaking caliper piston(s) or loose, damaged or disconnected brake lines. Inspect entire system and repair as necessary.

72 Brake pedal pulsates during brake application

1   Wheel bearings damaged, worn or out of adjustment (Chapter 1).
2   Caliper not sliding properly due to improper refitting or obstructions. Remove and inspect.
3   Rotor not within specifications. Remove the rotor and check for excessive lateral runout and parallelism. Have the rotors resurfaced or renew them. Also make sure that all rotors are the same thickness.
4   Out of round rear brake drums. Remove the drums and have them turned or renew them with new ones.

73 Brakes drag (indicated by sluggish engine performance or wheels being very hot after driving)

1   Output rod adjustment incorrect at the brake pedal.
2   Obstructed master cylinder compensator. Disassemble master cylinder and clean:
3   Master cylinder piston seized in bore. Overhaul master cylinder.
4   Caliper assembly in need of overhaul.
5   Brake pads or shoes worn out.
6   Piston cups in master cylinder or caliper assembly deformed. Overhaul master cylinder.
7   Rotor not within specifications (Section 72).

8   Parking brake assembly will not release.
9   Clogged brake lines.
10 Wheel bearings out of adjustment (Chapter 1).
11 Brake pedal height improperly adjusted.
12 Wheel cylinder needs overhaul.
13 Improper shoe to drum clearance. Adjust as necessary.

74 Rear brakes lock up under light brake application

1   Tyre pressures too high.
2   Tyres excessively worn (Chapter 1).

75 Rear brakes lock up under heavy brake application

1   Tyre pressures too high.
2   Tyres excessively worn (Chapter 1).
3   Front brake pads contaminated with oil, mud or water. Clean or renew the pads.
4   Front brake pads excessively worn.
5   Defective master cylinder or caliper assembly.

Suspension and steering

Note: *All service procedures for the suspension and steering systems are included in Chapter 10, unless otherwise noted.*

76 Vehicle pulls to one side

1   Tyre pressures uneven (Chapter 1).
2   Defective Tyre (Chapter 1).
3   Excessive wear in suspension or steering components (Chapter 1).
4   Wheel alignment incorrect.
5   Front brakes dragging. Inspect as described in Section 73.
6   Wheel bearings improperly adjusted (Chapter 1 or 8).
7   Wheel lug nuts loose.

77 Shimmy, shake or vibration

1   Tyre or wheel out of balance or out of round. Have them balanced on the vehicle.
3   Shock absorbers and/or suspension components worn or damaged. Check for worn bushes in the upper and lower links.
4   Wheel lug nuts loose.
5   Incorrect tyre pressures.
6   Excessively worn or damaged tyre.
7   Loosely mounted steering gear housing.
8   Steering gear improperly adjusted.
9   Loose, worn or damaged steering components.
10 Damaged idler arm.
11 Worn balljoint.

78 Excessive pitching and/or rolling around corners or during braking

1   Defective shock absorbers. Renew as a set.
2   Broken or weak leaf springs and/or suspension components.
3   Worn or damaged stabiliser bar or bushes.

79 Wandering or general instability

1   Improper tyre pressures.
2   Worn or damaged upper and lower link or tension rod bushes.
3   Incorrect front end alignment.
4   Worn or damaged steering linkage or suspension components.
5   Improperly adjusted steering gear.
6   Out of balance wheels.
7   Loose wheel lug nuts.
8   Worn rear shock absorbers.
9   Fatigued or damaged rear leaf springs.

80 Excessively stiff steering

1   Lack of lubricant in power steering fluid reservoir, where appropriate (Chapter 1).
2   Incorrect tyre pressures (Chapter 1).
3   Lack of lubrication at balljoints (Chapter 1).
4   Front end out of alignment.
5   Steering gear out of adjustment or lacking lubrication.
6   Improperly adjusted wheel bearings.
7   Worn or damaged steering gear.
8   Interference of steering column with turn signal switch.
9   Low tyre pressures.
10 Worn or damaged balljoints.
11 Worn or damaged steering linkage.
12 See also Section 79.

81 Excessive play in steering

1   Loose wheel bearings (Chapter 8).
2   Excessive wear in suspension bushes (Chapter 1).
3   Steering gear improperly adjusted.
4   Incorrect wheel alignment.
5   Steering gear mounting bolts loose.
6   Worn steering linkage.

82 Lack of power assistance

1   Steering pump drivebelt faulty or not adjusted properly (Chapter 1).
2   Fluid level low (Chapter 1).
3   Hoses or pipes restricting the flow. Inspect and renew parts as necessary.

Troubleshooting

4 Air in power steering system. Bleed system.
5 Defective power steering pump.

83 Steering wheel fails to return to straight-ahead position

1 Incorrect front end alignment.
2 Tyre pressures low.
3 Steering gears improperly engaged.
4 Steering column out of alignment.
5 Worn or damaged balljoint.
6 Worn or damaged steering linkage.
7 Improperly lubricated idler arm.
8 Insufficient oil in steering gear.
9 Lack of fluid in power steering pump.

84 Steering effort not the same in both directions (power system)

1 Leaks in steering gear.
2 Clogged fluid passage in steering gear.

85 Noisy power steering pump

1 Insufficient oil in pump.
2 Clogged hoses or oil filter in pump.
3 Loose pulley.
4 Improperly adjusted drivebelt (Chapter 1).
5 Defective pump.

86 Miscellaneous noises

1 Improper tyre pressures.
2 Insufficiently lubricated balljoint or steering linkage.
3 Loose or worn steering gear, steering linkage or suspension components.
4 Defective shock absorber.
5 Defective wheel bearing.
6 Worn or damaged suspension bushes.
7 Damaged leaf spring.
8 Loose wheel lug nuts.
9 Worn or damaged rear axleshaft spline.
10 Worn or damaged rear shock absorber mounting bushes.
11 Incorrect rear axle end play.
12 See also causes of noises at the rear axle and driveshaft.

87 Excessive tyre wear (not specific to one area)

1 Incorrect tyre pressures.
2 Tyres out of balance. Have them balanced on the vehicle.
3 Wheels damaged. Inspect and renew as necessary.
4 Suspension or steering components worn (Chapter 1).

88 Excessive tyre wear on outside edge

1 Incorrect tyre pressure.
2 Excessive speed in turns.
3 Front end alignment incorrect (excessive toe-in).

89 Excessive tyre wear on inside edge

1 Incorrect tyre pressure.
2 Front end alignment incorrect (toe-out).
3 Loose or damaged steering components (Chapter 1).

90 Tyre tread worn in one place

1 Tyres out of balance. Have them balanced on the vehicle.
2 Damaged or buckled wheel. Inspect and renew if necessary.
3 Defective tyre.

Chapter 1
Tune-up and routine maintenance

Contents

	Section		Section
Accelerator linkage check and lubrication	12	Ignition timing check	41
Air filter renewal	28	Introduction	2
Automatic transmission fluid change	36	Manual transmission lubricant change	34
Automatic transmission fluid level check	5	Manual transmission lubricant level check	20
Battery check, maintenance and charging	8	Pajero Maintenance schedule	1
Brake check	23	Positive Crankcase Ventilation (PCV) system check	38
Brake pedal height and freeplay check and adjustment	30	Power steering fluid level check	6
Chassis lubrication	16	Seat belt check	26
Clutch pedal height and freeplay check and adjustment	19	Spark plug renewal	39
Cooling system check	9	Spark plug wire check and renewal	40
Cooling system servicing (draining, flushing and refilling)	37	Suspension and steering check	17
Differential lubricant change	35	Throttle body mounting bolt torque check	27
Differential lubricant level check	22	Transfer case lubricant change	33
Drivebelt check, adjustment and renewal	25	Transfer case lubricant level check	21
Engine oil and filter change	13	Tune-up general information	3
Evaporative emissions system check	31	Tyre and tyre pressure checks	7
Exhaust system check	18	Tyre rotation	14
Fluid level checks	4	Under bonnet hose check and renewal	11
Fuel filter service	29	Valve clearance check and adjustment (Diesel engines only)	15
Fuel system check	24	Wiper blade inspection and renewal	10
Idle speed check and adjustment (2.8L diesel engine only)	32		

Specifications

Recommended lubricants and fluids[1]

Note: *Listed here are manufacturer recommendations at the time this manual was written. Manufacturers occasionally upgrade their fluid and lubricant specifications, so check with your local auto parts store for current recommendations.*

Engine oil
  Type
    Petrol engines
      To NT models .... API grade SG or higher
      NW models .... API grade SM or higher
    Diesel engines .... API grade CD or higher
  Viscosity .... See accompanying chart
  Capacity (with new oil filter)   **NL/NM/NP**   **NS/NT/NW**
    V6 petrol engine .... 4.9 litres   4.9 litres
    2.8L diesel engine .... 7.5 litres
    3.2L diesel engine .... 7.5 litres   9.8 litres

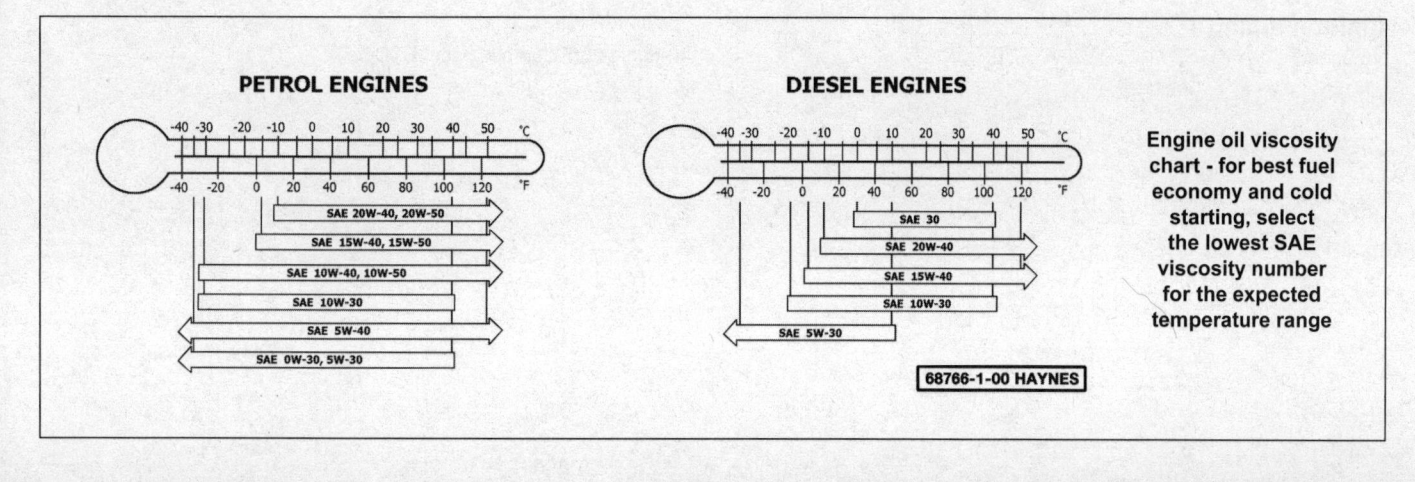

PETROL ENGINES

SAE 20W-40, 20W-50
SAE 15W-40, 15W-50
SAE 10W-40, 10W-50
SAE 10W-30
SAE 5W-40
SAE 0W-30, 5W-30

DIESEL ENGINES

SAE 30
SAE 20W-40
SAE 15W-40
SAE 10W-30
SAE 5W-30

Engine oil viscosity chart - for best fuel economy and cold starting, select the lowest SAE viscosity number for the expected temperature range

68766-1-00 HAYNES

Recommended lubricants and fluids[1] (continued)

Automatic transmission fluid

	NL	NM/NP	NS	NT	NW Petrol	NW Diesel
Capacity - dry (litres - approximate)[2]	8.5	9.3	9.7	10.9	9.7	10.9

Type
- NL .... Dexron II
- NM, NP, NS, NT & NW petrol .... Diamond ATF SP III or equivalent
- NW diesel .... Diamond ATF PA or equivalent

Manual transmission lubricant
- Type .... SAE 80/90W GL-5 gear lubricant
- Capacity (approximate) .... 3.2 litres

Differential lubricant
- Type
  - Standard .... SAE 80/90W GL-5 gear lubricant
  - Limited-slip differential .... LS 90
- Capacity (approximate)
  - Front .... 1.2 litres
  - Rear .... 1.6 litres

Transfer case lubricant
- Type .... 75W-85W GL-4 gear oil
- Capacity (approximate) .... 2.8 litres

Power steering fluid type .... Dexron II or Dexron III
Brake fluid type .... DOT 3 or 4 brake fluid
Clutch fluid type .... DOT 3 or 4 brake fluid

Coolant
- Type .... 50/50 mixture of ethylene glycol-based antifreeze and demineralised water
- Capacity (approximate)
  - Without rear heater .... 9.0 litres
  - With rear heater .... 10.5 litres

Chassis grease .... NLGI no. 2 chassis grease
Bonnet and door hinges .... Engine oil

Tune-up information

Firing order
- V6 engine 1-2-3-4-5-6

Idle speed
- 2.8L diesel engine
  - NL .... 800 ± 50 rpm
  - NM .... 750 ± 100 rpm
- 3.2L diesel engine
  - NM .... 750 ± 20 rpm
  - NW
    - Automatic transmission .... 650 ± 50 rpm
    - Manual transmission .... 600 ± 50 rpm
  - Except NM & NW
    - Automatic transmission .... 700 ± 30 rpm
    - Manual transmission .... 740 ± 30 rpm
- V6 petrol engines .... 700 ± 100 rpm

Spark plug type and gap[3]

- 3.5L V6 engine .... ND PK16PR-P11, Champion RC10PYP4 @ 1.1 mm
- 3.8L V6 engine
  - NP .... NGK BKR6ETUB or equivalent @ 0.7 to 0.8 mm
  - NS, NT, NW .... NGK IFR6B-K @ 0.7 to 0.8 mm

Ignition timing[3]

- V6 engine .... 10-degrees (5-degrees base) BTDC

Chapter 1 Tune-up and routine maintenance

Tune-up information (continued)

Valve clearances
2.8L diesel engine (engine at normal operating temperature)
   NL
      Inlet valves .... 0.20 mm
      Exhaust valves .... 0.30 mm
   NM
      Inlet valves .... 0.25 mm
      Exhaust valves .... 0.35 mm
3.2L diesel engine (engine cold)
   Inlet valves .... 0.10 mm
   Exhaust valves .... 0.15 mm
NS, NT and NW 3.8L petrol engine (engine cold)
   Inlet valves .... 0.10 mm
   Exhaust valves .... Hydraulic

Clutch
Pedal freeplay .... 4 to 13 mm
Pedal height .... 195.7 to 198.7 mm

Brake
Parking brake adjustment .... 4 to 6 clicks
Pedal height .... 187 to 190 mm
Pedal freeplay .... Less than 3 mm
Brake pad lining wear limit .... 2 mm

[1] All capacities approximate. Add as necessary to bring to appropriate level

[2] When refilling with automatic transmission fluid after overhaul or removing the pan, add fluid a little at a time, checking the fluid level after each addition. Do not drive the vehicle until you're certain the fluid level is correct. Normally, much more fluid is required after an overhaul than after a fluid change, since the torque converter is drained during an overhaul, but not during a normal fluid change.

[3] Refer to the Vehicle Emission Control Information label in the engine compartment: use the information there if it differs from that listed here

Torque specifications
                                                                                              Nm
Spark plugs 25
Engine oil drain plug 39
Manual transmission check/fill plug 32
Manual transmission drain plug 32
Differential check/fill and drain plugs 60
Throttle body mounting bolts (V6 petrol) 12
Transfer case check/fill and drain plugs 32
Wheel lug nuts .... 98 to 118

1-4 Chapter 1 Tune-up and routine maintenance

Typical 3.5L petrol engine compartment checking points

1. Evaporative emissions canister
2. Engine compartment fuse/relay centre
3. Windscreen washer fluid reservoir
4. Coolant reservoir
5. Battery
6. Engine oil dipstick
7. Radiator hose
8. Radiator cap
9. Drive belt
10. Engine oil filter
11. Brake master cylinder fluid reservoir
12. Air cleaner
13. Power steering fluid reservoir

Chapter 1 Tune-up and routine maintenance

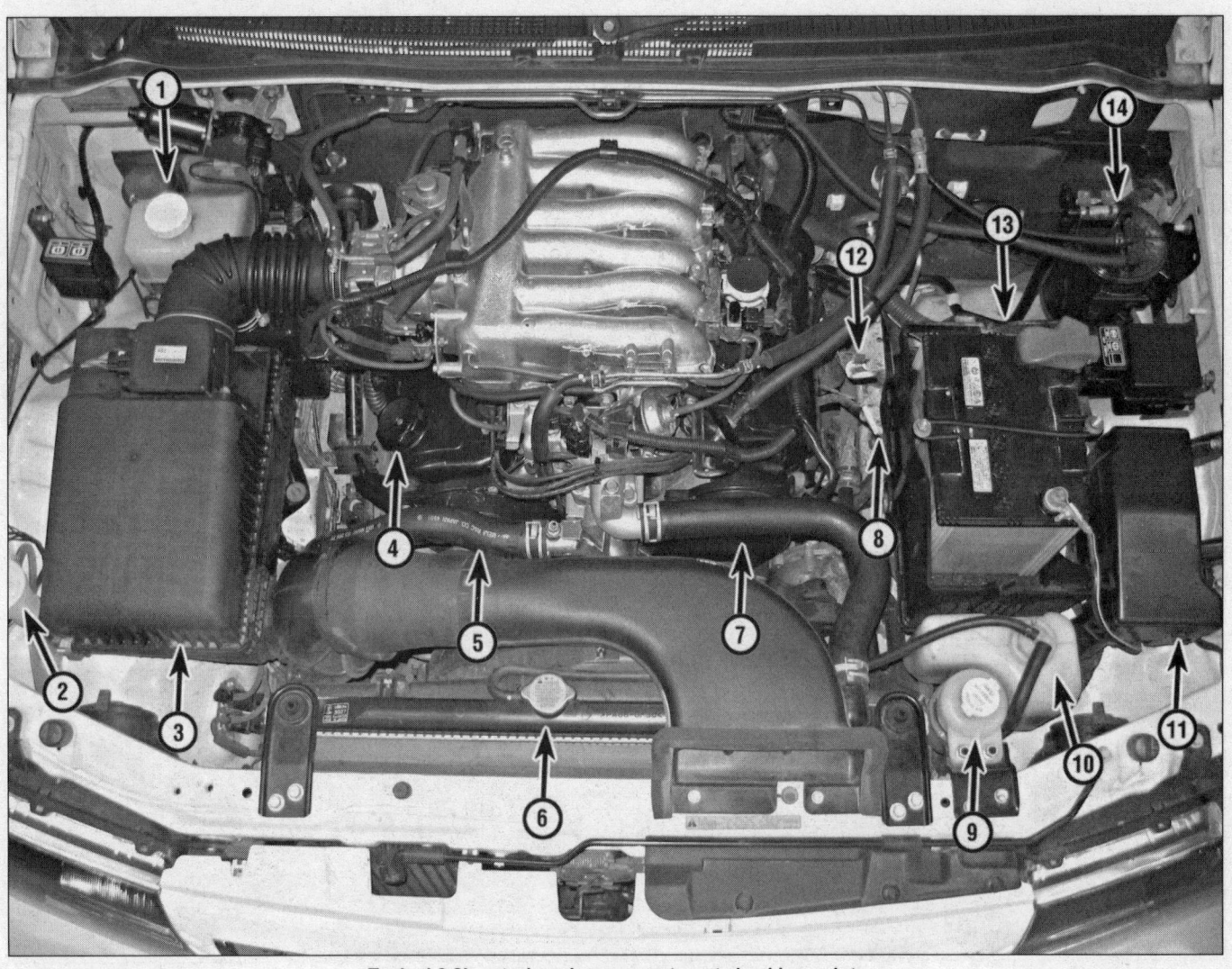

Typical 3.8L petrol engine compartment checking points

1 Brake master cylinder fluid reservoir
2 Windscreen washer fluid reservoir
3 Air cleaner
4 Engine oil filler cap
5 Lower radiator hose
6 Radiator cap
7 Upper radiator hose
8 Engine oil dipstick
9 Power steering pump reservoir
10 Coolant reservoir
11 Engine compartment fuse/relay centre
12 Automatic transmission fluid dipstick
13 Battery
14 Evaporative emissions canister

Typical 2.8L four-cylinder diesel engine compartment checking points

1 Engine compartment fuse/relay centre
2 Head lamp washer fluid reservoir
3 Coolant reservoir
4 Battery
5 Radiator hose
6 Radiator cap
7 Air cleaner
8 Power steering fluid reservoir
9 Windscreen wiper washer reservoir
10 Brake master cylinder fluid reservoir
11 Clutch master cylinder reservoir
12 Engine oil filler cap
13 Engine oil dipstick
14 Water separator (hidden)

Chapter 1 Tune-up and routine maintenance

Typical early 3.2L four-cylinder diesel engine compartment checking points

1. Brake master cylinder fluid reservoir
2. Windscreen wiper washer fluid reservoir
3. Air cleaner
4. Engine oil filler cap
5. Radiator cap
6. Radiator hose
7. Coolant reservoir
8. Engine compartment fuse/relay centre
9. Relay box
10. Fuel filter/water separator
11. Battery
12. Engine oil dipstick
13. Power steering fluid reservoir

Chapter 1 Tune-up and routine maintenance

Typical late 3.2L four-cylinder diesel engine compartment checking points

1. Brake master cylinder fluid reservoir
2. Windscreen wiper washer fluid reservoir
3. Air cleaner
4. Engine oil filler cap
5. Radiator cap
6. Radiator hose
7. Coolant reservoir
8. Engine compartment fuse/relay centre
9. Relay box
10. Fuel filter/water separator
11. Battery
12. Automatic transmission fluid dipstick
13. Engine oil dipstick
14. Power steering fluid reservoir

Chapter 1 Tune-up and routine maintenance

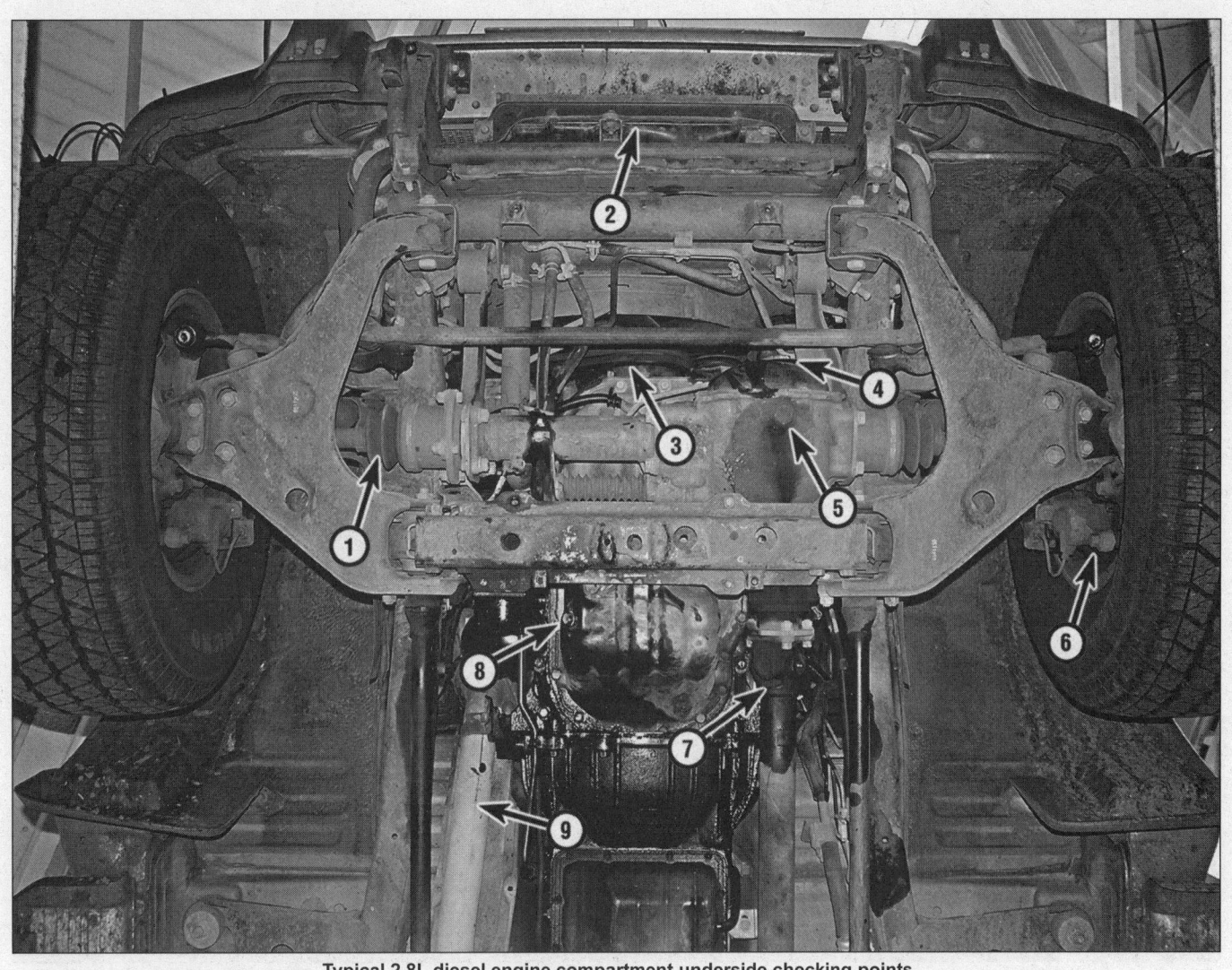

1-9

Typical 2.8L diesel engine compartment underside checking points

1 Driveaxle boot
2 Radiator
3 Engine drivebelt
4 Differential fill plug
5 Differential drain plug
6 Brake disc
7 Front driveshaft
8 Oil drain plug
9 Exhaust pipe

Typical 3.2L diesel engine compartment underside checking points

1. Driveaxle boot
2. Radiator
3. Brake disc
4. Steering gear boot
5. Differential fill plug
6. Engine oil drain plug
7. Front differential drain plug
8. Exhaust pipe
9. Front driveshaft

Chapter 1 Tune-up and routine maintenance

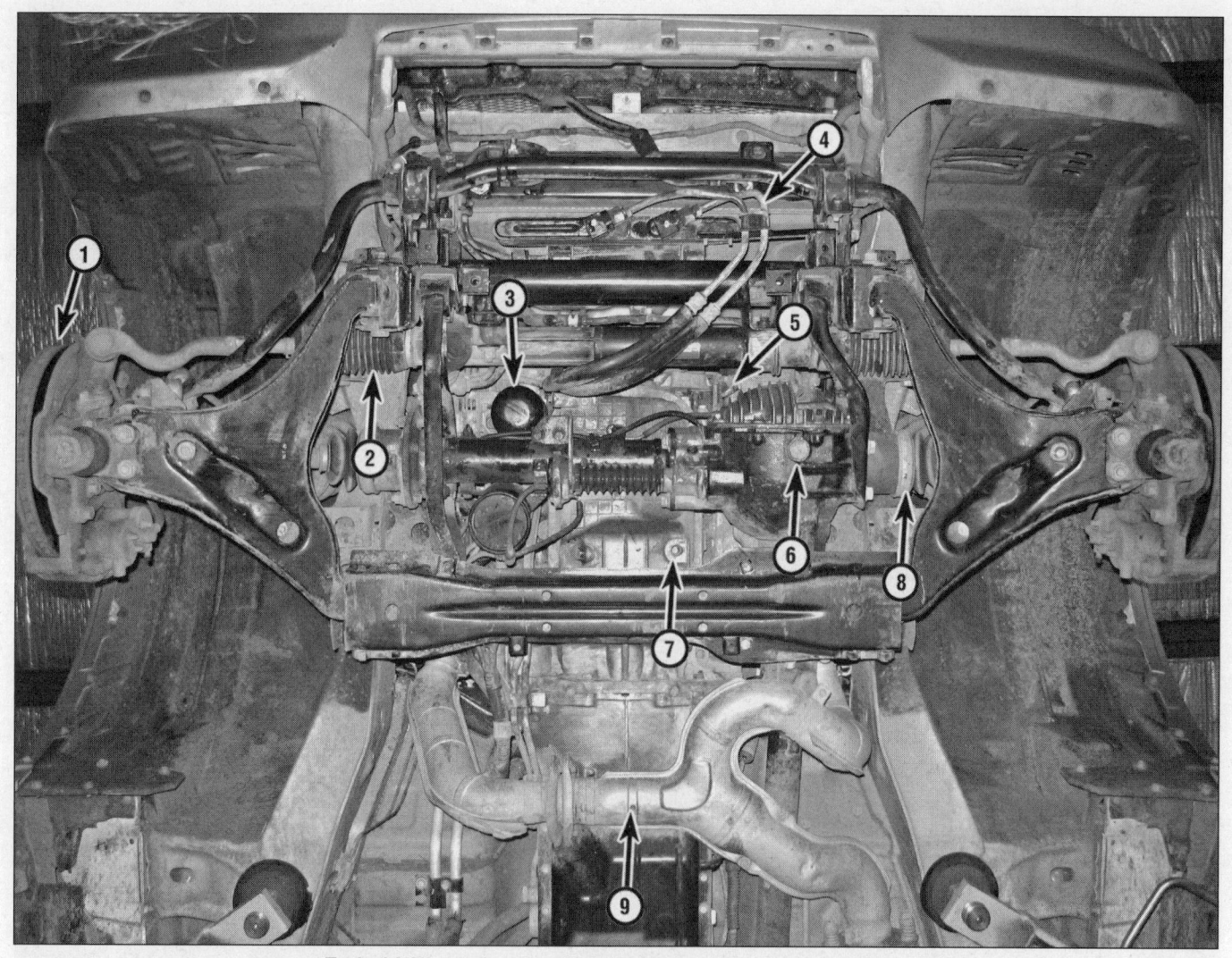

Typical 3.8L petrol engine compartment underside checking points

1 Brake disc
2 Steering gear boot
3 Oil filter
4 Oil cooler lines
5 Front differential fill plug
6 Front differential drain plug
7 Engine oil drain plug
8 Driveaxle boot
9 Exhaust pipe

Typical three link rear suspension underside component locations

1 Shock absorber
2 Fuel tank
3 Differential drain plug
4 Driveshaft
5 Muffler
6 Disc brake

Chapter 1 Tune-up and routine maintenance

Typical independent rear suspension underside component locations

1. Fuel tank
2. Stabiliser bar
3. Driveshaft
4. Muffler
5. CV-joint drive axle
6. Differential fill plug
7. Differential drain plug
8. Rear coil spring
9. Lower control arm
10. Shock absorber

1 Pajero Maintenance schedule

The following maintenance intervals are based on the assumption that the vehicle owner will be doing the maintenance or service work, as opposed to having a dealer service department do the work. Although the time/number of kilometres intervals are loosely based on factory recommendations, most have been shortened to ensure, for example, that such items as lubricants and fluids are checked/changed at intervals that promote maximum engine/driveline service life. Also, subject to the preference of the individual owner interested in keeping his or her vehicle in peak condition at all times, and with the vehicle's ultimate resale in mind, many of the maintenance procedures may be performed more often than recommended in the following schedule. We encourage such owner initiative.

When the vehicle is new it should be serviced initially by a factory authorised dealer service department to protect the factory warranty. In many cases the initial maintenance check is done at no cost to the owner (check with your dealer service department for more information).

Every 400 kilometres or weekly, whichever comes first

Check the engine oil level (Section 4)
Check the engine coolant level (Section 4)
Check the windscreen washer fluid level (Section 4)
Check the brake and clutch fluid levels (Section 4)
Check the automatic transmission fluid level (Section 5)
Check the power steering fluid level (Section 6)
Check the tyres and tyre pressures (Section 7)

Every 7,500 kilometres or 6 months, whichever comes first

All items listed above plus:
Change the engine oil and filter (Section 13) [1]

Note: *While the manufacturer doesn't specify replacing the oil filter every 7,500 km, we recommend replacing it every time the engine oil is changed.*

Every 15,000 kilometres or 12 months, whichever comes first

All items listed above plus:
Change the engine oil and filter (Section 13)
Check the engine drivebelts (Section 25)
Check and service the battery (Section 8)
Check the cooling system (Section 9)
Check and clean the air filter (Section 28)
Check the vacuum pump hoses (diesel engines) (see Section 23).
Check the manual transmission lubricant (Section 20) [2]
Check the transfer case lubricant level (Section 21) [2]
Check the differential lubricant level (Section 22) [2]
Inspect the suspension and steering components (Section 17) [2]
Inspect the fuel system (Section 24)
Inspect and renew if necessary all under bonnet hoses (Section 11)
Adjust the valves (diesel engine only) (Section 15) [1]
Inspect the exhaust system (Section 18) [2]
Check the seat belts (Section 26)
Lubricate the chassis components (Section 16)
Check and adjust if necessary, the clutch pedal freeplay (Section 19)

Every 30,000 kilometres or 24 months, whichever comes first

All items listed above plus:
Inspect the evaporative emissions system (Section 31)
Check and adjust, if necessary, the engine idle speed (early diesel models only) (Section 32)
Replace the brake fluid (see Section 23).
Inspect the inboard parking brake shoes and drums - models with rear disc brakes (see Chapter 9).
Replace the fuel filter (Section 29)
Adjust the valves (NW diesel engine only) (Section 15)
Check the brakes (Section 23) [2]

Every 45,000 kilometres or 36 months, whichever comes first

All items listed under 15,000 kilometres or 12 months, plus:
Renew the air filter (Section 28)
Service the cooling system (drain, flush and refill) (Section 37) [7]
Adjust the valves (Section 15) [6]
Check the ignition timing (early petrol models) (Section 41) [6]

Every 60,000 kilometres or 48 months, whichever comes first

All items listed under 30,000 kilometres or 24 months, plus:
Change the differential lubricant (Section 35) [3, 5]
Service the cooling system (drain, flush and refill) (Section 37) [6]

Every 90,000 kilometres or 72 months, whichever comes first

All items listed above plus:
Change the automatic transmission fluid and filter (petrol engines) (Section 36) [3]
Change the differential lubricant (Section 35) [3, 4]
Replace the timing belt (see Chapter 2A) [6]
Renew the spark plugs (Section 39) [6]
Inspect the spark plug wires (Section 40) [6]

Chapter 1 Tune-up and routine maintenance

Every 105,000 kilometres or 84 months, whichever comes first

All items listed under 15,000 kilometres or 12 months, plus:
Change the manual transmission lubricant (Section 34)
Change the transfer case lubricant (Section 33)³

1. NL to NS diesel models
2. This item is affected by "severe" operating conditions as described below. If your vehicle is operated under severe conditions, perform the indicated maintenance item at half the specified interval:

   Severe conditions are indicated if you mainly operate your vehicle under one or more of the following:
   In dusty areas
   Off road use
   Towing a trailer
   Idling for extended periods and/or low speed operation
   When outside temperatures remain below freezing and most trips are less than 6 kilometres

3. If operated under one or more of the following conditions, perform the indicated maintenance item at half the specified interval:
   In heavy city traffic where the outside temperature regularly reaches 32-degrees C or higher
   In hilly or mountainous terrain
   Frequent trailer pulling
   Frequent off road use
4. With standard diff
5. With limited slip diff (LSD)
6. Petrol models
7. Diesel models

2 Introduction

This Chapter is designed to help the home mechanic maintain the Mitsubishi Pajero with the goals of maximum performance, economy, safety and reliability in mind.

Included is a master maintenance schedule, followed by procedures dealing specifically with every item on the schedule. Visual checks, adjustments, component renewal and other helpful items are included. Refer to the accompanying illustrations of the engine compartment and the under side of the vehicle for the locations of various components.

Servicing your vehicle in accordance with the planned number of kilometres/time maintenance schedule and the step-by-step procedures should result in maximum reliability and extend the life of your vehicle. Keep in mind that it's a comprehensive plan - maintaining some items but not others at the specified intervals will not produce the same results.

As you perform routine maintenance procedures, you'll find that many can, and should, be grouped together because of the nature of the procedures or because of the proximity of two otherwise unrelated components or systems.

For example, if the vehicle is raised for chassis lubrication, you should inspect the exhaust, suspension, steering and fuel systems while you're under the vehicle. When you're rotating the tyres, it makes good sense to check the brakes since the wheels are already removed. Finally, let's suppose you have to borrow or rent a torque wrench. Even if you only need it to tighten the spark plugs, you might as well check the torque of as many critical fasteners as time allows.

The first step in this maintenance program is to prepare yourself before the actual work begins. Read through all the procedures you're planning to do, then gather up all the parts and tools needed. If it looks like you might run into problems during a particular job, seek advice from a mechanic or experienced do-it-yourselfer.

3 Tune-up general information

The term tune-up is used in this manual to represent a combination of individual operations rather than one specific procedure.

If, from the time the vehicle is new, the routine maintenance schedule is followed closely and frequent checks are made of fluid levels and high wear items, as suggested throughout this manual, the engine will be kept in relatively good running condition and the need for additional work will be minimised.

More likely than not, however, there will be times when the engine is running poorly due to lack of regular maintenance. This is even more likely if a used vehicle, which has not received regular and frequent maintenance checks, is purchased. In such cases, an engine tune-up will be needed outside of the regular routine maintenance intervals.

The first step in any tune-up or diagnostic procedure to help correct a poor running engine is a cylinder compression check. A compression check (see Chapter 2 Part D) will help determine the condition of internal engine components and should be used as a guide for tune-up and repair procedures. If, for instance, a compression check indicates serious internal engine wear, a conventional tune-up will not improve the performance of the engine and would be a waste of time and money. Because of its importance, the compression check should be done by someone with the right equipment and the knowledge to use it properly.

The following procedures are those most often needed to bring a generally poor running engine back into a proper state of tune.

Minor tune-up

Check all engine related fluids
Clean and check the battery (Section 8)
Check and adjust the drivebelts (Section 25)
Renew the spark plugs (Section 39)
Check the cylinder compression (Chapter 2D)
Inspect the spark plug and coil wires (Section 40)
Renew the air filter (Section 28)
Check and adjust the idle speed (Section 32)
Check the ignition timing (Section 41)
Renew the fuel filter (Section 29)
Check the PCV system (Section 38)
Adjust the valve clearances (Section 15)
Check and service the cooling system (Section 37)

Major tune-up

All items listed under Minor tune-up plus . . .
Check the EGR system (Chapter 6)
Check the charging system (Chapter 5)
Check the ignition system (Chapter 5)
Check the fuel system (Section 24 and Chapter 4)
Renew the spark plugs (Section 39)
Renew the spark plug wires (Section 40)

4 Fluid level checks

Note: *The following are fluid level checks to be done on a 400 kilometre or weekly basis. Additional fluid level checks can be found in specific maintenance procedures which follow. Regardless of how often the fluid levels are checked, watch for puddles under the vehicle - if leaks are noted, make repairs immediately.*

1 Fluids are an essential part of the lubrication, cooling, brake, clutch and windscreen washer systems. Because the fluids gradually

Chapter 1 Tune-up and routine maintenance

4.2a The engine oil dipstick on diesel engines are located next to the valve cover

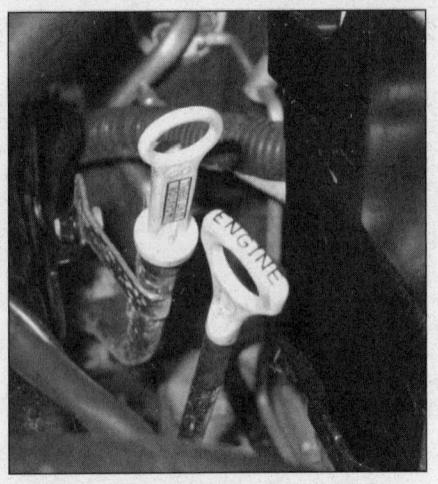

4.2b On petrol engines the dipstick is located on the passengers side

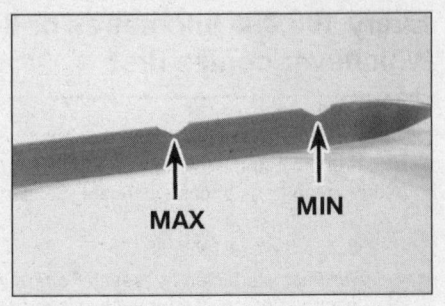

4.4 The oil level should be between the upper and lower notches - if it isn't, add enough oil to bring the level to or near the upper notch mark

become depleted and/or contaminated during normal operation of the vehicle, they must be periodically replenished. See *Recommended lubricants and fluids* at the beginning of this Chapter before adding fluid to any of the following components.

Note: *The vehicle must be on level ground when fluid levels are checked.*

Engine oil

Refer to illustrations 4.2a, 4.2b, 4.4 and 4.6

2   The engine oil level is checked with a dipstick that extends through a tube and into the sump at the bottom of the engine **(see illustrations)**.

3   The oil level should be checked before the vehicle has been driven, or about 15 minutes after the engine has been shut off. If the oil is checked immediately after driving the vehicle, some of the oil will remain in the upper engine components, resulting in an inaccurate reading on the dipstick.

4   Pull the dipstick from the tube and wipe all the oil from the end with a clean rag or paper towel. Insert the clean dipstick all the way back into the tube, then pull it out again. Note the oil at the end of the dipstick. Add oil as necessary to keep the level between the MAX and MIN marks or within the hatched area on the dipstick **(see illustration)**.

5   Don't overfill the engine by adding too much oil since this may result in oil fouled spark plugs, oil leaks or oil seal failures.

6   Oil is added to the engine after removing a threaded cap from the valve cover **(see illustration)**. An oil can spout or funnel may help to reduce spills.

7   Checking the oil level is an important preventive maintenance step. A consistently low oil level indicates oil leakage through damaged seals, defective gaskets or past worn rings or valve guides. If the oil looks milky in colour or has water droplets in it, the cylinder head gasket(s) may be blown or the head(s) or block may be cracked. The engine should be checked immediately. The condition of the oil should also be checked. Whenever you check the oil level, slide your thumb and index finger up the dipstick before wiping off the oil. If you see a small amount of dirt or metal particles clinging to the dipstick, the oil should be changed (see Section 13).

Engine coolant

Refer to illustration 4.8

Warning: *Don't allow antifreeze to come in contact with your skin or painted surfaces of the vehicle. Flush contaminated areas immediately with plenty of water. Don't store new coolant or leave old coolant lying around where it's accessible to children or pets - they're attracted by its sweet smell. Ingestion of even a small amount of coolant can be fatal! Wipe up garage floor and drip pan coolant spills immediately. Keep antifreeze containers covered and repair leaks in your cooling system immediately.*

8   All vehicles covered by this manual are equipped with a pressurised coolant recovery system. A white plastic coolant reservoir located in the engine compartment is connected by a hose to the radiator filler neck **(see illustration)**. If the engine overheats, coolant escapes through a valve in the radiator cap and travels through the hose into the reservoir. As the engine cools, the coolant is automatically drawn back into the cooling system to maintain the correct level.

9   The coolant level in the reservoir should be checked regularly.

4.6 Rotate the oil filler cap anti-clockwise remove it - always make sure the area to around the opening is clean before removing the cap; this prevents dirt from contaminating the engine

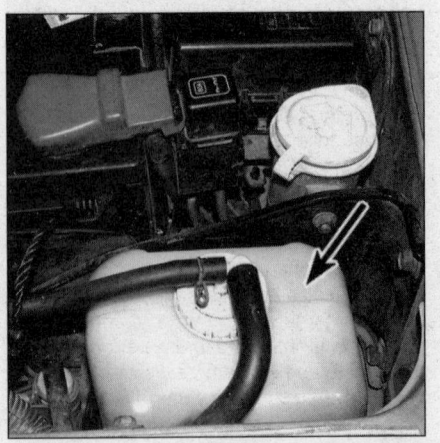

4.8 The coolant reservoir is located in the front corner of the engine compartment - the level must be maintained between the upper and lower marks

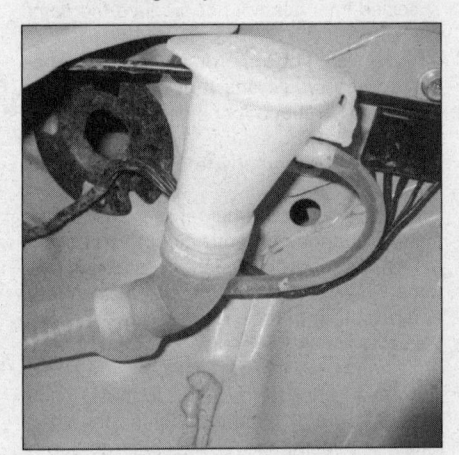

4.14a The windscreen washer fluid reservoir is located next to the coolant reservoir on most models

Chapter 1 Tune-up and routine maintenance

4.14b On headlight washer-equipped models, flip up the cap to add more fluid

4.17 Unscrew each cap from the battery and check the fluid level

4.18 The clutch master cylinder is located on the firewall (early model shown)

4.19 Keep the brake and clutch fluid levels near the upper or MAX marks on the reservoir - fluid can be added after unscrewing the cap (typical later model shown)

Warning: *Do not remove the radiator cap to check the coolant level when the engine is warm. The level in the reservoir varies with the temperature of the engine. When the engine is cold, the coolant level should be at or slightly above the lower mark on the reservoir. Once the engine has warmed up, the level should be at or near the upper mark. If it isn't, allow the engine to cool, then remove the cap from the reservoir and add a 50/50 mixture of ethylene glycol-based antifreeze and demineralised water.*

10 Drive the vehicle and recheck the coolant level. If only a small amount of coolant is required to bring the system up to the proper level, water can be used. However, repeated additions of water will dilute the antifreeze and water solution. In order to maintain the proper ratio of antifreeze and water, always top up the coolant level with the correct mixture. An empty plastic milk jug or bleach bottle makes an excellent container for mixing coolant. Do not use rust inhibitors or additives.

11 If the coolant level drops consistently, there may be a leak in the system. Inspect the radiator, hoses, filler cap, drain plugs and water pump (see Section 9). If no leaks are noted, have the radiator cap pressure tested by a service station.

12 If you have to remove the radiator cap, wait until the engine has cooled, then wrap a thick cloth around the cap and turn it to the first stop. If coolant or steam escapes, let the engine cool down longer, then remove the cap.

13 Check the condition of the coolant as well. It should be relatively clear. If it's brown or rust coloured, the system should be drained, flushed and refilled. Even if the coolant appears to be normal, the corrosion inhibitors wear out, so it must be renewed at the specified intervals.

Windscreen, headlight and rear washer fluid

Refer to illustrations 4.14a and 4.14b

14 Fluid for the windscreen washer system is stored in a plastic reservoir in the engine compartment **(see illustration)**. If necessary, refer to the underbonnet component illustration(s) at the beginning of this Chapter to locate the reservoir. Some models are equipped with headlight washers. The fluid reservoir is located on the left side of the engine compartment and should be kept filled to the upper mark **(see illustration)**. On vehicles with rear window washers, the fluid reservoir is located under a cover on the right side of the cargo area on NL models and in the back door on NM and later models.

15 In milder climates, plain water can be used in the reservoir, but it should be kept no more than 2/3 full to allow for expansion if the water freezes. In colder climates, use windscreen washer system antifreeze, available at any auto parts store, to lower the freezing point of the fluid. Mix the antifreeze with water in accordance with the manufacturer's directions on the container.

Caution: *Don't use cooling system antifreeze - it will damage the vehicle's paint.*

16 To help prevent icing in cold weather, warm the windscreen with the defroster before using the washer.

Battery electrolyte

Refer to illustration 4.17

17 To check the electrolyte level in the battery on conventional batteries, remove all of the cell caps **(see illustration)**. If the level is low, add distilled water until it's above the plates. Most aftermarket renewal batteries have a split-ring indicator in each cell to help you judge when enough water has been added - don't overfill the cells!

Brake and clutch fluid

Refer to illustrations 4.18 and 4.19

18 The brake master cylinder is mounted on the front of the power booster unit in the engine compartment. The clutch cylinder used on some models with manual transmissions is mounted adjacent to it on the firewall **(see illustration)**.

19 The fluid inside is readily visible. The level should be between the upper and lower marks on the reservoir **(see illustration)**. If a low level is indicated, be sure to wipe the top of the reservoir cover with a clean rag to prevent contamination of the brake and/or clutch system before removing the cover.

20 When adding fluid, pour it carefully into the reservoir to avoid spilling it onto surrounding painted surfaces. Be sure the specified fluid is used, since mixing different types of brake fluid can cause damage to the system. See *Recommended lubricants and fluids* at the front of this Chapter or your owner's manual.

Warning: *Brake fluid can harm your eyes and damage painted surfaces, so be very careful when handling or pouring it. Don't use brake fluid that's been standing open or is more than one year old. Brake fluid absorbs moisture from the air. Excess moisture can cause a dangerous loss of brake efficiency.*

21 At this time the fluid and master cylinder can be inspected for contamination. The system should be drained and refilled if deposits, dirt particles or water droplets are seen in the fluid.

22 After filling the reservoir to the proper level, make sure the cover is on tight to prevent fluid leakage.

23 The brake fluid level in the master cylinder will drop slightly as the pads and the brake shoes at each wheel wear down during normal operation. If the master cylinder requires repeated additions to keep it at the

Chapter 1 Tune-up and routine maintenance

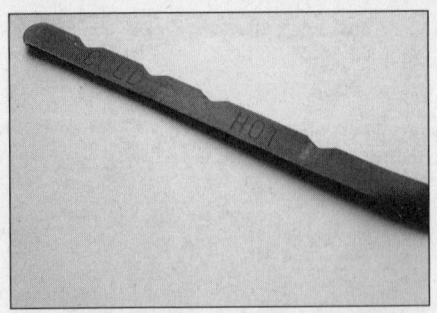

5.6 The automatic transmission fluid level must be between the two notches or marks on the dipstick with the engine at normal operating temperature

proper level, it's an indication of leakage in the brake system, which should be corrected immediately. Check all brake lines and connections (see Section 23 for more information).

24 If, upon checking the master cylinder fluid level, you discover one or both reservoirs empty or nearly empty, the brake system should be bled (see Chapter 9).

5 Automatic transmission fluid level check

Refer to illustration 5.6

1 The automatic transmission fluid level should be carefully maintained. Low fluid level can lead to slipping or loss of drive, while overfilling can cause foaming and loss of fluid.
2 With the parking brake set, start the engine, then move the shift lever through all the gear ranges, ending in Neutral. The fluid level must be checked with the vehicle level and the engine running at idle.

Note: *Incorrect fluid level readings will result if the vehicle has just been driven at high speeds for an extended period, in hot weather in city traffic, or if it has been pulling a trailer. If any of these conditions apply, wait until the fluid has cooled (about 30 minutes).*

3 With the transmission at normal operating temperature, remove the dipstick from the filler tube. The dipstick is located at the rear of the engine compartment on the passenger's side.
4 Wipe the fluid from the dipstick with a clean rag and push it back into the filler tube until the cap seats.
5 Pull the dipstick out again and note the fluid level.
6 The level should be between the two notches **(see illustration)**.
7 If additional fluid is required, add it directly into the tube using a funnel. It takes about 0.5 litre to raise the level from the lower notch to the FULL notch with a hot transmission, so add the fluid a little at a time and keep checking the level until it's correct.
8 The condition of the fluid should also be checked along with the level. If the fluid at the end of the dipstick is a dark reddish-brown

6.5a Unscrew the cap on the power steering fluid reservoir and check the fluid level on the dipstick

colour, or if it smells burned, it should be changed. If you are in doubt about the condition of the fluid, purchase some new fluid and compare the two for colour and smell.

6 Power steering fluid level check

Refer to illustrations 6.5a and 6.5b

1 Unlike manual steering, the power steering system relies on fluid which may, over a period of time, require replenishing.
2 The fluid reservoir for the power steering pump is located remotely from the pump on the drivers's side of the engine compartment on early models and the front of the engine compartment next to the radiator on later models

Note: *On 3.2L diesel engines the reservoir is located on top of the power steering pump.*

3 For the check, the front wheels should be pointed straight ahead and the engine should be off. The power steering fluid should be checked after the vehicle has been driven and the fluid is at normal operating tempera-

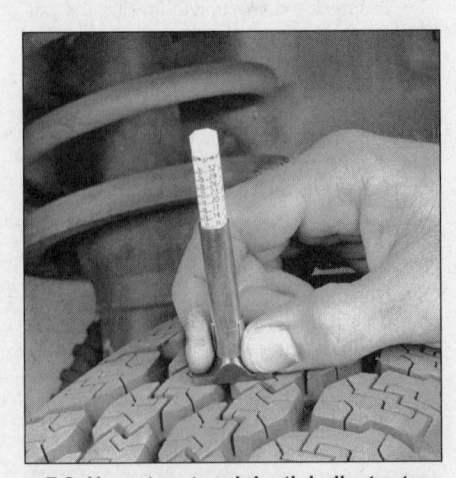

7.2 Use a tyre tread depth indicator to monitor tyre wear - they are available at auto parts stores and service stations and cost very little

6.5b The fluid level must be between the marks on the dipstick with the engine at normal operating temperature

ture and the steering rotated from lock-to-lock several times with the engine running.
4 Clean the cap and the area around the opening to prevent contamination of the fluid.
5 Twist off the reservoir cap which has a built-in dipstick attached to it **(see illustrations)**. Wipe off the dipstick with a clean rag, reinstall it and remove it to get an accurate reading. The fluid level should be between the MIN and MAX marks on the dipstick.
6 If additional fluid is required, pour the specified type directly into the reservoir, using a funnel to prevent spills.
7 If the reservoir requires frequent fluid additions, all power steering hoses, hose connections and the power steering pump should be carefully checked for leaks.

7 Tyre and tyre pressure checks

Refer to illustrations 7.2, 7.3, 7.4a, 7.4b and 7.8

1 Periodic inspection of the tyres may spare you the inconvenience of being stranded with a flat tyre. It can also provide you with vital information regarding possible problems in the steering and suspension systems before major damage occurs.
2 Tread wear can be monitored with a simple, inexpensive device known as a tread depth indicator **(see illustration)**.
3 Note any abnormal tread wear **(see illustration)**. Tread pattern irregularities such as cupping, flat spots and more wear on one side than the other are indications of front end alignment and/or balance problems. If any of these conditions are noted, take the vehicle to a tyre shop or service station to correct the problem.
4 Look closely for cuts, punctures and embedded nails or tacks. Sometimes a tyre will hold air pressure for a short time or leak down very slowly after a nail has embedded itself in the tread. If a slow leak persists, check the valve stem core to make sure it's tight **(see illustration)**. Examine the tread for

Chapter 1 Tune-up and routine maintenance

7.3 This chart will help you determine the condition of the tyres, the probable cause(s) of abnormal wear and the corrective action necessary

UNDERINFLATION

CUPPING

Cupping may be caused by:
- Underinflation and/or mechanical irregularities such as out-of-balance condition of wheel and/or tire, and bent or damaged wheel.
- Loose or worn steering tie-rod or steering idler arm.
- Loose, damaged or worn front suspension parts.

OVERINFLATION

INCORRECT TOE-IN OR EXTREME CAMBER

FEATHERING DUE TO MISALIGNMENT

an object that may have embedded itself in the tyre or for a "plug" that may have begun to leak (radial tyre punctures are repaired with a plug that's refitted in a puncture). If a puncture is suspected, it can be easily verified by spraying a solution of soapy water onto the puncture area **(see illustration)**. The soapy solution will bubble if there's a leak. Unless the puncture is unusually large, a tyre shop or service station can usually repair the tyre.

5 Carefully inspect the inner sidewall of each tyre for evidence of brake fluid leakage. If you see any, inspect the brakes immediately.

6 Correct air pressure adds wear to the lifespan of the tyres, improves performance and enhances overall ride quality. Tyre pressure cannot be accurately estimated by looking at a tyre, especially if it's a radial. A tyre pressure gauge is essential. Keep an accurate gauge in the vehicle. The pressure gauges attached to the nozzles of air hoses at petrol stations are often inaccurate.

7 Always check tyre pressure when the tyres are cold. Cold, in this case, means the vehicle has not been driven over a kilometre in the three hours preceding a tyre pressure check. A pressure rise of several kilopascals is not uncommon once the tyres are warm.

8 Unscrew the valve cap protruding from the wheel or hub cap and push the gauge firmly onto the valve stem **(see illustration)**. Note the reading on the gauge and compare the figure to the recommended tyre pressure shown on the placard either on the glove compartment door or one of the door pillars. Be sure to reinstall the valve cap to keep dirt and moisture out of the valve stem mechanism. Check all four tyres and, if necessary, add enough air to bring them up to the recommended pressure.

9 Don't forget to keep the spare tyre inflated to the specified pressure listed on the tyre placard.

8 Battery check, maintenance and charging

Refer to illustrations 8.1, 8.6, 8.7a, 8.7b and 8.7c

Warning: *Certain precautions must be followed when checking and servicing the battery. Hydrogen gas, which is highly flammable, is always present in the battery cells, so keep lighted tobacco and all other open flames and sparks away from the battery. The electrolyte inside the battery is actually dilute sulfuric acid, which will cause injury if splashed on your skin or in your eyes. It will also ruin clothes and painted surfaces. When removing the battery cables, always detach the negative cable first and hook it up last!*

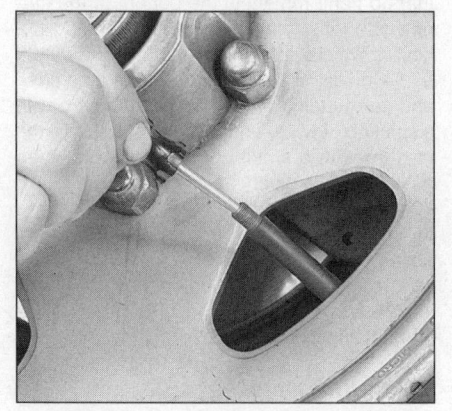

7.4a If a tyre loses air on a steady basis, check the valve core first to make sure it's snug (special inexpensive spanners are commonly available at auto parts stores)

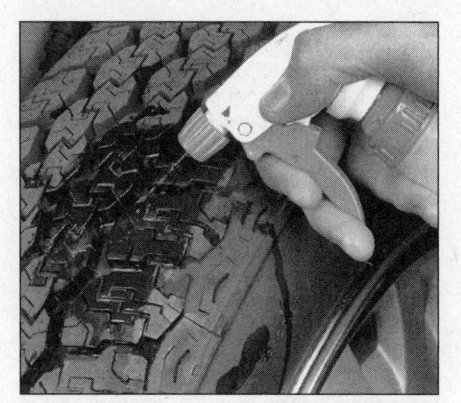

7.4b If the valve core is tight, raise the corner of the vehicle with the low tyre and spray a soapy water solution onto the tread as the tyre is turned slowly - leaks will cause small bubbles to appear

7.8 To extend the life of the tyres, check the air pressure at least once a week with an accurate gauge (don't forget the spare!)

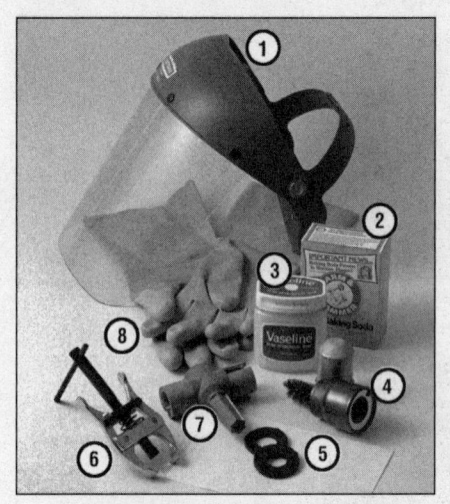

1•20 Chapter 1 Tune-up and routine maintenance

8.1 Tools and materials required for battery maintenance

1 **Face shield/safety goggles** - When removing corrosion with a brush, the acidic particles can easily fly up into your eyes
2 **Baking soda** - A solution of baking soda and water can be used to neutralise corrosion
3 **Petroleum jelly** - A layer of this on the battery posts will help prevent corrosion
4 **Battery post/cable cleaner** - This wire brush cleaning tool will remove all traces of corrosion from the battery posts and cable clamps
5 **Treated felt washers** - Placing one of these on each post, directly under the cable clamps, will help prevent corrosion
6 **Puller** - Sometimes the cable clamps are very difficult to pull off the posts, even after the nut/bolt has been completely loosened. This tool pulls the clamp straight up and off the post without damage.
7 **Battery post/cable cleaner** - Here is another cleaning tool which is a slightly different version of number 4 above, but it does the same thing
8 **Rubber gloves** - Another safety item to consider when servicing the battery; remember that's acid inside the battery!

8.6 Use a spanner to check the tightness of the battery cable bolts

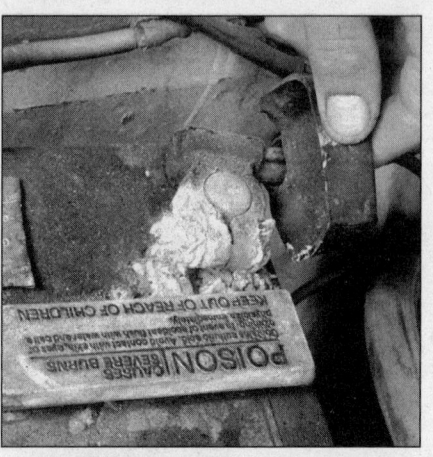

8.7a Battery terminal corrosion usually appears as light, fluffy powder

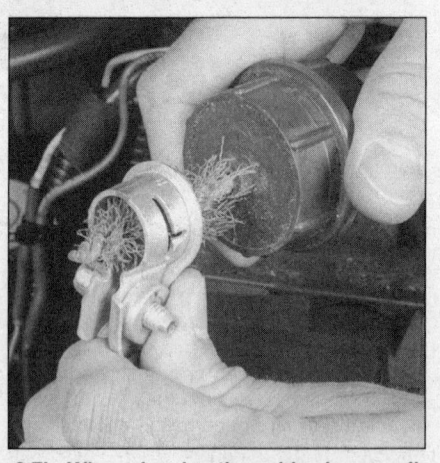

8.7b When cleaning the cable clamps, all corrosion must be removed (the inside of the clamp is tapered to match the taper on the post, so don't remove too much material)

8.7c Regardless of the type of tool used on the battery posts, a clean, shiny surface should be the result

Check and maintenance

1 Battery maintenance is an important procedure which will help ensure that you aren't stranded because of a dead battery. Several tools are required for this procedure **(see illustration)**.
2 When checking/servicing the battery, always turn the engine and all accessories off.
3 A sealed (sometimes called maintenance-free), battery is standard equipment on some vehicles. The cell caps cannot be removed, no electrolyte checks are required and water cannot be added to the cells. However, if a standard aftermarket battery has been refitted, the following maintenance procedure can be used.
4 Remove the caps and check the electrolyte level in each of the battery cells (see Section 4). It must be above the plates. There's usually a split-ring indicator in each cell to indicate the correct level. If the level is low, add distilled water only, then reinstall the cell caps.
Caution: *Overfilling the cells may cause electrolyte to spill over during periods of heavy charging, causing corrosion and damage to nearby components.*
5 The external condition of the battery should be checked periodically. Look for damage such as a cracked case.
6 Check the tightness of the battery cable bolts **(see illustration)** to ensure good electrical connections. Inspect the entire length of each cable, looking for cracked or abraded insulation and frayed conductors.
7 If corrosion (visible as white, fluffy deposits) **(see illustration)** is evident, remove the cables from the terminals, clean them with a battery brush and reinstall them **(see illustrations)**. Corrosion can be kept to a minimum by applying a layer of petroleum jelly or grease to the terminals.
8 Make sure the battery carrier is in good condition and the hold-down clamp is tight. If the battery is removed (see Chapter 5 for the removal and refitting procedure), make sure that no parts remain in the bottom of the carrier when it's reinstalled. When refitting the hold-down clamp, don't overtighten the nuts.
9 Corrosion on the carrier, battery case and surrounding areas can be removed with a solution of water and baking soda. Apply the mixture with a small brush, let it work, then rinse it off with plenty of clean water.
10 Any metal parts of the vehicle damaged by corrosion should be coated with a zinc-based primer, then painted.
11 Additional information on the battery and jump starting can be found in the front of this manual and in Chapter 5.

Charging

12 Remove all of the cell caps (if equipped) and cover the holes with a clean cloth to prevent spattering electrolyte. Disconnect the negative battery cable and hook the battery

Chapter 1 Tune-up and routine maintenance

charger leads to the battery posts (positive to positive, negative to negative), then plug in the charger. Make sure it is set at 12 volts if it has a selector switch.

13 If you're using a charger with a rate higher than two amps, check the battery regularly during charging to make sure it doesn't overheat. If you're using a trickle charger, you can safely let the battery charge overnight after you've checked it regularly for the first couple of hours.

14 If the battery has removable cell caps, measure the specific gravity with a hydrometer every hour during the last few hours of the charging cycle. Hydrometers are available inexpensively from auto parts stores - follow the instructions that come with the hydrometer. Consider the battery charged when there's no change in the specific gravity reading for two hours and the electrolyte in the cells is gassing (bubbling) freely. The specific gravity reading from each cell should be very close to the others. If not, the battery probably has a bad cell(s).

15 Some batteries with sealed tops have built-in hydrometers on the top that indicate the state of charge by the colour displayed in the hydrometer window. Normally, a bright-coloured hydrometer indicates a full charge and a dark hydrometer indicates the battery still needs charging. Check the battery manufacturer's instructions to be sure you know what the colours mean.

16 If the battery has a sealed top and no built-in hydrometer, you can hook up a digital voltmeter across the battery terminals to check the charge. A fully charged battery should read 12.6 volts or higher.

17 Further information on the battery and jump starting can be found in Chapter 5 and at the front of this manual.

9 Cooling system check

Refer to illustration 9.4

1 Many major engine failures can be attributed to a faulty cooling system. If the vehicle is equipped with an automatic transmission, the cooling system also cools the transmission fluid, prolonging transmission life.

2 The cooling system should be checked with the engine cold. Do this before the vehicle is driven for the day or after it has been shut off for at least three hours.

3 Remove the radiator cap by turning it counterclockwise until it reaches a stop. If you hear a hissing sound (indicating there's still pressure in the system), wait until it stops. Now press down on the cap with the palm of your hand and continue turning until it can be removed. Thoroughly clean the cap, inside and out, with clean water. Also clean the filler neck on the radiator. All traces of corrosion should be removed. The coolant inside the radiator should be relatively transparent. If it's rust coloured, the system should be drained and refilled (see Section 37). If the coolant level is not up to the top, add additional antifreeze/coolant mixture (see Section 4).

Check for a chafed area that could fail prematurely.

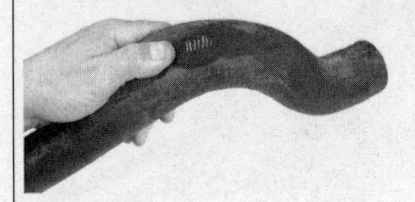

Check for a soft area indicating the hose has deteriorated inside.

Overtightening the clamp on a hardened hose will damage the hose and cause a leak.

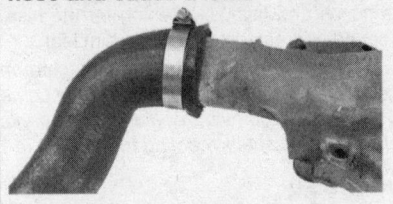

Check each hose for swelling and oil-soaked ends. Cracks and breaks can be located by squeezing the hose.

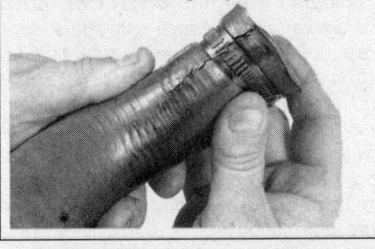

9.4 Hoses, like drivebelts, have a habit of failing at the worst possible time - to prevent the inconvenience of a blown radiator or heater hose, inspect them carefully as shown here

4 Carefully check the large upper and lower radiator hoses along with the smaller diameter heater hoses which run from the engine to the firewall. Inspect each hose along its entire length, renewing any hose that's cracked, swollen or deteriorated. Cracks may become more apparent if the hose is squeezed (see illustration). Regardless of condition, it's a good idea to renew hoses with new ones every two years. Make sure that all hose connections are tight. A leak in the cooling system will usually show up as white or rust coloured deposits on the areas adjoining the leak. If wire-type clamps are used at the ends of the hoses, it may be a good idea to renew them with more secure screw-type clamps.

5 Use compressed air or a soft brush to remove bugs, leaves, etc. from the front of the radiator or air conditioning condenser. Be careful not to damage the delicate cooling fins or cut yourself on them.

6 Every other inspection, or at the first indication of cooling system problems, have the cap and system pressure tested. If you don't have a pressure tester, most petrol stations and repair shops will do this for a minimal charge.

10.5 Depress the tab (arrow) and pull the blade assembly off the wiper arm

10 Wiper blade inspection and renewal

Refer to illustrations 10.5, 10.6a, 10.6b and 10.8

1 The windscreen wiper blades should be inspected periodically for damage, loose components and cracked or worn blade elements (the rubber portions).

2 Road film can build up on the blade elements and can affect their efficiency, so they should be washed regularly with a mild detergent solution.

3 The action of the wiping mechanism can loosen bolts, nuts and fasteners, so they should be checked and tightened, as necessary, at the same time the wiper blade elements are checked.

4 If the wiper blade elements are cracked, worn or warped, or no longer clean adequately, they should be renewed with new ones.

5 The wiper blade is removed by depressing the release tab at the centre of the wiper arm and pulling the blade off the arm (see illustration).

6 Bend the element end out of the way, use needle-nose pliers to pull the two support rods out, then slide the element out of the wiper bridge (see illustrations).

7 Slide the new element into place and insert the rods to lock it in place.

8 When fitting the wiper blade on the arm, place the plastic clip in position on the arm, then slide the blade into position over it until it locks (see illustration).

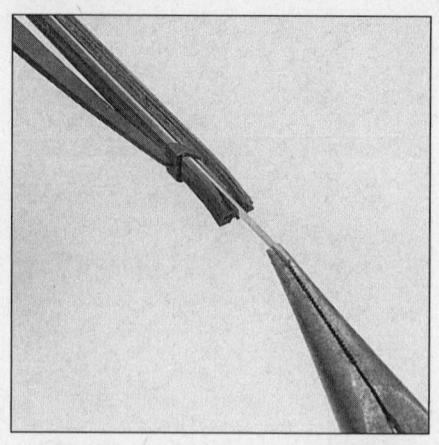

10.6a Use needle-nose pliers to pull the two support rods out of the blade element

10.6b With the rods out, it's an easy job to remove the element

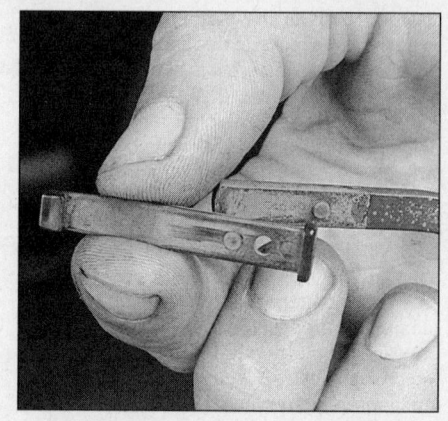

10.8 Place the plastic clip in position, then insert the blade onto the wiper arm

11 Under bonnet hose check and renewal

General

Caution: *Renewal of air conditioning hoses must be left to a dealer service department or air conditioning shop that has the equipment to depressurise the system safely. Never remove air conditioning components or hoses until the system has been depressurised.*

1 High temperatures in the engine compartment can cause the deterioration of the rubber and plastic hoses used for engine, accessory and emission systems operation. Periodic inspection should be made for cracks, loose clamps, material hardening and leaks. Information specific to the cooling system hoses can be found in Section 9.

2 Some, but not all, hoses are secured to the fittings with clamps. Where clamps are used, check to be sure they haven't lost their tension, allowing the hose to leak. If clamps aren't used, make sure the hose has not expanded and/or hardened where it slips over the fitting, allowing it to leak.

Vacuum hoses

3 It's quite common for vacuum hoses, especially those in the emissions system, to be colour coded or identified by coloured stripes moulded into them. Various systems require hoses with different wall thicknesses, collapse resistance and temperature resistance. When renewing hoses, be sure the new ones are made of the same material.

4 Often the only effective way to check a hose is to remove it completely from the vehicle. If more than one hose is removed, be sure to label the hoses and fittings to ensure correct refitting.

5 When checking vacuum hoses, be sure to include any plastic T-fittings in the check. Inspect the fittings for cracks and the hose where it fits over the fitting for distortion, which could cause leakage.

6 A small piece of vacuum hose (6.35 mm inside diameter) can be used as a stethoscope to detect vacuum leaks. Hold one end of the hose to your ear and probe around vacuum hoses and fittings, listening for the hissing sound characteristic of a vacuum leak.

Warning: *When probing with the vacuum hose stethoscope, be very careful not to come into contact with moving engine components such as the drivebelts, cooling fan, etc.*

Fuel hose

Warning: *There are certain precautions which must be taken when inspecting or servicing fuel system components. Work in a well ventilated area and don't allow open flames (cigarettes, appliance pilot lights, etc.) or bare light bulbs near the work area. Mop up any spills immediately and don't store fuel soaked rags where they could ignite. On vehicles equipped with fuel injection, the fuel system is under pressure, so if any fuel lines are to be disconnected, the pressure in the system must be relieved first (see Chapter 4 for more information).*

7 Check all rubber fuel lines for deterioration and chafing. Check carefully for cracks in areas where the hose bends and where it's attached to fittings.

8 High quality fuel line should be used for fuel line renewal.

Warning: *Never, under any circumstances, use unreinforced vacuum line, clear plastic tubing or water hose for fuel lines!*

9 Spring-type clamps are commonly used on fuel lines. They often lose their tension over a period of time, and can be "sprung" during removal. Renew all spring-type clamps with screw clamps whenever a hose is renewed.

Metal lines

10 Sections of metal line are often used for fuel line between the fuel pump and fuel injection unit. Check carefully to be sure the line has not been bent or crimped and look for cracks.

11 If a section of metal fuel line must be renewed, only seamless steel tubing should be used, since copper and aluminium tubing don't have the strength necessary to withstand normal engine vibration.

12 Check the metal brake lines where they enter the master cylinder and brake proportioning unit (if used) for cracks in the lines and loose fittings. Any sign of brake fluid leakage means an immediate thorough inspection of the brake system should be done.

Turbocharger hoses and lines

13 Close attention must be paid to the condition of the vacuum and oil lines connected to the turbocharger (if so equipped). A deteriorated vacuum hose can lead to engine damage due to over-boosting and a damaged oil line can prevent lubrication from reaching the turbocharger. This will result in instant turbocharger failure.

14 Closely examine all hoses and steel lines. Renew any that are suspect. If the oil supply line to the turbocharger has been disconnected for any reason, allow the engine to idle for one minute after re-starting.

12 Accelerator linkage check and lubrication

1 At the specified intervals, inspect the accelerator linkage and check it for free movement to make sure it is not binding.

2 Lubricate the linkage with a few drops of oil.

13 Engine oil and filter change

Refer to illustrations 13.3, 13.9, 13.14 and 13.18

1 Frequent oil changes are the most important preventive maintenance procedures that can be done by the home mechanic. As engine oil ages, it becomes diluted and contaminated, which leads to premature engine wear.

2 Although some sources recommend oil filter changes every other oil change, the minimal cost of an oil filter and the fact that it's easy to refit dictate that a new filter be used every time the oil is changed.

Chapter 1 Tune-up and routine maintenance

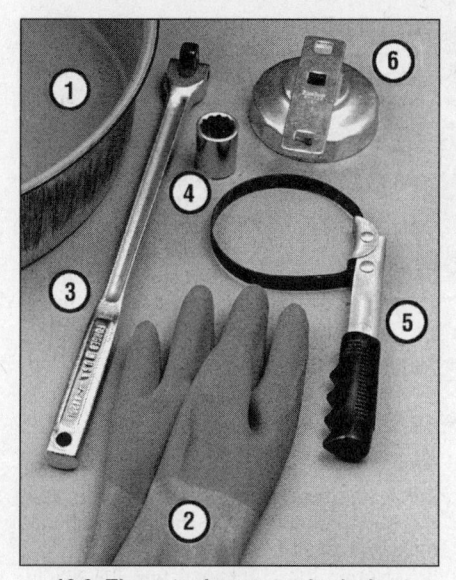

13.3 These tools are required when changing the engine oil and filter

1 **Drain pan** - *It should be fairly shallow in depth, but wide to prevent spills*
2 **Rubber gloves** - *When removing the drain plug and filter, you will get oil on your hands (the gloves will prevent burns)*
3 **Breaker bar** - *Sometimes the oil drain plug is tight and a long breaker bar is needed to loosen it*
4 **Socket** - *To be used with the breaker bar or a ratchet (must be the correct size to fit the drain plug - six-point preferred)*
5 **Filter wrench** - *This is a metal band-type wrench, which requires clearance around the filter to be effective*
6 **Filter spanner** - *This type fits on the bottom of the filter and can be turned with a ratchet or breaker bar (different size spanners are available for different types of filters)*

3 Gather all necessary tools and materials before beginning this procedure (**see illustration**).
4 You should have plenty of clean rags and newspapers handy to mop up any spills. Access to the underside of the vehicle is greatly improved if the vehicle can be lifted on a hoist, driven onto ramps or supported by jackstands.
Warning: *Do not work under a vehicle which is supported only by a bumper, hydraulic or scissors-type jack!*
5 If this is your first oil change, get under the vehicle and familiarise yourself with the locations of the oil drain plug and the oil filter. The engine and exhaust components will be warm during the actual work, so note how they're situated to avoid touching them when working under the vehicle.
6 Warm the engine to normal operating temperature. If the new oil or any tools are needed, use the warm-up time to obtain everything necessary for the job. The correct oil for your application can be found in *Recommended lubricants and fluids* at the beginning of this Chapter.
7 With the engine oil warm (warm engine oil will drain better and more built-up sludge will be removed with it), raise and support the vehicle. Make sure it's safely supported!
8 Move all necessary tools, rags and newspapers under the vehicle. Set the drain pan under the drain plug. Keep in mind that the oil will initially flow from the pan with some force; position the pan accordingly.
9 Being careful not to touch any of the hot exhaust components, use a wrench to remove the drain plug near the bottom of the sump (**see illustration**). Depending on how hot the oil is, you may want to wear gloves while unscrewing the plug the final few turns.
10 Allow the old oil to drain into the pan. It may be necessary to move the pan as the oil flow slows to a trickle.
11 After all the oil has drained, wipe off the drain plug with a clean rag. Small metal particles may cling to the plug and would immediately contaminate the new oil.
12 Clean the area around the drain plug opening and reinstall the plug. Tighten the plug to the torque listed at the beginning of this chapter.
13 Move the drain pan into position under the oil filter.
14 Use the filter wrench to loosen the oil filter (**see illustration**).
15 Completely unscrew the old filter. Be careful; it's full of oil. Empty the oil inside the filter into the drain pan.
16 Compare the old filter with the new one to make sure they're the same type.
17 Use a clean rag to remove all oil, dirt and sludge from the area where the oil filter mounts to the engine. Check the old filter to make sure the rubber gasket isn't stuck to the engine. If the gasket is stuck to the engine, remove it.
18 Apply a light coat of clean oil to the rubber gasket on the new oil filter (**see illustration**).
19 Attach the new filter to the engine, following the tightening directions printed on the filter canister or packing box. Most filter manufacturers recommend against using a filter wrench due to the possibility of overtightening and damage to the seal.
20 Remove all tools, rags, etc. from under the vehicle, being careful not to spill the oil in the drain pan, then lower the vehicle.
21 Move to the engine compartment and locate the oil filler cap.
22 Pour the fresh oil into the filler opening. A funnel may be used.
23 Pour three or four litres of fresh oil into the engine. Wait a few minutes to allow the oil to drain into the pan, then check the level on the oil dipstick (see Section 4 if necessary). If the oil level is above the L mark, start the engine and allow the new oil to circulate.
24 Run the engine for only about a minute and then shut it off. Immediately look under the vehicle and check for leaks at the sump drain plug and around the oil filter. If either one is leaking, tighten it a little more.
25 With the new oil circulated and the filter

13.9 Use the proper size spanner or socket to remove the oil drain plug to avoid rounding it off

13.14 The oil filter is usually on very tight and will require a special wrench for removal - DO NOT use the wrench to tighten the new filter

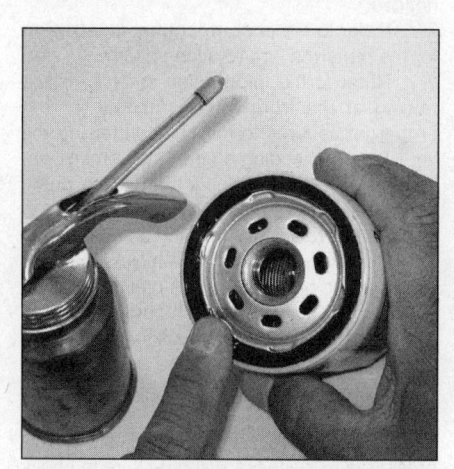

13.18 Lubricate the oil filter gasket with clean engine oil before fitting the filter on the engine

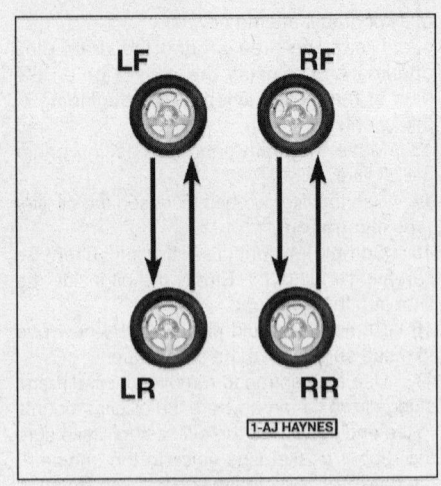

14.2 The recommended tyre rotation pattern for these vehicles

15.5 With the 2.8L engine at TDC on the compression stroke for number one cylinder, check the clearances measured directly below each cam for the valves indicated with dark arrows. Rotate the crankshaft one full revolution to check the valves with light arrows

now completely full, recheck the level on the dipstick and add more oil as necessary.
26 During the first few trips after an oil change, make it a point to check frequently for leaks and correct oil level.
27 The old oil drained from the engine cannot be reused in its present state and should be disposed of. Oil reclamation facilities, auto repair shops and petrol stations will normally accept the oil, which can be refined and used again. After the oil has cooled it can be poured into a container (capped plastic jugs or bottles, milk cartons, etc.) for transport to a disposal site.

14 Tyre rotation

Refer to illustration 14.2

1 The tyres should be rotated at the specified intervals and whenever uneven wear is noticed.
2 Refer to the **accompanying illustration** for the preferred tyre rotation pattern.
3 Refer to the information in *Jacking and towing* at the front of this manual for the proper procedures to follow when raising the vehicle and changing a tyre. If the brakes are to be checked, don't apply the parking brake as stated. Make sure the tyres are blocked to prevent the vehicle from rolling as it's raised.
4 Preferably, the entire vehicle should be raised at the same time. This can be done on a hoist or by jacking up each corner and then lowering the vehicle onto jackstands placed under the frame rails. Always use four jackstands and make sure the vehicle is safely supported.
5 After rotation, check and adjust the tyre pressures as necessary and be sure to check the lug nut tightness.
6 For additional information on the wheels and tyres, refer to Steering and Suspension (see Chapter 10).

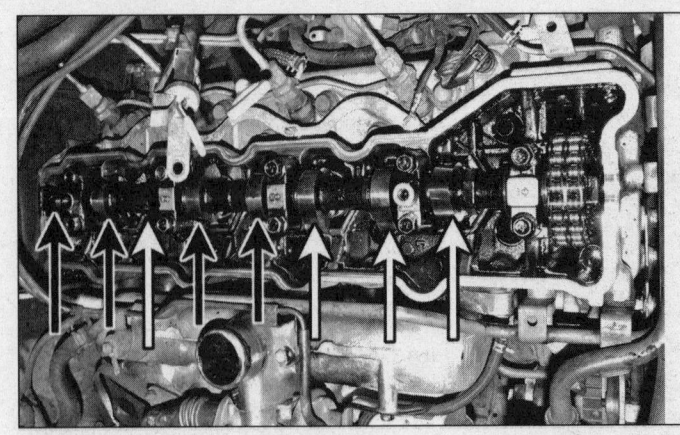

15 Valve clearance check and adjustment (Diesel engines only)

2.8L diesel engine

Refer to illustrations 15.5 and 15.6

1 Allow the engine to run until it has reached normal operating temperature.
2 Remove the valve cover (see Chapter 2B).
3 Remove the glow plug plate and the glow plugs (refer to Chapter 4).
4 Set the manual transmission in Neutral or the automatic transmission in PARK. With the parking brake set, rotate the crankshaft clockwise with a large ratchet and socket until the engine is at TDC on the compression stroke (see Chapter 2B). There is a protrusion on the camshaft which should be pointing upward when TDC on cylinder number one has been reached (see Chapter 2D).
5 Use a feeler gauge to check the valve clearances shown **(see illustration)**. Make note of all clearances measured. If any are outside of the allowable specifications, new shims will have to be purchased and refitted. Refer to the values listed in this Chapter's Specifications. Rotate the crankshaft one full revolution and check the valve clearances on the remaining four valves.
6 Perform the calculations to select new shims: The thickness of the new shim will be equal to the thickness of the existing shims, plus the clearance measured in Step 17, less the required clearance. Shims are made in 0.025 mm thickness differences. Their thickness is stamped on them ("2525" is equal to a thickness of 2.525 mm) **(see illustration)**.

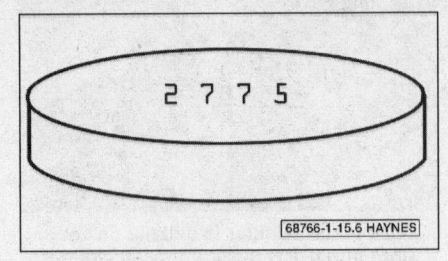

15.6 Each valve shim used on 2.8L diesel engines is marked with its thickness - this one is 2.775 mm thick

7 After selecting the appropriate shims, remove the camshaft (see Chapter 2B). Refit the shims needed, refit the camshaft and recheck the valve clearances.
8 Rotate the crankshaft one full revolution and perform the same operation on the remaining four valves **(see illustration 15.5)**.
9 After all valve clearances have been double checked, assemble the engine in the reverse order of disassembly.

3.2L diesel engine

Refer to illustrations 15.11 and 15.14

Caution: *Do not rotate the engine anticlockwise or damage will occur to the timing chain tensioner.*
10 The valve clearances must be checked and adjusted at the specified intervals with the engine cold.
11 Remove the engine cover fasteners **(see illustration)** and remove the cover.
12 Remove the EGR tubes, brackets and EGR assembly (see Chapter 6).
13 Remove the valve cover (see Chapter 2C) and glow plugs (see Chapter 4).
14 Place the number one piston at Top Dead Centre (TDC) on the compression stroke (see Chapter 2C) **(see illustration)**. There is a protrusion on the camshafts which should be pointing upward when number one piston is at TDC.
15 With the number one piston at TDC adjust inlet valves on cylinders No. 1, No. 2

15.11 Remove the engine cover fasteners (arrows) and remove the cover

Chapter 1 Tune-up and routine maintenance

15.14 Typical 3.2L diesel engine valve adjustment details

1 *Adjusting screw*
2 *Locknut*
3 *Rocker arm*
4 *Clearance check*
5 *TDC protrusion*

the appropriate size feeler gauge (see this Chapter's Specifications) between the roller rocker and the camshaft. Carefully tighten the adjusting screw until you can feel a slight drag on the feeler gauge as you withdraw it from camshaft and roller.
18 Hold the adjusting screw with a screwdriver (to keep it from turning) and tighten the locknut. Recheck the clearance to make sure it hasn't changed, then proceed to the next valve to be adjusted. Repeat the procedure until all the valves are properly adjusted.
19 Refit the valve cover, EGR assembly and engine cover.

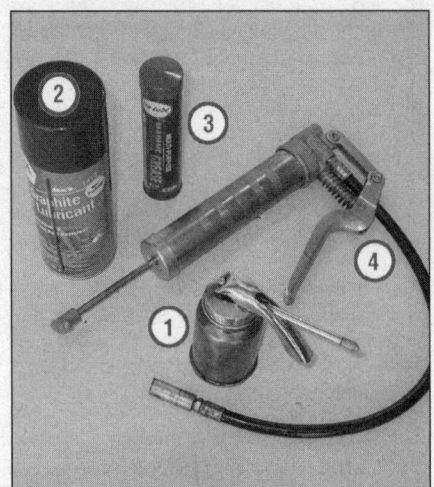

16 Chassis lubrication

Refer to illustrations 16.1 and 16.2
1 A grease gun and cartridge filled with the recommended grease are the only items required for chassis lubrication other than some clean rags and equipment needed to raise and support the vehicle safely **(see illustration)**.
2 There are several points on the vehicle's suspension, steering and drivetrain components that must be periodically lubricated with lithium-based multi-purpose grease, depending on model and year. Included are the upper and lower suspension balljoints, the swivel joints on the steering linkage and the front and rear driveshafts **(see illustration)**.
3 The grease point for each upper suspension balljoint (if equipped) is on top of the balljoint and is accessible by removing the front wheel and tyre. The steering linkage swivel joints on some models are designed to be lubricated and the driveshaft universal joints require lubrication as well.
4 For easier access under the vehicle, raise it with a jack and place jackstands under the frame. Make sure the vehicle is safely

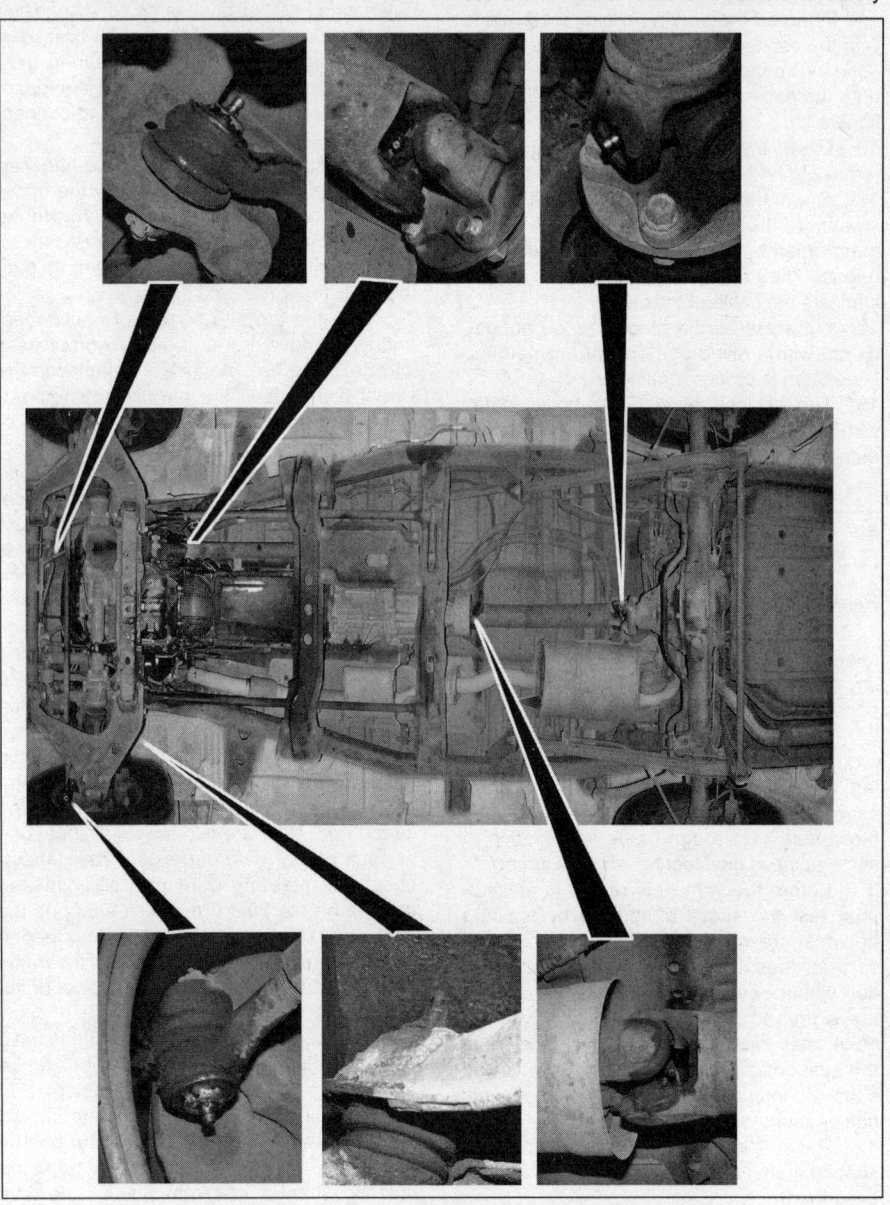

and exhaust valves No.1 and No. 3. Once those valves have been adjusted rotate the engine 360-degrees to number four cylinder TDC and adjust inlet valves on cylinders No. 3, No. 4 and exhaust valves No. 2 and No. 4.
16 The valve adjusting screws are located on the rocker arms.
17 Back off the locknut two full turns. Turn the adjusting screw anti-clockwise and insert

16.1 Materials required for chassis and body lubrication

1 **Engine oil** - *Light engine oil in a can like this can be used for door and bonnet hinges*
2 **Graphite spray** - *Used to lubricate lock cylinders*
3 **Grease** - *Grease, in a variety of types and weights, is available for use in a grease gun. Check the Specifications for your requirements*
4 **Grease gun** - *A common grease gun, shown here with a detachable hose and nozzle, is needed for chassis lubrication. After use, clean it thoroughly*

16.2 Typical chassis lubrication points

supported on the stands!

5 If grease fittings aren't already refitted, the plugs will have to be removed and fittings screwed into place.

6 Force a little of the grease out of the gun nozzle to remove any dirt, then wipe it clean with a rag.

7 Wipe the grease fitting and push the nozzle firmly over it. Squeeze the trigger on the grease gun to force grease into the component. Both the balljoints and swivel joints should be lubricated until the rubber reservoir is firm to the touch. Don't pump too much grease into the fittings or it could rupture the reservoir. If the grease seeps out around the grease gun nozzle, the fitting is clogged or the nozzle isn't seated all the way. Re-secure the gun nozzle to the fitting and try again. If necessary, renew the fitting.

8 Wipe excess grease from the components and the grease fittings.

9 While you're under the vehicle, clean and lubricate the parking brake cable along with the cable guides and levers. This can be done by smearing some of the chassis grease onto the cable and its related parts with your fingers.

10 Lower the vehicle to the ground for the remaining body lubrication process.

11 Open the bonnet and rear gate and smear a little chassis grease on the latch mechanisms. Have an assistant pull the release knob from inside the vehicle as you lubricate the cable at the latch.

12 Lubricate all the hinges (door, bonnet, hatch) with a few drops of light engine oil to keep them in proper working order.

13 The key lock cylinders can be lubricated with spray-on graphite, which is available at auto parts stores.

17 Suspension and steering check

Refer to illustration 17.11

1 Whenever the front of the vehicle is raised for any reason, it's a good idea to visually check the suspension and steering components for wear.

2 Indications of steering or suspension problems include excessive play in the steering wheel before the front wheels react, excessive swaying around corners or body movement over rough roads and binding at some point as the steering wheel is turned.

3 Before the vehicle is raised for inspection, test the shock absorbers by pushing down aggressively at each corner. If the vehicle doesn't come back to a level position within one or two bounces, the shocks are worn and should be renewed. As this is done listen for squeaks and other noises from the suspension components. Information on shock absorber and suspension components can be found in Chapter 10.

4 Raise the front end of the vehicle and support it on jackstands. Make sure it's safely supported!

5 Crawl under the vehicle and check for loose bolts, broken or disconnected parts and deteriorated rubber bushes on all suspension and steering components. Look for grease or fluid leaking from around the steering gear assembly and shock absorbers. If equipped, check the power steering hoses and connections for leaks.

6 The balljoint boots should be checked at this time. This includes not only the upper and lower suspension balljoints, but those connecting the steering linkage parts as well. After cleaning around the balljoints, inspect the seals for cracks and damage.

7 Grip the top and bottom of each wheel and try to move it in and out. It won't take a lot of effort to be able to feel any play in the wheel bearings. If the play is noticeable it would be a good idea to adjust it right away or it could confuse further inspections.

8 Grip each side of the wheel and try rocking it laterally. Steady pressure will, of course, turn the steering, but back-and-forth pressure will reveal a loose steering joint. If some play is felt it would be easier to get assistance from someone so while one person rocks the wheel from side to side, the other can look at the joints, bushes and connections in the steering linkage. Generally speaking, there are eight places where the play may occur. The two outer balljoints on the tie-rods are the most likely, followed by the two inner joints on the same rods, where they join to the centre rod. Any play in them means renewal of the tie-rod end. Next are two swivel bushes, one at each end of the centre gear rod. Finally, check the steering gear arm balljoint and the one on the idler arm which supports the centre rod on the side opposite the steering box. This unit is bolted to the side of the frame member and any play calls for renewal of the bushes.

9 To check the steering box, first make sure the bolts holding the steering box to the frame are tight. Then get another person to help examine the mechanism. One should look at, or hold onto, the arm at the bottom of the steering box while the other turns the steering wheel a little from side to side. The amount of lost motion between the steering wheel and the gear arm indicates the degree of wear in the steering box mechanism. This check should be carried out with the wheels first in the straight ahead position and then at nearly full lock on each side. If the play only occurs noticeably in the straight ahead position then the wear is most likely in the worm and/or nut. If it occurs at all positions, then the wear is probably in the sector shaft bearing. Oil leaks from the unit are another indication of such wear. In either case the steering box will need removal for closer examination and repair.

10 Moving to the vehicle interior, check the play in the steering wheel by turning it slowly in both directions until the wheels can just be felt turning. The steering wheel free play should be less than 35 mm. Excessive play is another indication of wear in the steering gear or linkage. The steering box can be adjusted for wear (see Chapter 10).

11 Inspect the front driveaxle CV joint boots for tears and leakage of grease **(see illustration)**.

12 Following the inspection of the front, a similar inspection should be made of the rear suspension components, again checking for loose bolts, damaged or disconnected parts and deteriorated rubber bushes.

18 Exhaust system check

Refer to illustration 18.2

1 With the engine cold (at least three hours after the vehicle has been driven), check the complete exhaust system from the manifold to the end of the tailpipe. The inspection should be done with the vehicle on a hoist to permit unrestricted access. If a hoist isn't available, raise the vehicle and support it securely on jackstands.

2 Check the exhaust pipes and connections for signs of leakage and/or corrosion indicating a potential failure. Make sure that all brackets and hangers are in good condition and tight **(see illustration)**.

3 Inspect the underside of the body for

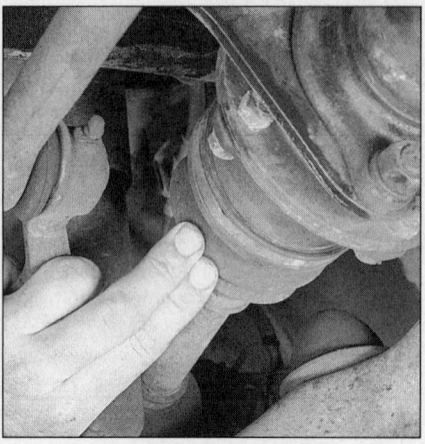

17.11 Push on the CV joint boot to check for cracks or lubricant leaks

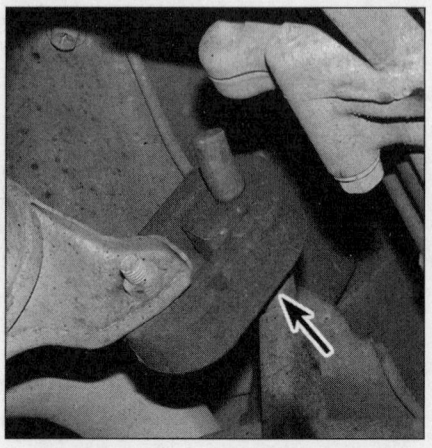

18.2 Check the exhaust system for rust, damage or worn rubber hangers

Chapter 1 Tune-up and routine maintenance   1-27

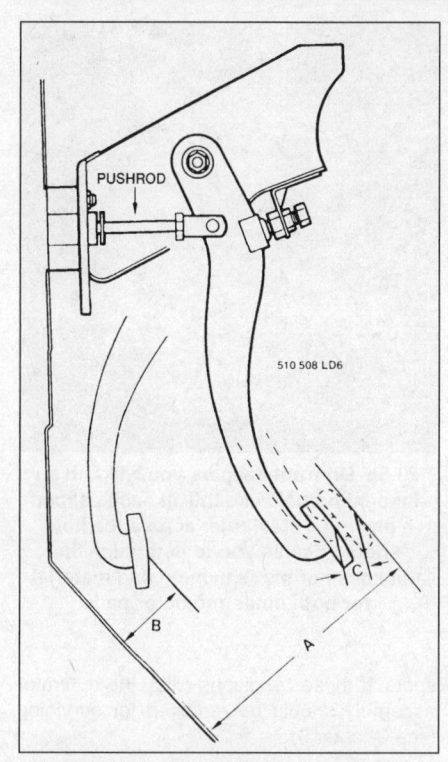

19.2 The clutch pedal height (A) is measured from the top of the pedal to the floor, clutch pedal disengaged height (B), is measured from the top of the pedal fully depressed to the toe board, the clutch pedal freeplay (C), measure the distance from the natural resting place of the pedal to the point at which resistance is felt

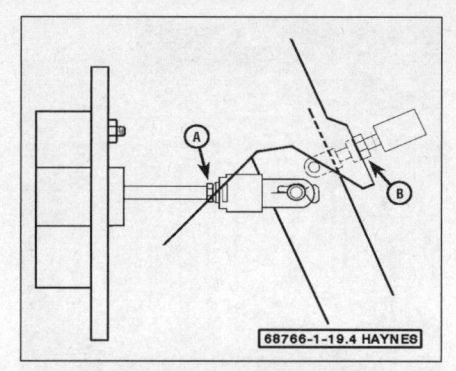

19.4 Adjust the pedal height and freeplay at the clutch master pushrod setting nut (A) or clutch pedal position switch (B) - don't push it toward the master cylinder during the adjustment

holes, corrosion, open seams, etc. which may allow exhaust gases to enter the passenger compartment. Seal all body openings with silicone sealant or body putty.

4 Rattles and other noises can often be traced to the exhaust system, especially the hangers, mounts and heat shields. Try to move the pipes, mufflers and catalytic converter. If the components can come in contact with the body or suspension parts, secure the exhaust system with new brackets and hangers.

19 Clutch pedal height and freeplay check and adjustment

Refer to illustrations 19.2 and 19.4

1 On vehicles equipped with a manual transmission, the clutch pedal height and freeplay must be correctly adjusted.
2 The height of the clutch pedal is the distance the pedal sits off the floor **(see illustration)**. The pedal height distance should be as listed in this Chapter's Specifications.
3 The freeplay is the pedal slack, or the distance the pedal can be depressed before it begins to have any effect on the clutch **(see illustration 19.2)**. The distance should be as listed in this Chapter's Specifications. If it isn't, it must be adjusted.
4 The freeplay and height are adjusted by loosening the setting nut or clutch pedal position switch lock nut **(see illustration)**, turning the rod or switch in or out to achieve the proper measurement and retightening the lock nut.

20 Manual transmission lubricant level check

Refer to illustration 20.1

1 Manual transmissions don't have a dipstick. The lubricant level is checked by removing a filler plug from the side of the transmission case **(see illustration)**. Locate the plug and use a rag to clean the plug and the area around it. If the vehicle is raised to gain access to the plug, be sure to support it safely on jackstands - DO NOT crawl under the vehicle when it's supported only by a jack!
2 With the engine and transmission cold, remove the plug. If lubricant immediately starts leaking out, thread the plug back into the transmission - the level is correct. If it doesn't, reach inside the hole with your little finger. The level should be even with the bottom of the plug hole.
3 If the transmission needs more lubricant, use a syringe or small pump to add it through the plug hole.
4 Thread the plug back into the transmission and tighten it securely. Drive the vehicle, then check for leaks around the plug.

21 Transfer case lubricant level check

Refer to illustration 21.2

1 If necessary, remove the transfer case rock guard (if equipped). The lubricant level is checked by removing a filler plug from the case. If the vehicle is raised to gain access to the plug, be sure to support it safely on jackstands - DO NOT crawl under the vehicle when it's supported only by a jack!
2 With the engine and transfer case cold, remove the fill plug **(see illustration)**. If lubricant immediately starts leaking out, thread the plug back into the case - the level is correct. If it doesn't, completely remove the plug and reach inside the hole with your little finger. The level should be even with the bottom of the plug hole.

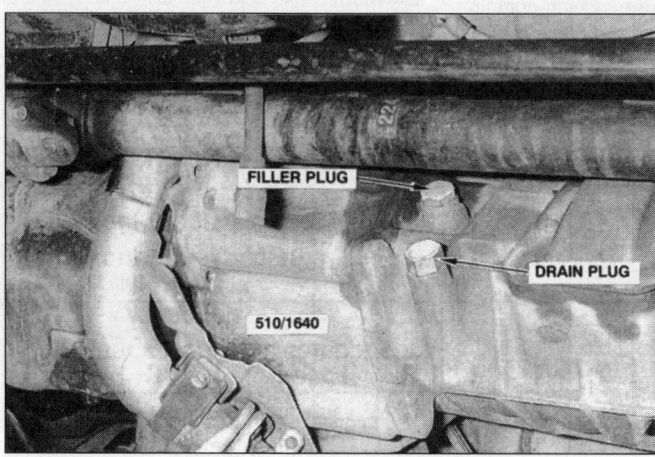

20.1 Manual transmission filler and drain plug locations

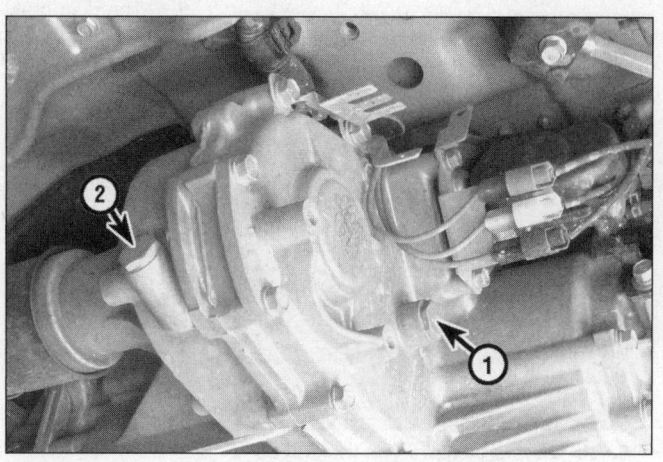

21.2 Transfer case drain plug (1) and filler plug (2) locations

Chapter 1 Tune-up and routine maintenance

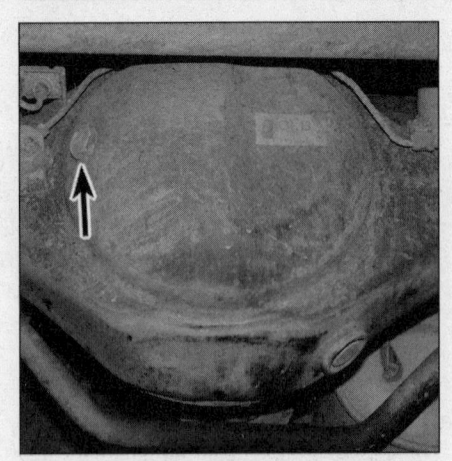

22.2a Typical early model rear differential check/fill plug location (arrow) - use a box-end spanner or socket when removing or refitting the plug to avoid rounding off the hex

3 If more lubricant is needed, use a syringe or small pump to add it through the opening.
4 Thread the plug back into the case and tighten it to the torque listed in this chapter's Specifications. Drive the vehicle, then check for leaks around the plug. Refit the rock guard.

22 Differential lubricant level check

Refer to illustrations 22.2a and 22.2b

1 The differential has a check/fill plug which must be removed to check the lubricant level. If the vehicle is raised to gain access to the plug, be sure to support it safely on jackstands - DO NOT crawl under the vehicle when it's supported only by a jack.
2 Remove the check/fill plug from the differential **(see illustrations)**.
3 The lubricant level should be at the bottom of the plug opening. If not, use a syringe to add the recommended lubricant until it just starts to run out of the opening.
4 Refit the plug and tighten it to the torque listed in this chapter's Specifications.

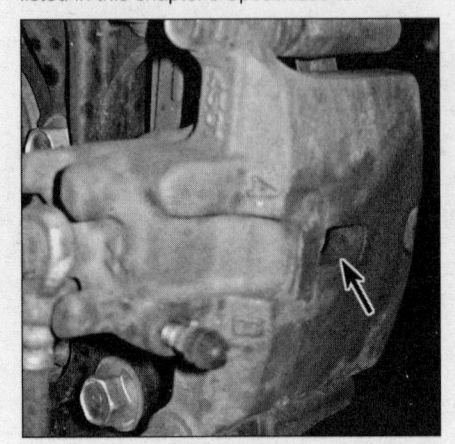

23.6b On rear calipers you will find an inspection hole like this in each caliper

22.2b Typical later model front differential check/fill plug (arrow)

23 Brake check

Refer to illustrations 23.6a, 23.6b and 23.11

Warning: *Brake system dust is hazardous to your health. DO NOT blow it out with compressed air and DO NOT inhale it. DO NOT use petrol or solvents to remove the dust. Use brake system cleaner or denatured alcohol only!*

Note: *For detailed photographs of the brake system, refer to Chapter 9.*

1 In addition to the specified intervals, the brakes should be inspected every time the wheels are removed or whenever a defect is suspected.
2 To check the brakes, the vehicle must be raised and supported securely on jackstands.

Disc brakes

3 Disc brakes are used on the front and rear wheels. Extensive rotor damage can occur if the pads are allowed to wear beyond the specified limit.
4 Raise the vehicle and support it securely on jackstands, then remove the wheels (see *Jacking and Towing* at the front of the manual if necessary).
5 The disc brake calipers, which contain the pads, are visible with the wheels removed. There's an outer pad and an inner pad in each caliper. All pads should be inspected.
6 Each caliper has an opening, which allows you to inspect the pads **(see illustrations)**. If the pad material has worn below the limit listed in this Chapter's Specifications, the pads should be renewed.
7 If you're unsure about the exact thickness of the remaining lining material, remove the pads for further inspection or renewal (see Chapter 9).
8 Before refitting the wheels, check for leakage and/or damage (cracks, splitting, etc.) around the brake hose connections. Renew the hose or fittings as necessary, referring to Chapter 9.
9 Check the condition of the rotor. Look for score marks, deep scratches and burned

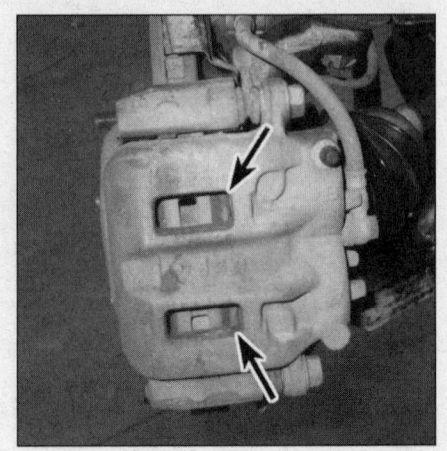

23.6a On front calipers you will find an inspection hole like this in each caliper - placing a steel ruler across the hole should enable you to determine the thickness of the remaining pad material for both inner and outer pads

spots. If these conditions exist, the hub/rotor assembly should be removed for servicing (see Chapter 9).

Parking brake

10 The parking brake is operated by a centre-mounted lever and locks the rear brake system. The easiest, and perhaps most obvious method of periodically checking the operation of the parking brake assembly is to park the vehicle on a steep hill with the parking brake set and the transmission in Neutral. If the parking brake cannot prevent the vehicle from rolling within 4 to 6 (lever) clicks, it's in need of adjustment (see Chapter 9).

Vacuum pump

11 Check the vacuum hoses and pipes between the vacuum pump and the brake booster, on models without a hydraulic brake booster **(see illustration)**.

Brake fluid

Warning: *Brake fluid can harm your eyes and damage painted surfaces, so use extreme*

23.11 Vacuum pump location on the 3.2 litre (4M41) diesel engine

Chapter 1 Tune-up and routine maintenance

caution when handling or pouring it. Do not use brake fluid that has been standing open or is more than one year old. Brake fluid absorbs moisture from the air. Excess moisture can cause a dangerous loss of braking effectiveness.

12 Inspect the brake fluid level and condition as described at the beginning of this chapter (see Section 4).

13 At the intervals specified in the Maintenance Schedule, the brake fluid should be renewed. This is a similar procedure to bleeding the brakes except the brakes are bled until clean fluid is expelled from each brake caliper or wheel cylinder (see Chapter 9).

24 Fuel system check

Warning: *Petrol is extremely flammable, so take extra precautions when you work on any part of the fuel system. Don't smoke or allow open flames or bare light bulbs near the work area, and don't work in a garage where a gas-type appliance (such as a water heater or clothes drier) is present. If you spill any fuel on your skin, rinse it off immediately with soap and water. When you perform any kind of work on the fuel tank, wear safety glasses and have a Class B type fire extinguisher on hand. On petrol fuel-injected models, no components should be disconnected until the pressure has been relieved (see Chapter 4).*

1 The fuel tank is located at the rear of the vehicle.

2 The fuel system should be checked with the vehicle raised on a hoist so the components underneath the vehicle are readily visible and accessible.

3 If the smell of petrol is noticed while driving or after the vehicle has been in the sun, the system should be thoroughly inspected immediately.

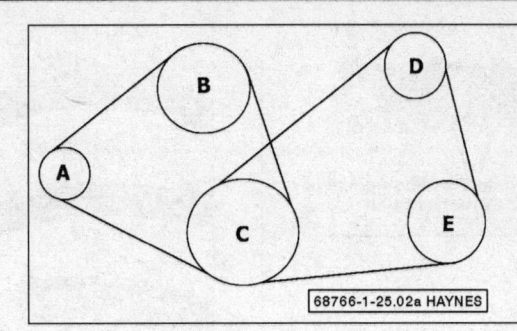

4 Remove the fuel tank cap and check for damage, corrosion and an unbroken sealing imprint on the gasket. Renew the cap with a new one if necessary.

5 With the vehicle raised, check the fuel tank and filler neck for punctures, cracks and other damage. The connection between the filler neck and the tank is especially critical. Sometimes a rubber filler neck will leak due to loose clamps or deteriorated rubber, problems a home mechanic can usually rectify.

Warning: *Do not, under any circumstances, try to repair a fuel tank yourself (except rubber components). A welding torch or any open flame can easily cause the fuel vapours to explode if the proper precautions are not taken!*

6 Carefully check all rubber hoses and metal lines leading away from the fuel tank. Look for loose connections, deteriorated hoses, crimped lines and other damage. Follow the lines to the front of the vehicle, carefully inspecting them all the way. Repair or renew damaged sections as necessary.

7 If a fuel odour is still evident after the inspection, refer to Section 31 and check the evaporative emissions system.

25.2a Typical drivebelt routing for the four-cylinder diesel engines
- A Alternator pulley
- B Water pump pulley
- C Crankshaft pulley
- D Tensioner pulley
- E Air conditioner compressor pulley

25 Drivebelt check, adjustment and renewal

1 The accessory drivebelts are located at the front of the engine. The belts drive the water pump, alternator, power steering pump and air conditioning compressor. The condition and tension of the drivebelts are critical to the operation of the engine and accessories. Excessive tension causes bearing wear, while insufficient tension produces slippage, noise, component vibration and belt failure. Because of their composition and the high stress to which they are subjected, drivebelts stretch and continue to deteriorate as they get older. As a result, they must be periodically checked and adjusted.

Check

Refer to illustrations 25.2a, 25.2b, 25.2c, 25.4a, 25.4b and 25.5

2 The number, type and routing of belts used on a particular vehicle depends on the engine, model year and accessories fitted **(see illustrations)**.

3 Various types of drivebelts are used on these models. Some components are driven by V-belts (these are the conventional type). Others are driven by V-ribbed belts. Some models use a single V-ribbed belt to drive all of the accessories. This is known as a "serpentine" belt because of the winding path it follows between various drive, accessory and idler pulleys.

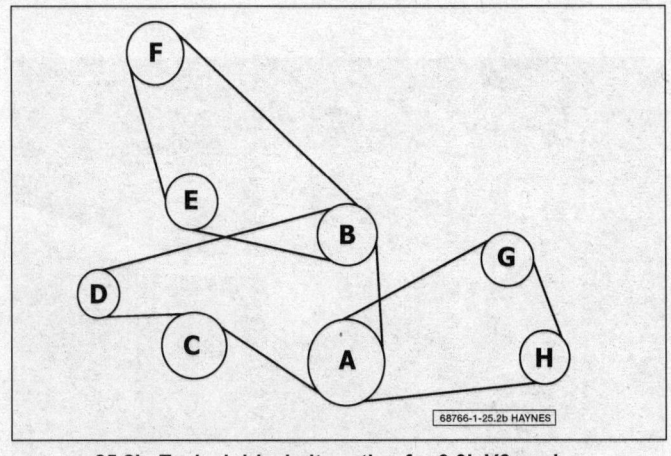

25.2b Typical drivebelt routing for 3.0L V6 engine
- A Crankshaft pulley
- B Cooling fan pulley
- C Tensioner pulley
- D Alternator pulley
- E Tensioner pulley
- F Power steering pump pulley
- G Tensioner pulley
- H Air conditioner compressor pulley

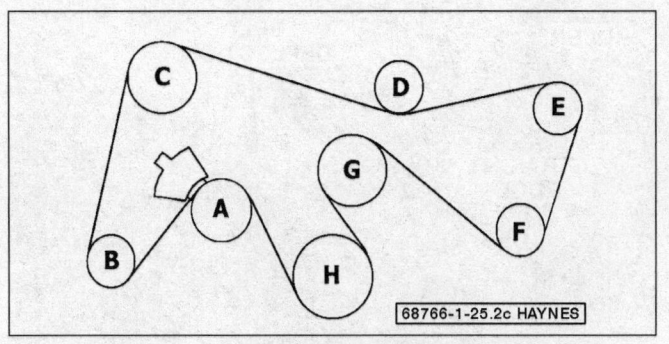

25.2c Typical drivebelt routing for 3.5 and 3.8L V6 engine
- A Serpentine belt tensioner
- B Alternator pulley
- C Idler pulley
- D Idler pulley
- E Power steering pump pulley
- F Air conditioner compressor pulley
- G Fan pulley
- H Crankshaft pulley

Chapter 1 Tune-up and routine maintenance

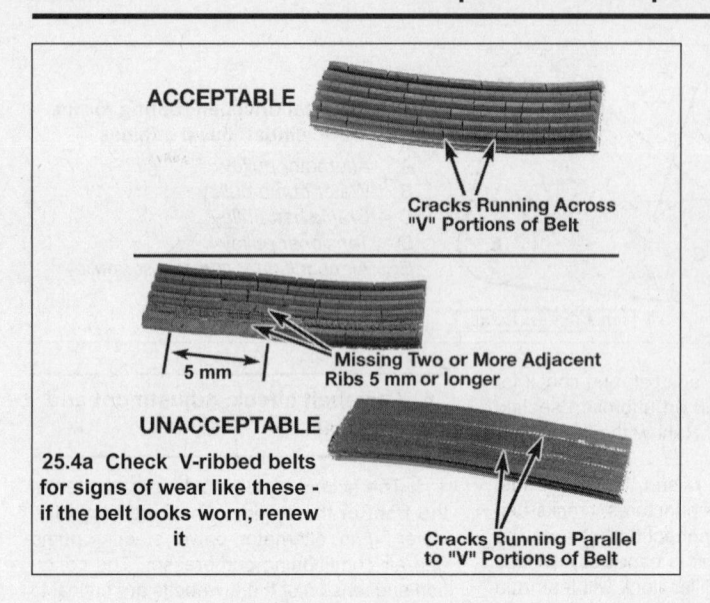

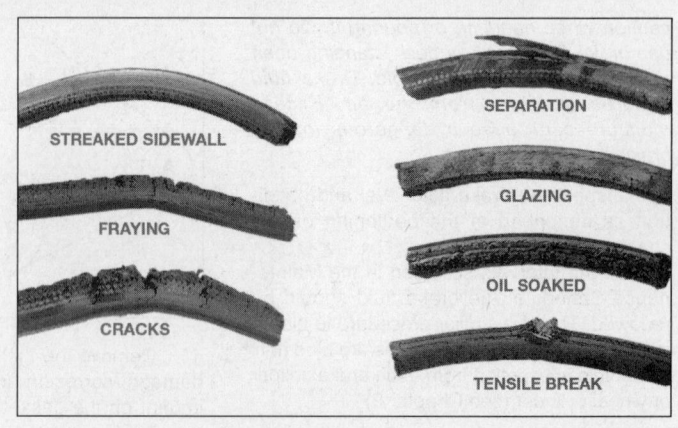

25.4a Check V-ribbed belts for signs of wear like these - if the belt looks worn, renew it

25.4b Here are some of the more common problems associated with drivebelts (check very carefully to prevent an untimely breakdown)

4 With the engine off, open the bonnet and locate the drivebelt(s) at the front of the engine. With a flashlight, check each belt for separation of the rubber plies from each side of the core, a severed core, separation of the ribs from the rubber, cracks, torn or worn ribs and cracks in the inner ridges of the ribs. Also check for fraying and glazing, which gives the belt a shiny appearance **(see illustrations)**. Cracks in the rib side of V-ribbed belts are acceptable, as are small chunks missing from the ribs. If a V-ribbed belt has lost chunks bigger than 13 mm from two adjacent ribs, or if the missing chunks cause belt noise, the belt should be renewed. Both sides of each belt should be inspected, which means you'll have to twist them to check the undersides. Use your fingers to feel a belt where you can't see it. If any of the above conditions are evident, renew the belt as described below.

5 To check the tension of the belts, the following "rule of thumb" method is recommended. Lay a straightedge across the longest free span (the distance between two pulleys) of the belt. Push down firmly on the belt at a point half way between the pulleys and see how much the belt moves (deflects). Measure the deflection with a ruler **(see illustration)**. The belt should deflect 6 to 8 mm if the distance from pulley centre-to-pulley centre is less than 300 mm; it should deflect from 9 to 12 mm if the distance from pulley centre-to-pulley centre is over 300 mm.

Adjustment

V-belts

Refer to illustrations 25.7a and 25.7b

6 Move the belt-driven accessory on the bracket, as follows:

7 For each accessory, there will be a locking bolt and a pivot bolt or nut **(see illustrations)**. Both must be loosened slightly to enable you to move the component.

8 Loosen the lock bolt then use the adjuster bolt to move the component away from the engine (to tighten the belt) or toward the engine (to loosen the belt).

9 Hold the accessory in position and check the belt tension. If it's correct, tighten the lock bolt until snug, then recheck the tension. If it's all right, tighten the lock bolt completely.

Renewal

V-ribbed belts

Refer to illustrations 25.10a and 25.10b

10 Follow the above procedures for drivebelt adjustment **(see illustrations)**, but loosen the belt until it will slip off the pulleys, then remove it. It may be necessary to remove forward belts to renew a rearward belt. Since belts tend to wear out at the same time, it's a good idea to renew all of them at the same time. Mark each belt and the corresponding pulley grooves so the belt can be reinstalled properly.

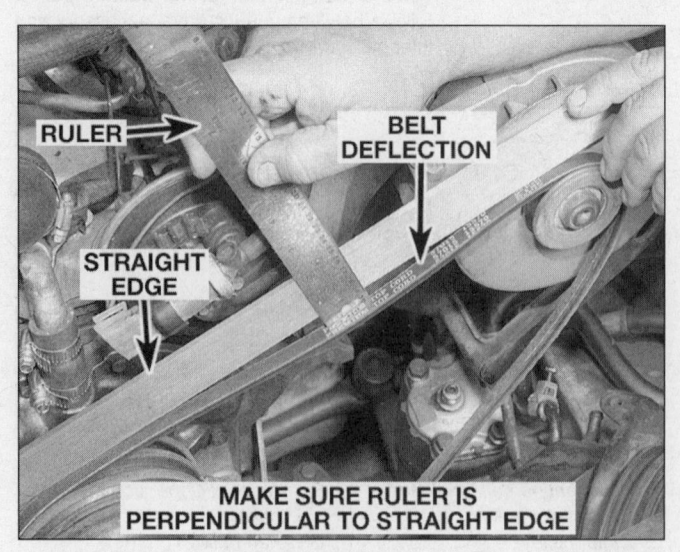

25.5 Measuring drivebelt deflection with a straightedge and ruler

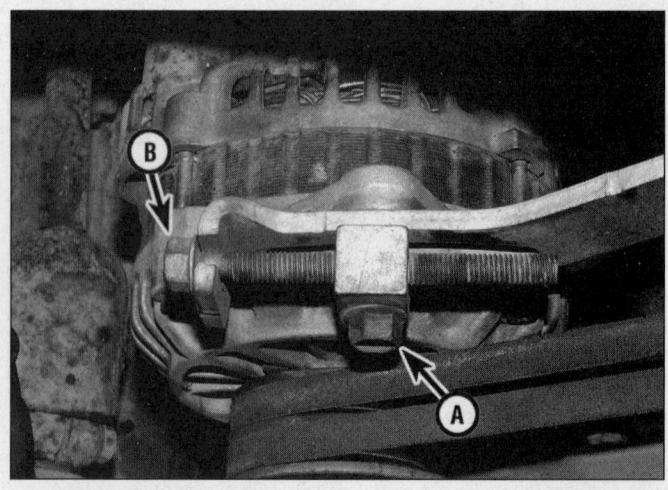

25.7a To adjust the alternator, loosen the locking bolt (A) and turn the adjuster bolt (B) out to remove the belts and in to tighten the belts

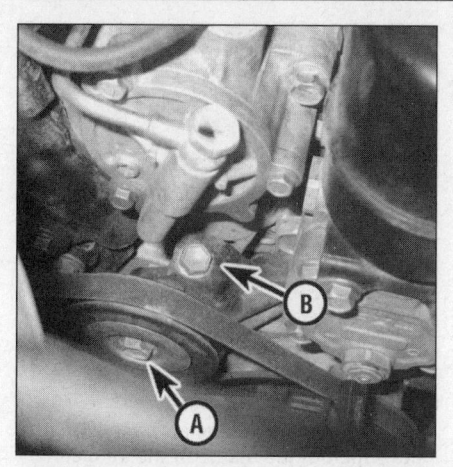

Chapter 1 Tune-up and routine maintenance

25.7b To adjust the power steering pump tensioner, loosen the centre locking bolt (A) and turn the adjuster bolt (B) out to remove the belt and in to tighten the belt

25.10a On 3.0L engines to adjust the power steering pump tensioner, loosen the centre locking bolt (A) and turn the adjuster bolt (B) in to remove the belt and out to tighten the belt

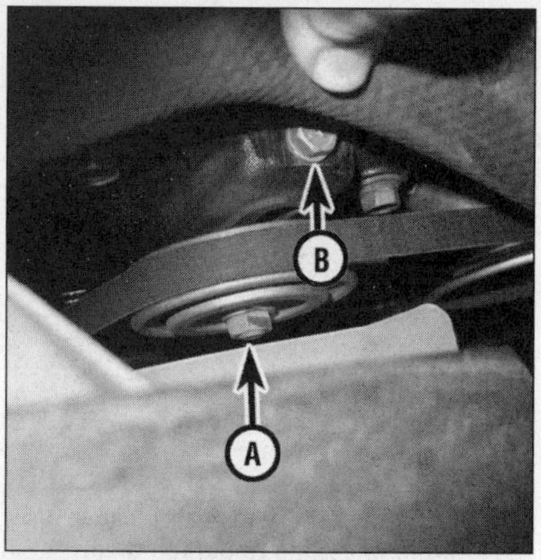

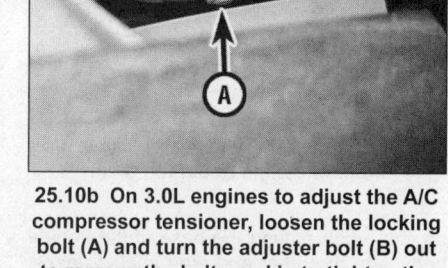

25.10b On 3.0L engines to adjust the A/C compressor tensioner, loosen the locking bolt (A) and turn the adjuster bolt (B) out to remove the belts and in to tighten the belts

Serpentine belt

Refer to illustrations 25.12 and 25.13

11 Note how the drive belt is routed, then remove the belt from the pulleys.
12 Insert a 1/2-inch drive ratchet or breaker bar into the tensioner square and rotate the handle anti-clockwise to release the drivebelt tension **(see illustration)**.
13 The tensioner can be locked into the released position by inserting a drill bit or punch through the tensioner and into the mounting body **(see illustration)** and remove the belt.
14 Fit the new drivebelt onto the crankshaft, power steering, alternator and air conditioning compressor pulleys as applicable, then rotate the tensioner and locate the drivebelt on the pulley. Make sure that the drivebelt is correctly seated in all of the pulley grooves, then release the tensioner.

Serpentine belt tensioner renewal

Refer to illustration 25.16

15 Remove the drivebelt as described previously.
16 Remove the tensioner mounting bolts **(see illustration)** then detach the tensioner from the engine.
17 Refitting is the reverse of removal. Be sure to tighten the tensioner bolts securely.

26 Seat belt check

1 Check the seat belts, buckles, latch plates and guide loops for any obvious damage or signs of wear.
2 Make sure the seat belt reminder light comes on when the key is turned on.
3 The seat belts are designed to lock up during a sudden stop or impact, yet allow free movement during normal driving. The retractors should hold the belt against your chest while driving and rewind the belt when the buckle is unlatched.
4 If any of the above checks reveal problems with the seat-belt system, renew parts as necessary.

27 Throttle body mounting bolt torque check

1 Bolts attach the throttle body to the air intake plenum. The bolts can sometimes work loose during normal engine operation and cause a vacuum leak.
2 To properly tighten the mounting bolts, a torque wrench is necessary. If you do not own one, they can usually be rented on a daily basis.
3 Remove the air cleaner or intake hose assembly (see Chapter 4).
4 Locate the mounting bolts at the base of the throttle body. Decide what special tools or adaptors will be necessary, if any, to tighten the bolts with a socket and torque wrench.
5 Tighten the bolts to the torque listed in this chapter's Specifications. Do not overtighten the bolts, as the threads may strip.
6 If you suspect a vacuum leak exists at the bottom of the throttle body obtain a short length of rubber hose. Start the engine and place one end of the hose next to your ear

25.12 Rotate the tensioner anti-clockwise to release the tension from the belt

25.13 Lock the tensioner bolt using a drill bit or centre punch

25.16 Remove the tensioner mounting bolt (A) and through bolt (B) and remove the tensioner

1-32 Chapter 1 Tune-up and routine maintenance

28.3a Pull up on the four air cleaner top attaching clips to detach them

28.3b Pull the air cleaner top back . . .

28.4 . . . and lift out the air filter element and wipe out the inside of the air cleaner housing with a clean rag

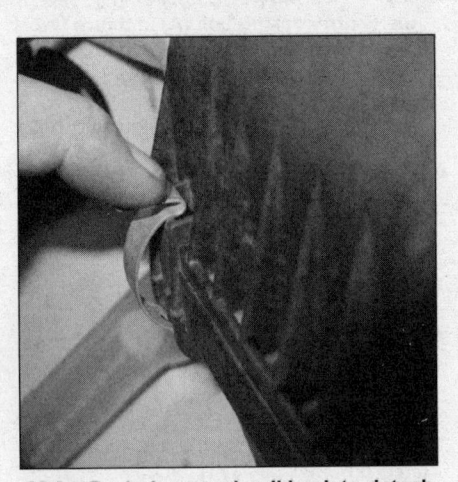

28.8a Push down and pull back to detach the clips

28.8b Lift the air cleaner top off and remove the filter

as you probe around the base of the throttle body with the other end. You should hear a hissing sound if a leak exists.

7 If, after the bolts are properly tightened, a vacuum leak still exists, the throttle body must be removed and a new gasket refitted. See Chapter 4 for more information.

8 After tightening the bolts, reinstall the air cleaner housing or intake hose.

28 Air filter renewal

1 At the specified intervals, the air filter should be renewed. A thorough program of preventive maintenance would also call for the filter to be inspected periodically between changes, especially if the vehicle is often driven in dusty conditions.

2 The air filter is located inside the air cleaner housing, which is mounted at the right front corner of the engine compartments.

Oval filter housing

Refer to illustrations 28.3a, 28.3b and 28.4

3 Release the four air cleaner top attaching clips **(see illustration)** and pull the air cleaner top **(see illustrations)**.

4 Remove the old filter element **(see illustration)**. If it is covered with dirt, it should be renewed.

5 Insert the filter element in the air cleaner housing and centre the filter.

6 Refit the air cleaner top and secure it with the clips.

7 Start the engine, making sure there are no air leaks around the housing top.

Rectangular filter housing

Refer to illustration 28.8a and 28.8b

8 Detach the clips **(see illustration)**, pull the cover up and lift the filter out of the housing **(see illustration)**. If the filter is covered with dirt, it should be renewed.

9 Wipe the inside of the air cleaner housing with a rag.

10 Place the old filter (if in good condition) or the new filter (if renewal is necessary) into the air cleaner housing making sure the filter is fully seated. Set the cover in place and attach the clips.

29 Fuel filter service

Warning: *Fuel is extremely flammable, so take extra precautions when you work on any part of the fuel system. Don't smoke or allow open flames or bare light bulbs near the work area, and don't work in a garage where a gas-type appliance (such as a water heater or clothes drier) is present. If you spill any fuel on your skin, rinse it off immediately with soap and water. When you perform any kind of work on the fuel tank, wear safety glasses and have a Class B type fire extinguisher on hand.*

Note: *On 2001 and later models the fuel filter and fuel pump are incorporated into the fuel pump module located in the fuel tank.*

1 This job should be done with the engine cold (after sitting at least three hours). Place a metal container, rags or newspapers under the filter to catch spilled fuel.

Warning: *Before attempting to remove the fuel filter, disconnect the negative cable from the battery and position it out of the way so it can't accidentally contact the battery post.*

2000 and earlier petrol models

Refer to illustration 29.3

2 Depressurise the fuel system (Chapter 4).

3 The fuel filter is located under the vehicle, adjacent to the fuel tank **(see illustration)**.

4 Raise the vehicle and support it securely on jackstands. Remove the filter protector plate (if equipped).

5 Using two spanners, remove the high-pressure hose.

6 Loosen the output hose bolt or fitting and detach it. If the hoses are in bad shape, now would be a good time to renew them.

7 Remove the bolts and detach the filter, noting the direction in which it was fitted.

8 Refit the new filter in the bracket, making sure the filter is properly oriented.

9 Connect the hoses to the new filter and tighten the bolts or fitting securely. On bolt-type (banjo) connections, use new sealing washers.

10 Start the engine and check carefully for leaks at the filter hose connections.

Chapter 1 Tune-up and routine maintenance

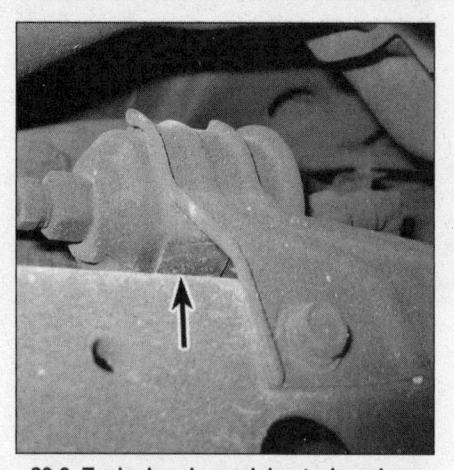

29.3 Typical early model petrol engines fuel filter location (arrow), use two spanners when removing the fuel hoses - an open end to steady the filter and a box-end to loosen the bolt without rounding it off

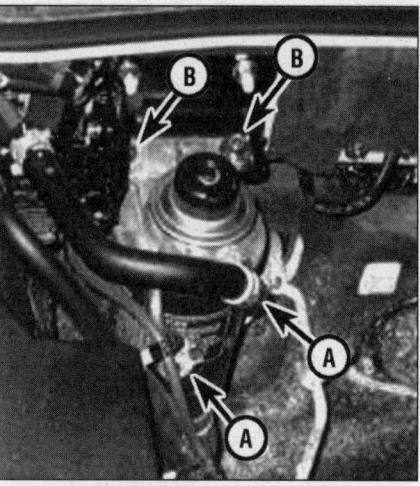

29.15 Remove the fuel lines (A) and then the fuel assembly mounting bolts (B)

29.17 Hold the filter securely and carefully unscrew the water sensor from the bottom of the filter using a pair of pliers, taking care not to damage the sensor

29.16 Use an oil filter wrench to loosen the filter from the housing, then unscrew the filter from the housing by hand

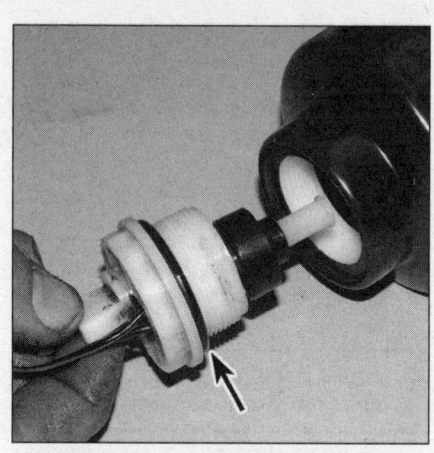

29.18 Fit a new O-ring (arrow) on the water sensor and screw the sensor into the new filter and tighten securely - make sure the O-ring was not damaged during installation

Diesel models

Fuel filter renewal

Refer to illustrations 29.15, 29.16 29.17 and 29.18

11 Remove the cap from the fuel tank.
12 Disconnect the wiring from the water sensor.
13 Place rags around and beneath the fuel filter to catch fuel that may spray or leak.
14 Disconnect the fuel hoses.
15 Remove the filter assembly mounting bolts and remove the **(see illustration)** filter assembly.
16 Using an oil filter wrench, remove the fuel filter canister **(see illustration)**.
17 Hold the canister firmly and screw the water sensor off of the canister **(see illustration)** and remove the O-ring from the sensor.
18 Fit a new O-ring onto the sensor **(see illustration)** and screw the sensor in to the new canister making sure the O-ring is not damaged. Refitting is the reverse of removal. Bleed the system (refer to Step 19).

Bleeding the fuel system

Refer to illustration 29.19 and 29.20

19 Loosen the small air plug located near the top of the filter assembly **(see illustration)**. Place rags under the filter.
20 Operate the manual pump **(see illustration)** until clear fuel with no bubbles runs from the bleed hole. Replace the air plug.
21 Operate the manual pump again until increased resistance is felt.

29.19 Place rags below the air bleed plug and loosen the plug to allow air to come out of the bleed screw

29.20 Depress the manual pump to force the air out of the system and prime the fuel lines, once all the air is out close the bleed screw and continue to pump the pump until there is a strong resistance felt

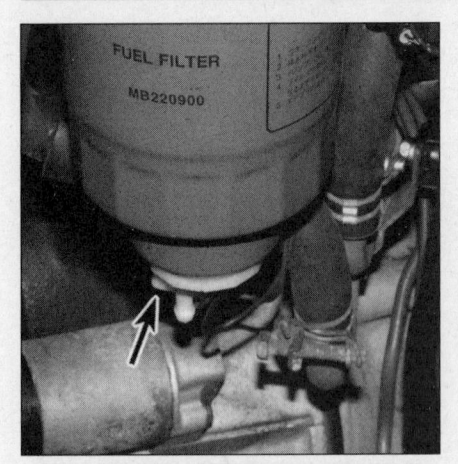

29.22 The water drain plug (arrow) is at the bottom of the fuel filter

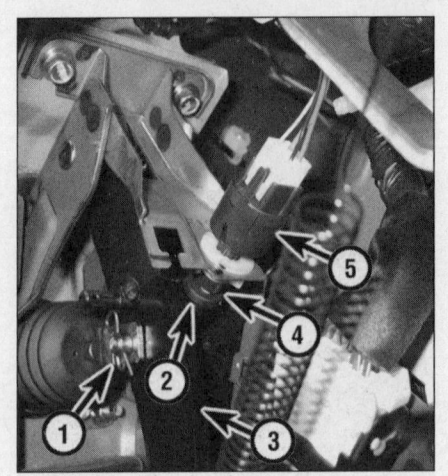

30.1 Brake pedal height adjustment details

1. Brake booster clip and adjustment rod
2. Stopper
3. Pedal
4. Brake light switch plunger
5. Stop light switch

31.2 The charcoal canister is attached to the fenderwell in the engine compartment - check the canister housing and hoses for damage

Draining water from the fuel filter

Refer to illustration 29.22

Note: *Drain the filter any time the fuel filter lamp on the instrument panel lights.*

22 Place rags under the filter. Loosen the drain plug at the bottom of the fuel filter a few turns **(see illustration)**.

23 Operate the hand pump at the top of the filter assembly until clear fuel runs out. Hand tighten the drain plug.

30 Brake pedal height and freeplay check and adjustment

Refer to illustration 30.1

1 Brake pedal height is the distance the pedal sits away from the floor **(see illustration)**. The distance should be as specified (see this Chapter's Specifications). If the pedal height is not within the specified range, loosen the locking nut and back the stop light switch off until it doesn't contact the brake pedal arm. Loosen the brake booster operating rod locking nut and turn rod in or out until the pedal height is correct. Retighten the locking nut.

2 Brake pedal freeplay is the distance the pedal can be depressed before it begins to have any effect on the brakes. Measure the freeplay with the engine off after stepping on the brake pedal five times. The freeplay should be as specified. If it isn't, loosen the locknut, back off the brake light switch and adjust the brake booster rod until the freeplay is correct, then retighten the locknut.

3 After adjustment, turn the stop light switch until it contacts the brake pedal arm, then back it off about one turn and tighten the locknut.

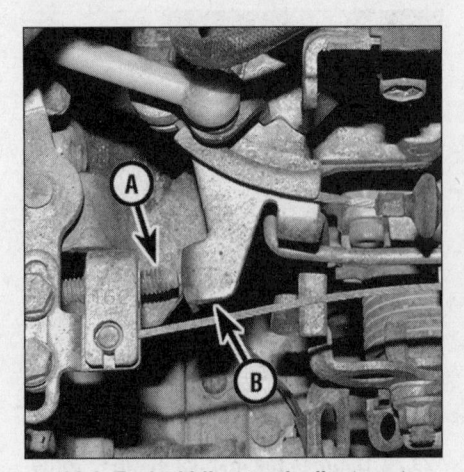

32.6 Typical idle speed adjustment details - 2.8L engine shown

A Adjusting screw
B Accelerator lever

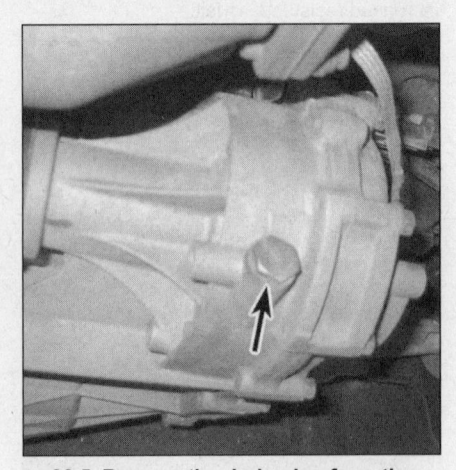

33.5 Remove the drain plug from the lower part of the case (arrow) and allow the old lubricant to drain completely

31 Evaporative emissions system check

Refer to illustration 31.2

1 The function of the evaporative emissions system is to draw fuel vapours from the fuel tank, store them in a charcoal canister and burn them during normal engine operation.

2 The most common symptom of a fault in the evaporative emissions system is a strong fuel odour in the engine compartment. If a fuel odour is detected, inspect the charcoal canister, located in the engine compartment. Check the canister and all hoses for damage and deterioration **(see illustration)**.

3 The canister is held to the fenderwell by a spring clip, secured around the outside of the canister body. The canister is removed by marking and disconnecting the hoses, disengaging the clamp and lifting the canister out.

4 The evaporative emissions control system is explained in more detail in Chapter 6.

32 Idle speed check and adjustment (2.8L diesel engine only)

Refer to illustration 32.6

1 Idle speed is critical to the performance of the engine itself as well as many accessories. A special diesel tachometer must be used when adjusting idle speed. The connection for these meters depends on the manufacturer, so follow the directions included with the tachometer.

2 Apply the parking brake and block the rear wheels. Be sure the transmission is in Neutral (manual transmission) or Park (automatic).

3 Turn off the air conditioner and all other accessories.

Chapter 1 Tune-up and routine maintenance

4   Start the engine and bring it to normal operating temperature.
5   Check the idle speed with the tachometer and compare your reading with that listed in the Specifications in this Chapter.
6   If the idle speed is incorrect, loosen the lock-nut and then turn the idle speed screw on the fuel injection pump to change it **(see illustration)**. Tighten the lock-nut securely.
7   Make sure the accelerator cable still has the proper amount of slack in it. If it does not, adjust the cable (refer to Chapter 4).

33 Transfer case lubricant change

Refer to illustration 33.5

1   Drive the vehicle for at least 15 minutes in 4WD to warm up the lubricant in the case.
2   Raise the vehicle and support it securely on jackstands.
3   Move a drain pan, rags, newspapers and tools under the vehicle.
4   Remove the filler plug (see Section 21).
5   Remove the drain plug **(see illustration)** from the lower part of the case and allow the old lubricant to drain completely.
6   Carefully clean and refit the drain plug after the case is completely drained. Tighten the plug to the torque listed in this Chapter's Specifications.
7   Fill the case with the specified lubricant until it's level with the lower edge of the filler hole.
8   Refit the filler plug and tighten it securely.
9   Check carefully for leaks around the drain plug after the first few kilometres of driving.

34 Manual transmission lubricant change

1   Drive the vehicle for a few kilometres to thoroughly warm up the transmission lubricant.
2   Raise the vehicle and support it securely on jackstands.
3   Move a drain pan, rags, newspapers and tools under the vehicle. With the drain pan and newspapers in position under the transmission, loosen the drain plug located in the bottom of the transmission case.
4   Once loosened, carefully unscrew it with your fingers until you can remove it from the transmission. Allow all of the oil to drain into the pan. If the plug is too hot to touch, use the wrench to remove it.
5   Clean the drain plug, then reinstall it in the transmission and tighten it to the specified torque.
6   Remove the transmission lubricant filler plug (see Section 20). Using a hand pump or syringe, fill the transmission with the correct amount and grade of lubricant, until the level is just at the bottom of the plug hole.
7   Reinstall the filler plug and tighten it to the torque listed in this chapter's Specifications.

35.3 Remove the drain plug (A) from the differential and allow the old lubricant to drain completely before refilling it through the fill plug (B) - front differential shown, rear differential similar

35 Differential lubricant change

Refer to illustration 35.3

Note: *The following procedure can be used for the rear differential as well as the front differential.*

1   Drive the vehicle for several kilometres to warm up the differential lubricant, then raise the vehicle and support it securely on jackstands.
2   Move a drain pan, rags, newspapers and a spanner or ratchet with an extension and socket under the vehicle.
3   With the drain pan under the differential, loosen the drain plug **(see illustration)**. It's the lower of the two plugs.
4   Once loosened, carefully unscrew it with your fingers until you can remove it from the case.
5   Allow all of the lubricant to drain into the pan, then renew the drain plug and tighten it to the torque listed in this Chapter's Specifications.
6   Feel with your hands along the bottom of the drain pan for any metal bits that may have come out with the lubricant. If there are any, it's a sign of excessive wear, indicating that the internal components should be carefully inspected in the near future.
7   Using a hand pump, syringe or funnel, fill the differential with the correct amount and grade of lubricant until the level is just at the bottom of the fill plug hole.
8   Reinstall the plug and tighten it to the torque listed in this chapter's Specifications.
9   Lower the vehicle. Check for leaks after the first few kilometres of driving.

36 Automatic transmission fluid change

Refer to illustration 36.6

1   At the specified time intervals, the transmission fluid should be drained and renewed. Since the fluid should be hot when it's drained, drive the vehicle for 15 or 20 minutes

36.6 Remove the transmission drain plug bolt (arrow) and allow the transmission fluid to drain - early model shown, later models similar

before proceeding.
2   Before beginning work, purchase the specified transmission fluid and filter (if equipped). Most models with drain plugs do not have filter, so it's important before starting the job to determine whether your model requires a renewal filter.
3   Other tools necessary for this job include jackstands to support the vehicle in a raised position, a drain pan capable of holding at least 9 litres, newspapers and clean rags.
4   Raise the vehicle and support it securely on jackstands.
5   Move the drain pan and necessary tools under the vehicle, being careful not to touch any of the hot exhaust components.
6   Place the pan under the drain plug **(see illustration)** in the transmission pan and remove the plug. Be sure the drain pan is in position, as fluid will come out with some force. Once the fluid is drained, reinstall the drain plug securely.
7   Lower the vehicle and add new automatic transmission fluid through the filler tube (see Section 5). The amount should be slightly less than the amount of fluid that was drained (you don't want to overfill it).
8   With the transmission in Park and the parking brake set, run the engine at a fast idle, but don't race it.
9   Move the gear selector through each range and back to Park, then check the fluid level (see Section 5). Add more fluid as required. Add the fluid a little at a time, continually checking the level so you don't overfill the transmission.
10 Check under the vehicle for leaks during the first few kilometres of driving.

37 Cooling system servicing (draining, flushing and refilling)

Refer to illustrations 37.4 and 37.12

Warning: *Antifreeze is a corrosive and*

37.4 The radiator drain plug (arrow) is located at the bottom of the radiator

37.12 On petrol engine models loosen the bleed screw (arrow) and allow all the air to bubble out as the new mixture is being added

38.5 Pull the PCV valve from the engine valve cover and remove the hose from the valve

poisonous solution, so be careful not to spill any of the coolant mixture on the vehicle's paint or your skin. If you do, rinse it off immediately with plenty of clean water. Consult local authorities regarding proper disposal of antifreeze before draining the cooling system. In many areas, reclamation facilities have been established to collect used oil and coolant mixtures.

1 Periodically, the cooling system should be drained, flushed and refilled to replenish the antifreeze mixture and prevent formation of rust and corrosion, which can impair the performance of the cooling system and cause engine damage. When the cooling system is serviced, all hoses and the radiator cap should be checked and renewed if necessary.
2 Apply the parking brake and block the wheels. If the vehicle has just been driven, wait several hours to allow the engine to cool down before beginning this procedure.
3 Once the engine is completely cool, remove the radiator cap. Place the heater temperature control in the maximum heat position.
4 Move a large container under the radiator drain to catch the coolant, then unscrew the drain plug (a pair of pliers may be required to turn it) (see illustration).
5 After the coolant stops flowing out of the radiator, move the container under the engine block drain plug(s) (on four-cylinder engines there is one plug on the side of the block; on V6 engines there are two plugs, located on each side of the block). Remove the plug(s) and allow the coolant in the block to drain.
6 While the coolant is draining, check the condition of the radiator hoses, heater hoses and clamps (refer to Section 9 if necessary).
7 Renew any damaged clamps or hoses.
8 Once the system is completely drained, flush the radiator with fresh water from a garden hose until it runs clear at the drain. The flushing action of the water will remove sediments from the radiator but will not remove rust and scale from the engine and cooling tube surfaces.
9 These deposits can be removed with a chemical cleaner. Follow the procedure outlined in the manufacturer's instructions. If the radiator is severely corroded, damaged or leaking, it should be removed (see Chapter 3) and taken to a radiator repair shop.
10 Remove the overflow hose from the coolant recovery reservoir. Drain the reservoir and flush it with clean water, then reconnect the hose.
11 Reinstall and tighten the radiator drain plug. Refit and tighten the block drain plug(s).
12 Slowly add new coolant (a 50/50 mixture of water and antifreeze) to the radiator until it's full. Add coolant to the reservoir up to the lower mark. On petrol engines loosen the bleed screw at the top of the engine (see illustration) and allow all the air to bubble out, as the coolant mixture is poured into the system. Once only coolant comes out of the bleed screw tighten the screw securely.
13 Leave the radiator cap off and run the engine in a well-ventilated area until the thermostat opens (coolant will begin flowing through the radiator and the upper radiator hose will become hot).
14 Turn the engine off and let it cool. Add more coolant mixture to bring the level back up to the lip on the radiator filler neck.
15 Squeeze the upper radiator hose to expel air, then add more coolant mixture if necessary. Refit the radiator cap.
16 Start the engine, allow it to reach normal operating temperature and check for leaks.

38 Positive Crankcase Ventilation (PCV) system check

Refer to illustrations 38.5 and 38.6

1 The Positive Crankcase Ventilation (PCV) system directs blow by gases from the crankcase back into the inlet manifold so they can be burned in the engine.
2 Rough idling or high idle speed and stalling are symptoms of faults in the PCV system.
3 The system on these models consists of a hose leading from the valve cover to the inlet manifold and a fresh air hose between the air cleaner assembly and the valve cover. Gases from the crankcase are carried by the hose through a PCV valve or orifice in the hose into the inlet manifold.
4 Check the system hoses for cracks, leaks and clogging. Clean the hoses if they are clogged and renew any which are damaged.
5 Remove the PCV valve (see illustration).
6 Start the engine and verify that air can be heard passing through the valve and a suction should be felt, indicating it is operating properly (see illustration).
7 If air will not pass through, renew the valve with a new one.
8 More information on the PCV system can be found in Chapter 6.

39 Spark plug renewal

Refer to illustrations 39.2, 39.5a, 39.5b, 39.6, 39.8, 39.10a and 39.10b

1 Renew the spark plugs with new ones at the intervals recommended in the Mainte-

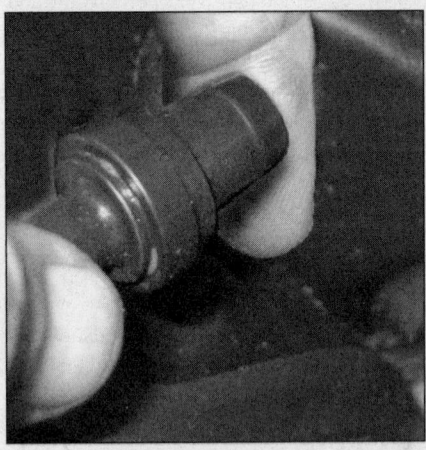

38.6 With the engine running, suction should be felt at the threaded end of the PCV valve

Chapter 1 Tune-up and routine maintenance

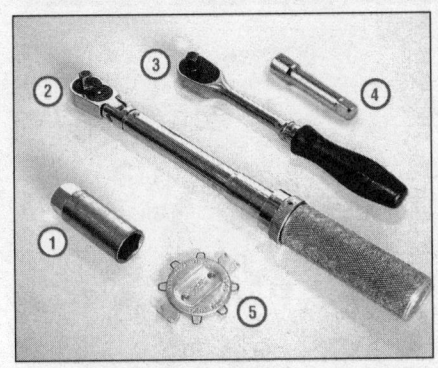

39.2 Tools required for renewing spark plugs

1 **Spark plug socket** - This will have special padding inside to protect the spark plug's porcelain insulator
2 **Torque wrench** - Although not mandatory, using this tool is the best way to ensure the plugs are tightened properly
3 **Ratchet** - Standard hand tool to fit the spark plug socket
4 **Extension** - Depending on model and accessories, you may need special extensions and universal joints to reach one or more of the plugs
5 **Spark plug gap gauge** - This gauge for checking the gap comes in a variety of styles. Make sure the gap for your engine is included

39.5a Spark plug manufacturers recommend using a wire type gauge when checking the gap - if the wire does not slide between the electrodes with a slight drag, adjustment is required

39.5b To change the gap, bend the side electrode only, as indicated by the arrows, and be very careful not to crack or chip the porcelain insulator surrounding the centre electrode

nance schedule.

2 In most cases, the tools necessary for spark plug renewal include a spark plug socket which fits onto a ratchet (spark plug sockets are padded inside to prevent damage to the porcelain insulators on the new plugs), various extensions and a gap gauge to check and adjust the gaps on the new plugs **(see illustration)**. A special plug wire removal tool is available for separating the wire boots from the spark plugs, but it isn't absolutely necessary. A torque wrench should be used to tighten the new plugs.

3 The best approach when renewing the spark plugs is to purchase the new ones in advance, adjust them to the proper gap and renew them one at a time. When buying the new spark plugs, be sure to obtain the correct plug type for your particular engine. This information can be found on the Emission Control Information label located under the bonnet and in the owner's manual. If differences exist between the plug specified on the emissions label and in the owner's manual, assume the emissions label is correct.

4 Allow the engine to cool completely before attempting to remove any of the plugs. While you're waiting for the engine to cool, check the new plugs for defects and adjust the gaps.

5 The gap is checked by inserting the proper thickness gauge between the electrodes at the tip of the plug **(see illustration)**. The gap between the electrodes should be the same as the one specified on the Emissions Control Information label. The wire should just slide between the electrodes with a slight amount of drag. If the gap is incorrect, use the adjuster on the gauge body to bend the curved side electrode slightly until the proper gap is obtained **(see illustration)**. If the side electrode is not exactly over the centre electrode, bend it with the adjuster until it is. Check for cracks in the porcelain insulator (if any are found, the plug shouldn't be used).

6 Remove the upper inlet manifold (see Chapter 2A). Remove the spark plug wire from one spark plug. Pull only on the boot at the end of the wire - don't pull on the wire **(see illustration)**.

7 If compressed air is available, use it to blow any dirt or foreign material away from the spark plug hole. A common bicycle pump will also work. The idea here is to eliminate the possibility of debris falling into the cylinder as the spark plug is removed.

8 Place the spark plug socket over the plug and remove it from the engine by turning it in a anti-clockwise direction **(see illustration)**.

9 Compare the spark plug to those shown in the photos located in the inside rear cover of this manual to get an indication of the general running condition of the engine.

10 Prior to refitting, apply a coat of anti-seize compound to the plug threads **(see illustration)**. Thread one of the new plugs into the hole until you can no longer turn it with your fingers, then tighten it with a torque wrench (if available) or the ratchet. It might be a good idea to slip a short length of rubber hose over the end of the plug to use as a tool to thread it into place **(see illustration)**. The hose will grip the plug well enough to turn it, but will start to slip if the plug begins to cross-thread in the hole - this will prevent damaged threads and the accompanying repair costs.

11 Before pushing the spark plug wire onto the end of the plug, inspect it following the procedures outlined in Section 40.

12 Attach the plug wire to the new spark plug, again using a twisting motion on the boot until it's seated on the spark plug.

13 Repeat the procedure for the remaining spark plugs, renewing them one at a time to prevent mixing up the spark plug wires.

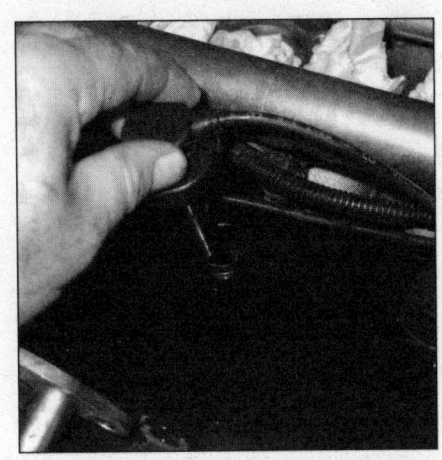

39.6 When removing the spark plug wires, pull only on the boot and use a twisting, pulling motion

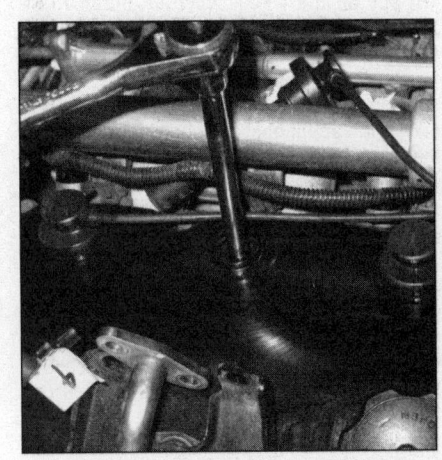

39.8 Use a socket wrench with a long extension to unscrew the spark plugs

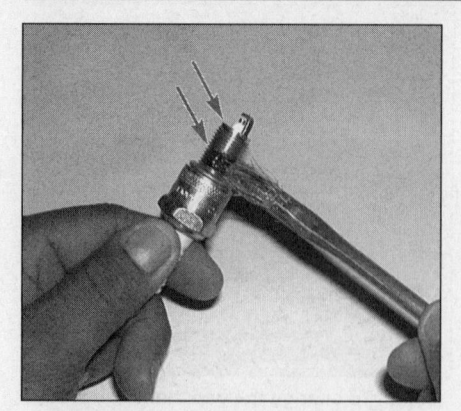

39.10a Apply a thin coat of anti-seize compound to the spark plug threads

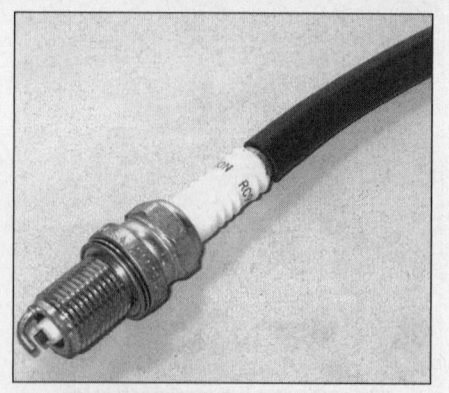

39.10b A length of 10 mm ID rubber hose will save time and prevent damaged threads when fitting the spark plugs

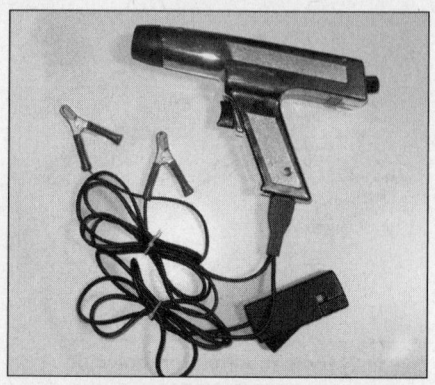

41.1 An inductive pick-up timing light which flashes a bright concentrated beam of light when the number one spark plug fires. Connect the leads according to the instructions supplied with the light to check the ignition timing

40 Spark plug wire check and renewal

1 The spark plug wires should be checked whenever new spark plugs are fitted.
2 Begin this procedure by making a visual check of the spark plug wires while the engine is running. In a darkened garage (make sure there is ventilation) start the engine and observe each plug wire. Be careful not to come into contact with any moving engine parts. If there is a break in the wire, you will see arcing or a small spark at the damaged area. If arcing is noticed, make a note to obtain new wires, then allow the engine to cool.
3 The spark plug wires should be inspected one at a time to prevent mixing up the order, which is essential for proper engine operation. Each original plug wire should be numbered to help identify its location. If the number is illegible, a piece of tape can be marked with the correct number and wrapped around the plug wire.
4 Disconnect the plug wire from the spark plug. A removal tool can be used for this purpose or you can grasp the rubber boot, twist the boot half a turn and pull the boot free. Do not pull on the wire itself **(see illustration 39.6)**.
5 Check inside the boot for corrosion, which will look like a white crusty powder.
6 Push the wire and boot back onto the end of the spark plug. It should fit tightly onto the end of the plug. If it doesn't, remove the wire and use pliers to carefully crimp the metal connector inside the wire boot until the fit is snug.
7 Using a clean rag, wipe the entire length of the wire to remove built-up dirt and grease. Once the wire is clean, check for burns, cracks and other damage. Do not bend the wire sharply, because the conductor within the wire might break.
8 Disconnect the wire from the ignition coil. Again, pull only on the rubber boot. Check for corrosion and a tight fit. Press the wire back into the ignition coil.
9 Inspect the remaining spark plug wires, making sure that each one is securely fastened at the coils and spark plug when the check is complete.
10 If new spark plug wires are required, purchase a set for your specific engine model. Pre-cut wire sets with the boots already refitted are available. Remove the wires one at a time to avoid mix-ups in the firing order.

41 Ignition timing check

Refer to illustrations 41.1 and 41.3

Note: *This ignition timing procedure only checks the base timing setting specified by the factory. Timing cannot be adjusted, therefore the purpose of this check is to verify that the computer is controlling the ignition timing and that the base setting is correct. In most cases, the ignition system can be checked (see Chapter 5) but if the base setting remains incorrect, the ECU (computer) is defective. Take the vehicle to the dealer service department to verify and repair the ignition system problem(s).*

1 Some special tools are required for this procedure **(see illustration)**. The engine must be at normal operating temperature.
2 Apply the parking brake and block the wheels to prevent movement of the vehicle. The transmission must be in Park (automatic) or Neutral (manual).
3 Locate the timing marks at the front of the engine (they should be visible from above after the bonnet is opened) **(see illustration)**. The crankshaft pulley has a notch in it and the timing belt cover has a protrusion with raised numbers. Clean the cover with solvent so the numbers are visible.
4 Use chalk or white paint to mark the notch in the crankshaft pulley.
5 Highlight the point on the cover that corresponds to the ignition timing specification listed in this Chapter's Specifications.
6 Hook up the timing light by following the manufacturer's instructions (an inductive pick-up timing light is preferred). Generally, the power leads are attached to the battery terminals and the pick-up lead is attached to the number one spark plug wire. The number one spark plug is the one closest to the front RHS of the engine.
Caution: *If an inductive pick-up timing light isn't available, don't puncture the spark plug wire to attach the timing light pick-up lead. Instead, use an adapter between the spark plug and plug wire. If the insulation on the plug wire is damaged, the secondary voltage will jump to ground at the damaged point and the engine will misfire.*
7 Make sure the timing light wires are routed away from the drivebelts and fan, then start the engine.
8 Allow the idle speed to stabilise, then point the flashing timing light at the timing marks - be very careful of moving engine components!
9 The mark on the crankshaft pulley will appear stationary. If it's aligned with the specified point on the timing cover, the ignition timing is correct.
10 If the timing is incorrect, have the ECU (computer) checked by a dealer service department or other qualified repair facility.
11 Turn off the engine and remove the timing light.

41.3 The timing marks are located at the front of the engine - highlight the marks in the crankshaft pulley and appropriate mark on the timing cover - 3.0L engine shown, all others similar

Chapter 2 Part A
V6 petrol engines

Contents

	Section
Camshaft oil seal - replacement	9
Camshafts - removal, inspection and refitting	11
CHECK ENGINE or SERVICE ENGINE SOON light on	See Chapter 6
Crankshaft front oil seal - renewal	8
Cylinder head - removal and refitting	12
Driveplate - removal and refitting	15
Engine mounts - check and renewal	17
Engine overhaul - general information	See Chapter 2D
Engine - removal and refitting	See Chapter 2D
Exhaust manifolds - removal and refitting	6
General information	1
Inlet manifold - removal and refitting	5
Oil pump - removal, inspection and refitting	14
Rear main oil seal - renewal	16
Repair operations possible with the engine in the vehicle	2
Rocker arm and hydraulic valve lash adjuster assembly - removal, inspection and refitting	10
Sump - removal and refitting	13
Timing belt - removal, inspection and refitting	7
Top Dead Centre (TDC) - for number one piston - locating	3
Valve cover - removal and refitting	4

Specifications

General

6G72 3.0L engine
- Displacement .... 2,972 cc
- Bore .... 91.1 mm
- Stroke .... 76.0 mm
- Compression ratio 8.9:1

6G74 3.5L engine
- Displacement .... 3,497 cc
- Bore .... 93.0 mm
- Stroke .... 85.8 mm
- Compression ratio 9.5:1

6G75 3.8L engine
- Displacement .... 3,828 cc
- Bore .... 95.0 mm
- Stroke .... 90.0 mm
- Compression ratio
  - NP 9.5:1
  - NS, NT 9.8:1

Firing order 1-2-3-4-5-6

Compression pressure

	NL	NM/NP	NS/NT	NW
Standard	1,270 kPa	1,177 kPa	1,710 kPa	1,530 kPa
Minimum	900 kPa	875 kPa	950 kPa	1,050 kPa
Maximum variation	98 kPa	98 kPa	98 kPa	98 kPa

Oil pressure (other models not specified)
- NS models .... Above 80 kPa @ idle
- NT/NW models .... Above 29 kPa @ idle; 294-686 kPa @ 3500 rpm

Cylinder numbers (as viewed from the drivers seat)
- Right side (No 1 is at the front of the engine) 1-3-5
- Left side (No 2 is at the front of the engine) 2-4-6

Cylinder numbering
⑤ ⑥
③ ④
① ②
Front

Camshaft

Cam lobe height

3.0 and 3.5 litre (SOHC) engines
- Inlet .... 37.71 mm
- Exhaust .... 37.14 mm

3.8 litre engines
- Inlet
  - Low speed .... 36.228 mm
  - High speed .... 37.209 mm
- Exhaust .... 37.874 mm
- Lobe wear limit .... 0.5 mm

3.5 litre (DOHC) engines
    Camshaft runout limit.. 0.10 mm
    Lobe height
        Intake... 35.20 mm
        Exhaust... 34.91 mm
    Lobe wear limit... 0.5 mm
Cam journal diameter
    Except DOHC... 45 mm
    DOHC .... 26 mm

Inlet and exhaust manifolds

	Except NW	NW
Inlet manifold warpage limit...	0.02 mm	0.20 mm
Exhaust manifold warpage limit...	0.02 mm	0.90 mm

Oil pump

	Standard	Limit
Body clearance...	0.10 to 0.18 mm	0.35 mm
Side clearance..	0.04 to 0.10 mm	
Tip clearance..	0.06 to 0.18 mm	

Timing belt

Automatic tensioner pushrod movement (@ 98 to 196 Newtons)........... 1.0 mm
Automatic tensioner protrusion... 12 mm

Piston

	Standard	Limit
Piston ring-to-ring groove clearance		
Top ring...	0.03 to 0.07 mm	0.10 mm
Second ring..	0.02 to 0.06 mm	0.10 mm
Piston ring end gap	**Standard**	**Limit**
Top ring...	0.25 to 0.40 mm	0.80 mm
Second ring..	0.35 to 0.50 mm	0.80 mm
Oil control ring...	0.10 to 0.35 mm	1.00 mm
Piston pin outside diameter...	22 mm	
Connecting rod big end side clearance...	0.10 to 0.25 mm	0.4 mm

Torque specifications

	Nm
Camshaft bearing cap bolts (DOHC)	
Front and rear...	20
No. 2, 3, 4..	11
Camshaft sprocket bolt...	78 to 98
Coolant crossover housing bolts..	18 to 20
Crankshaft pulley/vibration damper bolt	
Except 3.8L..	180 to 190
3.8L	185
Cylinder head bolts **(in sequence - see illustration 12.21)**	
Step 1...	108
Step 2...	Back off bolts to 0
Step 3...	108
Drivebelt tensioner bracket mounting bolts	
Small bolt..	20 to 28
Large bolt..	34 to 54
EGR tube-to-inlet manifold bolts..	16 to 20
EGR tube-to-manifold nut..	50 to 68
Exhaust manifold	
Exhaust manifold heat shield bolts..	13 to 15
Exhaust manifold-to-cylinder head nuts................................	44
Exhaust pipe-to-exhaust manifold nuts..................................	39 to 59
Flywheel/driveplate mounting bolts [1]..	72 to 76
Inlet manifold	
Upper inlet manifold bolts	
Except 3.8L...	16 to 20
3.8L..	21 to 23
Lower inlet manifold nuts **(see illustration 5.29)**	
Step 1 (Bolts A [right])...	5.0 to 8
Step 2 (Bolts D [left])...	21 to 23
Step 3 (Bolts A [right])...	21 to 23
Step 4 (Bolts D [left]) (confirm torque).....................	21 to 23
Step 5 (Bolts A [right]) (confirm torque)..................	21 to 23

Chapter 2 Part A V6 petrol engines

Torque specifications (continued)

	Nm
Oil pump	
Case mounting bolts	14
Cover retaining screws	8 to 12
Pick-up tube bolts	19
Relief valve plug	44
Oil filter adapter bolts	20 to 26
Oil pressure switch	8 to 12
Rocker arm shaft bolts (SOHC)	
Inlet side	28 to 34
Exhaust side	12 to 14
Sump bolts	
NL to NP models	5 to 7
NS, NT and NW models	6 to 12
Sump drain plug	39
Throttle body	6 to 12
Timing belt (see illustration 7.22a)	
Timing belt cover bolts	
Upper timing cover	
M6 bolt	11
M8 bolt	14
Lower timing cover	11
Auto-tensioner retaining bolts	23
Tensioner arm retaining bolt	44
Guide pulley retaining bolt	44
Tensioner pulley bolt	48
Valve cover bolts	3 to 4

[1] Apply a thread locking compound to the threads prior to refitting

1 General information

This Part of Chapter 2 is devoted to in-vehicle petrol engine repair procedures. Information concerning engine removal and refitting can be found in Part D of this Chapter.

The following repair procedures are based on the assumption that the engine is installed in the vehicle. If the engine has been removed from the vehicle and mounted on a stand, many of the steps outlined in this Part of Chapter 2 will not apply.

The Specifications included in this Part of Chapter 2 apply only to the procedures contained in this Part.

2 Repair operations possible with the engine in the vehicle

Many major repair operations can be accomplished without removing the engine from the vehicle.

Clean the engine compartment and the exterior of the engine with some type of degreaser before any work is performed. It will make the job easier and help keep dirt out of the internal areas of the engine.

Depending on the components involved, it may be helpful to remove the bonnet to improve access to the engine as repairs are performed (see Chapter 11 if necessary). Cover the fenders to prevent damage to the paint. Special pads are available, but an old bedspread or blanket will also work.

If vacuum, exhaust, oil or coolant leaks develop, indicating a need for gasket or seal replacement, the repairs can generally be made with the engine in the vehicle. The inlet and exhaust manifold gaskets, oil pan gasket, camshaft and crankshaft oil seals and cylinder head gasket are all accessible with the engine in place.

Exterior engine components, such as the inlet and exhaust manifolds, the sump, the oil pump, the water pump, the starter motor, the alternator and the fuel system components can be removed for repair with the engine in place.

Since the camshafts and cylinder head can be removed without pulling the engine, valve component servicing can also be accomplished with the engine in the vehicle. Replacement of the timing belt and sprockets is also possible with the engine in the vehicle.

In extreme cases caused by a lack of necessary equipment, repair or replacement of piston rings, pistons, connecting rods and rod bearings is possible with the engine in the vehicle. However, this practice is not recommended because of the cleaning and preparation work that must be done to the components involved.

3 Top Dead Centre (TDC) for number one piston - locating

Note: *The crankshaft timing marks on these engines aren't visible until after the timing belt cover has been removed. The number one cylinder can be positioned at TDC by using this procedure without removing the timing belt cover.*

1 Top Dead Centre (TDC) is the highest point in the cylinder that each piston reaches as it travels up-and-down when the crankshaft turns. Each piston reaches TDC on the compression stroke and again on the exhaust stroke, but TDC generally refers to piston position on the compression stroke.

2 Positioning a specific piston at TDC is an essential part of many procedures such as camshaft(s) removal, rocker arm removal, timing belt and sprocket replacement.

3 In order to bring any piston to TDC, the crankshaft must be turned using one of the methods outlined below. When looking at the front of the engine, normal crankshaft rotation is clockwise.

Warning: *Before beginning this procedure, be sure to set the parking brake, place the transmission in Park or Neutral and disable the ignition system by disconnecting the primary electrical connector from the ignition coil pack.*

a) *The preferred method is to turn the crankshaft with a large socket and breaker bar attached to the crankshaft balancer hub bolt that is threaded into the front of the crankshaft.*

b) *A remote starter switch, which may save some time, can also be used. Attach the switch leads to the S (switch) and B (battery) terminals on the starter solenoid. Once the piston is close to TDC, discontinue with the remote switch and use a socket and breaker bar as described in the previous paragraph.*

4.5 Typical valve cover retaining bolt locations

4.6 Remove the spark plug tube seals and, even if they look okay, replace them

4.7 Remove the old valve cover gasket and clean off all traces of old gasket material

c) *If an assistant is available to turn the ignition switch to the Start position in short bursts, you can get the piston close to TDC without a remote starter switch. Use a socket and breaker bar as described in Paragraph a) to complete the procedure.*

4 Remove all spark plugs as this will make it easier to rotate the engine by hand.

5 Insert a compression gauge (screw-in type with a hose) in the number 1 spark plug hole. Place the gauge dial where you can see it while turning the crankshaft balancer hub bolt.

Note: *The number one cylinder is located at the front right of the engine, on the driver side cylinder bank.*

6 Turn the crankshaft clockwise until you see compression building up on the gauge - you are on the compression stroke for that cylinder. If you did not see compression build up, continue with one more complete revolution to achieve TDC for the number one cylinder.

7 If your engine is equipped with a notch in the crankshaft pulley, align the notch in the pulley with the 0 or T mark on the timing belt cover. At this point the number one piston is at TDC on the compression stroke.

8 If your engine is not equipped with a timing scale or a notch in the crankshaft pulley, remove the compression gauge. Through the number one cylinder spark plug hole insert a length of wooden dowel or plastic rod and slowly push it down until it reaches the top surface of the piston crown.

Caution: *Don't insert a metal or sharp object into the spark plug hole as the piston crown may be damaged.* With the dowel or rod in place on top of the piston crown, slowly rotate the crankshaft clockwise until the dowel or rod is pushed upward, stops, and then starts to move back down. Now, rotate the crankshaft slightly anti-clockwise until the dowel or rod has reached it upper most travel. At this point the number one piston is at the TDC position.

9 After the number one piston has been positioned at TDC on the compression stroke, TDC for any of the remaining cylinders can be located by turning the crankshaft 120-degrees (1/3-turn) at a time and following the firing order (refer to the Specifications).

4 Valve cover - removal and refitting

Caution: *If the stereo in your vehicle is equipped with an anti-theft system, make sure you have the correct activation code before disconnecting the battery.*

SOHC
Removal

Refer to illustrations 4.5, 4.6 and 4.7

1 Disconnect the cable from the negative battery terminal (see Chapter 5).

2 Remove the upper inlet manifold (see Section 5).

3 Clearly label and disconnect the spark plug coils and wires (see Chapter 1). Also label and disconnect any electrical harnesses that connect to or cross over the valve cover.

4 Disconnect the breather hose and the PCV hose from the valve cover (see Chapter 6).

5 Remove the valve cover bolts **(see illustration)** and lift off the cover. If the cover sticks to the cylinder head, tap on it with a soft-face hammer or place a wood block against the cover and tap on the wood with a hammer.

Caution: *If you have to pry between the valve cover and the cylinder head, be extremely careful not to gouge or nick the gasket surfaces of either part. A leak could develop after reassembly.*

6 Remove the spark plug tube seals. Even if they look OK, they should be replaced **(see illustration)**.

7 Remove the old gasket **(see illustration)**. Thoroughly clean the valve cover and remove all traces of old gasket material. Gasket removal solvents are available from auto parts stores and may prove helpful. After cleaning the surfaces, degrease them with a rag soaked in lacquer thinner or acetone.

8 Fit the new spark plug seals onto the tubes.

9 Fit a new gasket on the cover, using anaerobic RTV sealant to hold it in place.

10 Tighten the valve cover bolts in 3 steps to the torque listed in this Chapter's Specifications using a criss-cross pattern starting in the middle of the cover and working outwards.

11 The remaining installation steps are the reverse of removal. When complete, run the engine and check for oil leaks.

DOHC engine

12 Detach the spark plug wires and cable brackets from the valve cover. Remove the centre covers and disconnect the wires from the spark plugs. Use numbered pieces of tape to label the wires so they can be returned to their original locations on reassembly.

13 Clearly label and then disconnect any emission hoses and cables which connect to or cross over the valve cover.

14 Remove the valve cover bolts and lift the covers off. If the cover sticks to the cylinder head, tap on it with a soft-face hammer or place a block of wood against the cover and tap on the wood with a hammer.

Caution: *If you have to prise between the valve cover and the cylinder head, be extremely careful not to gouge or nick the gasket surfaces of either part. A leak could develop after reassembly.*

15 After cleaning the surfaces, degrease them with a rag soaked in lacquer thinner or acetone.

Chapter 2 Part A V6 petrol engines

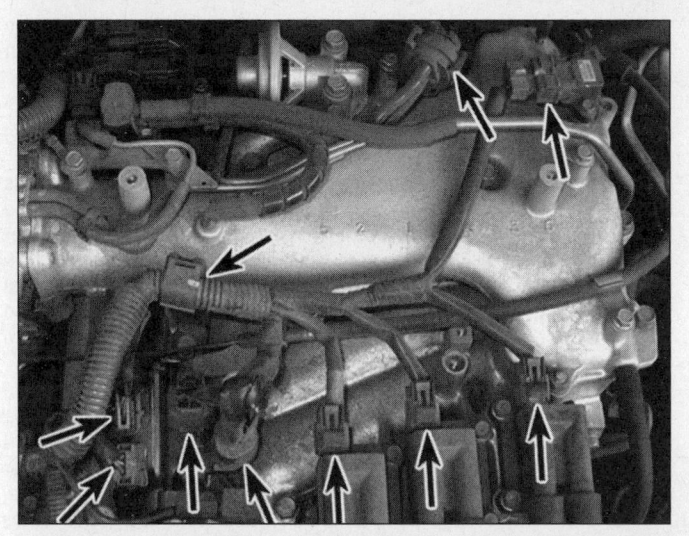

5.10 Disconnect the electrical connections from the upper inlet manifold (arrows) - typical 3.0L engine shown

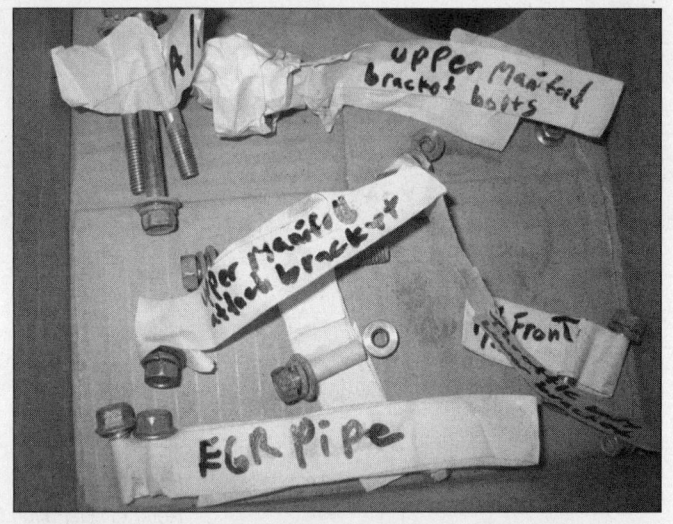

5.13 Clearly label all the bolts and brackets when you remove them

16 Refit a new gasket on the cover, using RTV to hold it in place. Place the cover on the engine and refit the cover bolts.
17 Tighten the bolts to the torque listed in this Chapter's Specifications. The remaining steps are the reverse of removal. When finished, run the engine and check for oil leaks.

Spark plug tube replacement

18 Remove the applicable valve cover.
19 Grasp the spark plug tube firmly with locking pliers, carefully twist it back and forth and simultaneously pull up, then remove the tube from the cylinder head.
20 Clean the locking agent from the tube and the recess in the cylinder head with solvent, then dry it thoroughly.
21 Apply a small amount of Loctite No. 271, or equivalent, around the lower end of the tube and refit the tube into the cylinder head. Carefully tap the tube into the recess with a wood block and mallet until it is fully seated in the cylinder head.

5 Inlet manifold - removal and refitting

Warning: *Wait until the engine is completely cool before beginning this procedure.*
Caution: *If the stereo in your vehicle is equipped with an anti-theft system, make sure you have the correct activation code before disconnecting the battery.*

Upper inlet manifold
Removal

Refer to illustrations 5.10, 5.13 and 5.14

1 Relieve the fuel pressure (see Chapter 4).
2 Disconnect the cables from the negative and positive battery terminals and remove the battery and battery tray (see Chapter 5).
3 Drain the engine coolant (see Chapter 1).
4 Remove the air cleaner (see Chapter 4).
5 Remove the air inlet duct from the throttle body (see Chapter 4).
6 Disconnect the accelerator cable (if equipped) from the throttle body (see Chapter 4).
7 If you're going to replace the upper inlet manifold, remove the throttle body (see Chapter 4). If you're just removing the upper inlet manifold to get to the lower inlet manifold or to perform some other service procedure, it's not necessary to remove the throttle body.
8 Remove all small brackets, fuel line, throttle cable and water out let.
9 Clearly label and disconnect all vacuum hoses, pipes and lines that would interfere with removal.
10 Clearly label and disconnect the following fuel, electrical **(see illustration)** and emission control electrical connectors and components (see Chapter 4, 5 or 6):

a) Airflow sensor connector.
b) Control wiring harness and power steering wiring harness combination connector.
c) Exhaust Gas Recirculation (EGR) solenoid valve connector.

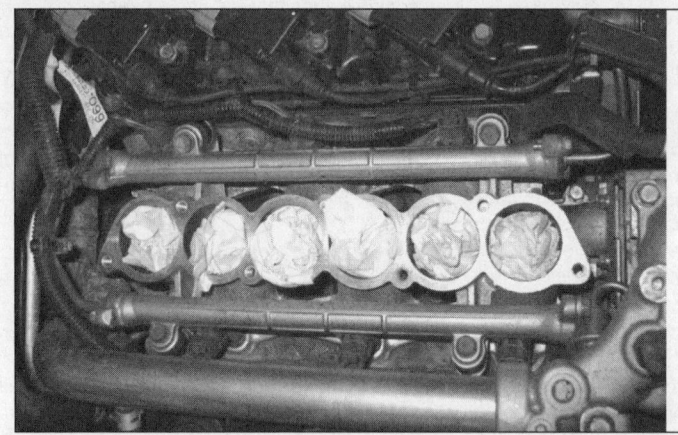

5.14 Carefully place rags into the lower manifold to prevent debris from falling into the engine - make sure you remove the rags when refitting the manifold

d) Evaporative emission (EVAP) purge solenoid valve connector.
e) Knock sensor connector.
f) Crankshaft Position (CKP) sensor connector.
g) Heated oxygen sensor connector.
h) Fuel injector connector.
i) Control wiring harness and injector wiring harness combination connector.
j) EGR solenoid valve, evaporative emission purge solenoid valve and vacuum valve.
k) EGR valve and EGR pipe **(see illustrations 6.4a and 6.4b)**.
l) Manifold differential pressure sensor.

11 Remove the ignition coils and power transistor (see Chapter 5).
12 Remove the bolts securing the upper inlet manifold side support stays.
13 Remove the upper inlet manifold bolts/nuts, remove the upper inlet manifold, then remove the manifold gasket.

Note: *The upper inlet bolts have different lengths, so keep them in the order and position they were removed from* **(see illustration)**. *If it sticks, tap the manifold with a soft-face hammer or carefully pry it from the lower inlet manifold.*

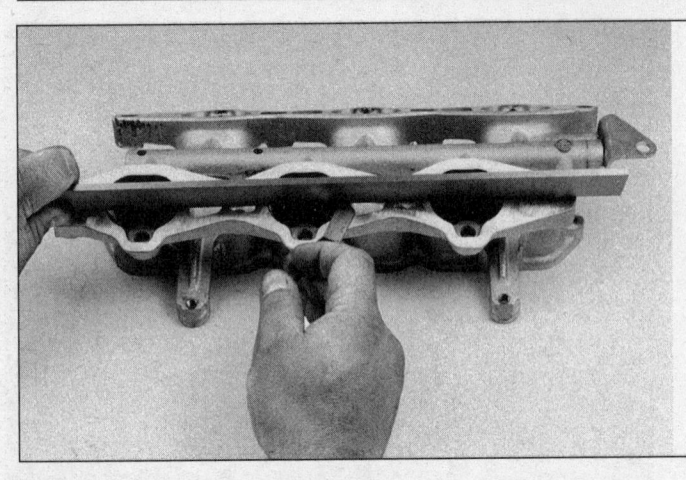

5.16 Check the intake manifold gasket surfaces for warpage

Caution: *Do not prise between gasket sealing surfaces.*

14 To minimize the chance of gasket debris or other contamination from getting into the engine, place clean rags into the lower inlet manifold passages **(see illustration)**.

15 Remove all traces of gasket material from both the upper and lower inlet manifold by carefully scraping them using a suitable gasket scraper.

Caution: *The inlet manifold components are made of aluminium and are easily nicked or gouged. Do not damage the gasket surfaces or a leak may result after the work is complete. Gasket removal solvents are available from auto parts stores and may prove helpful.*

Inspection

Refer to illustration 5.16

16 Using a precision straightedge and feeler gauge, check the upper and lower inlet manifold mating surfaces for warpage **(see illustration)**. If the warpage on any surface exceeds the limits listed in this Chapter's Specifications, the discrepant inlet manifold must be replaced or resurfaced by an automotive machine shop.

Refitting

Refer to illustration 5.18

17 Remove the rags from the lower inlet manifold. Use a shop vacuum to remove any contamination that may be present.

18 Refit the upper inlet manifold, using a new gasket. Tighten the bolts in 3 stages, working from the centre out **(see illustration)**, to the torque listed in this Chapter's Specifications.

19 The remaining Steps are the reverse of removal. Refill the cooling system (see Chapter 1).

Lower inlet manifold

Removal

20 Relieve the fuel pressure (see Chapter 4).

21 Remove the upper inlet manifold (see Steps 1 through 15).

22 Remove the fuel rail and injector assembly (see Chapter 4).

23 Loosen the lower inlet manifold nuts in the reverse order of the tightening sequence **(see illustration 5.29)**, 1/4 turn at a time until they can be removed by hand. Remove the washers.

24 Remove the lower inlet manifold from the engine. If it sticks, tap the manifold with a soft-face hammer or carefully pry it from the heads.

Caution: *Do not pry between gasket sealing surfaces.*

25 To minimize the chance of gasket debris or other contamination from getting into the engine, place clean rags into the cylinder head inlet passages.

26 Remove all traces of gasket material from the upper and lower inlet manifold and cylinder heads by carefully scraping them using a suitable gasket scraper.

Caution: *The inlet manifold components and cylinder heads are made of aluminium and are easily nicked or gouged. Do not damage the gasket surfaces or a leak may result after the work is complete. Gasket removal solvents are available from auto parts stores and may prove helpful.*

Inspection

27 Using a precision straightedge and feeler gauge, check the upper and lower inlet manifold gasket surfaces for warpage **(see illustration 5.16)**. Check the gasket surface on the cylinder head also. If the warpage on any surface exceeds the limits listed in this Chapter's Specifications, the discrepant component must be replaced or resurfaced by an automotive machine shop.

Refitting

Refer to illustration 5.29

28 Remove the rags from the cylinder head inlet passages. Use a shop vacuum to remove any contamination that may be present.

29 Refit the lower inlet manifold, using a new gasket. Tighten the nuts **(see illustration)** in five stages, following the sequence listed in this Chapter's Specifications, to the final torque.

30 Refit the fuel rail and fuel injector assembly (see Chapter 4).

5.18 Upper intake manifold circular tightening sequence - 3.8L engine shown

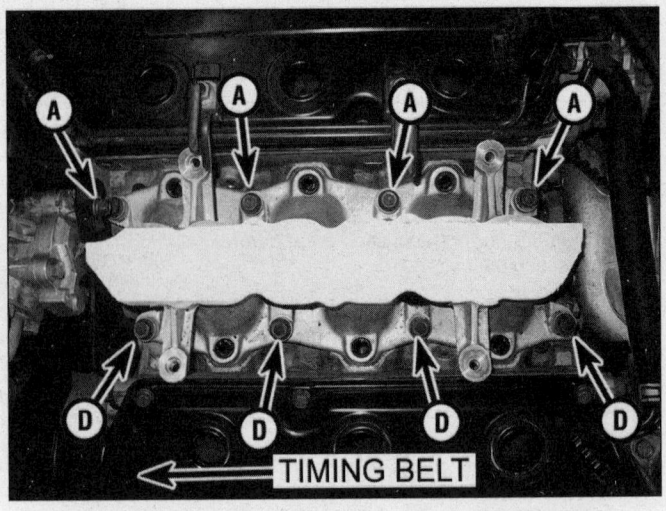

5.29 Lower intake manifold bolts - refer to this Chapter's Specifications for the tightening sequence and torque values

Chapter 2 Part A V6 petrol engines

6.4a Remove the upper EGR tube attaching bolts (arrows)

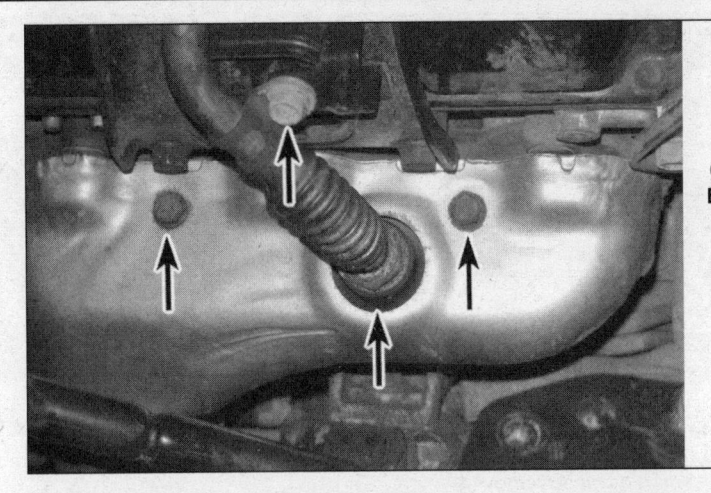

6.4b Remove the EGR tube support bracket bolt, and large nut, then remove the heat shield bolts and shield

31 Refit the upper inlet manifold, using a new gasket (see Steps 22 through 26).
32 The remaining Steps are the reverse of removal.
33 Refill the cooling system (see Chapter 1).

6 Exhaust manifolds - removal and refitting

Refer to illustrations 6.4a, 6.4b and 6.6

Warning: *Allow the engine to cool completely before beginning this procedure.*
Caution: *If the stereo in your vehicle is equipped with an anti-theft system, make sure you have the correct activation code before disconnecting the battery.*
Note 1: *This procedure can be used to remove one or both of the exhaust manifolds as required.*
Note 2: *The engine must be completely cool when this procedure is done.*

1 Disconnect the negative cable from the battery. Raise the vehicle and support it securely on jackstands.
2 Spray penetrating oil on the exhaust manifold fasteners and allow it to soak in. Disconnect the oxygen sensor electrical connector.
3 Remove the bolts and nuts that retain the front exhaust pipes to the manifolds and lower the pipes.
4 Remove the bolts and detach the EGR tube **(see illustrations)** from the left manifold.
5 Remove the bolts retaining the heat shield(s) to the manifold(s) near the cylinder head and slip it off the mounting studs **(see illustration 6.4b)**.
6 Remove the nuts that retain the manifold to the cylinder **(see illustration)** head and lift the exhaust manifold off.
7 Carefully inspect the manifolds and fasteners for cracks and damage.
8 Use a scraper to remove all traces of old gasket material and carbon deposits from the manifold and cylinder head mating surfaces. If the gasket was leaking, use a precision straightedge and feeler gauge, check the exhaust manifold gasket surfaces for warpage. Check the surface on the cylinder head also. If the warpage on any surface exceeds the limits listed in this Chapter's Specifications, the exhaust manifold and/or cylinder head must be replaced or resurfaced by an automotive machine shop.
9 Position new gaskets over the cylinder head studs.

Note: *If the new gasket is marked, refit the gasket with the numbers 1-3-5 on the top onto the right cylinder head and refit the gasket with the numbers 2-4-6 onto the left cylinder head.*

10 Refit the manifold and thread the mounting nuts into place.
11 Working from the centre out, tighten the nuts to the torque listed in this Chapter's Specifications in three or four equal steps.
12 Refit the remaining parts in the reverse order of removal. Use new gaskets when connecting the exhaust pipes.
13 Run the engine and check for exhaust leaks.

7 Timing belt - removal, inspection and refitting

Note: *If the timing belt failed with the engine operating, damage to the valves (and possibly to the pistons) most likely has occurred. One way this can be verified is by performing a compression check or a leak-down check on all cylinders, but in order to do so you'll have to first fit a new timing belt (and chances are you'll be wasting your time doing this, because most likely you'll just have to remove the belt and cylinder heads). Bent valves can sometimes be confirmed visually by removing the valve covers, camshafts and rocker arms and comparing the height of the valve stems. If one or more valve stems sit lower than the others, bent valves are indicated.*

SOHC engines

Removal

Refer to illustrations 7.1, 7.16, 7.19, 7.21, 7.22a, 7.22b, 7.22c, 7.22d, 7.23 and 7.25

Caution 1: *Do not turn the crankshaft or camshafts after the timing belt has been removed, as this will damage the valves from contact with the pistons. Do not try to turn the crank-*

6.6 Remove the nuts that retain the manifold to the cylinder head (arrows) and lift the exhaust manifold off

7.1 Remove the cover plug and verify the timing belt is not broken

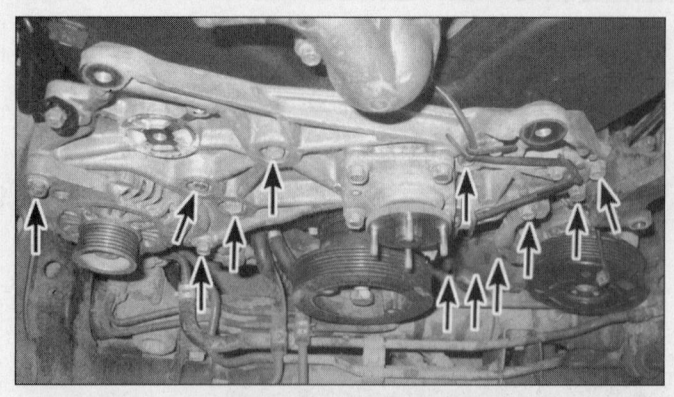

7.16 Remove the accessory mount assembly bolts (arrows), open the wire ties for the crank sensor and remove the assembly - The accessory mounting bolts are different sizes and should be marked when removed

7.19 Remove the upper timing belt cover bolts (arrows) and remove the cover

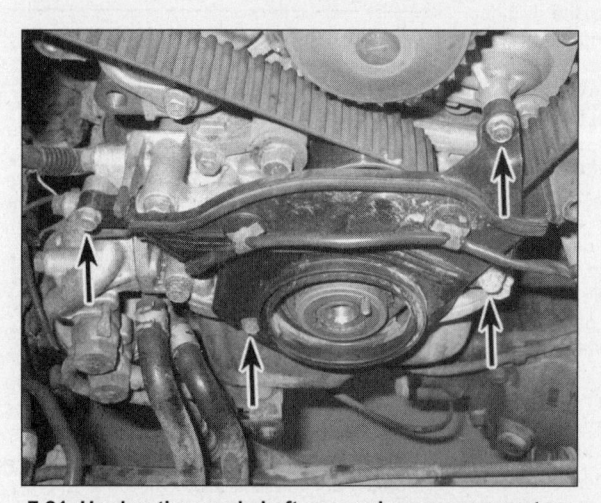

7.21 Unplug the crankshaft sensor harness connectors from the cover, then remove the lower timing belt cover bolts (arrows) and remove the cover

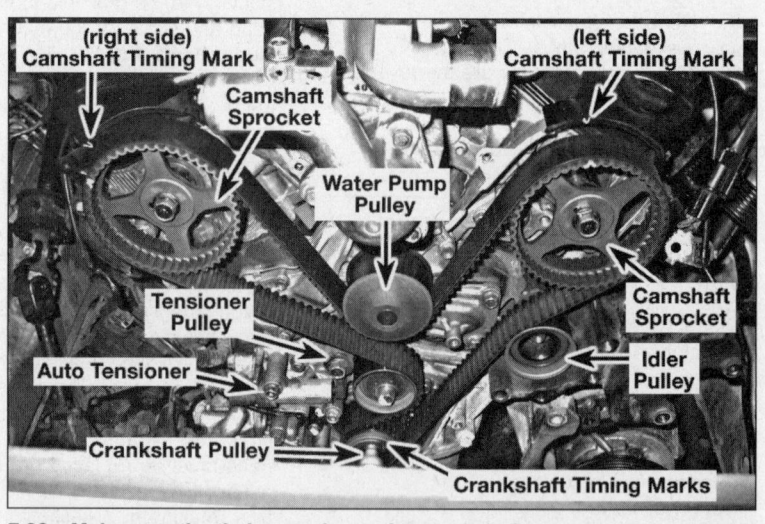

7.22a Make sure the timing marks on the crankshaft sprocket and camshaft sprockets align with their respective marks before removing the timing belt

7.22b Crankshaft timing belt sprocket timing marks (arrows)

shaft with the camshaft sprocket bolt(s) and do not rotate the crankshaft anti-clockwise as viewed from the timing belt end of the engine.
Caution 2: *If the stereo in your vehicle is equipped with an anti-theft system, make sure you have the correct activation code before disconnecting the battery.*

Note: *In order to perform this procedure, you'll need a special tool (MD 998767 or equivalent) to tension the timing belt. This tool number is available from automotive speciality tool companies.*

1 Verify the timing belt is not broken by looking into the belt cover viewing port **(see illustration)**. Position the number one piston at Top Dead Centre (see Section 3).
2 Disconnect the cables from the negative and positive battery terminals and remove the battery and battery tray (see Chapter 5).
3 Raise the vehicle, place it securely on jackstands, remove the skid plate and lower engine covers from under the engine.
4 Drain the coolant from the system (see Chapter 1) and remove the coolant reservoir (see Chapter 3).
5 Remove the air cleaner (see Chapter 4).

6 Remove the radiator shroud (see Chapter 3).
7 Remove the drivebelt (see Chapter 1).
8 Remove the cooling fan clutch and hub assembly (see Chapter 3).
9 Remove the valve covers (see Section 4).
10 Remove the drive belt auto tensioner (see Chapter 1).
11 Remove the accessory mount stay bracket from the drivers side of the engine.
12 Remove the power steering pump (see Chapter 10).
13 Remove the power steering pump (see Chapter 10) without disconnecting the lines and bracket.
14 Remove the air conditioning compressor (see Chapter 3).
15 Remove the air conditioning bracket bolt from the side of the block and pulley the bracket away so the accessory mount can be removed. Do not disconnect the refrigerant lines from the compressor.
16 Remove the alternator (see Chapter 5). Remove the accessory mount assembly bolts, open the wire ties for the crank sensor and remove the assembly **(see illustration)**.

Note: *The accessory mounting bolts are different sizes and should be marked when removed.*

17 Loosen the large bolt in the centre of the crankshaft pulley. To break it loose, attach a strap wrench to the pulley to hold the crank-

Chapter 2 Part A V6 petrol engines

7.22c Right side camshaft timing marks (arrows)

7.22d Left side camshaft timing marks (arrows)

7.23 If you plan to reuse the timing belt, paint an arrow on it to indicate the direction of rotation (clockwise) and which side faces out.

7.25 Unscrew the timing belt tensioner mounting bolts (arrows) and remove the tensioner

7.29 Carefully inspect the timing belt for damage or wear - bending it backwards will often make defects more apparent

shaft from turning and use a socket spanner to loosen the bolt and slowly draw the vibration damper off. **(see illustration 8.4)**.

18 After removing the crankshaft pulley, refit the crankshaft bolt using an appropriate spacer. This will enable you to turn the crankshaft later.

19 Remove the upper timing belt cover **(see illustration)**.

20 Remove the timing belt indicator bolts and remove the indicator bracket (if equipped).

21 Unplug the crankshaft sensor harness connectors from the cover, then remove the lower timing belt cover bolts and cover **(see illustration)**.

22 Make sure the timing marks on the crankshaft sprocket and camshaft sprockets align with their respective marks before removing the timing belt **(see illustrations)**.

23 If you plan to reuse the timing belt, paint an arrow on it to indicate the direction of rotation (clockwise) **(see illustration)** and which side faces out.

24 Loosen the centre bolt of the tensioner pulley and allow the pulley to rotate away from the belt. Carefully slip the timing belt off the sprockets and set it aside. If you plan to reuse the timing belt, place it in a plastic bag - do not allow the belt to come in contact with any type of oil or water as this will greatly shorten belt life.

25 Unscrew the timing belt tensioner mounting bolts and remove the tensioner **(see illustration)**.

Note: *The tensioner piston will extend when the assembly is removed.*

Inspection

Refer to illustration 7.29

26 With the timing belt covers removed, now is a good time to inspect the front crankshaft and camshaft seals for leakage. If leakage is evident, replace them (see Sections 8 and 9).

27 Inspect the water pump for evidence of leakage, usually indicated by a trail of wet or dried coolant. Check the pulley for excessive radial play and bearing roughness. Replace if necessary (see Chapter 3).

28 Rotate the tensioner pulley and guide pulley by hand and move them side-to-side to detect bearing roughness and/or excessive play. Visually inspect all timing belt sprockets for any signs of damage or wear. Replace as necessary.

29 Inspect the timing belt for cracks, separation, wear, missing teeth and oil contamination **(see illustration)**. Replace the belt if it's in questionable condition or the engine mileage is close to that referenced in the *Maintenance Schedule* (see Chapter 1).

7.33 Using a vice (lined with soft-jaws), compress the timing belt tensioner piston until the holes in the housing and piston align. Then place a small Allen wrench or drill bit, through the holes to keep the piston in position for installation

7.34 Binder clips can be used to retain the timing belt in position on the camshaft sprockets during installation

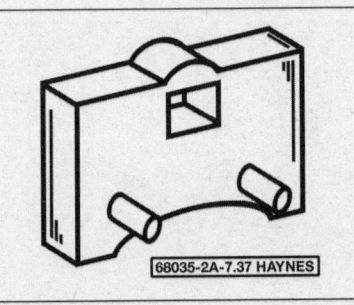

7.36 Using special tool MD 998767 (or equivalent) attached to a torque wrench, apply 4.4 Nm of torque to the tensioner pulley to properly tension the belt, then tighten the tensioner pulley bolt to the torque listed in this Chapter's Specifications. Remove the torque wrench and special tool from the tensioner.

30 Check the timing belt auto tensioner unit for leaks or any other obvious damage; replace if necessary.

Refitting

Refer to illustrations 7.33, 7.34, 7.36 and 7.37

31 Confirm that the timing marks on both camshaft sprockets are aligned with their respective marks on the rear timing belt covers **(see illustrations 7.22c and 7.22d)**. Reposition the camshafts if required.

Caution: *If it is necessary to rotate the camshafts to align the timing marks, first rotate the crankshaft slightly anti-clockwise (three notches on the sprocket) to ensure the valves do not contact the pistons.*

32 Position the crankshaft sprocket with the timing marks aligned **(see illustration 7.22b)**.

33 Before refitting, the timing belt tensioner piston must be compressed into the tensioner housing. Protect both ends of the tensioner and place the tensioner in a vice so the surface with the pin hole is facing up. Slowly compress the tensioner using the vice, then fit an appropriate size Allen wrench or drill bit through the body and into the piston to retain the piston in this position **(see illustration)**. Remove the tensioner from the vice and install it and the tensioner pulley arm assembly, tightening the mounting bolts to the torque listed in this Chapter's Specifications. Using special tool MD 998767 (or equivalent), turn the tensioner pulley into the timing belt, then tighten the tensioner pulley bolt temporarily.

34 Fit the new timing belt as follows: First onto the crankshaft sprocket and up around the idler pulley, then over the left side camshaft sprocket; clamp the belt to the sprocket with a binder clip **(see illustration)**. Now route the belt under the water pump pulley and over the right side camshaft sprocket, clamping it to the sprocket with a binder clip. Finally, pass the belt around the tensioner pulley. Once the belt is in place, remove the binder clips.

35 Using the crankshaft pulley bolt, turn the crankshaft 1/4-turn anti-clockwise, then clockwise 1/4 turn until the timing marks are all in alignment. Make sure the timing belt has no deflection between the left side camshaft sprocket and the crankshaft sprocket, all the slack is at the tensioner pulley and all the timing marks are aligned.

36 Loosen the tensioner pulley bolt and, using special tool MD 998767 (or equivalent) **(see illustration)**, apply 4.4 Nm to the tensioner pulley to properly tension the belt, then tighten the tensioner pulley bolt to the torque listed in this Chapter's Specifications. Remove the torque wrench and special tool from the tensioner.

37 Remove the Allen wrench or drill bit retaining the piston from the tensioner, then wait for five minutes. The timing belt tension is correct when the tensioner plunger extends from the tensioner body **(see illustration)** the amount listed in this Chapter's Specifications. If it doesn't, repeat Steps 35 and 36. Verify that the timing marks on the camshaft sprockets and crankshaft sprocket are still aligned with their respective timing marks **(see illustrations 7.22a through 7.22d)**.

38 Using the bolt in the centre of the crankshaft sprocket, slowly turn the crankshaft clockwise two complete revolutions.

Caution: *If you feel strong resistance while turning the crankshaft - STOP, the valves may be hitting the pistons from incorrect valve timing. Stop and re-check the valve timing.*

Note: *The camshafts and crankshaft sprocket marks will align every two revolutions of the crankshaft. Recheck the alignment of the timing marks* **(see illustrations 7.22a through 7.22d)**. *If the marks do not align properly, remove the timing belt tensioner, slip the belt off the camshaft sprockets, realign the marks, refit the belt and tensioner, then check the alignment again.*

39 The remaining Steps are the reverse of removal.

40 Tighten the crankshaft pulley bolt to the torque listed in this Chapter's Specifications.

DOHC engine

Removal

Refer to illustrations 7.55a, 7.55b, 7.56, 7.57a and 7.57b

41 Disconnect the cable from the negative terminal of the battery.

42 Position the number one piston at Top Dead Centre (see Section 3).

43 If equipped, unbolt the cruise control servo and set it aside, without disconnecting the wires or cables.

44 Drain the coolant from the system (see Chapter 1) and remove the coolant reservoir (see Chapter 3).

45 Remove the radiator shroud and the

7.37 Remove the Allen wrench or drill bit retaining the piston from the tensioner hole (A), then wait for five minutes. Measure the amount the pushrod extends (B) the amount listed in this Chapter's Specifications. If it doesn't, repeat Steps 35 and 36

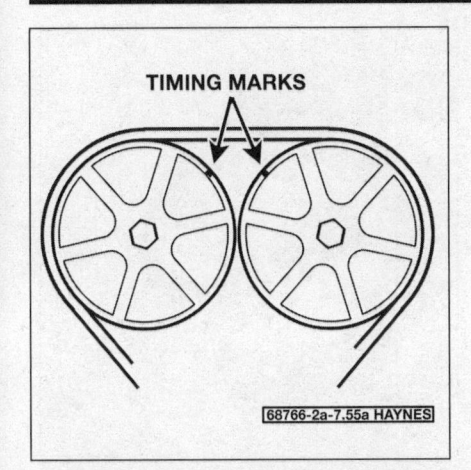

Chapter 2 Part A V6 petrol engines

7.55a The timing belt sprockets must be aligned with the timing marks

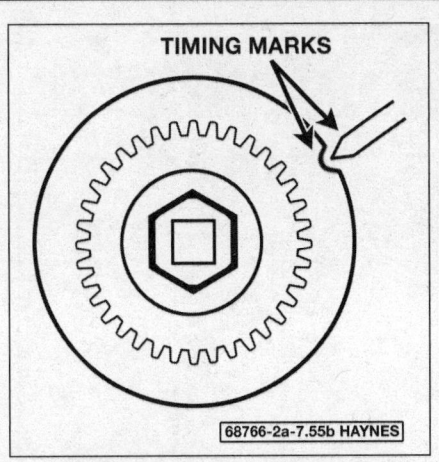

7.55b The crankshaft sprocket timing mark and pointer in proper alignment

7.56 If you'll be reusing the timing belt, mark an arrow on the belt in the direction of rotation so it may be refitted in the same direction

tion 8), the vibration damper and crankshaft sprocket flange.

Note: *Don't allow the crankshaft to rotate during removal of the pulley. If the crankshaft moves, the number one piston will no longer be at TDC.*

54 Remove the bolts securing the timing belt upper and lower covers. Note the various type and sizes of bolts by recording a diagram or making specific notes while the timing belt cover is being removed. The bolts must be refitted in their original locations.
55 Align the timing belt sprocket timing marks **(see illustrations)**.
56 Make a mark on the timing belt in the direction of rotation **(see illustration)** so it may be refitted in the same direction in the event the timing belt is reused. Loosen the centre bolt on the tensioner pulley, then remove the timing belt.

Caution: *Be sure that the timing marks are correctly aligned before removing the timing belt* **(see illustrations 7.55a and 7.55b)**.

57 If you plan to renew the camshaft(s) or camshaft oil seal(s), remove the camshaft sprocket(s). Using an adjustable wrench or an open-end wrench, hold the camshaft at the hexagon and remove the camshaft sprocket bolt **(see illustration)**. If the sprocket bolt cannot be loosened easily, place a block of wood between the head and the wrench **(see illustration)** to prevent damage to the head so more force can be used on the camshaft sprocket bolt. Remove the bolt and slide the sprocket off the camshaft.

Inspection

58 Rotate the tensioner pulley by hand and check for roughness and excessive play.
59 Inspect the timing belt for cracks, separation, wear, missing teeth and oil contamination. Renew the belt if it's in questionable condition.
60 Check the automatic tensioner for leaks or any obvious damage to the body. Also, check the rod end for wear or damage. Measure the rod protrusion for the correct length - it

radiator (see Chapter 3).
46 Remove the power steering pump (see Chapter 10) without disconnecting the lines.
47 Remove the air conditioning compressor (see Chapter 3), bracket and idler pulley. Do not disconnect the refrigerant lines from the compressor.
48 Raise the front of the vehicle and support it securely on jackstands.
49 Remove the splash pan from under the engine.
50 Position the number one piston at TDC on the compression stroke (see Section 3).
51 Remove the accessory mount, cooling fan and clutch assembly.
52 Remove the spark plugs (see Chapter 1).
53 Remove the crankshaft pulley (see Sec-

7.57a When loosening the camshaft sprocket bolt, hold the camshaft at the hexagon with an open-end wrench . . .

7.57b . . . and, if the bolt is very tight, position a wood block, as shown, to prevent damaging the cylinder head when the bolt breaks loose

8.4 Attach a strap wrench to the pulley to hold the crankshaft from turning and use a large socket and breaker bar to loosen the bolt

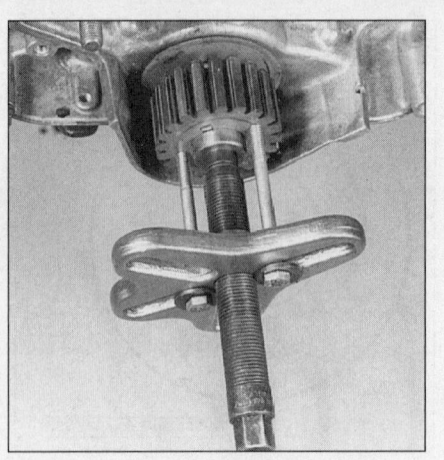

8.6 If the sprocket is stuck, drill and tap two holes and remove it with a bolt-type puller

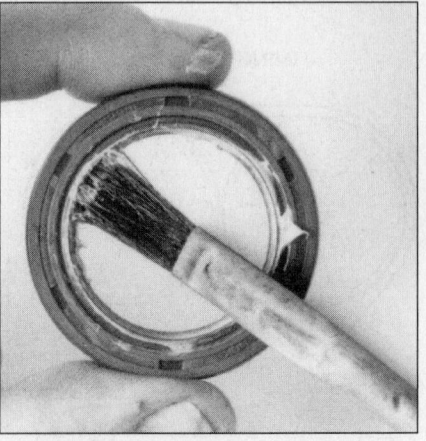

8.9 Apply a film of grease to the lips of the new seal before installing it (if you apply a small amount of grease to the outer edge, it will be easier to push into the bore)

should extend 12 mm beyond the body of the tensioner.

Refitting

61 Refit the timing belt sprockets, if they were removed. Tighten the bolts to the values listed in this Chapter's Specifications.
62 Align the timing marks located on the camshaft, crankshaft and sprockets **(see illustrations 7.55a and 7.55b)**.
63 Prepare the automatic tensioner for refitting. Place the tensioner in a vice that is equipped with soft jaws (or put a shop rag over the jaws to prevent damage to the tensioner). If the rod is easily retracted, renew it. The tensioner should have a fair amount of strength or resistance.
Caution: *Be sure the tensioner is in a level position when it is in the vice. Once the tensioner is compressed place a small Allen wrench, pin or something similar, through the hole to keep the rod retracted for reassembly on the engine* **(see illustration 7.33)**.
64 Refit the automatic tensioner onto the engine, keeping it in the compressed position.
65 Refit the tensioner pulley onto the tensioner arm. Position the two small holes in the tensioner pulley hub just to the left of the centre bolt. Tighten the centre bolt finger tight. Don't remove the Allen wrench from the tensioner yet.
66 Slide the sprocket onto the crankshaft and rotate it forward about three teeth, to slightly past the number 1 piston TDC mark. Then line up the timing marks on the left and right camshaft sprockets with the ones on the cylinder heads **(see illustrations 7.55a and 7.55b)**. Have an assistant hold the camshaft sprockets from moving with two spanners on the sprocket nuts.
67 Refit the timing belt in the following sequence:
a) *Refit the timing belt around the right bank camshaft sprockets, pull the timing belt onto the water pump pulley and hold it.*

b) *Pulling the belt with your right hand, refit it around the left bank sprockets.*
c) *Refit the belt around the idler pulley.*
d) *Align the crankshaft sprocket timing marks and turn the crankshaft sprocket one tooth anti-clockwise and refit the belt around the crankshaft sprocket.*
e) *Refit the belt on the tensioner pulley.*
f) *Turn the tensioner pulley so the pin hole faces up, press the pulley onto belt, then temporarily tighten the centre bolt. Make sure that all of the timing marks are now properly aligned* **(see illustrations 7.55a and 7.55b)**.
68 Adjust the timing belt tension in the following sequence:
a) *Turn the crankshaft 1/4 turn anti-clockwise, then clockwise to move all of the timing marks into alignment.*
b) *Loosen the tensioner centre bolt and attach Mitsubishi special socket tool no. MD998767 (or equivalent) to a torque wrench.*
Note: *The torque wrench must be capable of measuring small increments between 0 and 3 Nm. Apply 4.4 Nm to the tensioner* **(see illustration 7.36)**.
c) *While holding the 4.4 Nm tension on the timing belt tensioner, tighten the centre bolt to the torque listed in this Chapter's Specifications. Be careful not to rotate the tensioner while tightening the centre bolt.*
d) *Remove the Allen wrench or pin from the tensioner.*
e) *Rotate the crankshaft two complete turns and wait five minutes.*
Caution: *If you feel resistance while turning the crankshaft, the valves may be hitting the pistons from incorrect valve timing. Stop and re-check the valve timing. Measure how far the tensioner plunger protrudes from the tensioner body (the distance between the tensioner arm and the automatic tensioner body). It should be between 4.8 to 5.5 mm. Also, check that all timing marks are still aligned.*

69 If the tensioner protrusion is not as specified, repeat the belt adjustment procedure.
70 Refit the timing covers.
71 The remaining steps are the reverse of removal.

8 Crankshaft front oil seal - renewal

Refer to illustrations 8.4, 8.6, 8.9, 8.10a and 8.10b

Caution: *If the stereo in your vehicle is equipped with an anti-theft system, make sure you have the correct activation code before disconnecting the battery.*
1 Disconnect the negative cable from the battery.
2 Raise the front of the vehicle and support it securely on jackstands and remove the skid plate and lower engine cover (see Chapter 10).
3 Remove the drivebelts (see Chapter 1).
4 Attach a strap wrench to the pulley **(see illustration)** to hold the crankshaft from turning and use a socket spanner to loosen the bolt and slowly draw the vibration damper off.
5 Wedge two screwdrivers behind the crankshaft sprocket. Carefully prise the sprocket off the crankshaft and remove the

8.10a Fabricate a seal refitting tool from a piece of pipe and a large washer . . .

Chapter 2 Part A V6 petrol engines

8.10b . . . to push the seal into the bore - the pipe must bear against the outer edge of the seal as the bolt is tightened

Woodruff key. Some timing belt sprockets can be pried off easily with screwdrivers. Others are more difficult to remove because corrosion fuses them onto the nose of the crankshaft. If the pulley on your engine is difficult to prise off, don't damage the oil pump with the screwdrivers.

6   If the sprocket won't come loose, drill and tap two holes into the face of the sprocket (later modes already have these holes) and use a bolt-type puller to slip it off the crankshaft **(see illustration)**.

Caution: *Do not reuse a drilled sprocket - renew it.*

7   Turn the bolt of the puller until the pulley comes off. Remove the timing belt plate.
8   Carefully prise the oil seal out with a screwdriver or seal removal tool. Don't scratch or nick the crankshaft in the process!
9   Before refitting, apply a coat of multi-purpose grease to the inside of the seal **(see illustration)**.
10   There are several ways to fit a new seal into the pump body. The first is to fabricate a seal refitting tool with a short length of pipe of equal or slightly smaller outside diameter than the seal itself. File the end of the pipe that will bear down on the seal until it's free of sharp edges. You'll also need a large washer, slightly larger in diameter than the pipe, on which the bolt head can seat **(see illustration)**. Refit the oil seal by pressing it into position with the seal refitting tool **(see illustration)**. When you see and feel the seal stop moving, don't turn the bolt any more or you'll damage the seal. The second is to use a hammer and the appropriate size socket, drive the seal into the bore until it's flush with the oil pump housing.
11   Once the seal is fitted, slide the timing belt plate onto the nose of the crankshaft.
12   Make sure the Woodruff key is in place in the crankshaft.
13   Apply a thin coat of assembly lube to the inside of the timing belt sprocket and slide it onto the crankshaft.
14   Refitting of the remaining components is the reverse of removal. Be sure to refer to Section 7 for the timing belt refitting and adjustment procedure. Tighten all bolts to the torque values listed in this Chapter's Specifications.

9 Camshaft oil seal - renewal

Refer to illustrations 9.3 and 9.5

Caution: *Do not rotate the camshafts or crankshaft when the timing belt is removed or damage to the engine may occur.*

1   Remove the timing belt (see Section 7).
2   While keeping the camshaft from rotating, remove the camshaft sprocket bolt. Then using two large screwdrivers, lever the sprocket off the camshaft.

Note: *A strap-type damper/pulley holder tool is available at most auto parts stores and is recommended for this procedure, however, if you are not going to reuse the old timing belt, you can wrap a piece of it around the sprocket and use a chain wrench to hold the sprocket in place as shown.*

3   Carefully pry out the camshaft oil seal using a small hooked tool or screwdriver **(see illustration)**. Don't scratch the bore or damage the camshaft in the process (if the camshaft is damaged, the new seal will end up leaking).
4   Clean the bore and coat the outer edge of the new seal with engine oil or multi-purpose grease. Also lubricate the seal lip.
5   Using a socket with an outside diameter slightly smaller than the outside diameter of the seal and a hammer **(see illustration)**, carefully drive the new seal into the cylinder head until it's flush with the face of the cylinder head. If a socket isn't available, a short section of pipe will also work.

Note: *If engine location makes it difficult to use a hammer to fit the camshaft seal, fabricate a seal installation tool from a piece of pipe cut to the appropriate length, a bolt and a large washer **(see illustration 8.10a)**. Place the section of pipe over the seal and thread the bolt into the camshaft. The seal can now be pressed into the bore by tightening the bolt.*

6   Refit the camshaft sprocket, aligning the pin in the camshaft with the hole in the sprocket. Using an appropriate tool to hold the camshaft sprocket, tighten the camshaft sprocket bolt to the torque listed in this Chapter's Specifications.
7   Refit the timing belt (see Section 7).
8   Run the engine and check for oil leaks.

10 Rocker arm and hydraulic valve lash adjuster assembly - removal, inspection and refitting

SOHC engines

Removal

1   Disconnect the cable from the negative battery terminal (see Chapter 5).
2   Position the number one piston at Top Dead Centre (see Section 3).
3   Remove the valve cover(s) (see Section 4).
4   Prior to removing the rocker arm shafts,

9.3 Using a hooked tool or screwdriver, carefully pry the camshaft seal out of the bore - DO NOT nick or scratch the camshaft or seal bore

9.5 Using a hammer and the appropriate size socket, drive the camshaft seal into the bore until it is flush with the cylinder head

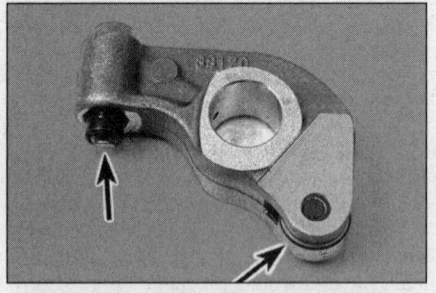

Chapter 2 Part A V6 petrol engines

10.8 Visually inspect the hydraulic lash adjuster and roller for damage and excessive play - check the rocker arm shaft bore for score marks or excessive wear

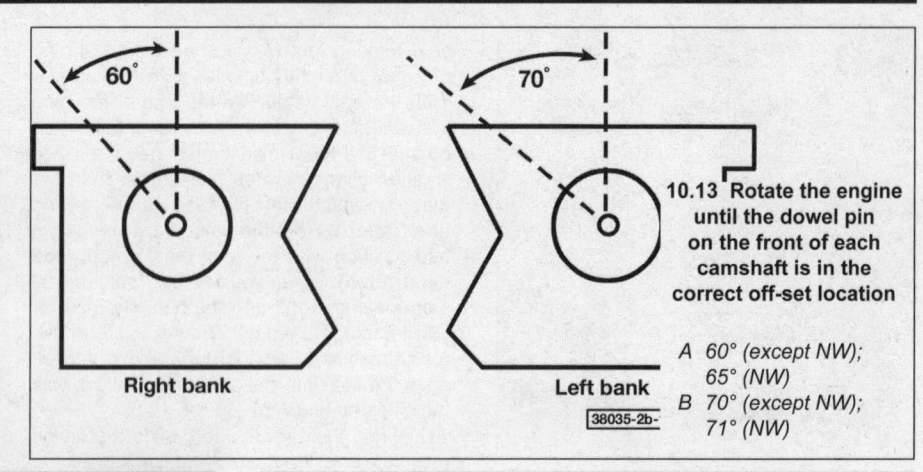

10.13 Rotate the engine until the dowel pin on the front of each camshaft is in the correct off-set location

A 60° (except NW); 65° (NW)
B 70° (except NW); 71° (NW)

10.14 The inlet rocker arm shaft springs must be installed as shown

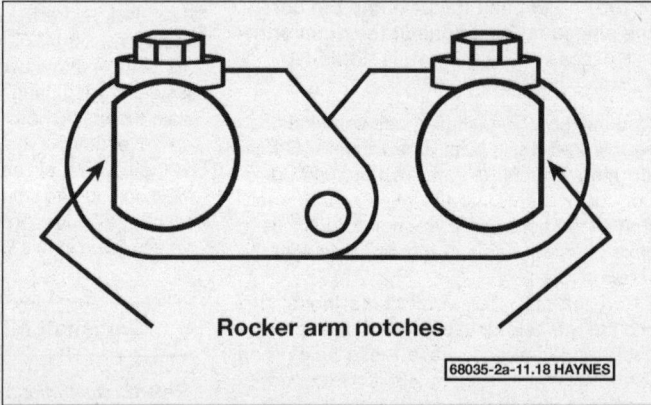

10.16 The rocker arm notches must be positioned opposite and facing out

identify each rocker arm and shaft as to its proper location (cylinder number and inlet or exhaust).

Caution: *Do not interchange the rocker arms onto a different shaft or shaft assemblies onto a different location as this could lead to premature wear.*

5 Loosen the rocker arm shaft bolts 1/4-turn at a time, until they can be loosened by hand, in the reverse order of the tightening sequence **(see illustration 10.17)**. Completely loosen the bolts, but do not remove them; leaving them in place will prevent the assembly from falling apart when it is lifted off the cylinder head.

Note: *Fit special hydraulic actuator holders (tool # MD998443 or equivalent) onto each lash adjuster to prevent the adjuster from falling into the engine. Use vinyl tape if the special tool holders are not available.*

6 Lift the rocker arms and shaft assemblies from the cylinder head and set them on the workbench.

7 It's okay to disassemble the rocker arm shaft components, but pay close attention to the relationship of the parts to each other.

Note: *To keep the rocker arms and related parts in order, it's a good idea to remove them and put them onto two lengths of wire in the same order as they're removed, marking each wire (which simulates the rocker shaft) as to which end would be the front of the engine.*

10.17 Rocker arm shaft bolt tightening sequence

Inspection

Refer to illustration 10.8

Note: *The roller is an integral part of each rocker arm and cannot be replaced separately. If defective, the complete arm must be renewed.*

8 Visually check the rocker arms for excessive wear or damage **(see illustration)**. Replace them if evidence of wear or damage is found.

9 Inspect each lash adjuster carefully for signs of wear and damage, particularly on the surface that contacts the valve tip. Use a small diameter wire to check the oil holes for restrictions.

10 Since the lash adjusters can become clogged, we recommend replacing the lash adjuster if you're concerned about their condition or if the engine is exhibiting valve "tapping" noises.

11 Inspect all rocker arm shaft components. Look for cracks, worn or scored surfaces or other damage. Replace any parts found to be damaged or worn excessively.

Refitting

Refer to illustrations 10.13, 10.14, 10.16 and 10.17

12 Prior to refitting, the lash adjusters must be partially full of engine oil - indicated by little or no plunger action when the adjuster is depressed. If there's excessive plunger travel, place the rocker arm assembly into clean engine oil and pump the plunger until the plunger travel is eliminated.

Chapter 2 Part A V6 petrol engines

10.21 On DOHC engines, once the camshaft has been removed, the rocker arms can be lifted off. If necessary, the lash adjuster below the rocker arm can also be removed - be sure to keep the rocker arms and lash adjusters in order so they can be returned to their original locations

Note: *If the plunger still travels within the rocker arm when full of oil, it's defective and the rocker arm assembly must be replaced.*

13 Rotate the engine until the dowel pin on the front of each camshaft is in the correct offset location **(see illustration)**. This will allow the camshaft lobes to be positioned down and away to ease the rocker arm and shaft refitting.

14 Refit the rocker arms and shaft springs (inlet shafts only), onto the shafts, making sure they are refitted in their original locations **(see illustration)**. Refit the inlet shaft first, then the exhaust shaft.

15 Refit the rocker shaft clips onto the rocker shafts with the open side of the clip sliding over the shaft, facing the valves.

16 Refit the rocker arm assemblies with the rocker arm shaft notches installed properly **(see illustration)**.

17 Tighten the rocker arm shaft bolts in the sequence shown **(see illustration)** in three steps to the torque listed in this Chapter's Specifications.

18 The remaining Steps are the reverse of removal. Run the engine and check for oil leaks and proper operation.

19 When re-starting the engine after replacing the rocker arm/lash adjusters, the adjusters will normally make tapping noises due to air in the lubrication system. To bleed air from the lash adjusters, start the engine and allow it to reach operating temperature, slowly raise the speed of the engine from idle to 3,000 rpm and back to idle over a one minute period. If, after several attempts, the adjuster(s) do not become silent, replace the defective rocker arm/lash adjuster assembly.

DOHC engine

Refer to illustration 10.21

20 Remove the camshafts (see Section 11).
21 Once the camshafts have been removed, the rocker arms can be lifted off **(see illustration)**.

Caution: *Each rocker arm must be placed back in the same location it was removed from, so mark each rocker arm or place them in a container (such as an egg carton) so they won't get mixed up. The lash adjusters can remain in the head at this time, unless they are being renewed.*

Inspection

22 Visually check the rocker arms for wear. Renew them if evidence of wear or damage is found.

23 The simplest way to check the adjusters is to warm the engine up to normal operating temperature and listen for tapping noises. After warm-up, raise the speed of the engine from idle to 3,000 rpm for one minute. If the adjuster(s) do not become silent, renew the defective ones. Another simple check can be made by removing the valve cover and pushing down on each adjuster. The adjuster should feel solid and not give. If an adjuster can be easily pushed down, it is faulty and should be renewed.

Removal

24 Remove the camshaft(s) (see Section 11).
25 Remove the rocker arms (see Section 4).
26 If the hydraulic lifters aren't already removed from the head, lift them out now.

Caution: *Be sure to keep the lifters in order so they can be placed back on the same camshaft lobe it was removed from.*

27 Inspect each adjuster carefully for signs of wear and damage, particularly on the ball tip that contacts the rocker arm. Since the lash adjusters frequently become clogged, we recommend renewing them if you're concerned about their condition or if the engine is exhibiting valve tapping noises.
28 Refitting is the reverse of removal.

Refitting

29 When reassembling the parts, be sure they all go back on in the same locations they were removed from.
30 The remainder of the reassembly is in the reverse order of disassembly. Run the engine and check for oil leaks and proper operation.

11 Camshaft - removal, inspection and refitting

Note: *On SOHC engines the camshaft(s) cannot be removed with the cylinder head(s) fitted on the engine.*

SOHC engines

Removal

Refer to illustration 11.5

1 Remove the valve covers (see Section 4).
2 Remove the rocker arm shaft assemblies (see Section 10).
3 Remove the cylinder head bolts and remove the cylinder heads (see Section 12).
4 On the right side cylinder head, carefully withdraw the camshaft from the rear of the cylinder head.

Caution: *Do not damage the camshaft lobes or bearing journals during removal.*

Note: *If you are removing both camshafts, identify each one as it is removed from the cylinder head so that it may be refitted back in its original location.*

5 On the left side cylinder head, remove the camshaft position sensor support bolts and remove the support. Remove the camshaft sensor retaining bolt and remove the bolt and sensor from the end of the camshaft and withdraw the camshaft **(see illustration)**.

Caution: *Do not damage the camshaft lobes or bearing journals during removal.*

11.5 Withdraw the camshaft from the rear of the cylinder head

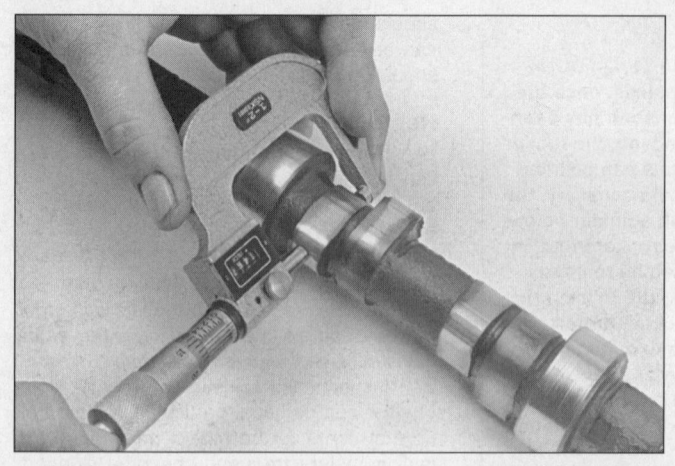

11.10 Check the camshaft lobes for wear with a micrometer

11.15 Prior to fitting the camshaft, lubricate the bearing journals, thrust surfaces and lobes with engine assembly lube or clean engine oil

11.20 If the bearing caps are difficult to remove, use the bolts as levers to help break the caps free

6 Remove the camshaft seal(s) from the cylinder head(s) (see Section 9).

Inspection

Refer to illustration 11.10

7 Using a suitable scraper, remove all traces of gasket material from all gasket surfaces.

Caution: *When removing gasket material from any surface, especially aluminium, be very careful not to scratch or gouge the gasket surface. Any damage to the surface may cause a leak after reassembly. Gasket removal solvents are available from auto parts stores and may prove helpful.*

8 Thoroughly clean the camshaft(s) with a rag soaked in lacquer thinner or acetone. Visually inspect the camshaft(s) for wear and/or damage to the lobe surfaces, bearing journals and seal contact surfaces. Visually inspect the camshaft bearing surfaces in the cylinder head(s) for scoring and other damage. Cylinder head replacement may be necessary if the camshaft bearing surfaces in the head are damaged or excessively worn.

9 Replace any component that fails the above inspections.

10 Using a micrometer, check the camshaft lobes for excessive wear by measuring the centre of the lobe (the area the rocker arm roller rides on) and comparing it with the edges of the lobes (the area the rocker arm roller does not ride on) **(see illustration)**. If any wear is indicated, check the corresponding rocker arm. Replace the camshaft and rocker arms if necessary.

Camshaft endplay measurement

11 Lubricate the camshaft(s) and cylinder head bearing journals with clean engine oil.

12 Carefully insert the camshaft into the cylinder head. Tighten the retaining bolts to the torque listed in this Chapter's Specifications.

13 Fit a dial indicator set up on the cylinder head and place the indicator tip on the camshaft at the sprocket end.

14 Using a screwdriver, carefully prise the camshaft to the rear of the cylinder head until it stops. Zero the dial indicator and pry the camshaft forward. The amount of indicator travel is the camshaft endplay. Compare the endplay measurement with the tolerance listed in this Chapter's Specifications. If the endplay is excessive, check the camshaft and cylinder head thrust bearing surfaces for wear and replace components as necessary.

Refitting

Refer to illustration 11.15

15 Very carefully clean the camshaft and bearing journals. Liberally coat the bearing journals, lobes and thrust bearing surfaces of the camshaft with engine assembly lube or engine oil **(see illustration)**.

16 Carefully insert the camshaft into the cylinder head. On the left side cylinder head, refit the camshaft position sensor, and support using a new O-ring, and tighten the bolts to the torque listed in Chapter 6.

17 Fit a new camshaft oil seal in the cylinder head (see Section 9).

18 Inspect the cylinder head bolts and refit the cylinder head(s) (see Section 12).

19 The remaining Steps are the reverse of removal. Check and adjust the ignition timing (see Chapter 5). Check for leaks and proper operation.

DOHC engine

Refer to illustration 11.20

Removal

20 Remove the timing belt and camshaft sprocket(s), then remove the camshaft bearing caps, loosening the bolts a little at a time to prevent distorting the camshaft(s) by loosening the caps from the ends of the shaft towards the centre. Once the bearing caps have all been loosened enough for removal, they may still be difficult to remove. Using the bearing cap bolts for extra leverage, move the cap back and forth to loosen the cap from the cylinder head **(see illustration)**. If they are still difficult to remove you can tap them gently with a soft face hammer so they can be lifted off.

Caution: *Store them in order so they can be returned to their original locations, with the same side facing forward. It's a good idea to mark the caps so there's no possibility of making a mistake. Carefully lift the camshaft(s) out of the cylinder head.*

Inspection

21 Remove the seal(s) from the camshaft(s) and thoroughly clean the camshaft(s) and the gasket surface. Visually inspect the camshaft

Chapter 2 Part A V6 petrol engines

12.16a Checking the cylinder head gasket surface for warpage

12.16b Checking the engine block head gasket surface for warpage

for wear and/or damage to the lobe surfaces, bearing journals and seal contact surfaces. Visually inspect the camshaft bearing surfaces in the cylinder head for scoring and other damage.

22 Measure the camshaft lobe heights and compare them to this Chapter's Specifications.

23 Measure the camshaft bearing journal diameters, then temporarily refit the bearing caps and measure the inside diameter of the camshaft bearing surfaces in the cylinder head, using a telescoping gauge. Subtract the journal measurement from the bearing measurement to obtain the camshaft bearing oil clearance. Compare this clearance with this Chapter's Specifications.

24 Renew the camshaft if it fails any of the above inspections. If the lobes are worn, renew the rocker arms along with the camshaft. Cylinder head renewal may be necessary if the camshaft bearing surfaces in the head are damaged or excessively worn.

Refitting

25 Very carefully clean the camshaft and bearing journals/caps. Liberally coat the journals, lobes and thrust portions of the camshaft with assembly lube or engine oil.

26 Carefully refit the camshaft(s) in the cylinder head.

27 Refit the lash adjusters and rocker arms if they haven't been refitted yet. Next refit the camshaft and camshaft bearing caps. Tighten them a little at a time, working from the centre journals out, doing one camshaft at a time, until the torque listed in this Chapter's Specifications is reached.

28 Coat a new camshaft oil seal with engine oil and press it into place with a hammer and deep socket.

29 Refit the camshaft sprocket(s) and tighten the bolts to the torque listed in this Chapter's Specifications.

30 Refit the timing belt (see Section 7).

31 Refit the remaining parts in the reverse order of removal.

32 Refit the valve cover and run the engine while checking for oil leaks.

12 Cylinder head - removal and refitting

Warning: *Allow the engine to cool completely before beginning this procedure.*

Caution: *If the stereo in your vehicle is equipped with an anti-theft system, make sure you have the correct activation code before disconnecting the battery.*

Removal

Refer to illustrations 12.16a and 12.16b

1 Position the number one piston at Top Dead Centre (see Section 3).

2 Disconnect the battery cables, starting with the negative battery terminal and then the positive battery terminal (see Chapter 5). Remove the battery and battery tray (see Chapter 5).

3 Drain the cooling system, remove the spark plugs and spark plug wires (see Chapter 1).

4 Remove the upper and lower inlet manifolds (see Section 5).

5 Remove the coolant crossover housing bolts and separate the assembly from the rear of the cylinder heads.

6 Remove the rocker arm shaft assemblies (see Section 10).

7 Remove the engine bracket from the front of the rear cylinder head.

8 Remove the exhaust manifold(s) (see Section 6).

9 Remove the timing belt (see Section 7).

10 Remove the camshaft sprocket(s) (see Section 9).

11 Clearly label and disconnect any hoses, lines, brackets or electrical connections that may interfere with cylinder head removal.

12 Loosen the cylinder head bolts, 1/4-turn at a time, in the reverse order of the tightening sequence **(see illustration 12.21)** until they can be removed by hand.

13 Carefully lift the cylinder head straight up and place it on wood blocks to prevent damage to the sealing surfaces. If the head sticks to the engine block, dislodge it by placing a wood block against the head casting and tapping the wood with a hammer or by prising the head with a prybar placed carefully on a casting protrusion.

14 Remove all traces of old gasket material from the block and head. Special gasket removal solvents that soften gaskets and make removal much easier are available at auto parts stores.

Caution: *The cylinder head is aluminium, be very careful not to gouge the sealing surfaces. When working on the block, place clean shop rags into the cylinders to help keep out debris. Use a vacuum cleaner to remove any contamination from the engine. Use a tap of the correct size to clean the threads in the*

12.19 When fitting the head gasket onto the block, make sure all passages in the block align with the holes in the gasket

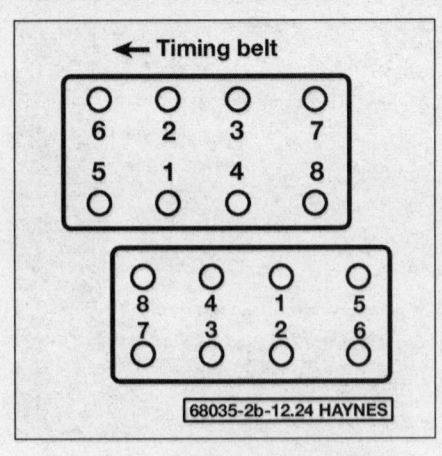

12.21 Cylinder head bolt tightening sequence

engine block. Clean and inspect all threaded fasteners for damage.

15 Inspect the cylinder head bolt threads for stretching, where the diameter of threads narrow due to bolt re-tensioning. If any cylinder head bolt exhibits damage or stretching, it must be replaced.

Note: *Be sure to check each cylinder head bolt for any signs of stretching or thread damage. Consult with a dealer parts department or machine shop/auto parts department. Replace any damaged cylinder head bolts with new head bolts.*

16 Using a precision straightedge and feeler gauge, check all gasket surfaces for warpage **(see illustrations)**.

17 If the warpage on any surface exceeds the limits listed in this Chapter's Specifications, the discrepant component must be replaced or resurfaced by an automotive machine shop.

Refitting

Refer to illustrations 12.19 and 12.21

18 Refit the camshaft(s) if removed (see Section 11).

19 Place a new gasket on the engine block **(see illustration)**. Use no sealer unless indicated by the gasket manufacturer. Note any directions printed on the gasket such as "Front" or "This side up." Place the cylinder head(s) in position on the engine block.

20 Refit the washers onto the cylinder head bolts with the rounded shoulders facing up. Apply clean engine oil to the cylinder head bolt threads and refit them into the cylinder head.

21 Tighten the cylinder head bolts in the sequence shown **(see illustration)** progressing in three stages to the torque listed in this Chapter's Specifications.

22 Refit the coolant crossover housing onto the rear of the cylinder heads. Be sure to fit a new O-ring onto the coolant inlet pipe. Torque the coolant crossover housing to the Specifications listed in this Chapter.

23 The remaining Steps are the reverse of removal.

24 Change the engine oil and filter, then refill the cooling system (see Chapter 1).

25 Start the engine and let it run until normal operating temperature is reached. Check for leaks and proper operation.

13 Sump - removal and refitting

Caution: *If the stereo in your vehicle is equipped with an anti-theft system, make sure you have the correct activation code before disconnecting the battery.*

Removal

1 Disconnect the cable from the negative battery terminal (see Chapter 5).

2 Raise the vehicle, place it securely on jackstands, remove the skid plate and lower cover from under the engine (see Chapter 10).

3 Drain the engine oil (see Chapter 1).

4 Remove the oil and transmission fluid dipstick tubes.

5 Remove the starter motor (see Chapter 5).

6 Remove both driveshafts from the front differential (see Chapter 8).

7 Unbolt the front differential from the crossmember assembly and lower the front differential (see Chapter 8).

8 Remove the transmission-to-oil pan support.

9 Remove the exhaust pipe assembly (see Chapter 4).

10 Remove the sump mounting bolts. If the sump is stuck, tap it with a soft-face hammer or place a wood block against the sump and tap the wood block with a hammer.

Caution: *If you're wedging something between the sump and the engine block to separate them, be extremely careful not to gouge or nick the gasket surface of either part; an oil leak could result.*

11 Remove the sump from the vehicle.

12 Remove the oil pump pick-up tube and screen if necessary for cleaning or repair.

13 Thoroughly clean all gasket sealing surfaces. Use a scraper to remove all traces of old gasket material. Gasket removal solvents are available at auto parts stores and may prove helpful. Check the sump sealing surface for distortion. Straighten or replace as necessary. After cleaning and straightening (if necessary), wipe the gasket surfaces of the sump and block clean with a rag soaked in lacquer thinner or acetone.

Refitting

Refer to illustrations 13.14 and 13.16

14 Apply a 4.0 mm bead of RTV sealant to the sump **(see illustration)**. Also apply a light coating of RTV sealant to the underside of the sump bolt heads.

15 Refit the oil pump pick-up tube if removed. Tighten the bolts to the torque listed in this Chapter's Specifications.

16 Place the sump against the engine block and refit the bolts **(see illustration)**. Tighten the bolts to the torque listed in this Chapter's Specifications using a circular pattern.

Caution: *Bolts numbered 13 and 14 are very long and easy to refit at an angle causing thread or seal housing damage.*

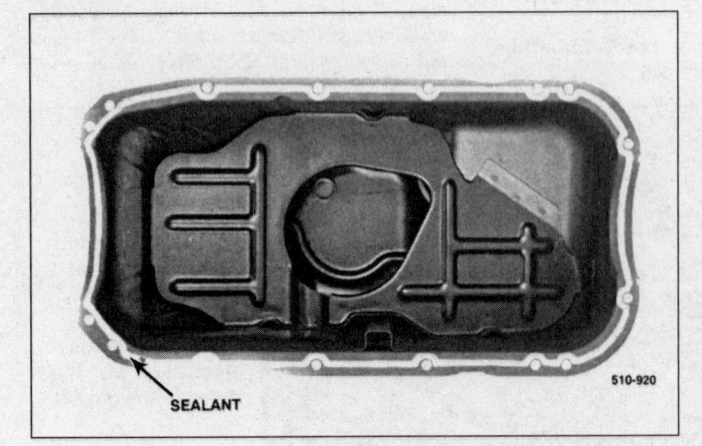

13.14 Apply a 4 mm bead of sealant to the sump as shown

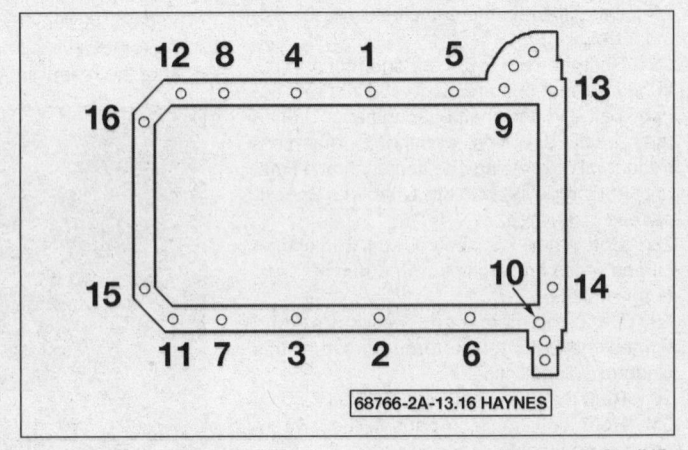

13.16 Tighten the sump in a circular pattern as shown - bolts #13 and #14 are very long and can easily be refitted at an angle

Chapter 2 Part A V6 petrol engines

14.9 Typical rotor cover screw mounting locations

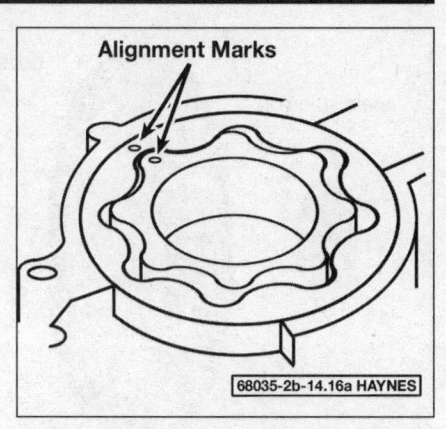

14.16a Install the rotors into the oil pump body with the match-marks aligned

17 The remaining Steps are the reverse of removal.
18 Lower the vehicle and fill the crankcase with the proper quantity and grade of engine oil (see *Recommended lubricants and fluids* at the beginning of Chapter 1) and run the engine, checking for leaks. Road test the vehicle and check for leaks again.

14 Oil pump - removal, inspection and refitting

Caution: *If the stereo in your vehicle is equipped with an anti-theft system, make sure you have the correct activation code before disconnecting the battery.*

Removal

Refer to illustration 14.9

1 Disconnect the cable from the negative battery terminal (see Chapter 5).
2 Raise the vehicle and support it securely on jackstands.
3 Remove the drivebelt (see Chapter 1).
4 Remove the timing belt (see Section 7) and crankshaft sprocket and Woodruff key (see Section 8).
5 Remove the sump (see Section 13).
6 If equipped, remove the air conditioning compressor bracket from the engine.

Warning: *The air conditioning system is under high pressure. Don't disconnect any of the refrigerant lines. After unbolting the air conditioning compressor from its bracket, position it out of the way and secure it with wire or rope.*

7 Remove the bolts and detach the oil pump assembly from the engine.

Caution: *If the pump doesn't come off by hand, tap it gently with a soft-faced hammer or pry on a casting boss.*

8 Remove the oil filter adapter and discard the gasket.
9 Remove the oil pump rotor cover **(see illustration)**.
10 New rotors are manufactured with arrows on them which are aligned at refitting. If both arrows are not clearly visible, use a permanent marker to match-mark the rotors so they can be refitted back in their original position. Remove the inner and outer rotor from the body.

Caution: *Be very careful with these components. Close tolerances are critical in creating the correct oil pressure. Any nicks or other damage will require replacement of the complete pump assembly.*

11 Using a hammer and drift, carefully and evenly drive the crankshaft front seal from the oil pump housing and discard it.
12 Disassemble the oil pressure relief valve assembly, taking note of the way the relief valve piston is refitted. Unscrew the relief valve plug and remove the bolt, washer, spring and relief valve.
13 Thoroughly clean all gasket sealing surfaces. Use a scraper to remove all traces of old gasket material. Gasket removal solvents are available at auto parts stores and may prove helpful. Check the oil pan sealing surface for distortion. Straighten or replace as necessary. After removing the residual gasket material, wipe the gasket surfaces of the oil pan and block clean with a rag soaked in lacquer thinner or acetone.

Inspection

Refer to illustrations 14.16a, 14.16b, 14.16c and 14.16d

14 Clean all oil pump components with solvent and inspect them for excessive wear and/or damage. Replace as required.

Note: *If either rotor is damaged, they must be replaced as a set.*

15 Inspect the oil pressure relief valve piston sliding surface and valve spring for damage.

Note: *If either the spring or the valve is damaged, they must be replaced as a set.*

16 Refit the rotors into the pump housing with the match-marks aligned. Check the

14.16b Use a feeler gauge to measure the inner rotor-to-outer rotor lobe clearance

14.16c Measuring the outer rotor-to-pump body clearance

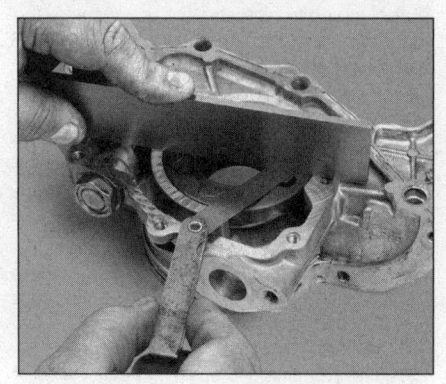

14.16d Place a precision straightedge over the rotors and measure the clearance between the rotors and the straightedge to determine the rotor-to-cover clearance

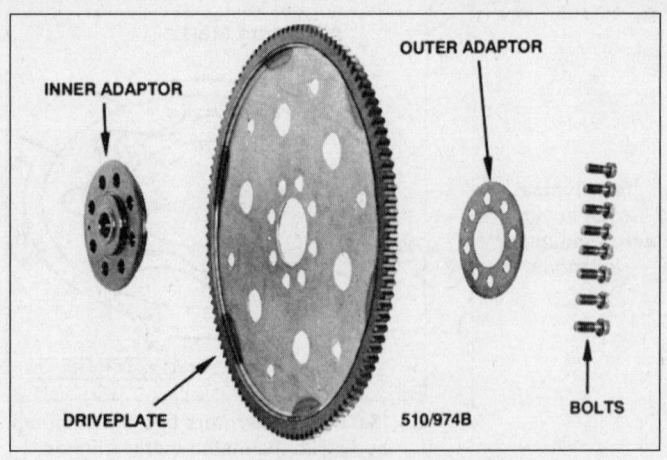

15.4 Typical driveplate component details

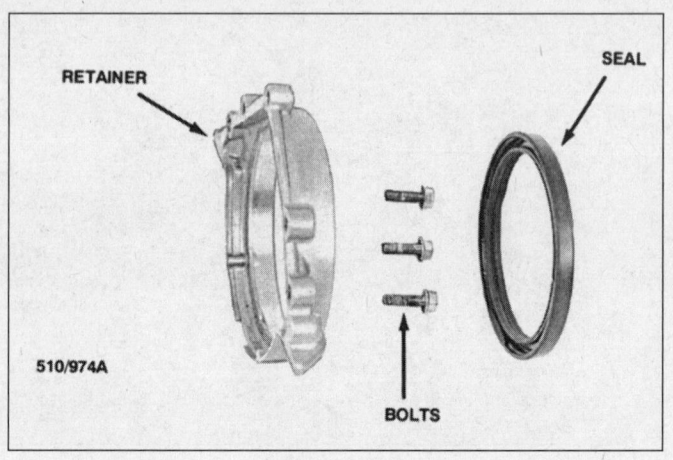

16.4 Typical rear crankshaft oil seal and seal retainer details

16.5 With the seal retainer supported on wood blocks, use a hammer and drift to drive the seal out of the retainer

oil pump rotor clearances using a precision straightedge and feeler gauges **(see illustrations)**. Compare the results to the tolerances listed in this Chapter's Specifications. Replace both rotors if any clearance is out of tolerance.

Refitting

17 Lubricate the relief valve piston, piston bore and spring with clean engine oil. Refit the relief valve piston into the bore maintaining original orientation followed by the spring and cap bolt. Tighten the plug bolt to the torque listed in this Chapter's Specifications.

Note: *If the relief valve piston is refitted incorrectly, serious engine damage could occur.*

18 Lubricate the oil pump rotor recess in the housing and the inner and outer rotors with clean engine oil. Refit the rotors into the pump housing with the match-marks aligned. Next, fill the rotor cavity with clean engine oil and refit the cover. Tighten the cover screws to the torque listed in this Chapter's Specifications.
19 Refit the new crankshaft front seal into the oil pump housing (see Section 8).
20 Refit a new gasket, and position the pump assembly on the block, aligning the inner rotor and crankshaft drive flats. Refit the mounting bolts.
21 If equipped, refit the air conditioning bracket onto the engine (one bolt secures both the air conditioning bracket and the oil pump housing).
22 Tighten the oil pump attaching bolts to the torque listed in this Chapter's Specifications.
23 Refit the Woodruff key, crankshaft timing belt sprocket (see Section 8) and timing belt (see Section 7).
24 Refit the sump (see Section 13).
25 The remaining Steps are the reverse of removal.
26 Allow the sealant to cure the amount of time indicated by the manufacturer before adding oil to the engine.

27 Change the oil filter then lower the vehicle and fill the crankcase with the proper quantity and grade of oil (see Chapter 1).
28 Start the engine and check for leaks.

15 Driveplate - removal and refitting

Removal

Refer to illustration 15.4

1 Remove the transmission (see Chapter 7).
2 To ensure correct alignment during refitting, match-mark the backing plate and driveplate to the crankshaft before removal.
3 Remove the bolts securing the driveplate to the crankshaft. A tool is available at most auto parts stores to hold the driveplate while loosening the bolts, if the tool is not available, wedge a screwdriver in the ring gear teeth to jam the driveplate.

Note: *On models equipped with the 3.2L diesel engines (4M41) the driveplate is a two piece unit consisting of the inertia ring and driveplate riveted together. If the rivets are damaged the unit must be replaced as a unit.*
4 Remove the driveplate from the crankshaft **(see illustration)**.
5 Clean the driveplate to remove any grease and oil. Inspect it for cracks, distortion and missing or excessively worn ring gear teeth. Replace if necessary.
6 Clean and inspect the mating surfaces of the driveplate and the crankshaft. Check the crankshaft rear main seal for leakage; if leakage is evident replace it before refitting the driveplate (see Section 16).

Installation

7 Position the driveplate and backing plate against the crankshaft. Align the previously applied match-marks. Before refitting the bolts, apply thread locking compound to the threads.
8 Hold the driveplate with the special holding tool, or wedge a screwdriver in the ring gear teeth to keep the driveplate from turning as you tighten the bolts in a criss-cross pattern to the torque listed in this Chapter's Specifications.
9 The remaining Steps are the reverse of removal.

Chapter 2 Part A V6 petrol engines

16.8 Drive the new seal into the retainer until it's flush - make sure it's square in the bore

17.10 Remove the engine mount nut-to-bracket (A) then remove the mount-to frame bolts (B) and manoeuvre the mount from the engine - typical left side mount shown, right side is similar

16 Rear main oil seal - renewal

Refer to illustrations 16.4, 16.5 and 16.8

1 The crankshaft rear main oil seal is pressed into a retainer and bolted to the rear of the engine block.
2 Remove the driveplate (see Section 15).
3 The crankshaft rear main oil seal can be replaced without removing the seal retainer. However, this method is NOT recommended because the lip of the seal is quite stiff and it's possible to cock the seal in the retainer bore or damage it during refitting. If you want to take the chance, carefully and evenly prise out the old seal using a flat blade screwdriver - do not damage the crankshaft sealing surface. Apply a light coating of clean engine oil to the crankshaft seal journal and the lip of the new seal then carefully tap the new seal into place using a hammer and socket. The seal lip is stiff, so carefully work it onto the seal journal of the crankshaft with a smooth object like the rounded end of a socket extension as you tap the seal into place. Don't force it or you may damage the seal.
4 The following method is recommended: remove the mounting bolts from the crankshaft rear seal retainer and oil sump rear bolts. Separate the retainer from the engine block **(see illustration)** and remove the retainer.
5 Using a hammer and drift, carefully drive the old seal out of the retainer and discard it **(see illustration)**.
6 Thoroughly clean all gasket sealing surfaces. Use a scraper to remove all traces of old gasket material. Gasket removal solvents are available at auto parts stores and may prove helpful. Check the oil pan sealing surface for distortion. Straighten or replace as necessary. After removing the residual gasket material, wipe the gasket surfaces clean using a rag soaked in lacquer thinner or acetone.
7 Thoroughly clean and inspect the seal bore and sealing surface on the crankshaft. Minor imperfections can be removed with fine emery cloth. If there is a groove worn in the crankshaft sealing surface (from contact with the seal), fitting a new seal will probably not stop the leak.
8 Fit the new seal into the retainer using a drift or socket or block of wood and a hammer. Drive it in until it's flush with the retainer **(see illustration)**.
9 Apply a 2 mm bead of RTV sealant to the retainer gasket sealing surface.
10 Lubricate the lip of the new seal and the crankshaft sealing surface with a light coat of clean engine oil.
11 Place the seal retainer in position on the engine block and refit the mounting bolts. The seal lip is stiff, so carefully work it onto the seal journal of the crankshaft with a smooth object like the rounded end of a socket extension as you tap the seal into place. Don't force it or you may damage the seal. Tighten the retainer bolts.
12 The remaining Steps are the reverse of removal.

17 Engine mounts - check and renewal

Caution: *If the stereo in your vehicle is equipped with an anti-theft system, make sure you have the correct activation code before disconnecting the battery.*

1 Engine mounts seldom require attention, but broken or deteriorated mounts should be renewed immediately or the added strain placed on the driveline components may cause damage or wear.

Check

2 During the check, the engine must be raised slightly to relieve the weight from the mounts.
3 Raise the vehicle and support it securely on jackstands, then position a jack under the engine sump. Place a large wood block between the jack head and the sump to prevent damage, then carefully raise the engine just enough to take the weight off the mounts.
Warning: *DO NOT place any part of your body under the engine when it's supported only by a jack!*
4 Inspect the mounts to see if the rubber is cracked, hardened or separated from the metal backing. Sometimes the rubber will split right down the centre.
5 Check for relative movement between the mount plates and the engine or frame. Use a large screwdriver or pry bar to attempt to move the mounts. If movement is noted, lower the engine and tighten the mount fasteners.
6 Rubber preservative may be applied to the mounts to slow deterioration.

Renewal

Refer to illustration 17.10

7 Disconnect the negative battery cable (see Chapter 5).
8 Raise the vehicle and support it securely on jackstands.
9 Place a floor jack under the engine with a wood block between the jack head and oil pan and raise the engine slightly to relieve the weight from the mount to be replaced.
10 Remove the fasteners and detach the mount from the frame and engine **(see illustration)**.
Caution: *Do not disconnect more than one mount at a time, except during engine/transaxle removal.*
11 Refitting is the reverse of removal. Use thread locking compound on the mount bolts and be sure to tighten them securely.

Notes

Chapter 2 Part B
2.8L diesel engine

Contents

	Section		Section
Camshaft - removal, inspection and refitting	11	Inlet manifold - removal and refitting	6
Compression check	See Chapter 2D	Oil pump - removal, inspection and refitting	14
Crankshaft front oil seal - renewal	10	Rear main oil seal - renewal	16
Cylinder head - removal and refitting	12	Repair operations possible with the engine in the vehicle	2
Drivebelt check, adjustment and renewal	See Chapter 1	Sump - removal and refitting	13
Engine mounts - check and renewal	17	Timing chain, sprockets and gears - removal, inspection and refitting	9
Engine oil and filter change	See Chapter 1		
Engine overhaul - general information	See Chapter 2D	Timing gear cover - removal and refitting	8
Engine - removal and refitting	See Chapter 2D	Top Dead Centre (TDC) for number one piston - locating	3
Exhaust manifold - removal and refitting	7	Valve cover - removal and refitting	4
Flywheel/driveplate - removal and refitting	15	Valve springs, retainers and seals - renewal	5
General information	1		

Specifications

General
Engine type	4M40T
Firing order	1 - 3 - 4 - 2
Cylinder numbers (drivebelt end-to-transmission end)	1 - 2 - 3 - 4
Bore and stroke	95 x 100 mm
Displacement	2,835 cc
Compression pressure	
Standard	2,840 kPa
Minimum	2,250 kPa
Maximum variation	290 kPa
Oil pressure	200 kPa @ idle

Camshaft
Endplay	
Standard	0.10 to 0.18 mm
Limit	0.30 mm
Runout maximum	0.020 mm
Bearing journal oil clearance	0.05 to 0.09 mm
Lobe lift	
Intake	9.89 mm
Exhaust	10.19 mm

Cylinder head
Warpage limit	0.2 mm
Inlet/exhaust manifold warpage limit	0.15 mm
Maximum allowable machining	0.2 mm

Oil pump

Gear-to-cover clearance
    Standard.. 0.05 to 0.10 mm
    Limit... 0.15 mm
Gear tip-to-case clearance
    Standard.. 0.15 to 0.26 mm
    Limit... 0.27 mm
Shaft clearance
    Standard.. 0.03 to 0.05 mm
    Limit... 0.15 mm

Piston protrusion above block deck

Non-turbocharged.. 0.55 to 0.77 mm
Turbocharged .... 0.45 to 0.67 mm

Timing gears and balance shafts

	Standard	Limit
Balance shaft-to-bush clearance	0.06 to 0.11 mm	0.16 mm
Left idler shaft-to-bush clearance	0.02 to 0.05 mm	0.1 mm
Right balance shaft gear and oil pump gear backlash	0.04 to 0.19 mm	0.3 mm
Oil pump gear and crankshaft gear backlash	0.04 to 0.18 mm	0.3 mm
Crankshaft gear and idler gear backlash	0.04 to 0.18 mm	0.3 mm
Idler gear and left idler gear backlash	0.04 to 0.19 mm	0.3 mm
Left idler gear and left balance shaft gear backlash	0.04 to 0.22 mm	0.4 mm
Idler gear and injection pump gear backlash	0.04 to 0.21 mm	0.4 mm
Balance shaft endplay	0.09 to 0.24 mm	0.3 mm
Idler gear and sprocket	0.05 to 0.20 mm	0.3 mm
Left idler gear	0.05 to 0.20 mm	0.3 mm

Crankshaft

	Standard	Limit
End play	0.1 to 0.28 mm	0.4 mm

Piston

	Standard	Limit
Piston ring-to-ring groove clearance		
Top ring	0.03 to 0.08 mm	0.15 mm
Second ring	0.07 to 0.10 mm	0.15 mm
Oil control ring	0.03 to 0.06 mm	0.15 mm
Piston ring end gap		
Top ring	0.30 to 0.45 mm	0.80 mm
Second ring (to 2001 models)	0.30 to 0.45 mm	0.80 mm
Second ring (from 2001 models)	0.40 to 0.55 mm	0.80 mm
Oil control ring	0.25 to 0.45 mm	1.00 mm
Piston pin clearance		
Pin to connecting rod	0.03 to 0.45 mm	0.1 mm
Pin to piston	0.007 to 0.021 mm	0.05 mm
Connecting rod big end side clearance	0.15 to 0.45 mm	0.6 mm

Torque specifications

	Nm
Balance shaft gear bolts	37
Camshaft bearing cap bolts	19 to 21
Camshaft sprocket bolt (left hand thread)	90
Crankshaft pulley bolt	323
Cylinder head bolts	
Large cylinder head bolts	
Step 1	100
Step 2	Fully loosen in reverse sequence
Step 3	50
Step 4	Tighten an additional 90-degrees
Step 5	Tighten an additional 90-degrees
Two small front cylinder head bolts	24
Exhaust manifold	
Manifold-to-cylinder head nuts	31
Manifold heat shield bolts	12 to 15
Manifold-to-exhaust pipe bolts	49
Flywheel-to-crankshaft bolts	125
Flexplate-to-crankshaft bolts	135
Inlet manifold bolts	18
Inlet manifold cover screws	10 to 12
Oil cooler banjo bolts	29 to 34
Oil cooler hoses-to-block banjo bolts	39 to 44

Chapter 2 Part B 2.8L diesel engine

Torque specifications

	Nm
Oil cooler mounting nuts	20
Oil cooler plugs	44
Oil pump cover-to-body screws	10
Timing chain tension lever bolt	41
Valve cover bolts	4
Motor mount-to-frame bolts	44

1 General information

This Part of Chapter 2 is devoted to in-vehicle repair procedures for the 2.8L model 4M40 four-cylinder diesel engine. All information concerning engine removal and refitting and engine overhaul can be found in Part D of this Chapter.

The following repair procedures are based on the assumption that the engine is in the vehicle. If the engine has been removed from the vehicle and mounted on a stand, many of the steps outlined in this Part of Chapter 2 will not apply.

The Specifications included in this Part of Chapter 2 apply only to the procedures contained in this Part.

The 2.8 litre engine is an inline vertical four, with a chain-driven overhead camshaft and a balance shaft counterbalancing system which cancels the engine's power pulses and produces relatively vibration-free operation. The crankshaft rides in renewable insert-type main bearings.

The pistons have two compression rings and one oil control ring. The semi-floating piston pins are press fitted into the small end of the connecting rod. The connecting rod big ends are also equipped with renewable insert-type plain bearings.

The engine is liquid-cooled, utilising a centrifugal impeller-type pump, driven by a belt from the camshaft, to circulate coolant around the cylinders and combustion chambers and through the inlet manifold.

Lubrication is handled by an oil pump mounted on the front of the engine. It is driven by the crankshaft. The oil is filtered continuously by a cartridge-type filter mounted on the side of the engine.

2 Repair operations possible with the engine in the vehicle

Many major repair operations can be accomplished without removing the engine from the vehicle.

Clean the engine compartment and the exterior of the engine with some type of degreaser before any work is done. It will make the job easier and help keep dirt out of the internal areas of the engine.

Depending on the components involved, it may be helpful to remove the bonnet to improve access to the engine as repairs are performed (refer to Chapter 11 if necessary). Cover the fenders to prevent damage to the paint. Special pads are available, but an old bedspread or blanket will also work.

If vacuum, exhaust, oil or coolant leaks develop, indicating a need for gasket or seal renewal, the repairs can generally be made with the engine in the vehicle. The inlet and exhaust manifold gaskets, oil sump gasket, crankshaft oil seals and cylinder head gasket are all accessible with the engine in place.

Exterior engine components, such as the inlet and exhaust manifolds, the oil sump, the water pump, the starter motor, the alternator and the fuel system components can be removed for repair with the engine in place.

Since the cylinder head can be removed without pulling the engine, camshaft and valve component servicing can also be accomplished with the engine in the vehicle. Renewal of the timing belt and sprockets is also possible with the engine in the vehicle.

In extreme cases caused by a lack of necessary equipment, repair or renewal of piston rings, pistons, connecting rods and rod bearings is possible with the engine in the vehicle. However, this practice is not recommended because of the cleaning and preparation work that must be done to the components involved.

3 Top Dead Centre (TDC) for number one piston - locating

Refer to illustration 3.7

1 Top Dead Centre (TDC) is the highest point in the cylinder that each piston reaches as it travels up-and-down when the crankshaft turns. Each piston reaches TDC on the compression stroke and again on the exhaust stroke, but TDC generally refers to piston position on the compression stroke.

2 Positioning the number one piston at TDC is an essential part of many procedures, such as camshaft, timing chain or distributor removal.

3 Before beginning this procedure, be sure to place the transmission in Park (automatic) or Neutral (manual) and apply the parking brake or block the rear wheels.

4 In order to bring any piston to TDC, the crankshaft must be turned using one of the methods outlined below. When looking at the front of the engine (timing belt end), normal crankshaft rotation is clockwise.

a) *The preferred method is to turn the crankshaft with a socket and ratchet attached to the bolt threaded into the front of the crankshaft.*

b) *A remote starter switch, which may save some time, can also be used. Follow the instructions included with the switch. Once the piston is close to TDC, use a socket and ratchet as described in the previous paragraph.*

c) *If an assistant is available to turn the ignition switch to the Start position in short bursts, you can get the piston close to TDC without a remote starter switch. Make sure your assistant is out of the vehicle, away from the ignition switch, then use a socket and ratchet as described in Paragraph a) to complete the procedure.*

Note: *It may be necessary to remove the glow plugs in order to rotate the engine (refer to Chapter 4).*

5 Remove the valve cover (refer to **Section 4**).

6 Rotate the engine until the notch on the crankshaft pulley is aligned with the '0' timing mark.

Caution: *Always turn the crankshaft clockwise.*

7 Check that the protrusion on the camshaft is pointing up **(see illustration)**. If it is, then the engine is at TDC on the compression stroke for number one cylinder. If it is not, then rotate the crankshaft one full turn until the marks are aligned and the protrusion is up.

8 To position the engine at TDC on number four cylinder (required when performing a valve adjustment), rotate the crankshaft one complete revolution, again aligning the notch and the '0' mark.

Chapter 2 Part B 2.8L diesel engine

4 Valve cover - removal and refitting

Caution: *If the stereo in your vehicle is equipped with an anti-theft system, make sure you have the correct activation code before disconnecting the battery.*

Removal

Refer to illustrations 4.6 and 4.7

1 Detach the cable from the negative battery terminal. Refer to Chapter 4 and remove any interfering turbocharger/intercooler components.
2 Disconnect the crankcase breather hose from the valve cover.
3 Disconnect any cables, air intake ducts or hoses which interfere with the valve cover removal.
4 Disconnect the accelerator cable from the valve cover and position it aside.
5 Wipe off the valve cover thoroughly to prevent debris from falling onto the exposed cylinder head or camshaft/valve train assembly.
6 Remove the valve cover bolts **(see illustration)**.
7 Carefully lift off the valve cover and gasket **(see illustration)**. If the cover is stuck to the cylinder head, tap it with a rubber mallet to break the seal. Do not prise between the cover and cylinder head or you'll damage the gasket mating surfaces.

Refitting

Refer to illustration 4.11

8 Clean the mating surfaces of the cylinder head and the valve cover. Clean the surfaces with a rag soaked in lacquer thinner or acetone.
9 Be sure to refit the semi-circular seals on top of the cylinder head. Apply beads of RTV sealant completely around the perimeter of the seals and also 10 mm on each side of them on the surface of the cylinder head.
10 Refit new seals on the valve cover bolts.
11 Refit a new gasket onto the valve cover. Refit the moulded rubber gasket onto the cover by pushing the new gasket into the slot **(see illustration)** that circles the valve cover perimeter. Refit new front and rear semi-circular seals with a bead of RTV sealant around them. Apply a bead of RTV sealant where the cylinder head and the front and rear semi-circular seals meet. Refit the valve cover and tighten the bolts to the torque listed in this Chapter's Specifications.

Caution: *Do not overtighten the valve cover.*

12 The remainder of refitting is the reverse of removal.

3.7 The protrusion (arrow) must face upward when the engine is correctly positioned at TDC for number one cylinder on the compression stroke

4.6 Remove the valve cover bolts and seals

5 Valve springs, retainers and seals - renewal

Note: *Broken valve springs and defective valve stem seals can be renewed without removing the cylinder heads. Two special tools and a compressed air source are normally required to perform this operation, so read through this Section carefully and rent or buy the tools before beginning the job.*

1 Refer to Section 4 and remove the valve cover from the cylinder head.
2 Remove the glow plug from the affected cylinder. Refer to Chapter 4.
3 Turn the crankshaft until the piston in the affected cylinder is at Top Dead Centre on the compression stroke (see Section 3). If you're renewing all of the valve stem seals, begin with cylinder number one and work on the valves for one cylinder at a time. Move from cylinder-to-cylinder following the firing order sequence (see this Chapter's Specifications).

4.7 Carefully lift off the valve cover and gasket. If the cover is stuck to the cylinder head, tap it with a rubber mallet to break the seal. Do not prise between the cover and cylinder head or you'll damage the gasket mating surfaces

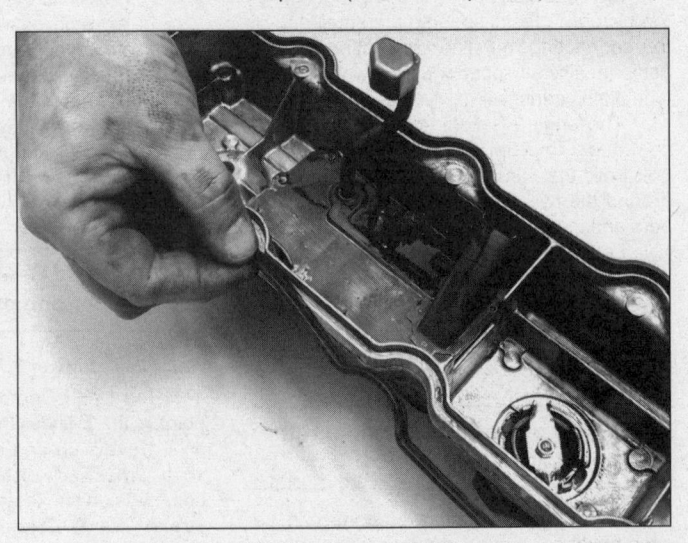

4.11 Fit the moulded rubber gasket onto the cover by pushing the new gasket into the slot

6.3 Remove the EGR tube mounting bolts/nuts, hose and waste gate hose

1 EGR tube mounting bolts/nuts
2 EGR hose
3 Waste gate hose
4 EGR hose bracket
5 Earth strap

6.4 Remove the turbo charger heat shield mounting bolts (arrows)

4 Thread an adaptor into the glow plug hole and connect an air hose from a compressed air source to it. Most auto parts stores can supply the air hose adaptor.
Note: *Many cylinder compression gauges utilise a screw-in fitting that may work with your air hose quick-disconnect fitting.*
5 Remove the camshaft (refer to Section 11). Remove the adjustment shim and the lifter.
6 Apply compressed air to the cylinder.
Warning: *The piston may be forced down by compressed air, causing the crankshaft to turn suddenly. If the spanner used when positioning the number one piston at TDC is still attached to the bolt in the crankshaft nose, it could cause damage or injury when the crankshaft moves.*
7 The valves should be held in place by the air pressure.
8 Stuff shop rags into the cylinder head holes around the valve spring area to prevent parts and tools from falling into the engine, then use a valve spring compressor to compress the spring.
Note: *A special valve spring compressor is required to perform this operation. Mitsubishi tools #MD998784 and MD998772 or their equivalents are needed. Remove the collets with small needle-nose pliers or a magnet.*
9 Remove the spring retainer, the valve spring, the lower retainer and then remove the valve guide seal.

Note: *If air pressure fails to hold the valve in the closed position during this operation, the valve face or seat is probably damaged. If so, the cylinder head will have to be removed for additional repair operations.*
10 Wrap a rubber band or tape around the top of the valve stem so the valve won't fall into the combustion chamber, then release the air pressure.
11 Inspect the valve stem for damage. Rotate the valve in the guide and check the end for eccentric movement, which would indicate that the valve is bent.
12 Move the valve up-and-down in the guide and make sure it doesn't bind. If the valve stem binds, either the valve is bent or the guide is damaged. In either case, the cylinder head will have to be removed for repair.
13 Reapply air pressure to the cylinder to retain the valve in the closed position, then remove the tape or rubber band from the valve stem.
14 Lubricate the valve stem with engine oil and refit a new guide seal.
15 Refit the spring and retainers in position over the valve.
16 Compress the valve spring and carefully position the collets in the groove. Apply a small dab of grease to the inside of each collet to hold it in place.
17 Remove the force from the spring tool and make sure the collets are seated.
18 Disconnect the air hose and remove the adaptor from the spark plug hole.

19 Refit the glow plugs.
20 Refer to Section 4 and refit the valve cover.
21 Start and run the engine, then check for oil leaks and unusual sounds coming from the valve cover area.

6 Inlet manifold - removal and refitting

Warning: *Diesel fuel is flammable, so take extra precautions when you work on any part of the fuel system. Don't smoke or allow open flames or bare light bulbs near the work area, and don't work in a garage where a gas-type appliance (such as a water heater) is present. If you spill any fuel on your skin, rinse it off immediately with soap and water. When you perform any kind of work on the fuel system, wear safety glasses and have a Class B type fire extinguisher on hand.*
Caution: *If the stereo in your vehicle is equipped with an anti-theft system, make sure you have the correct activation code before disconnecting the battery.*

Removal
Refer to illustrations 6.3 and 6.4

1 Detach the cable from the negative battery terminal.
2 Remove the intercooler and any other interfering ducts (see Chapter 4).
3 If the engine is equipped with EGR, remove the EGR hoses and tubes **(see illustration)**. The EGR valve can be left attached to the manifold if desired. Disconnect the boost hose from the waste gate and the inlet manifold.
4 Remove the turbocharger heat shield **(see illustration)** and the duct which connects the turbocharger to the inlet manifold. Remove the wastegate.
5 Remove the inlet manifold bolts and remove the manifold from the engine.

Refitting
6 Clean the inlet manifold and cylinder head surface, removing all traces of gasket material.
7 Check the mating surfaces of the manifold for flatness with a precision straightedge and feeler gauge.
8 Inspect the manifold for cracks and distortion.
9 If the manifold is cracked or warped, renew it or see if it can be re-surfaced/repaired at an automotive machine shop.
10 Check carefully for any stripped or broken inlet manifold bolts. Renew any defective bolts.
11 Place new gaskets onto the cylinder head.
12 Refit the inlet manifold and tighten the bolts finger-tight. Starting at the centre and working out in both directions, tighten the bolts in a criss-cross pattern until the torque listed in this Chapter's Specifications is reached.

13 The remainder of the refitting procedure is the reverse of removal.

7 Exhaust manifold - removal and refitting

Caution: *If the stereo in your vehicle is equipped with an anti-theft system, make sure you have the correct activation code before disconnecting the battery.*

Removal

1 Disconnect the negative battery cable from the battery.
2 Remove the inlet manifold (refer to Section 7).
3 Remove the interfering heat shields from the exhaust manifold **(see illustration 6.4)**.
4 Disconnect the turbocharger from the exhaust manifold (see Chapter 4).
5 Remove the exhaust manifold nuts and detach the exhaust manifold from the cylinder head.

Refitting

6 Inspect the exhaust manifold for cracks, damage or distortion.
7 Discard the old gaskets and use a scraper to clean the gasket mating surfaces on the exhaust manifold, turbocharger (or exhaust pipe) and cylinder head. Place new gaskets onto the cylinder head and turbocharger (or exhaust pipe).
8 Place the exhaust manifold in position on the cylinder head and refit the nuts. Starting at the centre, tighten the nuts in a criss-cross pattern until the torque listed in this Chapter's Specifications is reached.
9 The remainder of refitting is the reverse of removal.
10 Start the engine and check for exhaust leaks between the manifold and the cylinder head and between the manifold and the turbocharger (or exhaust pipe).

8 Timing gear cover - removal and refitting

Caution: *If the stereo in your vehicle is equipped with an anti-theft system, make sure you have the correct activation code before disconnecting the battery.*

Removal

1 Disconnect the cable from the negative terminal of the battery. Remove the air cleaner assembly and the intercooler assembly (see Chapter 4).
2 Remove the skid plate and lower cover, then drain the cooling system and engine oil (see Chapter 1).
3 Remove the drivebelts, fan and fan clutch assembly. Remove the vacuum pump, alternator, power steering pump and air conditioning compressor, if equipped, and lay them aside (see Chapter 3).

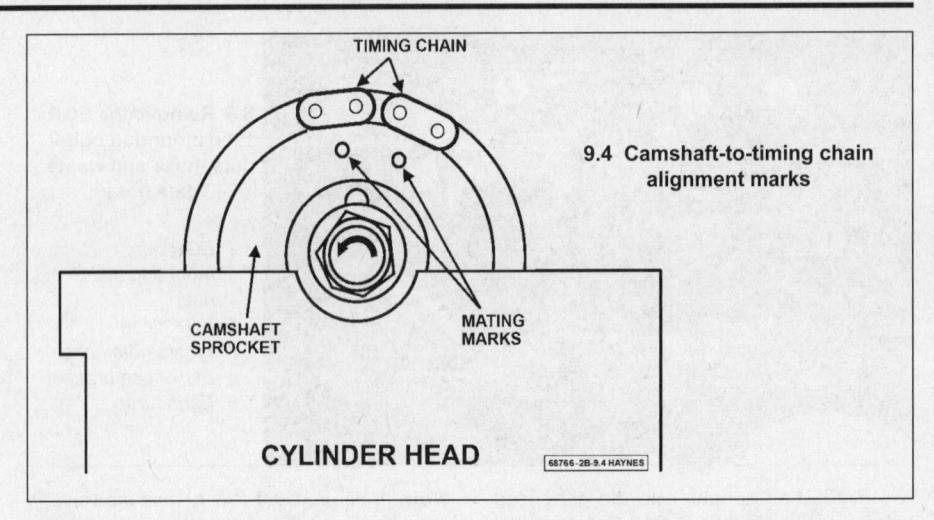

9.4 Camshaft-to-timing chain alignment marks

Warning: *The air conditioning system is under high pressure - do not disconnect the hoses!*

4 Remove the air conditioning mounting bracket and the water pump (see Chapter 3). Any other interfering components must be removed at this time.
5 Remove the crankshaft pulley bolt.

Note: *This bolt is very tight. If a pneumatic impact wrench is not available, it will be necessary to remove the flywheel inspection plate and wedge a screwdriver in the starter ring gear teeth to prevent the crankshaft from turning.*

6 Remove the crankshaft pulley by levering it off. If it is stuck to the crankshaft, use a special puller to remove it. Do not use the type of puller that attaches to the belt groove.
7 Disconnect the vacuum line and the wiring from the vacuum pump. Remove the vacuum pump and its O-rings from the timing cover.
8 Remove the bolts attaching the timing cover to the engine block, oil sump and the two front cylinder head bolts. Note the location of the bolts so they can be returned to the same locations from which they were removed. Tap the cover with a soft-faced hammer to break the gasket seal, then remove the cover from the engine block.

Caution: *Levering between the cover and the engine block can damage the gasket sealing surfaces.*

Caution: *If the cylinder head gasket is damaged during removal of the timing cover the cylinder head gasket must be renewed (see Section 12).*

Refitting

9 Thoroughly clean the front cover and engine block with acetone or lacquer thinner. Make sure the threaded holes in the engine block are clean and dry.
10 Apply a 3 mm bead of RTV sealant completely around the sealing surface of the cover, inboard of the bolt holes. Extend the bead to seal to the oil sump also.
11 Fit the front cover onto the engine. Refit and tighten the bolts in a crisscross pattern.
12 Apply a thin layer of clean moly-based grease to the seal contact surface of the crankshaft pulley, then slide it onto the crankshaft. Refit the bolt and tighten it to the torque listed in this Chapter's Specifications. It may again be necessary to secure the crankshaft to prevent it from turning.
13 The remainder of refitting is the reverse of removal.

9 Timing chain, sprockets and gears - removal, inspection and refitting

Caution: *If the stereo in your vehicle is equipped with an anti-theft system, make sure you have the correct activation code before disconnecting the battery.*

Removal

Refer to illustrations 9.4, 9.5 and 9.6

1 Disconnect the cable from the negative terminal of the battery. Drain the cooling system (see Chapter 1).
2 Position the engine on TDC for number one cylinder (refer to Section 3). Remove the valve cover (refer to Section 4).
3 Remove the front cover (refer to Section 8).
4 Check the alignment marks for the camshaft and timing chain **(see illustration)**.
5 Check the alignment marks for the idler gear and sprocket to the timing chain **(see illustration)**.

Note: *There are three bright white links on the chain, two links are for the camshaft and one link for the idler gear.*

6 Remove the timing chain tensioner assembly from the front of the cylinder head. Remove the camshaft sprocket.

Caution: *Do not rotate the crankshaft after this point. Hold the camshaft by the hex section* **(see illustration)**. *The bolt has a left hand thread.*

Note: *It is not necessary to remove the front cover in order to remove only the camshaft sprocket. Refer to the Section on camshaft removal.*

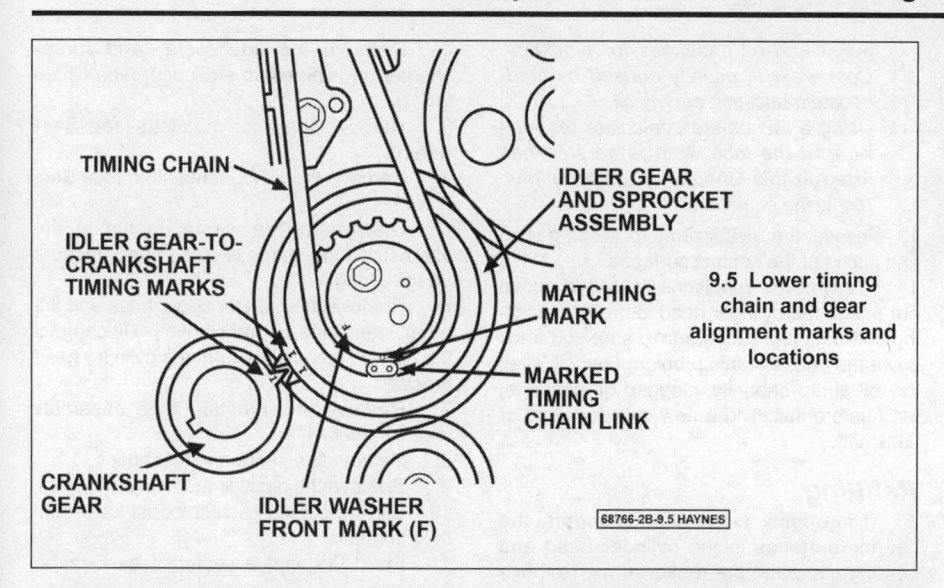

Chapter 2 Part B 2.8L diesel engine

9.5 Lower timing chain and gear alignment marks and locations

9.6 Remove the camshaft sprocket, hold the camshaft by the hex section then remove the bolt (the bolt is left hand thread) - the arrow on the bolt head indicates the direction for tightening the bolt

7 Remove the timing chain.

Note: *Tie the timing chain and camshaft sprocket together to prevent the mating marks from being misaligned.*

8 Remove the chain tensioner and guide plate assembly. The chain oil jet will be removed as part of this procedure.
9 Remove the oil pump/right balance shaft assembly.
10 Unbolt and remove the main idler gear assembly.

Note: *The "F" mark on the idler washer must face out toward the front of the engine.*

11 The fuel injection pump gear can be removed as part of the pump assembly.
12 Dismantle any assemblies which require further service.

Inspection

13 Check the chain tensioner components where they contact the chain for wear and damage. Also inspect the clearance at the tensioner lever shaft and its shaft. Renew any worn parts. Replace the timing chain if the vehicle has covered significant distance.
14 Check the fits of the balance shafts in their bushes. Special tools and expertise are required to renew the balance shaft bushes if they are excessively worn. The engine must be taken to a properly equipped repair shop. If the balance shafts are worn, they should be renewed at this time.
15 The other bushes in the idler gears can be renewed by a competent repair shop equipped with a hydraulic press.

Refitting

16 Make sure the crankshaft is positioned at Top Dead Centre (TDC) for number one cylinder (see Section 3).
17 Refit the idler gear and sprocket assembly. Align the '1' mark on the crankshaft gear between the two marks on the idler gear.
18 If the left balance shaft assembly has been dismantled, make certain that 'O' mark on the gear is facing the front. Refit the left balance shaft assembly.

Caution: *Several of these components use washers under the bolt heads which have an outer rounded edge. Make certain that this rounded edge faces toward the bolt head upon refitting.*

19 Refit the left idler gear assembly. Align the '3' and 'O' marks on it with those on the two mating gears. Refit the bolt - make certain that the bolt's washer has the 'F' facing the front.
20 Refit the right balance shaft/oil pump assembly. Make certain that the 'O' mark on the balance shaft gear is mated with the '6' mark on the oil pump gear. Align the '5' mark on the oil pump gear with the '5' mark on the crankshaft gear.
21 Make certain that the '1' marks on the crankshaft gear and idler gear are still aligned. Place the timing chain over the lower drive sprocket, aligning the single bright white link with the 'O' mark.
22 Put the other end of the timing chain around the camshaft sprocket, aligning the two bright white links with the two marks.
23 Refit the upper sprocket to the camshaft. Refit both tensioner assemblies.
24 Check the alignment of the fuel injection pump gear (refer to Chapter 4).
25 Rotate the crankshaft by hand through two complete revolutions. Again check the alignment of all marks. Check for proper tension of the timing chain.
26 Before installing the chain tensioner assembly into the cylinder head, turn the tensioner cam to force the plunger back into the tensioner body. Lock it in position with the hook.
27 Refit the tensioner with a new gasket. Release the hook to allow the tensioner to contact the chain tensioner.
28 The remainder of refitting is the reverse of removal.

10 Crankshaft front oil seal - renewal

1 Remove the drivebelts (see Chapter 1).

2 Raise the vehicle and support it securely on jackstands.
3 Remove the crankshaft pulley (see Section 8).
4 Carefully prise the seal out of the front cover with a seal removal tool or a screwdriver. If using a screwdriver, wrap the tip with electrical tape. Don't scratch the seal bore or damage the crankshaft in the process (if the crankshaft is damaged, the new seal will end up leaking).
5 Clean the bore in the timing chain cover and coat the outer edge of the new seal with engine oil or multi-purpose grease. Using a socket with an outside diameter slightly smaller than the outside diameter of the seal, carefully drive the seal into place with a hammer. If a socket is not available, a short section of a large diameter pipe will work. Check the seal after refitting to be sure the spring did not pop out.
6 Refitting is the reverse of removal.
7 Run the engine and check for leaks.

11 Camshaft - removal, inspection and refitting

Refer to illustration 11.8

Caution: *If the stereo in your vehicle is equipped with an anti-theft system, make sure you have the correct activation code before disconnecting the battery.*

Removal

1 Disconnect the cable from the negative battery terminal.
2 Remove the valve cover (see Section 4).
3 Position the number one piston at Top Dead Centre (see Section 3).
4 Use an electrician's plastic wire tie or a length of wire to tightly secure the timing chain to the camshaft sprocket.

5   Remove the camshaft sprocket bolt (see Section 11).
Caution: *Do not rotate the crankshaft after this point. Hold the camshaft by the hex section. The bolt has a left hand thread. Support the sprocket and chain with a fabricated holding device so they do not fall into the timing cover or off of the lower sprocket. If this happens, it will be necessary to reinstall the timing chain (see Section 9).*

6   Before removing the camshaft sprocket, remove the timing chain tensioner from the cylinder head (see Section 9).
7   Remove the camshaft sprocket from the camshaft.
8   Loosen the camshaft bearing cap bolts gradually and evenly a quarter turn at a time. Remove the five camshaft bearing caps **(see illustration)**.
9   Lift the camshaft off the cylinder head.

Inspection

10 To check camshaft runout:
a) Support the camshaft with a pair of V-blocks and attach a dial indicator with the stem resting against the centre bearing journal on the camshaft.
b) Rotate the camshaft and note the indicated runout.
c) Compare the results to the camshaft runout listed in this Chapter's Specifications.
d) If the indicated runout exceeds the specified runout, renew the camshaft.

11 Check the camshaft bearing journals and bearing caps for scoring and signs of wear.
12 Check the cam lobes for wear:
a) Check the toe and ramp areas of each cam for score marks and uneven wear. Also check for flaking and pitting.
b) If there is wear on the toe or the ramp, renew the camshaft, but first try to find the cause of the wear. Look for abrasive substances in the oil and inspect the oil pump and oil passages for blockage. Cam wear is usually caused by inadequate lubrication or dirty oil.
c) Using a micrometer, calculate the lobe wear. If the lobe wear is greater than listed in this Chapter's Specifications, renew the camshaft.

13 Inspect the rocker arms for wear, galling and pitting of the contact surfaces.
14 If any of the conditions described above are noted, the cylinder head is probably lacking sufficient lubrication, make sure you track down the cause of this problem (low oil level, low oil pump capacity, clogged oil passage, etc.) before installing a new cylinder head or camshaft.

Refitting

15 Thoroughly clean the camshaft, the bearing surfaces in the cylinder head and bearing caps and the rocker arms. Remove all sludge and dirt. Wipe off all components with a clean, lint-free cloth.
16 Lubricate the camshaft bearing surfaces in the cylinder head and the bearing journals and lobes on the camshaft with assembly lube or moly-base grease. Carefully lower the camshaft into position with the dowel pin pointing up.
Caution: *Failure to adequately lubricate the camshaft and related components can cause serious damage to bearing and friction surfaces during the first few seconds after engine start-up, when the oil pressure is low or nonexistent.*
17 Apply a thin coat of assembly lube or moly-base grease to the bearing surfaces of the camshaft bearing caps.
18 Refit the camshaft bearing caps. They are numbered with number one being closest to the front of the engine. They also have arrows pointing to the front of the engine. Tighten the bolts evenly and gradually to the torque listed in the Specifications in this Chapter.
19 Refit the camshaft sprocket/timing chain. Tighten the camshaft sprocket bolt to the torque listed in this Chapter's Specifications.
20 Refit the timing chain tensioner assembly with a new gasket (see Section 9).
21 Refit the valve cover. The remainder of refitting is the reverse of removal.

12 Cylinder head - removal and refitting

Caution 1: *Allow the engine to cool completely before beginning this procedure.*
Caution 2: *If the stereo in your vehicle is equipped with an anti-theft system, make sure you have the correct activation code before disconnecting the battery.*

Removal
Refer to illustration 12.15

1   Disconnect the negative cable from the battery.
2   Remove the intercooler and turbocharger on vehicles so equipped, (see Chapter 4).
3   Remove the inlet manifold (see Section 6).
4   Remove the exhaust manifold (see Section 7).
5   Disconnect the wiring, including the alternator wiring harness, and the oil pressure gauge wiring.
6   Remove the radiator upper hose and the other interfering coolant hoses. Disconnect the power steering line from the cylinder head bracket.
7   Remove the injection tube assembly (see Chapter 4).
8   Remove the interfering fuel hoses.
9   Remove the dipstick tube assembly.
10 Disconnect the vacuum/boost tubes and their brackets.
11 Drain the engine coolant (see Chapter 1).
12 Remove the valve cover (see Section 4).
13 Remove the timing chain tensioner and the camshaft sprocket (see Section 11).
Caution: *Do not rotate the crankshaft after this point. Hold the camshaft by the hex section when removing the sprocket bolt. The bolt has a left hand thread. Support the sprocket and chain with a fabricated holding device so they do not fall into the timing cover or off of the lower sprocket. If this happens, it will be necessary to reinstall the timing chain (see Section 9).*
14 Disconnect the glow plug harness wiring, the coolant temperature sensor and the earth cable.
15 Loosen the cylinder head bolts in 1/4-turn increments, following the reverse of the recommended tightening sequence, until they can be removed by hand **(see illustration)**.
16 Lift the cylinder head off the engine. If resistance is felt, don't prise between the cylinder head and engine block gasket mating surfaces - damage to the mating surfaces will result. Instead, prise against the casting protrusions on the sides of the cylinder head.
Caution: *Support the timing chain/sprocket so they do not fall and so the chain does not lose its mating with the lower sprocket.*
17 Set the cylinder head on wood blocks to prevent damage to the gasket sealing surfaces.
Caution: *Be careful not to disturb the timing belt and sprocket when lifting the cylinder head off. After the cylinder head is removed, secure the timing belt and sprocket to the engine, keeping tension on the belt. If the timing chain is disturbed it will become necessary to remove the front cover to restore timing. Do not rotate the crankshaft with the sprocket and chain removed from the camshaft.*
18 Check the cylinder head for warpage.

Refitting
Refer to illustrations 12.20, 12.21 and 12.26

19 A head gasket of the correct compressed

11.8 The camshaft bearing caps are numbered (arrow) and have an arrow pointing towards the front of the engine

Chapter 2 Part B 2.8L diesel engine

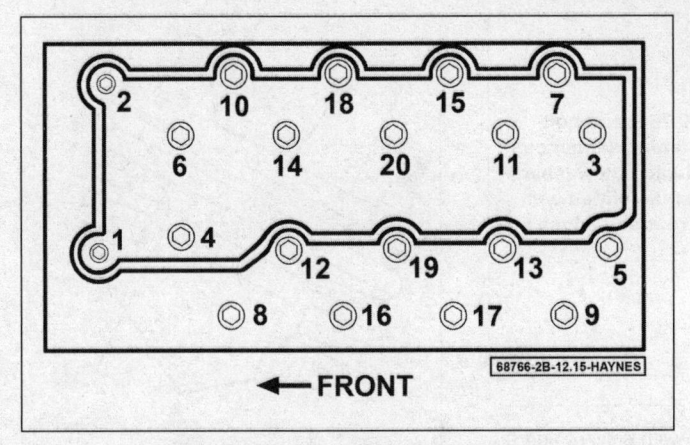

12.15 Head bolt loosening sequence

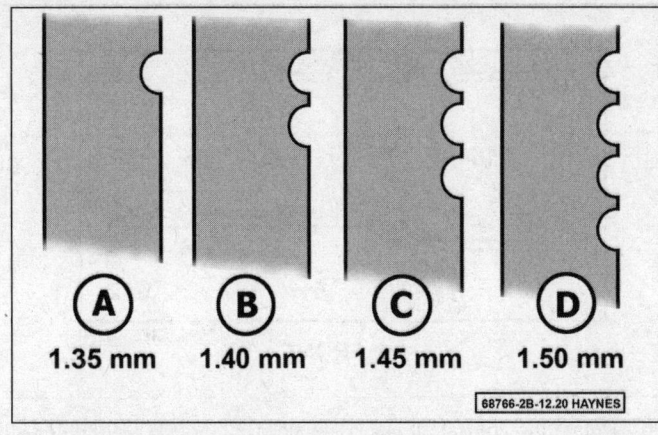

12.20 The thickness of each head gasket is identified by the number of notches at the rear

thickness must be chosen prior to installing the cylinder head. If no changes have been made which would change the distance that the pistons protrude above the block deck surface, then refit a new gasket of the same grade as the one removed. (These changes include a new connecting rod or piston). The classification mark is stamped on the top rear of the block deck.

Note: *If there is no mark stamped on the block, use a 'C' gasket.*

20 The various head gasket thicknesses are identified by the number of notches **(see illustration)**.

21 If a new piston or connecting rod has been refitted, have a very competent machine shop measure the piston protrusions and calculate the average. The chart can then be used to select the new gasket **(see illustration)**.

Note: *If one piston protrudes 0.03 mm or more than the average, use the next size thicker gasket.*

22 The mating surfaces of the cylinder head and engine block must be perfectly clean when the cylinder head is refitted.

23 Use a gasket scraper to remove all traces of carbon and old gasket material, then clean the mating surfaces with lacquer thinner or acetone. If there's oil on the mating surfaces when the cylinder head is refitted, the gasket may not seal correctly and leaks may develop. When working on the engine block, stuff the cylinders with clean shop rags to keep out debris. Use a vacuum cleaner to remove material that falls into the cylinders. Since the cylinder head is made of aluminium, aggressive scraping can cause damage. Be extra careful not to nick or gouge the mating surfaces with the scraper. Gasket removal solvents are available from most auto parts stores and may prove helpful.

24 Use a tap of the correct size to chase the threads in the cylinder head bolt holes. Clean and dry each bolt hole, if any fluid remains in a bolt hole, damage to the engine block may result when the bolts are tightened. Mount each cylinder head bolt in a vice and run a die down the threads to remove corrosion and restore the threads. Dirt, corrosion, sealant and damaged threads will affect torque readings.

25 Apply a dab of RTV sealant at each front cover-to-engine block joint and place a new gasket on the engine block. The gasket must have the correct marking. Check to see if there are any markings (such as 'TOP') on the gasket that say how it is to be refitted. Set the cylinder head in position.

26 Lightly oil the cylinder head bolt threads and refit the bolts. Tighten the cylinder head bolts in several increments, following the recommended sequence, to the torque listed in this Chapter's Specifications **(see illustration)**.

27 Refit the timing chain and camshaft sprocket. Tighten the camshaft sprocket bolt to the torque listed in this Chapter's Specifications.

28 Reinstall the remaining parts in the reverse order of removal.

29 Be sure to refill the cooling system and check all fluid levels.

Piston Protrusion		Cylinder head gasket	
Average piston protrusion	Crankcase identification Mark	Classification	Thickness when tightened
0.475 ± 0.028 mm (0.0187 ± 0.011 in.)	A	A (1 notch)	1.35 ± 0.03 mm (0.0531 ± 0.0012 in.)
0.532 ± 0.028 mm (0.0209 ± 0.011 in.)	B	B (2 notches)	1.40 ± 0.03 mm (0.0551 ± 0.0012 in.)
0.589 ± 0.028 mm (0.0232 ± 0.011 in.)	C	C (3 notches)	1.45 ± 0.03 mm (0.0571 ± 0.0012 in.)
0.646 ± 0.03 mm (0.0254 ± 0.011 in.)	D	D (4 notches)	1.50 ± 0.03 mm (0.0591 ± 0.0012 in.)

12.21 Head gasket selection chart for various average piston protrusions

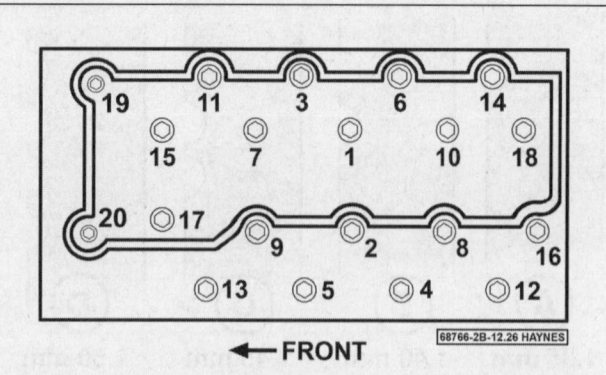

12.26 Head bolt tightening sequence. The head bolt washers must be refitted with their rounded edges up

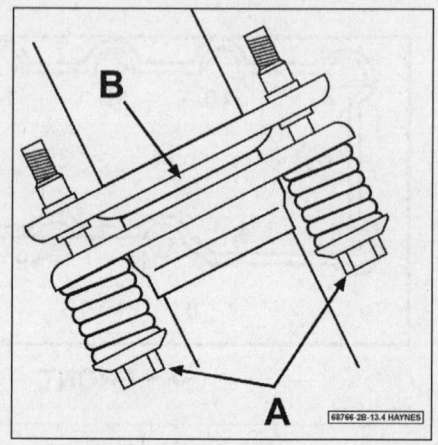

13.4 Remove the two springs and bolts (A) and allow the front pipe to drop down, make sure that the sealing ring (B) does not fall out when the pipe is removed

30 Rotate the crankshaft clockwise slowly by hand through two complete revolutions.
Caution: *If you feel any resistance while turning the engine over, stop and recheck the camshaft timing. The valves may be hitting the pistons.*
31 Start the engine and check the idle speed (see Chapter 1).
32 Run the engine until normal operating temperature is reached. Check for leaks and proper operation.

13 Sump - removal and refitting

Note: *The following procedure is based on the assumption that the engine is in the vehicle.*

Removal

Refer to illustration 13.4
1 Detach the cable from the negative battery terminal.
2 Raise the vehicle and support it securely on jackstands. Remove the skid plate and lower cover (see Chapter 10). Remove both drive axles, unbolt the front differential assembly from the crossmember assembly and lower the front differential (see Chapter 8).
3 Drain the oil and renew the oil filter (see Chapter 1).
4 Disconnect the exhaust pipe **(see illustration)** from the exhaust manifold or turbocharger, lower and support the exhaust pipe.
5 Remove the bolts securing the oil sump to the engine block. Tap on the sump with a soft-face hammer to break the gasket seal, then detach the oil sump from the engine. Don't prise between the engine block and oil sump mating surfaces.
Note: *If the sump is stuck to the crankcase, drive a short, stout knife blade between the two and then hammer it along the sump to break the seal.*
6 Using a gasket scraper, remove all traces of old gasket and/or sealant from the engine block and oil sump. Clean the mating surfaces with lacquer thinner or acetone. Make sure the threaded bolt holes in the engine block are clean.
7 Clean the oil sump with solvent and dry it thoroughly. Check the gasket flanges for distortion, particularly around the bolt holes. If necessary, place the sump on a wood block and use a hammer to flatten and restore the gasket surfaces.

Refitting
8 Apply a 4 mm bead of RTV silicone sealant around the perimeter of the sump in the groove. Be certain to lay the sealant inboard of the bolt holes.
9 Carefully place the oil sump in position within 15 minutes of applying the silicone.
10 Refit the bolts and tighten them in 1/4-turn increments to the torque listed in this Chapter's Specifications. Start with the bolts closest to the centre of the sump and work out in a spiral pattern. Don't overtighten them or leakage may occur.
11 The remainder of refitting is the reverse of removal. Add oil, run the engine and check for oil leaks.

14 Oil pump - removal, inspection and refitting

Removal
1 Disconnect the cable from the negative battery terminal.
2 Refer to Section 9 for the entire oil pump assembly removal procedure. The oil pump is removed as part of the right balance shaft/oil pump assembly.
3 To remove the balance shaft and dismantle the oil pump, place the assembly on a clean work bench. Remove the bolt from the smaller balance shaft drive gear and then remove the balance shaft.
4 Remove the screws from the rear of the oil pump housing. Remove the cover.
5 Remove the relief plug. Extract the small spring and the relief ball.

Inspection
6 Use a marker to mark the mating gear teeth before removing the driven gear. Use a feeler gauge to check the clearance between the tips of the gear teeth and the case.
7 Lay a straightedge across the pump case and use a feeler gauge to check the clearance between the gears and the cover. Compare your readings with those listed in the Specifications in this Chapter. Renew the oil pump if required.
8 Inspect the relief spring, bore and ball for signs of wear and damage. Renew any defective parts.
9 Lubricate the gears and bearing surfaces with clean engine oil. Refit the gears into the body with the mating marks aligned. Lubricate the oil pressure relief valve and refit the relief valve and spring assembly. Tighten the relief valve cap to the torque listed in this Chapter's Specifications. Refit the cover onto the pump body and tighten the screws securely.

Refitting
10 Pack the inner oil pump with petroleum jelly to assist in priming. Refit the oil pump cover after making certain that the alignment marks on the two gears are aligned. Tighten all fasteners to the torque listed in the Specifications in this Chapter.
11 The remainder of refitting is the reverse of removal.

15 Flywheel/driveplate - removal and refitting

Refer to Chapter 2A.

16 Rear main oil seal - renewal

Refer to Chapter 2A.

17 Engine mounts - check and renewal

Refer to Chapter 2A.

Chapter 2 Part C 3.2L diesel engine

Contents

	Section
Camshafts - removal, inspection and refitting	11
Compression check	See Chapter 2D
Crankshaft front oil seal - renewal	10
Cylinder head - removal and refitting	12
Drivebelt check, adjustment and renewal	See Chapter 1
Engine mounts - check and renewal	17
Engine oil and filter change	See Chapter 1
Engine overhaul - general information	See Chapter 2D
Engine - removal and refitting	See Chapter 2D
Exhaust manifold - removal and refitting	7
Flywheel/driveplate - removal and refitting	15
General information	1
Inlet manifold - removal and refitting	6

	Section
Oil pump - removal, inspection and refitting	14
Rear main oil seal - renewal	16
Repair operations possible with the engine in the vehicle	2
Sump - removal and refitting	13
Timing chain, sprockets and gears - removal, inspection and refitting	9
Timing gear cover - removal and refitting	8
Top Dead Centre (TDC) for number one piston - locating	3
Valve clearance - check and adjustment	See Chapter 1
Valve cover - removal and refitting	4
Valves - servicing	See Chapter 2D
Valve springs, retainers and seals - renewal	5

Specifications

General

Engine type	4M41	
Firing order	1 - 3 - 4 - 2	
Cylinder numbers (drivebelt end to transmission end)	1 - 2 - 3 - 4	
Bore and stroke	98.5 x 105 mm	
Displacement	3,200 cc	
Compression pressure	**Except NW**	**NW**
Standard	2,400 to 2,500 kPa	2,500 kPa
Minimum	2,200 kPa	1,750 kPa
Maximum variation	300 kPa	300 kPa
Oil pressure	Above 29 kPa @ idle; 294-686 @ 3500 rpm	

Camshaft [1]

Endplay	
Standard	0.10 to 0.18 mm
Limit	0.30 mm
Bearing journal oil clearance	0.05 to 0.09 mm
Lobe lift	
Intake	
Front	6.16 mm
Rear	6.10 mm
Exhaust	
Front	5.91 mm
Rear	6.16 mm

Cylinder head

Warpage limit	0.2 mm

Oil pump

Gear-to-cover clearance	**Except NW**	**NW**
Standard	0.05 to 0.10 mm	0.02 to 0.06 mm
Limit	0.15 mm	0.10 mm
Gear tip-to-case clearance		
Standard	0.15 to 0.26 mm	
Limit	0.27 mm	
Shaft clearance		
Standard	0.03 to 0.05 mm	
Limit	0.15 mm	

[1] At the time of publication, specification not available for NW models.

Piston

Piston diameter	98.5 mm	
Piston pin to connecting rod bushing clearance	0.03 to 0.05 mm	
Piston ring-to-ring groove clearance	**Standard**	**Limit**
Top ring		
Except NW models	0.110 to 0.160 mm	0.20 mm
NW models	0.069 to 0.0119 mm	0.20 mm
Second ring		
Except NW models	0.065 to 0.105 mm	0.15 mm
NW models	0.030 to 0.070 mm	0.15 mm
Oil control ring	0.025 to 0.065 mm	0.10 mm
Piston ring end gap	**Standard**	**Limit**
Top ring	0.20 to 0.30 mm	0.80 mm
Second ring	0.20 to 0.30 mm	0.80 mm
Oil control ring		
Except NW models	0.30 to 0.50 mm	0.80 mm
NW models	0.25 to 0.45 mm	0.80 mm
Piston protrusion above block deck [1]	-0.20 to -0.30 mm	
Connecting rod big end bearing side clearance	0.15 to 0.45 mm	0.6 mm

Timing gears and balance shafts

	Standard	Limit
Balance shaft-to-bush clearance		
NM and NP models	0.06 to 0.11 mm	0.16 mm
NS and NT models	0.070 to 0.136 mm	Not specified
NW models	0.069 to 0.110 mm	Not specified
Small left idler shaft-to-bush clearance	0.02 to 0.05 mm	0.1 mm
Large left idler shaft-to-bush clearance	0.025 to 0.066 mm	0.1 mm
Right balance shaft gear and oil pump gear backlash	0.04 to 0.19 mm	0.3 mm
Oil pump gear and crankshaft gear backlash		
NM and NP models	0.04 to 0.18 mm	0.3 mm
NS, NT and NW models	0.098 to 0.158 mm	Not specified
Crankshaft gear and idler gear backlash		
NM and NP models	0.04 to 0.18 mm	0.3 mm
NS, NT and NW models	0.082 to 0.142 mm	Not specified
Large left idler gear and small left idler gear backlash	0.04 to 0.19 mm	0.3 mm
Small left idler gear and left balance shaft gear backlash	0.04 to 0.22 mm	0.4 mm
Large idler gear and injection pump gear backlash (Early models)	0.04 to 0.21 mm	0.4 mm
Large idler gear and injection pump idler gear backlash (Late models)	0.096 to 0.156 mm	Not specified
Balance shaft endplay	0.09 to 0.24 mm	0.3 mm
Idler gear and sprocket endplay	0.05 to 0.20 mm	0.3 mm
Left idler gear endplay	0.05 to 0.20 mm	0.3 mm

Torque specifications

	Nm
Balance shaft gear bolts	
NM and NP models	37
NS, NT and NW models	35 (LH); 41 (RH)
Camshaft holder/cap bolts	19 to 21
Camshaft sprocket bolt (left hand thread)	90
Common rail (NS, NT and NW models)	20
Crankshaft pulley bolt	
NM and NP models	323
NS, NT and NW models	50; +90°; loosen; 50; +90°
Cylinder head	
Large bolts	
NM and NP models	
Step 1	100
Step 2	Fully loosen in reverse sequence
Step 3	50
Step 4	Tighten an additional 90-degrees
Step 5	Tighten an additional 90-degrees
NS, NT and NW models	
Step 1	98
Step 2	Fully loosen in reverse sequence
Step 3	49
Step 4	Tighten an additional 90-degrees
Step 5	Tighten an additional 90-degrees
Small bolts	
NM and NP models	57
NS, NT and NW models	58

Chapter 2 Part C 3.2L diesel engine

Torque specifications (continued) — **Nm**

Driveplate-to-crankshaft bolts
    Except NS models 135
    NS models 125
Engine cover screws 3
Engine mount
    Lower bolts
        NM and NP models 44
        NS and NT models 48
        NW models 44
    Upper nut
        NM, NP, NS, NT models .... Not specified
        NW models 60
Exhaust manifold
    Manifold heat shield bolts
        NM and NP models .... 12 to 15
        NS, NT and NW models 14
    Manifold-to-cylinder head nuts 30
    Manifold-to-exhaust pipe bolts
        NM and NP models 49
        NS, NT and NW models 41
Flywheel-to-crankshaft bolts
    NM, NP and NS models 123
    NT and NW models 132
Glow plugs .... 9; +30° to 40°
Injection pump mounting bolts
    NM and NP models .... Not specified
    NS, NT and NW models 24
Injection return pipe union bolt
    NM and NP models 13
    NS and NT models 15
    NW models 20
Injection supply pipe to injector
    NM and NP models 33
    NS, NT and NW models 35
Injector clamp bolt
    NM and NP models 21
    NS and NT models .... 10; +80° to 85°
    NW models .... 12; +90° to 95°
Inlet manifold bolts
    NM and NP models .... Not specified
    NS and NT models 17
    NW models 20
Oil cooler banjo bolts
    NM and NP models 48
    NS and NT models 33
    NW models .... Not specified
Oil cooler hoses-to-block banjo bolts
    NM and NP models 42
    NS and NT models 48
    NW models .... Not specified
Oil cooler plugs 44
Oil cooler mounting nuts/bolts 20
Oil pump cover-to body screws 10
Sump bolts
    NM, NP, NS and NT models 40
    NW models 24
Timing chain tension lever bolt
    NM and NP models 41
    NS, NT and NW models 38
Turbo (NW models)
    To-exhaust manifold nuts 59
    Oil line banjo bolt 17
    Oil line-to-turbo bolts 9
Vacuum pump
    Mounting bolts 24
    Oil line banjo bolts 20
Valve cover bolts 4

[1] At the time of publication, specification not available for NW models

1 General information

Chapter 2C is devoted to in-vehicle repair procedures for the 3.2L model 4M41 four-cylinder diesel engine. All information concerning engine removal and refitting and engine overhaul can be found in Chapter 2D.

The following repair procedures are based on the assumption that the engine is refitted in the vehicle. If the engine has been removed from the vehicle and mounted on a stand, many of the steps outlined in this Part of Chapter 2 will not apply.

The Specifications included in this Part of Chapter 2 apply only to the procedures contained in this Part.

The 3.2 litre engine is an inline vertical four cylinder, 4-valve direct injection, with chain-driven overhead dual camshafts and a balance shaft counterbalancing system which cancels the engine's power pulses and produces relatively vibration-free operation. The crankshaft rides in renewable insert-type main bearings.

The pistons have two compression rings and one oil control ring. The semi-floating piston pins are press fitted into the small end of the connecting rod. The connecting rod big ends are also equipped with renewable insert-type plain bearings.

The engine is liquid-cooled, utilising a centrifugal impeller-type water pump, driven by a belt from the camshaft, to circulate coolant around the cylinders and combustion chambers and through the inlet manifold.

Lubrication is handled by an oil pump mounted on the front of the engine. It is driven by the crankshaft. The oil is filtered continuously by a cartridge-type filter mounted on the side of the engine.

Models to NP use direct injection via a mechanical injection pump. Models from NS use a common rail injection system where fuel is supplied constantly to the injectors under pressure from a mechanical injection pump. Injection is controlled electronically via the engine management system.

2 Repair operations possible with the engine in the vehicle

Many major repair operations can be accomplished without removing the engine from the vehicle.

Clean the engine compartment and the exterior of the engine with some type of degreaser before any work is done. It will make the job easier and help keep dirt out of the internal areas of the engine.

Depending on the components involved, it may be helpful to remove the bonnet to improve access to the engine as repairs are performed (refer to Chapter 11 if necessary). Cover the fenders to prevent damage to the paint. Special pads are available, but an old bedspread or blanket will also work.

If vacuum, exhaust, oil or coolant leaks develop, indicating a need for gasket or seal renewal, the repairs can generally be made with the engine in the vehicle. The inlet and exhaust manifold gaskets, oil sump gasket, crankshaft oil seals and cylinder head gasket are all accessible with the engine in place.

Exterior engine components, such as the inlet and exhaust manifolds, the oil sump, the water pump, the starter motor, the alternator and the fuel system components can be removed for repair with the engine in place.

The cylinder head can be removed with the engine installed as can camshaft and valve component servicing. Renewal of the timing belt and sprockets is also possible with the engine in the vehicle.

In extreme cases caused by a lack of necessary equipment, repair or renewal of piston rings, pistons, connecting rods and rod bearings is possible with the engine in the vehicle. However, this practice is not recommended because of the cleaning and preparation work that must be done to the components involved.

3 Top Dead Centre (TDC) for number one piston - locating

Refer to illustrations 3.7a and 3.7b

1 Top Dead Centre (TDC) is the highest point in the cylinder that each piston reaches as it travels up-and-down when the crankshaft turns. Each piston reaches TDC on the compression stroke and again on the exhaust stroke, but TDC generally refers to piston position on the compression stroke.

2 Positioning the number one piston at TDC is an essential part of many procedures, such as camshaft, timing chain or injection pump removal.

3 Before beginning this procedure, be sure to place the transmission in Park (automatic) or Neutral (manual) and apply the parking brake or block the rear wheels.

4 In order to bring any piston to TDC, the crankshaft must be turned using one of the methods outlined below. When looking at the front of the engine (timing chain end), normal crankshaft rotation is clockwise.

   a) *The preferred method is to turn the crankshaft with a socket and ratchet attached to the bolt threaded into the front of the crankshaft.*
   b) *A remote starter switch, which may save some time, can also be used. Follow the instructions included with the switch. Once the piston is close to TDC, use a socket and ratchet as described in the previous paragraph.*
   c) *If an assistant is available to turn the ignition switch to the Start position in short bursts, you can get the piston close to TDC without a remote starter switch. Make sure your assistant is out of the vehicle, away from the ignition switch, then use a socket and ratchet as described in Paragraph a) to complete the procedure.*

Note: *It may be necessary to remove the glow plugs in order to rotate the engine (refer to Chapter 4).*

5 Remove the valve cover (see Section 4).
6 Rotate the engine until the notch on the crankshaft pulley is aligned with the "0" timing mark.

Caution: *Always turn the crankshaft clockwise.*

7 On early models, check that the protrusion on the camshafts are pointing up **(see illustration)**. On later models, check that the mark on the top of the camshaft front bearing

3.7a The protrusions (arrows) on the camshafts must face upward when the engine is correctly positioned at TDC for number one cylinder on the compression stroke

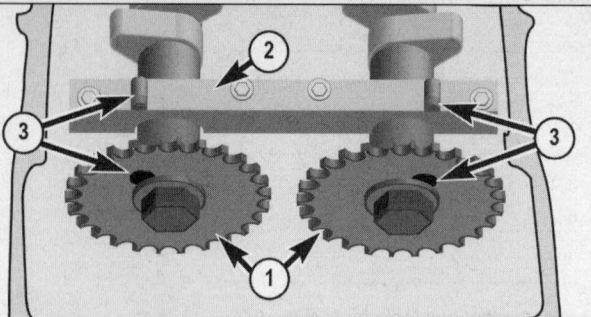

3.7b On later diesel engines, the timing marks are visible on the camshaft front bearing cap (1) and the timing chain sprockets (2) - TDC is set when the marks align as illustrated (3)

Chapter 2 Part C 3.2L diesel engine

cap is in line with the marks on each sprocket **(see illustration)**. If it is, then the engine is at TDC on the compression stroke for number one cylinder. If it is not, then rotate the crankshaft one full turn until the marks are aligned and the protrusion is up.

8 To position the engine at TDC on number four cylinder (required when performing a valve adjustment), rotate the crankshaft one complete revolution, again aligning the notch and the "0" mark.

4 Valve cover - removal and refitting

Caution: *If the stereo in your vehicle is equipped with an anti-theft system, make sure you have the correct activation code before disconnecting the battery.*

Removal

Refer to illustrations 4.4 and 4.6

1 Detach the cable from the negative battery terminal. Refer to Chapter 4 and remove any interfering turbocharger/intercooler components.
2 Disconnect the crankcase breather hose from the valve cover.
3 Disconnect any cables, air intake ducts or hoses which interfere with the valve cover removal.
4 Remove the EGR tube and mounting brackets **(see illustration)**.
5 Wipe off the valve cover thoroughly to prevent debris from falling onto the exposed cylinder head or camshaft/valve train assembly.
6 Remove the valve cover bolts **(see illustration)**.
7 Carefully lift off the valve cover and gasket. If the cover is stuck to the cylinder head, tap it with a rubber mallet to break the seal. Do not prise between the cover and cylinder head or you'll damage the gasket mating surfaces.

Refitting

8 Use a gasket scraper to remove all traces of old material from the gasket mating surfaces of the cylinder head and the valve cover. Clean the surfaces with a rag soaked in lacquer thinner or acetone.
9 Refit new seals on the valve cover bolts.
10 Refit a new gasket onto the valve cover. Refit the moulded rubber gasket onto the cover by pushing the new gasket into the slot that circles the valve cover perimeter. Refit the valve cover and tighten the bolts to the torque listed in this Chapter's Specifications.
Caution: *Do not overtighten the valve cover.*
11 The remainder of refitting is the reverse of removal.

5 Valve springs, retainers and seals - renewal

Note: *Broken valve springs and defective valve stem seals can be renewed without removing the cylinder heads. Two special tools and a compressed air source are normally required to perform this operation, so read through this Section carefully and rent or buy the tools before beginning the job.*

1 Refer to Section 4 and remove the valve cover from the cylinder head.
2 Remove the glow plug from the affected cylinder. Refer to Chapter 4.
3 Turn the crankshaft until the piston in the affected cylinder is at Top Dead Centre on the compression stroke (see Section 3). If you're renewing all of the valve stem seals, begin with cylinder number one and work on the valves for one cylinder at a time. Move from cylinder-to-cylinder following the firing order sequence (see this Chapter's Specifications).
4 Thread an adaptor into the glow plug hole and connect an air hose from a compressed air source to it. Most auto parts stores can supply the air hose adaptor.
Note: *Many cylinder compression gauges utilise a screw-in fitting that may work with your air hose quick-disconnect fitting.*
5 Remove the camshafts (refer to **Section** 11). Remove the rocker arms.
Note: *There are two different length rocker arms used, a long and short arm. Mark each one as they are removed to prevent them from being mixed up.*
6 Apply compressed air to the cylinder.
Warning: *The piston may be forced down by compressed air, causing the crankshaft to turn suddenly. If the spanner used when positioning the number one piston at TDC is still attached to the bolt in the crankshaft nose, it could cause damage or injury when the crankshaft moves.*
7 The valves should be held in place by the air pressure.
8 Stuff shop rags into the cylinder head holes around the valve spring area to prevent parts and tools from falling into the engine, then use a valve spring compressor to compress the spring.
Note: *A special valve spring compressor is required to perform this operation - contact your local Mitsubishi dealer. Remove the collets with small needle-nose pliers or a magnet.*
9 Remove the spring retainer, the valve spring, the lower retainer and then remove the valve guide seal.
Note: *If air pressure fails to hold the valve in the closed position during this operation, the valve face or seat is probably damaged. If so, the cylinder head will have to be removed for additional repair operations.*
10 Wrap a rubber band or tape around the top of the valve stem so the valve won't fall into the combustion chamber, then release the air pressure.
11 Inspect the valve stem for damage. Rotate the valve in the guide and check the end for eccentric movement, which would indicate that the valve is bent.
12 Move the valve up-and-down in the

4.4 Remove the EGR tube mounting brackets and retaining nuts and bolts (arrows)

4.6 Remove the valve cove mounting bolts (arrows) and remove the valve cover

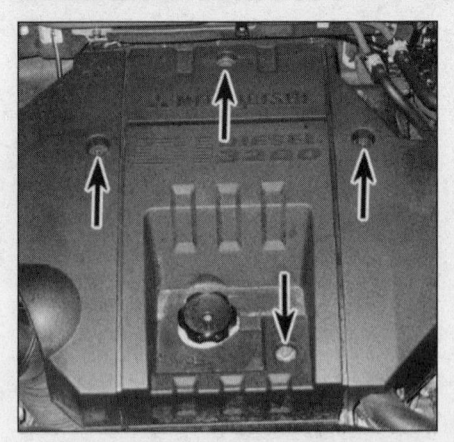

6.1 Remove the engine cover mounting bolts (arrows) and remove the cover

6.5 Disconnect the boost air temperature sensor electrical connector (arrow) and remove the sensor from the intake air fitting

6.7 Remove the fuel line clamps (arrows) and disconnect the fuel lines

guide and make sure it doesn't bind. If the valve stem binds, either the valve is bent or the guide is damaged. In either case, the cylinder head will have to be removed for repair.

13 Reapply air pressure to the cylinder to retain the valve in the closed position, then remove the tape or rubber band from the valve stem.

14 Lubricate the valve stem with engine oil and refit a new guide seal.

15 Refit the spring and retainers in position over the valve.

16 Compress the valve spring and carefully position the collets in the groove. Apply a small dab of grease to the inside of each collet to hold it in place.

17 Remove the force from the spring tool and make sure the collets are seated.

18 Disconnect the air hose and remove the adaptor from the glow plug hole.

19 Refit the glow plugs.

20 Refer to Section 4 and refit the valve cover.

21 Start and run the engine, then check for oil leaks and unusual sounds coming from the valve cover area.

6 Inlet manifold - removal and refitting

Warning: *Diesel fuel is extremely flammable, so take extra precautions when you work on any part of the fuel system. Don't smoke or allow open flames or bare light bulbs near the work area, and don't work in a garage where a gas-type appliance (such as a water heater) is present. If you spill any fuel on your skin, rinse it off immediately with soap and water. When you perform any kind of work on the fuel system, wear safety glasses and have a Class B type fire extinguisher on hand.*

Caution: *If the stereo in your vehicle is equipped with an anti-theft system, make sure you have the correct activation code before disconnecting the battery.*

Removal

Refer to illustrations 6.1, 6.5, 6.7 and 6.12

1 Remove the engine cover fasteners and remove the cover **(see illustration)**. Remove the skid plate and lower engine cover (see Chapter 10).

2 Detach the cable from the negative battery terminal. Remove the battery and battery tray (see Chapter 5).

3 Remove the fuel filter assembly (see Chapter 1).

4 Remove the EGR hoses and tubes (see Section 4).

5 Disconnect the boost air temperature sensor electrical connector and unscrew the sensor from the throttle body **(see illustration)**.

6 Remove the intake air fitting to the throttle body and remove the hose and throttle body.

7 Disconnect and plug the fuel lines **(see illustration)**.

8 Remove the engine oil and where fitted, the transmission fluid dipstick tubes mounting bolts and remove the tubes. Once the dipstick tubes have been removed a new O-ring must be fitted to the tubes.

9 Remove the breather hose-to-valve cover and remove the valve cover and gasket from the cylinder head (see Section 4).

10 Where fitted, remove the intake manifold cover attaching bolts and remove the cover.

11 Using two spanners, loosen and remove the injection pipe nuts-to-injection pump fitting. Remove the injection pipe clamps and brackets.

12 Disconnect the injection pipe from the injector nozzle and remove the pipe and seal **(see illustration)**.

Note: *It may be necessary to disconnect the glow plug plate from the glow plugs for more room.*

13 Where fitted, remove the filter from under the manifold.

14 Remove the spaces and disconnect the manifold attaching bolts and remove the manifold and gasket.

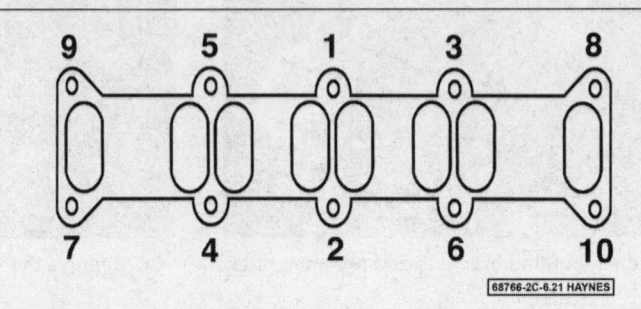

6.12 Remove the injection pipe from the injector nozzle and remove the seal

1 Injector pipe nut-to-injector connection
2 Injector seal
3 Glow plug plate

6.21 Starting at the centre and working out in both directions, tighten the bolts in a criss-cross pattern

Chapter 2 Part C 3.2L diesel engine

7.5 Remove the turbocharger cover mounting bolts (arrows) and remove the cover

7.10 Starting at the centre and working out in both directions, tighten the bolts in a circular pattern

Refitting

Refer to illustration 6.21

15 Clean the inlet manifold and cylinder head surface, removing all traces of gasket material.
16 Check the mating surfaces of the manifold for flatness with a precision straightedge and feeler gauge.
17 Inspect the manifold for cracks and distortion.
18 If the manifold is cracked or warped, renew it or see if it can be re-surfaced/repaired at an automotive machine shop.
19 Check carefully for any stripped or broken inlet manifold bolts. Renew any defective bolts.
20 Place new gasket onto the cylinder head.
21 Refit the inlet manifold and tighten the bolts finger-tight. Starting at the centre and working out in both directions, tighten the bolts in a criss-cross pattern (see illustration) until the torque listed in this Chapter's Specifications is reached.
22 The remainder of the refitting procedure is the reverse of removal.

Note: *Apply engine oil to the new injector nozzle seals and be careful not to damage it when fitting it to the cylinder head.*

7 Exhaust manifold - removal and refitting

Caution: *If the stereo in your vehicle is equipped with an anti-theft system, make sure you have the correct activation code before disconnecting the battery.*

Removal

Refer to illustration 7.5

1 Disconnect the negative battery cable from the battery.
2 Remove the engine cover (see illustration 6.1). Remove the skid plate and lower engine cover (see Chapter 10).
3 Remove the EGR tube (see illustration 4.4).
4 Remove the manifold heat protector.
5 Remove the turbocharger cover (see illustration).
6 Remove the three turbocharger-to-manifold nuts.
7 Remove the exhaust manifold mounting nuts and remove the manifold from the cylinder head.

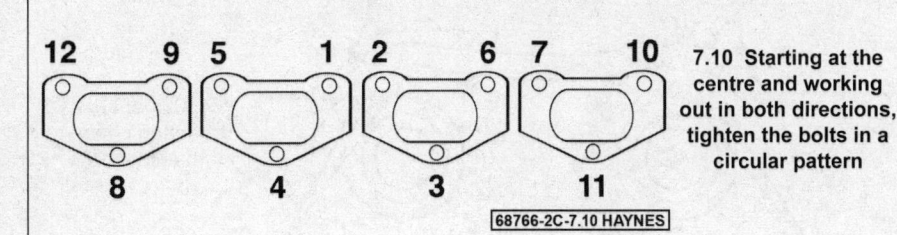

Refitting

Refer to illustration 7.10

8 Inspect the exhaust manifold for cracks, damage or distortion.
9 Discard the old gaskets and use a scraper to clean the gasket mating surfaces on the exhaust manifold, turbocharger (or exhaust pipe) and cylinder head. Place new gaskets onto the cylinder head and turbocharger (or exhaust pipe).
10 Place the exhaust manifold in position on the cylinder head and refit the nuts. Starting at the centre (see illustration), tighten the nuts in a circular pattern until the torque listed in this Chapter's Specifications is reached.
11 The remainder of refitting is the reverse of removal.
12 Start the engine and check for exhaust leaks between the manifold and the cylinder head and between the manifold and the turbocharger (or exhaust pipe).

8 Timing gear cover - removal and refitting

Caution: *If the stereo in your vehicle is equipped with an anti-theft system, make sure you have the correct activation code before disconnecting the battery.*

Removal

1 Disconnect the cable from the negative terminal of the battery. Remove the air cleaner assembly and the intercooler assembly (see Chapter 4).
2 Remove the skid plate and lower cover, then drain the cooling system and engine oil (see Chapter 1).
3 Remove the drivebelts, fan and fan clutch assembly. Remove the vacuum pump, alternator, power steering pump and air conditioning compressor, if equipped, and lay them aside (see Chapter 3).

Warning: *The air conditioning system is under high pressure - do not disconnect the hoses!*

4 Remove the air conditioning mounting bracket and the water pump (see Chapter 3). Any other interfering components must be removed at this time.
5 Remove the crankshaft pulley bolt.

Note: *This bolt is very tight. If a pneumatic impact wrench is not available, it will be necessary to remove the flywheel inspection plate and wedge a screwdriver in the starter ring gear teeth to prevent the crankshaft from turning.*

6 Remove the crankshaft pulley by levering it off. If it is stuck to the crankshaft, use a special puller to remove it. Do not use the type of puller that attaches to the belt groove.
7 Remove the timing gear case cover bolts and remove the case cover.
8 Remove the bolts attaching the timing cover and bearing block assembly to the engine block, oil sump and the two front cylinder head bolts. Note the location of the bolts so they can be returned to the same locations from which they were removed. Tap the cover with a soft-faced hammer to break the gasket seal, then remove the cover from the engine block. **Caution 1:** *Levering between the cover and the engine block can damage the gasket sealing surfaces.* **Caution 2:** *If the cylinder head gasket is damaged during removal of the timing cover the cylinder head gasket must be renewed (see Section 12).*

Refitting

9 Thoroughly clean the front cover and engine block with acetone or lacquer thinner. Make sure the threaded holes in the engine block are clean and dry.
10 Apply a 3 mm bead of RTV sealant completely around the sealing surface of the cover, inboard of the bolt holes. Extend the bead to seal to the oil sump also.
11 Fit the front cover onto the engine. Refit the bolts in a crisscross pattern and tighten them.
12 Apply a thin layer of clean moly-based grease to the seal contact surface of the crankshaft pulley, then slide it onto the crankshaft. Refit the bolt and tighten it to the torque listed in this Chapter's Specifications. It may again be necessary to secure the crankshaft to prevent it from turning.
13 The remainder of refitting is the reverse of removal.

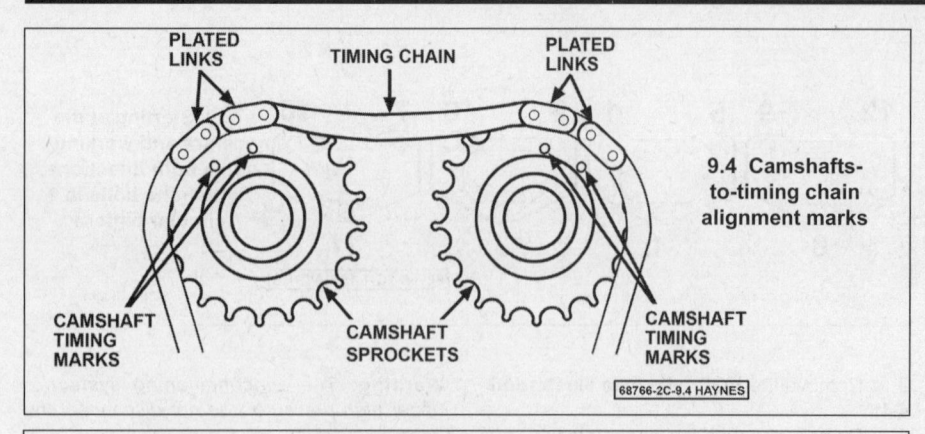

2C-8   Chapter 2 Part C 3.2L diesel engine

9.4 Camshafts-to-timing chain alignment marks

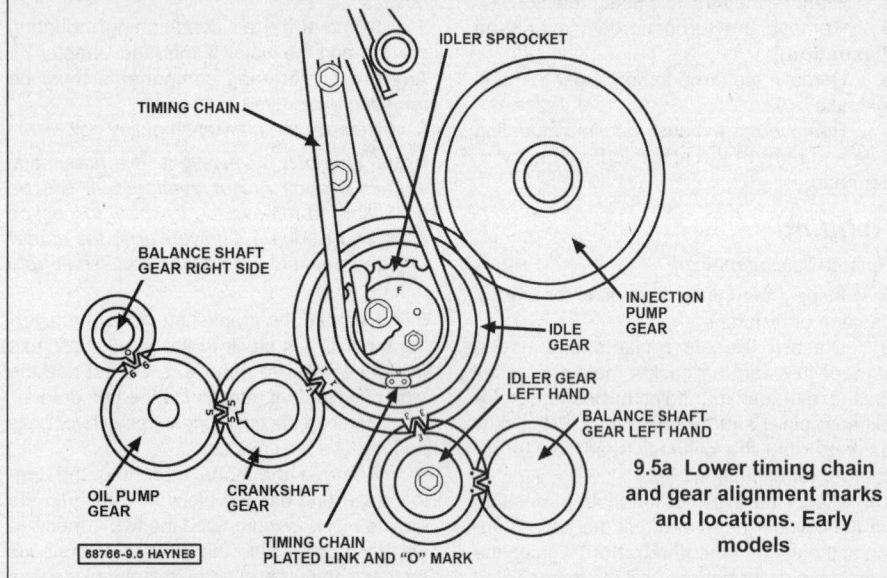

Labels: PLATED LINKS, TIMING CHAIN, PLATED LINKS, CAMSHAFT TIMING MARKS, CAMSHAFT SPROCKETS, CAMSHAFT TIMING MARKS

9.5a Lower timing chain and gear alignment marks and locations. Early models

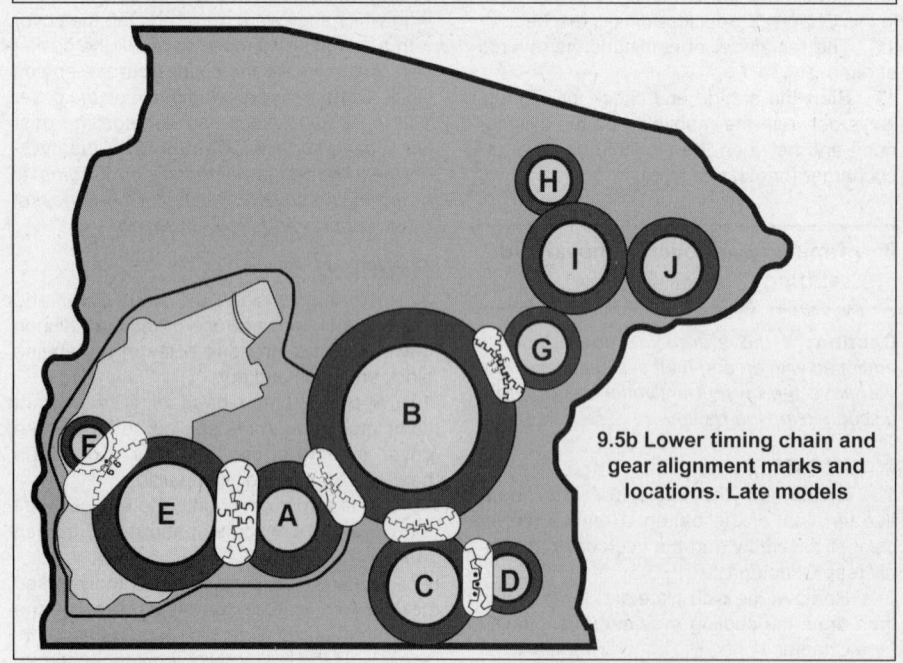

Labels: IDLER SPROCKET, TIMING CHAIN, BALANCE SHAFT GEAR RIGHT SIDE, INJECTION PUMP GEAR, IDLE GEAR, IDLER GEAR LEFT HAND, BALANCE SHAFT GEAR LEFT HAND, OIL PUMP GEAR, CRANKSHAFT GEAR, TIMING CHAIN PLATED LINK AND "O" MARK

9.5b Lower timing chain and gear alignment marks and locations. Late models

A Crankshaft sprocket
B Idler sprocket
C Left idler gear
D LH balance shaft sprocket
E Oil pump sprocket
F RH balance shaft sprocket
G Idler gear B sprocket
H Vacuum pump sprocket
I Injection pump sprocket
J Power steering pump sprocket

9 Timing chain, sprockets and gears - removal, inspection and refitting

Caution: *If the stereo in your vehicle is equipped with an anti-theft system, make sure you have the correct activation code before disconnecting the battery.*

Removal

Refer to illustrations 9.4, 9.5a, 9.5b and 9.6

1 Disconnect the cable from the negative terminal of the battery. Drain the cooling system (see Chapter 1).
2 Position the engine on TDC for number one cylinder (see Section 3). Remove the valve cover (see Section 4).
3 Remove the timing gear cover (see Section 8).
4 Check the alignment marks for the camshaft and timing chain **(see illustration)**.
5 Check the alignment marks for the idler gear and sprocket to the timing chain **(see illustration)**.

Note: *There are five bright white links on the chain, four links are for the camshafts and one link for the idler gear.*

6 Remove the timing chain tensioner assembly from the front of the cylinder head. Remove sprocket from both camshafts.

Caution: *Do not rotate the crankshaft after this point. Hold the camshafts by the hex section* **(see illustration)**. *The camshaft sprocket bolt has a left hand thread.*

Note: *It is not necessary to remove the front cover in order to remove only the camshaft sprockets. Refer to the Section on camshaft removal.*

7 Remove the timing chain.

Note: *Tie the timing chain and camshaft sprockets together to prevent the mating marks from being misaligned.*

9.6 Remove the camshafts sprockets, hold the camshaft by the hex section (arrow), then remove the bolt (the bolt is left hand thread) - the arrow on the bolt head indicates the direction for tightening the bolt

8 Remove the chain tensioner and guide plate assembly. The chain oil jet will be removed as part of this procedure.
9 Remove the oil pump/right balance shaft assembly.
10 Unbolt and remove the main idler gear assembly.
Note: *The "F" mark on the idler washer must face out toward the front of the engine.*
11 The fuel injection pump gear can be removed as part of the pump assembly.
12 Dismantle any assemblies which require further service.

Inspection

13 Check the chain tensioner components where they contact the chain for wear and damage. Also inspect the clearance at the tensioner lever shaft and its shaft. Renew any worn parts. Measure the clearance between the two sides of the timing chain as it is manually stretched. If the clearance is less than specified, renew it.
14 Check the fits of the balance shafts in their bushes. Special tools and expertise are required to renew the balance shaft bushes if they are excessively worn. The engine must be taken to a properly equipped repair shop. If the balance shafts are worn, they should be renewed at this time.
15 The other bushes in the idler gears can be renewed by a competent repair shop equipped with a hydraulic press.

Refitting

16 Make sure the crankshaft is positioned at Top Dead Centre (TDC) for number one piston (see Section 3).
17 Refit the idler gear and sprocket assembly. Align the "1" mark on the crankshaft gear between the two marks on the idler gear **(see illustrations 9.5a and 9.5b)**.
18 If the left balance shaft assembly has been dismantled, make certain the "O" mark on the gear is facing the front. Refit the left balance shaft assembly with the left idler gear and align the marks on the left idler gear and left balance shaft.
Caution: *Several of these components use washers under the bolt heads which have an outer rounded edge. Make certain that this rounded edge faces toward the bolt head upon refitting.*
19 Refit the idler gear assembly. Align the "3" and "1" marks on it with those on the two mating gears. Refit the bolt - make certain that the bolt's washer has the "F" facing the front.
20 Refit the right balance shaft/oil pump assembly. Make certain that the "O" mark on the balance shaft gear is mated with the "6" mark on the oil pump gear. Align the "5" mark on the oil pump gear with the "5" mark on the crankshaft gear.
21 Make certain that the "1" marks on the crankshaft gear and idler gear are still aligned. Place the timing chain over the lower drive sprocket, aligning the single bright white link with the "O" mark **(see illustration 9.5a)**.

Note: *On late models, the timing chain marks are in the same position as the early models. Therefore, it is safe to refer to the early model illustration 9.5a.*
22 Put the other end of the timing chain around the camshaft sprockets, aligning the four bright white links with the four marks **(see illustration 9.4)**.
23 Refit the upper sprockets to the camshaft. Refit both tensioner assemblies.
24 Check the alignment of the fuel injection pump gear (see Chapter 4).
25 Rotate the crankshaft by hand through two complete revolutions. Again check the alignment of all marks.
Note: *The idler gear marks will not align with the balance shafts, oil pump or crankshaft. Check that the balance shafts, crankshaft, camshafts and oil pump sprockets return to their original position. Check for proper tension of the timing chain along the opposite side to the tensioner.*
26 Before installing the chain tensioner assembly into the cylinder head, turn the tensioner cam to force the plunger back into the tensioner body. Lock it in position with the hook.
27 Refit the tensioner with a new gasket. Release the hook to allow the tensioner to contact the chain tensioner.
28 The remainder of refitting is the reverse of removal.

10 Crankshaft front oil seal - renewal

1 Remove the drivebelts (see Chapter 1).
2 Raise the vehicle and support it securely on jackstands.
3 Remove the crankshaft pulley (see Section 8).
4 Carefully prise the seal out of the front cover with a seal removal tool or a screwdriver. If using a screwdriver, wrap the tip with electrical tape. Don't scratch the seal bore or damage the crankshaft in the process (if the crankshaft is damaged, the new seal will end up leaking).
5 Clean the bore in the timing chain cover and coat the outer edge of the new seal with engine oil or multi-purpose grease. Using a socket with an outside diameter slightly smaller than the outside diameter of the seal, carefully drive the seal into place with a hammer. If a socket is not available, a short section of a large diameter pipe will work. Check the seal after refitting to be sure the spring did not pop out.
6 Refitting is the reverse of removal.
7 Run the engine and check for leaks.

11 Camshafts - removal, inspection and refitting

Refer to illustrations 11.7 and 11.8

Caution: *If the stereo in your vehicle is equipped with an anti-theft system, make sure you have the correct activation code before disconnecting the battery.*

Removal

1 Disconnect the cable from the negative battery terminal.
2 Remove the valve cover (see Section 4).
3 Position the number one piston at Top Dead Centre (see Section 3).
4 Check the camshafts for proper mark alignment **(see illustration 9.4)**. Use an electrician's plastic wire tie or a length of wire to tightly secure the timing chain to the camshaft sprockets.
5 Remove the camshaft sprocket bolts (see Section 9).
Caution: *Do not rotate the camshafts after this point. Hold the camshaft by the hex section. The bolt has a left hand thread. Support the sprockets and chain with a fabricated holding device so they do not fall into the timing cover or off of the lower sprocket. If this happens, it will be necessary to reinstall the timing chain (see Section 9).*
6 Before removing the camshaft sprockets, remove the timing chain tensioner from the cylinder head (see Section 9).
7 Remove the fuel leak-off bolts and gasket and remove the pipe **(see illustration)**.
8 Now remove the camshaft sprockets from both camshafts. Loosen the camshaft bearing cap bolts gradually and evenly a quarter turn at a time and remove the five camshaft bearing caps **(see illustration)**.

11.7 Fuel leak-off details

1 Fuel leak-off pipe retaining bolt
2 Fuel leak-off pipe gasket
3 Fuel leak-off pipe

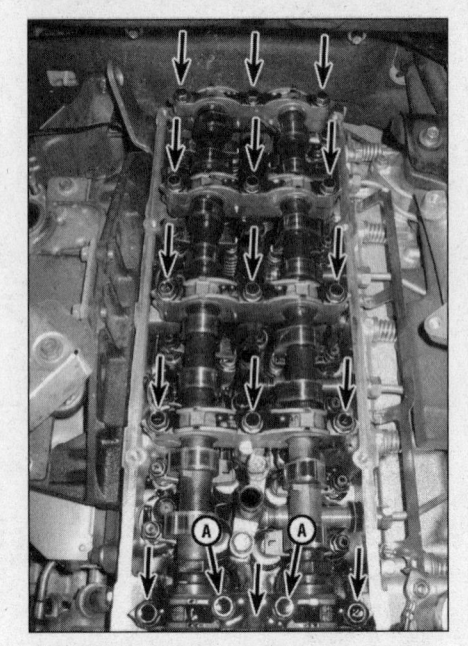

11.8 Remove the upper chain guide plate bolts (A) and remove the guide, then remove the camshaft cap/holder bolts (arrows) and remove the camshafts

9 Lift the intake and exhaust camshafts off the cylinder head and remove the camshaft holders.

Note: *The camshaft caps (upper half) and camshaft holders (lower half) hold the camshafts to the cylinder head. They are stamped on the side and must be refitted in the same location and can't be interchanged with each other.*

Inspection

10 To check camshaft runout:
a) *Support the camshaft with a pair of V-blocks and attach a dial indicator with the stem resting against the centre bearing journal on the camshaft.*
b) *Rotate the camshaft and note the indicated runout.*
c) *If the indicated runout is excessive, renew the camshaft.*

11 Check the camshaft bearing journals and bearing caps for scoring and signs of wear.
12 Check the cam lobes for wear:
a) *Check the toe and ramp areas of each cam for score marks and uneven wear. Also check for flaking and pitting.*
b) *If there is wear on the toe or the ramp, renew the camshaft, but first try to find the cause of the wear. Look for abrasive substances in the oil and inspect the oil pump and oil passages for blockage. Cam wear is usually caused by inadequate lubrication or dirty oil.*
c) *Using a micrometer, calculate the lobe wear. If the lobe wear is greater than listed in this Chapter's Specifications, renew the camshaft.*

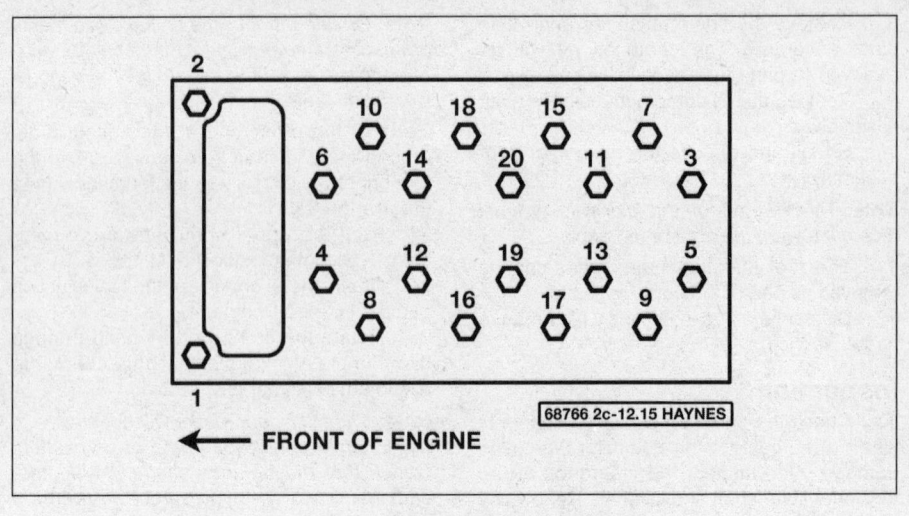

13 Inspect the rocker arms for wear, galling and pitting of the contact surfaces.
14 If any of the conditions described above are noted, the cylinder head is probably lacking sufficient lubrication, make sure you track down the cause of this problem (low oil level, low oil pump capacity, clogged oil passage, etc.) before installing a new cylinder head or camshaft.

Refitting

15 Thoroughly clean the camshafts, the bearing surfaces in the cylinder head, camshaft caps and holders, and the rocker arms. Remove all sludge and dirt. Wipe off all components with a clean, lint-free cloth.
16 Refit the camshaft holders to the cylinder head. The holders and caps are numbered on the sides and should be installed from the front of the cylinder head with holder stamped #1, to the back ending with holder stamped #5.
17 Lubricate the camshaft holder bearing surfaces in the cylinder head and the bearing journals and lobes on the camshaft with assembly lube or moly-base grease. Carefully lower the camshafts into position with the dowel pin pointing up.

Caution: *Failure to adequately lubricate the camshafts and related components can cause serious damage to bearing and friction surfaces during the first few seconds after engine start-up, when the oil pressure is low or nonexistent.*

18 Apply a thin coat of assembly lube or moly-base grease to the bearing surfaces of the camshaft bearing caps.
19 Refit the camshaft bearing caps. They are numbered with number one being closest to the front of the engine. Tighten the bolts evenly and gradually to the torque listed in the Specifications in this Chapter.
20 Refit the camshaft sprockets/timing chain. Tighten the camshaft sprocket bolts to the torque listed in this Chapter's Specifications.
21 Refit the timing chain tensioner assembly with a new gasket (see Section 9).
22 Refit the valve cover. The remainder of refitting is the reverse of removal.

12 Cylinder head - removal and refitting

Caution 1: *Allow the engine to cool completely before beginning this procedure.*
Caution 2: *If the stereo in your vehicle is equipped with an anti-theft system, make sure you have the correct activation code before disconnecting the battery.*

Removal

Refer to illustration 12.15

1 Disconnect the negative cable from the battery.
2 Remove the turbocharger (see Chapter 4).
3 Remove the inlet manifold (see **Section** 6).
4 Remove the exhaust manifold (see Section 7).
5 Disconnect the wiring, including the alternator wiring harness, and the oil pressure gauge wiring.
6 Remove the radiator upper hose and the other interfering coolant hoses. Disconnect the power steering line from the cylinder head bracket.
7 Remove the injection tube assembly (see Chapter 4).
8 Remove the interfering fuel hoses.
9 Remove the engine oil and transmission fluid dipstick tube assemblies.
10 Disconnect the vacuum/boost tubes and their brackets.
11 Drain the engine coolant (see Chapter 1).
12 Remove the valve cover (see Section 4).

12.15 Head bolt loosening sequence

	Notch specification chart
A	Thickness after installation of the head bolts - 0.70 mm
B	Thickness after installation of the head bolts - 0.75 mm
C	Thickness after installation of the head bolts - 0.80 mm
D	Thickness after installation of the head bolts - 0.85 mm

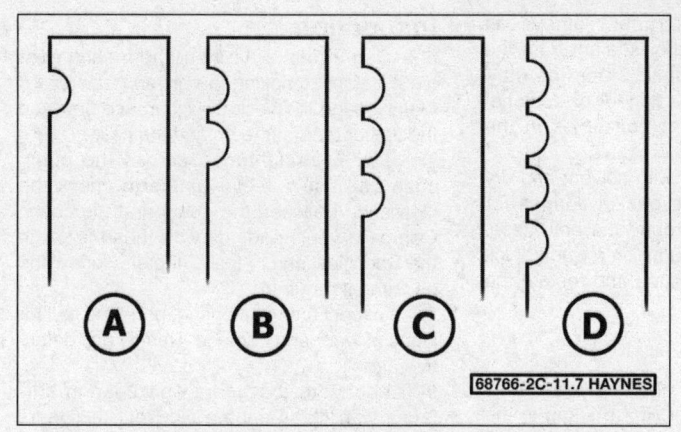

12.20 The thickness of each head gasket is identified by the number of notches at the front

12.21 Head gasket selection chart for various average piston protrusions

13 Remove the timing chain tensioner and the camshaft sprocket (see Section 9).

Caution: *Do not rotate the crankshaft after this point. Hold the camshafts by the hex section when removing the sprocket bolt. The bolt has a left hand thread. Support the sprockets and chain with a fabricated holding device so they do not fall into the timing cover or off of the lower sprocket. If this happens, it will be necessary to reinstall the timing chain (see Section 9).*

14 Disconnect the glow plug harness wiring, the coolant temperature sensor and the earth cable.

15 Loosen the cylinder head bolts in 1/4-turn increments, following the removal sequence, until they can be removed by hand (**see illustration**).

16 Lift the cylinder head off the engine. If resistance is felt, don't prise between the cylinder head and engine block gasket mating surfaces - damage to the mating surfaces will result. Instead, prise against the casting protrusions on the sides of the cylinder head.

Caution: *Support the timing chain/sprocket so they do not fall and so the chain does not lose its mating with the lower sprocket.*

17 Set the cylinder head on wood blocks to prevent damage to the gasket sealing surfaces.

Caution: *Be careful not to disturb the timing belt and sprocket when lifting the cylinder head off. After the cylinder head is removed, secure the timing belt and sprocket to the engine, keeping tension on the belt. If the timing chain is disturbed it will become necessary to remove the front cover to restore timing. Do not rotate the crankshaft with the sprocket and chain removed from the camshaft.*

18 Check the cylinder head for warpage.

Refitting

Refer to illustrations 12.20, 12.21 and 12.26

19 A head gasket of the correct compressed thickness must be chosen prior to installing the cylinder head. If no changes have been made which would change the distance that the pistons protrude above the block deck surface, then refit a new gasket of the same grade as the one removed. (These changes include a new connecting rod or piston). The classification mark is stamped on the top rear of the block deck.

Note: *If there is no mark stamped on the block, use a "C" gasket.*

20 The various head gasket thicknesses are identified by the number of notches (**see illustration**).

21 If a new piston or connecting rod have been refitted, have a very competent machine shop measure the piston protrusions and calculate the average. The chart can then be used to select the new gasket (**see illustration**).

Note: *If one piston protrudes 0.03 mm or more than the average, use the next size thicker gasket.*

22 The mating surfaces of the cylinder head and engine block must be perfectly clean when the cylinder head is refitted.

23 Use a gasket scraper to remove all traces of carbon and old gasket material, then clean the mating surfaces with lacquer thinner or acetone. If there's oil on the mating surfaces when the cylinder head is refitted, the gasket may not seal correctly and leaks may develop. When working on the engine block, stuff the cylinders with clean shop rags to keep out debris. Use a vacuum cleaner to remove material that falls into the cylinders. Since the cylinder head is made of aluminium, aggressive scraping can cause damage. Be extra careful not to nick or gouge the mating surfaces with the scraper. Gasket removal solvents are available from most auto parts stores and may prove helpful.

24 Use a tap of the correct size to chase the threads in the cylinder head bolt holes. Clean and dry each bolt hole; if any fluid remains in a bolt hole, damage to the engine block may result when the bolts are tightened. Mount each cylinder head bolt in a vice and run a die down the threads to remove corrosion and restore the threads. Dirt, corrosion, sealant and damaged threads will affect torque readings.

25 Apply a dab of RTV sealant at each front cover-to-engine block joint and place a new gasket on the engine block. The gasket must have the correct marking. Check to see if there are any markings (such as "TOP") on the gasket that say how it is to be refitted. Set the cylinder head in position.

26 Lightly oil the cylinder head bolt threads and refit the bolts. Tighten the cylinder head bolts in several increments, following the recommended sequence, to the torque listed in this Chapter's Specifications (**see illustration**).

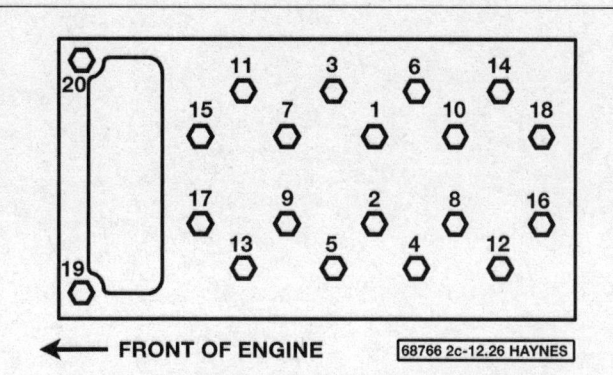

12.26 Head bolt tightening sequence. The head bolt washers must be refitted with their rounded edges up

27 Refit the timing chain and camshaft sprocket. Tighten the camshaft sprocket bolt to the torque listed in this Chapter's Specifications.
28 Reinstall the remaining parts in the reverse order of removal.
29 Be sure to refill the cooling system and check all fluid levels.
30 Rotate the crankshaft clockwise slowly by hand through two complete revolutions.
Caution: *If you feel any resistance while turning the engine over, stop and recheck the camshaft timing. The valves may be hitting the pistons.*
31 Start the engine and check the idle speed (see Chapter 1).
32 Run the engine until normal operating temperature is reached. Check for leaks and proper operation.

13 Sump - removal and refitting

Note: *The following procedure is based on the assumption that the engine is in the vehicle.*

Removal

1 Detach the cable from the negative battery terminal.
2 Raise the vehicle and support it securely on jackstands. Remove the skid plate and lower cover (see Chapter 10). Remove both drive axles, unbolt the front differential assembly from the crossmember assembly and lower the front differential (see Chapter 8).
3 Drain the oil and renew the oil filter (see Chapter 1). Remove the skid plate.
4 Disconnect the exhaust pipe from the exhaust manifold or turbocharger, lower and support the exhaust pipe.
5 Remove the bolts securing the oil sump to the engine block. Tap on the sump with a soft-face hammer to break the gasket seal, then detach the oil sump from the engine. Don't prise between the engine block and oil sump mating surfaces.
Note: *If the sump is stuck to the crankcase, drive a short, stout knife blade between the two and then hammer it along the sump to break the seal.*

6 Using a gasket scraper, remove all traces of old gasket and/or sealant from the engine block and oil sump. Clean the mating surfaces with lacquer thinner or acetone. Make sure the threaded bolt holes in the engine block are clean.
7 Clean the oil sump with solvent and dry it thoroughly. Check the gasket flanges for distortion, particularly around the bolt holes. If necessary, place the sump on a wood block and use a hammer to flatten and restore the gasket surfaces.

Refitting

8 Apply a 4 mm bead of RTV silicone sealant around the perimeter of the sump in the groove. Be certain to lay the sealant inboard of the bolt holes.
9 Carefully place the oil sump in position within 15 minutes of applying the silicone.
10 Refit the bolts and tighten them in 1/4-turn increments to the torque listed in this Chapter's Specifications. Start with the bolts closest to the centre of the sump and work out in a spiral pattern. Don't overtighten them or leakage may occur.
11 The remainder of refitting is the reverse of removal. Add oil, run the engine and check for oil leaks.

14 Oil pump - removal, inspection and refitting

Removal

1 Disconnect the cable from the negative battery terminal.
2 Refer to Section 9 for the entire oil pump assembly removal procedure. The oil pump is removed as part of the right balance shaft/oil pump assembly.
3 To remove the balance shaft and dismantle the oil pump, place the assembly on a clean work bench. Remove the bolt from the smaller balance shaft drive gear and then remove the balance shaft.
4 Remove the screws from the rear of the oil pump housing. Remove the cover.
5 Remove the relief plug. Extract the small spring and the relief ball.

Inspection

6 Use a marker to mark the mating gear teeth before removing the driven gear. Use a feeler gauge to check the clearance between the tips of the gear teeth and the case.
7 Lay a straightedge across the pump case and use a feeler gauge to check the clearance between the gears and the cover. Compare your readings with those listed in the Specifications in this Chapter. Renew the oil pump if required.
8 Inspect the relief spring, bore and ball for signs of wear and damage. Renew any defective parts.
9 Lubricate the gears and bearing surfaces with clean engine oil. Refit the gears into the body with the mating marks aligned. Lubricate the oil pressure relief valve and refit the relief valve and spring assembly. Tighten the relief valve cap securely.

Refitting

10 Pack the inner oil pump with petroleum jelly to assist in priming. Refit the oil pump cover after making certain that the alignment marks on the two gears are aligned. Tighten the cover screws to the torque listed in the Specifications in this Chapter.
11 The remainder of refitting is the reverse of removal.

15 Flywheel/driveplate - removal and refitting

Refer to Chapter 2A.

16 Rear main oil seal - renewal

Refer to Chapter 2A.

17 Engine mounts - check and renewal

Refer to Chapter 2A.

Chapter 2 Part D
General engine overhaul procedures

Contents

	Section
CHECK ENGINE light	See Chapter 6
Cylinder compression check	3
Engine - removal and refitting	7
Engine rebuilding alternatives	5
Engine removal - methods and precautions	6
General information - engine overhaul	1
Initial start-up and break-in after overhaul	8
Oil pressure check	2
Vacuum gauge diagnostic checks (petrol engines)	4

Specifications

General

Displacement
    6G72 petrol V6 engine .... 2,972 ml (3.0 litre)
    6G74 petrol V6 engine .... 3,497 ml (3.5 litre)
    6G75 petrol V6 engine .... 3,828 ml (3.8 litre)
    4M40 diesel engine .... 2,835 ml (2.8 litre)
    4M41 diesel engine .... 3,200 ml (3.2 litre)

Bore and Stroke
    6G72 petrol V6 engine .... 91.1 x 76.0 mm
    6G74 petrol V6 engine .... 93.0 x 85.8 mm
    6G75 petrol V6 engine .... 95.0 x 90.0 mm
    4M40 diesel engine .... 95.0 x 100 mm
    4M41 diesel engine .... 98.5 x 105 mm

Cylinder compression pressure .... Refer to Chapters 2A, 2B or 2C

Oil pressure
    Petrol engines (other models not specified)
        NS models .... Above 80 kPa @ idle
        NT and NW models .... Above 29 kPa @ idle 294-686 @ 3500 rpm
    Diesel engines .... Above 29 kPa @ idle; 294-686 @ 3500 rpm

Crankshaft endplay

	Standard	Limit
Petrol	0.05 to 0.25 mm	0.3 mm
Diesel	0.10 to 0.28 mm	0.4 mm

Torque specifications

Nm

Connecting rod bearing cap nuts
  Petrol engines
    3.5L and NP 3.8L engines
      Step 1 26
      Step 2 52
    NS and NT 3.8L engines
      Step 1 27
      Step 2 .... Tighten an additional 90-degree turn
  Diesel engine
    Step 1 50
    Step 2 .... Tighten an additional 90-degree turn
Main bearing cap bolts
  Petrol engines **(see illustration)**
    3.5L and NP 3.8L engines
      Bolt head marked 8 80
      Bolt head marked 10 95
    NS and NT 3.8L engine .... 74 ± 4
  Diesel engines **(see illustration)**
    Small bolts 25
    Large bolts
      Step 1 20
      Step 2 .... Tighten an additional 90-degree turn
      Step 3 .... Tighten an additional 90-degree turn

0.1 Petrol engine main bearing cap assembly

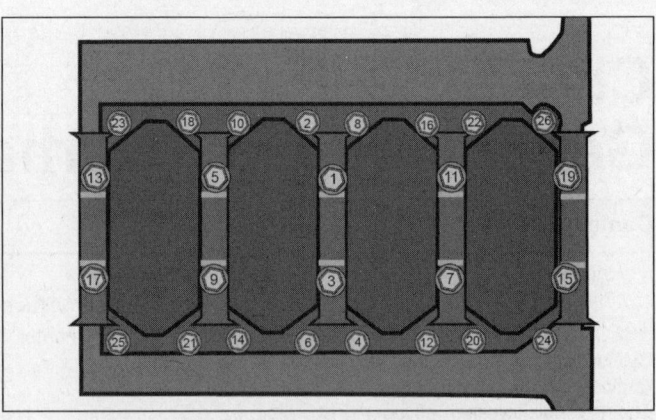

0.2 Diesel engine main bearing cap assembly

1 General information - engine overhaul

Overhauling an engine is a difficult and time-consuming task. Special tools and knowledge are required. For these reasons, we recommend that engine overhaul is best left to a professional engine rebuilder. A competent engine rebuilder will handle the inspection of your old parts and offer advice concerning the reconditioning or replacement of the original engine.

Be aware that some engine builders can only rebuild the engine you bring them, which can take several weeks, while other rebuilders have rebuilt exchange engines in stock. If time is an issue, an exchange engine may be the best solution. If an exchange engine is fitted, check with your state registry authority as some insist the engine number on the new engine is included on your registration and insurance details.

An engine overhaul involves restoring the internal parts to the specifications of a new engine. During an overhaul, the piston rings are replaced and the cylinder walls are reconditioned (rebored and/or honed). If a rebore is done by an automotive machine shop, new oversize pistons will also be installed. The main bearings and connecting rod bearings are generally replaced with new ones and, if necessary, the crankshaft may be reground to restore the journals. Generally, the valves are serviced as well, since they're usually in less-than-perfect condition at this point. The end result should be a like-new engine that will give many trouble-free miles.

For those with engine overhaul experience and access to the necessary tools who wish to undertake the overhaul themselves, engine specifications have been included at the start of this chapter. Also included in this chapter are general information and diagnostic testing procedures for determining the overall mechanical condition of your engine.

It is important to establish the condition of the cylinder block. Never purchase parts or have machine work done on other components until the block has been thoroughly inspected by a professional machine shop.

The following Sections have been written to help you determine whether your engine needs to be overhauled and how to remove and install it once you've determined it needs to be rebuilt. For information concerning in-vehicle engine repair, see Chapter 2A, Chapter 2B or Chapter 2C.

The Specifications included relate to engine overhaul. Refer to the previous Engine chapters for additional engine Specifications.

It's not always easy to determine when, or if, an engine should be completely overhauled, because a number of factors must be considered.

High mileage is not necessarily an indication that an overhaul is needed, while low mileage doesn't preclude the need for an overhaul. Frequency of servicing is probably the most important consideration. An engine that has had regular and frequent oil and filter changes, as well as other required maintenance, will most likely give many thousands of miles of reliable service. Conversely, a neglected engine may require an overhaul very early in its service life.

Excessive oil consumption is an indication that piston rings, valve seals and/or valve guides are in need of attention. Make sure that oil leaks aren't responsible before deciding that the rings and/or valve guides are bad. Perform a cylinder compression check to determine the extent of the work required (see Section 3).

Check the oil pressure with a gauge installed in place of the oil pressure sending unit and compare it to this chapter's Specifications (see Section 2). If it's extremely low, the bearings and/or oil pump are probably worn out.

Loss of power, rough running, knocking or metallic engine noises, excessive valve train noise and high fuel consumption rates may also point to the need for an overhaul, especially if they're all present at the same time. If a complete tune-up doesn't remedy the situation, major mechanical work is the only solution.

Note: *Critical cooling system components such as the hoses, drivebelts, thermostat and water pump should be replaced with new parts when an engine is overhauled. The radiator should be checked carefully to ensure that it isn't clogged or leaking (see Chapter 3). If you purchase a rebuilt engine or short block, some rebuilders will not warranty their engines unless the radiator has been professionally flushed.*

2 Oil pressure check

Refer to illustration 2.2

1 Low engine oil pressure can be a sign of an engine in need of rebuilding. A "low oil pressure" indicator (often called an "idiot light") is not a test of the lubrication system. Such indicators only come on when the oil pressure is dangerously low. Even a factory oil pressure gauge in the instrument panel is only a relative indication, although much better for driver information than a warning light. A better test is with a mechanical (not electrical) oil pressure gauge.

2 Locate the oil pressure indicator sending unit on the engine block:

a) On petrol engines, the oil pressure sending unit **(see illustration)** is located on the right front side of the engine block, on the oil pump.

b) On 4M40 (2.8L) diesel engines, the oil pressure sending unit is located at the front of the engine. On 4M41 (3.2L) diesel engines, the oil pressure sending unit is located on the right rear side of the engine on the oil cooler assembly.

3 Unscrew and remove the oil pressure sending unit and then screw in the hose for your oil pressure gauge. If necessary, fit an adapter fitting. Use Teflon tape or thread sealant on the threads of the adapter and/or the fitting on the end of your gauge's hose.

4 Connect an accurate tachometer to the engine, according to the tachometer manufacturer's instructions.

5 Check the oil pressure with the engine

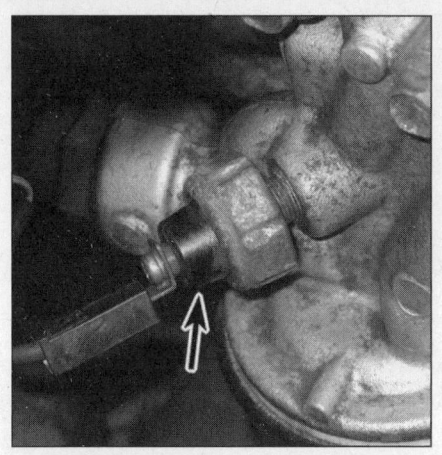

2.2 On petrol engines, the oil pressure sending unit (arrow) is located on the right front corner of the engine in the oil pump housing

running (normal operating temperature) at the specified engine speed, and compare it to this Chapter's Specifications. If it's extremely low, the bearings and/or oil pump are probably worn out.

3 Cylinder compression check

Petrol engines

Refer to illustrations 3.9, 3.10a and 3.10b

Note: *When doing a compression check, the ignition and fuel systems must be isolated to prevent the engine from starting while the compression gauge is installed. Due to the complexity of disabling the fuel and ignition system on these engines, it is recommended that a remote starter be used. A remote starter connects to the starter motor. One end connects to the large battery supply terminal and the other end connects to the small solenoid terminal. When the button on the remote starter is pressed, the starter motor will energise and rotate the engine. Doing the compression test this way means the ignition can remain Off preventing raw fuel being injected into the engine and passing through to the catalytic converter – damaging the converter. It also prevents the engine management system from setting fault codes about low fuel pressure or no ignition signals at the coils. A remote starter can be purchased from your local auto parts retailer.*

1 A compression check will tell you what mechanical condition the upper end of your engine (pistons, rings, valves, head gaskets) is in. Specifically, it can tell you if the compression is down due to leakage caused by worn piston rings, defective valves and seats or a blown head gasket.

Note: *The engine must be at normal operating temperature and the battery must be fully charged for this check.*

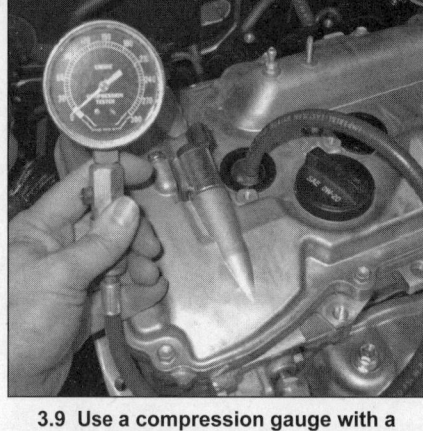

3.9 Use a compression gauge with a threaded fitting for the spark plug hole, not the type that requires hand pressure to maintain the seal (3.8L engine shown)

2 On petrol engines if not using a remote starter, depressurise the fuel system (see Chapter 4).

3 On petrol engines, begin by removing the upper intake manifold (see Chapter 2A).

4 Clean the area around the ignition coils or glow plugs before you remove them (compressed air should be used, if available). The idea is to prevent dirt from getting into the cylinders as the compression check is being done.

5 On diesel engines, remove the glow plugs (see Chapter 4).

6 On petrol engines, remove all of the spark plugs from the engine (see Chapter 1).

7 Remove the air intake duct from the throttle body, then block the throttle wide open.

8 If not using a remote starter, disconnect the wiring from each fuel injector (see Chapter 4). On petrol engines, also disable the fuel pump by removing the fuel pump fuse from the engine compartment fuse and relay box (see Chapter 4A).

9 Install a compression gauge in the spark plug, or glow plug hole **(see illustration)**.

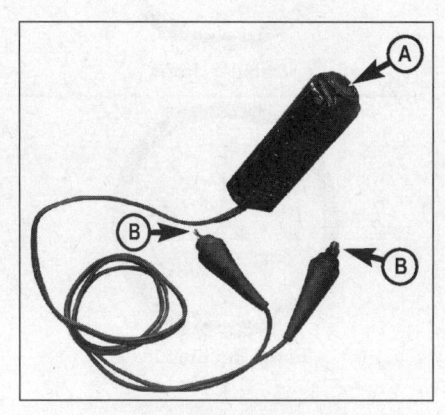

3.10a Typical remote starter switch (A) and alligator clips (B)

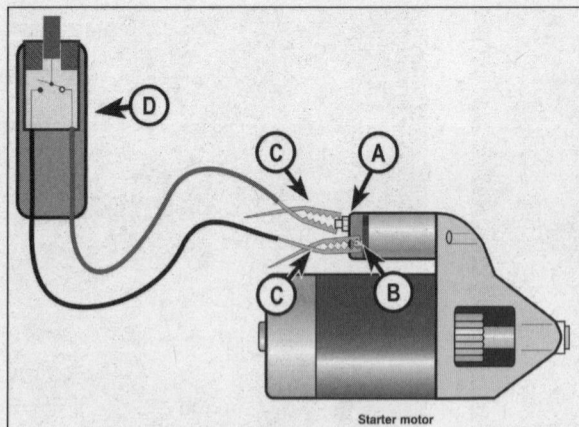

2D-4 Chapter 2 Part D General engine overhaul procedures

3.10b Illustration showing how to connect the remote starter switch. Connect one alligator clip to the large terminal on the starter motor that goes to the battery (A). Connect the second terminal to the solenoid terminal after disconnecting the wire from the solenoid (B). Ensure the alligator clips (C) are not touching. When the switch (D) is pressed, the starter motor will operate

Caution: *As the engine compression pressures are considerably higher on a diesel engine, a compression gauge specifically for a diesel engine must be used. This gauge must be capable of reading pressures above 4,000 kPa.*

10 If using a remote starter, connect it to the starter motor solenoid **(see illustrations)**.

11 Crank the engine over at least seven compression strokes and watch the gauge. The compression should build up quickly in a healthy engine. Low compression on the first stroke, followed by gradually increasing pressure on successive strokes, indicates worn piston rings. A low compression reading on the first stroke, which doesn't build up during successive strokes, indicates leaking valves or a blown head gasket (a cracked head could also be the cause). Deposits on the undersides of the valve heads can also cause low compression. Record the highest gauge reading obtained.

12 Repeat the procedure for the remaining cylinders and compare the results to this Chapter's Specifications.

13 Add some engine oil (about three squirts from a plunger-type oil can) to each cylinder, through the spark plug or glow plug hole, and repeat the test.

14 If the compression increases after the oil is added, the piston rings are definitely worn. If the compression doesn't increase significantly, the leakage is occurring at the valves or head gasket. Leakage past the valves may be caused by burned valve seats and/or faces or warped, cracked or bent valves.

15 If two adjacent cylinders have equally low compression, there's a strong possibility that the head gasket between them is blown. The appearance of coolant in the combustion chambers or the crankcase would verify this condition.

16 If one cylinder is slightly lower than the others, and the engine has a slightly rough idle, a worn lobe on the camshaft could be the cause.

17 If the compression is unusually high, the combustion chambers are probably coated with carbon deposits. If that's the case, the cylinder head(s) should be removed and decarbonised.

18 If compression is way down or varies greatly between cylinders, it would be a good idea to have a leak-down test performed by an automotive repair shop. This test will pinpoint exactly where the leakage is occurring and how severe it is.

19 After performing the test, don't forget to unblock the throttle plate.

4 Vacuum gauge diagnostic checks (petrol engines)

Refer to illustration 4.6

A vacuum gauge provides valuable information about what is going on in the engine at a low-cost. You can check for worn rings or cylinder walls, leaking cylinder head or inlet manifold gaskets, restricted exhaust, stuck or burned valves, weak valve springs, improper ignition or valve timing and ignition problems.

Unfortunately, vacuum gauge readings are easy to misinterpret, so they should be used in conjunction with other tests to confirm the diagnosis.

Both the gauge readings and the rate of needle movement are important for accurate interpretation. As vacuum increases (or atmospheric pressure decreases) the reading will increase. Also, for every 300 meters increase in elevation, the gauge readings will decrease about 25 mm (1 inch) of mercury.

Connect the vacuum gauge directly to inlet manifold vacuum, not to ported vacuum. Be sure no hoses are left disconnected during the test or false readings will result.

Before you begin the test, allow the engine to warm up completely. Block the wheels and set the parking brake. With the transmission in Park (automatic) or Neutral (manual), start the engine and allow it to run at normal idle speed.

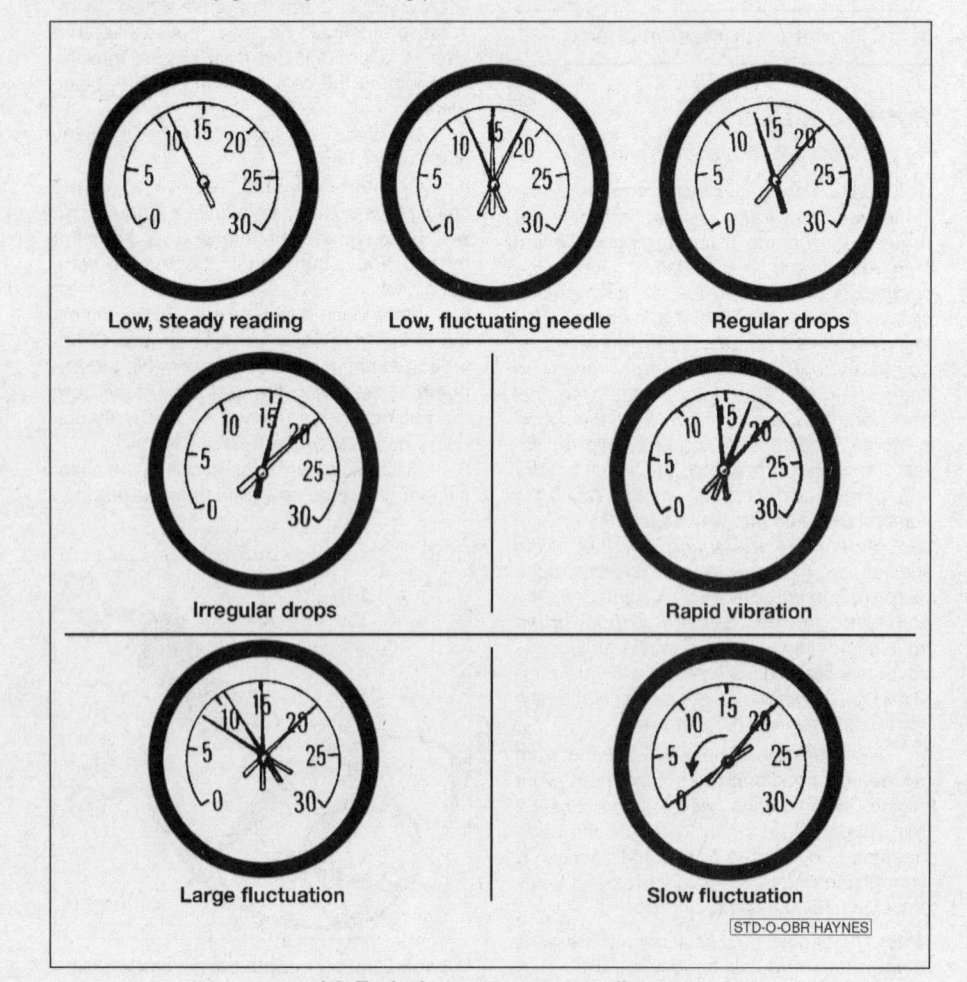

4.6 Typical vacuum gauge readings

Chapter 2 Part D General engine overhaul procedures

Warning: *Carefully inspect the fan blades for cracks or damage before starting the engine. Keep your hands and the vacuum tester clear of the fan and do not stand in front of the vehicle or in line with the fan when the engine is running.*

Read the vacuum gauge; an average, healthy engine should normally produce between 430 and 560 mm-Hg of vacuum with a fairly steady needle **(see illustration)**. Refer to the following vacuum gauge readings and what they indicate about the engines condition:

1 A low steady reading usually indicates a leaking gasket between the inlet manifold or throttle body, a leaky vacuum hose, late ignition timing or incorrect camshaft timing. Check ignition timing with a timing light and eliminate all other possible causes, utilising the tests provided in this Chapter before you remove the timing chain cover to check the timing marks.

2 If the reading is 75 to 200 mm-Hg below normal and it fluctuates at that low reading, suspect an inlet manifold gasket leak at an inlet port or a faulty injector.

3 If the needle has regular drops of about 50 to 100 mm-Hg at a steady rate the valves are probably leaking. Perform a compression or leak-down test to confirm this.

4 An irregular drop or down-flick of the needle can be caused by a sticking valve or an ignition misfire. Perform a compression or leak-down test and read the spark plugs.

5 A rapid vibration of about 100 mm-Hg vibration at idle combined with exhaust smoke indicates worn valve guides. Perform a leak-down test to confirm this. If the rapid vibration occurs with an increase in engine speed, check for a leaking inlet manifold gasket or cylinder head gasket, weak valve springs, burned valves or ignition misfire.

6 A slight fluctuation of 25 to 50 mm-Hg up and down, may mean ignition problems. Check all the usual tune-up items and, if necessary, run the engine on an ignition analyser.

7 If there is a large fluctuation, perform a compression or leak-down test to look for a weak or dead cylinder or a blown cylinder head gasket.

8 If the needle moves slowly through a wide range, check for a clogged PCV system, incorrect idle fuel mixture, throttle body or inlet manifold gasket leaks.

9 Check for a slow return after revving the engine by quickly snapping the throttle open until the engine reaches about 2,500 rpm and let it shut. Normally the reading should drop to near zero, rise above normal idle reading (about 125 mm-Hg over) and then return to the previous idle reading. If the vacuum returns slowly and doesn't peak when the throttle is snapped shut, the rings may be worn. If there is a long delay, look for a restricted exhaust system (often the muffler or catalytic converter). An easy way to check this is to temporarily disconnect the exhaust ahead of the suspected part and perform the test again.

5 Engine rebuilding alternatives

The do-it-yourselfer is faced with a number of options when purchasing a rebuilt engine. The major considerations are cost, warranty, parts availability and the time required for the rebuilder to complete the project. The decision to replace the engine block, piston/connecting rod assemblies and crankshaft depends on the final inspection results of your engine. Only then can you make a cost effective decision whether to have your engine overhauled or simply purchase an exchange engine for your vehicle.

Some of the rebuilding alternatives include:

Individual parts - If the inspection procedures reveal that the engine block and most engine components are in reusable condition, purchasing individual parts and having a rebuilder rebuild your engine may be the most economical alternative. The block, crankshaft and piston/connecting rod assemblies should all be inspected carefully by a machine shop first.

Short block - A short block consists of an engine block with a crankshaft and piston/connecting rod assemblies already installed. All new bearings are incorporated and all clearances will be correct. The existing camshafts, valve train components, cylinder head and external parts can be bolted to the short block with little or no machine shop work necessary.

Long block - A long block consists of a short block plus an oil pump, oil pan, cylinder head, valve cover, camshaft and valve train components, timing sprockets and chain or gears and timing cover. All components are installed with new bearings, seals and gaskets incorporated throughout. The installation of manifolds and external parts is all that's necessary.

Low mileage used engines - Some companies now offer low mileage used engines which are a very cost effective way to get your vehicle up and running again. These engines often come from vehicles which have been totalled in accidents or come from other countries which have a higher vehicle turn over rate. A low mileage used engine also usually has a similar warranty like the newly remanufactured engines.

Give careful thought to which alternative is best for you and discuss the situation with local automotive machine shops, auto parts dealers and experienced rebuilders before ordering or purchasing replacement parts.

6 Engine removal - methods and precautions

Refer to illustrations 6.1, 6.2, 6.3 and 6.4

If you've decided that an engine must be removed for overhaul or major repair work, several preliminary steps should be taken. Read all removal and installation procedures carefully prior to committing to this job. Make sure the engine hoist is rated in excess of the combined weight of the engine and transmission. A transmission jack is also very helpful. Safety is of primary importance, considering the potential hazards involved in removing the engine from the vehicle.

Locating a suitable place to work is extremely important. Adequate work space, along with storage space for the vehicle, will be needed. If a shop or garage isn't available, at the very least a flat, level, clean work surface made of concrete or asphalt is required.

Cleaning the engine compartment and engine before beginning the removal procedure will help keep tools clean and organized **(see illustrations 6.1 and 6.2)**.

If you're a novice at engine removal, get at least one helper. One person cannot easily do all the things you need to do to remove a big heavy engine and transmission assembly from the engine compartment. Also helpful is to seek advice and assistance from someone who's experienced in engine removal.

Plan the operation ahead of time. Arrange for or obtain all of the tools and equipment you'll need prior to beginning the job **(see illustrations 6.3 and 6.4)**. Some of the equipment necessary to perform engine

6.1 After tightly wrapping water-vulnerable components, use a spray cleaner on everything, with particular concentration on the greasiest areas, usually around the valve cover and lower edges of the block. If one section dries out, apply more cleaner

6.2 Depending on how dirty the engine is, let the cleaner soak in according to the directions and then hose off the grime and cleaner. Get the rinse water down into every area you can get at; then dry important components with a hair dryer or paper towels

2D-6　Chapter 2 Part D General engine overhaul procedures

6.3 Get an engine hoist that's strong enough to easily lift your engine in and out of the engine compartment (diesel engines are particularly heavy, so make sure that you obtain a heavy-duty hoist if you're planning to lift either of these engines out of the engine compartment); an adapter, like the one shown here (arrow), can be used to change the angle of the engine as it's being removed or installed

6.4 Get an engine stand sturdy enough to firmly support the engine while you're working on it. Stay away from three-wheeled models: they have a tendency to tip over more easily, so get a four-wheeled unit. The diesel engines are particularly heavy, so make sure that you obtain a heavy-duty stand capable of supporting one of these engines

removal and installation safely and with relative ease are (in addition to a vehicle hoist and an engine hoist) a heavy duty floor jack (preferably fitted with a transmission jack head adapter), complete sets of wrenches and sockets as described in the front of this manual, wooden blocks, plenty of rags and cleaning solvent for mopping up spilled oil, coolant and gasoline.

Plan for the vehicle to be out of use for quite a while. A machine shop can do the work that is beyond the scope of the home mechanic. Machine shops often have a busy schedule, so before removing the engine, consult the shop for an estimate of how long it will take to rebuild or repair the components that may need work.

7 Engine - removal and refitting

Refer to illustrations 7.5, 7.9, 7.19, 7.26, 7.28a, 7.28b and 7.28c

Warning: *DO NOT use a cheap engine hoist designed for lifting four-cylinder engines. Obtain a heavy-duty hoist designed for lifting heavy engines. And always be extremely careful when removing and refitting the engine. Serious injury can result from careless actions.*

Warning: *The models covered by this manual are equipped with Supplemental Restraint systems (SRS), more commonly known as airbags. Always disable the airbag system before working in the vicinity of the impact sensors, steering column or instrument panel to avoid the possibility of accidental deployment of the airbag, which could cause personal injury (see Chapter 12).*

Warning: *Petrol is extremely flammable, so take extra precautions when you work on any part of the fuel system. Don't smoke or allow open flames or bare light bulbs near the work area, and don't work in a garage where a gas-type appliance (such as a water heater or a clothes dryer) is present. Since petrol is carcinogenic, wear latex gloves when there's a possibility of being exposed to fuel, and, if you spill any fuel on your skin, rinse it off immediately with soap and water. Mop up any spills immediately and do not store fuel-soaked rags where they could ignite. The fuel system is under constant pressure, so, if any fuel lines are to be disconnected, the fuel pressure in the system must be relieved first (see Chapter 4 for more information). When you perform any kind of work on the fuel system, wear safety glasses and have a Class B type fire extinguisher on hand.*

Warning: *The air conditioning system is under high pressure, and refrigerant is expensive. Have a dealer service department or an automotive air conditioning shop discharge the system before beginning this procedure.*

Caution: *If the stereo in your vehicle is equipped with an anti-theft system, make sure you have the correct activation code before disconnecting the battery.*

1   On vehicles with air conditioning, remove the compressor and tie it out of the way.
Caution: *Don't disconnect the hoses unless the system has been discharged (see Warning 4).*
2   Relieve the fuel system pressure (see Chapter 4).
3   Disconnect the battery cables and then remove the battery(ies) (see Chapter 5).
4   Remove the bonnet (see Chapter 11) and then cover the fenders and cowl. Special pads are available to protect the fenders, but an old bedspread or blanket will also work.
5   Raise the vehicle and place it securely on jackstands **(see illustration)**.

6.5 A clutch alignment tool is necessary if you plan to install a rebuilt engine mated to a manual transmission

7.5 Place sturdy jackstands under the frame of the vehicle and set them both at uniform height

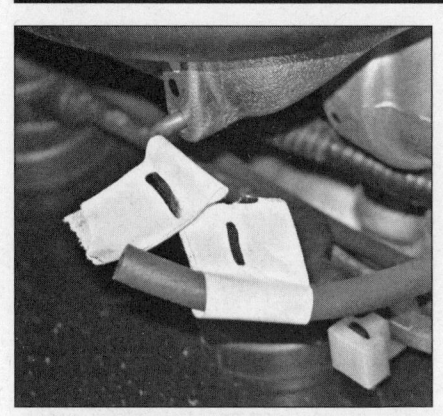

Chapter 2 Part D General engine overhaul procedures

7.9 Label both ends of each wire and hose before disconnecting it - do the same for vacuum hoses

Note: *On 4WD models, and on models with large tires, this step may not be necessary, because some models already have sufficient ground clearance to allow disconnection of the exhaust system, the engine mounts, etc. from underneath the vehicle. Raising these vehicles any higher might even make engine removal more difficult because it might position the vehicle too high to lift the engine out of the engine compartment with a hoist.*

6   Drain the engine oil and then remove the oil filter (see Chapter 1). Detach the engine oil dipstick tube bracket and then remove the engine oil dipstick tube.
7   Drain the cooling system (see Chapter 1).
8   Remove the air cleaner assembly, intercooler (if equipped) and the air intake duct (see Chapter 4).
9   Label all vacuum lines, emissions system hoses, wiring harness electrical connectors and ground straps to ensure correct refitting, then disconnect them. Pieces of masking tape with numbers or letters written on them work well **(see illustration)**. So does colored electrical tape. If there's any possibility of confusion, make a sketch of the engine compartment and clearly label the lines, hoses and wires. You can also use an inexpensive disposable or digital camera to take photos of connectors, grounds, harness routing, etc.
10 Disconnect the fuel lines running from the engine to the chassis (see Chapter 4). Plug or cap all open fittings/lines.
Warning: *Petrol is extremely flammable, so extra precautions must be taken when working on any part of the fuel system. DO NOT smoke or allow open flames or bare light bulbs near the vehicle. Also, don't work in a garage if a gas appliance is present.*
11 On petrol models, disconnect the throttle cable from the throttle linkage on the throttle body (early models) and then remove the throttle body (see Chapter 4). Disconnect the fuel lines from the fuel rail and then remove the fuel rail and the injectors (see Chapter 4). Remove the intake manifold (see Chapter 2A). Also remove all fuel and/or emission control components that might be damaged during engine removal (see Chapters 4 and 6).
12 On diesel models, remove the ducts between the intercooler and the turbocharger and between the turbocharger and the intake manifold covers, remove the turbocharger manifold, and then remove the turbocharger and the turbocharger pedestal (see Chapter 4). Disconnect the fuel lines from the cylinder heads. Remove the fuel filter/water separator (see Chapter 4).
13 Clearly label and then disconnect all coolant and heater hoses. Remove the cooling fan, shroud and radiator (see Chapter 3).
14 Remove the accessory drivebelt(s) (see Chapter 1) and then remove the alternator (see Chapter 5).
15 On vehicles with air conditioning, remove the condenser and the compressor (see Chapter 3). Look carefully at the air conditioning system plumbing. If some section(s) of the plumbing - particularly any section consisting of rigid metal lines - looks like it's going to impede engine removal and refitting, detach it from the engine and/or vehicle and set it aside. Secure it with wire if necessary to make sure that it won't be damaged by the engine when the engine is lifted out of the engine compartment.
16 On diesel engines, remove the intercooler (see Chapter 4). On some models equipped with an automatic transmission, there is an *external* oil cooler, which is located below the space occupied by an intercooler on diesel models. This auxiliary cooler, which is fitted in addition to the regular oil cooler that's integrated into the radiator, must also be removed (see Chapter 7B).
17 Remove the grille (see Chapter 11) and the upper radiator crossmember, which is secured by three bolts on each end. Removing the grille and the upper radiator crossmember gives you more room when manoeuvring the engine forward to clear the cowl, and it lowers the minimum height which the bottom of the engine must clear when it's hoisted out of the engine compartment.
18 Remove the power steering pump from its mounting bracket (see Chapter 10) and then secure it with wire so that it won't interfere with engine removal. On diesel engines, you'll have to remove the power steering pump pulley before you can unbolt the pump from its mounting bracket.
19 If you're going to be replacing the block, now is a good time to remove all large brackets such as the alternator, air conditioning compressor and power steering pump brackets **(see illustration)**.
20 Remove the part of the exhaust system that's routed underneath the engine, between the exhaust manifolds and the downstream catalytic converter (see Chapter 4). It's not absolutely necessary to remove the exhaust manifolds in order to remove the engine, but removing the manifolds will shave a little weight off the engine.
21 Remove the starter motor (see Chapter 5).
22 Remove the transmission (see Chapter 7).
23 Locate the lifting brackets on the engine. Roll a heavy-duty hoist into position and then attach it to the lifting brackets with a couple pieces of heavy-duty chain. Take up the slack in the sling or chain, but don't lift the engine.
Warning: *DO NOT use a cheap hoist designed to lift four-cylinder engines. Obtain a*

7.19 Label the bolts after removing them - take care to check each bolt when you remove it for length, thread pitch and size

7.26 Use long high-strength bolts (arrows) to hold the engine block on the engine stand - make sure they are tight before resting all the weight on the stand

7.28a Tap the edge of the welch plug into the block . . .

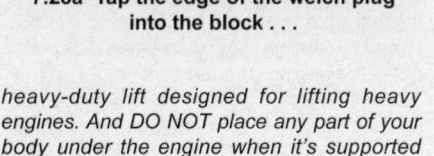

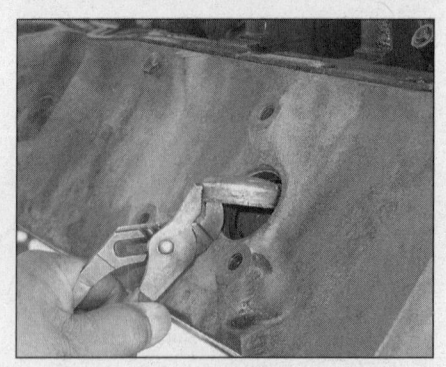

7.28b . . . then, use multi-grip pliers to lever the old welch plug from the block

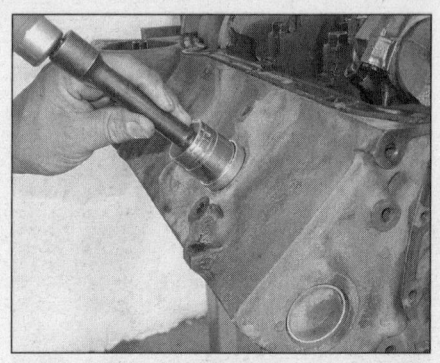

7.28c Use a socket that sits around the edge of the welch plug to tap it squarely into the block

heavy-duty lift designed for lifting heavy engines. And DO NOT place any part of your body under the engine when it's supported only by a hoist or other lifting device.

24 Remove the engine mount fasteners (see the "Engine mounts - check and renewal" section in Chapter 2A).

25 Recheck to be sure nothing is still connecting the engine to the transmission or vehicle. Disconnect anything still remaining. Raise the engine slightly and then inspect it thoroughly once more to make sure that *nothing* is still attached, then slowly lift the engine out of the engine compartment. Check carefully to make sure nothing is hanging on.

26 Remove the flywheel/driveplate (see Chapter 2A, 2B or 2C) and then mount the engine on an engine stand **(see illustration)**.

27 Inspect the engine and transmission mounts (see the "Engine mounts - check and renewal" section in Chapter 2A). If they're worn or damaged, replace them.

Refitting

28 Check the engine/transaxle mounts. If they're worn or damaged, replace them. Also check other components such as welch plugs, which are easy to change while the engine is removed **(see illustrations)**.

29 Install the flywheel/driveplate (see Chapter 2A, 2B or 2C).

30 If you're working on a vehicle with manual transmission, refit the clutch and pressure plate (see Chapter 8). Now is a good time to fit a new clutch.

31 Carefully lower the engine into the engine compartment and then reattach it to the engine mounts (see the "Engine mounts - check and renewal" section in Chapter 2A).

32 Refit the transmission (see Chapter 7) If you're working on a manual transmission model, apply a dab of high-temperature grease to the input shaft and guide it into the crankshaft pilot bearing until the bellhousing is flush with the engine block. If you're working on a vehicle with an automatic transmission, guide the torque converter into the crankshaft following the procedure outlined in Chapter 7B. Refit the transmission-to-engine bolts and tighten them securely.

Caution: *DO NOT use the bolts to force the transmission and engine together!*

33 Refit the remaining components in the reverse order of removal.

34 Add coolant, oil and transmission fluid as needed.

35 Run the engine and check for leaks and proper operation of all accessories, then refit the hood and test drive the vehicle.

36 Have the air conditioning system recharged and leak tested, if it was discharged.

8 Initial start-up and break-in after overhaul

Warning: *Have a fire extinguisher handy when starting the engine for the first time.*

1 Once the engine has been installed in the vehicle, double-check the engine oil and coolant levels.

2 It is good mechanical practice to crank the engine with the spark plugs or glow plugs removed to get oil circulating around the engine without the engine being under load. To do this, remove the spark plugs or glow plugs from the engine and crank it for about 10-seconds with a 15-second break and then repeat the procedure. Do this several times. While doing this it is imperative that the fuel injection system is disabled, on both petrol and diesel engines, as well as the ignition system on petrol engines. A procedure to crank the engine is covered in the engine compression check procedure (see Section 3).

Caution: *Ensure the fuel and ignition system is disabled before cranking the engine.*

3 Install the spark plugs or glow plugs, hook up the plug wires and restore the ignition system and fuel pump functions.

4 Start the engine. It may take a few moments for the fuel system to build up pressure, but the engine should start without a great deal of effort. On diesel engines, the fuel system will need to be bled (see Chapter 4B).

5 After the engine starts, it should be allowed to warm up to normal operating temperature. While the engine is warming up, make a thorough check for fuel, oil and coolant leaks.

6 Shut the engine off and recheck the engine oil and coolant levels.

7 Drive the vehicle to an area with minimum traffic, accelerate from 50 to 80 km/h, then allow the vehicle to slow to 50 km/h with the throttle closed. Repeat the procedure 10 or 12 times. This will load the piston rings and cause them to seat properly against the cylinder walls. Check again for oil and coolant leaks.

8 Drive the vehicle gently for the first 800 km (no sustained high speeds) and keep a constant check on the oil level. It is not unusual for an engine to use oil during the break-in period.

9 At approximately 800 to 1,000 km change the oil and filter.

10 For the next few hundred kilometres, drive the vehicle normally. Do not pamper it or abuse it.

11 After 3,000 km, change the oil and filter again and consider the engine broken in.

Chapter 3
Cooling, heating and air conditioning systems

Contents

	Section		Section
Air conditioning and heating system - check and maintenance	14	Cooling system servicing (draining, flushing and refilling)	See Chapter 1
Air conditioning compressor - removal and refitting	16	Engine cooling fan, clutch and pulley - check and renewal	5
Air conditioning condenser - removal and refitting	17	General information	1
Air conditioning condenser fan - removal and refitting	21	Heater/air conditioning control assembly - removal and refitting	19
Air conditioning evaporator - removal and refitting	18	Heater core - removal and refitting	12
Air conditioning receiver/drier (2000 and earlier models) - removal and refitting	15	Heating system - general information	10
Air conditioning system - general information	13	Oil cooler - removal and refitting	20
Antifreeze - general information	2	Radiator - removal and refitting	4
Blower motor - removal and refitting	11	Thermostat - check and renewal	3
Coolant reservoir - removal and refitting	6	Water pump - check	7
Coolant temperature gauge sender unit - check and renewal	9	Water pump - renewal	8

Specifications

General

Coolant type and capacity	See Chapter 1			
Thermostat opening temperature				
Petrol engines	82-degrees C			
Diesel engines				
Except NT, NW	76.5-degrees C			
NT, NW	82-degrees C			
Radiator cap pressure rating in kPa	NL	NM	NP	NS, NT, NW
Petrol engines	90	74 to 103	94 to 122	93 to 123
Diesel engines	74 to 103	74 to 103	74 to 103	93 to 123

Torque specifications

	Nm		
Cooling fan bolts/nuts	10 to 12		
Coolant temperature switch	10 to 12		
Coolant temperature sensor			
Petrol	20 to 40		
Diesel	30 to 39		
Fan clutch bolts	10 to 12		
Oil cooler			
Petrol engine	**NM and NP models**	**NS, NT, NW models**	
Oil cooler banjo bolts	29 to 34	33	
Oil cooler hoses-to-block banjo bolts	39 to 44	48	
Oil cooler plugs	44	44	
Oil cooler mounting nuts/bolts	20	10	
2.8L diesel engines			
Oil cooler banjo bolts	29 to 34		
Oil cooler hoses-to-block banjo bolts	39 to 44		
Oil cooler plugs	44		
Oil cooler mounting nuts	20		
3.2L diesel engines	**NM and NP models**	**NS, NT models**	**NW models**
Oil cooler banjo bolts	29 to 34	33	
Oil cooler hoses-to-block banjo bolts	39 to 44	48	
Oil cooler plugs	44	44	
Oil cooler mounting nuts/bolts	20	10	
Thermo switch	6 to 9		
Water pump bolts	23 to 25	Not specified	24 [1]

[1] *24 Nm - petrol engines; diesel engine - Not specified.*

1 General information

Engine cooling system

All vehicles covered by this manual employ a pressurised engine cooling system with thermostatically controlled coolant circulation. An impeller-type water pump mounted on the front of the block pumps coolant through the engine. The coolant flows around each cylinder and toward the rear of the engine. Cast-in coolant passages direct coolant around the intake and exhaust ports, near the spark plug areas and in close proximity to the exhaust valve guides.

A wax pellet-type thermostat is located in a housing near the front of the engine. During warm-up, the closed thermostat prevents coolant from circulating through the radiator. As the engine nears normal operating temperature, the thermostat opens and allows hot coolant to travel through the radiator, where it's cooled before returning to the engine.

The cooling system is sealed by a pressure type radiator cap, which raises the boiling point of the coolant and increases the cooling efficiency of the radiator. If the system pressure exceeds the cap pressure relief value, the excess pressure in the system forces the spring-loaded valve inside the cap off its seat and allows the coolant to escape through the overflow tube into a coolant reservoir. When the system cools the excess coolant is automatically drawn from the reservoir back into the radiator.

The coolant reservoir does double duty as both the point at which fresh coolant is added to the cooling system to maintain the proper fluid level and as a holding tank for overheated coolant.

This type of cooling system is known as a closed design because coolant that escapes past the pressure cap is saved and reused.

Heating system

The heating system consists of a blower fan and heater core located in the heater box, the hoses connecting the heater core to the engine cooling system and the heater/air conditioning control head on the dashboard. Hot engine coolant is circulated through the heater core. When the heater mode is activated, a flap door opens to expose the heater box to the passenger compartment. A fan switch on the control head activates the blower motor, which forces air through the core, heating the air.

Air conditioning system

The air conditioning system consists of a condenser mounted in front of the radiator, an evaporator mounted adjacent to the heater core, a belt-driven compressor mounted on the engine, a receiver/drier (early models) which contains a high-pressure relief valve and the plumbing connecting all of the above components.

A blower fan forces the warmer air of the passenger compartment through the evaporator core (sort of a radiator-in-reverse), transferring the heat from the air to the refrigerant. The liquid refrigerant boils off into low pressure vapour, taking the heat with it when it leaves the evaporator.

2 Antifreeze - general information

Warning: *Do not allow antifreeze to come in contact with your skin or painted surfaces of the vehicle. Rinse off spills immediately with plenty of water. If consumed, antifreeze can be fatal; children and pets are attracted by its sweet taste, so wipe up garage floor and drip pan coolant spills immediately. Keep antifreeze containers covered and repair leaks in your cooling system as soon as they are noticed.*

The cooling system should be filled with a water/ethylene glycol-based antifreeze solution, which will prevent freezing down to at -29-degrees C, or lower if local climate requires it. It also provides protection against corrosion and increases the coolant boiling point.

The cooling system should be drained, flushed and refilled at the specified intervals (see Chapter 1). Old or contaminated antifreeze solutions are likely to cause damage and encourage the formation of rust and scale in the system. Use distilled water with the antifreeze.

Before adding antifreeze, check all hose connections, because antifreeze tends to leak through very minute openings. Engines don't normally consume coolant, so if the level goes down, find the cause and correct it.

The exact mixture of antifreeze-to-water which you should use depends on the relative weather conditions. The mixture should contain at least 50 percent antifreeze, but should never contain more than 70 percent antifreeze. Consult the mixture ratio chart on the antifreeze container before adding coolant. Hydrometers are available at most auto parts stores to test the coolant. Use antifreeze which meets the vehicle manufacturer's specifications.

3 Thermostat - check and renewal

Warning: *Do not remove the radiator cap, drain the coolant or renew the thermostat until the engine has cooled completely.*

Check

1 Before assuming the thermostat is to blame for a cooling system problem, check the coolant level, water pump (see Section 7), drivebelt tension (see Chapter 1) and temperature gauge (or light) operation.

2 If the engine seems to be taking a long time to warm up (based on heater output or temperature gauge operation), the thermostat is probably stuck open. Renew the thermostat.

3 If the engine runs hot, use your hand to check the temperature of the upper radiator hose. If the hose isn't hot, but the engine is, the thermostat is probably stuck closed, preventing the coolant inside the engine from escaping to the radiator. Renew the thermostat.

Caution: *Don't drive the vehicle without a thermostat. The computer may stay in open loop and emissions and fuel economy will suffer.*

4 If the upper radiator hose is hot, it means that the coolant is flowing and the thermostat is open. Consult the *Troubleshooting* Section at the front of this manual for cooling system diagnosis.

Renewal

Refer to illustrations 3.10a, 3.10b and 3.13

5 Disconnect the negative battery cable from the battery.

6 Drain the cooling system (see Chapter 1). If the coolant is relatively new or in good condition (see Chapter 1), save it and reuse it.

7 Follow the upper radiator hose to the engine to locate the thermostat housing.

Note: *On diesel engines, the lower radiator hose connects to the thermostat housing.*

8 Loosen the hose clamp, then detach the hose from the fitting. If it's stuck, grasp it near the end with a pair of multi-grip pliers and twist it to break the seal, then pull it off. If the hose is old or deteriorated, cut it off and fit a new one.

9 If the outer surface of the large fitting that mates with the hose is deteriorated (corroded, pitted, etc.) it may be damaged further by hose removal. If it is, the thermostat housing cover will have to be renewed.

10 Remove the bolts and detach the housing cover **(see illustrations)**. If the cover is stuck, tap it with a soft-face hammer to jar it loose. Be prepared for some coolant to spill as the gasket seal is broken.

11 Note how it's fitted (which end is facing up), then remove the thermostat.

3.10a Location of the thermostat housing cover bolts - diesel engines

Chapter 3 Cooling, heating and air conditioning systems

3.10b Location of the thermostat housing cover bolts - later model 3.8L petrol engine shown, other petrol models similar

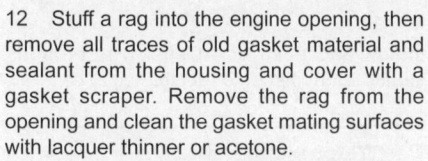

3.13 Be sure to fit a new rubber O-ring type gasket on the thermostat and that the jiggle valve is straight up

4.5a On later models disconnect the upper and lower fan shrouds from the main shroud

12 Stuff a rag into the engine opening, then remove all traces of old gasket material and sealant from the housing and cover with a gasket scraper. Remove the rag from the opening and clean the gasket mating surfaces with lacquer thinner or acetone.

13 Fit the new thermostat in the housing. Make sure the jiggle valve faces straight up - the spring end is normally directed into the engine **(see illustration)**.

14 Apply a thin, uniform layer of RTV sealant to both sides of the new gasket and position it on the housing.

15 Fit the cover and bolts. Tighten the bolts securely.

16 Reattach the hose to the fitting and tighten the hose clamp securely.

17 Refill the cooling system (see Chapter 1).

18 Start the engine and allow it to reach normal operating temperature, then check for leaks and proper thermostat operation (as described in Steps 2 through 4).

4 Radiator - removal and refitting

Refer to illustrations 4.5a, 4.5b, 4.6 and 4.8

Warning: *Wait until the engine is completely cool before beginning this procedure.*

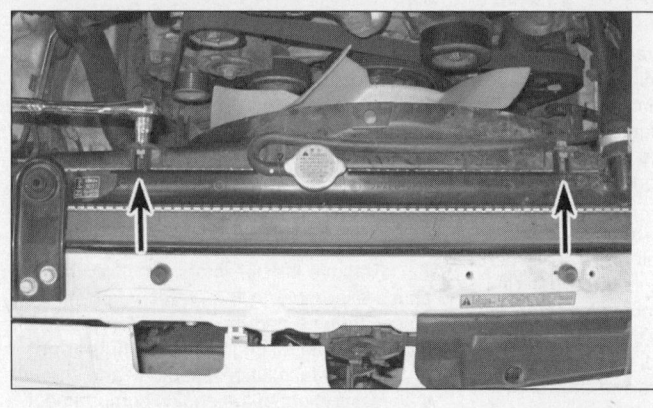

1 Disconnect the negative battery cable from the battery.

2 Drain the cooling system (see Chapter 1). If the coolant is relatively new or in good condition, save it and reuse it. If necessary for clearance, remove the air duct.

3 Loosen the hose clamps, then detach the radiator hoses from the fittings. If they're stuck, grasp each hose near the end with a pair of adjustable pliers and twist it to break the seal, then pull it off - be careful not to distort the radiator fittings! If the hoses are old or deteriorated, cut them off and fit new ones.

4.5b Remove the shroud mounting bolts (arrows)

4 Disconnect the reservoir hose from the radiator filler neck.

5 If equipped, disconnect the upper and lower fan shrouds from the main shroud **(see illustration)** and remove the shrouds. Remove the shroud mounting bolts **(see illustration)** and remove the shroud.

6 If the vehicle is equipped with an automatic transmission, disconnect the cooler hoses from the radiator **(see illustration)**. Use a drip pan to catch spilled fluid.

7 Plug the lines and fittings

8 Remove the radiator mounting bolts **(see illustration)**.

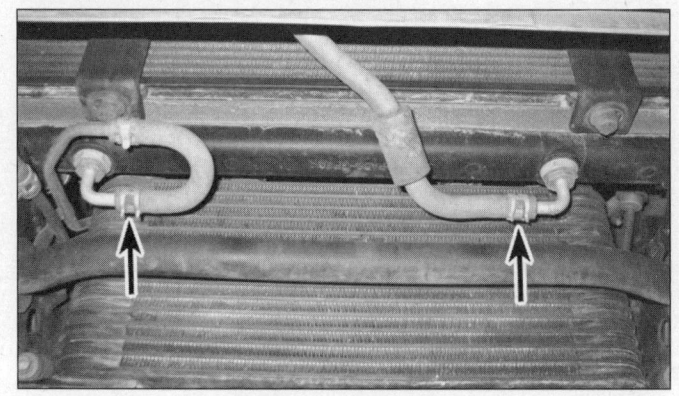

4.6 Disconnect the cooler hose clamps (arrows) from the radiator and remove the lines

4.8 Remove the radiator mounting bolts (arrows)

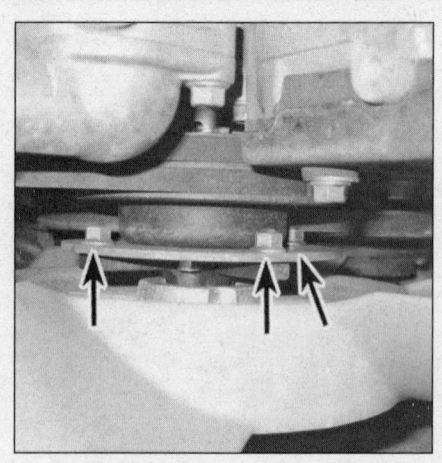

5.7 Remove the fan clutch attaching nuts (arrows)

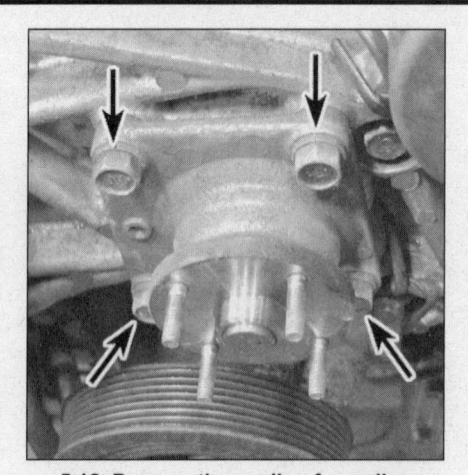

5.12 Remove the cooling fan pulley attaching bolts (arrows) and remove the assembly

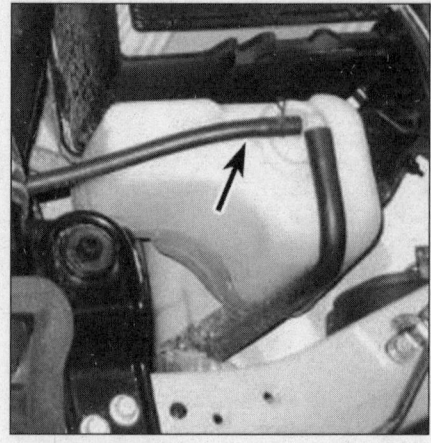

6.2 To remove the reservoir, carefully prise off the cap with the hose attached and lay the cap aside.

9 Carefully lift out the radiator. Don't spill coolant on the vehicle or scratch the paint.
10 With the radiator removed, it can be inspected for leaks and damage. If it needs repair, have a radiator shop or dealer service department perform the work as special techniques are required.
11 Bugs and dirt can be removed from the radiator with compressed air and a soft brush. Don't bend the cooling fins as this is done.
12 Check the radiator mounts for deterioration and make sure there's nothing in them when the radiator is refitted.
13 Refitting is the reverse of the removal procedure.
14 After refitting, fill the cooling system with the proper mixture of antifreeze and water. Refer to Chapter 1 if necessary.
15 Start the engine and check for leaks. Allow the engine to reach normal operating temperature, indicated by the upper radiator hose becoming hot. Recheck the coolant level and add more if required.
16 If you're working on an automatic transmission equipped vehicle, check and add fluid as needed.

5 Engine cooling fan, clutch and pulley - check and renewal

Warning: *To avoid possible injury or damage, DO NOT operate the engine with a damaged fan. Do not attempt to repair fan blades - renew a damaged fan with a new one.*

Check

1 Rock the fan back and forth by hand to check for excessive bearing play.
2 With the engine cold, turn the fan blades by hand. The fan should turn freely.
3 Visually inspect for substantial fluid leakage from the clutch assembly. If problems are noted, renew the clutch assembly.
4 With the engine completely warmed up, turn off the ignition switch.
5 Turn the fan by hand. Some drag should be evident. If the fan turns easily, renew the fan clutch.

Renewal

Refer to illustrations 5.7 and 5.12

6 Remove the fan shroud mounting screws and detach the shroud **(see illustration 4.8)**.
7 Remove the bolts/nuts attaching the fan/clutch assembly to the water pump hub on diesel engines and the cooling fan pulley on later model petrol engines **(see illustration)**.
8 Lift the fan/clutch assembly (and shroud, if necessary) out of the engine compartment.
9 Carefully inspect the fan blades for damage and defects. Renew it if necessary.
10 At this point, the fan may be unbolted from the clutch, if necessary. If the fan clutch is stored, position it with the radiator side facing down.
11 On 2000 and later petrol engines, the cooling fan is mounted to a fan pulley. Remove the fan/clutch as described in Step 7.
12 Remove the cooling fan pulley mounting bolts **(see illustration)** and remove the pulley and housing.
13 Refitting is the reverse of removal. Be sure to tighten the fan and clutch mounting nuts/bolts evenly and securely.

6 Coolant reservoir - removal and refitting

Refer to illustration 6.2

1 The coolant reservoir is located to the left of the radiator. It should be removed periodically and checked for cracks and other damage, and flushed with clean water.
2 To remove the reservoir, carefully prise off the cap with the hose attached **(see illustration)** and lay the cap aside.
3 Pull out the reservoir and simultaneously pull up and slide the reservoir off its mount.
4 To refit the reservoir, line it up with the mount and push down until it is properly seated. Don't forget to refit the cap.

7 Water pump - check

1 A failure in the water pump can cause serious engine damage due to overheating.
2 There are three ways to check the operation of the water pump while it's installed on the engine. If the pump is defective, it should be renewed with a new or rebuilt unit.
3 With the engine running at normal operating temperature, squeeze the upper radiator hose. If the water pump is working properly, a pressure surge should be felt as the hose is released.

Warning: *Keep your hands away from the fan blades!*

4 Water pumps are equipped with weep or vent holes. If a failure occurs in the pump seal, coolant will leak from the hole. In most cases you'll need a flashlight to find the hole on the water pump from underneath to check for leaks.
5 If the water pump shaft bearings fail, there may be a howling sound at the front of the engine while it's running. Shaft wear can be felt if the water pump pulley is rocked up and down. Don't mistake drivebelt slippage, which causes a squealing sound, for water bearing failure.

8 Water pump - renewal

Diesel engines

Removal

Warning: *Wait until the engine is completely cool before beginning this procedure.*

1 Drain the cooling system (see Chapter 1). If the coolant is relatively new or in good condition, save it and reuse it.
2 Remove the cooling fan and clutch assembly (see Section 5).

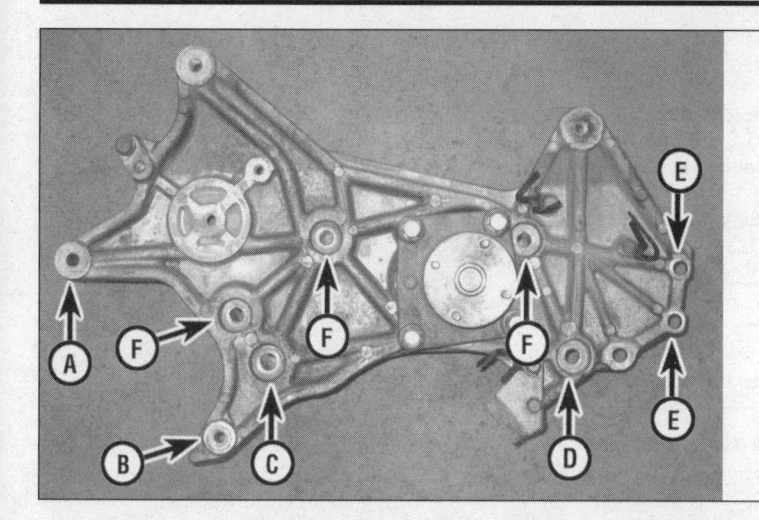

Chapter 3 Cooling, heating and air conditioning systems   3-5

8.24 On 2001 and later models remove the accessory mount attaching bolts (arrows) - the bolts are different lengths and thread pitches so make note of each bolt and its location

A Bolt size 10 x 106 mm, tightening torque 41+ 8 Nm
B Bolt size 8 x 30 mm, tightening torque 22 + 4 Nm
C Bolt size 12 x 100 mm, tightening torque 74 + 9 Nm
D Bolt size 10 x 100 mm, tightening torque 44+ 10 Nm
E Bolt size 10 x 30 mm, tightening torque 41+ 8 Nm
F Bolt size 10 x 100 mm, tightening torque 41+ 8 Nm

3 Disconnect and remove the lower radiator hose and heater hose.
4 Remove the drivebelts (see Chapter 1).
Note: *To remove the air conditioning belt, completely remove the adjustment bracket assembly.*
5 Remove the cooling fan and water pump pulley.
6 Remove the alternator bracket from the water pump (if required).
7 Remove the bolts and detach the water pump from the engine. Note the locations of the various lengths and different types of bolts as they're removed to ensure correct refitting.

Refitting

8 Clean the bolt threads and the threaded holes in the engine to remove corrosion and sealant.
9 Compare the new pump to the old one to make sure they're identical.
10 Remove all traces of old gasket material from the engine with a gasket scraper.
11 Clean the engine and new water pump mating surfaces with lacquer thinner or acetone.
12 On engines that use gaskets, apply a thin coat of RTV sealant to the engine side of the gasket and to the gasket mating surface of the new pump, then carefully mate the gasket and the pump. Slip a couple of bolts through the mounting holes to hold the gasket in place. On engines that use an O-ring instead of a gasket, apply no sealers or lubricants to the O-ring. Refit it dry.
13 Carefully attach the pump and gasket to the engine and thread the bolts into the holes finger tight. Note that on some engines the bolt on the left side of the pump (that attaches the alternator brace) is longer than the other bolts. Be sure to refit the bolt(s) with the correct length into the corresponding water pump holes.
14 Place the alternator bracket in position, refit the bolts and tighten all the bolts to the torque listed in this Chapter's Specifications in 1/4-turn increments. Don't overtighten them or the pump may be distorted.
15 Refit all parts removed for access to the pump.
16 Refill the cooling system and check the drivebelt tension (see Chapter 1). Run the engine and check for leaks.

Petrol engines

Caution: *If the stereo in your vehicle is equipped with an anti-theft system, make sure you have the correct activation code before disconnecting the battery.*

Removal

Refer to illustrations 8.24 and 8.28

Warning: *Wait until the engine is completely cool before beginning this procedure.*
17 Disconnect the negative battery cable from the battery.
18 Drain the cooling system (see Chapter 1). If the coolant is relatively new or in good condition, save it and reuse it.
19 Remove the radiator fan shroud (see Section 4).
20 Remove the drivebelts (see Chapter 1).
21 Remove the air conditioner tensioner pulley. On 2001 and later models, remove the front alternator mounting bolts (see Chapter 5) and tensioner assembly (see Chapter 1).
22 Remove the fan and fan clutch (see Section 5).
23 On 2001 and later models, remove the cooling fan bracket and pulley mount.
24 On 2001 and later models, loosen the air conditioning compressor mounting bolts and remove the accessory mount assembly mounting bolts **(see illustration)** then lift the assembly out. Mark the mounting bolts as they are removed - the bolts are different lengths and thread pitches.
25 Remove the crankshaft pulley (see Chapter 2A).
26 Remove the timing belt (see Chapter 2A).
27 Remove the lower radiator hose. If it's stuck, grasp it near the end with a pair of adjustable pliers and twist it to break the seal, then pull it off. If the hose is old or deteriorated, cut it off and fit a new one.
28 Remove the bolts and detach the water pump **(see illustration)**. Note the locations and various lengths and different types of bolts as they're removed to ensure correct refitting.

Refitting

Refer to illustration 8.33

29 Clean the bolt threads and the threaded holes in the engine to remove any corrosion and sealant.
30 Compare the new pump to the old one to make sure they're identical.

8.28 Typical water pump mounting bolt locations

3-6 Chapter 3 Cooling, heating and air conditioning systems

8.33 Fit a new O-ring in the groove at the front end of the coolant pipe (arrow) and lubricate the O-ring with coolant.

31 Remove all traces of old gasket material from the engine with a gasket scraper.
32 Clean the engine and new water pump mating surfaces with lacquer thinner or acetone.
33 Fit a new O-ring in the groove **(see illustration)** at the front end of the coolant pipe and lubricate the O-ring with coolant.
34 Apply a thin coat of RTV sealant to the engine side of the new gasket and to the gasket mating surface of the new pump, then carefully mate the gasket and the pump. Slip a couple of bolts through the pump mounting hole to hold the gasket in place.
35 Carefully attach the pump and gasket to the engine and thread the bolts into the holes finger tight. Be sure to refit the bolts with the correct length into the corresponding water pump holes.
36 Tighten all bolts to the torque listed in this Chapter's Specifications in 1/4-turn increments. Don't overtighten them or the pump may be distorted.
37 Refer to Chapter 2A for the refitting of the timing belt.
38 Refitting of all parts removed is the reverse of removal.
39 Refill the cooling system and check the drivebelt tension (see Chapter 1). Run the engine and check for leaks.

9 Coolant temperature gauge sender unit - check and renewal

Refer to illustration 9.1

Warning: *Wait until the engine is completely cool before beginning this procedure.*

1 The coolant temperature indicator system is composed of a light or temperature gauge mounted in the instrument panel and a coolant temperature sender unit mounted on the engine **(see illustration)**. Some vehicles have more than one sender unit, but only one is used for the indicator system.
2 If an overheating indication occurs, check the coolant level in the system and then make sure the wiring between the light or gauge and the sender unit is secure and all fuses are intact.
3 When the ignition switch is turned on and the starter motor is turning, the indicator light should be on (overheated engine indication).
4 If the light is not on, the bulb may be burned out, the ignition switch may be faulty or the circuit may be open. Test the circuit by connecting the sender unit wire to earth while the ignition is on (engine not running for safety). If the gauge deflects full scale or the light comes on, renew the sender unit.
5 As soon as the engine starts, the light should go out and remain out unless the engine overheats. Failure of the light to go out may be due to a shorted wire between the light and the sender unit, a defective sender unit or a faulty ignition switch. Check the coolant to make sure it's the proper type. Plain water may have too low a boiling point to activate the sender unit.
6 If the sender unit must be renewed, simply unscrew it from the engine and fit the new one. Use sealant on the threads. Make sure the engine is cool before removing the defective sender unit. There will be some coolant loss as the unit is removed, so be prepared to catch it. Check the level after the new one has been fitted.

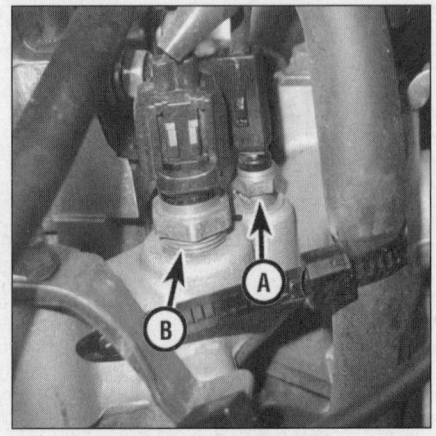

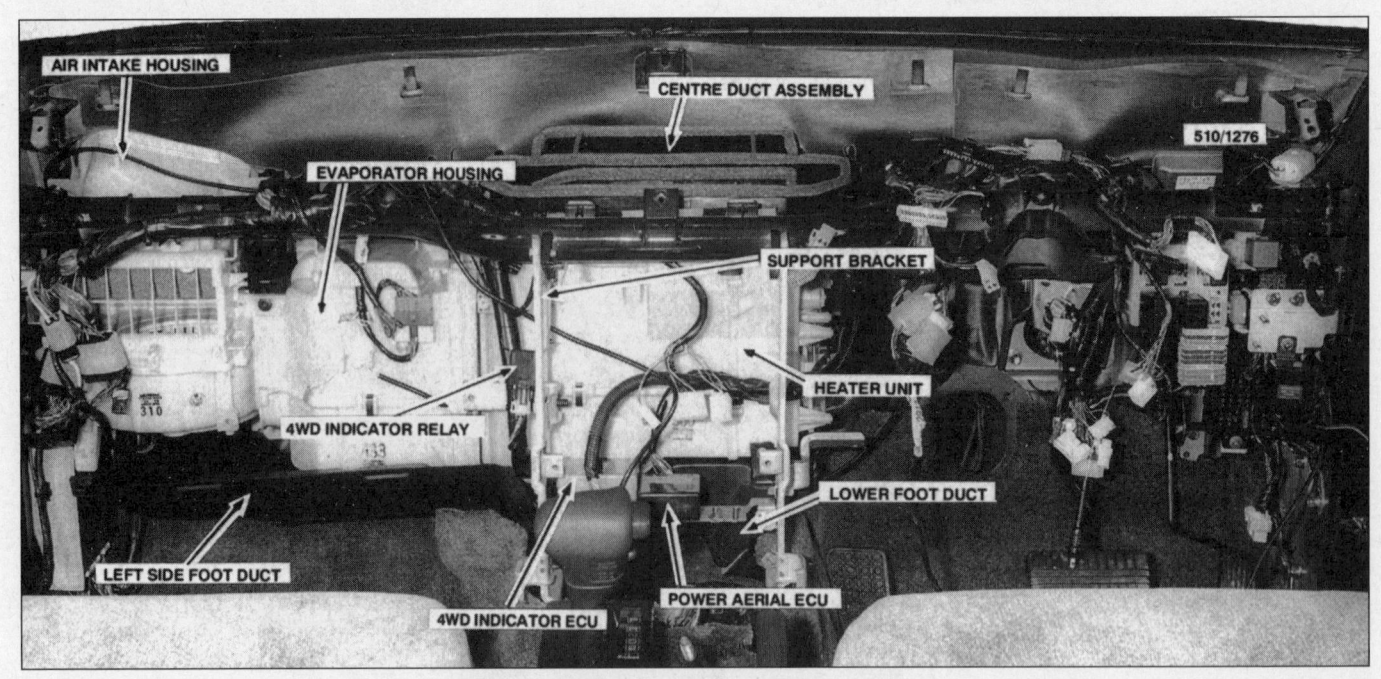

9.1 Typical location of the gauge coolant temperature sensor

A *Gauge coolant temperature sensor*
B *Engine temperature sensor (PCM)*

10.4 Typical heater system layout with air conditioning

Chapter 3 Cooling, heating and air conditioning systems

11.4 Disconnect the blower motor electrical connector (A) and the three retaining screws (arrows) - two of three screws shown

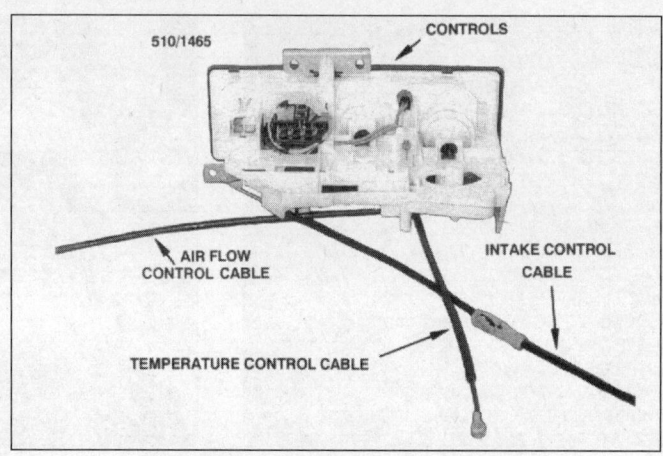

12.6 Typical heater control panel assembly

10 Heating system - general information

Refer to illustration 10.4

The main components of the heating system include the heater unit (which contains the heater core and cable-operated valves) the blower motor, the control assembly (mounted in the dash) and the air ducts which deliver the air to the various outlet locations.

Either outside air or interior (recirculated) air (depending on the settings) is drawn into the system through the blower unit. From there the blower motor forces the air into the heater unit.

The lever settings on the control assembly operate the valves in the heater unit, which determines the mix of heated and outside air by regulating how much air passes through the heater core. The hotter the setting the more air is passed through core.

The air ducts carry the heated air from the heater unit to the desired location **(see illustration)**. Again, valves within the duct system regulate where in the vehicle the air will be delivered.

The heater core is heated by engine coolant passing through it. The heater hoses carry the coolant from the engine to the heater core and then back again.

11 Blower motor - removal and refitting

Refer to illustration 11.4

Caution: *If the stereo in your vehicle is equipped with an anti-theft system, make sure you have the correct activation code before disconnecting the battery.*

1 Disconnect the negative battery terminal.
2 On 2000 and earlier models, remove the left hand side foot duct retaining screws and withdraw the foot duct.
3 Disconnect the wiring connector at the base of the fan motor.
4 Remove the three bolts attaching the motor to the heater assembly, unplug the electrical connectors, then lower the motor and fan **(see illustration)**.
5 Refitting is the reverse of removal.

12 Heater core - removal and refitting

Warning: *These models are equipped with airbags (Supplemental Restraint System [SRS]). The models are identified by the wording "SRS AIRBAG" on the steering wheel horn pad and instrument panel above the glovebox and the passenger's door (if equipped with a passenger's airbag). The airbag could accidentally deploy, causing serious injury and damage if any of the system wiring or components are disturbed. These components are located under the driver's seat, at the steering wheel, steering column and behind the dash. The yellow-covered wires connecting these locations must not be tampered with. Do not use test equipment on these wires. Refer to Chapter 12 for the disabling and enabling procedures.*

Warning: *The air conditioning system is under high pressure. DO NOT loosen any fittings or remove any components until after the system has been discharged. Air conditioning refrigerant should be properly discharged into an approved container at a dealership service department or an automotive air conditioning facility. Always wear eye protection when disconnecting air conditioning system fittings.*

Caution: *If the stereo in your vehicle is equipped with an anti-theft system, make sure you have the correct activation code before disconnecting the battery.*

Note: *The heater core removal procedure is extremely difficult. Attempt it only if you are certain that you have sufficient time and experience.*

All models

1 Disconnect the negative battery terminal.
2 Drain the cooling system (see Chapter 1).
3 Remove the centre console(s) (see Chapter 11).
4 Remove the centre trim panel (see Chapter 11).
5 Remove the instrument panel (see Chapter 11).

2000 and earlier models

Refer to illustrations 12.6 and 12.13

6 Disconnect the heater control cables **(see illustration)** at the heater assembly (not at the control assembly).
7 Remove the instrument panel (see Chapter 11).
8 Remove the main duct.
9 Remove the centre ventilator duct.
10 Remove the defroster duct.

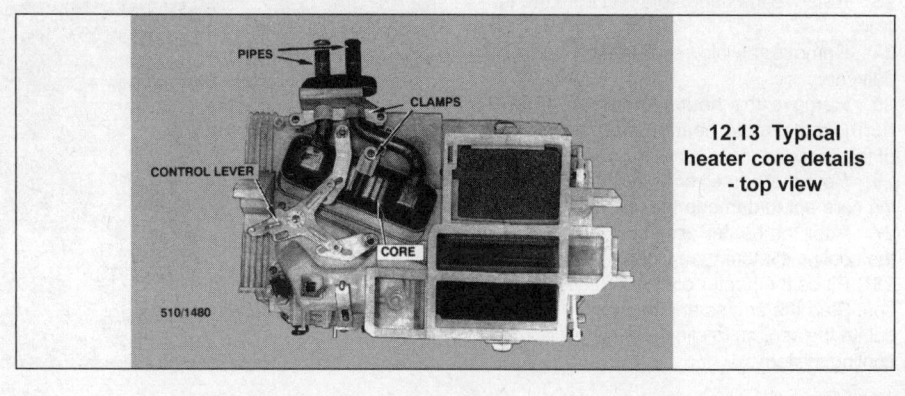

12.13 Typical heater core details - top view

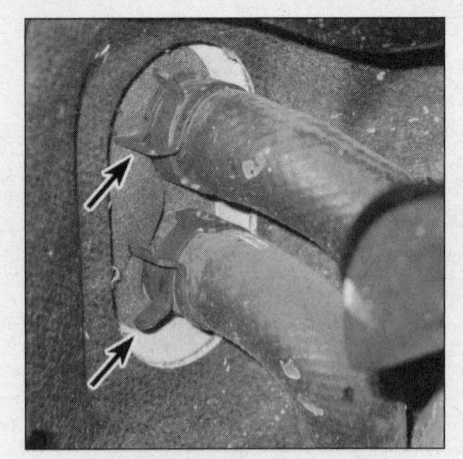

12.18 From inside the engine compartment disconnect the heater hose clamps (arrows) and cap the hoses

12.19 Remove the air conditioning lines mounting bolt (arrow) and remove the lines, then cap the lines.

12.21 Remove the foot ducts mounting screws (arrows) and remove the ducts - right side shown

11 Unbolt the centre reinforcements (four bolts at the bottom and four nuts at the top) and remove the heater unit.
12 If the heater unit is a split-type, remove the clips that hold the two halves of the heater unit together, then separate the halves and remove the heater core.
13 If the heater unit is not a split-type, remove the retaining bolt, control lever and remove the core from the case (see illustration).
14 Refitting is the reverse of removal.

2001 and later models

Refer to illustrations 12.18 12.19, 12.21 and 12.25

15 Have the air conditioning system discharged (see **Warning** above).
16 Remove the steering column (see Chapter 10).
17 Remove the drain hose.
18 From inside the engine compartment disconnect the heater hoses from the heater core and plug the hoses (see illustration).
19 Disconnect the air conditioning lines (see illustration) and cap the lines.
20 Disconnect the electrical connectors from the heater/evaporator case.
21 Remove the foot ducts (see illustration).
22 Remove the front deck crossmember assembly bolts and remove the crossmember.
23 Remove the flange bracket from the firewall.
24 Remove the blower assembly attaching bolts/nuts.
25 Remove the heater unit (see illustration). Remove the heater core from the side of the case.
26 Refit the heater core into the case, taking care not to damage the fins.
27 After the heater assembly is in place, fill the cooling system (see Chapter 1).
28 Place the heater control in the HOT position. Start the engine and allow it to run to circulate the coolant to eliminate any air from the cooling system.

29 Add coolant as the level drops. Once the level has stabilised, refit the radiator pressure cap and check for leaks.

13 Air conditioning system - general information

Warning: *The air conditioning system is under high pressure. Do not loosen any hose fittings or remove any components until after the system has been discharged by a service station or automotive air conditioning shop. Always wear eye protection when disconnecting air conditioning fittings.*

The air conditioning system used in these vehicles maintains proper temperature by cycling the compressor on and off according to the pressure within the system, and by maintaining a mix of cooled, outside and heated air, using the same blower, heater core and outlet duct system that the heating system uses.

A fast-idle control device regulates idle speed when the air conditioner is operating.

The main components of the system include a belt-driven compressor, a condenser (mounted in front of the radiator), a receiver/drier (2000 and earlier models) and an evaporator.

The system operates by air (outside or recirculated) entering the evaporator core by the action of the blower motor, where it receives cooling. When the air leaves the evaporator, it enters the heater/air conditioner duct assembly and, by means of a manually controlled deflector, either passes through or bypasses the heater core in the correct proportions to provide the desired vehicle temperature.

Distribution of this air into the vehicle is regulated by either a manually or electronically operated deflector, and is directed either to the floor vents, dash vents or defroster vents according to settings.

14 Air conditioning and heating system - check and maintenance

Refer to illustration 14.1

Warning: *The air conditioning system is under high pressure. Do not loosen any hose fittings or remove any components until after the system has been discharged by a dealer service department or service station. Always wear eye protection when disconnecting air conditioning system fittings.*

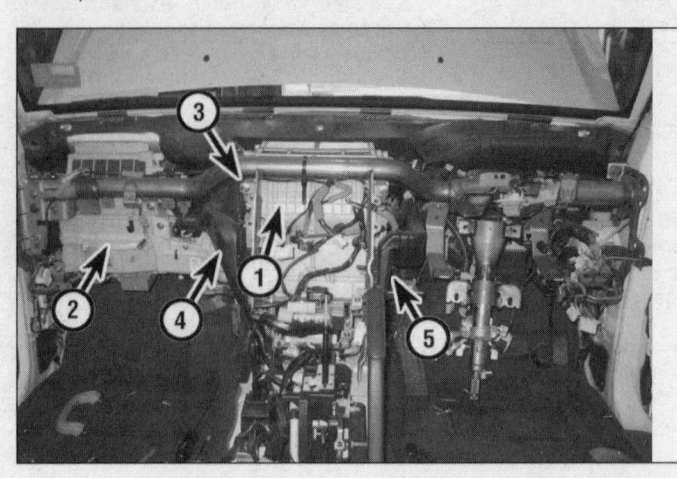

12.25 Typical later model heater/evaporator details

1 Heater/evaporator unit
2 Blower assembly
3 Front deck crossmember assembly
4 Foot duct (left)
5 Foot duct (right)

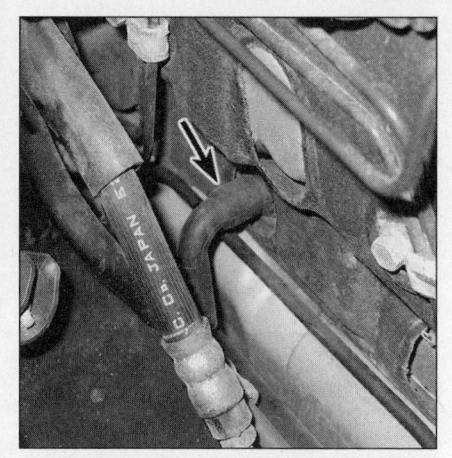

Chapter 3 Cooling, heating and air conditioning systems

14.1 Look for the evaporator drain hose on the firewall; to remove it for cleaning or for removing the evaporator, simply pull it off

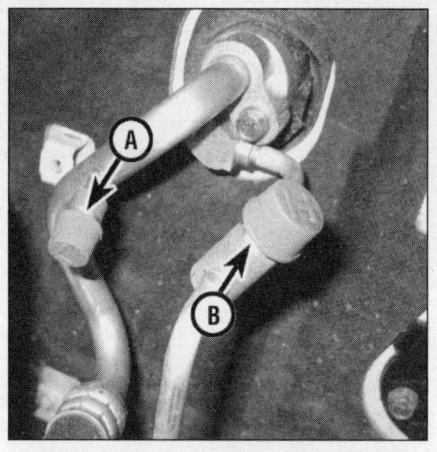

14.7a If the air conditioning system is properly charged, the low-pressure line (suction line) should feel cold and the high-pressure line (discharge line) should feel warm

A Low-pressure line (should feel cold)
B High-pressure line (should feel warm)

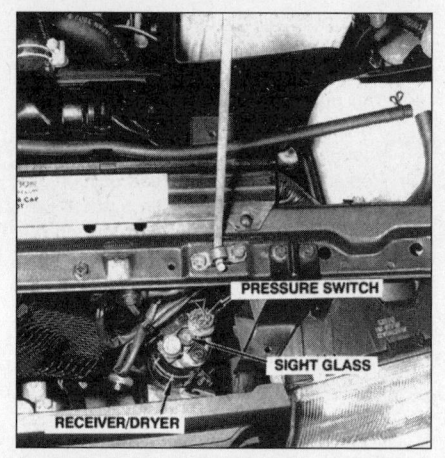

14.7b Watch the receiver/drier sight glass and see if it looks clear inside (which is normal) - if it's foamy inside, the system needs recharging

1 The following maintenance checks should be performed on a regular basis to ensure the air conditioner continues to operate at peak efficiency.
  a) Check the compressor drivebelt. If it's worn or deteriorated, replace it (see Chapter 1).
  b) Check the drivebelt tension and, if necessary, adjust it (see Chapter 1).
  c) Check the system hoses. Look for cracks, bubbles, hard spots and deterioration. Inspect the hoses and all fittings for oil bubbles and seepage. If there's any evidence of wear, damage or leaks, replace the hose(s).
  d) Inspect the condenser fins for leaves, bugs and other debris. Use a "fin comb" or compressed air to clean the condenser.
  e) Make sure the system has the correct refrigerant charge.
  f) Check the evaporator housing drain tube (see illustration) for blockage.

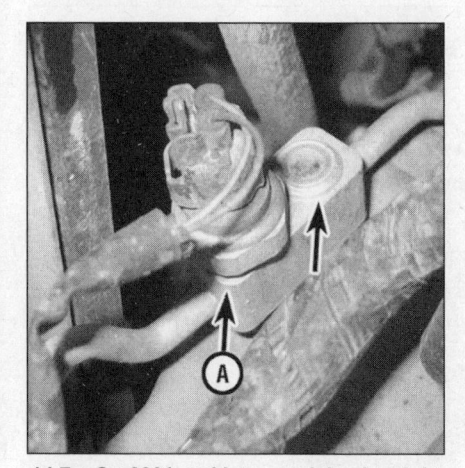

2 It's a good idea to operate the system for about 10 minutes at least once a month, particularly during the winter. Long term non-use can cause hardening, and subsequent failure, of the seals.
3 Because of the complexity of the air conditioning system and the special equipment necessary to service it, in-depth troubleshooting and repairs are not included in this manual (refer to the Haynes Automotive Heating and Air Conditioning Repair Manual). However, simple checks and component replacement procedures are provided in this Chapter.
4 The most common cause of poor cooling is simply a low system refrigerant charge. If a noticeable drop in cool air output occurs, the following quick check will help you determine if the refrigerant level is low.

Checking the refrigerant charge

Refer to illustrations 14.7a, 14.7b and 14.7c

5 Warm the engine up to normal operating temperature.
6 Place the air conditioning temperature selector at the coldest setting and the blower at the highest setting. Open the doors (to make sure the air conditioning system doesn't cycle off as soon as it cools the passenger compartment).
7 With the compressor engaged - the clutch will make an audible click and the center of the clutch will rotate - feel the lines going to and from the evaporator (see illustration). The high-pressure (small diameter) line should feel warm and the low-pressure (large diameter) line should feel cold. If so, the system is properly charged. Inspect the sight glass, if equipped, which is located on the receiver/drier (see illustration). If the refrigerant looks foamy, it's low. On 2001 and later models, there is no receiver/drier but there is

a sight glass (see illustration) located near the condenser in the liquid (high pressure) line.
8 Place a thermometer in the dashboard vent nearest the evaporator and operate the system until the indicated temperature is around 22 to 25-degrees C. If the ambient (outside) air temperature is very high, say 61-degrees C, the duct air temperature may be as high as 33-degrees C, but generally the air conditioning is 16 to 27-degrees C cooler than the ambient air (see illustration).

Note: *Humidity of the ambient air also affects the cooling capacity of the system. Higher ambient humidity lowers the effectiveness of the air conditioning system.*

Heating systems

9 If the carpet under the heater core is damp, or if antifreeze vapor or steam is coming through the vents, the heater core is leaking. Remove it (see Section 12) and install a new unit (most radiator shops will not repair a leaking heater core).

14.7c On 2001 and later models, the sight glass is located in the high pressure line near the condenser (arrow) and the dual pressure switch is mounted in the same block (A)

14.8 Insert a thermometer on the centre vent, turn on the air conditioning system and wait for it to cool down; depending on the humidity, the output air should 16 to 22-degrees cooler than the ambient air temperature

10 If the air coming out of the heater vents isn't hot, the problem could stem from any of the following causes:
  a) The thermostat is stuck open, preventing the engine coolant from warming up enough to carry heat to the heater core. Replace the thermostat (see Section 3).
  b) There is a blockage in the system, preventing the flow of coolant through the heater core. Feel both heater hoses at the firewall. They should be hot. If one of them is cold, there is an obstruction in one of the hoses or in the heater core, or the heater control valve is shut. Detach the hoses and back flush the heater core with a water hose. If the heater core is clear but circulation is impeded, remove the two hoses and flush them out with a water hose.
  c) If flushing fails to remove the blockage from the heater core, the core must be replaced (see Section 12).

Eliminating air conditioning odors

11 Unpleasant odors that often develop in air conditioning systems are caused by the growth of a fungus, usually on the surface of the evaporator core. The warm, humid environment there is a perfect breeding ground for mildew to develop.

12 The evaporator core on most vehicles is difficult to access, and factory dealerships have a lengthy, expensive process for eliminating the fungus by opening up the evaporator case and using a powerful disinfectant and rinse on the core until the fungus is gone. You can service your own system at home, but it takes something much stronger than basic household germ-killers or deodorizers.

13 Aerosol disinfectants for automotive air conditioning systems are available in most auto parts stores, but remember when shopping for them that the most effective treatments are also the most expensive. The basic procedure for using these sprays is to start by running the system in the RECIRC mode for ten minutes with the blower on its highest speed. Use the highest heat mode to dry out the system and keep the A/C switched Off.

14 Make sure that the disinfectant can comes with a long spray hose. Point the nozzle through the air recirculation door so that it protrudes inside the evaporator housing, and then spray according to the manufacturer's recommendations. Try to cover the whole surface of the evaporator core, by aiming the spray up, down and sideways. Follow the manufacturer's recommendations for the length of spray and waiting time between applications.

15 Once the evaporator has been cleaned, the best way to prevent the mildew from coming back again is to make sure your evaporator housing drain tube is clear (see illustration 14.1).

15 Air conditioning receiver/drier (2000 and earlier models) - removal and refitting

Warning: *The air conditioning system is under high pressure. DO NOT disassemble any part of the system (hoses, compressor, line fittings, etc.) until after the system has been depressurised by a dealer service department or service station.*

1 The receiver/drier, which acts as a reservoir for the refrigerant, is the canister-shaped object mounted either in the engine compartment or in front of the condenser (see illustration 14.7C).

2 Before removing the receiver/drier, the system must be discharged by an air conditioning technician (see **Warning** above). DO NOT attempt to do this yourself; the refrigerant used in the system can cause serious injuries and respiratory irritation.

3 Loosen the hose clamps and remove both hoses from the receiver/drier.

4 Loosen the clamp and pull up on the receiver/drier to remove it from its mount.

5 When refitting the receiver/drier, lubricate the inside surfaces of the hoses and the outside of the fittings with refrigerant oil. Be sure the hose clamps are properly located by the clamp finders and securely tightened.

6 Have the system evacuated, recharged and leak tested by the shop that discharged it.

16 Air conditioning compressor - removal and refitting

Warning: *The air conditioning system is under high pressure. DO NOT loosen any fittings or remove any components until after the system has been discharged. Air conditioning refrigerant should be properly discharged into an approved container at a dealership service department or an automotive air conditioning facility. Always wear eye protection when disconnecting air conditioning system fittings.*

Caution: *If the stereo in your vehicle is equipped with an anti-theft system, make sure you have the correct activation code before disconnecting the battery.*

1 Have the air conditioning system discharged (see **Warning** above).
2 Disconnect the negative battery cable from the battery.
3 Disconnect the compressor clutch wiring harness.
4 Remove the drivebelt (see Chapter 1).
5 Disconnect the refrigerant lines from the compressor. Plug the open fittings to prevent entry of dirt and moisture.
6 Unbolt the compressor from the mounting brackets and lift it out of the vehicle.
7 If a new compressor is being fitted, follow the directions with the compressor regarding the draining of excess oil prior to refitting.
8 The clutch may have to be transferred from the original to the new compressor.
9 Refitting is the reverse of removal. Renew all O-rings with new ones specifically made for air conditioning system use and lubricate them with refrigerant oil.
10 Have the system evacuated, recharged and leak tested by the shop that discharged it.

17 Air conditioning condenser - removal and refitting

Warning: *The air conditioning system is under high pressure. DO NOT disassemble any part of the system (hoses, compressor, line fittings, etc.) until after the system has been depressurised by a dealer service department or service station.*

1 Have the air conditioning system discharged (see **Warning** above).
2 Remove the battery (see Chapter 5).

19.8 Remove the control head mounting screws (arrows) and remove the head - 2000 and earlier model shown

Chapter 3 Cooling, heating and air conditioning systems

3 Drain the cooling system (see Chapter 1).
4 Remove the radiator (see Section 4).
5 Disconnect the refrigerant lines from the condenser.
6 Remove the mounting bolts from the condenser brackets.
7 Lift the condenser out of the vehicle and plug the lines to keep dirt and moisture out.
8 If the original condenser will be refitted, store it with the line fittings on top to prevent oil from draining out.
9 If a new condenser is being fitted, pour a small amount of refrigerant oil into it prior to refitting.
10 Refit the components in the reverse order of removal. Be sure the rubber pads are in place under the condenser.
11 Have the system evacuated, recharged and leak tested by the shop that discharged it.

18 Air conditioning evaporator - removal and refitting

Warning: *These models are equipped with airbags (Supplemental Restraint System [SRS]). The models are identified by the wording "SRS AIRBAG" on the steering wheel horn pad and instrument panel above the glovebox and the passenger's door (if equipped with a passenger's airbag). The airbag could accidentally deploy, causing serious injury and damage if any of the system wiring or components are disturbed. These components are located under the driver's seat, at the steering wheel, steering column and behind the dash. The yellow-covered wires connecting these locations must not be tampered with. Do not use test equipment on these wires. Refer to Chapter 12 for the disabling and enabling procedures.*

Warning: *The air conditioning system is under high pressure. DO NOT loosen any fittings or remove any components until after the system has been discharged. Air conditioning refrigerant should be properly discharged into an approved container at a dealership service department or an automotive air conditioning facility. Always wear eye protection when disconnecting air conditioning system fittings.*

Caution: *If the stereo in your vehicle is equipped with an anti-theft system, make sure you have the correct activation code before disconnecting the battery.*

Note: *The evaporator core removal procedure is extremely difficult. Attempt it only if you are certain that you have sufficient time and experience.*

1 The air conditioner evaporator is combined with the heater assembly and is mounted under the vehicle dashboard (see Section 12).
2 Before removing the evaporator, the system must be depressurised by an air conditioning technician. DO NOT attempt to do this yourself; the refrigerant used in the system can cause serious injuries and respiratory irritation.
3 Remove the glove box (see Chapter 11).
4 Loosen the hose clamps and remove the hoses from the evaporator fittings inside the engine compartment.
5 Disconnect the control cable from the damper lever at the right side of the evaporator.
6 Slide back the hose clamp and remove the drain hose from the spigot at the rear of the evaporator.
7 Peel off the sealing compound around the evaporator inlet and outlet tubes at the vehicle fire wall.
8 Remove the bolts attaching the evaporator to the dashboard and firewall and carefully move it down and out from the dashboard. Do not misplace the plastic duct that fits between the heater assembly and the evaporator.
9 Use a flat-bladed screwdriver to remove the clips from the evaporator housing and remove the evaporator.
10 Refitting is the reverse of removal. Be sure to position the plastic ducts before slipping the evaporator into place. When refitting the hoses, lubricate their surfaces and the outside of the fittings with refrigerant oil. The hoses must be positioned properly with the clamp finders and tightened securely. Do not forget to fit the drain hose and the sealing compound.
11 Have the system evacuated and recharged by the shop that discharged it.

19 Heater/air conditioning control assembly - removal and refitting

Caution: *If the stereo in your vehicle is equipped with an anti-theft system, make sure you have the correct activation code before disconnecting the battery.*

1 Disconnect the negative battery terminal.

NJ, NK, NL models

Refer to illustration 19.8

2 Open the glove compartment and prise the limit arms from the compartment lid. Allow the compartment to rest in the open position.
3 Mark the air intake control cable in relation to the retaining clip and disconnect the air intake housing **(see illustration 12.6)**.
4 Mark the temperature control cable in relation to the retaining clip and disconnect the cable from the left hand side of the heater unit.
5 Remove the lower dashboard panel (see Chapter 11).

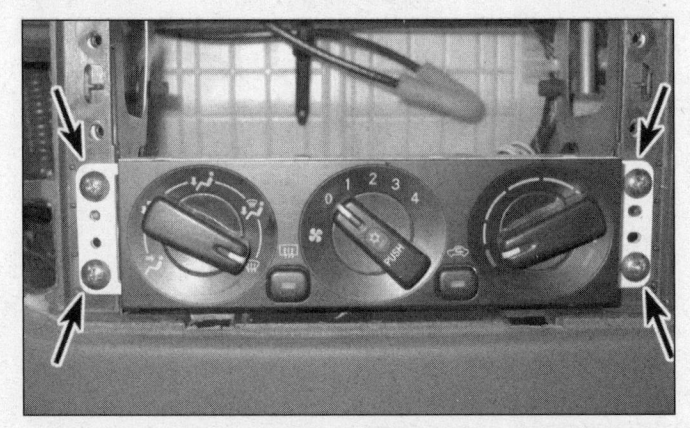

19.11 Remove the control head mounting screws (arrows) and pull the head forward from the dash

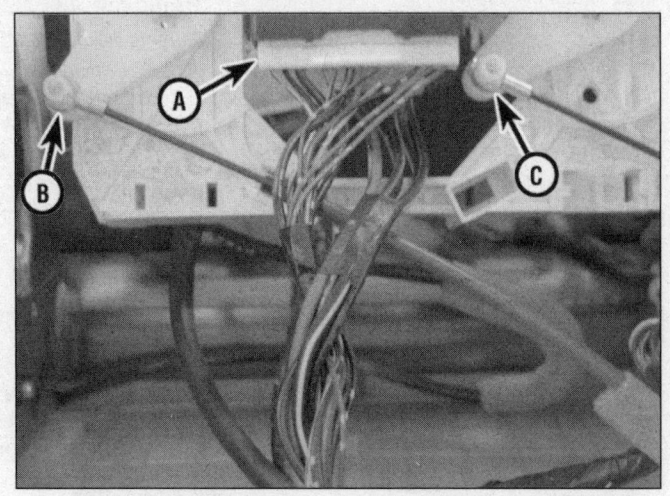

19.12 From underneath of the control head use a small pocket screwdriver to disconnect the cable and electrical connector

A Electrical connector
B Air outlet change over damper cable
C Air mix damper cable

Chapter 3 Cooling, heating and air conditioning systems

19.16a Removing the RH centre vent - pry from the sound system side to prevent breaking the vent

19.16b Once the majority of the clips are released, remove the vent, disconnecting any wiring

6 Mark the air flow cable in relation to the retaining clip and disconnect the cable from the right hand side of the heater unit.

7 Remove the radio trim panel and radio (see Chapter 12).

Note: Remove the radio only if more room is needed to remove the control head.

8 Remove the heater/air conditioning control head mounting screws and remove the assembly from the vehicle **(see illustration)**.

NM and NP models

Refer to illustrations 19.11 and 19.12

9 Remove the centre console (see Chapter 11).

10 Remove the centre trim panel (see Chapter 11).

11 Remove the control head mounting screws **(see illustration)** and pull the head forward.

12 From the underside of the control head **(see illustration)** disconnect the electrical harness and the cables.

13 Remove the control head from the dash.

14 Minor repairs, such as cleaning and lubrication of the pivots and cables, can be performed on the heater control assembly. But it would be a good idea to renew it if it is not operating properly.

15 Refitting is the reverse of the removal.

Remember to plug in the electrical connectors before refitting the instrument cluster trim panel.

NS, NT and NW models

Refer to illustrations 19.16a, 19.16b and 19.17

16 Using a trim tool, remove the centre vent assemblies **(see illustrations)**. When removing the driver side, disconnect the hazard lamp switch from the rear of the vent.

17 Grasp the bottom edge of the control assembly and pull from the dashboard **(see illustration)**.

18 Working at the rear of the controls, disconnect the wiring.

20 Oil cooler - removal and refitting

Petrol engines

Removal

Refer to illustration 20.4

1 The remote-mounted oil cooler is secured in front of the radiator and behind the grille on all other models.

2 Remove the skid plate and lower covers (see Chapter 10).

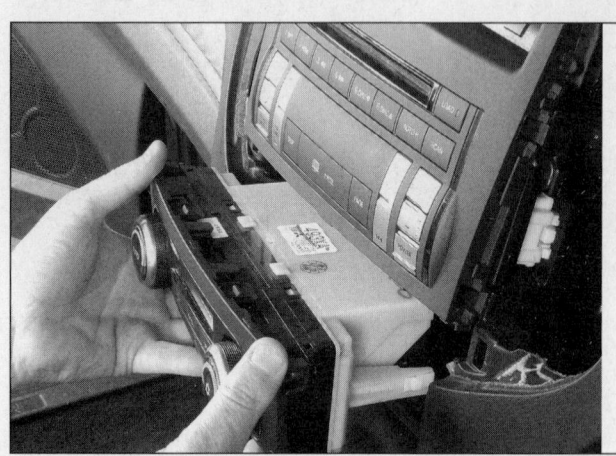

19.17 The ventilation system control assembly is retained by four clips

3 Place some rags beneath the oil cooler to catch spills.

4 Disconnect the cooler lines from the oil cooler assembly **(see illustration)**. If replacing a cooler line, disconnect the banjo bolt which attaches the oil cooler line to the oil cooler. Remove the sealing washers from each fitting.

5 Unbolt the oil cooler from the mounting brackets and lift it from the vehicle.

Refitting

6 Bolt the oil cooler to the mounting brackets.

7 Renew all the sealing washers on the oil line(s). Attach the line(s) to the cooler with the banjo bolt(s).

Note: There are marks on the ends of the lines which must face upward.

8 The remainder of the refitting is the reverse of removal.

Diesel engines

Removal

9 Remove any interfering engine compartment components.

10 Place rags beneath the oil cooler. Remove the oil filter (refer to Chapter 1).

11 Remove the bolts securing the oil cooler housing to the side of the engine.

12 Remove the nuts securing the cooler element to the oil cooler housing.

13 Remove the regulator and bypass plugs from the housing. Remove the washer, spring and plunger from the bore beneath each plug. Lay all of the components neatly in order so they can be returned to the same positions after they are inspected. Remove the water drain plug.

14 Inspect the cooler element for signs of damage and sludge. It can be cleaned, if required, using solvent.

15 Check the bypass and regulator components for wear and damage. Renew parts as required.

16 Thoroughly clean the housing and the side of the engine block.

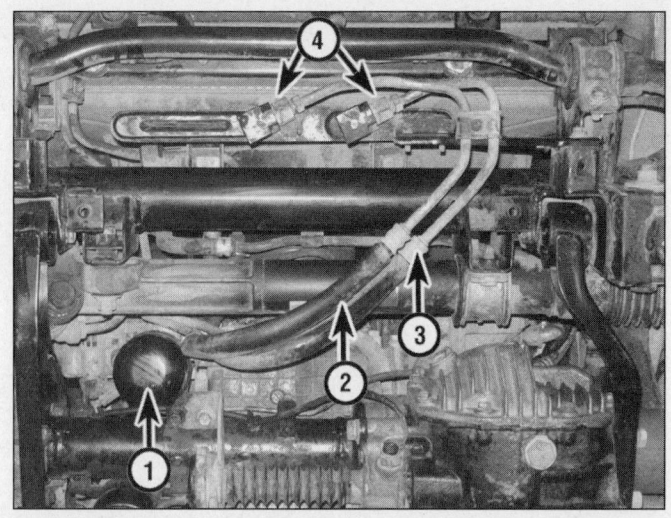

Chapter 3 Cooling, heating and air conditioning systems

20.4 Disconnect the oil cooler connectors from the oil cooler and remove the mounting bolts and cooler from the vehicle

1 Oil filter
2 Oil cooler return hose
3 Oil cooler feed hose
4 Oil cooler hose connectors

21.2 Remove the condenser fan mounting bolts (arrows) and remove the fan

Refitting

17 Renew all gaskets, O-rings and washers. Lubricate the O-rings with oil and refit the three on the engine block.
18 Assemble the oil cooler element to the cooler housing using new gaskets and O-rings.
19 Refit the three plugs in the cooler with their internal components using new washers.
20 Fill the oil filter with fresh engine oil before installing it. The remainder of the refitting is the reverse of removal.

21 Air conditioning condenser fan - removal and refitting

Refer to illustration 21.2

1 Remove the grille (see Chapter 11).
2 Remove the mounting bolts **(see illustration)** and pull the fan assembly forward.
3 Disconnect the electrical connector to the fan and remove the fan from the vehicle.
4 Refitting is the reverse of the removal.

Notes

Chapter 4
Fuel and exhaust systems

Contents

	Section
Accelerator cable - renewal and adjustment	9
Accelerator linkage check and lubrication	See Chapter 1
Air cleaner assembly - removal and refitting	8
Coolant temperature sensor (diesel) - check and renewal	26
Diesel fuel injection pump - removal and refitting	18
Diesel fuel injection pump timing adjustment	19
Exhaust system servicing - general information	31
Fuel cut solenoid - check and renewal	21
Fuel filter renewal	See Chapter 1
Fuel gauge sender unit (all models) - removal and refitting	5
Fuel hoses - renewal	10
Fuel injection system - check	12
Fuel injector(s) - check, removal and refitting	16
Fuel injector(s) (diesel) - removal and refitting	20
Fuel pressure regulator - removal and refitting	17
Fuel pressure relief procedure (petrol models)	2
Fuel pump - removal and refitting	4
Fuel pump/fuel pressure - check	3

	Section
Fuel rail assembly - removal and refitting	15
Fuel system check	See Chapter 1
Fuel tank cleaning and repair - general information	7
Fuel tank - removal and refitting	6
General information	1
Glow plug control unit - check and renewal	25
Glow plug relay - check and renewal	24
Glow plug(s) - check and renewal	23
Idle Speed Control (ISC) servo - check and renewal	14
Intercooler - removal and refitting	30
Multi-Point Injection (MPI) - general information	11
Preheat system - general information	22
Suction control valve - replacement	32
Throttle body mounting bolt torque check	See Chapter 1
Throttle body - removal and refitting	13
Turbocharger and intercooler - general information	27
Turbocharger - check	28
Turbocharger - removal and refitting	29

Specifications

Accelerator cable freeplay
Diesel engines	1 mm
Petrol engines	1 to 2 mm

Fuel pressure
Fuel-injected petrol models
Vacuum hose connected to pressure regulator	265 kPa at curb idle
Vacuum hose disconnected from regulator	324 to 343 kPa at curb idle

Fuel injector (petrol) resistance
NM and NP models	13 to 16 ohms
NS and NT models	10.5 to 13.5 ohms
Fuel injector (late 4M41 diesel) resistance	Approximately 0.45 ohms

Idle speed
Idle speed
    2.8L diesel engine
        NL .... 800 ± 50 rpm
        NM .... 750 ± 100 rpm
    3.2L diesel engine
        NM .... 750 ± 20 rpm
        Except NM
            Automatic transmission .... 700 ± 30 rpm
            Manual transmission .... 740 ± 30 rpm
        Except NM
            Automatic transmission .... 700 ± 30 rpm
            Manual transmission .... 740 ± 30 rpm
    V6 petrol engines .... 700 ± 100 rpm
Idle Speed Control (ISC) servo coil resistance .... 28 to 33 ohms @ 20-degrees C

Diesel injection pump adjustment
2.8L engines (4M40) .... 9-degrees ATDC
    Plunger stroke reading .... 0.97 to 1.03 mm
3.2L engines (NM and NP 4M41 models) .... 4-degrees BTDC

Diesel fuel cut solenoid resistance
2.8L engines (4M40) .... 8 to 10 ohms
3.2L engines (NM and NP 4M41 models) .... 6.8 to 9.2 ohms

Glow plug resistance (at room temperature)
2.8L engines (4M40) .... 0.6 ohms
3.2L engines
    NM and NP (4M41) models .... 1.1 ohms
    NS, NT and NW (4M41) models .... 0.5 to 1.5 ohms

Glow plug relay resistance
Except NS, NT and NW (4M41) models .... 3 ohms
NS, NT and NW (4M41) models .... 18 to 22 ohms

Diesel coolant temperature sensor resistance
NM and NP (4M41) models
    At 20-degrees C .... 2.3 to 2.6 K ohms
    At 80-degrees C .... 0.30 to 0.34 K ohms

NS, NT and NW (4M41) models
    At 20-degrees C .... 2.1 to 2.7 K ohms
    At 80-degrees C .... 0.26 to 0.36 K ohms

Turbocharger wastegate operating pressure
2.8L engines (4M40) .... 96 kPa
3.2L engines NM and NP (4M41) models .... 161 kPa
3.2L engines (4M41)
    NS models
        Automatic .... 177.3 to 195.9 kPa
        Manual .... 178.9 to 188.2 kPa
    NT models .... 177.3 to 195.9 kPa
    NW models .... 198.7 to 228.0 kPa
Wastegate begins to open (1-mm) at
    NS models .... 118.8 to 124.2 kPa
    NT models .... 46.2 to 50.0 kPa
    NW models .... 119 to 124 kPa

Chapter 4 Fuel and exhaust systems

Torque specifications

	Nm
Air intake plenum mounting bolts	
Petrol	
Except 3.8L	16 to 20
3.8L	21 to 23
Diesel	
2.8L	18
3.2L	
NM and NP models	44
NS and NT models	17
NW models	24
Diesel fuel injectors	
2.8L (4M40) engines	50 to 58
3.2L (4M41) engines	
Except NW models	
Step 1	10
Step 2	Tighten an additional 80°
NW models	
Step 1	12
Step 2	Tighten an additional 90°
Step 3	Tighten an additional 95°
Diesel fuel injection pump-to-engine	
2.8L (4M40) engines	19
3.2L NS, NT, NW (4M41) models	24
Diesel fuel injection pump sprocket nut	59 to 69
Diesel fuel return nuts-to-injectors	
2.8L (4M40) engines	31
3.2L NS and NT (4M41) models	15
Electric fuel pump flange nuts	3
Exhaust manifold bolts	31
Exhaust pipe-to-manifold nuts	
Except NW diesel	49
NW diesel	41
Fuel high-pressure hose attaching bolts	5
Fuel leak off pipe (3.2L engines NM and NP (4M41) models)	11 to 15
Glow plugs	
NL to NP models	
Step 1	10
Step 2	Tighten an additional 30°
NS to NW models	
Step 1	10
Step 2	Tighten an additional 30°
Step 3	Tighten an additional 40°
Glow plug nuts	
NL to NP models	1.3
NS to NW models	1.8
Throttle body bolts	
Petrol	
NL to NP models	10 to 14
NS to NW models	7 to 12
Diesel	11 to 15
Turbocharger mounting nuts	
NL to NP models	49 to 53
NS to NW models	49 to 69

1 General information, precautions and diesel fuel system cleaning

Diesel fuel system

Refer to illustration 1.1

The fuel system is comprised of a fuel tank, a fuel injection pump, an engine compartment-mounted fuel filter, fuel supply and return lines and four fuel injectors (see illustration).

2.8L (4M40) diesel engine

The fuel system consists of a rotary injection pump which supplies fuel to the injectors at a specified pressure but at a volume dependent upon engine load.

The volume injected is controlled by a variable speed mechanical governor which alters the discharge volume of the pumping plunger.

The system uses indirect injection, where fuel is sprayed into a precombustion chamber.

The injectors which screw into the cylinder head, are a pintle nozzle type. The conical shape of the bottom of the pintle needle forms the spray pattern.

The basic injection timing is set by the position of the injection pump on the engine. When the engine is running, the pump is advanced and retarded by the pump itself. It is influenced primarily by the accelerator position and engine speed.

3.2L (4M41) diesel engine

The fuel system consists of an electronically controlled injection pump which supplies fuel to the injectors at a specified pressure. On NM and NP models, there are two control units utilized in this system. The first is integral with the pump, and controls the fuel amount and pressure by a control sleeve, rotor spill ports and set of plungers that distributes the fuel under very high pressure. The second is the Engine Control Module or Powertrain Control Module (ECM/PCM) located behind the dashboard which provides the main control through various sensors on the engine.

On NS, NT and NW models, injection is controlled by electronically controlled injectors. Fuel is supplied to the injectors at a constant pressure via a fuel manifold (common rail) on the side of the engine. The ECM will energise a solenoid within each injector which then injects a specified amount of fuel into the engine. The amount of time the injector is energised will determine how much fuel is injected into the engine.

The injection pump is lubricated by the fuel it's pumping. This system is designed to allow the engine to run quietly and efficiently, while at the same time producing more power and less emissions than would be possible with a mechanical system.

The injectors are of the pintle nozzle type, which are installed to the cylinder head

1.1 Typical early 2.8L (4M40) diesel fuel system

1. Injection pump
2. Fuel cut solenoid
3. Injector delivery line
4. Injector
5. Glow plug and bridging strap

and spray fuel into the combustion chamber in the cylinder head. This is termed direct injection. The large hole in the pintle nozzle is not susceptible to blockage and the conical shape of the bottom of the pintle needle forms the spray pattern

The pump timing and idle speed is not adjustable and is completely computer controlled.

Both engines are equipped with a turbocharger and an intercooler to improve power.

The engines are stopped by means of a fuel cut solenoid which interrupts the flow of fuel to the injection pump when it is de-energized on early models, or by the computer not energising the injectors, on late models.

Petrol fuel system

The fuel system consists of the fuel tank, an electric fuel pump, an air cleaner, a fuel injection system and the hoses and lines which connect these components.

All models are fuel-injected. A multi-point (one injector per cylinder) Electronic Fuel Injection (EFI) system is used. All models use an in-tank electric fuel pump. For more information regarding the EFI system, refer to Section 11.

Precautions

Many of the operations described in this Chapter involve the disconnection of fuel lines which may cause fuel to leak. Before commencing work, refer to the **Warnings** and **Cautions** given below and the information in *Safety first* at the beginning of this manual.

Warning: *Fuel is flammable, so take extra precautions when you work on any part of the fuel system. Don't smoke or allow open flames or bare light bulbs near the work area. Don't work in a garage where a gas appliance such as a water heater or a clothes dryer is present. Since diesel fuel is carcinogenic, wear latex gloves when there is a possibility of being exposed to fuel. If you spill fuel on your skin, rinse it immediately with soap and water. Mop up any spills immediately and do not store fuel-soaked rags where they could ignite. When you perform any work on the fuel system, wear safety glasses and keep a Class B type fire extinguisher on hand.*

Warning: *Diesel fuel injectors operate at extremely high pressures and the jet of fuel produced at the nozzle is capable of piercing the skin with potentially fatal results. Never work with pressurized injectors - any pressure testing of the fuel system must be done by a diesel fuel systems specialist.*

Caution: *Under no circumstance should fuel be allowed to come in contact with coolant hoses - wipe off accidental spillage immediately. Hoses that have been contaminated with fuel for an extended period should be renewed. Diesel fuel systems are particularly sensitive to contamination from dirt, air and water. Pay particular attention to cleanliness when working on any part of the fuel system to prevent the entry of dirt. Thoroughly clean the area around fuel fittings before disconnecting them. Store dismantled components in sealed containers to prevent contamination and the formation of condensation. Use only lint-free rags and clean fuel for cleaning. Avoid using compressed air when cleaning components in place.*

Diesel fuel contamination

Before you renew an injection pump or some other expensive component, find out what caused the failure. If water contamination is present, buying a new pump or other component won't do much good. The following procedure will help you pinpoint whether water contamination is present:

a) Remove the fuel filter and inspect the contents for the presence of water or petrol (see Chapter 1).

b) If the vehicle has been stalling, performance has been poor or the engine has been knocking loudly, suspect fuel contamination. Petrol or water must be removed by flushing (see below).

c) If you find a lot of water in the fuel filter, remove the injection pump fuel return line and check for water there. If the pump has water in it, flush the system.

Chapter 4 Fuel and exhaust systems

d) Small quantities of surface rust won't create a problem. If contamination is excessive, the vehicle will probably stall.
e) Sometimes, contamination in the system becomes severe enough to cause damage to the internal parts in the pump. If the damage reaches this stage, have the damaged parts renewed and the pump rebuilt by an authorised fuel injection shop or buy a rebuilt pump.

Diesel fuel storage

Good quality diesel fuel contains inhibitors to stop the formation of rust in the fuel lines and the injectors. So long as there are no leaks in the fuel system, it is generally safe from water contamination. Diesel fuel is usually contaminated from water as a result of careless storage. There is little you can do about the storage practices of service stations where you buy diesel fuel, but if you keep a small supply of diesel fuel on hand at home, as many diesel owners do, follow these simple rules:

a) Diesel fuel ages and goes stale. Don't store containers of diesel fuel for long periods of time. Use it up regularly and replace it with fresh fuel.
b) Keep fuel storage containers out of direct sunlight. Variations in heat and humidity promote condensation inside fuel containers.
c) Don't store diesel fuel in galvanized containers. It may cause the galvanizing to flake off, contaminating the fuel and clogging filters when the fuel is used.
d) Label containers properly as containing diesel fuel.

Fighting fungi and bacteria in diesel fuel with biocides

If there is water in the fuel, fungi and/or bacteria can form in diesel fuel in warm or humid weather. Fungi and bacteria plug fuel lines, fuel filters and injection nozzles; they can also cause corrosion in the fuel system.

If you've had problems with water in the fuel system and you live in a warm and humid climate, have your dealer correct the problem. Then use a diesel fuel biocide to sterilize the fuel system in accordance with the manufacturer's instructions. Biocides are available from your dealer, service stations and auto parts stores. Consult your dealer for advice on using biocides in your area and for recommendations on which ones to use.

Cleaning the diesel fuel system

Water in the diesel fuel system

1 Disconnect the negative battery cable. Position it so that it cannot contact the positive cable.
2 Drain the fuel tank into an approved container and dispose of it properly.
3 Remove the fuel sender unit (see Section 5).
4 Thoroughly clean the fuel tank. If it is rusted inside, send it to a repair shop or renew it. Clean or renew the fuel pick-up screen in the fuel tank.
5 Reinstall the fuel tank but do not connect the fuel lines to it yet.
6 Remove the fuel filter (see Chapter 1).
7 Temporarily disconnect the fuel return line at the injection pump and again, using low air pressure, blow out the lines toward the rear of the vehicle.
8 Reconnect the main fuel and return lines at the tank. Fill the tank to a fourth of its capacity. Refit the cap.
9 Discard the fuel filter.
10 Connect the fuel line to the fuel filter housing.
11 Reconnect the battery cable.
12 Purge the fuel supply line by pressing the priming pump on top of the filter housing until clean fuel is flowing from the filter housing. Catch the fuel in a closed metal container.
13 Fit a new fuel filter.
14 Refit a hose from the fuel return line (from the injection pump) to a closed metal container with a capacity of at least eight litres.
15 Crank the engine until clear fuel appears at the return line. Don't crank the engine for more than 30 seconds at a time. If it is necessary to crank it again, allow a three minute interval before resuming.
16 Crank the engine until clear fuel appears at each nozzle. Don't crank the engine for more than 30 seconds at a time. If it is necessary to crank it again, allow a three minute interval before resuming. If the engine catches and starts, tighten the injector pipes at the injectors and allow the engine to run.

Petrol in the diesel fuel system

Warning: *Diesel fuel is flammable, so take extra precautions when you work on any part of the fuel system. Don't smoke or allow open flames or bare light bulbs near the work area. Don't work in a garage where a gas appliance such as a water heater or a clothes dryer is present. Since diesel fuel is carcinogenic, wear latex gloves when there is a possibility of being exposed to fuel. If you spill fuel on your skin, rinse it immediately with soap and water. Mop up any spills immediately and do not store fuel-soaked rags where they could ignite. When you perform any work on the fuel system, wear safety glasses and keep a Class B type fire extinguisher on hand.*

If petrol has been accidentally pumped into the fuel tank, it should be drained immediately. Petrol in the fuel in small amounts, up to 30 percent, isn't usually noticeable. At higher ratios, the engine may make a knocking noise which will get louder as the ratio of petrol increases. Here is how to rid the fuel system of petrol:

17 Drain the fuel tank into an approved container and fill the tank with clean, fresh diesel fuel.
18 Detach the fuel line between the fuel filter and the injection pump.
19 Connect a short pipe and hose to the fuel filter outlet and run it to a closed metal container.
20 Crank the engine to purge petrol out of the fuel pump and fuel filter. Do not crank the engine for more than 30 seconds at a time. Allow three minutes between interval to allow the starter to cool.
21 Remove the pipe and hose and refit the fuel line previously removed.
22 Try to start the engine. If it doesn't start, purge the injection pump and lines: Crack the fuel line fittings open a little, just enough for fuel to leak out. Depress the accelerator pedal to the floor and, holding it there, crank the engine until all petrol is removed, i.e. diesel fuel leaks from the fittings. Tighten the fittings. Limit cranking to 30 seconds with three minute intervals between cranking.

Warning: *Avoid sources of ignition and have a fire extinguisher nearby.*

2.1 Disconnect the fuel pump relay from the engine compartment relay box

1 Engine control relay
2 Fuel pump relay
3 Valve relay

4-6   Chapter 4 Fuel and exhaust systems

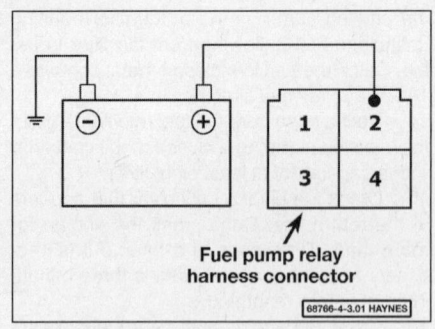

3.1 Apply battery voltage to the fuel pump relay harness connector terminal No.2

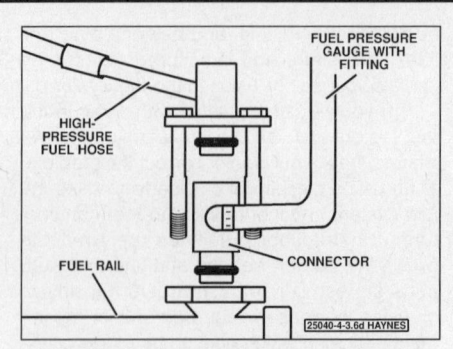

3.4b The fuel pressure gauge and gauge connector mount between the fuel rail and high pressure fuel line - note that the kit also contains extra long bolts to attach the connector to the fuel rail

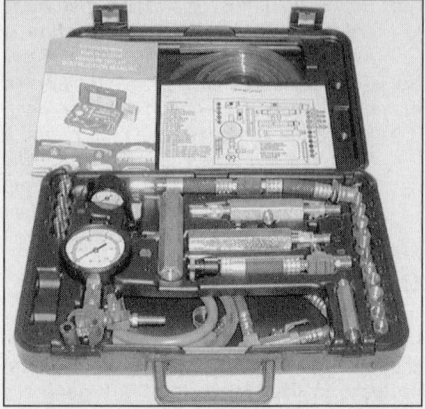

3.4a This aftermarket fuel pressure testing kit contains all the necessary fittings and adapters, along with the fuel pressure gauge, to test most automotive fuel systems

23   Start the engine and run it at idle for fifteen minutes.

Exhaust system

The exhaust system consists of the exhaust manifold(s), exhaust pipes, catalytic converter and muffler. For information regarding the removal and refitting of the exhaust manifold(s), refer to Chapters 2A, 2B or 2C. For information regarding exhaust system and catalytic converter servicing, refer to the last Section in this Chapter. For further information regarding the catalytic converter, refer to Chapter 6.

2 Fuel pressure relief procedure (petrol models)

Refer to illustration 2.1

Caution: *If the stereo in your vehicle is equipped with an anti-theft system, make sure you have the correct activation code before disconnecting the battery.*

1   Disconnect the fuel pump relay from the relay box in the engine compartment **(see illustration)**.
2   Start the engine, let it run until it stalls and turn off the ignition switch.
3   Detach the cable from the negative terminal of the battery and re-connect it after repairs are complete.

3 Fuel pump/fuel pressure (petrol models) - check

Warning: *Petrol is extremely flammable, so take extra precautions when you work on any part of the fuel system. Don't smoke or allow open flames or bare light bulbs near the work area, and don't work in a garage where a gas-type appliance (such as a water heater or clothes drier) is present. If you spill any fuel on your skin, rinse it off immediately with soap and water. When you perform any kind of work on the fuel system, wear safety glasses and have a Class B type fire extinguisher on hand.*

Caution: *If the stereo in your vehicle is equipped with an anti-theft system, make sure you have the correct activation code before disconnecting the battery.*

Fuel pump check

Refer to illustration 3.1

1   Turn the ignition switch to Off, open the fuel tank filler cap, and remove the relay cover and relay from the engine compartment **(see illustration 2.1)**. Apply battery voltage directly to the number two terminal of the fuel pump relay harness side connector **(see illustration)** and listen for the whirring sound of the electric pump through the filler port. Now squeeze the fuel high-pressure hose - you should be able to feel pressure in the hose. If you cannot hear whirring, the fuel pump or its circuit is defective. If you can hear whirring, but pressure does not develop in the fuel high-pressure hose, the fuel pump is defective.

Fuel pressure check

Refer to illustrations 3.4a, 3.4b, 3.12 and 3.13

2   Relieve the system fuel pressure (see Section 2), detach the cable from the negative battery terminal and reconnect the electrical connector for the fuel pump.
3   Disconnect the fuel high-pressure hose at the delivery pipe (see illustration 10.5b). Cover the connection with shop rags to absorb any fuel that leaks out.
4   Attach your fuel pressure gauge (it must have a range through 350 kPa) to the high pressure hose using a suitable adapter **(see illustrations)**.
5   Attach the gauge with adapter to the fuel delivery pipe.
6   Reconnect the battery terminal.
7   Apply battery voltage to the fuel pump relay harness connector **(see illustration 3.1)** and activate the fuel pump. Make sure there's no fuel leaking from the pressure gauge/adapter setup.
8   Start the engine and run it at curb idle speed, measure the fuel pressure with the vacuum hose connected to the pressure regulator and compare your reading to the pressure listed in this Chapter's Specifications.
9   Detach the vacuum hose from the pressure regulator, plug the hose, measure the fuel pressure again and compare this reading to the pressure listed in this Chapter's Specifications.
10   Race the engine two or three times in quick succession, then recheck the fuel pressure to verify it doesn't fall when the engine runs at idle.
11   Gently squeeze the fuel return hose with your fingers while repeatedly racing the engine to verify fuel pressure in the return hose. If the volume of fuel flow is insufficient, there won't be any fuel pressure in the return hose.
12   If the results of your readings aren't within the specified values, use the accompanying table **(see illustration)** to determine the prob-

Sympton	Probable cause	Remedy
Fuel pressure is too low	Clogged fuel strainer	Remove and clean or replace fuel strainer
	Faulty pressure regulator	Replace fuel pressure regulator
	Faulty fuel pump	Replace fuel pump
Fuel pressure is too high	Faulty pressure regulator	Replace fuel pressure regulator
	Clogged fuel return hose	Clean or replace fuel hose or pipe
Fuel pressure does not vary with engine speed	Leaking pressure regulator vacuum hose	Replace vacuum hose
	Faulty pressure regulator	Replace fuel pressure regulator

3.12 Fuel pressure troubleshooting table for fuel-injected engines

Sympton	Probable cause	Remedy
Fuel pressure drops slowly after engine is stopped	Leaking fuel injectors	Replace fuel injectors
	Faulty pressure regulator	Replace fuel pressure regulator
	Faulty fuel pump	Replace fuel pump
Fuel pressure drops sharply afer engine is stopped	Faulty pressure regulator	Replace fuel pressure regulator
	Faulty fuel pump	Replace fuel pump

3.13 Fuel pressure drop troubleshooting table for fuel-injected engines

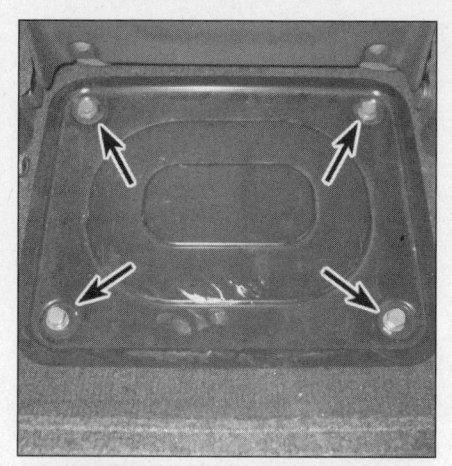

Chapter 4 Fuel and exhaust systems

4.2 Remove the floor cover mounting bolts (arrows) and remove the cover

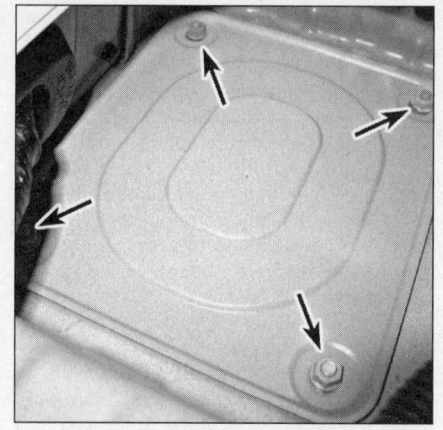

4.3 Remove the access cover mounting bolts (arrows) and remove the cover

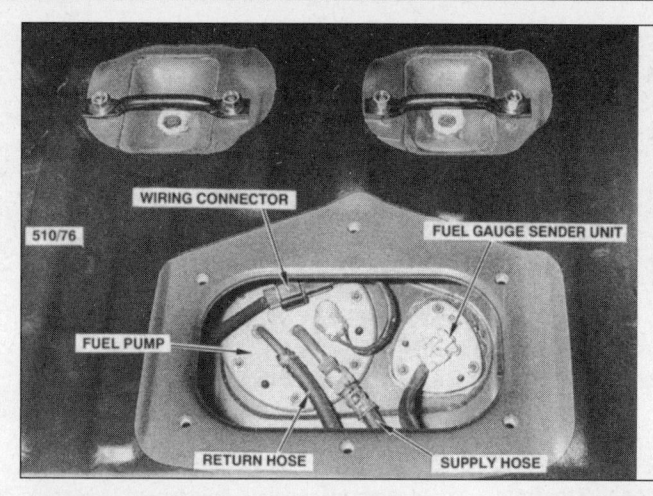

4.4a Typical 2000 and earlier fuel pump and fuel gauge sender details

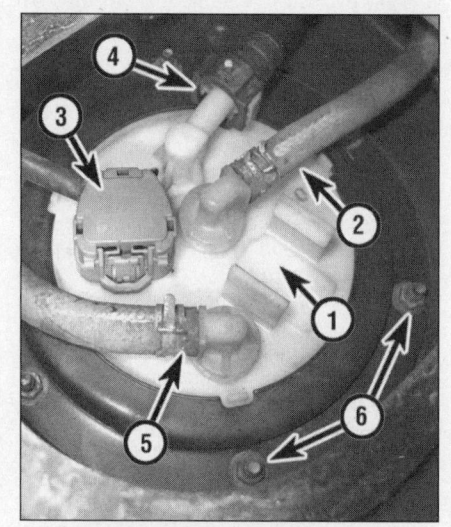

4.4b Typical 2001 and later fuel pump module assembly

1 Fuel pump module assembly
2 Fuel tank return hose
3 Harness connector
4 High pressure fuel hose
5 Fuel tank suction hose
6 Mounting bolts

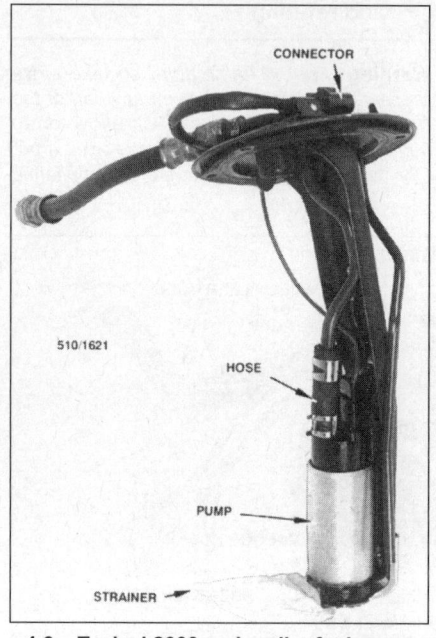

4.6a Typical 2000 and earlier fuel pump assembly details

4.6b Detach the inlet strainer from the fuel pump

able cause and make the necessary repairs.

13 Stop the engine and verify that the reading on the fuel pressure gauge doesn't drop. If it does drop, note the rate of drop and use the accompanying table **(see illustration)** to determine the cause and make the necessary repairs.

14 Relieve the system fuel pressure (see Section 2).

15 Cover the fuel high-pressure hose connection with a shop towel to absorb leaking fuel, disconnect the fuel high-pressure hose, remove the fuel gauge/adapter assembly, fit a new O-ring in the groove in the end of the high-pressure hose fitting and reconnect the hose. Tighten the attaching screws for the fuel high-pressure hose fitting to the torque listed in this Chapter's Specifications.

16 Apply battery voltage to the fuel pump relay harness connector, operate the pump and check the fuel high-pressure hose for leaks.

4 Fuel pump (petrol engines) - removal and refitting

Refer to illustrations 4.2, 4.3, 4.4a, 4.4b, 4.6a, 4.6b and 4.7

Warning: *Petrol is extremely flammable, so take extra precautions when you work on any part of the fuel system. Don't smoke or allow open flames or bare light bulbs near the work area, and don't work in a garage where a gas-type appliance (such as a water heater or clothes dryer) is present. If you spill any fuel on your skin, rinse it off immediately with soap and water. When you perform any kind of work on the fuel system, wear safety glasses and have a Class B type fire extinguisher on hand.*

1 On 2000 and earlier models access to the pump is from the luggage compartment. On 2001 and later models, fold the rear seats forward using the lever on the side of the seats.

2 On 2001 and later models, remove the floor cover mounting bolts and remove the cover **(see illustration)**.

3 Remove the access cover mounting bolts and remove the cover **(see illustration)**.

4 Disconnect the harness connector, high-pressure fuel line, and fuel tanks hoses **(see illustrations)**.

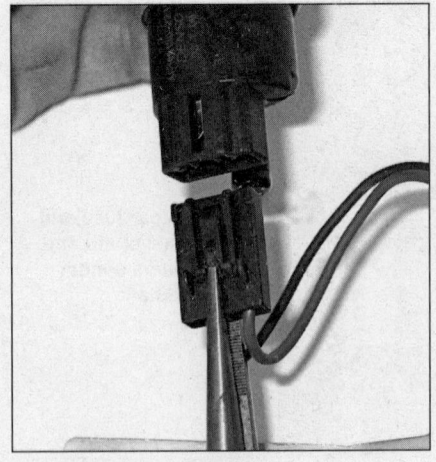

4-8 Chapter 4 Fuel and exhaust systems

4.7 Unplug the electrical connector from the fuel pump

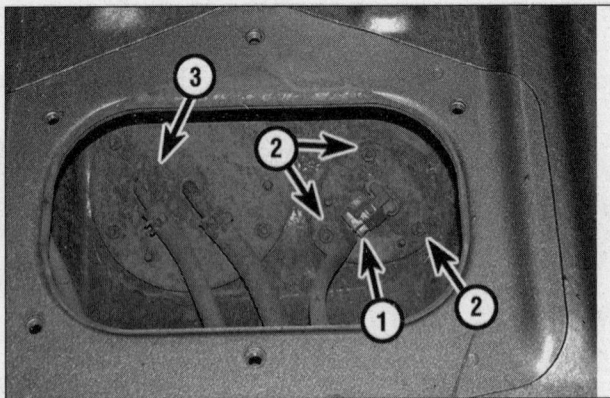

5.3 Typical fuel gauge sender unit details - early diesel model shown

1 Gauge sender electrical connector
2 Mounting nuts
3 Fuel delivery pipes

5 Remove the six mounting nuts and remove the fuel pump assembly from the vehicle.
6 Remove the fuel pump bracket and remove the cushion and inlet strainer **(see illustrations)**.
7 Disconnect the electrical connector from the pump **(see illustration)** and separate the pump from the grommet.
8 Refitting is the reverse of removal. Be sure the gasket between the fuel pump assembly and the fuel tank is in good shape. If not, renew it.

5 Fuel gauge sender unit (all models) - removal and refitting

Refer to illustration 5.3

Warning: *Fuel is flammable, so take extra precautions when you work on any part of the fuel system. Don't smoke or allow open flames or bare light bulbs near the work area. Don't work in a garage where a gas appliance such as a water heater or a clothes dryer is present. Since diesel fuel is carcinogenic, wear latex gloves when there is a possibility of being exposed to fuel. If you spill fuel on your skin, rinse it immediately with soap and water. Mop up any spills immediately and do not store fuel-soaked rags where they could ignite. When you perform any work on the fuel system, wear safety glasses and keep a Class B type fire extinguisher on hand.*

1 On 2000 and earlier models, remove the rear floor access cover bolts and remove the cover.
2 On 2001 and later models, slide the front seat back (or remove it) and remove the access cover bolts and cover.
3 Disconnect the harness connector and remove the sender unit mounting nuts **(see illustration)** and remove the sender from the vehicle.
Note: *It is not necessary to remove the fuel pump (petrol models) or fuel pipes (diesel models) to remove the gauge sender unit.*
4 Refitting is the reverse of removal. Be sure the gasket between the fuel pump assembly and the fuel tank is in good shape. If not, renew it.

6 Fuel tank (all models) - removal and refitting

Warning: *Fuel is flammable, so take extra precautions when you work on any part of the fuel system. Don't smoke or allow open flames or bare light bulbs near the work area. Don't work in a garage where a gas appliance such as a water heater or a clothes dryer is present. Since diesel fuel is carcinogenic, wear latex gloves when there is a possibility of being exposed to fuel. If you spill fuel on your skin, rinse it immediately with soap and water. Mop up any spills immediately and do not store fuel-soaked rags where they could ignite. When you perform any work on the fuel system, wear safety glasses and keep a Class B type fire extinguisher on hand.*

1 Before doing any work around the fuel tank, make sure that the ignition switch is off and remove the key from the ignition lock. Block the front wheels to keep the vehicle from rolling, then raise the rear of the vehicle and set it on jack stands.
2 Remove the tank filler cap so any pressure in the tank can escape.
3 Position a suitable container (large enough to hold the fuel that it is in the tank) under the tank. Remove the drain plug and allow the fuel to drain into the container. Be very careful when working around petrol; it is highly explosive. After the fuel has drained completely, refit the drain plug.

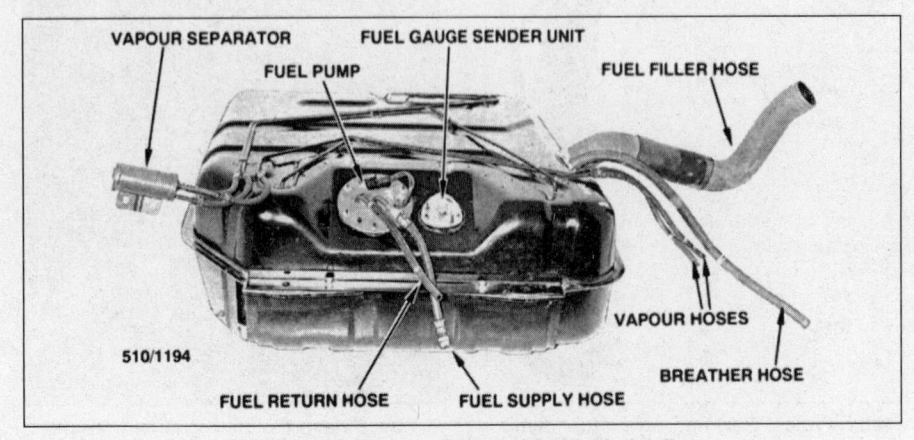

2000 and earlier models

Refer to illustrations 6.7 and 6.8

4 Loosen the hose clamps on the main, return and vapour fuel hoses, then pull the hoses off the tank.
5 Unplug the electrical wires from the fuel pump (see Section 4) and fuel level sender unit (see Section 5).
6 Remove the filler neck mud shield from the inside of the left rear wheel well. It is held in place with three bolts.
7 Loosen the hose clamps on the filler connecting hose (large) and the breather hose (small) where they attach to the tank **(see illustration)**. Pull the hoses off the tank. (Be careful not to damage them in the process).
8 Support the fuel tank, preferably with a portable jack and a block of wood. Remove the four mounting nuts **(see illustration)**, lower the tank carefully and move it out from under the vehicle.
9 Check the tank interior for rust and corrosion. If the tank is not extremely corroded, it can be cleaned and reused. Special solvents made especially for cleaning fuel tanks are available. If you use one, be sure to follow the

6.7 Typical early model petrol fuel tank details

VAPOUR SEPARATOR — FUEL GAUGE SENDER UNIT — FUEL PUMP — FUEL FILLER HOSE — VAPOUR HOSES — BREATHER HOSE — FUEL RETURN HOSE — FUEL SUPPLY HOSE

510/1194

Chapter 4 Fuel and exhaust systems

6.8 Remove the fuel tank mounting nuts and carefully lower the tank down

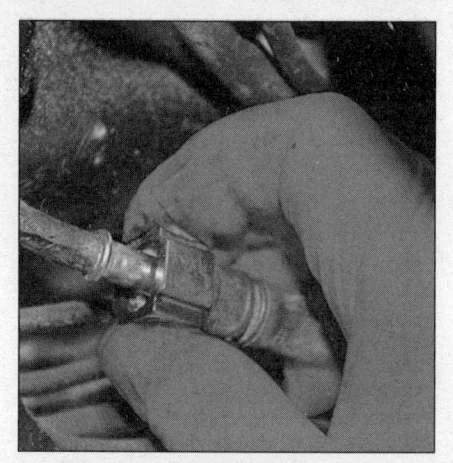

6.16 Disconnecting the high pressure fuel line quick connector on late models

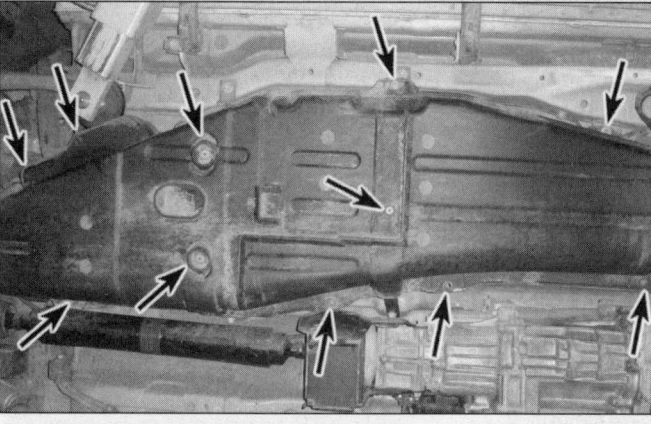

6.15 Remove the fuel tank shield nuts and bolts (arrows) - typical later model shown

directions on the container. The inside of the tank is plated with zinc so be sure to use a cleaner that will not harm it in any way.
10 If the tank is severely corroded, renew it.
11 Look for evidence of leaks and cracks. If any are found, take the tank to a repair shop to have it fixed.
12 Inspect all fuel and breather hoses for cracks and deterioration. Check all hose clamps for damage and proper operation.
13 Refitting of the tank is basically the reverse of removal. Be sure to double check all hoses for proper routing. Also, if you have not already done so, be sure to tighten the drain plug securely.
14 Fill the tank with fuel and check for leaks. After the engine has been run, make a second check for leaks, particularly at the hose fittings that were removed.

2001 and later models

Refer to illustrations 6.15, 6.16, 6.20a and 6.20b

15 Remove the tank under shield **(see illustration)** mounting bolts/nuts.
16 Loosen the hose clamps on the main, return and vapour fuel hoses, then pull the hoses off the tank. On late models, disconnect the quick connect fuel line **(see illustration)**.
17 Unplug the electrical wires from the fuel pump (see Section 4) and fuel level sender unit (see Section 5).
18 Remove the filler neck. Loosen the hose clamps on the filler connecting hose (large) and the breather hose (small) where they attach to the tank. Pull the hoses off the tank. (Be careful not to damage them in the process.)
19 Remove the transmission centre mount (see Chapter 7).
20 Support the fuel tank, preferably with a portable jack and a block of wood. Remove the mounting strap nuts **(see illustrations)** and bolts, lower the tank carefully and move it out from under the vehicle.
21 Look for evidence of leaks and cracks. If any are found, take the tank to a repair shop to have it fixed.
22 Inspect all fuel and breather hoses for cracks and deterioration. Check all hose clamps for damage and proper operation.
23 Refitting of the tank is basically the reverse of removal. Be sure to double check all hoses for proper routing. Also, if you have not already done so, be sure to tighten the drain plug securely.
24 Fill the tank with fuel and check for leaks. After the engine has been run, make a second check for leaks, particularly at the hose fittings that were removed.

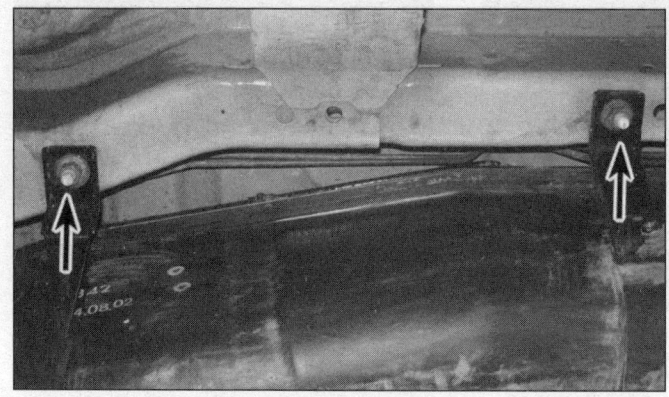

6.20a With the tank supported remove the fuel tank mounting strap nuts (arrows) . . .

6.20b . . . and mounting bolts (arrows and slowly lower the tank

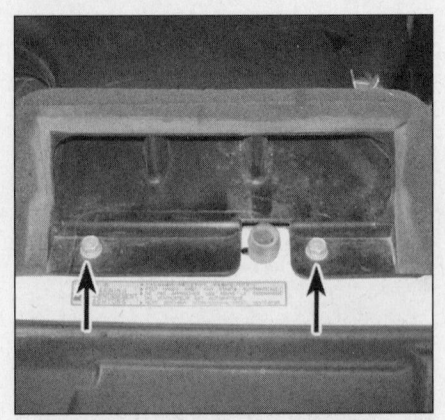

8.2a Remove the inlet air duct fasteners (arrows) . . .

8.2b . . . use a pocket screwdriver carefully prise the tab free and separate the inlet duct from the pre cleaner or lower air duct

8.3 Loosen the air intake hose clamp and separate the hose from the air cleaner

7 Fuel tank cleaning and repair - general information

1 All repairs to the fuel tank or filler neck should be carried out by a professional who has experience in this critical and potentially dangerous work. Even after cleaning and flushing of the fuel system, explosive fumes can remain and ignite during repair of the tank.

2 If the fuel tank is removed from the vehicle, it shouldn't be placed in an area where sparks or open flames could ignite the fumes coming out of the tank. Be especially careful inside garages where a gas-type appliance is located, because it could cause an explosion.

8 Air cleaner assembly - removal and refitting

Refer to illustrations 8.2a, 8.2b, 8.3, 8.5 and 8.6

1 The air cleaner assembly must be removed in order to perform many maintenance repair and adjustment procedures. It is very important to remove and refit it carefully and correctly to ensure proper engine operation.

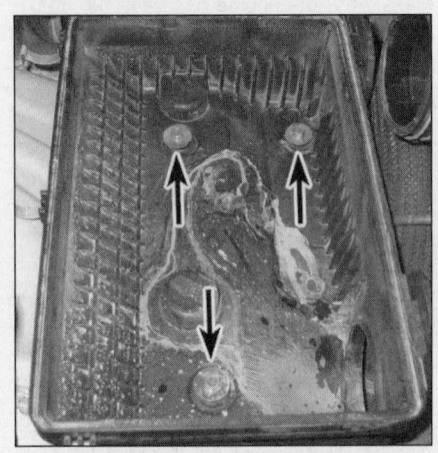

2 Remove the inlet air duct **(see illustrations)**.

3 Remove the air intake hose **(see illustration)**.

4 Remove the air cleaner top and filter (see Chapter 1).

5 Remove the air cleaner housing mounting bolts **(see illustration)** and remove the housing.

6 Remove the air cleaner mounting bracket bolts and grommets **(see illustration)**.

7 Refitting is the reverse of removal.

9 Accelerator cable - renewal and adjustment

Refer to illustration 9.3

Accelerator cable removal and refitting

1 Remove the air cleaner housing (see Section 8).

2 On petrol models, remove the cable bracket mounting bolts. Rotate the linkage and remove the cable from the throttle body.

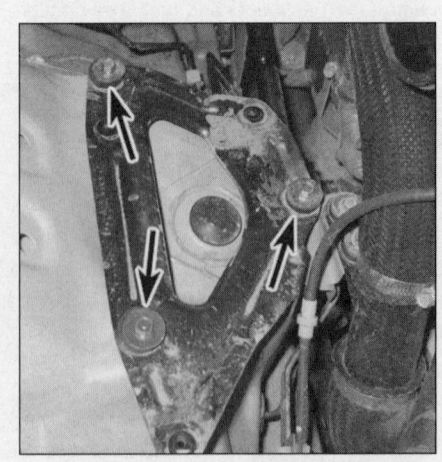

3 On diesel engines, loosen the adjustment nuts and cable clamp. Disconnect the inner and outer cables from the injection pump **(see illustration)**.

4 With the cable loosened from the engine, working inside the vehicle, under the dash, unhook the accelerator cable from the accelerator pedal assembly.

5 Detach the cable-to-firewall mounting bolts.

6 Refitting is the reverse of removal.

Accelerator cable adjustment

7 Before adjusting the accelerator cable freeplay on fuel-injected petrol engines, turn off the air conditioner and all lights, warm up the engine, verify the idle speed is correct, stop the engine (ignition switch off) and make sure there are no sharp bends in the accelerator cable. Then, before checking the cable freeplay, turn the ignition switch to On (with the engine stopped) and keep it in that position for 15 seconds. This 15-second key-on/engine off interval fully extends the probe for the idle speed control actuator.

8 The cable on fuel-injected petrol engines

8.5 Remove the air cleaner housing mounting bolts (arrows) and remove the housing

8.6 Remove the air cleaner mounting bracket bolts and grommets (arrows)

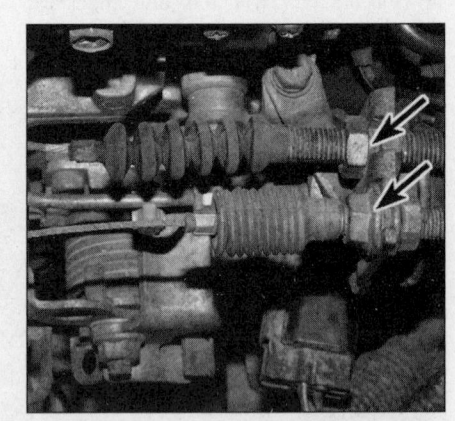

9.3 Typical early 2.8L (4M40) diesel engine accelerator cable adjustment nuts (arrows)

Chapter 4 Fuel and exhaust systems   4-11

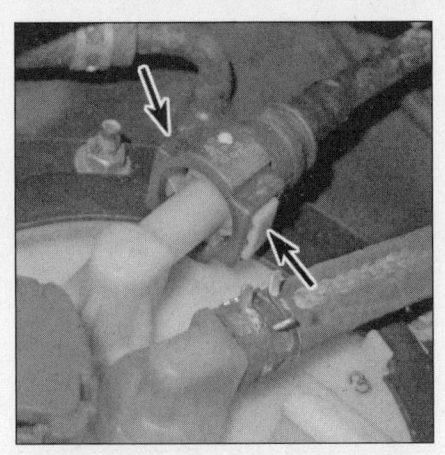

10.5a To disconnect the quick-release fittings, push the line towards the fitting and squeeze the two plastic tabs (arrows) then pull the line off

10.5b V6 petrol fuel supply hose (1), retained with a union type fitting and the return hose (2)

is adjusted basically the same way as diesel engines with two lock nuts mounted to a bracket. To ensure the correct gap between the throttle lever and its stopper, insert a feeler gauge between the lever and the stopper. The correct gap is listed in this Chapter's Specifications. Tighten adjustment bolts securely.
9   Now check the accelerator pedal: It should operate smoothly and the throttle valve must open fully by the time the accelerator pedal has been depressed as far as it will go.
10 Periodically, apply a thin coat of multi-purpose grease to the accelerator pedal pivot points.

10 Fuel hoses - renewal

Refer to illustration 10.5

Warning: *Fuel is extremely flammable, so take extra precautions when you work on any part of the fuel system. Don't smoke or allow open flames or bare light bulbs near the work area, and don't work in a garage where a gas-type appliance (such as a water heater or clothes dryer) is present. If you spill any fuel on your skin, rinse it off immediately with soap and water. When you perform any kind of work on the fuel system, wear safety glasses and have a Class B type fire extinguisher on hand.*

Caution: *If the stereo in your vehicle is equipped with an anti-theft system, make sure you have the correct activation code before disconnecting the battery.*

Note: *Since the fuel injection system is under considerable pressure, always renew all clamps released or removed with new ones.*

1   Periodically, check all rubber fuel hoses and metal fuel lines for cracks, bends, deformation, deterioration or clogging.
2   Remove the air cleaner assembly.
3   Relieve the fuel system pressure (see Section 2).
4   Disconnect the cable from the negative terminal of the battery (see Chapter 5).
5   Loosen the hose clamps or bolts (if equipped), wrap a cloth around each end of the hose to catch the residual fuel and twist and pull (clamped on type), pull straight off (bolt-on type), unscrew the hose (screw-in type) or squeeze the two plastic tabs and pull the line off (quick disconnect type) **(see illustrations)** to remove the hose.
6   When renewing hoses, always use original equipment-type renewal hose and use new hose clamps or O-rings. Pressure hoses for the fuel injection system are made from special materials to handle the high pressures - use only hoses made to the same high standards.
7   Connect the battery negative cable, start the engine and check for leaks.
8   Refit the air cleaner assembly.

11 Multi-Point Injection (MPI) - general information

All V6 models are equipped with an electronic fuel injection system known as Multi-Point Injection (MPI). Aside from slight differences in some emissions-related components, the earlier and later MPI systems are virtually identical. Both are computerised, electronically controlled fuel, ignition and emission control systems. Their important sub-systems include air induction, fuel delivery, fuel control, emission control and the engine control unit. Each system differs slightly in the type and location of these components.

Air induction system
The air induction system includes the air cleaner assembly, the throttle body, the ductwork between the air cleaner and the throttle body, the Throttle Position Sensor (TPS) and the Idle Speed Control (ISC) servo.

Fuel delivery system
The fuel delivery system provides fuel from the fuel tank into the fuel control system. It also returns any excess fuel back into the fuel tank. The system includes an in-tank electric fuel pump, fuel filter and return line.

Fuel control system
The fuel control system includes the fuel pressure regulator, the fuel rail and the fuel injectors. On MPI systems, the inlet manifold supplies air only; fuel is sprayed directly into the ports by the fuel injectors.

Emission controls and the engine control unit
The oxygen sensor, airflow sensor, intake air temperature sensor, engine coolant temperature sensor, Throttle Position Sensor (TPS), idle position switch, crank angle sensor and barometric pressure sensor are all important to the proper operation of the MPI system, but they're more closely related to emissions than to fuel. If you'd like to know more about related emission control systems, particularly the information sensors and the engine control unit, refer to Chapter 6.

12 Fuel injection system - check

Note: *The following procedure is based on the assumption that the fuel pressure is adequate (see Section 3).*

1   Check all earth wire connections for tightness. Check all wiring harness connectors related to the MPI system. Loose connectors and poor connections can cause many problems that resemble more serious malfunctions. Also check all vacuum connections and make sure all vacuum hoses are in good condition and not hardened, cracked or plugged.
2   Verify that the battery is fully charged; the engine control unit and the information sensors depend on an accurate supply voltage to function properly.
3   Check the air filter element - a dirty or partially blocked filter will severely impede performance and economy (see Chapter 1).
4   Check for blown fuses. If a blown fuse is found, renew it and see if it blows again. If it does, search the circuit for a short.
5   Look for leaks in the air intake duct between the air cleaner housing and the throttle body and at the gasket between the throttle body and the air intake plenum. Air leaks cause an excessively lean mixture. Also inspect all vacuum hoses connected to the throttle body and inlet manifold.
6   Remove the air intake duct from the throttle body and check for dirt, carbon or other residue build-up. If the throttle body is dirty (pay particular attention to the area just inside the throttle plate), clean it with carburettor cleaner and a toothbrush.
7   With the engine running, place a screwdriver against each injector, one at a time, and listen through the handle for the clicking sound made by the solenoid inside. This sound should be clearly audible at idle.

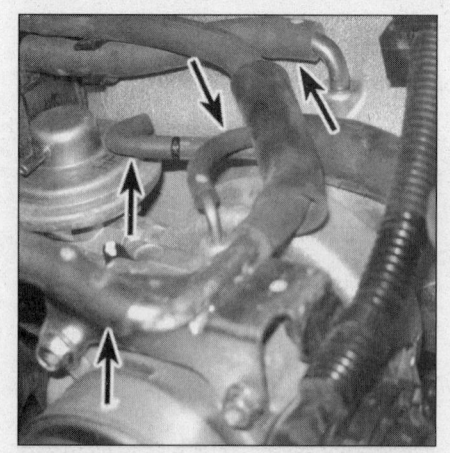

4-12   Chapter 4   Fuel and exhaust systems

13.2 Detach the vacuum hoses (arrows)

13.3 Loosen the hose clamp and detach the air intake hose from the throttle body

13.4 Late models use an electronically controlled throttle. As the throttle is operated electronically, there is no need for a throttle cable or an Idle Speed Control (ISC) servo. The wiring connector is labelled

13.7 Remove the throttle body mounting bolts (arrows), the throttle body and the gasket

an electronically controlled throttle, negating the need for a throttle cable or an ISC servo.

Caution: *If the stereo in your vehicle is equipped with an anti-theft system, make sure you have the correct activation code before disconnecting the battery.*

1   Disconnect the cable from the negative terminal of the battery (see Chapter 5) and disconnect the accelerator cable (see Section 9).
2   Detach the vacuum hose(s) **(see illustration)**.
3   Loosen the hose clamp and detach the air intake hose **(see illustration)**.
4   Unplug the Throttle Position Sensor (TPS) electrical connector. On late models, the same connector is also for the throttle control motor **(see illustration)**.
5   On early models, unplug the Idle Speed Control (ISC) servo electrical connector.
6   Place some absorbent shop towels under the connections for the coolant hoses, then detach both hoses. Some coolant will be lost.
7   Remove the throttle body mounting bolts **(see illustration)**, the throttle body and the gasket. Using a scraper, remove all traces of old gasket material from the throttle body and air intake plenum mating surfaces. Clean the surfaces with a rag soaked in lacquer thinner or acetone.
8   Refitting is the reverse of removal. Be sure to tighten the throttle body mounting

bolts to the torque listed in this Chapter's Specifications. Adjust the accelerator cable when you're through (see Section 9), and add coolant to renew the coolant lost when you disconnected the coolant hoses from the throttle body. Connect the negative battery cable.

13 Throttle body - removal and refitting

Refer to illustrations 13.2, 13.3 and 13.7

Note: *The Idle Speed Control (ISC) servo is fitted to early models only. Late models use*

14 Idle Speed Control (ISC) servo - check and renewal

Note: *The Idle Speed Control (ISC) servo is fitted to early models only. Late models use an electronically controlled throttle, negating the need for a throttle cable or an ISC servo.*

Check

Refer to illustrations 14.1 and 14.4

1   Listen to the ISC servo **(see illustration)** while an assistant turns the ignition switch to On (not to Start). The servo should make an audible sound.
2   If the servo is silent, inspect the electrical circuit. If the circuit is in good shape, the likely cause is a malfunction of the servo or the engine control unit.
3   Unplug the ISC servo electrical connector.

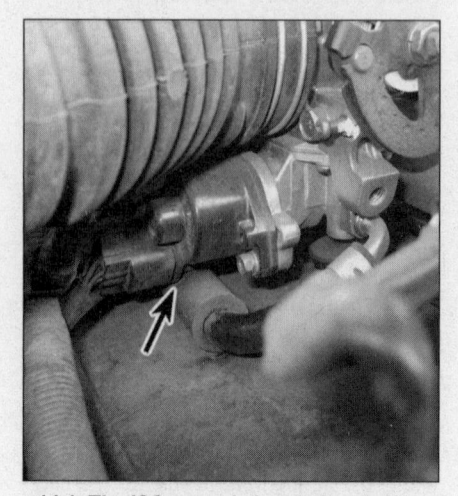

14.1 The ISC servo is located under the throttle body (arrow)

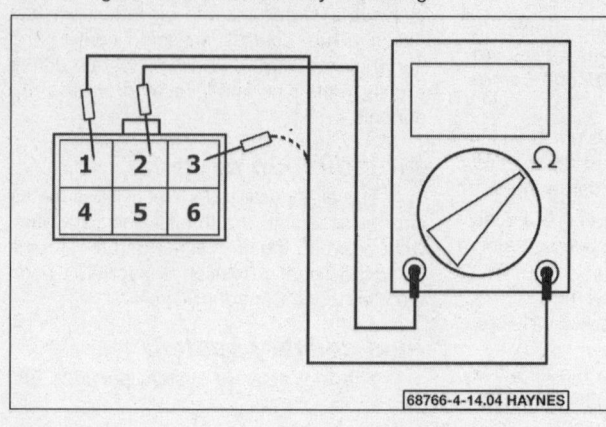

14.4 Using an ohmmeter or multimeter, check the continuity of the ISC servo connector at the indicated terminals and compare your measurements with the resistance listed in this Chapter's Specifications

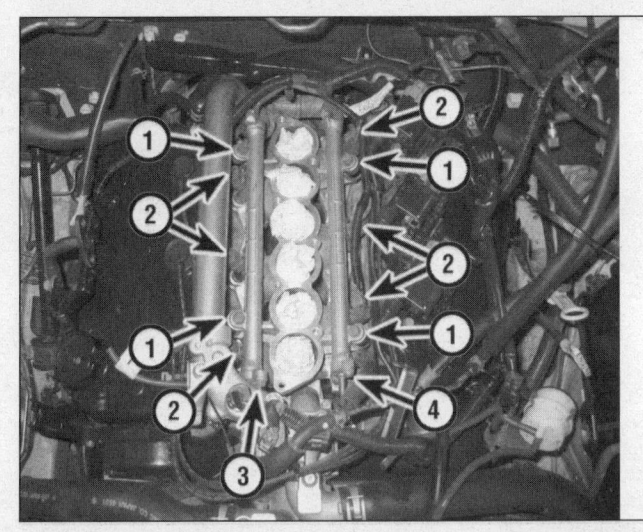

Chapter 4 Fuel and exhaust systems

15.5 Typical fuel rail and related components

1. Fuel rail mounting bolts
2. Fuel injectors
3. Fuel pressure regulator
4. High pressure fuel line connection

4 Measure the resistance between terminals 2 and 1, and between terminals 2 and 3 **(see illustration)** and compare your reading to the resistance listed in this Chapter's Specifications.

5 Measure the resistance between terminals 5 and 6, and between terminals 5 and 4 and compare your reading to the resistance listed in this Chapter's Specifications.

6 Remove the throttle body (see Section 13).

7 Remove the ISC servo (see below).

8 Hook up the positive terminal of a 6V DC battery to terminals 2 and 5.

9 Holding the ISC servo in hand with the pintle facing up, hook up the negative terminal of the 6V DC battery to each terminal of the connector in the following sequence and note whether there's any vibration (a very slight shaking of the servo) as the motor is activated.

1) Connect the battery negative terminal to connector terminals 3 and 6.
2) Connect the battery negative terminal to connector terminals 1 and 6.
3) Connect the battery negative terminal to connector terminals 1 and 4.
4) Connect the battery negative terminal to connector terminals 3 and 4.
5) Connect the battery negative terminal to connector terminals 3 and 6.
6) Repeat the above five steps in the reverse sequence (5 through 1).

10 If the servo vibrates slightly during these tests, it's okay; if it doesn't, renew it.

Renewal

11 Unplug the ISC servo electrical connector, if you haven't already done so.

12 Remove the two ISC servo mounting screws. The threads of these screws have been coated with adhesive, so make sure you don't strip out the heads trying to loosen them.

13 Remove the ISC servo unit.

14 Refitting is the reverse of removal. Be sure to tighten the screws securely.

15 Fuel rail assembly - removal and refitting

Refer to illustrations 15.5 and 15.10

Warning: *Petrol is extremely flammable, so take extra precautions when you work on any part of the fuel system. Don't smoke or allow open flames or bare light bulbs near the work area, and don't work in a garage where a gas-type appliance (such as a water heater or clothes dryer) is present. If you spill any fuel on your skin, rinse it off immediately with soap and water. When you perform any kind of work on the fuel system, wear safety glasses and have a Class B type fire extinguisher on hand.*

Caution: *If the stereo in your vehicle is equipped with an anti-theft system, make sure you have the correct activation code before disconnecting the battery.*

1 Relieve the fuel system pressure (see Section 2).

2 Disconnect the cable from the negative terminal of the battery (see Chapter 5).

3 Disconnect all hoses, cables and connectors from the throttle body (see Section 13)

4 Remove the throttle body and air intake plenum as an assembly (see Chapter 2A).

5 Cover the connection for the fuel high-pressure hose with a shop rag to absorb any spilled fuel (there's still residual pressure in the line, even after the fuel pressure has been relieved). Remove the fuel high-pressure hose attaching bolts **(see illustration)** and disconnect the hose. Discard the O-ring.

6 Loosen the hose clamp and disconnect the fuel return hose.

7 Detach the vacuum hose from the fuel pressure regulator and any other vacuum hoses in the way.

8 Pull up the retaining clip on each injector electrical connector and unplug the connector from the injector.

9 Remove the fuel rail mounting bolts and remove the fuel rail and the insulators. Pull gently up on the rail, using a rocking motion. Discard the O rings at the base of each injector.

10 Refitting is the reverse of removal. Be sure to fit new O rings to the base of each injector and replace any damaged insulators **(see illustration)**. Also, use a new O-ring for the fuel high-pressure hose connection and coat the O-ring with petrol before refitting. Tighten the fuel high-pressure hose attaching bolts to the torque listed in this Chapter's Specifications.

15.10 The plastic insulators must be installed between the fuel rail and the lower intake manifold

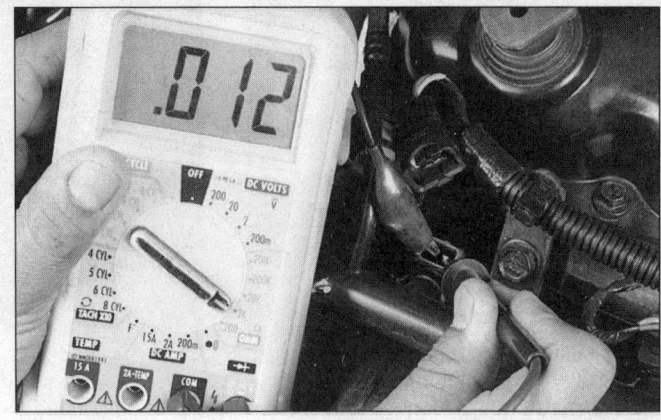

16.2 Measure the resistance between the injector terminals with an ohmmeter

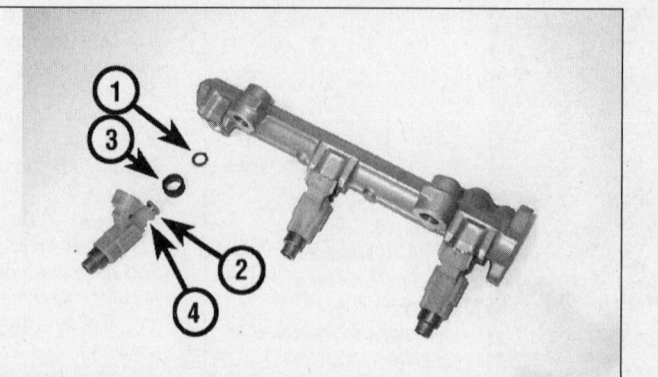

Chapter 4 Fuel and exhaust systems

16.5 Fuel injector and fuel rail assembly

1 Injector O-ring
2 O-ring groove at tip of injector
3 Injector seal
4 Seal fits on shoulder area near injector tip

16 Fuel injector(s) petrol engines - check, removal and refitting

Warning: *Petrol is extremely flammable, so take extra precautions when you work on any part of the fuel system. Don't smoke or allow open flames or bare light bulbs near the work area, and don't work in a garage where a gas-type appliance (such as a water heater or clothes dryer) is present. If you spill any fuel on your skin, rinse it off immediately with soap and water. When you perform any kind of work on the fuel system, wear safety glasses and have a Class B type fire extinguisher on hand.*

Check

Refer to illustration 16.2

1 With the engine running or cranking, listen to the sound from each injector with an automotive stethoscope and verify the injectors are all clicking the same. If you don't have a stethoscope, place the tip of a screwdriver against the injectors and press your ear against the handle of the screwdriver. Also feel the operation of each injector with your finger. It should sound/feel smooth and uniform and its sound/feel should rise and fall with engine rpm. If an injector isn't operating, or sounds/feels erratic, check the injector connector and the wire harness connector. If the connectors are snug, check for voltage to the injector, using a special injector harness test light (available at most auto parts stores).

2 If there's voltage to the injector but it isn't operating, or if it sounds or feels erratic, check the injector's resistance **(see illustration)**. Compare your measurement to the resistance listed in this Chapter's Specifications. If the indicated resistance is outside the specified range, renew the injector.

Removal and refitting

Refer to illustration 16.5

3 Remove the air intake plenum assembly (see Chapter 2A) and the fuel rail assembly (see Section 15).

4 Place the fuel rail assembly on a clean work surface so the fuel injectors are accessible. To remove an injector from the fuel rail, gently pull it straight out. Twisting it slightly as you pull may help. Discard the old O-ring and seal.

5 Refitting is the reverse of removal. Fit a new O-ring and seal onto each injector **(see illustration)**. Apply a light coat of fresh petrol to the O-ring to facilitate refitting. To refit an injector into the fuel rail, push it straight into its bore in the fuel rail, gently twisting it to the left and right as you push. Once the injector is fully seated, try to rotate it back and forth. It should turn smoothly if it's properly fitted. If it doesn't, the O-ring may be pinched or jammed; remove the injector and check the O-ring. If it's okay, refit the injector; if the O-ring is damaged, renew it before refitting the injector.

6 Refit the fuel rail assembly with the injectors installed in the fuel rail (see Section 15). Refit the air intake plenum assembly (see Chapter 2A).

17 Fuel pressure regulator (petrol models) - removal and refitting

Refer to illustrations 17.4, 17.6a and 17.6b

Warning: *Petrol is extremely flammable, so take extra precautions when you work on any part of the fuel system. Don't smoke or allow open flames or bare light bulbs near the work area, and don't work in a garage where a gas-type appliance (such as a water heater or clothes dryer) is present. If you spill any fuel on your skin, rinse it off immediately with soap and water. When you perform any kind of work on the fuel system, wear safety glasses and have a Class B type fire extinguisher on hand.*

Caution: *If the stereo in your vehicle is equipped with an anti-theft system, make sure you have the correct activation code before disconnecting the battery.*

1 Relieve the system fuel pressure (see Section 2).
2 Disconnect the cable from the negative battery terminal.
3 Remove the air intake plenum (see Chapter 2A).
4 Detach the vacuum line from the fuel pressure regulator **(see illustration)**.
5 Loosen the hose clamp, slide it back on the fuel return hose and disconnect the fuel return hose from the metal tube attached to the fuel pressure regulator.
6 Unbolt the fuel pressure regulator and detach it from the fuel rail. Discard the old O-ring **(see illustrations)**.

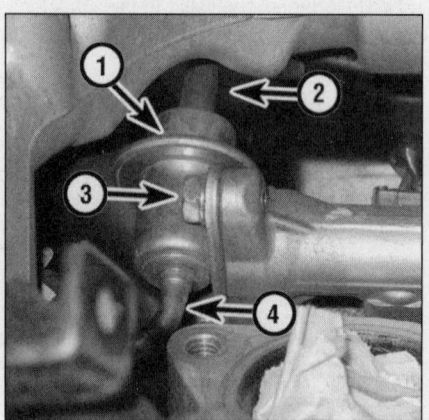

17.4 Detach the vacuum line from the fuel pressure regulator

1 Pressure regulator
2 Vacuum line
3 Mounting bolt (1 of 2 shown)
4 Pressure regulator return line

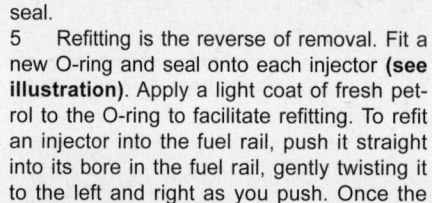

17.6a Remove and discard the old fuel pressure regulator O-ring

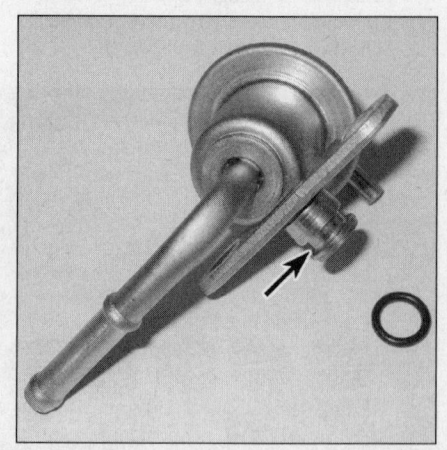

17.6b When installing a new O-ring, make sure that it's correctly installed in its groove; also, coat the new O-ring with a little clean engine oil or gasoline so that it'll slide freely into its bore in the fuel rail

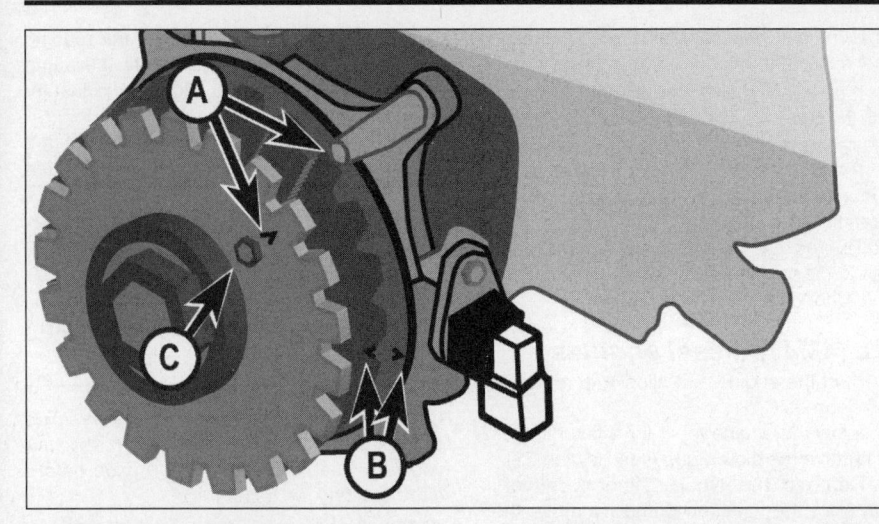

Chapter 4 Fuel and exhaust systems

18.21a Early 3.2L injection pump timing marks. These models can have either the marks labelled A or the marks labelled B. All models have the sub-gear lock bolt labelled C

7   Refitting is the reverse of removal. Use a new O-ring and coat it with a light coat of fresh petrol. Tighten the fuel pressure regulator mounting bolts to the torque listed in this Chapter's Specifications.

18 Diesel fuel injection pump - removal and refitting

Warning: *Diesel fuel is flammable, so take extra precautions when you work on any part of the fuel system. See Warnings in Section 1.*
Caution 1: *Do not attempt to disassemble the injection pump. All repairs to the pump should be carried out by a dealer service department or a diesel engine specialist.*
Caution 2: *If the stereo in your vehicle is equipped with an anti-theft system, make sure you have the correct activation code before disconnecting the battery.*
Note: *The timing the injection pump involves special measuring instruments. If you do not have access to these special tools, take the vehicle to a properly equipped diesel specialist.*

1   Disconnect the cable from the negative terminal of the battery (see Chapter 5).
2   Drain the engine coolant (refer to Chapter 1). Remove the intercooler, if so equipped.

3   Position the engine at TDC for number one cylinder on the compression stroke (see Chapter 2B or 2C).
4   Clean the pump area of debris that could fall into the front cover when the pump is removed.
5   Disconnect the wiring harness from the pump.

2.8L (4M40) engine

Removal

Caution: *Do not handle the pump by the accelerator or the fast-idle levers. Do not attempt to remove either of these levers.*
6   Disconnect the water hoses and fuel hoses at the pump.
7   Disconnect the accelerator cables (see Section 9).
8   Disconnect the boost hose.
9   Disconnect all of the fuel injection tubes. Be sure to hold the stationary part of the connection with a spanner to prevent it from rotating.
10   Remove the pump stay bolts and remove the stay.
11   Remove the pump mounting bolts from the timing cover side and lift the pump and O-ring from the engine.

Refitting

12   Refitting is the reverse of removal. The notch on the pump drive gear must align with the T mark.
13   To set the injection pump timing, refer to Section 19.
14   Tighten all fasteners to the torques listed in the Specifications in this Chapter. Be certain to hold the stationary parts of the connections with a spanner as you tighten them.
15   Bleed the fuel system (see Chapter 1). Adjust the idle speed (see Chapter 1).

3.2L (4M41) diesel engines

Removal

16   Disconnect all of the fuel injection tubes and hoses. Be sure to hold the stationary part of the connection with a spanner to prevent it from rotating.
17   Remove the pump stay bolts and remove the stay.
18   Remove the injection pump cover assembly.
19   Remove the pump mounting bolts from the timing cover side and lift the pump and O-ring from the engine.

Refitting

20   Install a M6X16 bolt to hold the injection pump sub gear to the injection pump gear.
21   Slide the injection pump into the timing cover and verify that the notch on the pump drive gear aligns with the notch of the flange plate. On late models, ensure that the marks are aligned as shown **(see illustrations)**.
22   Remove the M6X16 bolt holding the sub gear to the injection pump gear.
23   To set the injection pump timing, refer to Section 19 (see **Note** above).
24   Tighten all fasteners to the torque listed in the Specifications in this Chapter. Be certain to hold the stationary parts of the connections with a spanner as you tighten them.
25   Bleed the fuel system (see Chapter 1).

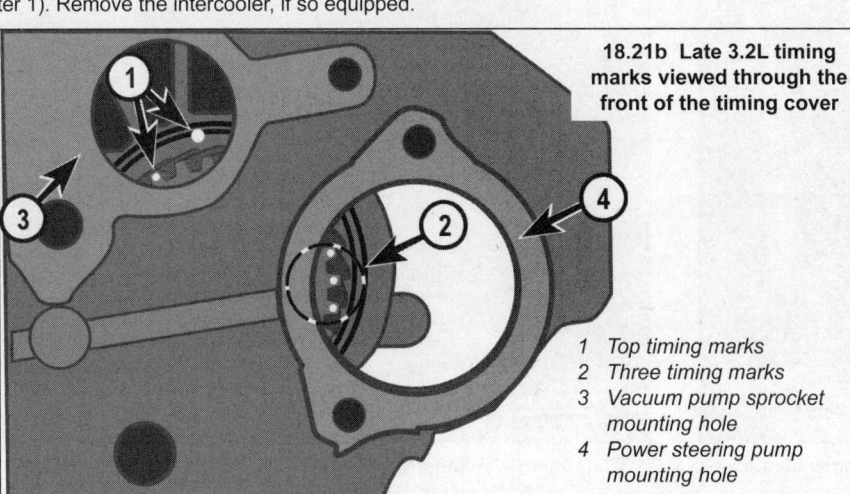

18.21b Late 3.2L timing marks viewed through the front of the timing cover

1   Top timing marks
2   Three timing marks
3   Vacuum pump sprocket mounting hole
4   Power steering pump mounting hole

19 Diesel fuel injection pump timing adjustment

Note: *This procedure involves special measuring instruments. If you do not have access to these special tools, take the vehicle to a properly equipped diesel specialist.*

2.8L (4M40) diesel engines

1 Start the engine and allow it to reach 80 to 95-degrees C.
2 Allow the engine to sit for a few minutes and remove the glow plugs (see Section 23).
3 Set No. 1 cylinder at TDC (see Chapter 2) and verify that the crankshaft pulley notch is pointing at the "0" mark of the timing gear case.
4 Remove the oil filler cap and verify that the notch on the camshaft is pointing up.
5 Obtain the required special tool (prestroke measuring adaptor MH063302 or its equivalent). Set the push rod so that it protrudes 12 mm from the end.
6 Connect a dial indicator to the special tool, lock the gauge down to the tool with the push rod still protruding 12 mm.
7 Remove the timing check plug from the centre of the injection pump. Attach the prestroke measuring tool and a dial indicator.
8 Rotate the engine so that the notch on the crankshaft pulley is at approximately 30-degrees before TDC. Set the dial indicator to zero.
9 Rock the crankshaft back and forth and verify that the dial indicator needle does not move. If it does set the engine to 30-degrees before TDC more accurately.
10 Rotate the engine clockwise until the crankshaft notch is at 9-degree ATDC position.

Note: *Always verify the information here with the information listed on the under-bonnet information decal or the owner's manual (each model uses a slightly different setting, however all are several degrees AFTER TDC). The dial indicator should read the value listed in the Specifications in this Chapter.*

11 If the reading is not within specifications, rotate the pump housing until it is correct. Tighten the fasteners and then re-check the reading.
12 Remove the dial indicator and the adaptor, then refit the plug, using a new gasket and tighten the plug securely.
13 Tighten the injector tubes or the glow plugs to the torque listed in the Specifications in this Chapter.

3.2L (4M41) diesel engines

14 Start the engine and allow it to reach 80 to 95-degrees C.
15 Allow the engine to sit for a few minutes and remove the glow plugs (see Section 23).
16 Remove the No.1 cylinder delivery valve from the injection pump. Remove the delivery valve gasket and fit the special tool # ME41133 to the delivery valve and refit the valve to the injection pump.
17 Place a drain pan under the vehicle. Using and old injection pipe, cut one end off and bend the pipe so fuel flow can be watched.
18 Obtain the required special tools (MD998754 and MB990767 or equivalents) and mount them to the crankshaft pulley. Rotate the crankshaft using the special tools and set No. 1 cylinder at TDC using the tools. Verify that the crankshaft pulley notch is pointing at the "0" mark of the timing gear case and remove the oil filler cap and verify that the notch on the camshafts are pointing up.
19 Rotate the engine so that the notch on the crankshaft pulley is at approximately 30-degrees BTDC.
20 Turn the ignition switch to the "OFF" position and connect the scan tool to the diagnostic connector.
21 Turn the ignition switch "ON" and follow the scan tool prompt (number 34).
22 Have an assistant pump the hand pump on the fuel filter (see Chapter 1) while turning the engine clockwise watching the fuel flow through the injection pipe.
23 When the fuel flow stops the timing should be at 4-degrees BTDC. If the reading is not within specifications, rotate the pump housing until it is correct. Tighten the fasteners and then re-check the reading.
24 Remove the special pipe made and fit a new gasket to the delivery valve and tighten the valve securely.
25 Tighten the injector tubes or the glow plugs to the torque listed in the Specifications in this Chapter.

20 Fuel injectors (diesel) - removal and refitting

Caution: *If the stereo in your vehicle is equipped with an anti-theft system, make sure you have the correct activation code before disconnecting the battery.*

Note: *Disassembly and testing of fuel injectors should be left to a shop with the proper equipment.*

1 Disconnect the cable from the negative terminal of the battery (see Chapter 5).
2 Remove any interfering components such as the engine cover, air cleaner assembly, the intercooler, etc.

2.8L (4M40) diesel engines

Refer to illustrations 20.3, 20.4 and 20.5

3 Disconnect the fuel return hose **(see illustration)**.
4 Disconnect the injection pipes from the injectors **(see illustration)**. Disconnect the fuel return tube. Be certain to hold the stationary part of the connection with a spanner to prevent it from rotating while you loosen the nut.
5 Use a deep socket and a ratchet to remove the injectors from the cylinder head **(see illustration)**.

Note: *Remove the injector gaskets from the cylinder head.*

6 Refitting is the reverse of removal. Tighten the injectors to the value listed in the Specifications in this Chapter.

20.3 Use a pair of pliers to remove the fuel return hose clamp and remove and plug the hose

20.4 Using a spanner disconnect the injection pipes from the injectors

Chapter 4 Fuel and exhaust systems

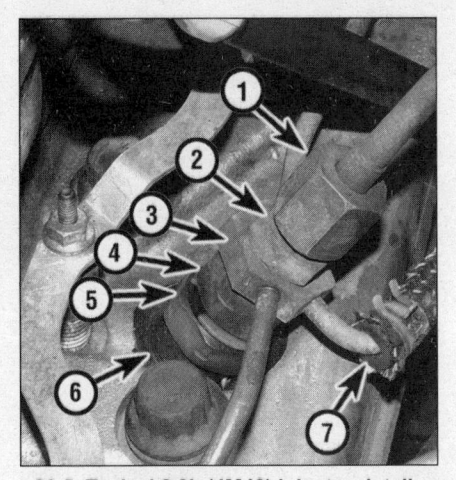

20.5 Typical 2.8L (4M40) injector details

1 Injection pipe
2 Lock nut
3 Fuel return pipe
4 Gasket
5 Injector nozzle assembly
6 Gasket
7 Fuel return hose

20.10 Disconnect the injection pipes from the injection pump and the injectors (arrow) and pull the pipes and seal from the cylinder head

20.12 Remove the fuel leak off pipe bolts (A) and gaskets, then remove the injector mounting bolts (B) and remove the injectors from the cylinder head

3.2L (4M41) diesel engines

Refer to illustrations 20.10 and 20.12

7 Remove the battery and tray see Chapter 5.
8 Remove the valve cover (see Chapter 2C).
9 Remove the fuel injection pipe clamps.
10 Disconnect the injection pipes from the injection pump and the injectors **(see illustration)** and pull the pipes and seal from the cylinder head.
11 Disconnect the fuel return pipe and hose.
12 Remove the fuel leak off pipe bolts **(see illustration)** and gaskets and remove the pipe from the top of the injectors.
13 On late models, disconnect the injector wiring connectors from each injector.
14 Remove the injector mounting bolts and remove the injectors from the cylinder head.
15 Refitting is the reverse of removal. Make sure to lube all the new injector O-rings and seals with engine oil before fitting them to the injector. Tighten the injectors bolts to the value listed in the Specifications in this Chapter.

21 Fuel cut solenoid - check and renewal

Refer to illustrations 21.2a and 21.2b

Caution: *If the stereo in your vehicle is equipped with an anti-theft system, make sure you have the correct activation code before disconnecting the battery.*

Check

1 Turn the ignition OFF.
2 Put a stethoscope to the fuel cut solenoid **(see illustrations)**. If a stethoscope is not available, a long screwdriver can be used. Hold the tip against the solenoid and the handle against your ear.
3 Have an assistant turn the ignition ON.
Warning: *Do not allow the engine to start while your body is near rotating components.*
4 Listen for a click as the ignition is energised. If no click is heard, disconnect the wiring harness from the solenoid and use test leads to apply earth and fused twelve volts. If no click is heard, renew the solenoid. If a click is heard, check the wiring circuit to the solenoid.
5 If the solenoid checks good, disconnect the wiring harness and use an ohmmeter to measure the resistance across the solenoid terminals. Compare your rearing to that listed in the Specifications in this Chapter.

Renewal

6 Disconnect the cable from the negative terminal of the battery (see Chapter 5).
7 Disconnect the wiring from the solenoid.
8 Remove the fuel cut solenoid from the injection pump.
9 Refitting is the reverse of removal.

22 Preheat system - general information

To assist cold starting, diesel engines are equipped with a preheat system. This is

21.2a The fuel cut solenoid is located at the rear of the injection pump (arrow) on the 2.8L (4M40) engine

21.2b The fuel cut solenoid is located at the front of the injection pump (arrow) on the 3.2L (4M41) engine

Chapter 4 Fuel and exhaust systems

23.2 Use a test light to make a quick check. Connect the clip end of the test light to the positive battery terminal and touch the light probe to the glow plug tip - the test light should illuminate

comprised of a glow plug for each cylinder, a glow plug control module, a coolant temperature sensor, a relay and a light on the instrument panel.

The glow plugs are small electrical heating elements, encapsulated in a metal or ceramic case with a probe at one end and an electrical connector at the other. Each cylinder has a glow plug threaded into it. When the glow plug is energized, the air and fuel passing over it is heated, allowing its optimum combustion temperature to be achieved more readily.

The duration of the preheating is governed by the preheat control unit which monitors the temperature of the engine via the coolant temperature sensor. It alters the preheating conditions to suit the engine temperature.

Preheating is triggered by the ignition key being turned ON. A dash-mounted lamp informs the driver that preheating is taking place. The lamp turns off when sufficient preheating has taken place to allow the engine to start. The control unit will switch off the glow plug's power if the engine is not started within a short time to prevent battery drain and glow plug burn-out.

After the engine has been started, the glow plugs continue to operate for a period of time. This helps to improve fuel combustion while the engine is warming up. This results in quieter, smoother running and reduced exhaust emissions.

23 Glow plugs - check and renewal

Check

Refer to illustration 23.2

1 Remove any interfering components such as the intercooler. Remove the glow plug electrical connection plate from all of the glow plugs.
2 Use a test light to make a quick check. Connect one the clip end of the test light to the positive battery terminal and touch the probe end to the glow plug tip **(see illustration)**. If the test light illuminates the glow plug works.
3 If the previous test works, use an ohmmeter to check the resistance between the uppermost tip of the glow plug and the base (earth). Compare your readings to that listed in the Specifications in this Chapter.
4 Renew any that are not within specifications.

Renewal

5 With the glow plug plate removed, clean any debris from around the glow plugs. Compressed air works best, but a rag will suffice.
6 Unscrew the glow plugs from the cylinder head. Be careful to not drop anything into the holes in the cylinder head. Seal the holes with tape to prevent any accidents.
7 Fit new glow plugs as required. Tighten them to the value listed in the Specifications in this Chapter.
8 Refit the glow plug plate.

24 Glow plug relay - check and renewal

Refer to illustrations 24.2 and 24.7

1 Disconnect the wiring from the relay.
2 Use an ohmmeter to check the continuity between terminal 1 and earth (use the bracket for an earth connection) on early models or between 1 and 4 on late models **(see illustration)**.
3 Compare your readings to that listed in the Specifications in this Chapter. There should be a small amount of resistance (neither an open circuit or a short).
4 Use fused test leads to connect terminal 1 to the positive battery terminal. Connect the negative battery terminal to the relay bracket.
5 Use an ohmmeter to check the continuity between terminals 3 and 2 on the relay. With power applied to the relay, there should be continuity (near zero resistance). When the test leads are disconnected, there should not be continuity (near infinite resistance).
6 If the relay fails either test, renew it.
7 Disconnect the wiring connectors **(see illustration)**, remove the mounting bolts and lift the relay from the engine compartment.
8 Refitting is the reverse of removal.

25 Glow control unit - renewal

Refer to illustration 25.1

Note: *The glow plugs are controlled by the engine/power train control module on NS and NT models, negating the need for a glow control module.*

24.7 Disconnect the wiring connectors (arrow), remove the mounting bolts and lift the relay from the engine compartment

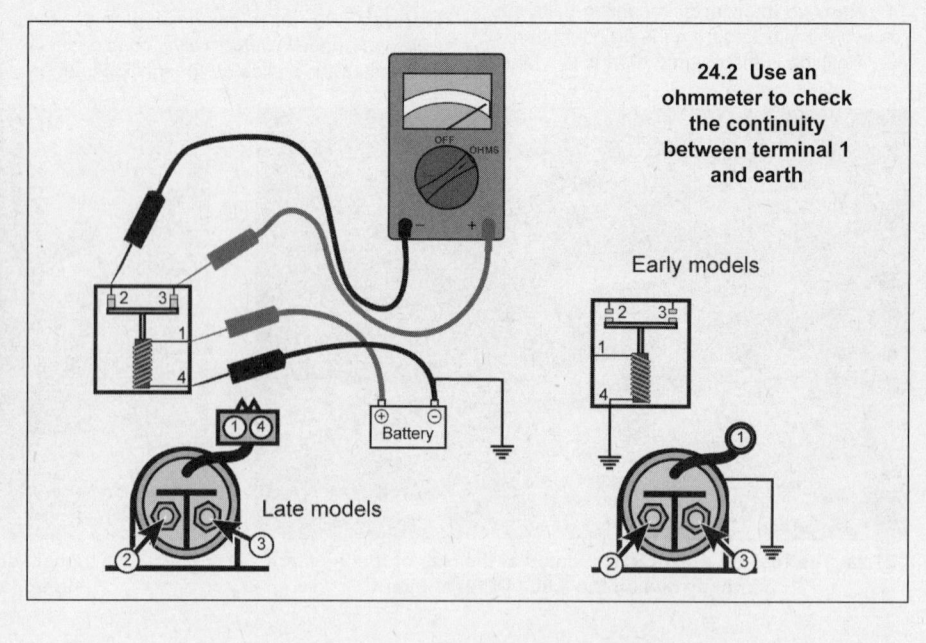

24.2 Use an ohmmeter to check the continuity between terminal 1 and earth

Chapter 4 Fuel and exhaust systems

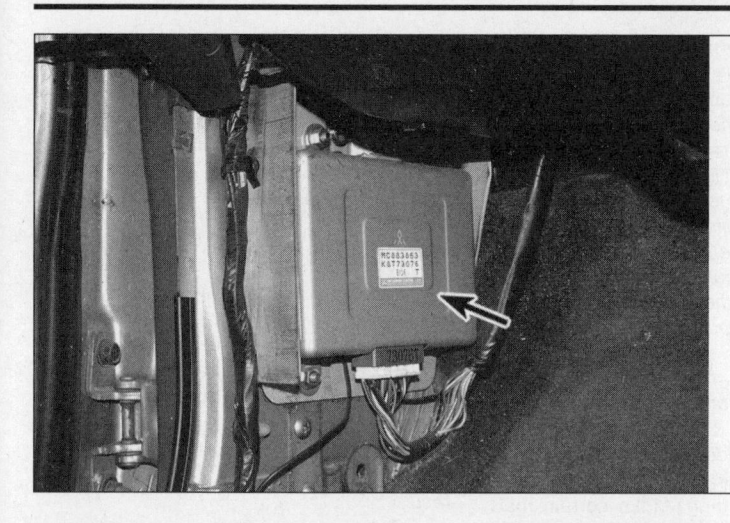

25.5 The glow control unit is located behind the passengers side kick panel (arrow) - typical early model with the 2.8L (4M40) engine shown

1 The glow control unit is located behind the passengers side kick panel (see illustration). Unplug the electrical connector, remove the bolts and detach the unit from the chassis. Refitting is the reverse of removal.

26 Coolant temperature sensor (diesel) - check and renewal

Check

Refer to illustration 26.4

1 Allow the engine to cool completely. Drain sufficient coolant from the radiator (see Chapter 1).
2 Remove the coolant temperature sensor from the engine, located just below the air boost sensor.
3 Put the sensor into a pan of water on a stove. Place a thermometer into the pan to monitor the water temperature.
4 Connect an ohmmeter to the terminals (see illustration). Observe the resistance and the water temperature as the pan is heated. Compare your readings to the values listed in the Specifications in this Chapter. If the values differ greatly, renew the sensor.

Renewal

Refer to illustration 26.7

5 Wait until the vehicle has completely cooled.
6 Place a container and rags under the sensor to catch coolant spillage. Alternatively, some coolant can be drained from the engine (refer to Chapter 1).
7 Unplug the electrical connector from the sensor (see illustration) and unscrew the sensor from the engine.
8 Apply sealer to the threads of the new sensor and place it close at hand.
9 Disconnect the wiring, then remove the sensor from the thermostat housing.
10 To minimize coolant loss, quickly fit the new sensor and tighten it securely.

27 Turbocharger and intercooler - general information

Only the diesel engines are available with turbochargers.

The turbocharger and intercooler increase power by using an exhaust gas driven turbine to pressurise the fuel/air mixture before it enters the combustion chambers. The amount of boost (inlet manifold pressure) is controlled by the wastegate (exhaust bypass valve). The wastegate is operated by a spring-loaded actuator assembly which controls the maximum boost level by allowing some of the exhaust gas to bypass the turbine.

After the inlet fuel/air mixture has been compressed by the turbocharger, its temperature rises greatly. It is then passed through an intercooler on some models to cool and condense it, thus providing more power. An intercooler works exactly like a radiator, using ambient air passing through a heat exchanger to cool the inlet charge.

A boost pressure signal is also supplied to the fuel injection pump so that it can alter the injection timing based upon boost pressure.

28 Turbocharger - check

General checks

1 While it is a simple device, the turbocharger is also a precision component which can be severely damaged by an interrupter oil or coolant supply as well as loose or damaged ducts.
2 Due to the specialised equipment and techniques required, checking and diagnosis of suspected problems dealing with the turbocharger should be left to a dealer service department. The home mechanic can, however, check the connections and linkages for security, damage and other obvious problems. Also, the home mechanic can check items that control the turbocharger, such as the wastegate. Refer to the wastegate check later in this Section.
3 Because each turbocharger has its own distinctive whine, a change in the noise level can be a sign of potential problems.
4 A high pitched whistling sound is a symptom of an inlet air or exhaust gas leak.

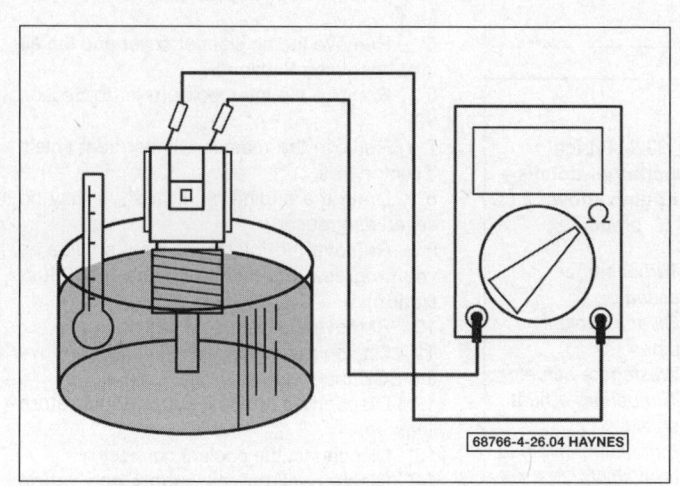

26.4 Ohmmeter connection details for checking the coolant temperature sensor

26.7 Unplug the electrical connector from the sensor and unscrew the sensor from the engine - early 2.8L engine shown

4-20 Chapter 4 Fuel and exhaust systems

5   If the unusual sound comes from the area of the exhaust turbine housing, the turbocharger can be removed and the turbine wheel inspected.

Caution: *All checks must be made with the engine OFF and cool to the touch. The turbocharger must be stopped or personal injury could result. Operating the engine without all of the turbocharger ducts and filters connected is also dangerous and can result in damage to the turbine wheel blades.*

6   With the engine turned OFF and completely cool, reach inside the inlet compressor housing and turn the compressor/turbine wheel to make sure that it spins very freely. If it doesn't, it's possible that the cooling and lubricating oil has sludged or clogged from overheating. Push in on the wheel and check for binding. The inlet compressor/exhaust turbine wheels should rotate freely with no binding or rubbing on the housing. If they do, the bearings are worn out.

7   Check the exhaust system for cracks and loose connections.

8   Because the turbocharger wheels rotate at speeds up to 140,000 rpm, severe damage can result from the interruption of coolant or lubrication to the bearings. Check for leaks in the oil and coolant lines. Also check that the oil return (drain-back) line is completely clear. If it is clogged, it can cause severe oil loss through the turbocharger seals. Burned oil on the turbocharger housing is a sign of this.

Caution: *It is important to allow the engine to idle for a period of time before turning it OFF if it has been operated at high speed immediately prior. If it is raced and then turned OFF, the turbocharger will be left spinning extremely fast when its lubrication stops. This can result in turbocharger failure. Additionally, if the engine has been rebuilt or had the oil removed for some other reason, be certain to prime the turbocharger with clean oil before starting the engine. Alternatively, you can operate the starter (while making certain that the engine will not start) until oil is supplied to the turbocharger.*

9   A boost level check can be made by connecting a pressure gauge to the wastegate hose using a tee fitting. Make certain that all connections are held securely with hose clamps, as substantial pressure is generated.

10   Carefully route the test hose and gauge through the engine compartment keeping clear of exhaust and rotating components. Run the gauge into the passenger area of the vehicle.

11   Have an assistant monitor the gauge while you make a full-throttle test in low gear. Maximum boost should occur at approximately 3,000 rpm.

12   If the engine produces excessive boost, then there is a problem with the wastegate.

13   If there is not sufficient boost, the problem could be due to a turbocharger system leak, an engine problem, a clogged intercooler, a wastegate malfunction or a defect in the turbocharger itself. Also check for a restricted exhaust system

Wastegate check

14   Disconnect the small hose from the wastegate. Connect a manual testing vacuum/pressure pump to the wastegate.

15   Slowly apply pressure to the wastegate and observe when the actuator begins to move.

Caution: *Do not apply more than the pressure listed in Specifications or damage could result.*

16   Compare your reading with that listed in the Specifications in this Chapter. If the wastegate operates at too low a pressure, then the engine will not produce enough power. If the wastegate begins to open at too high a pressure, then engine damage could result.

29 Turbocharger - removal and refitting

Refer to illustrations 29.3 and 29.9

Caution: *If the stereo in your vehicle is equipped with an anti-theft system, make sure you have the correct activation code before disconnecting the battery.*

Note: *The turbocharger on the 2.8L engine is oil cooled only and the 3.2L engine is water and oil cooled.*

1   Disconnect the cable(s) from the negative terminal of the battery(ies) (see Chapter 5).

2   Raise the front of the vehicle and support it securely on jackstands and remove the skid plate and lower engine cover (see Chapter 10).

3   Disconnect the front exhaust pipe **(see illustration)**.

4   Drain the engine coolant (refer to Chapter 1).

5   Remove the air cleaner cover and the air inlet hose (see Section 8).

6   Remove the intercooler (refer to Section 30).

7   Remove the master cylinder heat shield if it interferes.

8   Drain the engine oil (if fresh, it may be saved and reused).

9   Remove the interfering heat shields as you progress with this procedure **(see illustration)**.

10   Remove the two boost hoses.

11   On vehicles equipped with EGR, remove the EGR tube.

12   Disconnect the oil supply and return lines.

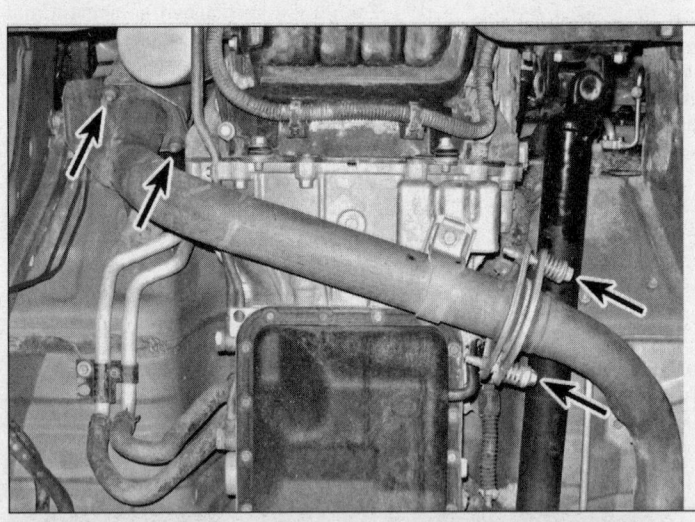

13   Disconnect the coolant connections.

14   Disconnect the oil supply and return lines.

29.3 Remove the front exhaust pipe upper nuts and lower bolts and springs (arrows) and remove the pipe.

29.9 Typical turbocharger details – 3.2L engine shown 2.8L similar

1 Turbocharger assembly
2 Oil and coolant pipes
3 Wastegate actuator
4 Turbocharger heat shield
5 Exhaust manifold heat shield

Chapter 4 Fuel and exhaust systems

30.1 Disconnect the air temperature sensor wiring harness (arrow) and the wiring to the intercooler fan motor

30.2 Disconnect the inlet and outlet air ducts at the turbocharger and inlet manifold

15   Remove the turbocharger along with the exhaust adaptor.

Note: *It maybe necessary to remove the turbocharger and exhaust manifold as a unit if you can't separate the turbocharger from the manifold (see Chapter 2B and 2C).*

16   With the assembly on the work bench, you can now disassemble the wastegate, the heat shields and then remove the exhaust adaptor from the turbocharger.

17   Place rags in all open inlet and exhaust ports to prevent the entry of debris. Seal all coolant and oil lines as well.

Refitting

18   Refitting is the reverse of removal. Make certain that all oil and coolant lines and ports are perfectly clean prior to assembly. Pour fresh oil into the turbocharger oil housing before attaching the oil lines.

30 Intercooler - removal and refitting

2000 and earlier models

Refer to illustrations 30.1, 30.2, 30.3 and 30.4

1   Disconnect the air temperature sensor wiring harness and the wiring to the intercooler fan motor **(see illustration)**.

2   Disconnect the inlet and outlet air ducts at the turbocharger and inlet manifold **(see illustration)**.

3   Remove the intercooler along with the support assembly **(see illustration)** and the various ducts and set it on a clean work bench.

4   Remove the hoses and tubes attached to the intercooler assembly **(see illustration)**.

It is important to make marks on each component as it is removed to indicate where it was refitted and in what orientation.

5   The intercooler can now be serviced or inspected.

Note: *If the inside of the intercooler has become partially clogged with sludge due to turbocharger wear, it can be cleaned at a radiator shop.*

6   Refitting is the reverse of removal.

2001 and later models

Refer to illustrations 30.10 and 30.12

7   Remove the air cleaner (see Section 8).

8   Raise the front of the vehicle and support it securely on jackstands and remove the skid plate and lower engine cover (see Chapter 10).

9   Remove the radiator shroud cover (see

30.3 Remove the intercooler along with the support assembly and the various ducts and set it on a clean work bench

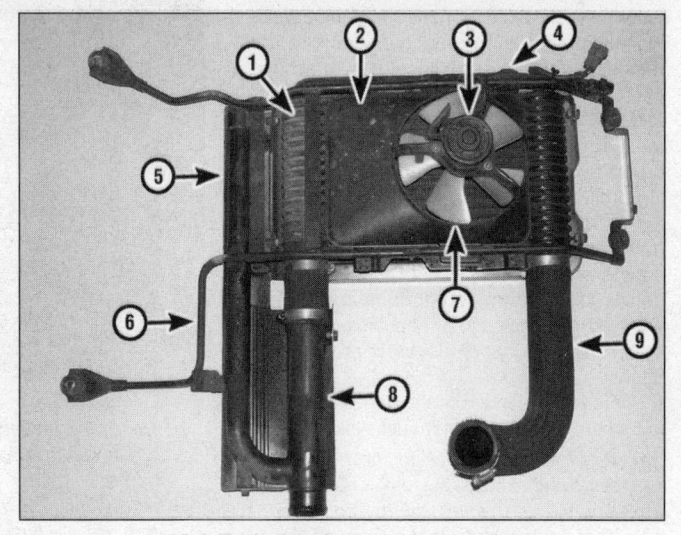

30.4 Typical early model intercooler

1 Intercooler
2 Fan shroud
3 Fan motor
4 Air temperature switch
5 Cover
6 Bracket assembly
7 Fan
8 Branch pipe
9 Inlet manifold hose

Chapter 3).
10 Remove the intercooler air hoses (see illustration).
11 Remove the intercooler air pipe and lower air hose.
12 Remove the intercooler mounting bolts and bush and remove the intercooler (see illustration).
13 Remove the air deflector plate mounting bolts and remove the plate.

31 Exhaust system servicing - general information

Refer to illustration 31.1

Warning: *Inspection and repair of exhaust system components should be done only with the engine and exhaust components completely cool. Also, when working under the vehicle, make sure it's securely supported on jackstands.*

1 The exhaust system (see illustration) consists of the exhaust manifold(s), the catalytic converter, the muffler, the tailpipe and all connecting pipes, brackets, hangers and clamps. The exhaust system is attached to the body with mounting brackets and rubber hangers. If any of the parts are improperly fitted, excessive noise and vibration will be transmitted to the body.

2 Conduct regular inspections of the exhaust system to keep it safe and quiet. Look for any damaged or bent parts, open seams, holes, loose connections, excessive corrosion or other defects which could allow exhaust fumes to enter the vehicle. Deteriorated exhaust system components shouldn't be repaired; they should be renewed with new parts.

3 If the exhaust system components are extremely corroded or rusted together, welding equipment will probably be required to remove them. The convenient way to accomplish this is to have a muffler repair shop remove the corroded sections with a cutting torch. If, however, you want to save money by doing it yourself (and you don't have a welding outfit with a cutting torch), simply cut off the old components with a hacksaw. If you have compressed air, special pneumatic cutting chisels can also be used. If you do decide to tackle the job at home, be sure to wear safety goggles to protect your eyes from metal chips and work gloves to protect your hands.

4 Here are some simple guidelines to follow when repairing the exhaust system:

a) Work from the back to the front when removing exhaust system components.
b) Apply penetrating oil to the component fasteners to make them easier to remove.
c) Use new gaskets, hangers and clamps when refitting exhaust system components.
d) Apply anti-seize compound to the threads of all exhaust system fasteners during reassembly.
e) Be sure to allow sufficient clearance between newly fitted parts and all points on the underbody to avoid overheating the floor pan and possibly damaging the interior carpet and insulation. Pay particularly close attention to the catalytic converter and heat shields.

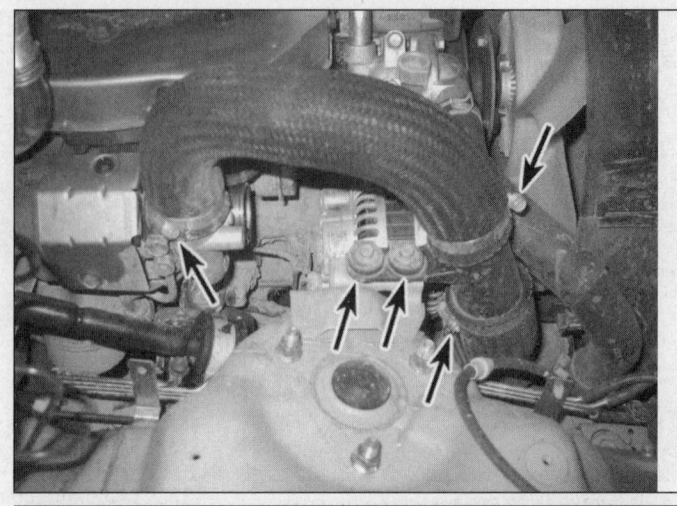

30.10 Remove the intercooler hose clamps and air pipe connector mounting bolts

30.12 Remove the intercooler mounting bolts (arrows) and bush and remove the intercooler

31.1 Typical exhaust systems used on 2001 and later models

1 Turbocharger exhaust adapter
2 Front exhaust pipe
3 Exhaust pipe connection
4 Catalytic converter

Chapter 4 Fuel and exhaust systems

32.3 Suction control valve (1) on the rear of the injection pump and the retaining bolts (2)

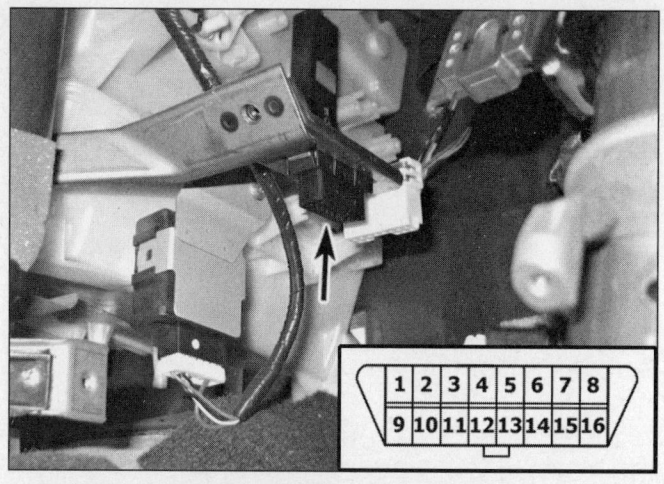

32.11 Arrow indicates the diagnosis connector between the steering column and heater box

32 Suction control valve - replacement

Refer to illustrations 32.3 and 32.11

Removal

1 Disconnect the negative (-) battery terminal (see Chapter 5).
2 Clean the area around the suction control valve with carburettor cleaner.

Caution: *Do not to let foreign material get into the injection pump during and after the suction control valve removal.*

3 Loosen the suction control valve bolts **(see illustration)**, and remove the valve from the injection pump.
4 Remove the gasket.
5 Remove the O-ring from the injection pump.
6 Installation is a reversal of the removal procedure.
7 Install the O-ring to the O-ring groove on the injection pump.
8 Install the gasket to the suction control valve.
9 Apply new engine oil to the O-ring in the injection pump groove, and insert the suction control valve by hand until it contacts with the injection pump.

Note: *When inserting the suction control valve, make sure that the suction control valve connector is in the direction shown in the illustration* **(see illustration 32.3)**.

10 Tighten the two suction control valve bolts evenly to 7 to 11 Nm.
11 Using a scan tool **(see illustration)**, reset the injection pump correction learning as follows:

Note: *The PCM learns the relationship between the suction control valve (linear solenoid valve) of the injection pump drive current and the fuel injection volume. The learning value is calculated from the suction control valve drive current and the rail pressure sensor output voltage. When the suction control valve or injection pump is replaced, this learning procedure must be executed. Re-learning is executed when the engine is idling after the learning value in the PCM has been reset by the scan tool.*

   a After the ignition switch is in "LOCK" (OFF) position, connect the scan tool to the diagnosis connector.
   b Switch ignition On - Do not start the engine.
   c Using the Special function menu, initialise the injection (or supply) pump.
   d After initializing, run the engine at idle under the following conditions.
     Accelerator pedal Off.
     Engine coolant temperature above 60°C.
     Fuel temperature above 30°C.
   e Confirm that the item No. 65 High pressure pump learned status on the scan tool data list is "2", indicating a successful reset.

Notes

Chapter 5
Engine electrical systems

Contents

	Section		Section
Alternator - removal and refitting	11	Ignition system - check	7
Battery cables - check and renewal	5	Ignition system - general information and precautions	6
Battery check and maintenance	See Chapter 1	Ignition timing check and adjustment	See Chapter 1
Battery - emergency jump starting	2	Spark plug renewal	See Chapter 1
Battery - removal and refitting	3	Spark plug wire check and renewal	See Chapter 1
Battery tray - removal and refitting	4	Starter motor - in-vehicle check	14
Charging system - check	10	Starter motor - removal and refitting	15
Charging system - general information and precautions	9	Starter motor/solenoid/gear reduction assembly - renewal	16
Drivebelt check, adjustment and renewal	See Chapter 1	Starting system - general information and precautions	13
General information	1	Voltage regulator/alternator brushes - renewal	12
Ignition coil(s) - check and renewal	8		

Specifications

Ignition system

Firing order	1-2-3-4-5-6			
Ignition coil(s)	NL	NM/NP 3.5L	NP 3.8L	NS/NT/NW
Primary resistance (ohms)	0.69 to 0.85	0.74 to 0.90	Not specified	Not specified
Secondary resistance (k/ohms)	15.3 to 20.7	20.1 to 27.3	8.5 to 11.5	Not specified
Spark plug wire resistance	22 K-ohms max			

1 General information

The engine electrical systems include all ignition, charging and starting components. Because of their engine-related functions, these components are discussed separately from chassis electrical devices such as the lights, the instruments, etc. (which are included in Chapter 12).

Always observe the following precautions when working on the electrical systems:

a) *Be extremely careful when servicing engine electrical components. They are easily damaged if checked, connected or handled improperly.*

b) *Never leave the ignition switch on for long periods of time with the engine off.*

c) *Don't disconnect the battery cables while the engine is running.*

d) *Maintain correct polarity when connecting a battery cable from another vehicle during jump starting.*

e) *Always disconnect the negative cable first and hook it up last or the battery may be shorted by the tool being used to loosen the cable clamps.*

It's also a good idea to review the safety-related information regarding the engine electrical systems located in the *Safety first!* Section near the front of this manual before beginning any operation included in this Chapter.

2 Battery - emergency jump starting

Refer to the *Booster battery (jump) starting* procedure at the front of this manual.

3 Battery - removal and refitting

Refer to illustration 3.1

1 Refer to the *Safety first!* Section at the front of this manual.

Caution: *Always disconnect the negative cable first and hook it up last or the battery may be shorted by the tool being used to loosen the cable clamps. Disconnect both*

5-2 Chapter 5 Engine electrical systems

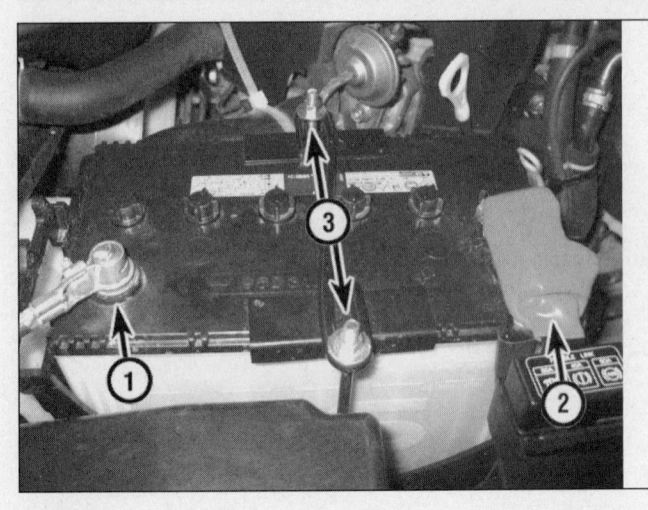

3.1 To remove the battery

1 Detach the cable from the negative terminal
2 Detach the cable from the positive terminal (under the protective cover)
3 Remove the nuts and detach the hold-down clamp

4.2 Remove the battery tray mounting bolts (arrows) and lift the tray out

cables from the battery terminals **(see illustration)**.
2 Remove the battery hold-down clamp.
3 Lift out the battery. Be careful - it's heavy.
4 While the battery is out, inspect the carrier (tray) for corrosion (see Chapter 1).
5 If you are renewing the battery, make sure that you get one that's identical, with the same dimensions, amperage rating, cold cranking rating, etc.
6 Refitting is the reverse of removal.

4 Battery tray - removal and refitting

Refer to illustration 4.2

1 Refer to the *Safety first!* Section at the front of this manual. Remove the battery as described in previous section.
2 Remove the battery tray mounting bolts and remove the tray **(see illustration)**.
Note: *If the battery tray is being replaced make sure the new one has all brackets that are riveted to the tray. If it doesn't you will need to cut off the rivets and transfer the brackets to the new tray.*
3 Refitting is the reverse of removal.

5 Battery cables - check and renewal

1 Periodically inspect the entire length of each battery cable for damage, cracked or burned insulation and corrosion. Poor battery cable connections can cause starting problems and decreased engine performance.
2 Check the cable-to-terminal connections at the ends of the cables for cracks, loose wire strands and corrosion. The presence of white, fluffy deposits under the insulation at the cable terminal connection is a sign that the cable is corroded and should be renewed. Check the terminals for distortion, missing mounting bolts and corrosion.
3 When removing the cables, always disconnect the negative cable first and

hook it up last or the battery may be shorted by the tool used to loosen the cable clamps. Even if only the positive cable is being renewed, be sure to disconnect the negative cable from the battery first (see Chapter 1 for further information regarding battery cable removal).
4 Disconnect the old cables from the battery, then trace each of them to their opposite ends and detach them from the starter solenoid and earth terminals. Note the routing of each cable to ensure correct refitting.
5 If you are renewing either one or both of the cables, take them with you when buying new cables. It is vitally important that you renew the cables with identical parts. Cables have characteristics that make them easy to identify: positive cables are usually red, larger in cross section and have a larger diameter battery post clamp; earth cables are usually black, smaller in cross-section and have a slightly smaller diameter clamp for the negative post.
6 Clean the threads of the solenoid or earth connection with a wire brush to remove rust and corrosion. Apply a light coat of battery terminal corrosion inhibitor, or petroleum jelly, to the threads to prevent future corrosion.
7 Attach the cable to the solenoid or earth connection and tighten the mounting nut/bolt securely.
8 Before connecting a new cable to the battery, make sure that it reaches the battery post without having to be stretched.
9 Connect the positive cable first, followed by the negative cable.

6 Ignition system - general information and precautions

When working on the ignition system, take the following precautions:
a) *Do not keep the ignition switch on for more than 10 seconds if the engine will not start.*
b) *Always connect a tachometer in accordance with the manufacturer's instructions. Some tachometers may be incom-*

patible with this ignition system. Consult a dealer service department before buying a tachometer for use with this vehicle.
c) *Never allow the primary terminals of the ignition coil to become earthed.*
d) *Do not disconnect the battery when the engine is running.*

The ignition system includes the ignition switch, the battery, the coils, the primary (low voltage) and secondary (high voltage) wiring circuits and the spark plugs.
The ignition system is distributorless (DIS). This system consists of the crankshaft position sensor, camshaft position sensor, ignition power transistor and separate ignition coils mounted on each spark plug.

7 Ignition system - check

Refer to illustrations 7.2a and 7.2b

Warning: *Because of the very high voltage generated by the ignition system (approximately 40,000 volts), use extreme care whenever performing an operation involving ignition components. This not only includes the coil and spark plug wires, but related items connected to the system as well, such as the electrical connectors, tachometer and any test equipment.*

Note: *The ignition system components on these models are expensive and difficult to diagnose. In the event of ignition system failure, if the checks do not clearly indicate the source of the ignition system problem, have the vehicle tested by a dealer service department or other qualified auto repair facility.*

1 If the engine turns over but won't start, disconnect the spark plug wire from any spark plug and attach it to a calibrated ignition tester (available at most auto parts stores).

Note: *Be sure to purchase the correct tester for the system the vehicle is equipped with. Alternatively, a spare spark plug can be used with a gap opened up to approximately 4 mm. Use a hose clamp and a bulldog clip to securely connect the spark plug threaded*

Chapter 5 Engine electrical systems

7.2a To use a calibrated ignition tester (available at most auto parts stores), simply disconnect a spark plug wire, attach the wire to the tester and clip the tester to a good earthing point - if there is enough power to fire the plug, sparks will be clearly visible between the electrode tip and the tester body as the engine is turned over

7.2b To test for spark at a high tension terminal that is connected directly (no spark plug wire) to a spark plug, remove the ignition coil, insert the calibrated ignition tester into the "boot" and clip the tester to a good ground and, on 2003 and later models (shown), be sure to ground the coil's metal housing to a good ground with a jumper wire

portion to earth on the vehicle.

2   Check for spark at the spark plug tester, or dummy spark plug while cranking the engine over. **(see illustration)**. Connect the clip on the tester to a bolt or metal bracket on the engine. **Note 1:** *2003 and later models have an ignition coil over cylinder No. 2 with a spark plug wire connecting it to its companion cylinder (No. 5), coil over cylinder No. 4 with a plug wire connecting it to its companion cylinder (No. 1) and another coil over cylinder No. 6 with a plug wire connecting it to its companion cylinder (No. 3). Because these coil assemblies actually fire two spark plugs simultaneously, you must check the spark at both high-tension terminals to test for sufficient secondary voltage. Testing at only one terminal will not conclusively tell you that one of these coils is operating correctly because there could be an open, or high resistance, in the circuit between the winding and the high tension terminal that you didn't test. So be sure to test both terminals of each coil on these models.* **Note 2:** *It is necessary to ground the coil assemblies on 2003 and later models because they're grounded through the coil mounting bolts. When you remove one of these coils to test for spark at the terminal that's plugged directly onto the top of the spark plug, run a jumper wire between the metal part of the coil (the boss for a mounting bolt) and a good ground such as the coil mounting bracket* **(see illustration)**.

3   A spark should be seen at the end of the spark plug.

Warning: *Keep clear of drivebelts and other moving engine components that could injure you.*

4   If sparks occur, sufficient voltage is reaching the plug to fire it (repeat the check at the remaining plug wires or ignition coils to verify the coils are not defective. However, the plugs themselves may be fouled, so remove them and check them as described in Chapter 1.

5   If no spark, or intermittent spark occur at one or more ignition coils, swap the coil with a cylinder that is sparking correctly and re-check. If spark is now available, a faulty ignition coil is indicated.

6   If there is no spark at any cylinder, check that power is available to the ignition coil wiring harness terminal 1 and earth is available at terminal 2. If power and earth are available with the ignition On, a faulty crankshaft position sensor, or camshaft position sensor are indicated.

8   Ignition coil(s) - check and renewal

Check

Note: *The following checks should be made with the engine cold. If the engine is hot, the resistance will be greater.*

2002 and earlier models

Refer to illustrations 8.4 and 8.5

1   Disconnect the electrical connector from the coil assembly.
2   Clearly label the spark plug wires and then disconnect them from the coil pack.
3   Unbolt the coil assembly and remove it.
4   Measure the primary resistance of each coil winding **(see illustration)**. Connect an ohmmeter between terminal 3 (power) and each of the other two terminals (ground path for each primary coil winding, switched on and off by the power transistor) and note the resistance. Compare the indicated resistance with the primary resistance listed in this Chapter's Specifications. If the primary resistance for either coil winding is incorrect, replace the coil assembly.
5   Measure the secondary resistance between the high-tension terminals of each coil winding **(see illustration)**. Connect an ohmmeter between the high-tension terminals for spark plug Nos. 1 and 4 and note the resistance. Repeat the check on terminals 6 and 3 and 5 and 2. Compare the indicated resistance with the secondary resistance listed in this Chapter's Specifications. If the secondary resistance for either coil winding is incorrect, replace the coil assembly.

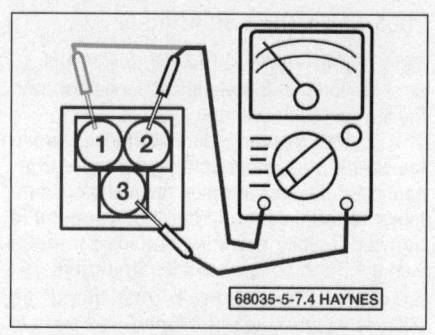

8.4 Ignition coil primary electrical connector terminal guide (2002 and earlier models)

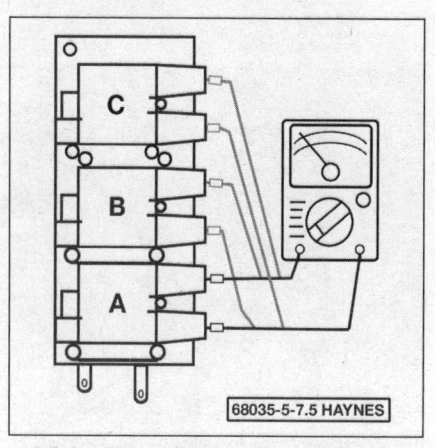

8.5 Ignition coil secondary resistance check (2002 and earlier models)

Chapter 5 Engine electrical systems

8.10a Ignition coil electrical connector terminal guide (2003 and later models)

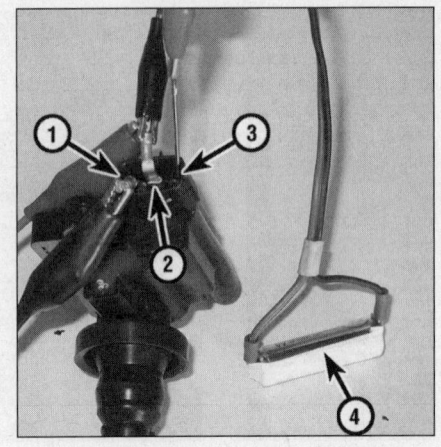

6 Refit the coil assembly and tighten the mounting bolts securely.
7 Reconnect the spark plug wires to the coil assembly (see Chapter 1).
8 Reconnect the coil electrical connector.

2003 and later 3.8L models

Refer to illustrations 8.10a, 8.10b and 8.11

9 Disconnect the electrical connector from the ignition coil assembly.
10 To check primary coil resistance (and to check the integral ignition power transistor), connect the negative probe of an *analog* ohmmeter to terminal 1 and the positive probe to terminal 2 while powering terminals 2 and 3 with a 1.5 volt battery **(see illustrations)**.
Caution: *The following test must be performed quickly (10 seconds or less) to prevent damage to the coil and to the ignition power transistor. When current is flowing from the battery to terminal 3 and from terminal 2 back to the battery, there should be continuity between terminals 1 and 2. When the battery circuit is opened, there should be no continuity between terminals 1 and 2. If the primary resistance is not as specified, replace the coil.*
11 To check coil secondary resistance, measure the resistance between the two high-tension terminals of the coil **(see illus-**

8.10b Here's the setup for testing the primary side of an ignition coil (2003 and later models)

1 Hook up the negative probe of an analog ohmmeter to terminal No. 1. Using spade connectors between the terminals and the alligator clips will "extend" the terminals so that you can clip onto them.
2 Hook up the positive ohmmeter probe to terminal No. 2 (with another spade connector). Then hook up the negative or ground wire for a 1.5-volt battery to this terminal (or to the spade connector, as shown).
3 Hook up the positive or power wire for the 1.5-volt battery to terminal No. 3.
4 You'll need a 1.5-volt battery and a couple of short leads to hook it up to terminals 2 and 3. We taped the ends of the leads to the battery so they'd stay put while we conducted the test.

tration). Note the indicated resistance and compare your measurement to the secondary resistance listed in this Chapter's Specifications. If the secondary resistance is incorrect, replace the coil.

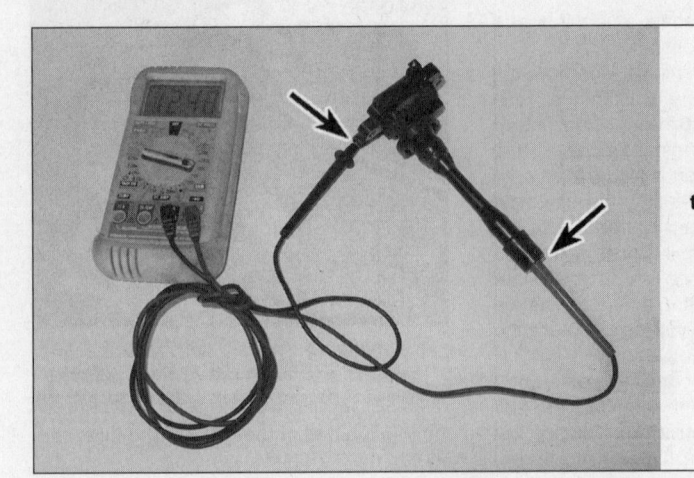

Replacement

Refer to illustrations 8.16 and 8.17

12 Disconnect the cable from the negative battery terminal.
13 Disconnect the electrical connector from the ignition coil(s) assembly.
14 Clearly label and detach the spark plug wires (see Chapter 1).
15 Remove the ignition coil mounting bolts and detach the coil pack from the engine.
16 Disconnect the electrical connector from the coil assembly **(see illustration)**.
17 Clearly label and detach the spark plug wire **(see illustration)** for the companion cylinder from the ignition coil assembly.
18 Remove the bolt(s) securing the coil/power transistor assemblies.
19 Refitting is the reverse of removal.

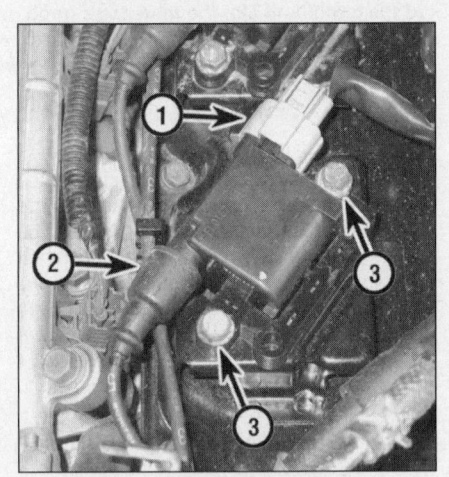

8.16 To disconnect the electrical connector from the ignition coil (2003 and later models)

1 Electrical connector
2 Coil wire
3 Mounting bolts

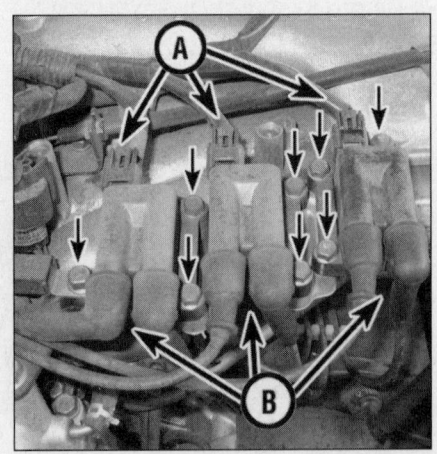

8.11 To measure the resistance on the secondary side of an ignition coil on 2003 and later models, hook up the probes of an ohmmeter to the two high tension terminals

8.17 Label the coil wires for each cylinder before removing the coils (2002 and earlier models) and remove the mounting bolts (arrows)

A Electrical connector
B Coil wires

Chapter 5 Engine electrical systems

9.1 Disconnect the electrical connectors to the power transistor (arrows)

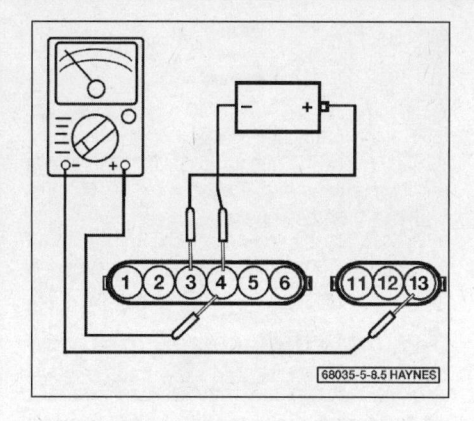

9.2 Power transistor test setup and electrical connector terminal guide for cylinders no.1 and no. 4

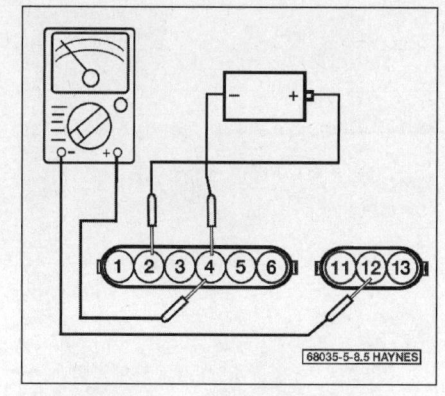

9.3 Power transistor test setup and electrical connector terminal guide for cylinders no. 2 and no. 5

9 Power transistor - check and replacement

Check

Refer to illustrations 9.1, 9.2, 9.3 and 9.4

Note: *On 2003 and later models, the power transistor is built into the coils and there is no check for these models.*

1 Disconnect the power transistor electrical connector(s) **(see illustration)**.
2 To check the power transistor for no. 1 and no. 4 cylinders, connect the probes of an *analog* ohmmeter between terminal 4 (on the big connector) and terminal 13 (on the small connector) **(see illustration)**. Then connect the negative side of a 1.5 volt battery to terminal 4 and the positive side of the battery to terminal 3 (both on the big connector).
Caution: *Don't connect the 1.5-volt battery for more than 10 seconds or the power transistor might be damaged. With the 1.5-volt battery connected, there should be continuity between terminals 4 and 13. But when the battery is disconnected, there should be no continuity between terminals 4 and 13. If the power transistor fails this check, replace it.*
3 To check the power transistor for no. 2 and no. 5 cylinders, connect the probes of an *analog* ohmmeter between terminal 4 (on the big connector) and terminal 12 (on the small connector) **(see illustration)**. Then connect the negative side of a 1.5 volt battery to terminal 4 and the positive side of the battery to terminal 2 (both on the big connector).
Caution: *Don't connect the 1.5-volt battery for more than 10 seconds or the power transistor might be damaged. With the 1.5-volt battery connected, there should be continuity between terminals 4 and 12. But when the battery is disconnected, there should be no continuity between terminals 4 and 12. If the power transistor fails this check, replace it.*
4 To check the power transistor for no. 3 and no. 6 cylinders, connect the probes of an *analog* ohmmeter between terminal 4 (on the big connector) and terminal 11 (on the small connector) **(see illustration)**. Then connect the negative side of a 1.5 volt battery to terminal 4 and the positive side of the battery to terminal 1 (both on the big connector).

Caution: *Don't connect the 1.5-volt battery for more than 10 seconds or the power transistor might be damaged. With the 1.5-volt battery connected, there should be continuity between terminals 4 and 11. But when the battery is disconnected, there should be no continuity between terminals 4 and 11. If the power transistor fails this check, replace it.*

Replacement

Refer to illustration 9.6

5 Remove the centre cover from the valve cover (covers up the spark plug wires, which are routed along the centre of the valve cover).
6 The power transistor is located on top of the engine, next to the ignition coil assembly. Disconnect the electrical connector from the power transistor, remove the bracket mounting bolts **(see illustration)**, then remove the power transistor-to-bracket mounting bolts and transistor.
7 Refitting is the reverse of the removal steps.

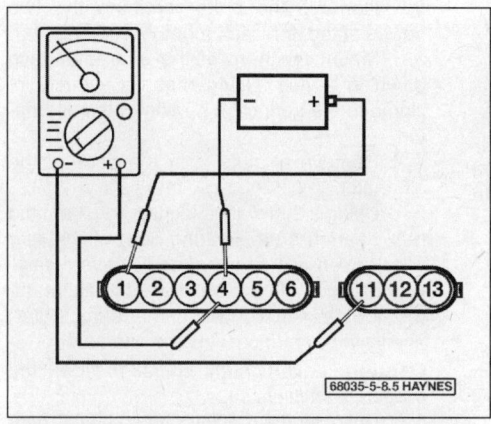

9.4 Power transistor test setup and electrical connector terminal guide for cylinders no. 3 and no. 6

9.6 Disconnect the electrical connectors to the transistor (1), remove the bracket retaining bolts (2), lift the transistor and bracket off of the engine, then remove the transistor from the bracket

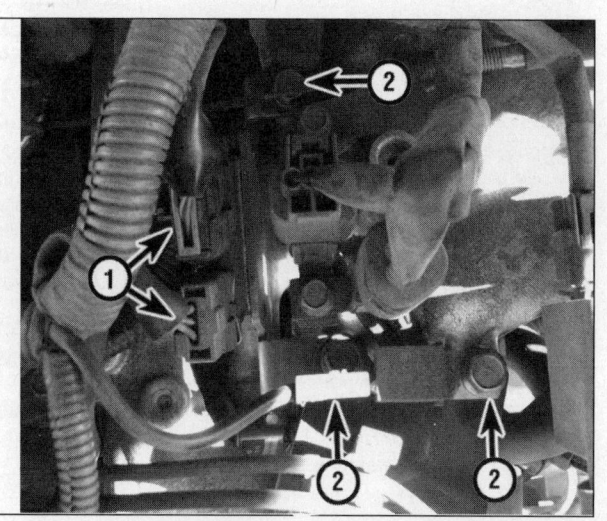

11.3 Loosen the adjustment bolt if equipped (arrow) and the pivot bolts to remove the drivebelt from the alternator pulley - 3.2L diesel engine shown, other engines similar

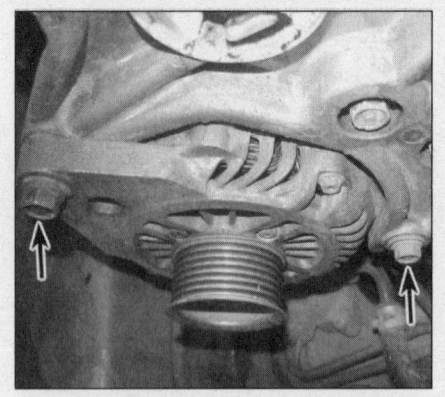

11.4 Remove the mounting bolts (arrows) - 3.8L petrol engine shown, other engines similar

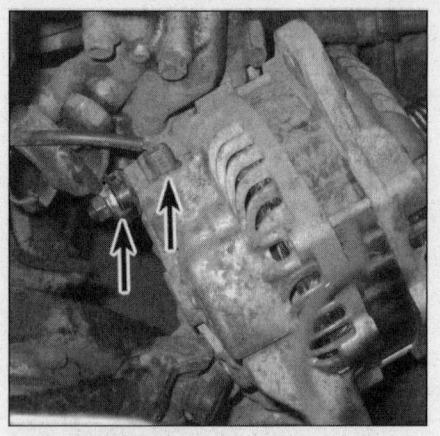

11.5 Disconnect the electrical connectors (arrows) from back of the alternator and remove the alternator

10 Charging system - check

1   If a malfunction occurs in the charging circuit, don't automatically assume that the alternator is causing the problem. First check the following items:

a) Check the drivebelt tension and condition (see Chapter 1). Renew it if it's worn or deteriorated.
b) Make sure the alternator mounting and adjustment bolts are tight.
c) Inspect the alternator wiring harness and the connectors at the alternator. They must be in good condition and tight.
d) Check the fusible link(s). If burned, determine the cause, repair the circuit and renew the link (the vehicle won't start and/or the accessories won't work if the fusible link blows). Sometimes a fusible link may look good, but still be bad. If in doubt, remove it and check for continuity.
e) Start the engine and check the alternator for abnormal noises (a shrieking or squealing sound indicates a bad bearing).
f) Check the specific gravity of the battery electrolyte. If it's low, charge the battery (doesn't apply to maintenance free batteries).
g) Make sure the battery is fully charged (one bad cell in a battery can cause overcharging by the alternator).
h) Disconnect the battery cables (negative first, then positive). Inspect the battery posts and the cable clamps for corrosion. Clean them thoroughly if necessary (see Chapter 1). Reconnect the cable to the positive terminal.
i) With the key off, connect a test light between the negative battery post and the disconnected negative cable clamp.
   1) If the test light does not come on, reattach the clamp and proceed to the next step.
   2) If the test light comes on, there is a short (drain) in the electrical system of the vehicle. The short must be repaired before the charging system can be checked.
   3) Disconnect the alternator wiring harness.
      (a) If the light goes out, the alternator is bad.
      (b) If the light stays on, pull each fuse until the light goes out (this will tell you which component is shorted).

2   Using a voltmeter, check the battery voltage with the engine off. If should be approximately 12-volts.
3   Start the engine and check the battery voltage again. It should now be approximately 14 to 15 volts.
4   Turn on the headlights. The voltage should drop, and then come back up, if the charging system is working properly.
5   If the voltage reading is more than the specified charging voltage, the voltage regulator may be malfunctioning. If the voltage is less, the alternator diode(s), stator or rectifier may be bad or the voltage regulator may be malfunctioning.

11 Alternator - removal and refitting

Refer to illustrations 11.3, 11.4 and 11.5

1   Detach the cable from the negative terminal of the battery.
2   Detach the electrical connector(s) from the alternator. Be sure to label each wire to avoid confusion during refitting.
3   Loosen the alternator adjustment and pivot bolts and detach the drivebelt **(see illustration)**.
4   Remove the mounting bolts and separate the alternator from the engine **(see illustration)**.
5   Disconnect the electrical connectors from the alternator **(see illustration)**.
6   If you're renewing the alternator, take the old one with you when purchasing a new unit. Make sure the new/rebuilt unit looks identical to the old alternator. Look at the terminals - they should be the same in number, size and location as the terminals on the old alternator. Finally, look at the identification numbers - they will be stamped into the housing or printed on a tag attached to the housing. Make sure the numbers are the same on both alternators.
7   Many new/rebuilt alternators DO NOT have a pulley fitted, so you may have to switch the pulley from the old unit to the new/rebuilt one. When buying an alternator, find out the shop's policy regarding pulleys - some shops will perform this service free of charge.
8   Refitting is the reverse of removal.
9   After the alternator is refitted, adjust the drivebelt tension (see Chapter 1).
10 Check the charging voltage to verify proper operation of the alternator (see section 10).

12 Voltage regulator/alternator brushes - renewal

Refer to illustration 12.6

1   Remove the alternator (see section 11).
2   Remove the bolts retaining the two halves of the alternator together.
3   Mount the front of the alternator face down in a vice. Using rags as a cushion, clamp to the front case portion of the alternator.
4   Remove all nuts from the back of the alternator.
5   Using a 200-watt soldering iron, heat the rear bearing area (bearing box) of the rear case. Insert two standard screwdrivers carefully between the two halves of the alternator (not too deep or you will damage the stator) and lever the rear case off the alternator.

Caution: *Lever gently or you'll break the delicate aluminium case.*

6   Unsolder the regulator/brush holder **(see illustration)**.

Note: *While applying heat to electrical*

Chapter 5 Engine electrical systems

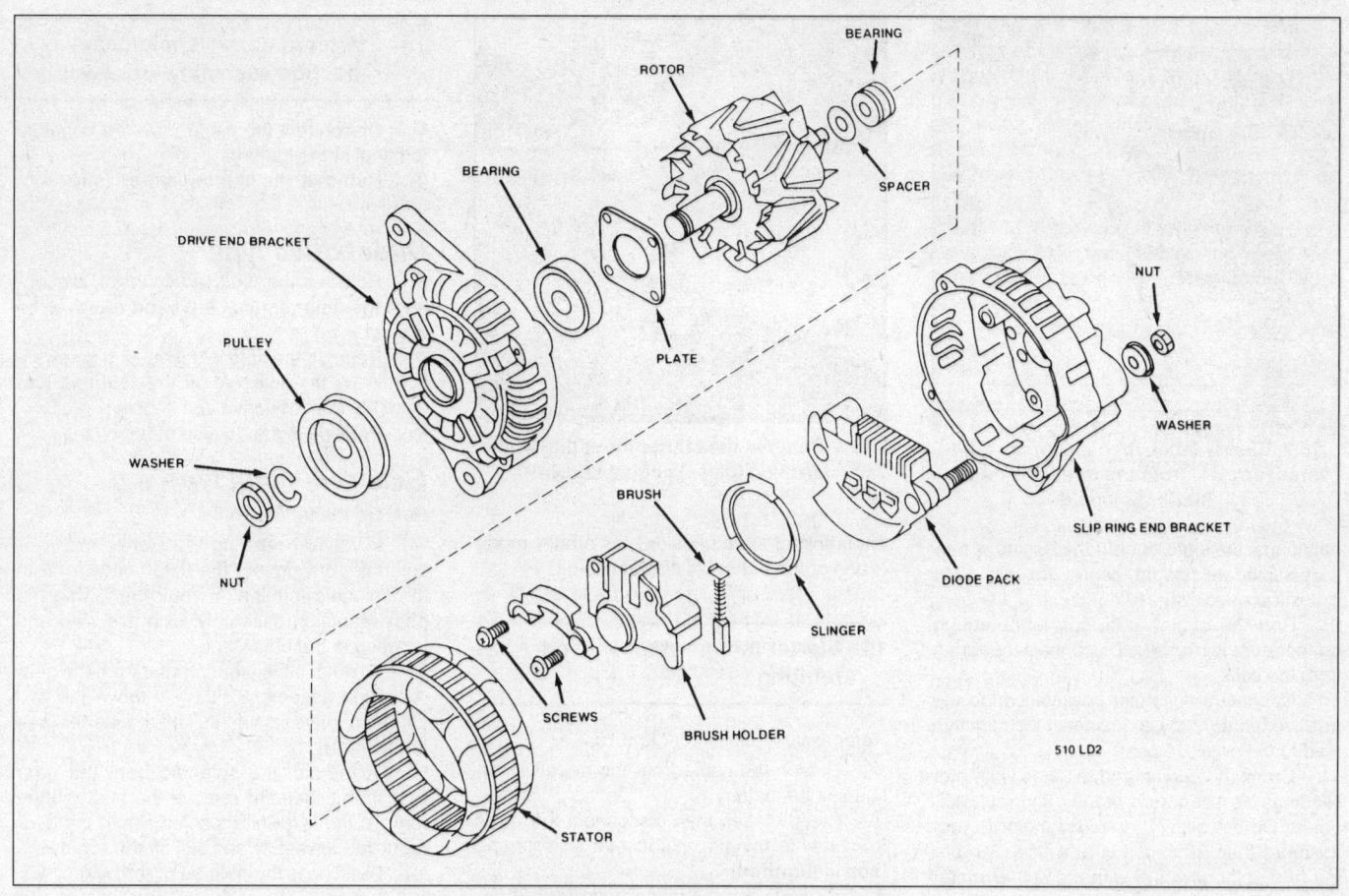

12.6 Typical exploded view of the alternator

components, it's a good idea to use a pair of needle-nose pliers as a heat sink. Don't apply heat for more than about five seconds.

7   Inspect the brushes for excessive wear and renew them if necessary by unsoldering.
8   When fitting new brushes, solder the pigtails so the brush limit line will be about 2 to 3 mm above the end of the brush holder.
9   To reassemble, compress the brushes into their holder and retain them with a straight piece of wire that can be pulled from the back of the alternator when reassembled.
10 To reassemble, reverse disassembly procedure.

13 Starting system - general information and precautions

The sole function of the starting system is to turn over the engine quickly enough to allow it to start.

The starting system consists of the battery, the starter motor, the starter solenoid and the wires connecting them. The solenoid is mounted directly on the starter motor.

The solenoid/starter motor assembly is fitted on the transmission bellhousing.

When the ignition key is turned to the Start position, the starter solenoid is actuated through the starter control circuit. The starter solenoid then connects the battery to the starter. The battery supplies the electrical energy to the starter motor, which does the actual work of cranking the engine.

Always observe the following precautions when working on the starting system:

a) *Excessive cranking of the starter motor can overheat it and cause serious damage. Never operate the starter motor for more than 30 seconds at a time without pausing to allow it to cool for at least two minutes.*
b) *The starter is connected directly to the battery and could arc or cause a fire if mishandled, overloaded or shorted out.*
c) *Always detach the cable from the negative terminal of the battery before working on the starting system.*

14 Starter motor - in-vehicle check

Note: *Before diagnosing starter problems, make sure the battery is fully charged.*

1   If the starter motor does not turn at all when the switch is operated, make sure that the shift lever is in Neutral or Park (automatic transmission) or that the clutch pedal is depressed (manual transmission).
2   Make sure that the battery is charged and that all cables, both at the battery and starter solenoid terminals, are clean and secure.
3   If the starter motor spins but the engine is not cranking, the overrunning clutch in the starter motor is slipping and the starter motor must be renewed.
4   If, when the switch is actuated, the starter motor does not operate at all but the solenoid clicks, then the problem lies with either the battery, the main solenoid contacts or the starter motor itself (or the engine is seized).
5   If the solenoid plunger cannot be heard when the switch is actuated, the battery is bad, the fusible link is burned (the circuit is open) or the solenoid itself is defective.
6   To check the solenoid, connect a jumper lead between the battery (+) and the ignition switch wire terminal (the small terminal) on the solenoid. If the starter motor now operates, the solenoid is not defective and the problem is in the ignition switch, neutral start switch or the wiring.
7   If the starter motor still does not operate, remove the starter/solenoid assembly for disassembly, testing and repair.
8   If the starter motor cranks the engine at an abnormally slow speed, first make sure that the battery is charged and that all termi-

5-8 Chapter 5 Engine electrical systems

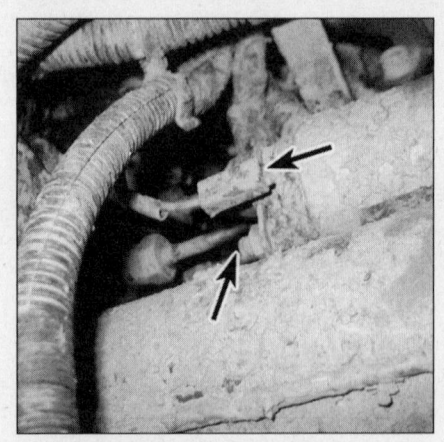

15.2 Clearly label, then disconnect the wires (arrows) from the terminals on the starter solenoid

15.3 Remove the starter mounting bolts (arrows) (diesel engine shown)

nal connections are tight. If the engine is partially seized, or has the wrong viscosity oil in it, it will crank slowly.

9   Run the engine until normal operating temperature is reached. Disconnect the wiring from the coils.
10   Connect a voltmeter positive lead to the positive battery post and connect the negative lead to the negative post.
11   Crank the engine and take the voltmeter readings as soon as a steady figure is indicated. Do not allow the starter motor to turn for more than 30 seconds at a time. A reading of 9 volts or more, with the starter motor turning at normal cranking speed, is normal. If the reading is 9 volts or more but the cranking speed is slow, the solenoid contacts are burned, there is a bad connection or the motor is faulty. If the reading is less than 9 volts and the cranking speed is slow, the starter motor is bad or the battery is discharged.

15 Starter motor - removal and refitting

Refer to illustrations 15.2 and 15.3

1   Detach the cable from the negative terminal of the battery.
2   Clearly label, then disconnect the wires from the terminals on the starter solenoid **(see illustration)**.
3   Remove the mounting bolts **(see illustration)** and remove the starter.
4   Refitting is the reverse of removal.

16 Starter motor/solenoid/gear reduction assembly - renewal

1   Disconnect the cable from the negative terminal of the battery.
2   Remove the starter motor (see section 15).

Direct drive type
3   Remove the field terminal nut, disconnect the field terminal lead and remove the washer.
4   Remove the solenoid mounting screws.
5   Work the solenoid off the shift fork and detach it from the drive end housing.
6   Refitting is the reverse of removal.

Gear reduction type
Refer to illustration 16.8

7   If you're renewing the starter motor or solenoid, disconnect the field coil wire from the solenoid terminal; if you're renewing the gear reduction assembly, skip this step and proceed to the next step.
8   To detach the starter motor from the gear reduction assembly, simply remove the two long through-bolts and pull off the starter **(see illustration)**.
9   To detach the solenoid from the gear reduction assembly, remove the starter, then remove the two Phillips screws from the gear reduction assembly and pull off the solenoid.
10   Refitting is the reverse of removal.

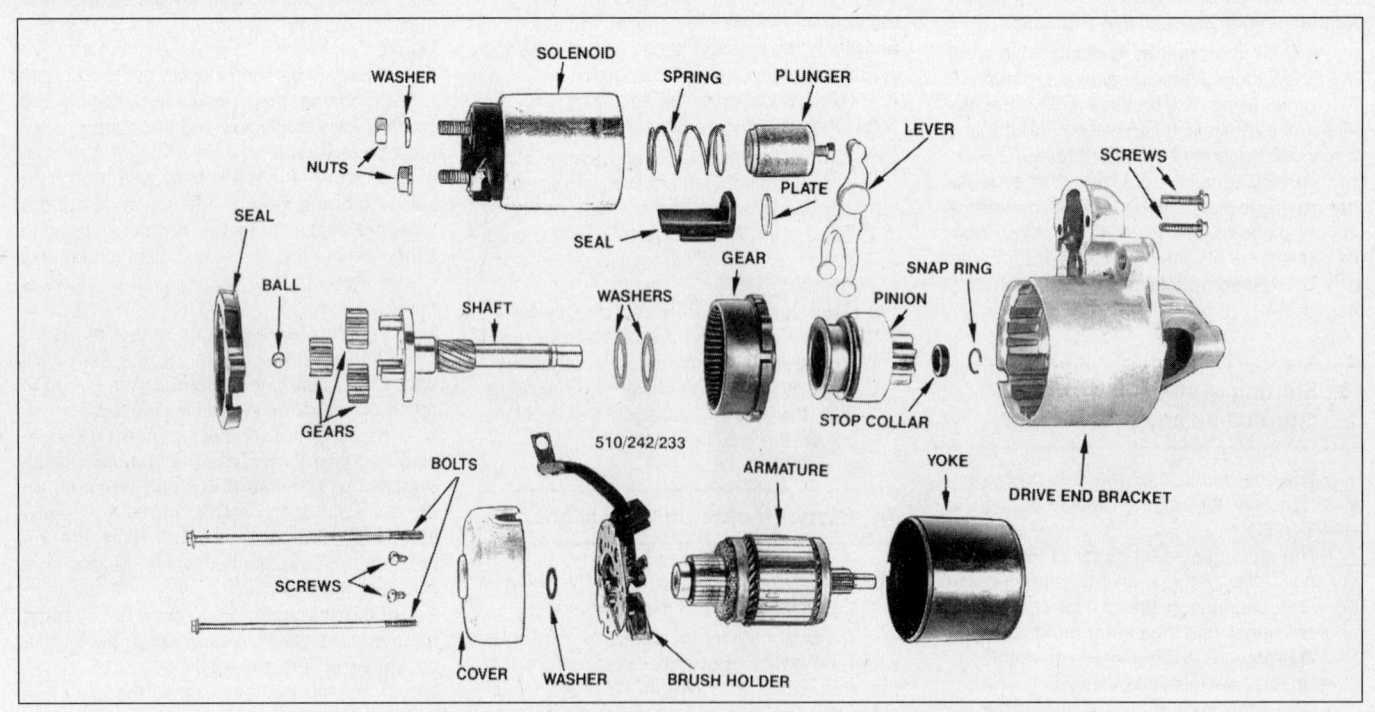

16.8 Typical exploded view of the gear reduction starter motor (early model shown)

Chapter 6
Emissions and engine control systems

Contents

	Section		Section
Accelerator Pedal Position (APPS) sensor - renewal	14	Knock sensor - renewal	10
Air flow sensor - renewal	5	On Board Diagnostic (OBD) system and trouble codes	2
Boost Air Temperature sensor (3.2L diesel engines) - renewal	13	Oxygen sensor (petrol engines) - renewal	9
Camshaft Position (CMP) sensor (petrol engines) - renewal	8	Positive Crankcase Ventilation (PCV) system	16
Catalytic converter	19	Powertrain Control Module (PCM) - check and renewal	3
CHECK ENGINE light	See Section 2	Power Steering Pressure Switch (PSP) - renewal	12
Crankshaft Position (CKP) sensor (petrol engines) - renewal	7	Suction control valve - replacement	See Chapter 4
Engine Coolant Temperature (ECT) sensor - renewal	6	Throttle Position sensor and control motor - renewal	15
Exhaust Gas Recirculation (EGR) system	17	Throttle Position sensor (TPS) - renewal	4
Evaporative emissions control (EVAP) system	18	Vehicle Speed sensor (VSS) - renewal	11
General information	1		

Specifications

Torque specifications

	Nm
Crankshaft sensor bolts	8 to 9
Camshaft sensor bolt	8 to 9
EGR mounting bolts/nuts	
Petrol	23
Diesel	48

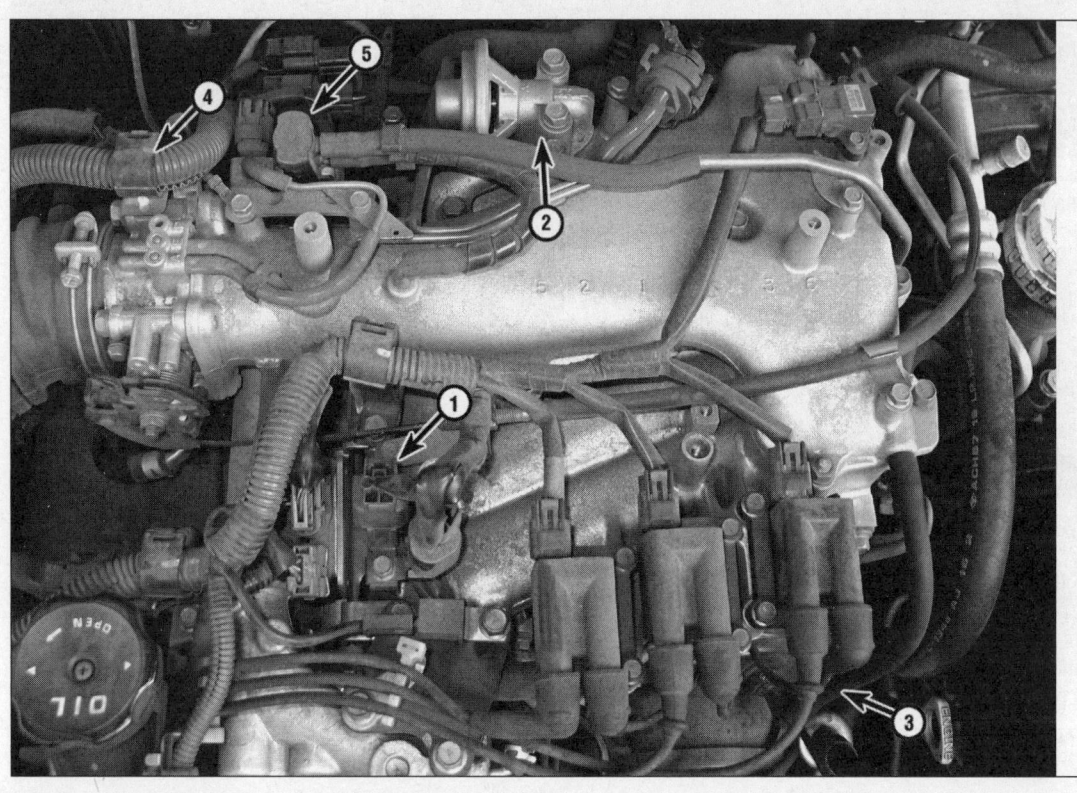

1.1a Typical engine emission control system components - 3.5L (6G74) V6 petrol engine

1. Engine coolant temperature (ECT) sensor
2. Exhaust gas recirculation (EGR) valve
3. Positive crankcase ventilation (PCV) valve
4. Throttle position sensor (TPS)
5. Canister purge valve

6-2 Chapter 6 Emissions and engine control systems

1.1b Typical engine emission control system components - 3.8L (6G75) V6 petrol engine

1. Engine coolant temperature (ECT) sensor
2. Positive crankcase ventilation (PCV) valve
3. Airflow sensor assembly
4. Exhaust gas recirculation (EGR) valve
5. Throttle position sensor (TPS)
6. EVAP canister

1.1c Typical engine emission control system components - 2.8L (4M40) 4cyl diesel engine

1. Exhaust gas recirculation (EGR) valve
2. Engine coolant temperature (ECT) sensor

Chapter 6 Emissions and engine control systems

6-3

1.1d Typical early engine emission control system components - 3.2L (4M41) 4cyl diesel engine

1 Exhaust gas recirculation (EGR) valve
2 Engine coolant temperature (ECT) sensor
3 Boost air temperature sensor

1.1d Typical late engine emission control system components - 3.2L (4M41) 4cyl diesel engine

1 Exhaust gas recirculation (EGR) cooler
2 EGR valve
3 Engine coolant temperature (ECT) sensor
4 Throttle body
5 Manifold absolute pressure (MAP) sensor

2.1 Digital multimeters can be used for testing all types of circuits; because of the high impedance, they are much more accurate than analog meters for measuring low-voltage computer circuits

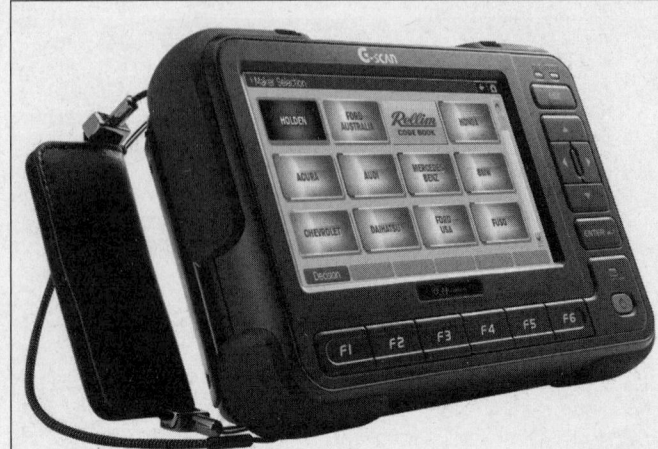

2.2 Scanners like this G-Scan are powerful diagnostic aids - programmed with comprehensive diagnostic information, they can tell you just about anything you want to know about your engine management system

1 General information

Refer to illustrations 1.1a, 1.1b, 1.1c and 1.1d

To prevent pollution of the atmosphere from incompletely burned and evaporating gases, and to maintain good driveability and fuel economy, a number of emissions control systems are incorporated on the vehicles covered by this manual **(see illustrations)**. The combination of systems used depends on the year in which the vehicle was manufactured, the locality to which it was originally delivered and the engine type. They include the:

On-Board Diagnostic (OBD) system
Electronic Fuel Injection (EFI) system (petrol models)
Exhaust Gas Recirculation (EGR) system
Evaporative Emissions Control (EVAP) system
Positive Crankcase Ventilation (PCV) system
Catalytic converter

All of these systems are linked, directly or indirectly, to the On Board Diagnostic (OBD) system. The Sections in this Chapter include general descriptions, checking procedures within the scope of the home mechanic and component renewal procedures (where applicable) for each of the systems listed above.

Before assuming that an emissions control system is malfunctioning, check the fuel and ignition systems carefully. The diagnosis of some emission control devices requires specialised tools, equipment and training. If checking and servicing become too difficult, or if a procedure is beyond your ability, consult your dealer service department or repair shop.

Note: *The most frequent cause of emissions system problems is simply a loose or broken vacuum hose or wiring connection. Therefore, always check the hose and wiring connections first.*

This does not necessarily mean, however, that the emissions control systems are particularly difficult to maintain and repair. You can quickly and easily perform many checks and do most (if not all) of the regular maintenance at home with common tune-up and hand tools.

Pay close attention to any special precautions outlined in this Chapter. It should be noted that the illustrations of the various systems may not exactly match the system fitted on your particular vehicle due to changes made by the manufacturer during production or from year to year.

A Vehicle Emissions Control Information (VECI) label is located in the engine compartment of all vehicles with which this manual is concerned. This label contains important emissions specifications and setting procedures, as well as a vacuum hose schematic with emissions components identified. When servicing the engine or emissions systems, the VECI label in your particular vehicle should always be checked for up-to-date information.

Note: *Check with your dealer about warranty coverage (within the first twelve months) before working on any emission related systems.*

2 On Board Diagnostic (OBD) system and trouble codes

Diagnostic tool information

Refer to illustrations 2.1 and 2.2

1   A digital multimeter is necessary for checking fuel injection and emission related components **(see illustration)**. A digital volt-ohmmeter is preferred over the older style analog multimeter for several reasons. The analog multimeter cannot display the volt-ohms or amps measurement in hundredths and thousandths increments. When working with electronic circuits which often are very low voltage, this accurate reading is most important. Another good reason for the digital multimeter is the high impedance circuit. The digital multimeter is equipped with a high resistance internal circuitry (10 million ohms). Because a voltmeter is hooked up in parallel with the circuit when testing, it is vital that none of the voltage being measured should be allowed to travel the parallel path set up by the meter itself. This dilemma does not show itself when measuring larger amounts of voltage (9 to 12 volt circuits) but if you are measuring a low voltage circuit such as the oxygen sensor signal voltage, a fraction of a volt may be a significant amount when diagnosing a problem. However, there are several exceptions where using an analog voltmeter may be necessary to test certain sensors.

2   Hand-held scanners are the most powerful and versatile tools for analysing engine management systems used on later model vehicles **(see illustration)**. A scan tool has the ability to help diagnose in-depth driveability problems and it allows freeze frame data to be retrieved from the PCM/ECM stored memory. Freeze frame data is a feature that records all related sensor and actuator activity on the PCM/ECM data stream, whenever an engine control or emissions fault is detected and a trouble code is set. This ability to look at the circuit conditions and values when the malfunction occurs provides a valuable tool when trying to diagnose intermittent driveability problems.

Note: *Some generic scanners are unable to extract all the codes for these models. Before purchasing a generic scan tool, contact the manufacturer of the scanner you're planning to buy and verify that it will work properly with the system you want to scan. If the tool is not available and intermittent driveability problems exist, have the codes extracted by a dealer service department or independent repair shop with a professional scan tool.*

General description

3   All petrol models and later diesel models are equipped with an On-Board Diagnostic (OBD) system. This system consists of an

Chapter 6 Emissions and engine control systems

2.29 The diagnostic connector (arrow) is located under the dash, between the steering column cover and the centre console - using a jumper wire, bridge terminals 1 and 4 of the diagnosis connector to enter self diagnosis mode on 3.5L petrol and 2.8L diesel engines

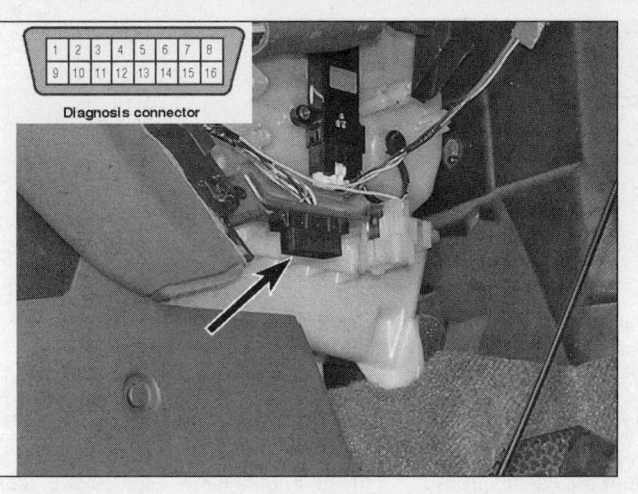

on-board computer known as the Powertrain Control Module (PCM), and information sensors, which monitors various functions of the engine and send data to the PCM. This system incorporates a series of diagnostic monitors that detect and identify the fuel injection and emissions control systems faults and store the information in the computer memory.

4 The PCM/ECM is the "brain" of the electronically controlled fuel and emissions system. It receives data from a number of sensors and other electronic components (switches, relays, etc.) Based on the information it receives, the PCM/ECM generates output signals to control various relays, solenoids (i.e. fuel injectors) and other actuators. The PCM/ECM is specifically calibrated to optimize the emissions, fuel economy and driveability of the vehicle.

5 When they're functioning correctly, emission control systems significantly reduce the levels of certain pollutants (carbon monoxide, hydrocarbons and oxides of nitrogen) emitted by automotive engines. The purpose of On Board Diagnostics (OBD) is to ensure that these systems continue to function correctly. The OBD system is an integral part of the engine management system, which consists of information sensors, output actuators and the Powertrain Control Module/Electronic Control Module (PCM or ECM). When the OBD system detects a malfunction, it notifies the driver by illuminating the CHECK ENGINE light, so that the vehicle can be serviced. It also stores enough information about the malfunction so that it can be identified and repaired.

6 The CHECK ENGINE light or Malfunction Indicator Light (MIL), is located in the instrument panel and should illuminate for three seconds as a bulb test each time the vehicle is started. When the PCM/ECM detects a fault in the emissions or engine control system it sets a trouble code in the PCM's memory. If the PCM/ECM detect a fault related to the vehicle emissions, it illuminates the CHECK ENGINE light which means an emissions component or system is in need of immediate service. In the event the PCM/ECM detects an active engine misfire, the CHECK ENGINE light will flash continuously.

If this occurs, turn the engine off as soon as possible and diagnose/correct the problem or severe catalytic converter damage may occur.

7 The EVAP system will cause the PCM/ECM to store the appropriate fault code and illuminate the CHECK ENGINE light on the instrument panel in the event of a sure leak. The most common cause of CHECK ENGINE light illumination is EVAP system pressure loss due to a loose or poor sealing fuel filler cap. Before accessing the trouble codes and trying to determine the faulty component, make sure your fuel cap seal is free from defects and tightened securely.

8 In addition to notifying the driver when an emissions fault has occurred, the CHECK ENGINE light can be used to display the stored trouble codes from the PCM's memory.

Information sensors

9 Air flow sensor - The Air Flow sensor measures the volume of the air being drawn into the engine. The Air Flow sensor also contains the Intake Air Temperature (IAT) sensor and the Barometric Pressure sensor (BARO). If any of these three components fails, the Air Flow sensor must be replaced.

10 Intake Air Temperature (IAT) sensor - The Intake Air sensor is a thermistor (a resistor which varies the value of its resistance in accordance with temperature changes). The IAT sensor provides the PCM/ECM with intake air temperature information. The PCM/ECM uses this information to control fuel flow, ignition timing and EGR system operation. The IAT sensor, along with the Barometric Pressure sensor, is an integral component of the Air Flow sensor and cannot be replaced separately.

11 Throttle position sensor (TP) - The TP sensor, which is located on the throttle body, on the end of the throttle shaft, is a potentiometer that produces a variable voltage signal in accordance with the opening angle of the throttle valve. This voltage signal tells the PCM/ECM when the throttle is closed, in a cruise position, or wide open, or anywhere in between. The PCM/ECM uses this information along with data from a number of other sensors, to calculate injector on-time. On models with an electronically controlled throttle, the throttle position sensor is incorporated in the same housing as the throttle control motor.

12 Engine coolant temperature (ECT) sensor - The ECT sensor is a thermistor (temperature-sensitive variable resistor) that sends a voltage signal to the PCM, which uses this data to determine the temperature of the engine coolant. The ECT sensor helps the PCM/ECM control air/fuel mixture ratio, ignition timing and EGR system control.

13 Crankshaft angle sensor (CKP) - The crankshaft sensor provides information on crankshaft position and the engine speed signal to the PCM.

14 Camshaft position sensor (CMP) - The camshaft position sensor produces a signal in which the PCM/ECM uses to identify number 1 cylinder and to time the firing sequence of the fuel injectors.

15 Vehicle speed sensor (VSS) - The VSS provides information to the PCM/ECM to indicate vehicle speed.

16 Barometric pressure sensor (BARO) - The barometric pressure sensor measures atmospheric pressure. The PCM/ECM uses this data from the sensor to determine the air density and altitude. The barometric sensor, along with the Intake Air Temperature (IAT) sensor is an integral part of the Air flow sensor, and cannot be replaced separately.

17 Oxygen sensor (O2S) - The O2S generates a voltage signal that varies with the difference between the oxygen content of the exhaust and the oxygen in the surrounding air. The PCM/ECM uses this information to fine tune the amount of fuel being injected into the engine. Late models also have a second oxygen sensor mounted after the catalytic converter. The signal from this sensor is used by the PCM/ECM to determine the condition of the catalytic converter.

18 Power steering pressure (PSP) switch - The PSP monitors the pressure inside the power steering system. When the pressure exceeds a certain threshold at idle or low speed manoeuvres, the switch sends a signal to the PCM, which raises the idle slightly to compensate for the extra load on the engine.

19 Boost Air Temperature sensor (diesel engines) - The boost sensor is a thermistor (a resistor which varies the value of its resistance in accordance with temperature changes). The Boost sensor is the diesels version of the IAT sensor, which provides the ECM with intake air temperature information. The PCM/ECM uses this information to control fuel flow, injector timing and EGR system operation.

20 Engine speed sensor (diesel engines) - The engine speed sensor uses a sensor plate mounted to the injection pump gear. The engine speed sensor read the projections off of the sensor plate and converts that into an electrical signal that is read by the PCM/ECU to control injection timing, and amounts of fuel that's injected.

Note: There are two engine speed sensors used, a main and a back-up. The back-up is only used if the main sensor fails.

21 **Accelerator pedal position sensor** - mounted to the pedal bracket. this sensor

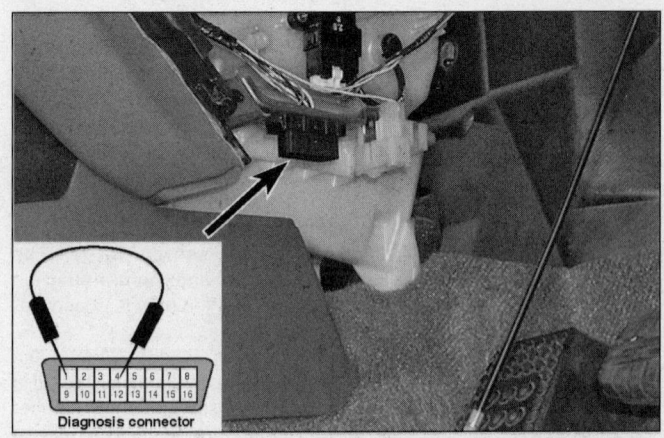

6-6   Chapter 6 Emissions and engine control systems

2.30a Use a jumper harness, connect terminals 1 and 4 of the diagnosis connector. With the ignition On, count the flashes from the Check Engine light

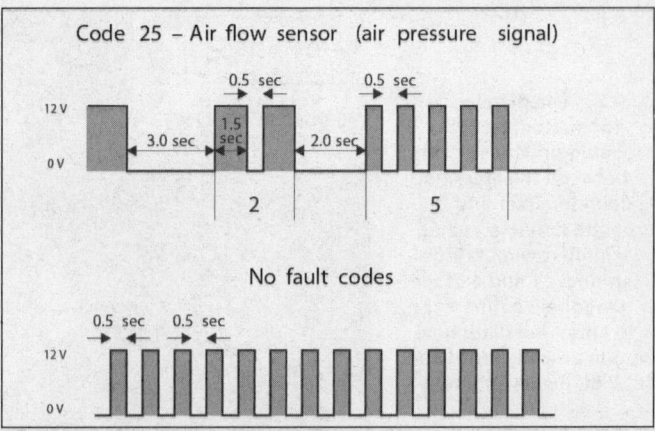

2.30b This table represents how the codes are displayed by the Check Engine lamp. Each code is represented by two groups of flashes separated by a 3 second pause.

measures the driver's demand (how far the throttle pedal is pressed). The signal is sent to the PCM/ECM where the PCM/ECM determines how far to open the throttle valve, via the throttle control motor.

Output actuators

22 EVAP purge control solenoid - The EVAP purge control solenoid, which is controlled by the PCM, allows the fuel vapours in EVAP canister to be drawn into the intake manifold for combustion when ordered to do so by the PCM.

23 Exhaust Gas Recirculation (EGR) solenoid - When the engine is put under a load (hard acceleration, passing, going up a hill, pulling a trailer, etc.) combustion chamber temperatures increase. When the chamber temperature exceeds 1,400 degrees CF, excessive amounts of oxides of nitrogen (NOx) are produced. NOx is a "precursor" (constituent) of photochemical smog. The EGR solenoid, which is controlled by the PCM, allows exhaust gases to recirculated back to the intake manifold where they dilute the incoming air/fuel mixture, which lowers the combustion temperature and decreases the amount of NOx produced during high-load conditions.

24 Fuel injectors (petrol) - The fuel injectors, which spray a fine mist of fuel into the intake ports, where it is mixed with incoming air, are inductive coils under PCM/ECM control. For more information about injectors, see Chapter 4).

25 Fuel injectors (late diesel) - Late diesel models use an electronic fuel injector to inject fuel under extremely high pressure into the combustion chamber. The amount of fuel and the time of the cycle (injection duration) are controlled by the engine PCM/ECM. The fuel is supplied to the injectors via pipes from the injection pump.

26 Idle Air Control (IAC) valve - The IAC valve controls the amount of air allowed to bypass the throttle plate when the throttle plate is at its (nearly closed) idle position. The IAC valve is controlled by the PCM. When the engine is placed under an additional load at idle (high power steering pressure or running the A/C compressor during low speed driving, for example) the engine can run roughly, stumble and even stall. To prevent this from happening, the PCM/ECM opens the IAC valve to increase idle speed enough to overcome the extra load imposed on the engine. For more information about IAC valve, see Chapter 4).

27 Power transistor - The power transistor triggers the ignition coil and determines proper spark advance based on inputs from the PCM. Refer to Chapter 5 for more information on the power transistor.

28 Throttle control motor - Late model petrol and diesel models use an electronically controlled throttle. This negates the need of a throttle cable. The throttle pedal has an accelerator pedal position sensor mounted to the pedal bracket which measures the driver's demand (how far the throttle pedal is pressed). This signal is sent to the PCM/ECM where the PCM/ECM determines how far to open the throttle valve based on signals from the Accelerator pedal position sensor. Also, the throttle position sensor, mounted to the throttle body, will signal back to the PCM/ECM the actual throttle valve position.

Obtaining and clearing Diagnostic Trouble Codes (DTCs)

Refer to illustration 2.29

29 To retrieve fault codes a scan tool is used. The scan tool is connected to the diagnosis connector, located in the driver compartment between the steering column and the centre console **(see illustration)**. On 3.5L petrol and 2.8L diesel models, fault codes can be retrieved without a scan tool and read at the Check Engine light using the following procedure.

Using the check engine light

Warning: *This procedure must not be attempted with 3.8L or 3.2L models*

Accessing the DTC's — 3.5L and 2.8L models

Refer to illustrations 2.30a and 2.30b

30 Fault codes can be retrieved by using a scan tool and following the scan tool prompts or by bridging diagnosis connector terminals 1 and 4 and reading the fault codes at the Check Engine lamp with the ignition switched On **(see illustration)**.

a) Each code is represented by two groups of flashes separated by a 3 second pause. The first group of flashes represents tens, the second group represents units. For example, two flashes, followed 2 seconds later by five flashes, would indicate code 25 **(see illustrations)**.
b) If more than one fault code is in memory, each code will be separated by a 3 second pause.
c) The sequence will be repeated as long as the diagnosis terminals are bridged.
d) If no fault codes are set, the Check Engine lamp will flash every 0.5 seconds.
e) Once you have outputted all of the stored DTC's, look them up on the accompanying chart.

31 After troubleshooting the source of each DTC, make any necessary repairs or replace the defective component(s).

Clearing the DTC's

32 Clear the DTCs as follows:

1) Disconnect the cable from the negative battery terminal for at least 10 seconds and then reconnect the cable.
2) Start the engine, warm it up and then run it at idle for 15 minutes and verify the Check Engine light does not come on.

Using a scan tool

Accessing the DTC's

33 Locate the diagnostic connector, which is located under the dash, between the steering column cover and the centre console **(see illustration 2.30a)**.

Chapter 6 Emissions and engine control systems

OBD trouble codes (3.5L petrol engines)

Trouble code	Circuit or system
12	Air flow sensor system
13	Intake air temperature sensor system
14	Throttle position sensor system
21	Engine coolant temperature sensor system
22	Crank angle sensor system
23	Camshaft position sensor system
24	Vehicle speed sensor system

Trouble code	Circuit or system
25	Barometric pressure sensor system
41	Injection system
44	Ignition coil and power transistor unit system (No.1 and No.4 cylinders)
52	Ignition coil and power transistor unit system (No.2 and No.5 cylinders)
53	Ignition coil and power transistor unit system (No.3 and No.6 cylinders)
54	Immobiliser system

OBD trouble codes (3.8L petrol engines)

Trouble code	Circuit or system
P0101	Mass Air flow circuit, system problem
P0102	Mass air flow sensor circuit, low input
P0106	Barometric pressure system problem
P0107	Barometric pressure sensor circuit, low input
P0108	Barometric pressure sensor circuit, high input
P0111	Intake air temperature system problem
P0112	Intake air temperature circuit, low input
P0113	Intake air temperature circuit, high input
P0116	Engine coolant circuit, system problem
P0117	Engine coolant temperature circuit, low input
P0118	Engine coolant temperature circuit, high input
P0121	Throttle position sensor circuit, system problem
P0122	Throttle position sensor circuit, low input
P0123	Throttle position sensor circuit, high input
P0125	Insufficient coolant temperature for closed loop fuel control
P0128	Coolant thermostat (Coolant temperature below thermostat regulating temperature)
P0130	Oxygen sensor circuit system problem (bank1 sensor 1)
P0131	Oxygen sensor circuit, low voltage (bank1 sensor 1)
P0132	Oxygen sensor circuit, high voltage (bank1 sensor 1)
P0133	Oxygen sensor circuit, slow response (bank1 sensor 1)
P0134	Oxygen sensor circuit - no activity found (bank1 sensor 1)
P0135	Oxygen sensor heater circuit malfunction (bank1 sensor 1)
P0136	Oxygen sensor circuit system problem (bank1 sensor 2)
P0137	Oxygen sensor circuit, low voltage (bank1 sensor 2)
P0138	Oxygen sensor circuit, high voltage (bank1 sensor 2)
P0139	Oxygen sensor circuit, slow response (bank1 sensor 2)

Trouble code	Circuit or system
P0141	Oxygen sensor circuit - no activity found (bank1 sensor 2)
P0150	Oxygen sensor circuit system problem (bank2 sensor 1)
P0151	Oxygen sensor circuit, low voltage (bank2 sensor 1)
P0152	Oxygen sensor circuit, high voltage (bank2 sensor 1)
P0153	Oxygen sensor circuit, slow response (bank2 sensor 1)
P0154	Oxygen sensor circuit - no activity found (bank2 sensor 1)
P0155	Oxygen sensor heater circuit malfunction (bank2 sensor 1)
P0156	Oxygen sensor circuit system problem (bank2 sensor 2)
P0157	Oxygen sensor circuit, low voltage (bank2 sensor 2)
P0158	Oxygen sensor circuit, high voltage (bank2 sensor 2)
P0159	Oxygen sensor circuit, slow response (bank2 sensor 2)
P0161	Oxygen sensor circuit - no activity found (bank2 sensor 2)
P0171	System too lean, left bank (bank 1)
P0172	System too rich, left bank (bank 1)
P0174	System too lean, right bank (bank 2)
P0175	System too rich, right bank (bank 2)
P0181	Fuel temperature sensor circuit system problem
P0182	Fuel temperature sensor circuit low input
P0183	Fuel temperature sensor circuit high input
P0201	Injector circuit - cylinder 1
P0202	Injector circuit - cylinder 2
P0203	Injector circuit - cylinder 3
P0204	Injector circuit - cylinder 4
P0205	Injector circuit - cylinder 5
P0206	Injector circuit - cylinder 6
P0222	Throttle position sensor (sub) circuit low input

OBD trouble codes (3.8L petrol engines) — continued

Trouble code	Circuit or system
P0223	Throttle position sensor (sub) circuit high input
P0300	Random/multiple misfire detected
P0301	Cylinder 1 misfire detected
P0302	Cylinder 2 misfire detected
P0303	Cylinder 3 misfire detected
P0304	Cylinder 4 misfire detected
P0305	Cylinder 5 misfire detected
P0306	Cylinder 6 misfire detected
P0325	Knock sensor circuit malfunction
P0335	Crankshaft position sensor circuit malfunction
P0340	Crankshaft position sensor circuit system problem
P0401	Exhaust gas recirculation flow insufficient detected
P0403	Exhaust gas recirculation control circuit
P0421	Warm up catalyst efficiency below threshold (bank 1)
P0431	Warm up catalyst efficiency below threshold (bank 2)
P0441	Evaporative emission control system incorrect purge flow
P0442	Evaporative emission control system leak detected (small)
P0443	Evaporative emission control system purge control circuit malfunction
P0446	Evaporative emission control system vent control circuit
P0451	Evaporative emission control system pressure sensor range
P0452	Evaporative emission control system pressure sensor low input
P0453	Evaporative emission control system pressure sensor high input
P0455	Evaporative emission control system leak detected (large)
P0456	Evaporative emission control system leak detected (very small)
P0461	Fuel level sensor circuit system problem
P0500	Vehicle speed sensor malfunction
P0506	Idle control system, rpm lower than expected
P0507	Idle control system, rpm higher than expected
P0513	Immobiliser malfunction
P0551	Power steering pressure sensor circuit problem
P0554	Power steering pressure sensor circuit intermittent
P0606	Powertrain control module main processor malfunction
P0638	Throttle actuator control motor circuit problem
P0642	Throttle position sensor power supply
P0657	Throttle actuator control motor relay circuit problem
P0660	Intake manifold tuning circuit problem

Trouble code	Circuit or system
P0705	Transmission range sensor (Park/Neutral position switch), circuit malfunction
P0712	Transmission fluid temperature sensor circuit low input
P0713	Transmission fluid temperature sensor circuit high input
P0715	Input/Turbine speed sensor circuit problem
P0720	Output speed sensor circuit problem
P0731	Gear 1 incorrect ratio
P0732	Gear 2 incorrect ratio
P0733	Gear 3 incorrect ratio
P0734	Gear 4 incorrect ratio
P0735	Gear 5 incorrect ratio
P0736	Gear R incorrect ratio
P0741	Torque converter clutch system stuck off
P0742	Torque converter clutch system stuck on
P0743	Torque converter clutch system electrical
P0748	Pressure control solenoid valve circuit
P0753	Shift solenoid "A" electrical
P0758	Shift solenoid "B" electrical
P0763	Shift solenoid "C" electrical
P0768	Shift solenoid "D" electrical
P0773	Shift solenoid "E" electrical
P1400	Manifold differential pressure sensor circuit problem
P1601	Communication problem between PCM/ECM and throttle actuator control module
P1603	Battery backup circuit problem
P1610	Immobiliser malfunction
P1751	A/T control relay malfunction
P2100	Throttle actuator control motor circuit open
P2101	Throttle actuator control motor magneto problem
P2102	Throttle actuator control motor circuit shorted low
P2103	Throttle actuator control motor circuit shorted high
P2108	Throttle actuator control processor problem
P2121	Accelerator pedal position sensor (main) circuit problem
P2122	Accelerator pedal position sensor (main) circuit low input
P2123	Accelerator pedal position sensor (main) circuit high input
P2126	Accelerator pedal position sensor (main) circuit problem
P2127	Accelerator pedal position sensor (main) circuit low input
P2128	Accelerator pedal position sensor (main) circuit high input
P2135	Throttle position sensor (main and sub) problem
P2138	Accelerator pedal position sensor (main and sub) problem

Chapter 6 Emissions and engine control systems

OBD trouble codes (2.8L diesel engines)

Trouble code	Circuit or system
11	Accelerator pedal position sensor (main) system
12	Boost pressure sensor system
13	Barometric sensor (built-in) system
14	Fuel temperature sensor system
15	Engine coolant temperature sensor system
16	Boost air temperature sensor system
17	Vehicle speed sensor system
18	Engine speed sensor (backup) system
21	Engine speed sensor system
23	Idle switch (accelerator pedal position sensor built-in) system
25	Timer piston position sensor system
26	Control sleeve position sensor system
27	Accelerator pedal position sensor (sub) system
41	Main throttle solenoid valve system
43	Timing control valve system
46	Injection correction ROM system
48	GE actuator (in the middle of control sleeve position sensor inoperative) system
49	Over boost (turbocharger waste gate malfunction)
54	Immobiliser system

OBD trouble codes (3.2L diesel engines)

Trouble code	Circuit or system
P0016	Crank angle sensor/camshaft position sensor phase problem
P0047	Variable geometry control solenoid valve circuit low input
P0048	Variable geometry control solenoid valve circuit high input
P0072	No. 2 intake air temperature sensor circuit low input
P0073	No. 2 intake air temperature sensor circuit high input
P0088	Common rail pressure malfunction
P0089	Suction control valve stuck
P0093	Fuel Leak Problem
P0102	Air flow sensor circuit low input
P0103	Air flow sensor circuit high input
P0106	Manifold absolute pressure sensor range/performance problem
P0107	Manifold absolute pressure sensor circuit low input
P0108	Manifold absolute pressure sensor circuit high input
P0112	No. 1 intake air temperature sensor circuit low input
P0113	No. 1 intake air temperature sensor circuit high input
P0117	Engine coolant temperature sensor circuit low input
P0118	Engine coolant temperature sensor circuit high input
P0122	Throttle position sensor circuit low input
P0123	Throttle position sensor circuit high input
P0182	Fuel temperature sensor circuit low input
P0183	Fuel temperature sensor circuit high input
P0191	Rail pressure sensor range/performance problem
P0192	Rail pressure sensor circuit low input
P0193	Rail pressure sensor circuit high input
P0201	No. 1 injector circuit malfunction
P0202	No. 2 injector circuit malfunction
P0203	No. 3 injector circuit malfunction
P0204	No. 4 injector circuit malfunction
P0299	Turbocharger under boost condition
P0301	No. 1 cylinder injector malfunction (No injection)
P0302	No. 2 cylinder injector malfunction (No injection)
P0303	No. 3 cylinder injector malfunction (No injection)
P0304	No. 4 cylinder injector malfunction (No injection)
P0335	Crank angle sensor system
P0336	Crank angle sensor range/performance problem
P0340	Camshaft position sensor system
P0341	Camshaft position sensor range/performance problem
P0403	Exhaust gas recirculation valve DC motor malfunction
P0405	Exhaust gas recirculation valve position sensor circuit low input
P0406	Exhaust gas recirculation valve position sensor circuit high input
P0502	Vehicle speed sensor low input
P0513	Immobiliser malfunction
P0551	Power steering fluid pressure switch system
P0603	EEPROM malfunction
P0604	Random access memory (RAM) malfunction
P0605	Read only memory (FLASH ROM) malfunction
P0606	Engine-ECM (main CPU) malfunction
P0607	Engine-ECM (sub CPU) malfunction
P0628	Suction control valve open

OBD trouble codes (3.2L diesel engines) — continued

Code	Description
P0629	Suction control valve battery short
P0630	Chassis number not programmed
P0638	Throttle valve control servo stuck
P0642	Analog sensor reference voltage No. 1 too low
P0643	Analog sensor reference voltage No. 1 too high
P0652	Analog sensor reference voltage No. 2 too low
P0653	Analog sensor reference voltage No. 2 too high
P1203	Capacitor insufficient charging
P1204	Capacitor excessive charging
P1272	Pressure limiter malfunction
P1273	Supply pump insufficient flow
P1274	Supply pump protection
P1275	Supply pump exchange
P1298	Variable geometry turbocharger control system malfunction (high pressure)
P1299	Variable geometry turbocharger control system malfunction (low pressure)
P1625	Injection quantity compensation valve error
P1626	Injection quantity compensation valve not coding
P2009	Swirl control solenoid valve circuit low input
P2010	Swirl control solenoid valve circuit high input
P2118	Throttle valve control DC motor current malfunction
P2122	Accelerator pedal position sensor (main) circuit low input
P2123	Accelerator pedal position sensor (main) circuit high input
P2127	Accelerator pedal position sensor (sub) circuit low input
P2128	Accelerator pedal position sensor (sub) circuit high input
P2138	Accelerator pedal position sensor (main and sub) range/performance problem
P2146	Injector common 1 (cylinder No. 1 and No. 4) circuit open
P2147	Injector common circuit earth short
P2148	Injector common circuit battery short
P2149	Injector common 2 (cylinder No. 2 and No. 3) circuit open
P2228	Barometric pressure sensor circuit low input
P2229	Barometric pressure sensor circuit high input
P2413	Exhaust gas recirculation system performance

34 With the key in the "OFF" position, connect the scan tool to the diagnostic connector, following all the instructions included with the scan tool. Turn the key to the "ON" position and read the codes and parameters of the display. If the information cannot be obtained readily, have the vehicle analysed by a dealer service department or other qualified repair shop.

Clearing the DTC's

35 With the scan tool attached to the diagnostic connector, follow the prompt of the screen to delete any stored DTC's.

Diagnostic Trouble Codes

36 The accompanying tables are a list of the Diagnostic Trouble Codes (DTCs) that can be accessed by a do-it-yourselfer working at home (there are many, many more DTCs available to dealerships with proprietary scan tools and software, but those cannot be accessed by volt-ohmmeter or generic scan tool). If, after you have checked and repaired the connectors, wire harness and vacuum hoses (if applicable) for an emission-related system, component or circuit, the problem persists, have the vehicle checked by a dealer service department or a qualified repair shop.

3 Powertrain Control Module (PCM/ECM) - check and renewal

PCM/ECM check

1 Remove the passenger side kick panel to gain access to the PCM.
2 Using the tips of the fingers, vigorously wiggle the wiring harness of the computer while the engine is running. If the computer is not functioning properly, the engine will stumble or stall and display glitches on the engine data stream obtained using a SCAN tool or other diagnostic equipment.
3 If the PCM/ECM fails this test, check the electrical connectors. Each connector is colour coded to fit the respective slot in the computer body. If there are no obvious signs of damage, have the unit checked at a dealer service department.

PCM/ECM renewal

Caution: *To prevent damage to the PCM, the ignition switch must be turned Off when disconnecting or connecting in the PCM/ECM connectors.*

Caution: *If the stereo in your vehicle is equipped with an anti-theft system, make sure you have the correct activation code before disconnecting the battery.*

4 Disconnect the cable from the negative battery terminal.

2000 and earlier models

5 Remove the wiring connectors from the PCM.
6 Carefully pull back the retaining clips and lift the PCM/ECM from the bracket without damaging the electrical connectors and wiring harness to the computer.
7 Refitting is the reverse of removal. Make certain to transfer the codes and numbers from the old unit to the new. Future computer work will be very difficult without this information.

Note: *If you are fitting a new PCM, it is necessary to have it properly coded.*

2001 and later models

Refer to illustration 3.11

8 Remove the main harness connections.
9 Remove the A/T control relay and connector.
10 Remove the Transmission Control Module (TCM) connector and remove the TCM.
11 Remove the ECM **(see illustration)**.

Note: *It may be necessary to remove the instrument panel for complete access to the ECM and mounting brackets.*

12 Refitting is the reverse of removal. Make certain to transfer the codes and numbers from the old unit to the new.

3.11 The engine-ECM (arrow) is in the passengers side corner behind the glove box

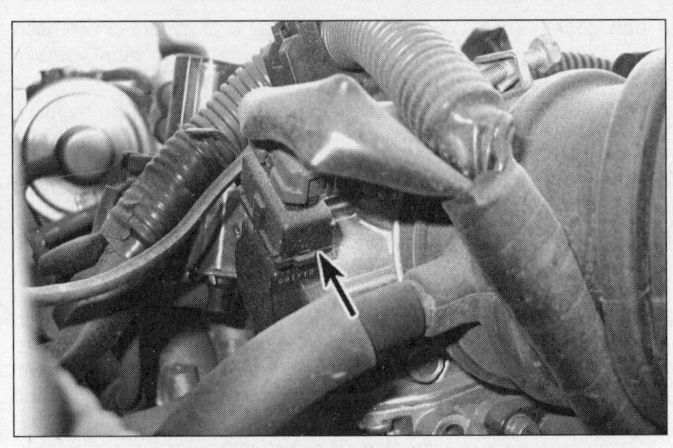

Chapter 6 Emissions and engine control systems

4.2 Disconnect the wiring harness from the sensor (arrow) by releasing the clip with a small screwdriver

5.2 Disconnect the electrical connector from the air flow sensor

4 Throttle Position sensor (TPS) - renewal

Refer to illustration 4.2

Caution: *If the stereo in your vehicle is equipped with an anti-theft system, make sure you have the correct activation code before disconnecting the battery.*

1   Detach the cable from the negative terminal of the battery.
2   Disconnect the wiring harness from the sensor **(see illustration)**, by releasing the clip with a small screwdriver.
3   Remove the two retaining screws.
4   Remove the TPS from the throttle body.
5   Refitting is the reverse of removal. Verify the TPS is mated with the throttle shaft properly before refitting fasteners.

5 Air flow sensor - renewal

Refer to illustration 5.2

Caution: *If the stereo in your vehicle is equipped with an anti-theft system, make sure you have the correct activation code before disconnecting the battery.*

Note: *The Barometric sensor, along with the Intake Air Temperature (IAT) sensor is an integral part of the Air flow sensor, and cannot be replaced separately.*

1   Detach the cable from the negative terminal of the battery.
2   Disconnect the wiring harness from the sensor **(see illustration)**.
3   Disconnect the air inlet hose clamp and pull the hose back.
4   Remove the four mounting nuts and remove the airflow sensor from the air cleaner.
5   Refitting is the reverse of removal. Tighten the nuts securely.

6 Engine Coolant Temperature (ECT) sensor - renewal

Refer to illustrations 6.1a, 6.1b, 6.1c, 6.1d and 6.5

Warning: *Wait until the engine is completely cool before beginning this procedure.*

1   The engine coolant temperature sensor is located on the intake manifold on petrol engines and the cylinder head on diesel engines **(see illustrations)**. The ECT sensor is a thermistor. The thermistor is a resistor which varies the value of its resistance in accordance with temperature changes. The change in resistance values will directly affect the voltage signal from the sensor to the PCM. As the sensor temperature decreases, the resistance values will increase. As the sensor temperature increases, the resistance value will decrease.

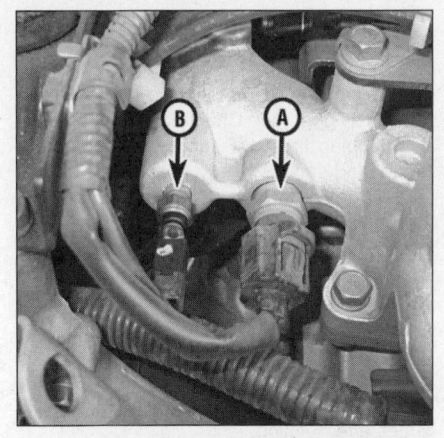

6.1a Typical location of the ECT (A) sensor and temperature gauge sender unit (B) - 3.5L petrol engine shown

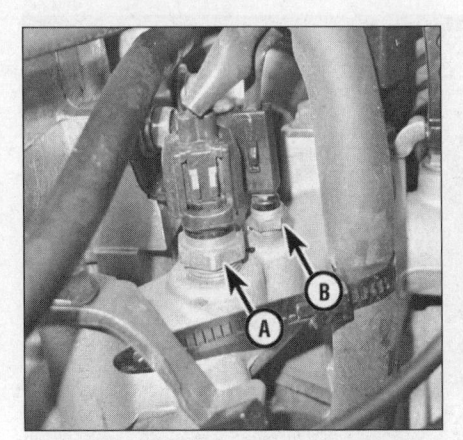

6.1b Typical location of the ECT (A) sensor and temperature gauge sender unit (B) - 3.8L petrol engine shown

6.1c Typical location of the ECT (arrow) sensor - 2.8L diesel engine shown

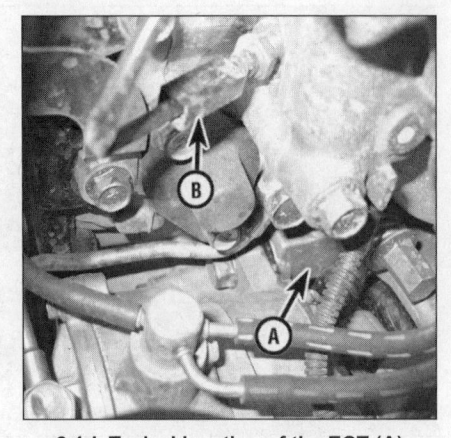

6.1d Typical location of the ECT (A) sensor and temperature gauge sending unit (B) - 3.2L diesel engine shown

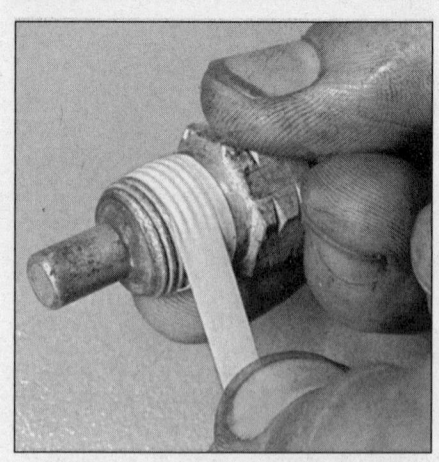

6.5 Wrap the threads of the ECT sensor with Teflon tape to prevent leakage

2 Make sure the ignition key is in the OFF position.
3 Drain approximately one litre from the cooling system (see Chapter 1).
4 Unplug the ECT sensor electrical connector and unscrew the sensor.
5 Wrap the threads of the new sensor with Teflon tape to prevent leakage and thread corrosion **(see illustration)**.
6 The remaining refitting steps are the reverse of removal.
Caution: *Handle the coolant sensor with care. Damage to this sensor will affect the operation of the entire engine control system.*
7 Tighten the ECT securely and check for codes after refitting.

7 Crankshaft Position (CKP) sensor (petrol engines) - renewal

Refer to illustration 7.4

Caution: *If the stereo in your vehicle is equipped with an anti-theft system, make sure you have the correct activation code before disconnecting the battery.*
1 Disconnect the cable from the negative terminal of the battery.
2 Remove the timing belt covers (see Chapter 2A).
3 Follow the CKP sensor harness to the top of the engine and disconnect the harness.
4 Remove the sensor mounting bolts **(see illustration)** and remove the sensor.
5 Refitting is the reverse of removal, making sure the sensor is installed in the exact position it was removed from.

8 Camshaft Position (CMP) sensor (petrol engines) - renewal

Caution: *If the stereo in your vehicle is equipped with an anti-theft system, make sure you have the correct activation code before disconnecting the battery.*
1 Disconnect the cable from the negative terminal of the battery.
2 The CMP is located at the rear of the cylinder head.
3 Disconnect the electrical connector from the top of the sensor.
4 Remove the sensor mounting bolt and remove the sensor.
5 Refitting is the reverse of removal, making sure the sensor O-ring is renewed.

9 Oxygen sensor (petrol engines) - renewal

Refer to illustration 9.2

Caution: *If the stereo in your vehicle is equipped with an anti-theft system, make sure you have the correct activation code before disconnecting the battery.*

Note: *The 3.8L (6G75) engines use multiple Oxygen sensors.*

Note: *Because the Oxygen sensor is fitted in the exhaust pipe, which contracts when cool, the sensor may be very difficult to loosen when the engine is cold. Rather than risk damage to the sensor (assuming you are planning to re-use it in another manifold), start and run the engine for a minute or two, then shut it off. Be careful not to burn yourself during the following procedure.*
1 Disconnect the cable from the negative terminal of the battery. Disconnect the electrical connector from the sensor.
2 Unscrew the sensor(s) from the exhaust pipe **(see illustration)**.
Caution: *Excessive force may damage the threads. If difficulty is experienced, try a penetrating lubricant to ease removal.*
3 Anti-seize compound must be used on the threads of the sensor to facilitate future removal. The threads of new sensors will already be coated with this compound, but if an old sensor is removed and fitted, recoat the threads as required.
4 Refitting is the reverse of removal.

10 Knock sensor - renewal

Caution: *If the stereo in your vehicle is equipped with an anti-theft system, make sure you have the correct activation code before disconnecting the battery.*
1 Disconnect the cable from the negative terminal of the battery.
2 Remove the upper and lower intake manifolds (see Chapter 2A).
3 Disconnect the knock sensor wiring harness.
4 The knock sensor is screwed into a bracket that is mounted to both sides of the crankcase. Unscrew the knock sensor from the bracket and remove it from the engine.
5 Refitting is the reverse of removal.

11 Vehicle Speed Sensor (VSS) - renewal

Refer to illustration 11.3

Caution: *If the stereo in your vehicle is equipped with an anti-theft system, make sure you have the correct activation code before disconnecting the battery.*

7.4 Remove the sensor mounting bolts (arrows) and remove the sensor

9.2 Froint oxygen sensor location

Chapter 6 Emissions and engine control systems

11.3 Vehicle Speed Sensor (VSS) location (arrow)

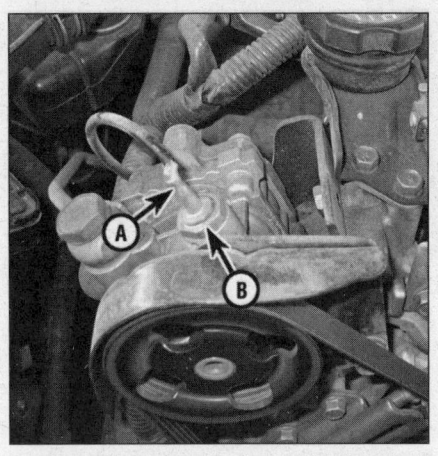

12.2a Disconnect the electrical connector (A) from the switch (B) and unscrew the switch - typical Power Steering Pressure Switch (PSP) on 3.5L petrol engine

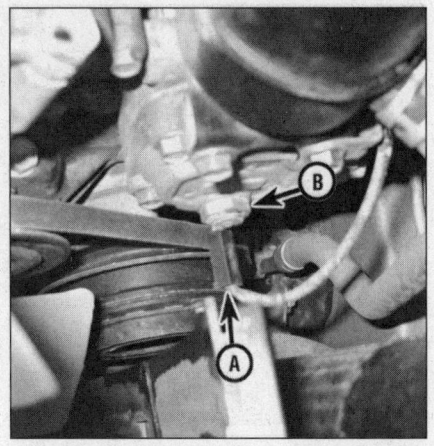

12.2b Disconnect the electrical connector (A) from the switch (B) and unscrew the switch - typical Power Steering Pressure Switch (PSP) on 3.2L diesel engine

1   Disconnect the cable from the negative terminal of the battery.
2   Raise the vehicle and support it securely on jackstands.
3   Disconnect the wiring harness from the sensor **(see illustration)**, by releasing the clip with a small screwdriver.
4   Remove the sensor mounting bolt and remove the sensor.
5   Refitting is the reverse of removal. Be sure to apply a little transmission fluid to the sensor O-ring first.

12 Power Steering Pressure Switch (PSP) - renewal

Refer to illustrations 12.2a and 12.2b

1   The power steering pressure switch is located on the power steering pump.
2   Disconnect the electrical connector to the PSP switch **(see illustrations)**.
3   Place a drain pan under the power steering pump.
4   Remove the power steering pump cap and withdraw some fluid.
5   Unscrew the switch from the pump and remove the switch.
Note: *Fluid will leak out when the switch is removed so have some fluid to replace any that's lost during removal.*
6   Refitting is the reverse of removal. Be sure to refill the system (see Chapter 1).
7   Bleed the air from the power steering pump (see Chapter 10).

13 Boost Air Temperature sensor (3.2L diesel engines) - renewal

Refer to illustration 13.2
Caution: *If the stereo in your vehicle is equipped with an anti-theft system, make sure you have the correct activation code before disconnecting the battery.*

1   Disconnect the cable from the negative terminal of the battery.
2   Disconnect the electrical connector to the sensor **(see illustration)**.
3   Unscrew the sensor from the intake air housing and remove the sensor and gasket.
4   Place the new gasket on to the sensor and install the sensor into the housing.
5   Refitting is the reverse of removal.

14 Accelerator Pedal Position (APPS) sensor - renewal

Refer to illustration 14.3
Warning: *All models have airbags. Always disconnect the negative battery cable, then the positive cable and wait two minutes before working in the vicinity of the impact sensors, steering column or instrument panel to avoid the possibility of accidental deployment of the airbag, which could cause personal injury (see Chapter 12).*

13.2 Disconnect the electrical connector (arrow) to the Boost Air Temperature sensor

Caution: *If the stereo in your vehicle is equipped with an anti-theft system, make sure you have the correct activation code before disconnecting the battery.*
1   Disconnect the cable from the negative terminal of the battery.
2   Carefully mark the accelerator pedal position sensor (APPS) to the bracket.
Note: *The APPS must be carefully removed and installed to the bracket, making sure that the sensor-to-bracket is marked so that it can be installed in the exact place. If this cannot be done take the vehicle to your local dealer and have the sensor installed and adjusted.*
3   Once the APPS has been marked, disconnect the electrical connector and remove the mounting screws **(see illustration)**, then carefully separate the sensor from the pedal bracket.
4   Refitting is the reverse of removal making sure the sensor is installed in the exact position it was removed from.

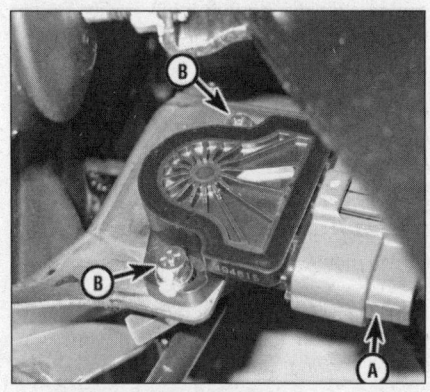

14.3 Once the APPS body has been carefully marked to the accelerator pedal bracket, disconnect the electrical connector (A) and remove the mounting screws (B), then carefully separate the sensor from the pedal bracket

15.1 Power for the throttle control motor is supplied by the labelled relay. On the relay cover the relay is labelled D

15.2 Disconnect the wiring from the sensor and check for power at terminal 2 of the wiring harness. Terminal identification is viewed as if looking into the rear of the connector

15 Throttle position sensor and control motor

Refer to illustrations 15.1 and 15.2

Note: *On late petrol models, throttle movement is controlled electronically by a throttle control motor. Within the throttle control motor assembly are two position sensors that relay to the PCM/ECM the actual throttle valve position. A sensor on the throttle pedal signals to the PCM/ECM the desired throttle position. The PCM/ECM then operates the throttle control motor, which opens the throttle valve to achieve the desired engine speed.*

The two position sensors share a common power supply and earth circuit. The main signal (from sensor terminal 1) and the sub signal (from sensor terminal 3) will indicate the actual throttle valve position to the PCM.

The position sensors are supplied 5 volts from the PCM/ECM to sensor terminal 2. The path to earth is completed at sensor terminal 4. The two signal circuits going to the PCM/ECM leave the sensor at terminals 1 (main signal) and 3 (sub signal). Terminals 5 and 6 are for the throttle control motor, which is controlled solely by the PCM.

The throttle control motor is controlled by the PCM. The power supply for the motor comes through the PCM/ECM from the throttle control servo relay **(see illustration)** *and is transmitted to the throttle control motor via the drivers within the PCM.*

1 Disconnect throttle position sensor and control motor wiring harness connector.
2 Check voltage at wiring harness connector terminal 2 **(see illustration)**. With ignition On, 5 volts should be available. If voltage is not as specified, check wiring and connections between throttle position sensor and PCM/ECM for continuity and shorts and PCM/ECM power supply and earth circuits. If no fault can be found, a faulty PCM/ECM is indicated.
3 Check for continuity to earth at wiring harness connector terminal 4. If continuity does not exist, check wiring and connections between throttle position sensor and PCM/ECM for continuity and shorts to voltage. PCM/ECM power supply and earth circuits. If no fault can be found, a faulty PCM/ECM is indicated.
4 Check control motor resistance between terminals 5 and 6 of throttle position sensor and control motor. Resistance should be 0.3 – 100 ohms at 20°C. If resistance is not as specified, a faulty throttle control motor is indicated.
5 Connect wiring to throttle position sensor and control motor.
6 Backprobe throttle position sensor and control motor terminal 1. Check voltage while slowly opening and closing the throttle valve with the ignition On Ensure voltage varies smoothly in relation to throttle movement. Ensure voltage is 0.2 – 0.8 volt when throttle is fully closed and voltage is 3.8 – 4.9 volts when throttle is fully open.
If voltages are not as specified, a faulty sensor is indicated.
7 Backprobe throttle position sensor and control motor terminal 3. Check voltage while slowly opening and closing the throttle with the ignition On. Ensure voltage varies smoothly in relation to throttle movement and that voltage is 2.2 – 2.8 volts when throttle is fully closed. and approximately voltage is 3.8 – 4.9 volts when throttle is fully open. If voltages are not as specified, a faulty sensor is indicated.

16 Positive Crankcase Ventilation (PCV) system - petrol engines only

Refer to illustration 16.1

1 The Positive Crankcase Ventilation (PCV) system **(see illustration)** reduces hydrocarbon emissions by scavenging crankcase vapours. It does this by circulating fresh air from the air cleaner through the crankcase, where it mixes with blow-by gases and is then rerouted through a PCV valve to the inlet manifold.
2 The main components of the PCV sys-

16.1 Typical PCV valve (arrow) and hose location

tem are the PCV valve and the vacuum hose connecting this component with the engine and the EVAP system.
3 To maintain idle quality, the PCV valve restricts the flow when the inlet manifold vacuum is high. If abnormal operating conditions arise, the system is designed to allow excessive amounts of blow-by gases to flow back through the crankcase vent tube into the air cleaner to be consumed by normal combustion.
4 Check and renewal of the PCV valve is covered in Chapter 1.

17 Exhaust Gas Recirculation (EGR) system

General information

1 This system meters small amounts of exhaust gases into the engine induction system through an EGR valve. From there the exhaust gases pass into the fuel/air mixture for the purpose of lowering combustion temperatures, thereby reducing the amount of oxides of nitrogen (NOx) formed.

Chapter 6 Emissions and engine control systems

17.7 Remove the vacuum line to the EGR - 3.8L (6G75) petrol engine

17.9a Typical EGR mounting bolt locations (arrows) - 2.8L (4M40) diesel engine

17.9b Typical EGR mounting bolt locations (arrows) - early 3.2L (4M41) diesel engine

2 The amount of exhaust gas admitted is regulated by the EGR valve which is in turn controlled by the PCM. The PCM/ECM uses information from several sensors to make its command to the EGR valve.
3 On all but late model diesels, the EGR valve is actuated by a vacuum control valve controlled by the PCM/ECM. On late model diesels **(see illustration 17.7c)**, the EGR is completely electronic.
4 Common problems with the EGR system include rough idling, stalling during deceleration and rough engine performance during light acceleration.

Check

5 Due to the requirement of special diagnostic equipment for the testing of this system, checking of the components should be handled by a dealer service department or other qualified repair facility.

EGR valve renewal

Refer to illustrations 17.7, 17.8a, 17.8b and 17.8c

6 The EGR valve is mounted to inlet manifold.
7 On early models, disconnect the vacuum line from the valve **(see illustration)**.

8 On late models, disconnect the wiring connector from the EGR valve **(see illustration)**.
9 Unbolt the EGR valve and remove it along with its gasket **(see illustrations)**.
10 Refitting is the reverse of removal.

EGR valve cooler renewal

Refer to illustration 17.12

11 Drain the cooling system (see Chapter 1).
12 Remove the bolts and remove the exhaust supply pipe from the turbo and cooler. **(see illustration)** Discard the gaskets.
13 Disconnect the coolant hoses from the cooler.
14 Remove the nuts and the crossover pipe bracket bolts.
15 Remove the mounting bolts and manoeuvre the crossover pipe from the top of the cooler and remove the cooler from the engine. Discard the crossover pipe gasket.
16 Refitting is the reverse of removal, ensuring new gaskets are used and the cooling system is filled (see Chapter 1). Check for coolant and exhaust leaks once the engine is running.

18 Evaporative emissions control (EVAP) system

Warning: *Petrol is flammable, so take extra precautions when you work on any part of the fuel system. Don't smoke or allow open flames or bare light bulbs near the work area. Don't work in a garage where a gas appliance such as a water heater or a clothes dryer is present. Since petrol is carcinogenic, wear latex gloves when there is a possibility of being exposed to fuel. If you spill fuel on your skin, rinse it immediately with soap and water. Mop up any spills immediately and do not store fuel-soaked rags where they could ignite. When you perform any work on the fuel system, wear safety glasses and keep a Class B type fire extinguisher on hand.*

General description

1 This system is designed to trap and store fuel vapours that evaporate from the fuel tank, throttle body and inlet manifold.
2 The Evaporative Emission Control System (EVAP) consists of the fuel filler cap, a charcoal-filled canister, the lines connecting the canister to the fuel tank, inlet manifold and

17.8 Electronic EGR valve components - late model 3.2 litre (4M41) diesel

1 EGR valve
2 EGR valve connector
3 EGR valve housing
4 Bolts
5 Crossover pipe bracket

17.12 EGR cooler fitted to late model 3.2 litre (4M41) diesel

1 Cooler assembly
2 Mounting bolts
3 Coolant pipes
4 Crossover pipe
5 Exhaust supply pipe into cooler

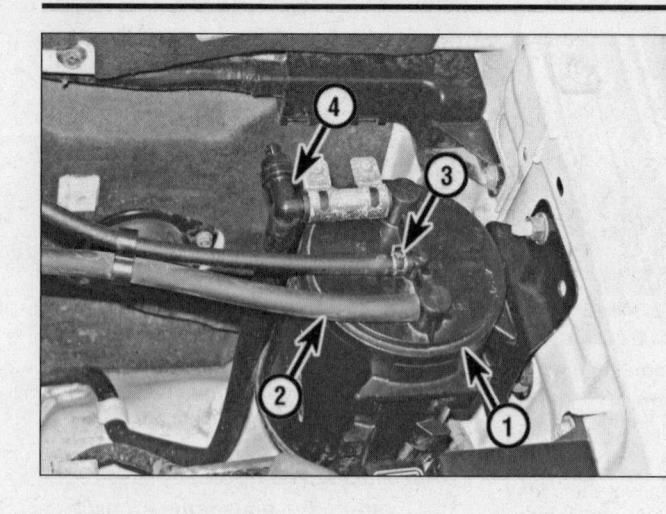

18.8 Clearly label, then detach, all vacuum and vapour lines from the canister - 3.8L engine shown, others similar

1 Carbon canister
2 Purge hose
3 Vapour hose
4 Vent hose

18.12 The purge control solenoid (arrow) is located on the rear of the upper manifold on 3.8L engines

a fresh air inlet line.

3 Fuel vapours are transferred from the fuel tank, throttle body and inlet manifold (or plenum) to a canister where they are stored when the engine is not operating. When the engine is running, the fuel vapours are purged from the canister by a purge control solenoid which is PCM/ECM controlled and consumed in the normal combustion process.

Check

4 Poor idle, stalling and poor driveability can be caused by an inoperative purge control solenoid, a damaged canister, split or cracked hoses or hoses connected to the wrong tubes.
5 Evidence of fuel loss or fuel odour can be caused by fuel leaking from fuel lines, a cracked or damaged canister, an inoperative bowl vent valve, an inoperative purge control valve, disconnected, misrouted, kinked, deteriorated or damaged vapour or control hoses or an improperly seated air cleaner or air cleaner gasket.
6 Inspect each hose attached to the canister for kinks, leaks and breaks along its entire length. Repair or renew as necessary.

Carbon canister

Removal

Refer to illustration 18.8

7 The canister is located at the rear corner of the engine compartment.
8 Clearly label, then detach, all vacuum and vapour lines from the canister **(see illustration)**.
9 Remove the canister from its bracket by sliding it up and pulling it out.

Refitting

10 Refitting is the reverse of removal.

Canister purge control solenoid

Removal

Refer to illustration 18.12

11 The purge control solenoid is located at the engine compartment.
12 Open the bonnet and locate the solenoid **(see illustration)**.
13 Disconnect the electrical connector from the solenoid.
14 Detach the vacuum lines, disconnect the mounting clip and remove the solenoid from the vehicle. On 3.8L engines the solenoid and mounting bracket must be replaced as a unit. Remove the mounting bracket bolts and replace the assembly.

Refitting

15 Refitting is the reverse of removal.

19 Catalytic converter

General description

Refer to illustration 19.1

1 The catalytic converter **(see illustration)** is an emission control device added to the exhaust system to reduce pollutants from the exhaust gas stream. These systems are equipped with a single bed monolith catalytic converter. This monolithic converter contains a honeycomb mesh which is also coated with two types of catalysts. One type is the oxidation catalyst while the other type is a three-way catalyst that contains platinum and palladium. The three-way catalyst lowers the levels of oxides of nitrogen (NOx) as well as hydrocarbons (HC) and carbon monoxide (CO) emissions. The oxidation catalyst lowers the levels of hydrocarbons and carbon monoxide.

Check

2 The test equipment for a catalytic converter is expensive and highly sophisticated. If you suspect the converter is malfunctioning, take it to a dealer service department or authorised emissions inspection facility for diagnosis and repair.
3 Whenever the vehicle is raised for service of underbody components, check the converter for leaks, corrosion and other damage. Check the welds/flange bolts that attach the front and rear ends of the converter to the exhaust system. If damage is discovered, the converter should be renewed.
4 Although catalytic converters don't break too often, they can become plugged. The easiest way to check for a restricted exhaust system (including the converter) on a petrol engine is to use a vacuum gauge to diagnose the effect of a blocked exhaust on intake vacuum.

a) Connect a vacuum gauge to an intake manifold vacuum source (see Chapter 2D).
b) Warm the engine to operating temperature, place the transmission in Park (automatic) or Neutral (manual) and apply the parking brake.
c) Note and record the vacuum reading at idle.
d) Quickly open the throttle to near full throttle and release it shut. Note and record the vacuum reading.
e) Perform the test three more times, recording the reading after each test.
f) If the reading after the fourth test is more than one-kPa lower than the reading recorded at idle, the exhaust system may be restricted (the catalytic converter could be plugged or an exhaust pipe or muffler could be restricted).

19.1 Check the catalytic converter (arrow) carefully for damage especially if the vehicle has been used in rough terrain - typical later model with diesel engine shown

Chapter 7 Part A
Manual transmission

Contents

	Section		Section
General information	1	Manual transmission - removal and refitting	5
Lubricant change	See Chapter 1	Oil seals - renewal	2
Lubricant level check	See Chapter 1	Shift lever - removal and refitting	3
Manual transmission overhaul - general information	6	Transmission mount - check and renewal	4

Specifications

General
Lubricant type .... See Chapter 1

Torque specifications   Nm
Transmission-to-engine bolts
    Diesel engines.. 48
        Starter motor bolts
            NL to NP models 48
            NS to NW models 30
        V6 engines
            12 x 40 mm bolts 79
            12 x 55 mm bolts 88
Transmission mounts
    NL to NP models 44
    NS to NW models 59

1 General information

All vehicles covered in this manual come equipped with a five-speed manual transmission or an automatic transmission. All information on the manual transmission is included in this part of Chapter 7. Information on the automatic transmission can be found in Part B (see Chapter 7B) and information on the transfer case can be found in Part C (see Chapter 7C).

The manual transmission used in these models is a five-speed unit, with fifth gear being an overdrive.

Due to the complexity, unavailability of new parts and the special tools necessary, internal repair by the home mechanic is not recommended. The information in this Chapter is limited to general information and removal and refitting of the transmission.

Depending on the expense involved in having a faulty transmission overhauled, it may be a good idea to renew the unit with either a new or rebuilt one. Your local dealer or transmission shop should be able to supply you with information concerning cost, availability and exchange policy. Regardless of how you decide to remedy a transmission problem, you can still save a lot of money by removing and refitting the unit yourself.

2 Oil seals - renewal

Refer to illustration 2.7

1   Oil leaks frequently occur due to wear of the extension housing oil seal. Renewal of this seal is relatively easy, since the repairs can usually be performed without removing the transmission or transfer case from the vehicle.

2   The housing oil seal is located at the extreme front and rear of the transfer case, where the driveshafts are attached. If leakage at the seal is suspected, raise the vehicle and support it securely on jackstands. If the seal is leaking, transmission lubricant will be built up

Chapter 7 Part A Manual transmission

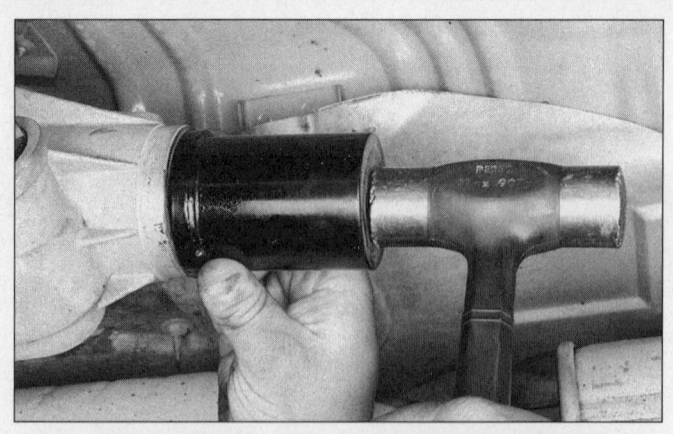

2.7 Use a large socket (shown) or a seal driver to drive the new seal into the extension housing of the transfer case. The outside diameter of the socket must be slightly smaller than the outside diameter of the seal, just enough to clear the edges of the seal bore

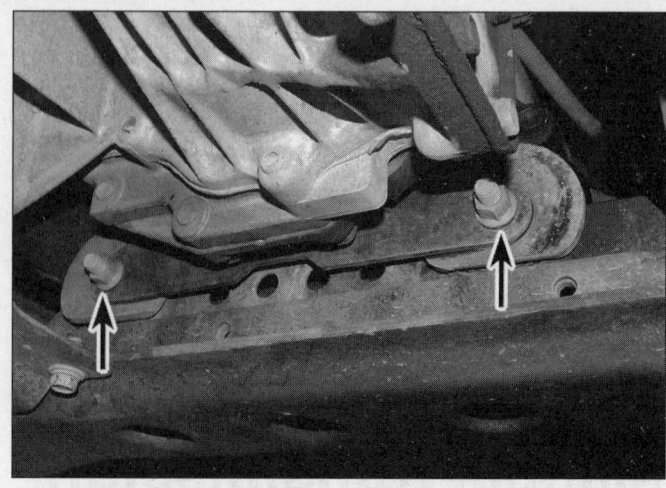

4.3 Remove the transmission mount through bolts and nuts (arrows)

on the front of the driveshaft and may be dripping from the front or rear of the transfer case.
3 Refer to Chapter 8 and remove the driveshaft.
4 Using a soft-faced hammer, carefully tap the dust shield (if equipped) to the rear and remove it from the transfer case. Be careful not to distort it.
5 Using a screwdriver or lever, carefully lever the oil seal out of the rear of the transfer. Do not damage the splines on the output shaft.
6 If the oil seal cannot be removed with a screwdriver or lever, a special oil seal removal tool (available at auto parts stores) will be required.
7 Using a large section of pipe or a very large deep socket as a drift, fit the new oil seal case **(see illustration)**. Drive it into the bore squarely and make sure it's completely seated.
8 Refit the dust shield (if equipped) by carefully tapping it into place. Lubricate the splines of the transmission output shaft and the outside of the driveshaft sleeve yoke with lightweight grease, then refit the driveshaft. Be careful not to damage the lip of the new seal.

3 Shift lever - removal and refitting

Removal

1 Disconnect the negative cable from the battery.
2 If your vehicle is equipped with a centre console, remove it (see Chapter 11).
3 Remove the screws that attach the shifter boot plate to the tunnel. Lift off the plate and pull back the rubber boot. It has a lip that fits over the sheetmetal of the tunnel; take care not to tear the boot as you pull it back.

4 Place the shift lever in the Neutral position. Remove the bolts attaching the shift lever assembly to the transmission and carefully lift out the lever. Plug or cover the hole with a clean rag.

Refitting

5 Apply a thin coat of RTV sealant to both sides of the two gaskets (one over and one under the shift lever stopper plate).
6 Apply multi-purpose grease to the shift lever bush and all shift lever sliding surfaces.
7 The remainder of refitting is the reverse of removal. Tighten the fasteners securely.

4 Transmission mount - check and renewal

Refer to illustration 4.3

Check

1 Insert a large screwdriver or lever into the space between the transmission extension housing and the crossmember and try to prise up slightly.
2 The transmission should not move from the crossmember. If there is any cracking or separation of the rubber from the mounting plate, renew the mount.

Renewal

3 Support the transmission with a jack. Place a block of wood on the jack head to serve as a cushion. Remove the fasteners attaching the mount to the crossmember and the transmission **(see illustration)**.
4 Raise the transmission slightly with the jack and remove the mount.
5 Refitting is the reverse of removal. Be sure to tighten the nuts/bolts to the torque listed in this chapter's Specifications.

5 Manual transmission - removal and refitting

Removal

1 Disconnect the negative battery cable from the battery.
2 Remove the air cleaner assembly (see Chapter 4), then remove the starter (see Chapter 5).
3 Raise the vehicle and support it securely on jackstands. Place a drain pan under the transmission, remove the drain plug and allow the transmission to lubricant to drain.
4 Remove the driveshaft(s) (see Chapter 8).
5 Remove the shift lever (see Section 3).
6 Disconnect the speedometer cable where it enters the transmission. Bend back the retaining strap (if equipped) that holds the speedometer cable housing to the frame crossmember and pull the speedometer cable away from the engine and transmission. Lay it on top of the left frame rail to keep it out of the way.
7 Push forward on the parking brake lever and disengage the cable from the lever. Loosen the parking brake cable housing clamp in front of the frame crossmember and slide the cable housing forward to free it from the support bracket on the crossmember. Lay the cable on top of the left frame rail to keep it out of the way. Remove the pin attaching the rear parking brake cable balancer to the parking brake lever.
8 Unplug the electrical connector for the back-up light switch (just behind the steering box). On early models, remove the bolts retaining the clutch release cylinder and any clips holding the pipes and hoses to the transmission. Remove the cylinder from the transmission housing and position clear of the work area. On late models with an internal release cylinder, place a container beneath the hydraulic line and disconnect it from the

Chapter 7 Part A Manual transmission

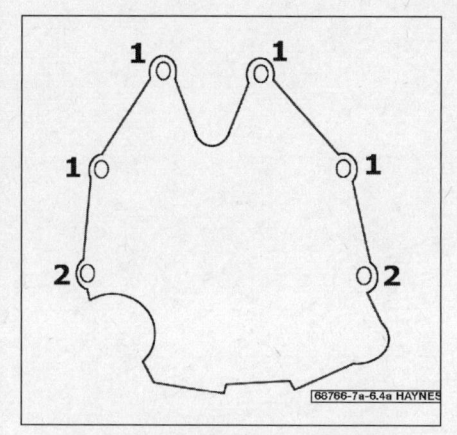

6.4a The transmission mounting bolts come in different lengths, mark each bolt as they are removed - typical petrol engine bolt identification

1 12 x 40 mm
2 12 x 55 mm

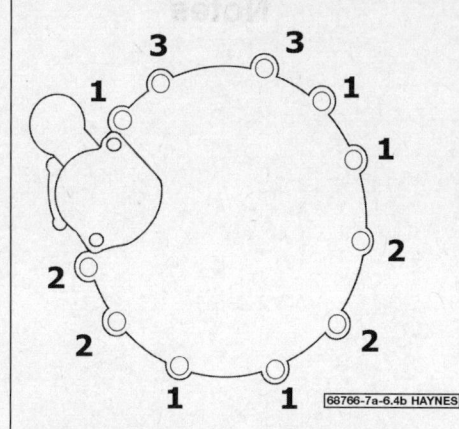

6.4b The transmission mounting bolts come in different lengths, mark each bolt as they are removed - typical diesel engine bolt identification

1 10/12 x 25 mm - depending on model
2 10 x 45 mm
3 10 x 50 mm

transmission. Plug the end of the hose and position clear of the work area.
9 Remove the splash shield from the front of the transmission. It is attached to the engine with two bolts and to the transmission with two bolts.
10 Remove the bolt attaching the exhaust pipe bracket to the transmission.
11 Support the engine with a hoist or, if a hoist isn't available, a floor jack placed under the engine sump (place a wood block on the jack head to serve as a cushion). Remove the bolts that attach the transmission bellhousing to the engine block.
12 Remove the two nuts that attach the transmission to the transmission support crossmember.
13 Support the transmission with a sturdy jack (preferably one equipped with wheels or casters). Remove the transmission support crossmember.
14 Carefully move the transmission/transfer case assembly straight back and away from the engine by moving the transmission supporting jack toward the rear of the vehicle. It would be very helpful to have an assistant at this point. You must pull the transmission/transfer case straight back until it is completely free from the engine or damage to the input shaft may result.
15 Slowly lower the jack and move the transmission/transfer case out from under the vehicle.

Refitting

16 Refitting is the reverse of removal. Be sure to check the clutch disc to make sure it is centre (see Chapter 8) before sliding the transmission into place. Also, before refitting, apply a coat of lithium-based grease to the end of the transmission input shaft and the splines.
17 With the help of an assistant, line up the clutch with the transmission input shaft. Make sure the engine and transmission/transfer case are in a straight line, not angled in relation to each other. Carefully slide the transmission forward until the bellhousing contacts the engine block. To properly engage the clutch disc and the transmission input shaft, you may have to rotate the crankshaft slightly (with a spanner on the bolt holding the pulley to the front of the crankshaft). Do not force the input shaft into the clutch. If the transmission does not move forward smoothly, either the clutch disc/input shaft splines are not lined up, or the transmission is cocked at an angle.
18 Once the transmission/transfer case assembly is in place, support it securely and tighten all of the mounting bolts to the torque listed in this Chapter's Specifications.
19 Don't forget to fill the transmission to the proper level with the recommended lubricant (see Chapter 1).
20 Be sure to bleed the clutch hydraulic system if the hydraulic lines have been opened (see Chapter 8).

6 Manual transmission overhaul - general information

Refer to illustrations 6.4a and 6.4b

Overhauling a manual transmission is a difficult job for the do-it-yourselfer. It involves the disassembly and reassembly of many small parts. Numerous clearances must be precisely measured and, if necessary, changed with select fit spacers and snap-rings. As a result, if transmission problems arise, it can be removed and refitted by a competent do-it-yourselfer, but overhaul should be left to a transmission repair shop. Rebuilt transmissions may be available - check with your dealer parts department and auto parts stores. At any rate, the time and money involved in an overhaul is almost sure to exceed the cost of a rebuilt unit.

Nevertheless, it's not impossible for an inexperienced mechanic to rebuild a transmission if the special tools are available and the job is done in a deliberate step-by-step manner so nothing is overlooked.

The tools necessary for an overhaul include internal and external snap-ring pliers, a bearing puller, a slide hammer, a set of pin punches, a dial indicator and possibly a hydraulic press. In addition, a large, sturdy workbench and a vise or transmission stand will be required.

During disassembly of the transmission, make careful notes of how each piece comes off, where it fits in relation to other pieces and what holds it in place **(see illustrations)**.

Before taking the transmission apart for repair, it will help if you have some idea what area of the transmission is malfunctioning. Certain problems can be closely tied to specific areas in the transmission, which can make component examination and renewal easier. Refer to the *Troubleshooting* Section at the front of this manual for information regarding possible sources of trouble.

Notes

Chapter 7 Part B
Automatic transmission

Contents

	Section		Section
Automatic transmission - removal and refitting	6	Oil seal renewal	See Chapter 7A
Diagnosis - general	2	Shift control cable - check and adjustment	3
Fluid and filter change	See Chapter 1	Throttle control cable (2000 and earlier models) - adjustment	4
Fluid level check	See Chapter 1	Transmission mounts - check and renewal	See Chapter 7A
General information	1	Transmission oil cooler - removal and refitting	7
Inhibitor switch - check and renewal	5		

Specifications

Torque specifications

	Nm
Starter mounting bolts	33
Torque converter-to-driveplate bolts	
NL to NP models	49
NS to NW	56
Transmission drain plug	32
Transmission oil cooler mounting bolts	12
Transmission oil cooler line banjo bolts	42
Transmission-to-engine bolts	
2.8L diesel engines	
10 x 25 mm bolts	49 to 55
10 x 45 mm bolts	19
10 x 50 mm bolts	43 to 55
3.2L diesel engines	48
Petrol engines	
12 x 40 mm bolts	74
12 x 55 mm bolts	88

1 General information

All vehicles covered in this manual come equipped with either a five-speed manual transmission or a 4-speed or 5-speed automatic transmission. All information on the automatic transmission is included in this Part of Chapter 7. Information on the manual transmission can be found in Chapter 7A.

Due to the complexity of the automatic transmissions covered in this manual and the need for specialised equipment to perform most service operations, this Chapter contains only general diagnosis, adjustment and removal and installation procedures.

If the transmission requires major repair work, it should be left to a dealer service department or an automotive or transmission repair shop. You can, however, remove and install the transmission yourself and save the expense, even if the repair work is done by a transmission shop.

2 Diagnosis - general

Note: *Automatic transmission malfunctions may be caused by five general conditions: poor engine performance, improper adjustments, hydraulic malfunctions, mechanical malfunctions or malfunctions in the computer or its signal network. Diagnosis of these problems should always begin with a check of the easily repaired items: fluid level* and condition (see Chapter 1), shift linkage adjustment and throttle linkage adjustment. Next, perform a road test to determine if the problem has been corrected or if more diagnosis is necessary. If the problem persists after the preliminary tests and corrections are completed, additional diagnosis should be done by a dealer service department or transmission repair shop. Refer to the Troubleshooting Section at the front of this manual for information on symptoms of transmission problems.

Preliminary checks

1 Drive the vehicle to warm the transmission to normal operating temperature.
2 Check the fluid level as described in Chapter 1:
  a) If the fluid level is unusually low, add enough fluid to bring the level within the designated area of the dipstick, then check for external leaks (see below).
  b) If the fluid level is abnormally high, drain off the excess, then check the drained fluid for contamination by coolant. The presence of engine coolant in the automatic transmission fluid indicates that a failure has occurred in the internal radiator walls that separate the coolant from the transmission fluid (see Chapter 3).
  c) If the fluid is foaming, drain it and refill the transmission, then check for coolant in the fluid or a high fluid level.
3 Check the engine idle speed.

Note: *If the engine is malfunctioning, do not proceed with the preliminary checks until it has been repaired and runs normally.*

4 Check the throttle control cable for freedom of movement. Adjust it if necessary (see section 4).

Note: *The throttle cable may function properly when the engine is shut off and cold, but it may malfunction once the engine is hot. Check it cold and at normal engine operating temperature.*

5 Inspect the shift linkage (see section 3). Make sure that it's properly adjusted and that the linkage operates smoothly.

Fluid leak diagnosis

6 Most fluid leaks are easy to locate visually. Repair usually consists of renewing a seal or gasket. If a leak is difficult to find, the following procedure may help.
7 Identify the fluid. Make sure it's transmission fluid and not engine oil or brake fluid (automatic transmission fluid is a deep red colour).
8 Try to pinpoint the source of the leak. Drive the vehicle several miles, then park it over a large sheet of cardboard. After a minute or two, you should be able to locate the leak by determining the source of the fluid dripping onto the cardboard.
9 Make a careful visual inspection of the suspected component and the area immediately around it. Pay particular attention to gasket mating surfaces. A mirror is often helpful for finding leaks in areas that are hard to see.
10 If the leak still cannot be found, clean the suspected area thoroughly with a degreaser or solvent, then dry it.
11 Drive the vehicle for several miles at normal operating temperature and varying speeds. After driving the vehicle, visually inspect the suspected component again.
12 Once the leak has been located, the cause must be determined before it can be properly repaired. If a gasket is renewed but the sealing flange is bent, the new gasket will not stop the leak. The bent flange must be straightened.
13 Before attempting to repair a leak, check to make sure that the following conditions are corrected or they may cause another leak.

Note: *Some of the following conditions cannot be fixed without highly specialised tools and expertise. Such problems must be referred to a transmission repair shop or a dealer service department.*

Gasket leaks

14 Check the pan periodically. Make sure the bolts are tight, no bolts are missing, the gasket is in good condition and the pan is flat (dents in the pan may indicate damage to the valve body inside).
15 If the pan gasket is leaking, the fluid level or the fluid pressure may be too high, the vent may be plugged, the pan bolts may be too tight, the pan sealing flange may be warped, the sealing surface of the transmission housing may be damaged, the gasket may be damaged or the transmission casting may be cracked or porous. If sealant instead of gasket material has been used to form a seal between the pan and the transmission housing, it may be the wrong sealant.

Seal leaks

16 If a transmission seal is leaking, the fluid level or pressure may be too high, the vent may be plugged, the seal bore may be damaged, the seal itself may be damaged or improperly refitted, the surface of the shaft protruding through the seal may be damaged or a loose bearing may be causing excessive shaft movement.
17 Make sure the dipstick tube seal is in good condition and the tube is properly seated. Periodically check the area around the speedometer gear or sensor for leakage. If transmission fluid is evident, check the O-ring for damage.

Case leaks

18 If the case itself appears to be leaking, the casting is porous and will have to be repaired or renewed.
19 Make sure the oil cooler hose fittings are tight and in good condition.

Fluid comes out vent pipe or fill tube

20 If this condition occurs, the transmission is overfilled, there is coolant in the fluid, the case is porous, the dipstick is incorrect, the vent is plugged or the drain-back holes are plugged.

3 Shift control cable - check and adjustment

Refer to illustration 3.2

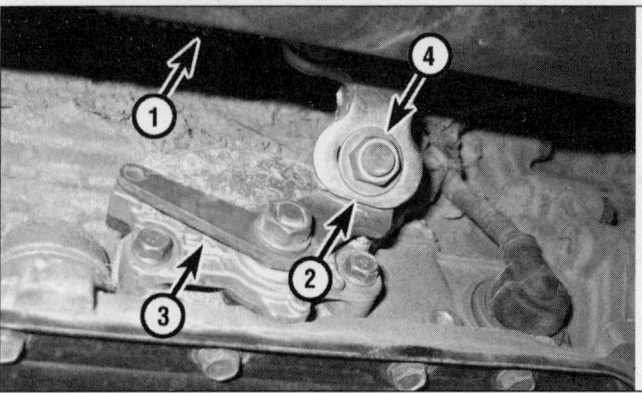

3.2 Place the shift control lever and the selector lever in the "N" position - cable details
1 Transmission control cable
2 Upper manual control lever adjusting nut
3 Inhibitor switch
4 Upper manual control lever

1 Move the shift lever to the 'N' neutral position on the floor console and from under the vehicle, loosen the upper manual control lever adjusting nut.

Note: *Verify the inhibitor switch is in the neutral position.*

2 To adjust the cable, lightly pull the cable forward and tighten the adjusting nut **(see illustration)**.
3 Move the shift lever through the gear ranges and verify that the transmission goes into the correct range and that the vehicle starts in the "P" and "N" positions.
4 If the cable doesn't go into the correct range readjust the control cable.

4 Throttle control cable (2000 and earlier models) - adjustment

Refer to illustration 4.3

1 The throttle control cable adjustment is very important to proper transmission operation. This adjustment positions a valve which controls shift speed, shift quality and part-throttle downshift sensitivity. If the linkage is adjusted so it is too short, slippage between

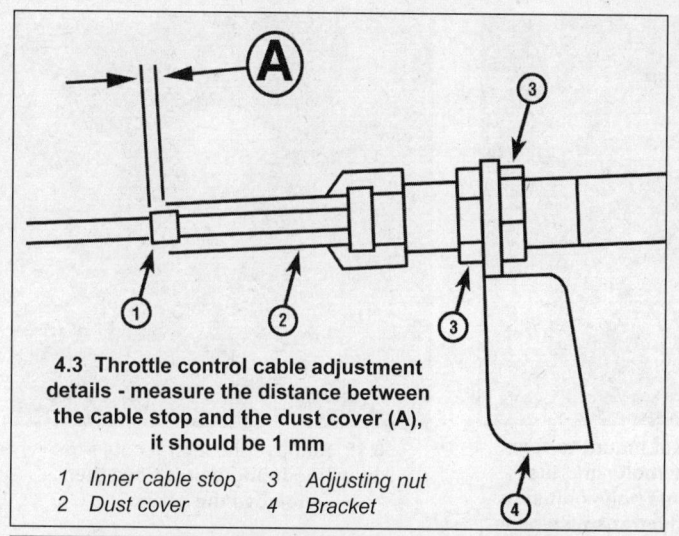

Chapter 7 Part B Automatic transmission   7B-3

4.3 Throttle control cable adjustment details - measure the distance between the cable stop and the dust cover (A), it should be 1 mm

1. Inner cable stop
2. Dust cover
3. Adjusting nut
4. Bracket

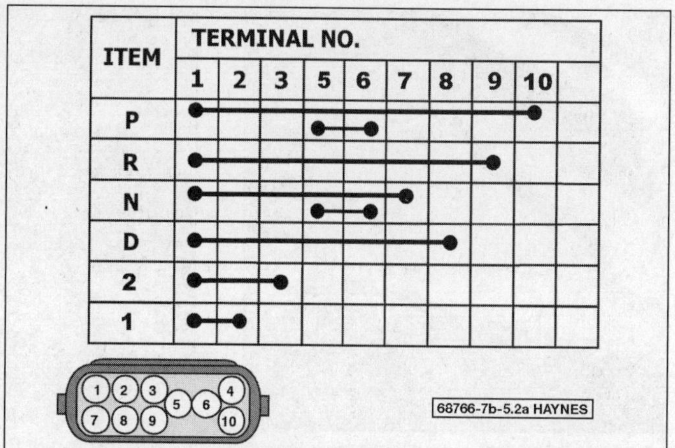

5.2a Inhibitor switch continuity table and terminal guide - 2000 and earlier models. Inset shows terminal identification

ITEM	TERMINAL NO.							
	1	2	3	5	6	7	8	9	10
P	●				●─●|			●
R	●							●	
N	●				●─●|			
D	●						●		
2						●─●|		
1	●		●						

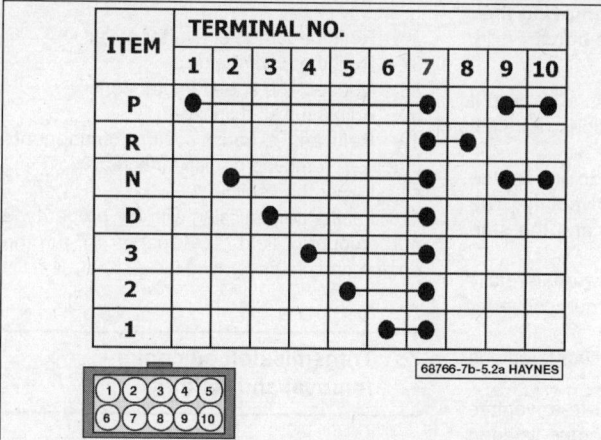

5.2b Inhibitor switch continuity table and terminal guide - 2001 and later models. Inset shows terminal identification

ITEM	TERMINAL NO.									
	1	2	3	4	5	6	7	8	9	10
P	●						●		●	
R							●			
N	●	●					●		●	
D			●				●			
3						●	●			
2					●		●			
1				●			●			

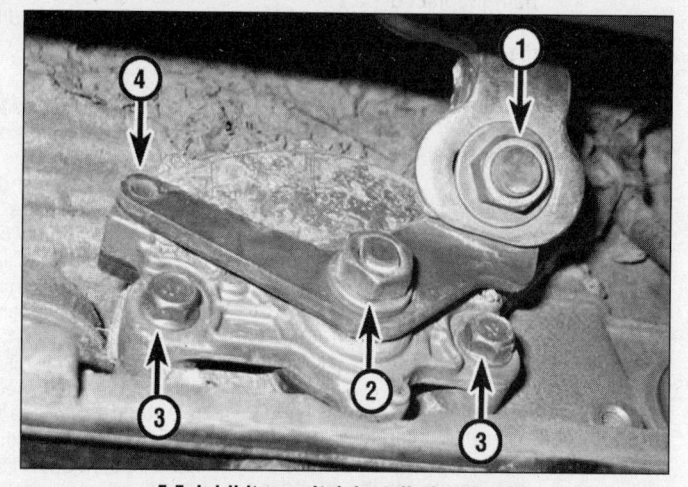

5.5 Inhibitor switch installation details

1. Upper manual control lever and adjusting nut
2. Lower manual control lever and lock nut
3. Inhibitor switch mounting bolts
4. Manual control lever-to-inhibitor switch alignment hole

shifts may occur. If the linkage is adjusted so it is too long, shifts may be delayed and part-throttle downshifts may be very erratic.

Warning: *When working under the vehicle be sure to support it on sturdy jackstands.*

2   Be sure the throttle lever and bracket are not bent or distorted.

3   Move the throttle to the full-open position and adjust the space between the cable stop and housing to 1 mm **(see illustration)**.

5 Inhibitor switch - check and renewal

Refer to illustrations 5.2a, 5.2b and 5.5

Check

1   The inhibitor switch completes the circuit from the ignition switch to the starter when the shift lever is in the Park or Neutral positions.

2   To check the switch, disconnect the electrical connector and, using an ohmmeter, check for continuity on the indicated terminals with the shift lever in the indicated positions **(see illustrations)**.

Renewal

3   Apply the parking brake securely and position the shift lever in the Neutral position. Raise the vehicle and support it securely on jackstands.

4   Disconnect the electrical connector from the inhibitor switch.

5   Remove the nut, washer and lever from the selector shaft **(see illustration)**.

6   Remove the mounting bolts and slide the switch off the selector shaft.

7   Fit the switch leaving the mounting bolts loose. Refit the shift lever, washer and nut. Tighten the nut securely.

8   Move the switch back and forth until the two raised bosses are aligned with the edges of the selector shaft (with the transmission in Neutral) and tighten the mounting bolts securely.

9   Adjust the shift control cable (see section 3).

10   Lower the vehicle and verify the engine starts in Park and Neutral only.

6 Automatic transmission - removal and refitting

Refer to illustrations 6.16, 6.17 and 6.18

Removal

1   Disconnect the negative cable from the battery.

2   Remove the knob from the transfer case shift lever (early models).

3   Raise the vehicle and support it securely on jackstands.

4   Drain the transmission fluid (see Chapter 1).

5   Remove the torque converter cover.

6   Mark the relationship of the torque converter to one of the studs so they can be refitted in the same position.

7   Remove the torque converter-to-driveplate bolts. Turn the crankshaft for access to each bolt. Turn the crankshaft in a clockwise direction only (as viewed from the front).

Chapter 7 Part B Automatic transmission

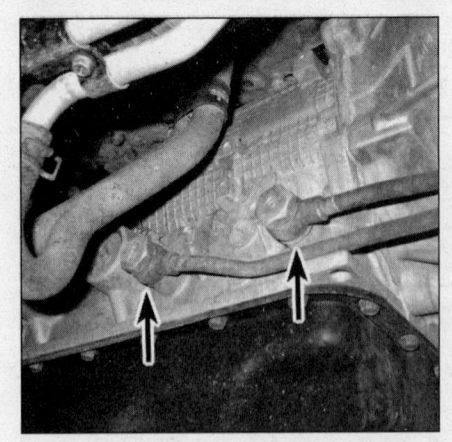

6.16 Disconnect and plug the oil cooler lines (arrows) - the oil cooler and lines should be flushed if the transmission is being replaced

6.17 Remove the rear mount-to-rear crossmember nuts/bolts and the crossmember-to-frame bolts (left side shown) - make sure the transmission is properly supported before removing the crossmember-to-frame bolts

6.18 Remove the lateral cable-to-body mounting bolt (arrow) then remove the cable

8 Remove the starter motor (see Chapter 5).
9 Remove the driveshaft(s) (see Chapter 8).
10 Disconnect the speedometer connection.
11 Detach the electrical connectors from the transmission.
12 Remove any exhaust components which will interfere with transmission removal (see Chapter 4).
13 Disconnect the throttle control linkage cable (early models).
14 Disconnect the shift cable.
15 Support the engine with a jack. Use a block of wood under the sump to spread the load. Support the transmission with a jack - preferably a jack made for this purpose. Safety chains will help steady the transmission on the jack.
16 Disconnect the transmission cooler lines **(see illustration)** and plug the lines.
17 Remove the rear mount-to-crossmember bolts and the crossmember-to-frame bolts **(see illustration)**.
18 Remove the two engine rear support-to-transmission extension housing bolts and lateral cable **(see illustration)** if equipped.
19 Raise the transmission enough to allow removal of the crossmember.
20 Remove the bolts securing the transmission to the engine.
21 Lower the transmission slightly and disconnect and plug the transmission fluid cooler lines.
22 Remove the transmission dipstick tube.
23 Move the transmission to the rear to disengage it from the engine block dowel pins and make sure the torque converter is detached from the driveplate. Secure the torque converter to the transmission so it won't fall out during removal.

Refitting

24 Prior to refitting, make sure the torque converter hub is securely engaged in the pump.
25 With the transmission secured to the jack, raise it into position. Be sure to keep it level so the torque converter does not slide forward.
26 Turn the torque converter to line up the studs with the holes in the driveplate. The mark on the torque converter and the stud made in Step 5 must line up.
27 Move the transmission forward carefully until the dowel pins and the torque converter are engaged.
28 Refit the transmission housing-to-engine bolts. Tighten them securely.
29 Refit the torque converter-to-driveplate bolts. Tighten the bolts to the torque listed in this Chapter's Specifications.
30 Connect the transmission fluid cooler lines. Refit the transmission mount crossmember and through-bolts. Tighten the bolts and nuts securely.
31 Remove the jacks supporting the transmission and the engine.
32 Refit the dipstick tube and cooler lines.
33 Refit the starter motor (see Chapter 5).
34 Connect the shift and throttle control cable.
35 Plug in the transmission electrical connectors.
36 Refit the torque converter cover.
37 Refit the driveshaft(s).
38 Connect the speedometer sensor.
39 Adjust the shift linkage.
40 Refit any exhaust system components that were removed or disconnected.
41 Lower the vehicle.
42 Fill the transmission with the proper type and amount of fluid (see Chapter 1), run the engine and check for fluid leaks.

7 Transmission oil cooler - removal and refitting

Refer to illustration 7.5

1 Remove the skid plate and lower cover (see Chapter 10).
2 Remove the front grille (see Chapter 11).
3 Place a drain pan under the cooler.
4 Disconnect the cooler lines from the cooler and plug the lines and cap the cooler fittings.
5 Remove the mounting bolts from the bracket and remove the cooler from the vehicle **(see illustration)**.
6 Refitting is the reverse of removal.

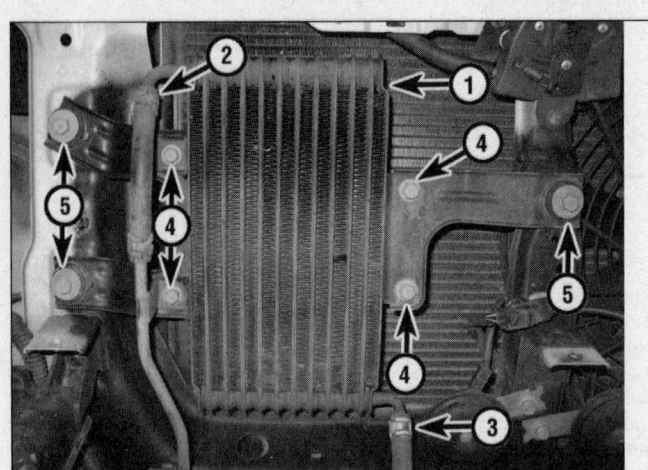

7.5 Transmission oil cooler installation details

1 *Transmission oil cooler*
2 *Oil return hose and clamp*
3 *Oil feed hose and clamp*
4 *Bracket-to-cooler bolts*
5 *Cooler mounting bracket bushings and bolts*

Chapter 7 Part C
Transfer case

Contents

	Section		Section
4WD indicator light switches - removal and refitting	3	Transfer case lubricant change	See Chapter 1
General information	1	Transfer case lubricant level check	See Chapter 1
Oil seal renewal	See Chapter 7A	Transfer case overhaul - general information	4
Shift lever - removal and refitting	2	Transmission mount - check and renewal	See Chapter 7A

Specifications

Torque specifications
	Nm
Four-wheel drive indicator switches	
NL to NP models	30
NS to NW models	35
Transfer case-to-transmission nuts and bolts	
NL to NP models	30
NS to NW models	35

1 General information

These models are equipped with a transfer case mounted on the transmission housing. Drive is passed through the transmission and transfer case to the front and rear axles by the driveshafts.

The transfer case is combined with the transmission to form one unit. With the appropriate support tools, the transfer case can be separated from the transmission by removing the transfer case-to-adapter plate bolts and removing the transfer case from the rear of the transmission adapter plate **(see illustrations 3.2c and 3.2d)**. Because of the special tools and techniques required, disassembly and overhaul of the transfer case should be left to a dealer service department or properly equipped shop. You can, however, remove and refit the transmission/transfer case yourself and save the expense, even if the repair work is done by a specialist.

2 Shift lever - removal and refitting

Refer to illustrations 2.2 and 2.4

1 On 2000 and earlier models the procedure for removing the transfer case shift lever is essentially the same as for removing the manual transmission shift lever (see Chapter 7A).

Note: *On 2001 and later models the shift lever is electronic and has no cable. All shifting is done by a motor mounted to the transfer unit.*

2 On 2001 and later models, unscrew the shift knob from the shift lever **(see illustration)**.

3 Remove the centre console (see Chapter 11).

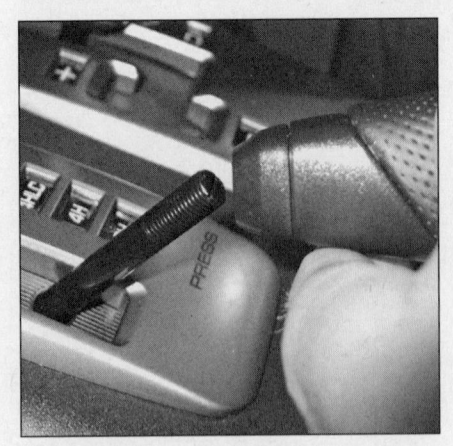

Chapter 7 Part C Transfer case

2.2 Turn the transfer shift knob anti-clockwise and remove it from the shift lever

2.4 Remove the shift switch lever mounting screws (arrows), disconnect the electrical connector and remove the switch

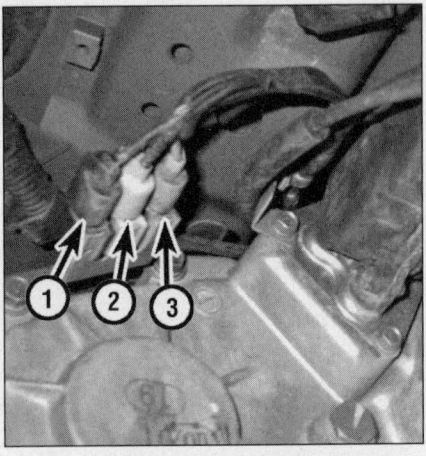

3.2b Typical late model location of the 4WD indicator switches

1 2WD/4WD detection switch connector
2 4H (Full time 4WD) switch connector
3 Centre differential lock detection switch connector

4 Remove the transfer select switch mounting bolts **(see illustration)**, disconnect the electrical connector and remove the switch.

5 Refitting is the reverse of removal. Be sure to tighten the transfer switch securely.

3 4WD indicator light switches - removal and refitting

Refer to illustrations 3.2a, 3.2b, 3.2c and 3.2d

1 Raise the vehicle and support it securely on jackstands (see Jacking and Towing).

2 On 2000 and earlier models, the 4WD indicator light switches are located on the top of the transfer case housing **(see illustration)**. On 2001 and later models the indicator switches are located on the left-hand side of the transfer case **(see illustration)**.

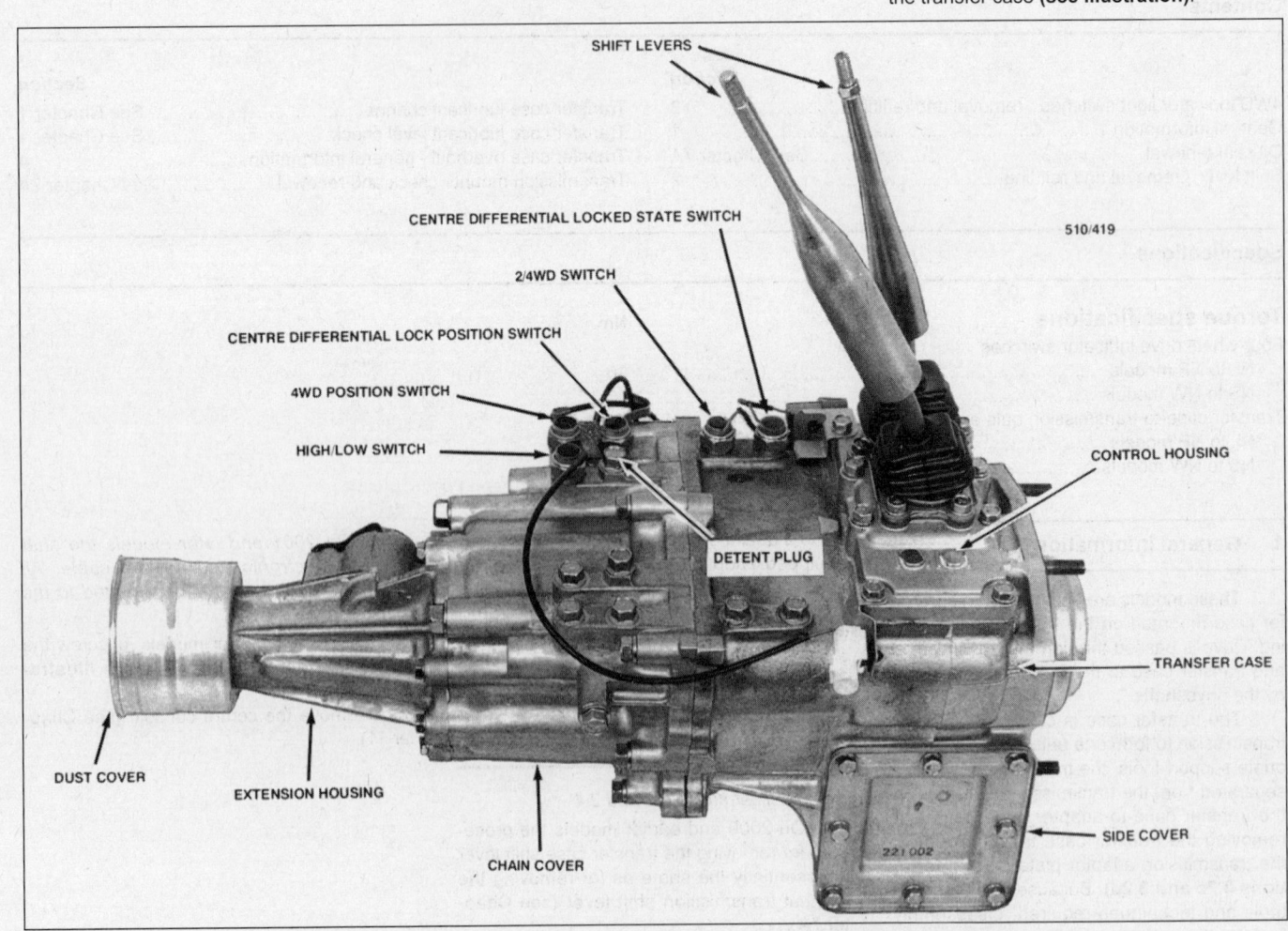

3.2a Typical early model location of the 4WD indicator light switches (arrows)

Labels: SHIFT LEVERS, CENTRE DIFFERENTIAL LOCKED STATE SWITCH, 2/4WD SWITCH, CENTRE DIFFERENTIAL LOCK POSITION SWITCH, 4WD POSITION SWITCH, HIGH/LOW SWITCH, DETENT PLUG, CONTROL HOUSING, TRANSFER CASE, SIDE COVER, CHAIN COVER, EXTENSION HOUSING, DUST COVER

Chapter 7 Part C Transfer case

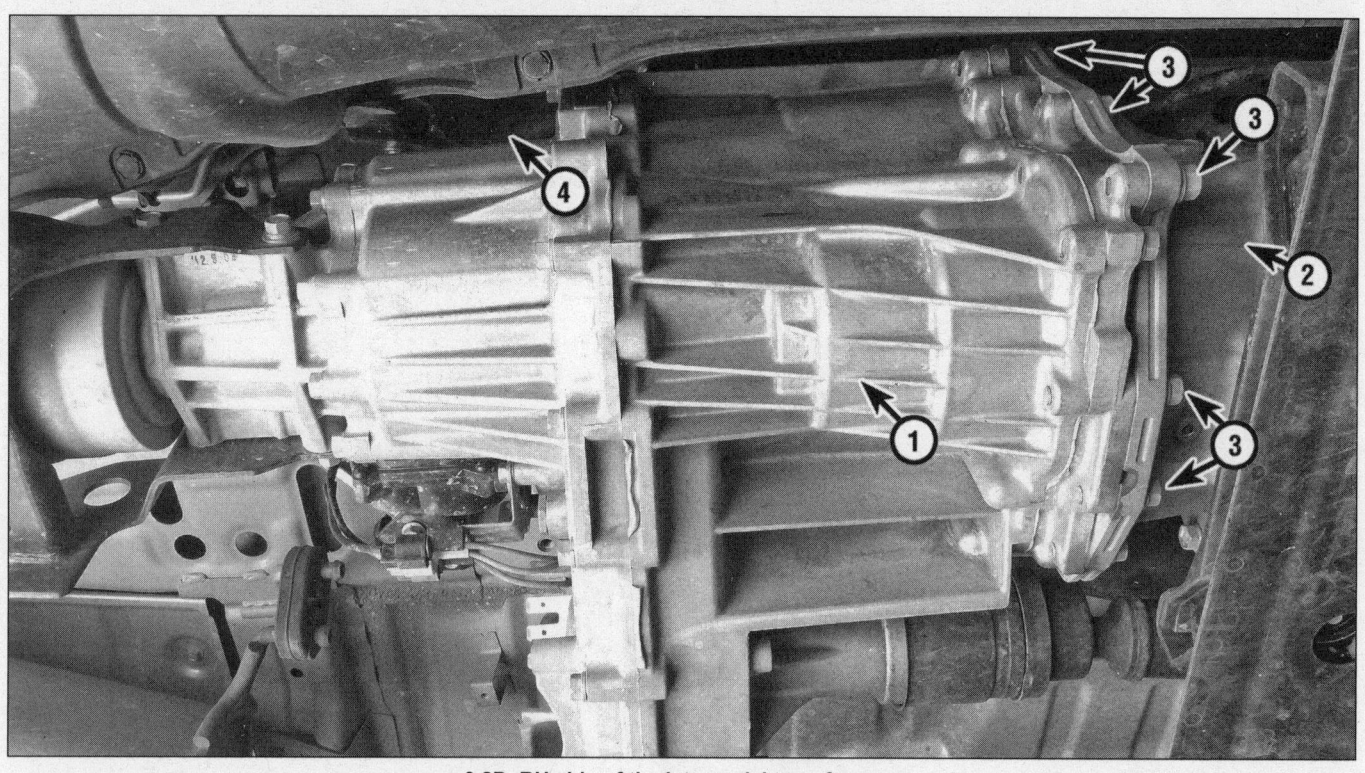

3.2D RH side of the late model transfer case

1 Transfer case
2 Adapter housing
3 Transfer case to adapter plate bolts and nuts
4 2WD operation detection switch and 4LLc (Direct low range 4WD) switch

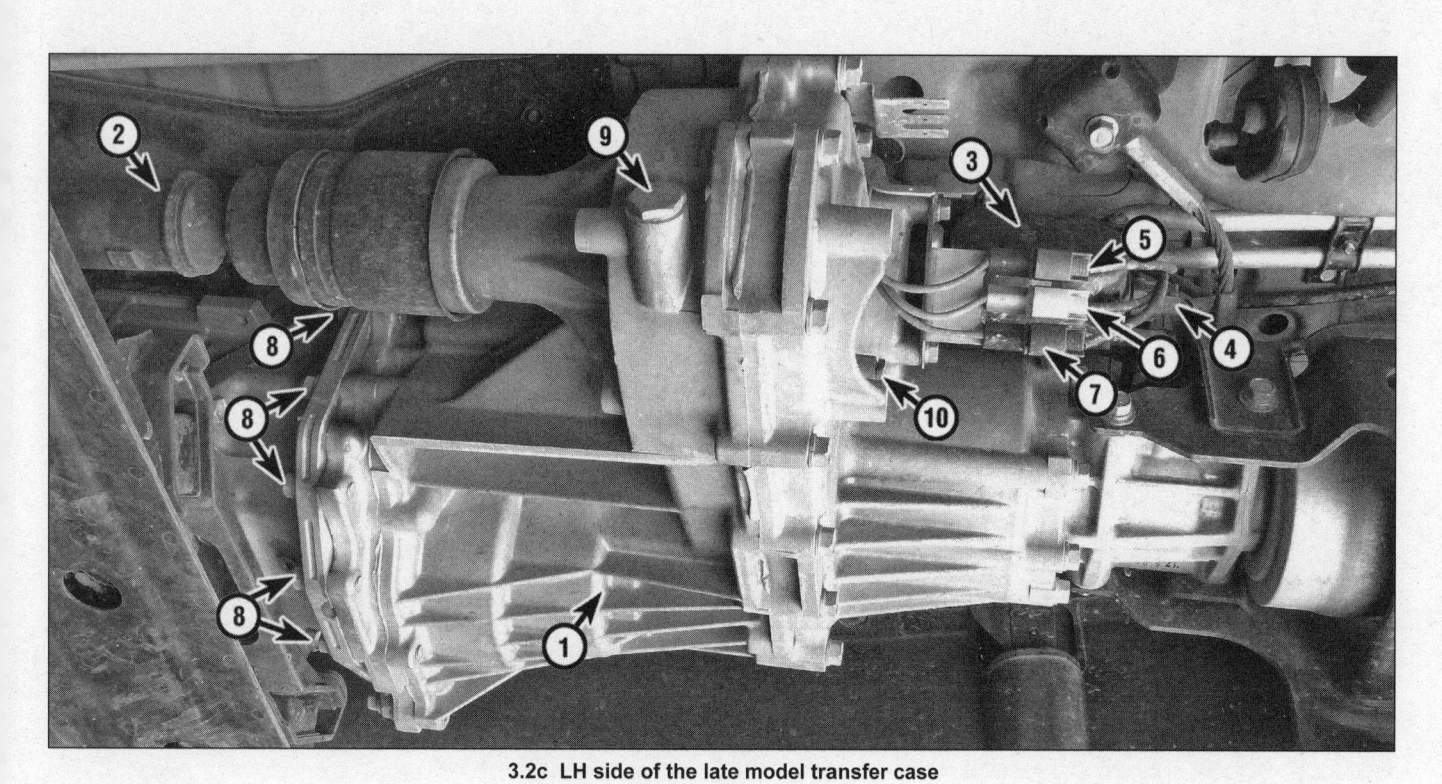

3.2c LH side of the late model transfer case

1 Transfer case
2 Front propeller shaft
3 Shift actuator
4 Shift actuator connector
5 2WD/4WD detection switch connector
6 4H position switch connector
7 Centre diff lock switch connector
8 Transfer case to adapter plate bolts and nuts
9 Transfer case drain plug
10 Transfer case filler plug

3 Unscrew the switch and remove the steel ball.
4 Refitting is the reverse of removal. Be sure to apply Teflon tape or a small amount of RTV sealant to the threads. Tighten the switch to the torque listed in this Chapter's Specifications.
5 Lower the vehicle.

4 Transfer case overhaul - general information

On these models the transmission/transfer case assembly is designed to be overhauled as a unit. Consequently, overhaul should be left to a repair shop specialising in both transmission and transfer cases. Rebuilt units may be available - check with your dealer parts department and auto parts stores. At any rate, some cost savings can be realised by removing the transmission/transfer case unit and taking it to the shop (see Chapter 7A) - manual transmission, or (see Chapter 7B) - automatic transmission.

Chapter 8
Clutch and driveline

Contents

	Section		Section
Clutch components - removal, inspection and refitting	3	Flywheel - removal and refitting	See Chapter 2
Clutch - description and check	2	Front axle disconnect solenoid and actuator -	
Clutch fluid level check	See Chapter 1	check and renewal	22
Clutch hydraulic system - bleeding	8	Front differential assembly - removal and refitting	18
Clutch master cylinder - removal and refitting	6	Front driveaxles - removal and refitting	20
Clutch pedal height and freeplay check and adjustment	See Chapter 1	Front hub assembly - removal, bearing repack, refitting and adjustment	19
Clutch release bearing - removal and refitting	4	General information	1
Clutch release cylinder - removal and refitting	7	Half shafts (independent rear suspension) - removal and refitting	16
Differential lubricant level check	See Chapter 1	Pilot bearing - inspection, removal and refitting	5
Driveaxle boot renewal and Constant Velocity (CV) joint overhaul	21	Pinion bearing oil seal - renewal	15
Driveline inspection	10	Rear axle assembly (banjo type axle housing) - removal and refitting	14
Driveshafts, differentials and axles - general information	9	Rear axleshafts, bearings and oil seals (banjo type axle housing) - removal and refitting	13
Driveshafts - removal and refitting	11	Universal joints (non-CFRP models) - renewal	12
Final drive assembly (independent rear suspension) - removal and refitting	17		

Specifications

Clutch
Hydraulic system fluid type	See Chapter 1
Clutch disc minimum lining thickness	0.3 mm
Clutch pedal freeplay	See Chapter 1

Driveline
U-joint journal endplay	0.06 mm
Driveaxle axial play	0.2 to 0.5 mm
Driveshaft boot installation length (measured from the centre of the inner and outer retaining clamp	
NL to NP	75 to 85 mm
NS and NT models	
RH side	75 to 85 mm
LH side	87 to 98 mm
NW models	
RH side	80 to 90 mm
LH side	88 to 98 mm

Torque specifications
	Nm
Clutch pressure plate-to-flywheel bolts	19
Clutch release lever shaft bolt	12
Driveshaft flange nuts and bolts	
NL to NP	49 to 59
NS to NW	50 to 70
Driveshaft-to-hub nut	
NL to NP	Not applicable
NS to NW	210 to 230

Torque specifications (continued)

	Nm
Rear axle	
Bearing retainer/brake backing plate-to-axle housing nuts (without IRS)	50 to 60
Differential mount bracket bolts (without IRS)	127 to 177
Differential pinion shaft nut	216
Dynamic damper mounting bolts	71 to 95
Half shaft hub nut (IRS)	
NL to NP models	226 to 284
NS to NW models	210 to 230
Half shaft flange bolts (IRS)	99 to 127
NL to NP models	99 to 127
NS to NW models	50 to 70
Hub and backing plate to knuckle (IRS)	
Bolt	
With 16-inch brake disc	69 to 85
With 17-inch brake disc	120 to 150
Nut	
With 16-inch brake disc	128 to 156
With 17-inch brake disc	190 to 220
Toe control tower bar bolts	38 to 54
Front axle	
Differential carrier bolts	
NL models	60 to 70
NM to NW models	80 to 98
Differential mount	
Bracket bolts (NL to NP models)	127 to 177
Mount nut (NS to NW models)	88 to 61
Differential pinion shaft nut	
NL to NP models	190 to 250
NS to NW models	187 to 245
Front crossmember bolts	
NL to NP models	119 to 137
NS to NW models	75 to 85
Hub body assembly bolts (1999 and earlier)	50 to 60
Rear differential mount bolts	19 to 27
Rear differential through bolt	50 to 68
Right front driveaxle flange bolts	50 to 60

Chapter 8 Clutch and driveline

1 General information

The information in this Chapter deals with the components from the rear of the engine to the front and rear wheels, except for the transmission and transfer case, which are dealt with in the previous Chapters. For the purposes of this Chapter, these components are grouped into four categories: clutch, driveshaft, front axle and rear axle. Separate Sections within this Chapter offer general descriptions and checking procedures for each of these groups.

Since nearly all the procedures covered in this Chapter involve working under the vehicle, make sure it's securely supported on sturdy jackstands or on a hoist where the vehicle can be easily raised and lowered.

2 Clutch - description and check

Refer to illustrations 2.1a and 2.1b

1 All models equipped with a manual transmission feature a single dry-plate, diaphragm spring-type clutch **(see illustrations)**. The actuation is through a hydraulic system.

2 When the clutch pedal is depressed, hydraulic fluid (under pressure from the clutch master cylinder) flows into the release cylinder. Because the release cylinder is connected to the clutch fork, the fork moves the release bearing into contact with the pressure plate release fingers, disengaging the clutch disc.

3 Terminology can be a problem regarding the clutch components because common names have in some cases changed from that used by the manufacturer. For example, the driven plate is also called the clutch plate or disc, the clutch release bearing is sometimes called a throwout or release bearing, the release cylinder is sometimes called the operating or slave cylinder.

4 Due to the slow wearing qualities of the clutch, it is not easy to decide when to go to the trouble of removing the transmission in order to check the wear on the friction lining. The only positive indication that something should be done is when it starts to slip or when squealing noises during engagement indicate that the friction lining has worn down to the rivets. In such instances it can only be hoped that the friction surfaces on the flywheel and pressure plate have not been badly worn or scored.

5 A clutch will wear according to the way in which it is used. Much intentional slipping of the clutch while driving - rather than the correct selection of gears - will accelerate wear. It is best to assume, however, that the disc will need renewal at around 150,000 kilometres.

6 Because of the clutch's location between the engine and transmission, it cannot be worked on without removing either the engine or transmission. If repairs which would require removal of the engine are not needed, the quickest way to gain access to the clutch is by removing the transmission as described in Chapter 7A.

7 Other than to renew components with obvious damage, some preliminary checks should be performed to diagnose a clutch system failure.

a) *The first check should be of the fluid level in the clutch master cylinder. If the fluid level is low, add fluid as necessary and re-test. If the master cylinder runs dry, or if any of the hydraulic components are serviced, bleed the hydraulic system as described in Section 8.*

b) *To check clutch spin down time, run the engine at normal idle speed with the transmission in Neutral (clutch pedal up - engaged). Disengage the clutch (pedal down), wait nine seconds and shift the transmission into Reverse. No grinding noise should be heard. A grinding noise would indicate component failure in the pressure plate assembly or the clutch disc.*

c) *To check for complete clutch release, run the engine (with the brake on to prevent movement) and hold the clutch pedal approximately 12 mm from the floor mat. Shift the transmission between 1st gear and Reverse several times. If the shift is not smooth, component failure is indicated. Measure the hydraulic release cylinder pushrod travel. With the clutch pedal completely depressed the release cylinder pushrod should extend substantially. If the pushrod will not extend very far or not at all, check the fluid level in the clutch master cylinder. The system may need to be bled (see Section 8).*

d) *Visually inspect the clutch pedal bush at the top of the clutch pedal to make sure there is no sticking or excessive wear.*

e) *Under the vehicle, check that the release fork is solidly mounted on the ball stud.*

Note: *Because access to the clutch components is an involved process, any time either the engine or transmission is removed, the clutch disc, pressure plate assembly and release bearing should be carefully inspected and, if necessary, renewed with new parts. Since the clutch disc is normally the item of highest wear, it should be renewed as a matter of course if there is any question about its condition.*

3 Clutch components - removal, inspection and refitting

Refer to illustrations 3.10 and 3.12

Warning: *Dust produced by clutch wear and deposited on clutch components is hazardous to your health. DO NOT blow it out with compressed air and DO NOT inhale it. DO NOT use petrol or petroleum-based solvents to remove the dust. Brake system cleaner should be used to flush the dust into a drain pan. After the clutch components are wiped clean with a rag, dispose of the contaminated rags and cleaner in a covered container.*

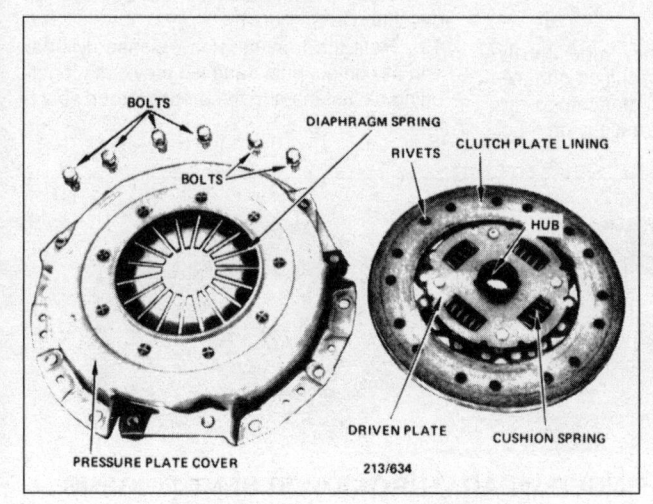

2.1a Typical clutch components

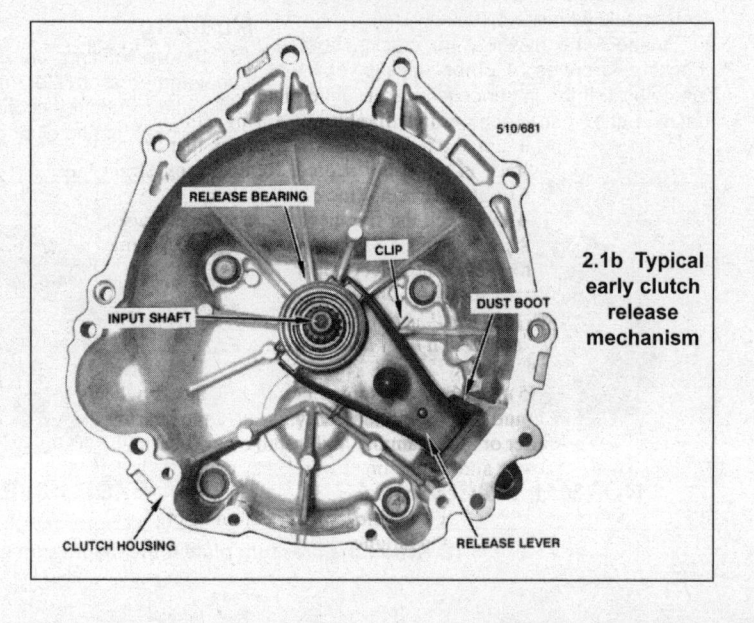

2.1b Typical early clutch release mechanism

Removal

1 Access to the clutch components is normally accomplished by removing the transmission, leaving the engine in the vehicle. If, of course, the engine is being removed for major overhaul, then the opportunity should always be taken to check the clutch for wear and renew worn components as necessary. The following procedures assume that the engine will stay in place.
2 Remove the release cylinder without disconnecting the hydraulic line (see Section 8). Support the cylinder out of the way by a piece of wire from the undercarriage.
3 Referring to Chapter 7 Part A, remove the transmission from the vehicle. Support the engine while the transmission is out. Preferably, an engine hoist should be used to support it from above. However, if a jack is used underneath the engine, make sure a piece of wood is used between the jack and sump to spread the load.

Caution: *The pickup for the oil pump is very close to the bottom of the sump. If the pan is bent or distorted in any way, engine oil starvation could occur.*

4 To support the clutch disc during removal, install a clutch alignment tool through the clutch disc hub.
5 Carefully inspect the flywheel and pressure plate for indexing marks. The marks are usually an X, an O or a white letter. If they cannot be found, apply marks yourself so the pressure plate and the flywheel will be in the same alignment during refitting.
6 Turning each bolt only 1/2-turn at a time, slowly loosen the pressure plate-to-flywheel bolts. Work in a diagonal pattern and loosen each bolt a little at a time until all spring pressure is relieved. Then hold the pressure plate securely and completely remove the bolts, followed by the pressure plate and clutch disc.

Inspection

7 Ordinarily, when a problem occurs in the clutch, it can be attributed to wear of the clutch disc assembly. However, all components should be inspected at this time.
8 Inspect the flywheel for cracks, heat checking, grooves or other signs of obvious defects. If the imperfections are slight, a machine shop can machine the surface flat

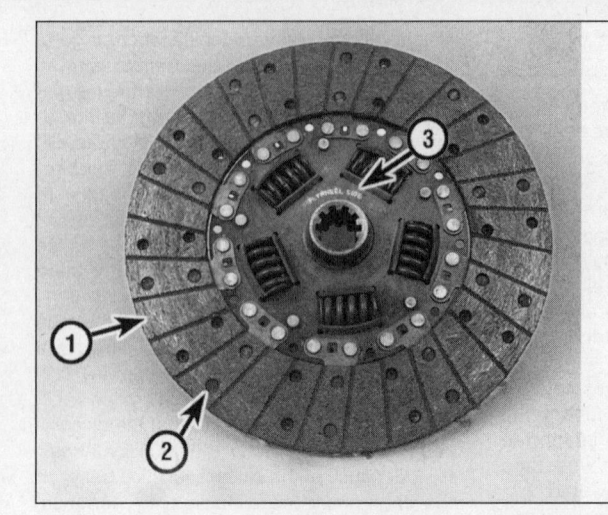

3.10 The clutch disc

1 *Lining* - This will wear down in use
2 *Rivets* - These secure the lining and will damage the pressure plate if allowed to contact it
3 *Marks* - "Flywheel side" or something similar

and smooth, which is highly recommended regardless of the surface appearance. Refer to Chapter 2 for the flywheel removal and refitting procedure.
9 Inspect the pilot bearing (if equipped) (see Section 5).
10 Inspect the lining on the clutch disc. There should be at least 0.3 mm of lining above the rivet heads. Check for loose rivets, warpage, cracks, distorted springs or damper bushes and other obvious damage **(see illustration)**. As mentioned above, ordinarily the clutch disc is renewed as a matter of course, so if in doubt about the condition, renew it with a new one.
11 Ordinarily, the release bearing is also renewed along with the clutch disc (see Section 4).
12 Check the machined surfaces of the pressure plate and the diaphragm spring fingers **(see illustration)**. If the surface is grooved or otherwise damaged, renew the pressure plate. Also check for obvious damage, distortion, cracking, etc. Light glazing can be removed with medium grit emery cloth. If a new pressure plate is indicated, new or factory-rebuilt units are available.

Refitting

13 Before refitting, carefully wipe the flywheel and pressure plate machined surfaces clean with a rubbing-alcohol dampened rag. It's important that no oil or grease is on these surfaces or the lining of the clutch disc. Handle these parts only with clean hands.
14 Position the clutch disc and pressure plate with the clutch held in place with an alignment tool. Make sure it's fitted properly (most renewal discs will be marked "flywheel side" or something similar - if not marked, refit the clutch with the damper springs or bushes toward the transmission).
15 Tighten the pressure plate-to-flywheel bolts only finger tight, working around the pressure plate.
16 Centre the clutch disc by ensuring the alignment tool is through the splined hub and into the pilot bearing in the crankshaft. Wiggle the tool up, down or side-to-side, as needed, to bottom the tool in the pilot bearing. Tighten the pressure plate-to-flywheel bolts a little at a time, working in a criss-cross pattern to prevent distorting the cover. After all of the bolts are snug, tighten them to the torque listed in this Chapter's Specifications. Remove the alignment tool.
17 Using high temperature grease, lubricate the inner groove of the release bearing (see Section 4). Also place grease on the fork fingers.
18 Refit the clutch release bearing as described in Section 4.
19 Refit the transmission, release cylinder and all components removed previously, tightening all fasteners to the proper torque specifications.

NORMAL FINGER WEAR   **EXCESSIVE FINGER WEAR**   **BROKEN OR BENT FINGERS**

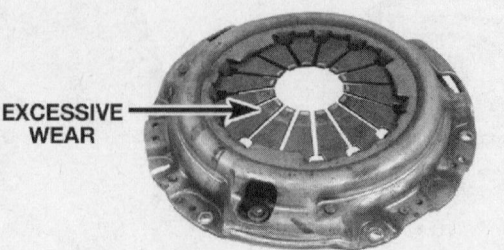

3.12 Renew the pressure plate if the diaphragm spring fingers exhibit these signs of wear

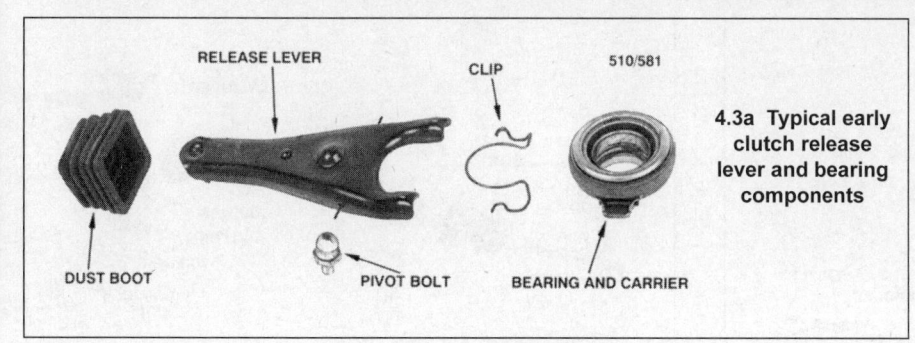

Chapter 8 Clutch and driveline

4.3a Typical early clutch release lever and bearing components

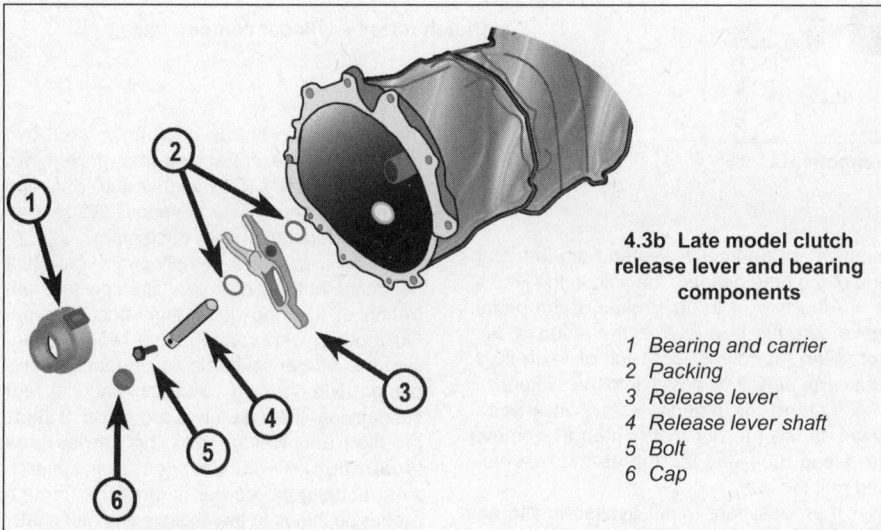

4.3b Late model clutch release lever and bearing components

1 Bearing and carrier
2 Packing
3 Release lever
4 Release lever shaft
5 Bolt
6 Cap

4 Clutch release bearing - removal and refitting

Refer to illustrations 4.3a and 4.3b

Removal

1 Disconnect the negative cable from the battery.
2 Remove the transmission (see Chapter 7A).
3 Detach the spring clip(s), then slide the release bearing off the transmission input shaft **(see illustrations)**.
4 On early models, detach the fork from the ballstud by pulling it straight off.
5 On late models, tap the cap from the bottom of the transmission housing. Remove the bolt and slide the release lever shaft from the transmission, gathering the two packing rings and removing the release lever.
6 Hold the bearing and turn the inner portion. If the bearing doesn't turn smoothly or if it's noisy, renew it with a new one. Wipe the bearing with a clean rag and inspect it for damage, wear and cracks. Don't immerse the bearing in solvent - it's sealed for life and to do so would ruin it.

Refitting

7 Lubricate the clutch fork ends where they contact the bearing lightly with moly-based grease. Apply a thin coat of the same grease to the inner diameter of the bearing and also to the transmission input shaft bearing retainer.
8 Refit the release bearing on the clutch fork so that both of the fork ends fit into the bearing tabs. Make sure the spring clip seats securely.
9 On early models, lubricate the clutch release fork ball socket with moly-based disulfide grease and push the fork onto the ball stud until it's firmly seated. Check to see that the bearing slides back and forth smoothly on the input shaft bearing retainer.
10 On late models, lubricate the release lever shaft as it passes through the release lever. Ensure the packing rings positioned either side of the lever and tighten the bolt to the torque listed in this chapters Specifications.
11 The remainder of the refitting is the reverse of the removal procedure, tightening all bolts to the specified torques.

5 Pilot bearing - inspection, removal and refitting

1 The clutch pilot bearing is a ball-type bearing used on some models which is pressed into the rear of the crankshaft. Its primary purpose is to support the front of the transmission input shaft. The pilot bearing should be inspected whenever the clutch components are removed from the engine. Due to its inaccessibility, if you are in doubt as to its condition, renew it with a new one.

Note: *If the engine has been removed from the vehicle, disregard the following steps which do not apply.*

2 Remove the transmission (see Chapter 7A).
3 Remove the clutch components (see Section 3).
4 Using a clean rag, wipe the bearing clean and inspect for any excessive wear, scoring or obvious damage. A flashlight will be helpful to direct light into the recess.
5 Check to make sure the pilot bearing turns smoothly and quietly. If the transmission input shaft contact surface is worn or damaged, renew the bearing with a new one.
6 Removal can be accomplished with a special puller but an alternative method also works very well.
7 Find a solid steel bar which is slightly smaller in diameter than the bearing. Alternatives to a solid bar would be a wood dowel or a socket with a bolt fixed in place to make it solid.
8 Check the bar for fit - it should just slip into the bearing with very little clearance.
9 Pack the bearing and the area behind it (in the crankshaft recess) with heavy grease. Pack it tightly to eliminate as much air as possible.
10 Insert the bar into the bearing bore and lightly hammer on the bar, which will force the grease to the backside of the bearing and push it out. Remove the bearing and clean all grease from the crankshaft recess.
11 To fit the new bearing, lubricate the outside surface with oil then drive it into the recess with a hammer and a socket with an outside diameter that matches the bearing outer race.
12 Pack the bearing with lithium base grease (NLGI No.2). Wipe off all excess grease so the clutch lining will not become contaminated.
13 Refit the clutch components, transmission and all other components removed to gain access to the pilot bearing.

6 Clutch master cylinder - removal and refitting

Refer to illustration 6.2

Caution: *Do not allow brake fluid to contact any painted surfaces of the vehicle, as damage to the finish may result.*

1 Disconnect the hydraulic line from the master cylinder and drain the fluid into a suitable container.
2 Remove the master cylinder flange mounting nuts and withdraw the unit from the engine compartment **(see illustration)**.
3 Position the clutch master cylinder against the firewall, inserting the pedal pushrod into the piston. Refit the nuts, tightening them securely.
4 Bleed the clutch hydraulic system following the procedure in Section 8, then check the pedal height and freeplay as described in Chapter 1.

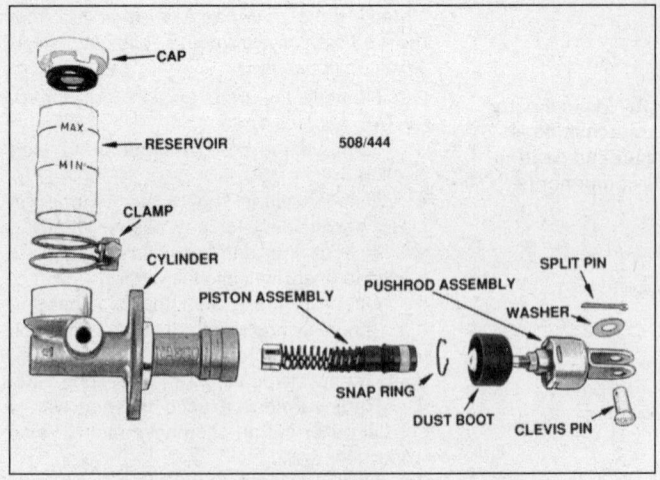

6.2 Typical early clutch master cylinder components

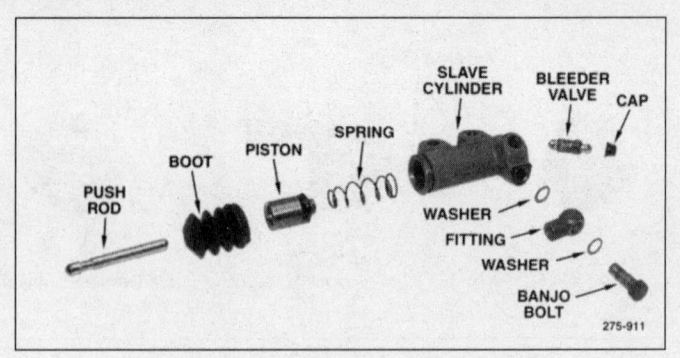

7.3 Clutch release cylinder components

7 Clutch release cylinder - removal and refitting

Refer to illustration 7.3

1 The clutch release cylinder is located on the side of the transmission bellhousing.
2 Raise the vehicle and support it securely on jackstands (see Jacking and Towing).
3 Disconnect the hydraulic line from the release cylinder. This is done by removing the bolt from the banjo fitting on the cylinder body (see illustration).
4 Remove the bolt(s) and pull off the release cylinder.
5 Refitting is the reverse of the removal procedure. Use new sealing washers at the banjo fitting. After the cylinder has been refitted, bleed the clutch hydraulic system as described in Section 8.

8 Clutch hydraulic system - bleeding

Caution: *Do not allow the brake fluid to contact any painted surface of the vehicle, as damage to the finish will result.*

1 Bleeding will be required whenever the hydraulic system has been dismantled and reassembled and air has entered the system.
2 First fill the fluid reservoir with clean brake fluid which has been stored in an airtight container. Never use fluid which has drained from the system or has bled out previously, as it may contain grit and moisture.
3 Attach a rubber or plastic bleed tube to the bleeder screw on the release cylinder and immerse the open end of the tube in a glass jar containing 25 to 50 mm of fluid.
4 Open the bleeder screw about half a turn and have an assistant quickly depress the clutch pedal completely. Tighten the screw and then have the clutch pedal slowly released with the foot completely removed. Repeat this sequence of operations until air bubbles are no longer ejected from the open end of the tube beneath the fluid in the jar.
5 After two or three strokes of the pedal, make sure the fluid level in the reservoir has not fallen too low. Keep it full of fresh fluid, otherwise air will be drawn into the system.
6 Tighten the bleeder screw on a pedal down stroke (do not overtighten it), remove the bleed tube and jar, top-up the reservoir and refit the cap.
7 If an assistant is not available, alternative 'one-man' bleeding operations can be carried out using a bleed tube equipped with a one-way valve or a pressure bleed kit, both of which should be used in accordance with the manufacturer's instructions.

9 Driveshafts, differentials and axles - general information

Refer to illustrations 9.5a and 9.5b

These models use two driveshafts; the primary shaft runs between the transfer case and the front differential and the rear driveshaft runs between the transfer case and the rear differential.

On 2001 and later models, the rear driveshaft has been changed. The new driveshaft is a Carbon Fibre Reinforced Plastic (CFRP) tube. This drive shaft is designed to allow the shaft to compress in the event of a collision. The CFRP driveshaft is not serviceable and must be replaced as a unit if the tube is dropped, cracked or chipped or if the joints are damaged.

On non CFRP tube driveshafts, all universal joints are of the solid type and can be renewed separately from the driveshaft. The driveshafts are finely balanced during production and whenever they are removed or disassembled, they must be reassembled and refitted in the exact manner and positions they were originally in, to avoid excessive vibration.

The front axle consists of a frame-mounted differential assembly and two driveaxles. The driveaxles incorporate two constant velocity (CV) joints each, enabling them to transmit power at various suspension angles independent from each other.

The rear axle assembly is a hypoid (the centreline of the pinion gear is below the centreline of the ring gear) semi-floating type. On models with conventional rear suspension the differential carrier is set into a 'banjo' design axle housing. With conventional rear suspension, the axle tubes are made of steel, pressed and welded into the carrier **(see illustration)**. On independent rear suspension models, the carrier is mounted through rubber bushings to the chassis and half shafts are used to transmit power to the wheels **(see illustration)**.

An optional limited slip rear axle is also available. This differential allows for normal operation until one wheel loses traction. The unit utilises multi-disc clutch packs and a speed sensitive engagement mechanism which locks both axleshafts together, applying equal rotational power to both wheels.

In order to undertake certain operations, particularly renewal of the axleshafts, it's important to know the axle identification number. It's located on a small metal tag on one of the cover bolts.

Many times a problem is suspected in the rear axle area when, in fact, it lies elsewhere. For this reason, a thorough check should be performed before assuming a rear axle problem.

The following noises are those commonly associated with rear axle diagnosis procedures:

a) *Road noise is often mistaken for mechanical faults. Driving the vehicle on different surfaces will show whether the road surface is the cause of the noise. Road noise will remain the same if the vehicle is under power or coasting.*
b) *Tyre noise is sometimes mistaken for mechanical problems. Tyres which are worn or low on air pressure are particularly susceptible to emitting vibrations and noises. Tyre noise will remain about the same during varying driving situations, where rear axle noise will change during coasting, acceleration, etc.*

Chapter 8 Clutch and driveline

9.5a Typical conventional rear axle

9.5b Typical later model independent rear suspension

c) *Engine and transmission noise can be deceiving because it will travel along the driveline. To isolate engine and transmission noises, make a note of the engine speed at which the noise is most pronounced. Stop the vehicle and place the transmission in Neutral and run the engine to the same speed. If the noise is the same, the rear axle is not at fault.*

Overhaul and general repair of the rear axle is beyond the scope of the home mechanic due to the many special tools and critical measurements required. Thus, the procedures listed here will involve axleshaft removal and refitting, axleshaft oil seal renewal, axleshaft bearing renewal and removal of the entire unit for repair or renewal.

10 Driveline inspection

1 Raise the rear of the vehicle and support it securely on jackstands (see Jacking and Towing).
2 Slide under the vehicle and visually inspect the condition of the driveshaft. Look for any dents or cracks in the tubing. If any are found, the driveshaft must be renewed.
3 Check for any oil leakage at the front and rear of the driveshaft. Leakage where the driveshaft enters the transmission indicates a defective rear transmission seal. Leakage where the driveshaft enters the differential indicates a defective pinion seal.
4 While still under the vehicle, have an assistant turn the rear wheel so the driveshaft will rotate. As it does, make sure that the universal joints are operating properly without binding, noise or looseness. Listen for any noise from the centre bearing, indicating it is worn or damaged. Also check the rubber portion of the centre bearing for cracking or separation, which will necessitate renewal.
5 The universal joint can also be checked with the driveshaft motionless, by gripping your hands on either side of the joint and attempting to twist the joint. Any movement at all in the joint is a sign of considerable wear. Lifting up on the shaft will also indicate movement in the universal joints.
6 Finally, check the driveshaft mounting bolts at the ends to make sure they are tight.
7 The above driveshaft checks should be repeated on the front driveshaft. In addition, check for grease leakage around the sleeve yoke, indicating failure of the yoke seal.
8 Check for leakage at each connection of the driveshafts to the transfer case and front differential. Leakage indicates worn oil seals.
9 At the same time, check for looseness in the joints of the front driveaxles.

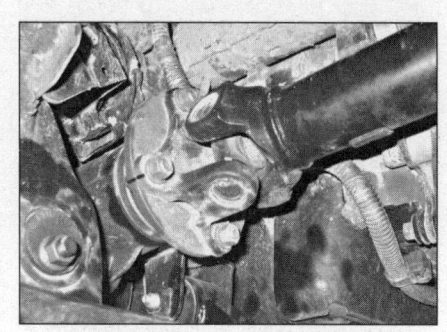

11 Driveshafts - removal and refitting

Front driveshaft

Refer to illustration 11.1

1 Raise the front of the vehicle and place it on jackstands (see Jacking and Towing). Mark the relationship of the front driveshaft flange to the front differential companion flange so they can be realigned upon refitting **(see illustration)**.
2 Lock the driveshaft from turning with a large screwdriver or lever, then remove the four nuts and bolts from the front flange.
3 Detach the flange from the front differential, withdraw the shaft from the transfer case and lower the driveshaft from the vehicle.
4 Refitting is the reverse of removal. Be sure to align all marks and tighten the flange bolts to the torque listed in this Chapter's Specifications.

Rear driveshaft

Non-CFRP type

Refer to illustration 11.7

5 Raise the rear of the vehicle and support it on jackstands (see Jacking and Towing).
6 Remove the nuts holding the centre support bearing bracket to the frame (three-joint type).
7 Mark the edges of the driveshaft rear flange and the differential companion flange so they can be realigned upon refitting **(see illustration)**.
8 Remove the four nuts and bolts.
9 Push the shaft forward slightly to disconnect the rear flange.
10 Pull the yoke from the transmission/transfer case while supporting the driveshaft with your hands.
11 While the driveshafts are removed, insert a plug in the transmission/transfer case to prevent lubricant leakage.
12 Refitting is the reverse of the removal procedure. During refitting, make sure all flange marks line up and the mounting bolts are fitted through the yoke to the companion flange.

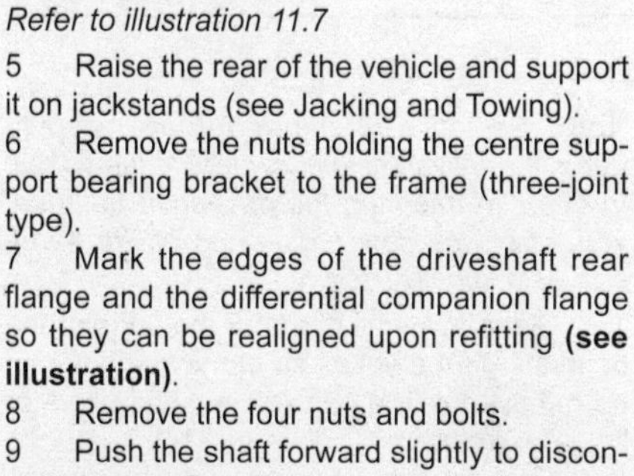

11.1 Mark the front driveshaft-to-differential flange relationship

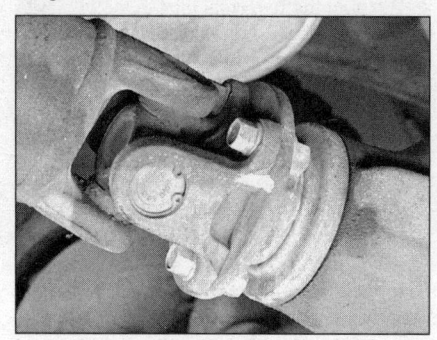

11.7 Mark the rear driveshaft-to-differential flange relationship - non-CFRP models

CFRP type

Refer to illustration 11.14

Caution: *The CFRP type driveshaft is made of carbon, fiberglass and plastic. The driveshaft can easily be damaged If dropped.*

13 Raise the rear of the vehicle and support it on jackstands (see Jacking and Towing).
14 Mark the edges of the driveshaft rear flange and the differential companion flange so they can be realigned upon refitting **(see illustration)**.
15 Remove the five nuts and bolts.
16 Push the shaft forward slightly to disconnect the rear flange.
17 Pull the yoke from the transmission/transfer case while supporting the driveshaft with your hands.
18 While the driveshafts are removed, insert a plug in the transmission/transfer case to prevent lubricant leakage.
19 Refitting is the reverse of the removal procedure. During refitting, make sure all flange marks line up and the bolts are fitted from the companion flange to the driveshaft.

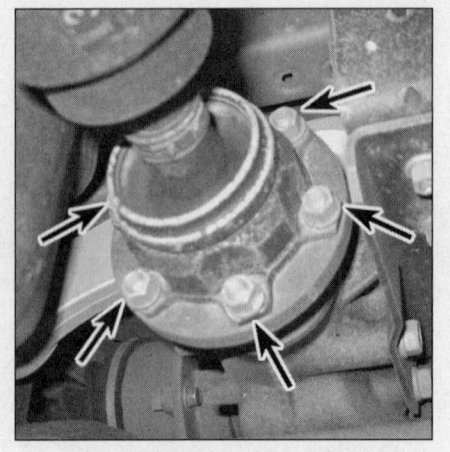

12 Universal joints (non-CFRP models) - renewal

Refer to illustrations 12.4 and 12.11

Note: *Selective fit snap-rings are used to retain the universal joint spiders in the yokes. In order to maintain the driveshaft balance, you must use new snap-rings of the same size as originally used.*

1 Clean away all dirt from the ends of the bearings on the yokes so the snap-rings can be removed with a pair of snap-ring pliers or long-nose pliers.
2 Support the universal joint in a vice equipped with soft jaws and remove the snap-rings. If they are very tight, tap the end of the bearing with a hammer to relieve the pressure.
3 You will need two sockets to remove the bearings from the yokes. One should be large enough to fit into the yoke where the snap-rings were fitted and the other should have an inside diameter just large enough for the bearings to fit into when they are forced out of the yoke.
4 Mount the universal joint in the vice with the large socket on one side of the yoke and the small socket on the other side, pushing against the bearing. Carefully tighten the vice until the bearing is pushed out of the yoke and into the large socket **(see illustration)**. If it can't be pushed all the way out, remove the universal joint from the vice and use a pair of pliers to finish removing the bearing.
5 Reverse the sockets and push out the bearing on the other side of the yoke. This time, the small socket will be pushing against the cross-shaped universal joint journal end.
6 Before pressing out the two remaining bearings, mark the universal joint journal (the cross) so it can be refitted in the same position during reassembly. Also mark the relationship of the yokes to each other.
7 The two remaining universal joints can be disassembled following the same procedure. Be sure to mark all components for each universal joint so they can be kept together and reassembled in the proper position.
8 When reassembling the universal joints, renew all needle bearings and dust seals with new ones.
9 Before reassembly, pack each grease cavity in the universal joint journals with a small amount of grease. Also, apply a thin coat of grease to the new needle bearing rollers and the roller contact areas on the universal joint journal.
10 Apply a thin coat of grease to the dust seal lips and fit the bearings and universal joint journals into the yoke using the vice and sockets that were used to remove the old bearings. Work slowly and be very careful not to damage the bearings as they are being pressed into the yokes.
11 Once the bearings are in place and properly seated, refit the snap-rings and check the clearance (U-joint journal endplay) with a feeler gauge **(see illustration)**. This is done with both snap-rings in place and the bearings and journal pressed toward one side of the yoke. Measure the clearance at the opposite side of the yoke. Compare this measurement with those in the Specifications Section at the beginning of this Chapter. If the measurement is greater than specified, fit a snap-ring of a different thickness and recheck the clearance. Repeat the procedure until the correct clearance is obtained. If possible, use snap-rings of the same thickness on each side of the yoke so the driveshaft balance isn't affected.

13 Rear axleshafts, bearings and oil seals (banjo type axle housing) - removal and refitting

Refer to illustrations 13.6, 13.8, 13.10 and 13.12

1 Loosen the lug nuts on the rear wheels.
2 Raise the rear of the vehicle, support it securely on jackstands and remove the rear wheels.
3 Remove the rear brake caliper anchor bolts and slide the brake caliper from the brake disc. Suspend the brake caliper using a wire to prevent damage to the brake hose. Remove the rotors from the axle shaft (see Chapter 9).
4 Remove the parking brake shoes and disconnect the parking brake cables from the backing plate (see Chapter 9). Clean all dirt from the area surrounding the carrier cover.
5 Unscrew and remove the nuts which attach the axleshaft bearing retainer plate to the brake backing plate.
6 Using a slide puller, remove the axle shaft. Remove and discard the O-ring from the end of the axle housing (if equipped). Don't damage the end of the housing.

Note: *If a slide hammer is not available, reverse the brake rotor on the axle flange and* **(see illustration)** *retain it loosely with the lug nuts. Use the brake rotor as a slide hammer but do not strike the rotor with a hammer.*

7 As the axleshaft is removed, it is possible that the bearing will become separated into three parts. This does not indicate that the bearing is unserviceable. If this happens, remove the two sections left behind from the axle tube.

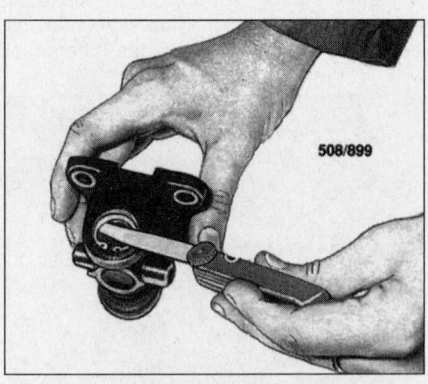

11.14 On CFRP models, mark the rear driveshaft-to-differential flange relationship and remove the five mounting nuts and bolts (arrows)

12.4 To press the universal joint out of the driveshaft, set it up in a vice with the small socket (on the left) pushing the joint and bearing cap into the large socket

12.11 Use a feeler gauge to check the snap-ring-to-bearing clearance (U-joint journal endplay)

Chapter 8 Clutch and driveline

13.6 Reverse the brake rotor and use as a puller

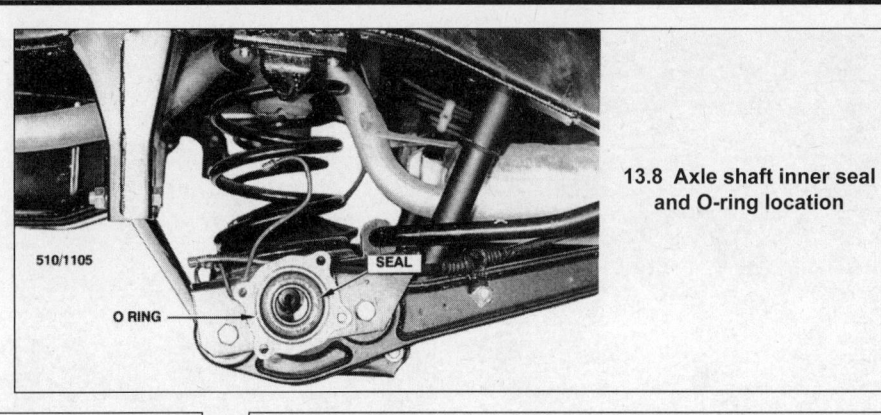

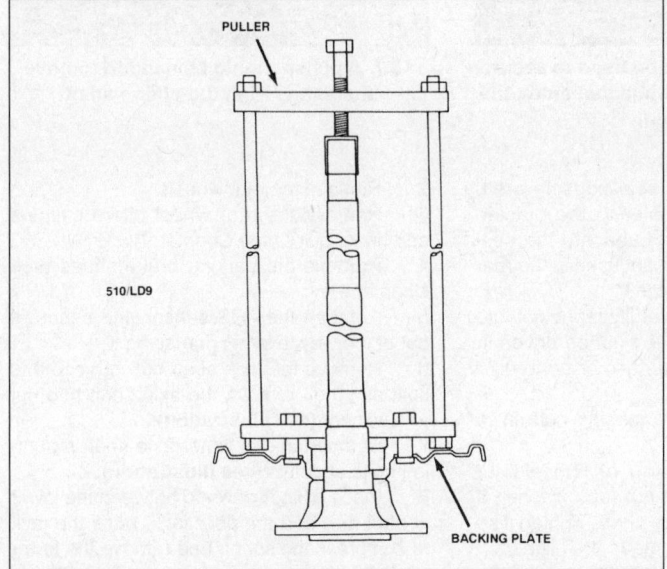

13.8 Axle shaft inner seal and O-ring location

13.10 Method of removing the axle shaft from the bearing case and backing plate

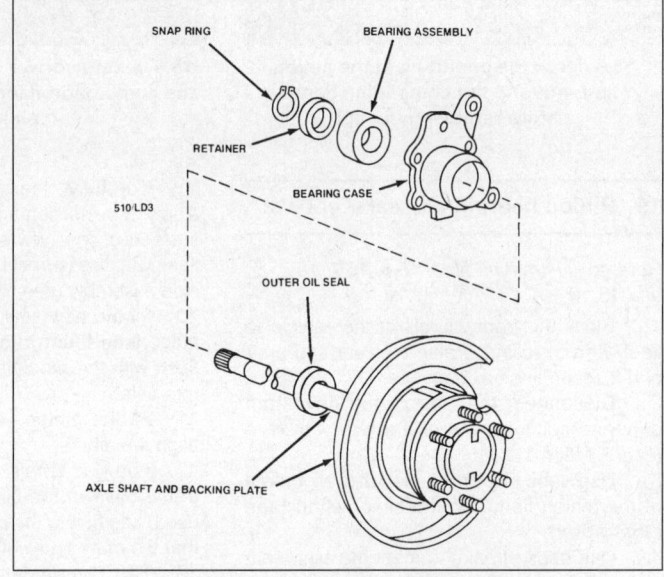

13.12 Typical rear axle and bearing details

8 Renew the inner seal and O-ring **(see illustration)**. With the axleshaft removed, hold it in the jaws of a vice so that the bearing retainer ring rests on the edges of the jaws.

9 Using a hammer and a sharp chisel, nick the retainer in two places. This will have the effect of spreading the retainer so that it will slide off the shaft. Do not damage the shaft in the process and never attempt to cut the retainer away with a torch, as the temper of the shaft will be ruined.

10 Using a suitable press or extractor, withdraw the bearing from the axleshaft **(see illustration)**.

11 Remove and discard the oil seal.

12 When fitting the new bearing, make sure that the retainer plate and the seal are refitted to the shaft first. Press on the bearing and the retaining ring tight up against it **(see illustration)**.

13 Before refitting the axleshaft assembly, smear wheel bearing grease onto the bearing end and in the bearing recess in the axle housing tube.

14 Apply rear axle oil to the axleshaft splines.

15 Hold the axleshaft horizontal and insert it into the axle housing. Feel when the shaft splines have picked up those in the differential side gears and then push the shaft fully into position, using a soft faced hammer on the end flange as necessary.

16 Bolt the retainer plate to the brake backplate, refit the brake rotor.

17 The remaining steps are the reverse of the removal procedure.

14 Rear axle assembly (banjo type axle housing) - removal and refitting

1 Loosen the rear wheel lug nuts, raise the vehicle and support it securely on jackstands placed underneath the frame. Remove the wheels.

2 Support the rear axle assembly with a floor jack placed underneath the differential.

3 Remove the shock absorber lower mounting nuts, detach the lower part of the shocks from the axle brackets and compress the shocks to get them out of the way (see Chapter 10).

4 Disconnect the driveshaft from the differential companion flange and hang it with a piece of wire from the underbody (see Section 11).

5 Disconnect the parking brake cables from the parking brake lever at each rear wheel (see Chapter 9).

6 Disconnect the rear flexible brake hose from the brake line above the rear axle housing. Disconnect the rear axle breather hose on top of the axle housing (if equipped). Plug the ends of the line and hose or wrap plastic bags tightly around them to prevent excessive fluid loss and contamination.

7 Support the rear axle assembly with a jack.

8 Remove the stabiliser bar bolts.

9 Remove the rear suspension lower arms and panhard rod.

10 Carefully lower the axle assembly to the floor with the jack, then remove it from under the vehicle. It would be a good idea to have an assistant on hand, as the assembly is very heavy.

11 Refitting is the reverse of the removal procedure. Be sure to tighten the bolts and nuts and the driveshaft companion flange bolts to the torques listed in this Chapter and the Specifications in Chapter 10. Bleed the brakes (see Chapter 9).

15.3 Mark the positions of the pinion shaft, nut and the companion flange before removing the nut

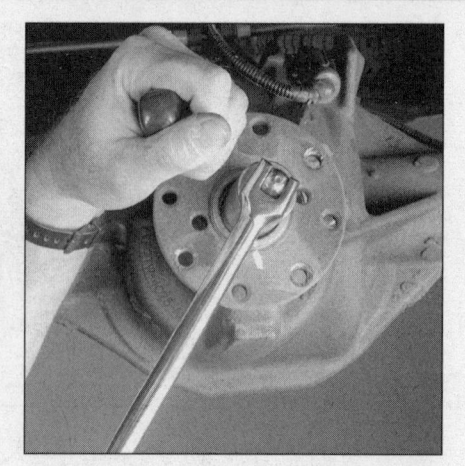

15.5 A screwdriver can be used to secure the companion flange while loosening the pinion nut

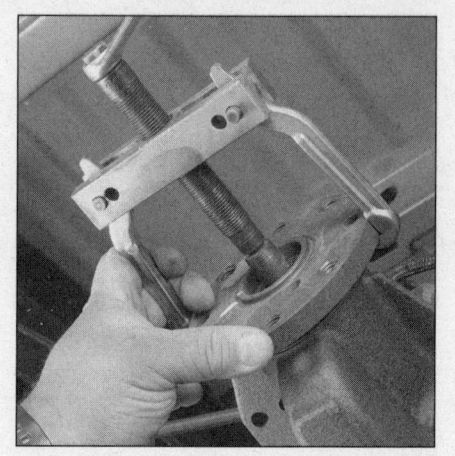

15.7 A puller should be used to remove the flange from the pinion shaft

15 Pinion bearing oil seal - renewal

Refer to illustrations 15.3, 15.5, 15.7, 15.8 and 15.10

1 Block the front wheels of the vehicle to keep it from rolling. Raise the rear and support it securely on axle stands.
2 Disconnect the rear of the driveshaft only and secure it out of the way with wire (see Section 11).
3 Use dabs of paint to mark the alignment of the pinion flange to the pinion shaft **(see illustration)**.
4 Use dabs of paint to mark the alignment of the pinion nut to the pinion flange in order to obtain the correct pinion bearing preload.
5 Lock the pinion flange with a large adjustable wrench or another type of holding device **(see illustration)**. Remove the pinion nut.
6 Place a drain pan beneath the rear axle.
7 Attach a puller to the flange and remove it **(see illustration)**. Do not hammer on the flange. This will damage the assembly.
8 Prise out the old oil seal and discard it **(see illustration)**.
9 Carefully clean the seal housing area. Apply non-hardening sealer to the outside surface of the new seal. Lubricate the seal itself with the correct lubricant used in the rear axle assembly (see Chapter 1).
10 Fit the new seal, carefully tapping it into place **(see illustration)**. It must be driven in flush with the mounting surface or up to 0.25 mm below.
11 Fit the pinion flange making certain to align the marks.
12 Apply a small amount of RTV sealer to the base of the pinion nut (and washer, if used) and fit it to the pinion shaft. Tighten it so that the marks previously made are aligned.
13 The remainder of installation is the reverse of removal.

16 Half shafts (independent rear suspension) - removal and refitting

Refer to illustrations 16.6, 16.7, 16.8 and 16.12

1 Raise the vehicle and support it securely on jackstands (see Jacking and Towing).
2 Remove the rear wheels.
3 Remove the rear wheel brake calipers and brake discs (see Chapter 9).
4 Remove the parking brake shoes (see Chapter 9).
5 Remove the ABS sensor and secure it out of the way to avoid damaging it.
6 Remove the axle shaft hub nut cap and split pin, then remove the axle shaft hub nut and washer **(see illustration)**.
7 Remove the six inner axle shaft mounting bolts and nuts **(see illustration)**.
8 Place a block of wood between the lower control arm and the floor jack, raise the jack to compress the spring and remove the lower control arm mounting bolts **(see illustration)**.
9 Slowly lower the jack down, tilt the knuckle down and slide the half shaft out of the knuckle.
10 The half shafts may now be removed from the centre section.

Caution: *The half shaft must be supported during this procedure in order to avoid allowing the C.V. joints to go past their range of motion. Do not prise on the tone wheel during this procedure. It may be necessary to insert a prise bar between the centre section and the half shaft if a puller is not available.*

15.8 Prise out the old seal with a seal removal tool

15.10 A seal driver or a large socket can be used to seat the new seal

Chapter 8 Clutch and driveline

16.6 Use a breaker bar and large prise bar to loosen the hub axle nut

16.7 Remove the six inner axle shaft mounting bolts and nuts (arrows) - five of six bolts shown

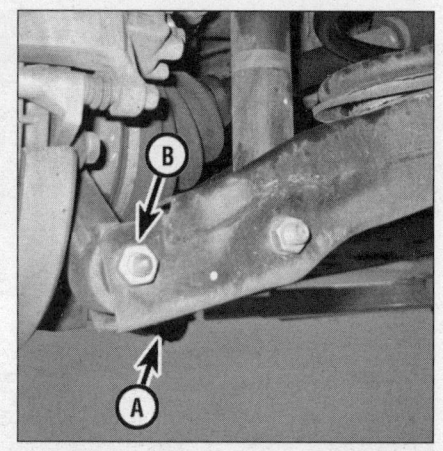

16.8 Place a floor jack with a block of wood under the lower control arm (A) and remove the lower control arm-to-knuckle nut and bolt (B)

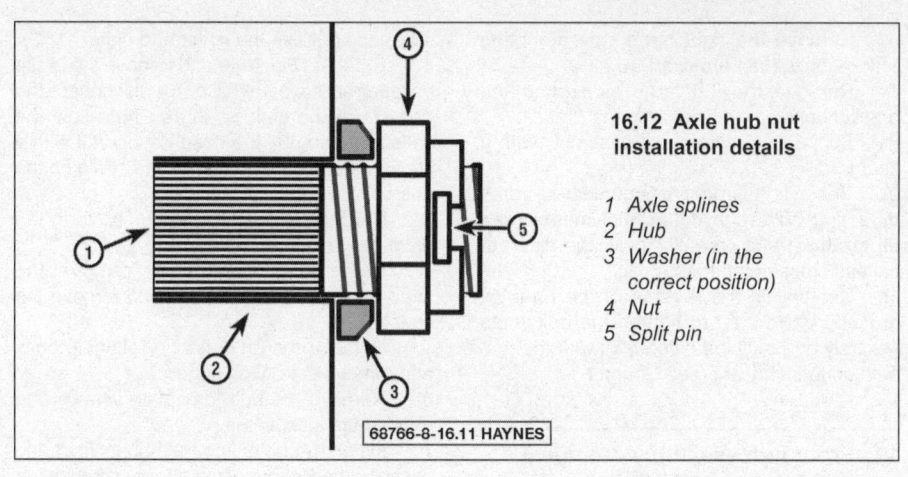

16.12 Axle hub nut installation details

1. Axle splines
2. Hub
3. Washer (in the correct position)
4. Nut
5. Split pin

17.1 Remove the dynamic damper mounting bolts (arrows)

Give the bar a sharp hammer blow to dislodge the half shaft.

11 Installation is the reverse of removal.

12 Install the hub nut washer with the taper to the outside **(see illustration)** and tighten the hub nut to the torque listed in this Chapter's Specification.

Note: *The control arm nuts are fitted toward the rear of the vehicle.*

17 Final drive assembly (independent rear suspension) - removal and refitting

Note: *On some early models it maybe necessary to remove the fuel tank to remove the final drive assembly (see Chapter 4).*

Removal

Refer to illustrations 17.1, 17.2, and 17.9

1 Remove the dynamic damper mounting bolts and remove the damper **(see illustration)**.

2 Remove the toe control tower bar mounting nuts and bolts and remove the bar **(see illustration)**.

3 Remove the exhaust pipe where it interferes with removal of the final drive assembly.

4 Disconnect the driveshaft at the rear and secure it out of the way with wire (see Section 11).

Caution: *Be certain to mark the alignment of the driveshaft to the pinion flange before disconnecting it.*

5 Remove both half shafts (see Section 6).

6 Remove the lower knuckle-to-arm mounting bolt on each side (see Chapter 10).

7 Disconnect the breather hose from the differential housing and differential lock (if equipped).

8 Disconnect the rear differential lock electrical harness connector (if equipped).

9 Loosen but do not remove the two rear bolts which secure the final drive assembly to the chassis **(see illustration)**.

10 Remove the front mounting bolts. Keep all washers and bushes in order so that they can be returned to their original locations.

11 Hold the final drive assembly with a sturdy floor jack or another reliable support.

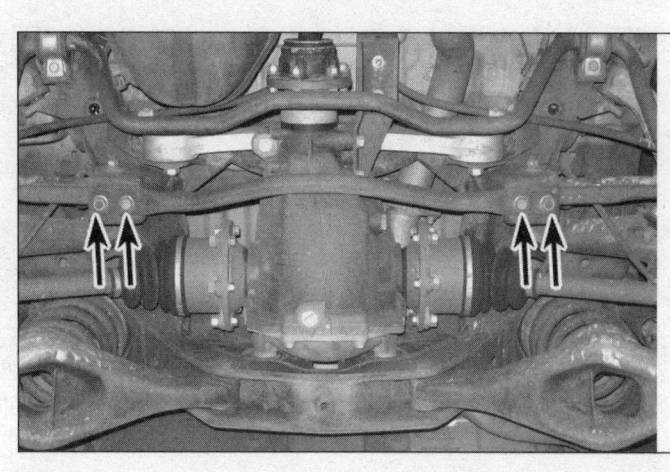

17.2 Remove the toe control tower bar mounting bolts (arrows)

17.9 Loosen the rear mounting bolts (arrows)

18.2 Remove the lower cover and skid plate mounting bolts (arrows) and remove the cover and plate

12 Remove the two rear mounting bolts **(see illustration 17.9)**.
13 Lower the unit, disconnect the vent hose from the top of the housing, then remove the entire assembly.

Refitting

14 Refitting is the reverse of removal. Be certain to align the match marks previously made. Tighten the bolts to the torques listed in this Chapter and Chapter 10 Specifications.

18 Front differential assembly - removal and refitting

Refer to illustrations 18.2, 18.6 and 18.9

1 Loosen the wheel lug nuts, raise the front of the vehicle and support it securely on jackstands (see Jacking and Towing). Remove the wheels.
2 Remove the lower cover and skid plate mounting bolts **(see illustration)** and remove the cover and plate.
3 Drain the lubricant from the differential (see Chapter 1).
4 Remove the front driveshaft (see Section 11).
5 Remove the driveaxles (see Section 20).
6 Remove the right hand side mounting bracket bolts **(see illustration)**.
7 Remove the left hand side mounting bracket bolts.
8 Support the differential assembly with a floor jack.
9 Remove the front crossmember-to-frame mounting bolts and differential mount **(see illustration)** and carefully lower the differential and crossmember as a unit.
10 Refitting is the reverse of the removal procedure. Be sure to tighten the bolts/nuts securely and refill the differential with the recommended lubricant (see Chapter 1).

19 Front hub assembly - removal, bearing repack, refitting and adjustment

Refer to illustrations 19.8, 19.16, 19.21, 19.22 and 19.27

1998 and earlier models

Removal

1 Raise the front of the vehicle and support it securely on jackstands (see Jacking and Towing). Remove the lower cover and skid plate mounting bolts **(see illustration 18.2)** and remove the cover and plate.
2 Refer to Chapter 9 and remove the brake caliper/pad assembly. Do not disconnect the hose from the caliper and do not allow the caliper to hang by the hose - support it with a section of stiff wire so there is no strain on the hose.
3 Carefully prise the grease cap from the drive flange.
4 Using snap ring pliers, remove the snap ring from the driveaxle and remove the spacer.
5 Remove the drive flange retaining bolts and remove the drive flange.
6 Remove the hub lock plate screws and remove the lock plate.
7 Install two bolts into the hub locknut and unscrew the locknut using a large screwdriver positioned between the bolts.
8 Slide the hub and disc assembly from the stub axle, taking care not to drop the outer bearing cone **(see illustration)**.
9 Using a lever or screwdriver, prise the seal from the inner end of the hub and discard the seal. Remove the inner bearing cone.

Note: *If the hub bearings are being removed for repacking only, it is not necessary to remove the inner and outer bearing cups.*

10 Support the hub assembly on two wood blocks and using a brass drift, drive the inner and outer bearing cups from the hub. The

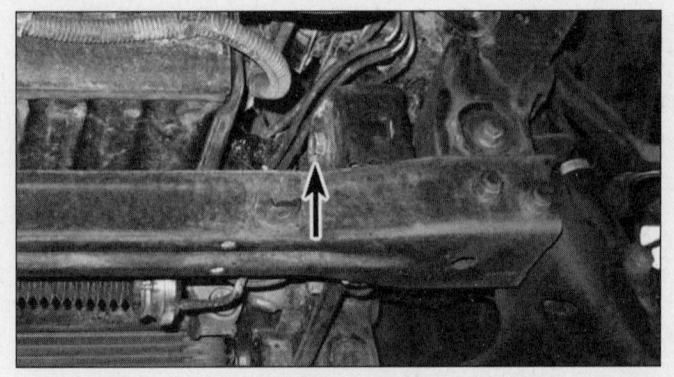

18.6 Remove the right hand side mounting bracket bolts (arrows)

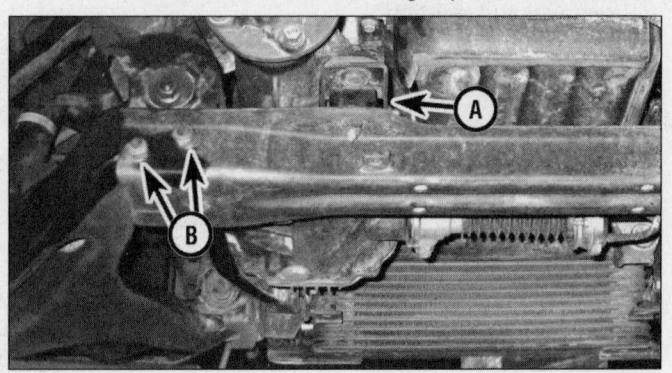

18.9 Remove the differential mount bolt and nut (A), and the front crossmember mounting bolts (B) - passengers side shown

Chapter 8 Clutch and driveline

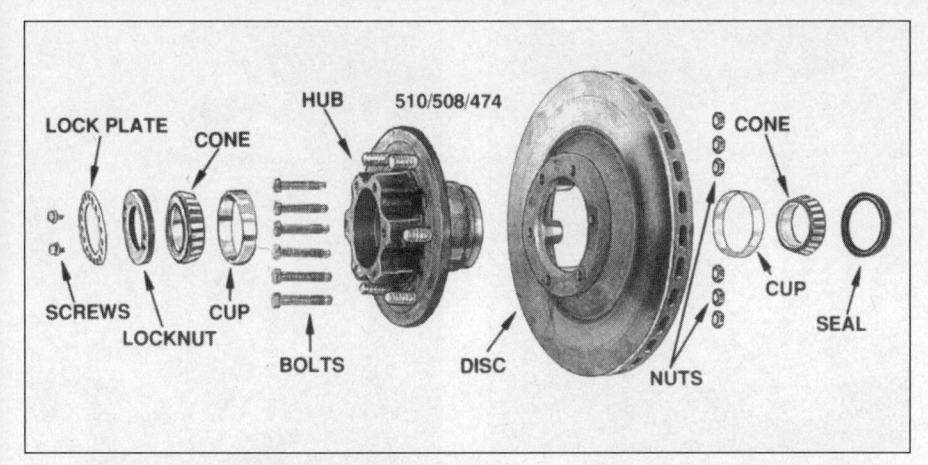

19.8 Typical 1999 and earlier model front hub and disc assembly exploded view

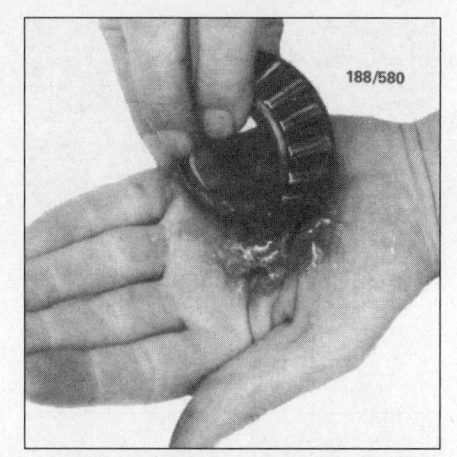

19.16 Pack the hub bearings by thoroughly working grease between the rollers and the inner race and roller cage

inner bearing cup is removed from the inner end of the hub and the outer bearing cup from the outer end of the hub.
11   If necessary mark the relationship between the hub and disc, removing the retaining nuts and bolts and separate the disc from the hub.
12   Clean all components in cleaning solvent and dry with compressed air if available.
Caution: *Do not spin the bearings with compressed air as damage to the bearings or injury to the operator may result.*
13   Check the roller bearings and cups for wear, pitting or damage and renew as necessary.
Note: *Individual bearing components should not be renewed separately. If any part of a bearing is faulty, the complete bearing must be renewed.*
14   If separated, assemble the disc and the hub ensuring that the mating marks are aligned and tighten the retaining nuts to the torque listed in this Chapters Specification section.

Bearing repack
15   Apply multipurpose grease to the outer surface of the bearing cups and using a brass drift, install the bearing cups into the hub so that their tapers face outwards and oppose each other.
16   Pack the inner and outer bearing cones with high melting point lithium based grease by thoroughly working the grease between the rollers, inner race and cage **(see illustration)**.
17   Install the inner bearing cone to the hub and install the hub seal until the body of the seal is level with the hub end face. Lubricate the seal lip with multipurpose grease.
18   Pack the cavity in the hub between the bearing cups with high melting point lithium grease and place the hub assembly on the stub axle.

Refitting and adjustment
19   Support the hub assembly in position and install the outer bearing cone. Install the locknut until it abuts the bearing cone.
20   Using a suitable adapter, tighten the locknut to 200 Nm to seat the bearings then loosen the locknut completely. Retighten the locknut to 25 Nm then loosen 30 to 40-degrees.
21   Connect a spring gauge to a wheel stud and adjust the locknut until the hub turning effort is 4 to 18 Nm **(see illustration)**.
22   Mount a dial gauge so that the plunger is against the hub face **(see illustration)** and measure the hub endplay. If the endplay exceeds 0.05 mm, remove the hub assembly and check that the bearings are correctly installed and lubricated.
23   Install the lock plate, aligning the tab with the keyway in the stub axle. If the holes in the locknut do not align with those in the lock plate, loosen the locknut until the holes align. Do not loosen the locknut more than 20-degrees.
24   Apply non hardening sealant to the hub and drive flange faces.
25   Install the drive flange to the driveaxle, install the retaining bolts and tighten the bolts to the torque listed in this Chapter's Specification.
26   Install the spacer and snap ring to the driveaxle.

19.21 Check the hub turning effort using a spring gauge

19.22 Measure the hub endplay using a dial gauge - Make sure the surface where the dial indicator rides on is clean

19.27 Use a feeler gauge to check for axle endplay

19.32 Remove the disc retaining screw and hub cap (arrow)

19.33 Use a breaker bar and large lever to loosen the hub axle nut

27   Measure the driveaxle endplay. Pull the driveaxle outwards and using a feeler gauge **(see illustration)**, measure the clearance between the spacer and the drive flange. If the clearance is not within 0.4 to 0.7 mm, install a spacer of suitable thickness.
28   Apply a non hardening sealant to the inner lip of the grease cap and install it into the drive flange.
29   Refit the brake caliper and wheel and lower the vehicle to the ground.

1999 and later models

Refer to illustrations 19.32, 19.33 and 19.34

Removal

30   Raise the front of the vehicle and support it securely on jackstands (see Jacking and Towing).
31   Refer to Chapter 9 and remove the brake caliper/pad assembly. Do not disconnect the hose from the caliper and do not allow the caliper to hang by the hose - support it with a section of stiff wire so there is no strain on the hose.
32   Remove the brake disc retaining screw **(see illustration)** and carefully prise the grease cap from the drive flange.
33   Remove the axle shaft hub nut cap and split pin, then remove the axle shaft hub nut and washer **(see illustration)**.
34   Turn the steering knuckle so the back side is visible, remove the four knuckle-to-hub mounting bolts **(see illustration)** and rotor protector (ABS models).
35   Using a plastic hammer or block of wood tap the hub assembly out of the steering knuckle.
36   Due to the special tools and expertise required to press the wheel bearing from the hub, the assembly should be taken to an automotive machine shop or other qualified repair facility to have the bearing replaced if it is worn.
37   Refitting is the reverse of the removal procedure.

Note: *Be sure to install the axle shaft washer correctly* **(see illustration 16.12)**.

20 Front driveaxles - removal and refitting

Refer to illustration 20.6

Removal

1   Raise the front of the vehicle and support it securely with jackstands (see Jacking and Towing). Remove the lower cover and skid plate mounting bolts **(see illustration 18.2)** and remove the cover and plate. Remove the wheels and the brake caliper assemblies (see Chapter 9). Do not disconnect the hoses from the calipers and do not allow the calipers to hang by the hoses - suspend them with pieces of stiff wire so there is no strain on the hoses.
2   Detach the ends of the axle shaft from the hub assemblies (see Section 19).
3   Remove each steering knuckle and front hub assembly as a unit (see Chapter 10).
4   To remove the left side (passenger's side) driveaxle, position a prybar or large screwdriver against the inner joint and carefully prise or 'pop' the joint out of the differen-

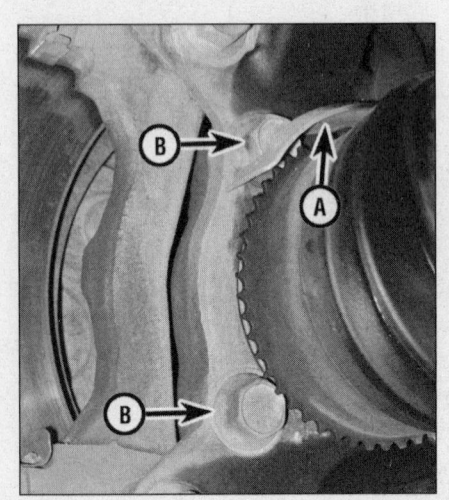

19.34 Remove the ABS rotor protector (A) and the hub mounting bolts (B) - two of four bolts shown

20.6 Remove the nuts and bolts (arrows) that attach the right driveaxle flange to the inner shaft, then carefully pull out the driveaxle - 3 of 4 nuts and bolts shown

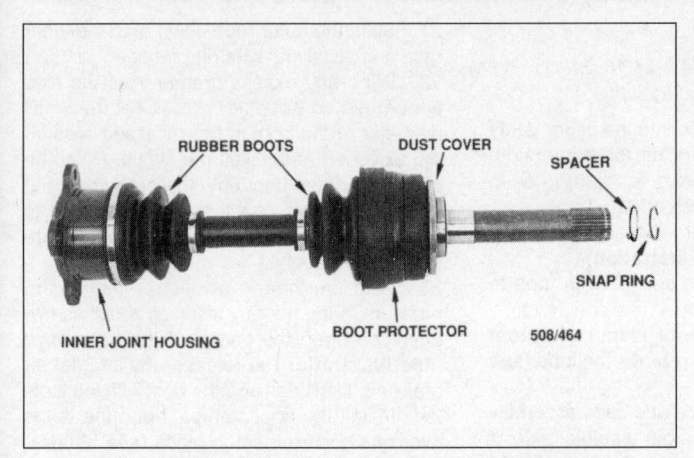

Chapter 8 Clutch and driveline

8-15

20.7 Typical right hand outer driveaxle components

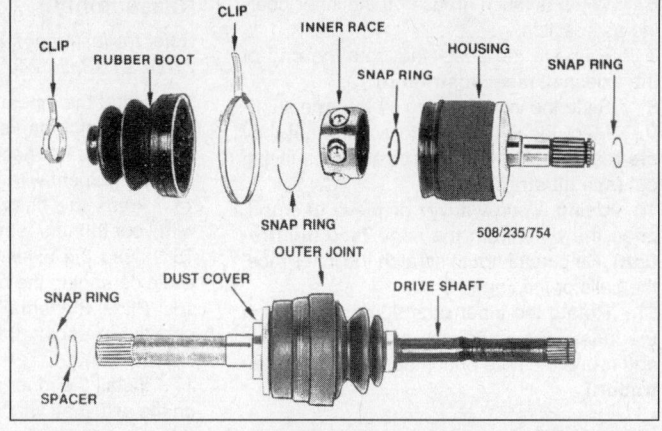

20.9 Typical exploded view of the left hand driveaxle

tial. Be careful not to damage the differential oil seal with the driveaxle inner splines as it is removed.

5   Use a jack to raise the right lower suspension arm, then remove the nuts and detach the shock absorber from the upper mount.

Caution: *Do not lower the jack until after the shock absorber has been reattached.*

6   Remove the nuts and bolts that attach the right driveaxle flange to the inner shaft **(see illustration)**, then carefully pull out the driveaxle. Remove the circlip from the inner end of the left driveaxle and renew it with a new one.

Refitting

Refer to illustrations 20.7 and 20.9

7   Attach the right driveaxle to the inner shaft flange **(see illustration)**, refit the bolts and nuts and tighten them to the torque listed in this Chapter's Specifications.

8   Attach the right shock absorber to the upper mount bracket and tighten the nuts.

9   Refit the left driveaxle **(see illustration)** in the differential and seat it by tapping on the outer end with a soft-face hammer.

10   Refit each steering knuckle and hub assembly and attach the balljoints, then adjust the driveaxle play as follows:

11   Refit the snap-ring on the end of the driveaxle, but do not refit the spacer/shim.

12   Mount a dial indicator on the front hub or brake disc and position the stem of the dial indicator against the end of the driveaxle as shown in **illustration 19.22**.

13   Move the driveaxle in and out and note the reading on the indicator. This is the axial (end) play.

Note: *On 1999 and later models, turn the driveaxle in both directions until resistance is felt (this is the centre of the turning stroke), then check the driveaxle play with the dial indicator.*

14   If the axial play is not as specified, select a shim/spacer from the sizes available that will produce the correct play.

21 Driveaxle boot renewal and Constant Velocity (CV) joint overhaul

Note: *If the CV joints exhibit signs of wear indicating need for an overhaul (usually due to torn boots), explore all options before beginning the job. Complete rebuilt driveaxles are available on an exchange basis, which eliminates much time and work. Whichever route you choose to take, check on the cost and availability of parts before disassembling the vehicle.*

Note: *Obtain a new rubber boot kit for each joint on the driveaxle before beginning disassembly. Do not disassemble the Birfield (outer) joints - if they are worn or damaged, new driveaxles are in order.*

Inner CV joint

Disassembly

Refer to illustrations 21.3, 21.4, 21.5, 21.7, 21.9, 21.10 and 21.11

1   Remove the driveaxles from the vehicle (see Section 20).

2   Mount the driveaxle in a vice. The jaws of the vice should be lined with wood or rags to prevent damage to the axleshaft.

3   Cut the boot clamps from the boot and discard them **(see illustration)**.

4   Slide the boot back on the axleshaft and prise the wire ring ball retainer from the outer race **(see illustration)**.

5   Pull the outer race off the inner bearing assembly **(see illustration)**.

21.3 Cut off the boot clamps and discard them

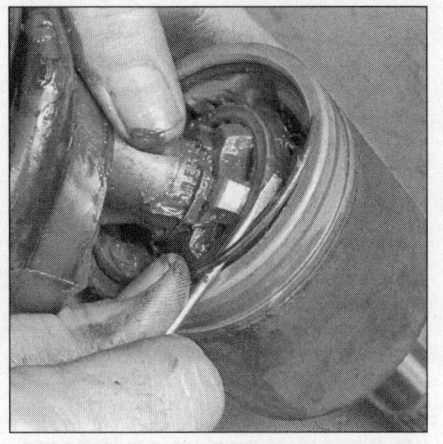

21.4 Prise the wire retainer ring from the CV joint housing with a small screwdriver

21.5 With the retainer removed, the outer race can be pulled off the bearing assembly

6 Wipe as much grease off the inner bearing as possible.
7 Remove the snap-ring from the end of the axleshaft (see illustration).
8 Slide the inner bearing off the axle shaft.
9 Mark the inner cage to ensure that they are reassembled with the correct sides facing out (see illustration).
10 Using a screwdriver or piece of wood, prise the balls from the cage (see illustration). Be careful not to scratch the inner race, the balls or the cage.
11 Rotate the inner race 90-degrees, align the inner race lands with the cage windows and rotate the race out of the cage (see illustration).

Inspection

Refer to illustrations 21.12a and 21.12b

12 Clean the components with solvent to remove all traces of grease. Inspect the cage and races for pitting, score marks, cracks and other signs of wear and damage. Shiny, polished spots are normal and will not adversely affect the CV joint performance (see illustrations).

Reassembly

Refer to illustrations 21.14, 21.16, 21.17, 21.20, 21.23, 21.24a and 21.24b

13 Insert the inner race into the cage. Verify that the matchmarks are on the same side. However, it's not necessary for them to be in direct alignment with each other.
14 Press the balls into the cage windows with your thumbs (see illustration).
15 Wrap the axleshaft splines with tape to avoid damaging the boot.
16 Slide the small boot clamp and boot onto the axleshaft, then remove the tape (see illustration).
17 Install the inner race and cage assembly on the axleshaft with a larger diameter side or "bulge" of the cage facing the axleshaft end (see illustration).
18 Install the snap-ring (see illustration 21.7).
19 Fill the outer race with CV joint grease (normally included with the new boot kit).
20 Pack the inner race and cage assembly with grease, by hand, until grease is worked completely into the assembly (see illustration).

21 Slide the outer race down onto the inner race and install the wire ring retainer.
22 Wipe any excess grease from the axle boot grove on the outer race. Seat the small diameter of the boot in the recessed area on the axleshaft and install the clamp. Push the other end of the boot onto the outer race and move the race in-or-out to adjust the joint to the proper length, as described in this Chapter's Specifications.
23 With the joint in position, equalise the pressure in the boot by inserting a dull screwdriver between the boot and the outer race (see illustration) to release any internal air pressure. Don't damage the boot with the tool.
24 Install the boot clamps, bend the tangs over and secure them in place (see illustrations).
25 Install the driveaxle (see Section 20).

Outer CV joint and boot

Refer to illustration 21.30

Note: *The outer CV joint is a non-serviceable item and is permanently retained to the driveaxle. If any damage or excessive wear occurs to the axle or the outer CV joint, the*

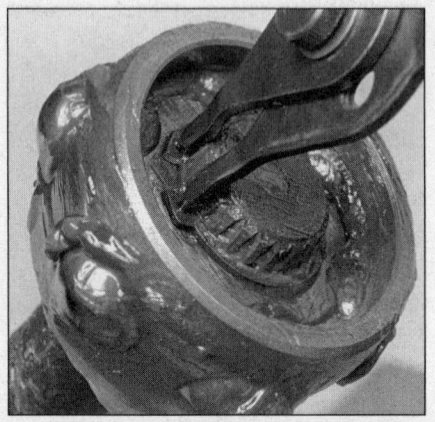

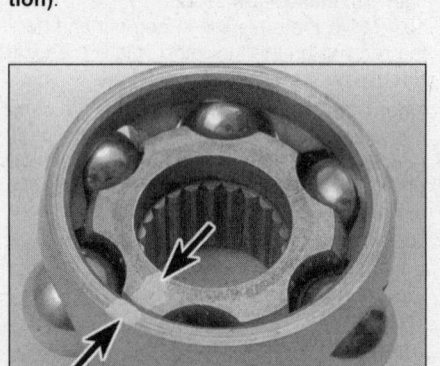

21.7 Remove the snap-ring from the end of the axleshaft

21.9 Make index marks on the inner race and cage so they'll both be facing the same direction when reassembled

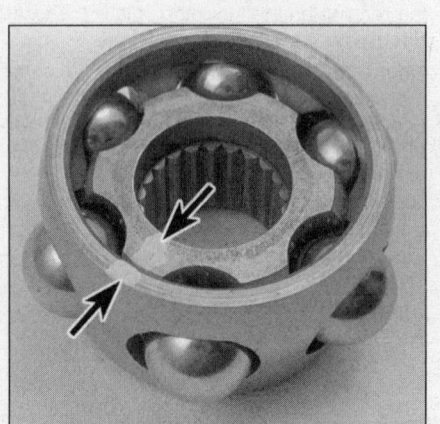

21.10 Pry the balls from the cage with a screwdriver (be careful not to nick or scratch them)

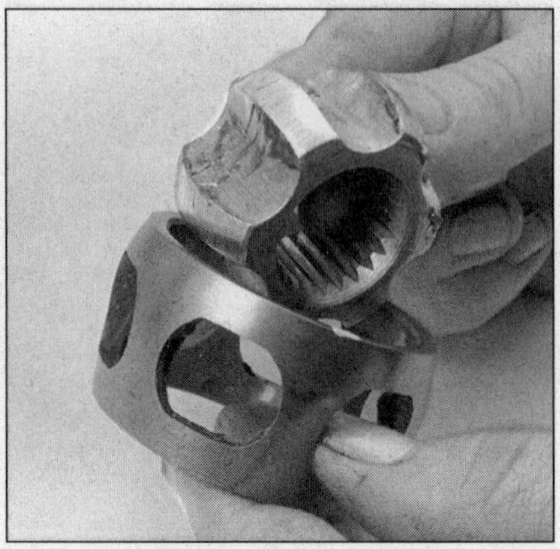

21.11 Tilt the inner race 90-degrees and rotate it out of the cage

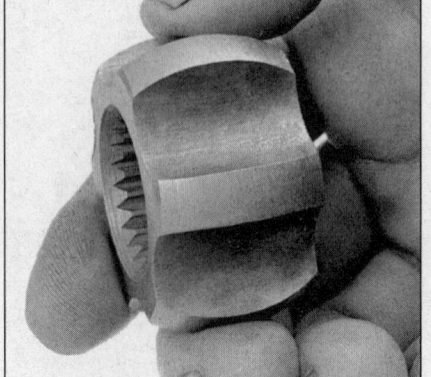

21.12a Inspect the inner race lands and grooves for pitting and score marks

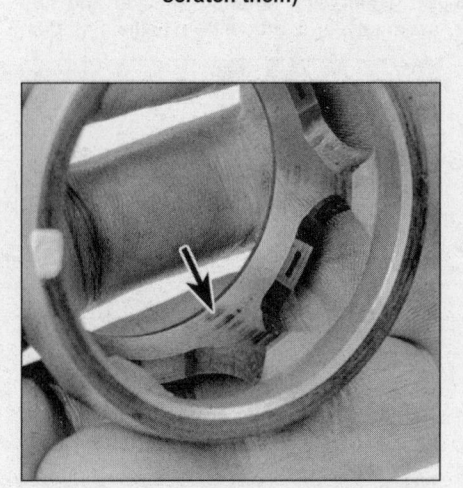

21.12b Inspect the cage for cracks, pitting and score marks (shiny spots are normal and don't affect operation)

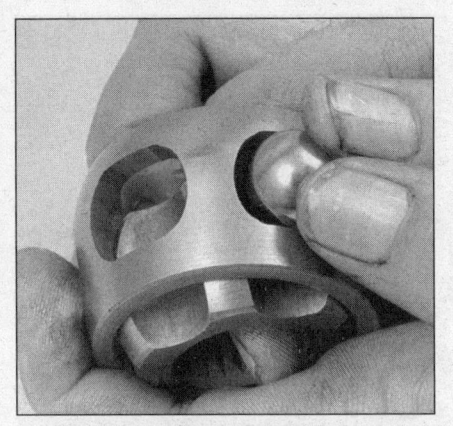

21.14 Press the balls into the cage through the windows

21.16 Wrap the splined area of the axle with tape to prevent damage to the boot

21.17 Install the inner race and cage assembly with the "bulge" facing the end of the axleshaft

21.20 Pack grease into the bearing until it's completely full

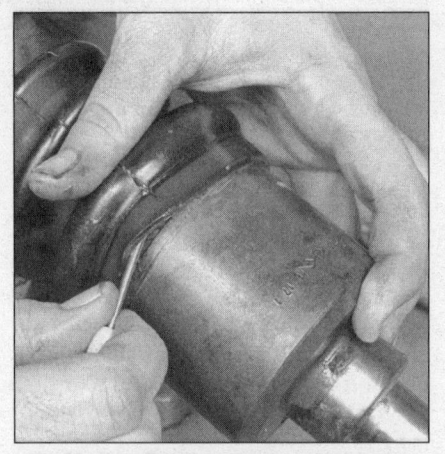

21.23 Equalise the pressure inside the boot by inserting a small screwdriver between the boot and the outer race

entire driveaxle assembly must be replaced (excluding the inner CV joint). Service to the outer CV joint is limited to boot replacement and grease repacking only.

26 Remove the driveaxle from the vehicle (see Section 20).
27 Mount the driveaxle in a vice. The jaws of the vice should be lined with wood or rags to prevent damage to the axleshaft.

28 Cut the boot clamps from both inner and outer boots and discard them (see illustration 21.3).
29 Remove the inner CV joint and boot (see Steps 4 through 11).
30 Remove the outer CV joint boot. Wash the outer CV joint assembly in solvent and inspect it as described in Step 12 (see illustration). Replace the axle assembly if any CV joint components are excessively worn. Install the new, outer boot and clamps onto the axleshaft (see illustration 21.16).

21.24a To install the new clamps, bend the tang down . . .

21.24b . . . and tap the tabs down to hold it in place

21.30 After the grease has been rinsed away and the cleaning solvent has been blown out with compressed air, rotate the outer joint housing through its full range of motion and inspect the bearing surfaces for wear or damage - if any of the balls, the race or cage look damaged, replace the driveaxle and outer joint

22.1 Typical free wheeling clutch assembly location (arrow)

22.7 Disconnect the vacuum lines and electrical connector (arrows)

31 Repack the outer CV joint with CV joint grease and spread grease inside the new boot as well.
32 Position the outer boot on the CV joint and install new boot clamps **(see illustrations 21.24a and 21.24b)**.
33 Reassemble the inner CV joint and boot (see Steps 15 through 24).
34 Install the driveaxle (see Section 20).

22 Front axle disconnect solenoid and actuator - check and renewal

Refer to illustration 22.1

1 The front axle is engaged into four-wheel drive by a vacuum-operated solenoid valve assembly and actuator which operates a free-wheeling clutch assembly **(see illustration)**.

Check

2 With the engine running, disconnect the hose from the vacuum source and check for strong vacuum.
3 Disconnect the electrical connectors from the solenoid valve assembly and check for 12 volts at the connector's blue-yellow wire. Check for continuity to earth at the yellow-green wire (with four-wheel drive engaged).
4 With the solenoid valves disconnected, check the resistance across the solenoid terminals. The resistance should be 36 to 46 ohms at 15-degrees C. If not within these specifications, renew the solenoid valve assembly.
5 Turn off the engine and check the vacuum hoses and pipes from the solenoid valve assembly to the actuator for kinks, cracks, or other damage.
6 Disconnect the vacuum hoses at the actuator and, with a hand vacuum pump, apply vacuum to one side and then the other of the actuator (be sure to cap the other side when applying vacuum). The actuator should shift the free-wheeling clutch in and out. If it doesn't, renew the actuator.

Renewal

Refer to illustrations 22.7 and 22.9

7 To renew the solenoid valve assembly, remove the vacuum hoses **(see illustration)** and electrical connectors from the solenoid valves.
8 Remove the fasteners and renew the solenoid valve assembly.
9 To renew the actuator, remove the vacuum hoses and pin connecting the shift rod to the actuator **(see illustration)**.
10 Remove the fasteners and renew the actuator assembly.

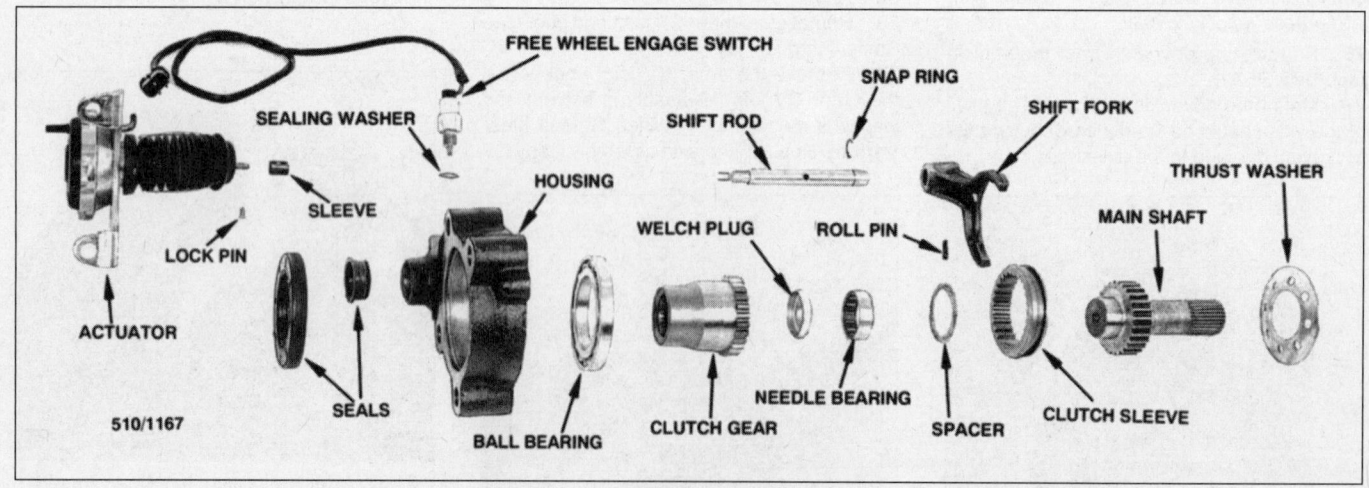

22.9 Exploded view of typical free wheeling clutch components

Chapter 9 Brakes

Contents

	Section
Anti-lock Brake System (ABS) - general information	12
Brake check	See Chapter 1
Brake disc - inspection, removal and refitting	4
Brake fluid level check	See Chapter 1
Brake light switch - check and renewal	14
Brake lines and hoses - inspection and renewal	6
Brake pedal height and freeplay check and adjustment	See Chapter 1
Brake hydraulic system - bleeding or replacing fluid	7
Disc brake caliper - removal and refitting	3

	Section
Disc brake pads - renewal	2
Front wheel bearing check, repack and adjustment	See Chapter 8
General information	1
Master cylinder - removal and refitting	5
Parking brake - adjustment	9
Parking brake cable(s) - renewal	10
Parking brake shoes - renewal	11
Power brake booster - check, removal and refitting	8
Vacuum pump (diesel engines) - removal and refitting	13

Specifications

General
Brake fluid type... DOT3 or DOT4
Master cylinder type
   Non ABS and 2000 and earlier ABS................. Tandem
   2001 and later ABS (HBB)................................. Single type
Brake booster
   Non ABS and 2000 and earlier ABS................. Vacuum assist
   2001 and later ABS (HBB)................................. Hydraulic assist
Brake booster pushrod-to-master cylinder piston clearance
   (with vacuum applied to booster)......................... 0.10 to 0.50 mm

Disc brakes
Brake pad minimum thickness................................. 2.0 mm
Disc minimum thickness*
   Front
      2000 and earlier...................................... 22.4 mm
      2001 to 2006.. 24.4 mm
      2007 and later.. 26.0 mm
   Rear
      2000 and earlier...................................... 16.4 mm
      2001 to 2006.. 20.4 mm
      2007 and later.. 16.0 mm

Disc brakes (continued)

Disc runout
  Front
    2000 and earlier... 0.1 mm
    2001 and later... 0.06 mm
  Rear
    2000 and earlier... 0.08 mm
    2001 and later... 0.06 mm
Rear disc (parking) brake
  Standard drum diameter
    2006 and earlier... 197 mm
    2007 and later.. 210 mm
  Maximum drum diameter [1]
    2006 and earlier... 198 mm
    2007 and later.. 211 mm

[1] Refer to the marks stamped on the drum (they supersede information printed here)

Torque specifications   Nm

Brake caliper guide pin mounting bolts
  Front
    2000 and earlier... 75
    2001 and later (where fitted).. 88
  Rear
    2006 and earlier... 44
    2007 and later.. 88
Caliper bracket mounting bolts
  Front
    2000 and earlier... 90
    2001 and later.. 104 to 122
  Rear
    2006 and earlier... 88
    2007 and later.. 113
Caliper inlet fitting... 30
Disc-to-hub bolts (2000 and earlier models)............................... 50 to 60
Master cylinder mounting nuts
  Non ABS and 2000 and earlier ABS..................................... 8 to 12
  2001 and later ABS (HBB)... 11 to 17
Power brake booster mounting nuts (non HBB)......................... 11 to 17
Vacuum pump oil line banjo bolts... 17

1 General information

The vehicles covered by this manual are equipped with hydraulically operated front and rear brake systems. The front and rear brakes are disc-type, using floating calipers.

Some early models are equipped with an Anti-lock Brake Syetem (ABS), whilst 2001 and later models are all equipped with ABS as a standard option.

Non ABS and 2000 and earlier ABS models, are equipped with a dual master cylinder which allows the operation of half of the system if the other half fails. This system also incorporates a proportioning valve which limits pressure to the rear brakes under heavy braking to prevent rear wheel lock-up. 2001 and later ABS models, are equipped with a hydraulic brake booster (HBB) which incorporates the master cylinder, pump motor, electronic control unit, accumulator and reservoir in one unit. Due to the complex nature of this system, all actual repair work must be done by a qualified automotive technician. For general information about this system see Section 12.

Non ABS and 2000 and earlier ABS models, are equipped with a power brake booster which utilises engine vacuum to assist in application of the brakes.

The parking brake operates the rear brakes only, through cable actuation.

There are some notes and cautions involving the brake system on these vehicle:
a) Use DOT3 or DOT4 brake fluid for these systems. Avoid mixing DOT3 and DOT4 brake fluids.
b) The brake pads and linings contain fibres which are hazardous to your health if inhaled. Whenever you work on the brake system components, carefully clean all parts with brake cleaner. Do not allow the fine dust to become airborne.
c) Safety should be paramount whenever any servicing of the brake components is performed. Do not use parts or fasteners which are not in perfect condition, and be sure that all clearances and torque specifications are adhered to. If you are at all unsure about a certain procedure, seek professional advice. Upon completion of any brake system work, test the brakes carefully in a controlled area before putting the vehicle into normal service. If a problem is suspected in the brake system, do not drive the vehicle until the fault is corrected.
d) Tyres, load and front end alignment are factors which also affect braking performance.
e) Due to the complex nature of the ABS system, all actual repair work must be done by a qualified automotive technician, for general information about the 2001 and later ABS system see (see Section 12).
f) If air has found its way into the hydraulic control unit, the system must be bled with the use of a scan tool. If the brake pedal feels spongy even after bleeding the brakes, or the ABS light on the instrument panel does not go off, or if you have any doubts whatsoever about the effectiveness of the brake system, have the vehicle towed to a dealer service department or other repair shop equipped with the necessary tools for bleeding the system.

2 Disc brake pads - renewal

Refer to illustration 2.4

Warning: *Disc brake pads must be renewed on both wheels at the same time - never*

Chapter 9 Brakes   9-3

2.4 Before removing the caliper, be sure to depress the pistons into the bottom of the bores in the caliper with a large G-clamp to make room for the new pads

2.5a Spray the disc, caliper and brake pads with brake system cleaner to remove the dust produced by brake pad wear

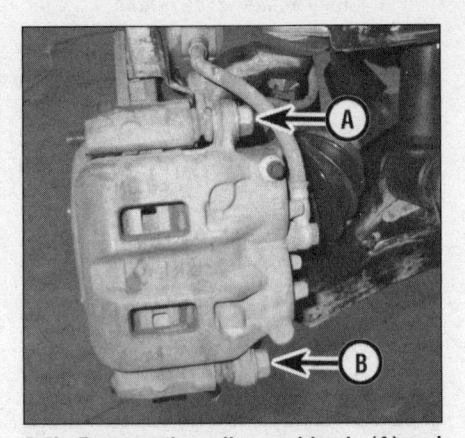

2.5b Remove the caliper guide pin (A) and guide pin lock bolt (B) . . .

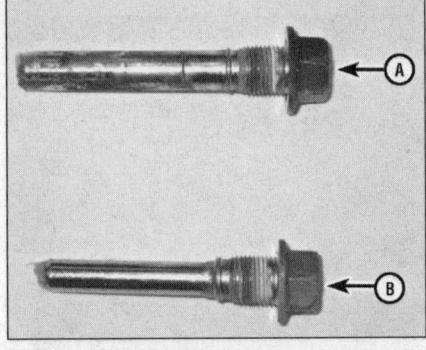

2.5c . . . noting the differences between the guide pin (A) and the guide pin lock bolt (B)

2.5d Remove the caliper from the pad assembly . . .

renew the pads on only one wheel. Also, the dust created by the brake system is harmful to your health. Never blow it out with compressed air and don't inhale any of it. An approved filtering mask should be worn when working on the brakes. Do not, under any circumstances, use petroleum-based solvents to clean brake parts. Use brake cleaner or denatured alcohol only!

Note: *When servicing the disc brakes, use only high-quality, nationally recognised name brand pads.*

1 Remove the master cylinder reservoir cap.
2 Loosen the front wheel lug nuts, raise the front of the vehicle and support it securely on jackstands. Remove the wheels. Work

on one brake assembly at a time, using the assembled brake for reference if necessary.
3 Inspect the disc brake carefully as outlined in Section 4. If machining is necessary, follow the information in that Section to remove the disc, at which time the pads can be removed as well.

2.5e . . . and use a piece of wire to tie it to the coil spring - never let the caliper hang by the brake hose

2.5f Remove the inner pad from the caliper bracket . . .

2.5g . . . and remove the outer pad from the bracket

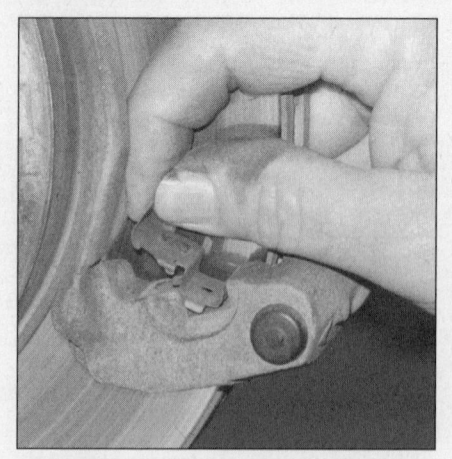

2.5h Remove the pad retainer clips from the caliper mounting bracket - 1 of 4 shown

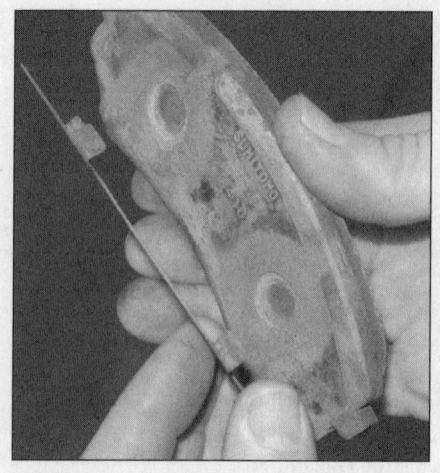

2.5i Separate the pad shim from each brake pad

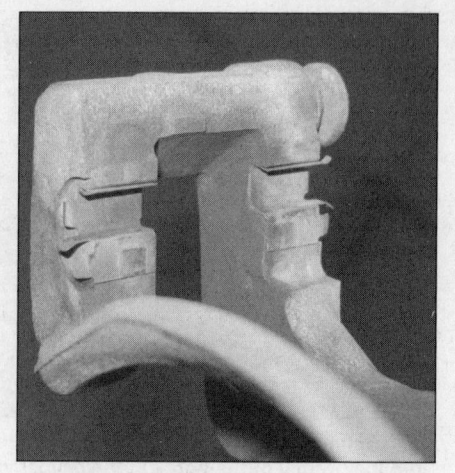

2.5j Make sure the pad retainer clips are fully seated once refitted

2.5k Fit the new outer pad and shim; make sure the "ears" on the upper and lower ends are full engaged with their respective grooves on the caliper bracket and the pad retainer clips

2.5l Fit the new inner pad and shim into the caliper bracket just like the outer pad with the wear indicator fitted on the lower "ear" (arrow)

2.5m Set the caliper down over the disc and new pads (if the pistons hit the inner pad, depress the pistons further into the caliper with your G-clamp). Refit the guide pins into the proper location (upper guide pin shown) and tighten the pins to the torque listed in this Chapter's Specifications

Early models

4 Using a large G-clamp, bottom the piston back into the caliper bore. The frame end of the G-clamp should be positioned on the backside of the caliper body and the screw should bear on the brake disc **(see illustration)**. As the piston is depressed to the bottom of the caliper bore, the fluid in the master cylinder will rise. Make sure that it doesn't overflow. If necessary, siphon off some of the fluid. Be careful not to spill fluid onto any of the painted surfaces - it will damage the paint.

Early models front pads

Refer to illustrations 2.5a through 2.5m

5 Follow the accompanying photos **(illustrations 2.5a through 2.5m)**, for the actual

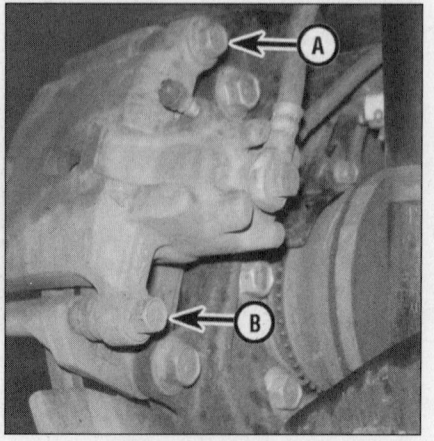

2.7a Remove the caliper guide pin (A) and guide lock pin (B) . . .

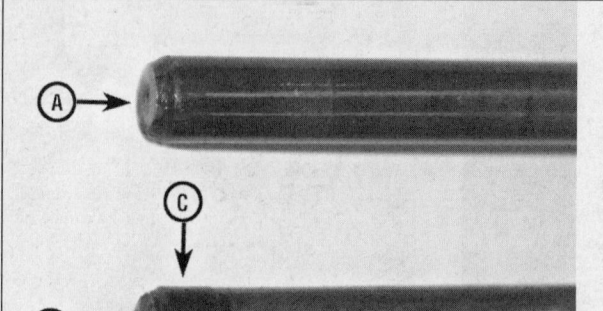

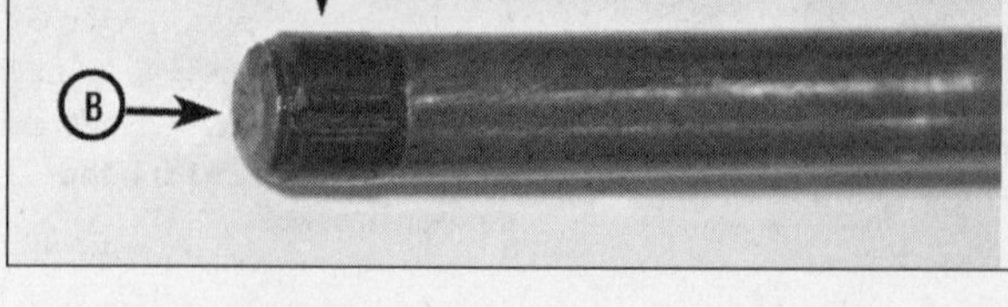

2.7b . . . noting the differences between the guide pin and the guide lock pin, check the lock pin for wear on the bush and renew if necessary

A Guide pin
B Guide lock pin
C Bush

Chapter 9 Brakes

2.7c Remove the caliper from the pad assembly and use a piece of wire to tie it to the coil spring - never let the caliper hang by the brake hose

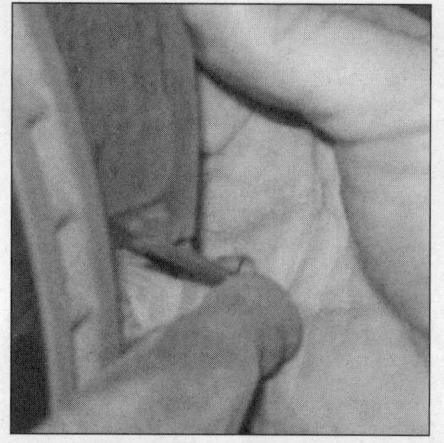

2.7d Remove the inner pad from the caliper mounting bracket, and remove the pad retainer clips from the caliper mounting bracket . . .

2.7e . . . and unclip the outer pad from the caliper

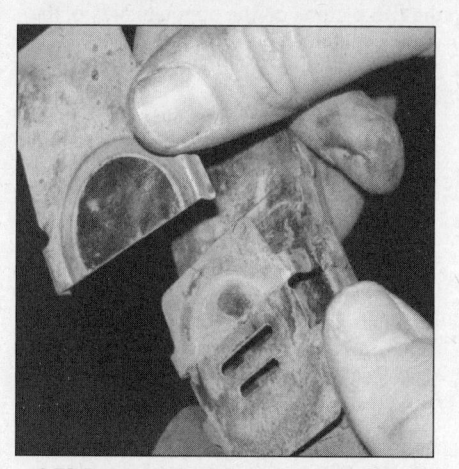

2.7f Remove the shims from the inner pad, noting how they come apart

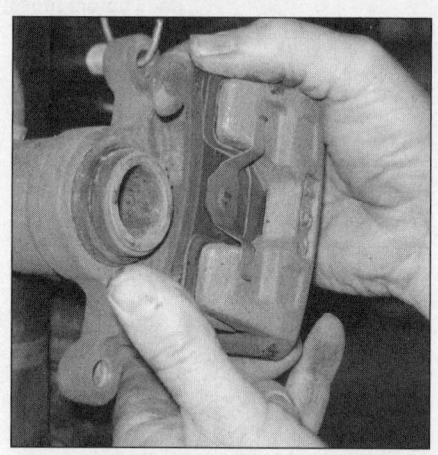

2.7g Slide the new outer pad onto the caliper, making sure the pad clips down into place

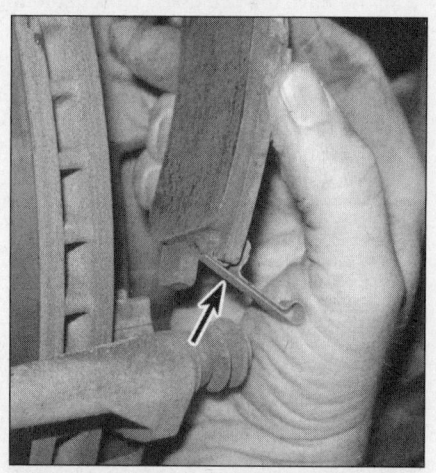

2.7h Refit the pad retainer clips onto the caliper mounting bracket and fit the new inner pad and shim(s) into the bracket with the wear indicator fitted on the lower "ear" (arrow). Set the caliper down over the disc and new pads (if the piston hits the inner pad, depress the piston further into the caliper with your G-clamp). Refit the guide pins into the proper location and tighten the pins to the torque listed in this Chapter's Specifications

pad replacement procedure. Be sure to stay in order and read the caption under each illustration.

6   After the job has been completed, firmly depress the brake pedal a few times to bring the pads into contact with the disc. Check the level of the brake fluid, adding some if necessary. Check the operation of the brakes carefully before placing the vehicle into normal service.

Rear pads

Refer to illustrations 2.7a through 2.7h

7   Wash the brake with brake system cleaner **(see illustration 2.4)**. Follow the accompanying photos **(illustrations 2.7a through 2.7h)**, for the actual pad replacement procedure. Be sure to stay in order and read the caption under each illustration.

Late model front pads

Refer to illustrations 2.8a through 2.8f

8   Follow the accompanying photos for the actual pad renewal procedure. Use **illustrations 2.8a through 2.8f** to renew the front brake pads. Be sure to stay in order and read the caption under each illustration.

All models

Note: *As the caliper piston is depressed to the bottom of the caliper bore, the fluid in the master cylinder will rise. Make sure that it doesn't overflow. If necessary, siphon off some of the fluid.*

Note: *When working on rear disc brakes, remove the pad support plates from the torque plate - they should be renewed if distorted in any way. Also, be sure to transfer the wear indicators from the old brake pads onto the new pads. If they are worn or bent, renew them with new parts.*

9   When refitting the caliper, be sure to tighten the mounting bolts to the torque listed in this Chapter's Specifications. After the job has been completed, firmly depress the brake pedal a few times to bring the pads into contact with the disc.

Warning: *Failure to do this will result in a temporary no brakes condition. Check the*

2.8a Late model front brake assembly showing pins (1) and clip (2)

Chapter 9 Brakes

2.8b Remove the two guide pins, gathering the anti-rattle spring at the same time

2.8c Use two screwdrivers to lever the pistons back into the caliper on one side. Once they are all the way in, insert the new pads before pressing the two pistons on the opposite side of the caliper

2.8d Remove the old disc pad, once the pistons are pushed all the way into the caliper bores

level of the brake fluid, adding some if necessary. Check the operation of the brakes carefully before placing the vehicle into normal service.

10 Refit the wheels and lower the vehicle. Road test the vehicle.

3 Disc brake caliper - removal and refitting

Warning: *Dust created by the brake system is harmful to your health. Never blow it out with compressed air and don't inhale any of it. An approved filtering mask should be worn when working on the brakes. Do not, under any circumstances, use petroleum-based solvents to clean brake parts. Use brake cleaner or denatured alcohol only!*

Note: *If an overhaul is indicated (usually because of fluid leakage), explore all options before beginning the job. New and factory rebuilt calipers are available on an exchange basis, which makes this job quite easy. If it's decided to rebuild the calipers, make sure that a rebuild kit is available before proceeding. Always rebuild the calipers in pairs - never rebuild just one of them.*

Removal

1 Remove the cap from the brake fluid reservoir, siphon off two-thirds of the fluid into a container and discard it.
2 Loosen the wheel lug nuts, raise the front of the vehicle and support it securely on jackstands. Remove the wheels.
3 Remove the brake hose inlet fitting bolt and detach the hose. Have a rag handy to catch spilled fluid and wrap a plastic bag tightly around the end of the hose to prevent fluid loss and contamination.
4 Remove the caliper pins and remove the caliper (see Section 2).

Refitting

5 Refit the upper mounting pin, swing the caliper down into position and tighten the upper mounting bolt and lower mounting bolt to the torque listed in the Specifications Section at the beginning of this Chapter.
6 Refit the flexible brake hose to the caliper. Be sure the hose does not interfere with any suspension or steering components.
7 Refit the wheel and tyre.

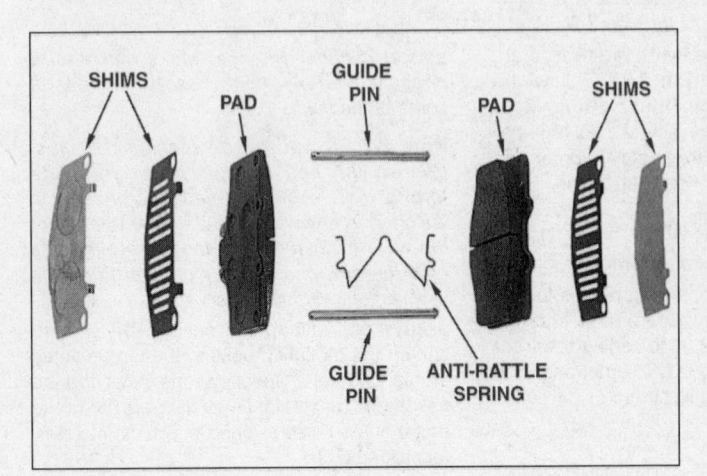

2.8e Ensure the shims are fitted to the new pads as illustrated

2.8f With the new pads installed, slide the guide pins into position along with the anti-rattle spring

Chapter 9 Brakes

4.4a Check the disc runout with a dial indicator positioned approximately 5 mm from the edge of the disc - if the reading exceeds the allowable runout, the disc will have to be resurfaced

4.4b Using a swirling motion, remove the glaze from the disc with emery cloth

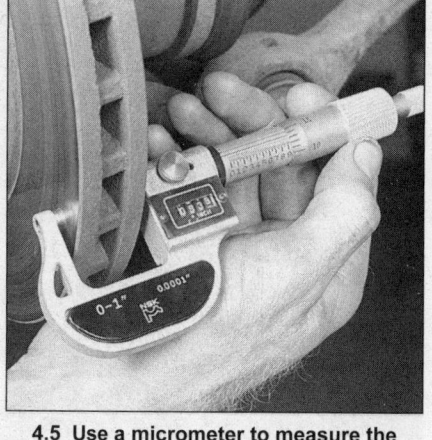

4.5 Use a micrometer to measure the thickness of the disc

4.6 Remove the caliper bracket mounting bolts (arrows) and remove the bracket - front bracket shown, rear caliper bracket similar

Inspection

1 Loosen the wheel lug nuts, raise the vehicle and support it securely on jackstands. Remove the wheel. On rear disc brakes, reverse and refit two wheel lugs nuts to hold the disc securely in place.

2 Remove the brake caliper as outlined in Sections 2 and 3. It's not necessary to disconnect the brake hose. After removing the caliper, suspend the caliper out of the way with a piece of wire from the underbody. Don't let the caliper hang by the hose and don't stretch or twist the hose.

3 Visually check the disc surface for score marks and other damage. Light scratches and shallow grooves are normal after use and may not always be detrimental to brake operation, but deep score marks - over approximately 0.4 mm - require disc removal and refinishing by an automotive machine shop. Be sure to check both sides of the disc. If pulsating has been noticed during application of the brakes, suspect excessive disc runout.

4 To check disc runout, place a dial indicator at a point about 5 mm from the outer edge of the disc **(see illustration)**. Set the indicator to zero and turn the disc. The indicator reading should not exceed the limit listed in this Chapter's Specifications. If it does, the disc should be refinished by an automotive machine shop.

Note: *Professionals recommend resurfacing of brake discs regardless of the dial indicator reading (to produce a smooth, flat surface, that will eliminate brake pedal pulsations and other undesirable symptoms related to questionable discs). At the very least, if you elect not to have the discs resurfaced, deglaze the brake pad surface with medium-grit emery cloth (use a swirling motion to ensure a non-directional finish)* **(see illustration)**.

5 The disc must not be machined to a thickness less than the specified minimum thickness. The minimum thickness is cast into the inside of the disc. The disc thickness can be checked with a micrometer **(see illustration)**.

Removal

Refer to illustrations 4.6, 4.7a and 4.7b

6 Remove the caliper mounting bracket bolts **(see illustration)** and lift the bracket off.

7 On 2000 and earlier models, remove the front hub/disc assembly. Unbolt the disc from the hub **(see illustration)**. On 2001 and later models remove the retaining screw **(see illustration)** and slide the rotor off of the hub assembly. On rear disc brakes, remove the retaining screw (if fitted) and/or the lug nuts previously fitted and lift off the disc.

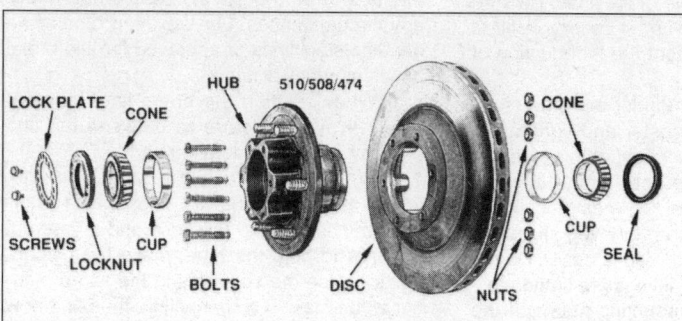

8 Bleed the brake system (see Section 7).

9 Lower the vehicle to the ground. Test the brakes carefully before placing the vehicle into normal operation.

4 Brake disc - inspection, removal and refitting

Refer to illustrations 4.4a, 4.4b and 4.5

Note: *The following procedure applies to both front and rear disc brakes.*

4.7a Front hub and disc exploded view - remove the bolts from the disc/hub assembly, then separate the two components (it may be necessary to tap the disc off with a hammer and block of wood)

4.7b Remove the disc retaining screw and slide the rotor off of the hub assembly - later model shown

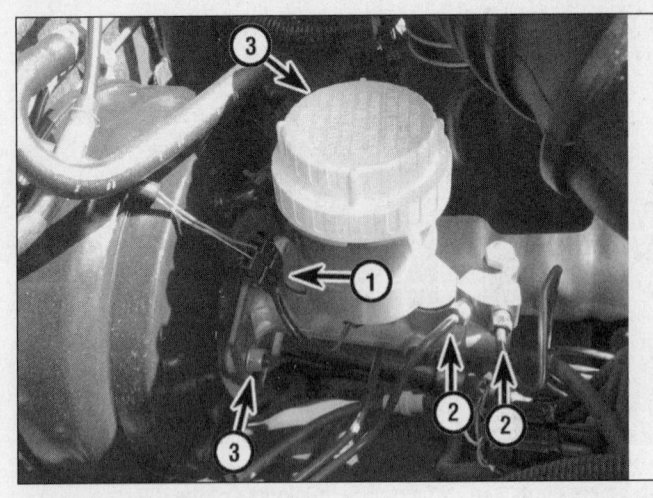

5.6 Brake master cylinder mounting details - early model non ABS shown

1 Brake fluid level switch electrical connector
2 Brake lines
3 Mounting nuts

5.8 The best way to bleed air from the master cylinder before fitting it on the vehicle is with a pair of bleeder tubes that direct brake fluid in to the reservoir during bleeding

Refitting

8 On 2000 and earlier models, refit the front disc and hub assembly and adjust the wheel bearing (see Chapter 8).
9 On 2001 and later models and rear-disc brakes, slide the disc back into place. Refit the retaining screw and tighten securely.
10 Refit the caliper mounting bracket, tightening the mounting bolts to the torques listed in this Chapter's Specifications. Position the pads in the bracket and refit the caliper (refer to Section 3 for the caliper refitting procedure, if necessary). Tighten the caliper bolts to the torque listed in this Chapter's Specifications.
11 Refit the wheel, then lower the vehicle to the ground. Depress the brake pedal a few times to bring the brake pads into contact with the disc. Bleeding of the system will not be necessary unless the brake hose was disconnected from the caliper. Check the operation of the brakes carefully before placing the vehicle into normal service.

5 Master cylinder - removal and refitting

Non ABS and 2000 and earlier ABS models

Removal

Refer to illustration 5.6

1 The master cylinder is located in the engine compartment, mounted to the power brake booster.
2 Remove as much fluid as you can from the reservoir with a syringe.
3 Place rags under the fluid fittings and prepare caps or plastic bags to cover the ends of the lines once they are disconnected.
Caution: *Brake fluid will damage paint. Cover all body parts and be careful not to spill fluid during this procedure.*
4 Loosen the tube nuts at the ends of the brake lines where they enter the master cylinder. To prevent rounding off the flats on these nuts, the use of a flare-nut spanner, which wraps around the nut, is preferred.
5 Pull the brake lines slightly away from the master cylinder and plug the ends to prevent contamination and disconnect any wiring from the master cylinder.
6 Remove the mounting nuts **(see illustration)** and pull the master cylinder off the studs and out of the engine compartment. Again, be careful not to spill the fluid as this is done.

Refitting

Refer to illustration 5.8

Note: *Avoid mixing DOT3 and DOT4 brake fluids.*

7 Before fitting a new master cylinder it should be bench bled. Because it will be necessary to apply pressure to the master cylinder piston and, at the same time, control flow from the brake line outlets, it is recommended that the master cylinder be mounted in a vice, with the jaws of the vice clamping on the mounting flange.
8 Insert a pair of master cylinder bleeder tubes to the outlet ports of the master cylinder **(see illustration)**.
9 Fill the reservoir with brake fluid of the recommended type (see Chapter 1).
10 Slowly push the piston assembly into the master cylinder bore to expel the air from the master cylinder. A large Phillips screwdriver can be used to push on the piston assembly - air will be expelled from the pressure chambers and into the reservoir. Because the tubes are submerged in fluid, air can't be drawn back into the master cylinder when you release the pistons.
11 Repeat the procedure until only brake fluid is expelled from the brake lines. Be sure to keep the master cylinder reservoir filled with brake fluid to prevent the introduction of air into the system.
12 Refit the master cylinder over the studs on the power brake booster and tighten the attaching nuts only finger tight at this time.
13 Thread the brake line fittings into the master cylinder. Since the master cylinder is still a bit loose, it can be moved slightly in order for the fittings to thread in easily. Do not strip the threads as the fittings are tightened.
14 Fully tighten the mounting nuts and brake fittings.
15 Fill the master cylinder reservoir with fluid, then bleed the brake system as described in Section 9. To bleed the cylinder on the vehicle, have an assistant pump the brake pedal several times and then hold the pedal to the floor. Loosen the fitting nuts to allow air and fluid to escape. Repeat this procedure on both fittings until the fluid is clear of air bubbles. Test the operation of the brake system carefully before placing the vehicle in normal service.

2001 and later ABS models

Due to the complex nature of this system, all actual repair work must be done by a qualified automotive technician.
For general information about the 2001 and later ABS system see Section 12.

6 Brake lines and hoses - inspection and renewal

Note: *Avoid mixing DOT3 and DOT4 brake fluids.*

1 About every six months the flexible hoses which connect the steel brake lines with the front and rear brakes should be inspected for cracks, chafing of the outer cover, leaks, blisters, and other damage.
2 Spare steel and flexible brake lines are commonly available from dealer parts departments and auto parts stores. Do not, under any circumstances, use anything other than genuine steel lines or approved flexible brake hoses as renewal items.
3 When refitting the brake line, leave at least 19 mm of clearance between the line and any moving or vibrating parts.
4 When disconnecting a hose and line, first remove the spring clip. Then, using a normal spanner to hold the hose and a flare-nut spanner to hold the tube, make the disconnection. Use the spanners in the same manner when making a connection, then fit a new clip.

Note: *Make sure the tube passes through the centre of its grommet.*

5 When disconnecting two hoses, use normal spanners on the hose fittings. When connecting two hoses, make sure they are not bent, twisted or strained.
6 Steel brake lines are usually retained along their span with clips. Always remove these clips completely before removing a fixed brake line. Always refit these clips, or new ones if the old ones are damaged, when renewing a brake line, as they provide support and keep the lines from vibrating, which can eventually break them.
7 Remember to bleed the hydraulic system after renewing a hose or line.

7 Brake hydraulic system - bleeding or replacing fluid

Warning: *Wear eye protection when bleeding the brake system. If the fluid comes in contact with your eyes, immediately rinse them with water and seek medical attention.*
Note: *Bleeding the hydraulic system is necessary to remove any air that manages to find its way into the system when it's been opened during removal and refitting of a hose, line, caliper, wheel cylinder or master cylinder.*
Note: *Avoid mixing DOT3 and DOT4 brake fluids.*
Note: *The brake fluid should be changed at the intervals indicated in Chapter 1. The procedure for changing the brake fluid and bleeding the system are similar.*

Non ABS and 2000 and earlier ABS models

Refer to illustration 7.8

1 It will probably be necessary to bleed the system at all four brakes if air has entered the system due to low fluid level, or if the brake lines have been disconnected at the master cylinder.
2 If a brake line was disconnected only at a wheel, then only that caliper must be bled.
3 If a brake line is disconnected at a fitting located between the master cylinder and any of the brakes, that part of the system served by the disconnected line must be bled.
4 Remove any residual vacuum from the brake power booster by applying the brake several times with the engine off.
5 Remove the master cylinder reservoir cover and fill the reservoir with brake fluid. Refit the cover.
Note: *Check the fluid level often during the bleeding operation and add fluid as necessary to prevent the fluid level from falling low enough to allow air bubbles into the master cylinder.*
6 Have an assistant on hand, as well as a supply of new brake fluid, a clear container partially filled with clean brake fluid, plastic, rubber or vinyl tubing to fit over the bleeder valve and a spanner to open and close the

7.8 When bleeding the brakes, a hose is connected to the bleeder valve at the caliper or wheel cylinder and then submerged in brake fluid - air will be seen as bubbles in the hose and container when the valve is opened - all air must be expelled before moving the next wheel

bleeder valve.
7 Beginning at the left rear wheel, loosen the bleeder valve slightly, then tighten it to a point where it is snug but can still be loosened quickly and easily.
8 Place one end of the tubing over the bleeder valve and submerge the other end in brake fluid in the container **(see illustration)**.
9 Have the assistant pump the brakes slowly a few times to get pressure in the system, then hold the pedal firmly depressed.
10 While the pedal is held depressed, open the bleeder valve just enough to allow a flow of fluid to leave the valve. Watch for air bubbles to exit the submerged end of the tube. When the fluid flow slows after a couple of seconds, close the valve and have your assistant release the pedal.
11 Repeat Steps 9 and 10 until no more air is seen leaving the tube, then tighten the bleeder valve and proceed to the right front wheel, the right rear wheel and the left front wheel, in that order, and perform the same procedure. Be sure to check the fluid in the master cylinder reservoir frequently.
12 Never use old brake fluid. It contains moisture which will lower the boiling point of the brake fluid and also deteriorate the brake system rubber components.
13 Refill the master cylinder with fluid at the end of the operation.

2001 and later ABS models

Warning: *If air has found its way into the hydraulic control unit, the system must be bled with the use of a scan tool. If the brake pedal feels "spongy" even after bleeding the brakes, or the ABS light on the instrument panel does not go off, or if you have any doubts whatsoever about the effectiveness of the brake system, have the vehicle towed to a dealer service department or other repair shop equipped with the necessary tools for bleeding the system.*

Caution: *Do not allow too much brake fluid to be drained at any one bleeding.*
Note: *The master cylinder is combined with the hydraulic unit, pump motor and hydraulic booster which is referred to as the Hydraulic brake booster (HBB).*

14 It will probably be necessary to bleed the system at all four brakes if air has entered the system due to low fluid level, or if the brake lines have been disconnected at the master cylinder.
15 If a brake line was disconnected only at a wheel, then only that caliper must be bled.
16 If a brake line is disconnected at a fitting located between the master cylinder and any of the brakes, that part of the system served by the disconnected line must be bled.
17 Remove the HBB reservoir cover and fill the reservoir with brake fluid. Refit the cover.
Note: *Check the fluid level often during the bleeding operation and add fluid as necessary to prevent the fluid level from falling low enough to allow air bubbles into the system.*
18 Once the reservoir on the Hydraulic brake booster unit (HBB) has been filled, turn the ignition switch to the "LOCK" position, and bleed the front calipers starting from the right then the left as described in Steps 9 and 10.
19 Turn the key to the "ON" position and listen for the hydraulic pump to begin running. Check the level of the reservoir. If the reservoir is low add fluid as needed to stop the pump motor and refit the filler cap.
20 With the key still in the "ON" position depress the pedal several times. Turn the key to the "LOCK" position and recheck the level in the reservoir.
21 If the fluid is not clear wait a minute or two for the fluid level to turn clear. If it doesn't turn clear repeat Step 18.
22 Turn the key to the "ON" position and bleed the rear calipers from the right then the left as described in Steps 9 and 10.
23 Turn the key to the "LOCK" position and recheck the level in the reservoir. Depress the brake pedal until the pedal effort becomes difficult to depress.
24 Turn the key to the "ON" position and depress the brake pedal fast, twenty times then verify that the pump motor stops. Turn the key to the "LOCK" position and depress the brake pedal forty times until the pedal effort becomes difficult to depress again.
25 Turn the key to the "ON" position and verify that the pump motor stops within 25 seconds. If the motor doesn't stop bleed the system again.
26 Check the fluid level and add fluid to bring the level up to the MAX mark on the reservoir.
27 Check the operation of the brakes carefully before placing the vehicle into normal service.

Warning: *Do not operate the vehicle if you are in doubt about the effectiveness of the brake system. It is possible for air to become trapped in the anti-lock brake system hydraulic control unit, so, if the brake pedal feels "spongy" even after repeated bleeding*

8.7 Locate the pushrod clevis (arrow) connecting the booster to the brake pedal and disconnect the clevis pin, then separate the booster from the pedal

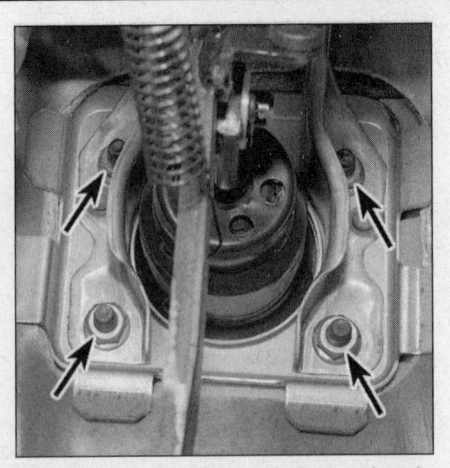

8.11 Remove the four nuts (arrows) and washers holding the brake booster to the firewall

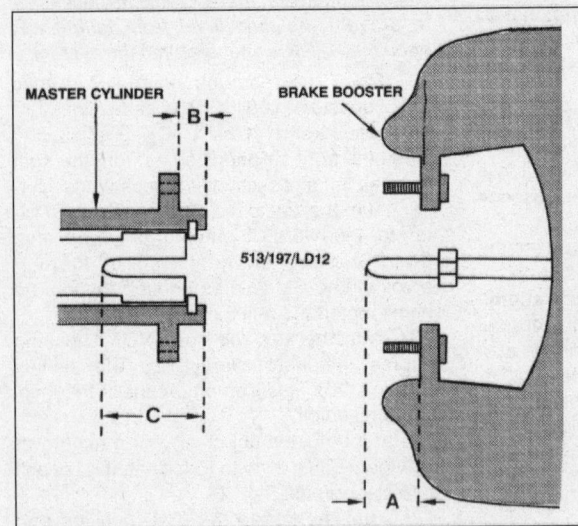

8.14 The clearance between the booster pushrod and the master cylinder piston must be within the specified range. If there's excessive clearance, the brake pedal travel will be excessive; if there's no clearance, the brakes may drag. To adjust the length of the booster pushrod, hold the serrated portion of the rod with a pair of pliers and then turn the adjusting nut in or out, as necessary, to achieve the desired setting - Pushrod clearance = (C-B) - A

8   Remove the clevis pin retaining clip with pliers and pull out the pin.
9   Holding the clevis with pliers, disconnect the clevis locknut with a spanner. The clevis is now loose.
10 Disconnect the hose leading from the engine to the booster. Be careful not to damage the hose when removing it from the booster fitting.
11 Remove the four nuts **(see illustration)** and washers holding the brake booster to the firewall. You may need a light to see these, as they are up under the dash area.
12 Slide the booster straight out from the firewall until the studs clear the holes and pull the booster, brackets and gaskets from the engine compartment area.

Refitting

Refer to illustration 8.14

13 Refitting procedures are basically the reverse of those for removal. Tighten the booster mounting nuts to the torque listed in this Chapter's Specifications. Tighten the clevis locknut securely.
14 If the power booster unit is being renewed, the clearance between the master cylinder piston and the pushrod in the vacuum booster must be measured and, if necessary, adjusted **(see illustration)**. Using a depth micrometer or vernier calipers, measure the distance from the seat (recessed area) in the master cylinder to the master cylinder mounting flange. Next, connect a hand held vacuum pump to the power booster vacuum fitting and apply 67 kPa (petrol); 94 kPa (diesel) of vacuum to the booster. Measure the distance from the end of the vacuum booster pushrod to the mounting face of the booster (where the master cylinder mounting flange seats). Determine the clearance from the measurements and compare it to the value listed in this Chapter's Specifications. Turn the adjusting screw on the end of the power booster pushrod until the clearance is within the specified limit.
15 Refit the master cylinder.
16 After the final refitting of the master cylinder and brake hoses and lines, the brake pedal height and freeplay must be adjusted (see Chapter 1) and the system must be bled (see Section 7).

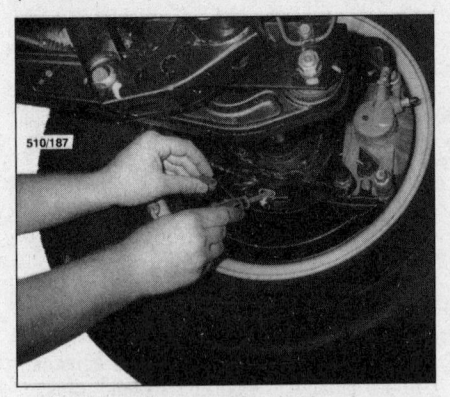

or the BRAKE or ANTI-LOCK light stays on, have the vehicle towed to a dealer service department or other repair shop equipped with the necessary tools for bleeding the system.

8 Power brake booster - check, removal and refitting

Non ABS and 2000 and earlier ABS models

Operating check

1   Depress the brake pedal several times with the engine off and make sure that there is no change in the pedal reserve distance.
2   Depress the pedal and start the engine. If the pedal goes down slightly, operation is normal.

Airtightness check

3   Start the engine and turn it off after one or two minutes. Depress the brake pedal several times slowly. If the pedal goes down farther the first time but gradually rises after the second or third depression, the booster is airtight.
4   Depress the brake pedal while the engine is running, then stop the engine with the pedal depressed. If there is no change in the pedal reserve travel after holding the pedal for 30 seconds, the booster is airtight.

Removal

Refer to illustrations 8.7 and 8.11

5   Power brake booster units should not be disassembled. They require special tools not normally found in most service stations or shops. They are fairly complex and, because of their critical relationship to brake performance, it is best to renew a defective booster unit with a new or rebuilt one.
6   To remove the booster, first remove the brake master cylinder as described in Section 5. On some vehicles it is not necessary to disconnect the brake lines from the master cylinder, as there is enough room to reposition the cylinder to allow booster removal.
7   Locate the pushrod clevis connecting the booster to the brake pedal **(see illustration)**. This is accessible from the interior in front of the driver's seat.

9.4 Retract the parking brake shoes - early model shown, later model similar

Chapter 9 Brakes

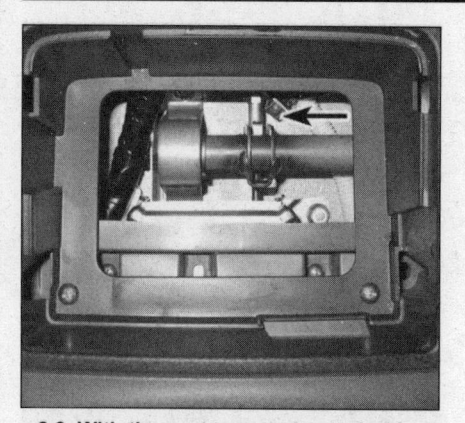

9.9 With the centre console cup holder removed you can see the parking brake equaliser adjuster nut (arrow)

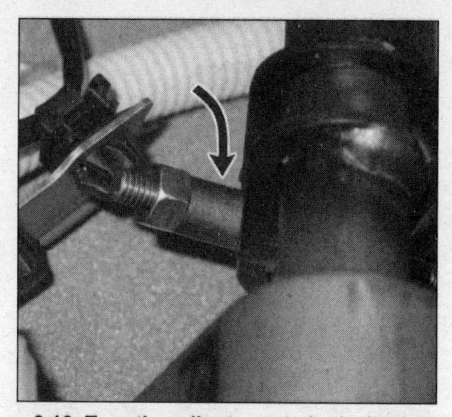

9.10 Turn the adjuster nut clockwise to tighten the cables

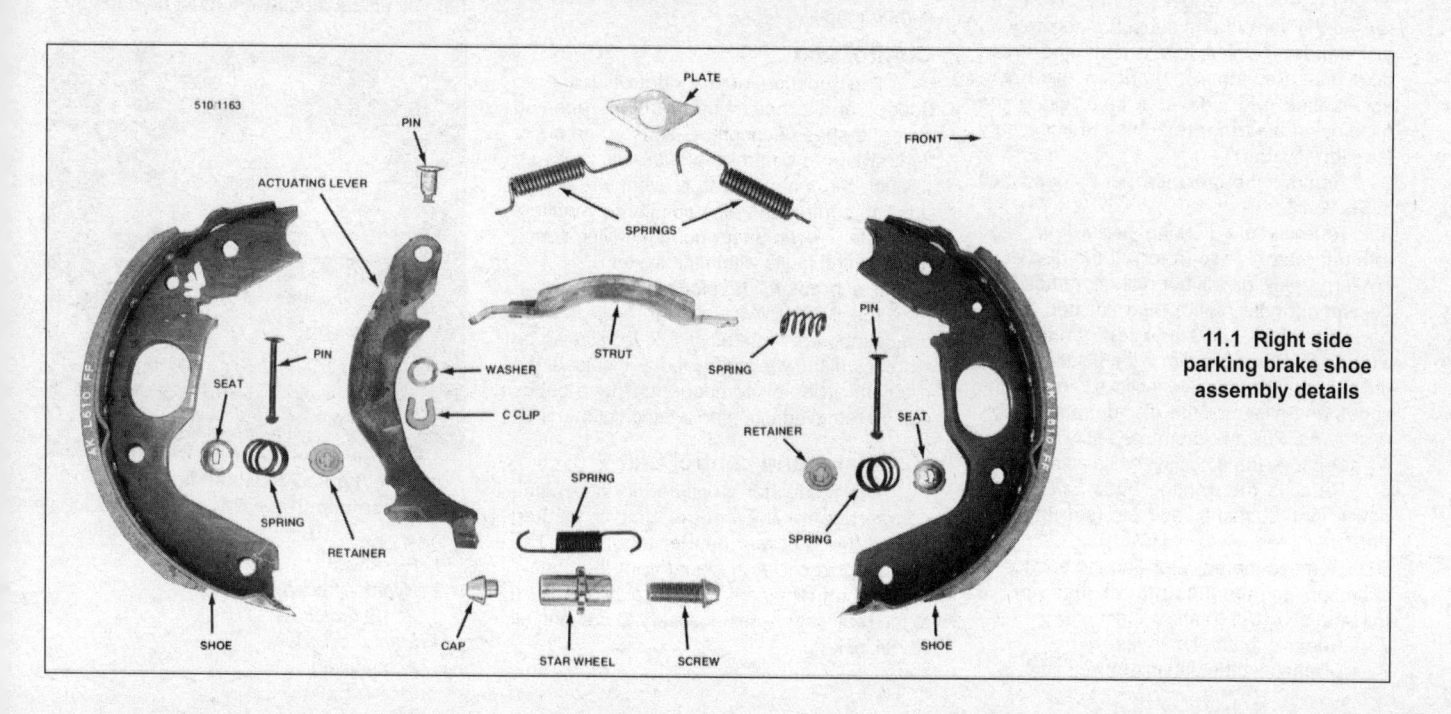

10.4 Remove the parking brake cables mounting brackets (arrow) and remove the cable - 1 of 4 shown

2001 and later ABS models

Due to the complex nature of this system, all actual repair work must be done by a qualified automotive technician.

For general information about the 2001 and later ABS system see Section 12.

9 Parking brake - adjustment

Refer to illustrations 9.4, 9.9 and 9.10

1 If the parking brake doesn't keep the vehicle from rolling when the parking brake lever is pulled up 4 to 6 clicks, adjust the parking brake.
2 Raise the vehicle and support it securely on jackstands.
3 Chock the front wheels, release the parking brake and place the transmission in neutral.
4 Working underneath the vehicle, remove the plug from the access hole in the brake backing plate and insert a narrow, flat bladed screwdriver into the access hole and engage the teeth on the star wheel **(see illustration)**.
5 Rotate the star wheel to expand the parking brake shoes until the disc cannot be rotated.
6 Rotate the star wheel in the opposite direction three to four notches and install the plug to the backing plate.
7 Using the same procedure, adjust the brake shoes on the opposite wheel.
8 Firmly apply the parking brake lever with a force of 196N and check that the lever travels 4 to 6 clicks of the ratchet, indicating that the parking brake cable adjustment is correct.
9 If the handbrake cable requires adjustment, remove the cup holders from the centre console **(see illustration)**.
10 Turn the nut on the equaliser end of the cables. Make sure the equaliser is even as the nut is tightened **(see illustration)**.
11 Remove all slack from the parking brake cables. After adjustment apply the parking brake several times and check that handle travel is 4 to 6 clicks. Make sure the rear brakes don't drag when the parking brake is released. Check to see that the parking brake light on the dash glows when the handle is applied.
12 Refit the cup holder to the centre console and verify that the parking brake will hold the vehicle on a moderate incline. If it still won't keep the vehicle from rolling, inspect the rear parking brakes as described in Section 11 of this Chapter.

10 Parking brake cable(s) - renewal

Refer to illustration 10.4

1 Raise the vehicle and support it securely on jackstands.

11.1 Right side parking brake shoe assembly details

11.5 Remove the parking brake shoe hold-down spring, washer and pin (arrow)

11.6 Remove the adjuster and the anchor-to-shoe springs (arrow), then remove the strut and strut-to-shoe spring.

12.10 Typical ABS-ECU location - centre console removed for clarity
1 *HBB warning buzzer*
2 *ABS-ECU*

2 Disassemble the rear brakes and remove the ends of the parking brake cables from the parking brake levers (see Section 11).
3 Remove the centre console (see Chapter 11).
4 Separate the parking brake cables at the adjuster, then remove the bolts and the cables **(see illustration)** from underneath the vehicle.
5 Refitting is the reverse of the removal procedure.
6 Following refitting, adjust the parking brake (see Section 9).

11 Parking brake shoes - renewal

Refer to illustrations 11.1, 11.5 and 11.6

1 Loosen rear wheel lug nuts, raise the rear of the vehicle and support it securely on jackstands. Remove the wheels and brake disc (see Section 4). Work on the brake assemblies one side at a time, using the assembled brake for reference, if necessary **(see illustration)**.
2 Remove the brake caliper as described in Section 3.
3 Release the parking brake lever and rotate the brake disc (rotor). If the disc does not turn freely, or will not pull off, remove the adjustment hole rubber plug (located on the back side of the backing plate). Turn the star-wheel anti-clockwise with a flat-bladed screwdriver approximately 3 to 4 clicks to retract the shoes and allow for the disc/drum assembly to slide off. Pull disc/drum assembly off.
4 Remove the adjusting wheel spring.
5 Remove the parking brake shoe hold-down spring, washer and pin **(see illustration)**.
6 Remove the adjuster and the anchor-to-shoe springs **(see illustration)**, then remove the strut and strut-to-shoe spring.
7 Remove the brake shoes.
8 Disconnect the parking brake cable.

9 Remove the lever assembly from the rear brake shoe.
10 Refitting is the reverse of removal. Repeat the operation on the other wheel. Don't forget to tighten the lug nuts to the torque specified in Chapter 1. Road test the vehicle carefully on a level road, away from traffic, before placing it into normal service again.

12 Anti-lock Brake System (ABS) - general information

2000 and earlier ABS models

The anti-lock brake system prevents wheel lock-up by sensing the drop in wheel speed and modulating hydraulic pressure to the brakes accordingly. It consists of several components:

Control unit

The function of the control unit is to accept and process information received from the speed sensors, G-sensor and brake light switch to control the hydraulic pressure through the modulator to prevent wheel lock up. The control unit also constantly monitors the system, even under normal driving conditions, to find faults within the system.
If a problem develops within the system, the BRAKE warning light will glow on the dashboard. A diagnostic code will also be stored, which, when retrieved will indicate the problem areas or component. These codes can be retrieved using an analog voltmeter.

Modulator and control unit

The modulator is located in the engine compartment. The control unit is located behind the right rear quarter trim panel. The modulator receives a signal from the control unit, it then regulates the hydraulic pressure to the rear wheels as necessary to prevent full wheel lock-up.

G-sensor

The G-sensor is located behind the centre console. The G-sensor senses the force and speed of deceleration and sends a signal to the control unit.

Speed sensors

The speed sensors are located at each wheel, behind the brake disc. The speed sensor sends a signal to the control unit indicating the wheel rotational speed.

Brake light switch

The brake light switch powers the control unit when the brake pedal is applied. Without this signal the anti-lock system would not activate.

2001 and later ABS models

Due to the complex nature of this system, all actual repair work must be done by a

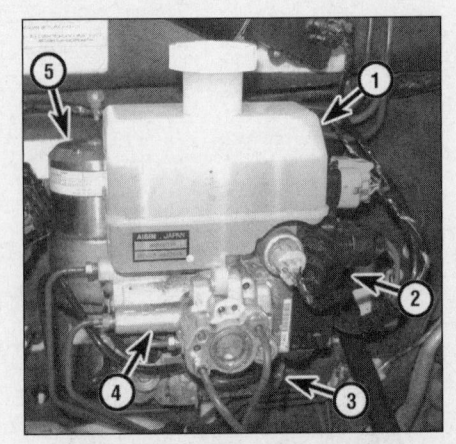

12.12 Typical 2001 and later "HBB" Hydraulic Brake Booster details
1 *Reservoir*
2 *Hydraulic control unit*
3 *Pump motor*
4 *Master cylinder*
5 *Accumulator*

Chapter 9 Brakes

12.13 The G-sensor (arrow) is located under the centre console - centre console removed for clarity

12.14a Typical front ABS speed sensor (arrow)

12.14b Typical rear ABS speed sensor (arrow)

qualified automotive technician.

The ABS system is standard on all vehicles, it is designed to aid in steering control and performance and hard braking situations. The later model ABS system controls the brake pressure to each wheel independently from each other wheel through the Electronic Brake Force Distribution system (EBD) which controls the optimum brake force to the rear wheels by electronic control.

ABS-ECU

Refer to illustration 12.10

The function of the ABS-ECU (see illustration) is to accept and process information received from the speed sensors, G-sensor and brake light switch to control the hydraulic pressure through the HBB to prevent wheel lock up. The ABS-ECU also constantly monitors the system, even under normal driving conditions, to find faults within the system.

If a problem develops within the system, the BRAKE warning light will glow on the dashboard. A diagnostic code will also be stored, which, when retrieved will indicate the problem areas or component.

Hydraulic brake booster (HBB)

Refer to illustration 12.12

The HBB is located in the engine compartment (see illustration). The hydraulic control unit, master cylinder, pump motor and accumulator are incorporated into the HBB assembly. The control unit receives a signal from the ABS-ECU, it then regulates the hydraulic pressure to the front and rear wheels as necessary to control braking applications as needed and to prevent full wheel lock-up.

G-sensor

Refer to illustration 12.13

The G-sensor is located underneath the centre console (see illustration). The G-sensor senses the force and speed of deceleration and sends a signal to the control unit.

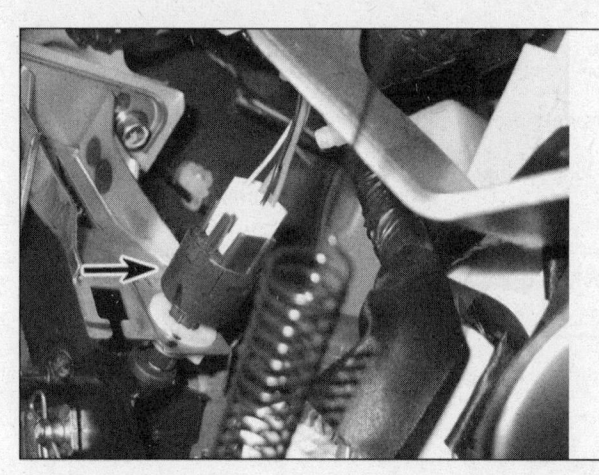

12.15 Typical brake light switch location (arrow)

Speed sensors

Refer to illustrations 12.14a and 12.14b

The speed sensors (see illustrations) are located at each wheel, behind the brake disc. The speed sensor sends a signal to the control unit indicating the wheel rotational speed.

Brake light switch

Refer to illustration 12.15

The brake light switch powers the control unit when the brake pedal is applied (see illustration). Without this signal the anti-lock system would not activate.

Diagnosis and repair - all models

If a dashboard light comes on and stays on while the vehicle is in operation, the ABS system requires immediate attention. Although special electronic ABS diagnostic testing tools are necessary to properly diagnose the system, you can perform a few preliminary checks before you taking the vehicle to a dealer service department.

a) Check the brake fluid level in the reservoir.
b) Verify that the computer electrical connectors are securely connected.
c) Check the electrical connectors at the hydraulic control unit.
d) Check the fuses.
e) Follow the wiring harness to each wheel and verify that all connectors are secure and that the wiring is not damaged.

13 Vacuum pump (diesel engines) - removal and refitting

Refer to illustration 13.4

Removal

1 Remove the intercooler assembly and any other interfering upper engine compartment component.
2 Disconnect the vacuum hose from the pump.
3 Remove the oil pressure switch, the sealing washers and the oil line to the vacuum pump.
4 Unbolt and remove the vacuum pump from the front of the engine (see illustration). Remove the O-rings from the pump.

13.4 Vacuum pump location on the 3.2 litre (4M41) engine

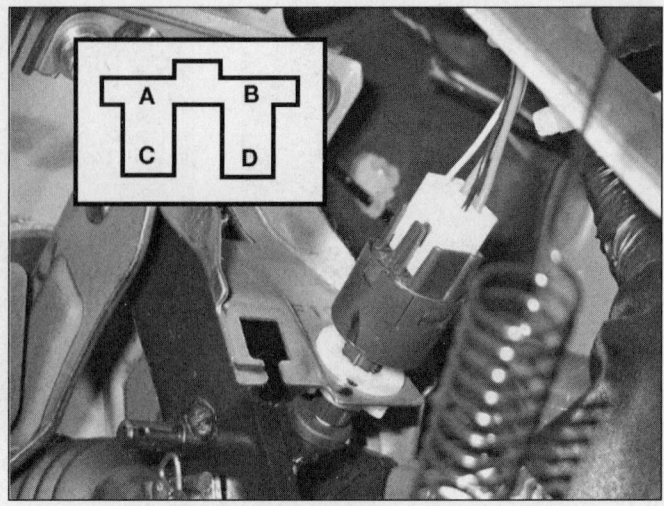

14.1 Check for resistance between terminals A and B with the plunger fully released

Refitting

5 Renew both of the O-rings on the pump. Bolt the pump to the engine.
6 Renew the sealing washers on the oil line/oil pressure switch assembly.
7 The remainder of the refitting is the reverse of removal.

14 Brake light switch - check and renewal

Check

Refer to illustration 14.1

1 Connect an ohmmeter between terminals A and B of the stop light switch **(see illustration)**.
2 Depress the plunger all the way in, there should be no continuity.
3 Release the plunger and there should be continuity. If either test fails renew the switch.

Removal

4 Disconnect the electrical connector from the brake light switch.
5 Remove the switch by turning the switch approximately 1/4 turn anti-clockwise and remove the switch.

Refitting

6 Screw the switch into the bracket and adjust the switch see Chapter 1.
7 The remainder of refitting is the reverse of removal.

Chapter 10
Suspension and steering systems

Contents

	Section
Ball joints - check and renewal	9
Chassis lubrication	See Chapter 1
Front end alignment - general information	26
Front hub assembly - removal, bearing repack, refitting and adjustment	See Chapter 8
Front shock absorber (1999 and earlier models) - removal and refitting	3
Front shock absorber (2000 and later models) - removal and refitting	4
Front shock absorber/spring assembly (2000 and later models) - renewal	5
Front stabiliser bar - renewal	2
Front steering knuckle - removal and refitting	10
Front suspension lower control arm - removal and refitting	8
Front suspension upper control arm - removal and refitting	7
General information	1
Power steering fluid level check	See Chapter 1
Power steering pump - removal and refitting	24
Power steering system - bleeding	25
Rear knuckle (Independent rear suspension) - removal and refitting	19

	Section
Rear lower control arm (Independent rear suspension) - removal and refitting	17
Rear shock absorber - removal and refitting	11
Rear stabiliser bar - removal and refitting	15
Rear suspension coil spring - removal and refitting	14
Rear suspension lateral rod (banjo type axle housing) - removal and refitting	13
Rear suspension trailing arms - removal and refitting	12
Steering and suspension check	See Chapter 1
Steering freeplay - adjustment	23
Steering gear - removal and refitting	22
Steering linkage - removal and refitting	21
Steering wheel - removal and refitting	20
Toe control arm (Independent rear suspension) - removal and refitting	18
Torsion bar - removal, refitting and adjustment	6
Tyre and tyre pressure checks	See Chapter 1
Tyre rotation	See Chapter 1
Upper control arm and ball joint (Independent rear suspension) - removal and refitting	16
Wheels and tyres - general information	27

Specifications

General
Bump stop tip-to-bracket clearance (see illustration 6.10) .... 18 mm (torsion bar suspension models) — See Section 6

Torque specifications
Nm

Front suspension

	NL to NP	NS models	NT/NW models
Lower arm shaft-to-crossmember (pivot shaft) nut or bolt	123	145	145
Lower ball joint-to-lower arm bolt	95	125	125
Lower ball joint-to-steering knuckle nut	147	100	75 (NT); 100 (NW)
Lower shock absorber mounting bolt/nut (1999 and earlier)	95		
Lower shock absorber mounting bolt/nut (2000 and later)	162	133	133
Shock absorber damper mounting nut (2000 and later)	22	26	26
Shock absorber mounting nuts (2000 and later)	44	44	44
Stabiliser bar link nuts	108	130	130
Stabiliser bar mounting bracket bolts	44	44	44
Torsion bar anchor arm nut B	108		
Torsion bar locknut	45		
Upper arm shaft-to-frame bolt	147	108	108
Upper ball joint-to-lower arm bolt	26 to 34		
Upper ball joint-to-steering knuckle nut	75	75	75
Upper shock absorber mounting nut (1999 and earlier)	15		

Torque specifications (continued)

	Nm		
Rear suspension	**NL to NP**	**NS models**	**NT/NW models**
Coil spring type			
Lateral rod nuts	235		
Lower shock absorber bolt	216		
Stabiliser bar bracket bolts	34		
Trailing arm-to-axle bolts	235		
Trailing arm-to-frame nut	235		
Upper shock absorber nut	22		
Independent rear suspension			
Ball joint-to-upper control arm bolts	98	82	82
Lower control arm-to-frame bolts/nuts	123	145	145
Lower control arm-to-knuckle bolts/nuts	152	145	145
Shock absorber-to-lower control arm bolts/nuts	152	100	100
Stabiliser bar link ball stud nuts	104	50	50
Stabiliser bar mounting bracket bolts	44	44	44
Stabiliser link ball stud-to-upper control arm nut	104	50	50
Toe control arm ball stud nuts	67	75	75 (NT); 78 (NW)
Toe control arm bolts/nuts	123	145	145
Toe control tower bar nuts bolts	46	46	46
Trailing arm bolts	231	148	148
Upper ball joint-to-knuckle nut	150	118	118
Upper control arm-to-frame bolts/nuts	167	124	124
Upper shock absorber mounting nut	44	30	30
Steering	**NL to NP**	**NS models**	**NT/NW models**
Flexible coupling-to-steering gear pinch bolt	18	18	18
Idler arm bracket-to-frame bolts	55 to 65		
Idler arm-to-pivot shaft nut	137		
Pitman arm-to-relay rod nut	44		
Pitman arm-to-steering gear nut	30 to 35		
Power steering pump banjo bolt	57	57	57
Power steering pump mounting bolts	22	39[1]; 29[2]	39[1]; 29[2] (NT) N/S[3] 23[2] (NW)
Rack and pinion steering gear mounting bolts	69	117	82
Rack and pinion steering gear mounting nuts	69	82	118
Rack and pinion steering gear pinch bolt	15	15	15/18
Steering gear-to-frame bolts (Ball and nut type)	54 to 64		
Steering wheel lock nut	41	41	41
Steering wheel/air bag module lock bolt	50	9	9
Tie-rod end-to-relay rod nut	45		
Tie-rod end-to-steering knuckle nut (Ball and nut type)	45		
Tie-rod end-to-steering knuckle nut (Rack and pinion type)	39	47	47

[1] Petrol; [2] Diesel; [3] Not specified

1 General information

Refer to illustrations 1.1a, 1.1b, 1.2a and 1.2b

Two different front suspensions were used on the vehicles covered by this manual. On 2000 and earlier models, an independent type, made up of upper and lower arms, torsion bars, ball joint-mounted steering knuckles and shock absorbers. Some models are equipped with a stabiliser bar to limit body roll during cornering. On 2001 and later models, a coil spring double wishbone independent type suspension, made up of upper and lower control arms with coil over shock absorbers and stabiliser bar (see illustration).

Two different types of rear suspension are used on the vehicles covered by this manual. On 2000 and earlier models, the rear suspension consists of the rear axle housing (banjo type), coil springs with a trailing arm (see illustration) and track rod arrangement to locate the axle. On 2001 and later models, the rear suspension is a multi-link double wishbone independent suspension (see illustration) consisting of the rear differential carrier, upper and lower control arms, coil springs, shock absorbers, toe control arm, stabiliser bar and trailing arms. Information regarding axles and the rear axle housing can be found in Chapter 8.

Two different steering systems are used on the vehicles covered by this manual. On 1999 and earlier models, the steering system is composed of a steering column, steering gear, Pitman arm, relay rod, two tie-rod assemblies and an idler arm. On 2000 and later models the steering system is composed of a steering column, rack and pinion steering gear, and inner and outer tie rods. Both type have power assisted steering, which includes a belt-driven pump and associated hoses to provide hydraulic pressure to the steering gear.

Frequently, when working on the suspension or steering system components, you may come across fasteners which seem impossible to loosen. These fasteners on the underside of the vehicle are continually subjected to water, road grime, mud, etc., and can become rusted or "seized," making them extremely difficult to remove. In order to unscrew these stubborn fasteners without damaging them (or other components), be sure to use lots of penetrating oil and allow it to soak in for a while. Using a wire brush to clean exposed threads will also ease removal of the nut or bolt and prevent damage to the threads. Sometimes a sharp blow with a hammer and punch is effective in breaking the bond between a nut and bolt threads, but care must be taken to prevent the punch from slipping off the fastener and ruining the threads. Heating the stuck fastener and surrounding area with a torch sometimes helps too, but isn't recommended because of the obvious dangers associated with fire. Long breaker bars and extension pipes will increase leverage. Never use an extension pipe on a ratchet - the ratcheting mechanism could be damaged. Fasteners that require drastic measures to unscrew should always be renewed.

Chapter 10 Suspension and steering systems

1.1a Typical 2000 and earlier front suspension layout

1 Torsion bar
2 Lower control arm
3 Lower ball joint
4 Outer tie-rod end
5 Inner tie-rod end
6 Stabiliser bar
7 Steering relay rod

1.1b Typical 2001 and later front suspension layout

1 Steering gear
2 Coil spring
3 Stabiliser bar
4 Outer tie rod
5 Lower ball joint
6 Lower control arm
7 Stabiliser link
8 Knuckle

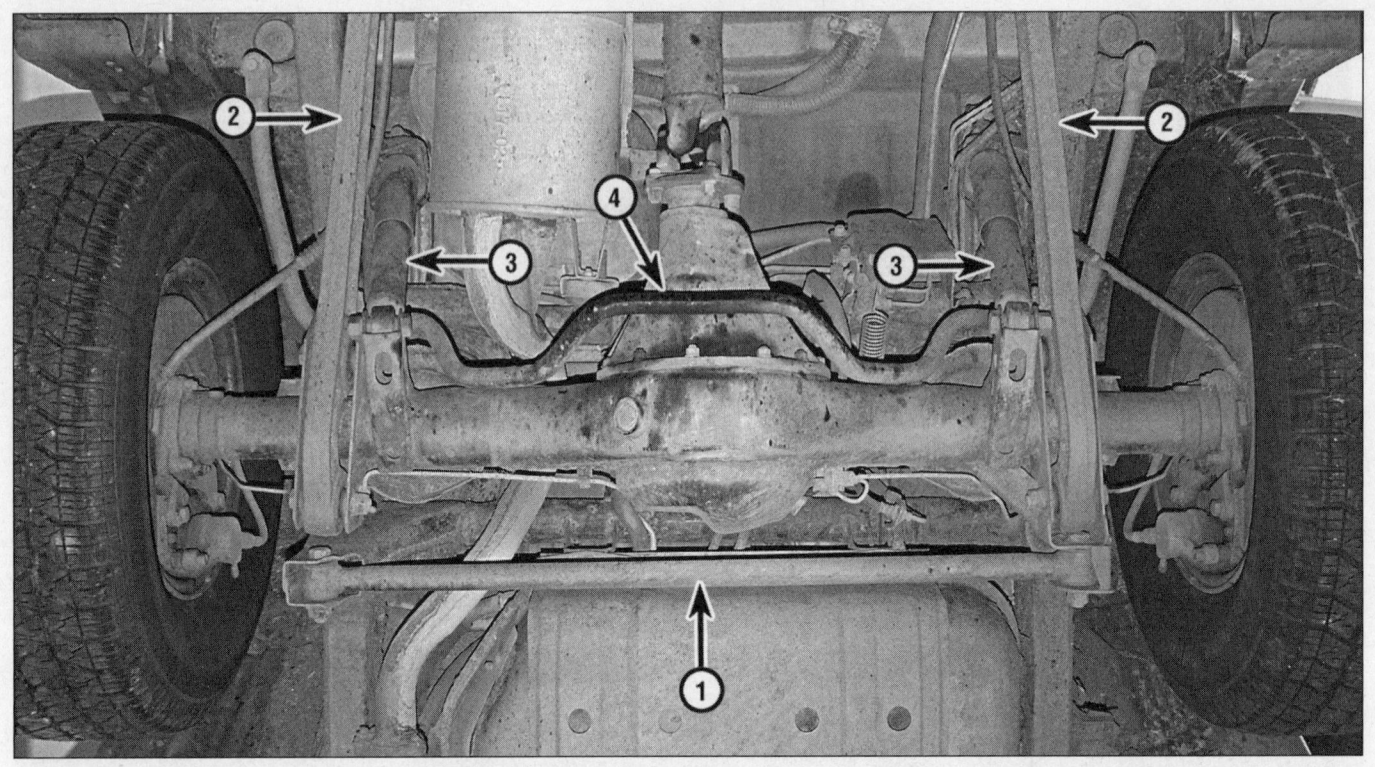

10-4 Chapter 10 Suspension and steering systems

1.2a Typical 2000 and earlier rear suspension layout

| 1 Lateral rod | 2 Lower arm | 3 Shock absorbers | 4 Stabiliser bar |

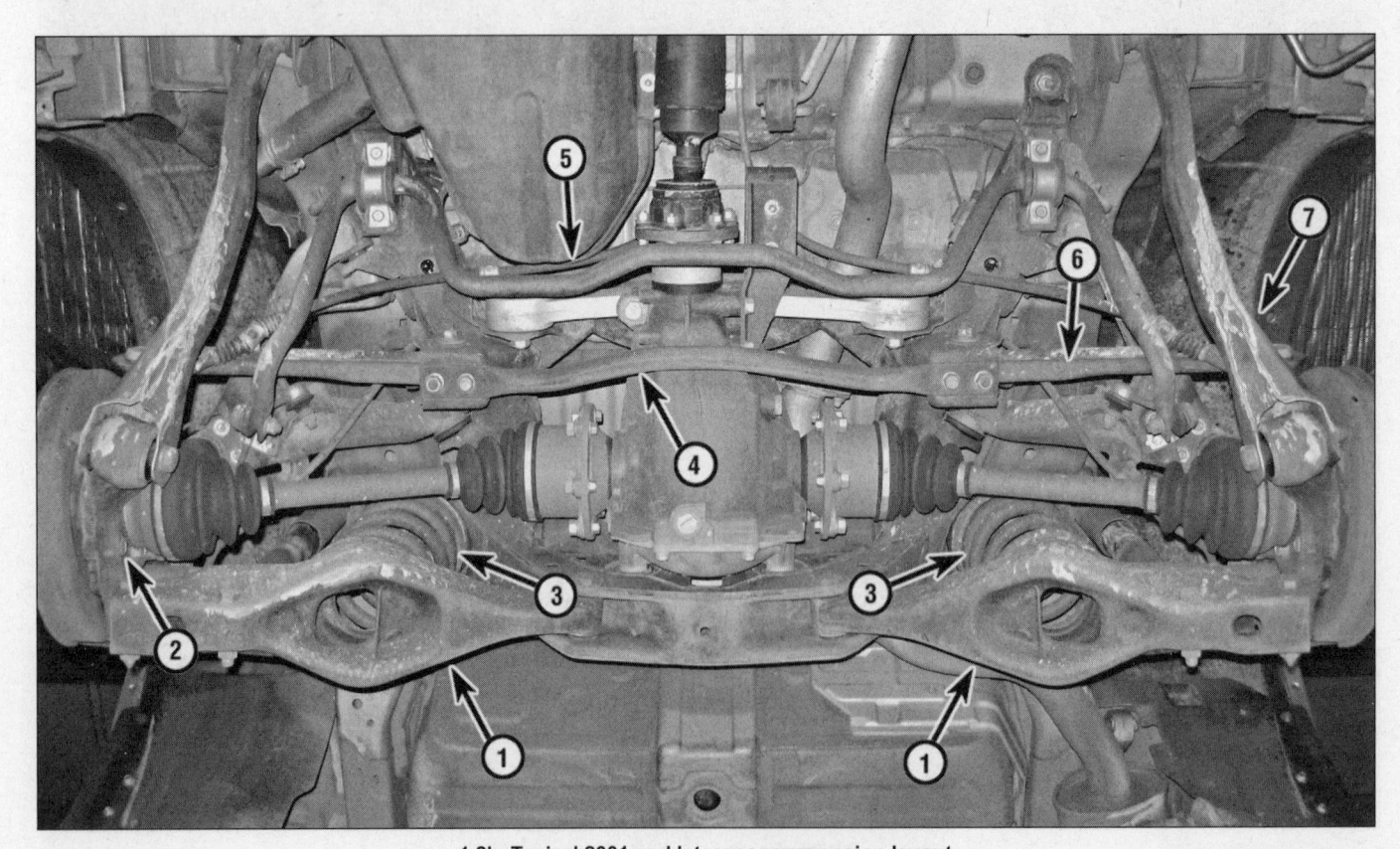

1.2b Typical 2001 and later rear suspension layout

1 Lower control arm
2 Knuckle
3 Coil springs
4 Toe control tower bar
5 Stabiliser bar
6 Toe control arm
7 Trailing arm

Chapter 10 Suspension and steering systems

2.2 Remove the lower cover (A) and skid plate (B) mounting bolts (arrows) and remove the cover and plate - later model shown, earlier models similar

2.3 Remove the stabiliser bar lower link-to-control arm mounting nut (arrow) and separate the stabiliser bar from the control arm - later model shown, earlier models similar

Since most of the procedures that are dealt with in this Chapter involve jacking up the vehicle and working underneath it, a good pair of jackstands will be needed. A hydraulic floor jack is the preferred type of jack to lift the vehicle, and it can also be used to support certain components during various operations.

Warning: *Never, under any circumstances, rely on a jack to support the vehicle while working on it. Whenever any of the suspension or steering fasteners are loosened or removed they must be inspected and, if necessary, renewed with new ones of the same part number or of original equipment quality and design. Torque specifications must be followed for proper reassembly and component retention. Never attempt to heat or straighten any suspension or steering component. Always renew them.*

2 Front stabiliser bar - removal and refitting

Refer to illustrations 2.2, 2.3 and 2.4

Warning: *Whenever any of the suspension or steering fasteners are loosened or removed, they must be inspected and, if necessary, renewed with new ones of the same part number or of original equipment quality and design. Torque specifications must be followed for proper reassembly and component retention.*

Removal

1 Raise the front of the vehicle and support it securely on jackstands (see Jacking and Towing). Apply the parking brake.
2 Remove the lower cover and skid plate **(see illustration)**.
3 Remove the stabiliser bar-to-lower arm link nuts **(see illustration)**.
4 Remove the stabiliser bar bracket bolts **(see illustration)** and detach the bar from the vehicle.
5 Pull the brackets off the stabiliser bar and inspect the bushes for cracks, hardening and other signs of deterioration. If the bushes are damaged, renew them.

Refitting

6 Position the stabiliser bar bushes on the bar. Push the brackets over the bushes and raise the bar up to the frame. Install the bracket bolts but don't tighten them completely at this time.
7 Install the stabiliser bar-to-lower arm nuts and tighten the nuts to the specified torque.
8 Lower the vehicle and tighten the bracket, bolts and link nuts to the specified torque.

3 Front shock absorber (1999 and earlier models) - removal and refitting

Refer to illustrations 3.3 and 3.5

Warning: *Whenever any of the suspension or steering fasteners are loosened or removed, they must be inspected and, if necessary, renewed with new ones of the same part number or of original equipment quality and design. Torque specifications must be followed for proper reassembly and component retention.*

1 Raise the front of the vehicle and support it securely on jackstands (see Jacking and Towing).
2 Remove the front wheels and the lower cover and skid plate **(see illustration 2.2)**.
3 Remove the nuts holding the shock absorber to the upper mount **(see illustration)**. Clamp a pair of locking pliers to the flats at the top of the shock rod to prevent it from turning.

Note: *If the vehicle has remote-controlled variable shock absorbers, the actuator assembly is bolted to the top of the shock absorber stud end. To remove the actuator, loosen the two bolts that hold the actuator to the mounting bracket, then remove the upper shock absorber hold-down nut and actuator mounting bracket. Remove the lower shock*

2.4 Remove the four stabiliser bar mounting bolts (arrows) and remove the stabiliser bar - right side of the stabiliser bar shown, left side is the same

3.3 Remove the locking and mounting nuts on the upper end of the shock absorber shaft

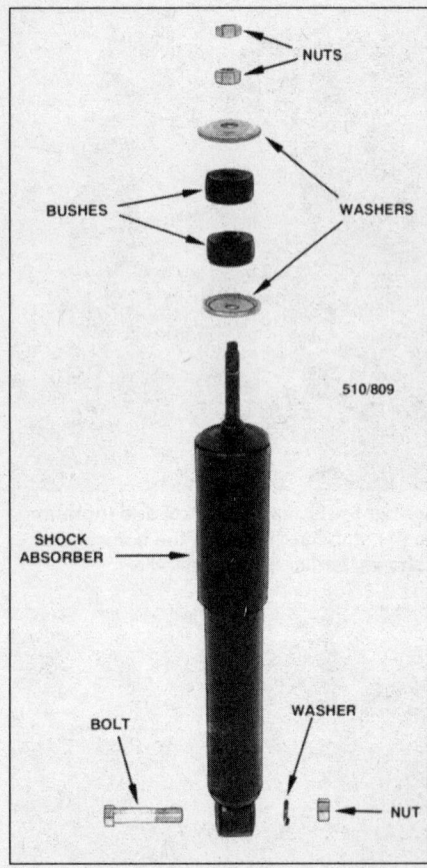

3.5 Exploded view of typical early model shock absorber

absorber hold-down nut and actuator washer assembly with the stud pin. Be careful not to bend the stud pin on the washer assembly.

4 Remove the upper washer and rubber cushion from the shaft of the shock absorber.

5 Remove the shock absorber-to-lower control arm through bolt and nut, then fully compress the shock absorber and lift it up and over the arm to remove it **(see illustration)**.

6 Refitting is the reverse of the removal procedure. Make sure the washers and bushes are assembled in the proper order. Tighten the bolts and nuts to the specified torque.

4 Front shock absorber/spring assembly (2000 and later models) - removal and refitting

Refer to illustrations 4.6 and 4.7

Warning: *Whenever any of the suspension or steering fasteners are loosened or removed, they must be inspected and, if necessary, renewed with new ones of the same part number or of original equipment quality and design. Torque specifications must be followed for proper reassembly and component retention.*

1 Detach the cable from the negative terminal of the battery.

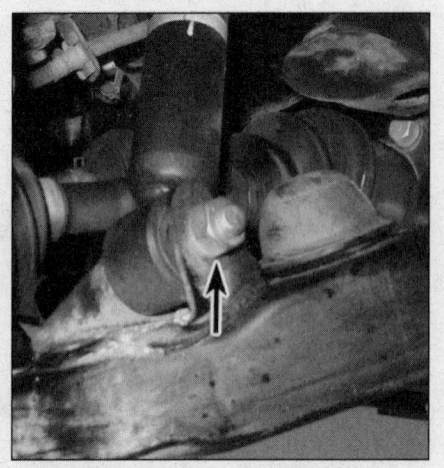

4.6 Remove the shock absorber-to-lower control arm through bolt (arrow) and separate the shock absorber from the control arm - it may be necessary to raise the control arm with a trolley jack to remove the through bolt

2 If removing the right side shock absorber/spring assembly, remove the air cleaner housing (see Chapter 4). If removing the left side, remove the battery and battery tray (see Chapter 5).

3 Raise the front of the vehicle and support it securely on jackstands (see Jacking and Towing).

4 Remove the front wheels and the lower cover and skid plate **(see illustration 2.2)**.

5 Remove the upper control arm (see Section 7).

6 Remove the lower shock absorber-to-lower control arm mounting bolt **(see illustration)**.

7 Remove the three upper shock absorber mounting nuts **(see illustration)** and carefully manoeuvre the assembly from the vehicle.

8 Refitting is the reverse of the removal procedure. Make sure the washers and bushes are assembled in the proper order. Tighten the bolts and nuts to the specified torque.

5 Front shock absorber/spring assembly (2000 and later models) - renewal

Warning: *Whenever any of the suspension or steering fasteners are loosened or removed, they must be inspected and, if necessary, renewed with new ones of the same part number or of original equipment quality and design. Torque specifications must be followed for proper reassembly and component retention.*

1 If the shock absorbers or coil springs exhibit the telltale signs of wear (leaking fluid, loss of damping capability, chipped, sagging or cracked coil springs) explore all options before beginning any work. The shock absorber assemblies are not serviceable and must be renewed if a problem develops.

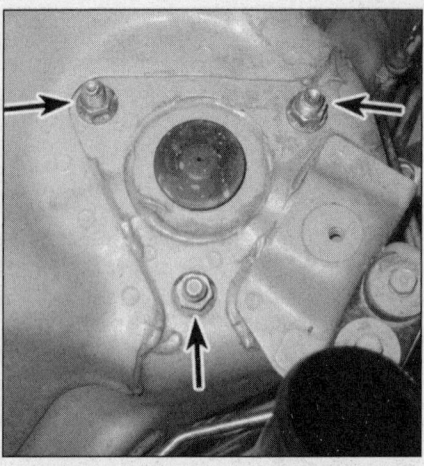

4.7 Support the shock absorber and spring assembly with one hand (or have an assistant hold it for you) and remove the mounting nuts (arrows)

Warning: *Disassembling a shock absorber assembly is a potentially dangerous undertaking and utmost attention must be directed to the job, or serious injury may result. Use only a high quality spring compressor and carefully follow the manufacturer's instructions furnished with the tool. After removing the coil spring from the assembly, set it aside in a safe, isolated area.*

Disassembly

Refer to illustrations 5.3, 5.4, 5.5, 5.6 and 5.7

2 Remove the shock absorber/spring assembly following the procedure described in the previous Section. Mount the assembly in a vice. Line the vice jaws with wood or rags to prevent damage to the unit and don't tighten the vise excessively.

3 Following the tool's manufacturer's instructions, fit the spring compressor (which can be obtained at most auto parts stores or

5.3 Fit the spring compressor in accordance with the tool manufacturer's instructions and compress the spring until all pressure is relieved from the upper spring set (you can verify the spring is loose by wiggling it)

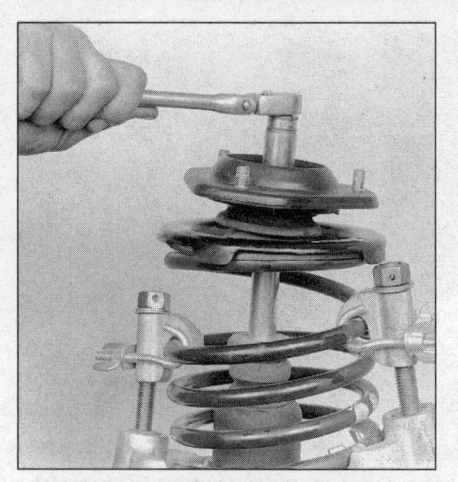

Chapter 10 Suspension and steering systems

5.4 Remove the damper shaft nut

5.5 Lift the insulator off the shaft

5.6 Remove the upper spring seat and the upper pad from the damper shaft

equipment yards on a daily hire basis) on the spring and compress it sufficiently to relieve all pressure from insulator **(see illustration)**. This can be verified by wiggling the spring.
4 Loosen the damper shaft nut with a socket **(see illustration)**.
5 Remove the nut and insulator **(see illustration)**. Inspect the bearing in the insulator for smooth operation. If it doesn't turn smoothly, renew the insulator. Inspect the rubber portion of the insulator for cracking and general deterioration. If there is any separation of the rubber, renew it.
6 Lift the upper spring seat and upper pad from the damper shaft **(see illustration)**. Check the spring seat for cracking and hardness, renew it if necessary.
7 Carefully lift the compressed spring from the assembly **(see illustration)** and set it in a safe place.
Warning: *Never place your head near the end of the spring!*
8 Slide the rubber bumper and dust cover off the damper shaft.

Reassembly

Refer to illustrations 5.10 and 5.11

9 If the lower insulator is being renewed, set it into position with the dropped portion seated in the lowest part of the seat. Extend the damper rod to its full length and refit the rubber bumper and dust cover.
10 Carefully place the coil spring onto the lower insulator, with the end of the spring resting in the lowest part of the insulator **(see illustration)**.
11 Refit the upper pad and upper spring seat, making sure that the flats in the hole in the seat match up with the flats on the damper shaft **(see illustration)**.
12 Refit the insulator onto the damper shaft.
13 Fit the new lock nut and tighten it to the torque listed in this Chapter's Specifications.
14 Refit the shock absorber/coil spring assembly following the procedure outlined previously (see Section 4).

6 Torsion bar - removal, refitting and adjustment

Refer to illustrations 6.2, 6.3, 6.4 and 6.10

Warning: *Whenever any of the suspension or steering fasteners are loosened or removed, they must be inspected and, if necessary, renewed with new ones of the same part number or of original equipment quality and design. Torque specifications must be followed for proper reassembly and component retention.*

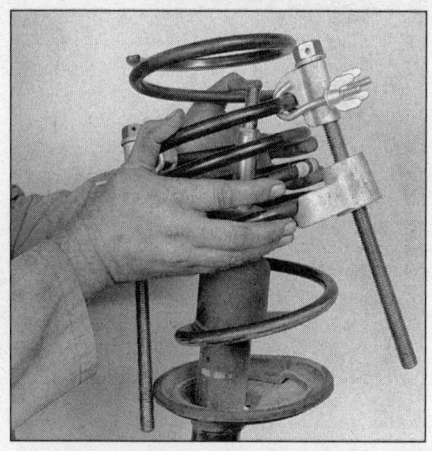

5.7 Remove the compressed spring from the assembly - keep the ends of the spring pointed away from your body

Removal

1 Loosen the wheel lug nuts, raise the front of the vehicle and support it securely on jackstands (see Jacking and Towing). Remove the front wheels and the lower cover and skid plate **(see illustration 2.2)** then remove the brake caliper assembly (see Chapter 9).

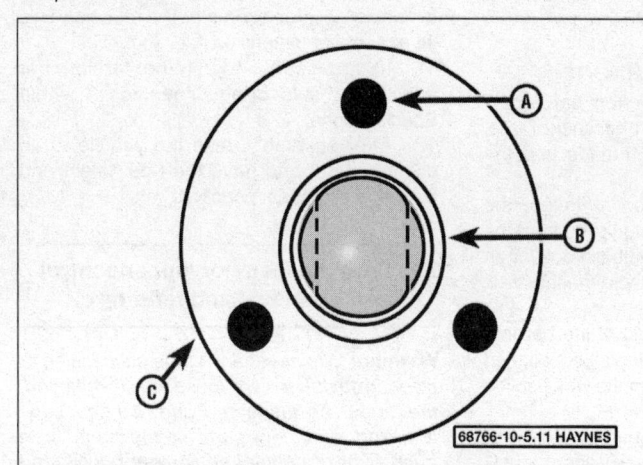

5.10 When refitting the spring, make sure the ends fits into the recessed portion of the lower seat

5.11 The flat on the damper shaft must match up with the flat in the upper spring seat

A Mounting studs
B Damper slot alignment
C Upper spring bracket

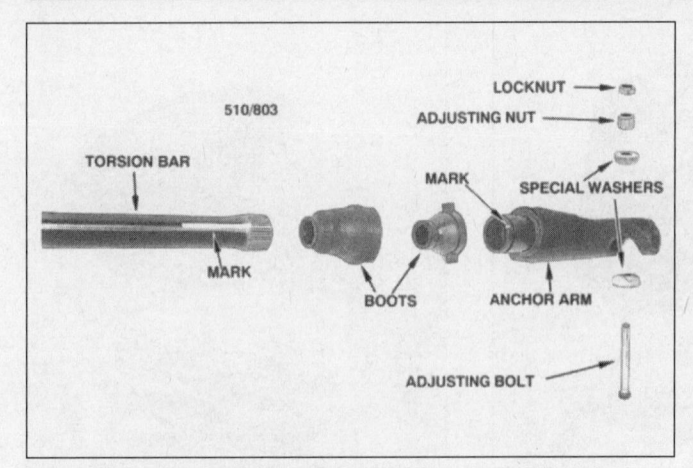

6.2 Torsion bar and rear anchor arm components showing the manufacturers reference marks

6.3 Mark the torsion bar before removing it, but DO NOT scratch it or make a mark with a centre-punch

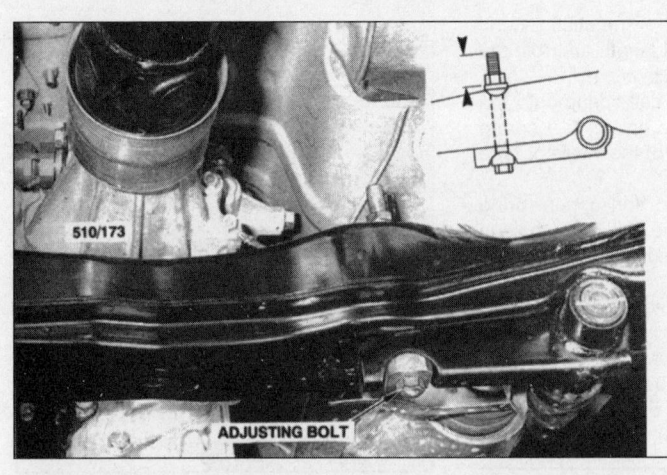

6.4 Make sure the adjusting bolt measurements are as specified as the torsion bar is installed

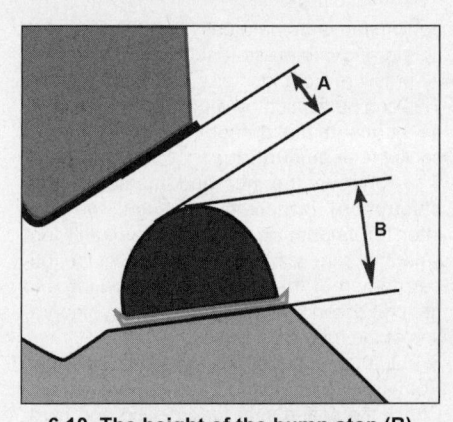

6.10 The height of the bump stop (B) should be 50 mm. The clearance between the bump stop and the bracket (A) should be 18 mm with the vehicle weight on the suspension, if it isn't as specified, the torsion bars may require further adjustment

2 Remove the anchor arm dust covers **(see illustration)**.
3 Mark the torsion bar directly opposite the mark on the anchor arm **(see illustration)**. **Caution:** *Do not punch or scratch the torsion bar - use paint to make the mark.*
4 Measure the distance from the underside of the torsion bar adjusting bolt head to the bottom face of the nut on each side **(see illustration)** and note the measurement to assist with assembly.
5 Loosen the lock nut and adjusting nut at the anchor arm assembly until the torsion bar can be slipped out of the anchor arms.

Refitting and adjustment

6 When refitting the torsion bar, apply grease to the torsion bar and anchor arm splines, the adjusting bolt threads and the inside of the dust boots.
7 If both bars have been removed, the right torsion bar can be distinguished from the left by checking the end of the bar. Look for an L or an R stamped into the end of each bar (R is right, L is left).
8 Position the marked end of the bar into the anchor arm with the mating marks aligned (if a new bar is installed, align the white spline with the mark on the anchor arm).
9 Assemble the torsion bar and the rear anchor arm and tighten the adjusting nut until the distance from the adjusting nut bottom face to the top of the bolt is the same as the measurements made in Step 4 **(see illustration 6.4)**.
10 Reinstall the hub, wheel and brake caliper, then lower the vehicle and measure the distance from the lower control arm to the top of the bump stop **(see illustration)**. A new bump stop should be 50 mm high (dimension B). Measure the distance between the bump stop and the bracket (dimension A) which should be 18 mm. If dimension B is less than 50 mm, add the missing bump stop height to dimension A. For example, if dimension B is 48 mm, make dimension A 20 mm.
11 If necessary, adjust the torsion bar adjusting nut to bring dimension A within Specifications.
12 After assembly, take the vehicle to an alignment shop to have the ride height and front end alignment checked.

7 Front suspension upper control arm - removal and refitting

Warning: *Whenever any of the suspension or steering fasteners are loosened or removed, they must be inspected and, if necessary, renewed with new ones of the same part number or of original equipment quality and design. Torque specifications must be followed for proper reassembly and component retention.*

Removal

All models
1 Loosen the wheel lug nuts, raise the front of the vehicle and support it securely on jackstands (see Jacking and Towing). Apply the parking brake. Remove the front wheels and the lower cover and skid plate **(see illustration 2.2)**.

Torsion bar suspension
Refer to illustration 7.4

2 Support the lower arm with a jack. The support point must be as close to the ball joint as possible to give maximum leverage on the lower arm.
3 Remove the split pin and nut and separate the upper ball joint from the steering knuckle, but be careful not to let the steering knuckle/brake caliper assembly fall outward, as this may damage the brake hose (see Section 9).

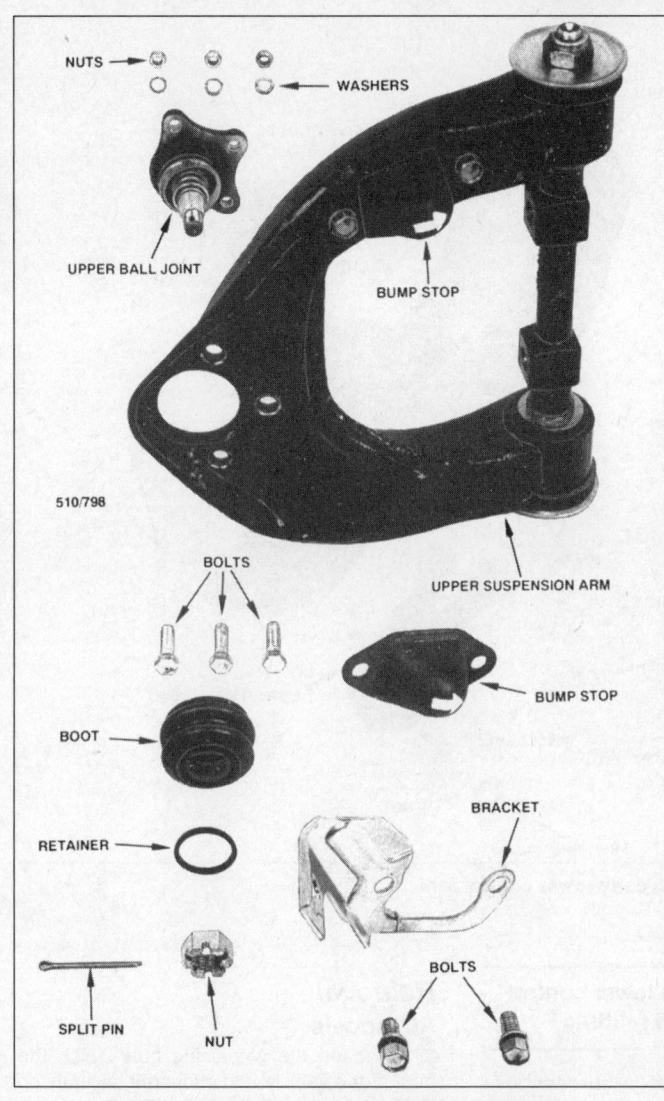

Chapter 10 Suspension and steering systems

7.4 Upper control arm and related components

7.7 Remove the ABS wheel sensor clip, bracket and hydraulic brake line clip (arrows)

7.8 Remove the upper ball joint-to-upper control arm mounting bolts (arrows) and separate the control arm from the ball joint

4 Remove the upper arm-to-frame bolts, noting the positions of any alignment shims. They must be reinstalled in the same locations to maintain wheel alignment **(see illustration)**.

5 Detach the upper arm from the vehicle. Inspect the bushes for deterioration, cracks and other damage, renewing them if necessary. It may be necessary to loosen the body mount nuts and raise the front of the body with a jack to provide sufficient clearance to allow removal of the upper arm.

Shock absorber/coil spring suspension

Refer to illustrations 7.7, 7.8 and 7.9

6 Remove the ABS wheel sensor bracket and mounting bolt.

7 Disconnect the hydraulic brake line clip **(see illustration)**.

8 Remove the upper ball joint-to-upper control arm mounting bolts **(see illustration)** and separate the control arm from the ball joint

9 Remove the upper control arm-to-frame attaching bolts and nuts **(see illustration)**.

10 Detach the upper arm from the vehicle. Inspect the bushes for deterioration, cracks and other damage, renewing them, if necessary. It may be necessary to loosen the body mount nuts and raise the front of the body with a jack to provide sufficient clearance to allow removal of the upper arm.

7.9 Remove the upper control arm-to-frame attaching bolts and nuts (arrows)

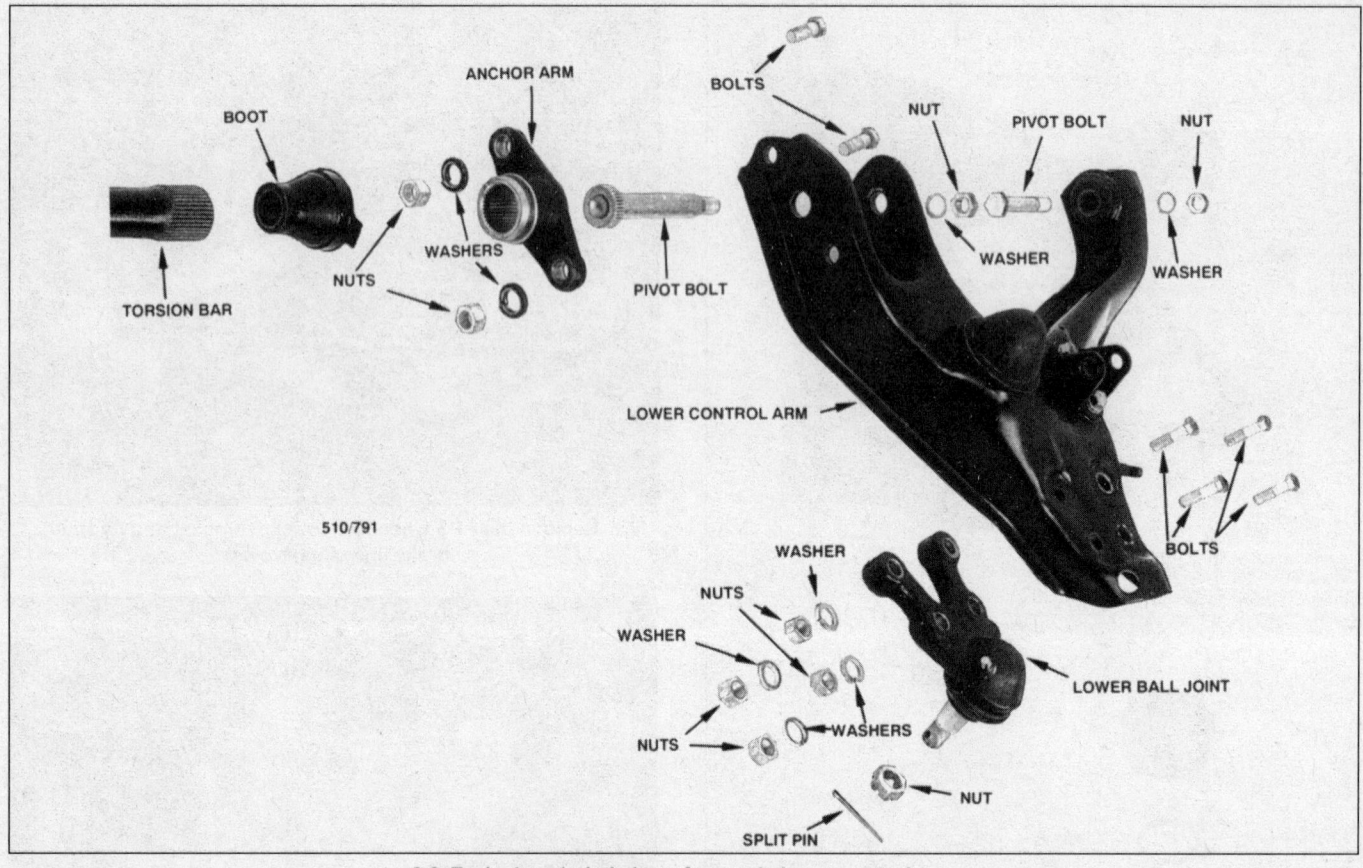

8.2 Typical exploded view of an early lower control arm

Refitting

Torsion bar suspension

11 Position the arm on the frame and install the bolts. Install any alignment shims that were removed. Tighten the bolts to the torque listed in this Chapter's Specifications.

12 Connect the ball joint to the steering knuckle and tighten the nut to the torque listed in this Chapter's Specifications.

13 Tighten the torsion bar anchor bolt(s) and adjust the bumper stop-to-bracket clearance as described in Section 6, Step 10.

Shock absorber/coil spring suspension

14 Refit the control arm to the frame and install the bolts/nuts, tightening them to the torque listed in this Chapter's Specifications.

15 Refit the ball joint-to-control arm bolts and tighten them to the torque listed in this Chapter's Specifications.

16 Refit the ABS wheel sensor bracket and hydraulic brake line clip.

All models

17 Install the wheel and lug nuts and lower the vehicle. Tighten the lug nuts to the torque specified in Chapter 1.

18 Drive the vehicle to an alignment shop to have the front end alignment checked and, if necessary, adjusted.

8 Front suspension lower control arm - removal and refitting

Warning: *Whenever any of the suspension or steering fasteners are loosened or removed, they must be inspected and, if necessary, renewed with new ones of the same part number or of original equipment quality and design. Torque specifications must be followed for proper reassembly and component retention.*

8.9a Mark the rear lower control arm mounting bolt (arrow) to eccentric cam location before removing

Removal

All models

1 Loosen the wheel lug nuts, raise the front of the vehicle and support it securely on jackstands (see Jacking and Towing). Apply the parking brake. Remove the front wheels and the lower cover and skid plate (see illustration 2.2).

Torsion bar suspension

Refer to illustration 8.2

2 Remove the torsion bar (see Section 6) and unbolt the lower ball joint from the control arm. Remove the lower arm pivot nuts and shafts and lower the arm from the vehicle (see illustration).

Shock absorber/coil spring suspension

Refer to illustrations 8.9a and 8.9b

3 Remove the front driveaxles (see Chapter 8).

4 Remove the stabiliser link mounting nut (see Section 2).

5 Remove the shock absorber-to-lower control arm mounting bolt (see Section 4).

6 Disconnect the outer tie rod from the steering knuckle (see Section 21).

7 Unbolt the upper ball joint from the upper control arm (see Section 7) and allow the knuckle to tilt outwards.

Chapter 10 Suspension and steering systems

8.9b Remove the front lower control arm mounting nut and bolt (arrows)

9.6a With the lower ball joint stud nut loosened (but not removed), install a small puller on the steering knuckle boss as shown, pop the ball stud loose from the knuckle, then remove the nut and separate the ball joint from the knuckle

9.6b With the upper ball joint stud nut loosened (but not removed), use a pickle fork tool to separate the upper ball joint from the knuckle; unless you're very careful, the pickle fork will probably damage the ball joint seal, but there's no other way to split the upper ball joint unless you want to remove the driveaxle!

8   Remove the lower arm ball joint mounting bolts and separate the ball joint from the arm (see Section 9).
9   Mark the lower control arm eccentric cam bolt **(see illustration)** and remove the lower control arm bolts **(see illustration)** and the lower control arm.

Refitting
10   Inspect the lower arm bushes for deterioration, cracking and other damage. If the bushes are in need of renewal, take the lower arm to an automotive machine shop to have the old bushes pressed out and new ones pressed in.

Torsion bar suspension
11   Connect the ball joint to the lower arm and install the bolts and nuts. Position the arm at normal ride height and tighten the pivot shaft nuts to the torque listed in the Specifications Section at the beginning of this Chapter. Install the torsion bar (see Section 6).

Shock absorber/coil spring suspension
12   Refit the lower control arm and bolts to the marked position and temporarily tighten the mounting bolts.
13   Refitting is the reverse of the removal procedure. Install the wheel and lug nuts. Allow the wheels to touch the ground and tighten the lower control arm mounting bolts to the torque listed in the Specification Section.

All models
14   Lower the vehicle completely and tighten the lug nuts.
15   Drive the vehicle to an alignment shop to have the front end alignment checked and, if necessary, adjusted.

9 Ball joints - check and renewal

Warning: *Whenever any of the suspension or steering fasteners are loosened or removed, they must be inspected and, if necessary,* renewed with new ones of the same part number or of original equipment quality and design. Torque specifications must be followed for proper reassembly and component retention.

Check
1   Raise the vehicle and support it securely on jackstands (see Jacking and Towing). Apply the parking brake. Remove the front wheels and the lower cover and skid plate **(see illustration 2.2)**. Place the jack under one of the control arms and lift it until the chassis is about to lift of the jack stand.
2   Visually inspect the rubber seal for cuts, tears or leaking grease. If any of these conditions are noticed, the ball joint should be renewed.
3   Place a large lever under the upper ball joint and attempt to push the upper control arm up. Next, position the lever between the steering knuckle and the arm and apply downward pressure. If any movement is seen or felt during either of these checks, a worn ball joint is indicated.
4   Have an assistant slowly raise and lower the jack and while touching the ball joint stud castellated nut, check for any looseness. Movement indicates a worn out ball joint stud or a widened hole in the steering knuckle boss. If the latter problem exists, the steering knuckle should be renewed as well as the ball joint.

Renewal
Refer to illustrations 9.6a and 9.6b

5   With the vehicle raised and supported, position a floor jack under the lower arm - it must stay there throughout the entire operation. Remove the wheel. Remove the ball joint split pin and loosen the castellated nut a couple of turns, but don't remove it (it will prevent the ball joint and steering knuckle from separating violently).

6   Using a ball joint separating tool, separate the ball joint from the steering knuckle. There are several types of ball joint tools available, but the kind that pushes the ball joint stud out of the knuckle boss works best **(see illustrations)**. The wedge, or "pickle fork" type works fairly well, but it tends to damage the ball joint seal. Some two-jaw pullers will do the job, also.
7   Remove the castellated nut and disconnect the ball joint from the steering knuckle. If necessary, remove the steering knuckle (see Section 10) and the driveaxle (see Chapter 8).
8   The ball joint is retained to the suspension arm by bolts and nuts. Remove the bolts and nuts, then detach the ball joint from the arm. Take note of how the ball joint is positioned on the arm - the new one must be installed the same way **(see illustrations 7.4 and 7.8)**.
9   Position the new ball joint on the arm and install the nut or bolts, tightening them to the torque listed in this Chapter's Specifications.
10   Insert the ball joint stud into the steering knuckle boss, install the castellated nut and tighten it to the specified torque. Install a new split pin. If necessary, tighten the nut an additional amount to line up the slots in the nut with the hole in the ball joint stud (never loosen the nut to align the hole).
11   Install the wheel and lug nuts. Lower the vehicle and tighten the lug nuts to the torque specified in Chapter 1.

10 Front steering knuckle - removal and refitting

Warning: *Whenever any of the suspension or steering fasteners are loosened or removed, they must be inspected and, if necessary,*

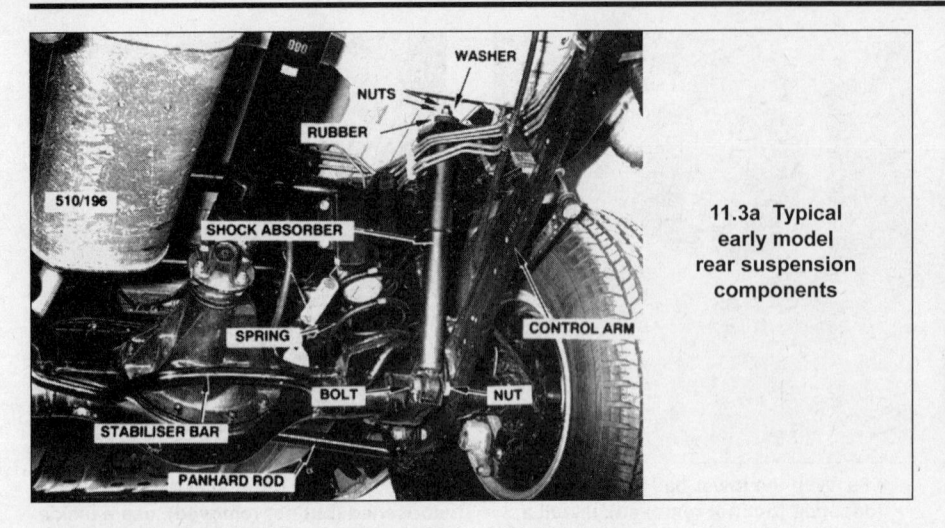

11.3a Typical early model rear suspension components

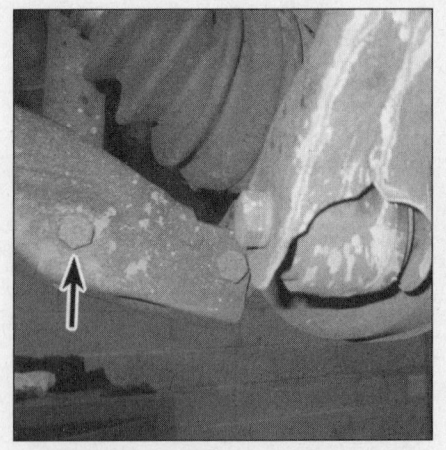

11.3b Remove the lower shock absorber mounting bolt (arrow) and nut - later model shown, earlier models similar

11.4 Typical upper shock absorber mounting nut, washers and bush (arrow) - later model shown, earlier models similar

renewed with new ones of the same part number or of original equipment quality and design. Torque specifications must be followed for proper reassembly and component retention.

Removal

1 Loosen the wheel lug nuts, raise the vehicle and support it securely on jackstands placed under the frame. Apply the parking brake. Remove the front wheels and the lower cover and skid plate **(see illustration 2.2)**.
2 Remove the brake caliper and place it on top of the upper arm or wire it up out of the way. Remove the brake disc and caliper mounting bracket from the steering knuckle (see Chapter 9 if necessary).
3 Remove the front hub and remove the driveaxle split pin, lock nut and push the driveaxle into the knuckle (see Chapter 8).
4 Separate the tie-rod end from the knuckle arm (see Section 21).
5 Remove the split pins from the upper and lower ball joint studs and back off the nuts one turn each.
6 Remove the shock absorber (see Section 3).
7 Using a special tool, separate the suspension arms from the steering knuckle **(see illustrations 9.6a and 9.6b)**. There are several types of tools available, but the kind that pushes the ball joint stud out of the knuckle boss works the best. The wedge, or pickle fork type works fairly well, but it tends to damage the ball joint seal. Some two-jaw pullers will do the job, also. Once the ball joints have been released from the tapered holes in the knuckle, remove the nuts completely and carefully detach the knuckle. Be careful not to damage the CV joint boots when detaching the driveaxle.

Refitting

8 Place the knuckle between the upper and lower suspension arms and insert the ball joint studs into the knuckle, beginning with the lower ball joint. Install the nuts and tighten them to the torque listed in this Chapter's Specifications. Install new split pins, tightening the nuts slightly to align the slots in the nuts with the holes in the ball joint studs, if necessary.
9 Install the shock absorber.
10 Connect the tie-rod end to the knuckle arm and tighten the nut to the torque listed in this Chapter's Specifications. Be sure to use a new split pin.
11 Install the strut rod and connect the stabiliser bar.
12 Install the brake caliper mounting bracket and caliper (see Chapter 9).
13 Install the wheel and lug nuts. Lower the vehicle to the ground and tighten the nuts to the torque specified in Chapter 1.

11 Rear shock absorber - removal and refitting

Refer to illustrations 11.3a, 11.3b and 11.4

Warning: *Whenever any of the suspension or steering fasteners are loosened or removed, they must be inspected and, if necessary, renewed with new ones of the same part number or of original equipment quality and design. Torque specifications must be followed for proper reassembly and component retention.*

1 If the shock absorber is to be renewed with a new one, it is recommended that both shocks on the rear of the vehicle be renewed at the same time.
2 Raise and support the rear of the vehicle according to the jacking and towing procedures at the front of this manual. Use a jack to raise the differential until the tyres clear the ground, then place jackstands under the axle housing. Do not attempt to remove the shock absorbers with the vehicle raised and the axle unsupported.
3 Unscrew and remove the lower shock absorber mounting nut to disconnect it at the spring seat **(see illustrations)**.
4 Unscrew and remove the upper mounting nut at the frame and remove the shock absorber **(see illustration)**.
Note: *If the vehicle is equipped with remote-controlled variable shock absorbers, remove the actuator assembly before removing the shock absorber.*

5 If the unit is defective, it must be renewed. Renew worn rubber bushes.
6 Install the shocks in the reverse order of removal, but let the vehicle be free standing on the ground before tightening the mounting nuts.
7 Bounce the rear of the vehicle a couple of times to settle the bushes into place, then tighten the nuts to the torques listed in the Specifications at the beginning of this chapter.

12 Rear suspension trailing arms - removal and refitting

Refer to illustrations 12.4a and 12.4b

Warning: *Whenever any of the suspension or steering fasteners are loosened or removed, they must be inspected and, if necessary, renewed with new ones of the same part number or of original equipment quality and design. Torque specifications must be followed for proper reassembly and component retention.*

1 Raise the vehicle and support it securely on jackstands (see Jacking and Towing).

Chapter 10 Suspension and steering systems

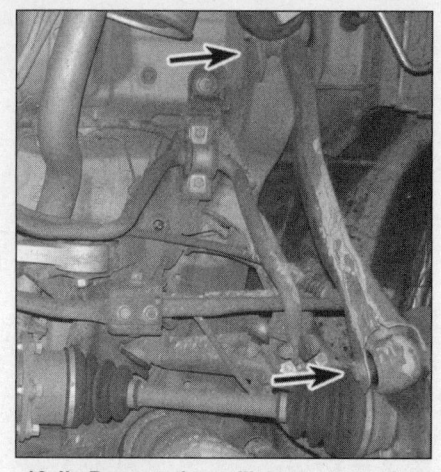

12.4a Exploded view of typical trailing arm - early model with banjo axle housing

12.4b Remove the trailing arm mounting bolts (arrows) - Independent rear suspension shown

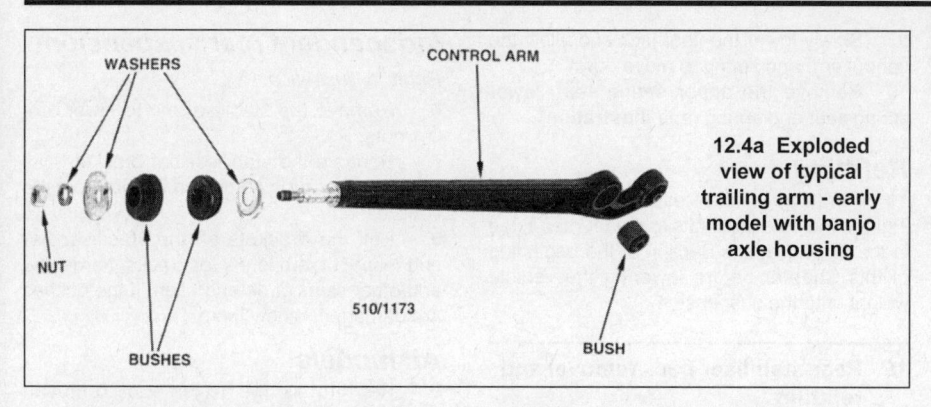

2 Remove the parking brake cable bolt.
3 Support the differential housing with a floor jack.
Note: *On Independent rear suspensions place the floor jack under the lower control arm on the side that the trailing arm is being replaced.*
4 Remove the nuts and bolts and detach the trailing arm from the vehicle **(see illustrations)**.
5 Refitting is the reverse of removal. Tighten the nuts and bolts to the torques listed in the Specifications Section at the beginning of this Chapter before lowering the vehicle weight onto the suspension.

13 Rear suspensioan lateral rod (banjo type axle housing) - removal and refitting

Refer to illustration 13.3

Warning: *Whenever any of the suspension or steering fasteners are loosened or removed, they must be inspected and, if necessary, renewed with new ones of the same part number or of original equipment quality and design. Torque specifications must be followed for proper reassembly and component retention.*
1 Raise the vehicle and support it securely on jackstands (see Jacking and Towing).
2 Remove the trailing arm(s) (see Section 12).
3 Remove the lateral rod mounting bolts **(see illustration)**.
4 Remove the nuts and bolts and detach the lateral rod.
5 Inspect the bushes for cracks, hardening and other signs of deterioration. If the bushes are damaged, renew them.
6 Refitting is the reverse of removal. Tighten the nuts and bolts to the torques listed in the Specifications Section at the beginning of this Chapter before lowering the vehicle weight onto the suspension.

14 Rear suspension coil spring - removal and refitting

Warning: *Whenever any of the suspension or steering fasteners are loosened or removed, they must be inspected and, if necessary, renewed with new ones of the same part number or of original equipment quality and design. Torque specifications must be followed for proper reassembly and component retention.*

Removal
All models
1 Raise the front of the vehicle and support it securely on jackstands (see Jacking and Towing).
2 Support the axle with a jack.

Banjo type axle housing
Refer to illustration 14.5
3 Remove the right side lateral rod nut and bolt (see Section 13).
4 Remove the lower left shock absorber bolt (see Section 11).

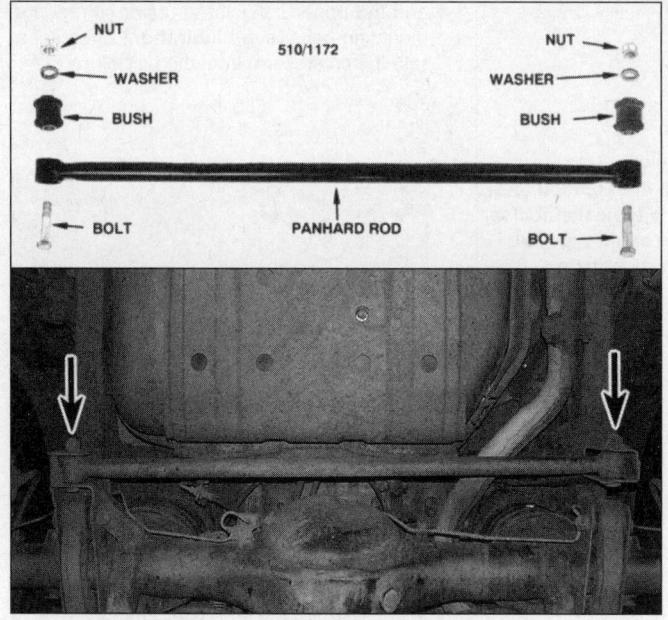

13.3 Remove the lateral rod mounting bolts and nuts (arrows) and remove the rod

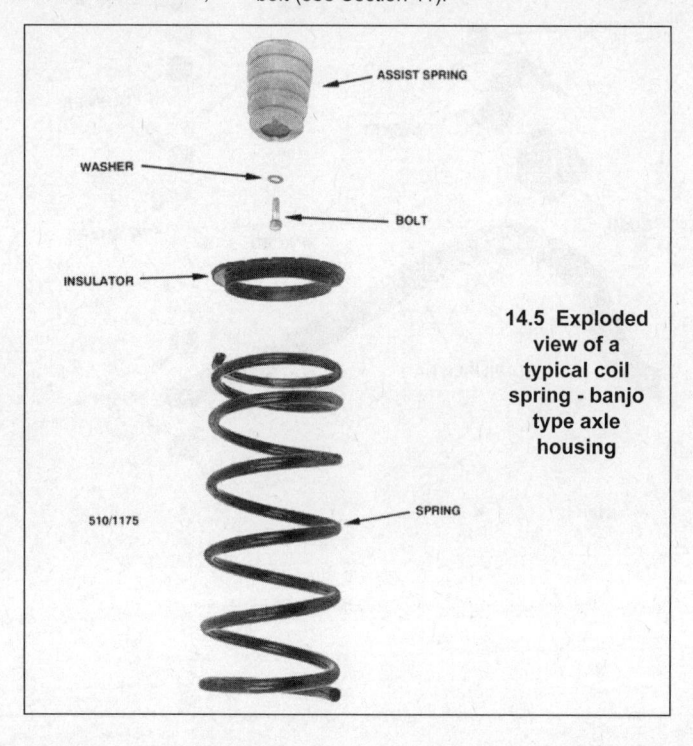

14.5 Exploded view of a typical coil spring - banjo type axle housing

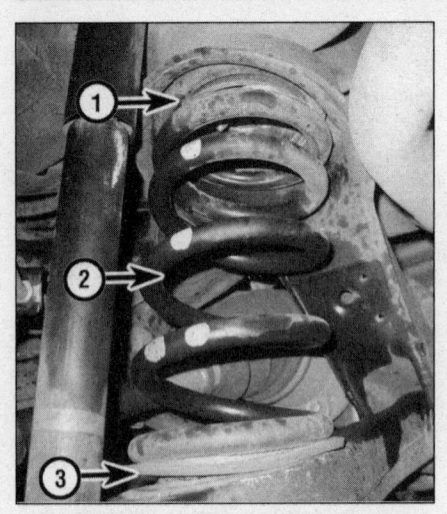

10-14 Chapter 10 Suspension and steering systems

9 Slowly lower the floor jack and allow the control arm and spring to move down.
10 Remove the upper spring seat, lower spring seat and spring **(see illustration)**.

Refitting

11 Refitting is the reverse of removal. Tighten the nuts and bolts to the torques listed in the Specifications Section at the beginning of this Chapter before lowering the vehicle weight onto the suspension.

15 Rear stabiliser bar - removal and refitting

Warning: *Whenever any of the suspension or steering fasteners are loosened or removed, they must be inspected and, if necessary, renewed with new ones of the same part number or of original equipment quality and design. Torque specifications must be followed for proper reassembly and component retention.*

1 Raise the vehicle and support it securely on jackstands (see Jacking and Towing).

Banjo type axle housing

Refer to illustration 15.4

2 Remove the parking brake cable attaching bolt.
3 Remove the lower left shock absorber bolt (see Section 11).
4 Remove the stabiliser bar bracket bolts and detach the brackets and bushes **(see illustration)**.
5 Remove the stabiliser link bolts and detach the bar from the vehicle.

Independent rear suspension

Refer to illustration 15.7

6 Remove the stabiliser bar-to-lower arm link nuts.
7 Remove the stabiliser bar bracket bolts **(see illustration)** and detach the bar from the vehicle.
8 Pull the brackets off the stabiliser bar and inspect the bushes for cracks, hardening and other signs of deterioration. If the bushes are damaged, renew them.

All models

9 Refitting is the reverse of removal. Before lowering the vehicle weight onto the suspension, tighten the bracket bolts to the torque listed in the Specifications Section at the beginning of this Chapter. Tighten the nuts on the stabiliser link bolts securely.

16 Upper control arm and ball joint (Independent rear suspension) - removal and refitting

Removal

Upper control arm

Refer to illustration 16.6

1 Loosen the wheel lug nuts, raise the rear of the vehicle and support it securely on jackstands (see Jacking and Towing).
2 Remove the ABS wheel sensor bracket and mounting bolt.
3 Disconnect the hydraulic brake line clip.
4 Remove the bumper stop mounting nut and remove the stop.
5 Remove the stabiliser bar (see Section 15).
6 Remove the upper ball joint split pin and the upper ball joint to upper control arm mounting bolts **(see illustration)**, then separate the control arm from the ball joint

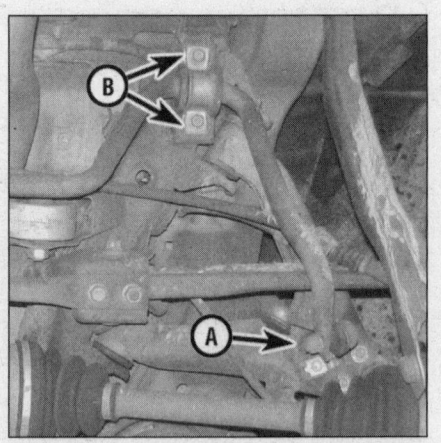

14.10 Remove the spring from the lower control arm

1 Upper spring seat
2 Spring
3 Lower spring seat

5 Lower the axle and remove the springs and insulator **(see illustration)**.

Independent rear suspension

Refer to illustration 14.10

6 Place a floor jack under the lower control arm with a block of wood between the jack and the control arm to support the arm.
7 Remove the lower shock absorber mounting bolt (see Section 11).
8 Remove the outer lower control arm-to-knuckle mounting bolt (see Section 17).

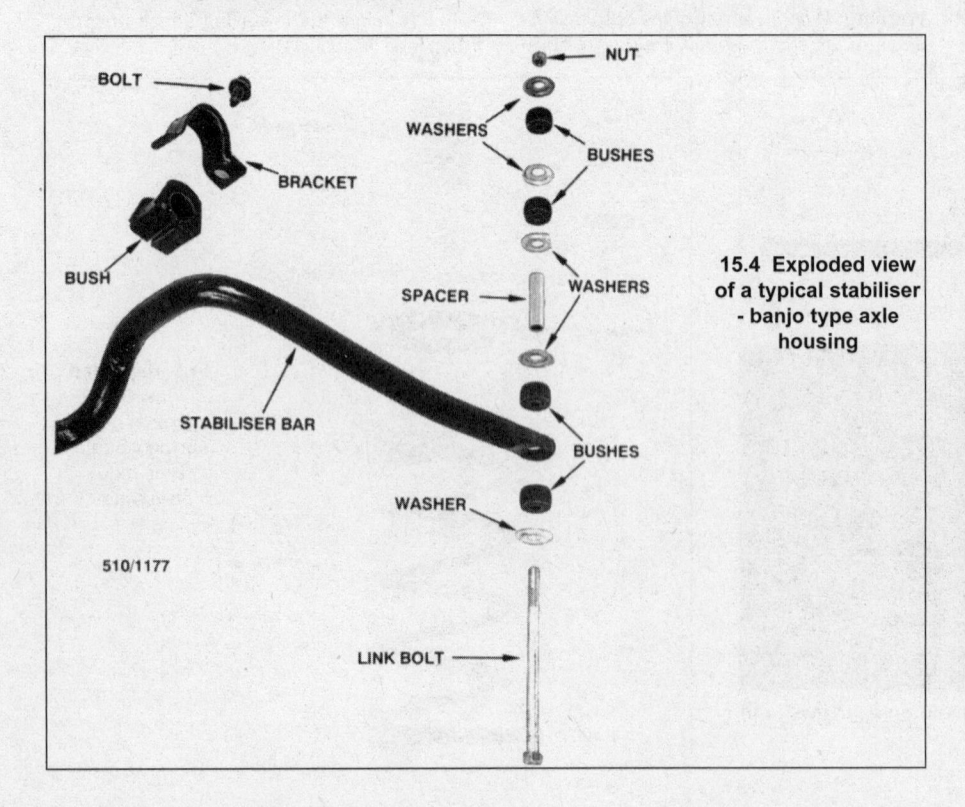

15.4 Exploded view of a typical stabiliser - banjo type axle housing

15.7 Remove the stabiliser link nut (A) and the remove the stabiliser bar bolts (B), then remove the bracket, bush and bar

Chapter 10 Suspension and steering systems

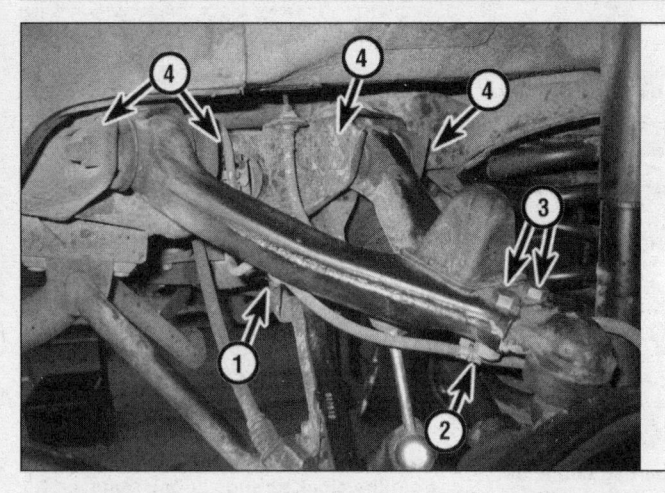

16.6 Remove the brake line, clip, bump stopper, ball joint mounting bolts and upper control arm mounting bolts

1 Brake line clip
2 ABS line clips
3 Ball joint bolts
4 Upper control arm mounting bolts/nuts

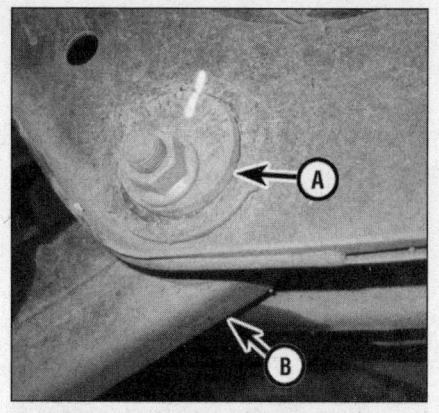

17.8. Mark and remove the camber adjustment bolt (A) and remove the lower control arm (B)

18.4 Remove the toe control arm ball joint-to-knuckle connector nut (arrow) and separate the joint.

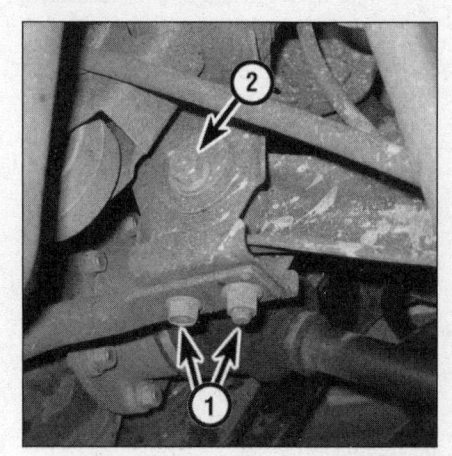

18.5 Inner toe control arm details

1 Toe control tower bar mounting nuts/bolts
2 Toe adjustment eccentric cam bolt

Ball joint

7 With the vehicle raised and supported, position a floor jack under the lower arm - it must stay there throughout the entire operation. Remove the wheel. Remove the ball joint split pin and loosen the castellated nut a couple of turns, but don't remove it (it will prevent the ball joint and rear knuckle from separating violently).

8 Using a ball joint separating tool, separate the ball joint from the rear knuckle. There are several types of ball joint tools available, but the kind that pushes the ball joint stud out of the knuckle boss works the best. The wedge, or "pickle fork" type works fairly well, but it tends to damage the ball joint seal. Some two-jaw pullers will do the job, also.

9 Remove the castellated nut and disconnect the ball joint from the rear knuckle. If necessary, remove the rear knuckle (see Section 19) and the driveaxle (see Chapter 8).

Refitting
Ball joint

10 The ball joint is retained to the suspension arm by bolts and nuts. Remove the bolts and nuts, then detach the ball joint from the arm. Take note of how the ball joint is positioned on the arm - the new one must be installed the same way.

11 Position the new ball joint on the arm and install the nut or bolts, tightening them to the torque listed in this Chapter's Specifications.

12 Insert the ball joint stud into the steering knuckle boss, install the castellated nut and tighten it to the specified torque. Install a new split pin. If necessary, tighten the nut an additional amount to line up the slots in the nut with the hole in the ball joint stud (never loosen the nut to align the hole).

Upper control arm

13 Refit the control arm to the frame and install the bolts/nuts, tightening them to the torque listed in this Chapter's Specifications.

14 Refit the ball joint-to-control arm bolts and tighten them to the torque listed in this Chapter's Specifications.

15 Refit the ABS wheel sensor bracket and hydraulic brake line clip.

16 Install the wheel and lug nuts and lower the vehicle. Tighten the lug nuts to the torque specified in Chapter 1.

17 Drive the vehicle to an alignment shop to have the alignment checked and, if necessary, adjusted.

17 Rear lower control arm (Independent rear suspension) - removal and refitting

Refer to illustration 17.8

1 Raise the vehicle and support it securely on jackstands
2 Support the axle with a jackstand.
3 Place a floor jack under the lower control arm with a block of wood between the jack and the control arm to support the arm.
4 Remove the lower shock absorber mounting bolt (see Section 11).
5 Remove the outer lower control arm-to-knuckle mounting bolt.
6 Slowly lower the floor jack and allow the control arm and spring to move down.
7 Remove the upper spring seat, lower spring seat and spring (see Section 14).
8 Mark the lower control arm eccentric cam bolt **(see illustration)** and remove the lower control arm inner bolt. Remove the lower control arm.
9 Refitting is the reverse of removal. Tighten the nuts and bolts to the torques listed in the Specifications Section at the beginning of this Chapter before lowering the vehicle weight onto the suspension.
10 Drive the vehicle to an alignment shop to have the alignment checked and, if necessary, adjusted.

18 Toe control arm (Independent rear suspension) - removal and refitting

Refer to illustrations 18.4 and 18.5

Warning: *Whenever any of the suspension or steering fasteners are loosened or removed, they must be inspected and, if necessary,* renewed with new ones of the same part number or of original equipment quality and design. Torque specifications must be followed for proper reassembly and component retention.

1 Raise the vehicle and support it securely on jackstands

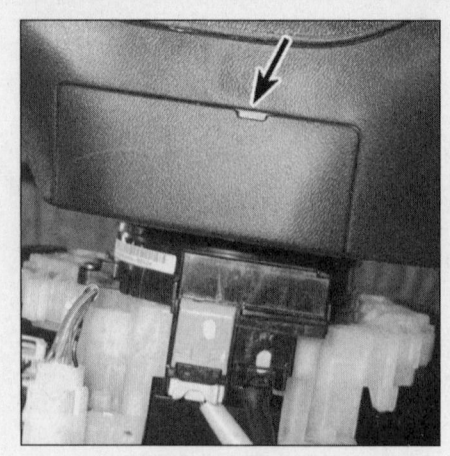

10-16 Chapter 10 Suspension and steering systems

20.11 Remove the lower steering wheel cover (arrow)

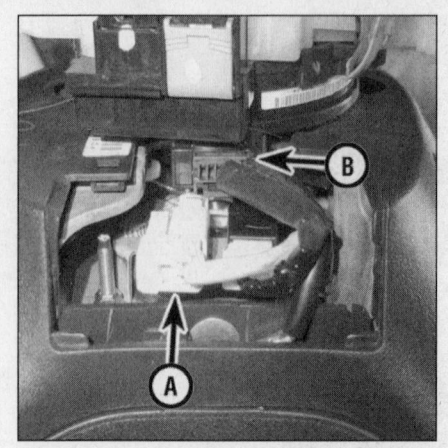

20.12a Disconnect the air bag connector (A) and horn switch connector (B)

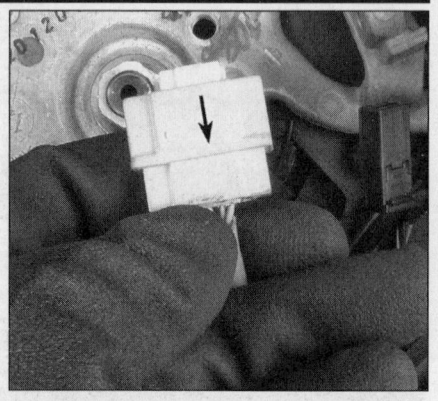

20.12b On late models, slide the outer sleeve on the airbag connector in the direction of the arrow to disconnect it from the clock spring - airbag removed for clarity

2 Remove the parking brake cable mounting bolt from the toe control arm.
3 Remove the toe control tower bar mounting bolts (4) and remove the bar.
4 Remove the toe control arm ball joint-to-knuckle connector nut **(see illustration)** and separate the joint.
5 Mark the eccentric cam bolt **(see illustration)** and remove the inner toe control arm inner bolt. Remove the toe control arm.
6 Refitting is the reverse of removal. Tighten the nuts and bolts to the torques listed in the Specifications Section at the beginning of this Chapter before lowering the vehicle weight onto the suspension.
7 Drive the vehicle to an alignment shop to have the alignment checked and, if necessary, adjusted.

19 Rear knuckle (Independent rear suspension) - removal and refitting

Warning: *Whenever any of the suspension or steering fasteners are loosened or removed, they must be inspected and, if necessary, renewed with new ones of the same part number or of original equipment quality and design. Torque specifications must be followed for proper reassembly and component retention.*

Removal
1 Loosen the wheel lug nuts, raise the vehicle and support it securely on jackstands placed under the frame.
2 Remove the brake caliper and place it on top of the upper arm or wire it up out of the way. Remove the brake disc and caliper mounting bracket from the steering knuckle (see Chapter 9 if necessary).
3 Remove the front hub and remove the driveaxle split pin, lock nut and push the drive-axle into the knuckle (see Chapter 8).
4 Separate the toe control arm end from the knuckle arm (see Section 18).
5 Remove the split pins from the upper ball joint stud and back off the nuts one turn each (see Section 16).

6 Remove the shock absorber (see Section 11).
7 Remove the lower control arm-to knuckle bolt (see Section 17).
8 Using a special tool, separate the upper control arm from the knuckle **(see illustrations 9.6a and 9.6b)**. There are several types of tools available, but the kind that pushes the ball joint stud out of the knuckle boss works the best. The wedge, or pickle fork type works fairly well, but it tends to damage the ball joint seal. Some two-jaw pullers will do the job, also. Once the ball joint has been released from the tapered holes in the knuckle, remove the nuts completely and carefully detach the knuckle.

Refitting
9 Place the knuckle between the upper and lower suspension arms and insert the upper ball joint stud into the knuckle. Install the nut and tighten it to the torque listed in this Chapter's Specifications. Refit the lower control arm bolt and tighten it to the torque listed in this Chapter's Specification.
10 Install the shock absorber.
11 Connect the toe control arm to the knuckle and tighten the nut to the torque listed in this Chapter's Specifications.
12 Install the stabiliser bar.
13 Install the brake caliper mounting bracket and caliper (see Chapter 9).
14 Install the wheel and lug nuts. Lower the vehicle to the ground and tighten the nuts to the torque specified in Chapter 1.
15 Drive the vehicle to an alignment shop to have the alignment checked and, if necessary, adjusted.

20 Steering wheel - removal and refitting

Non Air Bag models

Removal
1 Disconnect the cable from the negative battery terminal.

2 Using a small screwdriver, remove the horn pad screw from the underside of the steering wheel.
3 Unscrew the steering wheel nut.
4 Remove the horn pad and disconnect the electrical connector.
5 Mark the steering wheel hub and the column shaft with paint to ensure correct repositioning during reassembly.
6 Remove the wheel using a puller.
Caution: *Do not hammer on the wheel or the shaft to separate them.*

Refitting
7 Realign the steering wheel and the column shaft using the paint marks. Install and tighten the retaining nut to the torque listed in this Chapter's Specifications, then attach the horn plate and button or centre pad.
8 Connect the negative battery cable.

Air bag models
Removal
Refer to illustrations 20.11, 20.12a, 20.12b, 20.13, 20.14 and 20.15

Warning: *Later models are equipped with a Supplemental Restraint System (SRS), more commonly known as airbags. Always disable the airbag system before working in the vicinity of any airbag system component to avoid the possibility of accidental deployment of the airbag(s), which could cause personal injury (see Chapter 12). Do not use a memory saving device to preserve the PCM or radio memory when working on or near airbag system components.*

Warning: *With driver's side airbag, put the wheels in the straight-ahead position and lock the steering column. The steering column must not be rotated while the steering wheel is removed.*

Caution: *If the stereo in your vehicle is equipped with an anti-theft system, make sure you have the correct activation code before disconnecting the battery.*

9 Disconnect the cable from the negative and positive terminals of the battery and wait at least one minute for the back-up power

Chapter 10 Suspension and steering systems

20.13 Insert an 8 mm Allen head socket through the steering wheel cover and remove the locking bolt - air bag module removed for clarity

20.14 On late models, the airbag is held by a screw on each side of the steering wheel

20.15 Mark the wheel and shaft (1) to ensure the wheel is returned to its original position and then remove the nut (2)

supply to deplete. Position the front wheels in the straight-ahead position. See **Warnings** above.
10   Remove the steering column covers (see Chapter 11).
11   Use a small screwdriver to prise the lower cover off of the steering wheel **(see illustration)**.
12   Carefully unplug the wiring **(see illustrations)** from the airbag module and horn switch.

Early models
13   Slide an 8-mm Allen head socket into the side of the steering wheel and remove the locking bolt **(see illustration)**.
14   Carefully remove the airbag module and steering wheel.

Late models
14   Remove the two screws from each side of the steering wheel **(see illustration)** and lift the airbag assembly from the steering wheel.
15   Mark the steering wheel hub and the column shaft with paint to ensure correct repositioning during reassembly.
16   Remove the wheel using a puller.
Caution: *Do not hammer on the wheel or the shaft to separate them.*

Refitting
Warning: *Make sure the airbag clockspring is centre (follow any instructions printed on the clockspring assembly).*

17   To refit the wheel, centre the steering wheel and slip the wheel onto the shaft.
18   Connect the wiring to the airbag assembly, horn switch and refit the cover. Tighten all nuts and bolts to the torque given in this Chapter's Specifications.
19   Connect the battery cables.

21 Steering linkage - removal and refitting

Warning: *Whenever any of the suspension or steering fasteners are loosened or removed, they must be inspected and, if necessary, renewed with new ones of the same part number or of original equipment quality and design. Torque specifications must be followed for proper reassembly and component retention.*

1   All steering linkage removal and refitting procedures should be performed with the front end of the vehicle raised and placed securely on jackstands (see Jacking and Towing).
2   Before removing any steering linkage components, obtain a ball joint separator. It may be a screw-type puller or a wedge-type (pickle fork) tool, although the wedge-type tool tends to damage the ball joint seals. It is possible to jar a ball joint taper pin free from its eye by striking opposite sides of the eye simultaneously with two large hammers, but the space available to do so is usually very limited.
3   After fitting any of the steering linkage components, the front wheel alignment should be checked by a reputable front end alignment shop.

Pitman arm
Refer to illustration 21.6

4   Remove the nut securing the Pitman arm to the steering gear sector shaft.
5   Scribe or paint match marks on the arm and shaft.
6   Using a puller **(see illustration)**, disconnect the Pitman arm from the shaft splines.
7   Remove the split pin and castle nut securing the Pitman arm to the relay rod.

21.6 Separate the Pitman arm from the steering gear, use a Pitman arm puller

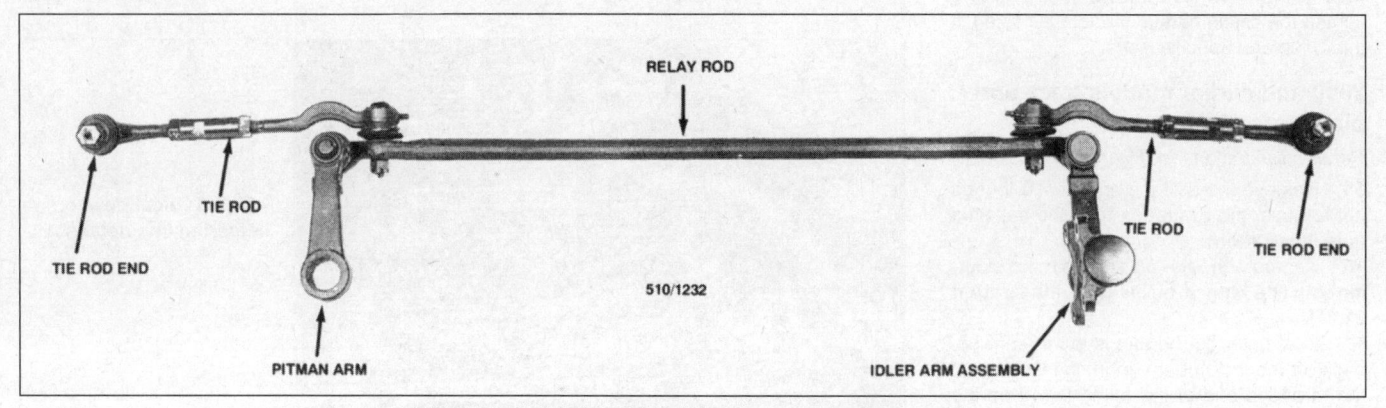

21.10 Typical 1999 and earlier steering linkage assembly

21.11 Using a small puller, separate the tie-rod end ball stud from the steering knuckle arm

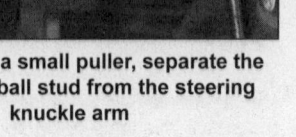

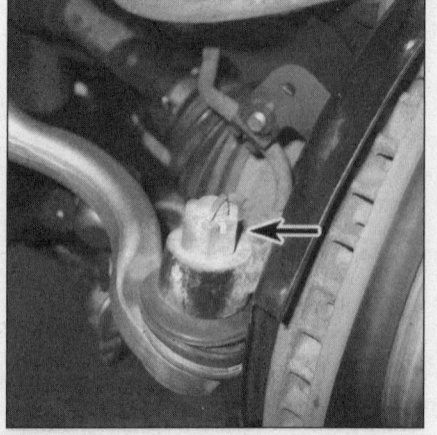

21.15 Remove the split pin and loosen the castle nut (arrow) from the outer tie-rod

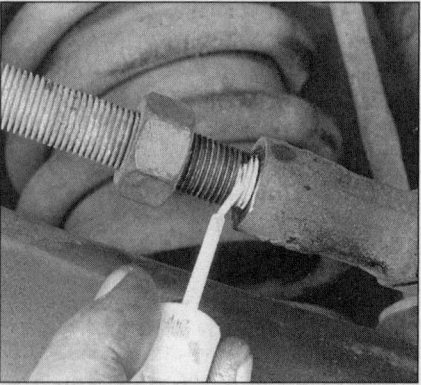

21.17 Make sure you place a mark on the threaded inner tie-rod in line with the end of the threaded portion of the outer tie-rod end; thus, when you refit the tie-rod end and screw it in until the inner end is aligned with this mark, front toe-in will still be the same as before

8 Using a puller, disconnect the Pitman arm from the relay rod.
9 Refitting is the reverse of the removal procedure. Be sure to tighten the nuts to the torques listed in this Chapter's Specifications and install a new split pin.

Tie-rod

1999 and earlier models

Refer to illustrations 21.10 and 21.11

10 Remove the split pins and castle nuts securing the tie-rod to the relay rod and knuckle arm **(see illustration)**.
11 Separate the tie-rod from the relay rod and knuckle arm with a puller **(see illustration)**.
12 If a tie-rod end is to be renewed, loosen the lock nut and mark the relationship of the tie-rod end to the tie-rod with white paint. When fitting the new rod end, thread it onto the tie-rod until it reaches the mark, then turn the lock nut until it contacts the rod end. Don't tighten it fully at this time.
13 Turn the tie-rod ends so they are at approximately 90-degree angles to each other, then tighten the jam nuts to lock the ends in position.
14 The remaining refitting steps are the reverse of those for removal. Make sure to tighten the castle nuts to the torques listed in this Chapter's Specifications.

2000 and earlier models (rack and pinion steering)

Refer to illustrations 21.15 and 21.17

15 Remove the split pin and loosen, but do not remove, the castle nut from the ball stud **(see illustration)**.
16 Separate the tie-rod end from the steering knuckle with a puller **(see illustration 21.11)**.
17 If an outer tie-rod end is to be renewed, back off the locknut and mark the location of the threaded end of the outer tie-rod on the inner **(see illustration)**, so that when the new tie-rod is screwed onto the inner tie-rod the toe-in won't be affected. Unscrew the outer tie-rod.
18 Lubricate the threaded portion of the tie-rod with chassis grease. Screw the new tie-rod end onto the tie-rod until the threaded end reaches the mark you made on the threads. Don't tighten the locknut yet.
19 Connect the tie-rod end to the steering knuckle and refit the castle nut. Tighten the nut to the torque listed in this Chapter's Specifications and fit a new split pin. If the ballstud spins when attempting to tighten the nut, force it into the tapered hole with a large pair of pliers. If necessary, tighten the nut slightly to align a slot in the nut with the split pin hole in the ballstud. Fit the new split pin.
20 Tighten the tie-rod end locknut securely.
21 Refit the wheel and lug nuts, lower the vehicle and tighten the lug nuts to the torque listed in the Chapter 1 Specifications. Drive the vehicle to an alignment shop to have the toe-in checked and, if necessary, adjusted.

Idler arm

22 Remove the nut securing the idler arm to the bracket.
23 Remove the split pin and castle nut securing the idler arm to the relay rod.
24 Using a puller, disconnect the idler arm from the relay rod.
25 Slide the idler arm off the bracket shaft and remove it from the vehicle.
26 Refitting is the reverse of the removal procedure. Be sure to tighten the nuts to the specified torque and install a new split pin. Drive the vehicle to an alignment shop to have the toe-in checked and, if necessary, adjusted.

22 Steering gear - removal and refitting

Warning: *Whenever any of the suspension or steering fasteners are loosened or removed, they must be inspected and, if necessary, renewed with new ones of the same part number or of original equipment quality and design. Torque specifications must be followed for proper reassembly and component retention.*

Note: *If you find that the steering gear is defective, it is not recommended that you overhaul it. Because of the special tools needed to do the job, it is best to let your dealer service department overhaul it for you (or renew it with a factory rebuilt unit).*

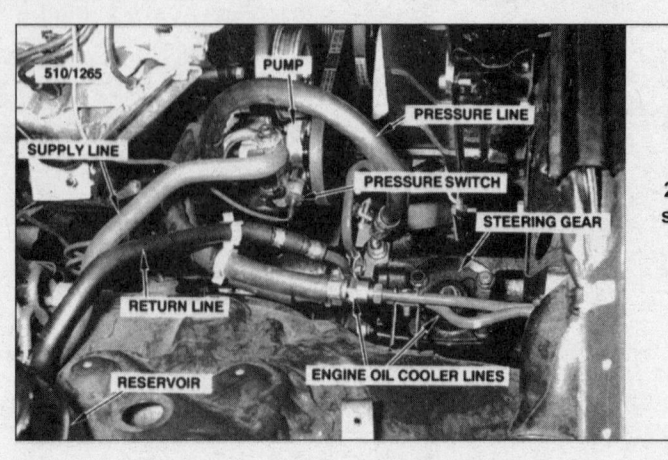

22.3 Typical power steering line details

Chapter 10 Suspension and steering systems

22.7 Disconnect the power steering pressure hose and return line (arrows) from the steering rack

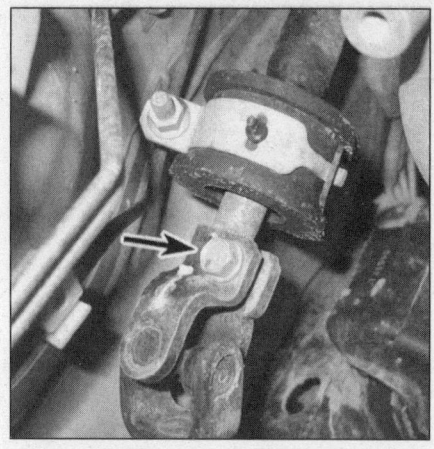

22.8 Remove the pinch bolt (arrow)

However, you can remove and install it yourself by following the procedure outlined here. The removal and refitting procedures for manual steering and power steering gear housings are identical except that the inlet and outlet lines must be removed from the steering gear housing on power steering-equipped models before the housing can be removed. The steering system should be filled and power steering systems should be bled after the gear is reinstalled (see Section 25).

1   Park the vehicle with the front wheels pointing straight ahead. Apply the parking brake. Loosen the wheel lug nuts, raise the front of the vehicle and support it securely on jackstands (see Jacking and Towing). Remove the front wheels and the lower cover and skid plate **(see illustration 2.2)**.

Ball and nut type steering gear

Refer to illustration 22.3

2   Place an alignment mark on the steering shaft flexible coupling and the gear housing worm shaft to assure correct reassembly, then remove the coupling pinch bolt.
3   Disconnect the power steering line connections from the steering gear **(see illustration)**. Plug the lines so the fluid will not drain.
4   Disconnect the Pitman arm and the left tie-rod from the relay rod (see Section 21).
5   Remove the bolts securing the gear housing to the chassis and lower the gear from the vehicle.
6   Refitting is the reverse of the removal procedure. Be sure to tighten all nuts and bolts to the torques listed in this Chapter's Specifications.

Rack and pinion type steering gear

Refer to illustrations 22.7, 22.8 and 22.11

7   Place a drain pan under the right side of the steering gear. Remove the power steering pressure and return lines from the steering gear **(see illustration)**. Cap the ends to prevent excessive fluid loss and contamination. Disconnect the wiring from the steering gear pressure switch.
8   Mark the relationship of the intermediate shaft coupling and the steering gear input shaft **(see illustration)** and remove the pinch bolt.
9   Disconnect the tie-rod ends from the steering knuckles (see Section 21).
10   Disconnect the right hand side differential mounting bracket (see Chapter 8).
11   Support the steering gear and remove the steering gear-to-frame mounting bolts **(see illustration)**. Lower the unit, separating the intermediate shaft from the steering gear input shaft, and remove the steering gear from the vehicle.
12   Raise the steering gear into position and connect the intermediate shaft, aligning the marks.

Note: *Make sure the steering gear is centre before refitting it.*

13   Refit the steering gear mounting bolts and tighten them to the torque listed in this Chapter's Specifications.
14   Connect the tie-rod ends to the steering knuckles (see Section 21).
15   Refit the intermediate shaft pinch bolt and tighten it to the torque listed in this Chapter's Specifications.
16   Connect the power steering pressure and return lines to the steering gear. Fill the power steering pump reservoir with the recommended fluid (see Chapter 1).
17   Refit the differential mounting bracket (see Chapter 8).
18   Lower the vehicle and bleed the system as outlined in Section 25.
19   If the steering gear has been renewed, take the vehicle to an alignment shop to have the toe-in adjusted and the steering wheel centred.

23 Steering freeplay - adjustment

Refer to illustration 23.6

1   Raise the vehicle with a jack so that the front wheels are off the ground and place the vehicle securely on jackstands (see Jacking and Towing).
2   Point the wheels straight ahead.
3   Using a spanner, loosen the locknut on the steering gear.
4   Turn the adjusting screw clockwise to decrease wheel freeplay and counterclockwise to increase it.

Note: *Turn the adjusting screw in small increments, checking the steering wheel freeplay between them.*

22.11 Steering rack mounting bolt locations

23.6 Loosen the locknut with a spanner and use a screwdriver to turn the adjusting screw - when tightening the locknut, be sure to hold the screw to keep it from turning

24.4 Disconnect the power steering pump pressure switch connector

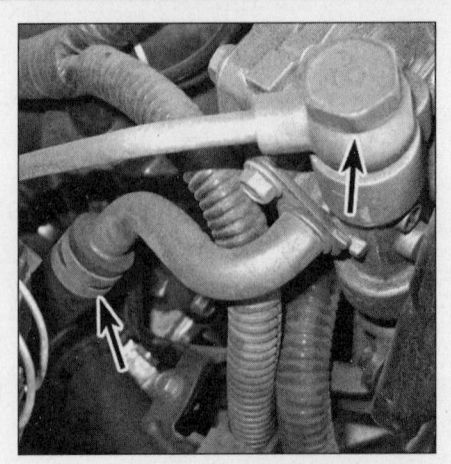

24.5 Remove the pump return line and banjo fitting (pressure line)

24.6a Remove the two front pump mounting bolts through the pulley

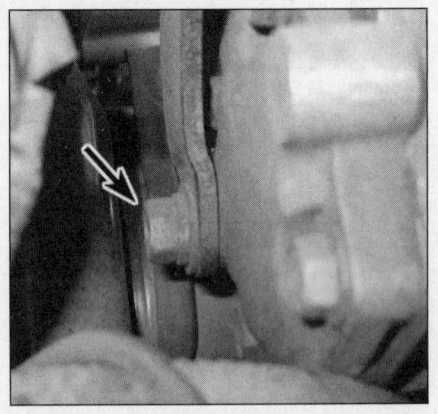

24.6b Remove the rear pump mounting bolt (arrow) and remove the pump from the bracket

24.9 Disconnect the electrical connector (arrow) to the power steering pressure switch.

5   Turn the steering wheel halfway around in both directions, checking that the freeplay is correct and that the steering is smooth.
6   Hold the adjusting screw so that it will not turn and tighten the locknut **(see illustration)**.
7   Remove the jackstands and lower the vehicle.

24 Power steering pump - removal and refitting

Warning: *Whenever any of the suspension or steering fasteners are loosened or removed, they must be inspected and, if necessary, renewed with new ones of the same part number or of original equipment quality and design. Torque specifications must be followed for proper reassembly and component retention.*

Note: *If you find that the steering pump is defective, it is not recommended that you overhaul it. Because of the special tools needed to do the job, it is best to let your dealer service department overhaul it for you*

(or renew it with a factory rebuilt unit). However, you can remove it yourself using the procedure which follows.

Removal

Petrol engines

Refer to illustrations 24.4, 24.5, 24.6a and 24.6b

1   On 3.5 and 3.8L engines, remove the battery and tray (see Chapter 5).
2   Position a container to catch the pump fluid. Drain the power steering fluid from the reservoir using a suction gun.
3   Remove the drivebelt (see Chapter 1).
4   Disconnect the electrical connector **(see illustration)** to the power steering pressure switch (automatic transmission models).
5   Remove the pressure line banjo fitting and return hose **(see illustration)**. As each is disconnected, cap or tape over the hose opening and then secure the end in a raised position to prevent leakage and contamination. Cover or plug the pump openings so dirt won't enter the unit.
6   Remove the two front power steering pump mounting bolts **(see illustration)** and the rear mounting bolt **(see illustration)**.
7   Remove the pump from the mounting bracket and then remove the pump.

Diesel engines

Refer to illustrations 24.9 and 24.10

8   Remove the engine covers (see Chapter 1) and position a container to catch the pump fluid.
9   Disconnect the electrical connector **(see illustration)** to the power steering pressure switch.
10 Remove the pressure line banjo fitting and return hose **(see illustration)**. As each

24.10 Remove the pressure line banjo fitting and return hose clamp (arrow) - cap or tape over the hose opening and then secure the end in a raised position to prevent leakage and contamination

Chapter 10 Suspension and steering systems

is disconnected, cap or tape over the hose opening and then secure the end in a raised position to prevent leakage and contamination. Cover or plug the pump openings so dirt won't enter the unit.
11 Remove the two pump mounting bolts from the back side of the timing gear case.
12 Pull the pump out of the timing gear case and renew the O-ring.

Refitting

13 Refitting is the reverse of the removal procedure. Be sure to tighten all nuts and bolts to the torques listed in this Chapter's Specifications. When fitting the pressure line, make sure there is sufficient clearance.
14 On petrol engine models adjust the drivebelt tension, see Chapter 1.
15 Fill the power steering fluid reservoir with the specified fluid and bleed the power steering system (see Section 25).
16 Check for fluid leaks.

25 Power steering system - bleeding

1 Check the fluid in the reservoir and add fluid of the specified type if it is low.
2 Jack up the front of the vehicle and place it securely on jackstands (see Jacking and Towing).
3 With the engine off, turn the steering wheel fully in both directions two or three times.
4 Recheck the fluid in the reservoir and add more fluid if necessary.
5 Start the engine and turn the steering wheel fully in both directions two or three times. The engine should be running at 1000 rpm or less.
6 Remove the jackstands and lower the vehicle completely.
7 With the engine running at 1000 rpm or less, turn the steering wheel fully in both directions two or three times.
8 Return the steering wheel to the centre position.
9 Check that the fluid is not foamy or cloudy.
10 Measure the fluid level with the engine running.
11 Turn off the engine and again measure the fluid level. It should rise no more than 5 mm when the engine is turned off.
12 If a problem is encountered, repeat Steps 7 through 11.
13 If the problem persists, remove the pump (see Section 24), and have it repaired by a dealer service department.

26 Front end alignment - general information

Refer to illustration 26.1

A front end alignment refers to the adjustments made to the front wheels so they are in proper angular relationship to the suspension and the ground. Front wheels that are out of proper alignment not only affect steering control, but also increase tyre wear.

The front end adjustments normally required are camber, caster and toe-in (see illustration).

Getting the proper front wheel alignment is a very exacting process, one in which complicated and expensive machines are necessary to perform the job properly. Because of this, you should have a technician with the proper equipment perform these tasks. We will, however, use this space to give you a basic idea of what is involved with front-end alignment so you can better understand the process and deal intelligently with the shop that does the work.

Toe-in is the turning in of the front wheels. The purpose of a toe specification is to ensure parallel rolling of the front wheels. In a vehicle with zero toe-in, the distance between the front edges of the wheels will be the same as the distance between the rear edges of the wheels. The actual amount of toe-in is normally only a small number of millimetres. Toe-in adjustment is controlled by the tie-rod end position on the inner tie-rod. Incorrect toe-in will cause the tyres to wear improperly by making them scrub against the road surface.

Camber is the tilting of the front wheels from the vertical when viewed from the front of the vehicle. When the wheels tilt out at the top, the camber is said to be positive (+). When the wheels tilt in at the top the camber is negative (-). The amount of tilt is measured in degrees from the vertical and this measurement is called the camber angle. This angle affects the amount of tyre tread which contacts the road and compensates for changes in the suspension geometry when the vehicle is cornering or travelling over an undulating surface.

Caster is the tilting of the front steering axis from the vertical. A tilt toward the rear is positive caster and a tilt toward the front is negative caster. Caster angle affects the self-

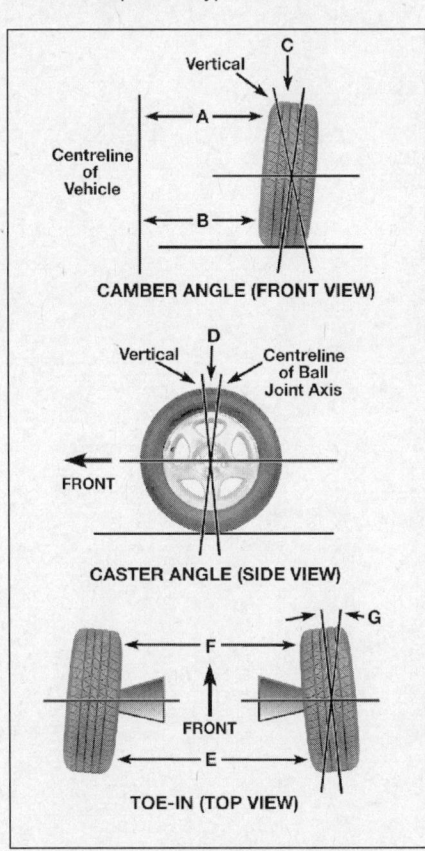

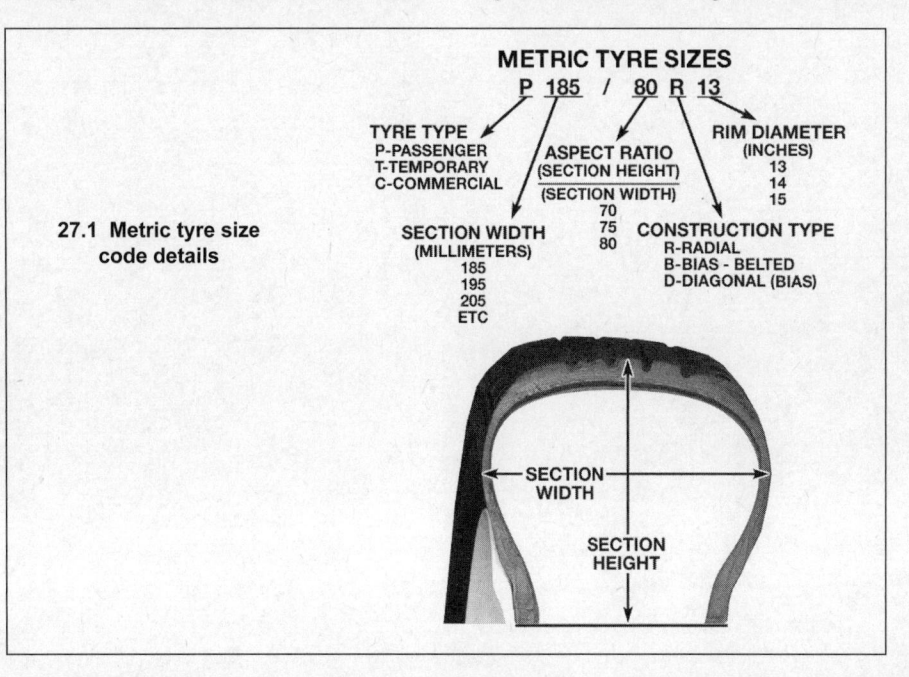

26.1 Front end alignment details

1 A minus B = C (degrees camber)
2 E minus F = -toe-in (measured in millimetres)
3 G = toe-in (expressed in degrees)

27.1 Metric tyre size code details

centreing action of the steering, which governs straight-line stability. Caster is adjusted by moving shims from one end of the upper arm mount to the other.

27 Wheels and tyres - general information

Refer to illustration 27.1

All models covered by this manual are equipped with metric-sized radial tyres **(see illustration)**. Use of other size or type of tyres may affect the ride and handling of the vehicle. Don't mix different types of tyres, such as radials and bias belted, on the same vehicle as handling may be seriously affected. It's recommended that tyres be renewed in pairs on the same axle, but if only one tyre is being renewed, be sure it's the same size, structure and tread design as the other.

Because tyre pressure has a substantial effect on handling and wear, the pressure on all tyres should be checked at least once a month or before any extended trips (see Chapter 1).

Wheels must be renewed if they are bent, dented, leak air, have elongated bolt holes, are heavily rusted, out of vertical symmetry or if the lug nuts won't stay tight. Wheel repairs that use welding or peening are not recommended.

Tyre and wheel balance is important to the overall handling, braking and performance of the vehicle. Unbalanced wheels can adversely affect handling and ride characteristics as well as tyre life. Whenever a tyre is refitted on a wheel, the tyre and wheel should be balanced by a shop with the proper equipment.

Wheels can be damaged by an impact with a curb or other solid object. If the wheels are bent, the result is a hazardous condition that must be corrected. To check the wheels, raise the vehicle and set it on jackstands (see Jacking and Towing). Visually inspect the wheels for obvious signs of damage such as cracks and deformation.

Chapter 11 Body

Contents

	Section		Section
Body - maintenance...	2	General information...	1
Body repair - major damage...	6	Hinges and locks - maintenance..	7
Body repair - minor damage...	5	Instrument panel and related trim - removal and refitting....	18
Bonnet - removal, refitting and adjustment........................	9	Outside mirror - removal and refitting.................................	17
Bumpers - removal and refitting...	11	Radiator grille - removal and refitting..................................	10
Centre console - removal and refitting...............................	19	Rear cargo door - removal, refitting and adjustment..........	14
Door latch, lock cylinder and handles - removal, refitting and adjustment..	15	Seat belts - check...	23
		Seats - removal and refitting..	22
Door - removal, refitting and adjustment............................	13	Steering column cover - removal and refitting....................	20
Door trim panel - removal and refitting...............................	12	Upholstery and carpets - maintenance...............................	4
Door window and regulator - removal and refitting.............	16	Vinyl trim - maintenance...	3
Front fender - removal and refitting....................................	21	Windscreen and fixed glass - renewal................................	8

1 General information

These models feature a separate boxed steel frame and body. Certain components are particularly vulnerable to accident damage and can be unbolted and renewed. Among these parts are the body mouldings, doors, bumpers, bonnet and all glass.

Only general body maintenance practices and body panel repair procedures within the scope of the do-it-yourselfer are included in this Chapter.

2 Body - maintenance

1 The condition of your vehicle's body is very important, because the resale value depends a great deal on it. It's much more difficult to repair a neglected or damaged body than it is to repair mechanical components. The hidden areas of the body, such as the wheel wells, the frame and the engine compartment, are equally important, although they don't require as frequent attention as the rest of the body.
2 Once a year, or every 20,000 kilometres, it's a good idea to have the under-side of the body steam cleaned. All traces of dirt and oil will be removed and the area can then be inspected carefully for rust, damaged brake lines, frayed electrical wires, damaged cables and other problems.
3 At the same time, clean the engine and the engine compartment with a steam cleaner or water soluble degreaser.
4 The wheel wells should be given close attention, since undercoating can peel away and stones and dirt thrown up by the tyres can cause the paint to chip and flake, allowing rust to set in. If rust is found, clean down to the bare metal and apply an anti-rust paint.
5 The body should be washed about once a week. Wet the vehicle thoroughly to soften the dirt, then wash it down with a soft sponge and plenty of clean soapy water. If the surplus dirt is not washed off very carefully, it can wear down the paint.
6 Spots of tar or asphalt thrown up from the road should be removed with a cloth soaked in solvent.
7 Once every six months, wax the body and chrome trim. If a chrome cleaner is used to remove rust from any of the vehicle's plated parts, remember that the cleaner also removes part of the chrome, so use it sparingly.

3 Vinyl trim - maintenance

Don't clean vinyl trim with detergents, caustic soap or petroleum-based cleaners. Plain soap and water works just fine, with a soft brush to clean dirt that may be ingrained. Wash the vinyl as frequently as the rest of the vehicle. After cleaning, application of a high-quality rubber and vinyl protectant will help prevent oxidation and cracks. The protectant can also be applied to weatherstripping, vacuum lines and rubber hoses, which often fail as a result of chemical degradation, and to the tyres.

4 Upholstery and carpets - maintenance

1 Every three months remove the floor mats and clean the interior of the vehicle (more frequently if necessary). Use a stiff whisk broom to brush the carpeting and loosen dirt and dust, then vacuum the upholstery and carpets thoroughly, especially along seams and crevices.
2 Dirt and stains can be removed from carpeting with basic household or automotive carpet shampoos available in spray cans. Follow the directions and vacuum again, then use a stiff brush to bring back the "nap" of the carpet.
3 Most interiors have cloth or vinyl upholstery, either of which can be cleaned and maintained with a number of material-specific cleaners or shampoos available in auto supply stores. Follow the directions on the product for usage, and always spot-test any upholstery cleaner on an inconspicuous area (bottom edge of a back seat cushion) to ensure that it doesn't cause a colour shift in the material.
4 After cleaning, vinyl upholstery should be treated with a protectant.

Note: *Make sure the protectant container indicates the product can be used on seats - some products may make a seat too slippery.*

Caution: *Do not use protectant on vinyl-covered steering wheels.*

5 Leather upholstery requires special care. It should be cleaned regularly with saddlesoap or leather cleaner. Never use alcohol, petrol, nail polish remover or thinner to clean leather upholstery.
6 After cleaning, regularly treat leather upholstery with a leather conditioner, rubbed in with a soft cotton cloth. Never use car wax on leather upholstery.
7 In areas where the interior of the vehicle is subject to bright sunlight, cover leather seating areas of the seats with a sheet if the vehicle is to be left out for any length of time.

5 Body repair - minor damage

See photo sequence

Repair of scratches

1 If the scratch is superficial and does not penetrate to the metal of the body, repair is

These photos illustrate a method of repairing simple dents. They are intended to supplement *Body repair - minor damage* in this Chapter and should not be used as the sole instructions for body repair on these vehicles.

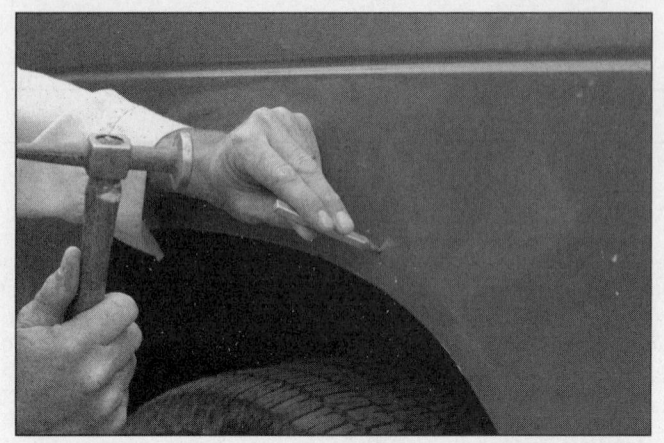

1 If you can't access the backside of the body panel to hammer out the dent, pull it out with a slide-hammer-type dent puller. In the deepest portion of the dent or along the crease line, drill or punch hole(s) at least one inch apart . . .

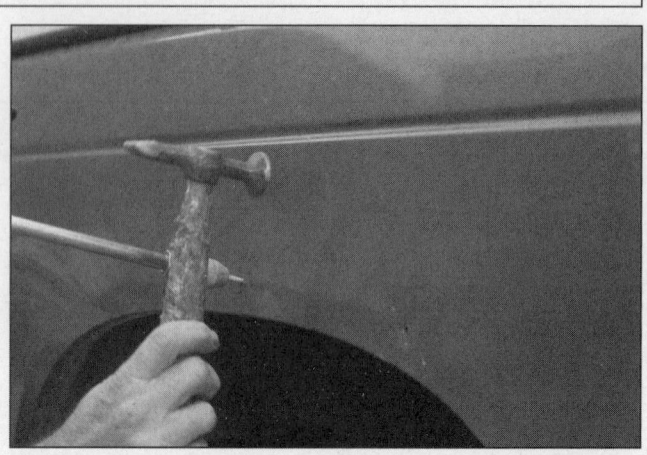

2 . . . then screw the slide-hammer into the hole and operate it. Tap with a hammer near the edge of the dent to help 'pop' the metal back to its original shape. When you're finished, the dent area should be close to its original contour and about 1/8-inch below the surface of the surrounding metal

3 Using coarse-grit sandpaper, remove the paint down to the bare metal. Hand sanding works fine, but the disc sander shown here makes the job faster. Use finer (about 320-grit) sandpaper to feather-edge the paint at least one inch around the dent area

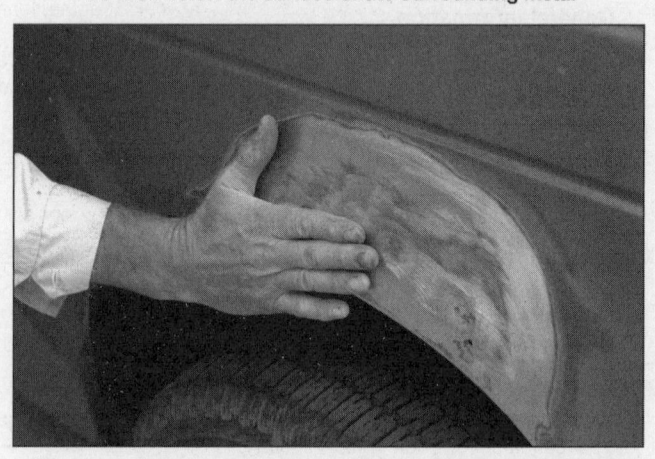

4 When the paint is removed, touch will probably be more helpful than sight for telling if the metal is straight. Hammer down the high spots or raise the low spots as necessary. Clean the repair area with wax/silicone remover

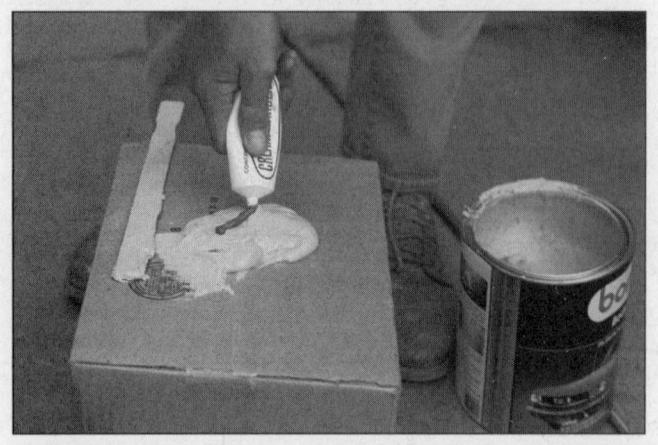

5 Following label instructions, mix up a batch of plastic filler and hardener. The ratio of filler to hardener is critical, and, if you mix it incorrectly, it will either not cure properly or cure too quickly (you won't have time to file and sand it into shape)

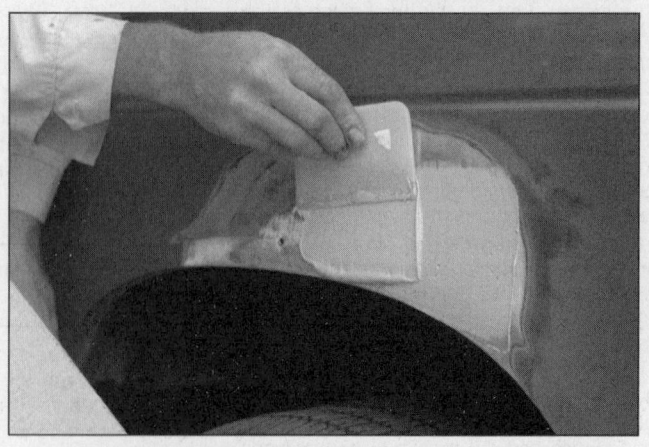

6 Working quickly so the filler doesn't harden, use a plastic applicator to press the body filler firmly into the metal, assuring it bonds completely. Work the filler until it matches the original contour and is slightly above the surrounding metal

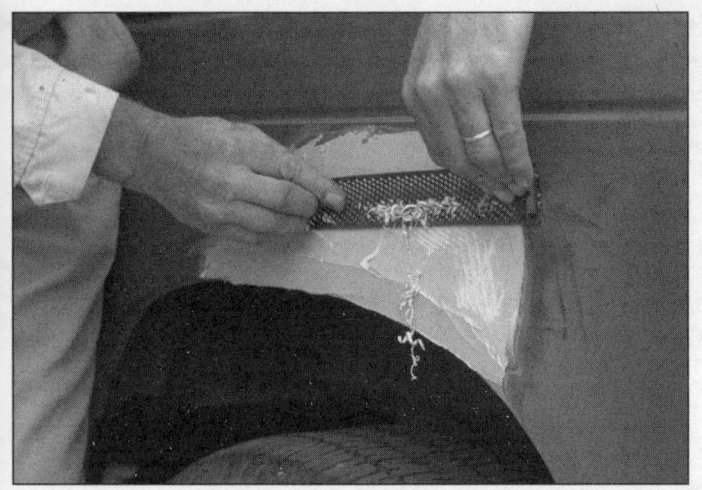

7 Let the filler harden until you can just dent it with your fingernail. Use a body file or Surform tool (shown here) to rough-shape the filler

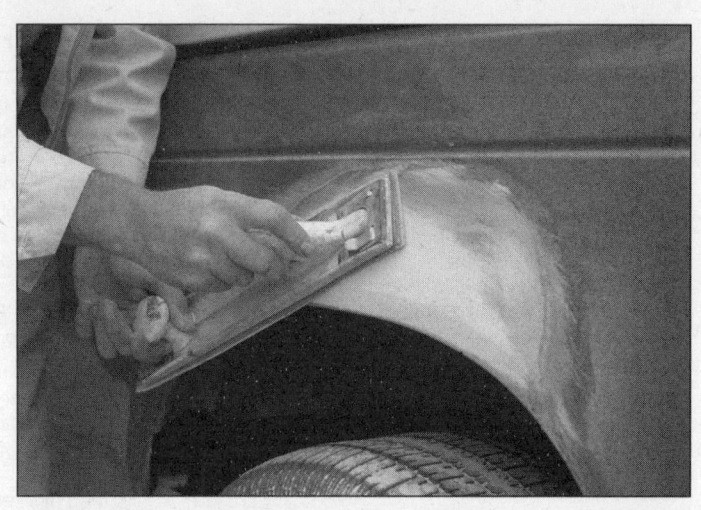

8 Use coarse-grit sandpaper and a sanding board or block to work the filler down until it's smooth and even. Work down to finer grits of sandpaper - always using a board or block - ending up with 360 or 400 grit

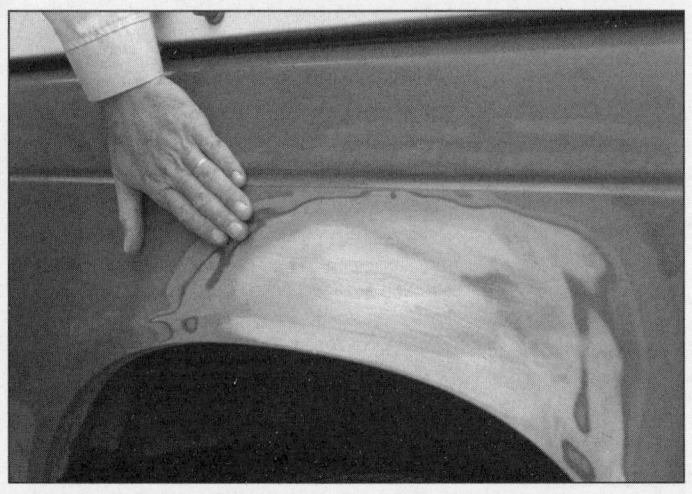

9 You shouldn't be able to feel any ridge at the transition from the filler to the bare metal or from the bare metal to the old paint. As soon as the repair is flat and uniform, remove the dust and mask off the adjacent panels or trim pieces

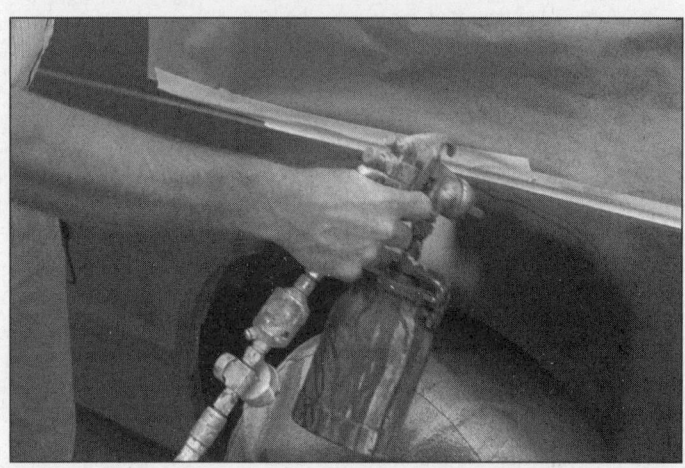

10 Apply several layers of primer to the area. Don't spray the primer on too heavy, so it sags or runs, and make sure each coat is dry before you spray on the next one. A professional-type spray gun is being used here, but aerosol spray primer is available inexpensively from auto parts stores

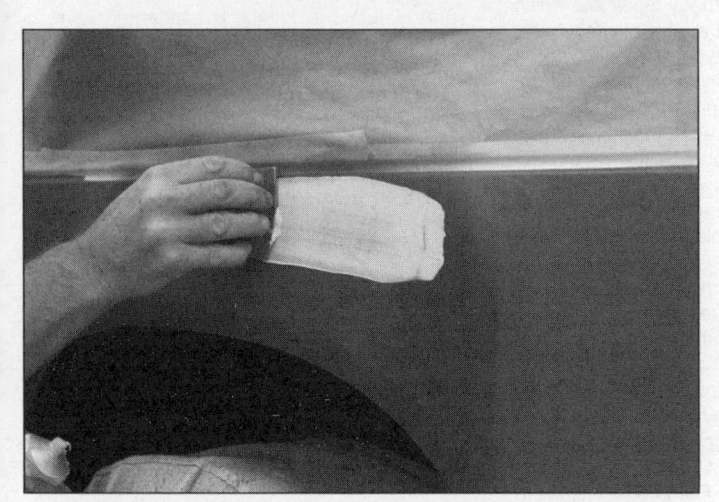

11 The primer will help reveal imperfections or scratches. Fill these with glazing compound. Follow the label instructions and sand it with 360 or 400-grit sandpaper until it's smooth. Repeat the glazing, sanding and respraying until the primer reveals a perfectly smooth surface

12 Finish sand the primer with very fine sandpaper (400 or 600-grit) to remove the primer overspray. Clean the area with water and allow it to dry. Use a tack rag to remove any dust, then apply the finish coat. Don't attempt to rub out or wax the repair area until the paint has dried completely (at least two weeks)

very simple. Lightly rub the scratched area with a fine rubbing compound to remove loose paint and built up wax. Rinse the area with clean water.

2   Apply touch-up paint to the scratch, using a small brush. Continue to apply thin layers of paint until the surface of the paint in the scratch is level with the surrounding paint. Allow the new paint at least two weeks to harden, then blend it into the surrounding paint by rubbing with a very fine rubbing compound. Finally, apply a coat of wax to the scratch area.

3   If the scratch has penetrated the paint and exposed the metal of the body, causing the metal to rust, a different repair technique is required. Remove all loose rust from the bottom of the scratch with a pocket knife, then apply rust inhibiting paint to prevent the formation of rust in the future. Using a rubber or nylon applicator, coat the scratched area with glaze-type filler. If required, the filler can be mixed with thinner to provide a very thin paste, which is ideal for filling narrow scratches. Before the glaze filler in the scratch hardens, wrap a piece of smooth cotton cloth around the tip of a finger. Dip the cloth in thinner and then quickly wipe it along the surface of the scratch. This will ensure that the surface of the filler is slightly hollow. The scratch can now be painted over as described earlier in this section.

Repair of dents

4   When repairing dents, the first job is to pull the dent out until the affected area is as close as possible to its original shape. There is no point in trying to restore the original shape completely as the metal in the damaged area will have stretched on impact and cannot be restored to its original contours. It is better to bring the level of the dent up to a point which is about 3 mm below the level of the surrounding metal. In cases where the dent is very shallow, it is not worth trying to pull it out at all.

5   If the back side of the dent is accessible, it can be hammered out gently from behind using a soft-face hammer. While doing this, hold a block of wood firmly against the opposite side of the metal to absorb the hammer blows and prevent the metal from being stretched.

6   If the dent is in a section of the body which has double layers, or some other factor makes it inaccessible from behind, a different technique is required. Drill several small holes through the metal inside the damaged area, particularly in the deeper sections. Screw long, self tapping screws into the holes just enough for them to get a good grip in the metal. Now the dent can be pulled out by pulling on the protruding heads of the screws with locking pliers.

7   The next stage of repair is the removal of paint from the damaged area and from 2.5 cm or so of the surrounding metal. This is easily done with a wire brush or sanding disk in a drill motor, although it can be done just as effectively by hand with sandpaper. To complete the preparation for filling, score the surface of the bare metal with a screwdriver or the tang of a file or drill small holes in the affected area. This will provide a good grip for the filler material. To complete the repair, see the Section on filling and painting.

Repair of rust holes or gashes

8   Remove all paint from the affected area and from 2.5 cm or so of the surrounding metal using a sanding disk or wire brush mounted in a drill motor. If these are not available, a few sheets of sandpaper will do the job just as effectively.

9   With the paint removed, you will be able to determine the severity of the corrosion and decide whether to renew the whole panel, if possible, or repair the affected area. New body panels are not as expensive as most people think and it is often quicker to fit a new panel than to repair large areas of rust.

10   Remove all trim pieces from the affected area except those which will act as a guide to the original shape of the damaged body, such as headlight shells, etc. Using metal snips or a hacksaw blade, remove all loose metal and any other metal that is badly affected by rust. Hammer the edges of the hole inward to create a slight depression for the filler material.

11   Wire brush the affected area to remove the powdery rust from the surface of the metal. If the back of the rusted area is accessible, treat it with rust inhibiting paint.

12   Before filling is done, block the hole in some way. This can be done with sheet metal riveted or screwed into place, or by filling the hole with wire mesh.

13   Once the hole is blocked off, the affected area can be filled and painted. See the following subsection on filling and painting.

Filling and painting

14   Many types of body fillers are available, but generally speaking, body repair kits which contain filler paste and a tube of resin hardener are best for this type of repair work. A wide, flexible plastic or nylon applicator will be necessary for imparting a smooth and contoured finish to the surface of the filler material. Mix up a small amount of filler on a clean piece of wood or cardboard (use the hardener sparingly). Follow the manufacturer's instructions on the package, otherwise the filler will set incorrectly.

15   Using the applicator, apply the filler paste to the prepared area. Draw the applicator across the surface of the filler to achieve the desired contour and to level the filler surface. As soon as a contour that approximates the original one is achieved, stop working the paste. If you continue, the paste will begin to stick to the applicator. Continue to add thin layers of paste at 20-minute intervals until the level of the filler is just above the surrounding metal.

16   Once the filler has hardened, the excess can be removed with a body file. From then on, progressively finer grades of sandpaper should be used, starting with a 180-grit paper and finishing with 600-grit wet or dry paper. Always wrap the sandpaper around a flat rubber or wooden block, otherwise the surface of the filler will not be completely flat. During the sanding of the filler surface, the wet-or-dry paper should be periodically rinsed in water. This will ensure that a very smooth finish is produced in the final stage.

17   At this point, the repair area should be surrounded by a ring of bare metal, which in turn should be encircled by the finely feathered edge of good paint. Rinse the repair area with clean water until all of the dust produced by the sanding operation is gone.

18   Spray the entire area with a light coat of primer. This will reveal any imperfections in the surface of the filler. Repair the imperfections with fresh filler paste or glaze filler and once more smooth the surface with sandpaper. Repeat this spray-and-repair procedure until you are satisfied that the surface of the filler and the feathered edge of the paint are perfect. Rinse the area with clean water and allow it to dry completely.

19   The repair area is now ready for painting. Spray painting must be carried out in a warm, dry, windless and dust free atmosphere. These conditions can be created if you have access to a large indoor work area, but if you are forced to work in the open, you will have to pick the day very carefully. If you are working indoors, dousing the floor in the work area with water will help settle the dust which would otherwise be in the air. If the repair area is confined to one body panel, mask off the surrounding panels. This will help minimise the effects of a slight mismatch in paint colour. Trim pieces such as chrome strips, door handles, etc., will also need to be masked off or removed. Use masking tape and several thicknesses of newspaper for the masking operations.

20   Before spraying, shake the paint can thoroughly, then spray a test area until the spray painting technique is mastered. Cover the repair area with a thick coat of primer. The thickness should be built up using several thin layers of primer rather than one thick one. Using 600-grit wet-or-dry sandpaper, rub down the surface of the primer until it is very smooth. While doing this, the work area should be thoroughly rinsed with water and the wet-or-dry sandpaper periodically rinsed as well. Allow the primer to dry before spraying additional coats.

21   Spray on the top coat, again building up the thickness by using several thin layers of paint. Begin spraying in the centre of the repair area and then, using a circular motion, work out until the whole repair area and about 5.0 cm of the surrounding original paint is covered. Remove all masking material 10 to 15 minutes after spraying on the final coat of paint. Allow the new paint at least two weeks to harden, then use a very fine rubbing compound to blend the edges of the new paint into the existing paint. Finally, apply a coat of wax.

Chapter 11 Body

9.2 Use a scribe or marking pen to mark the hinge locations

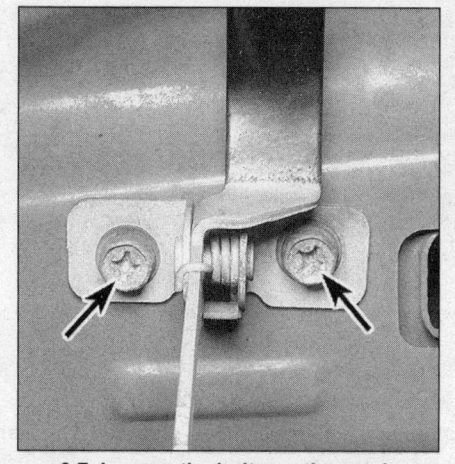

9.7 Loosen the bolts on the catch assembly (arrows) to adjust the position - be sure to mark the edges first so it can be returned to the original location

9.10 Loosen the mounting bolts (arrows) and adjust the latch assembly

6 Body repair - major damage

1 Major damage must be repaired by an auto body shop specifically equipped to perform unibody repairs. These shops have the specialised equipment required to do the job properly.

2 If the damage is extensive, the body must be checked for proper alignment or the vehicle's handling characteristics may be adversely affected and other components may wear at an accelerated rate.

3 Due to the fact that all of the major body components (bonnet, fenders, etc.) are separate units, any seriously damaged components should be renewed rather than repaired. Sometimes the components can be found in a wrecking yard that specialises in used vehicle components, often at considerable savings over the cost of new parts.

7 Hinges and locks - maintenance

Once every 10,000 kilometres, or every twelve months, the hinges and latch assemblies on the doors, bonnet and cargo door should be given a few drops of light oil or lock lubricant. The door latch strikers should also be lubricated with a thin coat of grease to reduce wear and ensure free movement. Lubricate the door and cargo door locks with spray-on graphite lubricant.

8 Windscreen and fixed glass - renewal

Renewal of the windscreen and fixed glass requires the use of special fast-setting adhesive/caulk materials and some specialised tools and techniques. These operations should be left to a dealer service department or a shop specialising in glass work.

9 Bonnet - removal, refitting and adjustment

Refer to illustrations 9.2, 9.7, 9.10 and 9.11

Note: *The bonnet is heavy and somewhat awkward to remove and refit - at least two people should perform this procedure.*

Removal and refitting

1 Use blankets or pads to cover the cowl area of the body and the fenders. This will protect the body and paint as the bonnet is lifted off.

2 Scribe or mark alignment marks around the hinge plate to insure proper alignment during refitting **(see illustration)**.

3 Disconnect any cables or wire harnesses which will interfere with the removal.

4 Have an assistant support the weight of the bonnet. Remove the hinge-to-bonnet nuts or bolts.

5 Lift off the bonnet.

6 Refitting is the reverse of removal.

Adjustment

7 Fore-and-aft and side-to-side adjustment of the bonnet is done by moving the bonnet in relation to the hinge plate after loosening the bolts and by loosening the catch adjusting screws and repositioning it **(see the accompanying illustration and illustration 9.2)**.

8 Scribe a line or paint the edges around the entire hinge plate so you can judge the amount of movement.

9 Loosen the bolts and move the bonnet into correct alignment. Move it only a little at a time. Tighten the hinge bolts and carefully lower the bonnet to check the alignment.

10 If necessary after refitting, the entire bonnet latch assembly can be adjusted in-and-out as well as from side-to-side on the bonnet so the bonnet closes securely and is flush with the fenders. To do this, scribe a line around the bonnet latch mounting bolts

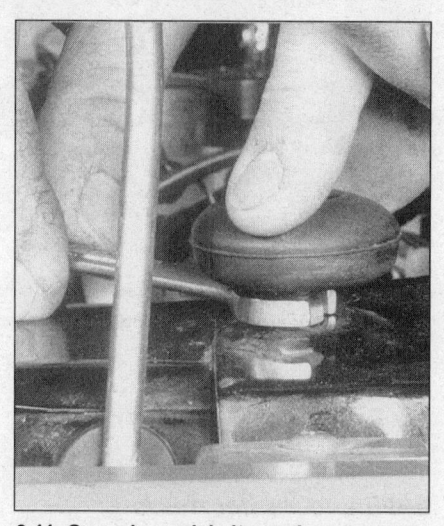

9.11 On early models it may be necessary to loosen the jam nuts before adjusting the bonnet bumper height

to provide a reference point for the side-to-side movement. Then loosen the bolts and reposition the latch assembly as necessary to adjust the side-to-side movement and use a screwdriver to turn the height adjustment screw to adjust the bonnet up-and-down **(see illustration)**. Following adjustment, retighten the mounting bolts and adjustment screw locknut.

11 Finally, adjust the bonnet bumpers on the bonnet so the bonnet, when closed, is flush with the fenders **(see illustration)**.

Note: *On 2000 and later model there are four bonnet bumpers, two in front of the radiator and one behind each headlight assembly mounted on the core support.*

12 The bonnet latch assembly, as well as the hinges, should be periodically lubricated with white lithium-base grease to prevent sticking and wear.

10.1 Typical 1999 and earlier model grille mounting details

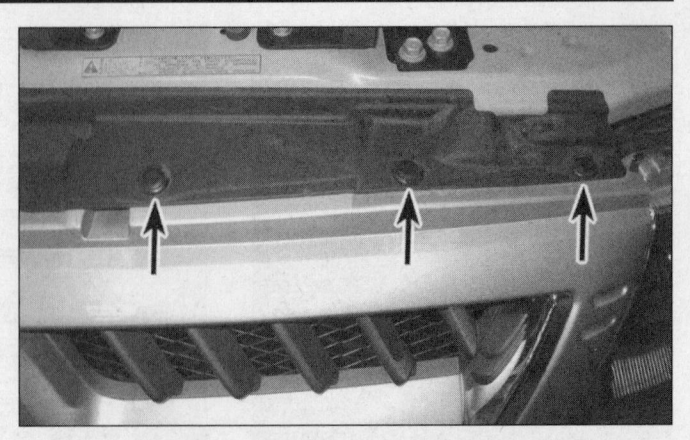

10.4 Use a pocket screwdriver and pop the centre pin up and remove the radiator cover clips (arrows)

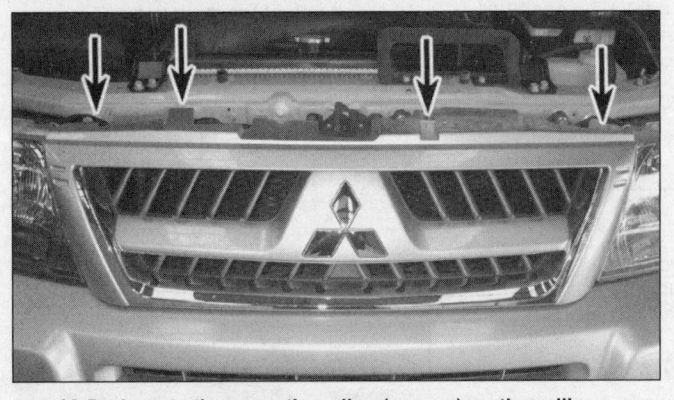

10.5a Locate the mounting clips (arrows) on the grille . . .

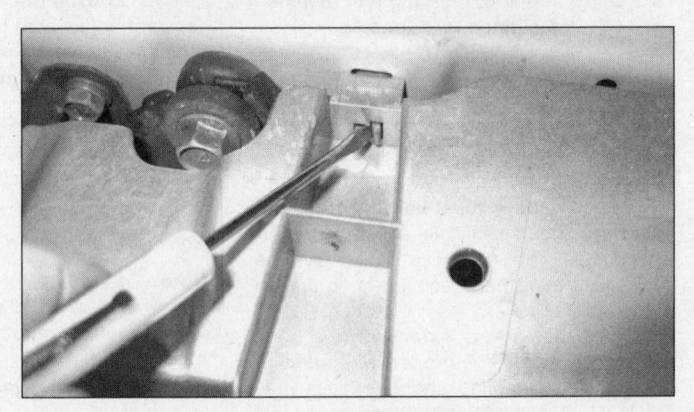

10.5b . . . release the grille mounting clips by moving the clip end to the unlock position

10 Radiator grille - removal and refitting

1999 and earlier models

Refer to illustration 10.1

1   The radiator grille is held in place by clips and, on some models, screws. Remove any screws and disengage the grille retaining clips with a small screwdriver **(see illustration)**.
2   Once all the retaining clips are disengaged, pull the grille out and remove it.
3   To refit the grille, press it in place until the clips lock it in position.

2000 and later models

Refer to illustrations 10.4, 10.5a, 10.5b, 10.5c and 10.5d

4   Remove the radiator cover push clips **(see illustration)** and remove the radiator cover.
5   Disconnect the grille attaching clips **(see illustrations)**.
6   Pull the grill slightly forward and lift the grill out.

11 Bumpers - removal and refitting

Warning: *Models covered by this manual are equipped with Supplemental Restraint System (SRS), more commonly known as airbags. Always disable the airbag system before working in the vicinity of any airbag system component to avoid the possibility of accidental deployment of the airbag, which could cause personal injury (see Chapter 12).*

10.5c NW radiator grille clip locations

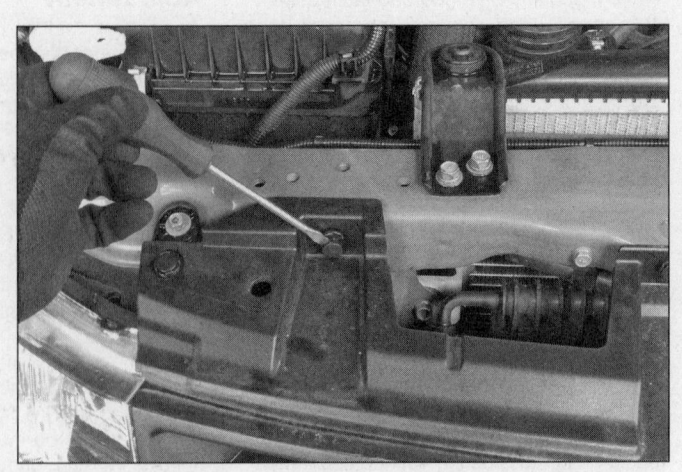

10.5d Removing one of the NW grill clips with a screwdriver

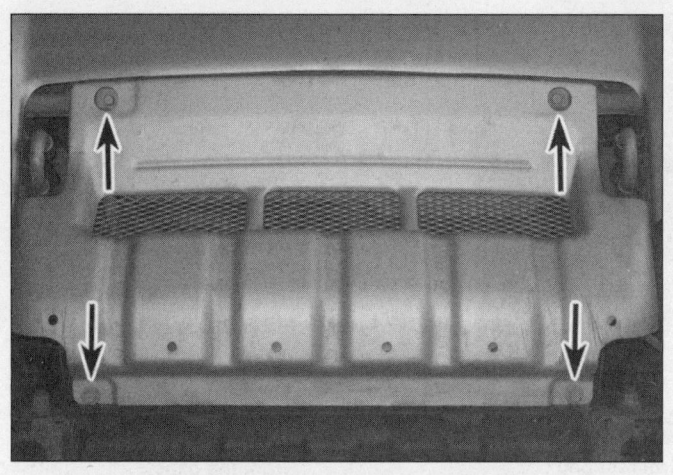

Chapter 11 Body

11.7 Remove the skid plate mounting bolts (arrows)

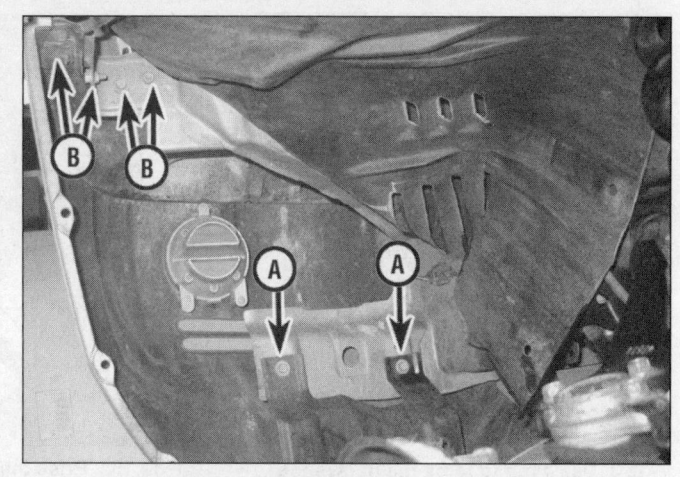

11.9 Remove the front bumper stay mounting bolts (A) and lower facia bolts (B)

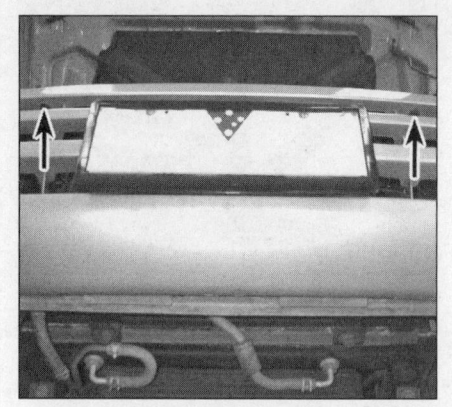

11.11a Remove the front bumper facia lower mounting bolts . . .

11.11b . . . and the upper facia mounting bolts

5 Tighten the retaining bolts securely.

2000 and later models

Refer to illustrations 11.7, 11.9, 11.11a and 11.11b

6 Remove the radiator cover and grille (see Section 10).
7 Remove the skid plate bolts and remove the skid plate **(see illustration)**.
8 Remove the front lower fender splash shield mounting clips (see Section 20).
9 Remove the front bumper stay mounting bolts **(see illustration)** and lower facia bolts.
10 Disconnect the fog lamp electrical connectors (if equipped).
11 Remove the front bumper facia mounting bolts **(see illustrations)**.
12 Refitting is the reverse of removal.
13 Tighten the retaining bolts securely.

Rear

Refer to illustration 11.17

14 Remove the rear mudguards mounting screws and remove the guards.
15 Remove the rear combination lamps (see Chapter 12).
16 With the combination lamps removed, remove the mounting screws that were hidden by the lamps.
17 Remove the top bumper cover mounting screws **(see illustration)** and remove the cover.
18 Remove the lower cover mounting screws from the bottom of the bumper.
19 Remove the bumper cover mounting screws from the ends of the cover from inside the wheel well.
20 Carefully remove the bumper.

Note: *Later models have a two piece bumper, a cover and a reinforcement.*

21 On later models, remove the cover as previously described. Remove the bumper reinforcement mounting bolts and remove the reinforcement.
22 Installation is the reverse of removal.

12 Door trim panel - removal and refitting

1999 and earlier models

Refer to illustration 12.3

Caution: *If the stereo in your vehicle is equipped with an anti-theft system, make sure you have the correct activation code before disconnecting the battery.*

1 Disconnect the negative (-) battery terminal (see Chapter 5).
2 Remove all door trim panel retaining screws and door pull/armrest assemblies.
3 Remove the window crank, using a wire

Front

1999 and earlier models

1 Disconnect any wiring or other components that would interfere with bumper removal.
2 Support the bumper with a jack or jackstand. Alternatively, have an assistant support the bumper as the bolts are removed.
3 Remove the retaining bolts and detach the bumper.
4 Refitting is the reverse of removal.

11.17 Remove the top cover mounting screws (arrows) and remove the cover – later model shown

Chapter 11 Body

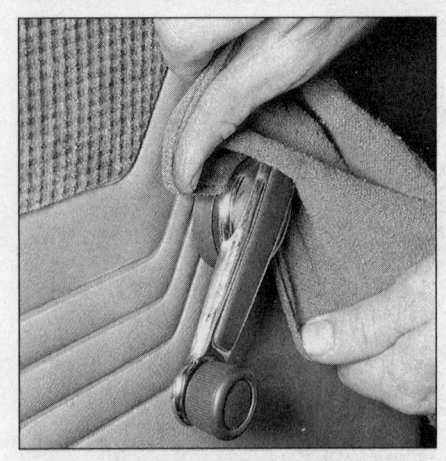

12.3 Use a rag to force the horseshoe shaped clip off the shaft

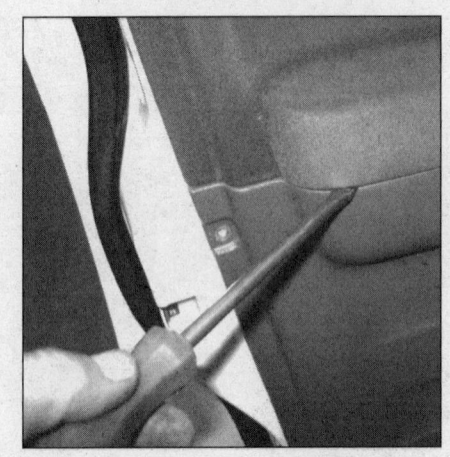

12.10a Prise the arm rest pad ...

12.10b ... and the power window switch from the panel

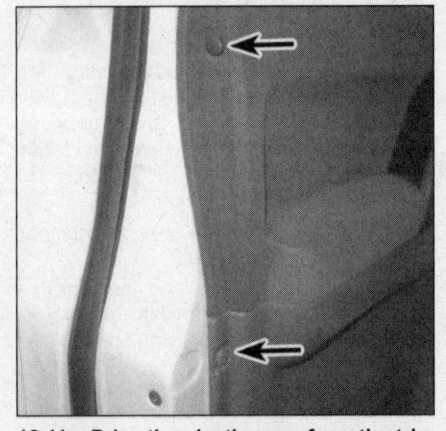

12.11a Prise the plastic caps from the trim panel retaining screws and remove the screws (arrows)

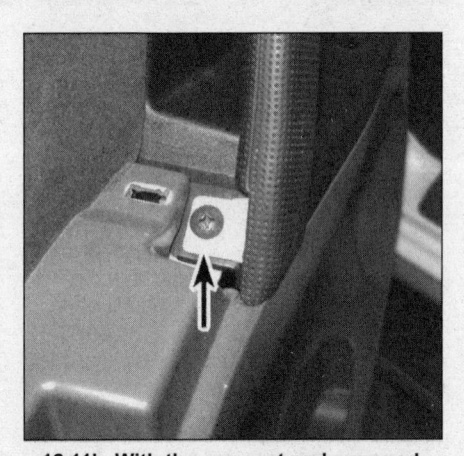

12.11b With the arm rest pad removed, remove the trim panel screw (arrow)

12.12 Insert a putty knife between the trim panel and the door and disengage the retaining clips, work around the outer edge until the panel is free

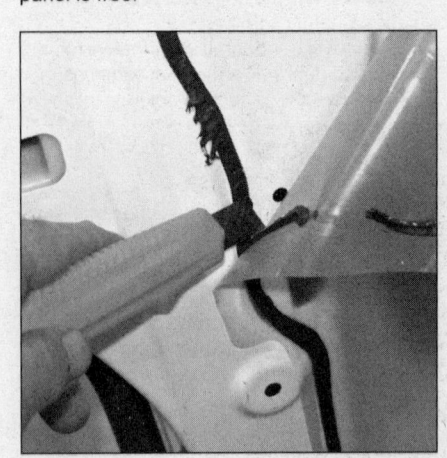

12.14 For access to the inner door, carefully peel back the plastic watershield - it may be necessary to cut the adhesive to prevent the shield from tearing

hook or crank removal tool (or a rag) to pull out the retaining clip **(see illustration)**.

4 Insert a putty knife between the trim panel and the door and disengage the retaining clips. Work around the outer edge until the panel is free.

5 Once all of the clips are disengaged, detach the trim panel, unplug any wire harness connectors and remove the trim panel from the vehicle.

6 For access to the inner door, carefully peel back the plastic watershield **(see illustration 12.14)**.

7 Prior to refitting of the door panel, be sure to refit any clips in the panel which may have come out during the removal procedure and remain in the door itself.

8 Plug in the wire harness connectors and place the panel in position in the door. Press the door panel into place until the clips are seated and refit the armrest/door pulls. Refit the clip and press the manual regulator window crank onto the shaft until it locks.

2000 and later models

Refer to illustrations 12.10a, 12.10b, 12.11a, 12.11b, 12.12 and 12.14

Caution: *If the stereo in your vehicle is equipped with an anti-theft system, make sure you have the correct activation code before disconnecting the battery.*

9 Disconnect the negative (-) battery terminal (see Chapter 5).

10 Prise the arm rest pad, power window switch **(see illustrations)** and inside door handle cover from the panel.

11 Remove all door trim panel retaining screws **(see illustrations)**.

12 Insert a putty knife between the trim panel and the door and disengage the retaining clips **(see illustration)**. Work around the outer edge until the panel is free.

13 Once all of the clips are disengaged, detach the trim panel, unplug any wire harness connectors and remove the trim panel from the vehicle.

14 For access to the inner door, carefully peel back the plastic watershield **(see illustration)**.

15 Prior to refitting of the door panel, be sure to refit any clips in the panel which may have come out during the removal procedure and remain in the door itself.

16 Plug in the wire harness connectors and place the panel in position in the door. Press the door panel into place until the clips are seated and refit the armrest/door pulls. Refit the clip and press the manual regulator window crank onto the shaft until it locks.

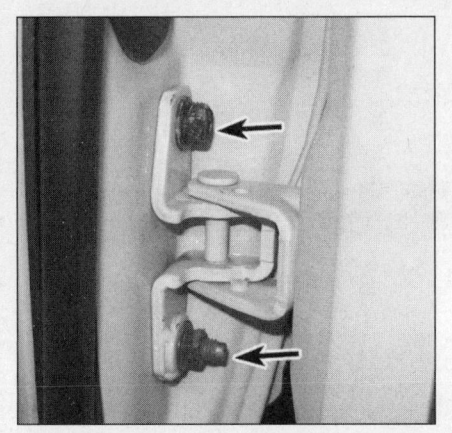

Chapter 11 Body

13.4 Remove the hinge mounting nuts and bolts (arrows) - lower hinge shown

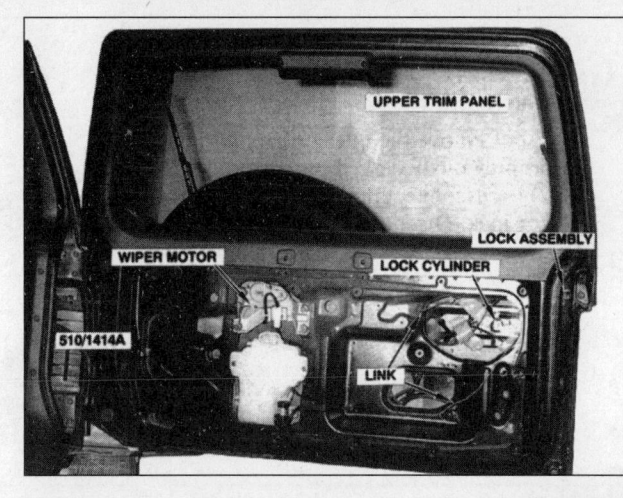

14.4 Typical rear cargo door details

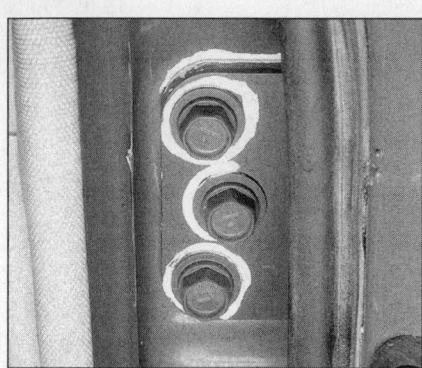

14.3 Scribe or use a marker to make marks around the bolts and hinges on the cargo door

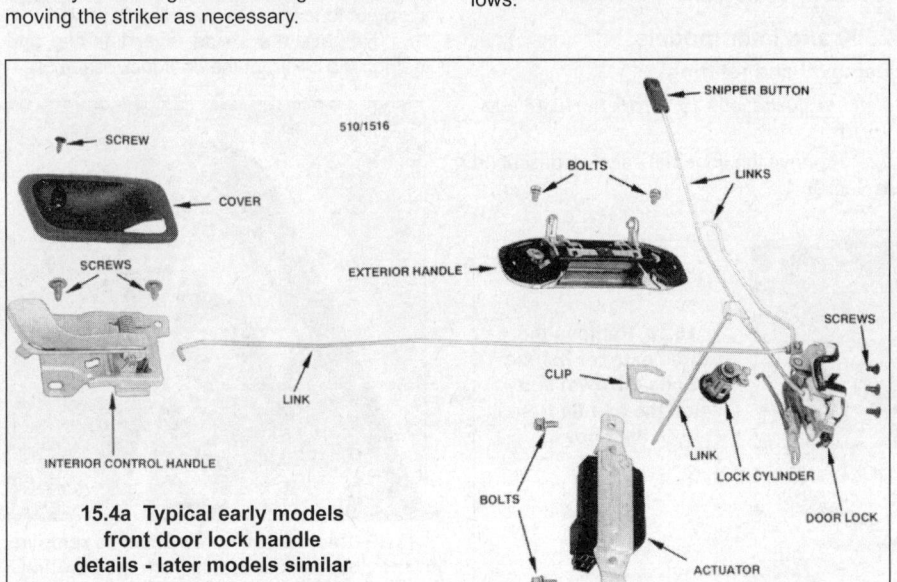

15.4a Typical early models front door lock handle details - later models similar

13 Door - removal, refitting and adjustment

Refer to illustration 13.4

1 Remove the door trim panel (see Section 12). Disconnect any wire harness connectors and push them through the door opening so they won't interfere with door removal.
2 Place a jack or jackstand under the door or have an assistant on hand to support it when the hinge bolts are removed.

Note: *If a jack or jackstand is used, place a rag between it and the door to protect the door's painted surfaces.*

3 Scribe around the door hinges.
4 Remove the hinge-to-door bolts **(see illustration)** and carefully lift off the door.
5 Refitting is the reverse of removal.
6 Following refitting of the door, check the alignment and adjust it, if necessary. The door lock striker can be adjusted both up-and-down and sideways to provide positive engagement with the lock mechanism. This is done by loosening the mounting screws and moving the striker as necessary.

14 Rear cargo door - removal, refitting and adjustment

Refer to illustrations 14.3 and 14.4

Removal and refitting

1 Disconnect any wire harness connectors and push them through the door opening so they won't interfere with door removal.
2 Place a jack or jackstand under the door or have an assistant on hand to support it when the hinge bolts are removed. **Note 1:** *If a jack or jackstand is used, place a rag between it and the door to protect the door's painted surfaces.* **Note 2:** *Remove the spare tyre to help lighten the door weight.*
3 Scribe around the door bolts **(see illustration)**.
4 Remove the hinge-to-door bolts and carefully lift off the door **(see illustration)**.
5 Refitting is the reverse of removal.

Adjustment

6 Following refitting of the door, check the alignment and adjust it if necessary as follows:

a) Up-and-down and side-to-side adjustments are made by loosening the hinge-to-body bolts and moving the door as necessary.
b) The door lock striker can also be adjusted both up-and-down and sideways to provide positive engagement with the lock mechanism. This is done by loosening the mounting screws and moving the striker as necessary.

15 Door latch, lock cylinder and handles - removal, refitting and adjustment

Front door

1999 and earlier models

Refer to illustrations 15.4a, 15.4b and 15.7

Removal and refitting

1 Remove the door trim panel as described in Section 12.
2 Remove the plastic watershield, taking care not to tear it.
3 Remove the inside lever link clip and detach the link from the door lock assembly.
4 Remove the screws that retain the interior handle assembly and lift it out **(see illustrations)**.

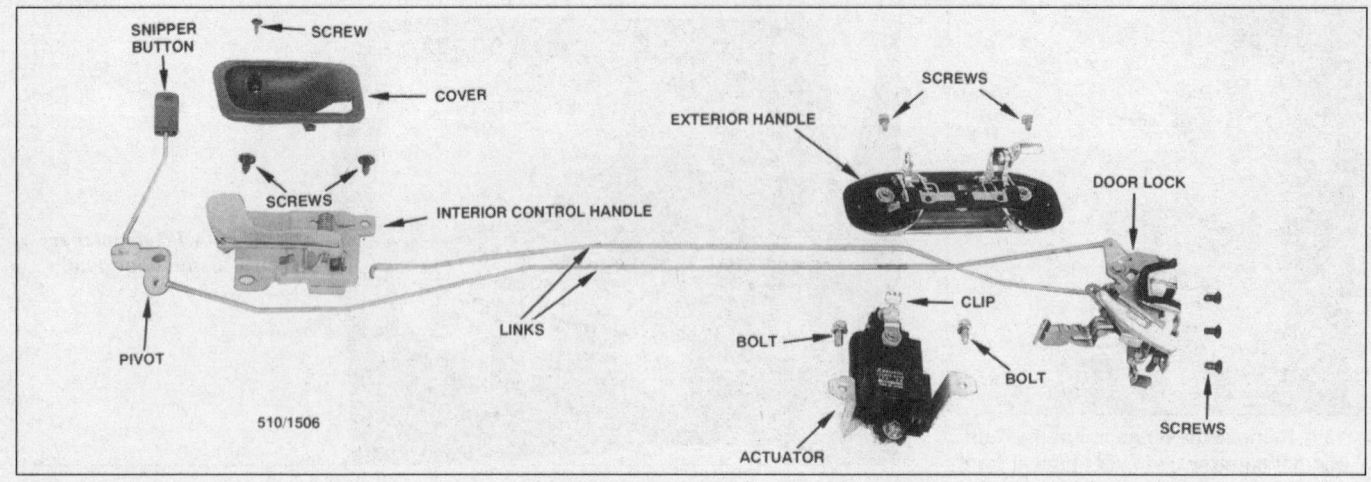

15.4b Typical early model rear door lock handle details - later models similar

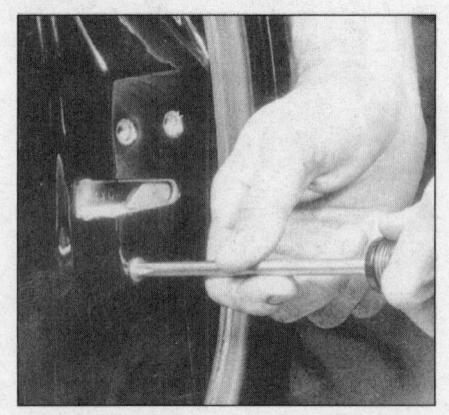

15.7 Remove the screws holding the latch assembly to the door

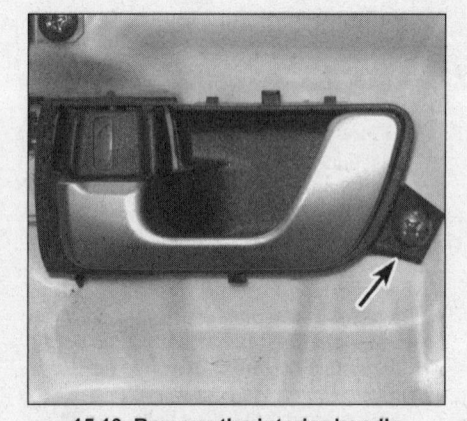

15.13 Remove the interior handle retaining screw (arrow) and pull the handle from the door

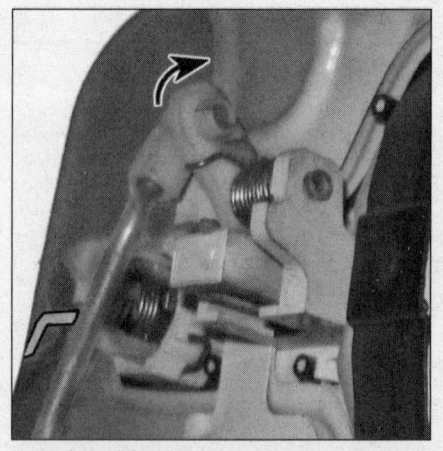

15.16 Disconnect the lock rod clip by rotating the clip up and pulling the rod out

5 Remove the glass run channel.
6 Disengage the door lock rod from the door latch assembly.
7 Remove the door latch assembly mounting screws and lift out the door latch assembly **(see illustration)**.
8 If necessary, remove the two nuts retaining the exterior handle and lift it out.
9 Remove the door lock cylinder through the outside of the door.
10 Refitting is the reverse of removal.

Note: *During refitting, apply grease to the sliding surface of all levers and springs.*

Adjustment

11 To adjust the outside door handle freeplay, remove the retaining clip from the actuating rod and turn the connector up or down to remove the freeplay.

2000 and later models

Removal and refitting

Refer to illustrations 15.13, 15.16, 15.18 and 15.19

12 Remove the door trim panel as described in Section 12.

13 Remove the screw that retains the interior handle assembly, lift it out **(see illustration)** and detach the cable and rod.
14 Remove the plastic watershield, taking care not to tear it (see Section 12).
15 Remove the inside lever link clip and detach the link from the door lock assembly.

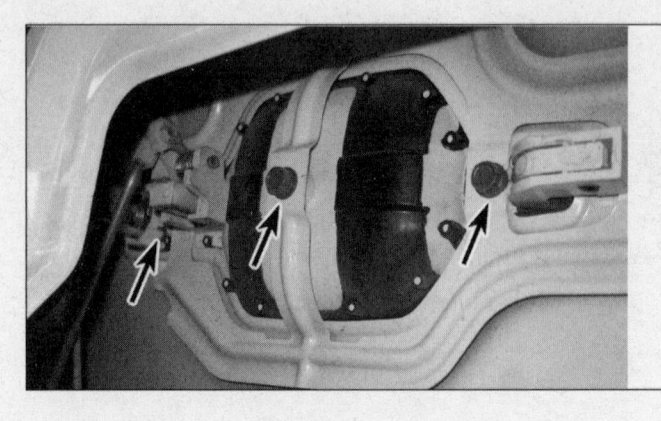

15.18 Remove the three exterior handle bolts (arrows) and pull the handle from the door

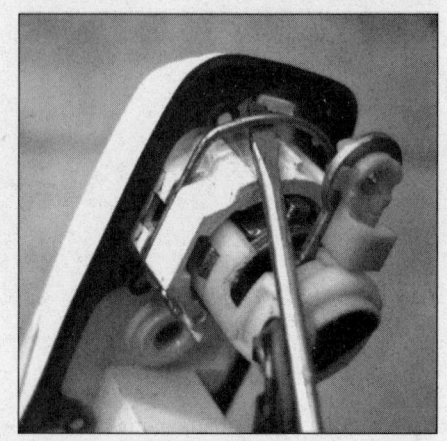

15.19 Use a small screwdriver to remove the door lock actuator from the exterior handle

Chapter 11 Body

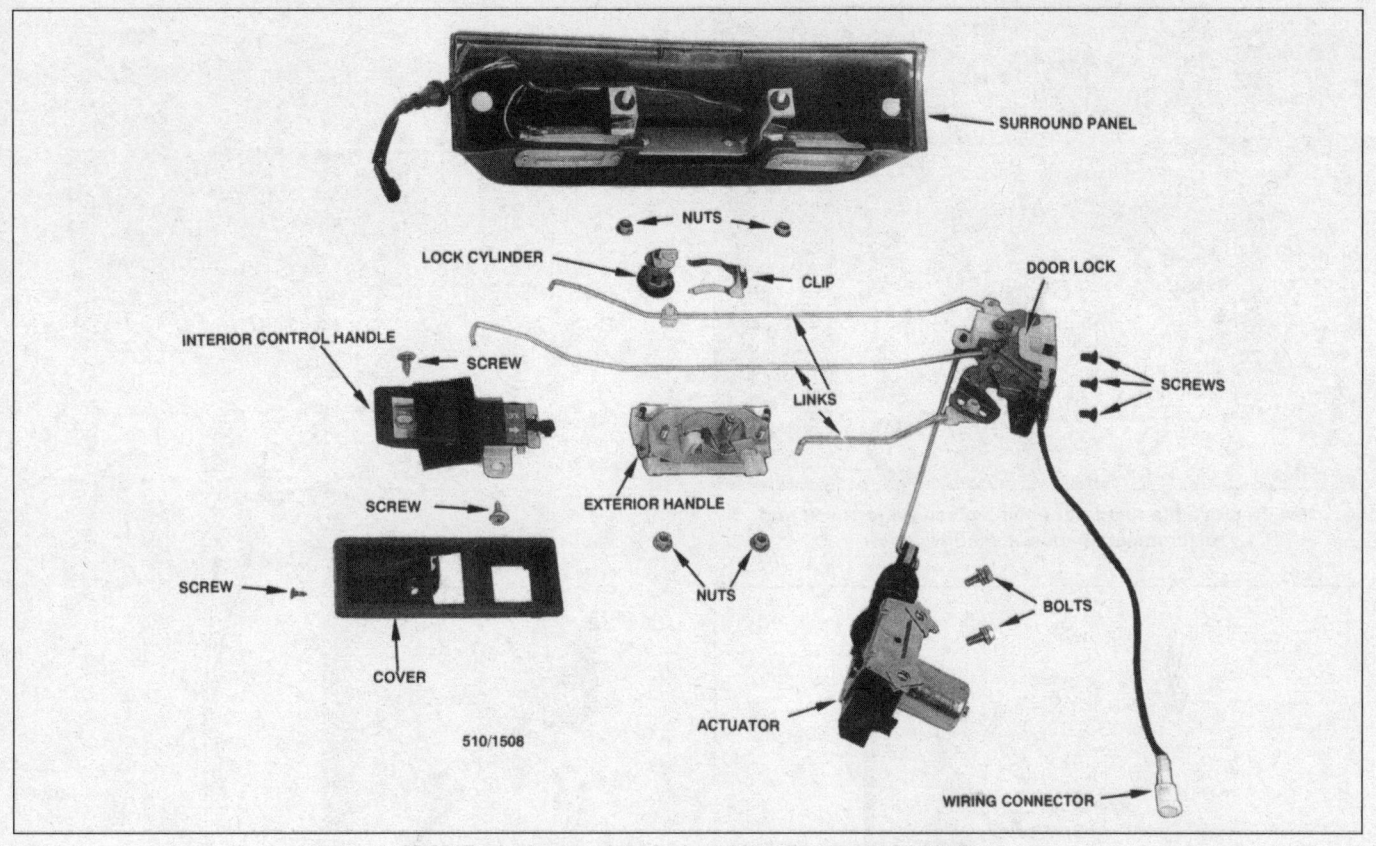

11-11

15.23 Typical cargo door lock and handle assembly details

16 Disengage the door lock rod from the door latch assembly **(see illustration)**.
17 Remove the door latch assembly mounting screws and lift out the door latch assembly **(see illustration 15.7)**.
18 Remove the three bolts retaining the exterior handle **(see illustration)**, disconnect the lock cylinder electrical connector and lift the assembly out.
19 Remove the door lock cylinder retaining clip **(see illustration)** and remove the lock cylinder through the outside of the door.
20 Refitting is the reverse of removal.

Note: *During refitting, apply grease to the sliding surface of all levers and springs.*

Cargo door

Refer to illustration 15.23

Removal and refitting

21 Remove the door trim panel as described in Section 12.
22 Remove the plastic watershield, taking care not to tear it.
23 Remove the inside lever link clip and detach the link from the door lock assembly **(see illustration)**.
24 Remove the screws that retain the interior handle assembly and lift it out.
25 Disengage the door lock rod from the door lock assembly.
26 Remove the door lock assembly mounting screws and lift out the door lock assembly.

27 If necessary, remove the two nuts retaining the exterior handle and lift it out.
28 Squeeze the retaining clip with pliers and push the door lock cylinder through to the outside of the door and remove it.
29 Refitting is the reverse of removal.

Note: *During refitting, apply grease to the sliding surface of all levers and springs.*

Adjustment

30 To adjust the outside door handle freeplay, remove the retaining clip from the actuating rod and turn the connector up or down to remove the freeplay.

16 Door window and regulator - removal and refitting

Refer to illustrations 16.2, 16.4, 16.5a and 16.5b

1 Remove the door trim panel and plastic watershield (see Section 12).
2 Remove the screws from the window bottom channel assembly and lower the window glass **(see illustration)**.
3 Prise the two glass seals from the window opening. Remove the window glass by tilting it to detach the regulator arm from the glass channel and then sliding the glass up and out of the door.

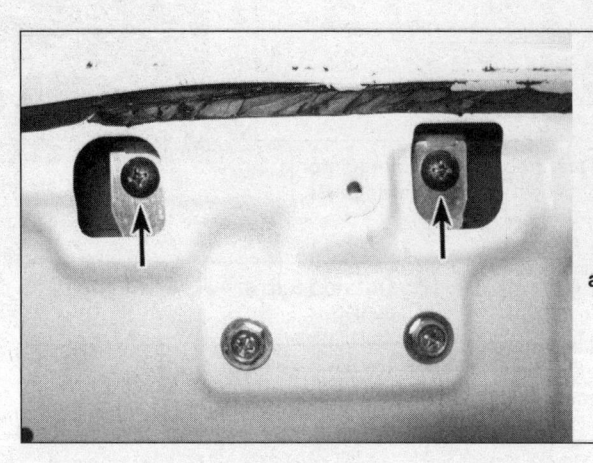

16.2 Remove the screws (arrows) from the window bottom channel assembly and lower the window glass

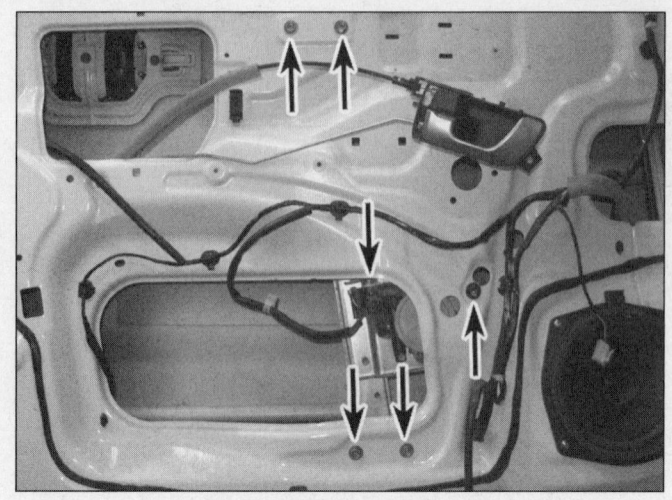

16.4 Remove the regulator retaining screws (arrows) and disconnect the power window motor

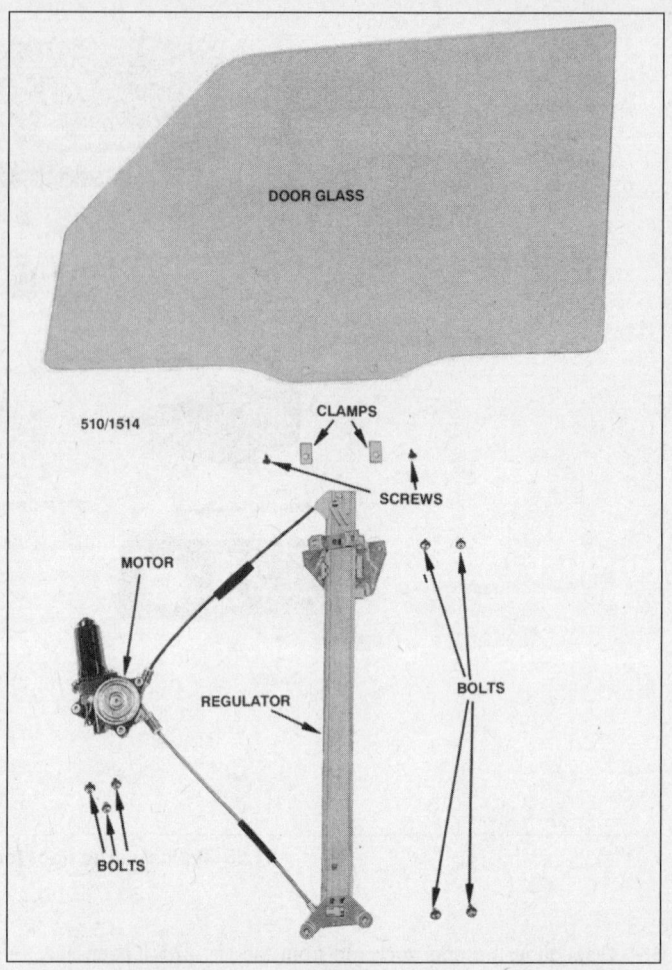

16.5a Typical power widow front door glass and regulator components - earlier model shown, later models similar

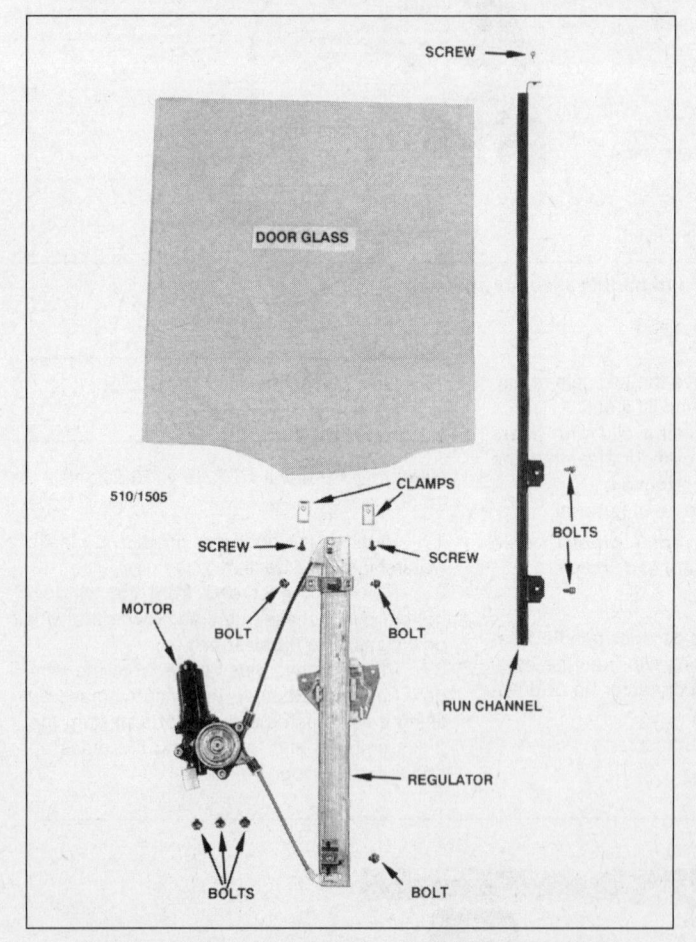

16.5b Typical power widow rear door glass and regulator components - earlier model shown, later models similar

17.1 Carefully prise the mirror cover off the door

4 Remove the regulator retaining screws **(see illustration)** and disconnect the power window motor.
5 Detach the regulator and guide it out of the opening in the door **(see illustrations)**.
6 Refitting is the reverse of removal.

17 Outside mirror - removal and refitting

Refer to illustrations 17.1 and 17.2

1 Open the door and use a small screwdriver to prise the screw cover from the door **(see illustration)**. Note the location of the plastic retaining clips.
2 Remove the screws **(see illustration)**, disconnect the electrical connector on the power mirror and lift the mirror off the door.
3 Refitting is the reverse of removal.

Chapter 11 Body   11-13

17.2 Disconnect the electrical connectors and remove the mirror fasteners (arrows)

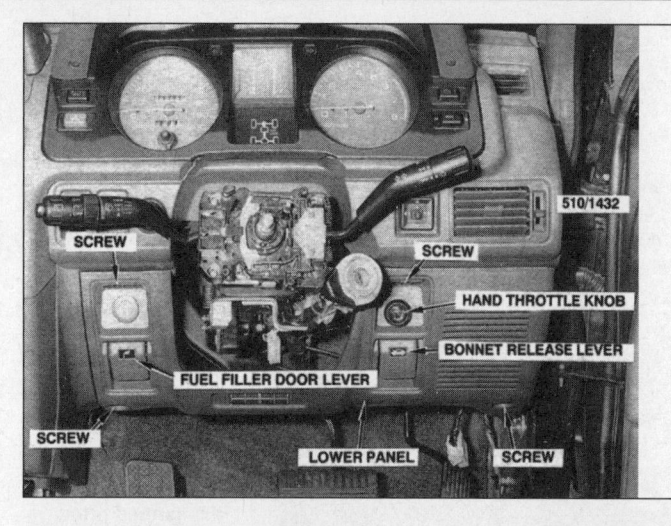

18.2 Typical 1999 and earlier model lower panel details

18 Instrument panel and related trim - removal and refitting

Warning: *Models covered by this manual are equipped with Supplemental Restraint System (SRS), more commonly known as airbags. Always disable the airbag system before working in the vicinity of any airbag system component to avoid the possibility of accidental deployment of the airbag, which could cause personal injury (see Chapter 12).*

Caution: *If the stereo in your vehicle is equipped with an anti-theft system, make sure you have the correct activation code before disconnecting the battery.*

1   Disconnect the negative (-) battery terminal (see Chapter 5).

1999 and earlier models

Refer to illustrations 18.2, 18.5, 18.8, 18.16 and 18.17

2   Remove the instrument panel lower cover **(see illustration)** and disconnect the bonnet and fuel filler door release handles.

3   On the passenger's side, remove the corner instrument panel cover retaining screw and remove the cover.

4   Unclip the glove box stoppers, lower the glove box and remove the mounting screws to remove the glove box.

5   Remove the centre trim panel mounting screws and carefully prise the panel out **(see illustration)**.

6   Remove the heater/air conditioning control and cables (see Chapter 3).

7   Remove the radio and speakers (see Chapter 12).

8   Remove the instrument cluster surround panel **(see illustration)** and remove the instrument cluster (see Chapter 12).

18.5 Remove the centre trim panel retaining screws (arrows)

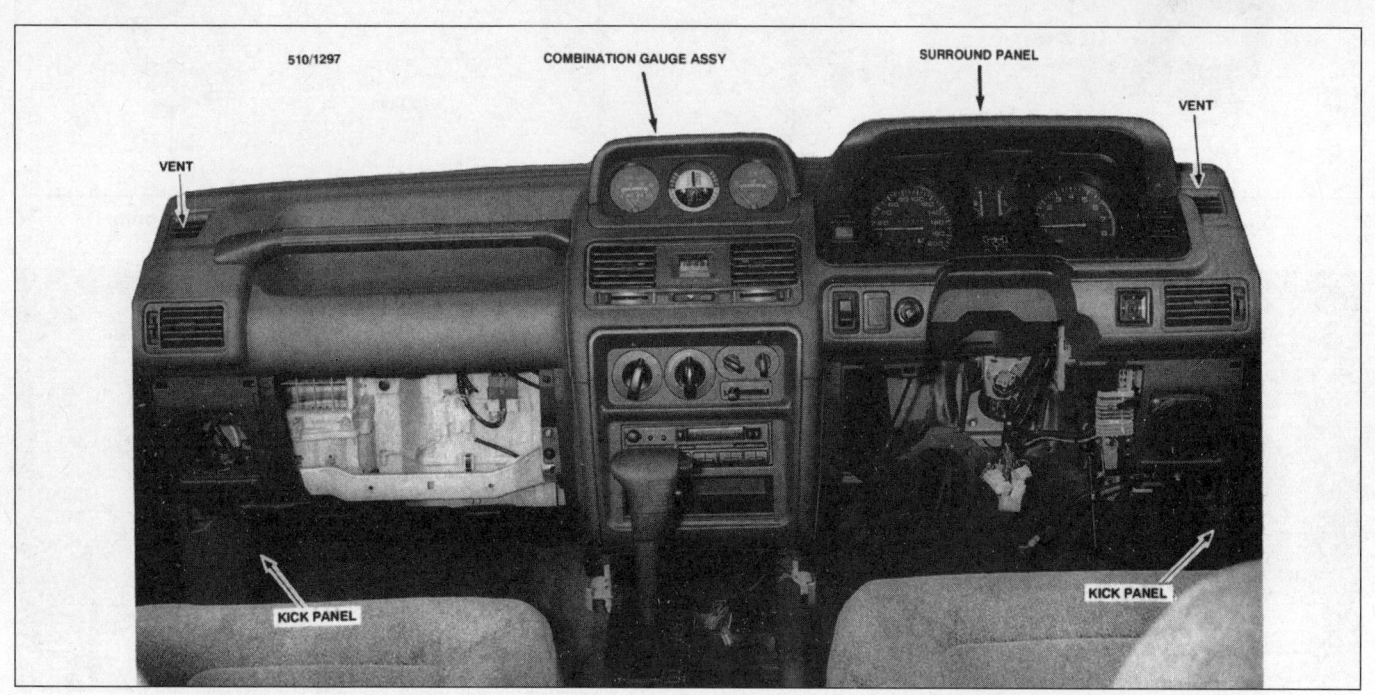

18.8 Typical 1999 and earlier model partially dismantled details

9 Remove the steering column covers (see Section 20).
10 Prise the clock or cover plug from the panel.
11 Prise the side defroster vent covers from the instrument panel.
12 Remove the instrument panel switches (see Chapter 12).
13 On air conditioned models disconnect the ventilation control wire (note its position for refitting).
14 Disconnect the main harness connector from the right side of the instrument panel.
15 Remove and lower the steering column.
16 Remove the instrument panel retaining bolts **(see illustration)** and screws and the pillar trim panels.
17 Make a last-minute inspection to verify that all electrical connectors are disconnected **(see illustration)**, all wiring harnesses are detached, and all fasteners are removed. With help from an assistant carefully pull the instrument panel off and remove it from the vehicle.
18 Refitting is the reverse of removal.

2000 and later models

Refer to illustrations 18.21a, 18.21b, 18.21c, 18.21d, 18.21e, 18.21f, 18.24, 18.25, 18.26, 18.27, 18.28, 18.30, 18.31, 18.33, 18.35, 18.36 and 18.38

19 Remove the centre floor console (see Section 19).
20 Remove the CD player unit (see Chapter 12).
21 Remove the centre trim panel mounting screw **(see illustration)** and carefully prise the centre panel out.
22 Remove the centre display unit and radio unit (see Chapter 12).
23 Remove the air conditioning control assembly (see Chapter 3).
24 Unclip the lower glove box stoppers **(see illustration)**, remove the glove box and disconnect the glove box lamp switch.

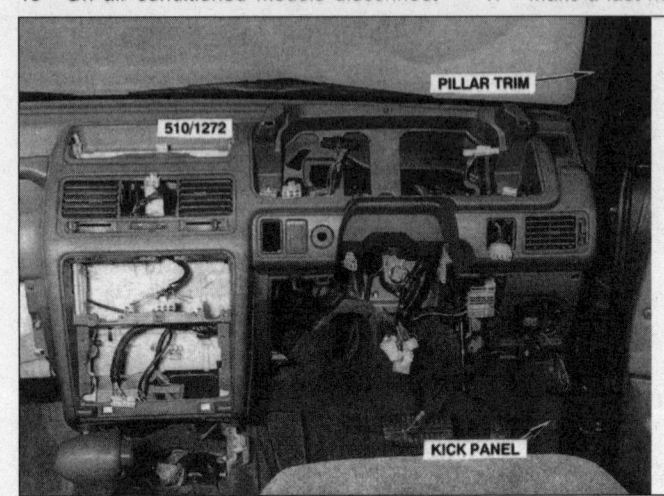

18.16 Typical 1999 and earlier model instrument panel partially dismantled prior to removal

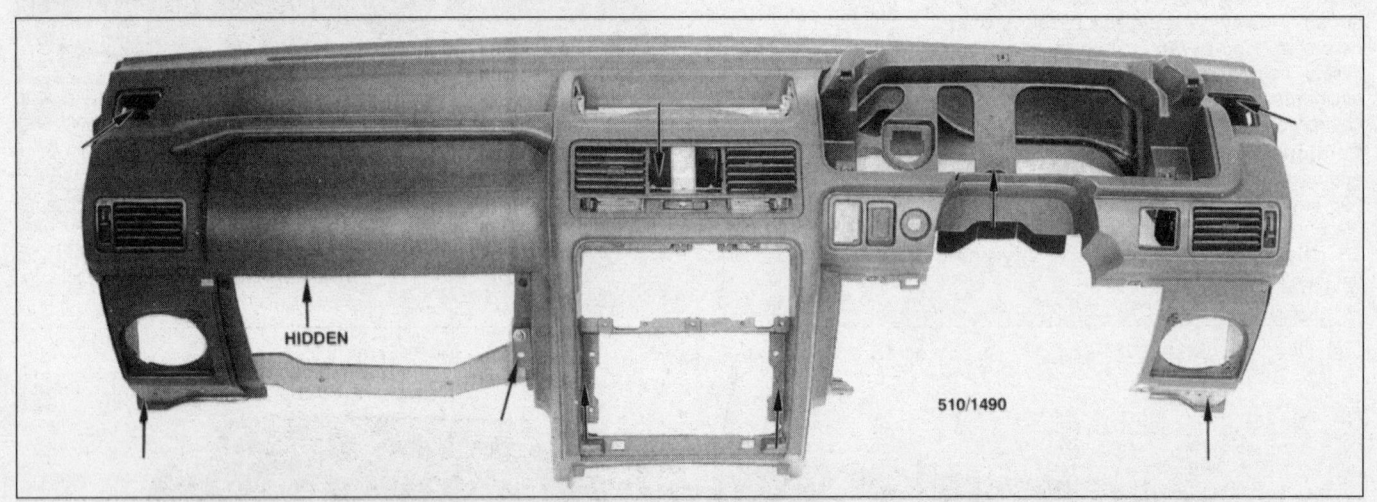

18.17 Typical 1999 and earlier model instrument panel - arrows indicate the locations of the retaining screws and bolts

18.21a Remove the centre trim panel mounting screws (arrows) and carefully prise the centre panel out - NM/NP models

18.21b Removing the RH centre vent - pry from the sound system side to prevent breaking the vent - NT/NW models

Chapter 11 Body   11-15

18.21c Once the majority of the clips are released, remove the vent, disconnecting any wiring - NT/NW models

18.21d The ventilation system control assembly is retained by four clips - NT/NW models

18.21e Use a screwdriver to release the clips holding the audio system facia to the dashboard

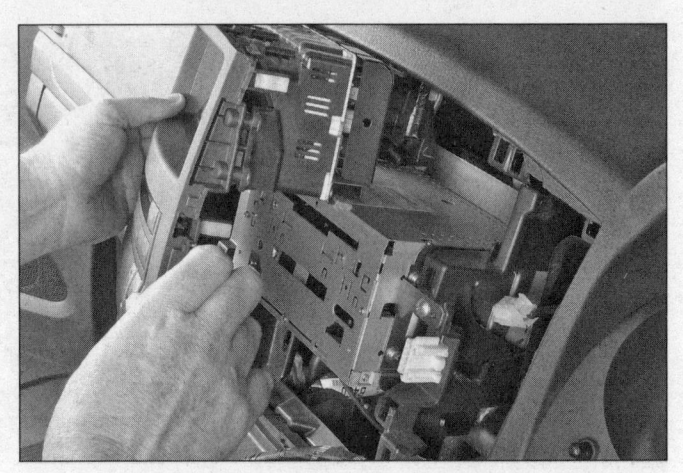

18.21f Remove the audio system facia from the dashboard

25 Remove the upper glove box mounting screws **(see illustration)** and remove the glove box.
26 Disconnect the passenger side air bag module harness connector **(see illustration)** and remove the module to frame bolts.

Caution: *See Chapter 12 for air bag warnings and information.*
27 Remove the instrument panel side covers **(see illustration)**.
28 Prise the air outlet assemblies from the instrument panel **(see illustration)**.
29 Remove the instrument cluster trim panel and cluster (see Chapter 12).
30 Remove the lower panel (knee bolster) mounting screws **(see illustration)** and lower the panel.
31 Disconnect the electrical switches, bonnet and fuel door release levers from the lower panel **(see illustration)**.

18.24 Rotate the lower glove box stoppers to release them

18.25 Remove the upper glove box mounting screws (arrows) and remove the glove box.

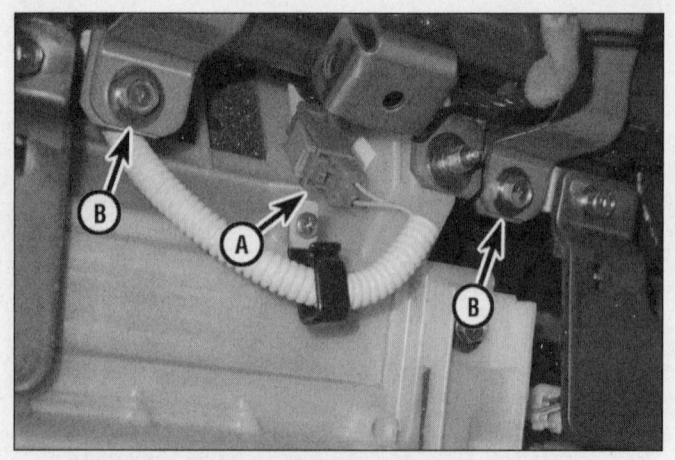

18.26 Disconnect the passenger side air bag module harness connector (A) and remove the module to frame bolts (B)

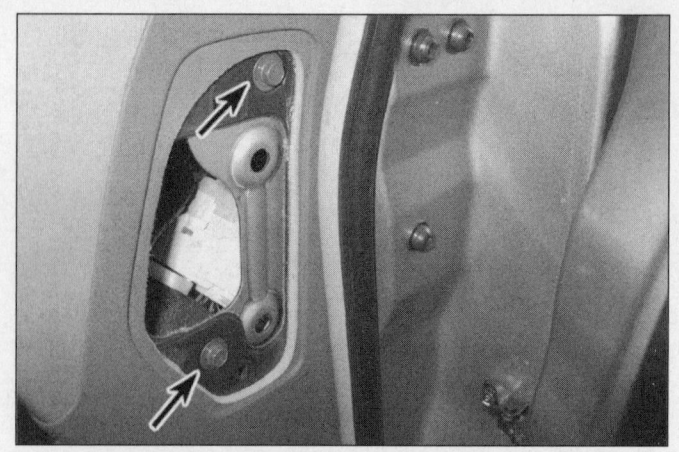

18.27 Remove the instrument panel side cover and the instrument panel side bolts (right side shown, left side similar)

18.28 Prise the air outlet assemblies from the instrument panel noting how the clips are fitted

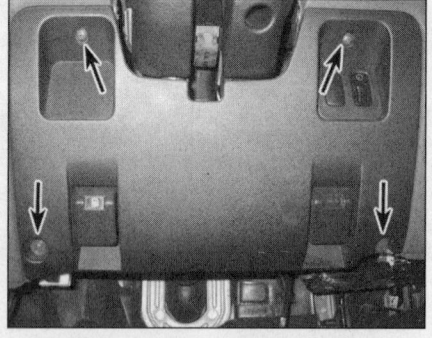

18.30 Remove the lower panel (knee bolster) mounting screws (arrows) and lower the panel

18.31 Remove the release lever mounting screw (arrows) and disconnect the cable to remove it from the panel

32 Remove the steering column covers (see Section 20) and kick panels.
33 Disconnect all electrical connectors and remove the stay mounting nuts/bolts **(see illustration)**.
34 Remove the lower corner panel.
35 Remove the upper pillar handle mounting screws **(see illustration)** and remove the handles and pillar trim.
36 Remove the four steering column mounting bolts and lower the steering column **(see illustration)**.
37 Disconnect all the electrical connections at each side of the instrument panel.
38 Remove the instrument panel retaining bolts **(see illustration)** and screws and the pillar trim panels.
39 Make a last-minute inspection to verify that all electrical connectors are disconnected, all wiring harnesses are detached, and all fasteners are removed. With help from an assistant, carefully pull the instrument panel off and remove it from the vehicle.
40 Refitting is the reverse of removal.

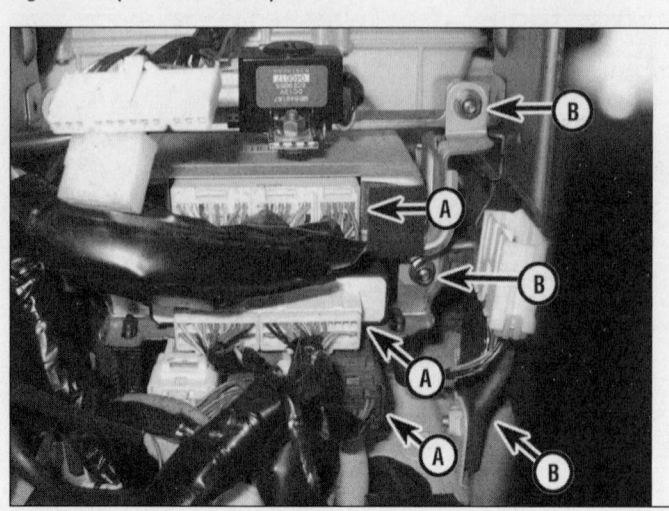

18.33 Disconnect all electrical connectors (A) and remove the stay mounting nuts/bolts (B) - right side shown left side similar

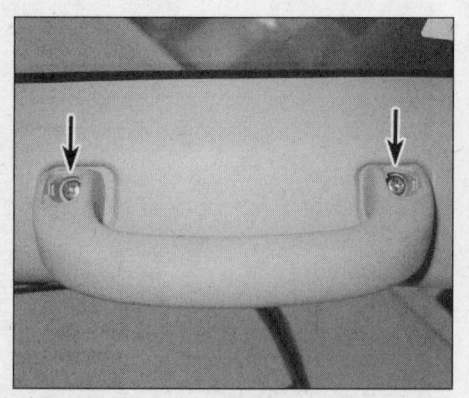

18.35 Prise the screw covers from the upper pillar handle and remove the mounting screws (arrows)

Chapter 11 Body

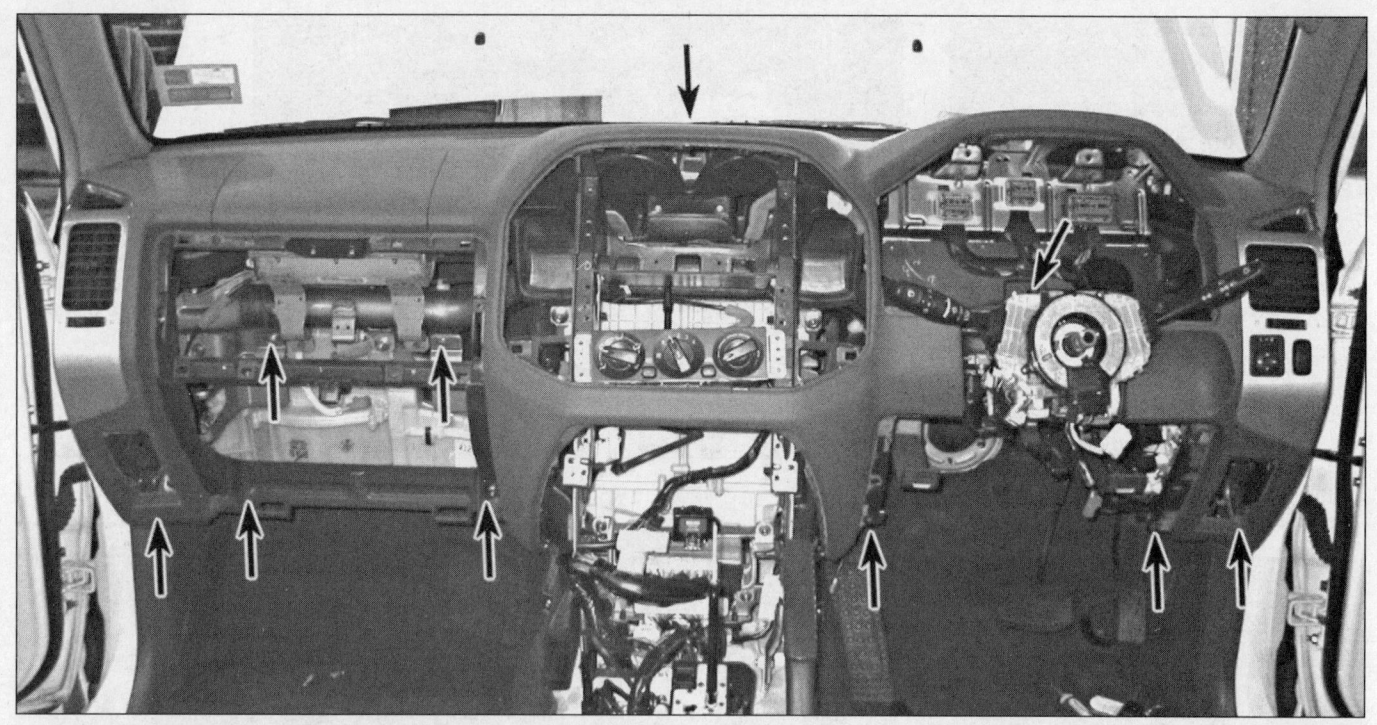

11-17

18.38 Remove the instrument panel retaining bolts (arrows) and screws, then remove the instrument panel

18.36 Remove the four steering column mounting bolts (arrows) and lower the steering column

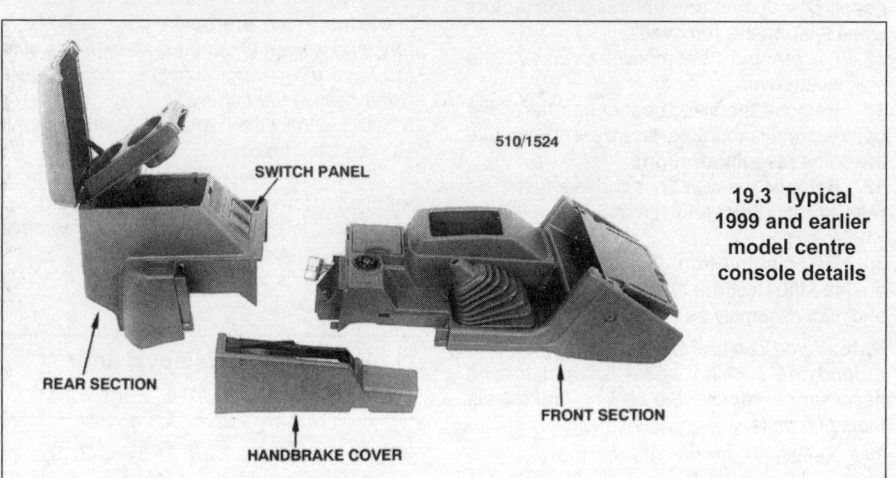

19.3 Typical 1999 and earlier model centre console details

19 Centre floor console - removal and refitting

Warning: *Models covered by this manual are equipped with Supplemental Restraint System (SRS), more commonly known as airbags. Always disable the airbag system before working in the vicinity of any airbag system component to avoid the possibility of accidental deployment of the airbag, which could cause personal injury (see Chapter 12).*

Caution: *If the stereo in your vehicle is equipped with an anti-theft system, make sure you have the correct activation code before disconnecting the battery.*

1999 and earlier models

Refer to illustration 19.3

1 Disconnect the negative (-) battery terminal (see Chapter 5).
2 Remove the shift knob from the shift lever.
3 Remove the panel screws from the console base **(see illustration)**.
4 Lift the console from the passenger compartment.
5 Refitting is the reverse of removal.

2000 and later models

Refer to illustrations 19.9, 19.11, 19.12 and 19.13

Note: *Remove the front seat (see Section 22). It is not absolutely necessary to remove the front seats to remove the centre console, but doing this will save you time and effort while doing this repair.*

Chapter 11 Body

19.9 Remove the indicator panel mounting screws (arrows) and remove the panel - disconnect any electrical connectors when the panel is removed

19.11 Remove the switch panel and the lower centre panel mounting screws (arrows) and remove the panel

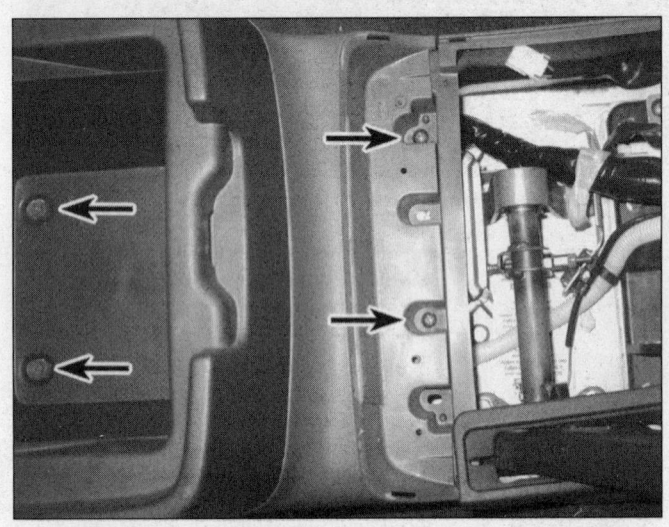

19.12 Remove the rear floor console fasteners (arrows) and remove the unit as a whole

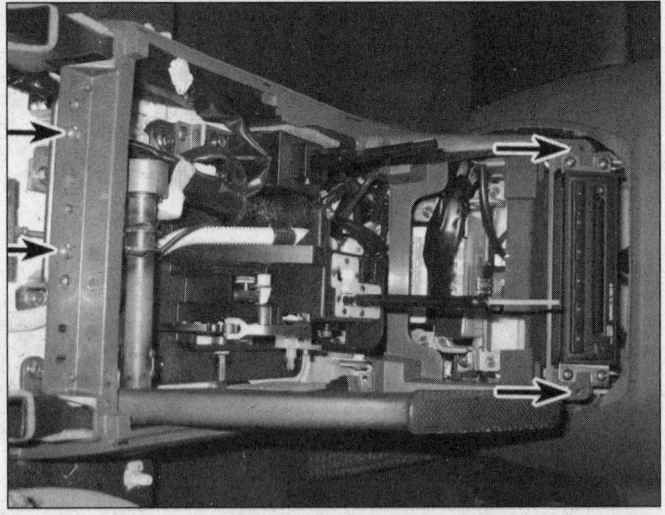

19.13 Remove the front floor console fasteners (arrows) and remove the console and duct assembly as a whole up and around the parking brake lever

6 Disconnect the negative (-) battery terminal (see Chapter 5).
7 Remove the cup holder and parking brake lever cover.
8 Remove the transfer and transmission shift knob (see Chapter 7).
9 Remove the indicator panel mounting screws **(see illustration)** and remove the panel. Disconnect any electrical connectors when the panel is removed.
10 On manual transmissions remove the shift lever cover.
11 Remove the switch panel and the lower centre panel mounting screws and remove the panel **(see illustration)**.
12 Remove the rear floor console fasteners **(see illustration)** and remove the unit as a whole.
13 Remove the front floor console fasteners **(see illustration)** and remove the console and duct assembly as a whole.

Note: *If you can't lift the front centre console around the parking brake lever it maybe necessary to remove the parking brake lever mounting bolts.*

14 Refitting is the reverse of removal.

20 Steering column cover - removal and refitting

Refer to illustration 20.2

Caution: *If the stereo in your vehicle is equipped with an anti-theft system, make sure you have the correct activation code before disconnecting the battery.*

1 Disconnect the negative (-) battery terminal (see Chapter 5).
2 Remove the retaining screws and remove the lower cover **(see illustration)**.
3 Lower the steering column and remove the upper shroud.
4 Refitting is the reverse of removal.

21 Front fender - removal and refitting

Refer to illustrations 21.3, 21.5 and 21.8

1 Raise the vehicle, support it securely on jackstands and remove the front wheel.

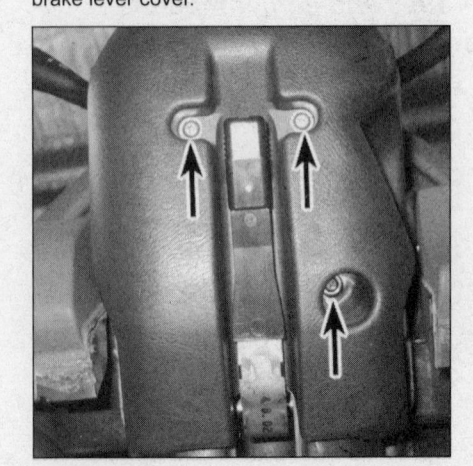

20.2 Remove the retaining screws (arrows) and remove the lower cover

Chapter 11 Body

21.3 Remove the splash shield fasteners and remove the splash shield

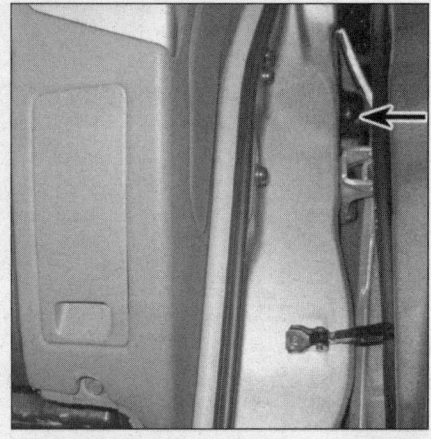

21.5 Open the door and remove the upper and lower fender mounting bolts - upper bolt shown

2   Remove the front bumper and skid plate (see Section 11).
3   Remove the splash shield mounting clips and bolts and remove the shield **(see illustration)**.
4   Remove the front and side turn signal lamps (see Chapter 12).
5   Open the door and remove the fender mounting bolt(s) **(see illustration)**.
6   With the bumper removed, remove the bolt from the lower corner of the fender.
7   On 2000 and later models remove the two mounting bolts from the bottom of the fender (under the vehicle).
8   Remove the top fender mounting bolts **(see illustration)**.
9   Detach the fender. It's a good idea to have an assistant support the fender while it's being moved away from the vehicle to prevent damage to the surrounding body panels.
10 Refitting is the reverse of removal.
11 Tighten all nuts, bolts and screws securely.

21.8 Remove the top (arrows) fender mounting bolts and remove the fender

22 Seats - removal and refitting

Front seats

Refer to illustration 22.1

1   Remove the retaining bolts, disconnect any electrical connectors and lift the seats

22.1 Typical front seat mounting details

from the vehicle **(see illustration)**. On front bench seats, you'll also have to remove the seat belt stalks.
2   Refitting is the reverse of removal.

Rear seats

Refer to illustration 22.5a, 22.5b and 22.5c

3   Firmly push the front edge of the seat

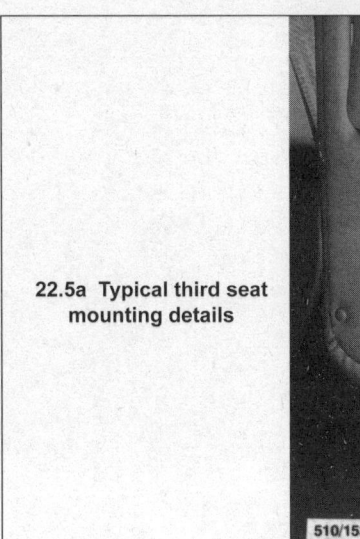

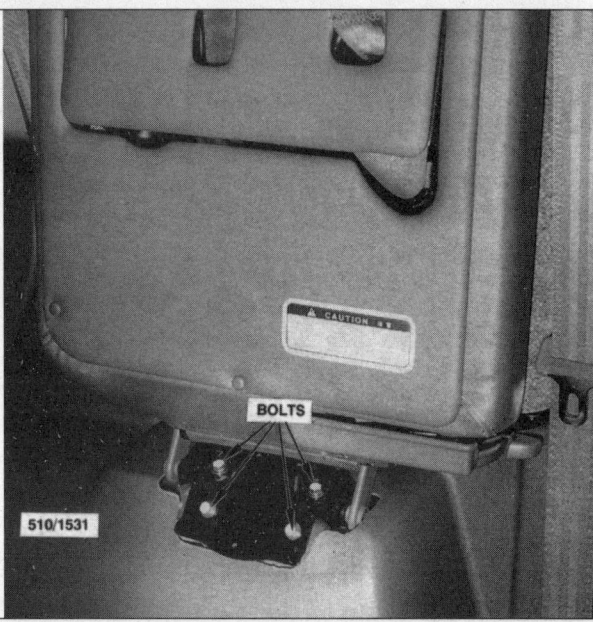

22.5a Typical third seat mounting details

22.5b Typical rear seat mounting details - 2000 and earlier models

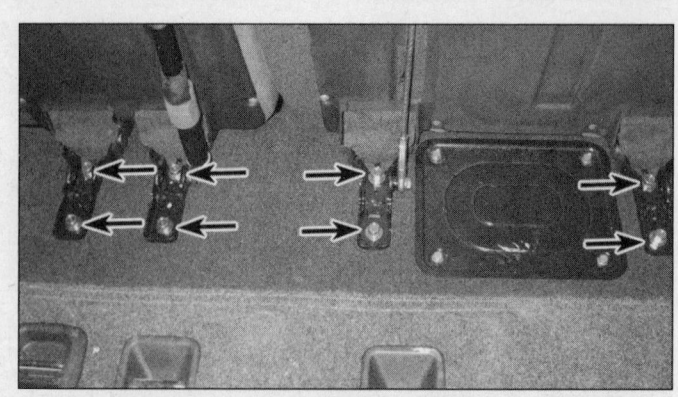

22.5c Remove the seat mounting bolts (arrows) to remove the rear seats - 2001 and later models

cushion rearward and disengage the retaining clips. Lift the front edge upward and remove the cushion.
4　Release the locks and pull the seat backs forward. Remove the trim securing the carpet to the seat back.
5　Remove the seat mounting bolts **(see illustrations)**.
6　Refitting is the reverse of removal..

23　Seat belts - check

Refer to illustration 23.1
1　Check the seat belts **(see illustration)**, buckles, latch plates and guide loops for any obvious damage or signs of wear.
2　Make sure the seat belt reminder belt light comes on when the key is turned on.
3　The seat belts are designed to lock up during a sudden stop or impact, yet allow free movement during normal driving. Retractors should hold the belt against your chest while driving and rewind the belt when the buckle is unlatched.
4　If any of the above checks reveal problems with the seat belt system, replace parts as necessary.

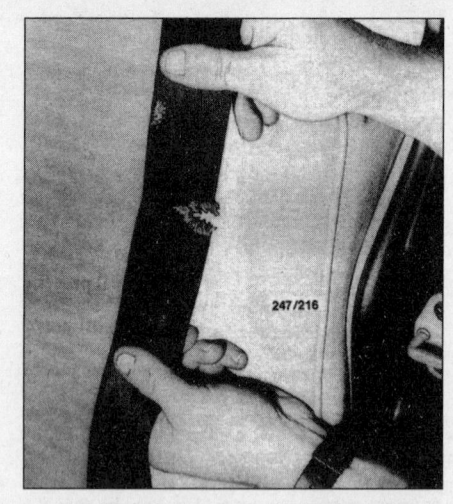

23.1 Check the seat belt webbing for fraying, cuts, burns or other damage

Chapter 12
Chassis electrical system

Contents

	Section		Section
Airbags - general information	24	Horn - check and renewal	23
Audio system - removal and refitting	20	Ignition switch and lock cylinder - removal and refitting	8
Bulb - renewal	13	Instrument cluster - removal and refitting	15
Centre display (2000 and later models) - removal and refitting	19	Power door lock system - description and check	18
Circuit breakers - general information	5	Power seats - description and check	22
Cruise control system - description and check	16	Power window system - description and check	17
Electrical troubleshooting - general information	2	Radio aerial - removal and refitting	21
Fuses - general information	3	Relays - general information	6
Fusible links - general information	4	Steering column switches and airbag clock spring - removal and refitting	9
General information	1		
Headlight housing - removal and refitting	12	Turn signal/hazard flasher - check and renewal	7
Headlights - adjustment	11	Wiper motor - removal and refitting	14
Headlights - renewal	10	Wiring diagrams - general information	25

1 General information

The electrical system is a 12-volt, negative earth type. Power for the lights and all electrical accessories is supplied by a lead/acid-type battery which is charged by the alternator.

This Chapter covers repair and service procedures for the various electrical components not associated with the engine. Information on the battery, alternator and starter motor can be found in Chapter 5.

It should be noted that when portions of the electrical system are serviced, the negative battery cable should be disconnected from the battery to prevent electrical shorts and/or fires.

2 Electrical troubleshooting - general information

A typical electrical circuit consists of an electrical component, any switches, relays, motors, fuses, fusible links or circuit breakers related to that component and the wiring and connectors that link the component to both the battery and the chassis. To help you pinpoint an electrical circuit problem, wiring diagrams are included at the end of this book.

Before tackling any troublesome electrical circuit, first study the appropriate wiring diagrams to get a complete understanding of what makes up that individual circuit. Trouble spots, for instance, can often be narrowed down by noting if other components related to the circuit are operating properly. If several components or circuits fail at one time, chances are the problem is in a fuse or earth connection, because several circuits are often routed through the same fuse and earth connections.

Electrical problems usually stem from simple causes, such as loose or corroded connections, a blown fuse, a melted fusible link or a bad relay. Visually inspect the condition of all fuses, wires and connections in a problem circuit before troubleshooting it.

If testing instruments are going to be utilised, use the diagrams to plan ahead of time where you will make the necessary connections in order to accurately pinpoint the trouble spot.

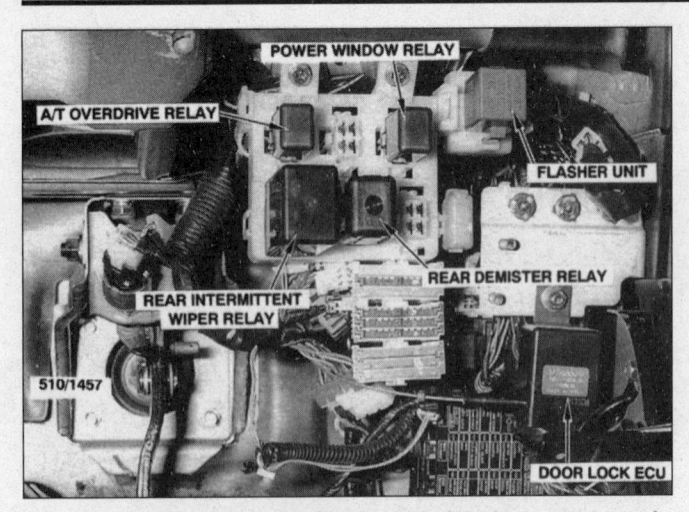

3.1a The fuse block is located in the end of the instrument panel - 1999 and earlier model shown

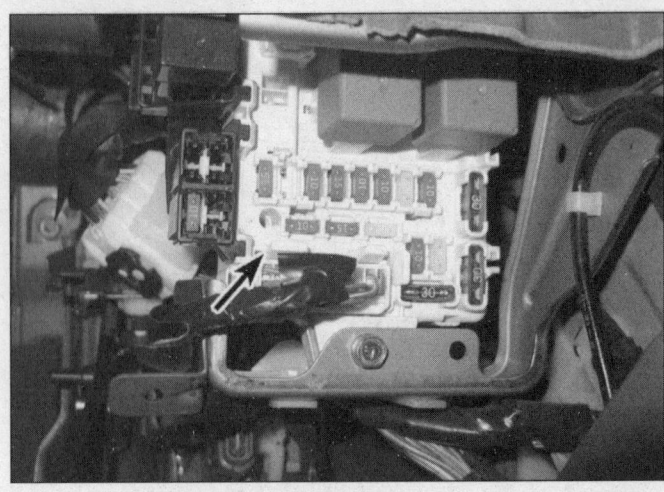

3.1b The fuse block is located in the end of the instrument panel - 2000 and later model shown

The basic tools needed for electrical troubleshooting include a circuit tester or voltmeter (a 12-volt bulb with a set of test leads can also be used), a continuity tester, which includes a bulb, battery and set of test leads, and a jumper wire, preferably with a circuit breaker incorporated, which can be used to bypass electrical components. Before attempting to locate a problem with test instruments, use the wiring diagram(s) to decide where to make the connections.

Voltage checks

Voltage checks should be performed if a circuit is not functioning properly. Connect one lead of a circuit tester to either the negative battery terminal or a known good earth. Connect the other lead to a connector in the circuit being tested, preferably nearest to the battery or fuse. If the bulb of the tester lights, voltage is present, which means that the part of the circuit between the connector and the battery is problem free. Continue checking the rest of the circuit in the same fashion. When you reach a point at which no voltage is present, the problem lies between that point and the last test point with voltage. Most of the time the problem can be traced to a loose connection.

Note: *Keep in mind that some circuits receive voltage only when the ignition key is in the accessory or run position.*

Finding a short

One method of finding shorts in a circuit is to remove the fuse and connect a test light or voltmeter in its place to the fuse terminals. There should be no voltage present in the circuit. Move the wiring harness from side-to-side while watching the test light. If the bulb goes on, there is a short to earth somewhere in that area, probably where the insulation has rubbed through. The same test can be performed on each component in the circuit, even a switch.

Earth check

Perform an earthing point test to check whether a component is properly earthed. Disconnect the battery and connect one lead of a self-powered test light, known as a continuity tester, to a known good earth. Connect the other lead to the wire or earth connection being tested. If the bulb goes on, the earth is good. If the bulb does not go on, the earth is not good.

Continuity check

A continuity check is done to determine if there are any breaks in a circuit - if it is passing electricity properly. With the circuit off (no power in the circuit), a self-powered continuity tester can be used to check the circuit. Connect the test leads to both ends of the circuit (or to the "power" end and a good earth), and if the test light comes on the circuit is passing current properly. If the light doesn't come on, there is a break somewhere in the circuit. The same procedure can be used to test a switch, by connecting the continuity tester to the switch terminals. With the switch turned On, the test light should come on.

Finding an open circuit

When diagnosing for possible open circuits, it is often difficult to locate them by sight because oxidation or terminal misalignment are hidden by the connectors. Merely wiggling a connector on a sensor or in the wiring harness may correct the open circuit condition. Remember this when an open circuit is indicated when troubleshooting a circuit. Intermittent problems may also be caused by oxidised or loose connections.

Electrical troubleshooting is simple if you keep in mind that all electrical circuits are basically electricity running from the battery, through the wires, switches, relays, fuses and fusible links to each electrical component (light bulb, motor, etc.) and to an earthing point, from which it is passed back to the battery. Any electrical problem is an interruption in the flow of electricity to and from the battery.

3 Fuses - general information

Refer to illustrations 3.1a, 3.1b, 3.1c and 3.3

1 The electrical circuits of the vehicle are protected by a combination of fuses, circuit breakers and fusible links. The fuse block is located in the end of the instrument panel under a cover on the right side of the panel **(see illustration)**. On later models the fuse blocks are located under the dash on the right

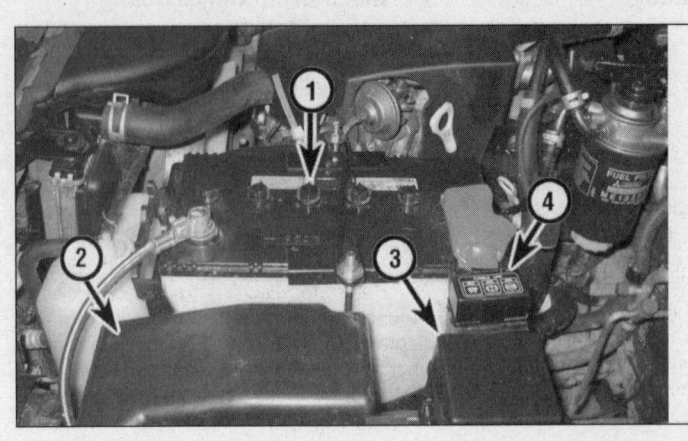

3.1c Typical later model power distribution centre located in the engine compartment

1. Battery
2. Engine fuse block (power distribution centre)
3. Relay box
4. Fusible links

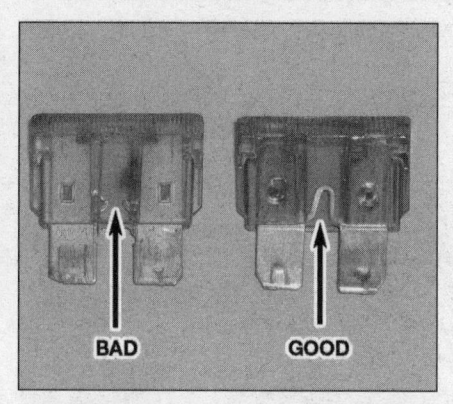

Chapter 12 Chassis electrical system

3.3 When a fuse blows, the element between the terminals melts (fuse on the left is blown)

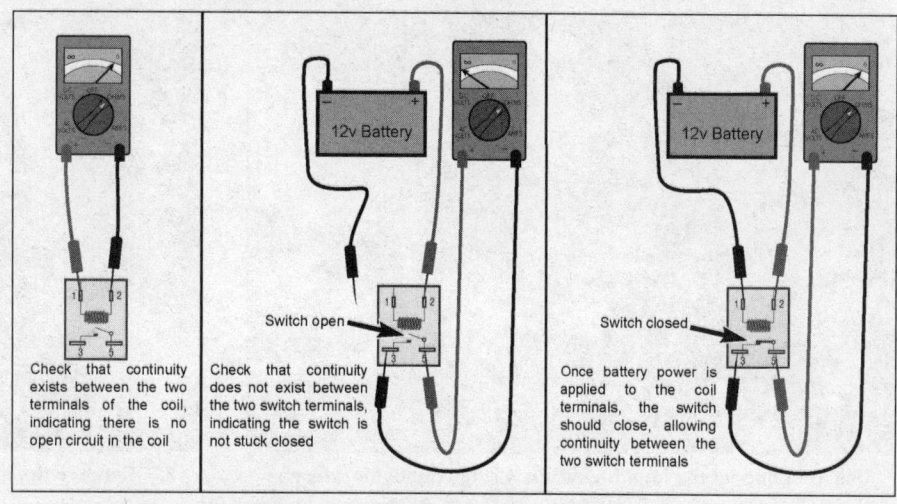

Check that continuity exists between the two terminals of the coil, indicating there is no open circuit in the coil

Check that continuity does not exist between the two switch terminals, indicating the switch is not stuck closed

Once battery power is applied to the coil terminals, the switch should close, allowing continuity between the two switch terminals

4.1 Illustration shows how a typical four-terminal normally open relay operates and is tested using a power supply and an ohmmeter

side and in the engine compartment (see illustrations).

2   Each of the fuses is designed to protect a specific circuit, and the various circuits are identified on the fuse panel itself.

3   Miniaturized fuses are employed. These compact fuses, with blade terminal design, allow fingertip removal and refitting. If an electrical component fails, always check the fuse first. A blown fuse is easily identified through the clear plastic body. Visually inspect the element for evidence of damage (see illustration). If a continuity check is called for, the blade terminal tips are exposed in the fuse body.

4   Be sure to renew blown fuses with the correct type. Fuses of different ratings are physically interchangeable, but only fuses of the proper rating should be used. Renewing a fuse with one of a higher or lower value than specified is not recommended. Each electrical circuit needs a specific amount of protection. The amperage value of each fuse is moulded into the fuse body.

5   If the renewed fuse immediately fails, don't renew it again until the cause of the problem is isolated and corrected. In most cases, the cause will be a short circuit in the wiring caused by a broken or deteriorated wire.

4 Fusible links - general information

Some circuits are protected by fusible links. The links are used in circuits which are not ordinarily fused, such as the ignition circuit.

Although the fusible links appear to be a heavier gauge than the wire they are protecting, the appearance is due to the thick insulation. All fusible links are four wire gauges smaller than the wire they are designed to protect.

Fusible links cannot be repaired, but a new link of the same size wire can be put in its place. The procedure is as follows:

a) Disconnect the negative cable from the battery.
b) Disconnect the fusible link from the wiring harness.
c) Plug in the connectors at each end of the new fusible link.
d) Connect the battery negative cable. Test the circuit for proper operation.

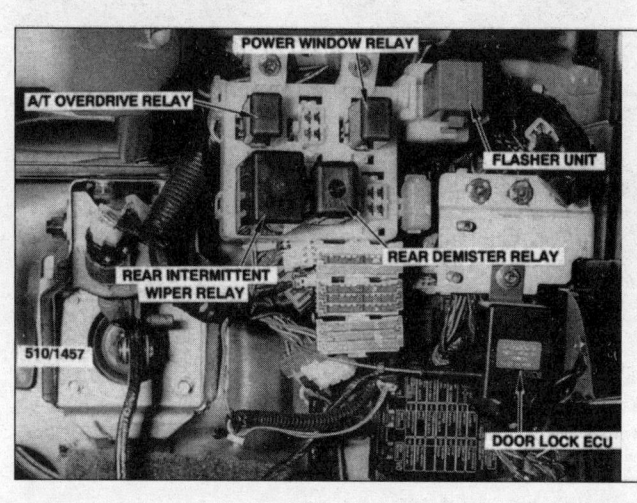

5 Circuit breakers - general information

Circuit breakers protect components such as power windows, power door locks and headlights. Some circuit breakers are located in the fuse box.

On some models the circuit breaker resets itself automatically, so an electrical overload in a circuit breaker protected system will cause the circuit to fail momentarily, then come back on. If the circuit does not come back on, check it immediately. Once the condition is corrected, the circuit breaker will resume its normal function. Some circuit breakers must be reset manually.

6 Relays - general information

Refer to illustration 7.1

1   Several electrical accessories in the vehicle use relays to transmit the electrical signal to the component. If the relay is defective, that component will not operate properly.

2   The various relays are grouped together in several locations (see illustrations 3.1a, 3.1b and 3.1c).

3   If a faulty relay is suspected, it can be removed and tested by a dealer service department or a repair shop. Defective relays must be renewed as a unit.

7 Turn signal/hazard flasher - check and renewal

Refer to illustration 7.1

Note: *On 2000 and later models the turn signal/hazard flasher is controlled by the ETACS (electronic time and alarm control system) located under the dash next to the fuse panel.*

7.1 Typical early model turn signal/hazard flasher location

Chapter 12 Chassis electrical system

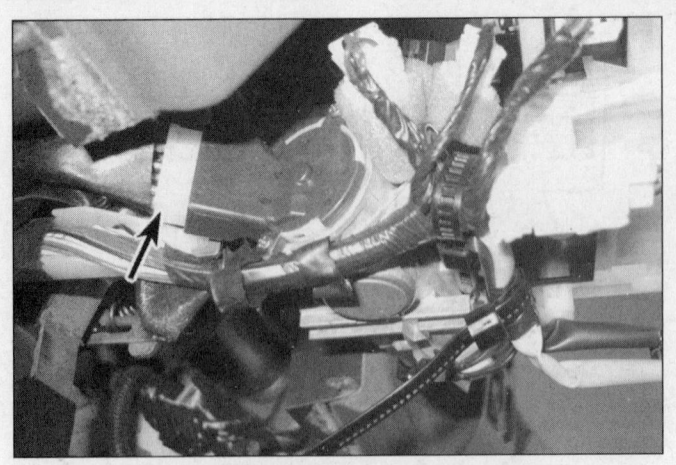

8.5 Disconnect the ignition switch wiring connector (arrow)

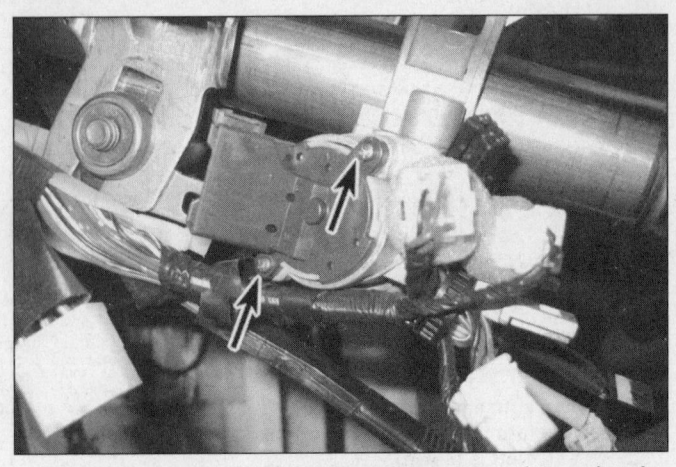

8.6 Remove the ignition switch retaining screws (arrows) and remove the switch

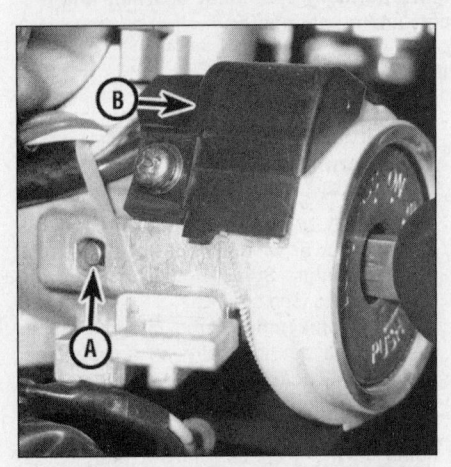

8.8 Remove the key reminder switch (B) and insert a small wire (approximately 1.5 mm) into the hole in the lock cylinder body (A) then remove the lock cylinder

1   The turn signal/hazard flasher, a small box or canister-shaped unit located under the driver's side of the instrument panel **(see illustration)**, flashes the turn signals.

2   When the flasher unit is functioning properly, an audible click can be heard during its operation. If the turn signals fail on one side or the other and the flasher unit does not make its characteristic clicking sound, a faulty turn signal bulb is indicated.
3   If both turn signals fail to blink, the problem may be due to a blown fuse, a faulty flasher unit, a broken switch or a loose or open connection. If a quick check of the fuse box indicates that the turn signal fuse has blown, check the wiring for a short before fitting a new fuse.
4   To renew the flasher, simply pull it out and press in a new one.
5   Make sure that the renewed unit is identical to the original. Compare the old one to the new one before fitting it.
6   Refitting is the reverse of removal.

8   Ignition switch and lock cylinder - removal and refitting

Warning: *The models covered by this manual have a Supplemental Restraint System (SRS), more commonly known as airbags.* *Always disconnect the negative battery cable, then the positive battery cable and wait two minutes before working in the vicinity of impact sensors or steering column to avoid the possibility of accidental deployment of the airbag, which could cause personal injury (see Section 24). Do not use electrical test equipment on any of the airbag system wiring or tamper with them in any way.*

Caution: *If the stereo in your vehicle is equipped with an anti-theft system, make sure you have the correct activation code before disconnecting the battery.*

1   Disconnect the negative battery terminal.
2   Remove the steering wheel (see Chapter 10).
3   Remove the steering column covers (see Chapter 11).
4   Remove the column switch assembly (see Section 9).

Ignition switch

Refer to illustration 8.5 and 8.6

5   Disconnect the ignition switch wiring connector **(see illustration)**.
6   Remove the ignition switch retaining

8.10 Remove the steering column bolts (arrows) and lower the steering column

8.11 Use a hammer and small chisel to cut grooves in the shear-off bolt heads (arrows) and unscrew the bolts with a screwdriver and remove the body

Chapter 12 Chassis electrical system

9.10 Depress the tabs (arrows) and slide the switch from the clock spring assembly

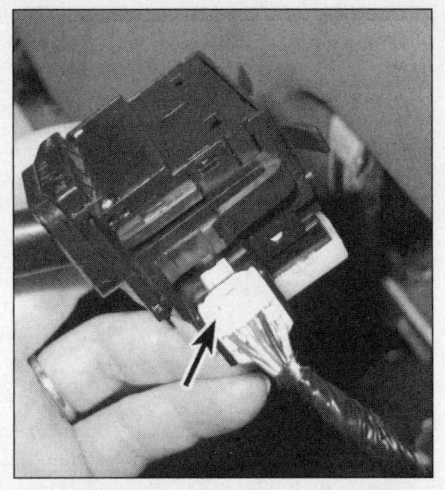

9.11 Disconnect the electrical connector from the switch (arrow) and remove the switch from the vehicle

screws **(see illustration)** and remove the switch.

Key lock cylinder

Refer to illustration 8.8

7   Turn the key to the to the ACC (accessories) position.
8   Insert a small wire (approximately 1.5 mm) into the hole in the lock cylinder body **(see illustration)**.
9   Push on the wire and pull the lock cylinder straight out and remove it from the steering column.

Key lock cylinder body

Refer to illustrations 8.10 and 8.11

10 Remove the steering column bolts and lower the steering column **(see illustration)**.
11 Use a hammer and small chisel to cut grooves in the shear-off bolt heads **(see illustration)**, unscrew the bolts with a screwdriver and remove the switch.
12 Tighten the shear head bolts until the head breaks off.
13 Refitting is the reverse of removal.

9 Steering column switches and airbag clock spring - removal and refitting

Warning: *Models covered by this manual are equipped with Supplemental Restraint System (SRS), more commonly known as airbags. Always disable the airbag system before working in the vicinity of any airbag system component to avoid the possibility of accidental deployment of the airbag, which could cause personal injury (see Section 24).*
Caution: *If the stereo in your vehicle is equipped with an anti-theft system, make sure you have the correct activation code before disconnecting the battery.*

Steering column switches

1   Disconnect the negative battery cable from the battery.
2   Remove the steering column covers (see Chapter 11).
3   Remove the steering wheel (see Chapter 10).

1999 and earlier models

4   Use wire cutters to remove the cable band.
5   Remove the screws holding the steering column switch.
6   Remove the steering column switch.

2000 and later models

Refer to illustrations 9.10 and 9.11

7   Disconnect the negative battery cable.
Warning: *Disconnect the cable(s) from the negative battery terminal(s) and wait at least two minutes for the airbag power supply to be depleted (see Section 24).*
8   Remove the steering column covers (see Chapter 11).
9   Remove the steering wheel and airbag module (see Chapter 10).

10 Remove the steering column switch(s) by depressing the tabs **(see illustration)** and slide the switch from the switch body.
11 Disconnect the electrical connector from the switch **(see illustration)**.
12 Remove the clock spring (see Steps 15 through 21).
13 Using a small pocket screwdriver prise the end of the switch body out to allow it to slide off of the steering column.
14 Refitting is the reverse of removal.

Airbag clock spring

Refer to illustrations 9.20 and 9.21

15 Set the steering wheel and wheels in a straight ahead position, then remove the ignition key.
16 Disconnect the negative battery cable.
Warning: *Disconnect the cable(s) from the negative battery terminal(s) and wait at least two minutes for the airbag power supply to be depleted (see Section 24).*
17 Remove the steering column covers (see Chapter 11).
18 Remove the steering wheel and airbag module (see Chapter 10).
19 Remove the steering column switches (see Steps 7 through 11).
20 Verify that the clock spring alignment marks are in the correct position **(see illustration)**.
21 Remove the clock spring retaining screws **(see illustration),** disengage the claw clips from the column switch and remove the clock spring.
Caution: *Do not allow the clock spring to rotate when it is removed or damage to the clock spring may occur.*
22 Before refitting the clock spring make sure it is aligned properly. The arrows on the switch must be aligned and the electrical connector cavity must be at the 6 o'clock position. Take note of any other alignment marks which may be present on the airbag clock spring, and of any other instructions which maybe printed on the clock spring. If the clock spring is not aligned properly, rotate the hub of the clock spring fully clockwise (don't apply too

9.20 Clock spring alignment marks (arrows)

9.21 Remove the clock spring retaining screws (arrows), disengage the claw clips from the column switch body and remove the clock spring

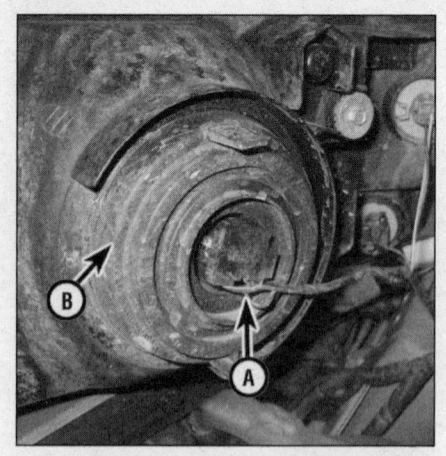

10.1 Disconnect the electrical connector to the bulb (A), then remove the rubber cover (B) to expose the retaining clip

10.2 Detach the spring retainer and pull the bulb straight out of the housing

much force) and then turn it back about 3 times anti-clockwise to align the mating marks **(see illustration 9.20)**.
23   Refit the clock spring on to the steering column body with the electrical cavity at the 6 o'clock position, press the clock spring onto the switch body and verify the alignment marks are correct. Refit the mounting screws and tighten them securely.
24   The remaining steps are the reverse of removal.

10   Headlights - renewal

Refer to illustrations 10.1 and 10.2

1   Disconnect the electrical connector **(see illustration)** at the bulb, then pull out the socket cover and connector.
2   Detach the spring retainer **(see illustration)** and rotate it out of the way, then withdraw the bulb assembly from the headlight housing.
3   Insert the new bulb assembly into the headlight housing, secure it with the spring retainer, refit the socket cover and plug in the connector.

Note: *To renew the left side bulb it's necessary to remove the engine coolant reservoir.*

Caution: *Never hold a halogen bulb with your bare hands, a dirty rag, etc. The oils on the glass will cause the bulb to create a hot spot and fail prematurely. If any oil or dirt gets on the glass, clean it thoroughly with lacquer thinner or alcohol before refitting.*

11   Headlights - adjustment

Refer to illustration 11.6

Note: *The headlights must be aimed correctly. If adjusted incorrectly they could blind the driver of an oncoming vehicle and cause a serious accident or seriously reduce your ability to see the road. The headlights should be checked for proper aim every 12 months and any time a new headlight is fitted or front end body work is performed. It should be emphasized that the following procedure is only an interim step which will provide temporary adjustment until the headlights can be adjusted by a properly equipped shop.*

1   Headlights have two spring loaded adjusting screws, one on the top controlling up-and-down movement and one on the side controlling left-and-right movement.
2   There are several methods of adjusting the headlights. The simplest method requires a blank wall 8 meters in front of the vehicle and a level floor.
3   Position masking tape vertically on the wall in reference to the vehicle centreline and the centrelines of both headlights.
4   Position a horizontal tape line in reference to the centreline of all the headlights.

Note: *It may be easier to position the tape on the wall with the vehicle parked only a few centimetres away.*

5   Adjustment should be made with the vehicle sitting level, the fuel tank half-full and no unusually heavy load in the vehicle.
6   Starting with the low beam adjustment, position the high-intensity zone so it's five centimetres below the horizontal line and five centimetres to the side of the headlight vertical line **(see illustration)**, away from oncoming traffic. Adjustment is made by turning the top adjustment screw clockwise to raise the beam and anti-clockwise to lower it. The adjusting screw on the side is used in the same manner to move the beam left or right.
7   With the high beams on, the high-intensity zone should be vertically centred with the exact centre just below the horizontal line.

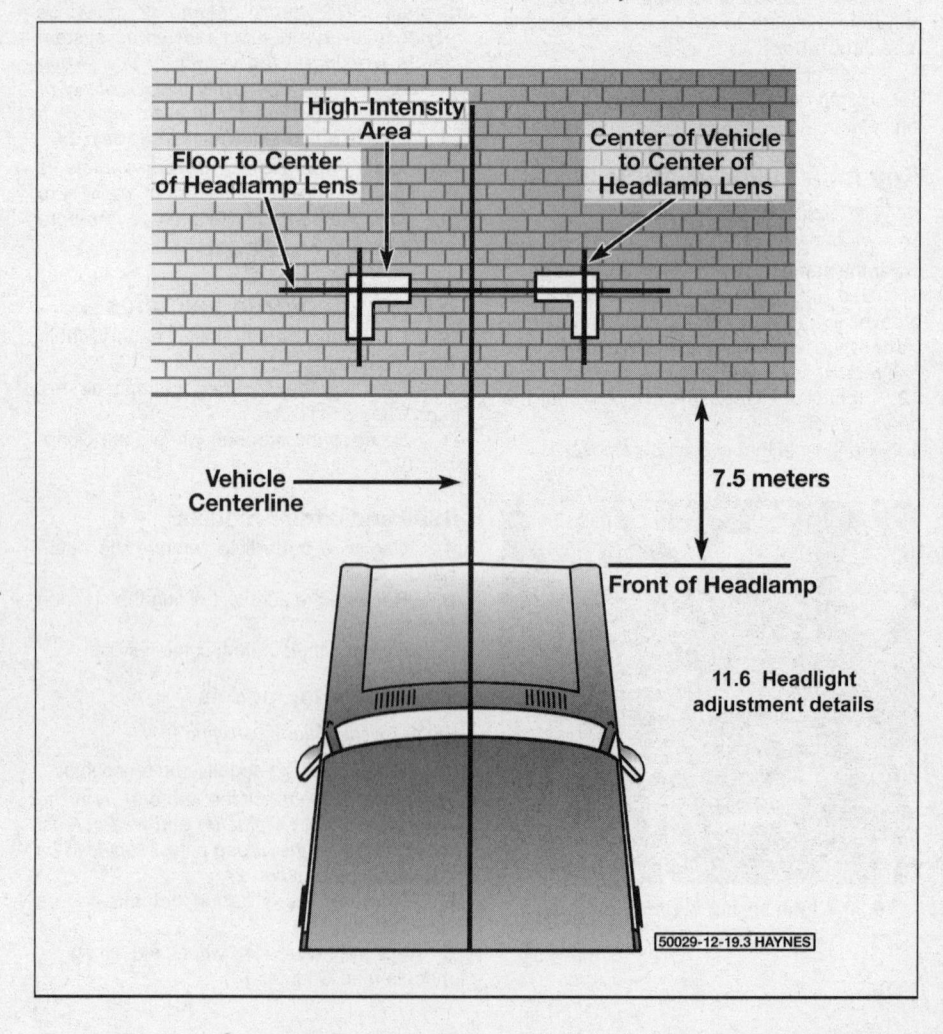

11.6 Headlight adjustment details

Chapter 12 Chassis electrical system

12.6 Remove the headlight assembly fasteners and then lift it from the vehicle - 1999 and earlier models

12.11 Remove the headlamp assembly retaining bolts (arrows) and remove the assembly - 2000 and later models

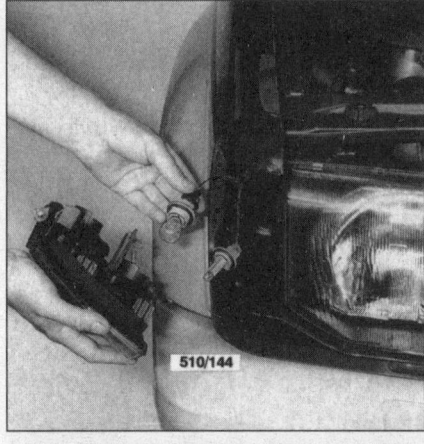

13.1a Remove the turn signal mounting screws, pull the light forward and unscrew the bulb from the rear of the lamp - 1999 and earlier models

12.9 With the inner splash shield pulled back remove the corner headlamp retaining nut (arrow) - 2000 and later models

10 Disconnect the wiring harness from the lights.
11 Remove the headlamp assembly retaining bolts **(see illustration)** and remove the assembly
12 Refitting is the reverse of removal.

13 Bulb - renewal

Refer to illustrations 13.1a, 13.1b, 13.1c, 13.1d, 13.1e, 13.1f, 13.1g, 13.1h, 13.1i, 13.1j, 13.1k and 13.1l

1 The lenses of many lights are held in place by screws, which makes it a simple procedure to gain access to the bulbs **(see illustrations)**.
2 On some lights, such as the interior dome light, the lenses are held in place by clips. The lenses can be removed either by unsnapping them or by using a small screwdriver to prise them off.

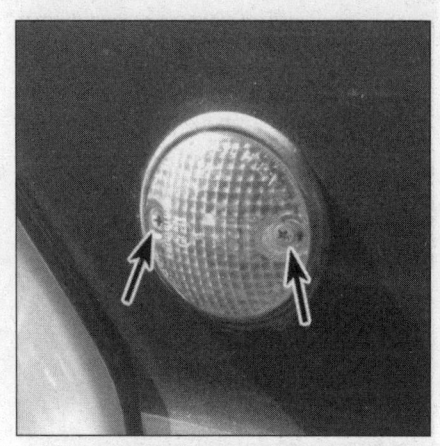

Note: *It may not be possible to position the headlight aim exactly for both high and low beams. If a compromise must be made, keep in mind that the low beams are the most used and have the greatest effect on driver safety.*

8 Have the headlights adjusted by a dealer service department or service station at the earliest opportunity.

12 Headlight housing - removal and refitting

Warning: *The models covered by this manual have a Supplemental Restraint System (SRS), more commonly known as airbags. Always disconnect the negative battery cable, then the positive battery cable and wait two minutes before working in the vicinity of impact sensors or steering column to avoid the possibility of accidental deployment of the airbag, which could cause personal injury (see Section 24). Do not use electrical test equipment on any of the airbag system wiring or tamper with them in any way.*

Caution: *If the stereo in your vehicle is equipped with an anti-theft system, make sure you have the correct activation code before disconnecting the battery.*

1 Disconnect the negative cable from the battery.

1999 and earlier models

Refer to illustration 12.6

2 Remove the grille (see Chapter 11).
3 Disconnect the wiring harness from the lights.
4 Remove the grille assembly (see Chapter 11).
5 Remove the turn signal assembly (see Section 13).
6 Remove the screws from the headlight assembly and then lift it from the vehicle **(see illustration)**.

2000 and later models

Refer to illustrations 12.9 and 12.11

7 Remove the front grille (see Chapter 11).
8 Remove the front portion of the inner fender splash shield (see Chapter 11).
9 Remove the corner retaining nut **(see illustration)**.

13.1b Remove the side turn signal lamp retaining screws, then remove the lamp and unscrew the bulb - 1999 and earlier models

Chapter 12 Chassis electrical system

3 Several types of bulbs are used. Some are removed by pushing in and turning them anti-clockwise. Others can simply be unclipped from the terminals or pulled straight out of the socket.

4 To gain access to the instrument panel lights, the instrument cluster will first have to be removed (see Section 15).

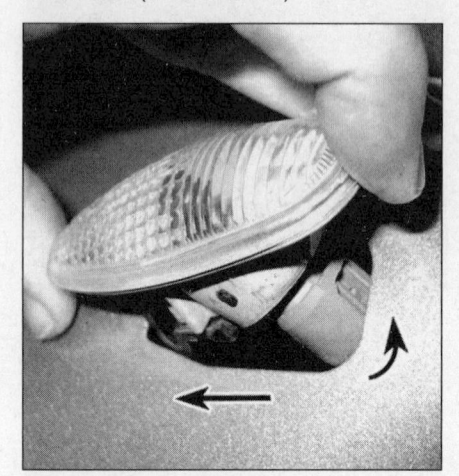

13.1c On 2000 and later models, push the side turn signal lamp forward then pull the back side out and remove the lamp - unclip the bulb from the lamp

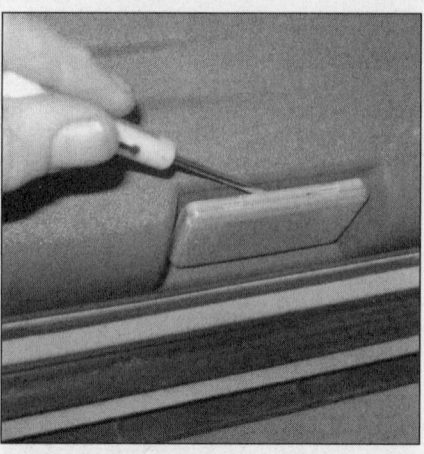

13.1d On interior lamps carefully prise the lens cover off . .

13.1e . . . and pull the bulb out from the two contacts

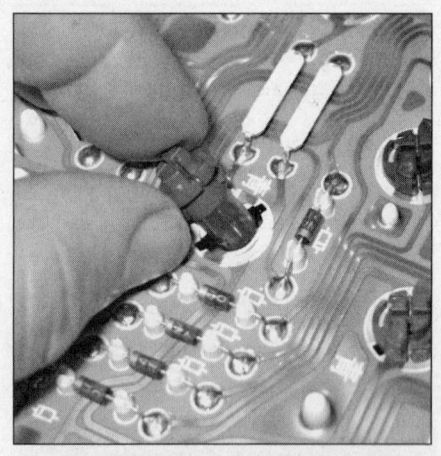

13.1f With the instrument cluster removed, rotate the bulb anti-clockwise and remove it from the circuit board

13.1g Remove the rear combination lamp retaining screws (arrows)

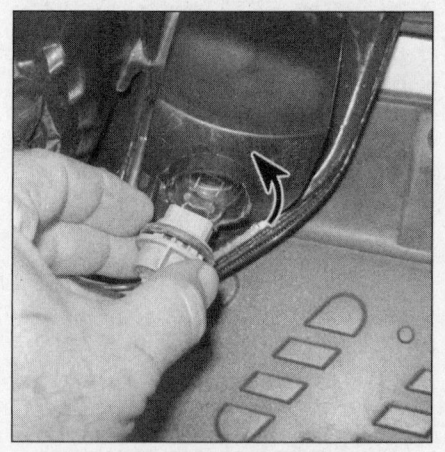

13.1h Rotate the socket anti-clockwise and unplug the bulb from the socket

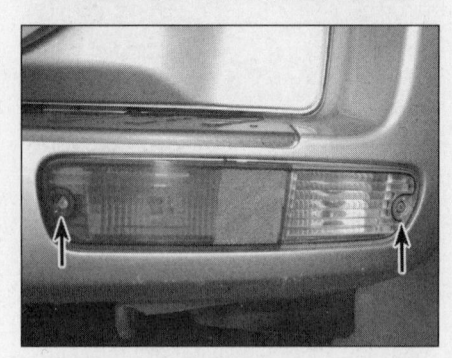

13.1i Remove the two rear lamp retaining screws and disconnect the bulb from the socket

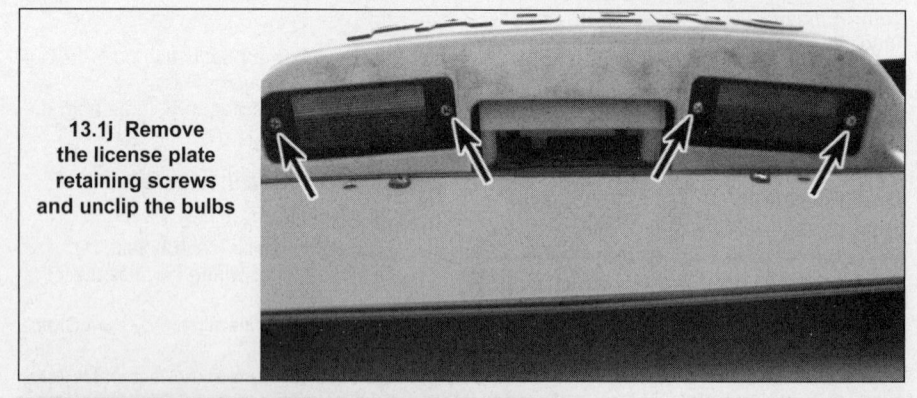

13.1j Remove the license plate retaining screws and unclip the bulbs

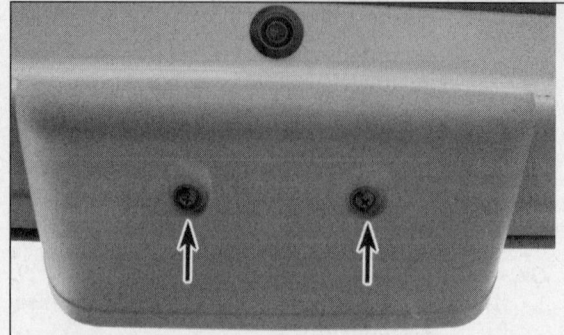

13.1k On the high-mount brake light remove the trim screws (arrows) and remove the cover

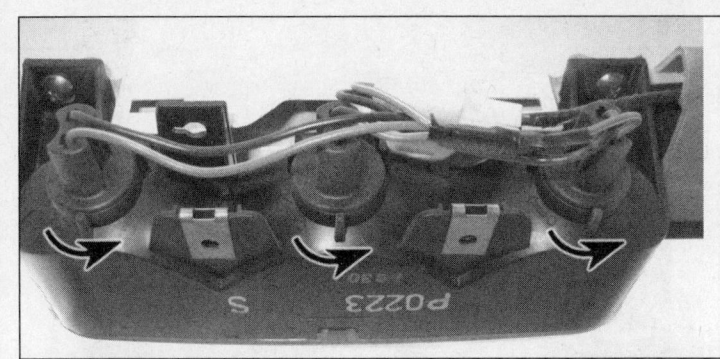

Chapter 12 Chassis electrical system

13.1l With the cover removed, rotate the bulb sockets anti-clockwise and remove the socket, then pull the bulb from the socket

13.1m On NT models, to access the rear fog lamp and number plate lamps, remove the covers from inside the tailgate and remove the two bolts holding the spare tyre cover. Open the cover to access the lamps

13.1n Removing one of the number plate lamp bulb holders by rotating it anticlockwise, then pull the bulb from the socket

13.1o Removing the rear flog lamp bulb holder by rotating it anticlockwise, then pull the bulb from the socket

3 Remove the three bolts attaching the motor to the vehicle firewall **(see illustration)**.
4 Pull up on the wiper arm until the actuator arm joint is visible in the access hole, then prise the motor out of the actuator arm joint with a screwdriver.

Wiper washer motor and tank (2000 and later models)

Refer to illustrations 14.6 and 14.10

5 Remove the inner fender splash shield (see Chapter 11).
6 Disconnect the wiper washer motor electrical connector and motor from the tank **(see illustration)**.
7 To remove the washer tank, remove the front bumper (see Chapter 11).
8 Remove the front head light assembly (see Section 12).
9 Disconnect the fluid line connections and electrical connector to the motor **(see illustration 14.6)**.
10 Remove the tank mounting nuts and bolts **(see illustration)**.

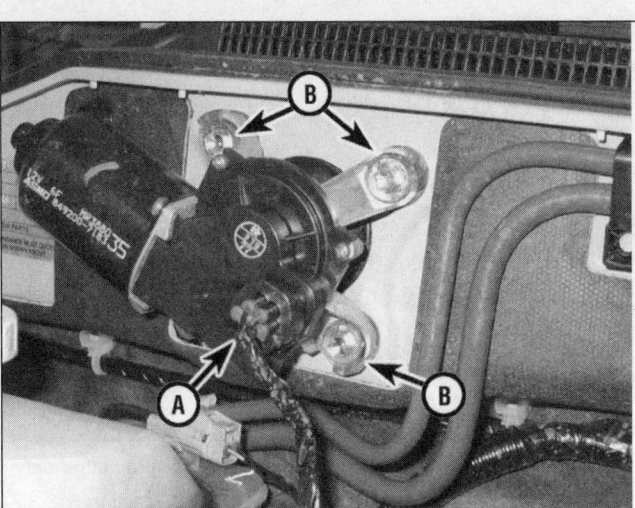

14 Wiper motor - removal and refitting

Warning: *Models covered by this manual are equipped with Supplemental Restraint System (SRS), more commonly known as airbags. Always disable the airbag system before working in the vicinity of any airbag system component to avoid the possibility of accidental deployment of the airbag, which could cause personal injury (see Section 24).*

Caution: *If the stereo in your vehicle is equipped with an anti-theft system, make sure you have the correct activation code before disconnecting the battery.*

1 Remove the negative battery cable from the battery.

Front

Refer to illustration 14.3

2 Unplug the electrical connector leading from the wiper motor.

14.3 Disconnect the wiper motor electrical connector (A), then remove the three bolts attaching the motor to the vehicle firewall (B)

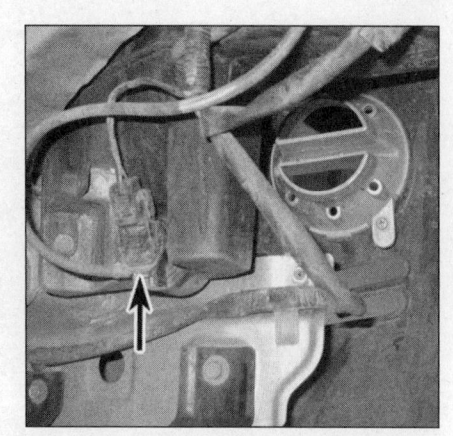

14.6 Disconnect the wiper washer motor electrical connector (arrow) and motor from the tank

14.10 Remove the tank mounting nuts and bolts (arrows)

14.14 Typical rear wiper motor details

Rear

Refer to illustration 14.14

11 Remove the rear door trim panel (see Chapter 11).
12 Remove the rear wiper arm mounting nut and remove the arm and grommet.
13 Unplug the electrical connector leading from the wiper motor.
14 Remove the three bolts attaching the motor to the door **(see illustration)** and remove the motor.
15 Refitting is the reverse of removal.

15 Instrument cluster - removal and refitting

Refer to illustrations 15.2 and 15.3

Warning: *Models covered by this manual are equipped with Supplemental Restraint System (SRS), more commonly known as airbags. Always disable the airbag system before working in the vicinity of any airbag system component to avoid the possibility of accidental deployment of the airbag, which could cause personal injury (see Section 24).*

Caution: *If the stereo in your vehicle is equipped with an anti-theft system, make sure you have the correct activation code before disconnecting the battery.*

1 Disconnect the negative cable from the battery.
2 Remove any screws and detach the cluster cover **(see illustration)**.
3 Remove the screws holding the instrument cluster in place **(see illustration)**.
4 Pull the instrument cluster out, disconnect the electrical connectors, then remove the cluster from the vehicle.
5 Refitting is the reverse of removal.

16 Cruise control system - description and check

1 The cruise control system maintains vehicle speed with a vacuum actuated servo motor located in the engine compartment, which is connected to the throttle linkage by a cable. The system consists of the electronic control module, brake switch, control switches, a relay, the vehicle speed sensor and associated wiring. Listed below are some general procedures that may be used to locate common cruise control problems.
2 Locate and check the fuse (see Section 3).
3 Have an assistant operate the brake lights while you check their operation (voltage from the brake light switch deactivates the cruise control).
4 If the brake lights don't come on or don't shut off, correct the problem and retest the cruise control.
5 Inspect the cable linkage between the cruise control actuator and the throttle linkage.
6 Visually inspect the wires connected to the cruise control actuator and check for damage and broken wires.
7 The vehicle speed sensor is located in the instrument cluster on the back of the speedometer. Remove the cluster and unplug the electrical connector. Use an ohmmeter to determine that the continuity and discontinuity alternates between terminals 1 and 2 four times when the speedometer shaft is rotated. If the continuity doesn't vary as the shaft rotates, the sensor is defective.
8 Test drive the vehicle to determine if the

15.2a Remove the cover mounting screws (arrows) and carefully prise the cover from the instrument panel - early models

15.2b On NT and NW models, the cover is retained by clips only

Chapter 12 Chassis electrical system

15.3a Remove the instrument cluster screws (arrows) and remove the cluster - early models

15.3b Remove the instrument cluster screws (arrows) and remove the cluster - late models

cruise control is now working. If it isn't, take it to a dealer service department or an automotive electrical specialist for further diagnosis and repair.

17 Power window system - description and check

1 The power window system consists of the control switches, the motors, glass mechanisms (regulators), and associated wiring.
2 Power windows are wired so they can be lowered and raised from the master control switch by the driver or by remote switches located at the individual windows. Each window has a separate motor which is reversible. The position of the control switch determines the polarity and therefore the direction of operation. The system is equipped with a relay that controls current flow to the motors.
3 The power window system operates when the ignition switch is ON. In addition, these models have a window lockout switch at the master control switch which, when activated, disables the switches at the rear windows and, sometimes, the switch at the passenger's window also. Always check these items before troubleshooting a window problem.
4 These procedures are general in nature, so if you can't find the problem using them, take the vehicle to a dealer service department or other qualified repair shop.
5 If the power windows don't work at all, check the fuse or circuit breaker.
6 If only the rear windows are inoperative, or if the windows only operate from the master control switch, check the rear window lockout switch for continuity in the unlocked position. Renew it if it doesn't have continuity.
7 Check the wiring between the switches and fuse panel for continuity. Repair the wiring, if necessary.
8 If only one window is inoperative from the master control switch, try the other control switch at the window.

Note: *This doesn't apply to the drivers door window.*
9 If the same window works from one switch, but not the other, check the switch for continuity.
10 If the switch tests OK, check for a short or open in the wiring between the affected switch and the window motor.
11 If one window is inoperative from both switches, remove the trim panel from the affected door and check for voltage at the motor while the switch is operated.
12 If voltage is reaching the motor, disconnect the glass from the regulator (see Chapter 11). Move the window up and down by hand while checking for binding and damage. Also check for binding and damage to the regulator. If the regulator is not damaged and the window moves up and down smoothly, renew the motor (see Chapter 11). If there's binding or damage, lubricate, repair or renew parts, as necessary.
13 If voltage isn't reaching the motor, check the wiring in the circuit for continuity between the switches and motors. Check that the relay is earthed properly and receiving voltage from the switches. Also check that the relay sends voltage to the motor when the switch is turned on. If it doesn't, renew the relay.
14 Test the windows after you are done to confirm proper repairs.

18 Power door lock system - description and check

The power door lock system operates the door lock actuators mounted in each door. The system consists of the switches, actuators and associated wiring. Since special tools and techniques are required to diagnose the system, it should be left to a dealer service department or a repair shop. However, it is possible for the home mechanic to make simple checks of the wiring connections and actuators for minor faults which can be easily repaired. These include:

a) *Check the system fuse and/or circuit breaker.*
b) *Check the switch wires for damage and loose connections.*
c) *Check the switches for continuity.*
d) *Remove the door panel(s) and check the actuator wiring connections to see if they're loose or damaged. Inspect the actuator rods (if equipped) to make sure they aren't bent or damaged. Inspect the actuator wiring for damaged or loose connections. The actuator can be checked by applying battery power momentarily. A discernible click indicates that the solenoid is operating properly.*

19 Centre display (2000 and later models) - removal and refitting

Refer to illustration 19.3

Warning: *Models covered by this manual are equipped with Supplemental Restraint System (SRS), more commonly known as airbags. Always disable the airbag system before working in the vicinity of any airbag system component to avoid the possibility of accidental deployment of the airbag, which could cause personal injury (see Section 24).*

Caution: *If the stereo in your vehicle is equipped with an anti-theft system, make sure you have the correct activation code before disconnecting the battery.*

1 Disconnect the negative cable from the battery.
2 Remove the centre trim panel mounting screws and carefully prise the centre trim panel from the instrument panel (see Chapter 11).
3 Remove the centre display mounting screws **(see illustration)** and pull the display forward.
4 Lift the centre display and unplug the electrical connectors.
5 Refitting is the reverse of removal.

Chapter 12 Chassis electrical system

19.3 Remove the centre display mounting screws (arrows) and remove the display - RV meter shown

20.2 Remove the centre console trim panel retaining screws (arrows) and remove the panel

20 Audio system - removal and refitting

Warning: *Models covered by this manual are equipped with Supplemental Restraint System (SRS), more commonly known as airbags. Always disable the airbag system before working in the vicinity of any airbag system component to avoid the possibility of accidental deployment of the airbag, which could cause personal injury (see Section 24).*

Caution: *If the stereo in your vehicle is equipped with an anti-theft system, make sure you have the correct activation code before disconnecting the battery.*

1 Disconnect the negative cable from the battery.

1999 and earlier models

Radio

Refer to illustrations 20.2 and 20.3

2 Remove the centre console trim panel **(see illustration)**.
3 Remove the radio mounting screws **(see illustration)**.

4 Lift the radio out and unplug the electrical connectors.
5 Refitting is the reverse of removal.

2000 and later models

Audio unit/CD player

Refer to illustration 20.7

6 Remove the centre trim panel (see Chapter 11).
7 Remove the audio unit mounting screws **(see illustration)**.
8 Separate the audio unit from the command centre and unplug the electrical connectors.
9 Refitting is the reverse of removal.

CD changer

Refer to illustration 20.11

10 Remove the lower centre console (see Chapter 11).
11 Remove the CD changer mounting screws **(see illustration)**.
12 Separate the CD changer from the instrument panel and unplug the electrical connectors.
13 Refitting is the reverse of removal.

Speakers

Refer to illustration 20.15

14 Remove the door trim panel (see Chapter 11) or wagon lift gate panel, or the dashboard extension panel.
15 Remove the retaining screws attaching the speaker to the door **(see illustration)** or to it's mounting bracket.
16 On speakers in the package shelf, remove the speaker retaining nuts.
17 Disconnect the speaker wiring, and remove the speaker from the vehicle.
18 Refitting is the reverse of removal.

Security code

Refer to illustration 20.21

19 Turn the ignition to On or Accessory.
20 Turn the radio on and "CODE" will illuminate on the radio display.
21 Using buttons numbered 1 through 4 enter the 4-digit security code from the security code information card **(see illustration)**.
22 Once the security code appears in the display press the CD button and this should be followed by a radio frequency. The unit is active and will operate.
23 If an error is made while entering the

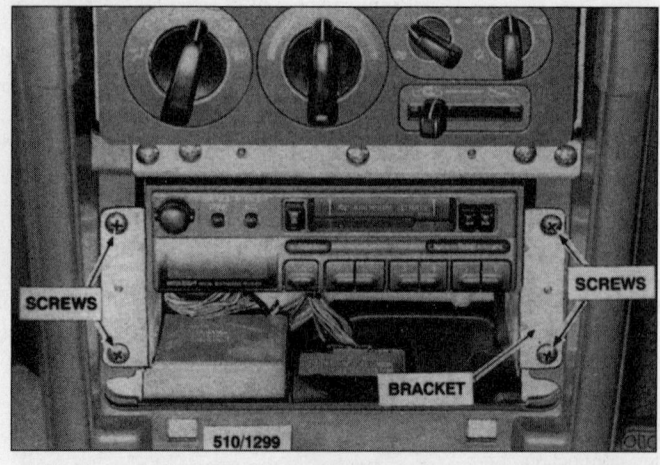

20.3 Remove the radio assembly mounting screws and remove the radio

20.7a Remove the audio unit mounting screws (arrows) and remove the unit

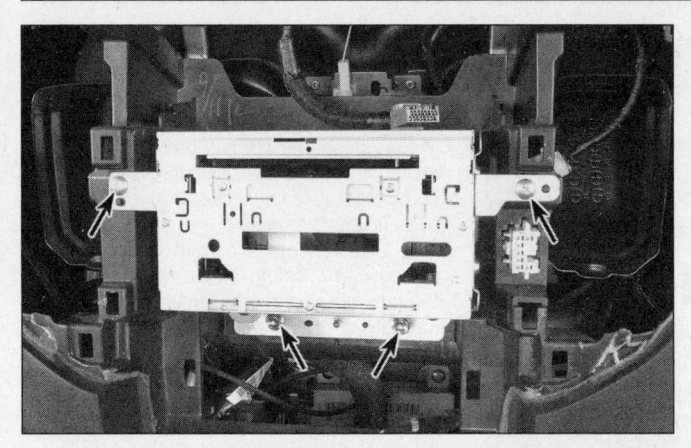

Chapter 12 Chassis electrical system

20.7b NT/NW audio system retaining screws, viewed with the facia panel removed

20.11 Remove the CD changer mounting screws (arrows) and remove the changer

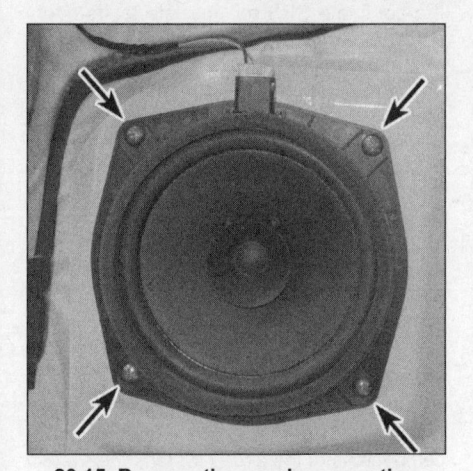

20.15 Remove the speaker mounting screws (arrows), lift the speaker then disconnect the wiring from the speaker

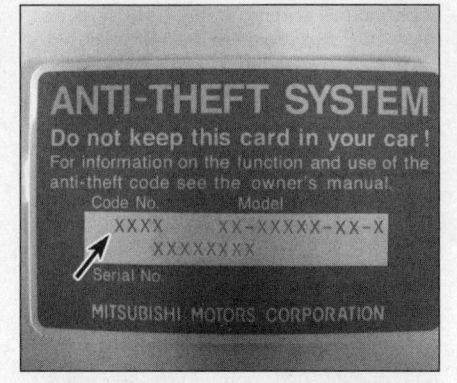

20.21 The radio security code (arrow) is printed on a card from the factory, if it is missing you can only obtain this information from a dealer service department

21.5 Using circlip pliers to turn the lock ring anti-clockwise to remove the base

security code, ERR appears in the display. Wait until CODE appears, and then enter the correct security code.
24 If you make three errors while entering the code, you must wait three minutes before repeating the process.

21 Radio aerial - removal and refitting

Refer to illustration 21.5

Caution: *If the stereo in your vehicle is equipped with an anti-theft system, make sure you have the correct activation code before disconnecting the battery.*

1 Disconnect the cable from the negative battery terminal.
2 Remove the centre trim panel and remove the radio (see Section 20).
3 Disconnect the aerial antenna from the radio.

Note: *Tie a cord to the end of the antenna and pull the antenna out. Tie the cord to the new antenna cable and pull the antenna through the body using the cord.*

4 Remove the drivers side kick panel.
5 Remove the ring nut **(see illustration)** and the base.
6 Remove the antenna motor mounting nuts and remove the antenna motor.
7 The remainder of the refitting is the reverse of removal.

22 Power seats - description and check

1 Power seats allow you to adjust the position of the seat with little effort. Some models feature a six-way seat that goes forward and backward, up and down and tilts forward and backward. Other models feature a ten-way seat that also includes a power lumbar support and seat back recliner.
2 The six-way seats are powered by three reversible motors mounted in one housing that are controlled by switches on the side of the seat. Each switch changes the direction of seat travel by reversing polarity to the drive motor. Ten-way seats have two additional motors: the lumbar support motor and a seat back recliner motor. The lumbar support motor is mounted in the seat base and connected to the lumbar mechanism by operating cables. The seat back motor is part of the seat back motor/drive assembly which is mounted on the outer side of the seat.
3 Diagnosis is a simple matter, using the following procedures.
4 Look under the seat for any object which may be preventing the seat from moving.
5 If the seat won't work at all, check the fuse or circuit breaker.
6 With the engine off to reduce the noise level, operate the seat controls in all directions and listen for sound coming from the seat motors.
7 If the seat won't work at all, check the fuse or circuit breaker.

Note: *The ignition must be ON for the power seats to work.*

8 If the motor runs or clicks but the seat doesn't move, check the seat drive mechanism for wear or damage and correct as necessary.
9 If the motor doesn't work or make noise, check for voltage at the motor while an assistant operates the switch.
10 If the motor is getting voltage but doesn't run, test it off the vehicle with jumper wires. If it still doesn't work, renew it.

11 If the motor isn't getting voltage, check for voltage at the switch. If there's no voltage at the switch, check the wiring between the fuse panel and the switch. If there's voltage at the switch, check the switch for continuity in all its operating positions. Renew the switch if there's no continuity.
12 If the switch is good, check for a short or open in the wiring between the switch and motor. If there's a relay between the switch and motor, check that it's earthed properly and there's voltage to the relay. Also check that there's voltage going from the relay to the motor when the switch is operated. If there's not, and the relay is earthed properly, renew the relay.
13 Test the completed repairs.

23 Horn - check and renewal

Warning: *The models covered by this manual have a Supplemental Restraint system (SRS), more commonly known as airbags. Always disconnect the negative battery cable, then the positive battery cable and wait two minutes before working in the vicinity of impact sensors or steering column to avoid the possibility of accidental deployment of the airbag, which could cause personal injury (see Section 24). Do not use electrical test equipment on any of the airbag system wiring or tamper with them in any way.*
Caution: *If the stereo in your vehicle is equipped with an anti-theft system, make sure you have the correct activation code before disconnecting the battery.*

Check

1 Disconnect the electrical connector from the horn.
2 Test the horn by connecting battery voltage to the two terminals with a pair of jumper wires.
3 If the horn doesn't sound, renew it. If it does sound, the problem lies in the switch, relay or the wiring between components.

Renewal

Refer to illustration 23.6
4 Remove the grille (refer to Chapter 11).
5 Disconnect the wiring from the horn.
6 Remove the horn mounting bolt, bracket and horn **(see illustration)**.
7 Refitting is the reverse of removal.

24 Airbags - general information

Later models are equipped with a Supplemental Restraint System (SRS), more commonly known as airbags. This system is designed to protect the driver and the front seat passenger from serious injury in the event of a frontal collision. It consists of an airbag module in the centre of the steering wheel and the right side of the instrument panel, three crash sensors mounted at the

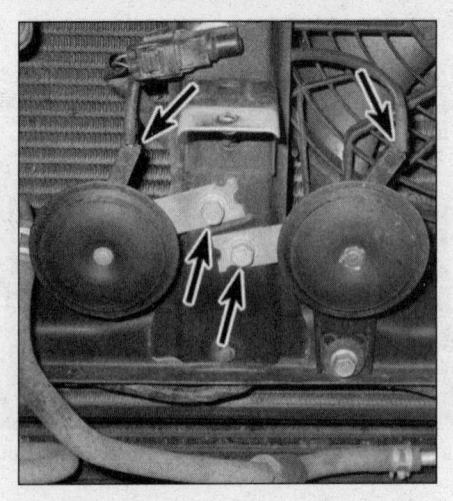

23.6 Disconnect the horn electrical connectors and mounting bolts (arrows), then remove the horn

front and the interior of the vehicle and a diagnostic monitor which also contains a backup power supply located in the passenger compartment.

Airbag module

Driver's-side airbag

The driver's-side airbag module contains a housing incorporating the cushion (airbag) and inflation unit mounted in the centre of the steering wheel. The inflation assembly is mounted on the back of the housing over a hole through which gas is expelled, inflating the bag almost instantaneously, when an electrical signal is sent from the system. A coil assembly on the steering column under the module carries this signal to the module.
This coil assembly can transmit an electrical signal regardless of the steering wheel position. The igniter in the airbag converts the electrical signal to heat and ignites the sodium azide/copper oxide powder, producing nitrogen gas, which inflates the bag.
Refer to Chapter 10 for information on the removal of the driver side air bag.

Passenger-side airbag

The passenger-side airbag is mounted above the glove compartment and is designated by the letters SRS (Supplemental Restraint System). It consists of an inflator containing an igniter, a bag assembly, a reaction housing and a trim cover.
The passenger airbag is considerably larger than the steering wheel mounted unit and is supported by the steel reaction housing. The trim cover is textured, painted to match the instrument panel and has a moulded seam which splits when the bag inflates. As with the steering wheel mounted airbag, an electrical signal ignites the sodium azide/iron oxide powder which inflates the bag with the nitrogen gas.
Refer to Chapter 11 for information on the removal of the passenger air bag.

Sensors

The system has three sensors: two forward sensors at the front of the vehicle and a safing sensor inside the diagnostic monitor in the passenger compartment. The sensors are basically pressure sensitive switches that complete an electrical circuit during an impact of sufficient G forces.
The sensors are hard wired with the airbags. The safing sensor and one of the forward crash sensors must close simultaneously in order for the airbag(s) to deploy. When this occurs, current flows from the battery, through the closed sensors and to the igniter in each airbag.

Electronic diagnostic monitor

The electronic diagnostic monitor checks the complete SRS for possible faults every time the vehicle is started. If the system is operating properly, the "AIR BAG" light turns on for eight seconds and then turns off. If a fault is discovered, the light will remain on, it will flash, or the system will beep. Should any of these alerts occur, or if the "AIR BAG" light fails to illuminate at all, the vehicle should be taken to your dealer immediately for service.
The electronic diagnostic monitor also contains a backup power supply so the airbag(s) can still deploy even if battery power is cut off in the crash.

Disabling the system

When working in the vicinity of the steering wheel, steering column or near other components of the airbag system, the system should be disarmed. To do this, perform the following steps:
a) *Turn the ignition switch to OFF.*
b) *Detach the cable from the negative battery terminal, then the positive cable, and wait 2 minutes for the electronic module backup power supply to be depleted.*

Enabling the system

a) *Turn the ignition switch to OFF.*
b) *Connect the positive battery cable first, and then the negative cable.*

25 Wiring diagrams - general information

Since it isn't possible to include all wiring diagrams for every year covered by this manual, the following diagrams are those that are typical and most commonly needed.
When checking a circuit, make sure that all connectors are clean, with no broken or loose terminals. When unplugging a connector, do not pull on the wires. Pull only on the connector housings themselves.

Chapter 12 Chassis electrical system

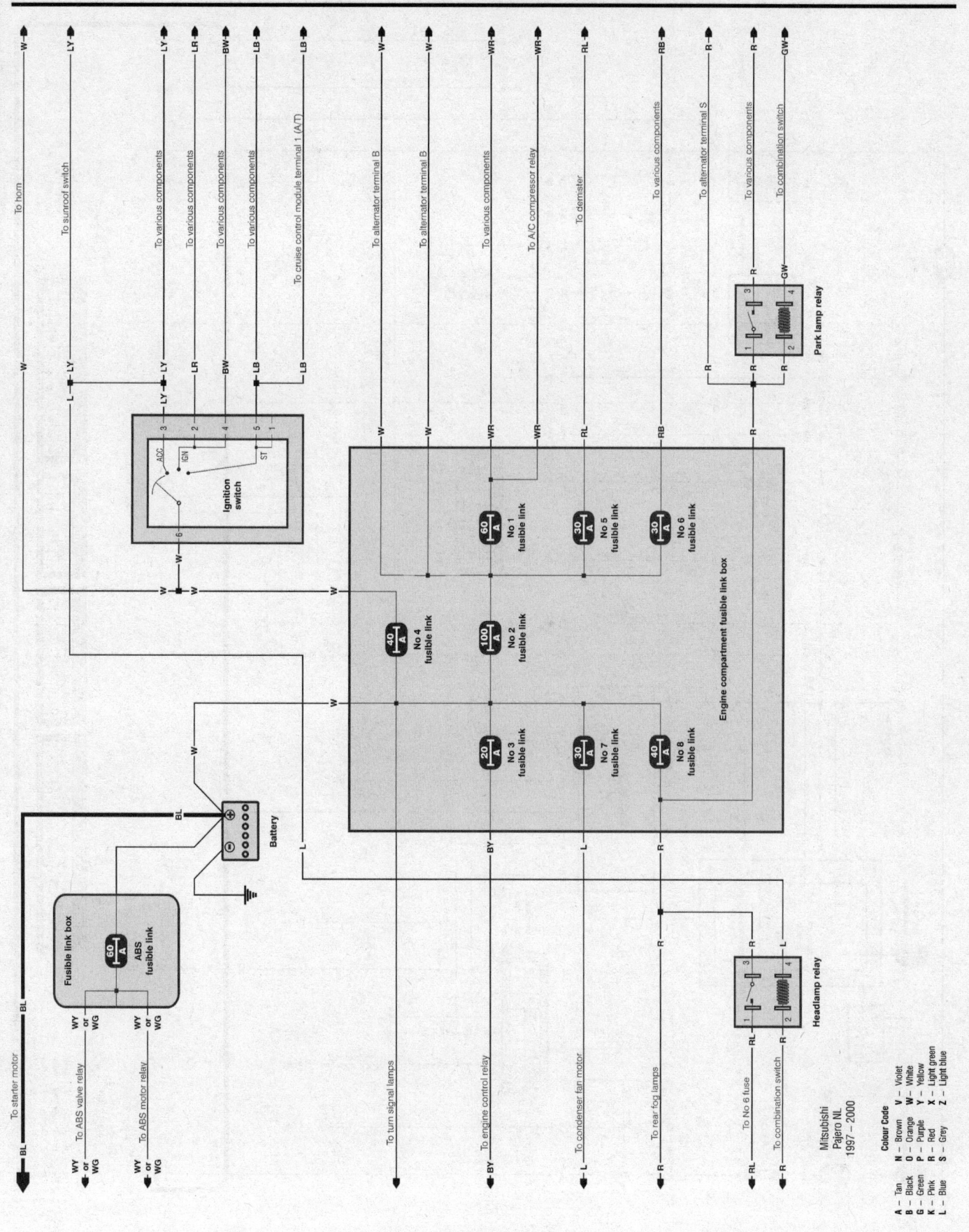

Power distribution, NL models

Mitsubishi Pajero NL 1997 – 2000

Colour Code

- A – Tan
- B – Black
- G – Green
- K – Pink
- L – Blue
- N – Brown
- O – Orange
- P – Purple
- R – Red
- S – Grey
- V – Violet
- W – White
- Y – Yellow
- X – Light green
- Z – Light blue

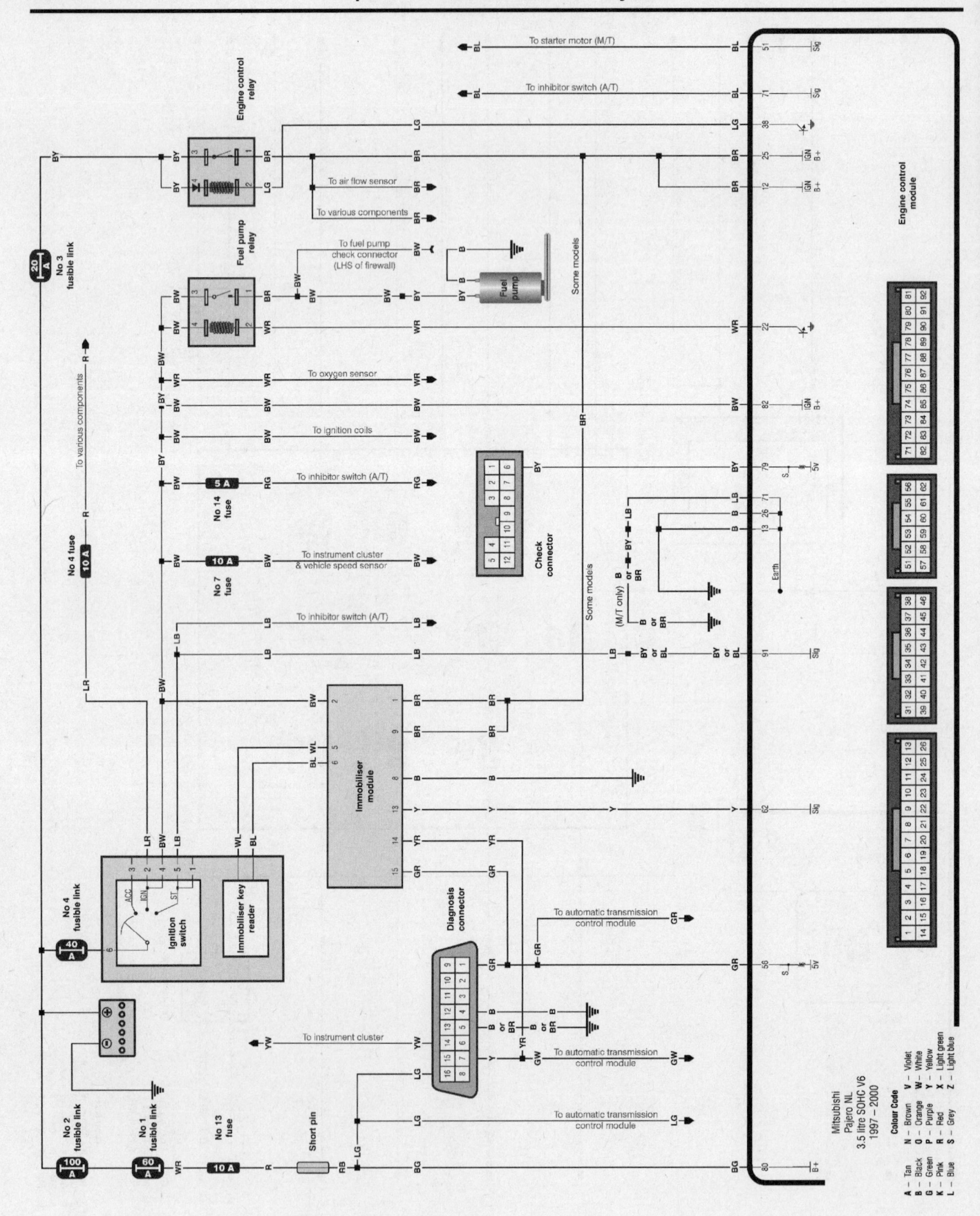

EFI and engine management system — petrol, NL models

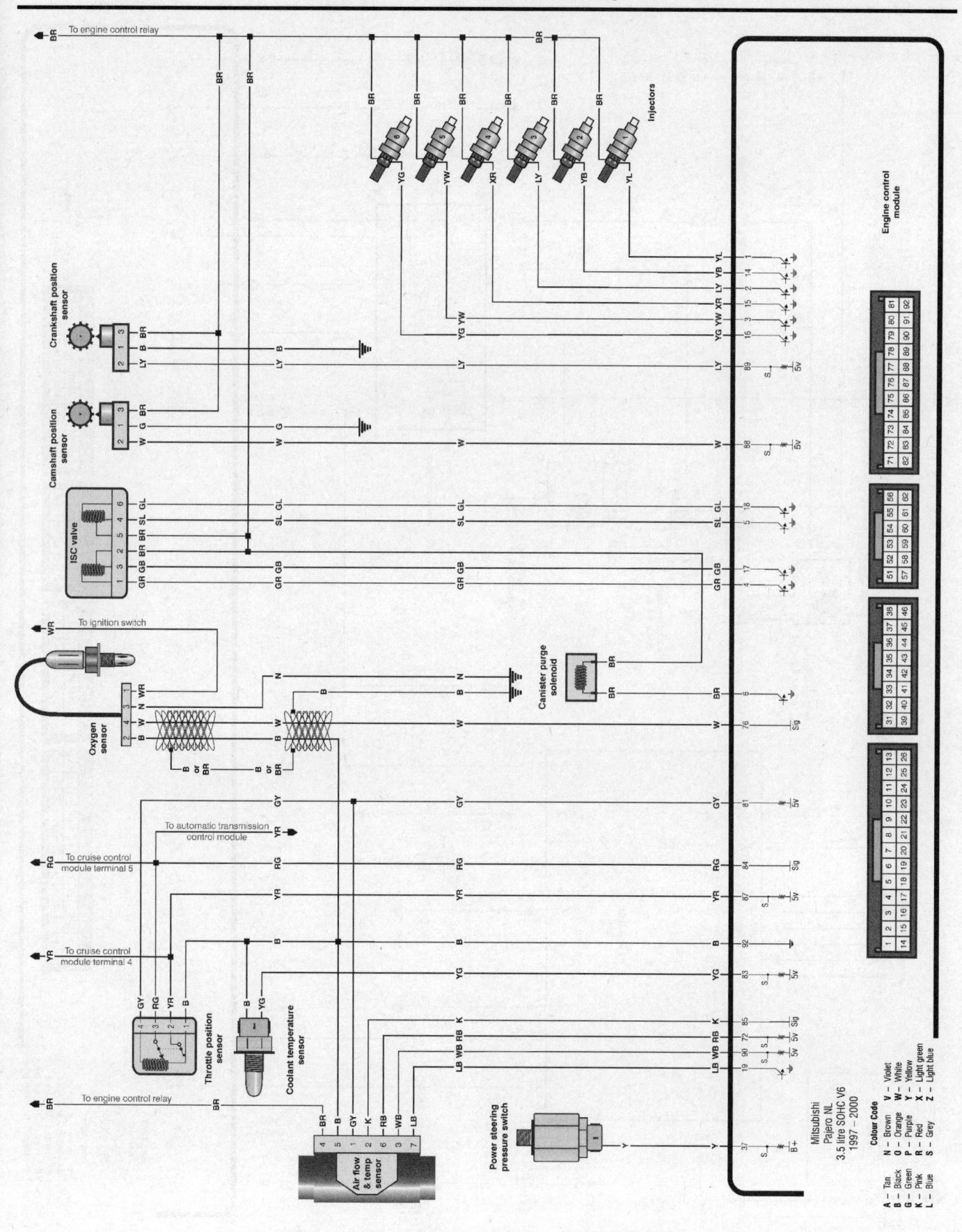

Chapter 12 Chassis electrical system

EFI and engine management system — petrol, NL models

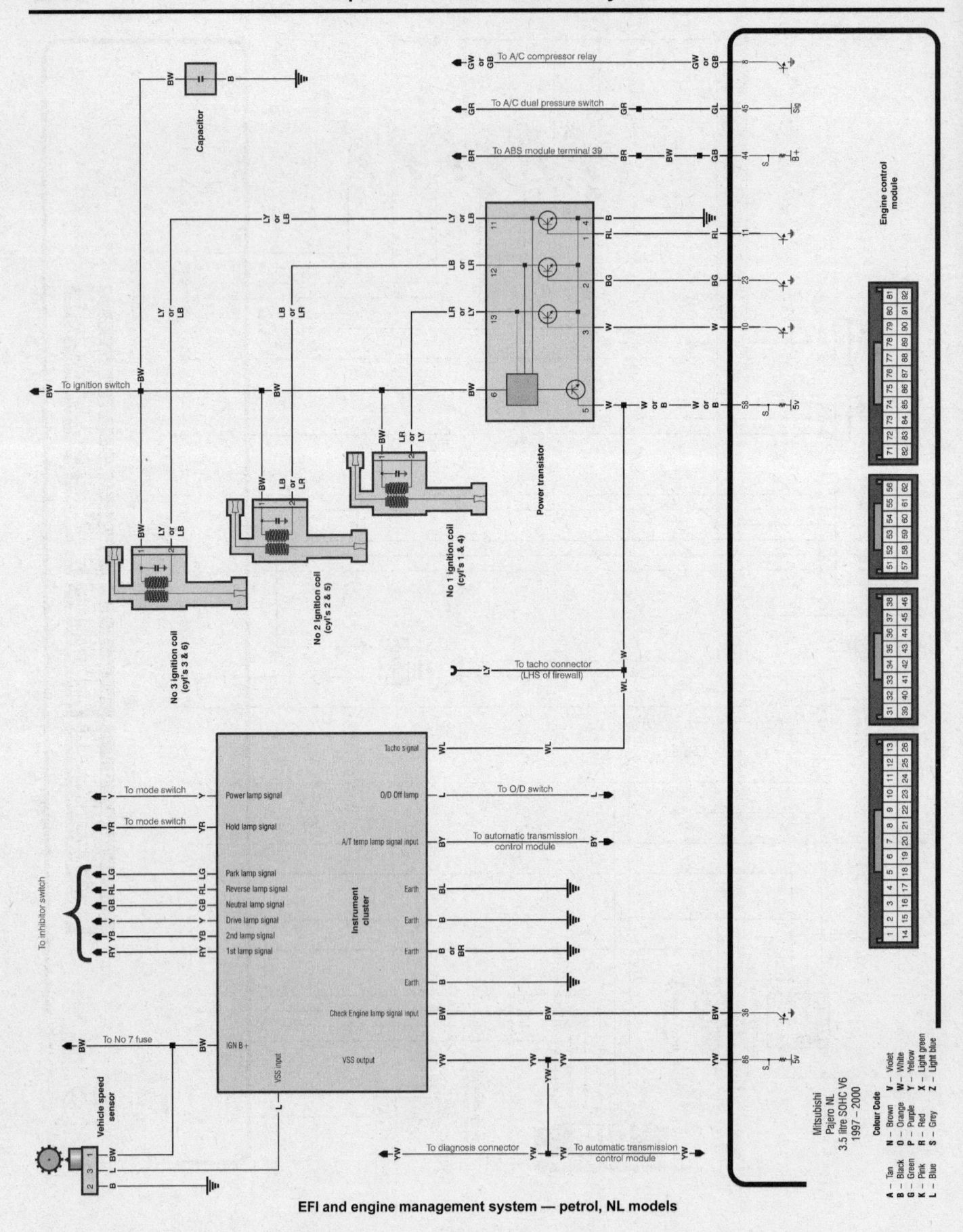

EFI and engine management system — petrol, NL models

Chapter 12 Chassis electrical system

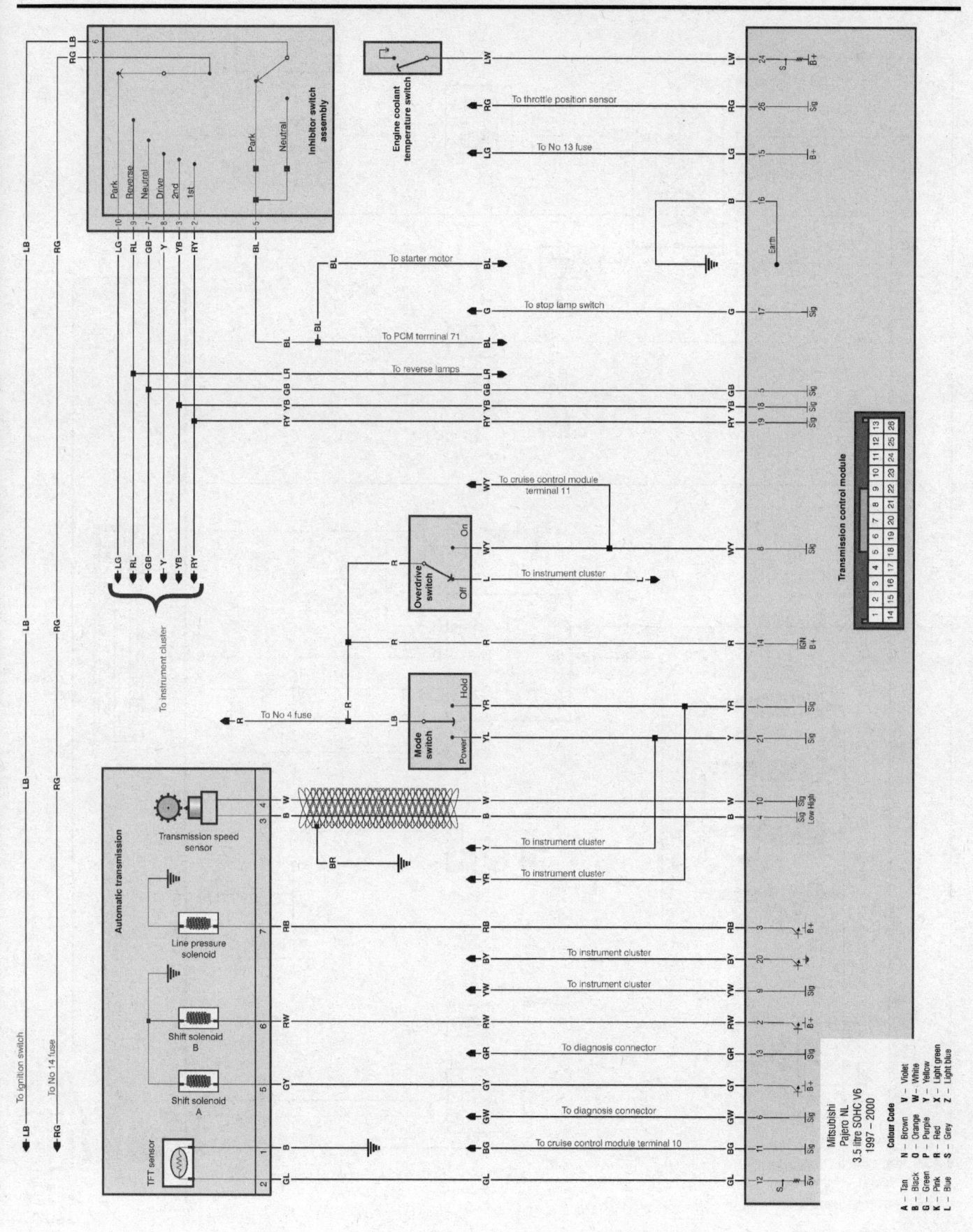

Automatic transmission — petrol, NL models

Chapter 12 Chassis electrical system

Engine management system, intercooler fan — diesel, NL models

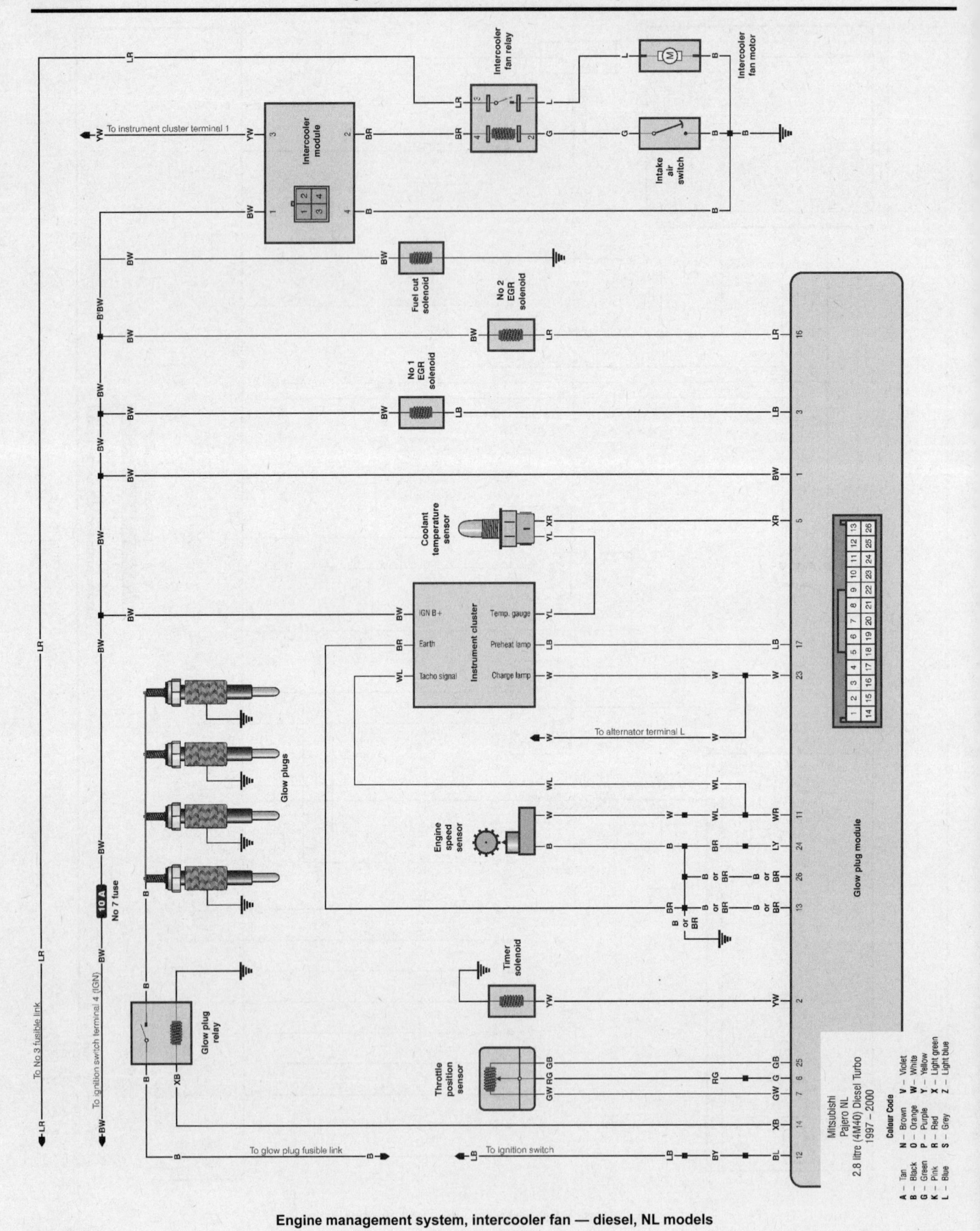

Chapter 12 Chassis electrical system

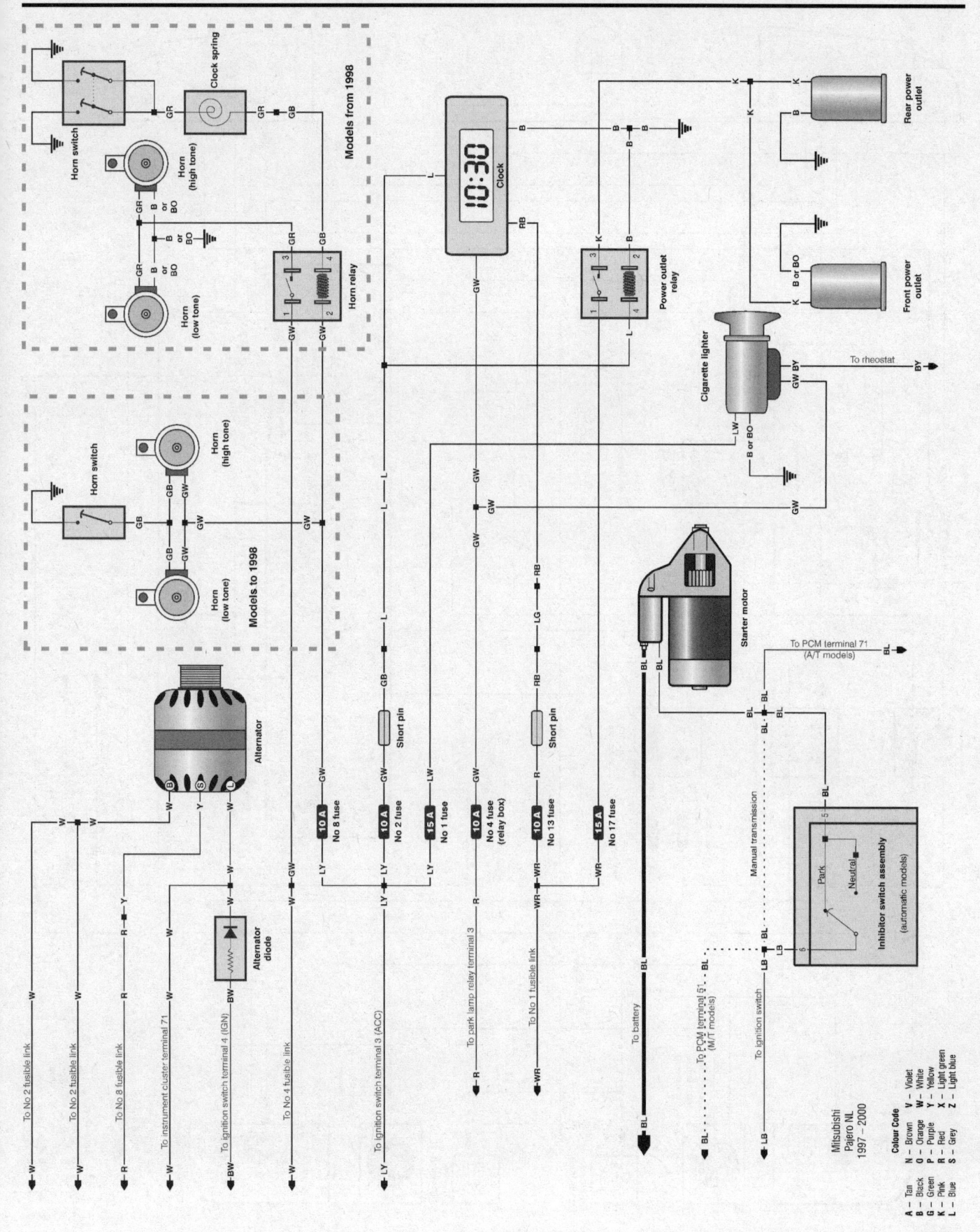

12-21

Starting system, charging system, cigarette lighter, power outlets, horn, clock, NL models

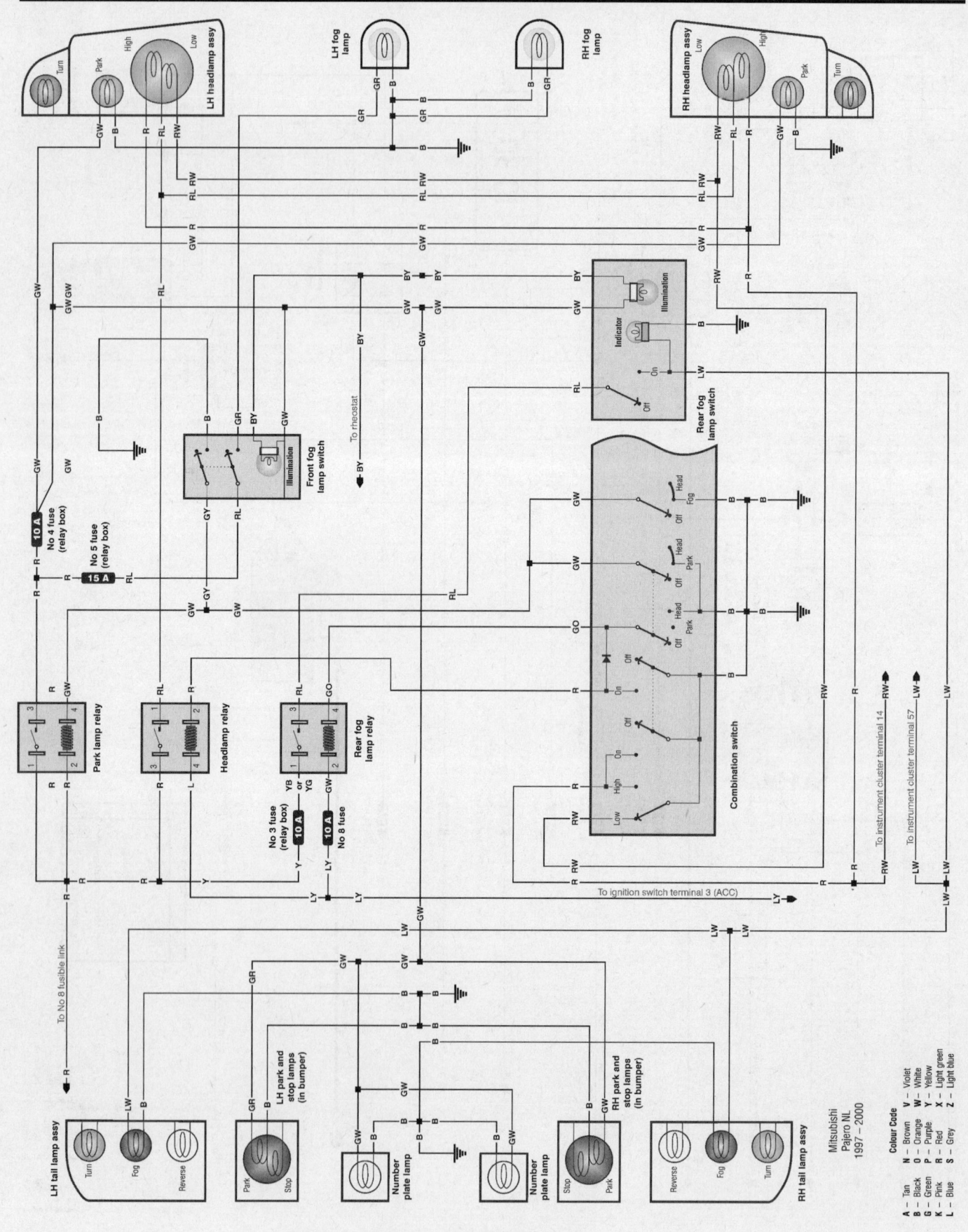

Headlamps, tail lamps, front and rear fog lamps, NL models

Chapter 12 Chassis electrical system

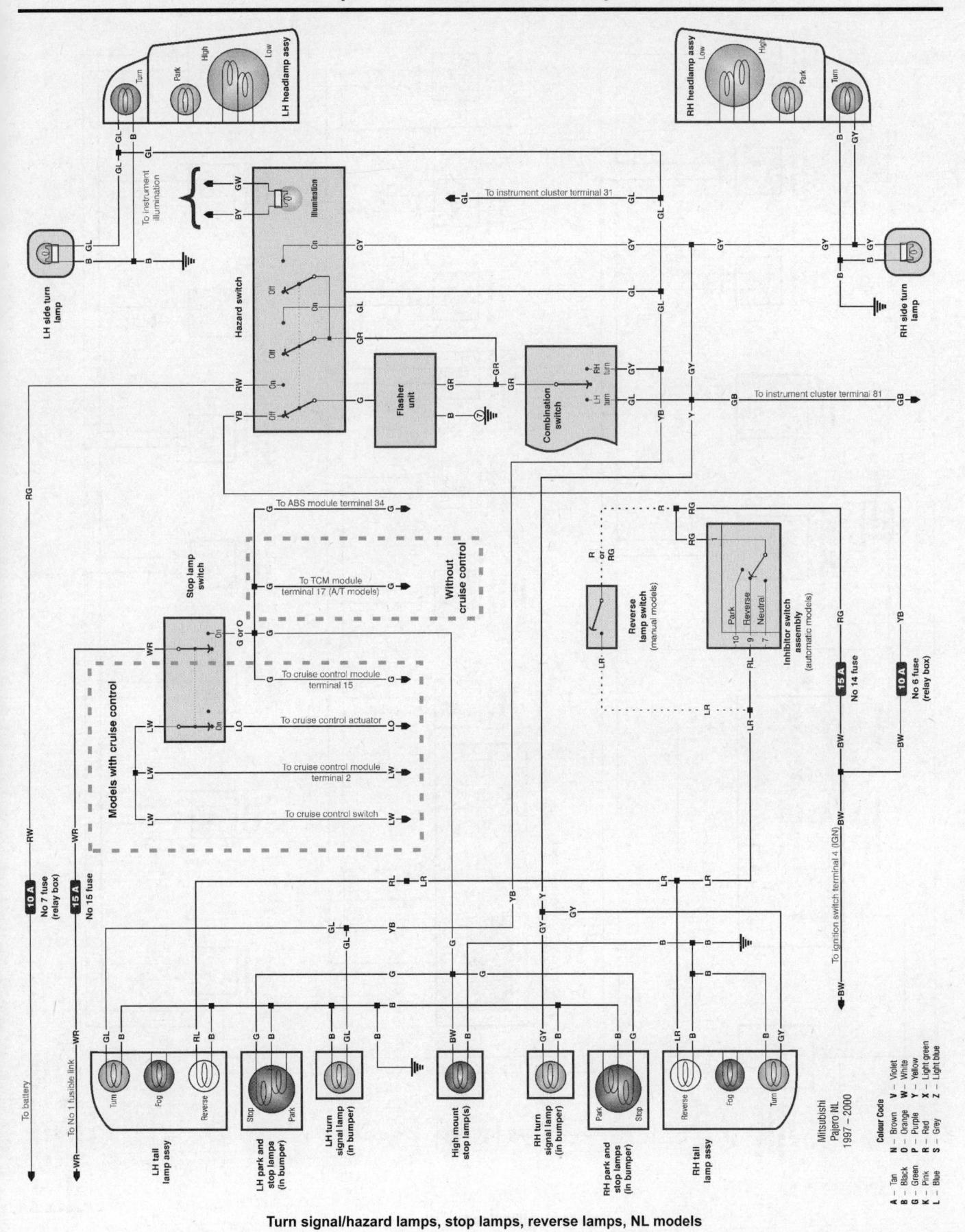

12-23

Turn signal/hazard lamps, stop lamps, reverse lamps, NL models

Mitsubishi Pajero NL 1997–2000

Colour Code
A – Tan
B – Black
G – Green
K – Pink
L – Blue
N – Brown
O – Orange
P – Purple
R – Red
S – Grey
V – Violet
W – White
Y – Yellow
X – Light green
Z – Light blue

12-24　Chapter 12　Chassis electrical system

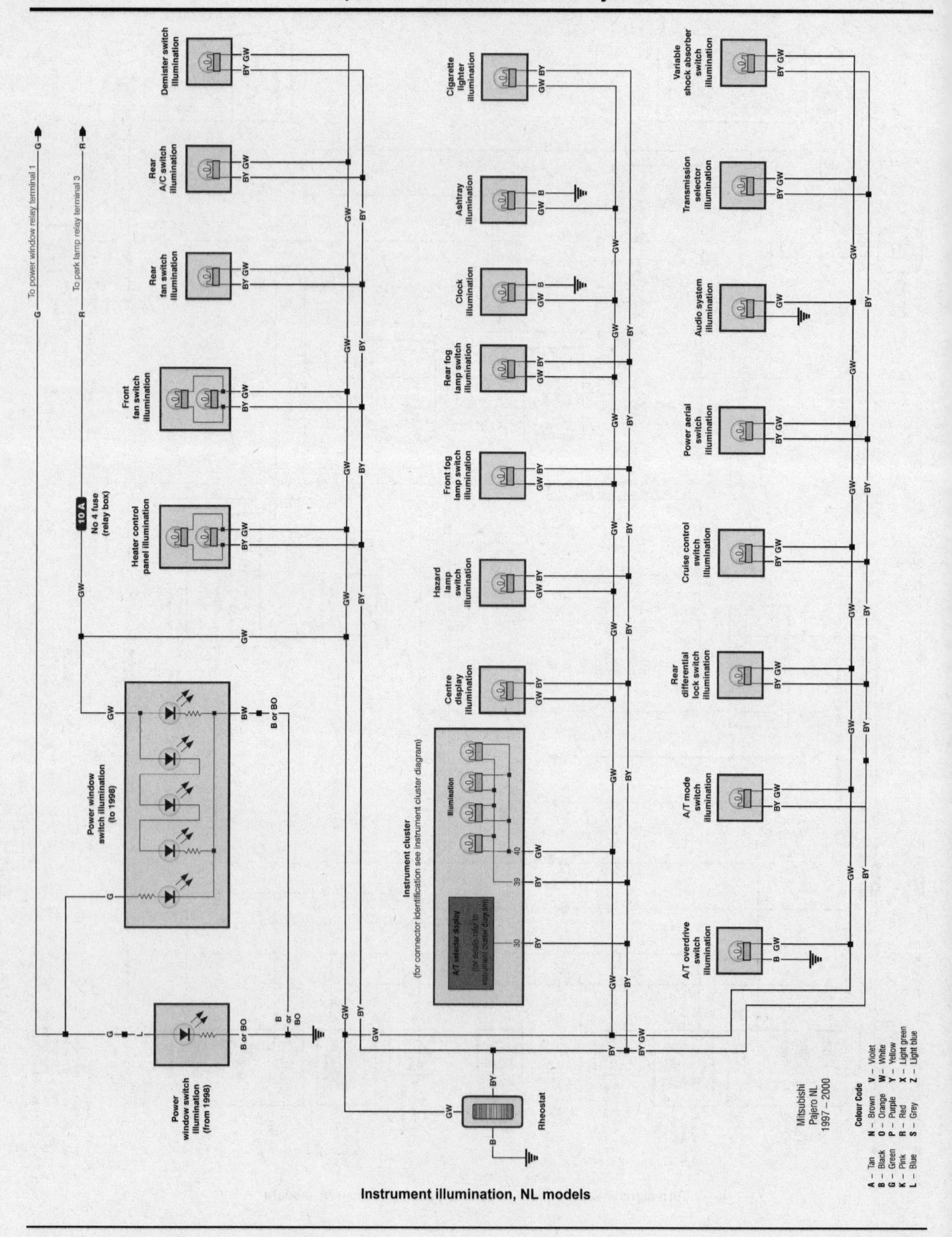

Instrument illumination, NL models

Mitsubishi Pajero NL 1997–2000

Colour Code
A – Tan
B – Black
G – Green
K – Pink
L – Blue
N – Brown
O – Orange
P – Purple
R – Red
S – Grey
V – Violet
W – White
Y – Yellow
X – Light green
Z – Light blue

Chapter 12 Chassis electrical system

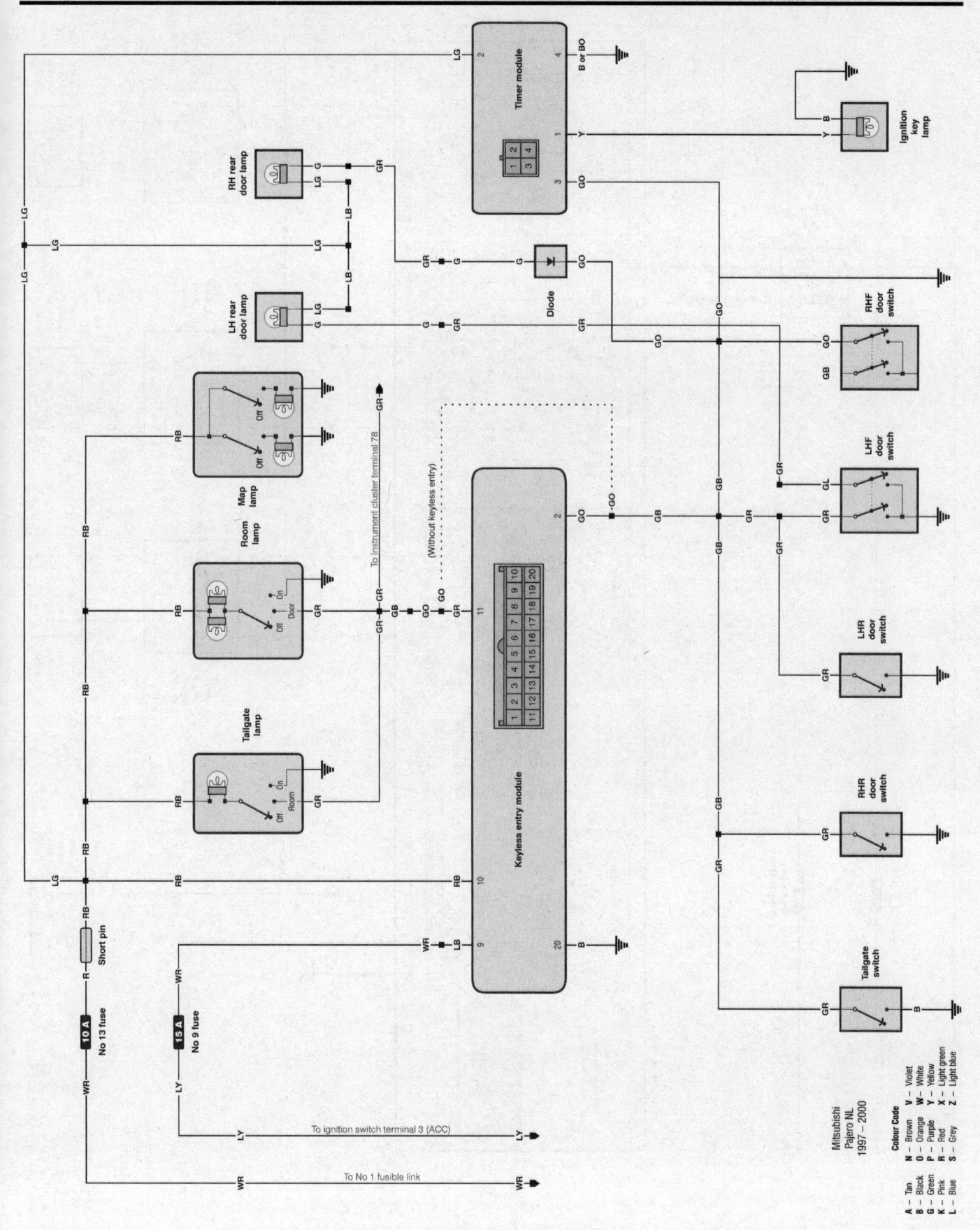

Keyless entry, interior lighting, NL models

Mitsubishi Pajero NL 1997 – 2000

Colour Code

- A – Tan
- B – Black
- G – Green
- K – Pink
- L – Blue
- N – Brown
- O – Orange
- P – Purple
- R – Red
- S – Grey
- V – Violet
- W – White
- Y – Yellow
- Z – Light green
- (Light blue)

Chapter 12 Chassis electrical system

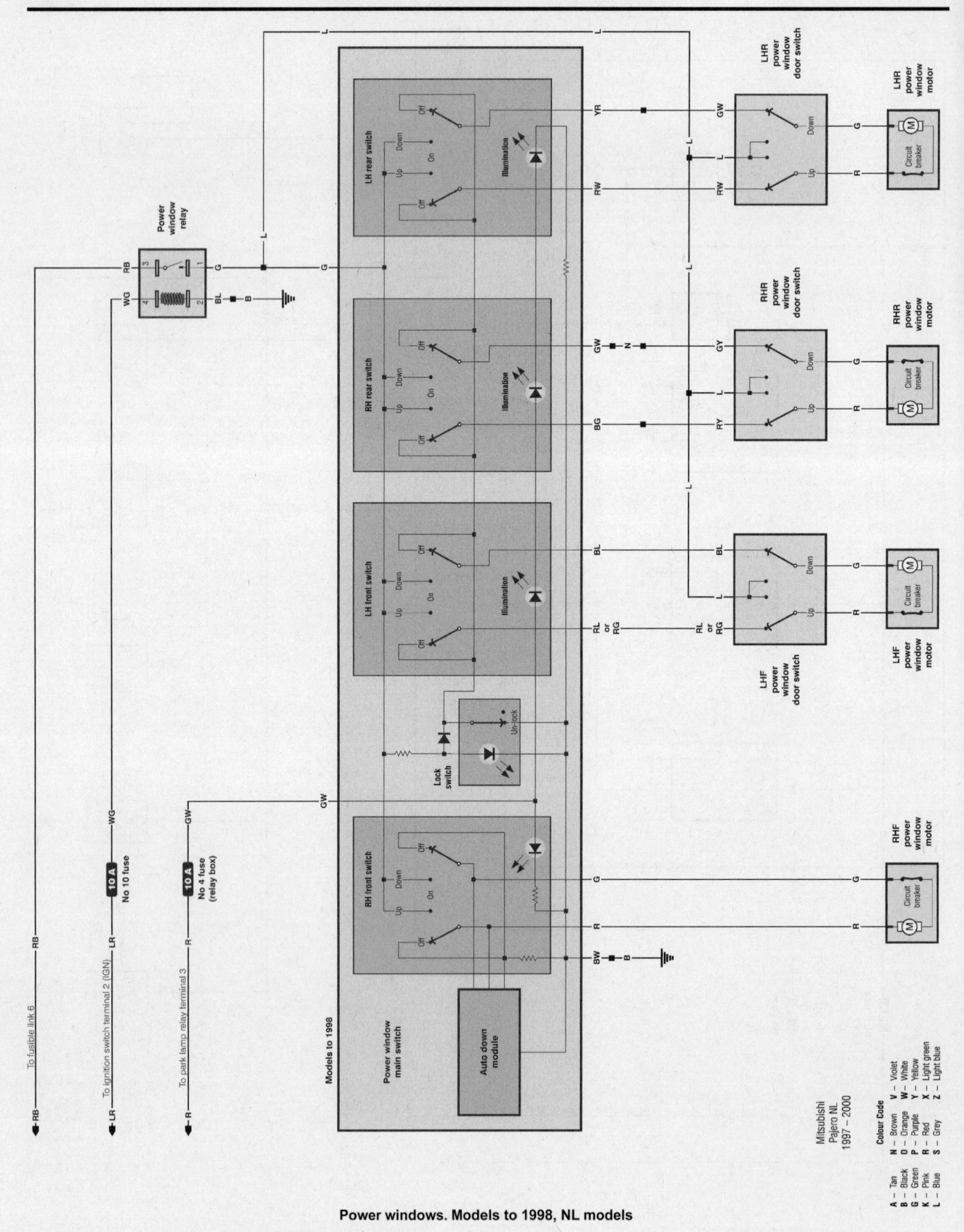

Power windows. Models to 1998, NL models

Chapter 12 Chassis electrical system

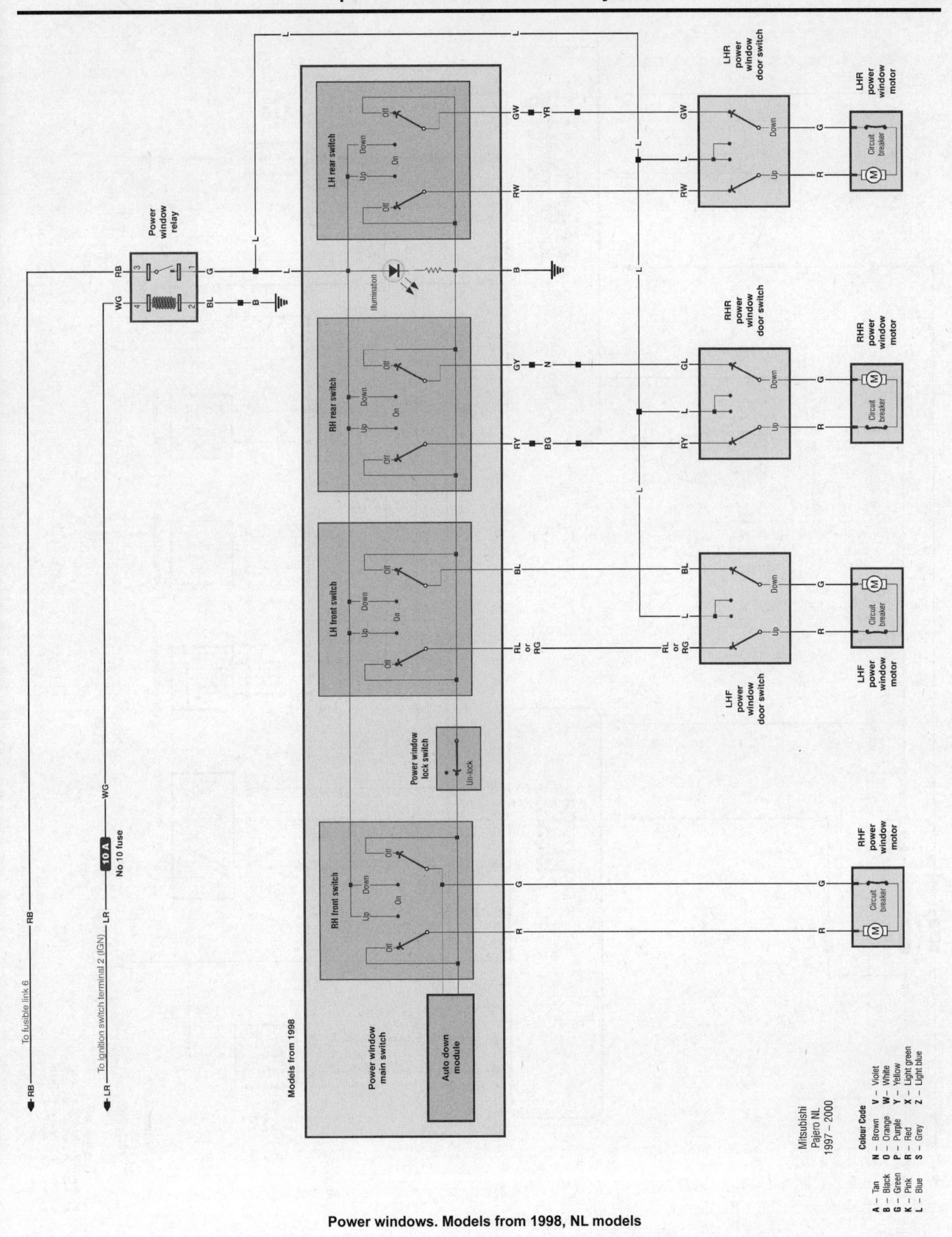

Power windows. Models from 1998, NL models

Chapter 12 Chassis electrical system

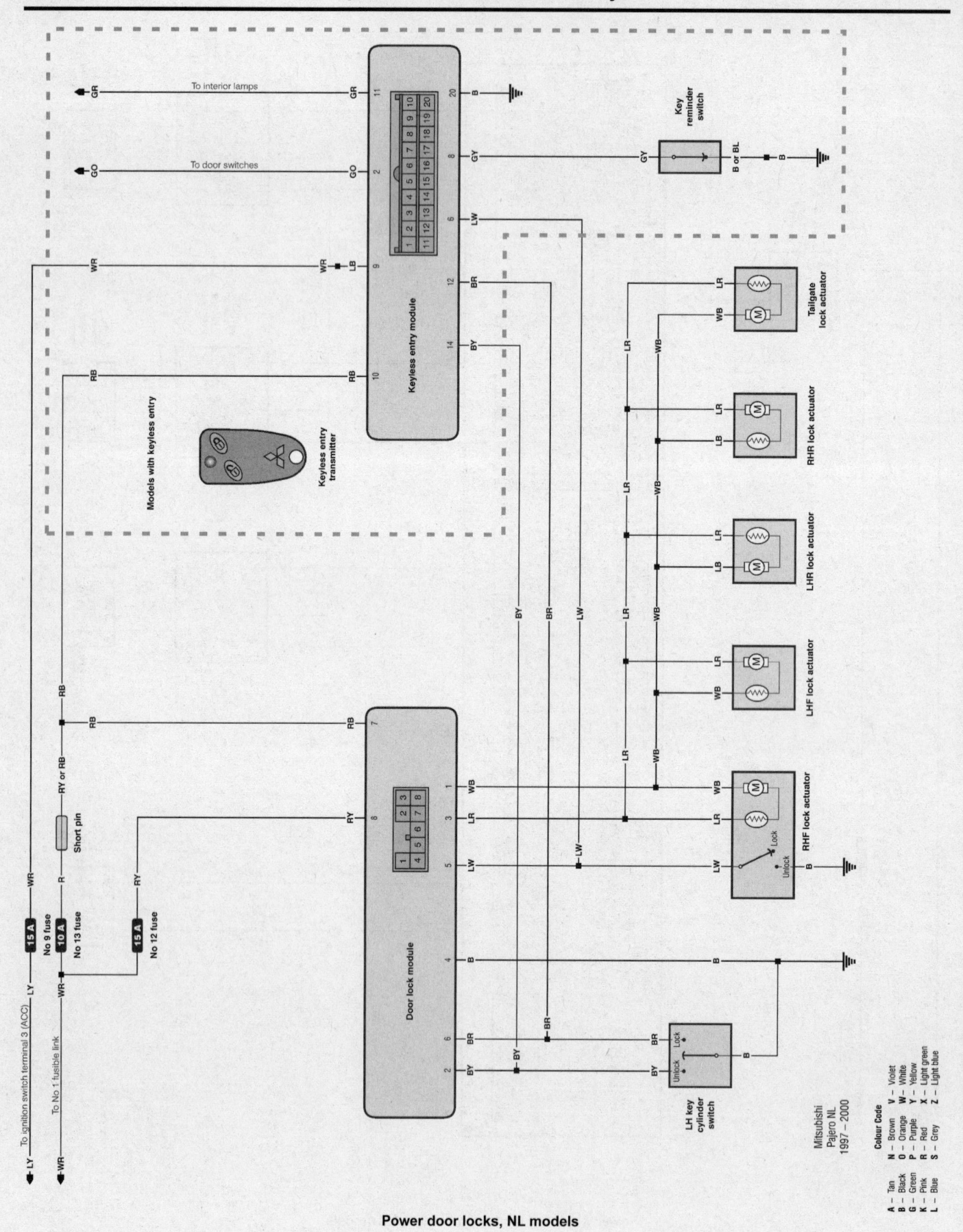

Power door locks, NL models

Mitsubishi Pajero NL 1997–2000

Colour Code:
- A – Tan
- B – Black
- G – Green
- K – Pink
- L – Blue
- N – Brown
- O – Orange
- P – Purple
- R – Red
- S – Grey
- V – Violet
- W – White
- Y – Yellow
- X – Light green
- Z – Light blue

Chapter 12 Chassis electrical system

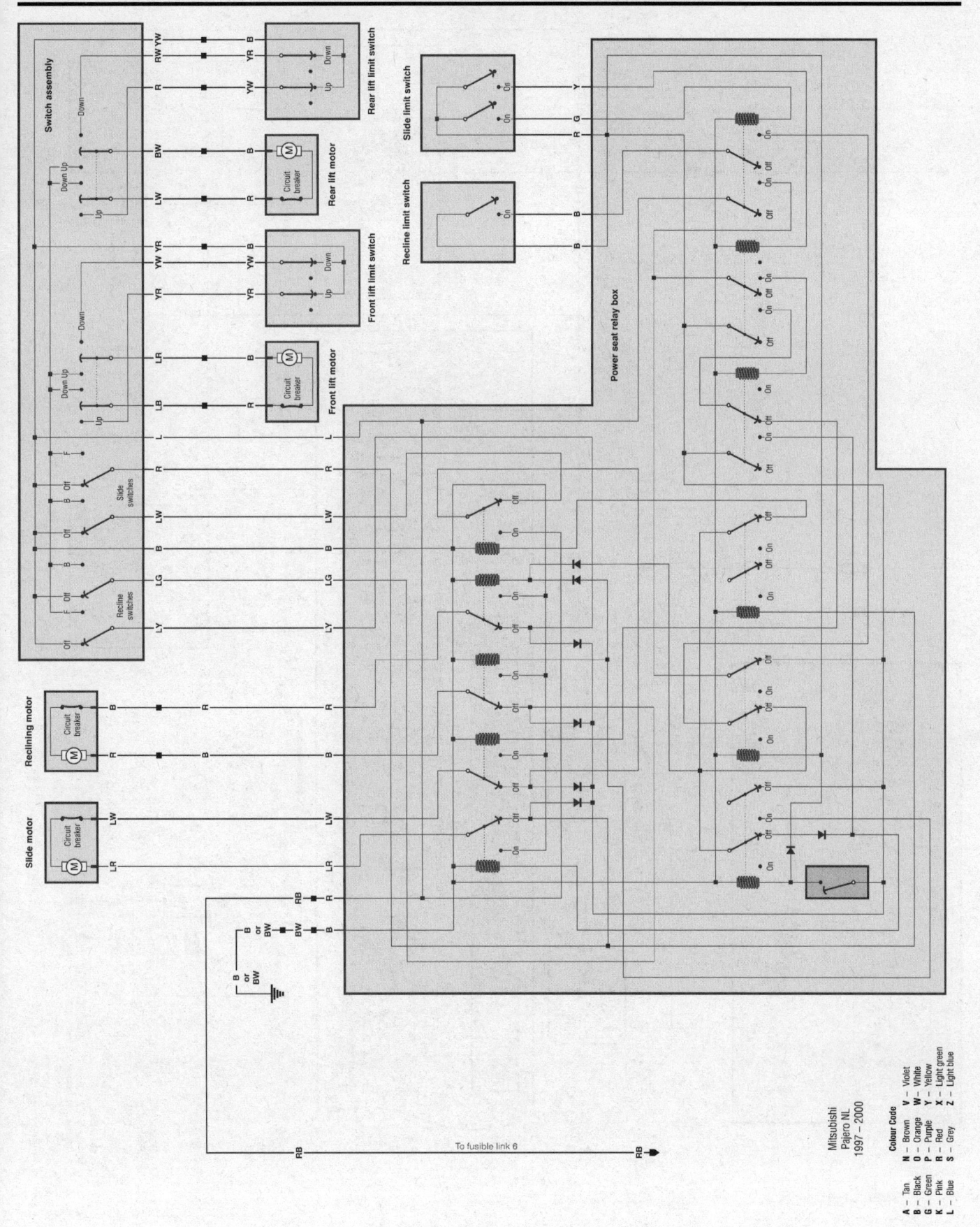

12-29

Power mirrors, NL models

12-30 Chapter 12 Chassis electrical system

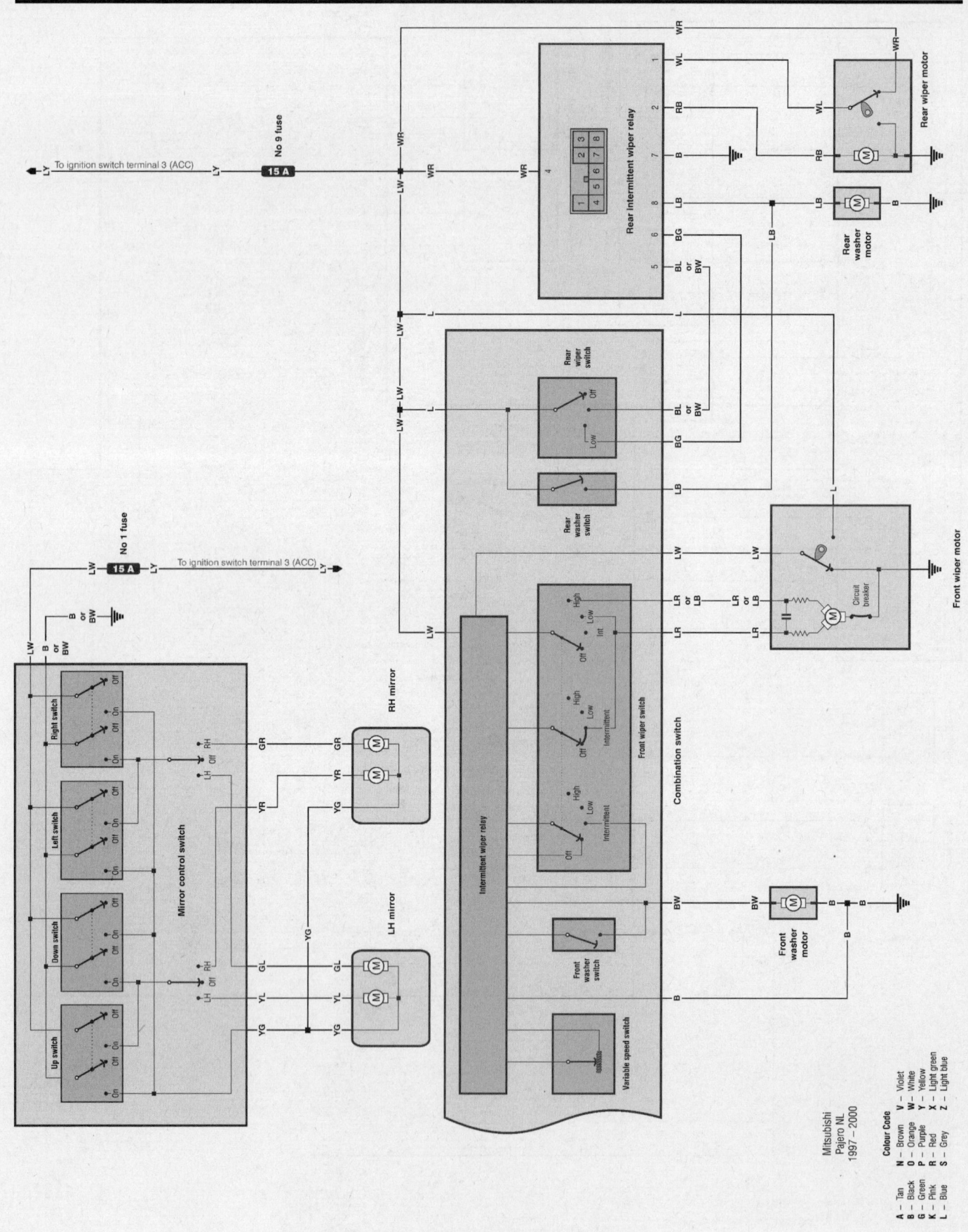

Power seats, wipers and washers, NL models

Mitsubishi Pajero NL 1997–2000

Colour Code
A – Tan
B – Black
G – Green
K – Pink
L – Blue
N – Brown
O – Orange
P – Purple
R – Red
S – Grey
V – Violet
W – White
Y – Yellow
X – Light green
Z – Light blue

Chapter 12 Chassis electrical system

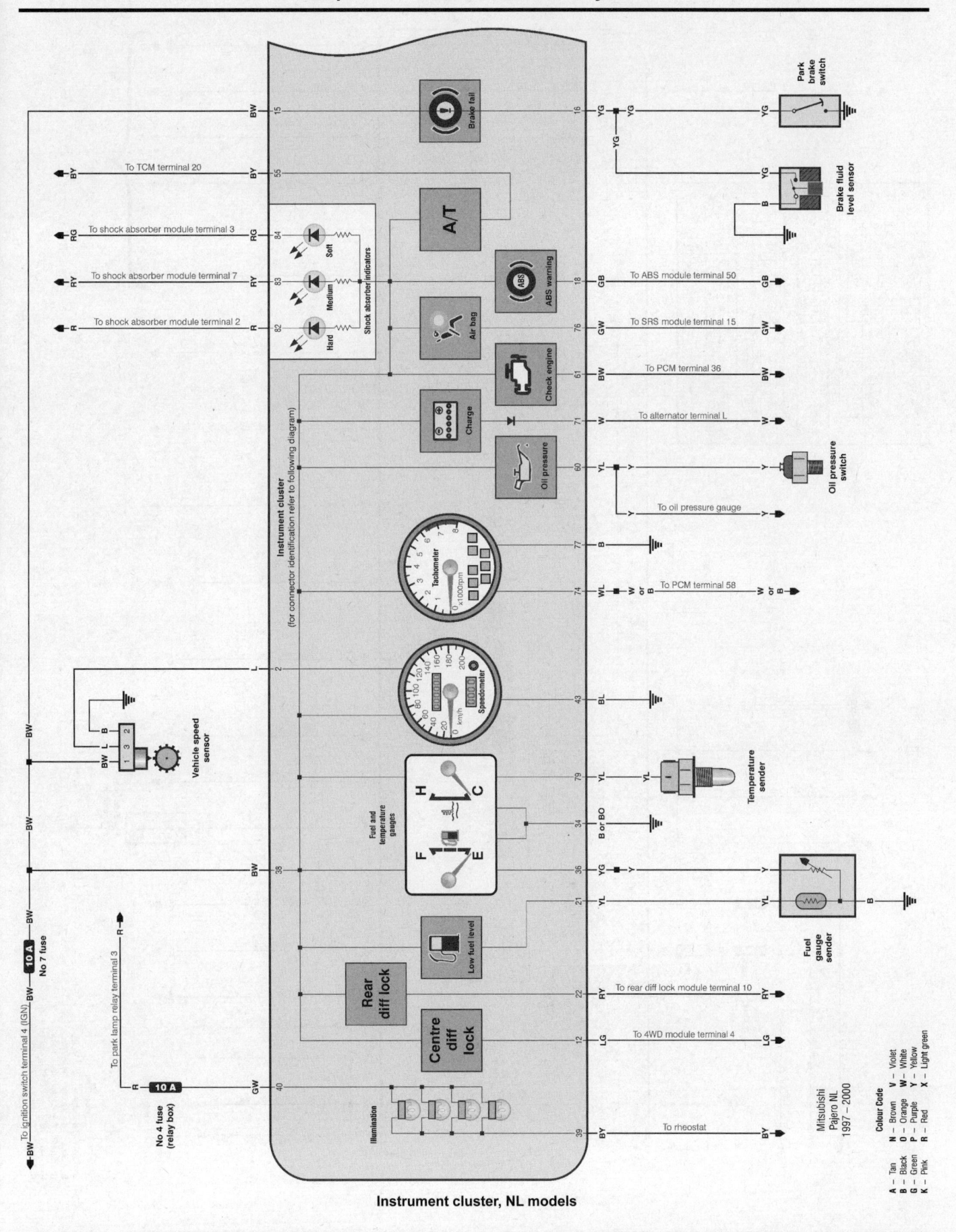

Instrument cluster, NL models

Mitsubishi Pajero NL 1997 – 2000

Colour Code
A – Tan
B – Black
G – Green
K – Pink
N – Brown
O – Orange
P – Purple
R – Red
V – Violet
W – White
Y – Yellow
L – Light green

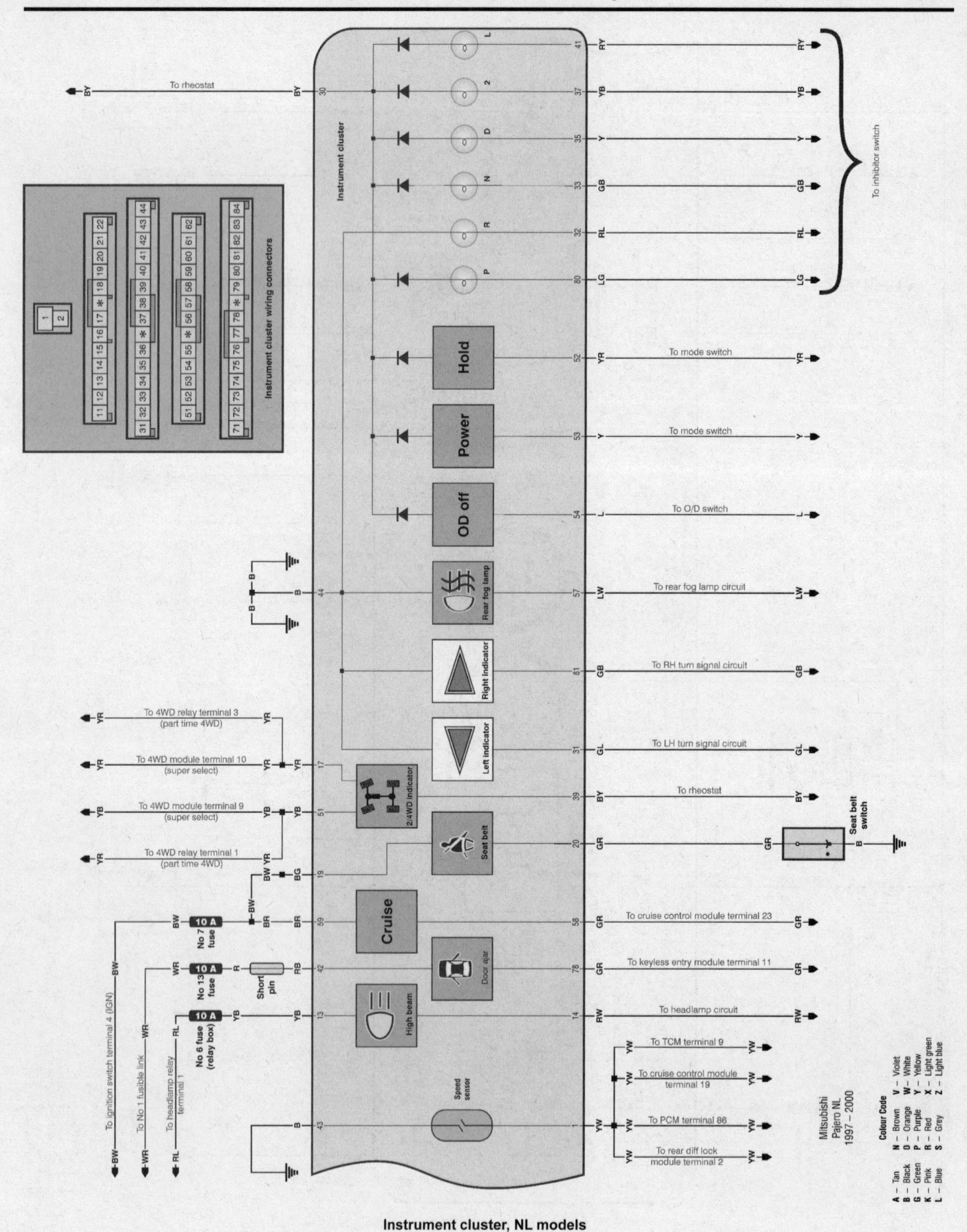

Instrument cluster, NL models

Mitsubishi Pajero NL 1997 – 2000

Colour Code

- A – Tan
- B – Black
- G – Green
- K – Pink
- L – Blue
- N – Brown
- O – Orange
- P – Purple
- R – Red
- S – Grey
- V – Violet
- W – White
- Y – Yellow
- X – Light green
- Z – Light blue

Chapter 12 Chassis electrical system

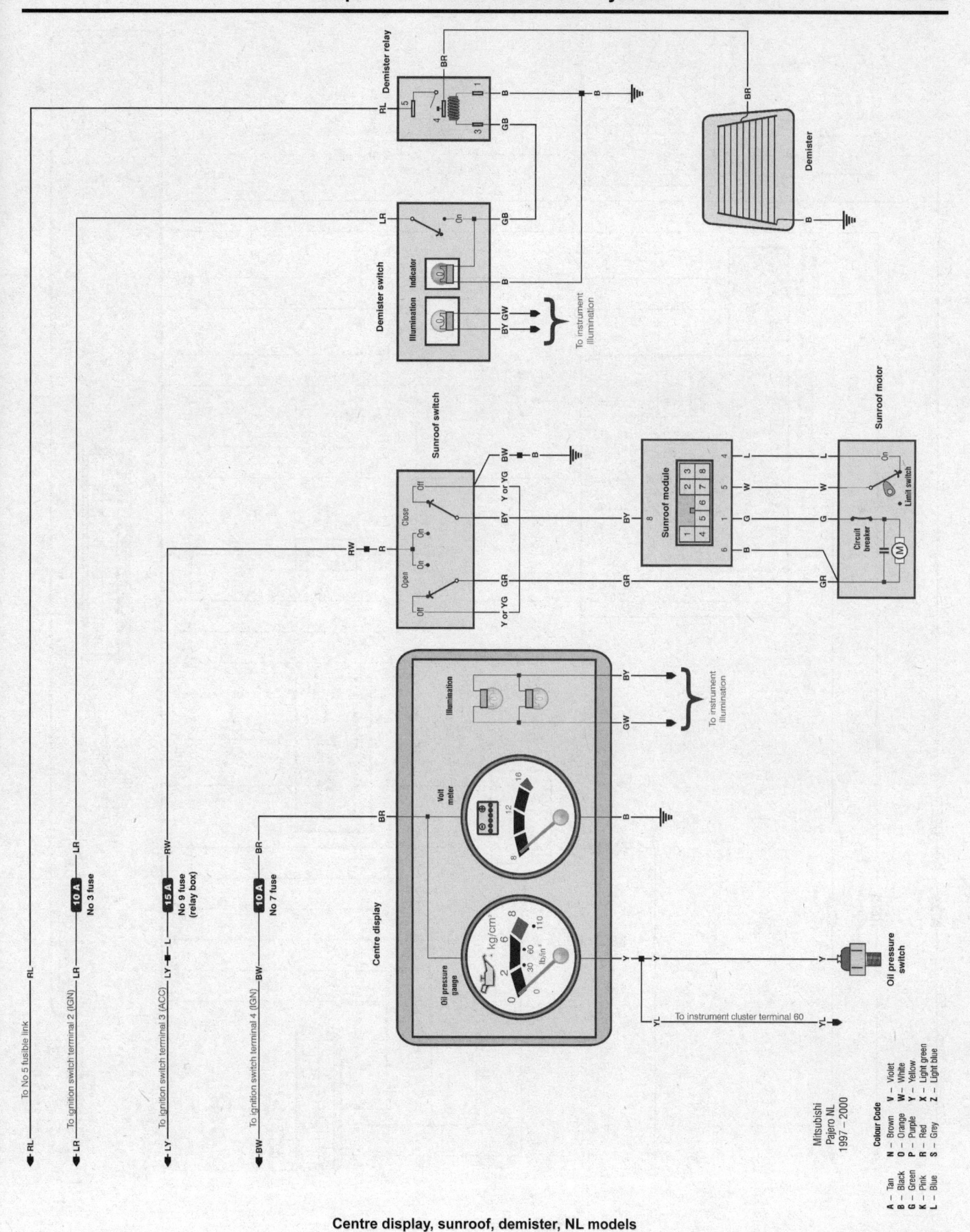

Centre display, sunroof, demister, NL models

12-34 Chapter 12 Chassis electrical system

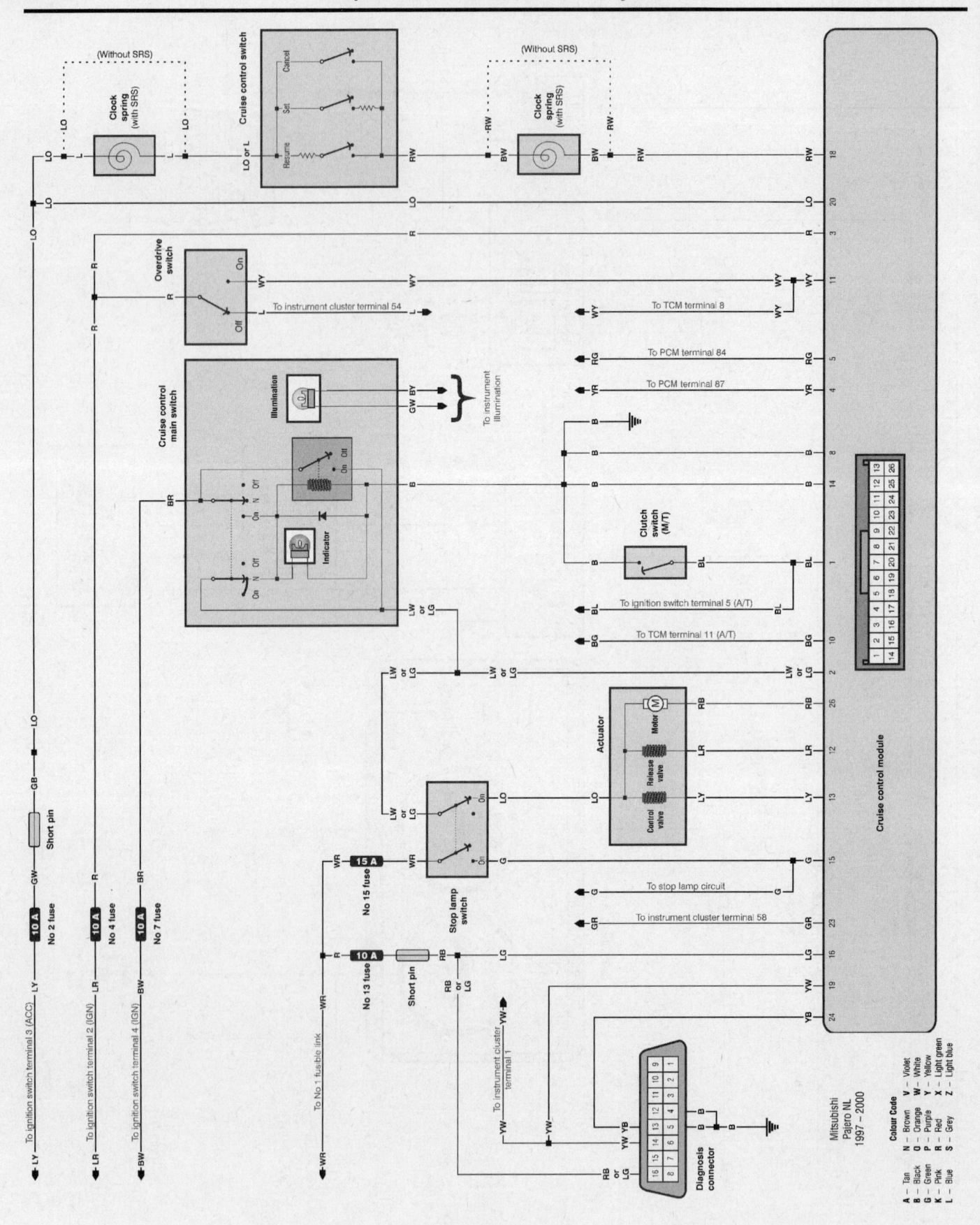

Cruise control, NL models

Mitsubishi Pajero NL 1997–2000

Colour Code:
- A – Tan
- B – Black
- G – Green
- K – Pink
- L – Blue
- N – Brown
- O – Orange
- P – Purple
- R – Red
- S – Grey
- V – Violet
- W – White
- Y – Yellow
- X – Light green
- Z – Light blue

Chapter 12 Chassis electrical system

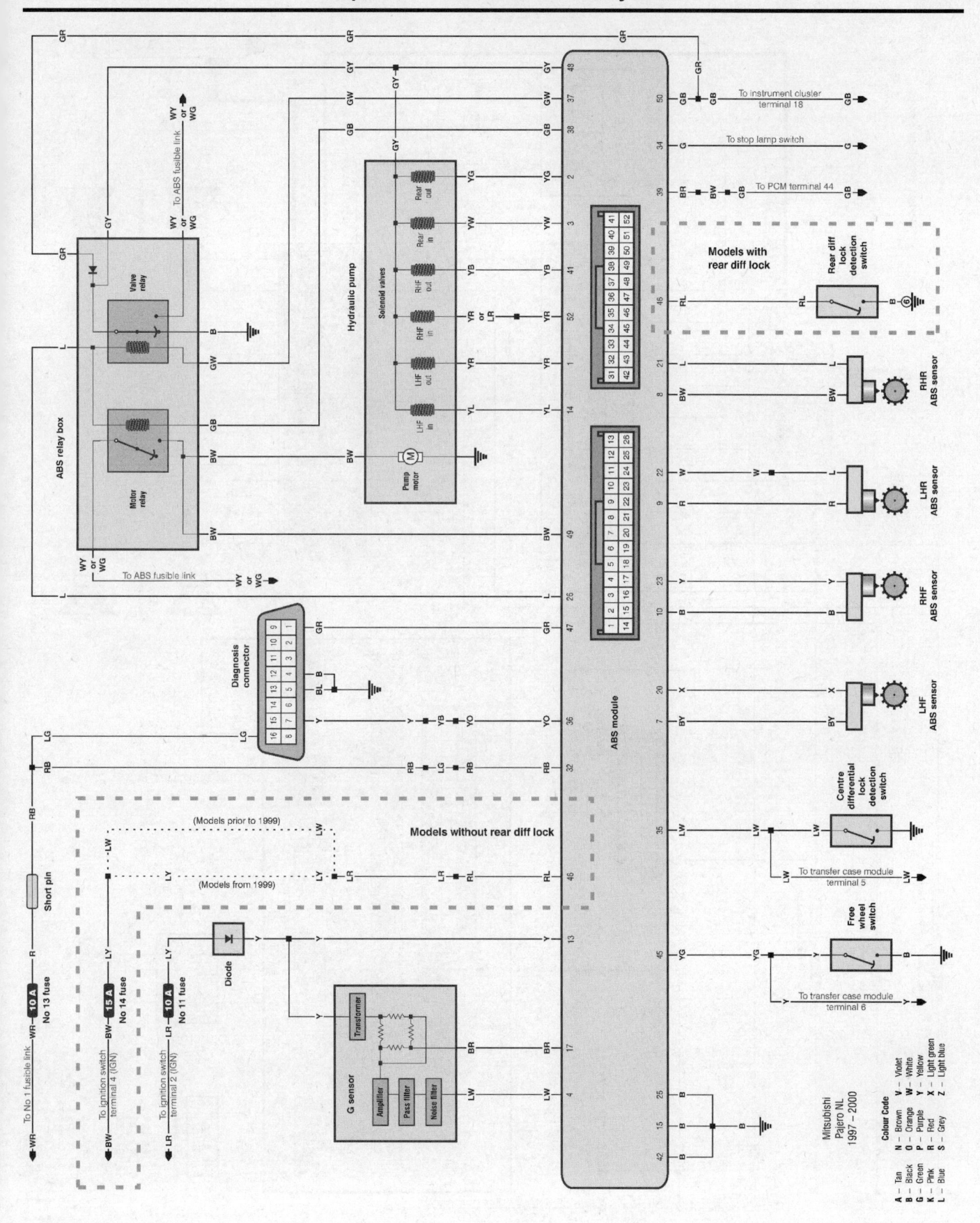

12-35

Antilock braking system (ABS), NL models

Chapter 12 Chassis electrical system

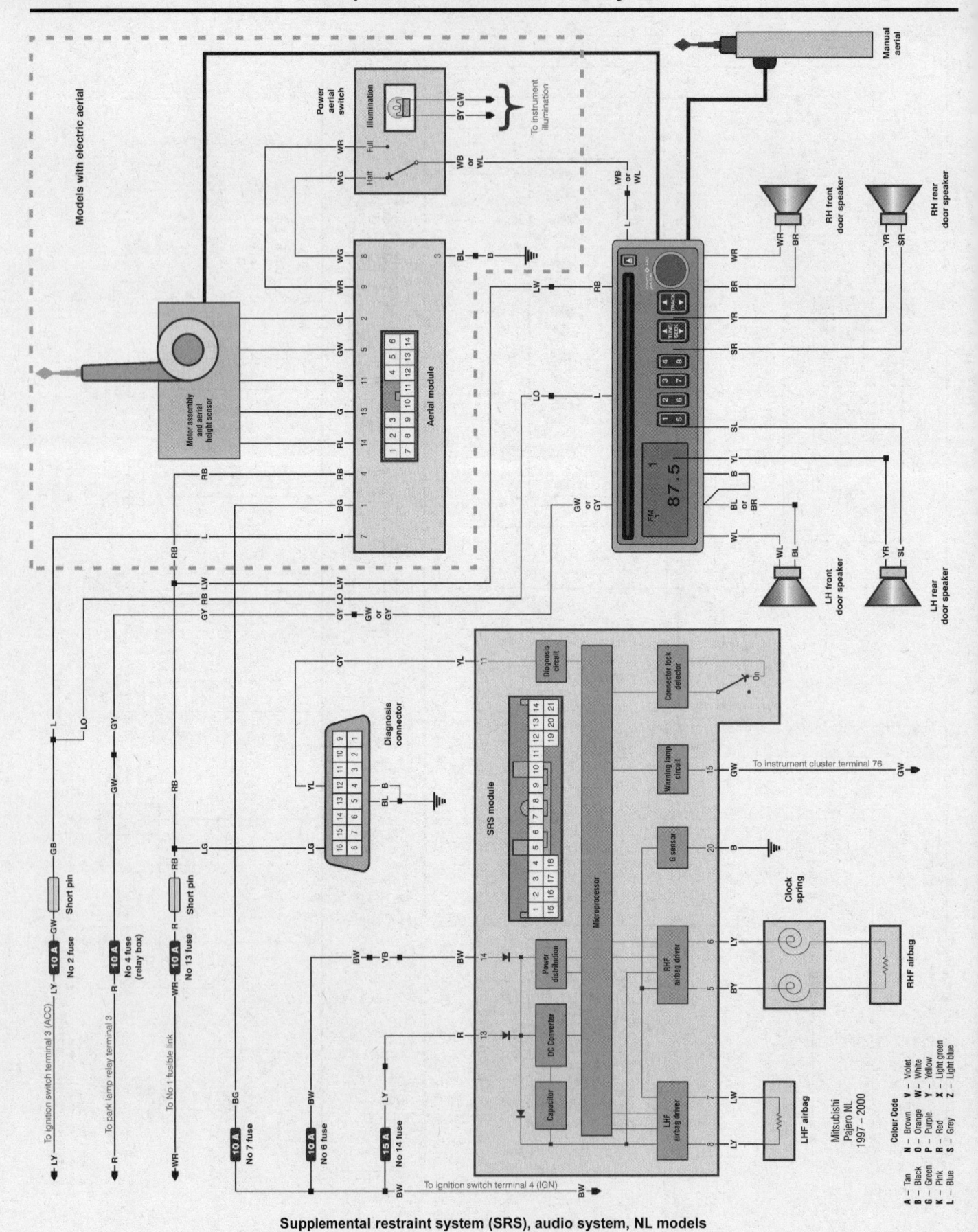

Supplemental restraint system (SRS), audio system, NL models

Mitsubishi Pajero NL 1997 – 2000

Colour Code

- A – Tan
- B – Black
- G – Green
- K – Pink
- L – Blue
- N – Brown
- O – Orange
- P – Purple
- R – Red
- S – Grey
- V – Violet
- W – White
- Y – Yellow
- X – Light green
- Z – Light blue

Chapter 12 Chassis electrical system

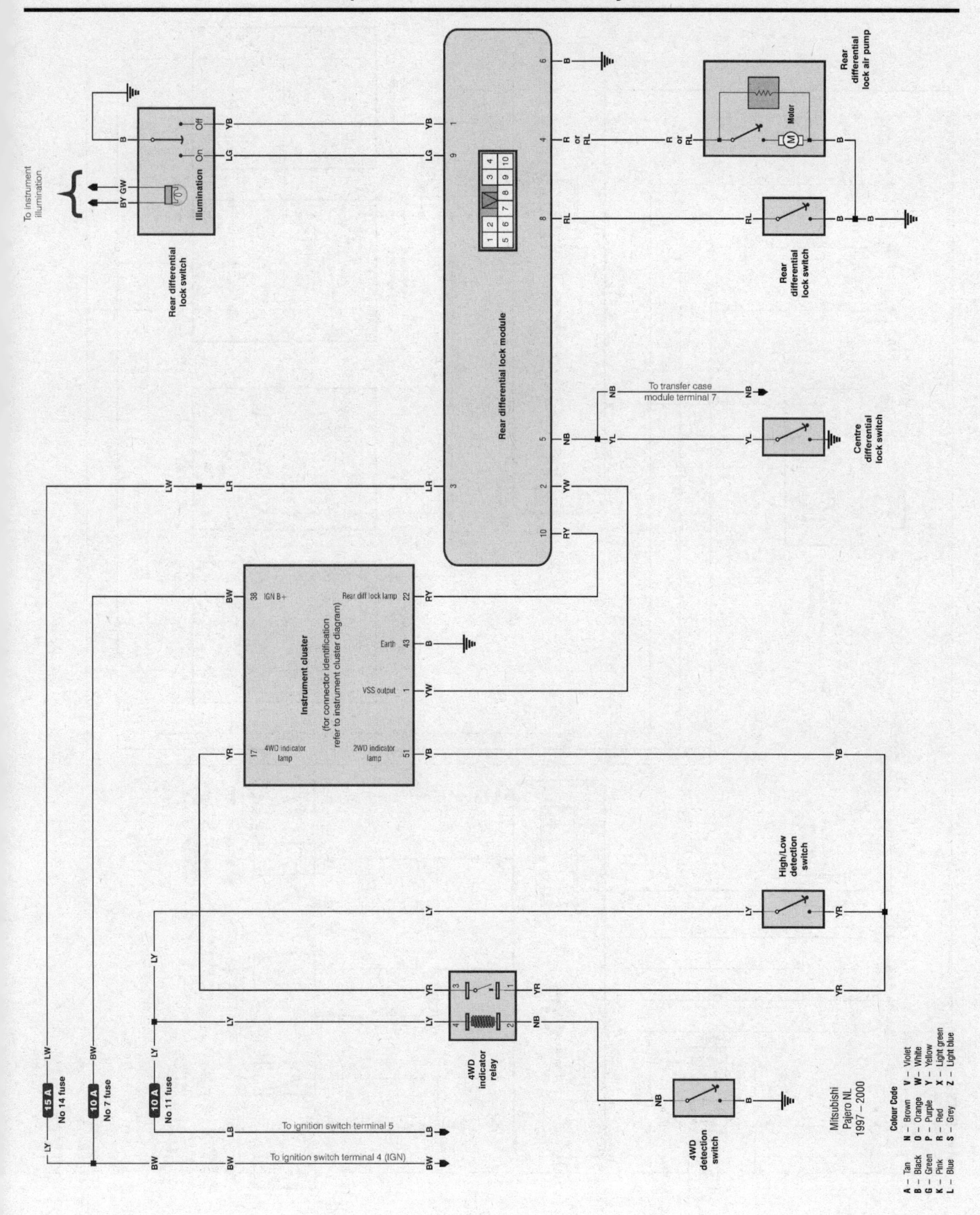

4WD indicator lamps, rear differential lock, NL models

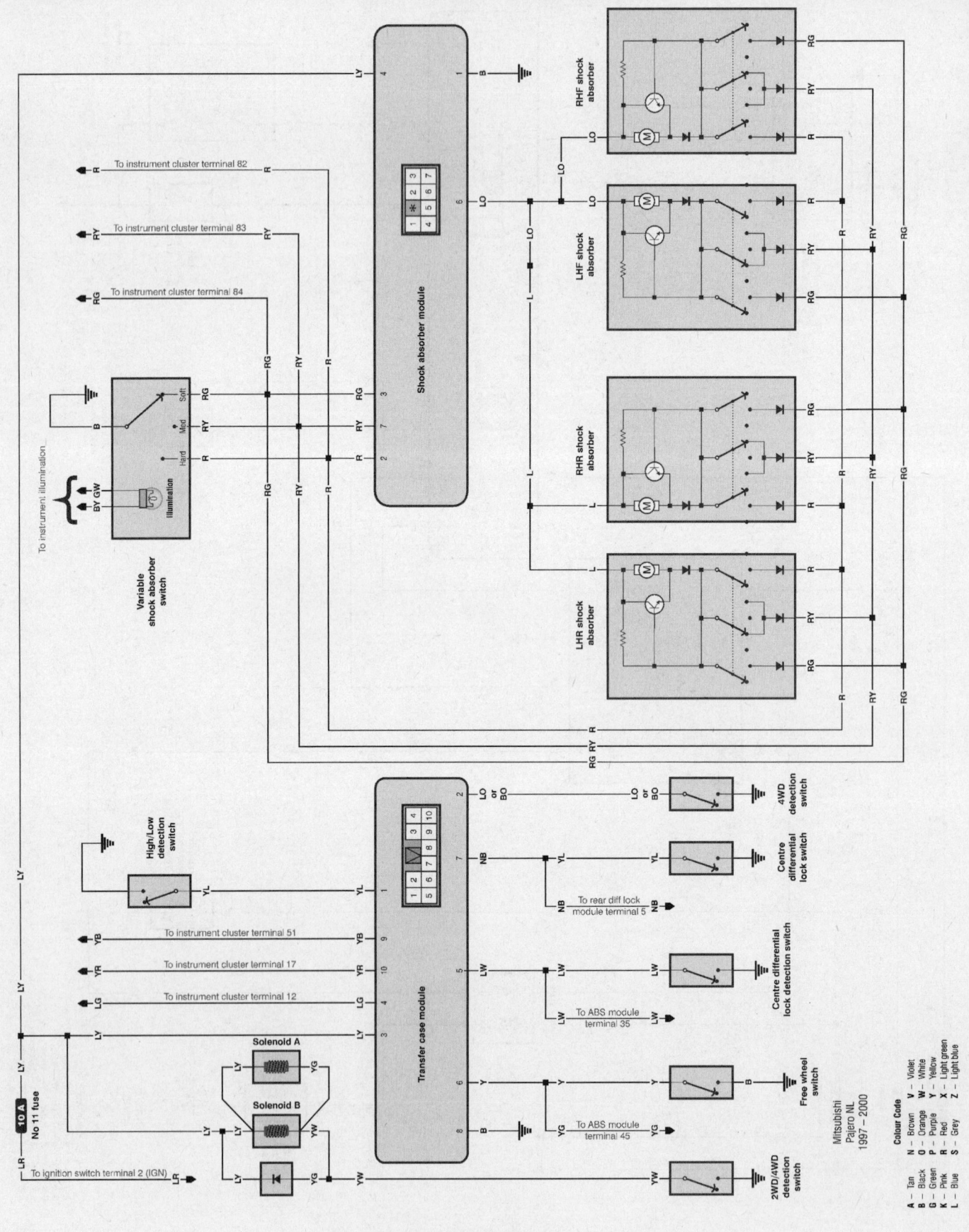

4WD selection system, suspension, NL models

Chapter 12 Chassis electrical system

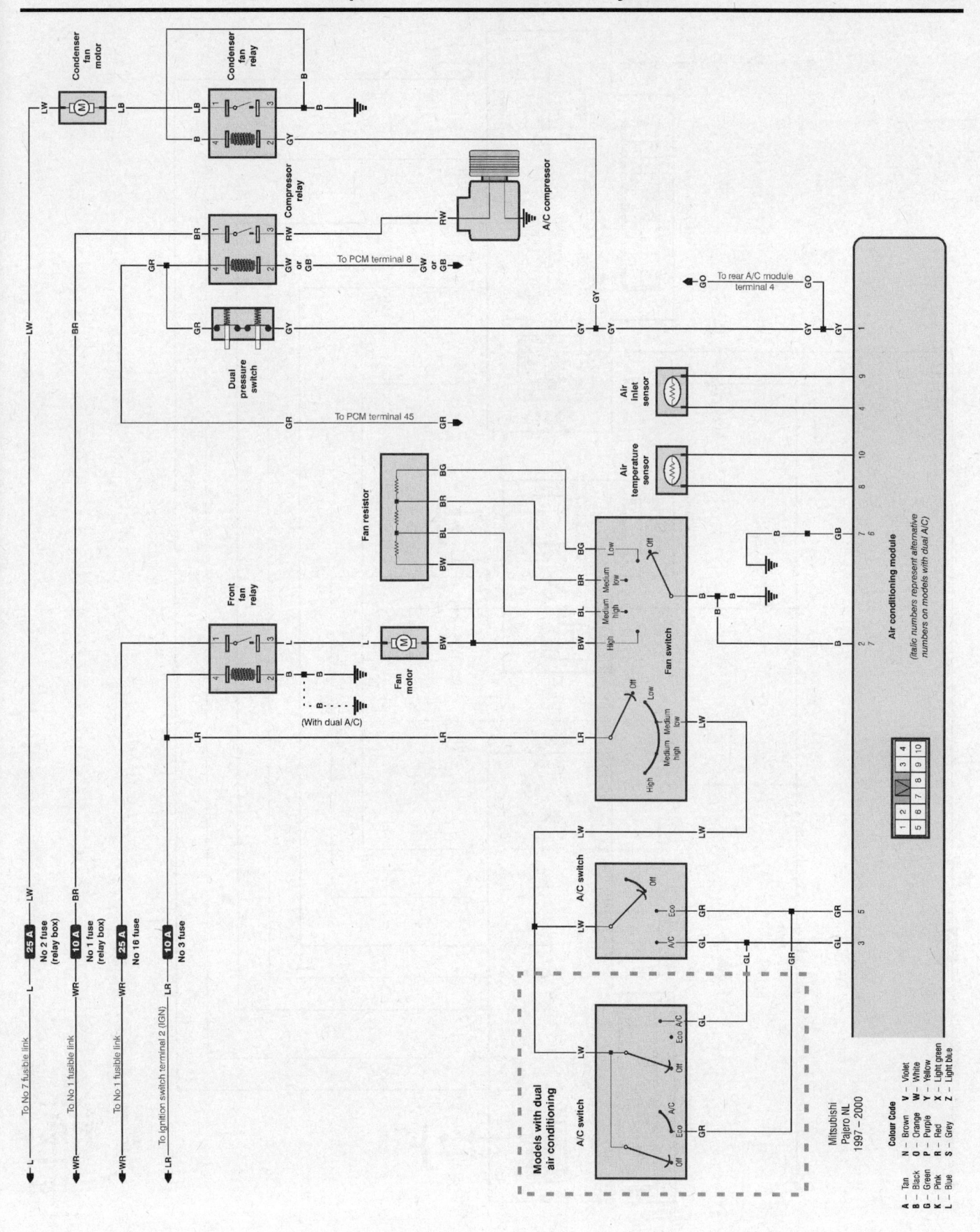

Air conditioning (front), condenser fan, NL models

Chapter 12 Chassis electrical system

Air conditioning (rear), NL models

Mitsubishi Pajero NL 1997 – 2000

Colour Code

A – Tan	N – Brown	V – Violet	
B – Black	O – Orange	W – White	
G – Green	P – Purple	Y – Yellow	
K – Pink	R – Red	X – Light green	
L – Blue	S – Grey	Z – Light blue	

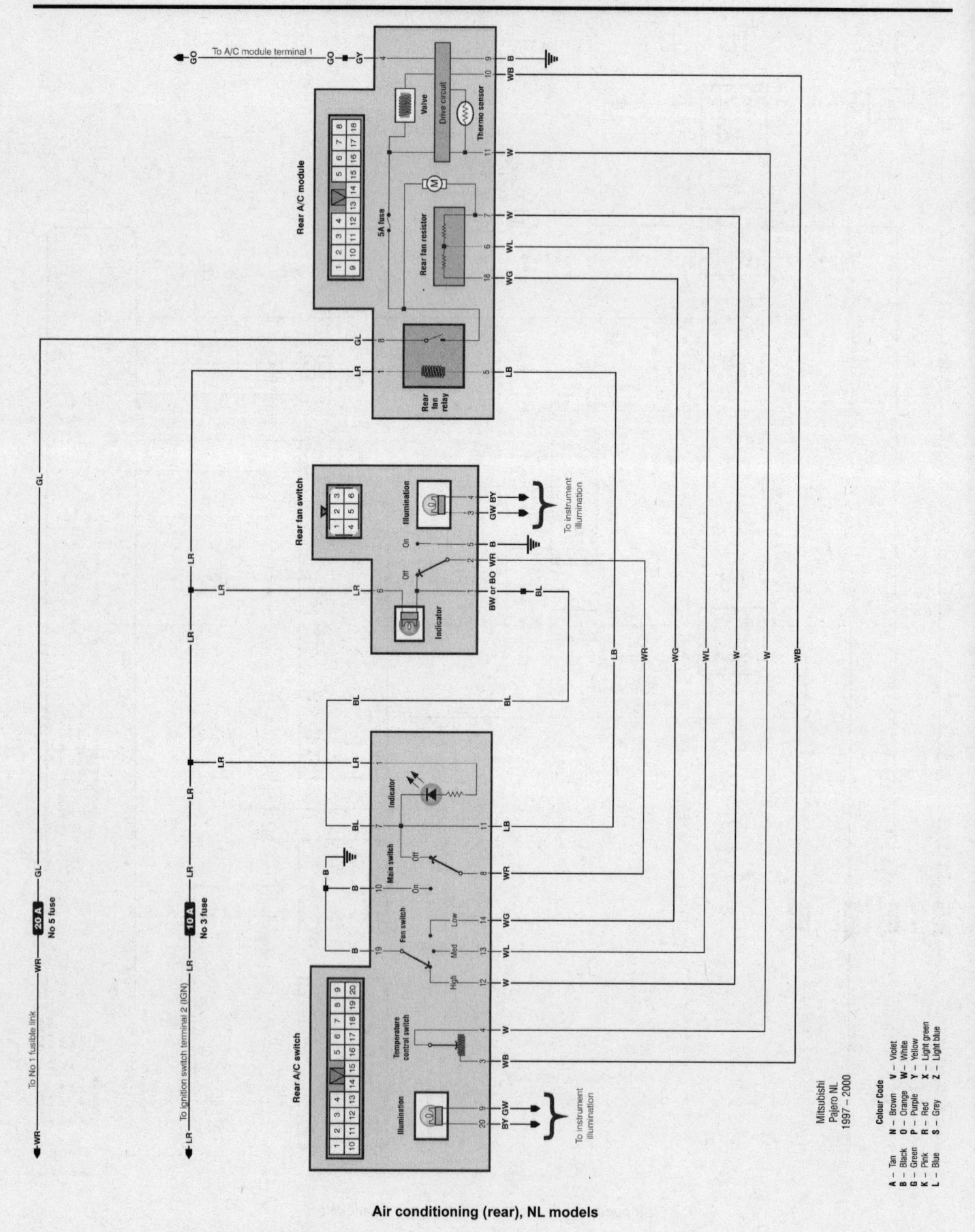

Chapter 12 Chassis electrical system

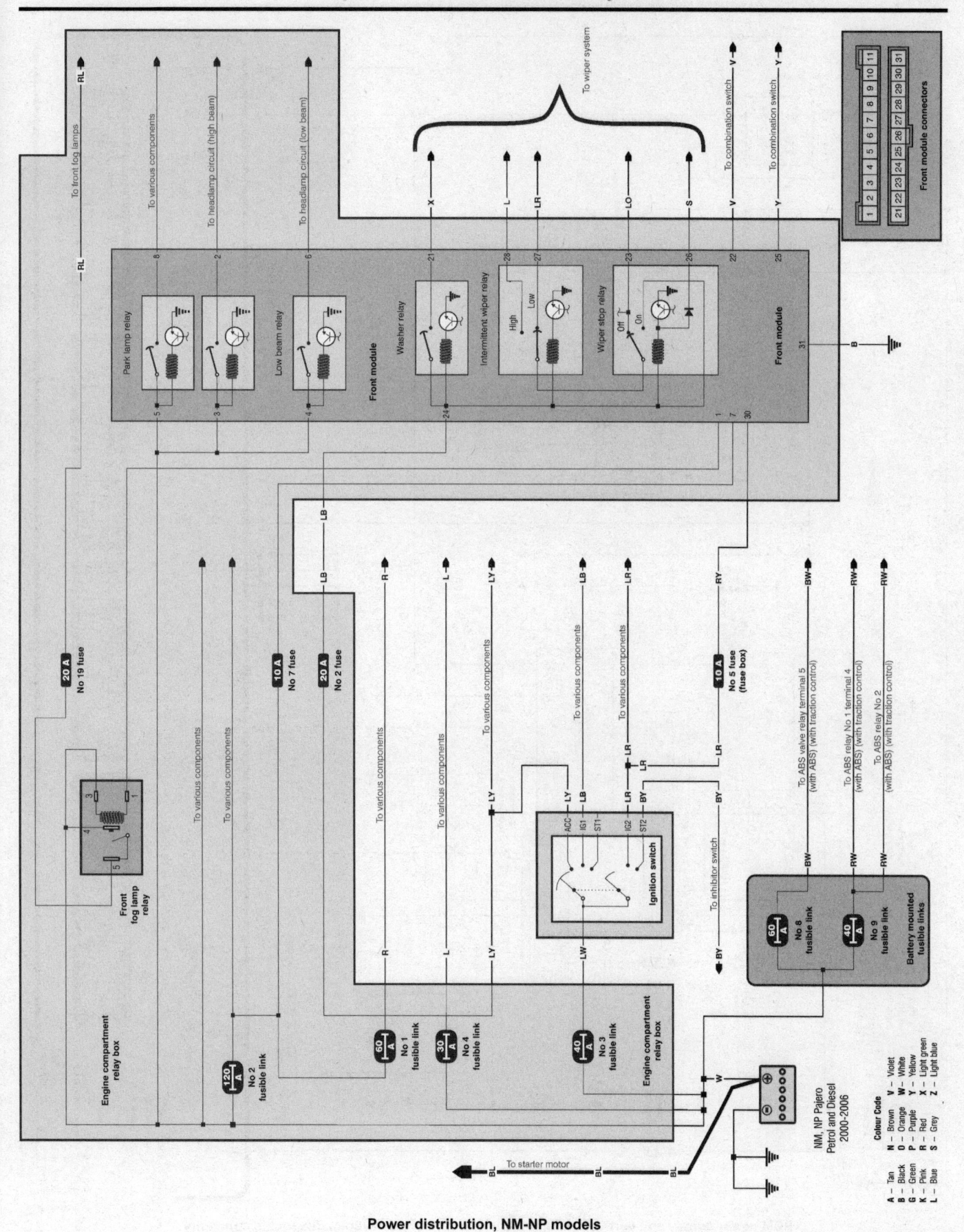

Power distribution, NM-NP models

12-42 Chapter 12 Chassis electrical system

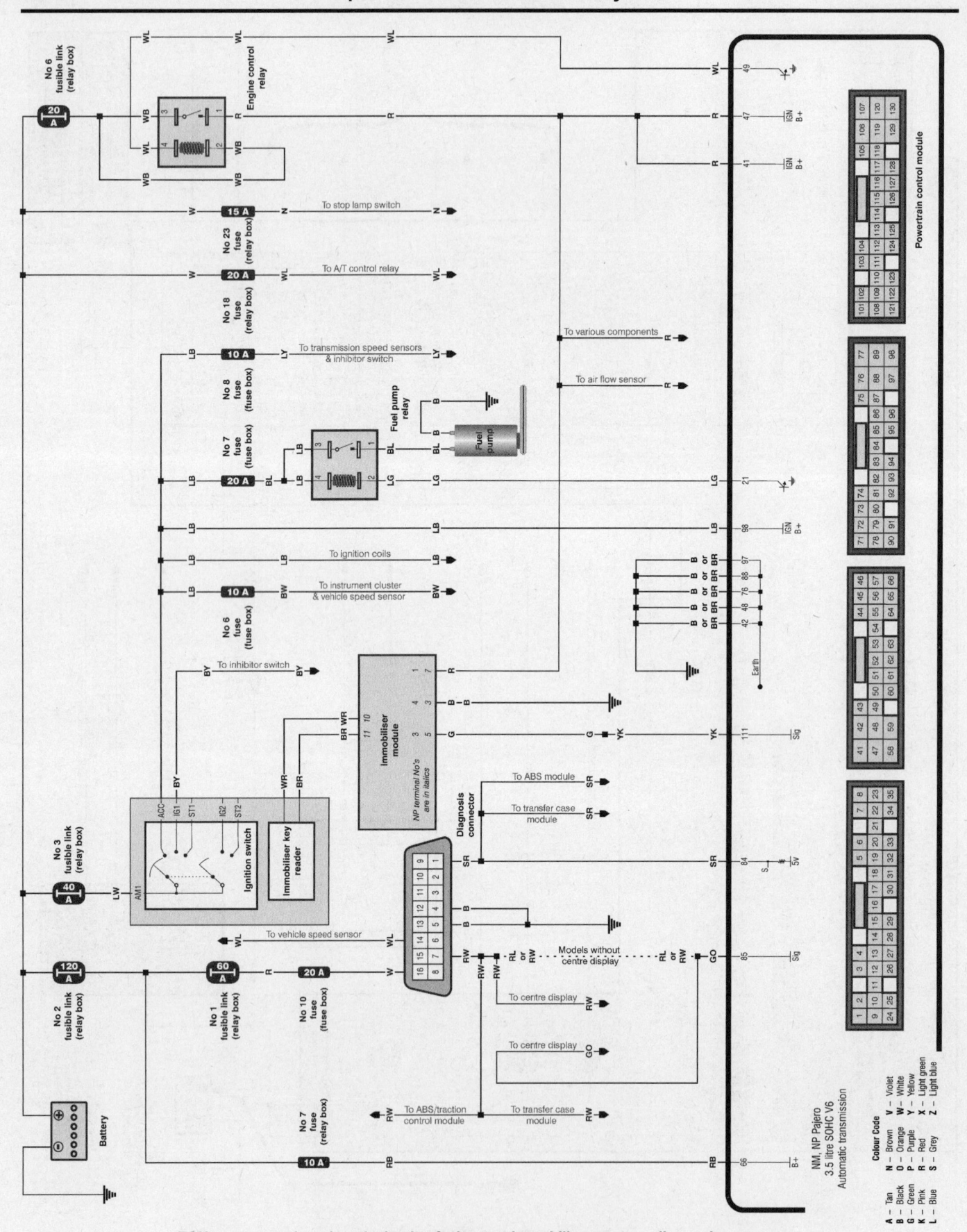

**PCM power supply and earth circuits, fuel pump, immobiliser system, diagnosis connector.
Automatic transmission — petrol, NM-NP models**

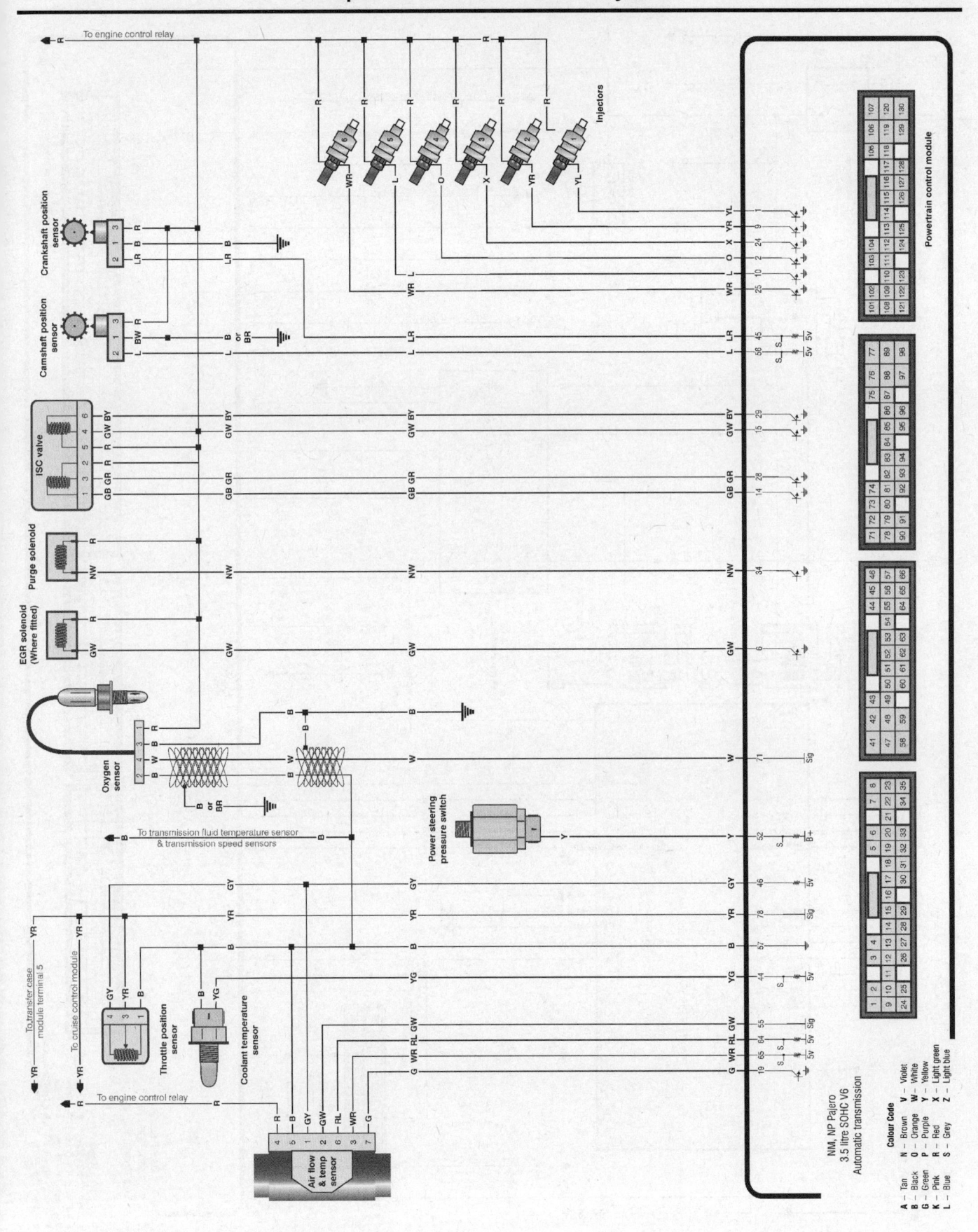

Chapter 12 Chassis electrical system

Various engine management input sensors, ISC valve, fuel injectors. Automatic transmission — petrol, NM-NP models

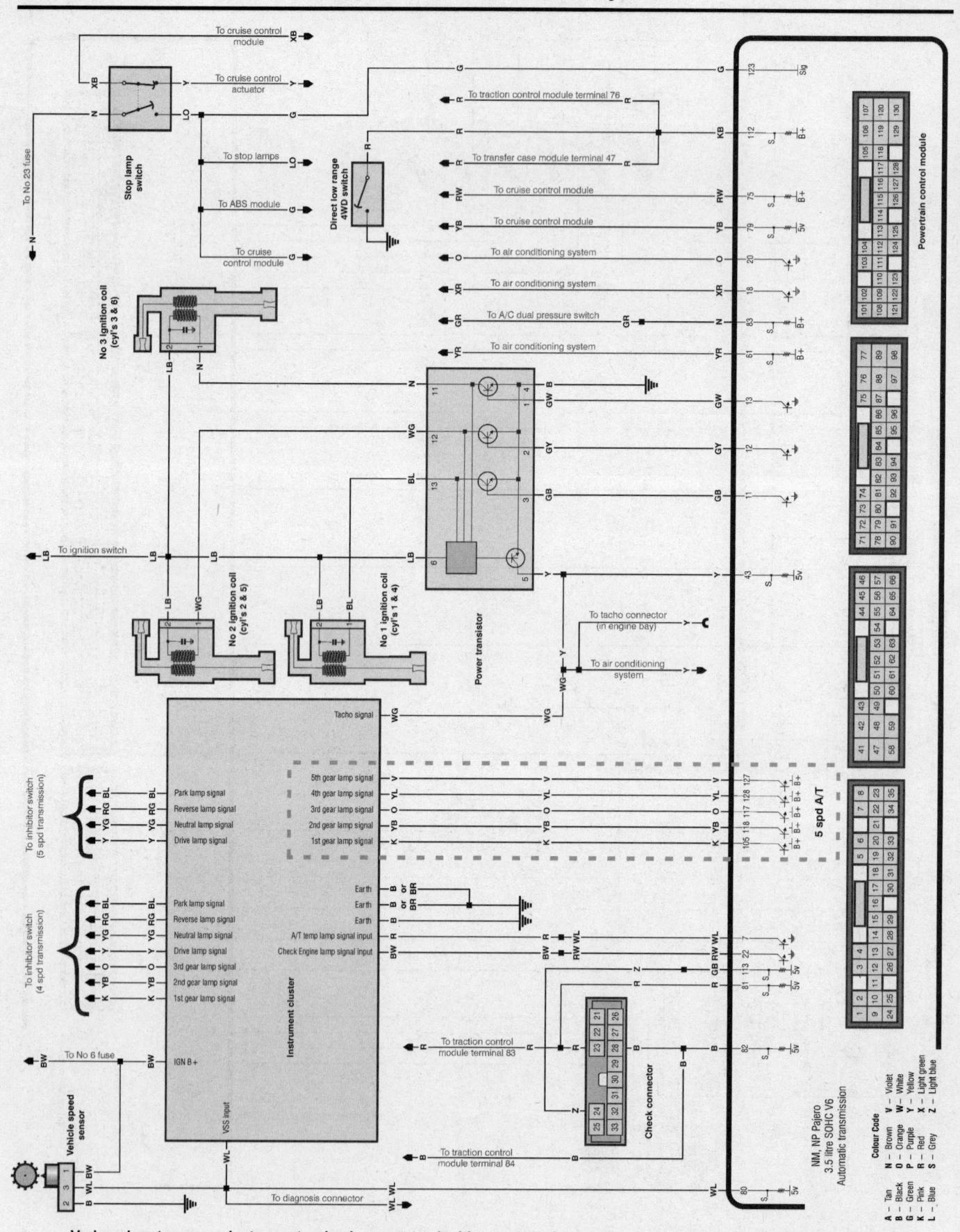

Various input sensors, instruments, check connector, ignition system. Automatic transmission — petrol, NM-NP models

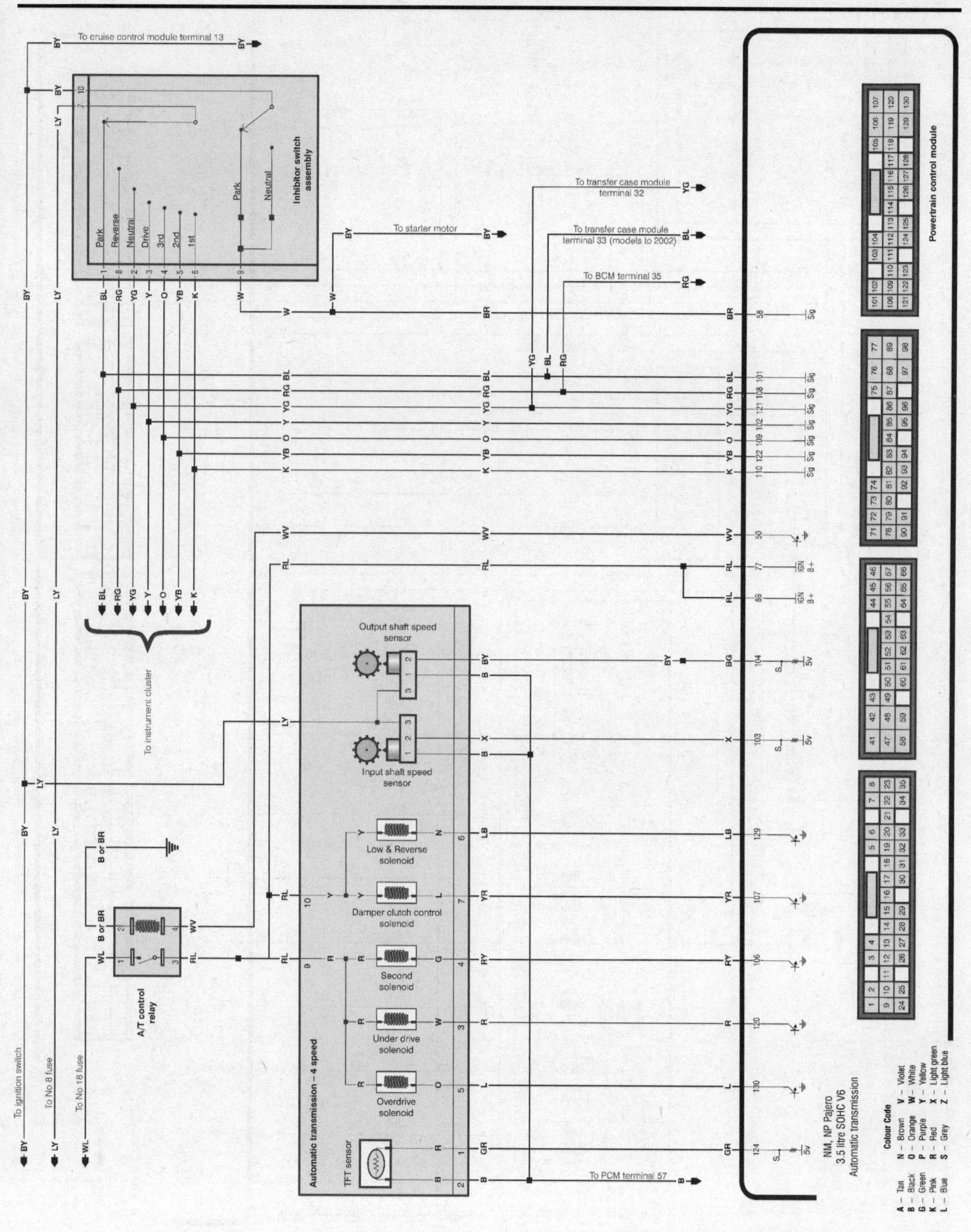

Chapter 12 Chassis electrical system

Four speed automatic transmission, inhibitor switch. Automatic transmission — petrol, NM-NP models

Five speed automatic transmission, inhibitor switches, shift switch assembly.
Automatic transmission — petrol, NM-NP models

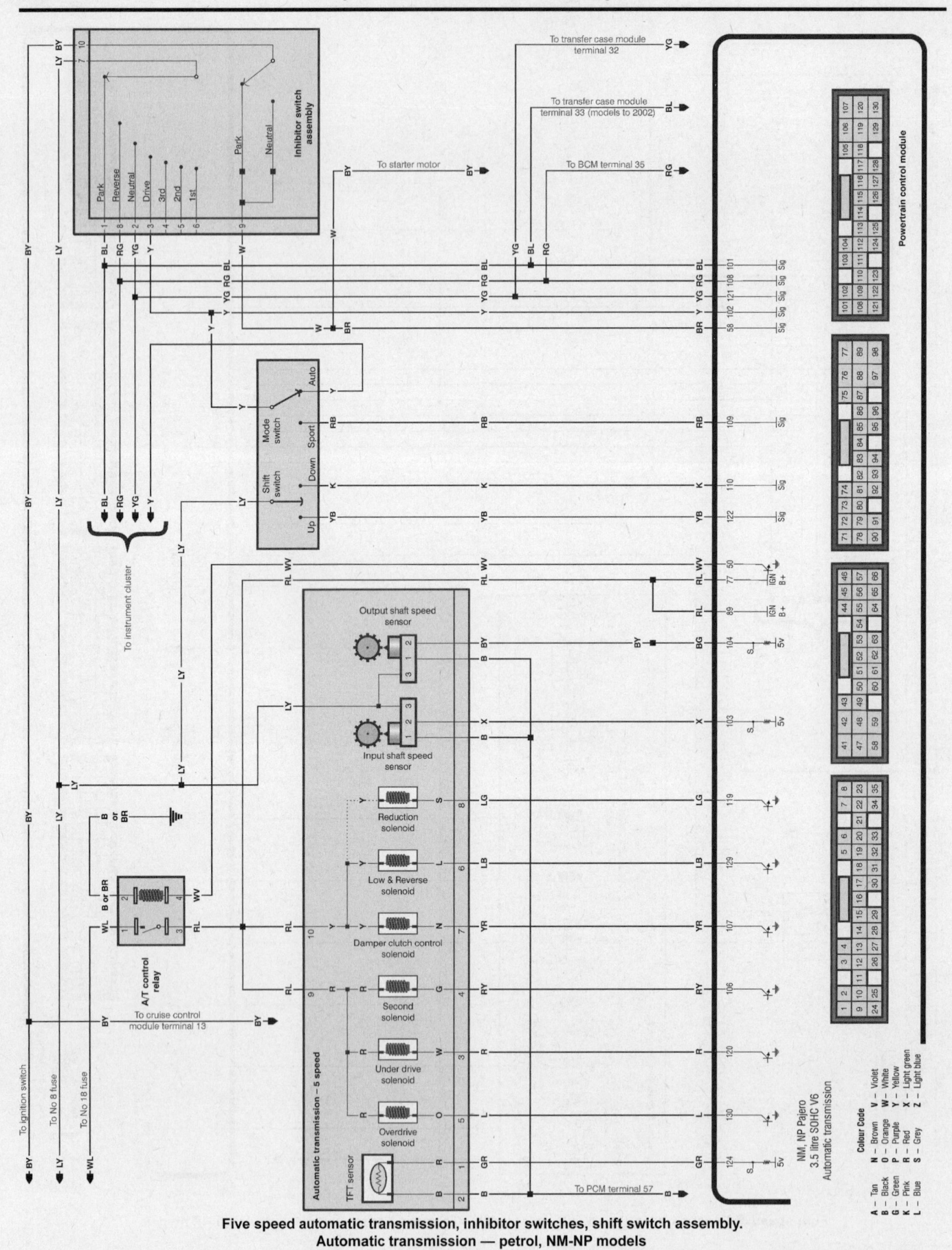

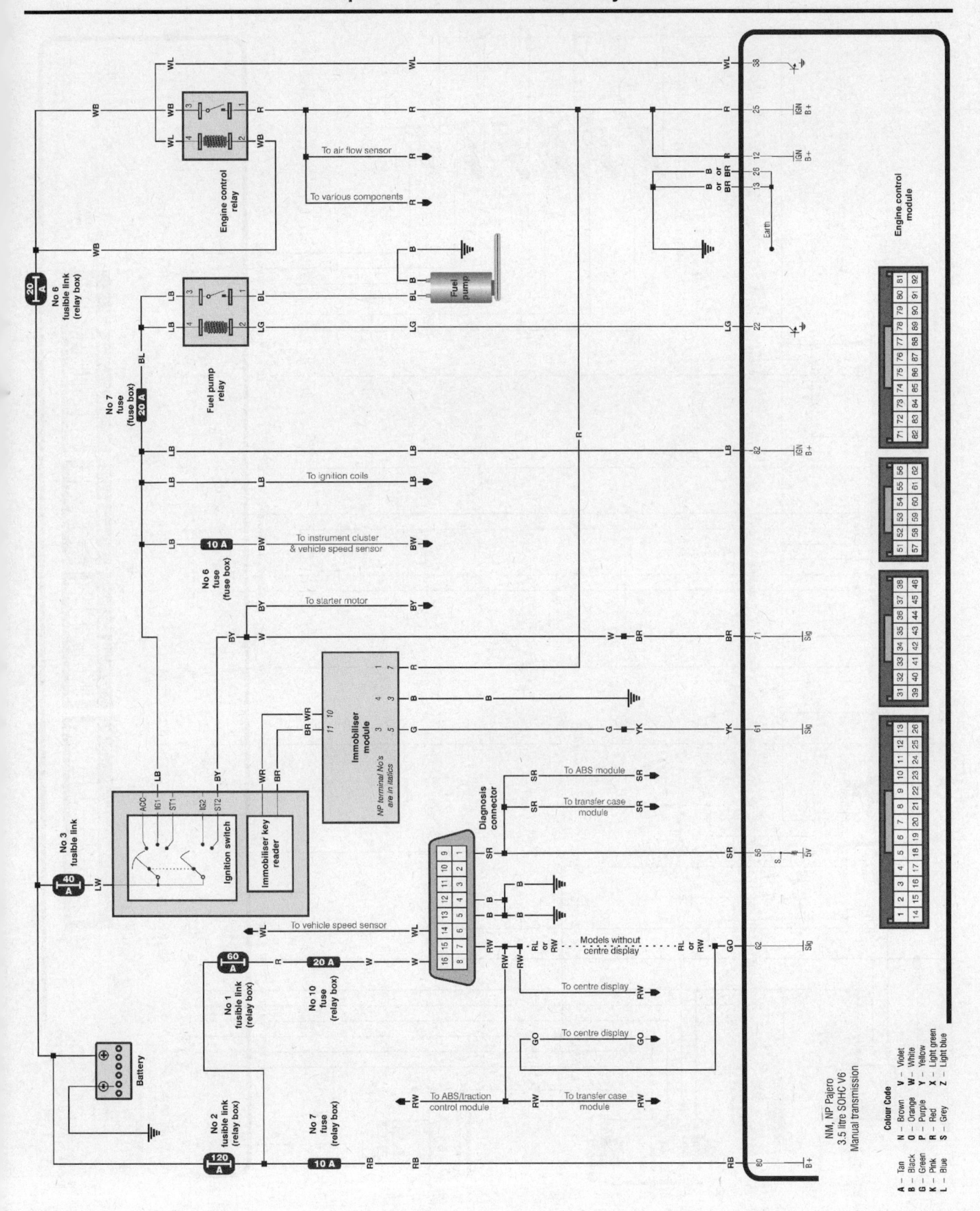

Chapter 12 Chassis electrical system

**PCM power supply and earth circuits, fuel pump, immobiliser system, diagnosis connector.
Manual transmission — petrol, NM-NP models**

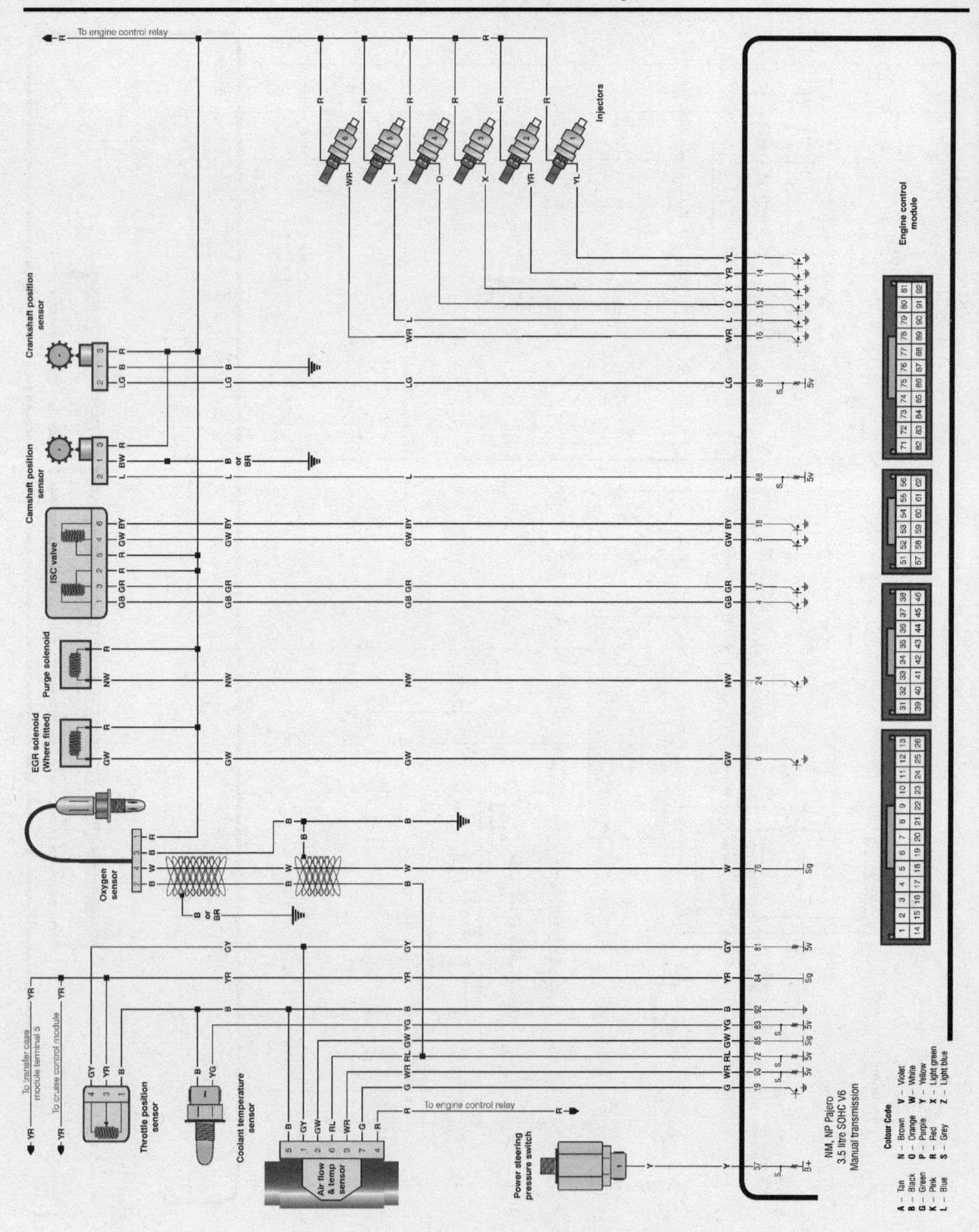

12-48 Chapter 12 Chassis electrical system

Various engine management input sensors, ISC valve, fuel injectors. Manual transmission — petrol, NM-NP models

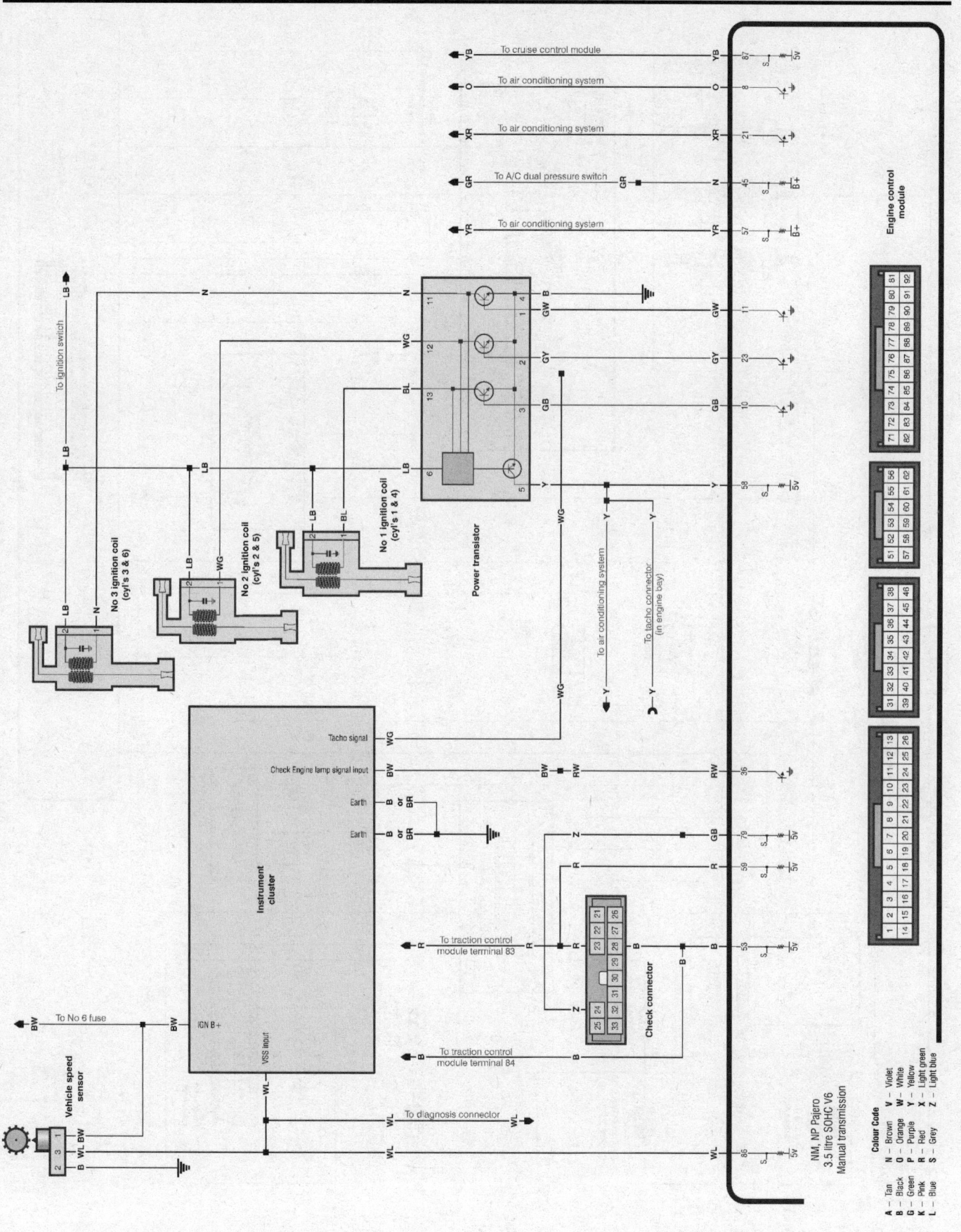

Chapter 12 Chassis electrical system

12-49

Vehicle speed sensor, instruments, check connector, ignition system. Manual transmission — petrol, NM-NP models

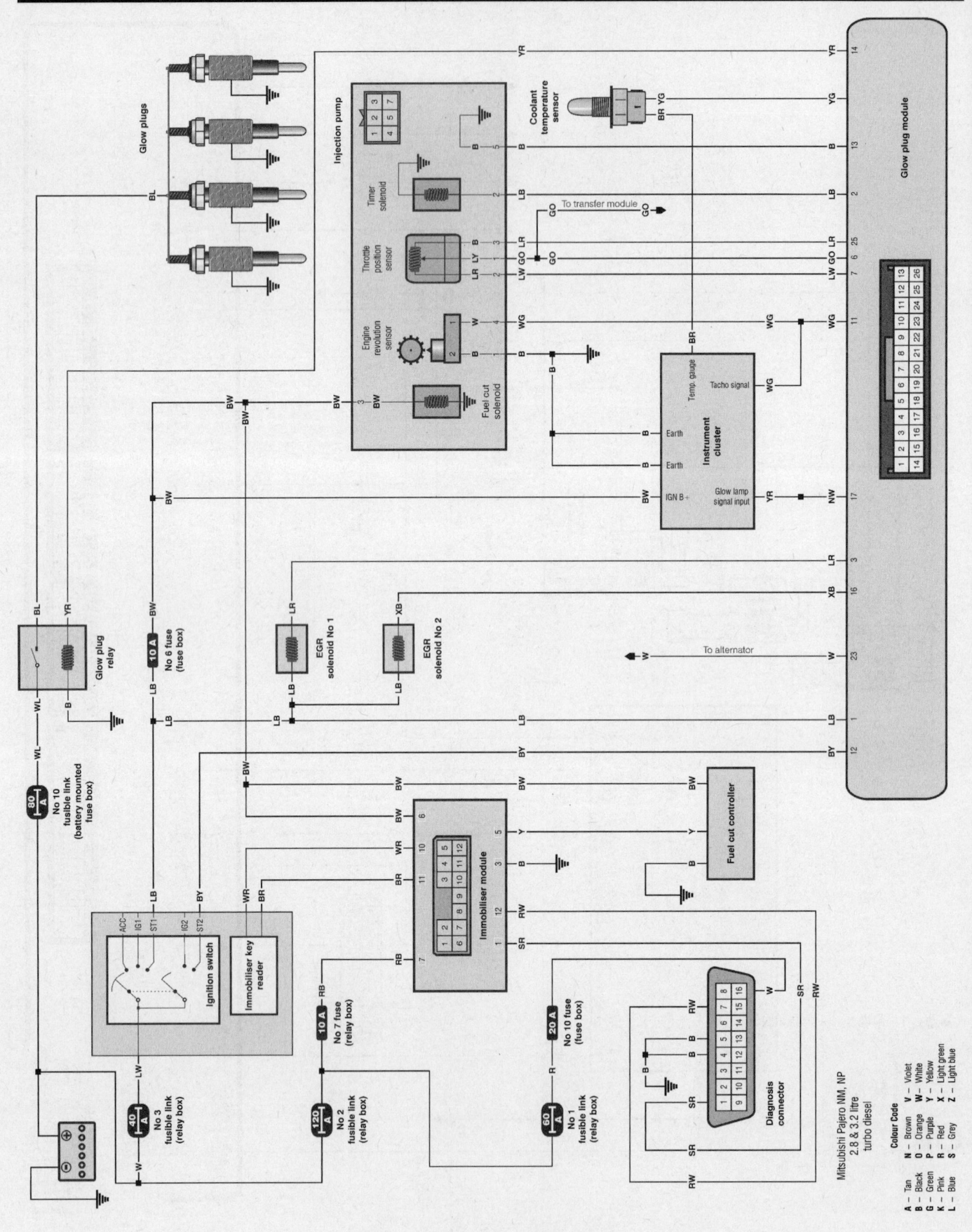

Engine control system. 4M40 models

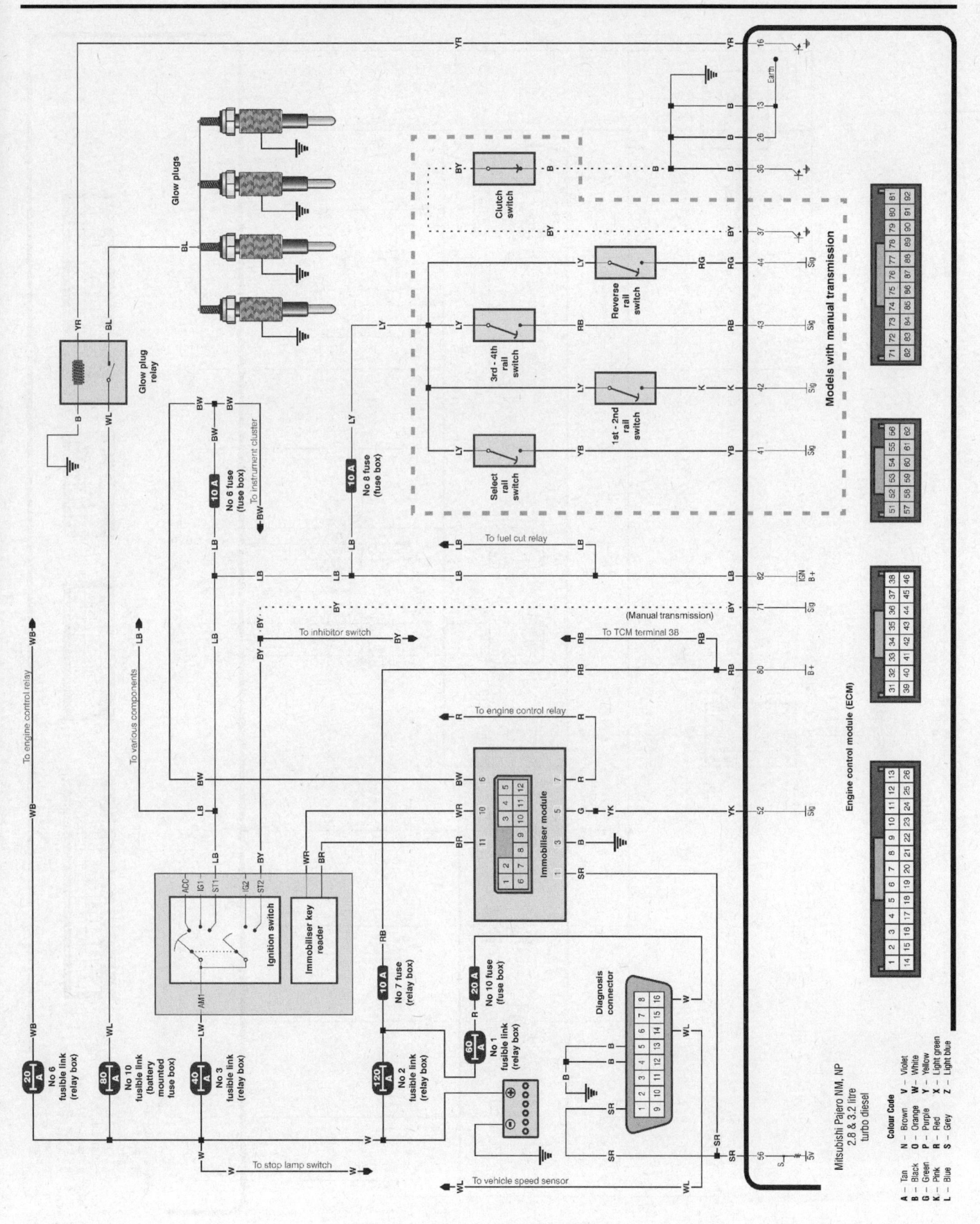

Chapter 12 Chassis electrical system

12-51

Engine control system. 4M41 models

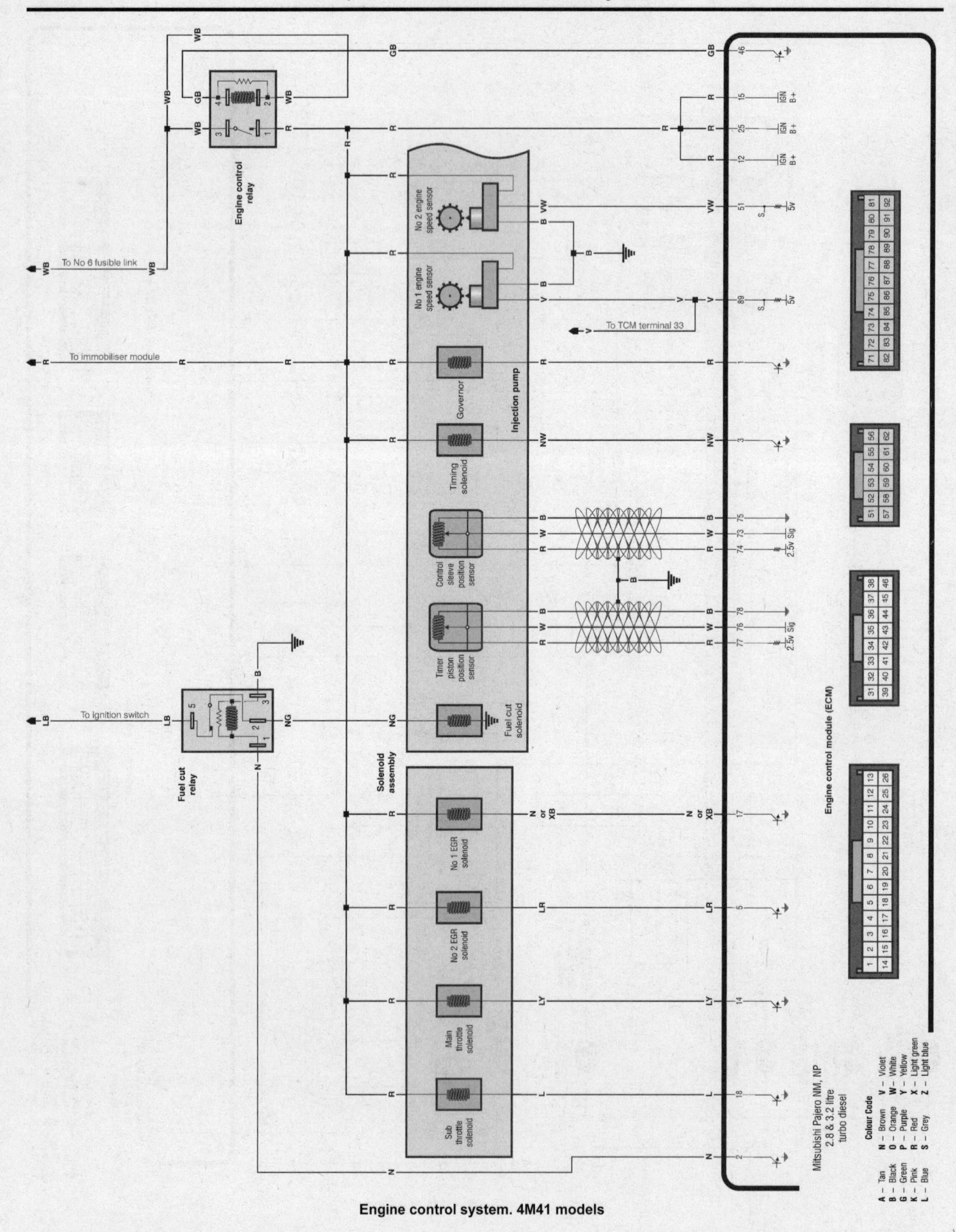

Engine control system. 4M41 models

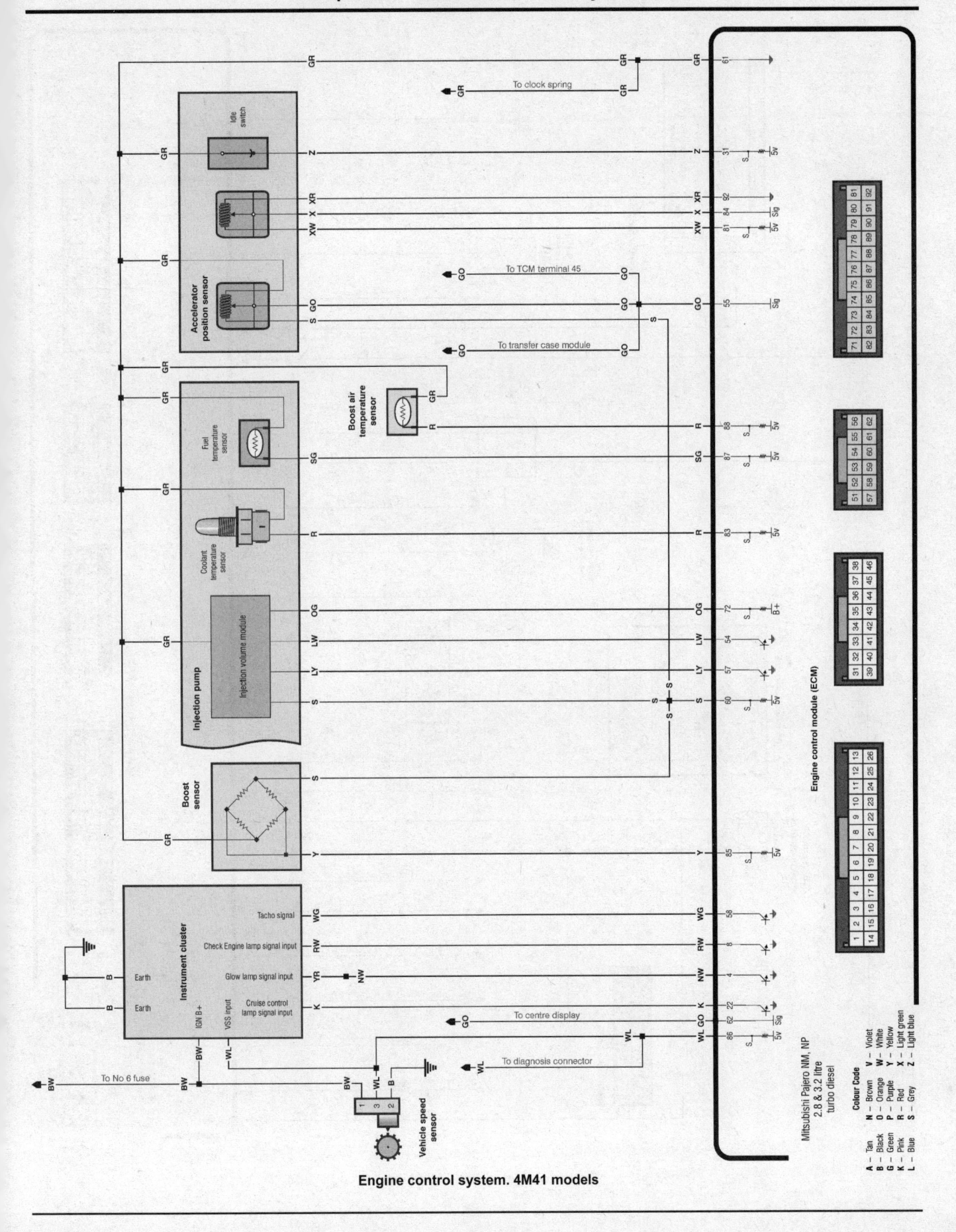

Chapter 12 Chassis electrical system

12-53

Engine control system. 4M41 models

Mitsubishi Pajero NM, NP 2.8 & 3.2 litre turbo diesel

Colour Code
A – Tan   N – Brown   V – Violet
B – Black   O – Orange   W – White
G – Green   P – Purple   Y – Yellow
K – Pink   R – Red   X – Light green
L – Blue   S – Grey   Z – Light blue

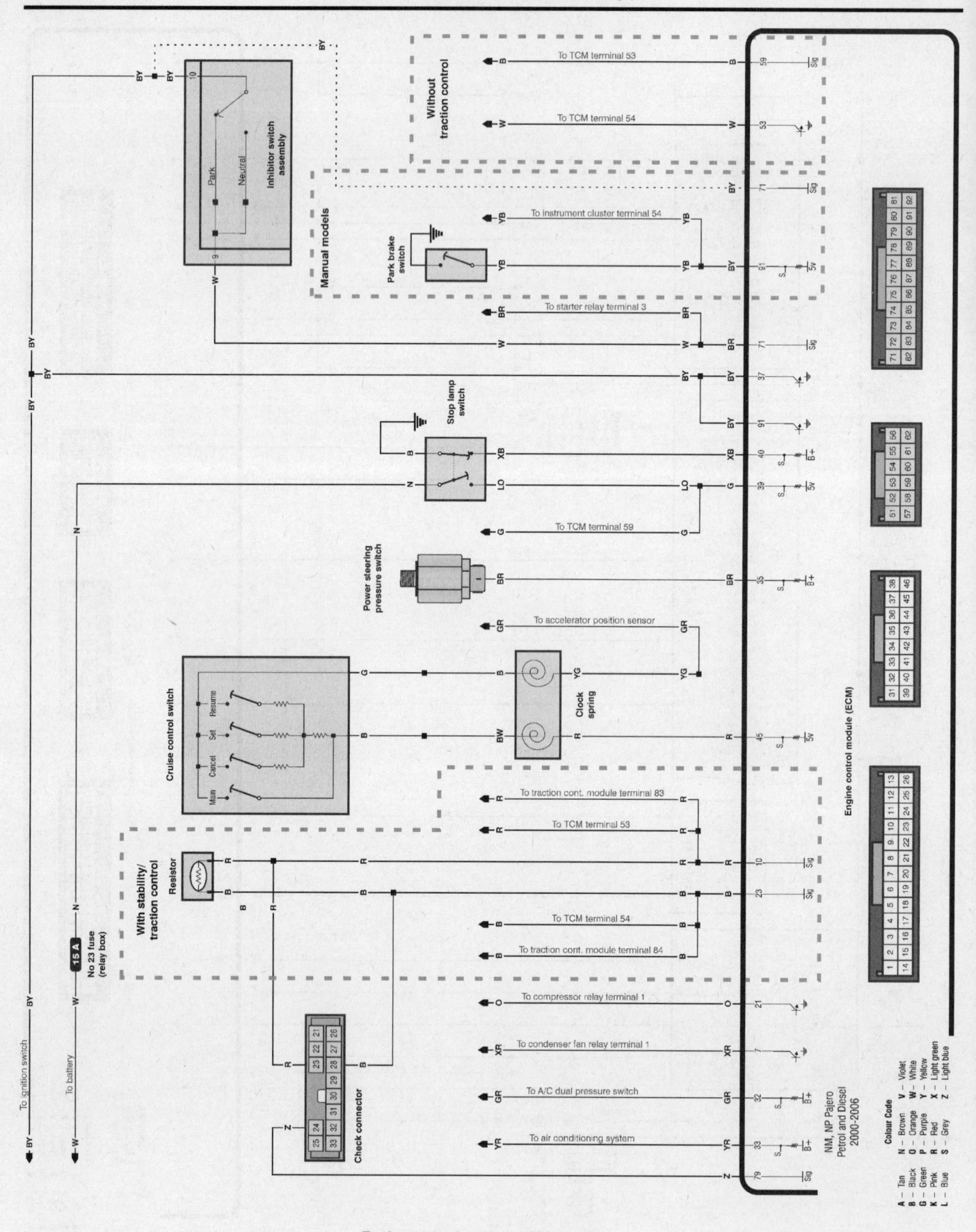

Chapter 12 Chassis electrical system

Engine control system. 4M41 models

Chapter 12 Chassis electrical system

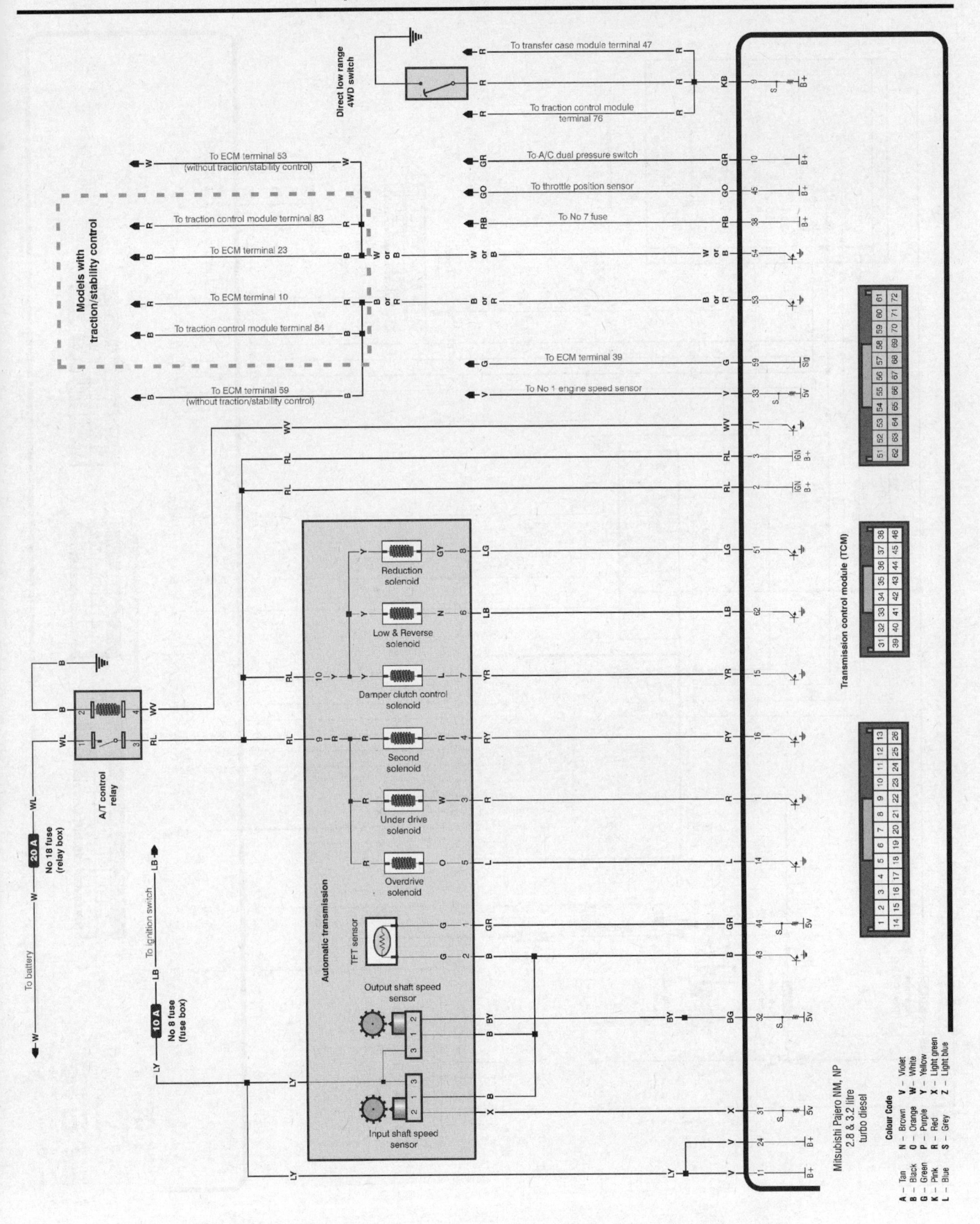

Automatic transmission control module, automatic transmission. Diesel, NM-NP models

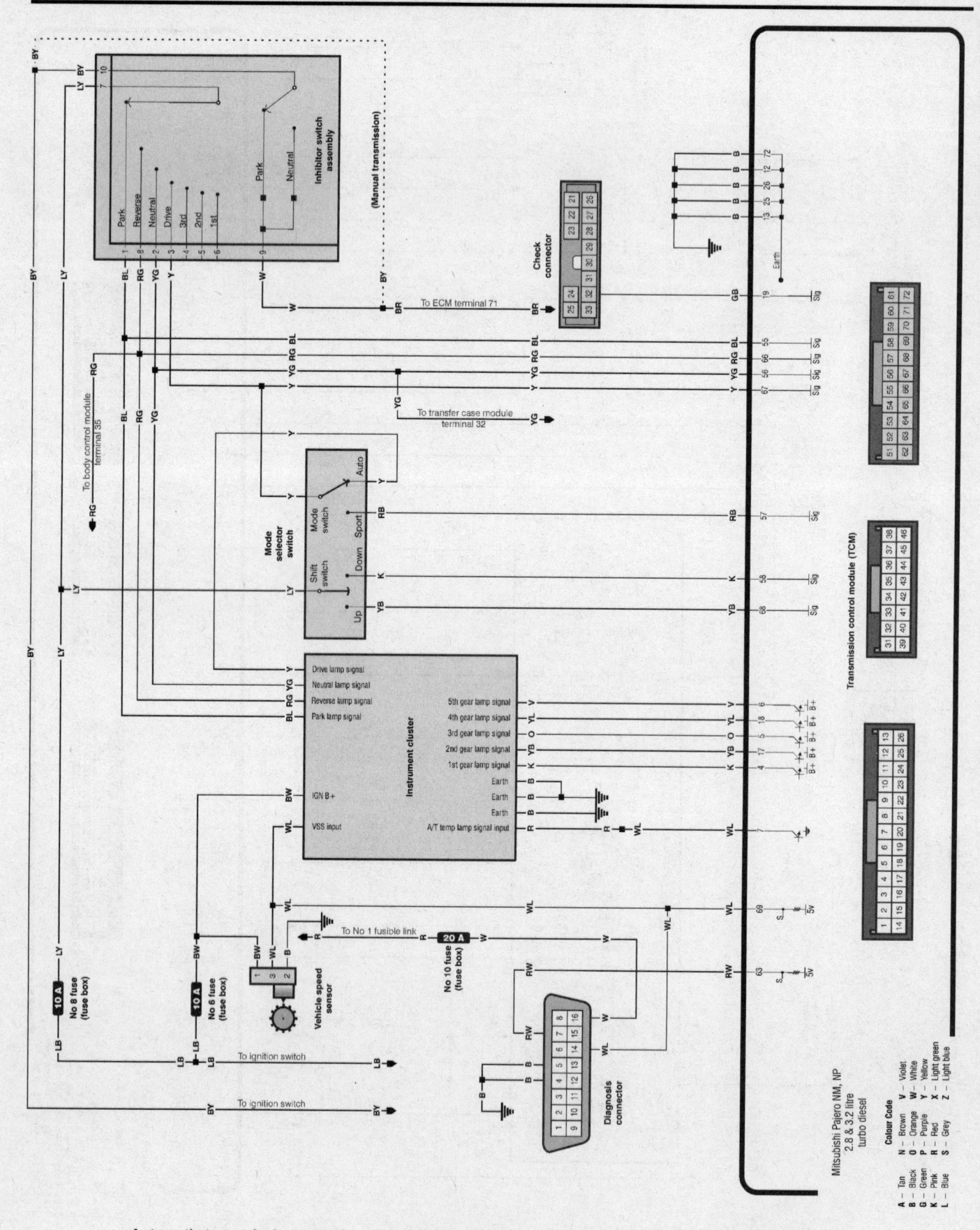

Automatic transmission control module, instruments, sports shift, inhibitor switch. Diesel, NM-NP models

Chapter 12 Chassis electrical system

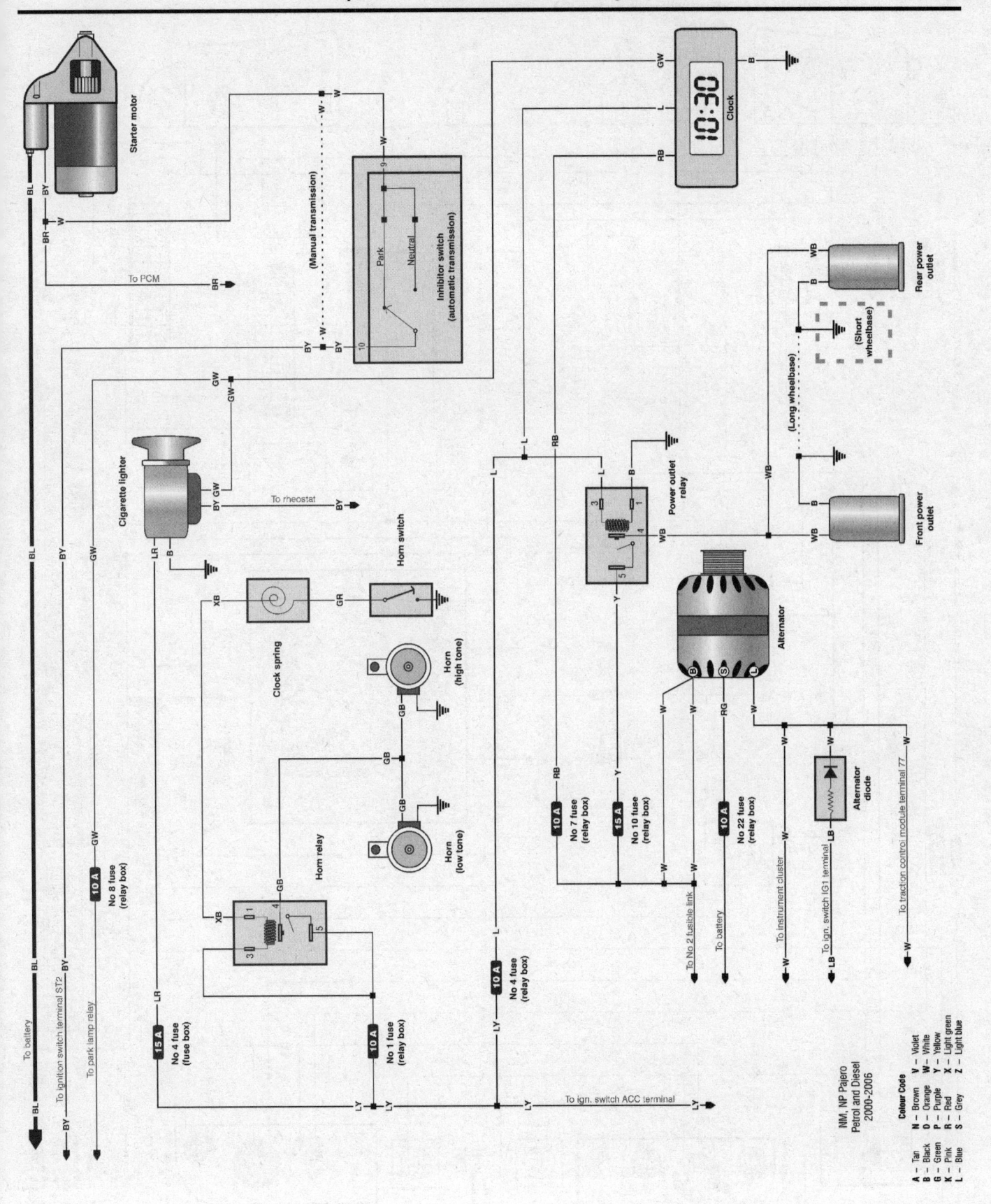

12-57

Starting system, charging system, horn, cigarette lighter, power outlets, clock, NM-NP models

Chapter 12 Chassis electrical system

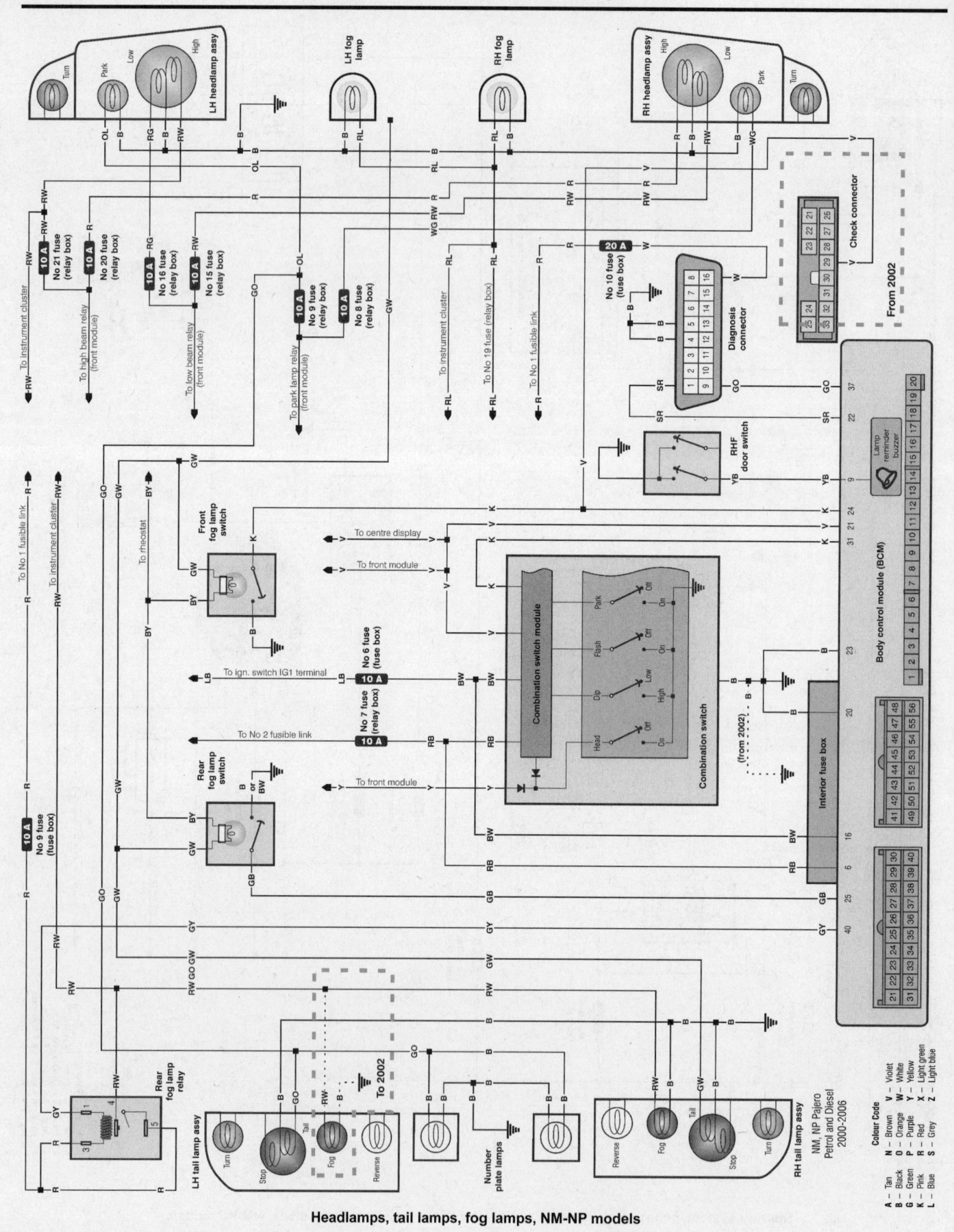

Headlamps, tail lamps, fog lamps, NM-NP models

Chapter 12 Chassis electrical system

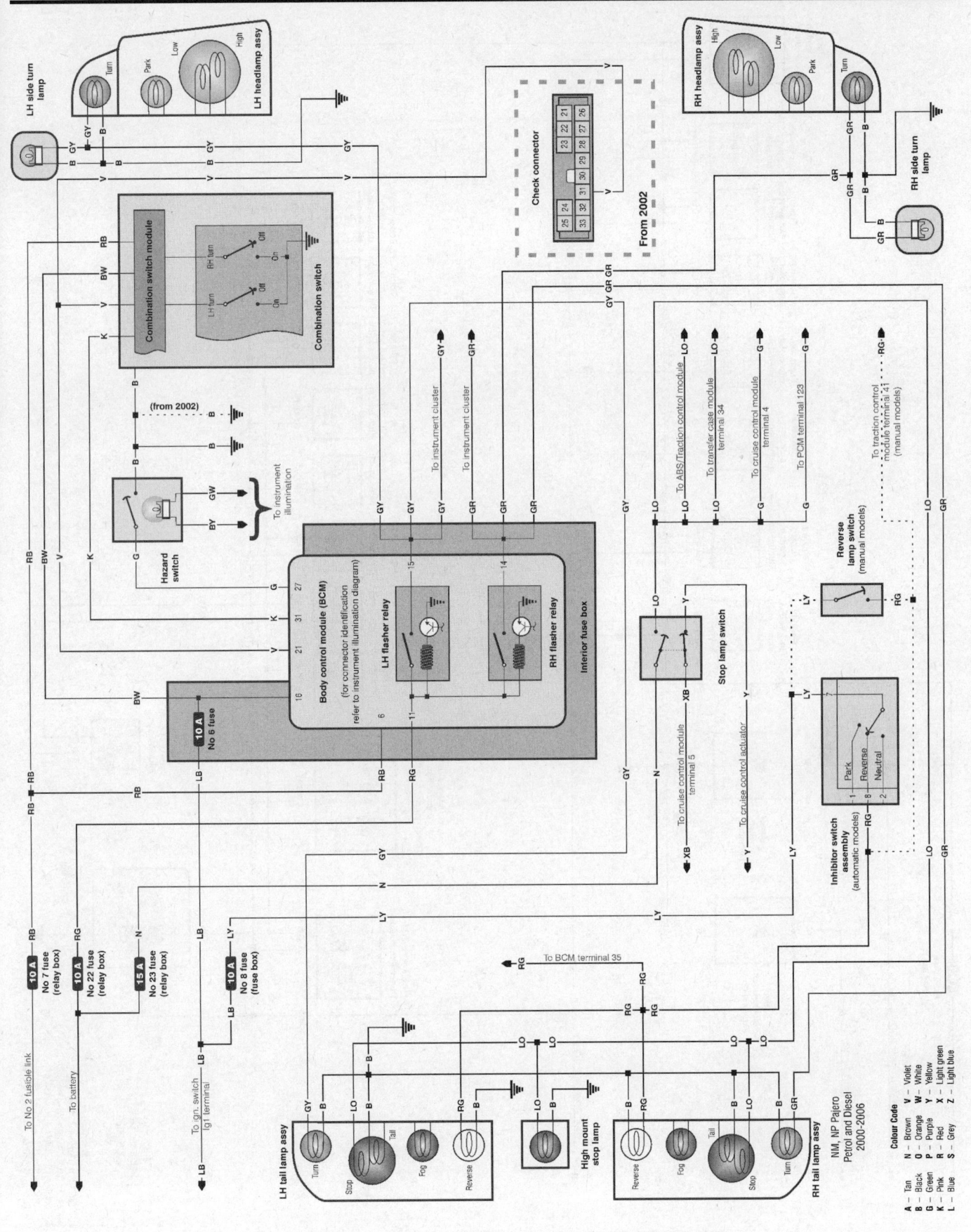

12-59

Turn signal/hazard lamps, stop lamps, reverse lamps, NM-NP models

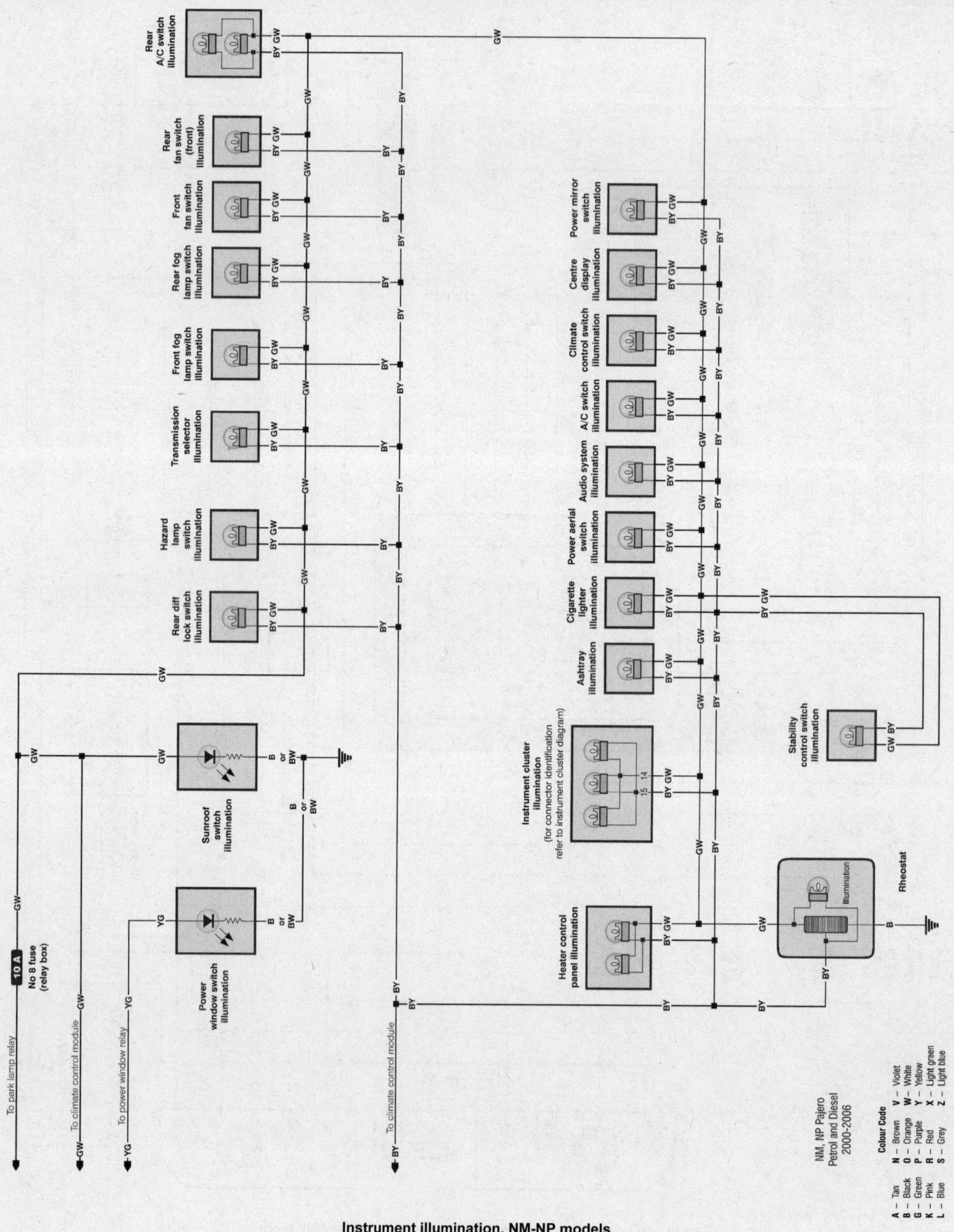

Instrument illumination, NM-NP models

Chapter 12 Chassis electrical system

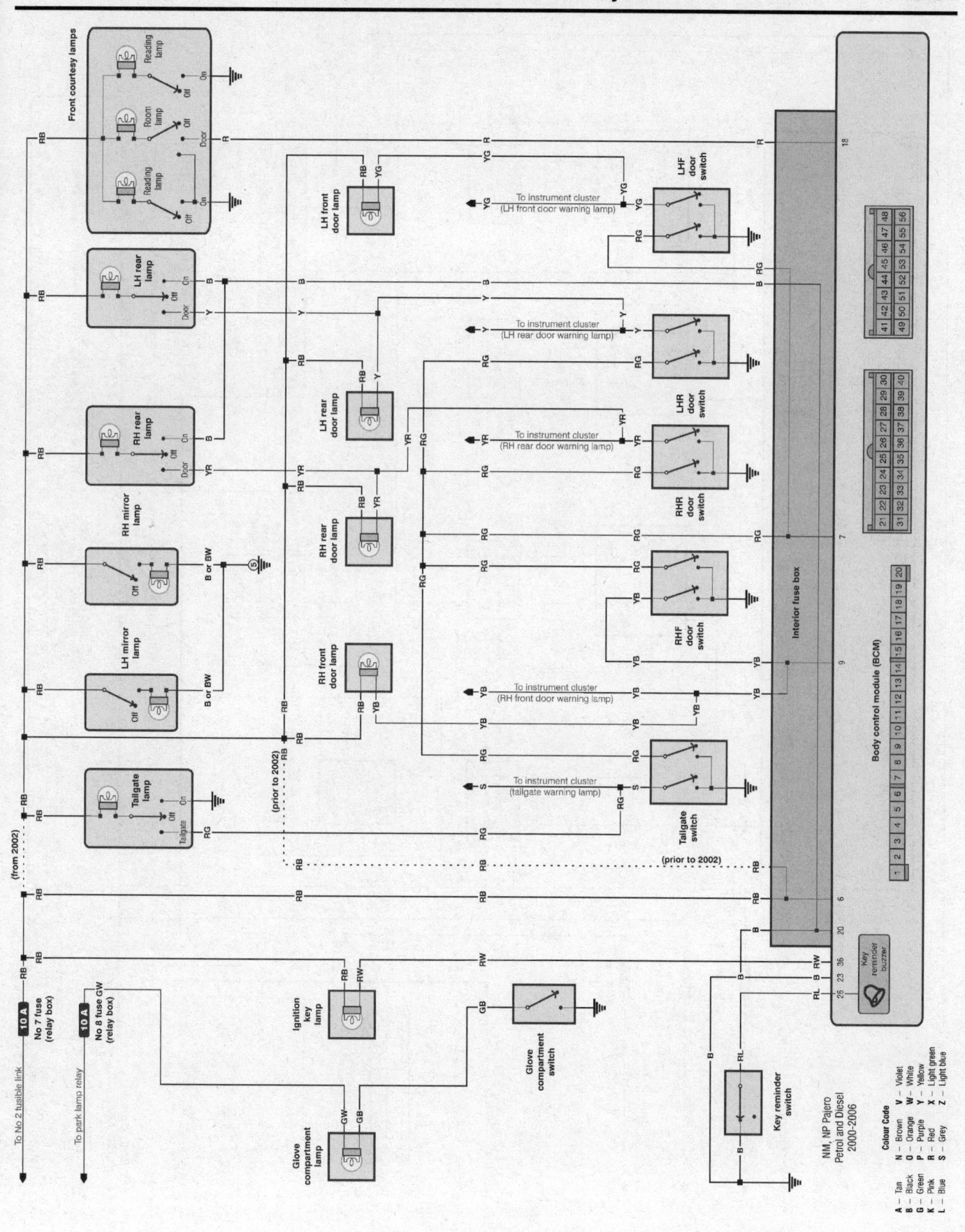

12-61

Interior lighting, NM-NP models

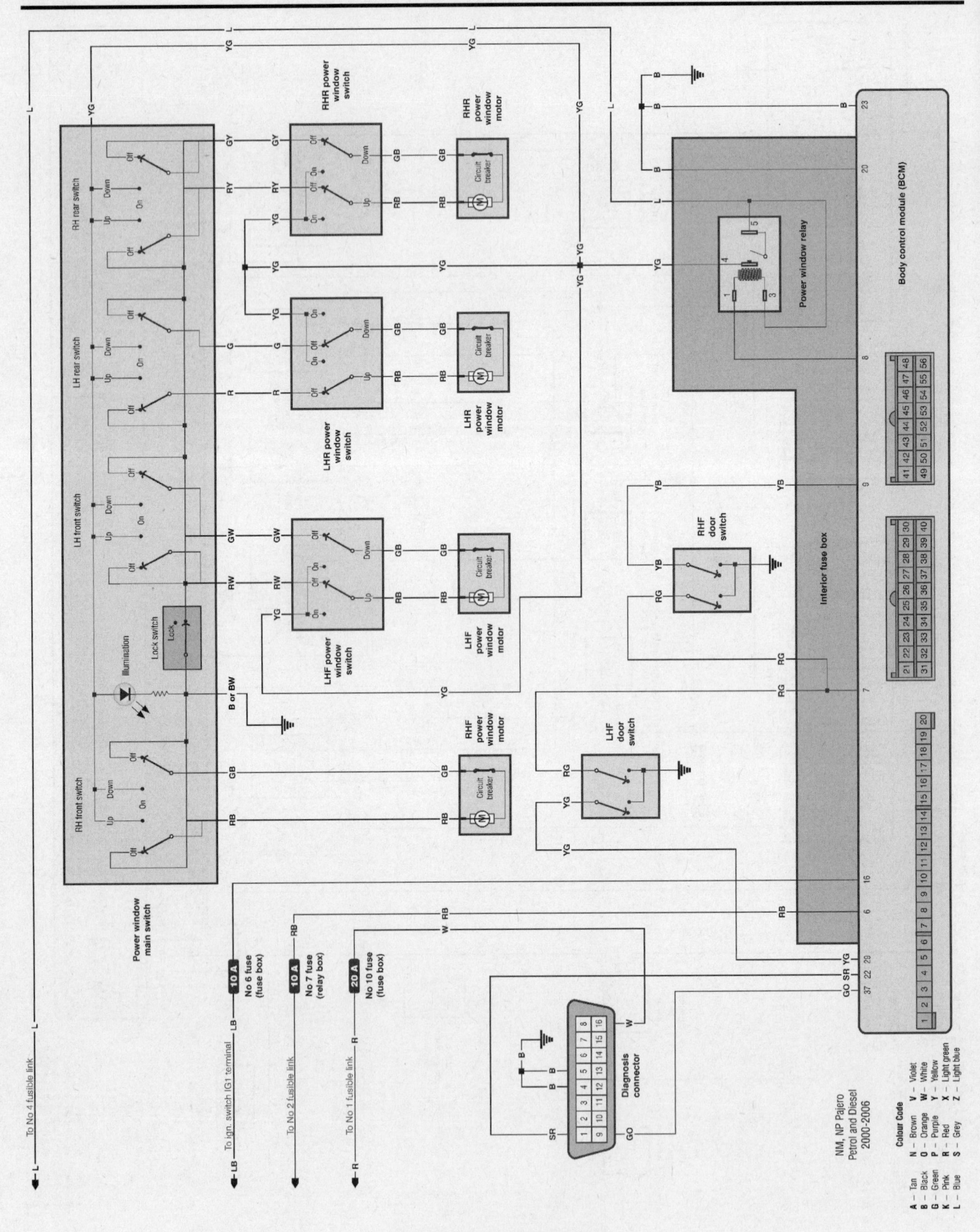

Power windows, NM-NP models

Chapter 12 Chassis electrical system

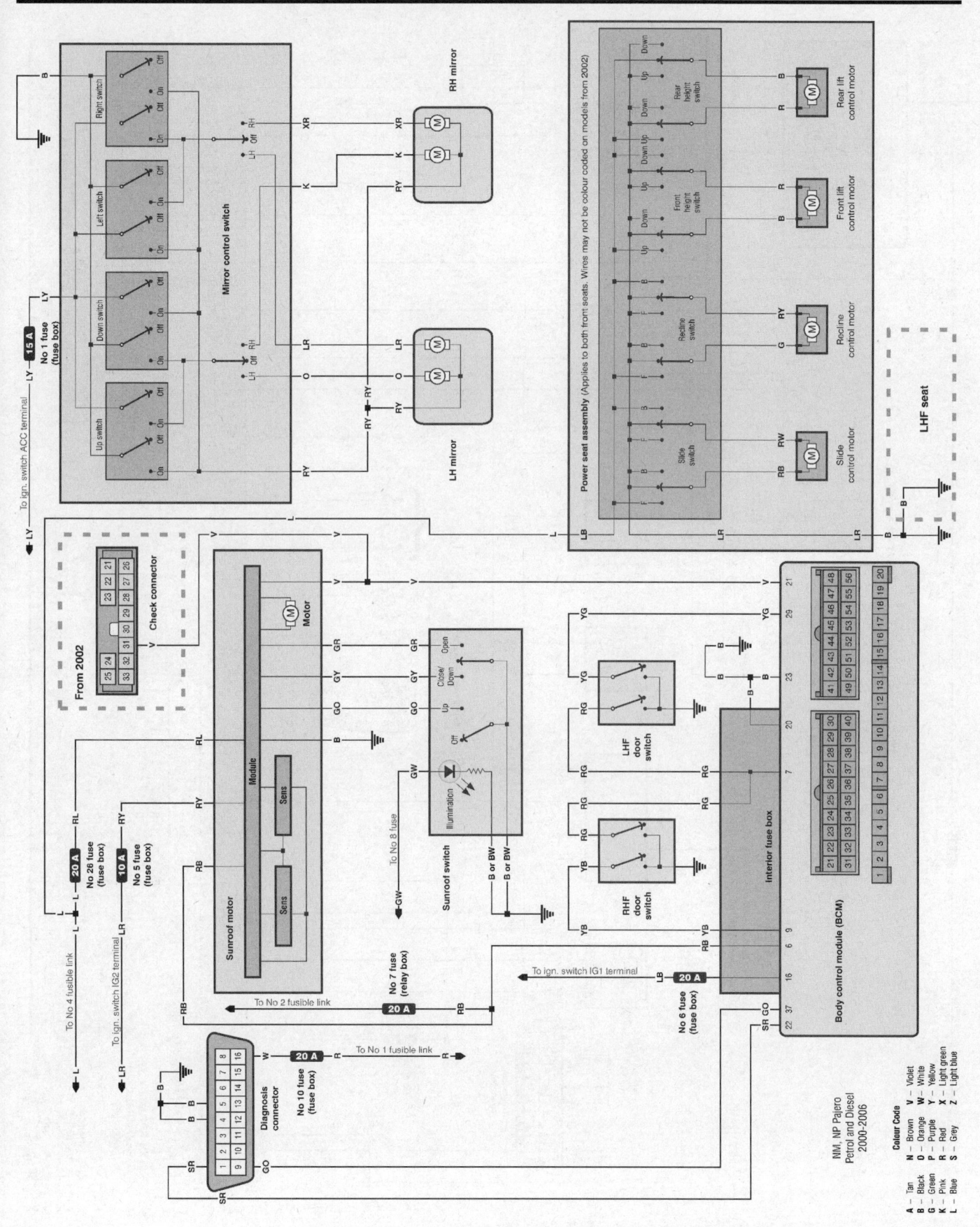

Power mirrors, power seats, sunroof, NM-NP models

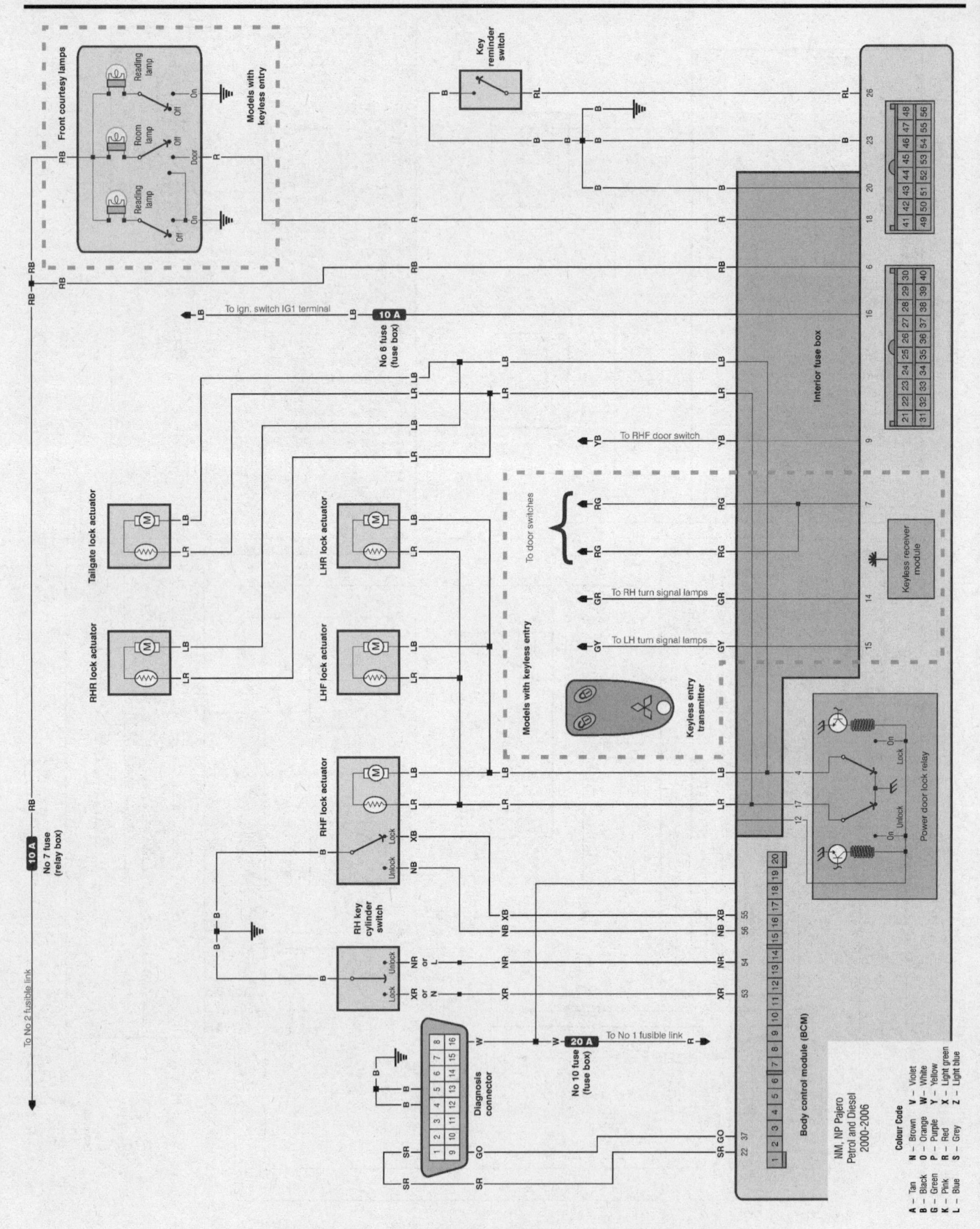

Power door locks, keyless entry, map reading lamps, NM-NP models

Chapter 12 Chassis electrical system

12-65

Wipers and washers, NM-NP models

NM, NP Pajero
Petrol and Diesel
2000-2006

Colour Code:
- A – Tan
- B – Black
- G – Green
- K – Pink
- L – Blue
- N – Brown
- O – Orange
- P – Purple
- R – Red
- S – Grey
- V – Violet
- W – White
- Y – Yellow
- X – Light green
- Z – Light blue

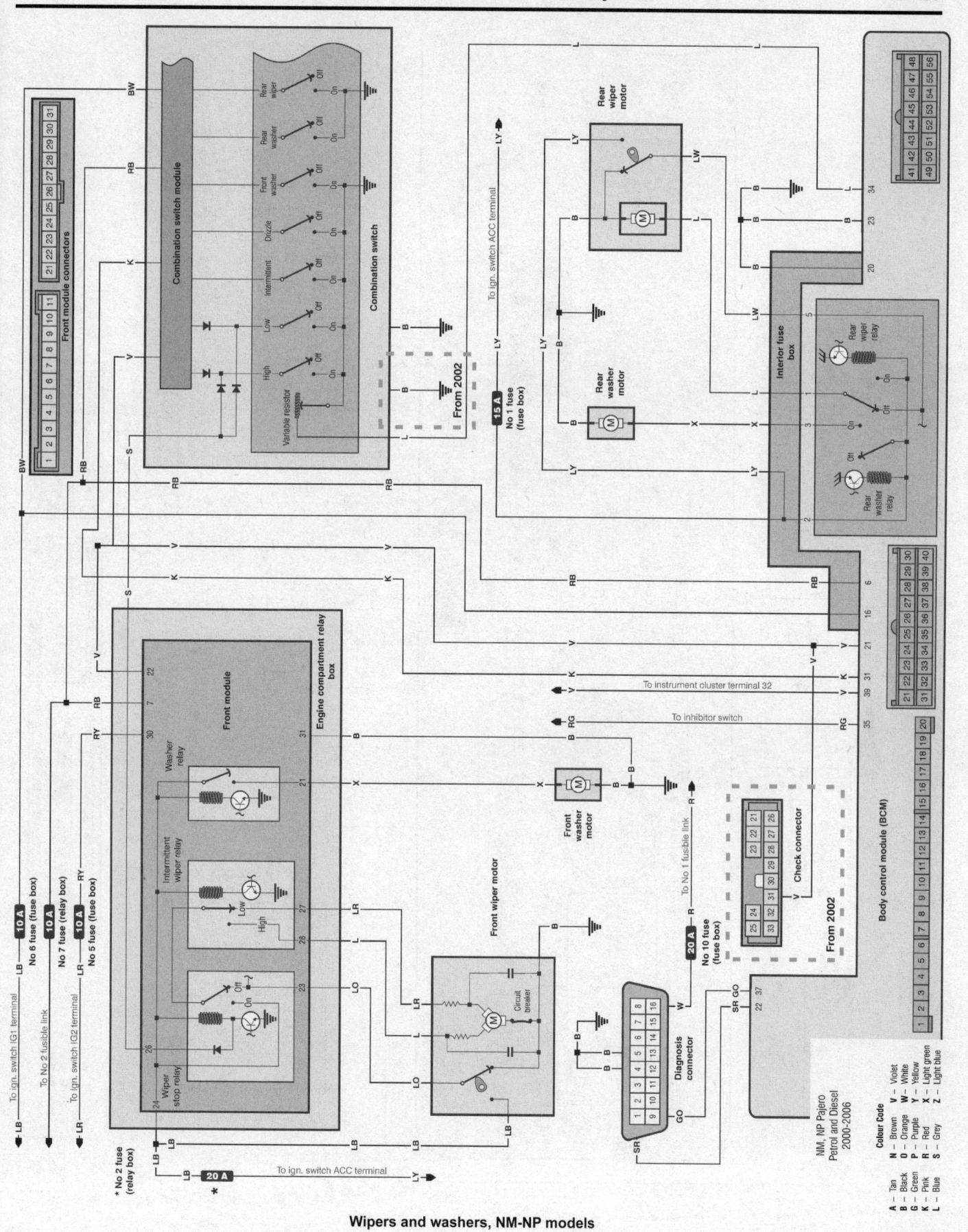

Chapter 12 Chassis electrical system

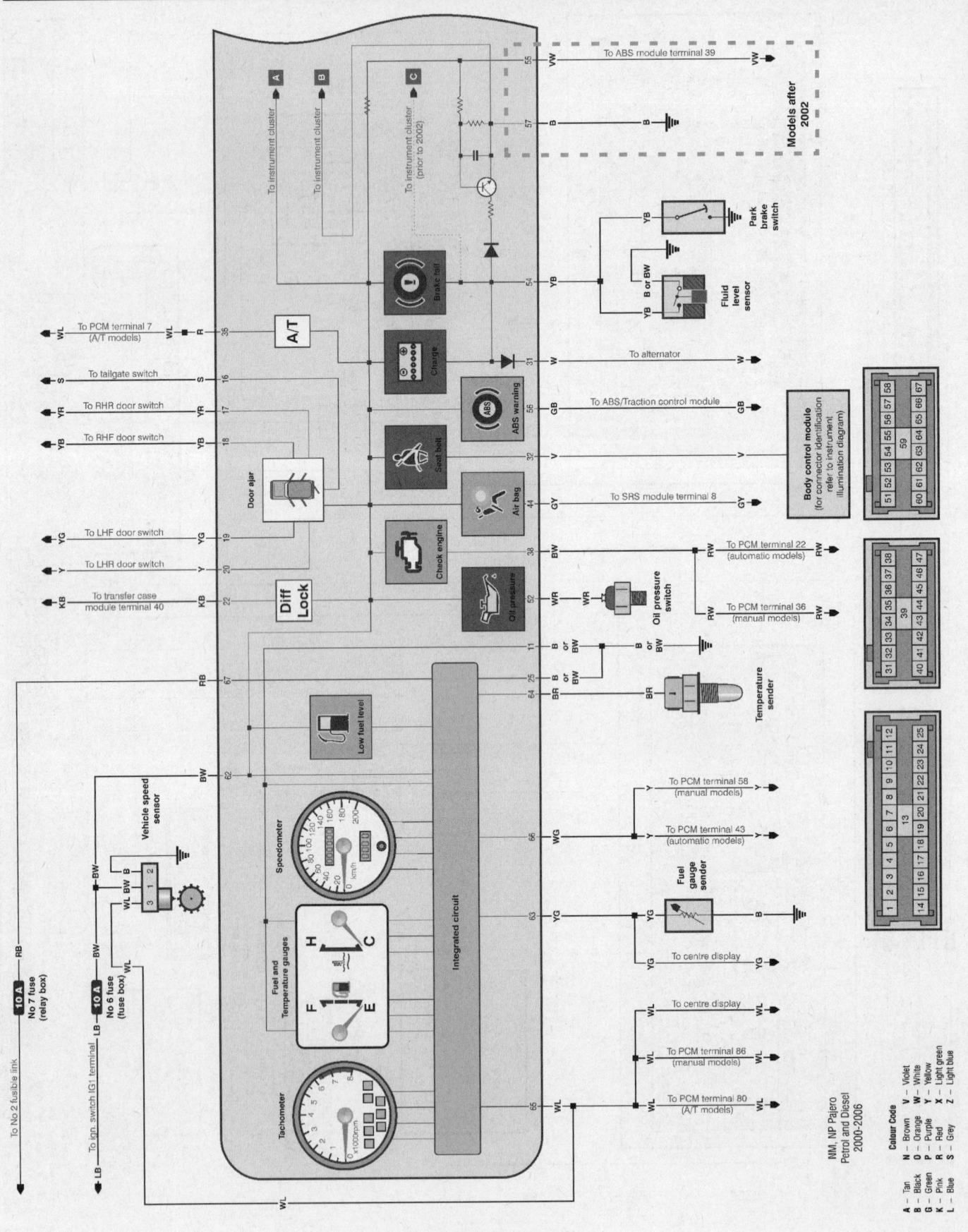

Instrument cluster, NM-NP models

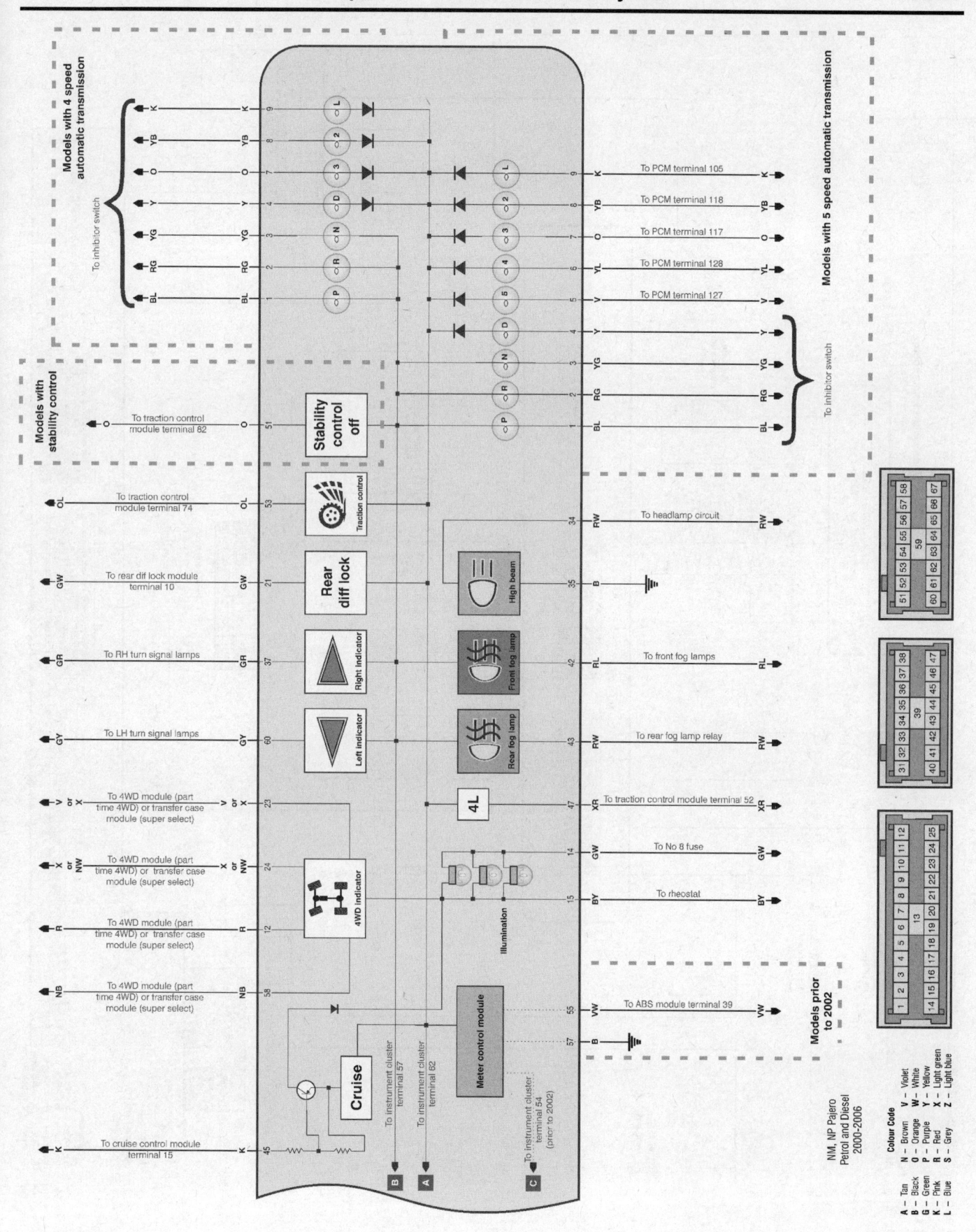

Chapter 12 Chassis electrical system

Instrument cluster, NM-NP models

NM, NP Pajero Petrol and Diesel 2000-2006

Colour Code

- A – Tan
- B – Black
- G – Green
- K – Pink
- L – Blue
- N – Brown
- O – Orange
- P – Purple
- R – Red
- S – Grey
- V – Violet
- W – White
- Y – Yellow
- X – Light green
- Z – Light blue

Chapter 12 Chassis electrical system

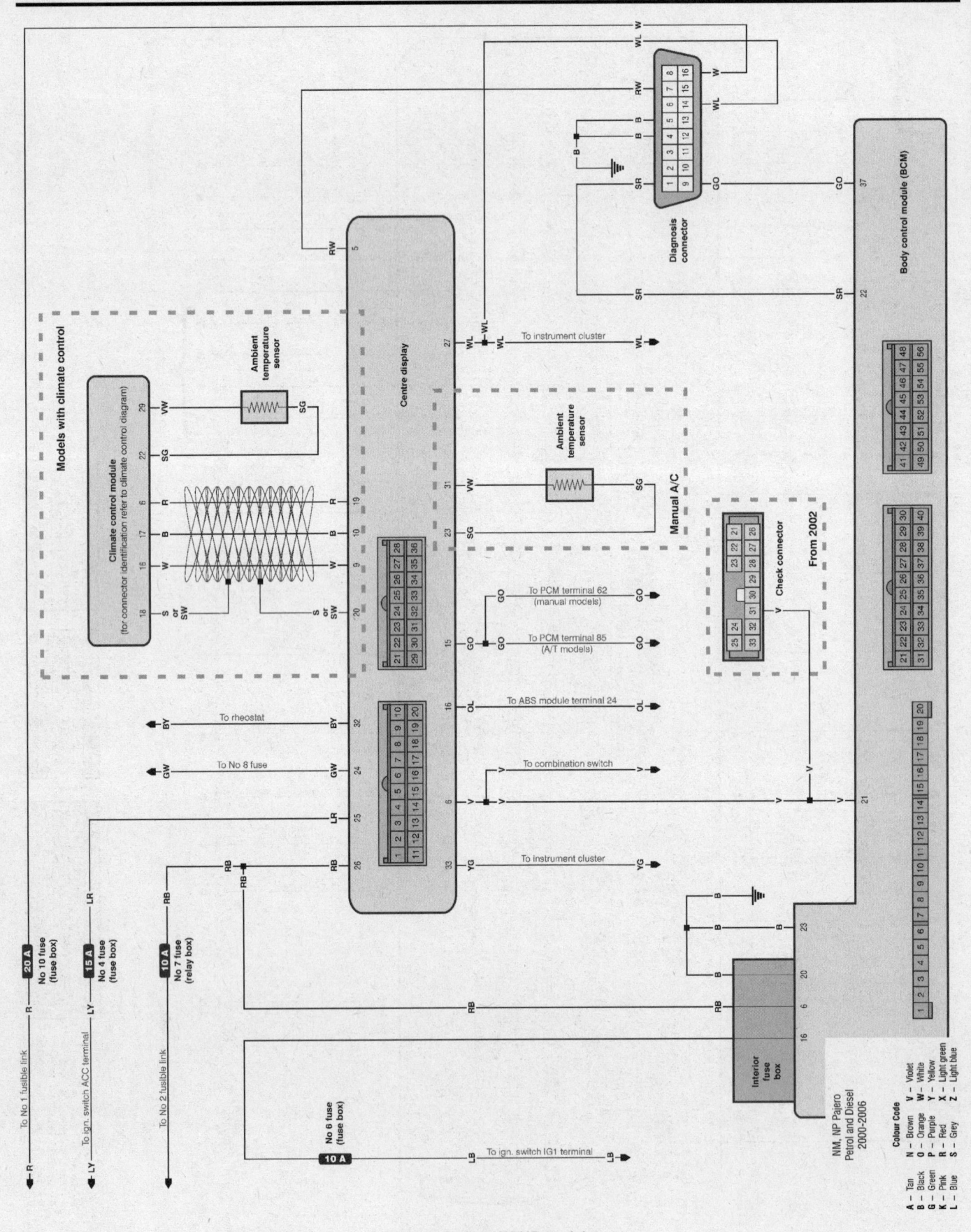

Centre display, NM-NP models

Chapter 12 Chassis electrical system

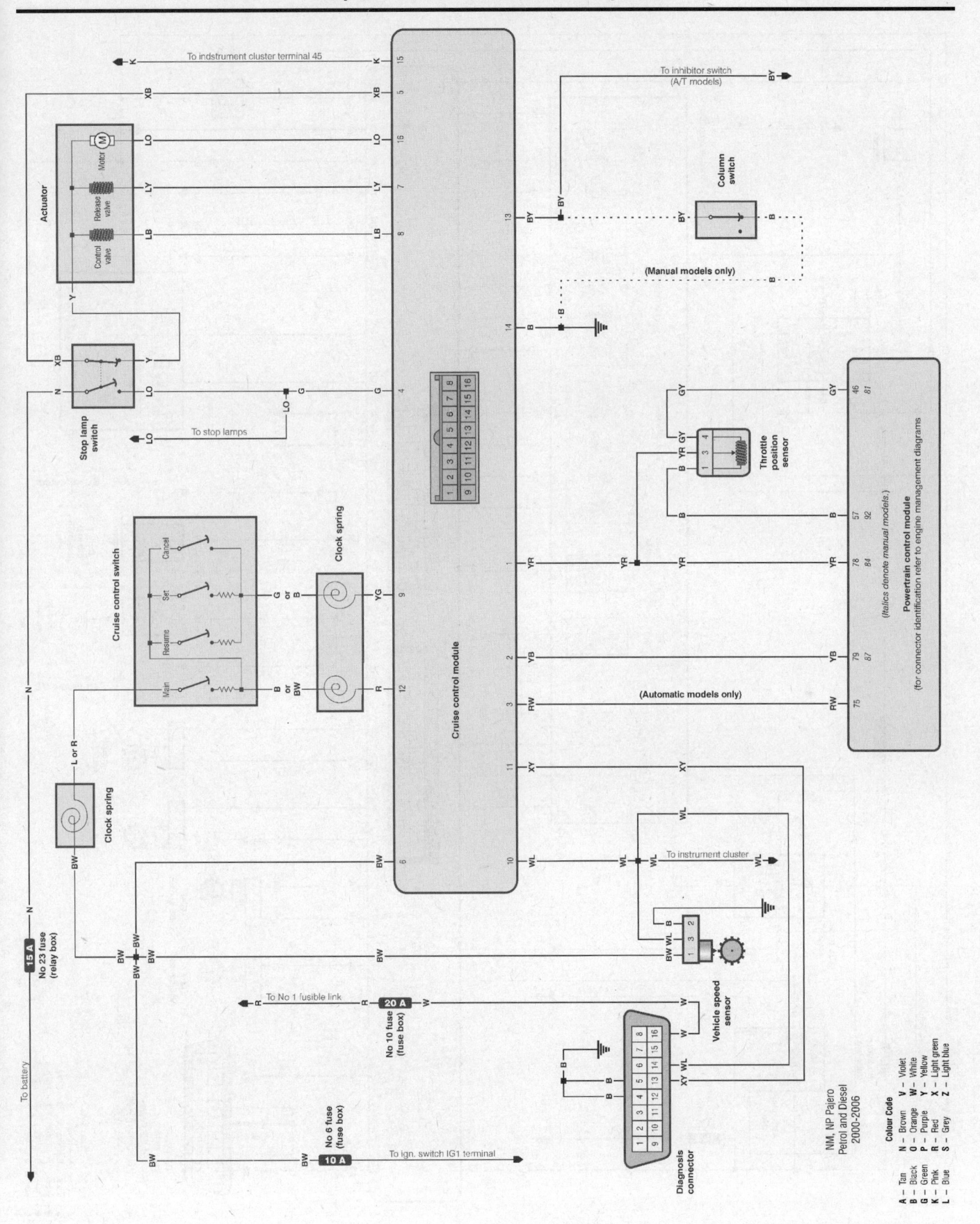

12-69

Cruise control, NM-NP models

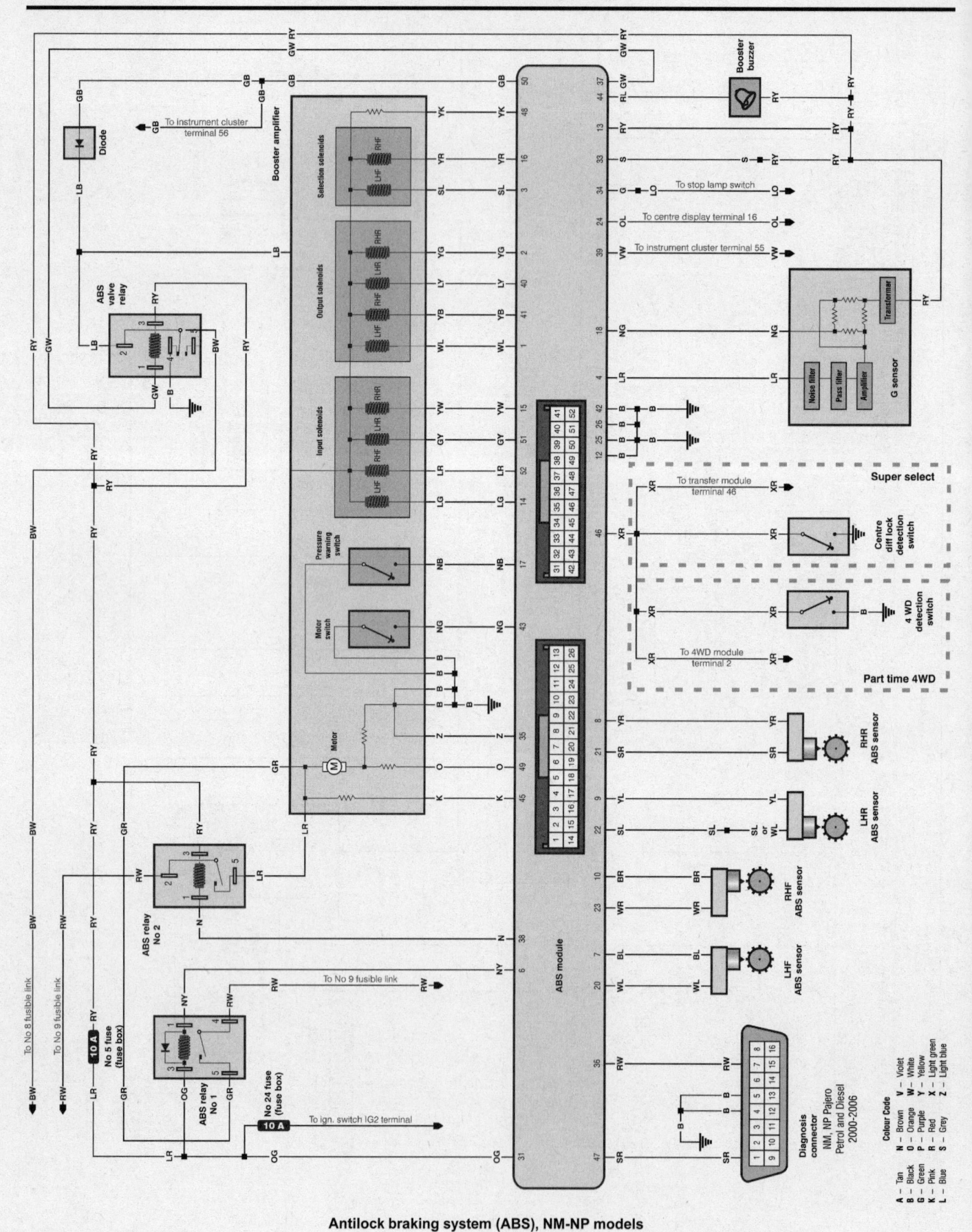

Antilock braking system (ABS), NM-NP models

Chapter 12 Chassis electrical system

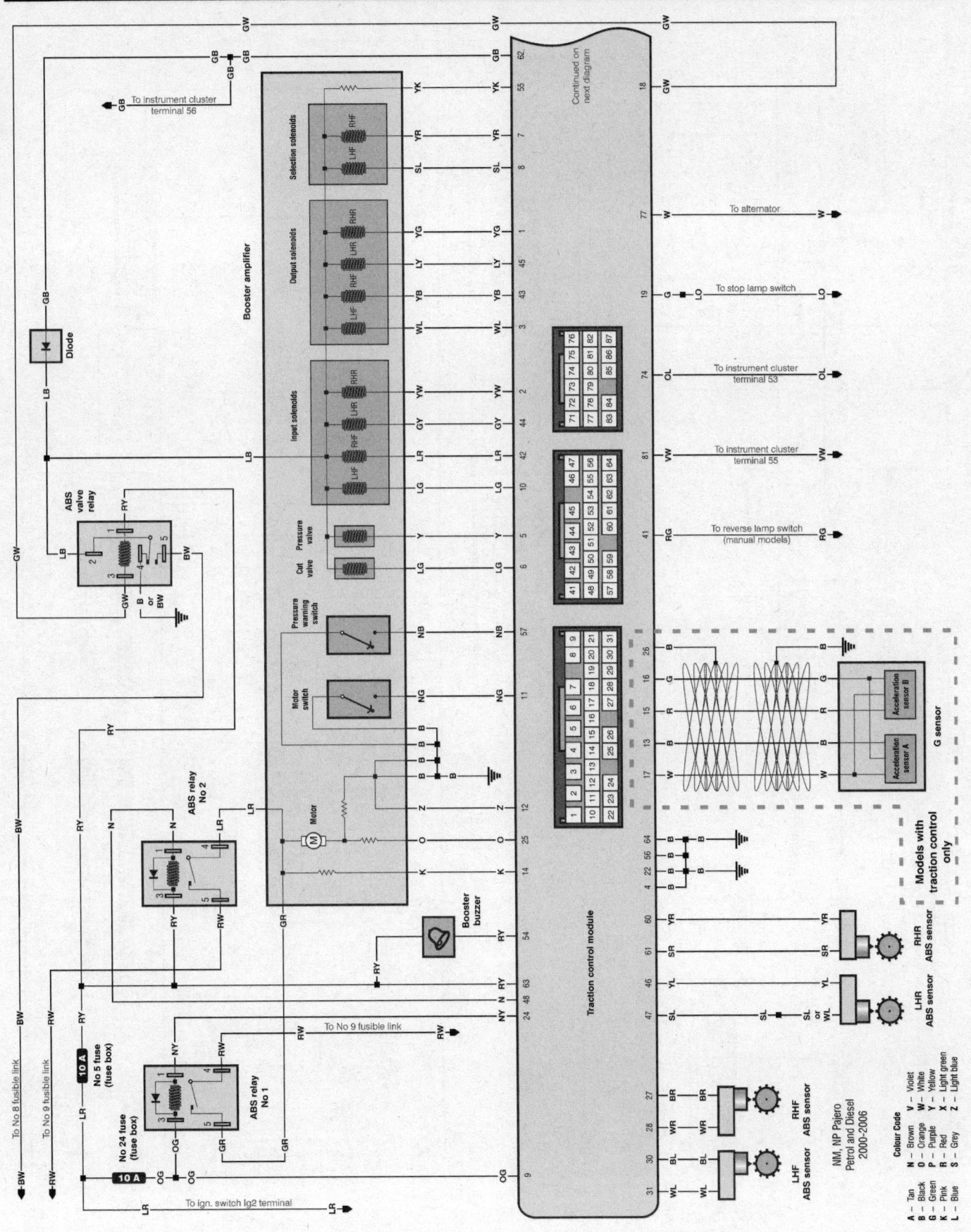

Antilock braking system (ABS), traction control system, NM-NP models

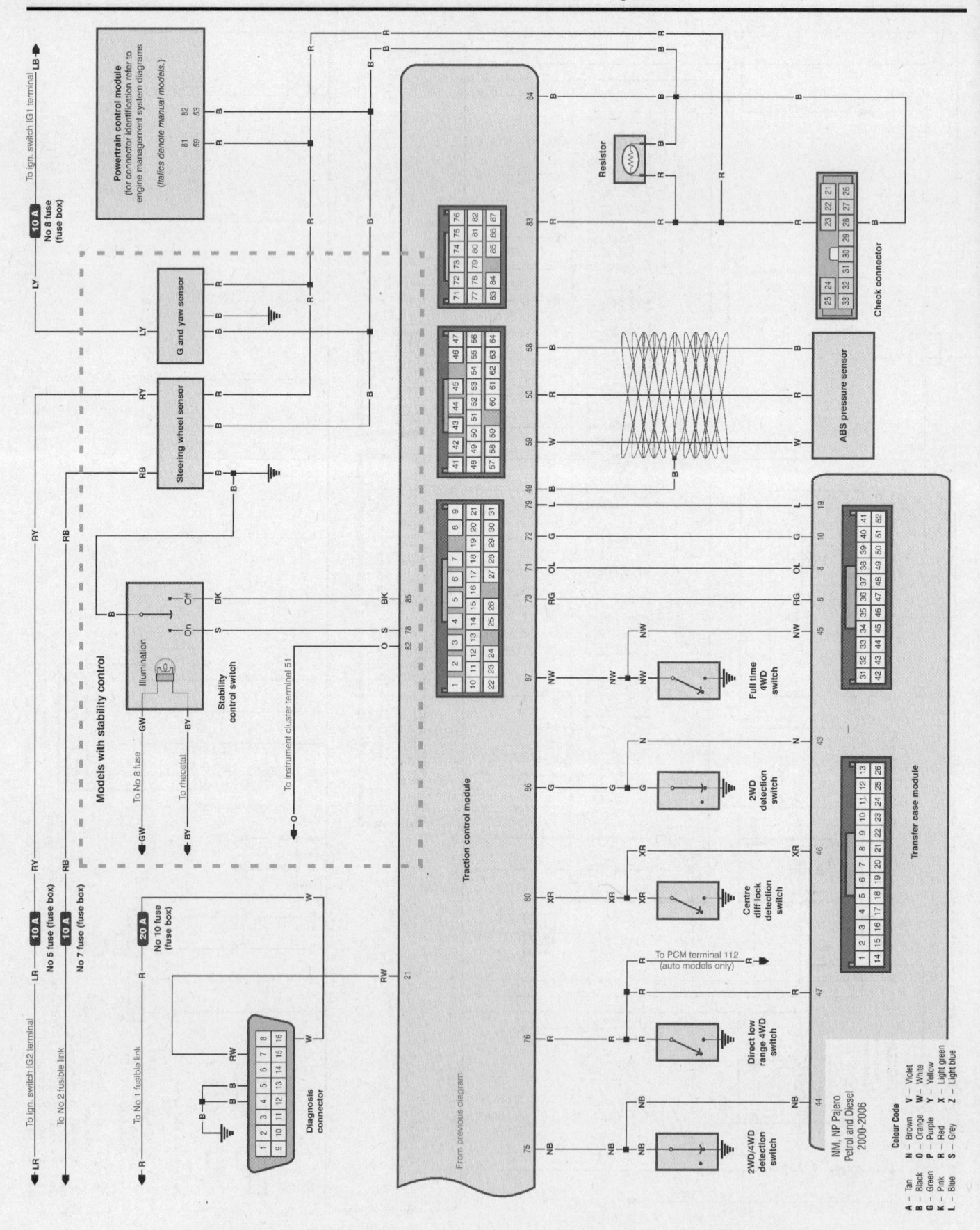

Antilock braking system (ABS), traction control system, stability control, NM-NP models

Chapter 12 Chassis electrical system

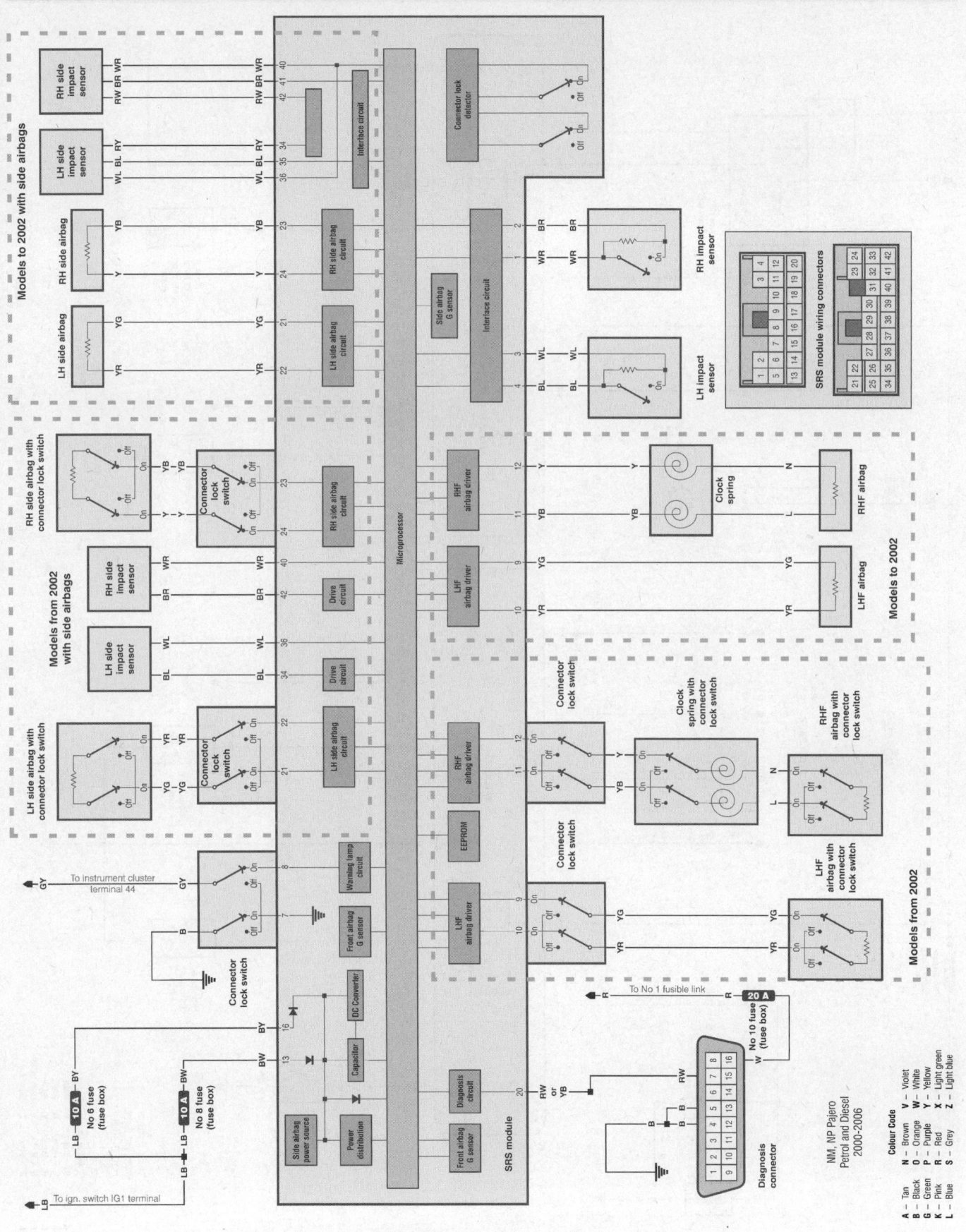

12-73

Supplement restraint system (SRS), NM-NP models

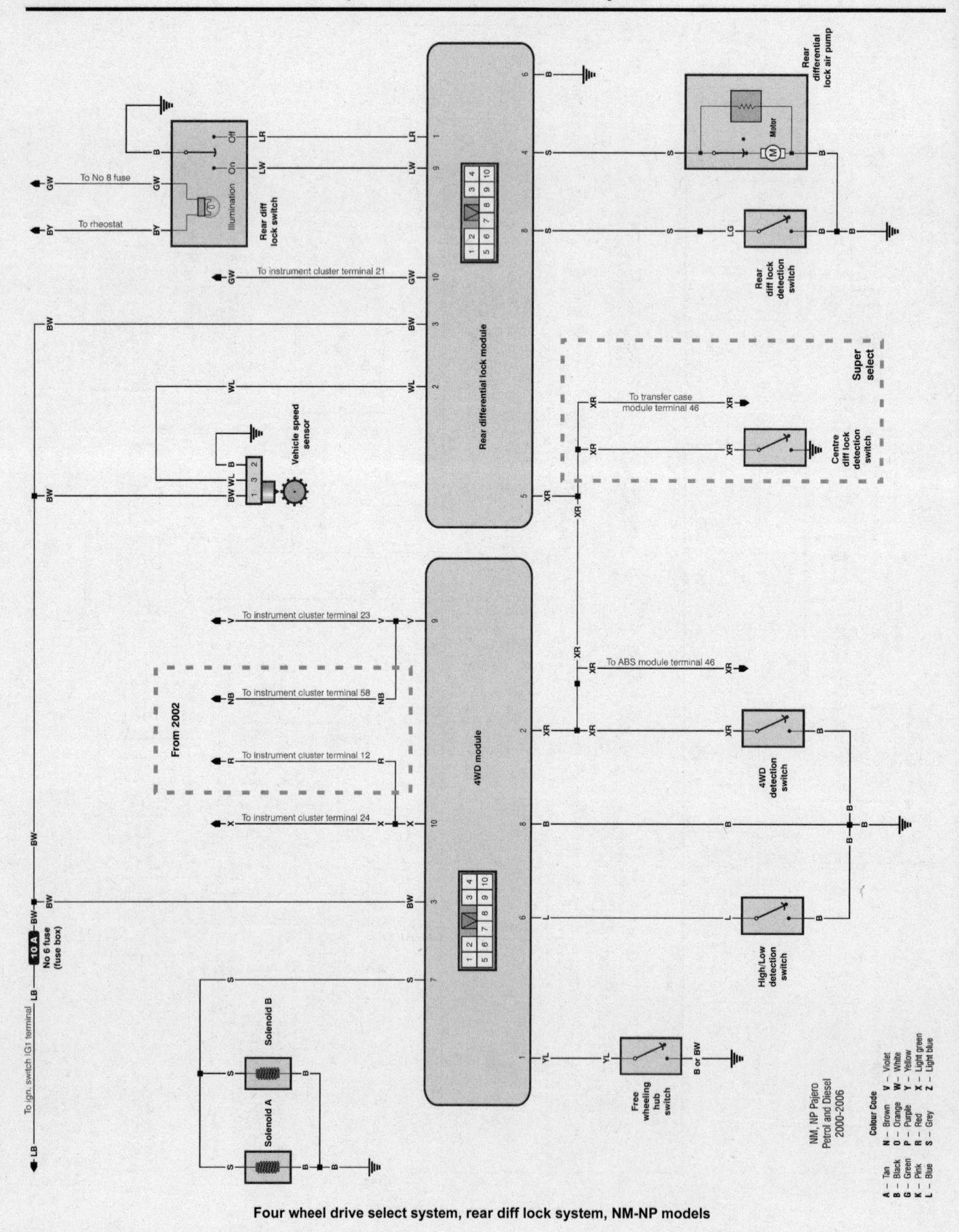

Four wheel drive select system, rear diff lock system, NM-NP models

Chapter 12 Chassis electrical system

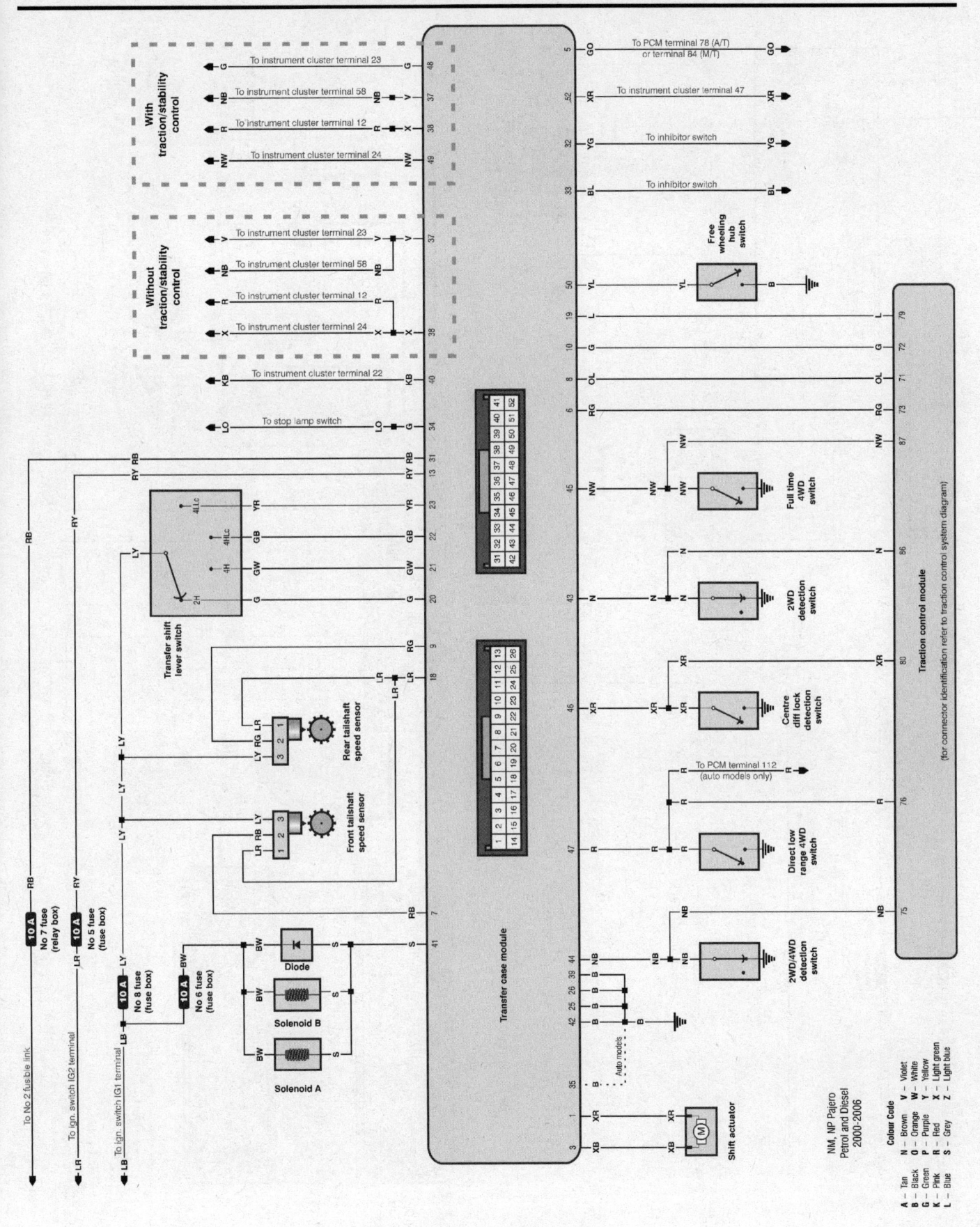

Super select system, NM-NP models

12-76 Chapter 12 Chassis electrical system

Audio system, NM-NP models

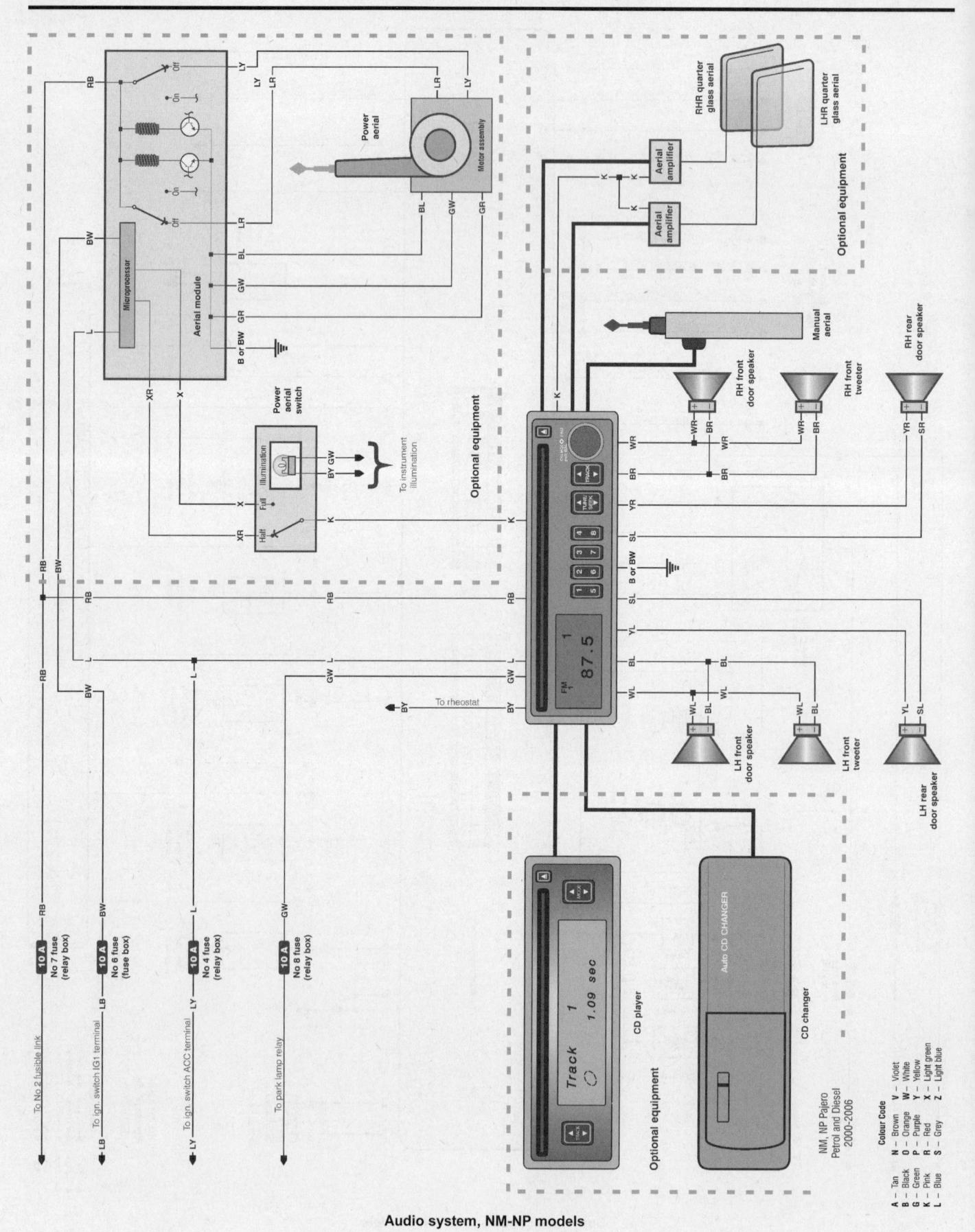

Chapter 12 Chassis electrical system

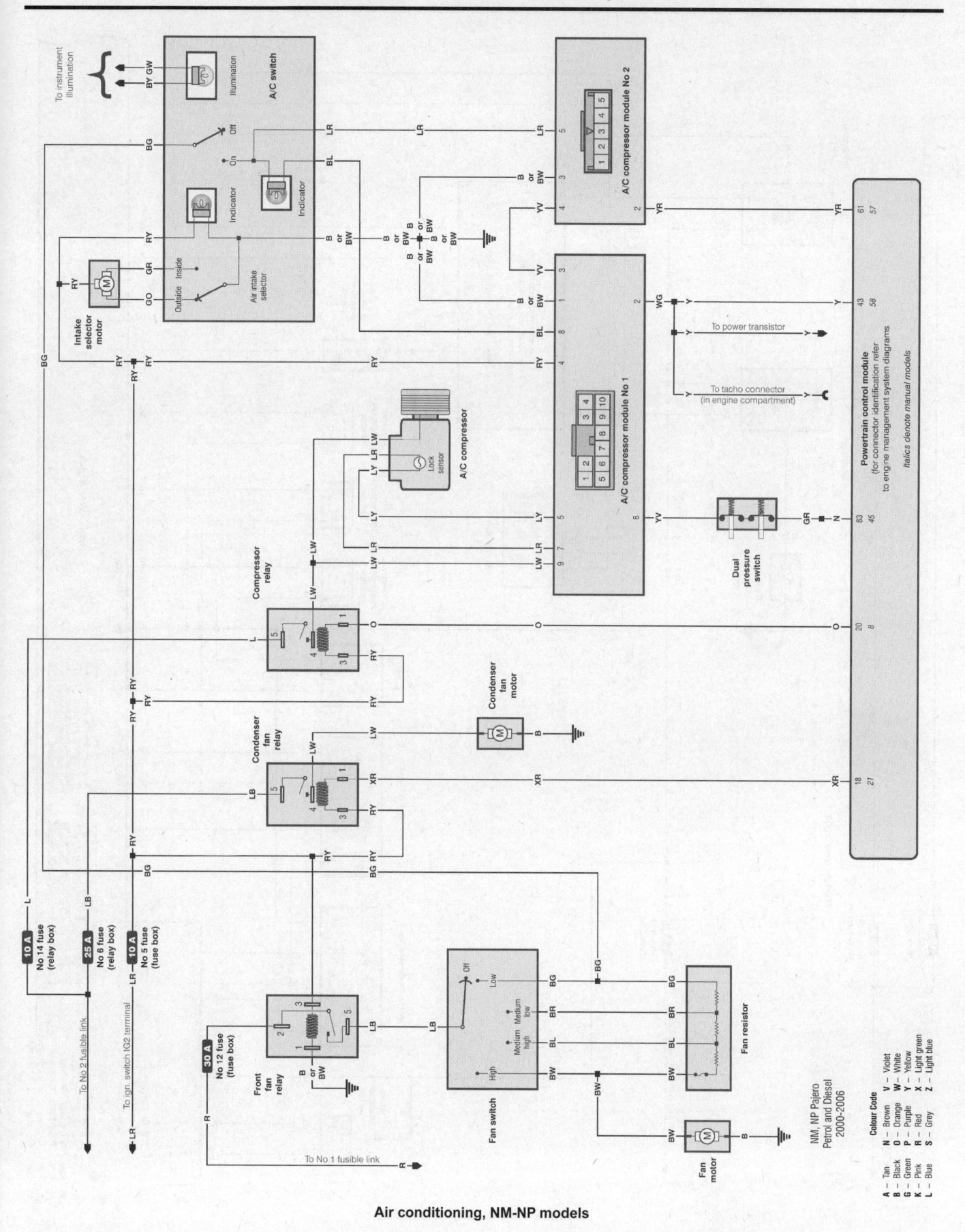

Air conditioning, NM-NP models

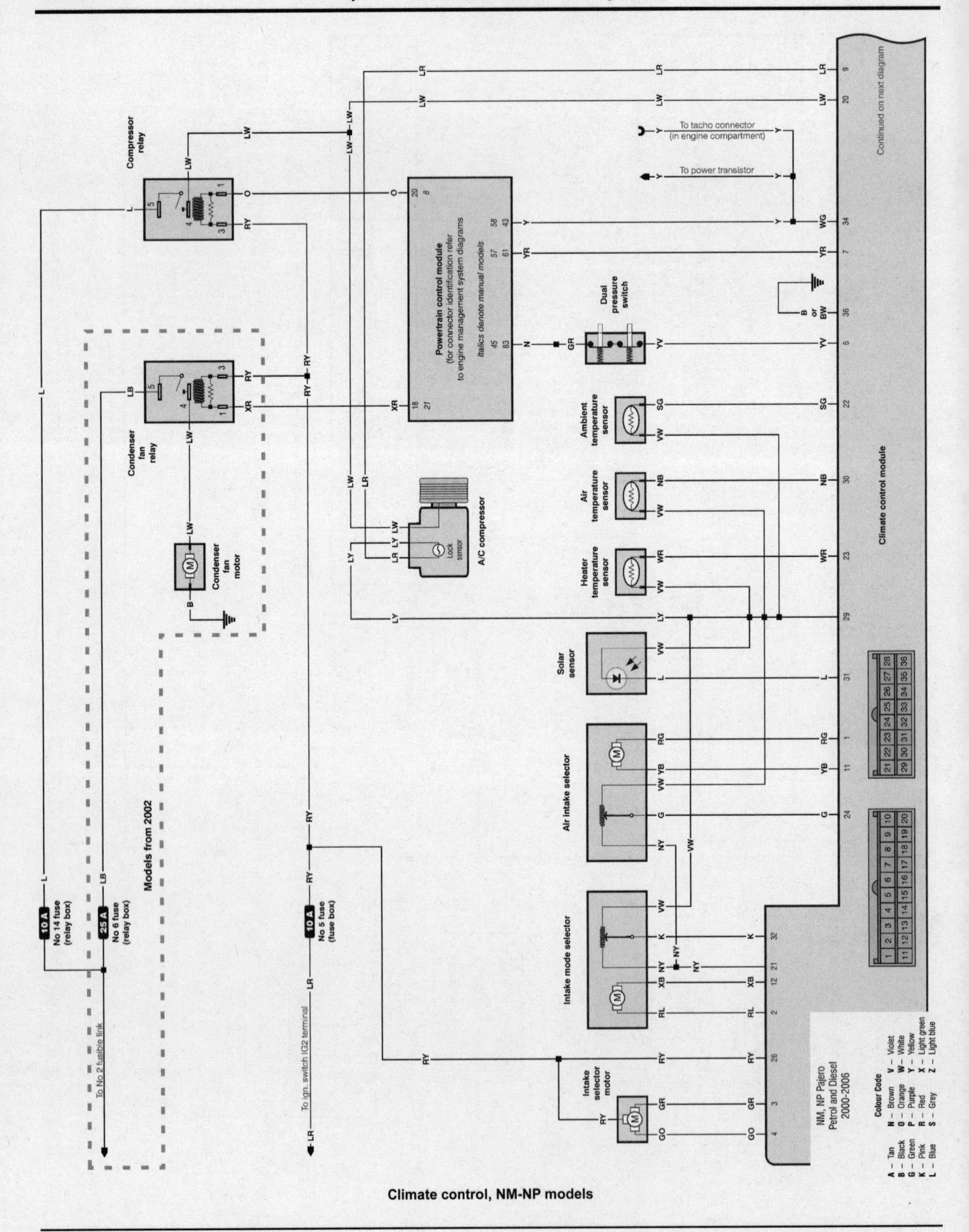

Climate control, NM-NP models

Chapter 12 Chassis electrical system

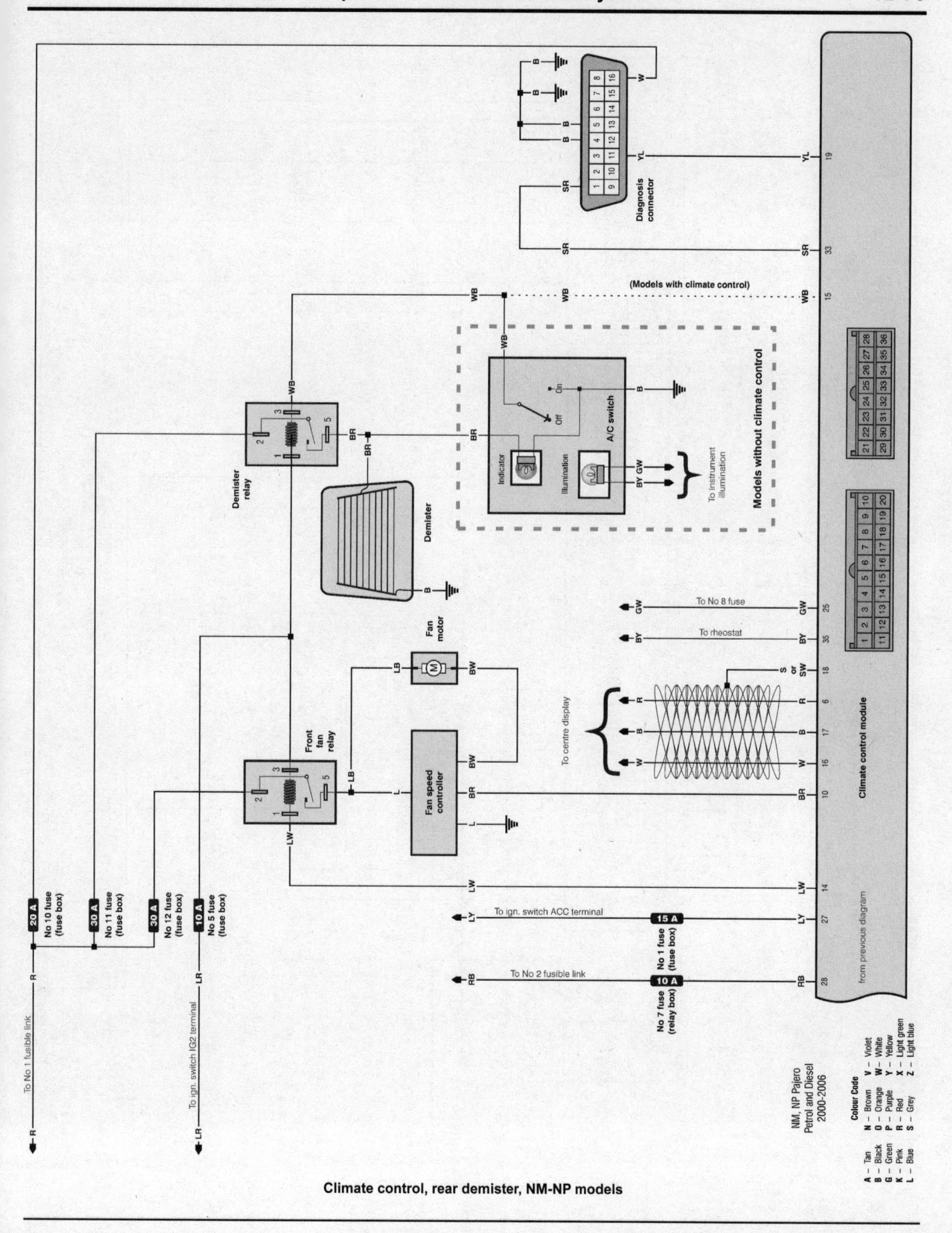

Climate control, rear demister, NM-NP models

12-80 Chapter 12 Chassis electrical system

Rear air conditioning system, NM-NP models

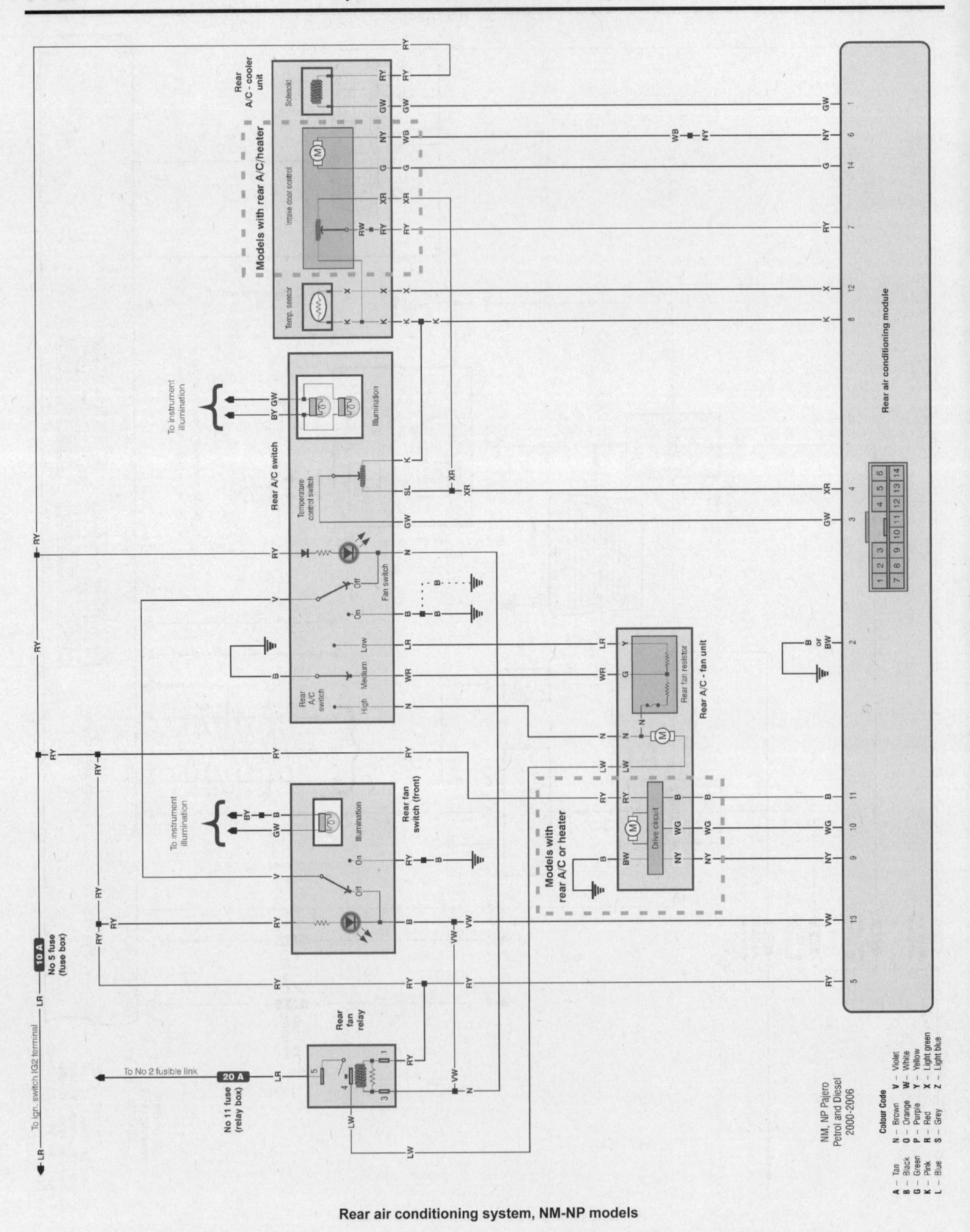

Chapter 12 Chassis electrical system

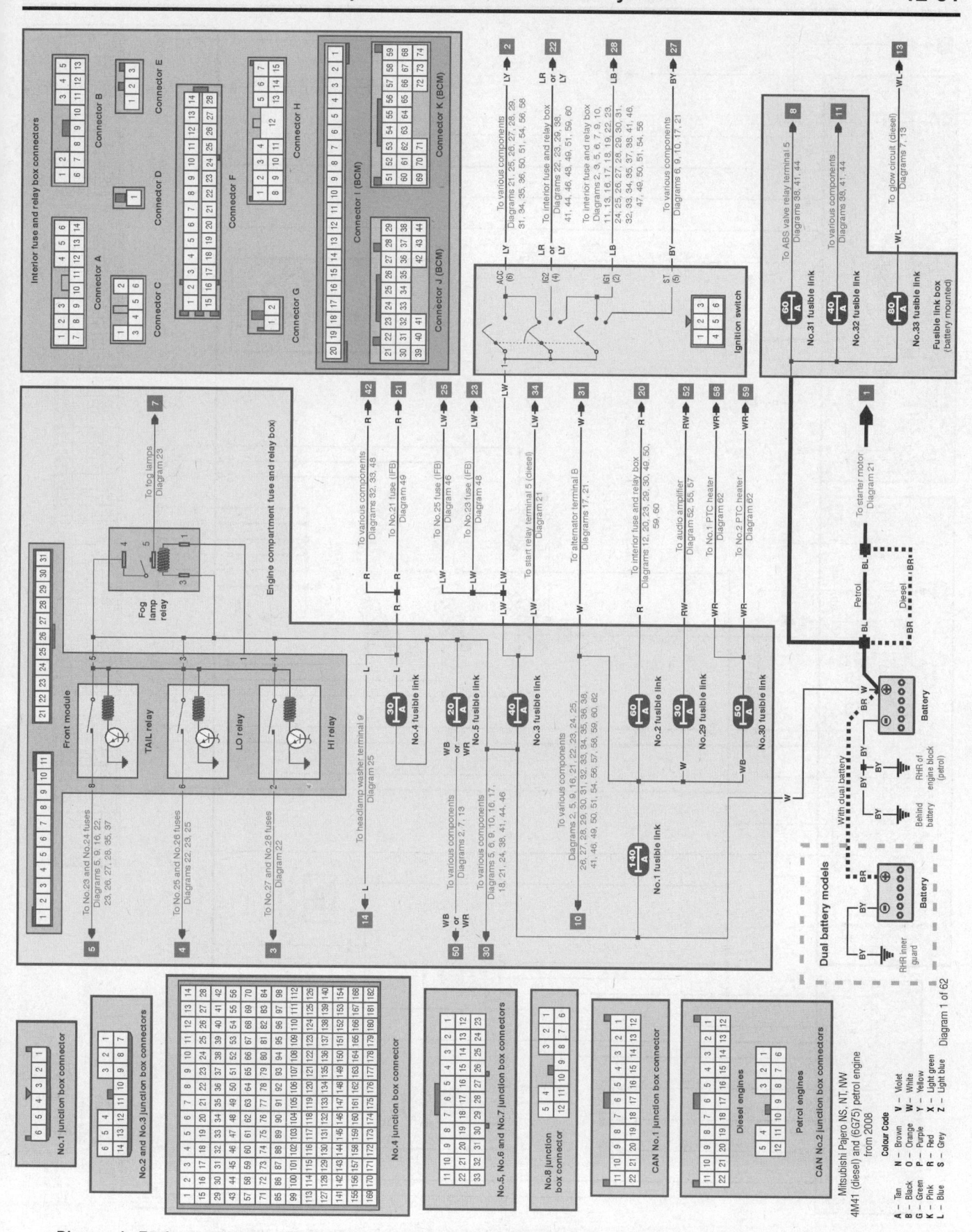

12-81

Diagram 1 - Engine compartment fuse and relay box, ignition switch, fusible link box, interior fuse and relay box connectors - NS, NT and NW models

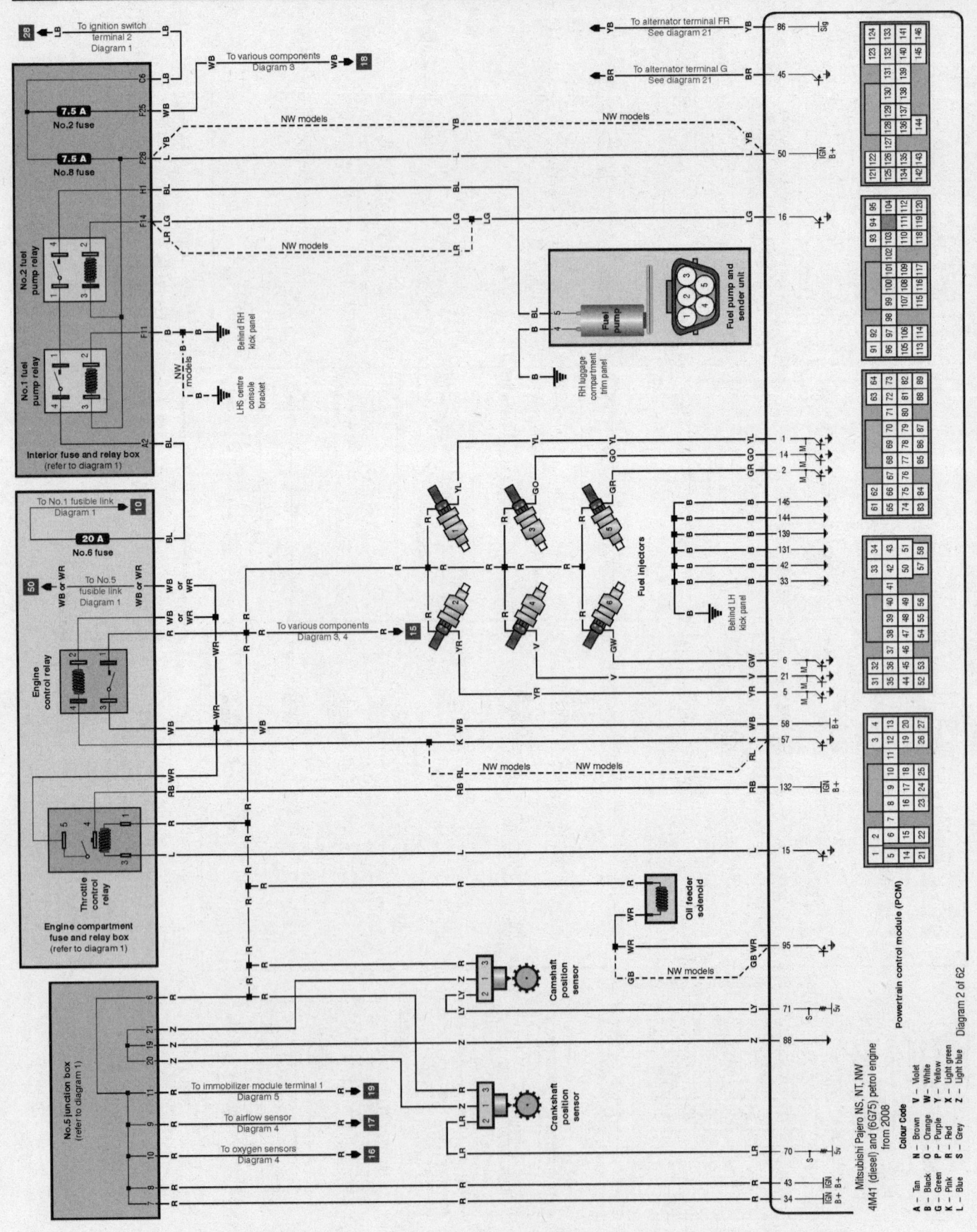

Diagram 2 - PCM power supply, earth circuits, injectors, fuel pump - NS, NT and NW petrol models

Chapter 12 Chassis electrical system

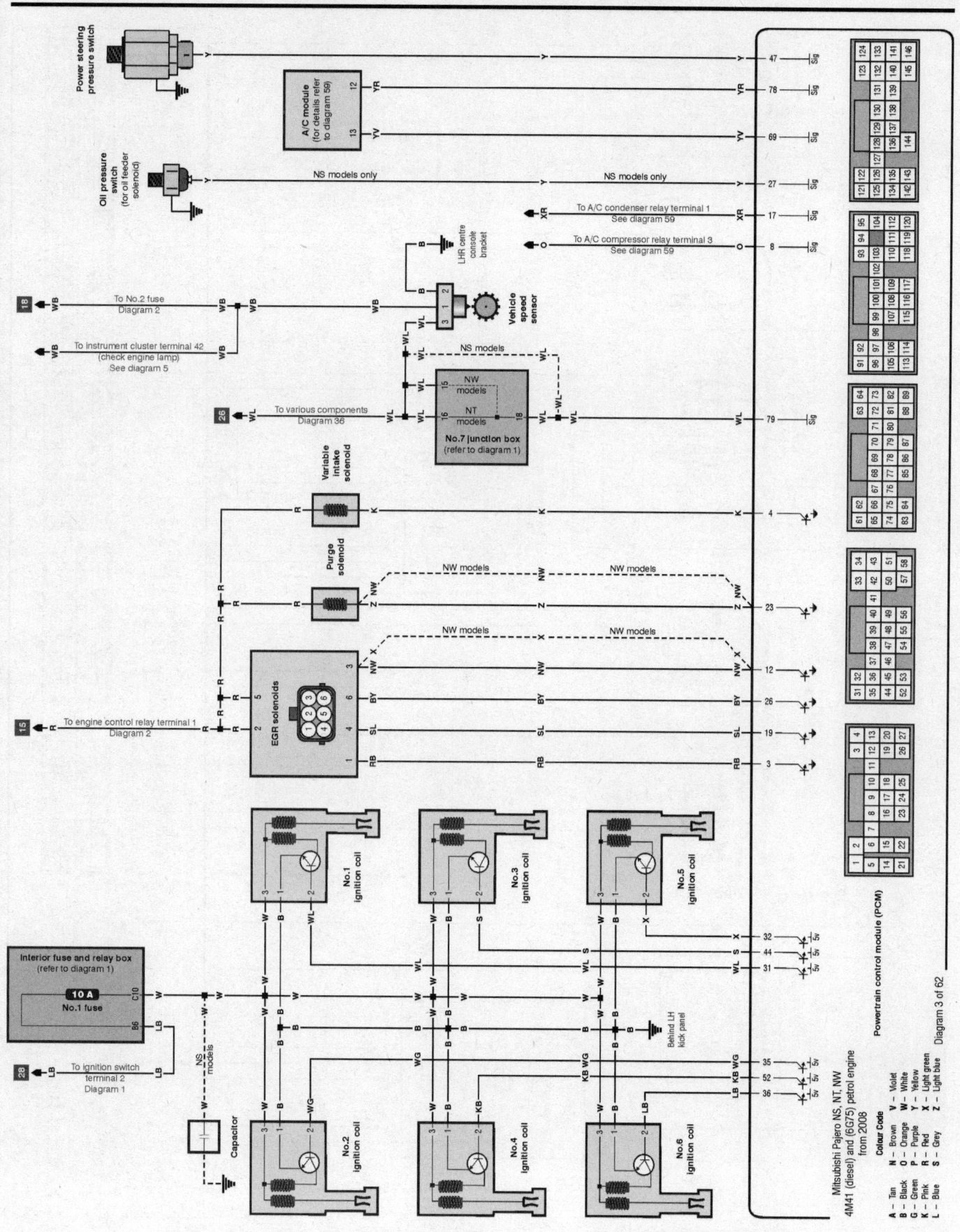

12-83

Diagram 3 - Ignition system, various sensors and solenoids - NS, NT and NW petrol models

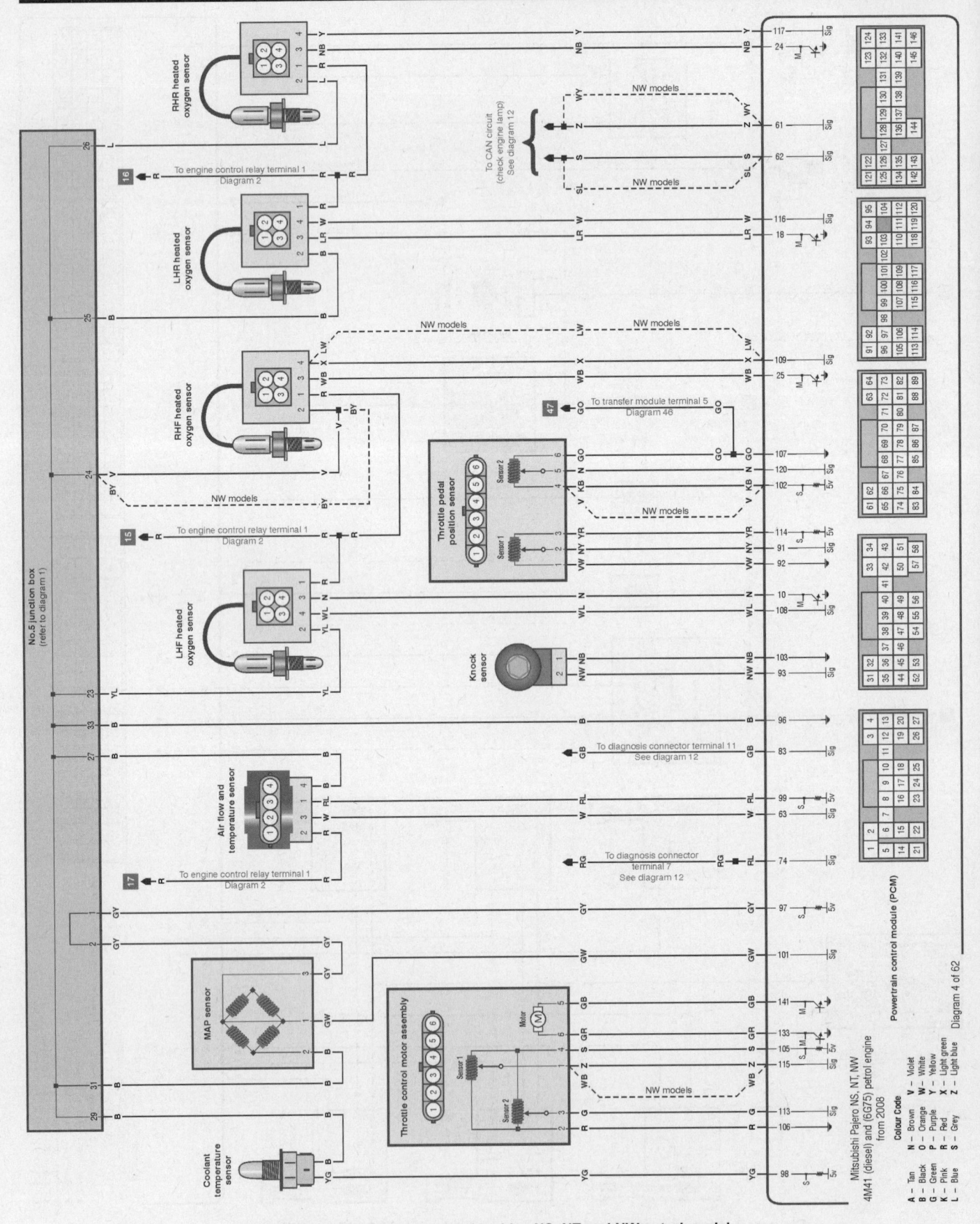

Diagram 4 - Various sensors, solenoids - NS, NT and NW petrol models

Chapter 12 Chassis electrical system

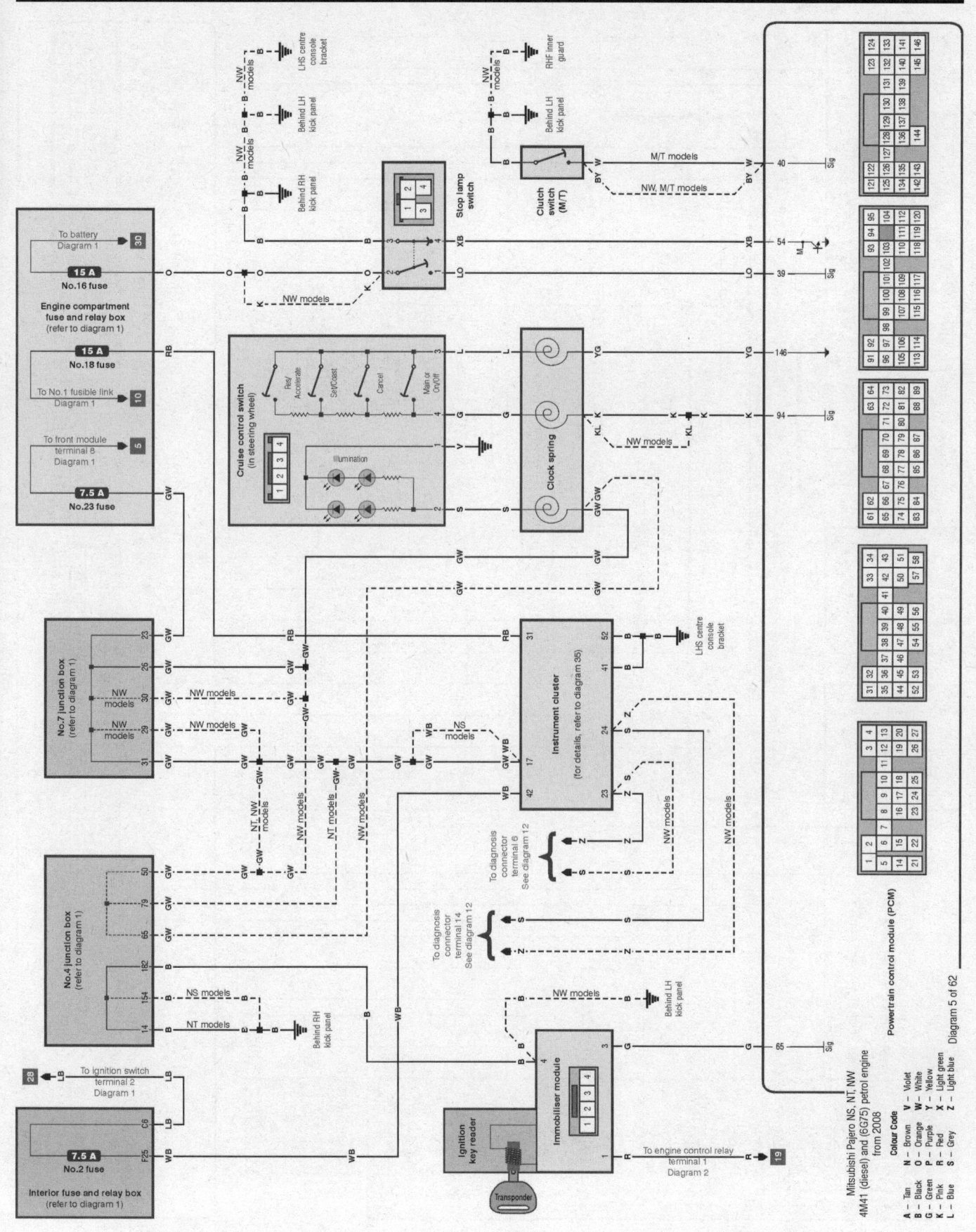

Diagram 5 - Cruise control, instrument cluster, immobiliser system - NS, NT and NW petrol models

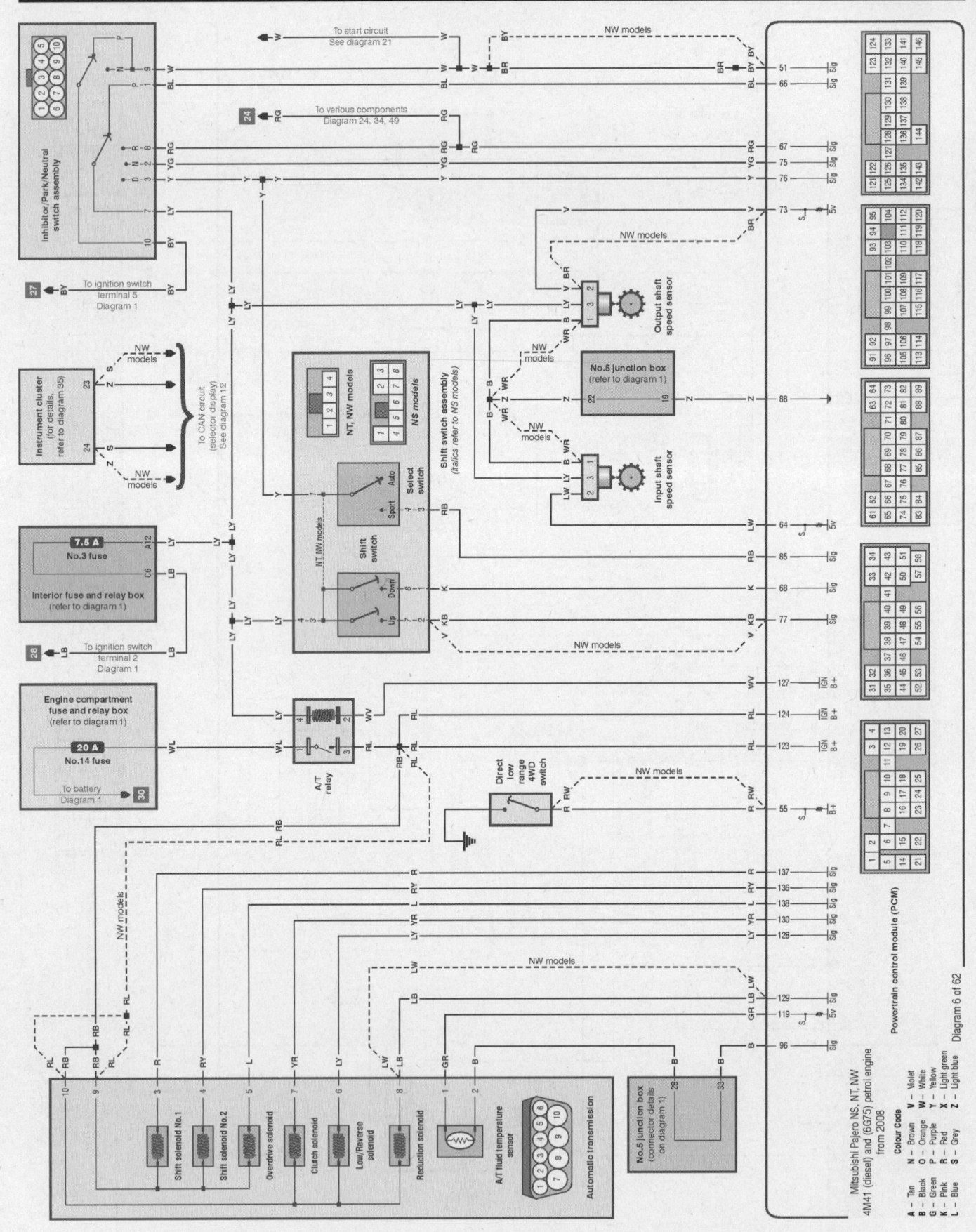

Diagram 6 - Automatic transmission, inhibitor switch - NS, NT and NW petrol models

Chapter 12 Chassis electrical system

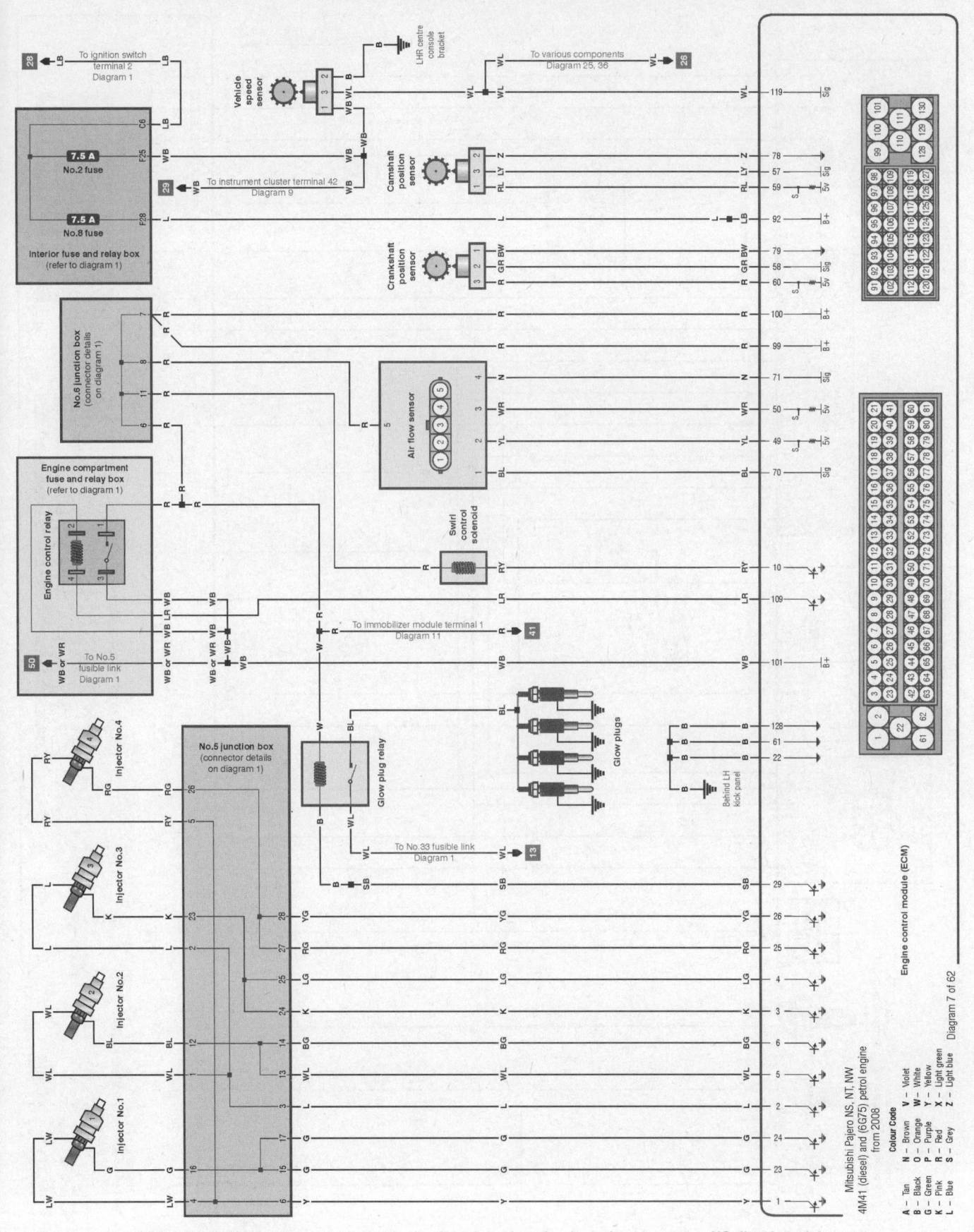

12-87

Diagram 7 - ECM power supply, earth circuits, glow plug circuit, various sensors - NS diesel models

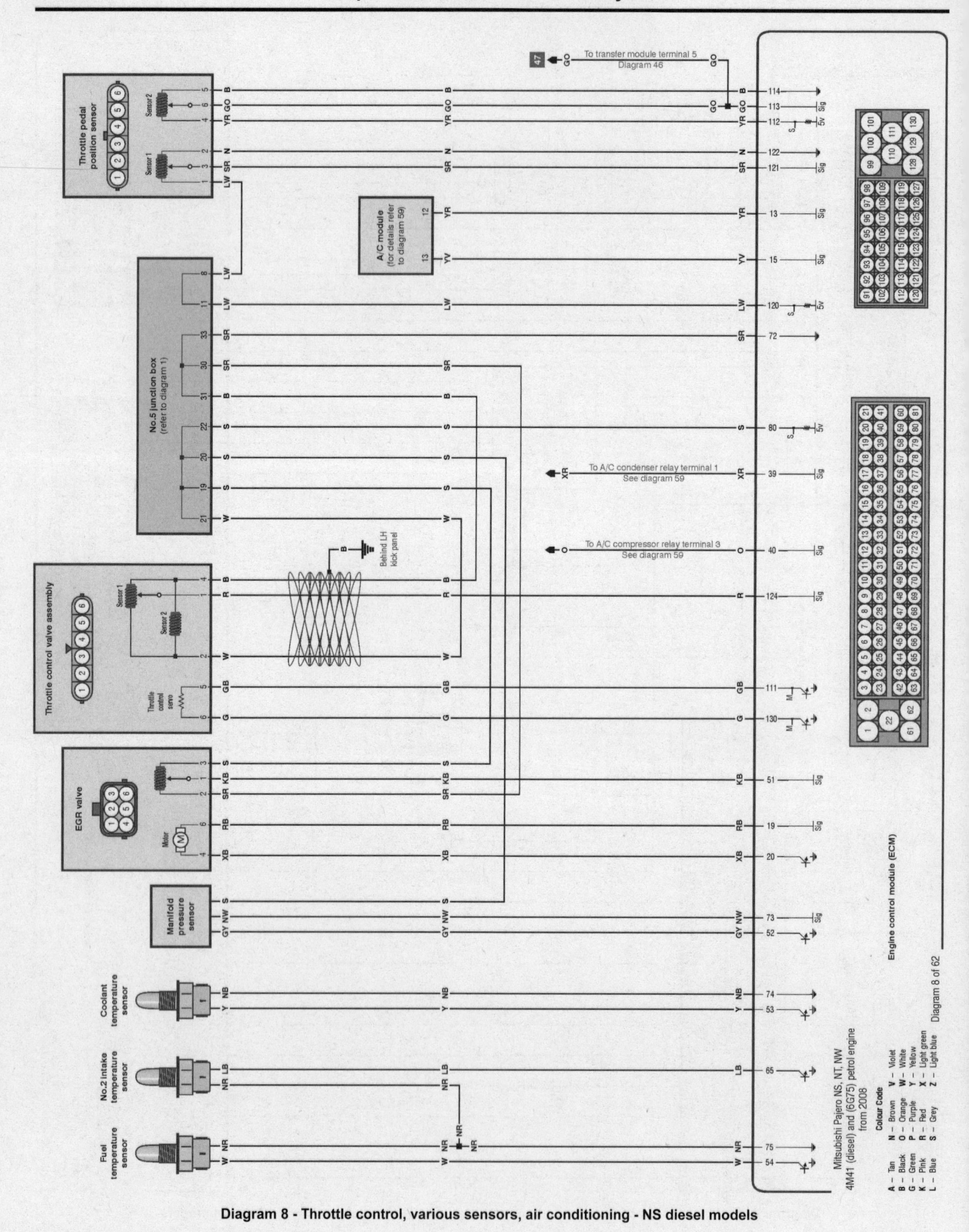

Diagram 8 - Throttle control, various sensors, air conditioning - NS diesel models

Chapter 12 Chassis electrical system

Diagram 9 - Various sensors, cruise control, instrument cluster - NS diesel models

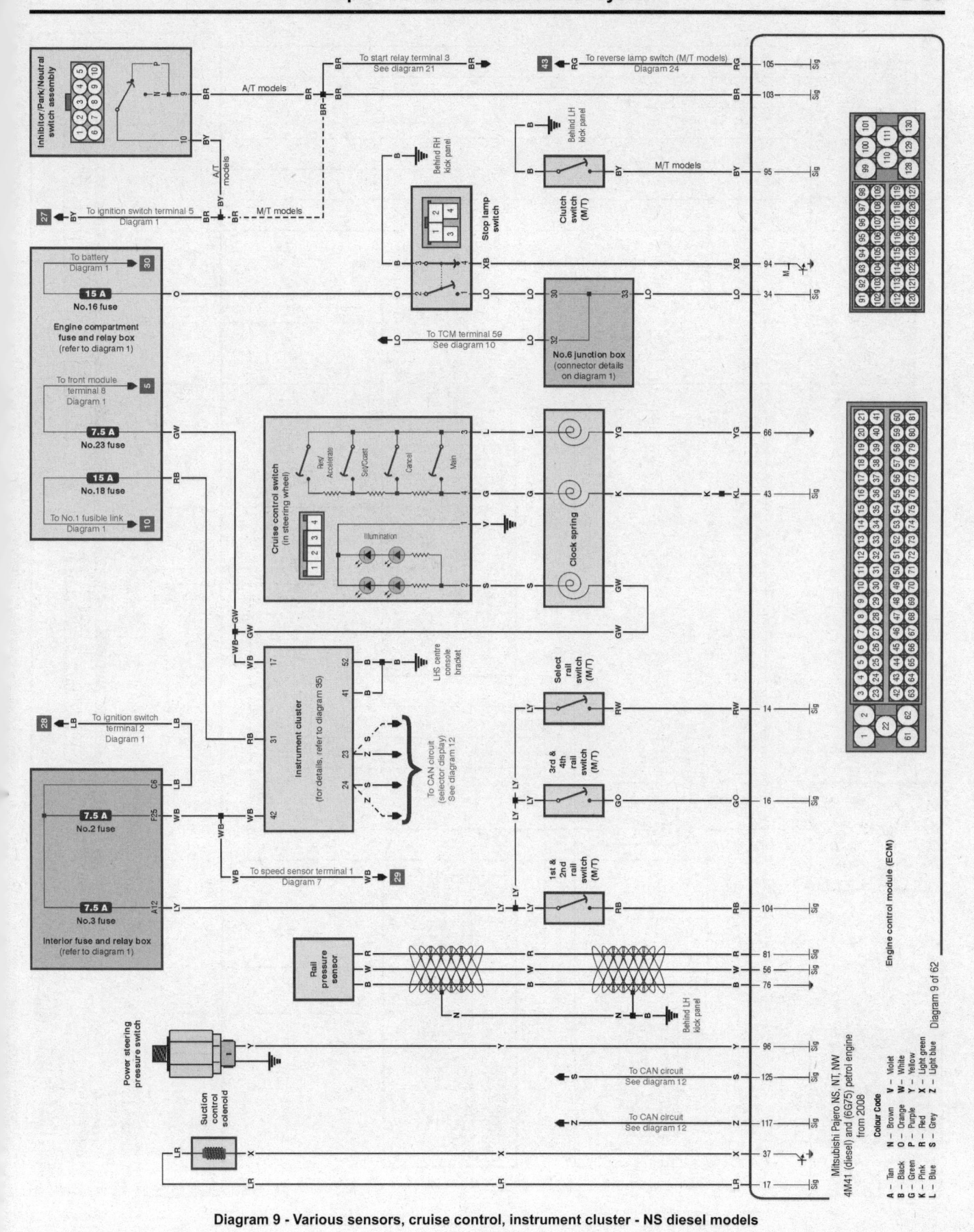

12-90   Chapter 12 Chassis electrical system

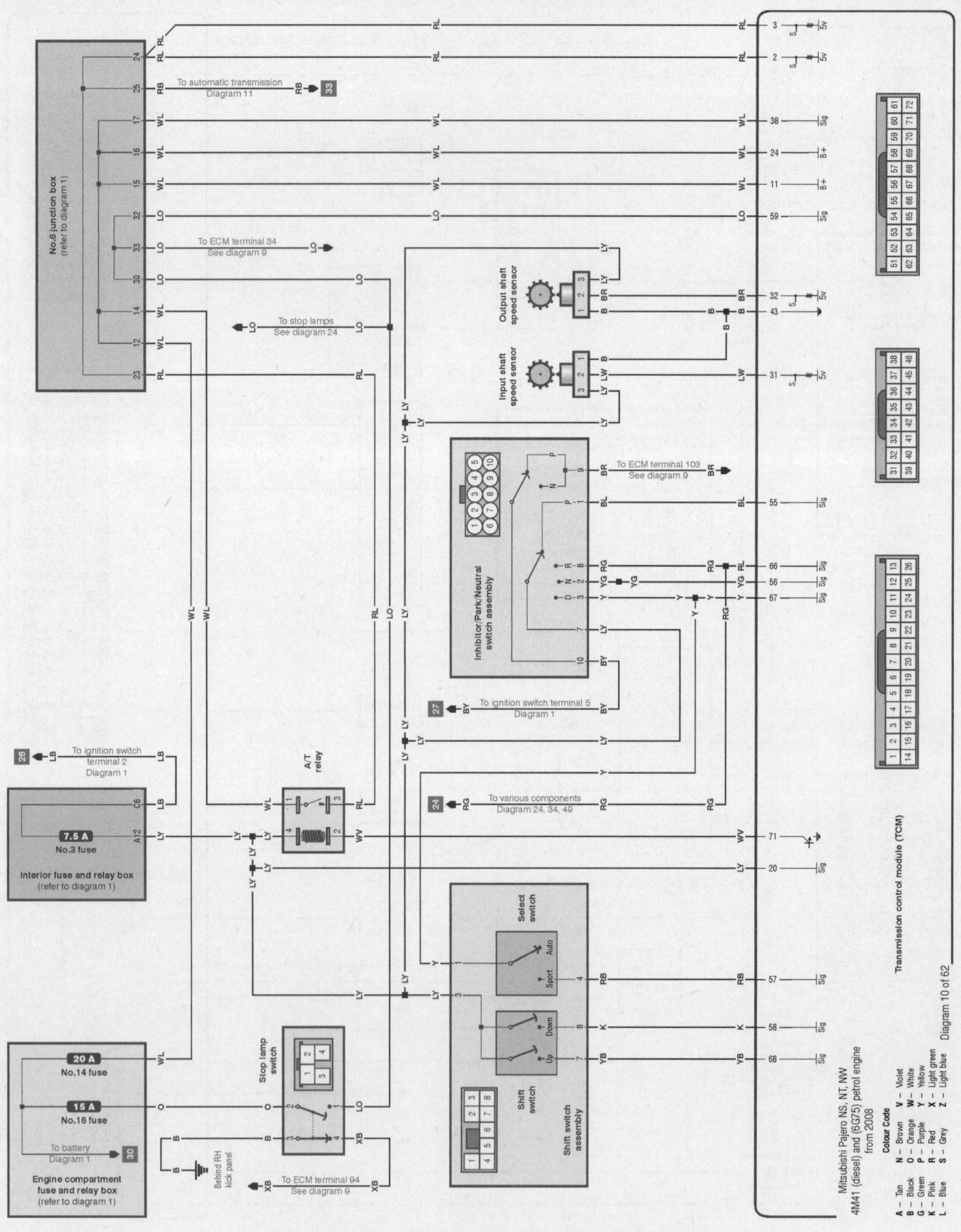

Diagram 10 - Automatic transmission, inhibitor switch - NS diesel models

Chapter 12 Chassis electrical system

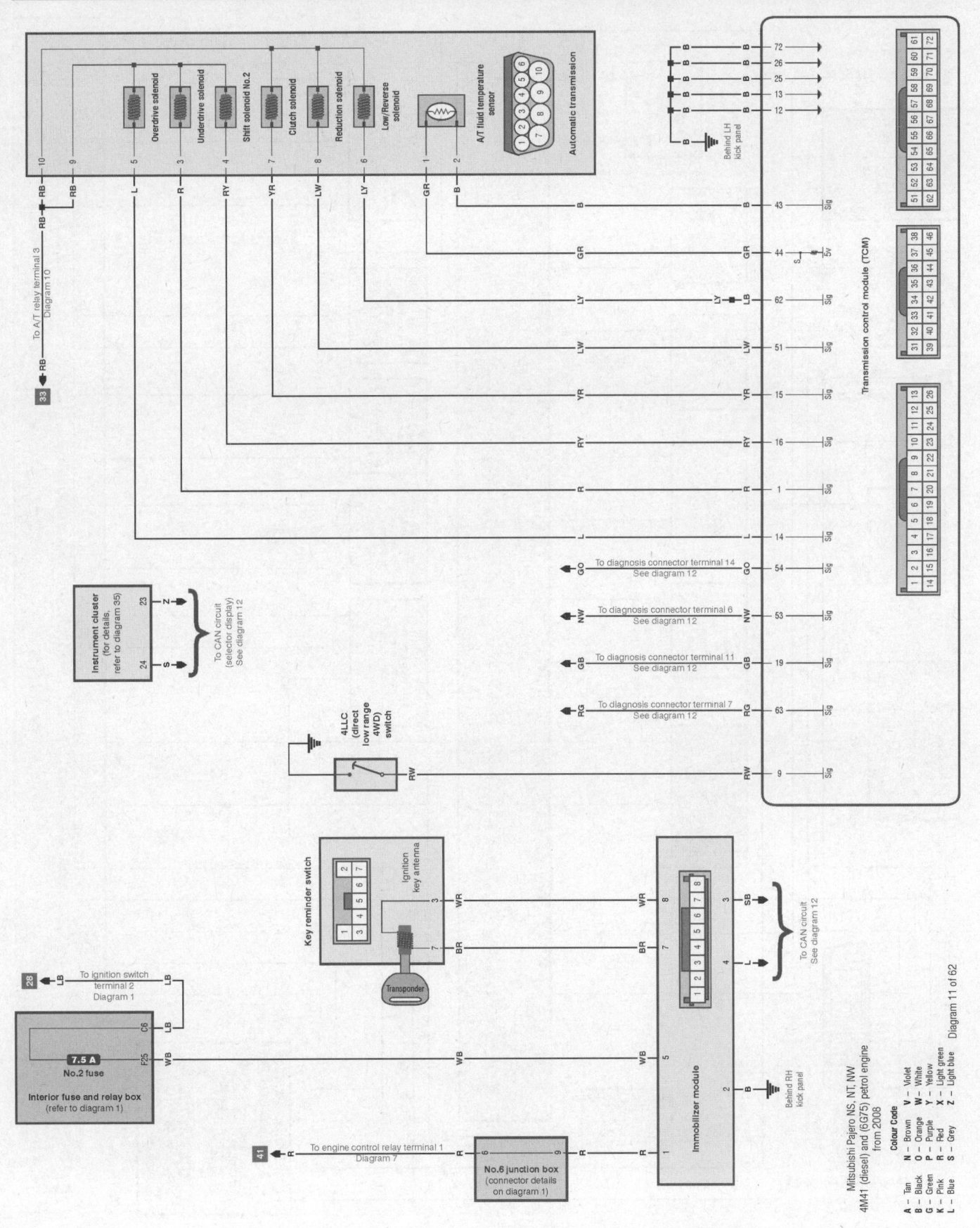

Diagram 11 - Automatic transmission, immobilizer system - NS diesel models

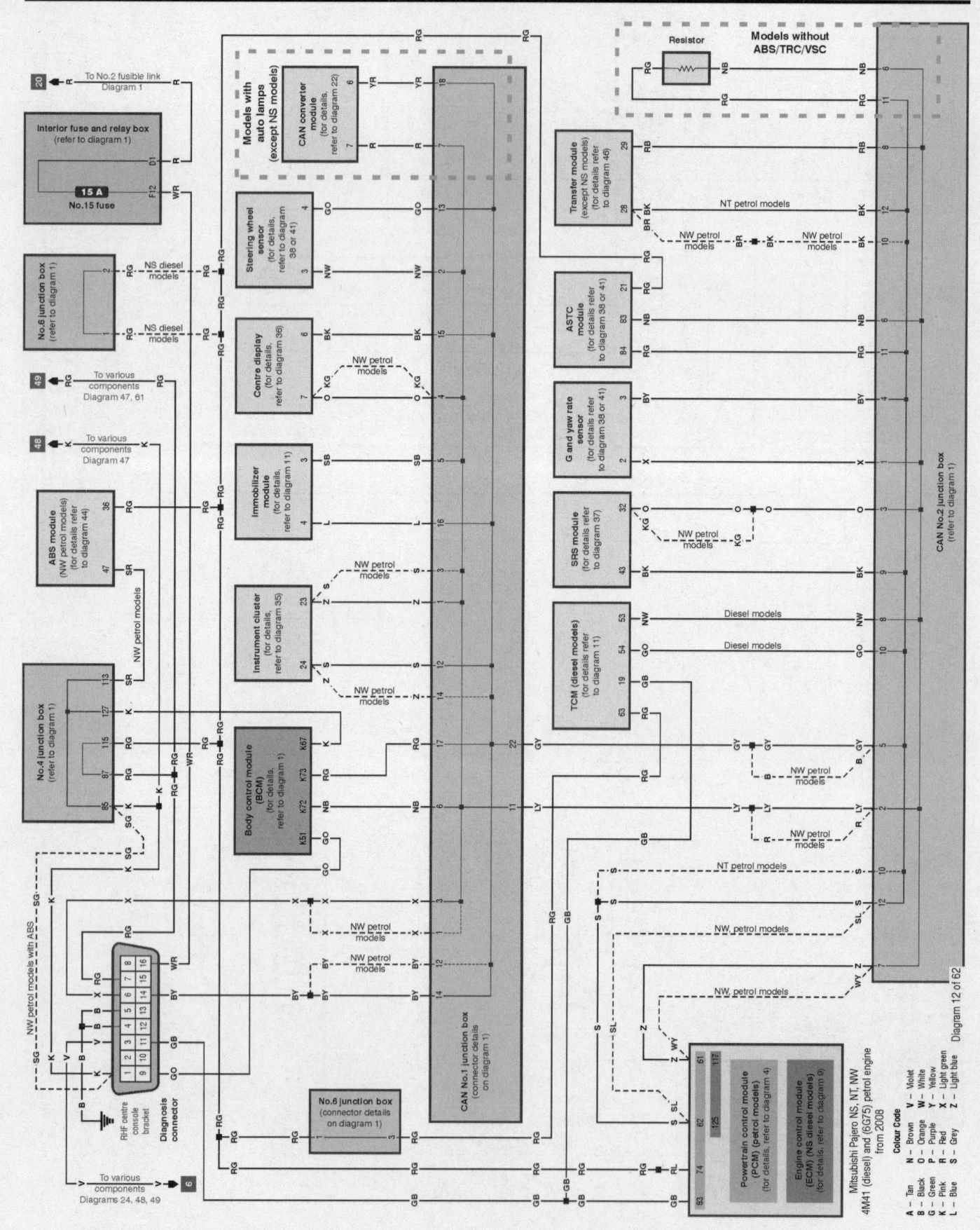

Diagram 12 - Communication area network (CAN), diagnosis connector - NS, NT, NW petrol models and NS diesel models

Chapter 12 Chassis electrical system

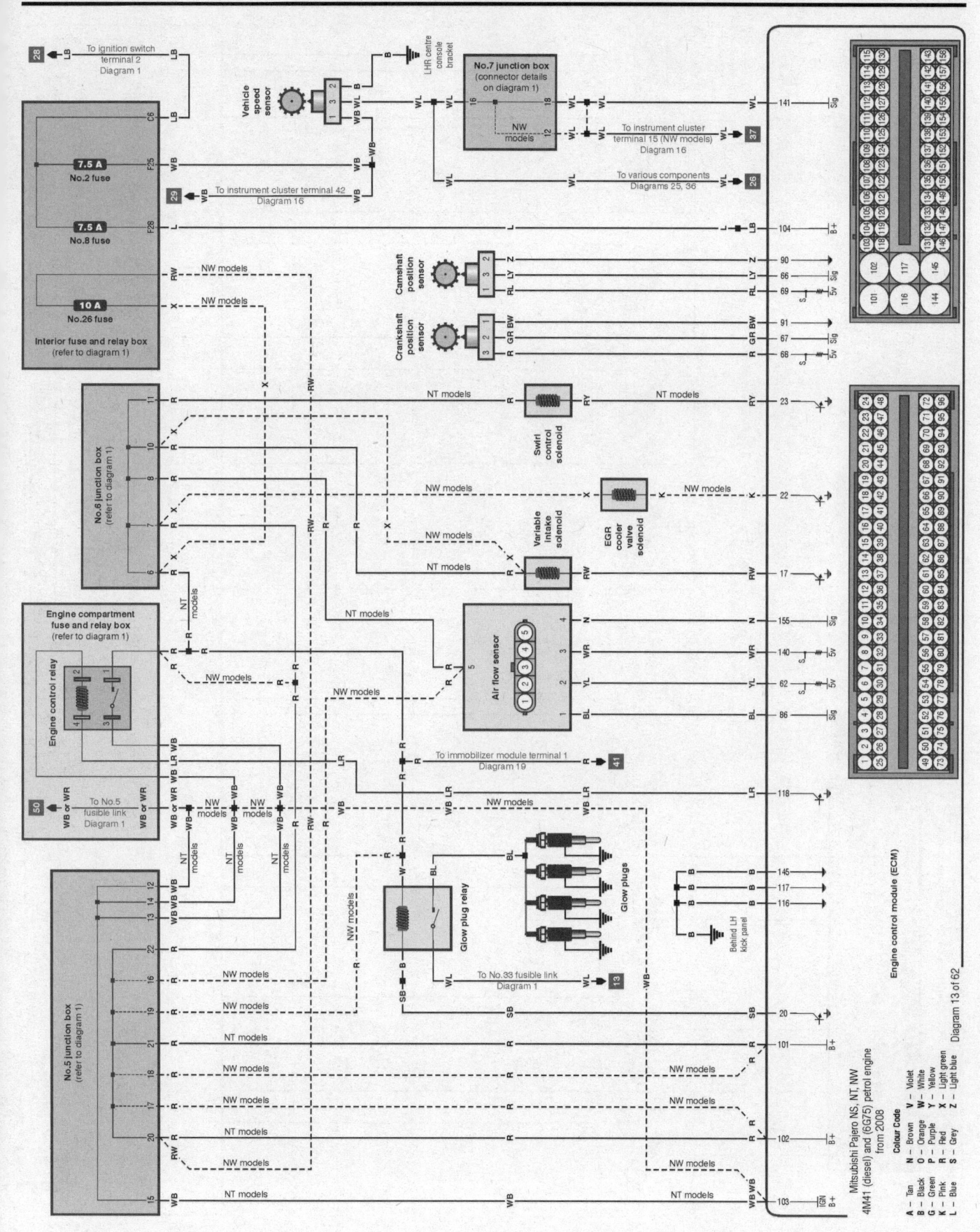

12-93

Diagram 13 - PCM power supply, earth circuits, glow plug circuit, various sensors and solenoids - NT, NW diesel models

12-94 Chapter 12 Chassis electrical system

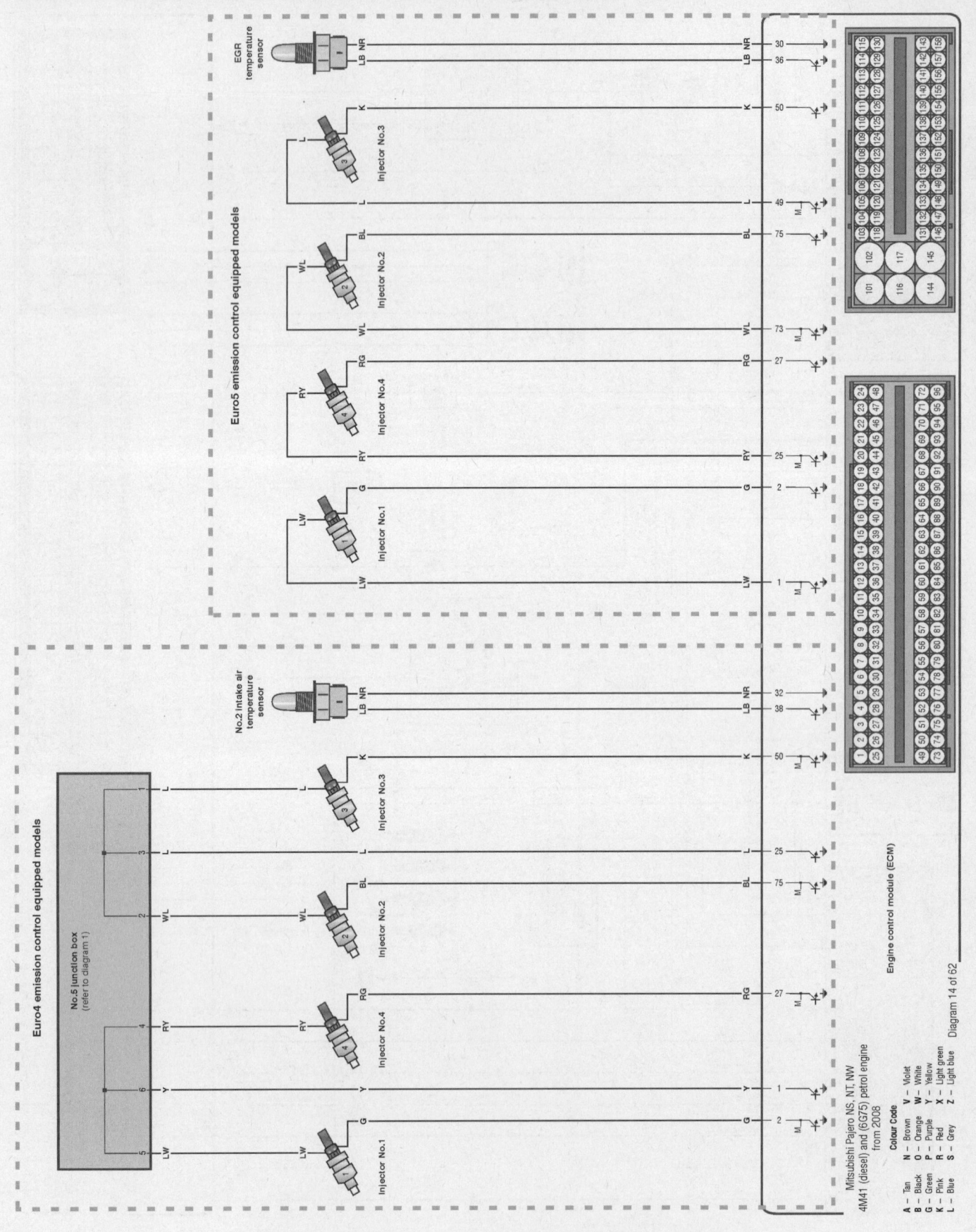

Diagram 14 - Fuel injectors, various sensors - NT, NW diesel models

Chapter 12 Chassis electrical system

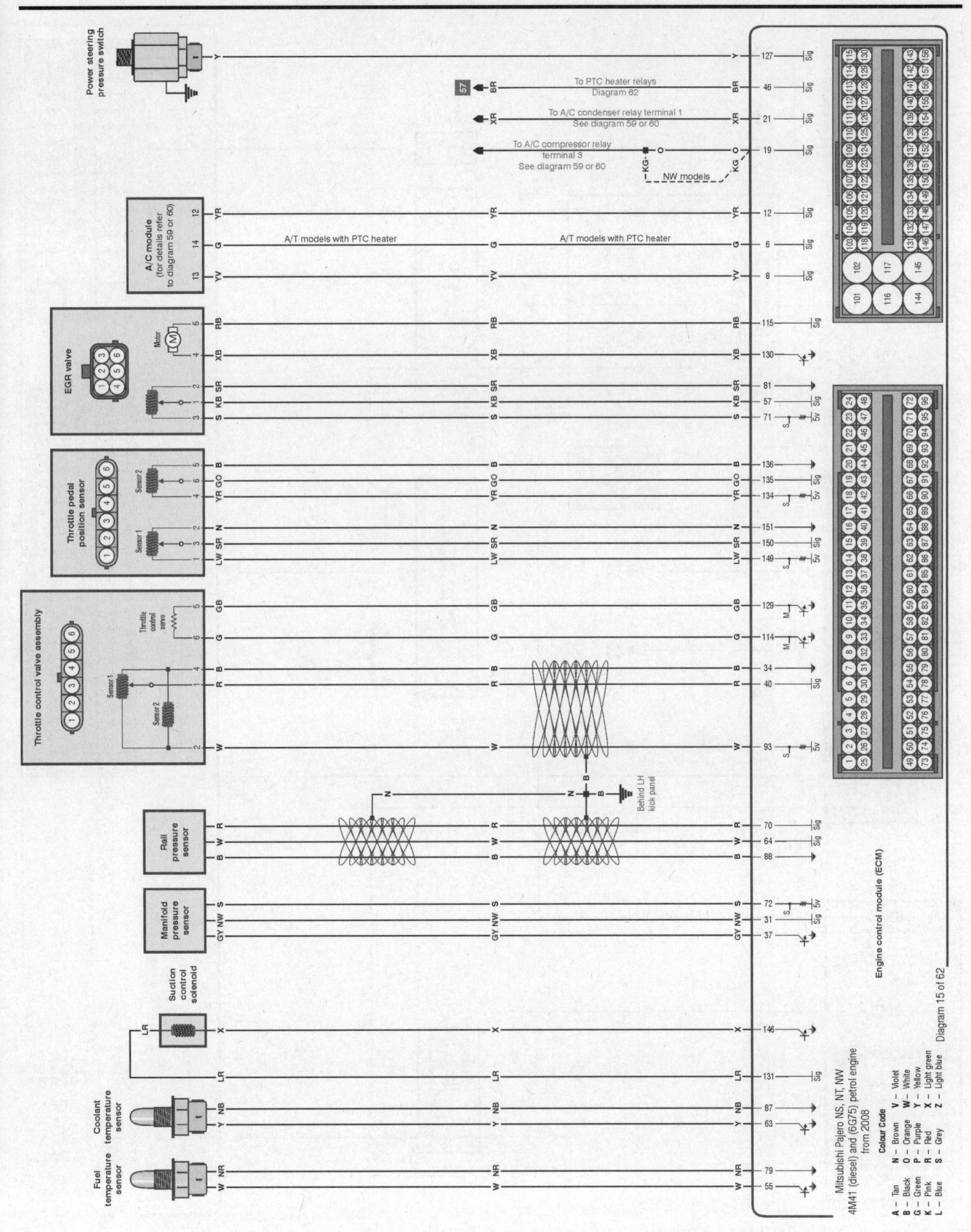

12-95

Diagram 15 - Throttle control, air conditioning, various sensors - NT and NW diesel models

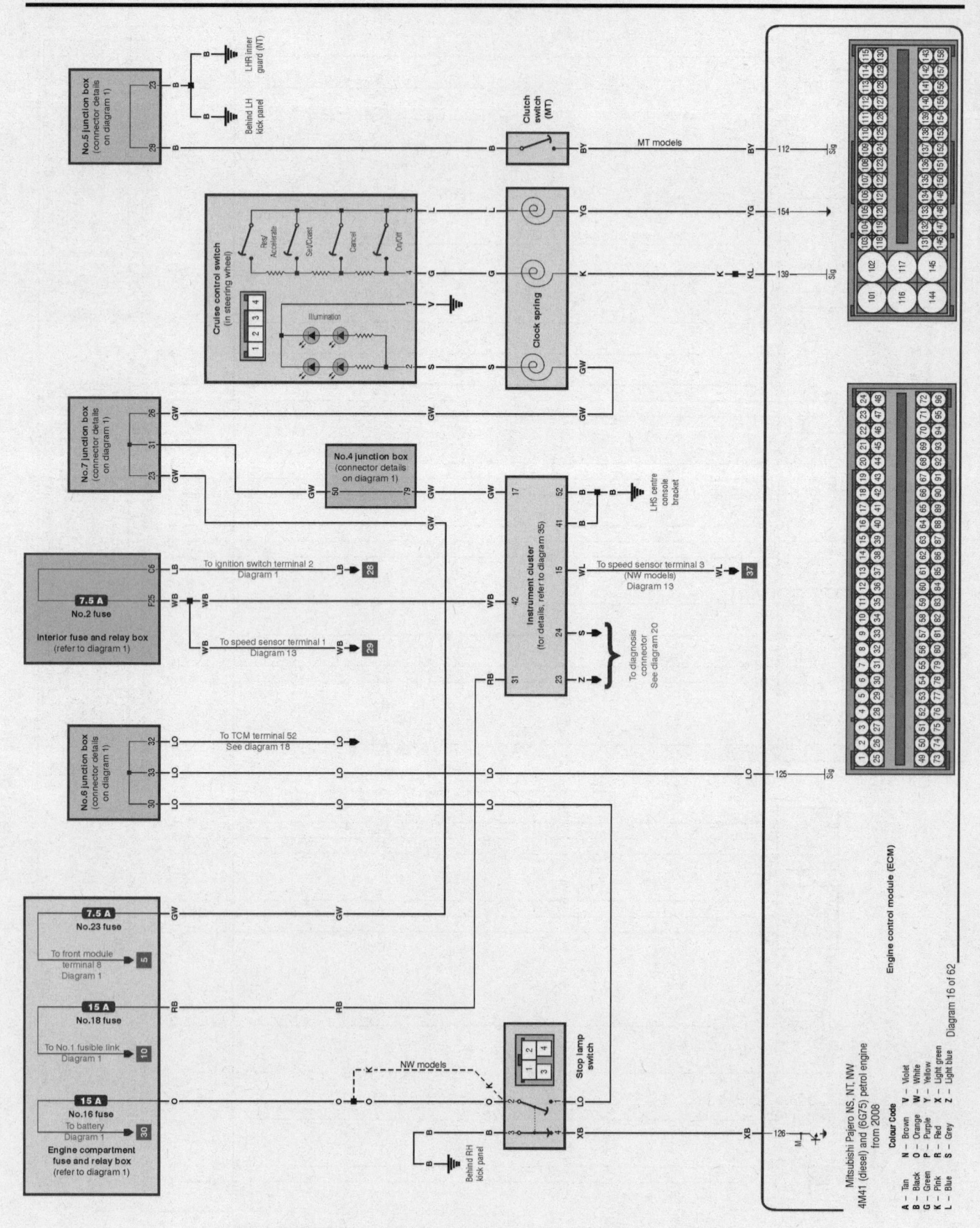

Diagram 16 - Cruise control, instrument cluster - NT and NW diesel models

Chapter 12 Chassis electrical system

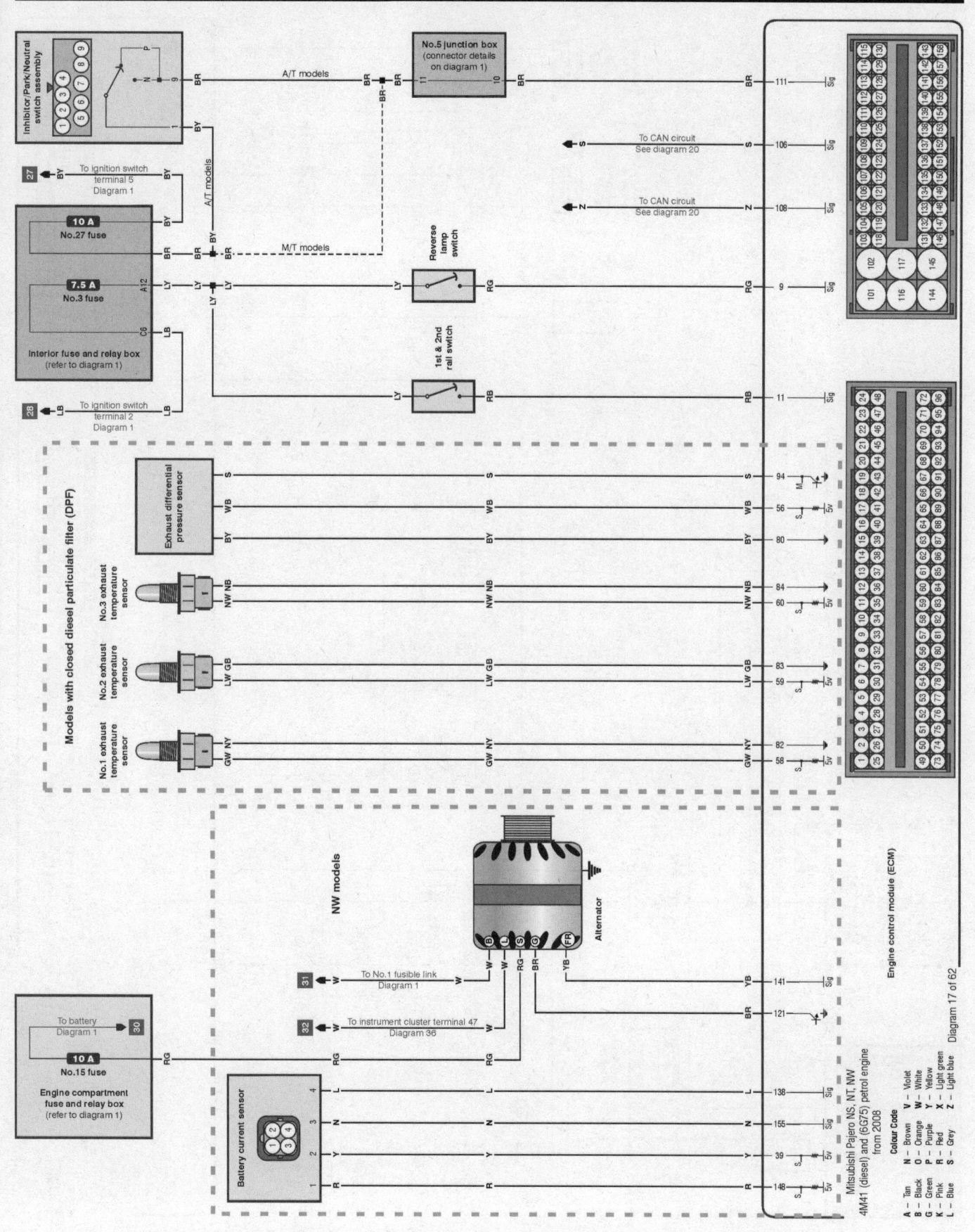

12-97

Diagram 17 - Charge system (NW diesel models), various sensors and switches - NT and NW diesel models

Chapter 12 Chassis electrical system

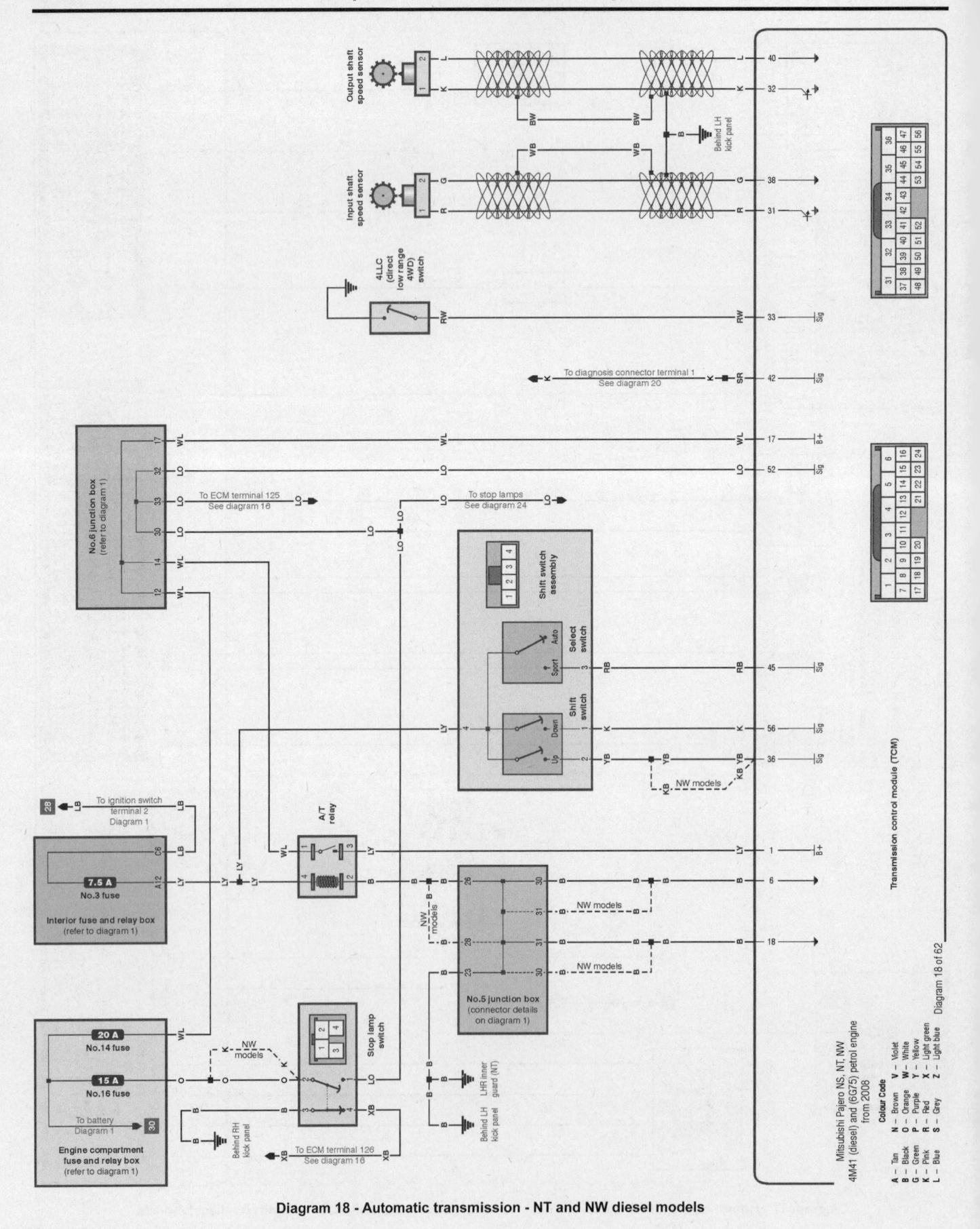

Diagram 18 - Automatic transmission - NT and NW diesel models

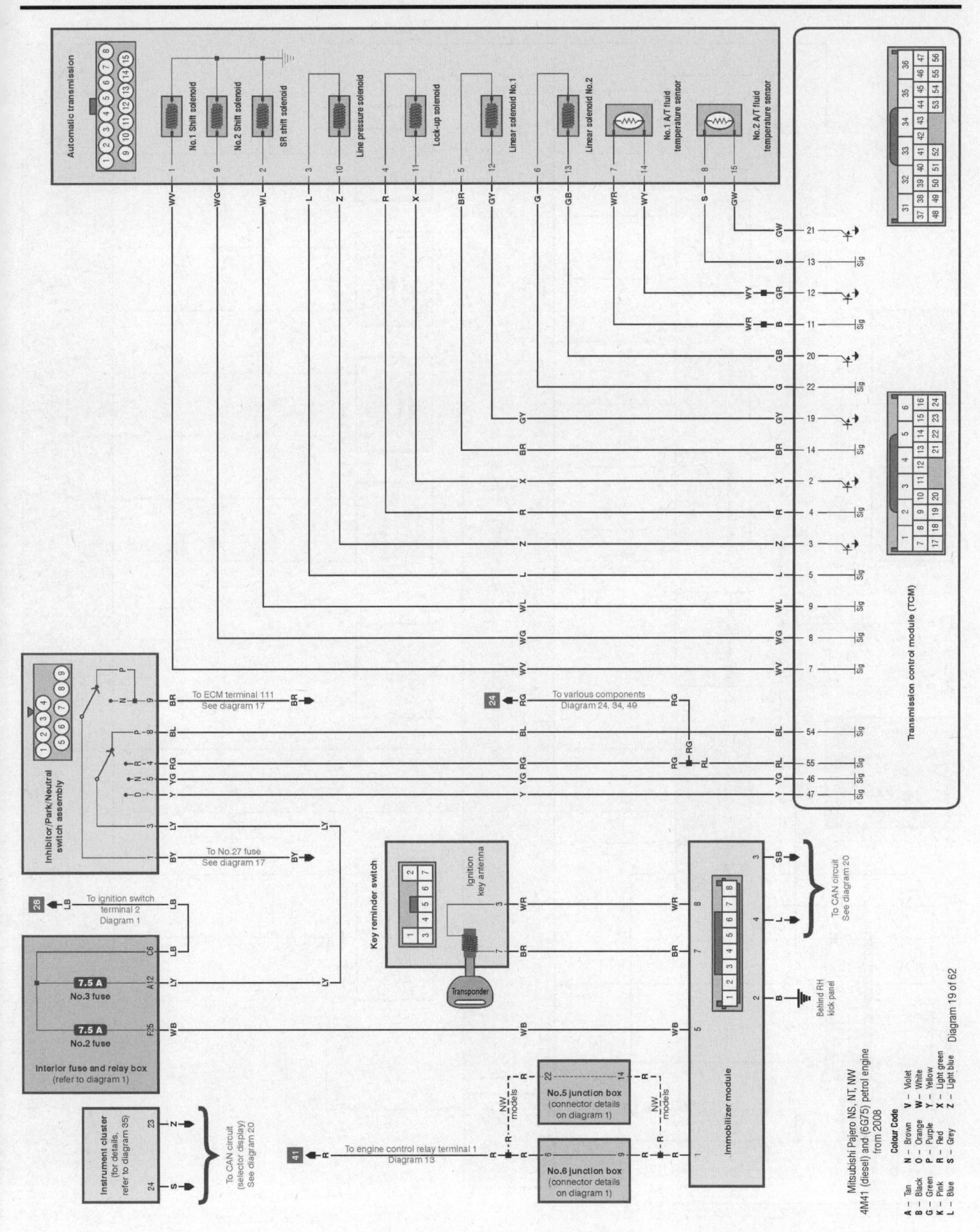

Diagram 19 - Automatic transmission, inhibitor switch, immobilizer system - NT and NW diesel models

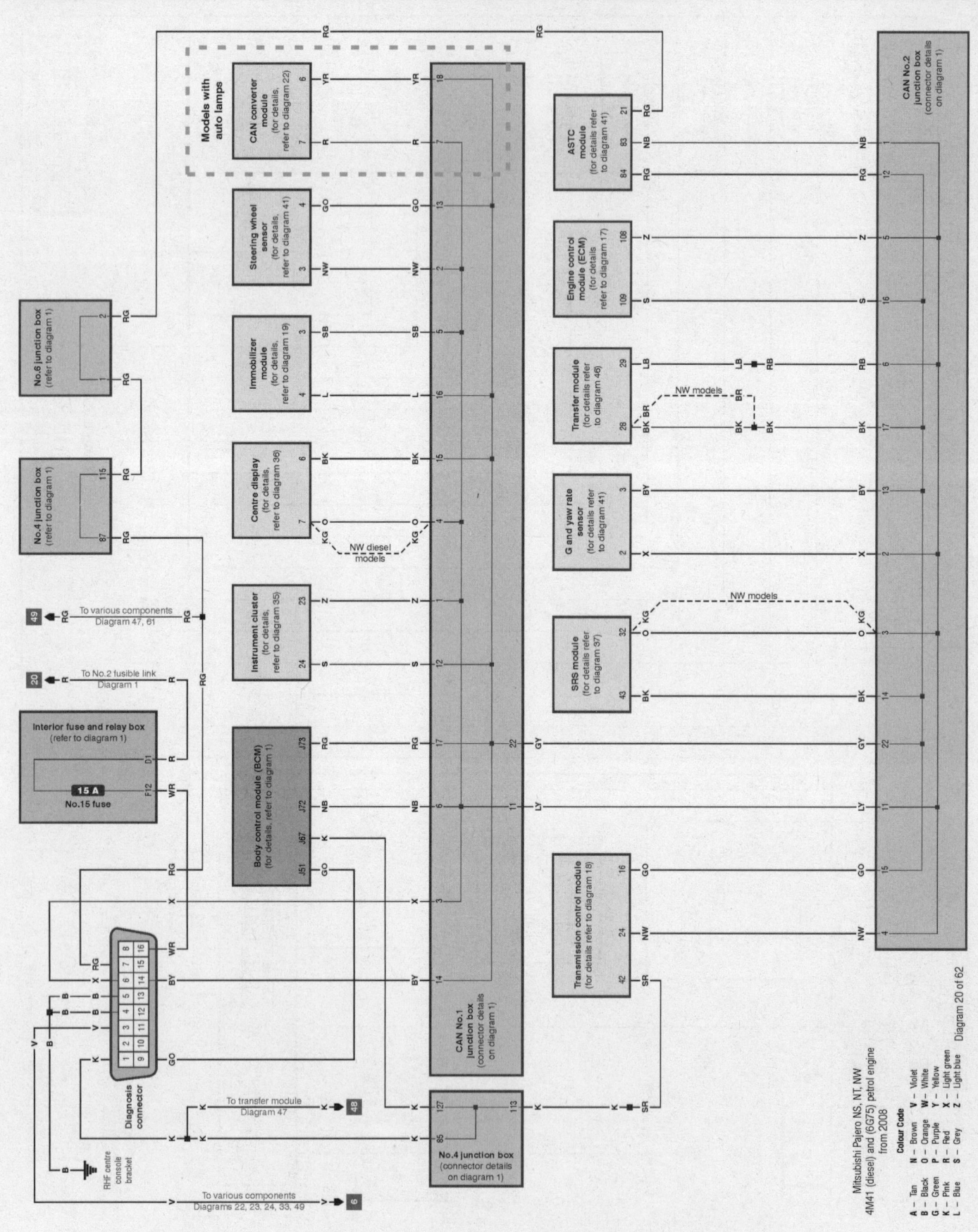

Diagram 20 - Communication area network (CAN), diagnosis connector - NT and NW diesel models

Chapter 12 Chassis electrical system

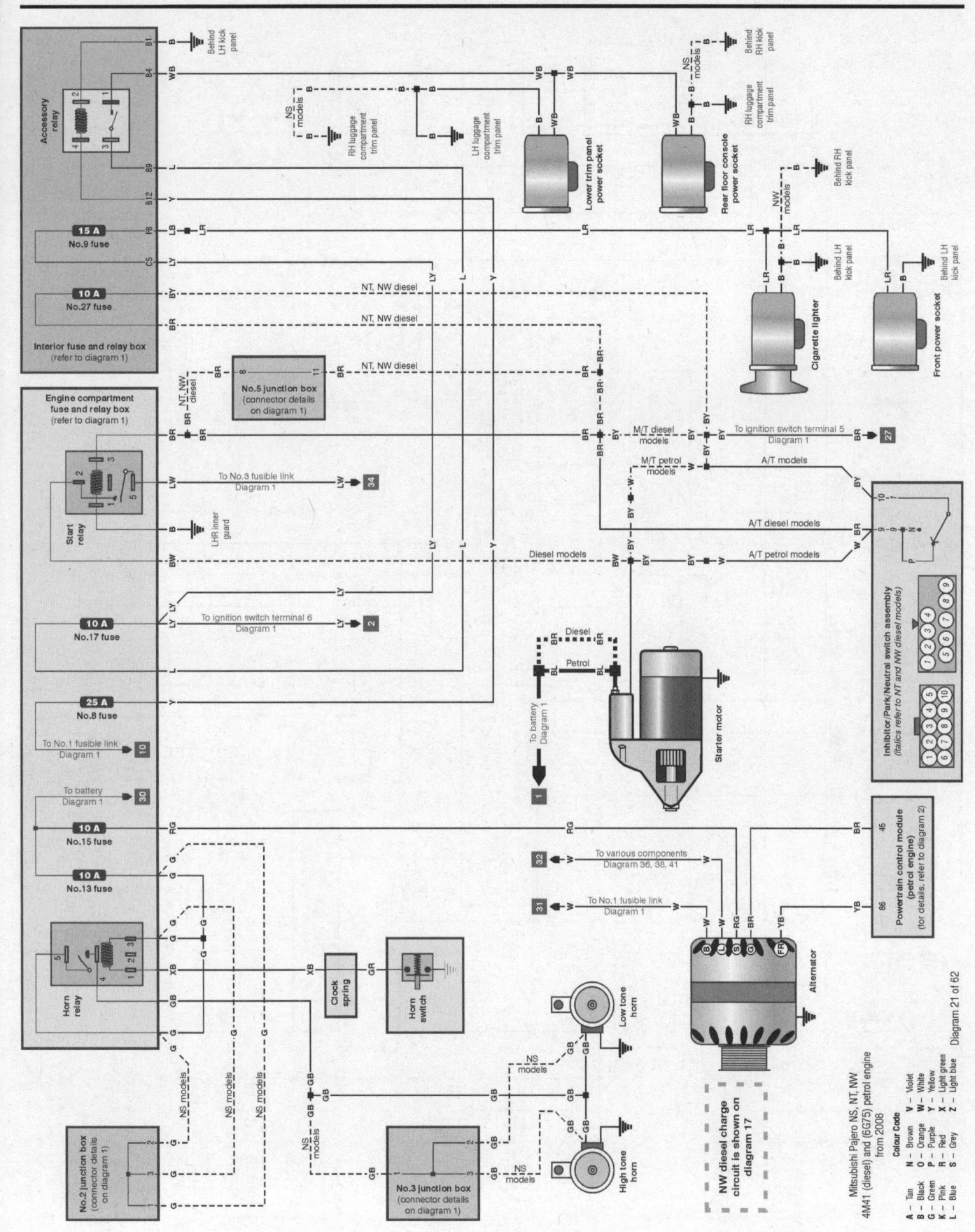

Diagram 21 - Charging, starting, horn, cigarette lighter, power sockets - NS, NT and NW models

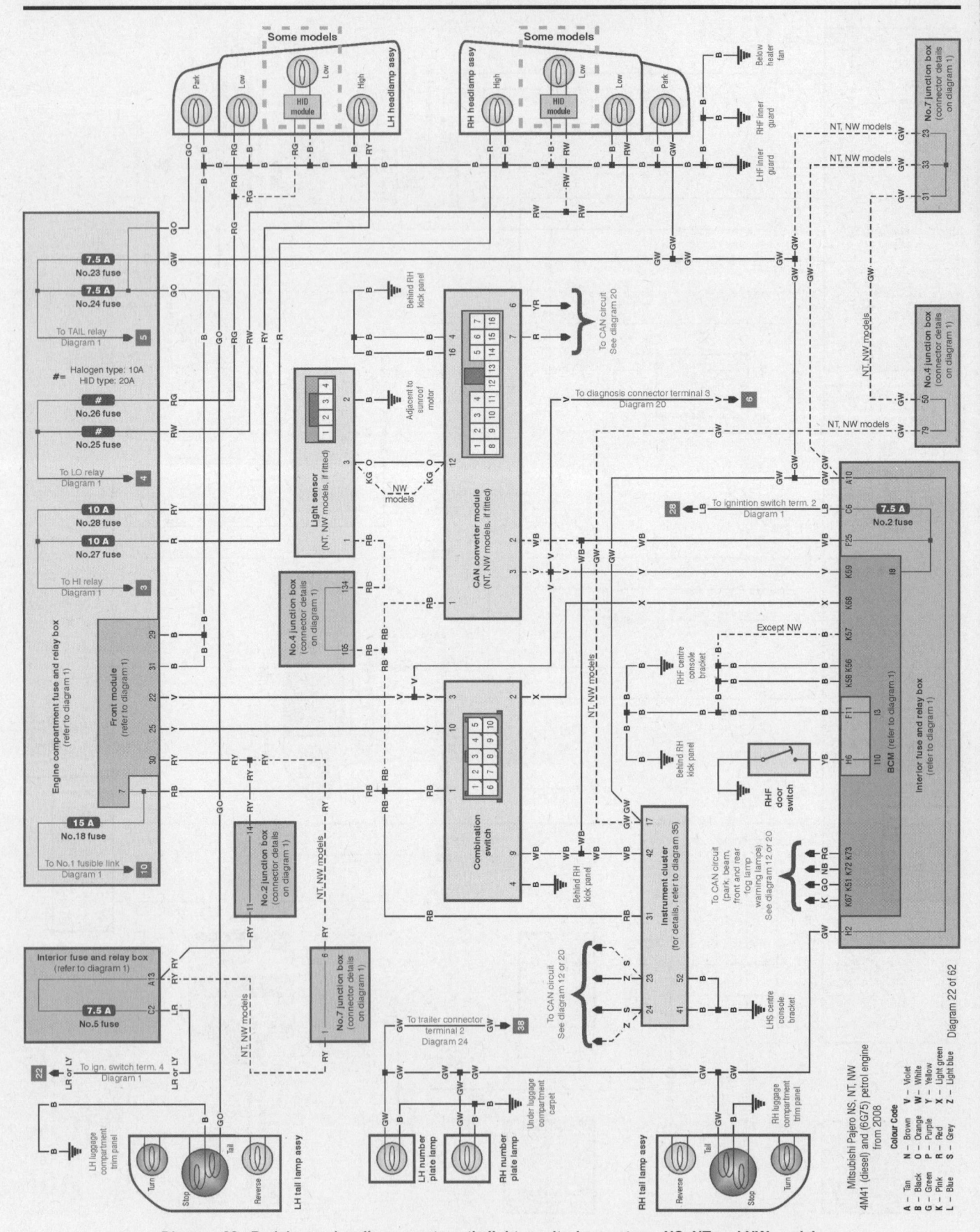

Diagram 22 - Park lamps, headlamps, automatic light monitoring system - NS, NT and NW models

Chapter 12 Chassis electrical system

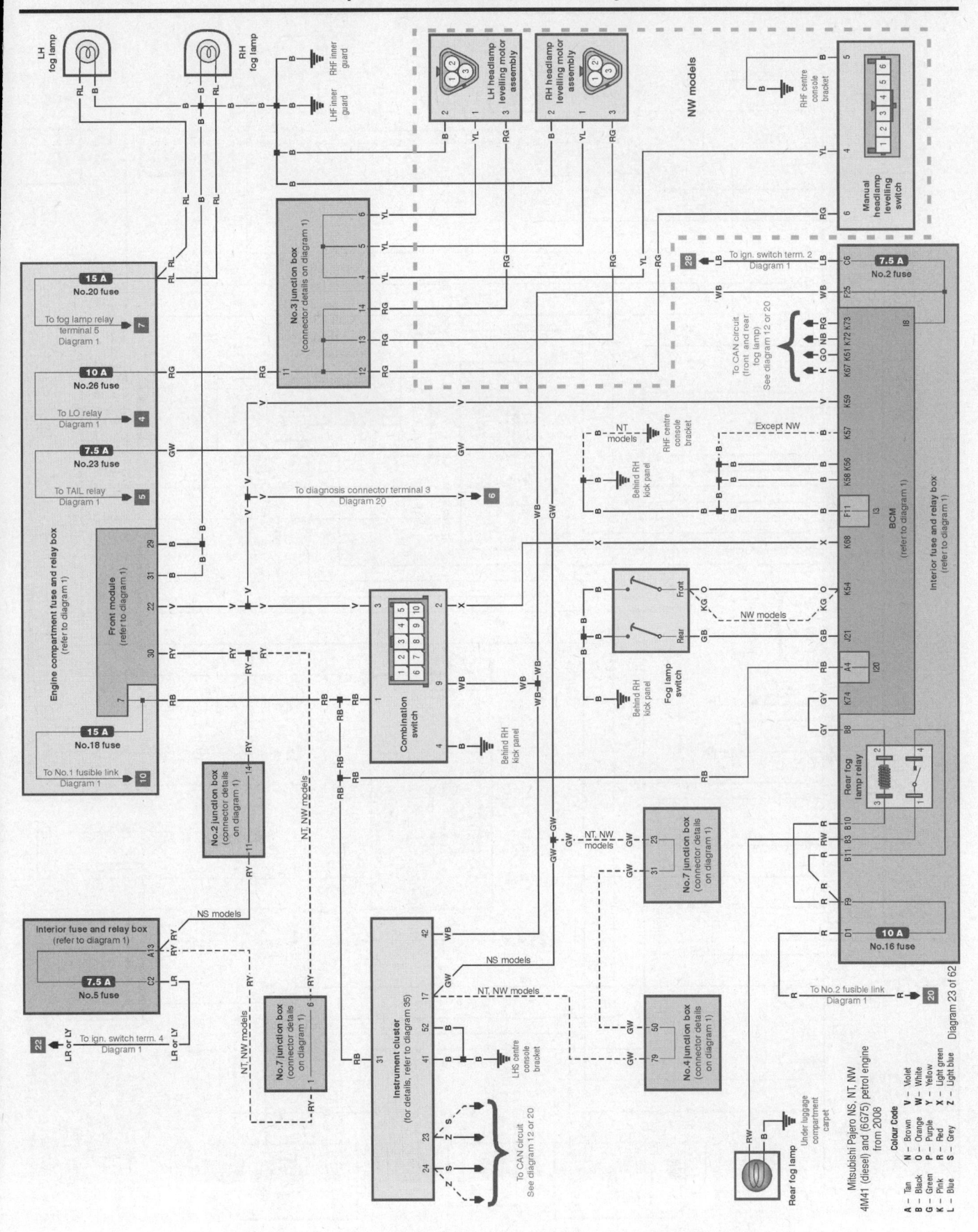

Diagram 23 - Front and rear fog lamps, manual headlamp levelling - NW models

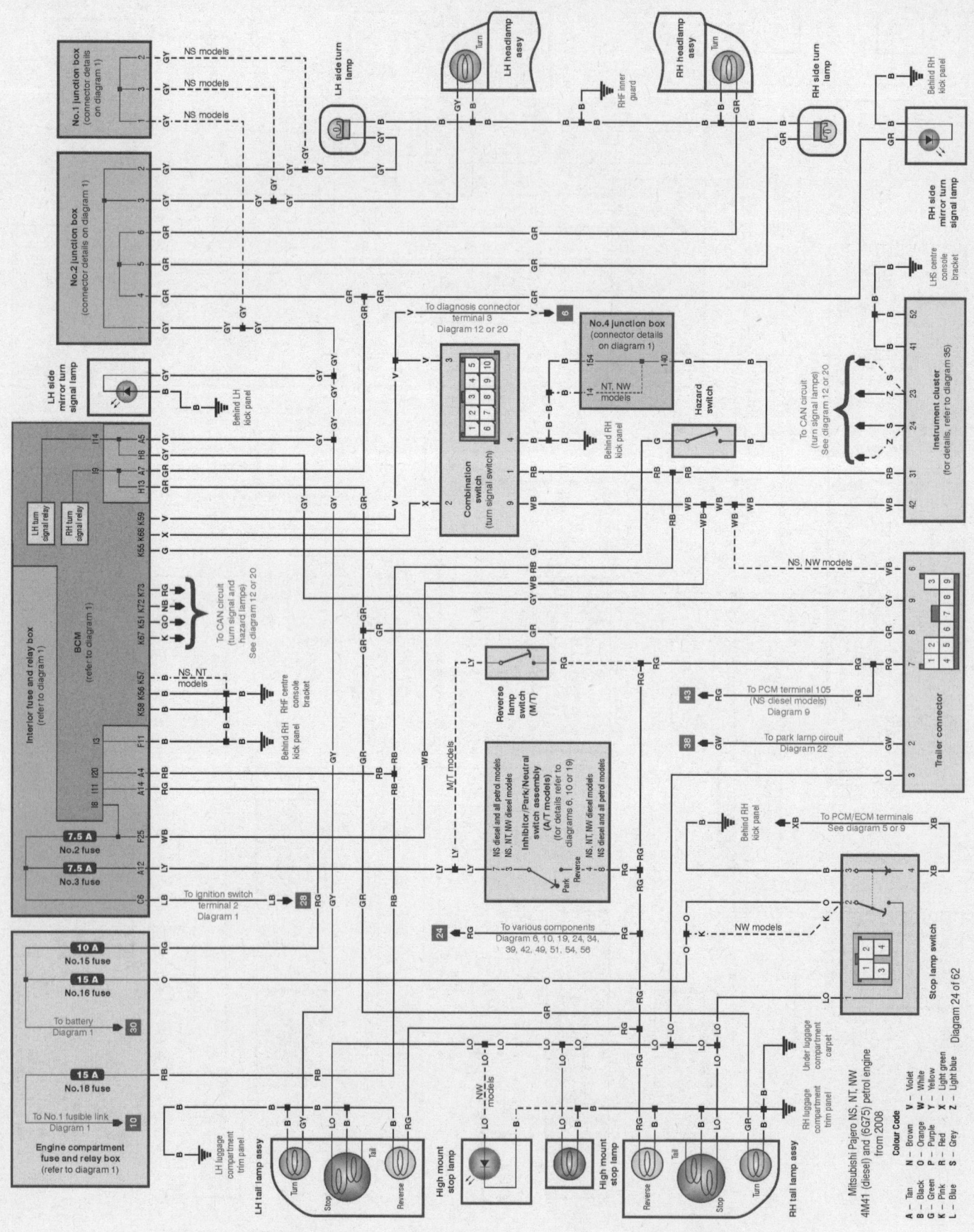

Diagram 24 - Stop lamps, turn signal/hazard lamps, reverse lamps - NS, NT and NW models

Chapter 12 Chassis electrical system

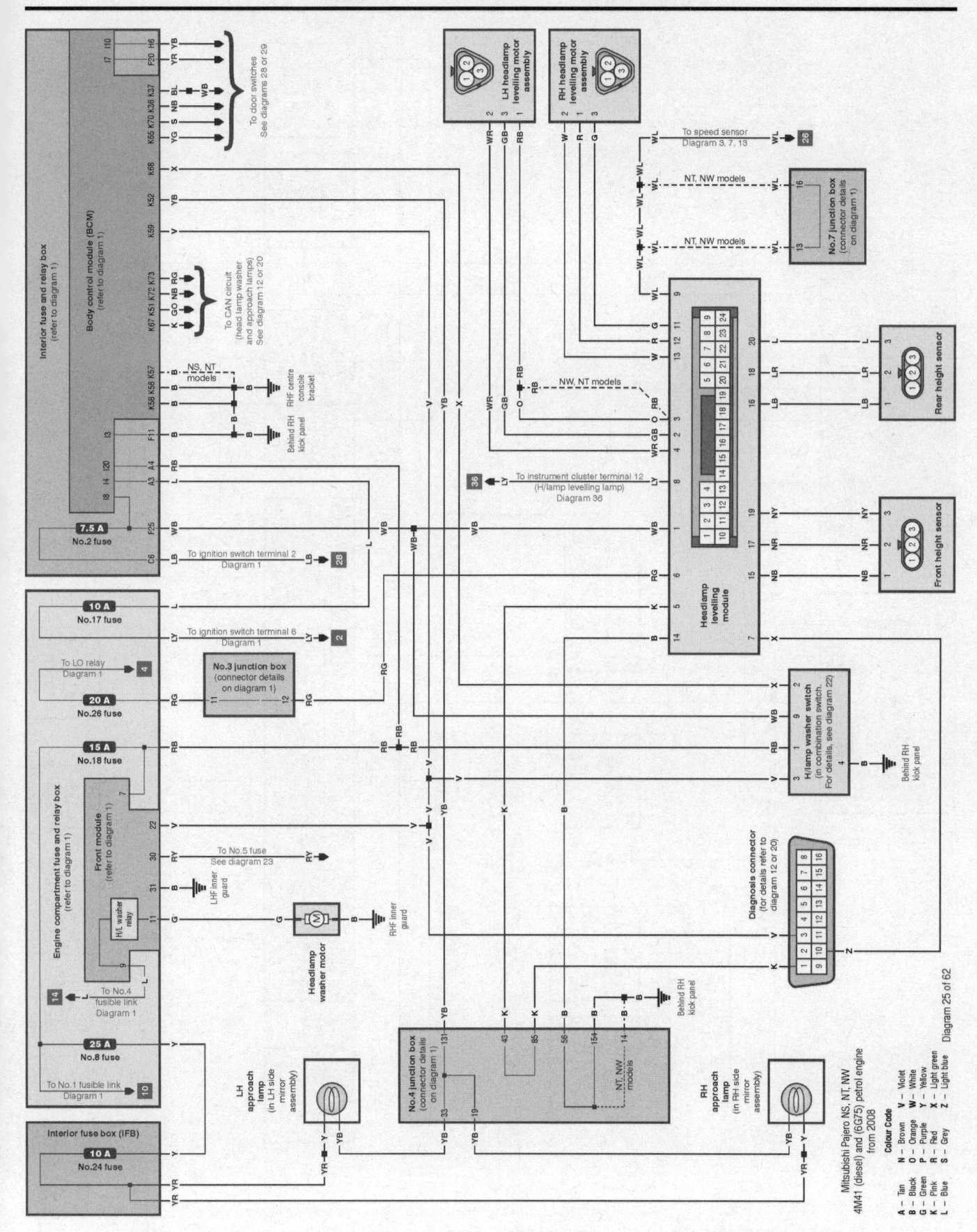

Diagram 25 - Approach lamps, headlamp washer, headlamp levelling systems - NS, NT and NW models

12-106 Chapter 12 Chassis electrical system

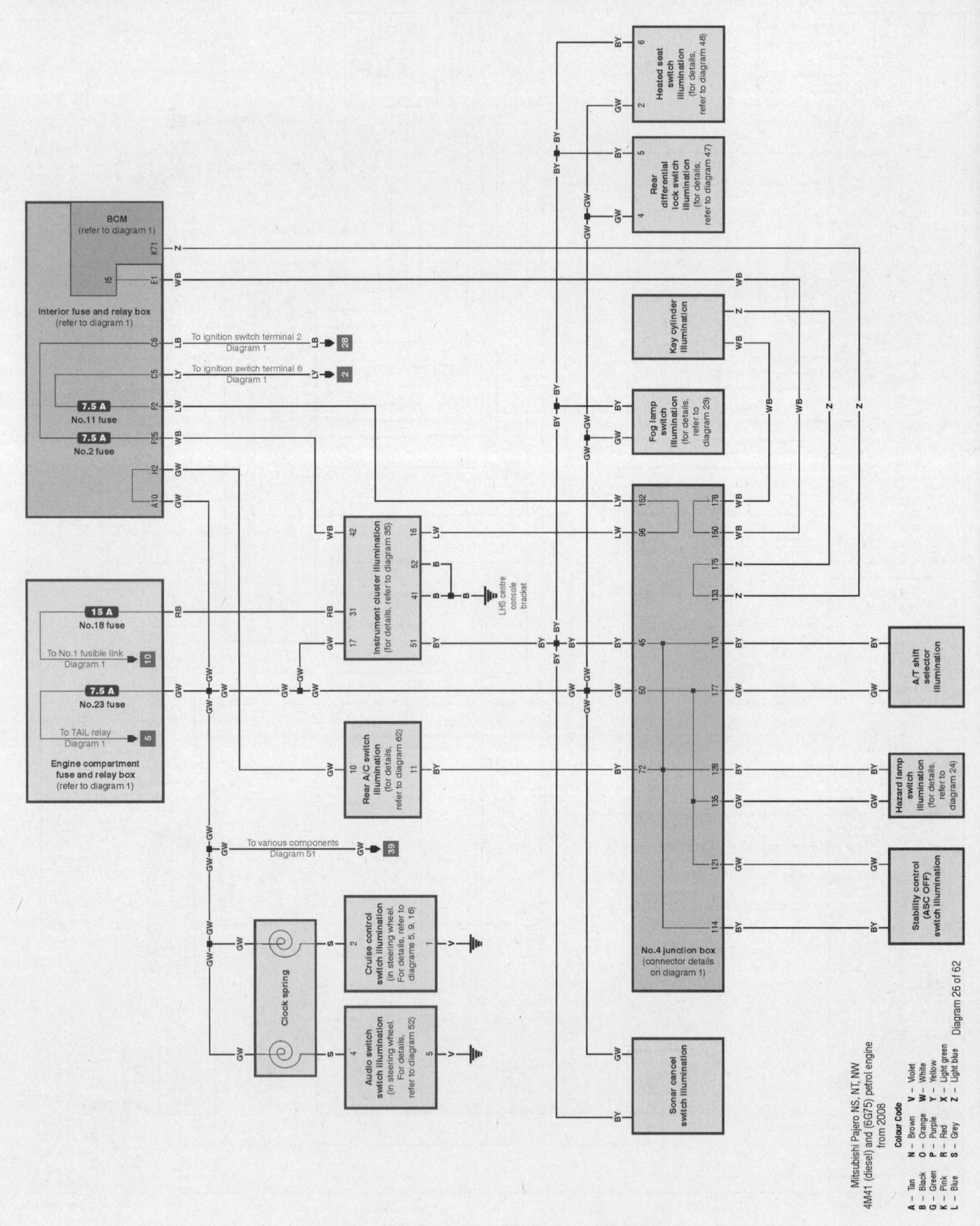

Diagram 26 - Instrument illumination - NS models

Chapter 12 Chassis electrical system

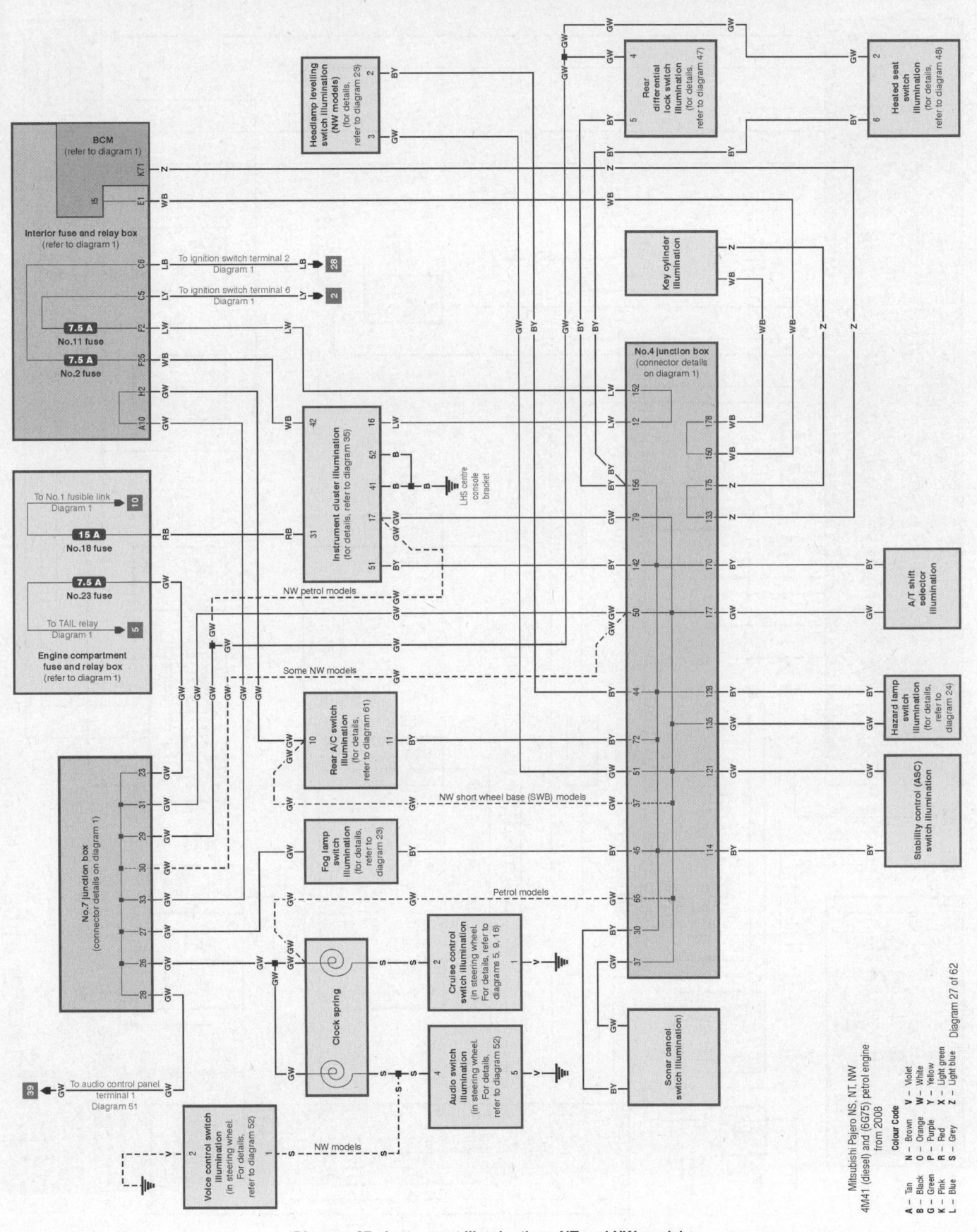

Diagram 27 - Instrument illumination - NT and NW models

Chapter 12 Chassis electrical system

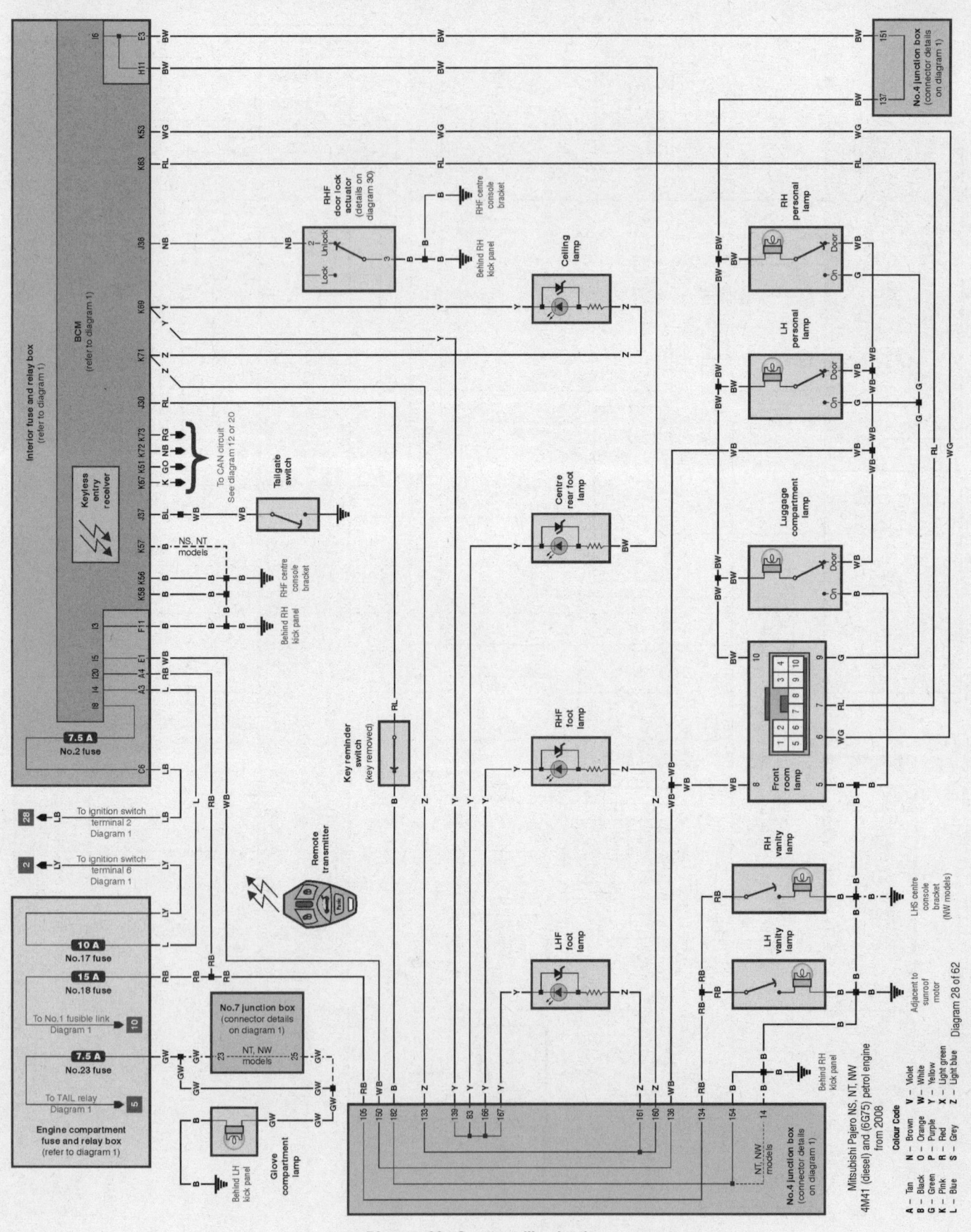

Diagram 28 - Courtesy illumination

Chapter 12 Chassis electrical system

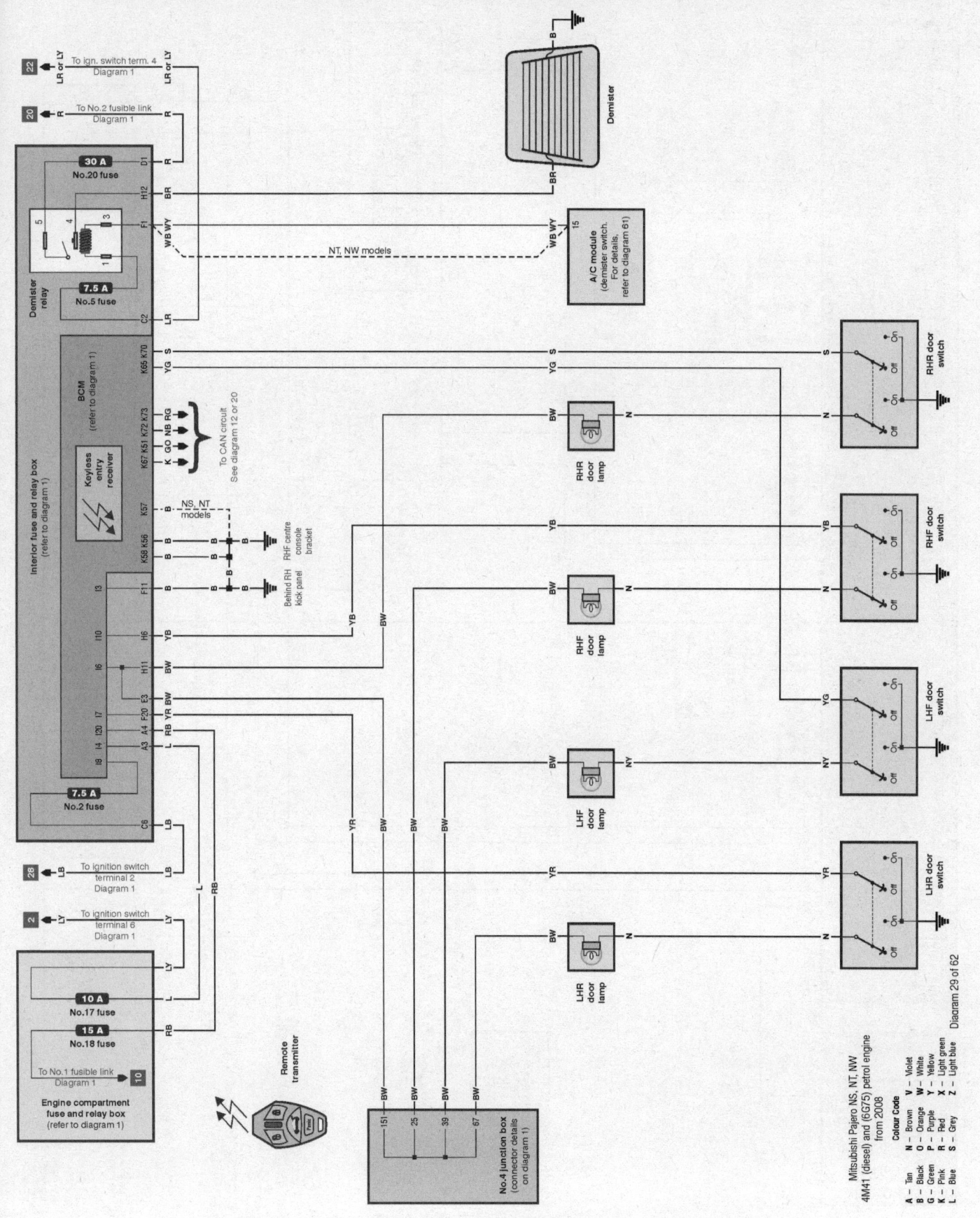

12-109

Diagram 29 - Courtesy illumination, rear window demister - NS, NT and NW models

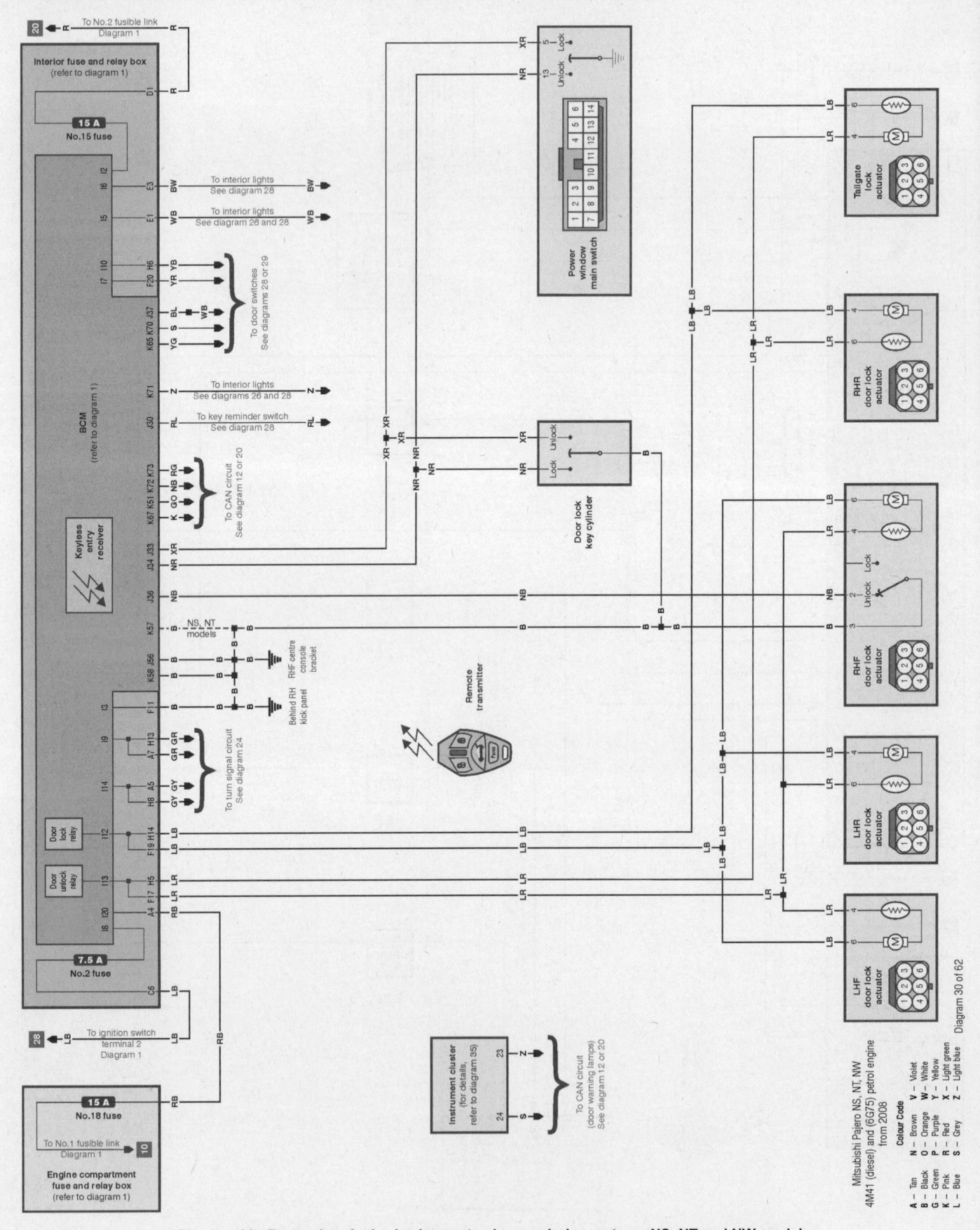

Diagram 30 - Power door locks, keyless entry, key reminder system - NS, NT and NW models

Chapter 12 Chassis electrical system

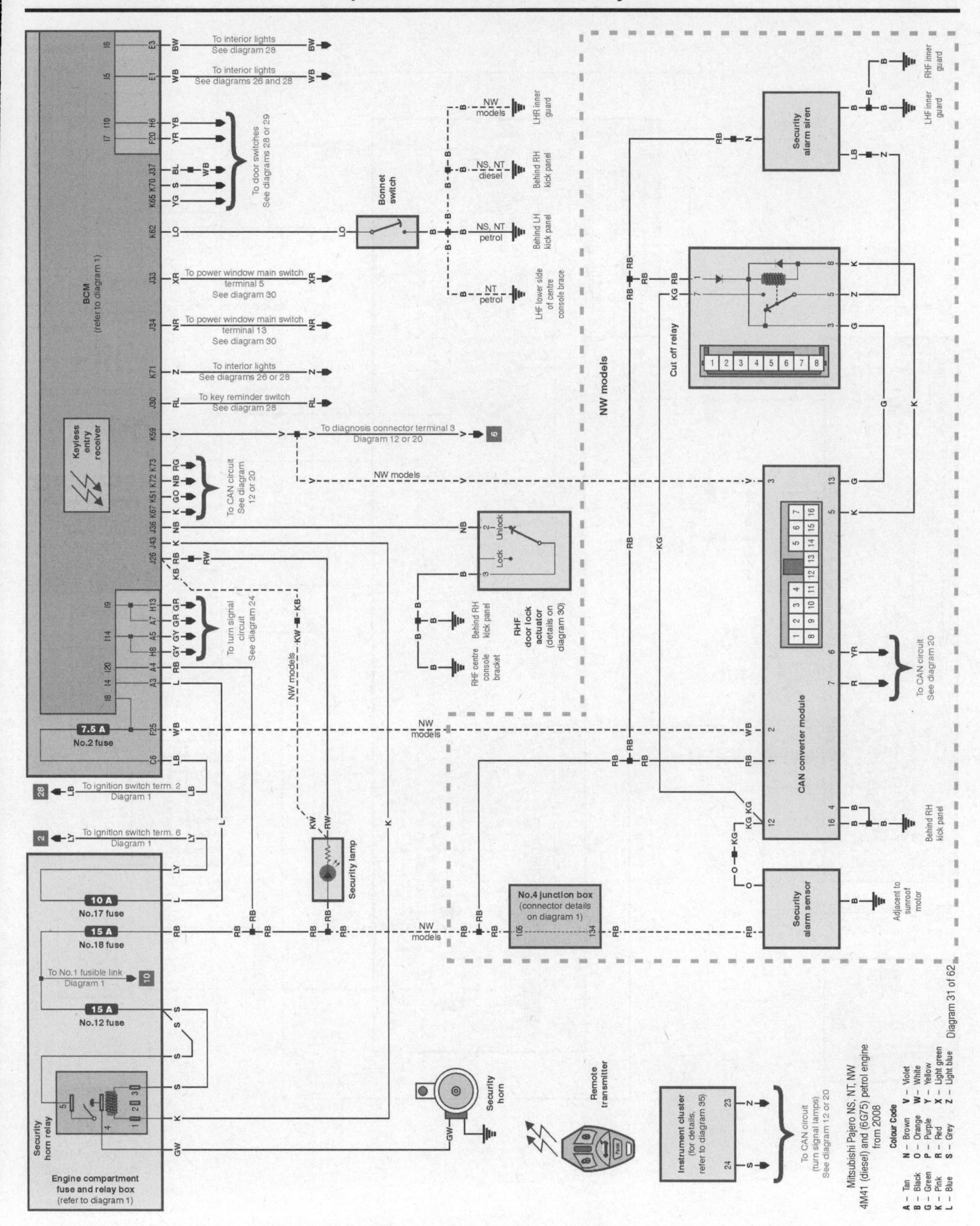

12-111

Diagram 31 - Theft alarm - NS, NT and NW models

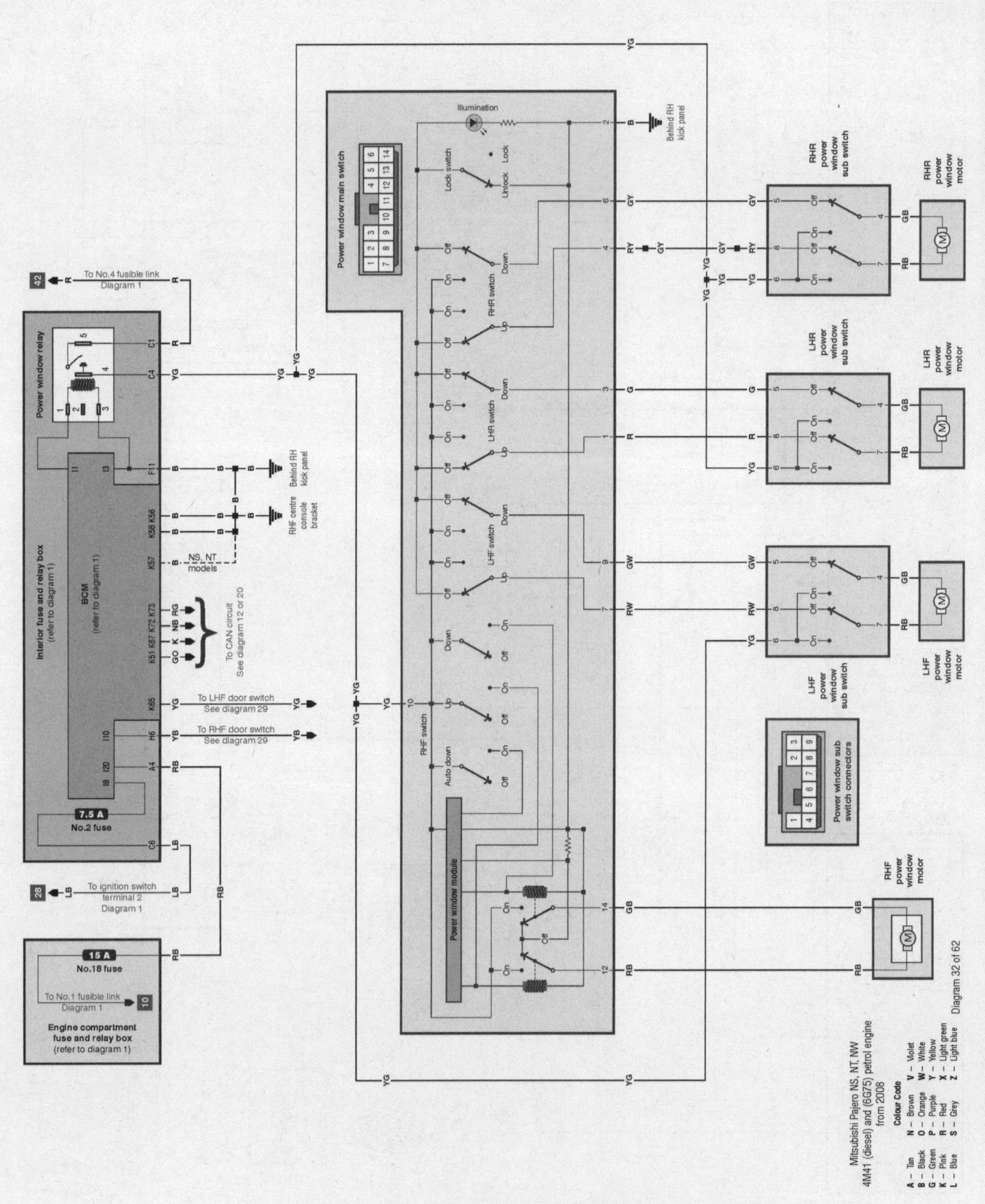

Diagram 32 - Power windows - NS and NT models

Chapter 12 Chassis electrical system

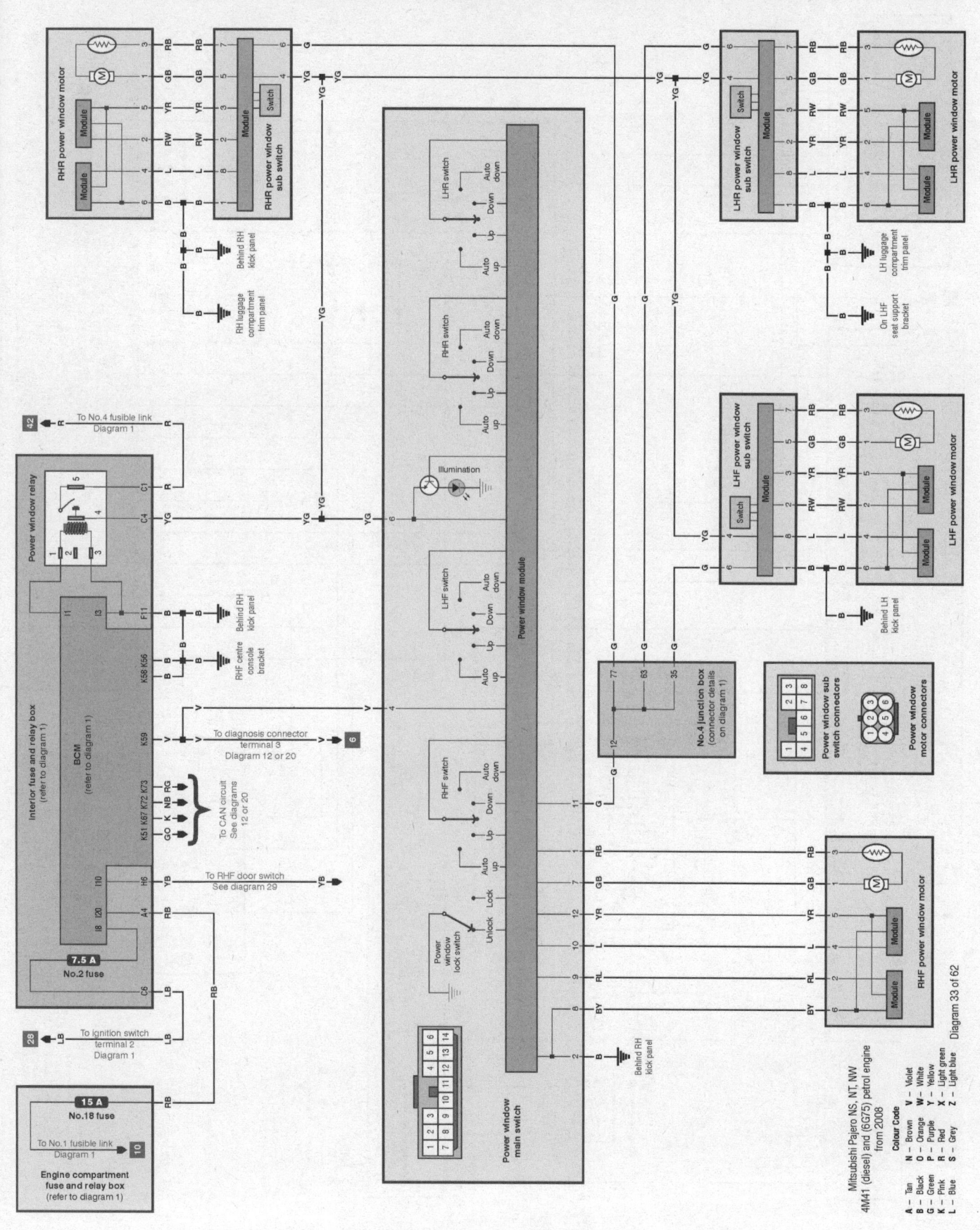

Diagram 33 - Power windows - NW models

12-114　Chapter 12　Chassis electrical system

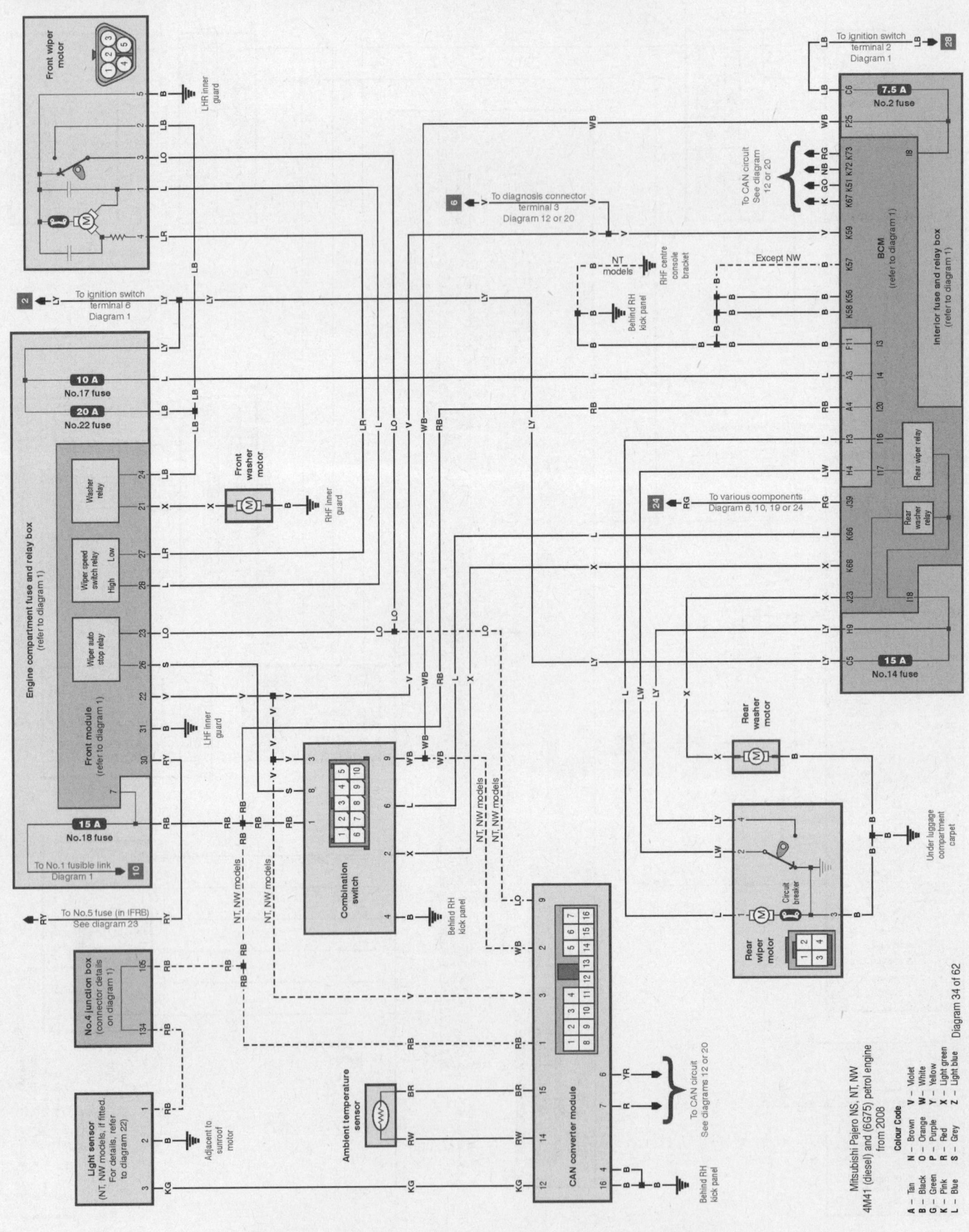

Diagram 34 - Front and rear wipers and washer - NS, NT and NW models

Chapter 12 Chassis electrical system

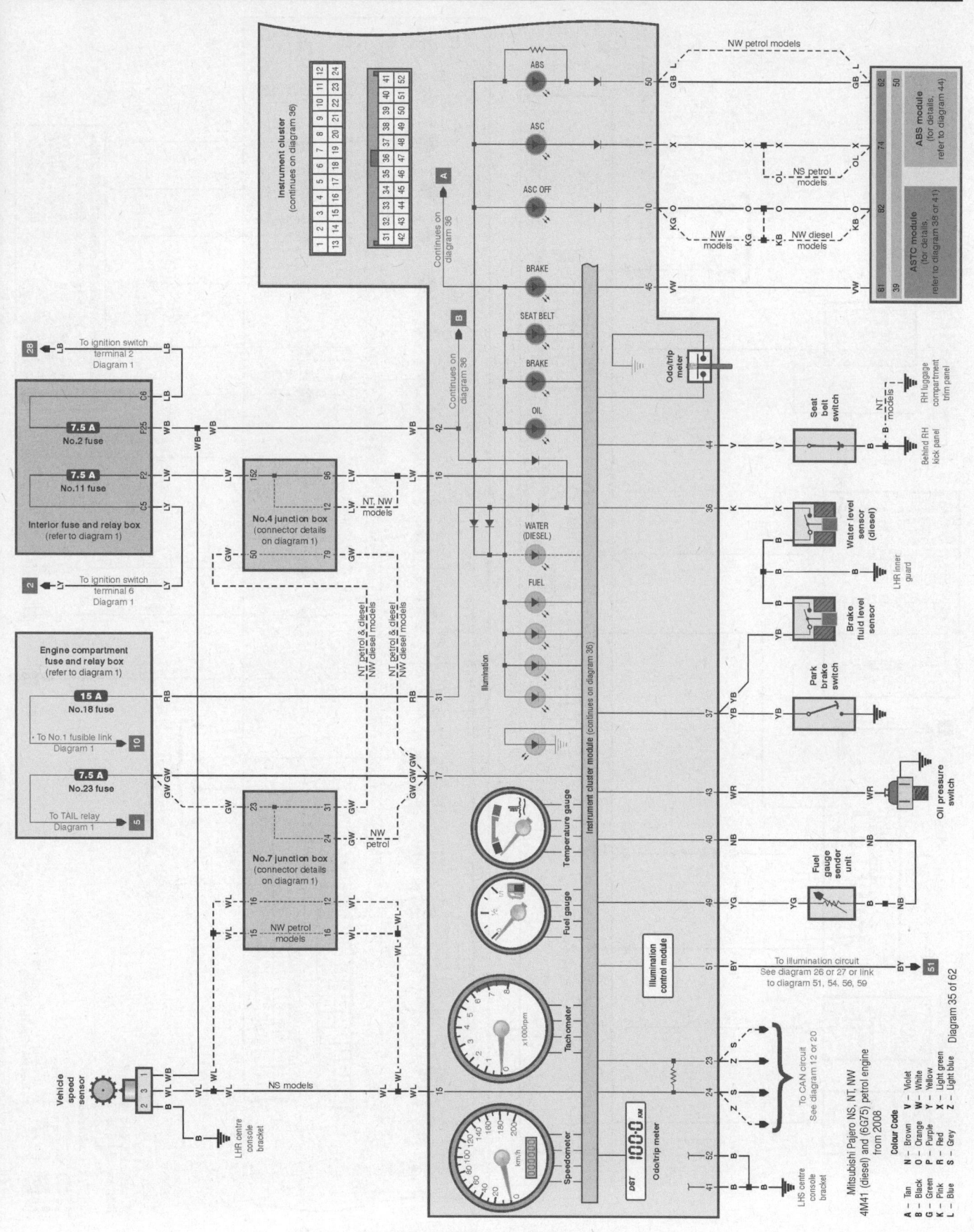

Diagram 35 - Instrument cluster - NS, NT and NW models

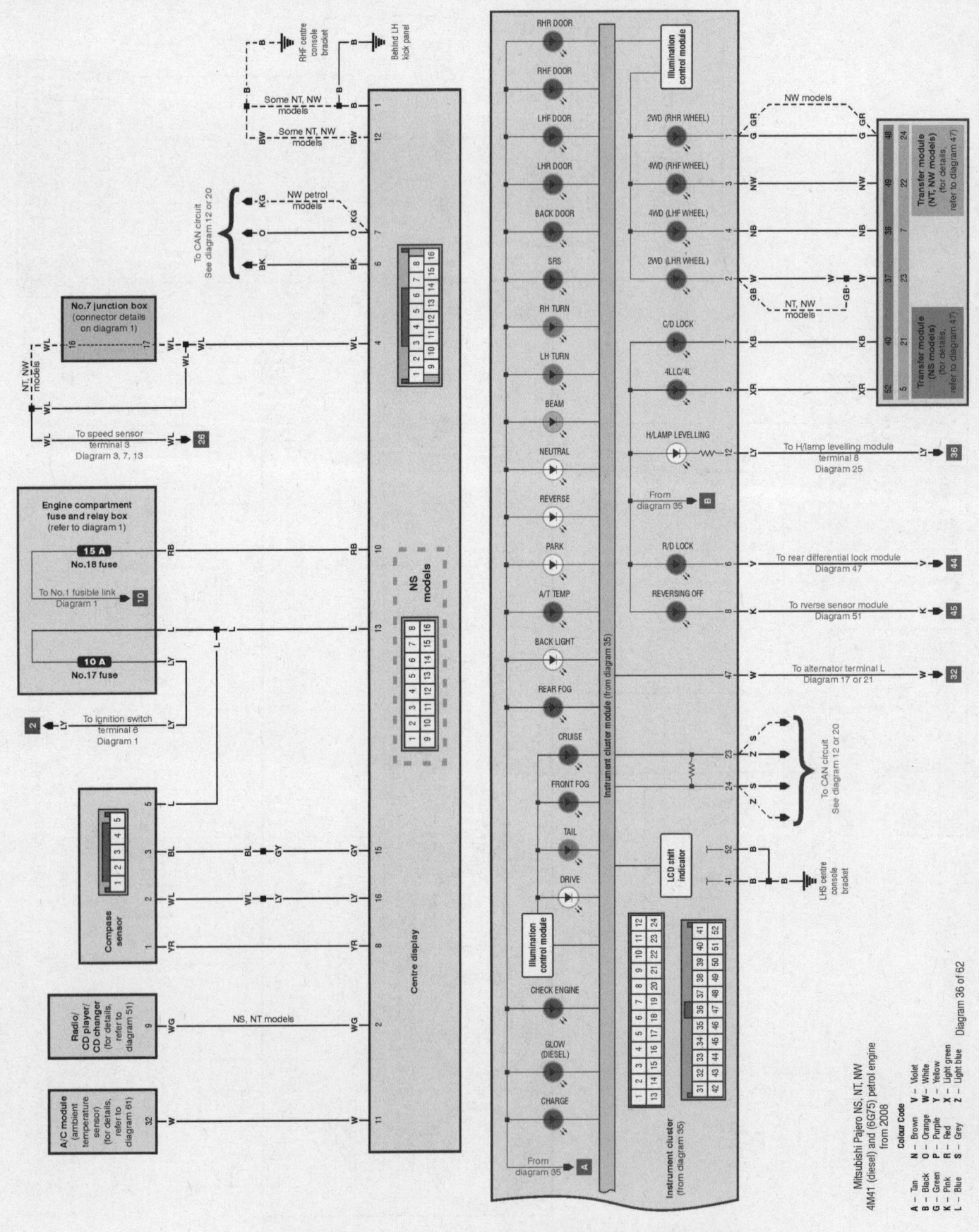

Diagram 36 - Instrument cluster, centre display - NS, NT and NW models

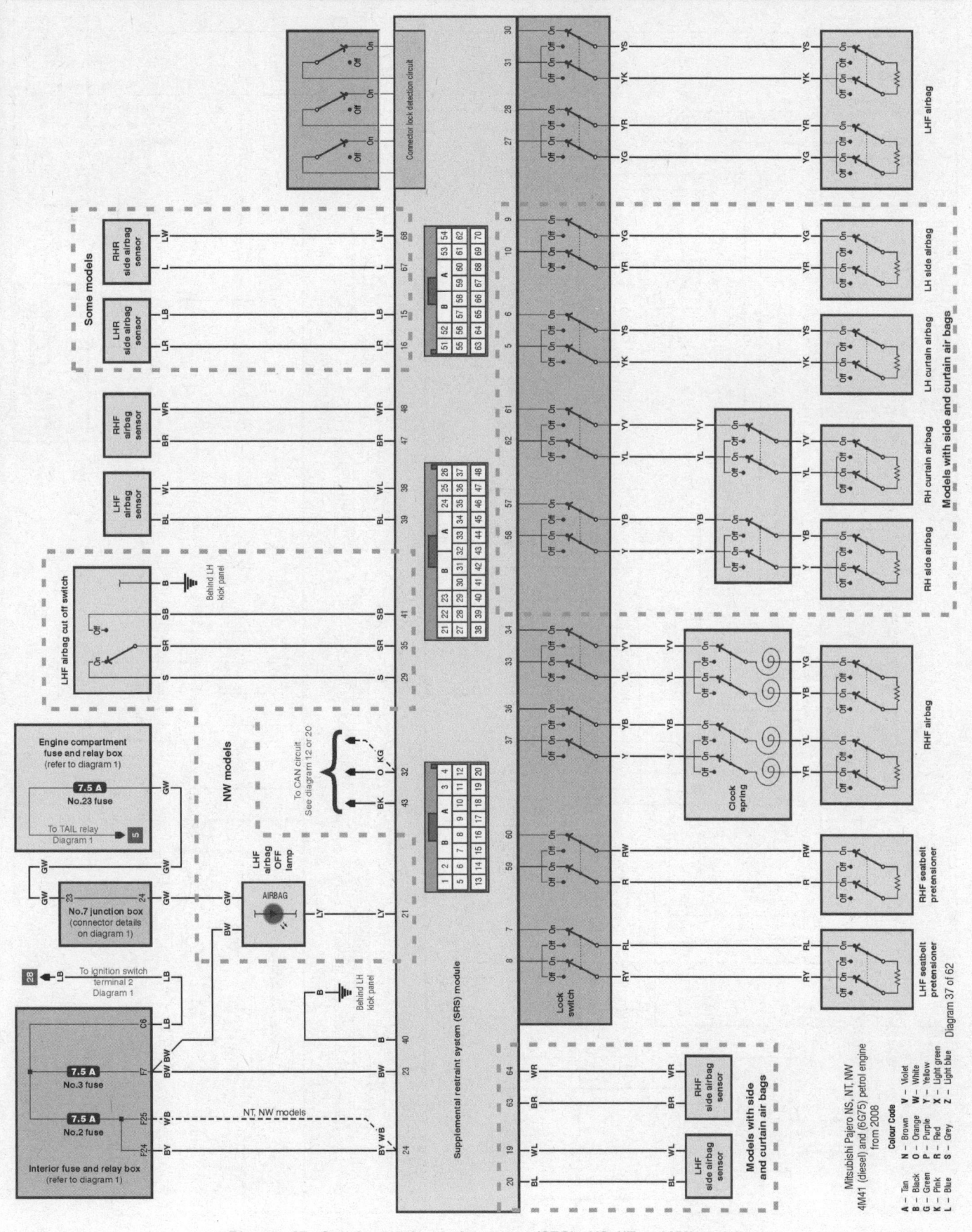

Diagram 37 - Supplemental restraint system (SRS) - NS, NT and NW models

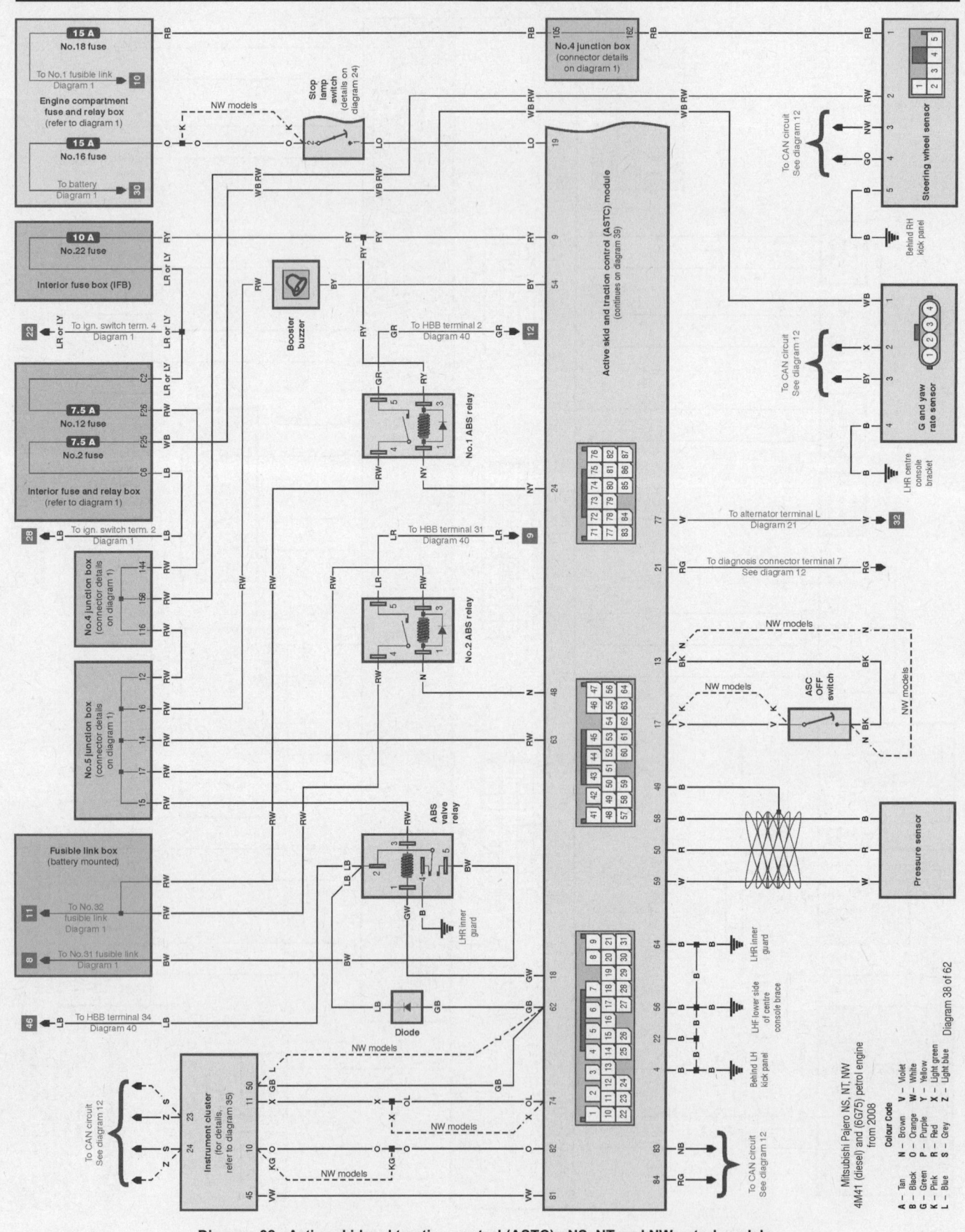

Diagram 38 - Active skid and traction control (ASTC) - NS, NT and NW petrol models

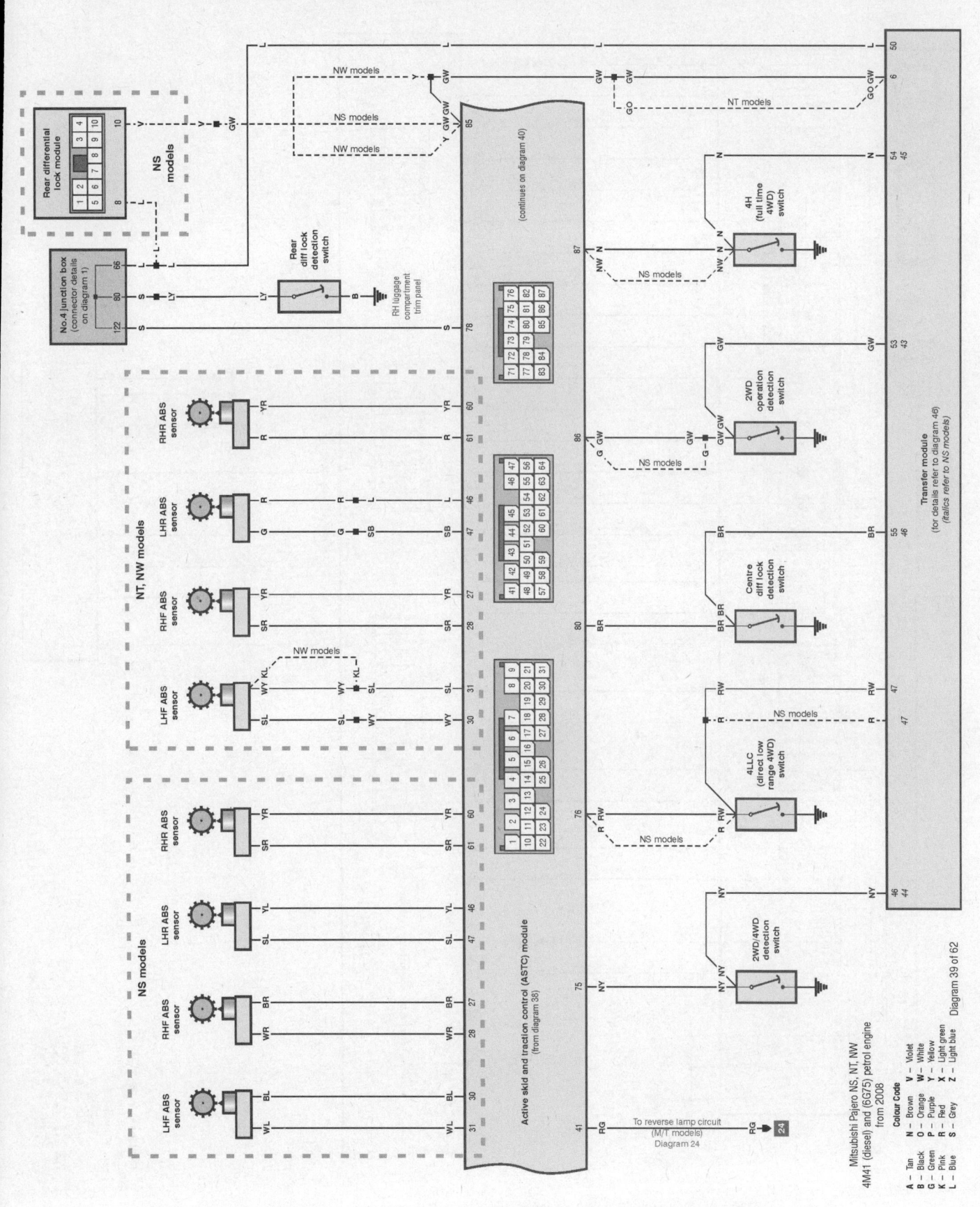

Diagram 39 - Active skid and traction control (ASTC) - NS, NT and NW petrol models

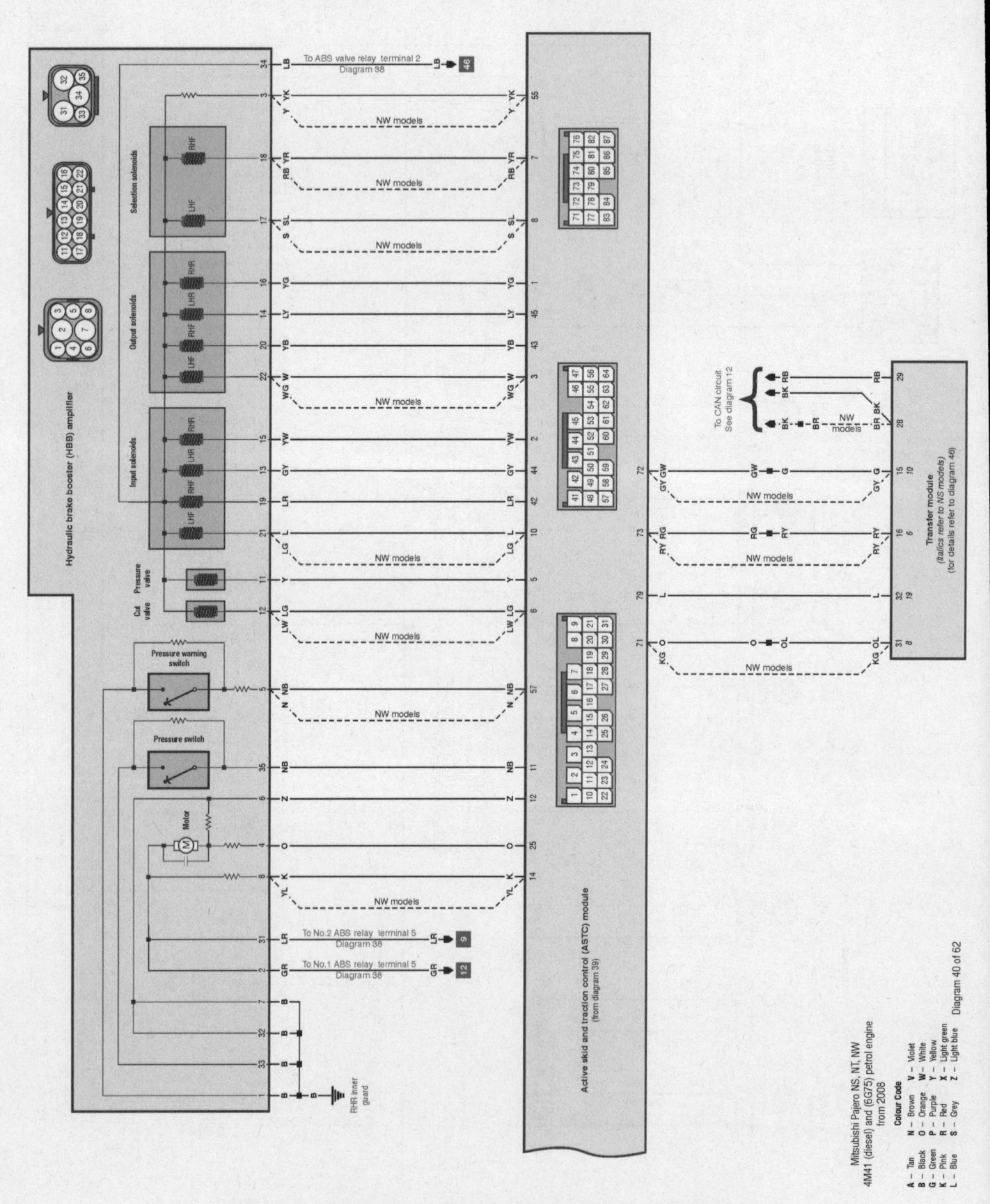

Diagram 40 - Active skid and traction control (ASTC) - NS, NT and NW petrol models

Chapter 12 Chassis electrical system 12-121

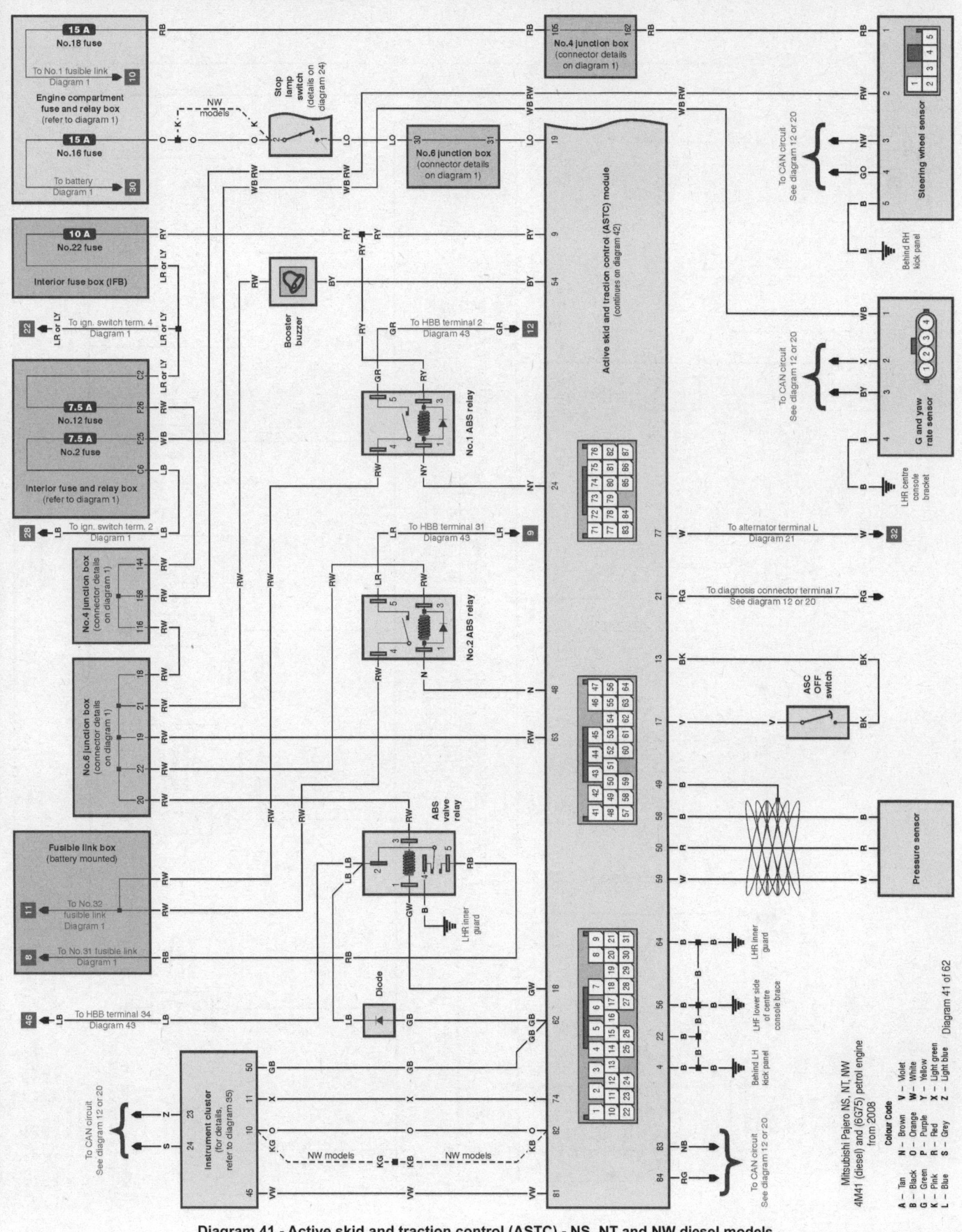

Diagram 41 - Active skid and traction control (ASTC) - NS, NT and NW diesel models

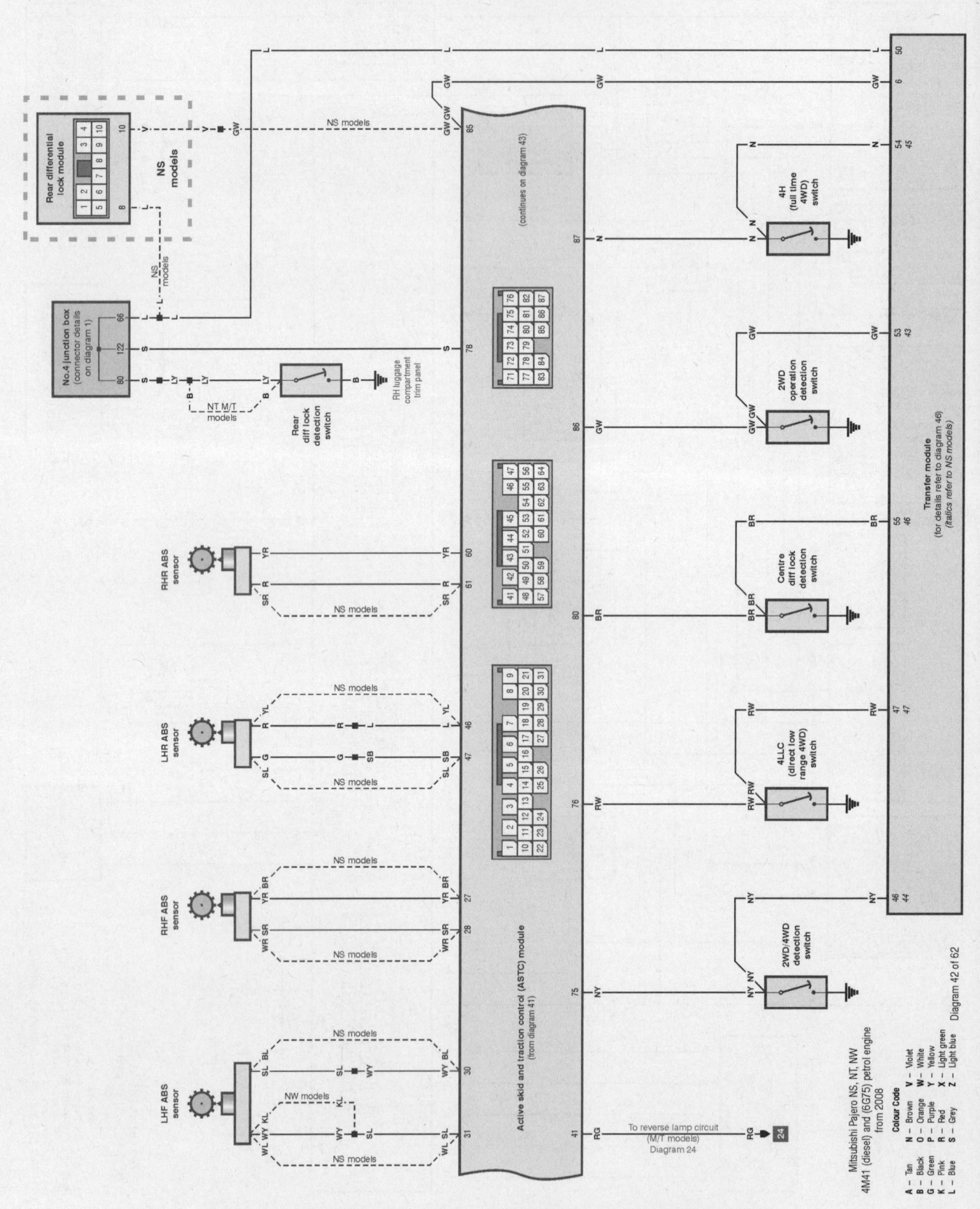

Diagram 42 - Active skid and traction control (ASTC) - NS, NT and NW diesel models

Chapter 12 Chassis electrical system

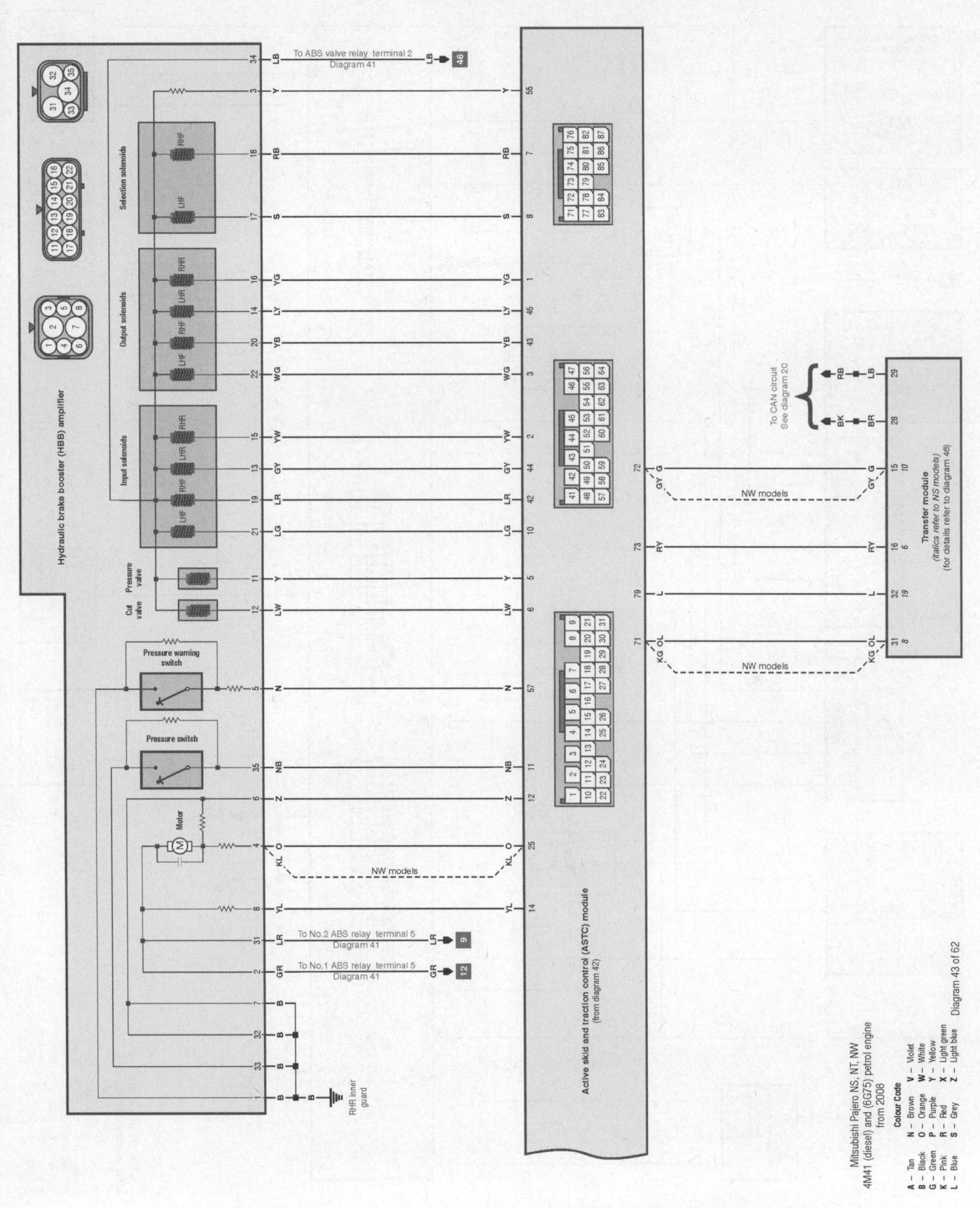

12-123

Diagram 43 - Active skid and traction control (ASTC) - NS, NT and NW diesel models

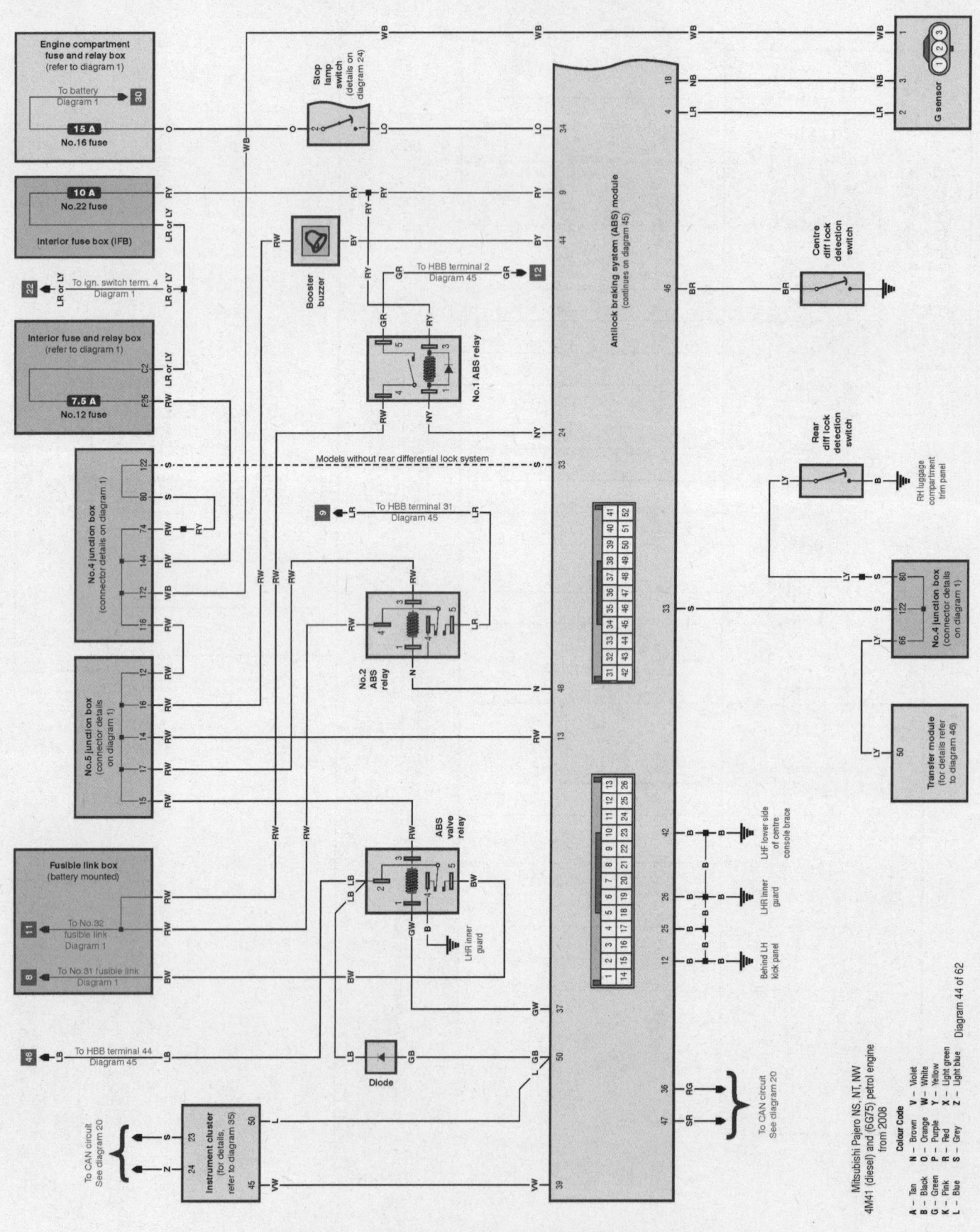

Diagram 44 - Antilock braking system (ABS) - NW petrol models

Chapter 12 Chassis electrical system

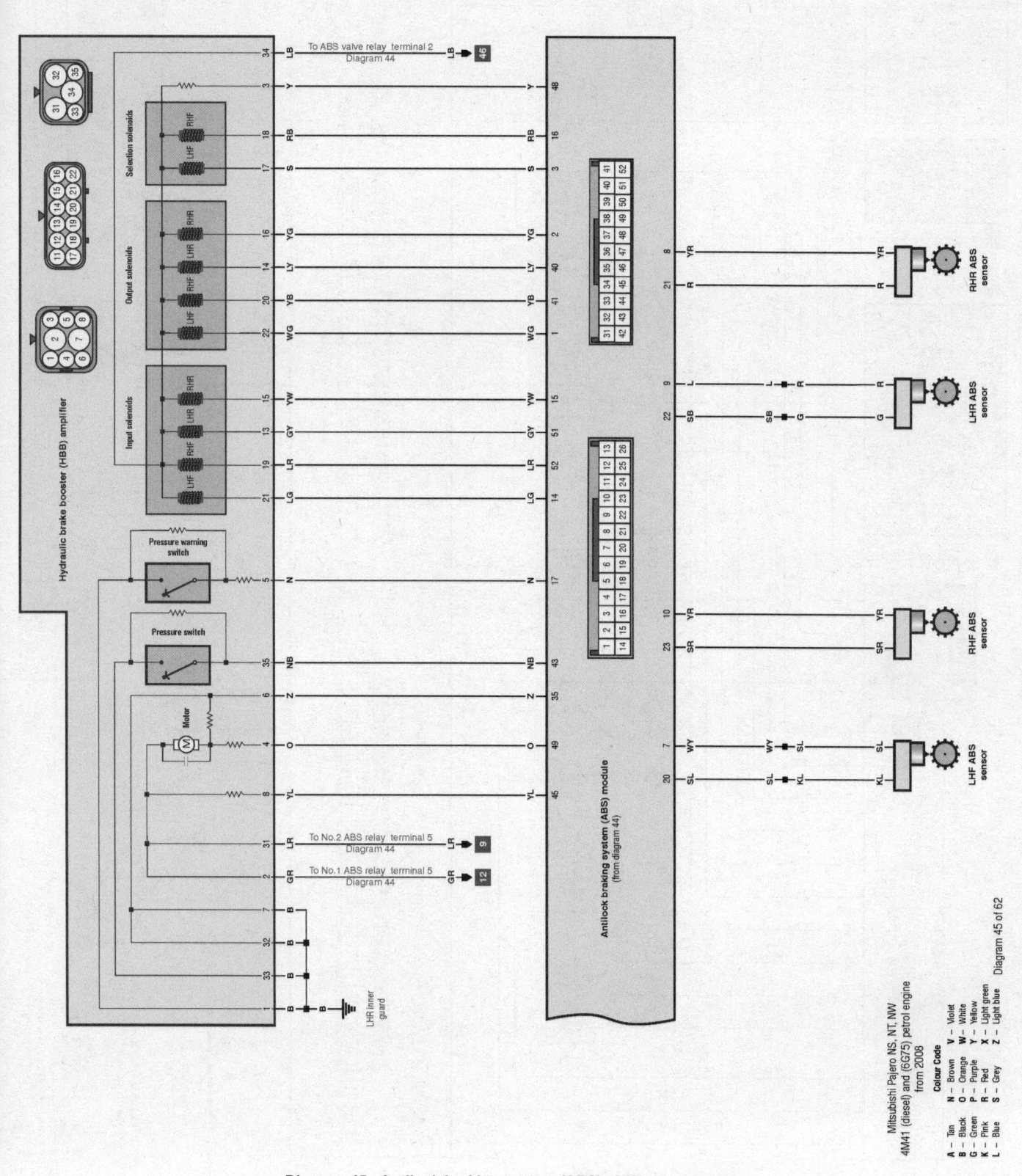

12-125

Diagram 45 - Antilock braking system (ABS) - NW petrol models

Mitsubishi Pajero NS, NT, NW 4M41 (diesel) and (6G75) petrol engine from 2008

Diagram 45 of 62

Colour Code

A – Tan
B – Black
G – Green
K – Pink
L – Blue
N – Brown
O – Orange
P – Purple
R – Red
S – Grey
V – Violet
W – White
Y – Yellow
X – Light green
Z – Light blue

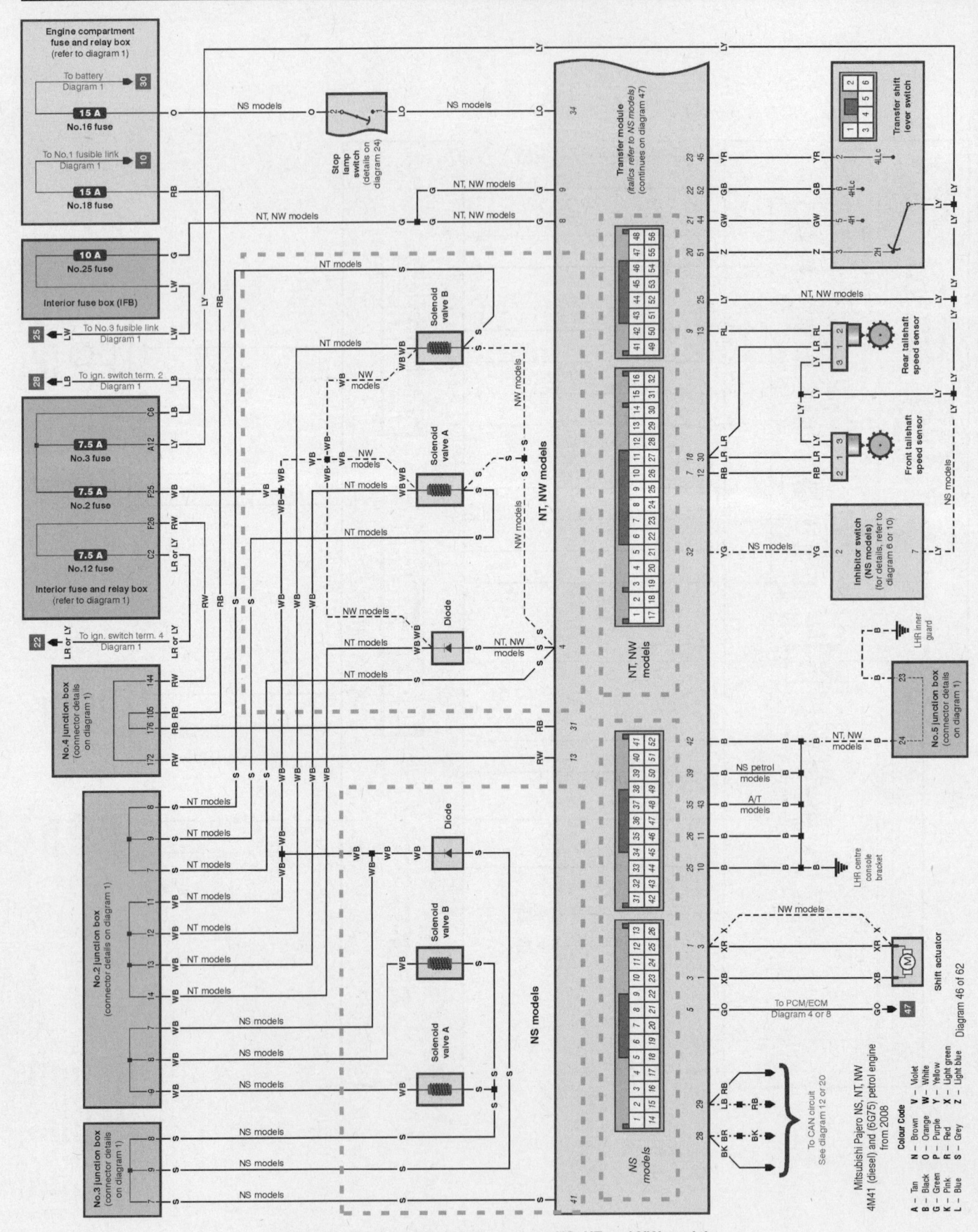

Diagram 46 - Super select 4WD system - NS, NT and NW models

Chapter 12 Chassis electrical system

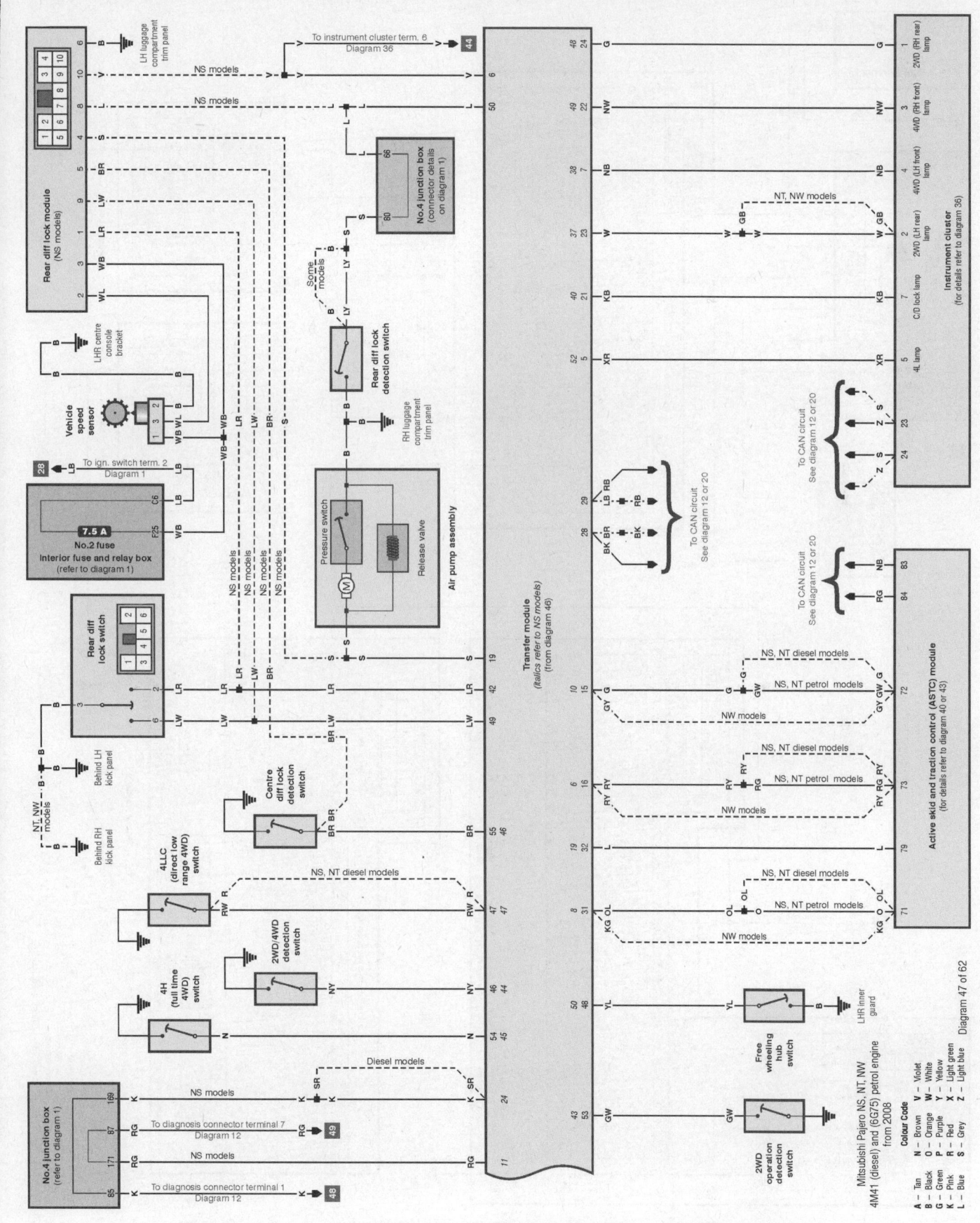

Diagram 47 - Super select 4WD system, rear differential lock system - NS, NT and NW models

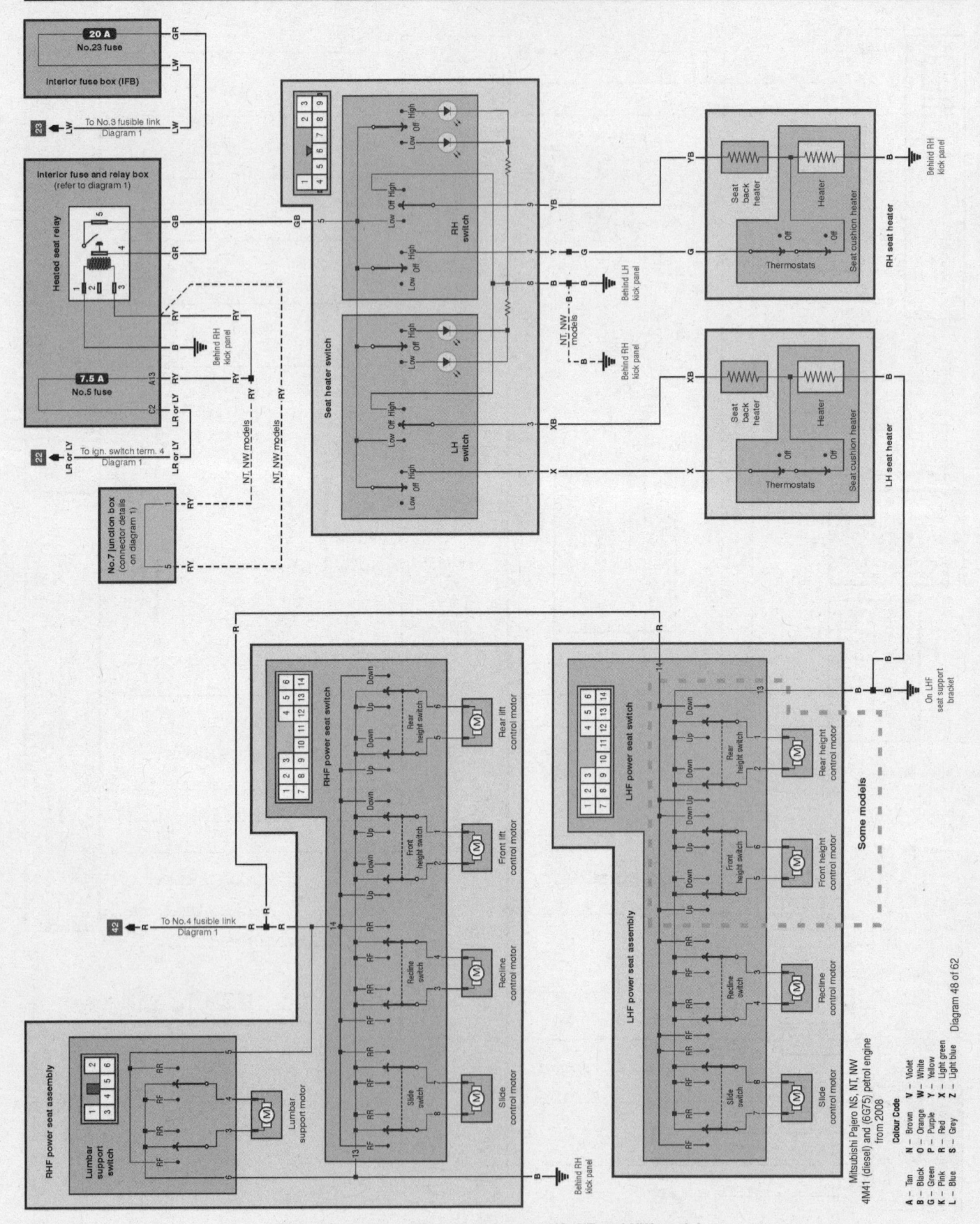

Diagram 48 - Power seats, seat heater - NS, NT and NW models

Chapter 12 Chassis electrical system

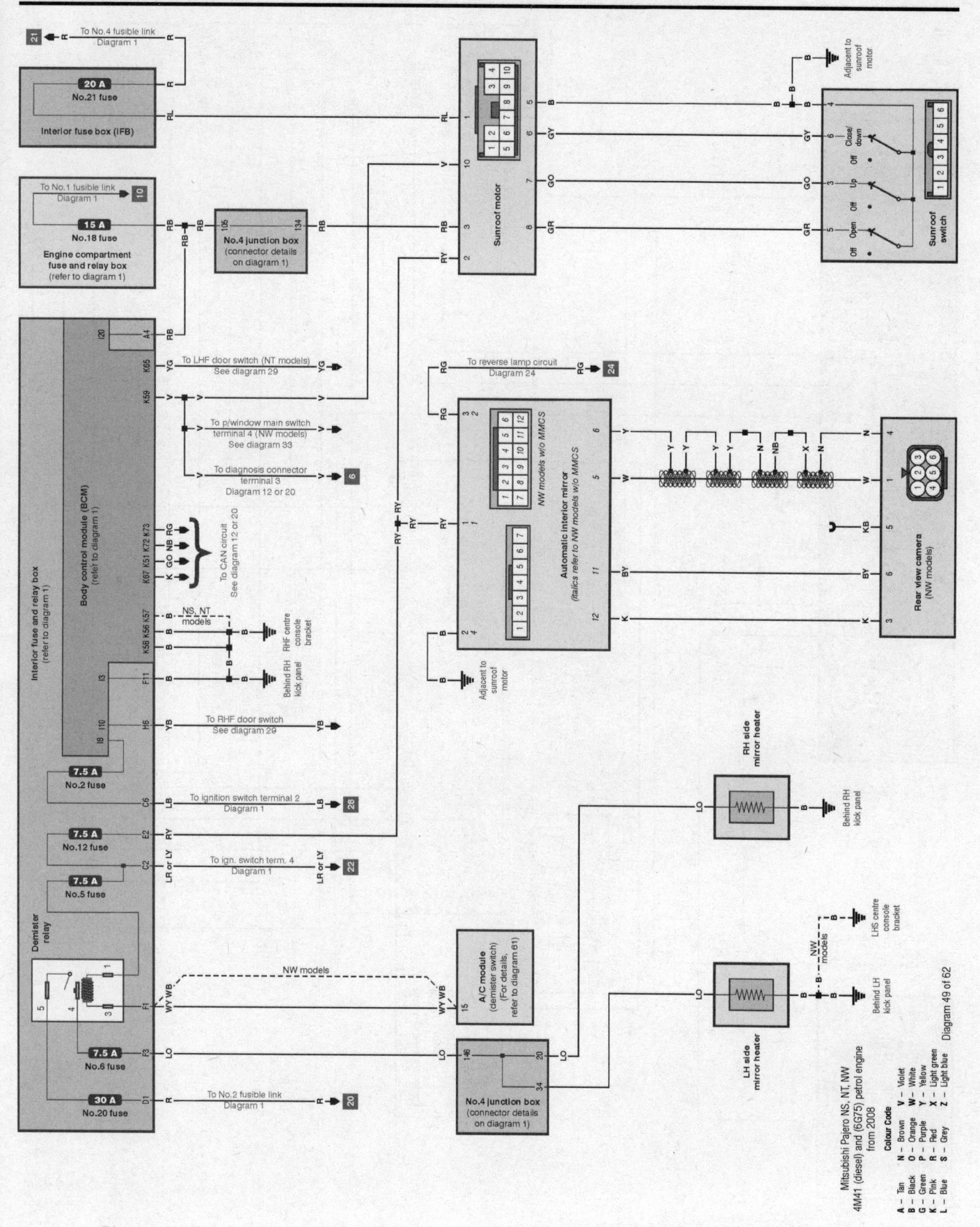

Diagram 49 - Exterior mirror heater, automatic interior mirror, rear view camera, sunroof - NS, NT and NW models

Chapter 12 Chassis electrical system

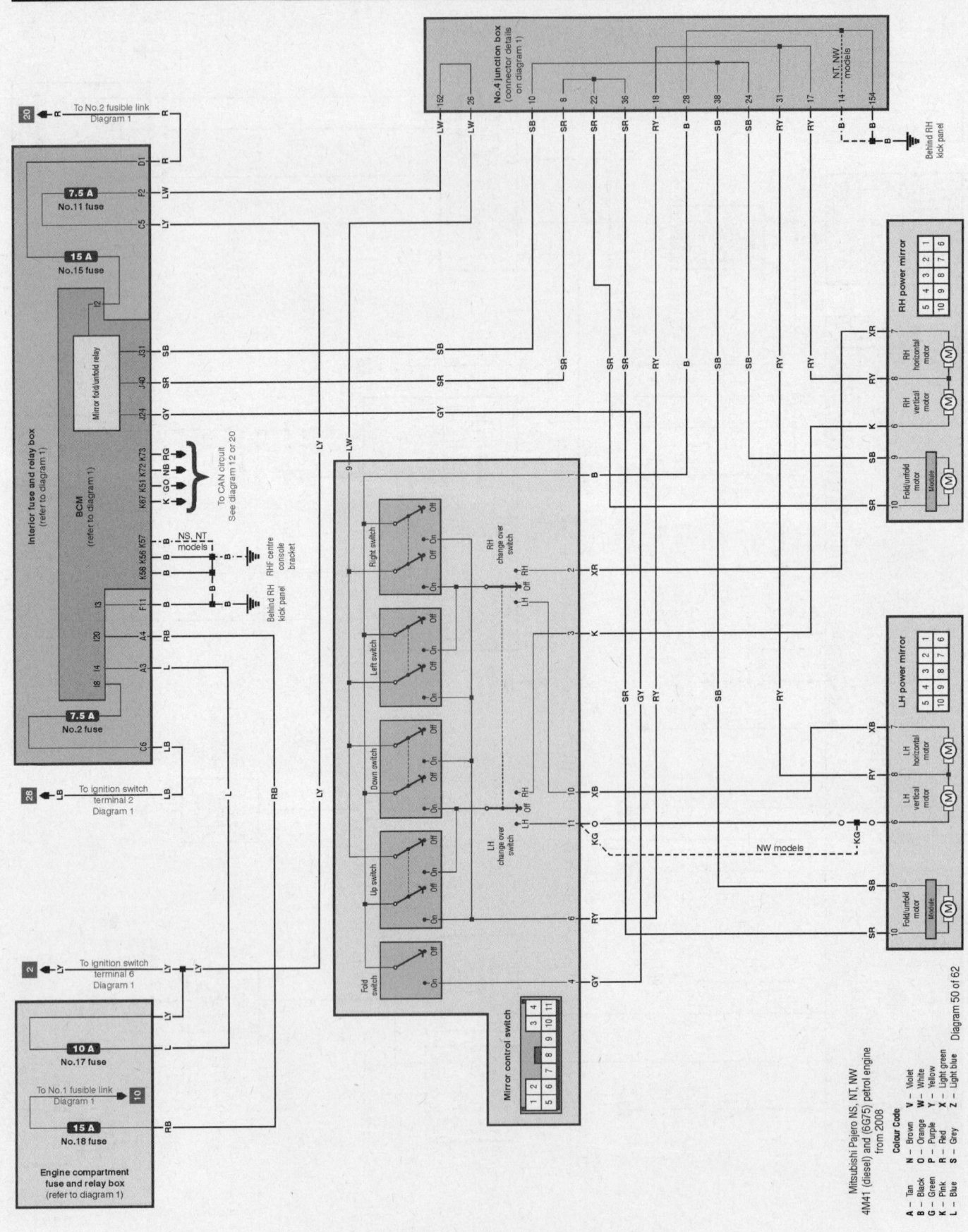

Diagram 50 - Power mirrors - NS, NT and NW models

Chapter 12 Chassis electrical system

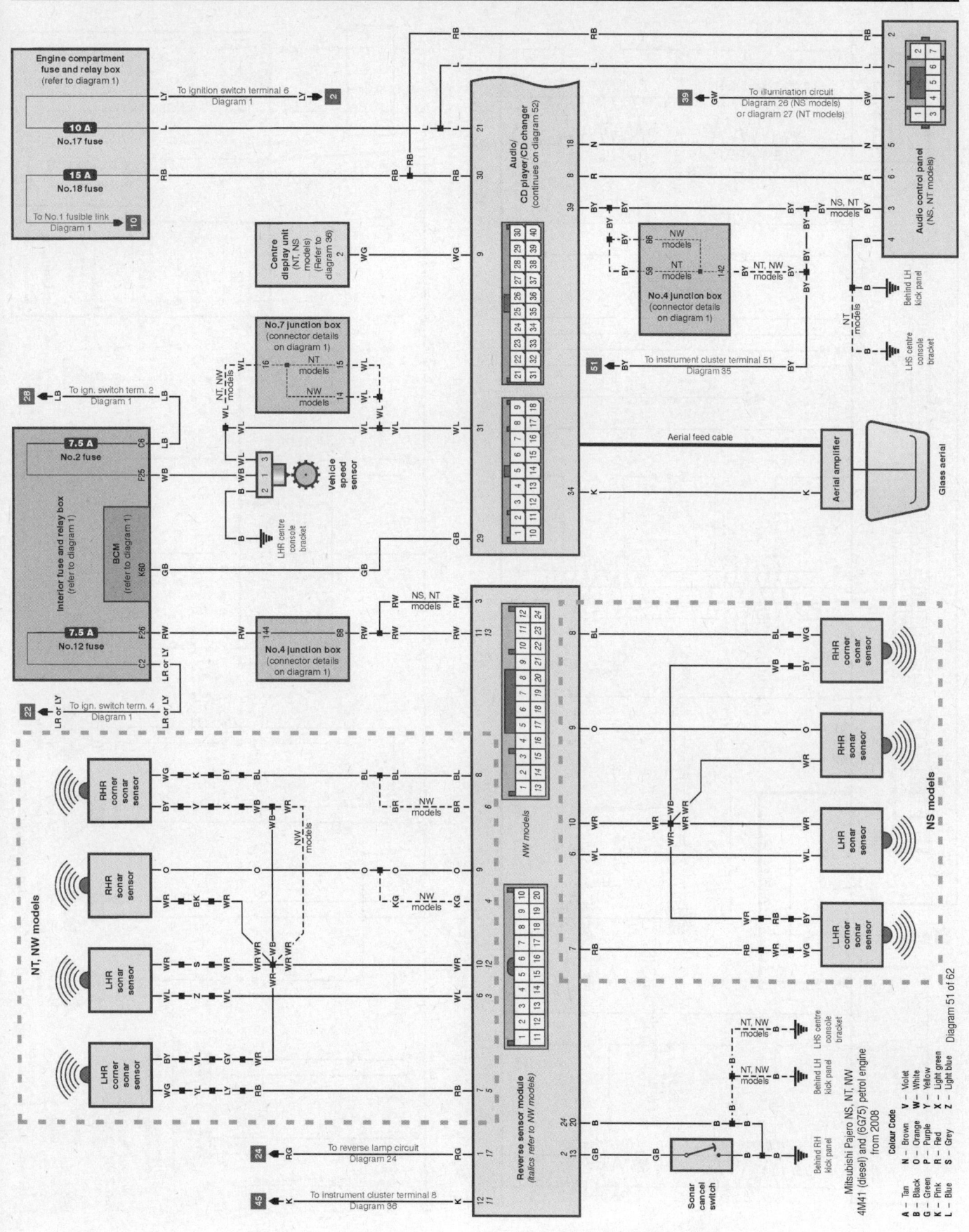

Diagram 51 - Reverse sensor, audio system - NS, NT and NW models

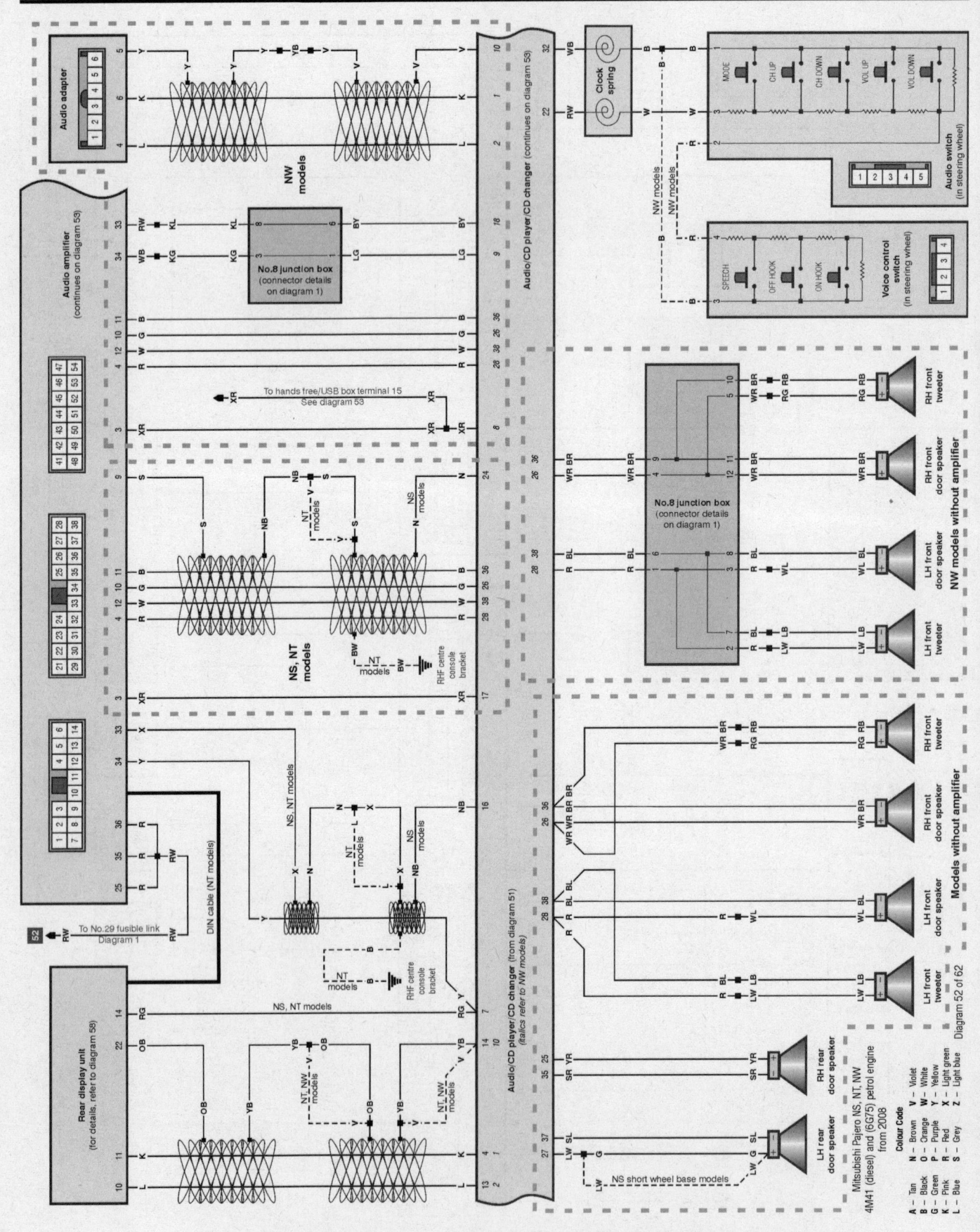

Diagram 52 - Audio system, audio amplifier - NS, NT and NW models

Chapter 12 Chassis electrical system

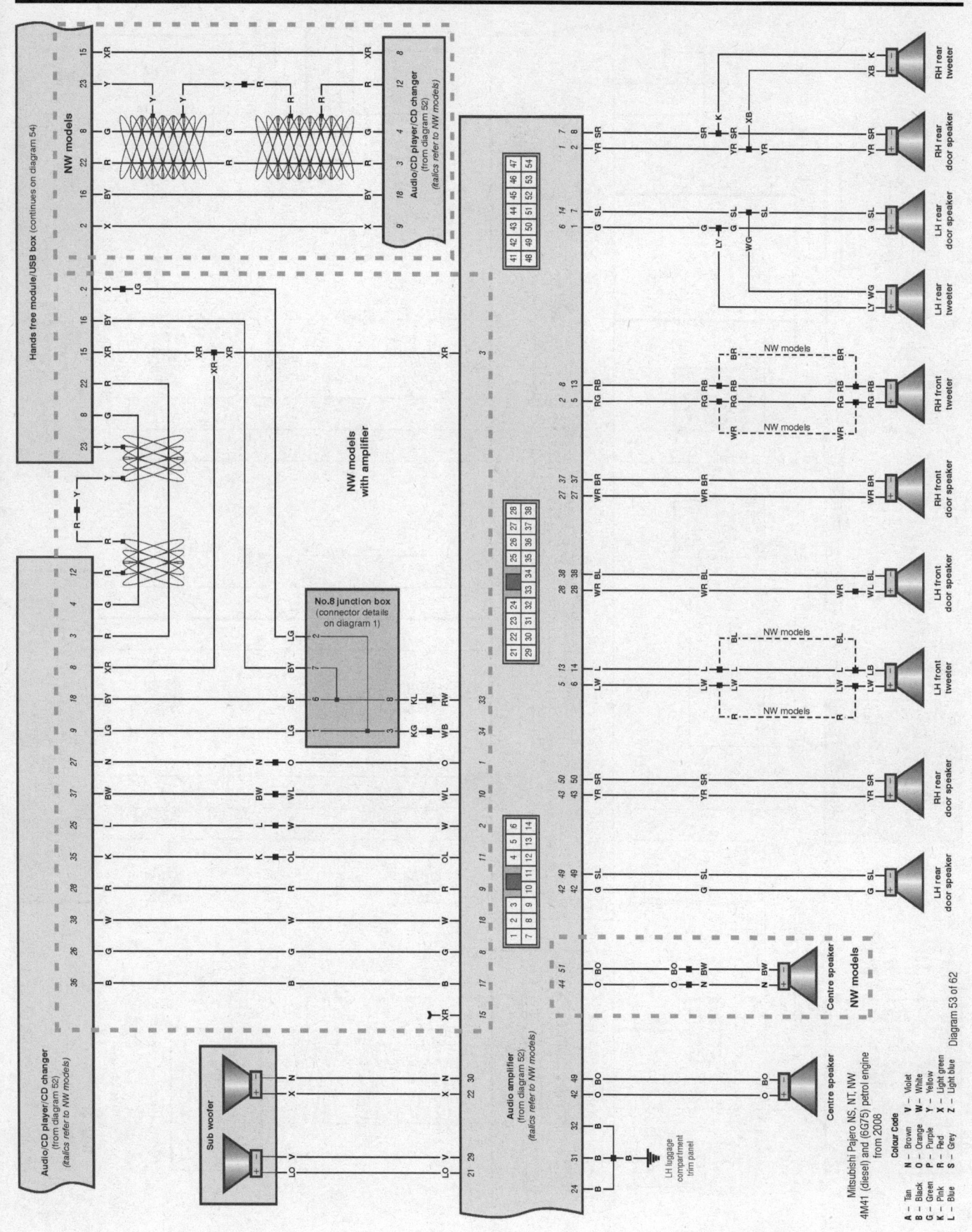

Diagram 53 - Audio system with amplifier, hands free/USB system - NS, NT and NW models

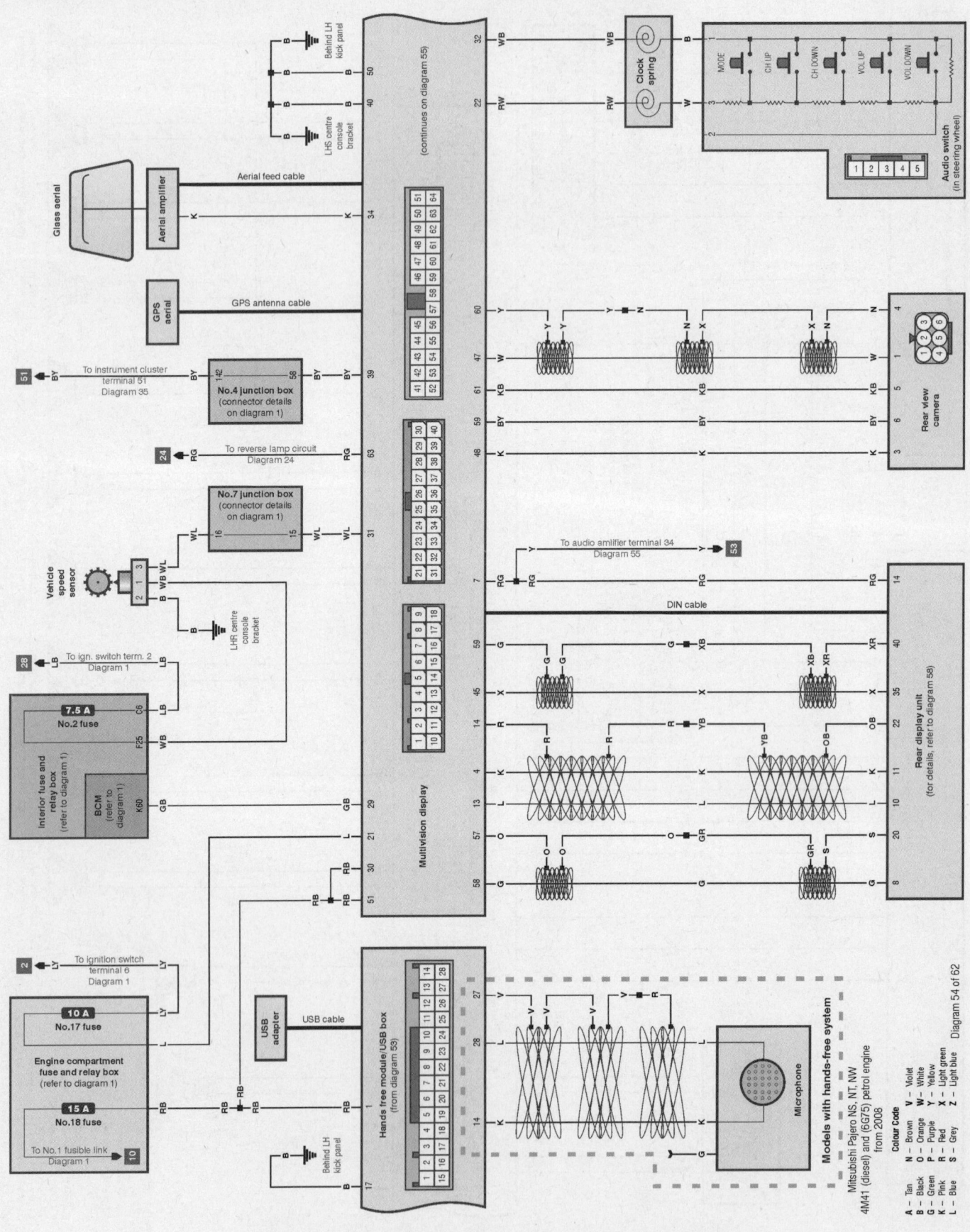

Diagram 54 - Hands free/USB system, multivision display - NT models

Chapter 12 Chassis electrical system

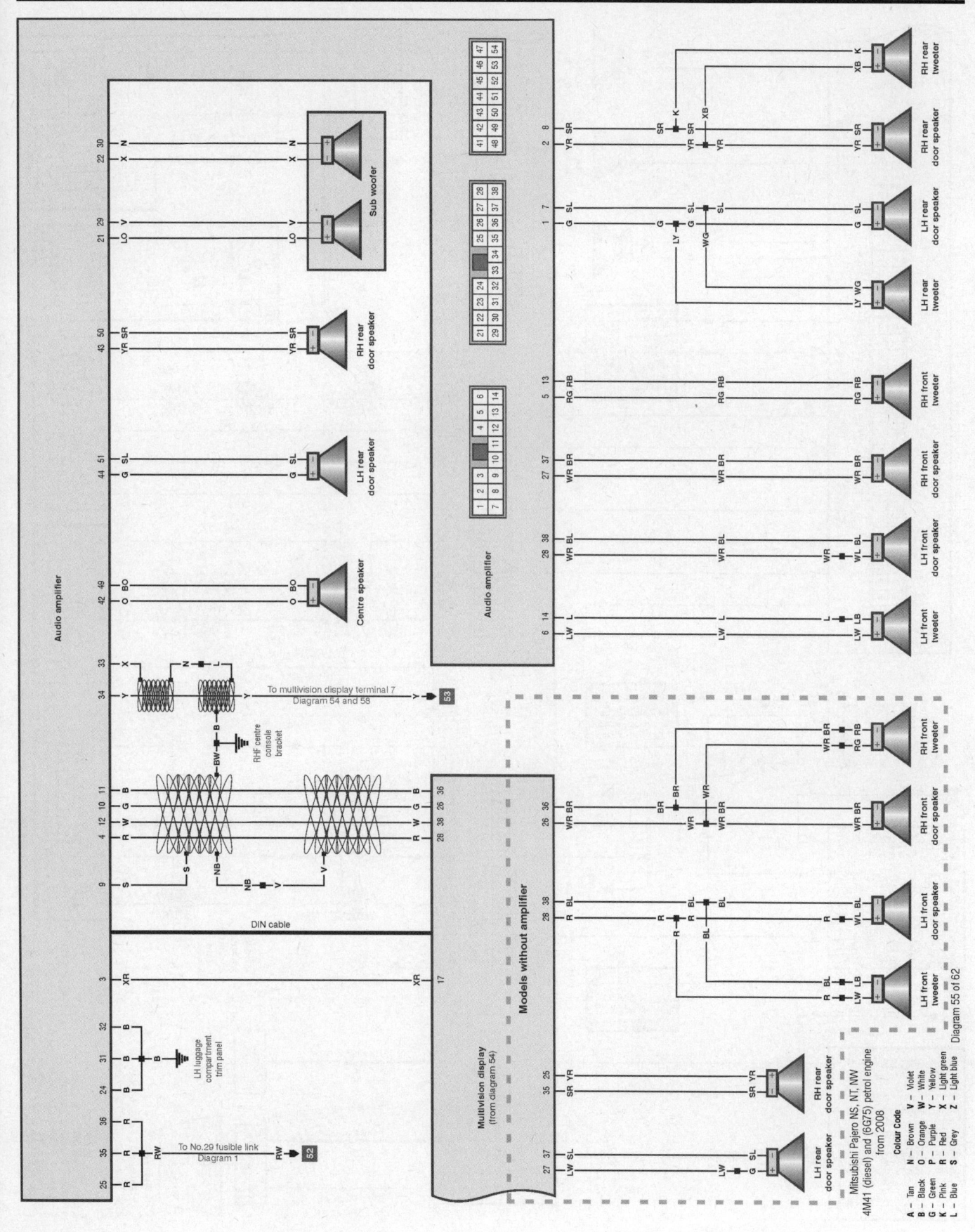

Diagram 55 - Multivision display with audio amplifier - NT models

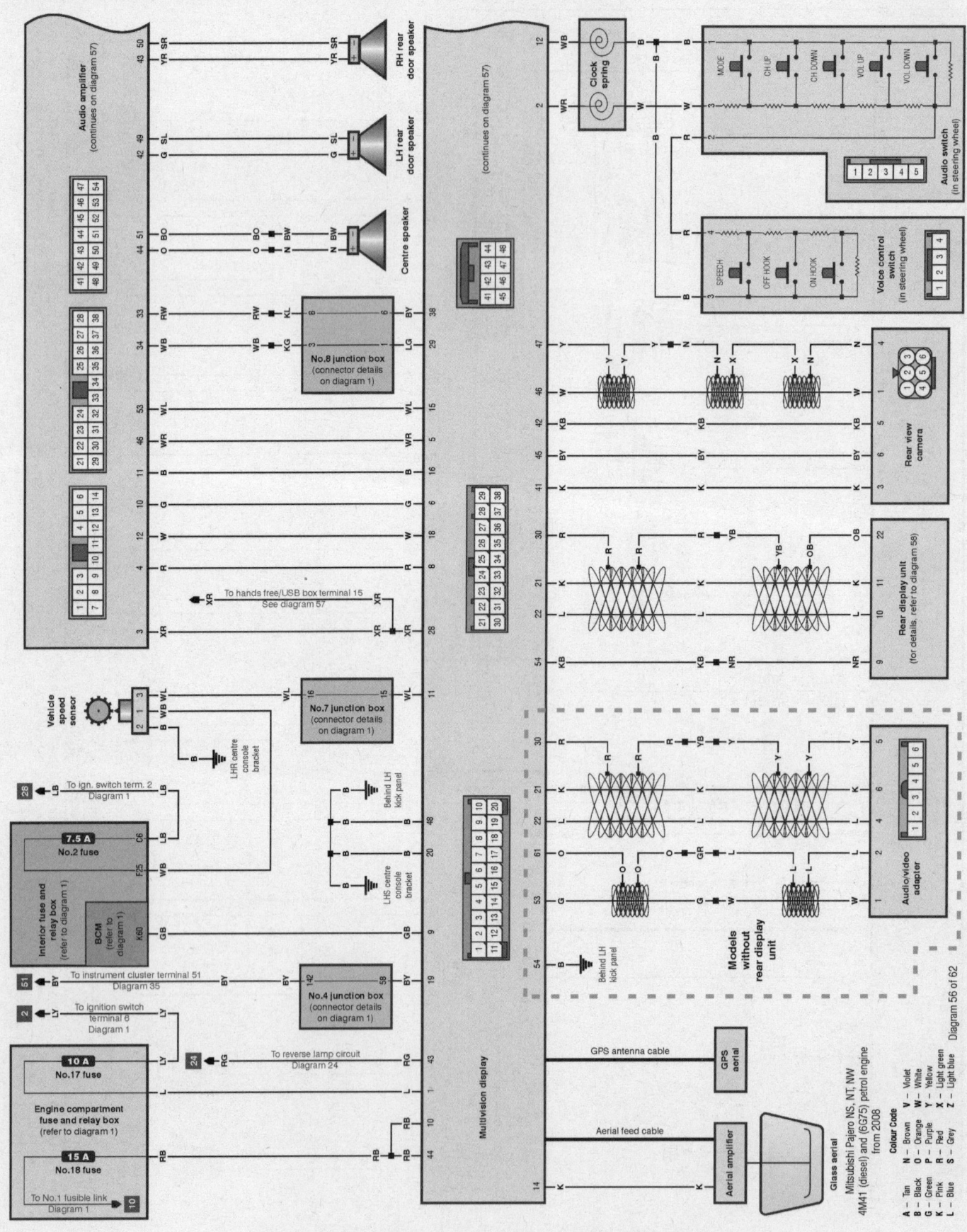

Diagram 56 - Multivision display with audio amplifier - NW models

Chapter 12 Chassis electrical system 12-137

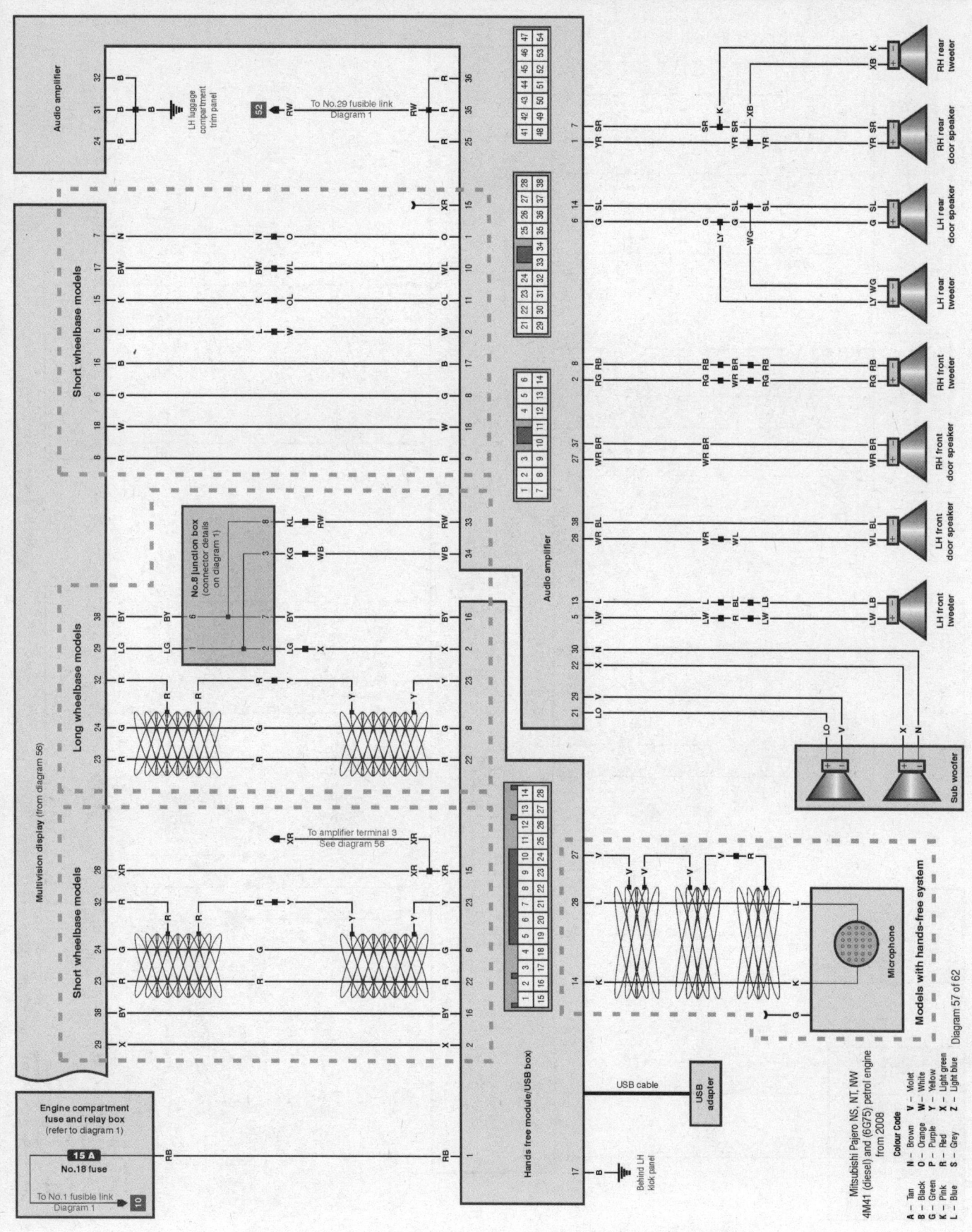

Diagram 57 - Hands free/USB system, multivision display - NW models

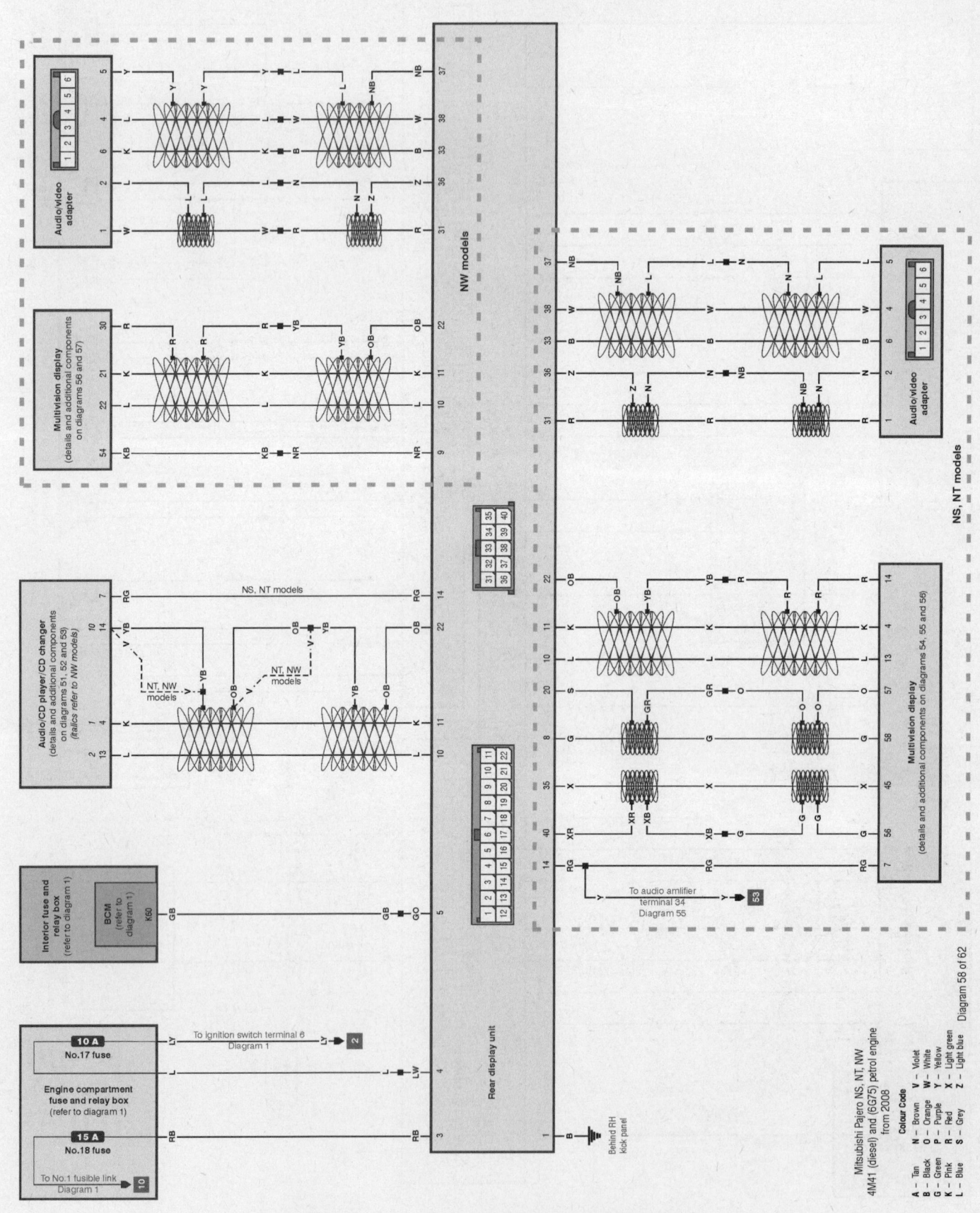

Diagram 58 - Rear display system - NS, NT and NW models

Chapter 12 Chassis electrical system

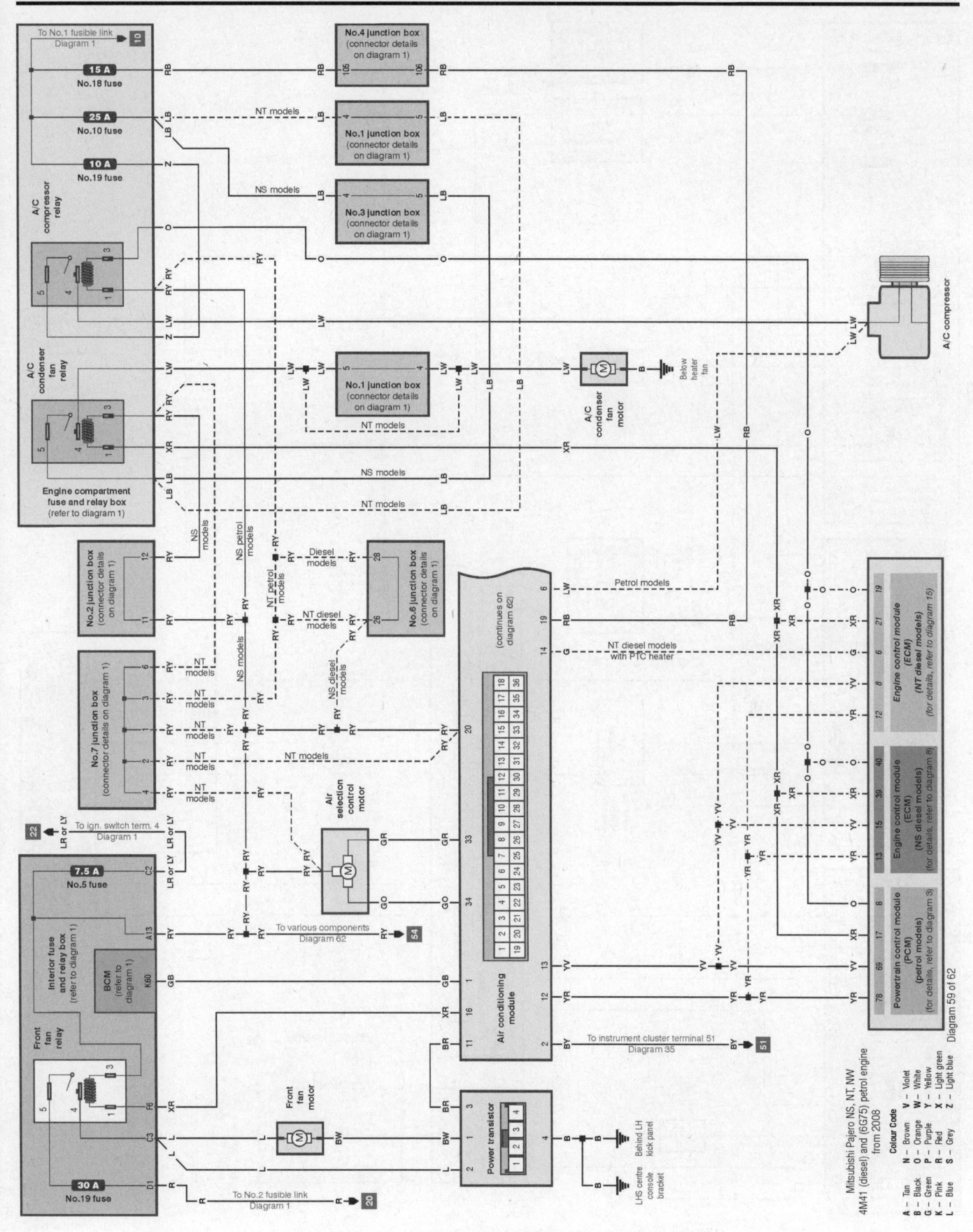

12-139

Diagram 59 - Automatic air conditioning - NS and NT models

12-140 Chapter 12 Chassis electrical system

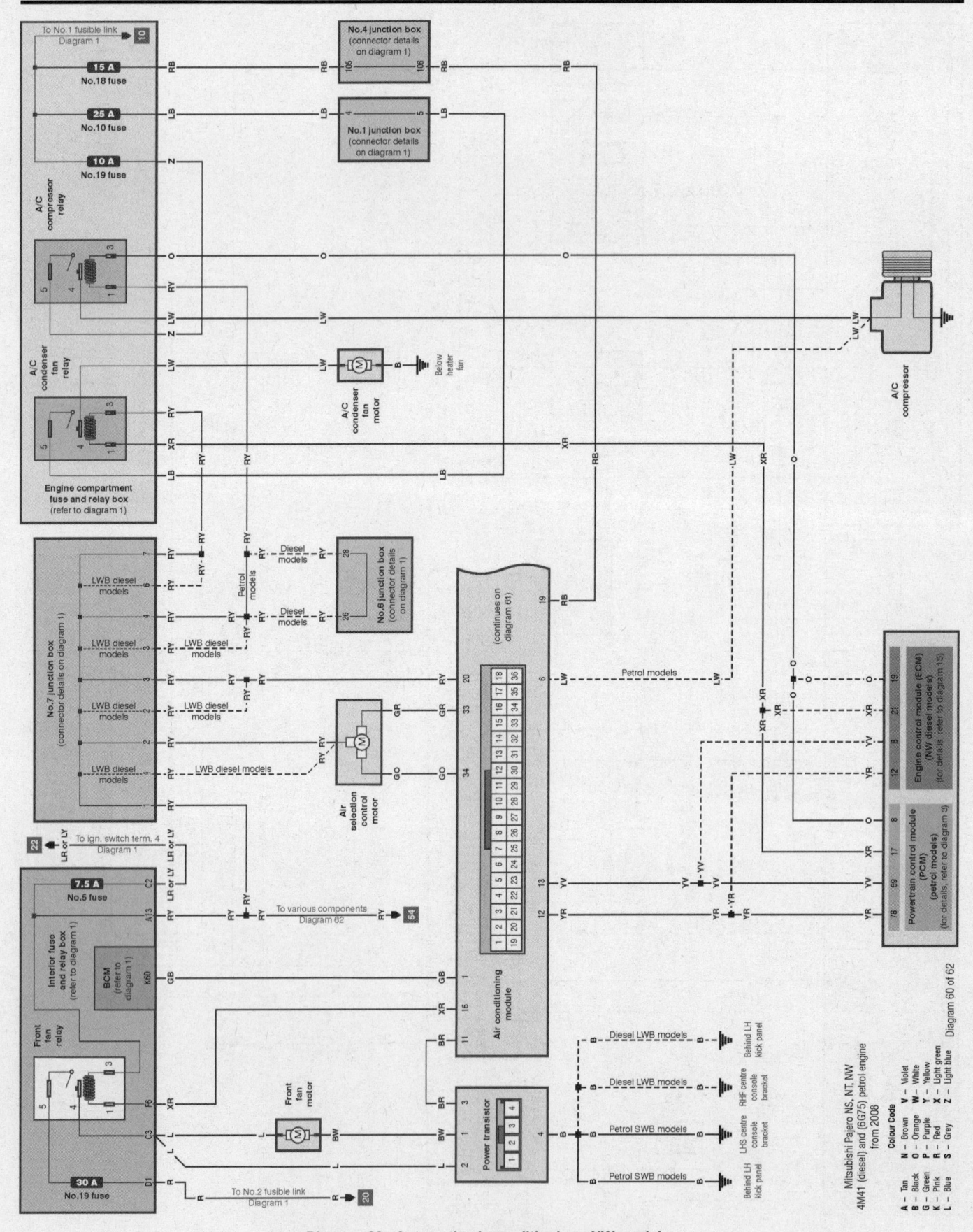

Diagram 60 - Automatic air conditioning - NW models

Chapter 12 Chassis electrical system

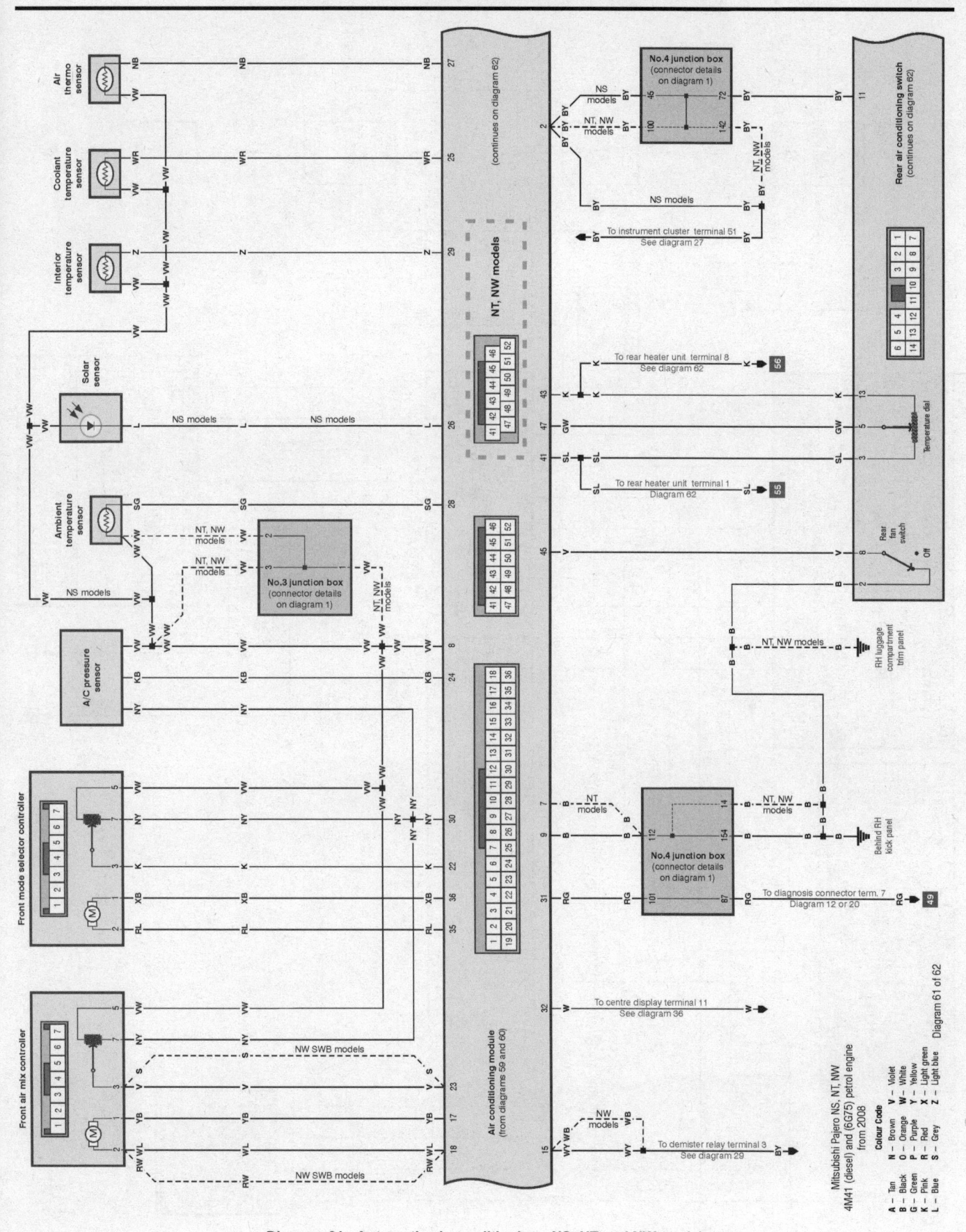

Diagram 61 - Automatic air conditioning - NS, NT and NW models

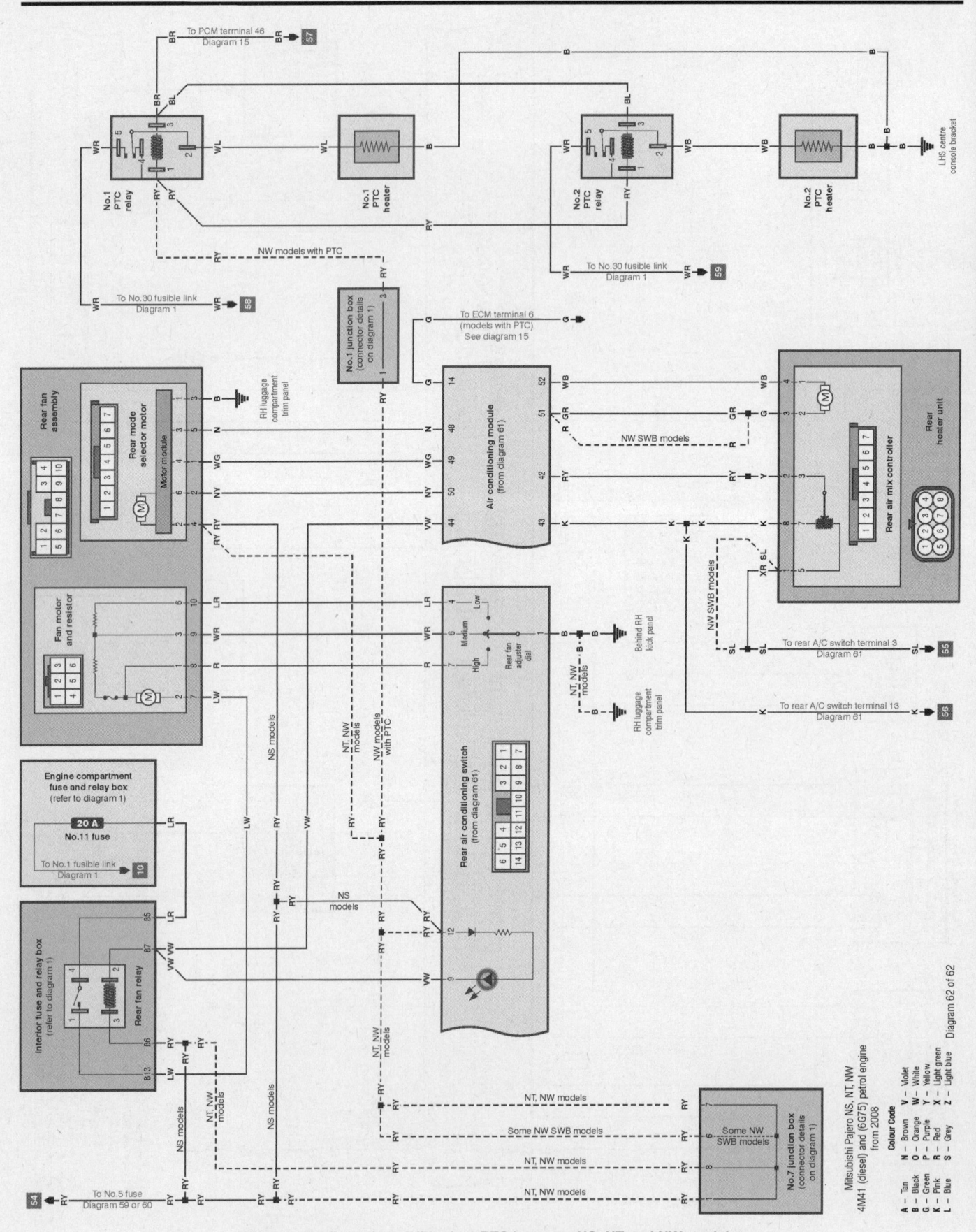

Diagram 62 - Rear air conditioning, PTC heaters - NS, NT and NW models

Index

A

Accelerator
    Linkage check and lubrication, 1-22
    Cable - renewal and adjustment, 4-10
    Accelerator Pedal Position (APPS) sensor - renewal, 6-13
Airbags, 12-14
Air cleaner assembly - removal and refitting, 4-10
Air conditioning and heating system
    Check and maintenance, 3-9
    Compressor - removal and refitting, 3-10
    Condenser fan - removal and refitting, 3-13
    Condenser - removal and refitting, 3-10
    Control assembly - removal and refitting, 3-11
    Evaporator - removal and refitting, 3-11
    General information, 3-7
    Heater core - removal and refitting, 3-7
    Receiver/drier (2000 and earlier models) - removal and refitting, 3-10
Air filter renewal, 1-32
Air flow sensor- renewal, 6-11
Alternator, 5-6
Antifreeze - general information, 3-2
Anti-lock Brake System (ABS) - general information, 9-12
Audio system - removal and refitting, 12-12
Automatic transmission
    Fluid change, 1-35
    Fluid level check, 1-18
    Removal and refitting
        Refitting, 7B-4
        Removal, 7B-3
    Shift control cable - check and adjustment, 7B-2
    Transmission mount - check and renewal, 7A-2
    Transmission oil cooler - removal and refitting, 7B-4

B

Ball joints - check and renewal, 10-11
Battery
    Cables - check and renewal, 5-2
    Check, maintenance and charging
        Charging, 1-20
        Check and maintenance, 1-20
    Emergency jump starting, 5-1
    Removal and refitting, 5-1
    Tray - removal and refitting, 5-2
Bleeding the fuel system, 1-33
Blower motor - removal and refitting, 3-7
Body
    Maintenance, 11-1
    Repair - major damage, 11-5
    Repair - minor damage, 11-4
Bonnet - removal, refitting and adjustment, 11-5
Boost Air Temperature sensor (3.2L diesel engines) - renewal, 6-13
Brakes
    Check, 1-28
    Brake fluid, 1-28
    Disc brakes, 1-28
    Parking brake, 1-28
    Vacuum pump, 1-28
    Disc - inspection, removal and refitting
        Caliper - removal and refitting, 9-6
        Inspection, 9-7
        Pads - renewal, 9-2
        Refitting, 9-8
        Removal, 9-7
    Hydraulic system - bleeding or replacing fluid, 9-9
    Light switch - check and renewal, 9-14
    Lines and hoses - inspection and renewal, 9-8
    Master cylinder - removal and refitting, 9-8
    Parking brake
        Adjustment, 9-11
        Cable(s) - renewal, 9-11
        Shoes - renewal, 9-12
    Pedal height and freeplay check and adjustment, 1-34
Bulb - renewal, 12-7
Bumpers - removal and refitting, 11-6

C

Camshaft
    Oil seals - renewal (V6 petrol engines), 2A-13
    Position (CMP) sensor (petrol engines) - renewal, 6-12
    Removal, inspection and refitting
        V6 petrol engines
            DOHC engine, 2A-16
            SOHC engines, 2A-15
        2.8L diesel engine
            Inspection, 2B-8
            Refitting, 2B-8
            Removal, 2B-7
        3.2L diesel engine
            Inspection, 2C-10
            Refitting, 2C-10
            Removal, 2C-9
Catalytic converter, 6-16
Centre display (2000 and later models) - removal and refitting, 12-11
Centre floor console - removal and refitting, 11-17
Charging system - check, 5-6
Chassis lubrication, 1-25
Circuit breakers - general information, 12-3
Clutch
    Components - removal, inspection and refitting, 8-3
    Description and check, 8-3
    Hydraulic system - bleeding, 8-6
    Master cylinder - removal and refitting, 8-5
    Pilot bearing - inspection, removal and refitting, 8-5
    Pedal height and freeplay check and adjustment, 1-27
    Release bearing - removal and refitting, 8-5
    Release cylinder - removal and refitting, 8-6

Index

Compliance plate, 0-6
Coolant temperature gauge sender unit - check and renewal, 3-6
Coolant temperature sensor (diesel) - check and renewal, 4-19
Cooling system
    Check, 1-21
    Reservoir - removal and refitting, 3-4
    Servicing (draining, flushing and refilling), 1-35
Crankshaft front oil seal - renewal
    2.8L diesel engine, 2B-7
    3.2L diesel engine, 2C-9
    V6 petrol engines, 2A-12
Crankshaft Position (CKP) sensor (petrol engines) - renewal, 6-12
Cruise control system - description and check, 12-10
Cylinder compression check, 2D-3
Cylinder head - removal and refitting
    2.8L diesel engine, 2B-8
    3.2L diesel engine, 2C-10
    V6 petrol engines, 2A-17

D

Diesel fuel injection pump
    Removal and refitting, 4-15
    Timing adjustment, 4-16
Differential
    Lubricant change, 1-35
    Lubricant level check, 1-28
Disc brakes
    Caliper - removal and refitting, 9-6
    Pads - renewal, 9-2
Door
    Latch, lock cylinder and handles - removal, refitting and adjustment
        Cargo door, 11-11
        Front door
            1999 and earlier models, 11-9
            2000 and later models, 11-10
            Adjustment, 11-10
    Removal, refitting and adjustment, 11-9
    Trim panel - removal and refitting
        1999 and earlier models, 11-7
        2000 and later models, 11-8
    Window and regulator - removal and refitting, 11-11
Driveaxle boot renewal and Constant Velocity (CV) joint overhaul
    Inner CV joint, 8-15
    Outer CV joint and boot, 8-16
Drivebelt check, adjustment and renewal, 1-29
Driveline inspection, 8-7
Driveplate/flywheel - removal and refitting
    2.8L diesel engine, 2B-10
    3.2L diesel engine, 2C-12
    V6 petrol engines, 2A-20
Driveshafts
    Differentials and axles - general information, 8-6
    Removal and refitting, 8-7

E

Electrical troubleshooting - general information, 12-1
Engine Coolant Temperature (ECT) sensor - renewal, 6-11
Engine cooling fan, clutch and pulley - check and renewal, 3-4
Engine
    Identification number, 0-6
    Mounts - check and renewal
        2.8L diesel engine, 2B-10
        3.2L diesel engine, 2C-12
        V6 petrol engines, 2A-21
    Oil and filter change, 1-22
    Rebuilding alternatives, 2D-5
    Removal and refitting, 2D-8
    Removal - methods and precautions, 2D-5
    Sump - removal and refitting
        2.8L diesel engine, 2B-10
        3.2L diesel engine, 2C-12
        V6 petrol engines, 2A-18
    Vacuum gauge diagnostic checks (petrol engines), 2D-4
    Vacuum pump (diesel engines) - removal and refitting
        Refitting, 9-14
        Removal, 9-13
    Valve clearance check and adjustment
        2.8L diesel engine, 1-24
        3.2L diesel engine, 1-24
    Valve cover - removal and refitting
        V6 petrol engines, 2A-4
            DOHC engine, 2A-4
            SOHC, 2A-4
        2.8L diesel engine, 2B-4
        3.2L diesel engine, 2C-5
    Valve springs, retainers and seals - renewal
        2.8L diesel engine, 2B-4
        3.2L diesel engine, 2C-5
Evaporative emissions control (EVAP) system, 6-15
Exhaust Gas Recirculation (EGR) system, 6-14
Exhaust
    Manifold - removal and refitting
        3.2L diesel engine, 2C-7
        2.8L diesel engine, 2B-6
        V6 petrol engines, 2A-7
    System check, 1-26
    System servicing - general information, 4-22

F

Final drive assembly (independent rear suspension) - removal and refitting, 8-11
Fluid level checks
    Battery electrolyte, 1-17
    Brake and clutch fluid, 1-17
    Engine coolant, 1-16
    Engine oil, 1-16
    Power steering fluid level check, 1-18
    Windscreen, headlight and rear washer fluid, 1-17
Flywheel/driveplate/ - removal and refitting
    2.8L diesel engine, 2B-10
    3.2L diesel engine, 2C-12
    V6 petrol engines, 2A-20
Four-wheel-drive (4WD) indicator light switches - removal and refitting, 7C-2
Front axle
    Differential assembly - removal and refitting, 8-12
    Disconnect solenoid and actuator - check and renewal, 8-18
    Driveaxles - removal and refitting, 8-14
Front end alignment - general information, 10-21
Front fender - removal and refitting, 11-18
Front hub assembly - removal, bearing repack, refitting and adjustment
    1998 and earlier models, 8-12
    1999 and later models, 8-14

Front shock absorber
    1999 and earlier models - removal and refitting, 10-5
    And spring assembly (2000 and later models) - removal and refitting, 10-6
Front stabiliser bar - removal and refitting, 10-5
Front steering knuckle - removal and refitting, 10-11
Front suspension lower control arm - removal and refitting, 10-10
Front suspension upper control arm - removal and refitting, 10-8
Fuel system
    Cut solenoid - check and renewal, 4-17
    Filter service, 1-32
        2000 and earlier petrol models, 1-32
        Diesel models
            Bleeding the fuel system, 1-33
            Draining water from the fuel filter, 1-34
            Fuel filter renewal, 1-33
    Gauge sender unit (all models) - removal and refitting, 4-8
    Hoses - renewal, 4-11
    Injection system - check, 4-11
    Injectors (diesel) - removal and refitting
        2.8L (4M40) diesel engines, 4-16
        3.2L (4M41) diesel engines, 4-17
    Injector(s) petrol engines - check, removal and refitting, 4-14
    Injection pump - Diesel
        Removal and refitting, 4-15
        Timing adjustment, 4-16
    Precautions and diesel fuel system cleaning
        Cleaning the diesel fuel system
            Petrol in the diesel fuel system, 4-5
            Water in the diesel fuel system, 4-5
        Diesel fuel contamination, 4-4
        Diesel fuel storage, 4-5
        Diesel fuel system
            2.8L (4M40) diesel engine, 4-4
            3.2L (4M41) diesel engine, 4-4
        Exhaust system, 4-6
        Fighting fungi and bacteria in diesel fuel with biocides
        Petrol fuel system, 4-4
    Pressure regulator (petrol models) - removal and refitting, 4-14
    Pressure relief procedure (petrol models), 4-6
    Pump/fuel pressure (petrol models) - check, 4-6
    Pump (petrol engines) - removal and refitting, 4-7
    Rail assembly - removal and refitting, 4-13
    Suction control valve - replacement, 4-23
    System check, 1-29
    Tank (all models) - removal and refitting, 4-8
    Tank cleaning and repair - general information, 4-10
Fuses - general information, 12-2
Fusible links - general information, 12-3

G

Glow control unit - renewal, 4-18
Glow plug relay - check and renewal, 4-18
Glow plugs - check and renewal, 4-18

H

Half shafts (independent rear suspension) - removal and refitting, 8-10
Headlights, 12-6
Heater/air conditioning, 3-7
Hinges and locks - maintenance, 11-5
Horn - check and renewal, 12-14

I

Idle speed
    Check and adjustment (2.8L diesel engine only), 1-34
    Control (ISC) servo - check and renewal, 4-12
Ignition
    Coil(s) - check and renewal, 5-3
        Check
            2002 and earlier models, 5-3
            2003 and later 3.8L models, 5-4
        Replacement, 5-4
    Switch and lock cylinder - removal and refitting
        Ignition switch, 12-4
        Key lock cylinder, 12-5
        Key lock cylinder body, 12-5
    System
        Check, 5-2
        General information and precautions, 5-2
    Ignition timing check, 1-38
Inhibitor switch - check and renewal, 7B-3
Initial start-up and break-in after overhaul, 2D-8
Inlet manifold - removal and refitting
    2.8L diesel engine, 2B-5
    3.2L diesel engine, 2C-6
    V6 petrol engines
        Lower inlet manifold, 2A-6
        Upper inlet manifold, 2A-5
Instrument cluster - removal and refitting, 12-10
Instrument panel and related trim - removal and refitting
    1999 and earlier models, 11-13
    2000 and later models, 11-14
Intercooler - removal and refitting, 4-21

J

Jacking, 0-16
    Floor jack and chassis stands, 0-16
    Vehicle jack - changing the wheel, 0-16
Jump starting, 5-1

K

Knock sensor - renewal, 6-12

M

Manual transmission
    Lubricant
        Change, 1-35
        Level check, 1-27
    Oil seals - renewal, 7A-1
    Overhaul - general information, 7A-3
    Removal and refitting
        Refitting, 7A-3
        Removal, 7A-2
    Shift lever - removal and refitting, 7A-2
    Transmission mount - check and renewal, 7A-2
Master cylinder
    Brake - removal and refitting, 9-8
    Clutch - removal and refitting, 8-5
Multi-Point Injection (MPI) - general information, 4-11

O

Oil cooler - removal and refitting, 3-12
Oil pressure check, 2D-3
Oil pump - removal, inspection and refitting
    2.8L diesel engine, 2B-10
    3.2L diesel engine, 2C-12
    V6 petrol engines, 2A-19
On Board Diagnostic (OBD) system and trouble codes
    Diagnostic tool information, 6-4
    Diagnostic Trouble Codes, 6-10
    General description, 6-4
    Information sensors, 6-5
    OBD trouble codes
        2.8L diesel engines, 6-9
        3.2L diesel engines, 6-9
        3.5L petrol engines, 6-7
        3.8L petrol engines, 6-7
    Obtaining and clearing Diagnostic Trouble Codes (DTCs), 6-6
    Output actuators, 6-6
Outside mirror - removal and refitting, 11-12
Oxygen sensor (petrol engines) - renewal, 6-12

P

Parking brake
    Adjustment, 9-11
    Brake cable(s) - renewal, 9-11
    Brake shoes - renewal, 9-12
Pinion bearing oil seal - renewal, 8-10
Positive Crankcase Ventilation (PCV) system
    Check, 1-36
    Petrol engines only, 6-14
Power brake booster - check, removal and refitting
    2001 and later ABS models, 9-11
    Non ABS and 2000 and earlier ABS models, 9-10
Power door lock system - description and check, 12-11
Power seats - description and check, 12-13
Power steering
    Fluid level check, 1-18
    Pressure Switch (PSP) - renewal, 6-13
    Pump - removal and refitting, 10-20
    System - bleeding, 10-21
Powertrain Control Module (PCM/ECM) - check and renewal, 6-10
Power transistor - check and replacement, 5-5
Power window system - description and check, 12-11
Preheat system - general information, 4-17

R

Radiator grille - removal and refitting, 11-6
Radiator - removal and refitting, 3-3
Radio aerial - removal and refitting, 12-13
Rear axle
    Assembly (banjo type axle housing) - removal and refitting, 8-9
    Shafts, bearings and oil seals (banjo type axle housing) - removal and refitting, 8-8
Rear cargo door - removal, refitting and adjustment, 11-9
    Adjustment, 11-9
    Removal and refitting, 11-9
Rear knuckle (Independent rear suspension) - removal and refitting, 10-16
    Refitting, 10-16
    Removal, 10-16

Rear lower control arm (Independent rear suspension) - removal and refitting, 10-15
Rear main oil seal - renewal
    2.8L diesel engine, 2B-10
    3.2L diesel engine, 2C-12
    V6 petrol engine, 2A-21
Rear shock absorber - removal and refitting, 10-12
Rear stabiliser bar - removal and refitting, 10-14
Rear suspension
    Lateral rod (banjo type axle housing) - removal and refitting, 10-13
    Coil spring - removal and refitting, 10-13
    Trailing arms - removal and refitting, 10-12
Relays - general information, 12-3
Rocker arm and hydraulic valve lash adjuster assembly - removal, inspection and refitting, 2A-13
    DOHC engine, 2A-15
    SOHC engines, 2A-13

S

Seat belts
    Check, 1-31, 11-20
    Removal and refitting, 11-19
Shift control cable (automatic transmission) - check and adjustment, 7B-2
Shift lever - removal and refitting
    Manual transmission, 7A-2
    Transfer case, 7C-1
Spark plug
    Renewal, 1-36
    Tube replacement, 2A-5
    Wire check and renewal, 1-38
Starter motor
    General information and precautions, 5-7
    In-vehicle check, 5-7
    Removal and refitting, 5-8
    /solenoid/gear reduction assembly - renewal, 5-8
Steering
    Column cover - removal and refitting, 11-18
    Column switches and airbag clock spring - removal and refitting
        Airbag clock spring, 12-5
        Steering column switches
            1999 and earlier models, 12-5
            2000 and later models, 12-5
    Freeplay - adjustment, 10-19
    Gear - removal and refitting, 10-18
    Linkage - removal and refitting
        Idler arm, 10-18
        Pitman arm, 10-17
        Tie-rod
            1999 and earlier models, 10-18
            2000 and earlier models (rack and pinion steering), 10-18
    Wheel - removal and refitting, 10-16
Suction control valve - replacement, 4-23
Sump, engine - removal and refitting
    2.8L diesel engine, 2B-10
    3.2L diesel engine, 2C-12
    V6 petrol engines, 2A-18
Suspension and steering check, 1-26

Index

T

Thermostat, engine - check and renewal, 3-2
Throttle body
    Mounting bolt torque check, 1-31
    Removal and refitting, 4-12
Throttle control cable (2000 and earlier models) - adjustment, 7B-2
Throttle position sensor (TPS)
    And control motor, 6-14
    Renewal, 6-11
Timing belt - removal, inspection and refitting
    DOHC engine, 2A-10
    SOHC engines, 2A-7
Timing chain, sprockets and gears - removal, inspection and refitting
    2.8L diesel engine, 2B-6
    3.2L diesel engine, 2C-8
Timing gear cover - removal and refitting
    2.8L diesel engine, 2B-6
    3.2L diesel engine, 2C-7
Toe control arm (Independent rear suspension) - removal and refitting, 10-15
Top Dead Centre (TDC) for number one piston - locating
    2.8L diesel engine, 2B-3
    3.2L diesel engine, 2C-4
    V6 petrol engines, 2A-3
Torsion bar - removal, refitting and adjustment, 10-7
Transfer case
    Lubricant change, 1-35
    Shift lever - removal and refitting, 7C-1
    Lubricant level check, 1-27
    Overhaul - general information, 7C-3
Transmission mount - check and renewal, 7A-2
Transmission oil cooler - removal and refitting, 7B-4
Tune-up general information, 1-15
Turbocharger and intercooler, 4-19
Turn signal/hazard flasher - check and renewal, 12-3
Tyre and tyre pressure checks, 1-18
Tyre rotation, 1-24

U

Under bonnet hose check and renewal, 1-22
    Fuel hose, 1-22
    General, 1-22
    Metal lines, 1-22
    Turbocharger hoses and lines, 1-22
    Vacuum hoses, 1-22
Universal joints (non-CFRP models) - renewal, 8-8
Upholstery and carpets - maintenance, 11-1
Upper control arm and ball joint (Independent rear suspension) - removal and refitting, 10-14

V

Vacuum gauge diagnostic checks (petrol engines), 2D-4
Vacuum pump (diesel engines) - removal and refitting, 9-13
Valve clearance check and adjustment, 1-24
Valve cover - removal and refitting
    V6 petrol engines, 2A-4
    2.8L diesel engine, 2B-4
    3.2L diesel engine, 2C-5

Valve springs, retainers and seals - renewal
    2.8L diesel engine, 2B-4
    3.2L diesel engine, 2C-5
Vehicle Speed Sensor (VSS) - renewal, 6-12
Vinyl trim - maintenance, 11-1
Voltage regulator/alternator brushes - renewal, 5-6

W

Water pump
    Check, 3-4
    Renewal
        Diesel engines, 3-4
        Petrol engines, 3-5
Wheels and tyres - general information, 10-22
Windscreen and fixed glass - renewal, 11-5
Wiper blade inspection and renewal, 1-21
Wiper motor - removal and refitting, 12-9
Wiring diagrams
    General information, 12-14
    4WD indicator lamps, rear differential lock, NL models, 12-37
    4WD selection system, suspension, NL models, 12-38
    Active skid and traction control (ASTC) - NS, NT, NW diesel models, 12-121 to 12-123
    Active skid and traction control (ASTC) - NS, NT, NW petrol models, 12-118 to 12-120
    Air conditioning (front), condenser fan, NL models, 12-39
    Air conditioning (rear), NL models, 12-40
    Air conditioning, NM-NP models, 12-77
    Air conditioning system (rear), NM-NP models, 12-80
    Air conditioning (rear), PTC heaters - NS, NT, NW models, 12-142
    Air conditioning (automatic) - NS and NT models, 12-139
    Air conditioning (automatic) - NS, NT, NW models, 12-141
    Air conditioning (automatic) - NW models, 12-140
    Antilock braking system (ABS) - NW petrol models, 12-124, 12-125
    Antilock braking system (ABS), NL models, 12-35
    Antilock braking system (ABS), NM-NP models, 12-70
    Antilock braking system (ABS), traction control system, NM-NP models, 12-71
    Antilock braking system (ABS), traction control system, stability control, NM-NP models, 12-72
    Approach lamps, headlamp washer, headlamp levelling systems - NS, NT, NW models, 12-105
    Audio system with amplifier, hands free/USB system - NS, NT, NW models, 12-133
    Audio system, audio amplifier - NS, NT, NW models, 12-132
    Audio system, NM-NP models, 12-76
    Automatic transmission - NT, NW diesel models, 12-98
    Automatic transmission - petrol, NL models, 12-19
    Automatic transmission control module, automatic transmission. Diesel, NM-NP models, 12-55
    Automatic transmission control module, instruments, sports shift, inhibitor switch. Diesel, NM-NP models, 12-56
    Automatic transmission, immobilizer system - NS diesel models, 12-91
    Automatic transmission, inhibitor switch - NS diesel models, 12-90
    Automatic transmission, inhibitor switch - NS, NT, NW petrol models, 12-86
    Automatic transmission, inhibitor switch, immobilizer system - NT, NW diesel models, 12-99
    Centre display, NM-NP models, 12-68
    Centre display, sunroof, demister, NL models, 12-33
    Charge system (NW diesel models), various sensors and switches - NT, NW diesel models, 12-97
    Charging, starting, horn, cigarette lighter, power sockets - NS, NT, NW models, 12-101
    Climate control, NM-NP models, 12-78

Climate control, rear demister, NM-NP models, 12-79
Communication area network (CAN), diagnosis connector - NS, NT, NW petrol models and NS diesel models, 12-92
Communication area network (CAN), diagnosis connector - NT, NW diesel models, 12-100
Courtesy illumination, 12-108
Courtesy illumination, rear window demister - NS, NT, NW models, 12-109
Cruise control, instrument cluster - NT, NW diesel models, 12-96
Cruise control, instrument cluster, immobiliser system - NS, NT, NW petrol models, 12-85
Cruise control, NL models, 12-34
Cruise control, NM-NP models, 12-69
ECM power supply, earth circuits, glow plug circuit, various sensors - NS diesel models, 12-87
EFI and engine management system - petrol, NL models, 12-16, 12-18
Engine compartment fuse and relay box, ignition switch, fusible link box, interior fuse and relay box connectors - NS, NT, NW models, 12-81
Engine control system. 4M40 models, 12-50
Engine control system. 4M41 models, 12-51
Engine control system. 4M41 models, 12-52
Engine control system. 4M41 models, 12-53
Engine control system. 4M41 models, 12-54
Engine management system, intercooler fan - diesel, NL models, 12-20
Exterior mirror heater, automatic interior mirror, rear view camera, sunroof - NS, NT, NW models, 12-129
Five speed automatic transmission, inhibitor switches, shift switch assembly. Automatic transmission - petrol, NM-NP models, 12-46
Four speed automatic transmission, inhibitor switch. Automatic transmission - petrol, NM-NP models, 12-45
Four wheel drive select system, rear diff lock system, NM-NP models, 12-74
Front and rear fog lamps, manual headlamp levelling - NW models, 12-103
Front and rear wipers and washer - NS, NT, NW models, 12-114
Fuel injectors, various sensors - NT, NW diesel models, 12-94
Hands free/USB system, multivision display - NT models, 12-134
Hands free/USB system, multivision display - NW models, 12-137
Headlamps, tail lamps, fog lamps, NM-NP models, 12-58
Headlamps, tail lamps, front and rear fog lamps, NL models, 12-22
Ignition system, various sensors and solenoids - NS, NT, NW petrol models, 12-83
Instrument cluster - NS, NT, NW models, 12-115
Instrument cluster, centre display - NS, NT, NW models, 12-116
Instrument cluster, NL models, 12-31, 12-32
Instrument cluster, NM-NP models, 12-66, 12-67
Instrument illumination - NS models, 12-106
Instrument illumination - NT, NW models, 12-107
Instrument illumination, NL models, 12-24
Instrument illumination, NM-NP models, 12-60
Interior lighting, NM-NP models, 12-61
Keyless entry, interior lighting, NL models, 12-25
Multivision display with audio amplifier - NT models, 12-135
Multivision display with audio amplifier - NW models, 12-136
Park lamps, headlamps, automatic light monitoring system - NS, NT, NW models, 12-102
PCM power supply and earth circuits, fuel pump, immobiliser system, diagnosis connector. Automatic transmission - petrol, NM-NP models, 12-42

PCM power supply and earth circuits, fuel pump, immobiliser system, diagnosis connector. Manual transmission - petrol, NM-NP models, 12-47
PCM power supply, earth circuits, glow plug circuit, various sensors and solenoids - NT, NW diesel models, 12-93
PCM power supply, earth circuits, injectors, fuel pump - NS, NT, NW petrol models, 12-82
Power distribution, NL models, 12-15
Power distribution, NM-NP models, 12-41
Power door locks, keyless entry, key reminder system - NS, NT, NW models, 12-110
Power door locks, keyless entry, map reading lamps, NM-NP models, 12-64
Power door locks, NL models, 12-28
Power mirrors - NS, NT, NW models, 12-130
Power mirrors, NL models, 12-29
Power mirrors, power seats, sunroof, NM-NP models, 12-63
Power seats, seat heater - NS, NT, NW models, 12-128
Power seats, wipers and washers, NL models, 12-30
Power windows - NS and NT models, 12-112
Power windows - NW models, 12-113
Power windows, NM-NP models, 12-62
Power windows. Models from 1998, NL models, 12-27
Power windows. Models to 1998, NL models, 12-26
Rear display system - NS, NT, NW models, 12-138
Reverse sensor, audio system - NS, NT, NW models, 12-131
Starting system, charging system, cigarette lighter, power outlets, horn, clock, NL models, 12-21
Starting system, charging system, horn, cigarette lighter, power outlets, clock, NM-NP models, 12-57
Stop lamps, turn signal/hazard lamps, reverse lamps - NS, NT, NW models, 12-104
Super select 4WD system - NS, NT, NW models, 12-126
Super select 4WD system, rear differential lock system - NS, NT, NW models, 12-127
Super select system, NM-NP models, 12-75
Supplement restraint system (SRS), NM-NP models, 12-73
Supplemental restraint system (SRS) - NS, NT, NW models, 12-117
Supplemental restraint system (SRS), audio system, NL models, 12-36
Theft alarm - NS, NT, NW models, 12-111
Throttle control, air conditioning, various sensors - NT, NW diesel models, 12-95
Throttle control, various sensors, air conditioning - NS diesel models, 12-88
Turn signal/hazard lamps, stop lamps, reverse lamps, NL models, 12-23
Turn signal/hazard lamps, stop lamps, reverse lamps, NM-NP models, 12-59
Various engine management input sensors, ISC valve, fuel injectors. Automatic transmission - petrol, NM-NP models, 12-43
Various engine management input sensors, ISC valve, fuel injectors. Manual transmission - petrol, NM-NP models, 12-48
Various input sensors, instruments, check connector, ignition system. Automatic transmission - petrol, NM-NP models, 12-44
Various sensors, cruise control, instrument cluster - NS diesel models, 12-89
Various sensors, solenoids - NS, NT, NW petrol models, 12-84
Vehicle speed sensor, instruments, check connector, ignition system. Manual transmission - petrol, NM-NP models, 12-49
Wipers and washers, NM-NP models, 12-65